PENGUIN BOOKS

EC LAW

Stephen Weatherill received his schooling in Hull and Bradford, before being awarded MA and MSc degrees by the Universities of Cambridge and Edinburgh respectively. He held lecturing posts at the Universities of Reading and Manchester and is now Professor of European Law in the Department of Law at the University of Nottingham. He has delivered papers on European Community law to many academic and professional audiences in the UK and in other member states of the Community. He is the author of *Cases and Materials on EC Law* (2nd edn, 1994) and has contributed to several other works connected with the development of Community law. He is also the author of several articles in leading legal journals, including the *Yearbook of European Law*, the *Common Market Law Review* and the *European Law Review*.

Paul Beaumont received his schooling in East Kilbride, Scotland, before graduating LL.B. from the University of Glasgow. A Commonwealth Scholarship was awarded to him, and he graduated LL.M. at Dalhousie University, Halifax, Nova Scotia. He has taught at the University of Aberdeen since 1983 and is now Professor of European Union and Private International Law there. In addition to teaching European Community law at Aberdeen, he has given papers on the subject in the United Kingdom, Canada and Sweden. He is the co-author with Professor A. E. Anton FBA of two books published by W. Green, the second edition of Anton's *Private International Law* (1990) and the second edition of *Civil Jurisdiction in Scotland: Brussels and Lugano Conventions* (1995). A quarterly columnist on European Law for the *Scottish Law Gazette* since 1985, he is also a regular contributor on current developments in Community law for the *International and Comparative Law Quarterly*.

EC LAW

Stephen Weatherill and
Paul Beaumont

SECOND EDITION

PENGUIN BOOKS

PENGUIN BOOKS

Published by the Penguin Group
Penguin Books Ltd, 27 Wrights Lane, London w8 5tz, England
Penguin Books USA Inc., 375 Hudson Street, New York, New York 10014, USA
Penguin Books Australia Ltd, Ringwood, Victoria, Australia
Penguin Books Canada Ltd, 10 Alcorn Avenue, Toronto, Ontario, Canada m4v 3b2
Penguin Books (NZ) Ltd, 182–190 Wairau Road, Auckland 10, New Zealand

Penguin Books Ltd, Registered Offices: Harmondsworth, Middlesex, England

First published 1993
Second edition 1995
3 5 7 9 10 8 6 4 2

Set in 9.5/11.5 pt Monophoto Bembo
Typeset by Datix International Limited, Bungay, Suffolk
Printed in England by Clays Ltd, St Ives plc

Contents

Preface

It would not be possible to write a single-volume book that covered the whole field of Community law and policy in any depth. Therefore, in this book, we have selected those aspects that represent the principal institutional, constitutional and substantive areas of the Community legal order. Thus there is substantial coverage of the political institutions of the Community, the varied and complex legislative procedures, economic and monetary union (including the Danish and United Kingdom opt-outs), subsidiarity, social policy, the four freedoms in the context of '1992', competition policy and, generally, of a Community that is active in ever wider fields.

We have not devoted separate chapters to environmental, transport, agriculture, external relations, regional and fisheries policies, partly because they are not usually covered in EC law courses, but have mentioned some aspects of them where appropriate. The treatment has expanded in this second edition. There is a chapter on social policy not only because of its relevance to many courses on EC law, but also because it allows for the discussion of more general themes relevant to the Community's regulatory competence, which ought to provide insights into the other common policies we have not been able to cover in depth.

We are conscious that there is a great diversity in the content of EC law courses taught in Britain and elsewhere. This book will be sufficiently comprehensive both for courses that concentrate on institutional and constitutional issues, with limited reference to substantive law, and for courses that study substantive law in depth while reducing emphasis on the institutional structure of the Community. Moreover, it is apparent that some EC law courses are fragmenting, with separate courses on, for example, competition law, becoming increasingly common. We hope that this book is broad enough to reflect those developments too.

It would be futile to present Community law as a static set of rules. The structure of the Community and its legal order continues to evolve. The substantive law of integration has many facets and, increasingly, the major new challenges in the law relate to regulation of the market once it has been integrated. This emphasis on the nature of a general law of the

vii

economy is likely to accelerate once the excitement generated by the completion of the internal market at the end of 1992 begins to recede into history. Similarly, the institutional and constitutional arrangements within the Community are confronted by challenges that demand more attention to the appropriate level for law-making (European, national or regional). The Community operates increasingly in a world of minimum harmonization, 'opt-outs' and subsidiarity. Demands for increased democratic legitimacy in the Community and the pressures to embrace Eastern European countries pose further major questions for its established structures.

Such developments take the field of inquiry of the Community lawyer far beyond the traditional emphasis on supremacy, direct effort, the four freedoms and competition policy as the pillars of Community law. While an understanding of these matters (the *acquis communautaire*) remains essential to a study of Community law and is the basis of this book's analysis, our aim throughout has been to show how the Community is in a process of continual evolution and to make reference to the tensions within established legal structures. We use the principles of Community law as the basis for our explanation and, where possible, explain how the application of those principles may evolve. That shifting process is the essential nature of Community law.

We do not overlook the criticism that the Community has attracted from many quarters, nor are we constrained by a purely legal focus. We have, for example, placed the legal structures in their political context, demonstrated the role of law in achieving economic objectives and considered the intrusion of the Community into the social policy of the member states. In many areas a book of this nature can be no more than a starting point for debate and we will be well satisfied if we have provided a clear and informed explanation and stimulated further discussion.

The law stated in this book is as at 1 January 1995. We have been able to take account of the accession of Austria, Finland and Sweden to the European Community on that date. More generally we have endeavoured fully to update the first edition which stated the law as at 1 April 1992. In a few places it has been possible to take account of developments early in 1995. At the end of the book is a Select Further Reading list, which should be used as a supplement to each chapter.

Within the project we regard ourselves as co-authors. Nominally, Stephen Weatherill acted as Editor, but this means no more than that his involvement with Penguin slightly predates that of Paul Beaumont and that he has prepared the tables and index. On deciding what shall be included in the book and how it shall be written, the process has been totally non-hierarchical. Paul Beaumont has been primarily responsible for Chapters 2–12; Stephen Weatherill for Chapters 13–20 and 22–27; Chapters 1 and 21 evolved. However, we have read and commented in depth on each other's chapters so we accept responsibility as a team for the book that has emerged from this cross-border, albeit British, project.

Our thanks are due to the late Kenneth Simmonds, who was most supportive at the very inception of this project. Karl Newman was equally helpful along the way. The staff of Penguin Books have been happy to allow us a free hand in choosing the style of the book, for which we are grateful.

On a more personal level, Stephen Weatherill gives special thanks to Catherine Redgwell. Paul Beaumont thanks the staff at UKREP for helpful briefings and documents, and the members of the Legal Service in the Commission and the Council and the MEPs who took time to speak to him. He also thanks his wife, Marion, and their two children, David and Anna, for their patience and love.

Stephen Weatherill
Paul Beaumont

Tables of Cases

EUROPEAN COURT OF JUSTICE

NUMERICAL LIST

Case 258/84 Nippon Seiko v Council [1987] ECR 1923, [1989] 2 CMLR 76 **249, 250**

Case 247/84 Leon Motte [1985] ECR 3887, [1987] 1 CMLR 663 **466**

Cases 279, 280, 285, 286/84 Rau v Commission [1987] ECR 1069, [1988] 2 CMLR 704 **260**

Case 304/84 Ministère Public v Muller [1986] ECR 1511, [1987] 2 CMLR 469 **466**

Case 307/84 Commission v France [1986] ECR 1725, [1987] 3 CMLR 555 **568**

Case 309/84 Commission v Italy [1986] ECR 599, [1987] 2 CMLR 657 **204**

Case 311/84 Centre Belge-Télémarketing v CLT [1985] ECR 3261, [1986] 2 CMLR 558 **753, 754**

Case 5/85 AKZO v Commission [1986] ECR 2585, [1987] 3 CMLR 716 **52, 53, 766**

Case 21/85 Maas v Bundesanstalt für Landwirtschaftliche Marktordnung [1986] ECR 3537, [1987] 3 CMLR 794 **260**

Case 35/85 Procureur de la République v Tissier [1986] ECR 1207, [1987] 1 CMLR 551 **293**

Case 45/85 Verband der Sachversicherer v Commission [1987] ECR 405, [1988] 4 CMLR 264 **672, 685**

Case 53/85 AKZO v Commission [1986] ECR 1965, [1987] 1 CMLR 231 **224, 265, 764, 768, 770, 777–8**

Case 54/85 Ministère Public v Mirepoix [1986] ECR 1067, [1987] 2 CMLR 44 **467, 471**

Case 59/85 Netherlands v Reed [1986] ECR 1283, [1987] 2 CMLR 448 **261, 550, 552**

Case 66/85 Lawrie-Blum v Land Baden-Wurttemburg [1986] ECR 2121, [1987] 3 CMLR 389 **547, 569**

Cases 67, 68, 70/85 Van der Kooy v Commission [1988] ECR 219 **243**

Case 69/85 Wünsche v Germany [1986] ECR 947 **292**

Case 71/85 Netherlands v Federatie Nederlandse Vakbeweging [1986] ECR 3855 **340**

Case 78/85 Group of the European Right v Parliament [1986] ECR 1753, [1988] 3 CMLR 645 **227**

Cases 80, 159/85 Nedelandse Bakkerij v Edah [1986] ECR 3359, [1988] 2 CMLR 113 **531**

Case 85/85 Commission v Belgium [1986] ECR 1149, [1987] 1 CMLR 787 **194, 199**

Cases 89, 104, 116–17, 125–9/85 A. Åhlström and Others v Commission (Woodpulp) [1988] ECR 5193, [1988] 4 CMLR 901 **246, 672, 679, 690, 691**

Cases C-89/85, C-104/85, C-114/85, C-116/85, C-117/85, C-125–9/85

ALPHABETICAL LIST

lxxx

OPINIONS

SPECIAL AGREEMENTS

COURT OF FIRST INSTANCE

NUMERICAL LIST

Cases T-1, T-2, T-3/89 Rhône-Poulenc, Petrofina, Atochem *v* Commission [1991] ECR II-867, 1087, 1177; T-4, T-6, T-7, T-8/89 BASF AG, Enichem Anic, SA Hercules, DSM NV *v* Commission [1991] ECR II-1523, 1624, 1711, 1833; Cases T-9, T-10, T-11, T-12, T-13, T-14, T-15/89 Hüls AG, Hoechst AG, Shell Ltd, SA Solvay, ICI plc, Montedipe SpA,

ALPHABETICAL LIST

EUROPEAN COURT OF HUMAN RIGHTS

CASES BEFORE NATIONAL COURTS

BELGIUM

FRANCE

GERMANY

IRELAND

ITALY

UNITED STATES

Tables of Treaties and Legislation

THE TREATY ON EUROPEAN UNION

Article	Page	Article	Page
A	10	K	566
D	48, 88, 103	K.3(2)(c)	333
F(2)	257, 171	K.6	102
G	11, 12	L	88, 257, 771
J.3	78, 90	N	91, 320
J.4	78	N.1	75
J.7	102	N.2	18, 126
J.8	90	O	82, 130, 132
		R.2	18

See the *EC Treaty* table for the impact of the Treaty on European Union on the EEC Treaty, which it converts into the EC Treaty.

THE EC TREATY

It is impossible to preserve a rigid division between the EEC Treaty and the EC Treaty. The latter is really simply an amended version of the former. However, using separate tables seems the most convenient solution to this difficult problem.

References in this table cover Treaty provisions where cited in the text specifically as provisions in the EC Treaty, as created by the Treaty on European Union signed at Maastricht; and where cited without elaboration, being unchanged by the Treaty signed at Maastricht and where no point is being made in the text about the impact of Treaty amendments. Provisions referred to explicitly because of their role under the EEC Treaty, prior to the amendments agreed at Maastricht, are contained in the table on the EEC Treaty.

DIRECTIVES

Merger regulation

EEC TREATY

References to the EEC Treaty as amended by the Single European Act. This list contains only references to the EEC Treaty as such, where a specific point is being made that it is the pre-Maastricht arrangements that are under discussion. General references to the Treaty are contained in the EC Treaty list. See also the separate list indicating where the EC Treaty article does not correspond to the EEC Treaty article.

EC provisions that do not correspond to their EEC equivalents (not including reference to new provisions introduced by the Treaty on European Union)

EEC Article	EC Article
7	6
8a	7a
8	7
127	125
128	now part of 127
129	198d
130	198e
130o	130n
149(1)	189a(1)
149(2)	189c
149(3)	189a(2)

EURATOM

Article	Page
31	105, 180
108	93
188	319
Reg. 3954/87	180

ECSC

Article	Page
21	93
66	806
80	683

ACT OF ACCESSION OF THE UNITED KINGDOM

UK STATUTES

EUROPEAN CONVENTION ON HUMAN RIGHTS

Abbreviations

AC   Appeal Cases
AG   Advocate-General
AJCL   *American Journal of Comparative Law*
AJDA   *Actualités Juridiques de Droit Administratif*
AJIL   *American Journal of International Law*
All ER   *All England Law Reports*
Am Ec Rev   *American Economic Review*
Anglo-Am LR   *Anglo-American Law Review*
BLB   *Business Law Brief*
BVerfGe   Bundesverfassungsgericht
CAP   Common Agricultural Policy
CDE   *Cahiers de Droit Européen*
CFI   Court of First Instance
Ch   Chancery
CLJ   *Cambridge Law Journal*
CLP   *Current Legal Problems*
CMLR   *Common Market Law Reports*
CMLRev   *Common Market Law Review*
Co Law   *The Company Lawyer*
Col J Transnat L   *Columbia Journal of Transnational Law*
Col L   *Columbia Law Review*
COREPER   Committee of Permanent Representatives
Corn ILJ   *Cornell International Law Journal*
Corn LR   *Cornell Law Review*
Denning LJ   *Denning Law Journal*
E Bus LR   *European Business Law Review*
EC   European Community
ECB   European Central Bank
ECHR   European Court of Human Rights
ECJ   European Court of Justice
ECLJ   *European Consumer Law Journal*
ECLR   *European Competition Law Review*
ECR   *European Court Reports*

ECSC   European Coal and Steel Community
ECU   European Currency Unit
EEA   European Economic Area
EEC   European Economic Community
EEIG   European Economic Interest Grouping
EFTA   European Free Trade Association
EIPR   *European Intellectual Property Review*
EJIL   *European Journal of International Law*
ELRev   *European Law Review*
EMI   European Monetary Institute
EMS   European Monetary System
EMU   Economic Monetary Union
ERM   Exchange Rate Mechanism
Euratom   European Atomic Energy Community
Fordham Corp L Inst   *Annual Proceedings of the Fordham Corporate Law Institute*
Foro. it   *Foro Italiano*
GATT   General Agreement on Tariffs and Trade
Geo Wash LR   *George Washington Law Review*
GYIL   *German Yearbook on International Law*
Harvard Intl LJ   *Harvard International Law Journal*
Harv LR   *Harvard Law Review*
ICCLR   *International Company and Commercial Law Review*
ICLQ   *International and Comparative Law Quarterly*
ILJ   *Industrial Law Journal*
ILM   *International Legal Materials*
Int Lawyer   *International Lawyer*
IRLR   *Industrial Relations Law Reports*
J Env L   *Journal of Environmental Law*
JBL   *Journal of Business Law*
JCMS   *Journal of Common Market Studies*
JCP   *Journal of Consumer Policy*
JSPTL   *Journal of the Society of Public Teachers of Law*
JSWFL   *Journal of Social Welfare and Family Law*
JWTL   *Journal of World Trade Law*
LIEI   *Legal Issues of European Integration*
LQR   *Law Quarterly Review*
McGill LJ   *McGill Law Journal*
Melb ULR   *Melbourne University Law Review*
MEP   Member of the European Parliament
MLR   *Modern Law Review*
NATO   North Atlantic Treaty Organization
NDLRev   *Notre Dame Law Review*

NJW   *Neue Juristische Wochenschrift*
NILQ   *Northern Ireland Legal Quarterly*
OECD   Organization for Economic Cooperation and Development
OEEC   Organization for European Economic Cooperation
OJ   *Official Journal*
Ox JLS   *Oxford Journal of Legal Studies*
Ox Rev Ec Pol   *Oxford Review of Economic Policy*
PL   *Public Law*
PubProc LRev   *Public Procurement Law Review*
QB   Queens Bench
Rev Droit Européen   *Revue de Droit Européen*
Rev Trim Droit Européen   *Revue Trimistrielle de Droit Européen*
RMC   *Revue du Marché Commun*
RSDIC   *Revue Suisse de Droit International de Concurrence*
SAD   Single Administrative Document
Scand SL   *Scandinavian Studies in Law*
SEA   Single European Act
SLG   *Scottish Law Gazette*
SLT   *Scots Law Times*
SJ   *Solicitors Journal*
StatLRev   *Statute Law Review*
Syd LR   *Sydney Law Review*
Tul LR   *Tulane Law Review*
UNCTAD   United Nations Conference on Trade and Development
U Pa LR   *University of Pennsylvania Law Review*
Utilities LR   *Utilities Law Review*
Valparaiso ULR   *Valparaiso University Law Review*
WLR   *Weekly Law Reports*
WEU   Western European Union
WQ   Written Question
Yale J Intl Law   *Yale Journal of International Law*
Yale LJ   *Yale Law Journal*
YEL   *Yearbook of European Law*

CHAPTER I

The Development of the European Community

THE HISTORY OF THE COMMUNITY

There is nothing new about the desire to unite Europe. Figures from history as diverse as the Roman emperors, Genghis Khan, Napoleon and Hitler have in turn coveted the common objective of taking the Continent as their own. Some such attempts have failed, others have enjoyed limited success over varying periods of time. None has brought lasting peace and prosperity to all the inhabitants of Europe. The European Community aims to achieve that objective through cooperation between previously independent and sometimes hostile states. Europe is to be united by the consent of its citizens for the benefit of its citizens.

THE IMMEDIATE POST-WAR PERIOD

The modern history of European integration begins immediately after the Second World War. The states of Europe shared a common interest in restructuring the Continent. Europe lay devastated by a conflict that had claimed many millions of lives. That horrific struggle was itself the culmination of a hundred years and more of turmoil within the changing patchwork of European states. The persistent misery of local and regional conflict induced a willingness to seek fresh solutions independent of the old, discredited nation-state structure. The post-war climate nurtured an audience receptive to the evolving belief that Europe should pursue the path of integration.

The ambitions of this vision were quickly confronted by the obstacles of political reality. Even as the war ended in 1945, the Continent was divided into two power blocs, and it was soon apparent that the plans for European integration could embrace only Western Europe. The eastern half of the Continent fell under the Soviet domination from which it emerged only at the end of the 1980s. Financial support was forthcoming from the United States for the process of cooperative reconstruction within Europe.

This 'Marshall Plan' (taking the name of the imaginative US Secretary of State of the time) was rejected by the states of Eastern Europe. The influence of the Soviet Union and its fear of exposing itself to American economic domination were doubtless the primary explanation for this refusal. Meanwhile, the United Kingdom held aloof from the ambitious plans for European integration that were being prepared elsewhere and clung to the idea that international cooperation, though desirable, should be pursued by fully independent states. There was nothing radical about this belief. It emerged in the Organization for European Economic Cooperation (OEEC), which was set up in response to the Marshall Plan.[1] It was also reflected in the Council of Europe, which was established in 1949 and brought together governments in a forum for negotiation and cooperation. This organization is still in existence today and has performed many valuable tasks, notably the nurturing of the European Convention on Human Rights. However, it fell short of the ambitions of the European integrationists, principally because it acts by unanimity among nation-states or not at all. This characterizes it as an intergovernmental organization.

THE TREATY OF PARIS: THE EUROPEAN COAL AND STEEL COMMUNITY

Jean Monnet, a French businessman turned administrator,[2] and Robert Schuman, the French Foreign Minister, were among the most active of the integrationists. Their collaboration led to the first stage in the modern European Community. In May 1950 Schuman revealed a plan for the fusion of the coal and steel industries of France and Germany, with an invitation to other countries to participate.[3] Six states began the progress towards European unity. In 1951 France, the fledgling Federal Republic of Germany, Italy, the Netherlands, Belgium and Luxembourg signed the Treaty of Paris, which brought into existence the European Coal and Steel Community (ECSC) at the start of 1952. The character of the ECSC was very different from the traditional model of an international organization. It was not merely a forum for joint discussion or intergovernmental decision-making. The Paris Treaty established new institutions, independ-

1 This organization became the Organization for Economic Cooperation and Development (OECD) in 1961.
2 Monnet, *Memoirs*; see also *Proceedings of the Centenary Symposium on Jean Monnet*, Luxembourg, EC Official Publications, 1989.
3 See Fontaine, *Europe – A Fresh Start: The Schuman Declaration 1950–90*, Luxembourg, EC Official Publications, 1990.

ent of the six member states, with power to supervise the development of the coal and steel industries of the states party to the treaty. Responsibility for coal and steel had passed out of the hands of six nation-states and into the hands of international institutions. It is this 'transfer' of legislative and administrative powers that was regarded as the vital step towards integration taken in the Treaty of Paris. Over forty years later the debate about the extent to which states are prepared to transfer 'sovereign' powers to the European institutions remains the political flashpoint of Community affairs.

The choice of coal and steel as the starting point of European integration was no accident. These were the war-making industries. The participants placed them under common control partly as a means of ensuring that no state possessed the capacity independently to prepare for war. The 'German problem' loomed large for all involved in the process. All Europe would benefit from the economic regeneration of Germany, the heart of the Continent. The task was to promote this restructuring within the security of a wider European framework. From its very inception the movement for European integration was inspired by much more than purely economic objectives. The political restructuring of the Continent and the basic desire to avoid further conflict were high on the agenda. The Preamble to the Treaty of Paris referred to the creation of an economic community as 'the basis for a broader and deeper community among peoples long divided by bloody conflicts'. European integration concerns much more than economics, yet, even today, some politicians underestimate the breadth of the Community's interests.

THE (FAILED) EUROPEAN DEFENCE COMMUNITY

The next step in the integrationists' plan proved overambitious. The creation of a unified European Army within a European Defence Community was mooted. Like the ECSC this was in part a plan to secure the rehabilitation of Germany within a wider European framework. Negotiations progressed, with the strong support of the United States, and a treaty was signed in 1952. However, it was not ratified and by 1954 the impetus was lost. With French support rapidly disappearing, the plan collapsed. Defence matters were left to be discussed in a framework based on pure intergovernmental cooperation. The most important manifestations of this approach remain the North Atlantic Treaty Organization (NATO) and the Western European Union (WEU). Yet the determination to integrate Western Europe was not destroyed by this failure. It was merely deflected, towards the sphere of economic relations.

THE TREATIES OF ROME: THE EEC AND EURATOM

The Messina Conference of 1955 prepared the ground for more broadly based economic integration. An intergovernmental committee was set up, chaired by the Belgian foreign minister, Paul-Henri Spaak. Its report, in April 1956, examined the economic attraction of integration and elaborated proposals for institutional support. By 1957 the six participant states were ready to take a further step. The two Treaties of Rome were signed, creating, from the start of 1958, two further communities. These were the European Economic Community (EEC) and the European Atomic Energy Community (Euratom). Like the Paris Treaty, which established the ECSC, these treaties were characterized by the creation of autonomous institutions possessing the power to develop the new structure independently of the participant states. Three European Communities were thus in existence. In 1967 the Merger Treaty came into effect with the purpose of rationalizing their administration. The members of the Commissions of the EEC and Euratom, of the High Authority of the ECSC and of the Councils of all three communities were the same people, albeit wearing different hats. Thereafter, there were still formally three separate treaties and three separate European Communities, but for all practical purposes they were administered on a day-to-day basis as one. The Treaty on European Union agreed at Maastricht in December 1991 established the 'European Community' (EC) as the formal legal title of what had been the European Economic Community, but the three separate communities continue to exist.

Whereas the Coal and Steel Treaty and the Euratom Treaty were limited in the scope of the activities to which they applied, the treaty establishing the EEC was of significantly broader scope. According to Article 3 of the EEC Treaty, its activities included the elimination of trade restrictions, such as customs duties and quantitative restrictions, and the abolition of obstacles to the free movement of persons, services and capital between member states. Common policy-making in the spheres of agriculture and transport was envisaged. A system for ensuring that competition should not be distorted was to be instituted. More broadly still, Article 3h referred to 'the approximation of the laws of Member States to the extent required for the proper functioning of the common market'. Externally, a common customs tariff and a common commercial policy towards third countries were to be established. The EEC Treaty created procedures whereby legislation could be adopted in pursuance of these activities by the three leading political institutions of the Community: the Commission, the Assembly and the Council. The legislative procedures placed the Commission as the initiator in most cases, and conferred on the Assembly, which formally became the Parliament in 1987, limited powers of influence. The Council was the dominant institution in the legislative process, for in the majority of cases it held responsibility for the final adoption of legislation. The Council comprised representatives of the member states drawn from the governments of those states. In many cases it acted only by unanimity.

The aspirations of the founding fathers of the treaties were rather grand. They envisaged gradual progress towards European unity. The Preamble to the Paris Treaty of 1951 declared that the parties were 'resolved to substitute for age-old rivalries the merging of their essential interests' and that they recognized 'that Europe can be built only through practical achievements which will first of all create real solidarity'. The Preamble to the EEC Treaty of 1957 states a determination 'to lay the foundations of an ever closer union among the peoples of Europe' and a resolve to pool resources 'to preserve and strengthen peace and liberty'. Monnet and Schuman believed in the development of a process of integration, rather similar to a snowball that rolls down a hill gathering more and more snow as its descent accelerates. They thought that integration in one particular sector of the economy would spill over into integration in other sectors.[4] Modern states are so closely interdependent that any element of cooperation tends to induce further cooperation. So, they believed, coal and steel were simply a start. The eventual triumph of European integration would follow, as the weight of economic forces dictated an integrationist political response. With the advantage of hindsight, this view might now seem rather naïve. Political inertia regularly shows itself capable of shrugging off apparently irresistible forces – temporarily, if not indefinitely. Yet the early integrationists' views were not so misconceived, even though they may have underestimated the importance of political initiatives within the process. The internationalization of the European and global economy carries with it certain inevitable consequences concerning joint regulation and decision-making. The great political debates of the present decade often concentrate on the identification of matters that can be dealt with satisfactorily at national level and matters that have moved so far into the transnational domain that national political decision-making is inefficient, even irrelevant. Environmental pollution provides a classic example of a problem that does not respect national frontiers and that may, accordingly, require, at least in part, a concerted response. Aspects of the issue of the appropriate level of decision-making in the European Community have in recent times been ventilated in discussion of the implications of the 'principle of subsidiarity'.[5]

4 Political scientists have subjected this and similar theories to extensive analysis. See, e.g., Lindberg, *European Economic Integration*; Mitrany, *A Working Peace System*; Haas, *The Uniting of Europe*.
5 See pp. 12–15, 34.

THE GROWTH OF THE COMMUNITY

The Community entered the 1960s preparing to take advantage of the generally healthy global economic climate. This was a time of low unemployment and high economic growth. The six states naturally enjoyed an increase in trade between themselves, as in many cases they traded with each other in preference to former partners. That was not all. The advantages of creating an economic bloc going beyond the territory of an individual state were becoming apparent. Economies of scale accrued to the six states. Improved competitiveness followed. The establishment of the Community had not simply pooled wealth, it had created it. The EEC Treaty timetables for the reduction and eventual elimination of barriers to trade were met on and, in some cases, before the agreed deadlines. The European integration project seemed to be well on the way to being judged a success.

The impression of a flourishing Community posed important questions for those states that were on the outside looking in. The United Kingdom was torn in several directions. Its ambitions to remain one of the world's great superpowers had scarcely outlasted the Second World War, but it had not yet discovered its new role. A number of factors left the United Kingdom on the outside of the Community. It continued to owe allegiance to the Commonwealth and therefore did not necessarily wish to make a whole-hearted commitment to Europe. The desire for new national and international institutions that had gripped much of post-war Europe was less pressing in the United Kingdom, which could, after all, point to its own existing institutions as victorious and in no need of modification. Choosing to remain outside the developing Community, the United Kingdom took refuge in the European Free Trade Association (EFTA), a much less ambitious scheme, which had as its focus mere intergovernmental cooperation in purely economic matters. EFTA, which comprised several West European states not members of the EEC, proved inadequate for the United Kingdom, which was in economic terms its largest member by far. By the early 1960s the Conservative Party had determined that the United Kingdom could no longer remain on the periphery of Western Europe. Entry into the Community was no simple matter. Two sets of negotiations during the 1960s, including one conducted by a Labour Government, proved fruitless because of French opposition. Eventually, the United Kingdom, under a Conservative Government with Edward Heath as Prime Minister, acceded to the Community treaties and became a member state from the beginning of 1973. A 1975 referendum, held under a Labour Government, brought a near 2:1 majority in favour of continued membership. It now seems that the not infrequent disagreements about Europe in

British politics are conducted by the leading figures in the main political parties without bringing into question the basic fact of British membership of the Community.

In 1973 the Community of six became the Community of nine. The United Kingdom was joined as a new member by Denmark and the Republic of Ireland; Norway's application was withdrawn after a referendum showed popular rejection of accession. The three new member states were given transitional periods in which to align their economies to the demands of the Community system. This involved, for example, the progressive reduction and elimination of tariff barriers and quota systems. These transitional periods expired in 1977 and the states have long been accepted as full members. The Community extended its geographical ambit eastwards in 1981 when Greece joined, and in 1986 the total number of states reached twelve with the Iberian enlargement – the accession of Spain and Portugal. The continuing eagerness to join the 'Community club' is a strong indication that the Community is seen as a success, at least by outsiders. Many expected the accession of Spain and Portugal to signal a pause of a decade or more in the enlargement of the Community while the group of twelve took stock of its plans for new initiatives. The pace of development in what was formerly known as Eastern Europe soon forced a revision of that cautious prediction. In 1990 the former German Democratic Republic became part of the Community, albeit as an extension of the Federal Republic rather than as a thirteenth member state.

The momentum was maintained. The attraction of the EC to the remaining EFTA states was sufficiently strong to induce the states of EFTA and the states of the EC to negotiate an agreement to create an European Economic Area (EEA). The pattern of the EEA was based on an extension of the internal market framework to all the participant states.[6] The EEA came into being at the start of 1994 after crossing some unexpected hurdles. In 1991 the European Court ruled a draft agreement incompatible with the EC legal order in an opinion in which the Court was strikingly assertive about its mission to protect the Treaty, a 'constitutional charter of a Community based on the rule of law'.[7] The agreement was renegotiated and subsequently approved in an amended form by the Court.[8] The Swiss people voted by referendum in December 1992 against their country's participation. This required further readjustment before the

---

6 For an in-depth analysis, see Blanchet, Piipponen, Westman-Clément, *The Agreement on the European Economic Area* (1994). See also Cremona, 'The Dynamic and Homogenous EEA: Byzantine Structures and Variable Geometry' (1994) 19 ELRev 508.

7 Opinion 1/91 [1991] ECR I-6079. See Ch. 10, p. 321.

8 Opinion 1/92 [1992] ECR I-2821.

entry into force of the EEA at the start of 1994. The EC twelve and five EFTA states were party to the agreement. Part of the motivation for setting up the EEA was to enhance the economic advantages of integrated markets, but several of the EFTA states perceived the EEA as a useful stepping stone to full EC membership. In the event, Austria, Finland and Sweden spent only one year as members of the EEA outside the Community and they became full members at the start of 1995, raising the total membership to fifteen. Norway too had negotiated terms for accession but, once again, a negative verdict was delivered by the Norwegian people. Norway was then left with Iceland and Liechtenstein in the sparsely populated non-EC EEA. Further EC enlargement seems highly probable, perhaps by 2000. A number of states, including those of former Eastern Europe, have association agreements with the Community which are designed, in differing ways, to prepare the ground for eventual full membership.

THE SINGLE EUROPEAN ACT

The EEC Treaty of Rome survived without major amendment for almost thirty years after it came into force in 1958. However, the Single European Act, signed in 1986, and in effect as of 1 July 1987, made a number of important adjustments to the structure of the Community by expanding its formal competences and adjusting its institutional structure. Article 8a of the Act inserted into the Treaty a commitment to 'adopt measures with the aim of progressively establishing the internal market over a period expiring on 31 December 1992'. This placed on a formal footing the Commission's proposals unveiled by its President, Jacques Delors, in its programme for 1985, which had been presented to the Parliament and subsequently endorsed by the Council. The realization of the internal market by the end of 1992 in accordance with Article 8a demanded significant legislative activity by the Community.

The Act altered some voting procedures under the Treaty.[9] The requirement of unanimity in Council was replaced in some areas by qualified majority voting, in order to facilitate the passage of legislation. For example, many of the measures needed to complete the internal market by the end of 1992 required only qualified majority vote, which denied the ability of a single state or a small minority of states to block such initiatives. The Act also introduced amendments to the Community's legislative procedure, enhancing to a limited extent the powers of the most

9 These matters are examined more fully in Chs. 2–5.

overtly democratic element in the institutional structure, the Assembly[10] which was officially renamed the Parliament. The 'cooperation procedure', where it applied, introduced a 'second reading' of legislation by Parliament. The Parliament's rejection of a proposal at that stage alters voting requirements in Council from qualified majority to unanimity. This is negative in that the Parliament cannot insert its own views; and, moreover, it cannot prevent a unanimous Council overriding its objections. However, Parliament's influence is increased, especially where it is able to form an alliance with the Commission and at least one member state. In such circumstances, provided a qualified majority of states is determined to secure legislation in the field in question, it will be incumbent on the Council to accommodate the Parliament's views in a compromise solution.

The Act also introduced new Community competences. Titles inserted into the Treaty included Economic and Social Cohesion, Research and Technological Development, and the Environment. To some extent these provisions did little more than confirm initiatives upon which the Community had already embarked, but the Act placed these developments on a formal footing.[11] Similarly, the Single European Act introduced into the Treaty the first formal reference to the European Monetary System,[12] which had been in operation since 1979. Finally, the Act added separate provisions dealing with political cooperation. The member states had been consulting each other more or less informally about foreign policy for many years, having initiated the process at the Hague Summit of 1969. In practice, foreign ministers met in the framework of what became known as European political cooperation. This evolving process of collaboration was placed on a more formal footing in the Single European Act, although in this sphere intergovernmental collaboration, rather than integration, remains the norm.

10 It should not be overlooked that the Council too is comprised of democratically elected individuals.
11 Usher, 'The Development of Community Powers after the Single European Act', in White and Smythe (eds.), *European and International Law*.
12 See also Ch. 21.

THE TREATY ON EUROPEAN UNION AGREED AT MAASTRICHT

The Single European Act was both a reaction to political readiness to deepen the process of European integration and in itself an impulse in the direction of deepening. In December 1991 the heads of government and of state of the member states[13] met in Maastricht in the Netherlands and agreed further major changes to the Community structure. The new Treaty was signed on 7 February 1992. A target date of 1 January 1993 was set for ratification by all the member states after they had appropriate national approval, but this target was not achieved and the Treaty came into force on the first day of the month following the ratification of the Treaty by the last of the signatory states. Germany was twelfth and last to ratify, in October 1993, and consequently the Treaty on European Union entered into force on 1 November 1993.

The Treaty on European Union has two elements. The first stands alone, separate from the existing Community legal order, whereas the second effects a substantial amendment of the Treaty of Rome and in so doing alters its name from the EEC Treaty to the EC Treaty – officially, the Treaty establishing the European Community. So, after Maastricht, there are four treaties: the Treaty on European Union, the European Community Treaty, the European Coal and Steel Community Treaty and the European Atomic Energy Community Treaty. There are all too many potential sources of confusion, but one such source is removed by the expedient of identifying the provisions of the Treaty on European Union by the letters A–S. Numbers are preserved for the other three treaties. The Articles of the EEC and EC Treaties are referred to by their number, followed by the relevant initials, e.g., Article 1 EEC, Article 1 EC. The numbering of the provisions of the EC Treaty follows closely the pattern of the EEC Treaty as amended by the Single European Act. The Maastricht amendments have been fitted in with minimal disturbance to the existing numbers, which have become very familiar over a period of many years. There are only a few exceptions, of which the most notable may be the transformation of Article 8a EEC, which concerns the establishment of the internal market, into Article 7a EC.[14]

The Treaty on European Union is in large measure a statement of political intent, containing relatively few legally specific commitments. For example, Article A declares, *inter alia*: 'This Treaty marks a new stage in the process of creating an ever closer union among the peoples of

---

13 For composition of the European Council, see pp. 36, 87.
14 Other examples include Arts. 7, 8 EEC, now Arts. 6, 7 EC; Art. 128 EEC is subsumed in Art. 127 EC; Arts. 129 and 130 EEC become Art. 198d and 198e EC.

Europe, in which decisions are taken as closely as possible to the citizen.' The Union is wider than the European Community, although it is stated to be founded upon it. The Treaty on European Union contains two fields of activity that will be pursued by the Union although they are not pursued by the European Community. These are called, first, Common Foreign and Security Policy, which is the successor to European political cooperation; and, second, Justice and Home Affairs. Both matters are to be dealt with outside the scope of EC law as such and, in this sense, the European Union lacks a unitary structure.[15] Neither of these two fields of activity is the subject of separate treatment in this book, which is confined to EC law. Likewise, this book is not concerned with the ECSC and Euratom. Prior to the Maastricht Treaty amendments, the term 'European Community' was popularly used to denote the EEC, ECSC and Euratom together. This book examines the European Community as it is legally defined after Maastricht, as the successor to the EEC.

Article G of the Treaty on European Union provides the bridge to the EC Treaty. It contains eighty-six paragraphs, which amend large parts of the EEC Treaty. A properly consolidated version of the EC Treaty thus comprises the EEC Treaty amended by both the Single European Act and the Treaty on European Union.[16]

The centrepiece of the new provisions is found in Articles 102a–109m EC. These are the complex provisions that establish a timetable for progress towards economic and monetary union.[17] The broad purpose of this objective is set out in another new provision, Article 3a EC:

1. ... the activities of the Member States and the Community shall include, as provided in this Treaty and in accordance with the timetable set out therein, the adoption of an economic policy which is based on the close co-ordination of Member States' economic policies, on the internal market and on the definition of common objectives, and conducted in accordance with the principle of an open market economy with free competition.

2. Concurrently with the foregoing, and as provided in this Treaty and in accordance with the timetable and the procedures set out therein, these activities shall include the irrevocable fixing of exchange rates leading to the introduction of a single currency, the ECU, and the definition and conduct of a single monetary policy and exchange-rate policy the primary objective of both of which shall be to maintain price stability and, without prejudice to this objective, to support the

---

15 See Curtin, 'The Constitutional Structure of the Union: A Europe of Bits and Pieces' (1993) 30 CMLRev. 17; Select Further Reading, pp. 887–8.
16 There are other less fundamental amendments to be taken into account, such as the Treaties of Accession and the Merger Treaty.
17 See Ch. 21.

general economic policies in the Community, in accordance with the principle of an open market economy with free competition.

3. These activities of the Member States and the Community shall entail compliance with the following guiding principles: stable prices, sound public finances and monetary conditions and a sustainable balance of payments.

Under the Maastricht Treaty the EC's legislative procedures are adjusted once again.[18] These amendments are extremely complicated. There is an increase in the different procedures whereby Community legislation may be adopted, involving combinations of different institutional interrelation and different voting procedures in Council. The choice of one procedure rather than another in particular areas of Community competence depends on a careful reading of the text. However, perhaps the most striking feature of the Maastricht amendments is the introduction of a power of veto vested in the Parliament, albeit in limited areas of Community competence only. This seems likely to signal a notable increase in the Parliament's power and influence.

The Treaty adds several new fields of activity, including the following titles: Culture, Public Health, Consumer Protection, Trans-European Networks, Industry, and Development Cooperation. Moreover, it strengthens the provisions of the titles on Economic and Social Cohesion and the Environment, which were inserted by the Single European Act.

Important amendments and additions are made to the opening Articles of the Treaty, which establish some of its key principles and objectives. The first paragraph of Article G of the Treaty on European Union declares that the term 'European Economic Community' shall be replaced by the term 'European Community'. This is doubtless primarily of symbolic rather than substantive value, but, even as a symbol, it demonstrates the important wider focus of the Community's activities. The question of allocation of responsibility between different levels of administration in the Community is addressed by a new provision, Article 3b:

... In areas which do not fall within its exclusive competence, the Community shall take action, in accordance with the principle of subsidiarity, only if and in so far as the objectives of the proposed action cannot be sufficiently achieved by the Member States and can, therefore, by reason of the scale or effects of the proposed action, be better achieved by the Community.

This should be read in the light of the declaration in the Preamble to the Treaty on European Union that the states are 'resolved to continue the process of creating an ever closer union among the peoples of Europe, in which decisions are taken as closely as possible to the citizen in accordance with the principle of subsidiarity'.[19] The introduction of subsidiarity has changed the culture within the Community institutions which now consider the principle systematically before embarking on new legislation. The Commission takes the principle seriously, reviewing all draft legislation for compliance with subsidiarity and publishing the outcome in an explanatory memorandum and the key points in a recital in the Preamble to the legislation.

The Commission has developed guidelines on the application of subsidiarity, referred to in the three paragraphs of Article 3b EC. The first paragraph says that 'the Community shall act within the limits of the powers conferred upon it by this Treaty and of the objectives assigned to it therein'. There is nothing new in this paragraph, as the Community has always been restricted to acting where the Treaty gives it a legal basis to do so. The Commission guideline merely confirms that a draft measure should be examined to establish the Treaty objective to be achieved and whether it can be justified in relation to that objective and that the necessary legal basis for its adoption exists.

The second paragraph, quoted above, introduces the subsidiarity principle. The first point noted in the Commission guidelines is that this paragraph does not apply to matters falling within the Community's exclusive competence. There is no agreement as to the scope of the Community's exclusive competence but it must surely be relatively narrow. The question of whether the objectives of the proposed action cannot be sufficiently achieved by the member states and can be better achieved by the Community should be examined in the light of the following guidelines.

– the issue under consideration has transnational aspects which cannot be satisfactorily regulated by action by member states; and/or
– actions by member states alone or lack of Community action would conflict with the requirements of the Treaty (such as the need to correct distortion of competition or avoid disguised restrictions on trade or strengthen economic and social cohesion) or would otherwise significantly damage member states' interests; and/or
– the Council must be satisfied that action at Community level would produce clear benefits by reason of its scale or effects compared with action at the level of the member states (the reasons for that conclusion must be substantiated by qualitative or, wherever possible, quantitative indicators).

The Commission also conceded that the objective of presenting a single position of the member states *vis-à-vis* third countries is not in itself a

19 See also pp. 34, 143, 145 and 484.

justification for internal Community action in the area concerned.

These guidelines are inevitably somewhat general, but they do help to make the Community question whether it should act even where it does have the competence to do so. The Commission is taking fewer but, it believes, better-targeted initiatives.[20]

The third paragraph of Article 3b states: 'Any action by the Community shall not go beyond what is necessary to achieve the objectives of this Treaty.' The Commission has identified the origin of this paragraph as being the principle of proportionality developed by the Court of Justice. The paragraph is not restricted to Community action outwith its exclusive competence. The Commission's guidelines require that any burdens imposed by Community action should be minimized and should be proportionate to the objective to be achieved. Community measures should leave as much scope for national decision as possible and should respect well-established national arrangements and the organization and working of member states' legal systems. Consideration should be given to setting minimum standards at Community level and allowing member states to set higher national standards. Of particular importance is the statement by the Commission that 'other things being equal, directives should be preferred to regulations and framework directives to detailed measures. Non-binding measures such as recommendations should be preferred where appropriate.' This signals an important move away from detailed Community law that is directly applicable towards looser measures which have to be implemented and fleshed out by member states and even towards soft law (measures that have no binding force but that seek to influence).

In practical terms the Commission is committed to consulting more widely before proposing legislation and to a more systematic use of consultation documents (green papers). The Commission is also required to submit an annual report to the European Council and European Parliament on the application of the subsidiarity principle.[21] The Council will systematically examine every Commission proposal to see if it conforms with Article 3b. The working groups and Coreper will be expected, where appropriate, to describe in their reports on legislative proposals how Article 3b has been applied. In the cooperation and conciliation and veto procedures the Council will inform the European Parliament of its position concerning the observance of Article 3b. Parliament will pay particular attention to whether legislative proposals respect the prin-

20 See the decline in principal legislation proposals: over 180 in 1990, over 100 in 1991, over 80 in 1992, over 70 in 1993 and over 40 in the first ten months of 1994, see COM (94) 533 final, p. 4.
21 The first report was made on 25 November 1994, see COM (94) 533 final.

ciple of subsidiarity.[22] The commitment of the political institutions to respecting subsidiarity is reflected in the 1993 Inter-Institutional Agreement on Procedures for Implementing the Principle of Subsidiarity.[23]

It seems that up to now the Commission has been the political institution which has taken subsidiarity most seriously. Admittedly it had, by the end of 1994, withdrawn only eleven legislative proposals, none of which were of major significance, but it had simplified a number of other proposals some of which were of general importance. It also takes an over-broad approach to the Community's exclusive competence. However, the Parliament opposed the withdrawal of most of the measures that the Commission has withdrawn to date[24] and the Commission has commented critically on the Council's attitude to subsidiarity: 'principle and practice are often far apart with Member States meeting within the Council often adopting positions on individual cases at variance with their respect in principle for Article 3b'.[25]

It is extremely difficult to see how judges can decide whether a measure complies with Article 3b(2) without second-guessing the political judgment of the Community institutions. It seems likely that the Court of Justice will confine itself to a form of procedural, rather than substantive, review, i.e. requiring a reasoned statement in the Preamble to legislation as to how it is compatible with Article 3b(2).

Article 8 EC is a new provision.[26] It declares that every person holding the nationality of a member state shall be a citizen of the Union. This is a surprising provision in several respects. It is not surprising to find such a political declaration in the Treaty on European Union, but the reference to citizenship of the *Union* suggests that it might have been appropriate to leave it in that Treaty alone. Yet the member states have chosen to incorporate the status of citizen of the Union into the EC Treaty. Some of the attributes of the citizen are coterminous with those enjoyed by the economically active national of a member state prior to Maastricht.[27] Article 8a EC, for example, refers to 'the right to move and reside freely within the territory of the Member States, subject to the limitations and conditions laid down in this Treaty and by the measures adopted to give it effect'. However, some provisions reach beyond existing entitlements. For

22 See European Parliament Rules of Procedure, June 1994, Rule 54.
23 See the text in Westlake, *The Commission and the Parliament* (1994) pp. 145–6.
24 See resolution of 15 September 1993 noted in *Commission Report to the European Council on the Adaptation of Community legislation to the Subsidiarity Principle*, 24 November 1993, COM (93) 545 final.
25 *Report to the European Council on the Application of the Subsidiarity Principle 1994*, 25 November 1994, COM (94) 533 final.
26 Art. 8 EEC has become Art. 7 EC.
27 See Ch. 18.

example, Article 8b EC provides that a citizen resident in a state other than that of which he or she is a national 'shall have the right to vote and to stand as a candidate at municipal elections' in the state of residence under the same conditions as nationals of that state. The right is subject to legislative measures being adopted unanimously in Council which, as required by the Treaty, occurred before the end of 1994.[28] Citizenship of the Union is a dynamic concept, but its conversion into a concrete set of rights and duties that bears comparison with citizenship of a member state seems, as yet, remote.

The Treaty on European Union is also supplemented by a large number of protocols, some of which develop or explain the provisions of the Treaty, and some of which reflect the reservations of individual states. The former category includes the Protocol on the Statute of the European System of Central Banks and of the European Central Bank; and on the Statute of the European Monetary Institute.[29] The latter category includes the protocol that incorporates the United Kingdom's unwillingness to move to the third stage of economic and monetary union without a separate decision to do so by its government and Parliament[30] and the protocol declaring that nothing in the Treaty 'shall affect the application in Ireland of Article 40.3.3 of the Constitution of Ireland'. This refers to the protection of the unborn child recognized by the Irish Constitution.[31] A further protocol has elements of both amplification and reservation. An agreement on the implementation of further measures in the field of social policy is limited to eleven member states and recognizes the United Kingdom's decision not to participate.[32]

THE PROCESS OF RATIFICATION OF THE TREATY ON EUROPEAN UNION

The process of securing the ratification of the Treaty on European Union by all twelve member states received a jolt when the Danish people voted narrowly against ratification in June 1992. Later that month the Irish people voted in favour of ratification and a favourable response was also recorded, albeit narrowly, in the French referendum of September 1992, conducted against a background of turbulence on international capital

28 Ch. 18, p. 544.
29 See Ch. 21.
30 ibid.
31 See Ch. 19, pp. 580–81. The relevant constitutional provisions were subsequently amended.
32 See Ch. 20, p. 644.

markets. Political will remained firmly behind the Treaty. On 12 December 1992 the heads of state and government meeting in the European Council at Edinburgh reached an agreement designed to lead to resolution of the Danish problem in anticipation of a second referendum in that country. There were severe impediments to finding a satisfactory solution. The Danes were determined to secure legally binding solutions to their problems, but the other member states were not prepared to alter the Treaty agreed at Maastricht, for that would then have forced the ratification process to begin again. An ingenious and effective solution was arrived at. The European Council adopted a legally binding decision. Its precise legal status is a matter for debate. It is understood that the head of the Council Legal Service explained to the European Council that the decision would be legally binding as a matter of international law, but that it would not require the ratification process to be started afresh. The decision makes no reference to any specific legal basis in any of the Treaties of the European Communities. It appears to be a decision on the intergovernmental plane and as such escapes the jurisdiction of the European Court.

The decision does not attempt to alter the Treaty on European Union in any way. It clarifies its meaning in four key areas of special interest to Denmark; citizenship, economic and monetary union, defence policy, and justice and home affairs.[33] The elements dealing with Citizenship confirm that Citizenship of the Union does not in any way take the place of national citizenship. On economic and monetary union, a Danish opt-out from the third stage, already enshrined in a Protocol to the Treaty on European Union, is reasserted. Similarly, on defence policy and on justice and home affairs the Edinburgh decision carefully repeats what had already been agreed at Maastricht with regard to the limits of Danish obligations to participate. For all its imprecise legal status, the decision was in essence an exercise in changing the political climate in Denmark by correcting misperceptions about the Maastricht Treaty and in assuring the other member states that the Treaty had not been altered and that therefore fresh ratifications were not required.

Almost all the political parties in Denmark agreed to support a yes vote in a second referendum in 1993. The favourable vote was duly secured by a majority that was small, but rather larger than that in the no vote of 1992.

In the United Kingdom, the European Communities (Amendment) Act 1993 received the Royal Assent on 20 July 1993 after a tortuous path through Parliament. However, the main drama was yet to come because

---

33 For a thorough inquiry into the nature and purpose of the decision in each of these areas, see the first edition of this book, pp. 773–9.

section 7 of the Act said that the Act could not come into force until each House of Parliament had come to a Resolution considering the question of adopting the Protocol on Social Policy. The main opposition parties wanted the Government to accept the Agreement on Social Policy contained in the Protocol but John Major, the Prime Minister, had regarded the UK's non-participation in the Agreement as one of the triumphs of his negotiating at Maastricht.[34]

On 22 July 1993 the House of Lords approved a Resolution supporting Government policy on the Social Policy Protocol but the Government was defeated in the House of Commons. This prompted John Major to make the adoption of the Resolution a confidence issue and on the next day he obtained a comfortable majority.[35] The ratification of the Treaty on European Union was then held up by an action for judicial review brought by Lord Rees-Mogg.[36] After he decided not to appeal against the decision of the Divisional Court, the UK ratified the Treaty on 2 August 1993.[37]

Germany was the last of the twelve member states to ratify. A major reason for the delay was a direct challenge to the constitutionality of German ratification brought by a German citizen before the Bundesverfassungsgericht, the Federal Constitutional Court, in Karlsruhe.[38] Only after the court had ruled that ratification was compatible with the German constitution was German ratification possible.[39] Germany ratified the Treaty in October 1993 and in accordance with Article R(2) it came into force on the first day of the following month, 1 November 1993.

According to Article N(2), a conference of representatives of the governments of the member states shall be convened in 1996. It is stated that that intergovernmental conference (IGC) shall examine those provisions for which revision is provided, but the agenda for the IGC will doubtless be a good deal longer than is explicitly foreseen in the Treaty on European Union. The looming 1996 IGC is certain to be of fundamental importance to the future shaping of the Union.

---

34 See further Ch. 20, pp. 644–6.

35 *Hansard*, HC Vol. 229, col. 725.

36 *R v Secretary of State for Foreign and Commonwealth Affairs, ex parte Rees-Mogg* [1993] 3 CMLR 101. Cf. the follow-up decision in Scotland, *Monckton v Lord Advocate, The Times*, 12 May 1994.

37 For more detail on this case and on the United Kingdom's ratification of the TEU and implementation of the relevant parts of it into UK law, see Beaumont and Moir, *European Communities (Amendment) Act 1993 with the Treaty of Rome (as amended)* (1994).

38 English translation, *Brunner v European Union Treaty* [1994] 1 CMLR 57.

39 The ruling of *BVerfG* is notable for an expressed intent to check the *vires* of Community action; see Ch. 12, pp. 376–7.

THE OBJECTIVES OF THE COMMUNITY

The history of the Community demonstrates that the objectives of the Community are wide ranging. The title originally chosen for the most important of the three entities, the 'European Economic Community', leaves no doubt that the economy was the central declared concern of the participants. However, the emergence of the European integration movement from the devastation of the Second World War indicates that the whole process was permeated by desires that were more deep rooted than the mere liberation of the factors of production. The formal adoption of the title 'European Community' in the Treaty on European Union agreed at Maastricht confirmed a determination to ensure that the growth of the Community was not confined by a narrow conception of economic activity.

THE TASK AND THE ACTIVITIES OF THE COMMUNITY

Article 2 EC is a broadly phrased declaration of the Community's intent, which was extended by the amendments agreed at Maastricht:

The Community shall have as its task, by establishing a common market and an economic and monetary union and by implementing the common policies or activities referred to in Articles 3 and 3a, to promote throughout the Community a harmonious and balanced development of economic activities, sustainable and non-inflationary growth respecting the environment, a high degree of convergence of economic performance, a high level of employment and of social protection, the raising of the standard of living and quality of life, and economic and social cohesion and solidarity among Member States.

Articles 3 EC and 3a EC list Community activities. Some of those included in the EEC Treaty of Rome are referred to above.[40] The Maastricht Treaty added further activities to those in Article 3 EC, and includes a specific reference to the creation of an internal market. Further activities now incorporated within Article 3 EC include a policy in the sphere of the environment, the promotion of research and technological development and a contribution to the strengthening of consumer protection. Article 3a EC, inserted at Maastricht, concerns economic and monetary policy.[41]

40 See p. 4.
41 See p. 11.

THE NATURE OF THE COMMON MARKET

The choice of the creation of a common market as a central element in the Community's endeavours provides a yardstick for measuring its achievements. A common market is an ambitious project. It involves the removal of barriers to trade, direct and indirect, between the member states. Beyond that *negative* aspect, it must also embrace *positive* decision-making to establish rules and regulations that apply throughout the territory of the participant states, without regard for the old national boundaries.[42] These are the internal aspects of the common market. Externally, it involves the establishment of a common policy towards third countries wishing to import goods into the common market. The common market should present a unified face to the outside world. Broadly, the creation of a common market implies the creation of a territory encompassing several states that economically has the characteristics of just one state. The Court itself has referred to the objective of 'the creation of a single market achieving conditions similar to those of a domestic market'.[43] The Court placed this objective in its broader context in its 'Opinion on the Draft Agreement relating to the Creation of a European Economic Area'.[44] It declared that the Treaty aimed to achieve economic integration leading to the establishment of an internal market and economic and monetary union. It drew from Article 1 of the Single European Act the objective of making concrete progress towards European unity. The substantive provisions on free movement and competition were simply means to that end. This decision firmly asserted the link between economic integration and political integration, and the role of law as an instrument in developing that process.

The economic advantages of such an arrangement flow from the release of economies of scale and the stimulation of competition. Producers can supply consumers throughout the common market, instead of only the consumers of their home state. Existing manufacturing facilities can be used more efficiently. Opportunities for specialization are enhanced. It should be possible to attract investment more readily. The eventual winner is the consumer, who should, in principle, be able to choose from a wider range of better-quality, lower-priced goods. Efficient allocation of re-

---

42 On the nature of negative and positive integration, see Tinbergen, *International Economic Integration*.

43 Case 26/76 *Metro* v *Commission* [1977] ECR 1875; see also Case 270/80 *Polydor* v *Harlequin* [1982] ECR 329.

44 Opinion 1/91, [1991] ECR I-6079, [1992] 1 CMLR 245.

sources is secured by the interplay of the forces of supply and demand in the free market.

The common market envisaged by Article 2 EC should be distinguished from other forms of economic cooperation and integration.[45] A *free-trade area* involves the free movement of goods between the participating states. However, the states remain free to decide their own policies for trade outside the free-trade bloc. Tariffs may differ. This may tempt a producer outside the free-trade area to try to evade the high tariffs of state A by importing products into the bloc via a low-tariff state B and then moving them on to state A. However, the participants in a free-trade area will not permit this: they typically restrict free trade to goods originating within one of the participant states; third-party goods are excluded. The free-trade area is accordingly limited in its ambition, because of the unwillingness of the participant states to coordinate their external trade policy.

In a *customs union* the states are prepared to take that further step. A common external tariff is established. There is no distortion attributable to the importer's choice of point of entry into the customs union. Accordingly, all goods that have reached the market of the customs union are entitled to free movement within it, irrespective of their origin. The customs union draws the states together more closely than a free-trade area, for it requires negotiation in pursuit of the establishment of the common external tariff and then permits free trade in all goods in circulation within the area, not simply goods originating in one of the participant states.

The common market typically takes two further steps. First, it envisages a broader scope to the right of free movement. Within a common market, goods, persons, services and capital ought, in principle, to be entitled to free circulation, so that, in theory, they can be allocated to their most economically efficient use at the most economically efficient location. A further aspect of this broader freedom may also emerge in an extended interpretation of the nature of barriers to trade. The control of technical non-tariff barriers to trade is frequently a well-developed element of a common market. Secondly, a common market typically envisages common policy-making by the participating states in relation to both external and internal matters. In this respect the common market may assume elements of a political character, which takes it into realms to which a customs union does not aspire. This development may in turn require institutional arrangements to be put in place.

---

45 Jackson, *World Trade*; McGovern, *International Trade Regulation*. See also refs. under 'The Objectives of the Community' in Select Further Reading. For a collection of relevant essays see Jacquemin and Sapir (eds.), *The European Internal Market*.

OBSTACLES TO THE ACHIEVEMENT OF THE COMMON MARKET

After more than thirty years of development, the Community has not yet achieved the status of a common market. It enjoyed much early success in meeting the timetable for its transformation into an economically integrated area. Wisely, the drafters of the EEC Treaty had incorporated dates at which specified steps would be taken in the pursuit of integration. Article 8 EEC declared that 'the common market shall be progressively established during a transitional period of twelve years', which comprised three stages of four years each. This placed the end of the transitional period at the end of 1969. The elimination of trade barriers was achieved step by step through the course of this period. Article 13 EEC, for example, required that 'customs duties on imports in force between Member States shall be progressively abolished by them during the transitional period in accordance with Articles 14 and 15', which set the timetable. The success in eliminating trade barriers was such that the customs union was achieved in 1968, eighteen months in advance of the scheduled date. The accession of new member states is achieved through similar staged progression. For the three states that acceded in 1973, the United Kingdom, Ireland and Denmark, transitional arrangements relating to tariffs and quotas ran until the end of June 1977. Reference to the transitional period still appears in many important Treaty provisions, but it has now lost its general relevance.

However, after the first flush of success, the Community began to find progress increasingly elusive. Apparently insuperable obstacles confronted attempts to reach agreement on the removal of the more tenacious barriers to trade, such as those arising from the different tax regimes of the member states. Practices such as state subsidies in support of domestic industry and public purchasing that favoured domestic producers and suppliers remained rife, even though it is fundamentally incompatible with a common market to use nationality rather than quality as the criterion for purchase. Moreover, the scope of common policy-making was, in practice, much narrower than envisaged by the Treaty, leaving important decisions in the hands of individual states. The Community's phase of dynamic early development was at an end. The Community seemed paralysed during the 1970s and early 1980s.[46]

Two factors account for this slide into stagnation. First, economic optimism of the early years of the Community had been replaced by the

---

46 There were exceptions; e.g., the first direct elections of the European Parliament and the creation of the European Monetary System in 1979 and the social policy directives of the 1970s (see Ch. 20).

global economic depression, attributable in large part to the oil price rises of the early 1970s. The Community was severely afflicted by the decline in the health of the economy, manifested by rises in both inflation and unemployment. The short-term panacea of national protectionism, often motivated by domestic political pressures, on occasion proved a more attractive response than the more intangible, longer term benefits offered by integration within the Community.

Second, the political will needed to sustain the Community was in decline. Decisions were too often not being taken in the Community institutions. In part, this was attributable to the heterogeneity of interest comprised within the Community, which made agreement on controversial topics very difficult to achieve. This problem deepened as the Community was enlarged and, indeed, it is a problem that is faced anew as the Community continues to enlarge in the 1990s. However, when the problem first appeared in the 1960s, a solution seemed at hand. The drafters of the EEC Treaty had foreseen the likely difficulty in reaching unanimous agreement and had provided for it: after a stipulated transitional period a range of major decisions would be taken by qualified majority vote in the Council (the body responsible for the adoption of legislation), not by unanimity. No state would hold a veto. In this way, difficult decisions on which a minority of states held contrary views would none the less be adopted and the Community would not be tied to the pace of the slowest participant. This system of majority voting was a key feature of the anticipated development of the Community. The inability of a single state to deny the wishes of the majority clearly manifested the diminution in national sovereignty that each state accepted in joining the Community. However, the structure did not develop in practice in the manner planned by the Treaty.

Once the due date for the introduction of qualified majority voting in many areas was reached, the French opposition to the disappearance of the national veto proved so entrenched that France simply withdrew from the administration of the Community for a period of several months. This spell is wryly referred to as 'la politique de la chaise vide'. This crisis was resolved only when a compromise formula was reached in Luxembourg in January 1966. The so-called 'Luxembourg Accords' were no more than an agreement to disagree.[47] France declared its belief that a veto over Community policy-making existed where a state felt that its vital national interests were at stake. The other states simply noted this view without accepting it and the Community resumed everyday work with the participation of all six states. The Accords may have lacked formal legal status, but the effect

47 See Ch. 3.

on Community practice was profound. Spoken or unspoken, the Luxembourg Accords and the national veto operated to inhibit the passage of decisions by majority vote. Difficult decisions were not taken. The Community had failed to develop into a body equipped with autonomous powers to act in the face of the opposition of a minority of its states. This restricted its role to intergovernmental cooperation dependent on unanimous support for action.

THE NATURE OF THE INTERNAL MARKET

In the early 1980s the Commission took the view that the Community had to be reawakened. The inspired choice of stimulus was the plan to complete the 'single market' or the 'internal market' by the end of 1992.[48]

The 'internal market' was defined in Article 8a EEC, a provision inserted by the Single European Act, as 'an area without internal frontiers in which the free movement of goods, persons, services and capital is ensured in accordance with the provisions of this Treaty'.[49] This is an uncompromising agenda. It sets an objective of removing all internal frontiers between the member states, with a view to ensuring that trade between England and France becomes in principle as simple as trade between England and Scotland. As far as the economy is concerned, national boundaries should become irrelevant.

This plan has vitally important economic significance and is fascinating for the lawyer too, but, above all, '1992' was an attempt to get the Community 'up off its backside and running', to quote Lord Cockfield, a British member of the Commission, who was one of the architects of the project. Millions of people who had little idea what the 1992 plans actually involved were none the less suddenly aware of the existence and importance of the Community. The Community leapt from obscurity to the front page of every serious newspaper in Western Europe and beyond.

The Commission needed support for the merits of this plan if it was to demonstrate that 1992 was more than a public-relations exercise designed to boost the profile of the Brussels bureaucrat. Such support was supplied by Paolo Cecchini, an Italian economist, who produced a vast report that quantified the benefits on offer if the member states of the Community would agree to surrender the range of barriers to trade that they had

---

48 For discussion of aspects of the project, see Bieber, Dehousse, Pinder and Weiler (eds.), *1992*; Lodge (ed.), *The European Community*; Dehousse, '1992 and Beyond: the Institutional Dimension of the Internal Market Programme' [1989/1] LIEI 109. See also Select Further Reading, p. 887.
49 Now contained in Art. 7a EC.

maintained in spite of their long-standing but apparently discarded commitment to a common market.[50] Cecchini showed that a genuinely barrier-free market would liberate a wave of competitive energy that would sweep away national complacency and replace it with much more efficient European-based structures. Manufacturers would produce for over 340 million consumers and could cut their unit costs of production accordingly: these are economies of scale. Goods could be made at their most cost-effective location in the Community without the constraints of national boundaries. Consumers would enjoy a wider and better choice. Naturally, Cecchini foresaw that a period of disruptive industrial restructuring could be expected. The Community might presently possess twelve widget producers, one for each state, where, in fact, only three are needed. The creation of the internal market would shake out a great deal of inefficient 'dead wood'. Short-term unemployment seems inevitable, but Cecchini argued that the creation of new employment opportunities would far outweigh such short-term losses. Cecchini produced some rough guides to the benefits he perceived. The Community's gross domestic product would increase by some 6 per cent, which amounts to a gain of approximately £140 billion; 5 million new jobs would be created; prices of consumer goods would fall by, on average, some 6 per cent. So 1992 was about boosting the Community's profile, but it was also about money.

Commission President Jacques Delors first presented the '1992 idea' to the Parliament in early 1985, and the Commission's plan for the completion of the internal market by the end of 1992 first appeared in developed form in its White Paper on the subject,[51] published in June 1985 and approved by the Milan Council later that month. This classified the trade barriers that stood in the way of the realization of a single market within the Community according to three types: fiscal, physical and technical. The White Paper identified 300 measures that needed to be adopted before the internal market could become a reality, a figure subsequently adjusted to 282. The Council having accepted the plan, the Commission prepared the necessary legislative proposals, initially under the enthusiastic stewardship of Lord Cockfield, who was the Commissioner responsible until the end of 1988. From 1985 onwards the Commission devoted a great deal of energy to preparing the legislation, guiding it through the legislative procedures involving, where appropriate, the Parliament and ultimately the Council, and then supervising implementation, where necessary, by the member states.

Of course, despite the political support for the plan, it would have failed

50 For a summary, see Paolo Cecchini, *The European Challenge*.
51 COM (85) 310.

if, as before, the difficult decisions had simply been blocked in Council by a single dissentient member state exercising its national veto. A formal change in Community decision-making procedures was needed. Thus the 1987 Single European Act was a crucial complement to the 1985 White Paper. One of its most important tasks was to amend the EEC Treaty to adjust the Community's institutional balance in some areas in favour of majority voting. Article 100a was introduced in derogation from Article 100, which had required unanimity in Council, to permit the adoption by qualified majority vote of measures needed to achieve the objectives set out in Article 8a EEC. The purpose was to ease the passage of difficult decisions relating to the completion of the internal market by the end of 1992. This was essential, above all, in order to provide business with sufficient confidence about the successful outcome of the drive to complete the internal market to make the necessary investment decisions that, more than any legislative act, will serve to ensure that market integration is attained.

The internal market is not a new concept. The economic analysis offered by Cecchini is no different in principle from that which had inspired the original proponents of the common market more than thirty years earlier. Indeed, the internal market may seem rather less ambitious in its scope than the common market to which the Community originally committed itself in 1958. The internal market seems to give a priority to the removal of trade barriers without an equal commitment to the complementary introduction of common policies. But it seems only fair to judge the 1992 project against the state of the Community in the early 1980s, not against what have proved to be elusive, even abstract, goals. Its specific timetable for the removal of trade barriers has revived the process of market integration. The 1992 project has succeeded in ensuring that the Community is once again a leading actor in the development of European politics.

The impact of the completion of the internal market will vary sector by sector.[52] In a sector already open to cross-border competition it may not radically alter the competitive structure of the market. In some industries the economies of scale on offer by virtue of participation in the Community market may already have been achieved. By contrast, in sectors that were previously stubbornly protected by high barriers to cross-border trade and that involve products that are readily transportable across borders the impact may be very substantial and rapid restructuring may be anticipated. It is, of course, essential for business to plan ahead.[53] Market integration

52 This was recognized and explored by Cecchini, *The European Challenge*. See also Mayes (ed.), *The European Challenge*.
53 See, e.g., Dudley, *1992*.

presents opportunities in the form of the accessibility of new markets, but it also poses threats in the shape of competitors from other member states eager to invade existing markets.

BEYOND THE INTERNAL MARKET

It was always misleading to suppose that the completion of the internal market could be defined solely by changes in the law at midnight on 31 December 1992. In law, the basis of the project was the *acquis communautaire* described in this book and, in particular, the provisions guaranteeing free movement of the factors of production contained in the original Treaty of Rome. True, a significant number of legislative measures were required to build on these Treaty provisions in order to achieve the completion of the internal market and many of these measures were due to come into force at the start of 1993. However, others had already come into force in advance of 31 December 1992 and some, although a small minority, were not yet in force. Moreover, the reality of the completion of the internal market remained and remains dependent on national implementation of Community rules. The speed of implementation at national level has accelerated, but still falls some way short of 100 per cent and varies state by state. The internal market is accordingly in an advanced stage of evolution but still requires some refinement. Even after the successful completion of the internal market, the rules of the market continue to require supervision both by the Commission and by private individuals who enjoy directly effective rights conferred by Community law. The Commission has long insisted on the importance of private enforcement of Community law and this technique was further encouraged by a report published at the end of 1992 by a committee chaired by Peter Sutherland, which seeks to enhance awareness of rights under Community law. The Commission has focused with increasing rigour on securing the effective application of the legal rules that underpin the internal market.[54]

In fact, it is rather misleading to assess the process of completion of the internal market simply by reference to a specific date and a list of measures that have or have not been adopted and have or have not been implemented. The reality of market integration will be achieved through commercial planning and decision-making. Firms that restructure their product distribution networks and their corporate take-over strategies along European instead of national lines will be the real motors of

54 Ch. 16, p. 480.

integration. The distinctively 'national' firm ought to decline in economic relevance in tandem with the decline of the distinctively national market. Ultimately, the purchasing patterns of consumers will demonstrate the existence of an integrated market. There is overwhelming evidence that this process is far advanced. This is the heart of market integration.

The 1992 process, as a reinvigoration, was a beginning, not an end in itself. Long before the end of 1992 the Community was already setting itself new objectives. A committee comprising the twelve governors of the member states' central banks and three independent monetary experts was set up by the European Council in 1988 under the chairmanship of the Commission President, Jacques Delors.[55] It reported in 1989 and the so-called 'Delors Report' set forth, *inter alia*, a three-stage programme for the achievement of economic and monetary union.[56] The European Council accepted this as the next target after the completion of the single market, and intense efforts were devoted to preparing the necessary political and legislative initiatives. These came to fruition at the end of 1991 in the increased commitments to deeper integration that were agreed at Maastricht.

The Treaty on European Union made significant revisions to the existing EEC Treaty and converted it into the European Community (EC) Treaty. The centrepiece of these amendments was the establishment of a programme for a three-stage progress to economic and monetary union. In the third stage a single currency, the ECU, will be established.[57] There are several perceived advantages of this move towards yet closer integration. By eliminating exchange-rate fluctuation between member states, commercial confidence and certainty is promoted. Such stability should prove efficient and it should stimulate economic growth. Transaction costs of currency conversion are eliminated. The Community's ability to deal in its own single currency will also have important international implications, both in terms of protection secured by a strong single currency against external economic pressures and as a means of reinforcing the Community's capacity to dictate trading conditions. The establishment of monetary union between the member states is also likely to bolster the efficacy of the Community's policy-making initiatives, for they will be backed by a stable currency that is not susceptible to being undermined by the erratic economic behaviour of a single state. The corollary to this is the diminution in individual states' capacity to pursue economic policies independently of their Community partners. Individual

55 See Ch. 3.
56 See more fully Ch. 21.
57 The United Kingdom negotiated a protocol permitting it to opt out of this stage; the same is true of Denmark, see p. 659.

states will lose control of interest rates, exchange rates and money supply to the independent European Central Bank. States will be prevented from accumulating excessive government budget deficits by the threat of sanctions imposed by the Council. These are changes that will present a vivid demonstration of the scope of the transfer of powers within the Community structure.

The Community has thus continued to prove itself able to maintain its momentum by elaborating specific plans of action. Thus, when the states of Eastern Europe achieved freedom from Soviet domination in 1989, the Community was immediately seen as the key structure within which discussions about the future shape of the Continent could take place. New goals could be set in order to accommodate the aspirations of a Europe that had suddenly expanded. The majority of the states of former Eastern Europe aspire to Community membership in the medium term. These developments extend beyond economics. The Community found itself with responsibility thrust upon it.

The contrast with 1945 is remarkable. The economy of Europe is once more strong. The single market due for completion in 1992 was already able to compete on equal terms with the economies of North America and the Far East. The economic integration of Europe appears ready to go wider and deeper. Europe will doubtless never regain its nineteenth-century pre-eminence in the world, but once more it has a vital role to play – this time, as an integrated bloc. From this perspective, the Community has achieved many of its objectives. It has converted nation-states with declining global influence into participants in a powerful economic entity. From this perspective, the effect of Community membership, despite the views of some critics, is not a diminution in national sovereignty, but instead a means of sharing in enhanced sovereignty. Integration yields more than an aggregation of power; it creates power. Integrating Europe is a means of preserving and expanding rapidly disappearing power in an increasingly international economic climate.

THE SUBSTANTIVE LAW OF THE COMMUNITY[58]

The aspirations of the Community are broad. They encompass economic, social and political matters. The European Community Treaty constitutes a set of legal rules that are designed to bring about these objectives. The

[58] This section provides an overview of the law examined in depth in Chs. 13–27.

law is being used as an instrument of economic and social integration. Given this function, it is unhelpful to view Community law merely as a set of rules independent of their background. The legal system of the Community must be assessed in the light of the broader objectives of the Community. Indeed, as will be seen, the law of the Community has contributed in no small measure to the development of the Community and to the gradual achievement of its objectives.

LAW OF ECONOMIC INTEGRATION

The heart of the Community is the pursuit of economic integration. Accordingly, the heart of the substantive law of the EC Treaty is the range of provisions that prohibit the erection or maintenance of barriers to trade between member states. They are the ground rules for the construction of the economically integrated territory that is replacing the separate economies of the member states.

The Treaty rules have as their focus the establishment of the 'four freedoms': the free movement of goods, the free movement of persons, the free movement of services and the free movement of capital. The Treaty prevents individual member states restricting the free movement of these 'factors of production' across national boundaries, except in narrowly defined circumstances. The release of the factors of production ensures the economic energy required to develop a market that is governed by considerations of demand and efficiency, instead of by artificial national boundaries.

The first of the four freedoms, the free movement of goods, has generated the most litigation.[59] Liberating the market in manufactured goods has been at the forefront of economic integration. Fiscal trade barriers are controlled by Articles 12 EC and 95 EC. Article 12 EC outlaws the imposition of customs duties between member states. Article 95 EC forbids the imposition of taxation on imported goods, which discriminates in favour of home-produced goods. So, for example, the UK found itself obliged to amend a taxation system that favoured beer, a typical British product, over wine, which is typically imported.[60] Member states have not lost the power to develop their own tax regimes, but they are subject to the obligation that the system be 'tax-neutral' as far as origin of Community goods is concerned.

Article 30 EC forbids physical and technical barriers to trade. It has

---

59 See Chs. 13–17.
60 Case 170/78 *Commission* v *UK* [1983] ECR 2263, [1983] 3 CMLR 512, p. 410 below.

proved to be one of the most vigorous instruments for the dismantling of national laws that restrict trade. Holding goods at frontiers in order to subject them to inspections has been held an unlawful restriction on the free movement of goods. Governments may not encourage their consumers to favour home-produced goods. Article 30 EC has even been used to tackle national rules that restrict the free movement of goods despite their apparent equal application to home-produced goods and imports. German beer purity laws, which stipulated the permissible ingredients for beer to be sold in the Federal Republic, were struck down by the European Court in 1987.[61] The rules applied to all beer, wherever it was made, but the effect was to exclude from the German market beers made according to the different traditions of the other member states. The result of this approach is that once a product has been lawfully made in one member state, it is in principle entitled to access to the markets of all the other member states, thereby securing economic integration and conferring on the consumer the ultimate choice of product on grounds of quality, not origin. Only exceptionally can a state uphold a restriction on trade; recognized derogations include the protection of public morality and public health.

The second of the four freedoms, the free movement of persons,[62] is secured for workers by Article 48 EC and for the self-employed by Article 52 EC. The existence of rights to cross frontiers vested in individuals extends the role of the Community beyond that of a bloc limited to trade in goods, and is a vivid manifestation of the fact that the Community is about people.

The freedom to provide services[63] is contained in Article 59 EC and complements the right of establishment in Article 52 EC. Both provisions are of particular value to companies and other commercial concerns wishing to take advantage of the wider market. There will, however, remain differences between, for example, the company law regimes of different states. These differences will hinder free movement, but may be justified in law if shown to exist for legitimate reasons.

The free movement of capital[64] is covered in Article 67 EC. This has long been the least regarded of the freedoms, but in the context of the proposals for economic and monetary union, the place of capital liberalization has assumed central importance.

Several of these provisions are subject to exceptions, albeit narrowly

---

61 Case 178/84 *Commission* v *Germany* [1987] ECR 1227, [1988] 1 CMLR 780, p. 496 below.
62 See Chs. 18–19.
63 See Ch. 19.
64 See Ch. 21.

construed. Threats to public health may justify the control of imports. More generally, a state may be able to point to matters of national commercial, social or consumer protection policy that justify the maintenance of national measures that operate as barriers to trade between member states. The Treaty mechanism for dismantling these lawful trade barriers is harmonization. In the Community harmonization means the establishment of a common, unified Community system that replaces the divergent, market-partitioning national systems. The development of harmonization legislation is therefore an important method of opening up the market by removing the residual areas of lawful barriers to trade. It is also, of course, a field where the Community takes a positive role in creating its own policy, which visibly supersedes national competence. The failure to pass harmonization legislation was one of the great stumbling blocks of the Community during the 1970s and early 1980s, and progress in this field was vital to the reinvigoration of the Community in the approach to 1992. Consequently, the Single European Act of 1987 ensured that most harmonization legislation designed to complete the single/internal market could be passed by qualified majority vote, rather than requiring unanimity.[65]

THE COMPETITION RULES

The substantive legal rules mentioned so far are primarily addressed to the state: governments and other public bodies are forbidden from maintaining trade barriers. But Community law is of much wider significance; it reaches into the private sector. It would be fruitless to prevent states from partitioning the market along national lines if private firms were simply to step in and take their place by carving up the territory of the Community for their own purposes. Therefore, the EC Treaty includes a competition policy.[66] The basic competition rules are contained in Articles 85 EC and 86 EC, which ensure supervision of the activities of commercial undertakings in the market. They are designed to control anticompetitive behaviour, and, particularly, to put a stop to any attempt to treat the market as a divisible collection of states instead of a single market.

Article 85 EC concerns cartels and anticompetitive practices. It contains a basic prohibition on agreements that distort patterns of trade in the common market, although there remains the possibility of exemption of agreements shown to yield specified economic advantages. Article 86 EC provides for supervision of the activities of a single firm, rather than a

---

65 The style of harmonization has also changed. Ch. 17 examines the new approach to technical harmonization.
66 See Chs. 22–7.

cartel. A firm in a 'dominant position' must not 'abuse' that position of economic strength. The administration and enforcement of the competition rules is the province of the Commission, subject to review by the Court of First Instance. The Commission enjoys strikingly broad powers to intervene in order to put an end to unlawful practices and to impose fines on participating firms. The competition rules also apply to the state when it participates in the economy. Public monopolies and nationalized industries are subject to the competition rules notwithstanding their link to the state, and the Commission has had no hesitation in challenging unfair practices in these sectors. These rules are supplemented by those guaranteeing supervision of state aids, found in Article 92 EC.

COMMUNITY POLICY-MAKING

The removal of trade barriers in order to liberalize free trade is plainly central to the Community's endeavours. However, the Community legal order extends beyond prohibitions to a range of important positive aspects, such as the role of harmonization and the competition rules. The Community is involved in the creation of common policies to provide regulation of the free market that the EC Treaty has created. The most developed of the Community's common policies is also its most notorious: the Common Agricultural Policy (CAP).[67] Its problems aside,[68] this is an important example of how policy-making has been transferred from the individual member states to the Community institutions, although the administration of the CAP remains a matter for national authorities. Other common policies, in the area of fisheries and transport, for example, are gradually taking shape as the regulatory competence of the Community begins to mature.[69]

The Single European Act put several areas of developing Community activity on to a formal legal basis. Thus, policy in the areas of economic and social cohesion, research and development, and the environment have been the subject of explicit coverage in the Treaty since 1987. The Treaty on European Union agreed at Maastricht took this process still further by extending existing competences and adding new ones in the areas of culture, public health, consumer protection, trans-European networks, industry, and development cooperation. Above all, the Maastricht Treay

67 The CAP is not examined separately in this book. See, e.g., Snyder, *Law of the Common Agricultural Policy*.
68 Difficulty in achieving a satisfactory balance between producer and consumer interests is endemic to any system of agricultural policy, national or international.
69 For a survey, see Mathijsen, *European Union Law*, Part 3.

established the procedures whereby economic and monetary union will be attained.

This book devotes special attention to the development of a Community social policy,[70] a key component in the creation of a positive aspect to the Community. A social policy is concerned with providing protection for individuals to complement the liberalization of the market. If the negative aspects of Community law are concerned with securing the integration of the market, then the positive aspects are concerned with the consequences of that integration. Fierce political debate has surrounded the question of a Community social policy. The United Kingdom has adopted a particularly sceptical line over the desirability of such initiatives and refused to participate in the Agreement on Social Policy entered into by the other eleven member states at Maastricht. Both the Agreement and the United Kingdom 'opt-out' are recorded in a Protocol to the Treaty on European Union.

Questions about the Community's regulatory competence are in many respects concerned with the allocation of responsibilities to different levels within its developing structure. That is to say, defining the Community's regulatory competence cannot be divorced from defining the member states' regulatory competence. The Treaty agreed at Maastricht made a formal commitment to the principle of subsidiarity. It is referred to in the Preamble, in which the states resolved that decisions shall be 'taken as closely as possible to the citizen in accordance with the principle of subsidiarity'.[71] This notion seems more political than legal. The Community, like the United States before it, needs to develop its own method of assimilating national and regional diversity within broader integrated structures. The United Kingdom insisted that the word 'federal' be excluded from the Treaty on European Union and, given the lack of mutual understanding between states with different legal and political traditions as to the meaning of federalism, there is much to be said for the view that the introduction of the word would have been more hindrance than help.[72] Indeed, an examination of federal systems throughout the world reveals many different models. Significantly more power is vested in the central institutions in the United States than in, for example, Belgium.[73] However, whatever label or formula might be used, the Community finds itself in need of a clearer idea of how to achieve a balance of power between institutions at different levels in the administrative structure.

70 See Ch. 20.
71 See also Art. 3b EC, pp. 12–15.
72 Lord Mackenzie Stuart, formerly the President of the European Court, has observed that 'the words "federal" and "federation" have no precise meaning . . . Can we not ban these words from all discussion?' (Letter to *The Times*, 22 June 1991). He was particularly concerned that ambiguous words should not be used in legal texts.
73 See Cappelletti, Seccombe, Weiler (eds.), *Integration through Law*.

Internal unity is impossible without external unity. The true common market presents a uniform face to the outside world.[74] Goods entering the territory of the common market from third countries must pay the same tariff and be subject to the same rules no matter which member state's ports they happen to arrive at. To achieve this external unity, the Community has developed a common customs tariff. However, the external implications of the EC extend beyond its physical frontiers. In some areas that fall within Community competence, the Community has replaced the individual member states as the responsible body for negotiating with third parties. This has led to the establishment of important common external Community policies as well as common policies in the internal sphere. Thus the negotiation of some commercial agreements with third parties is the job of the Community, as part of the development of a common commercial policy. The Community has participated in discussions within the General Agreement on Tariffs and Trade (GATT), in the United Nations Conference on Trade and Development (UNCTAD) and in the OECD. It enjoys exclusive power to impose anti-dumping duties and countervailing duties on goods that it considers to be penetrating the Community market at an unfairly low price.[75] The Agreement on the World Trade Organization, the culmination of the Uruguay Round, was concluded by the Community and the member states as a matter of joint competence.[76] The Community also takes seriously its responsibilities to the states of the developing world; the Lome Conventions have proved particularly important instruments in this context.

THE EC's INSTITUTIONAL STRUCTURE[77]

The key feature of the European Community, which distinguishes it from most international organizations, is the existence of a sophisticated set of institutions enjoying autonomous powers to advance its interests. The Treaty of Rome established a set of institutions that have as their task the supervision of the process of economic integration. They hold the power to pass legislation to bring about the desired objectives. The evolution of the EC has seen many formal and informal changes in the role and

---

74 For an overview, see Pinder, *European Community*, Ch. 9.
75 See Ch. 8, esp. pp. 234–7 and 244.
76 See Ch. 10, pp. 322–4.
77 This section provides an overview of the law examined in depth in Chs. 2–5.

interrelation of the institutions. A brief sketch of the role of the four principal EC institutions follows.

THE INSTITUTIONS

The Council is the representative of the interest of the individual member states.[78] The membership of the Council alters depending on the nature of the subject-matter under discussion. If agricultural affairs are under discussion, the agriculture ministers of each state will comprise the Council; budgetary matters bring the finance ministers to the table. Where matters of general EC interest are at issue, the national foreign ministers will form the Council. At least twice a year heads of government of fourteen member states and the President of France meet as the European Council. Each state holds the presidency of the council for a six-month period in rotation. The most important feature of the Council, then, is that its membership is drawn from the ranks of national government ministers. They come to the Community table bearing their own national interests, albeit in the Community framework, at the forefront of their thinking.

The Commission, by contrast, is the representative of the Community interest.[79] Based largely in Brussels, it exists to administer the EC on a day-to-day basis. It supervises the correct application of the treaties, and, if necessary, takes steps against states acting in breach of them.[80] It is led by a president, an office held during the drive towards the completion of the internal market by a Frenchman, Jacques Delors, who was succeeded in 1995 by Jacques Santer, a Luxembourg national. The Commissioners are drawn from the member states and are appointed by the governments of the states. However, once appointed, the Commissioner's allegiance is to the Community. A national of one member state, he or she is working on behalf of all the member states. The work of the Commission is divided among directorates-general, which develop and execute policy in particular areas of Community competence. These directorates-general are staffed by EC civil servants drawn from all the member states.

The Parliament contains 626 directly elected members.[81] In an attempt to embellish its European credentials, the members (MEPs) sit by political affiliation, rather than by nationality. The largest group has long been the Socialists, although no group has ever come close to commanding an overall majority. The Parliament is not of the model familiar to observers

78 See Ch. 3.
79 See Ch. 2.
80 See Ch. 7.
81 See Ch. 4.

of national parliaments in Western Europe. Its formal powers under the EEC Treaty were severely limited. It had certain rights of participation in the legislative process and of supervision of the Commission. It also exerted a rather tenuous informal influence over the Commission and Council. The feeble powers of the Parliament, which is, after all, the only Community institution directly elected by the people of Europe, left the Community glaringly exposed to allegations that it was democratically flawed. In recognition of this failing, the Parliament had conferred upon it a cautious raising of its profile in the Single European Act and, again, in the Treaty on European Union, where it obtained for the first time a right of veto over legislative proposals in some areas. The pressure for radical improvements in the Community's democratic voice remains high on the institutional agenda.

The fourth and final major institution is the Court, based in Luxembourg.[82] The Court is composed of judges drawn from national legal professions, but, of course, once appointed, they sit as judges of the Community Court, untainted by national bias. Proceedings before the Court are largely written, not oral. The Court is assisted by an advocate-general, who presents an opinion on the case, prior to the Court's ruling, thereby providing the judges with learned, though not binding, assistance. The Court delivers only one, collegiate judgment. Even in its earliest years the Court showed itself prepared actively to develop Community law and it has made a major contribution to the impact of Community law in the national legal orders of the member states. In 1989 a Court of First Instance was introduced as a means of reducing the heavy workload of the original Court.

THE LEGISLATIVE PROCEDURE[83]

The passage of EC legislation is the field in which the interrelationships of the Community institutions are at their most delicate. The balance of powers within the legislative process is, in fact, a useful guide to the health and vitality of an independent European Community.

Particular Treaty provisions possess their own procedures for the making of relevant legislation. The respective roles of the Council, Commission and Parliament differ in technical ways, often for no apparent good reason. However, a general pattern may be discerned. This places the Commission as the body responsible for the initiation of Community policy, which endows it with certain strategic advantages, but it is not normally the ultimate legislator. The Parliament then enjoys a right to be consulted in relation to a number of legislative provisions. Its role in this

82 See Ch. 6.
83 See Ch. 5.

respect has been extended by the Single European Act and the Treaty on European Union, but it remains unable to impose its view on the other institutions, save for the veto conferred in limited areas at Maastricht. The Council normally has the power to decide whether to pass the measure as a new piece of Community legislation.

This model obviously provides that the Council normally acts as the ultimate legislator. The Council, as explained above, is the body in which the national interest is represented, whereas the Commission and Parliament are usually taken to act in pursuit of the wider Community interest. This indicates the formidable practical constraints to the growth of an autonomous Community with the vitality necessary to pursue policies of general Community interest. The Council's place as the central component in the legislative process means that its voting procedures determine whether or not Community legislation designed to advance integration will be adopted. Until the early 1980s a unanimous vote was required in Council for the passage of major legislation. This was either because the relevant Treaty provision required unanimity in Council or, where the Treaty required qualified or simple majority voting, due to a member state invoking its non-legal 'veto' under the notorious Luxembourg Accord. The Single European Act contributed to the modification of this situation by establishing that in order to complete the internal market by the end of 1992, voting procedures in Council for most internal market legislation would be altered from unanimity to qualified majority. Member states have thus accepted that they may be outvoted in Council and bound by legislation that they find unappealing. They have done this in the confident expectation that the economic benefits of 1992 are worth the burden of some unattractive legislation. The Luxembourg Accord veto could still be invoked, but it has been used very rarely indeed since the passing of the Single European Act. For the Community, the switch away from unanimous voting is an important shift in the institutional balance, because dissent in Council cannot now so readily block Community legislation. In this way, the autonomy of the Community and its ability to pass legislation in the general Community interest despite minority dissent have been enhanced.

COMMUNITY LEGISLATION

The legislative process yields three major types of Community legislation:[84] the regulation, the directive and the decision. The regulation is the most

---

84 See Ch. 5.

powerful strand of Community legislation. It has the force of law in all member states once made. The directive sets out a general policy goal, but leaves it to each member state to implement the directive in its own national order. Thus, whereas a regulation is already law in every member state when it emerges from the Community legislative process, a directive is intended to have legal effect once it has been transformed into national law by national means. The third strand of Community legislation, the decision, is more akin to an administrative rather than a legislative measure. For example, the Commission may issue a decision to a single member state or to a firm directing it to terminate a practice unlawful under Community law. The decision is binding, but it is not a measure of general application.

The European Court stands ready to hear applications for judicial review of Community legislation.[85] It is possible to attack regulations, directives and decisions on several grounds of illegality. Article 173 EC provides the Court with the juridiction to review the legality of any legislative act. Member states may thus challenge the acts of the Community institutions. Private individuals too may challenge measures that affect their interests, although, in common with most administrative law systems, there are restrictive laws of standing that must be satisfied before such an action can be pursued.

THE CONSTITUTIONAL PRINCIPLES OF COMMUNITY LAW

THE SUPREMACY OF COMMUNITY LAW

The relationship between Community and national law is left unexplained in the EC Treaty. At an early stage in the development of the Community legal order the European Court declared Community law to be 'supreme'; that is, Community law prevails in the event of conflict with national law.[86] The Court considers that the principle of supremacy is inherent, if not explicit, in the very structure of the Treaty. If national law could be upheld against Community law, the states could simply go their own way, ignoring the obligations of Community membership and thereby destroying the unity at the heart of the process of economic integration in the common market. If it is to work, then Community law can only be

85 See Ch. 8.
86 See Ch. 12.

supreme. The Court's view was expressed without equivocation in its decision in *Costa v ENEL*:

... the law stemming from the Treaty, an independent source of law, could not, because of its special and original nature, be overridden by domestic legal provisions, however framed, without being deprived of its character as Community law and without the legal basis of the Community itself being called into question.[87]

THE DIRECT EFFECT OF COMMUNITY LAW[88]

Community law may be 'directly effective'; that is, it may be pleaded by litigants before domestic courts. Like the principle of supremacy, the principle of direct effect is not to be found in the EC Treaty, but has instead been deduced by the European Court as a necessary legal device for achieving the objectives of the Treaty. In *Van Gend en Loos* the Court ruled that

... the Community constitutes a new legal order of international law for the benefit of which the States have limited their sovereign rights, albeit within limited fields, and the subjects of which comprise not only Member States but also their nationals. Independently of the legislation of Member States, Community law therefore not only imposes obligations on individuals but is also intended to confer upon them rights which become part of their legal heritage.[89]

The cumulative effect of the two key principles of supremacy and of direct effect lends Community law immense practical vitality in domestic litigation. Direct effect ensures that an individual litigant is able to raise a relevant point of Community law before a national court; supremacy then ensures that the Community law right will prevail over the national rule in the event of conflict.

ARTICLE 177 EC: THE PRELIMINARY REFERENCE PROCEDURE

The preliminary reference procedure[90] established by Article 177 EC allows collaboration between a national court and the European Court when a point of Community law is raised before the national court. The

---

87 Case 6/64 [1964] ECR 585, 594.
88 See Ch. 11.
89 Case 26/62 [1963] ECR 1, 12.
90 See Ch. 9.

principles of direct effect and of supremacy are not, on their own, sufficient to create a truly coherent legal order. A national court might be quite willing to apply Community law, but find itself bemused by its complexities. Worse, a national court might confidently apply Community law on its own initiative while simultaneously a national court in another member state is applying the same provision in an entirely different manner. If that happens, Community law will mean one thing in one state and something quite different in another. Unity in a common market would simply not occur.

Where a point of Community law is raised before a national court, that court is competent under Article 177 EC to seek assistance from the European Court on how to interpret it. This allows the European Court to deliver authoritative rulings on the meaning of Community law in order to preclude the development of divergent interpretations in different states. The Court in Luxembourg can oversee the development and application of the Community legal order. However, the European Court does not actually decide the case in hand. Its interpretation of Community law is returned to national level, where the case is then disposed of accordingly. The two levels of courts thus collaborate in the development of Community law.

CONCLUSION

Treaties, several of which have contributed to the development of the Community, are recognized instruments of international law under which states assume obligations. In Community law, however, there is a commitment to integration that transcends the traditional flavour of mutual obligations under international treaties. As the Court observed in *Van Gend en Loos*, the states have 'limited their sovereign rights'. The Court has consistently and energetically espoused the view that the Community legal order has its own distinctive characteristics. It is neither national law, nor international law; it is *sui generis*; it is Community law. The combination of the constitutional principles of the Community legal order led the Court in December 1991 to declare that the EC Treaty constitutes the constitutional charter of a Community based on the rule of law.[91]

91 Opinion 1/91, note 44 above. See Mancini, 'The Making of a Constitution for Europe' (1989) 26 CMLRev 595.

CHAPTER 2

Commission

COMPOSITION

The Commission of the European Community is made up of twenty Commissioners, one of whom is the President, appointed by common accord of the governments of the member states.[1] The Council can alter the number of members of the Commission by unanimous vote. No qualifications are prescribed for Commissioners other than that they must have general competence, their independence must be beyond doubt and they must be nationals of a member state. No more than two may be nationals of any one state.[2] In practice, the five largest states – France, Germany, Italy, Spain and the United Kingdom – are able to select two of their nationals as Commissioners, and the other member states select just one.

In the United Kingdom this has meant that the Prime Minister of the day appoints one Commissioner from his or her party and one from the largest opposition party in the House of Commons. Up to now this has meant one Conservative and one Labour politician. The other member states that have two Commissioners have not always adopted the practice of having one from the Government party and one from the leading opposition party. The leading German opposition party, the Social Democrats, did not have a Commissioner chosen from their ranks between 1987 and 1994, and both the German Commissioners during that period came from different parties in the centre-right coalition Government.[3] In the Ortoli Commission of 1973 the German Christian Democrats did not have

1 See Art. 157 EC. At Maastricht the Dutch presidency proposed a reduction in the number of members of the Commission to one per member state, but this was not agreed. Instead the intergovernmental conference agreed in a declaration that the member states would examine the questions relating to the number of members of the Commission before the end of 1992. No changes were made and the accession of Austria, Finland and Sweden on 1 January 1995 merely led to an increase in the size of the Commission from 17 to 20; see Arts. 9 & 30 of Council Decision 95/1, OJ 1995 L1/1.
2 See Art. 157(1) EC.
3 From January 1995 a prominent German trade unionist, Monika Wulf-Mathies, was appointed as one of the two German Commissioners.

a Commissioner, and both Commissioners came from the centre-left coalition Government. Likewise, the French Commissioners of that period were drawn from the Gaullist Government or from another party on the centre-right.[4]

Some of the British Commissioners have been very senior politicians who have held one or more of the great offices of state. Roy Jenkins, now Lord Jenkins of Hillhead, was President of the Commission from 1977 to 1981, having been Chancellor of the Exchequer (1967–70) and Home Secretary (1965–7, 1974–6) in Labour Governments. He has been the only major British politician still at the peak of his career when he went to the Commission, and he was enticed by the carrot of being the President. Sir Leon Brittan was appointed a Commissioner in 1989, having held, among other Cabinet jobs, that of Home Secretary (1983–5) in a Conservative Government. Other British Commissioners have been Cabinet ministers of lesser rank, such as Christopher Soames, later Lord Soames, who had been Secretary of State for War (1958–60) and Minister for Agriculture (1960–64) in a Conservative Government, and George Thomson, now Lord Thomson, who had been Chancellor of the Duchy of Lancaster (1966–7, 1969–70) and Secretary of State for Commonwealth Affairs (1967–8) in a Labour Government, both of whom were Commissioners from 1973 to 1977. Lord Cockfield, a Commissioner from 1985 to 1989, had been Secretary of State for Trade (1982–3) and Chancellor of the Duchy of Lancaster (1983–4) in a Conservative Government, and Bruce Millan, a Commissioner from 1989 to 1995, had previously been Secretary of State for Scotland (1976–9) in a Labour Government. Some Commissioners have even been junior ministers or humble backbenchers: Ivor Richard, now Lord Richard, was a parliamentary under-secretary in the Ministry of Defence (1969–70) in a Labour Government before serving as a Commissioner (1981–5); Stanley Clinton Davis, now Lord Davis, was a parliamentary under-secretary in the Department of Trade (1974–9) in a Labour Government, before becoming a Commissioner (1985–9); and Christopher Tugendhat was a Conservative MP (1970–76) before serving as a Commissioner (1977–85). Neil Kinnock, who took up office in January 1995, never held Government office but was Leader of Her Majesty's Opposition from 1983 to 1992.

The fact that two-thirds of the British Commissioners have previously been Cabinet ministers is not significantly out of line with the position in other member states. The Commission of 1981–5 was headed by a former Prime Minister of Luxembourg, Gaston Thorn, and also contained seven

4 See Van Miert, 'The Appointment of the President and the Members of the European Commission' (1973) 10 CMLRev 257, 260–61.

former Cabinet ministers. Thus eight of the fourteen members were of Cabinet rank.[5] It was not until January 1989 that the Commission ceased to be exclusively male, with the appointment of two women. Five of the twenty Commissioners appointed in 1995 are women.

Commissioners are appointed for five years.[6] This is renewable, but few British Commissioners have served more than one term,[7] although others would, it seems, have liked to serve for longer, but have earned the disapproval of the Government of the day and have not been reappointed.[8] Community law prescribes that Commissioners shall be

completely independent in the performance of their duties. In the performance of these duties, they shall neither seek nor take instructions from any Government or from any other body. They shall refrain from any action incompatible with their duties. Each Member State undertakes to respect this principle and not to seek to influence the members of the Commission in the performance of their tasks.[9]

Thus Commissioners are protected from Government influence during their term of office. They retain their individual political philosophies, but each Commissioner is not expected to conform to the policy of the Government of the member state of which he or she is a national. However, Commissioners who are out of tune with the Government of the member state of which they are nationals may well find that their appointment is not renewed. There is a danger that Commissioners will, at least in their public statements, avoid major policy differences with their Government in order to have their appointment renewed. There is, however, little or no evidence of this. Recent United Kingdom Commissioners drawn from the Conservative Party have very publicly disagreed with the Conservative Government on such issues as harmonization of indirect taxes and on monetary union. For example, Lord Cockfield, as Commissioner responsible for the internal market, had championed the proposal of the harmonization of indirect tax rates, which was included in

5 See Tugendhat, *Making Sense of Europe*, p. 141. There is some evidence that in the earlier days of the Community some Commissioners of limited ability were appointed as a means of removing them from the national political scene; see Van Miert (1973) 10 CMLRev 257, 263.

6 See Art. 158(1) EC.

7 Christopher Tugendhat served 8 years, Bruce Millan 6 years and Sir Leon Brittan is scheduled to serve at least 11 years.

8 Ivor Richard was not reappointed in 1985, although it is believed the Leader of the Opposition wished that he should remain the Labour politician on the Commission. Lord Cockfield was not reappointed in 1989 and it is widely believed that Margaret Thatcher, the Prime Minister, thought he had 'gone native'; see George, *An Awkward Partner*, p. 197.

9 Art. 157(2) EC.

the Commission's White Paper *Completing the Internal Market*,[10] but was consistently opposed by the British Government.[11] Sir Leon Brittan advocated an independent European Central Bank of a federal nature administering a single currency as part of monetary union and urged the British Government not to reject monetary union and end up in the slow lane of a two-speed European Community.[12] At the time the British Government was advocating a hard ECU, a parallel rather than a single currency, and was opposed to the idea of handing over control of monetary policy to an independent central bank.[13]

It is possible for a Commissioner to maintain a dignified public silence as to his or her personal views and merely to represent the collegiate view of the Commission. Such a Commissioner would be acting in a way consistent with the notion of collective responsibility. This would seem to be a more appropriate role for a Commissioner than engaging in advocacy of a personal vision of the future of Europe. If Commissioners made it clear that they were simply representing the Commission's collective view, which they may have disagreed with in the privacy of the Commission deliberations, on issues such as harmonization of indirect tax rates and monetary union, they would not leave themselves exposed to accusations that they have 'gone native' and would enhance the strength of the Commission's views by standing on that ground rather than on that of their own personal political weight.

PRESIDENT

The Community treaties say little about the role of the President of the Commission. In fact, prior to the amendments made at Maastricht it was merely stated that the President and six Vice-Presidents of the Commission were appointed by common accord of the Governments of member states for a two-year period, which could be renewed.[14] While the role of the six Vice-Presidents was a cosmetic one to give the senior Commissioners a grand title, the role of the President has grown in significance. At Maastricht a new procedure for appointment of the President and the members

---

10 COM (85) 310.
11 See George, *An Awkward Partner*, pp. 195–7.
12 See *The Times*, 28 March 1990 and 18 July 1990.
13 See the Major plan, announced in a speech to the German Industry Forum by John Major, Chancellor of the Exchequer, on 20 June 1990 and reported in *The Times*, 21 June 1990.
14 Art. 14 Merger Treaty.

of the Commission was agreed.[15] The Governments of the member states will nominate by common accord the person they intend to appoint as President. Significantly, the Governments will be obliged to consult the European Parliament first.[16] Rule 32 of the European Parliament's Rules of Procedure[17] provides that the nominee will be requested to make a statement to Parliament and that, following a debate, Parliament is to approve or reject the nomination by a majority of the votes cast.[18] If the Parliament rejects the nomination then the President of the Parliament will request the Governments of the member states to withdraw their nomination and present a new one to Parliament. The Governments would not be bound by such a request but it is unlikely that a nominee would proceed in the face of opposition from the Parliament. Thus the Parliament probably has a *de facto* veto on who is to be nominated as President of the Commission. The nominee for President is then consulted by the Governments of the member states before they nominate the people they intend to appoint as Commissioners. The nominated President and members of the Commission will be voted on as a body, not individually, by the European Parliament. Rule 33 of the European Parliament's Rules of Procedure envisages that the nominated President and nominated members of the Commission will provisionally allocate the portfolios and that the nominees will appear before the appropriate committees of Parliament according to their prospective fields of responsibility. The nominees are not required to submit to this grilling by the committees but in fact the nominees for the 1995 Commission did so. This is an example of the European Parliament gaining more power than is envisaged by the EC Treaty by clever use of its Rules of Procedure. It was generally considered that the committee hearings in early 1995 were relatively tame. All they can do is report their conclusions to the President of the Parliament. Although a few of the nominees were subject to adverse criticism the Parliament has no power to vote on them individually. After all the hearings have been concluded the nominee for President of the Commission presents the programme of the nominated Commission at a sitting of Parliament. After a debate the Parliament votes its approval or disapproval by a simple majority of the votes cast.[19] On 18 January 1995 the Santer

15 Art. 158(2) EC.
16 This is something that had been done in practice although it was not required by law.
17 European Parliament Rules of Procedure (9th ed., June 1994).
18 In July 1994 at a European Council meeting in Brussels the Heads of Government of the member states nominated Jacques Santer, then Prime Minister of Luxembourg, as the new President of the Commission. M. Santer did make a statement before the Parliament and was approved by 260 votes to 238, with 23 abstentions (see Bull E.U. 7, 8/94, 1.6.3).
19 Although Art. 158(2) EC does not specify what the voting requirements are, Rule

Commission was approved by 416 votes for, 103 votes against and 59 abstentions. The concerns about the competence or institutional attitude of a minority of the nominees provoked only a small minority of the MEPs into voting against the Commission as a whole. It would seem that the Parliament's *de facto* veto over the nominees for President is much more significant than its *de jure* veto over the nominated Commission as a whole. It is politically very unlikely that the Parliament would ever be dissatisfied with enough of the Commission nominees to block the appointment of them all.[20] If approved by the Parliament, the President and members of the Commission will be appointed by common accord of the Governments of the member states. The requirement to have six Vice-Presidents of the Commission was removed at Maastricht and replaced by a discretion given to the Commission to appoint one or two Vice-Presidents from amongst its members.[21]

The President chairs the meetings of the Commission and proposes the allocation of portfolios to individual Commissioners after informal preliminary discussion with colleagues. The decision, however, is a collective one, and there can still be heated discussion in the Commission before final agreement is reached.[22] In October 1994 in a contentious meeting of the nominated Commission in Luxembourg, Sir Leon Brittan failed in his bid to have relations with Eastern Europe and the former Soviet Union included in his portfolio. Instead the Commission backed Jacques Santer's allocation of those relations to Hans van den Broek, the former Dutch Foreign Minister.[23] The President has a seat by right at the annual international summits of the group of seven leading industrial countries[24] and at the European Council.[25] He presents the Commission's annual

33(5) of the Parliament's Rules of Procedure specifies that a majority of votes cast is sufficient.

20 The Conference of the Representatives of the Governments of the Member States formally decided to appoint the new Commission for a five-year period beginning on 23 January 1995, in Decision 95/12; see OJ 1995 L19/51.

21 See Art. 161 EC. The new 1995 Commission appointed Sir Leon Brittan and Manuel Marin as Vice-Presidents.

22 This was particularly so in 1970, 1977 and 1981 (see Tugendhat, *Making Sense of Europe*, pp. 140–41), but it would seem that President Jacques Delors has been able to allocate the portfolios with little difficulty.

23 See *The Times*, 31 October 1994.

24 This has been the case since the late 1970s when the then President, Roy Jenkins, attended to represent the European Community notwithstanding the fact that four of the participating states (France, Germany, Italy and the United Kingdom) were member states of the Community. The other participating states are Canada, Japan and the United States.

25 It was clear from the first session of the European Council in Dublin on 10–11 March 1975 that the President of the Commission attended the European Council and was privy to the 'fireside chats' of the heads of government and of state of the member states

legislative programme to the European Parliament early in the calendar year, and replies to the debate on the programme.[26]

From the merger of the separate Commissions for the EEC and Euratom and of the High Authority of the ECSC into one Commission in July 1967 until the late 1980s an informal agreement operated whereby a President was appointed for two or, at most, four years and the nationality of the President rotated around the member states. This was partly due to the French hostility to Walter Hallstein, a German Christian Democrat, who had been the first President of the EEC Commission from January 1958 to July 1967, and saw the Commission as an embryonic federal government for Europe. The Gaullist French Government of the time opposed such grand designs and wanted to limit the authority of the presidency by curtailing the period of office.[27] The first President of the merged Commission was Jean Rey, a Belgian Liberal. He was succeeded in 1970 by an Italian Christian Democrat, Franco-Maria Malfatti, who did not complete his two-year mandate.[28] The French Gaullist François-Xavier Ortoli was President from January 1973 to January 1977, and he was succeeded by Roy Jenkins of the United Kingdom and Gaston Thorn of Luxembourg, each serving a four-year term.

The pattern was broken by Jacques Delors, a French Socialist. He served as President for ten years from January 1985 to January 1995. On a strict rotation of nationalities the President appointed in 1985 should have come from Denmark or Ireland, which had never held the presidency, or from Germany, Belgium, the Netherlands or Italy, which had all occupied the presidency but before the previous French President, M. Ortoli. The reasons for this change in pattern are fully known only by the members of the Governments of the member states who agreed to appoint M. Delors and to renew his mandate.[29] It could be that the French raised no objections to a prominent personality as Commission President, even for such a long period, because the Socialists were in power and the person

---

away from the Foreign Ministers. (See Bulmer and Wessels, *The European Council*, pp. 50, 112.) The President's position in the European Council was guaranteed by Art. 2 of the Single European Act, and Art. D of the Treaty on European Union confirms the equality of the heads of government and of state of the member states and the President of the Commission at the European Council. They are 'assisted by the ministers of foreign affairs of the Member States and by a member of the Commission'.

26 See e.g., *The Commission's Programme for 1990*, EC Bull. Supp. 1/90 and Jacques Santer's presentation to the Parliament on 15 February 1995.

27 See Van Miert, (1973) 10 CMLRev 257, 266.

28 A Dutch Socialist, Sicco Mansholt, was appointed President for the remainder of Malfatti's two-year period.

29 The renewals of Delors's mandate beyond the normal four years were made at the European Council meetings in Hanover in 1988, in Dublin in 1990, and in Lisbon in 1992.

concerned was 'one of them'.[30] Why the other member states gave up their 'prior claim' to the presidency is unknown, but perhaps they were not able to offer a politician of sufficient stature who wanted to do the job. The extension of Delors's mandate is also hard to explain. The British Government was certainly unsympathetic to some of Delors's ideas about the Community,[31] but may have been persuaded that he should have the opportunity to carry through the completion of the internal market, a cause the British Government and the other member states thoroughly approved of, by the beginning of 1993. It was Delors who had suggested this target date in presenting the Commission's legislative programme to the European Parliament early in 1985.[32] The willingness to surrender some national interests in dropping a strict rotation of the presidency and in allowing an individual politician to stamp his mark on the development of Europe by having a protracted period as President are two of the signs of the renewed commitment to the Community that emerged in the late 1980s. The search for a successor to Jacques Delors did not involve a reversion to the idea of giving a country who has not had a President the opportunity to have one. Following the veto by John Major of the nomination of the Belgian Prime Minister, Jean Luc-Dehaene, it was agreed to nominate the Luxembourg Prime Minister, Jacques Santer, even though a former Luxembourg Prime Minister had been President of the Commission in the early 1980s. Santer is likely to be a much less visionary President of the Commission than Jacques Delors but whether there is much to choose between him and Jean Luc-Dehaene is debatable. Jacques Santer will serve as President at least until January 2000.

The position of the President is enhanced by the fact that the Governments of the member states have to agree on who it should be, and he or she is consulted by those Governments before they nominate the members of the Commission.[33] The nominee for President is voted on by the Parliament separately and therefore clearly has its confidence whereas

30 Delors had been the French Finance Minister from 1981 to 1984 in the Socialist Government.
31 Delors had said, in a speech to the European Parliament, in July 1988 that 'in ten years 80 per cent of economic legislation — and perhaps tax and social legislation — will be directed from the Community'; see OJ 1988, Annex, Debates of the European Parliament, 1988–9, no. 2–367/140. Mrs Thatcher, in a BBC radio interview, said this statement went 'over the top' and served only to 'frighten people'. The disagreement between Delors's and Thatcher's vision of Europe is discussed in George, *An Awkward Partner*, pp. 192–8.
32 See *The Thrust of Commission Policy*, EC Bull. Supp. 1/85, 14–15 January 1985. In June 1992 John Major was willing to back Delors as President until 1995 due to the lack of a suitable alternative candidate who would command the support of the other member states.
33 See Van Miert, (1973) 10 CMLRev 257 and Art. 158(2) EC.

individual members of the Commission are not voted on individually but only collectively. In theory, the Commission is not appointed by the Council. This emphasizes that it is independent of the Council and not its creature. In practice, the members of the Council or European Council meet in the margin of a Council or European Council meeting to appoint the Commission; the same people wearing their Government representatives' hats rather than their members-of-the-Council hats.[34]

The President of the Commission can be responsible for promoting major ideas that are later adopted by the Council or European Council. Roy Jenkins can be regarded as one of the fathers of the European Monetary System because he revived the concept of economic and monetary union in a speech in Florence on 27 October 1977.[35] Certainly it took the leadership of the German Chancellor, Helmut Schmidt, and the French President, Giscard d'Estaing, to launch the specific proposal of the EMS at the European Council in Copenhagen in April 1978 and to carry the idea through to agreement.[36] As noted above, Jacques Delors and his fellow Commissioners were the architects of the proposal to complete the internal market by the end of 1992. The idea of the internal market goes back to the original EEC Treaty itself, but the plan to establish a timetable for its completion and to set out the legislative measures needed to achieve it was presented to the European Parliament by the Commission headed by President Delors in its programme for 1985.[37] The European Council endorsed the 1992 goal for completion of the internal market at their meeting on 29 and 30 March 1985. Subsequently, the EEC Treaty was amended by the Single European Act partly to facilitate the completion of the internal market. These two examples show that major progress in the Community cannot be achieved without the approval of the European Council, but they also show that the Commission, or at least its President, can be influential in promoting ideas that are adopted by the European Council.

34 See eg. Decision 95/3 of 1 January 1995, OJ 1995 L1/222.
35 See Tugendhat, *Making Sense of Europe* p. 137.
36 See Bulmer and Wessels, *The European Council*, pp. 63, 81–3.
37 EC Bull. Supp. 1/90.

DISMISSAL

Individual members of the Commission, including the President and Vice-Presidents, can be dismissed (compulsorily retired) during their term of office only by the Court of Justice on an application by the Council or the Commission. The Court will do this only if the Commissioner no longer fulfils the conditions required for the performance of his or her duties or has been guilty of serious misconduct.[38] Only one Commissioner Albert Borschette, has been dismissed in this way, and that was because he was in a coma and was not going to recover. He died shortly after being replaced by Raymond Vouel.[39]

The whole Commission could be dismissed by the European Parliament if a motion of censure were to be carried by a two-thirds majority of the votes cast, provided it constituted a majority of the members of the European Parliament.[40] This power has never been used. This may be because it is not selective and compels Parliament to dismiss Commissioners it is happy with as well as those it might wish to get rid of. Another factor is that the new Commission would be appointed by common accord of the Governments of the member states in the same way as outlined above. Hence, until the Maastricht Treaty amendments the Parliament had no say in the appointment of the new Commission and the only remedy would have been to dismiss it too.[41] More positively, the Parliament is usually content with the work of the Commission, and its battle for greater legislative power is with the Council and the member states.

DECISION-MAKING

The Commission meetings are held in private. Sometimes the Commission invites the official responsible for a proposal to attend. Commission decisions are arrived at by a majority vote,[42] though in practice attempts

38 See Art. 160 EC.
39 See Comm. Dec. 76/619 (OJ 1976 L201/31) and Kapteyn and Verloren van Themaat, *Law of the European Communities*, p. 110, note 39.
40 Art. 144. See Ch. 4, p. 100 for the attempts to use this power.
41 After the Maastricht amendments, the Commission as a whole has to be approved by the Parliament: Art. 158(2). Art. 144 is amended to clarify that the new Commission appointed to replace the Commission sacked by the Parliament is appointed only for the remainder of the latter's term of office.
42 Art. 163.

are made to reach consensus. The Commission has the power to adopt rules of procedure,[43] and the importance of compliance with these is shown by *BASF AG and Others* v *Commission*.[44] In this case Article 12 of the then Rules of Procedure, which required the original text of Commission measures to be annexed to the minutes in which their adoption was recorded, was not complied with in adopting Commission Decision 89/190. The Commission was unable to produce an authenticated version of the decision, which was then declared non-existent by the Court of First Instance. The Court of Justice decided that the failure to follow the correct procedure in adopting the decision was not of 'such obvious gravity that the decision must be treated as legally non-existent'.[45] However, the Court of Justice decided that a failure to authenticate the decision in the way required by the Commission's Rules of Procedure constituted an infringement of an essential procedural requirement and therefore the decision was annulled. Only simple corrections of spelling and grammar may be made to the text of an act after its formal adoption by the college of Commissioners. The college must agree not only the operative part of the act but also the statement of reasons.[46]

Once a decision has been taken, any Commissioners who voted against it are expected to support the Commission decision in public. The principle of collective responsibility was confirmed by the European Court in *AKZO Chemie* v *Commission*. 'All the members of the college of Commissioners bear collective responsibility on the political level for all decisions adopted.'[47] Each Commissioner has a personal staff, known as his or her cabinet, and the *chefs de cabinets* have an important role in preparing the items for consideration at meetings of the Commission.[48] A *chef de cabinet* may attend the meetings of the Commission in the absence of the Commissioner and, at the invitation of the President, state the views of the absent member.[49] Non-controversial matters are dealt with by a written procedure whereby each Commissioner is sent a written proposal that will be adopted if none of them raises any objections within the period stated, usually a week.[50] In 1992 the written procedure was used 2,200 times.[51]

---

43 Art. 162(2). The Commission's Provisional Rules of Procedure of 6 July 1967 (OJ Spec. Edn 2nd Ser. (VII) p. 14) were replaced by the Rules of Procedure of the Commission of 17 February 1993 (OJ 1993 L230/15) which came into force on 11 September 1993.
44 Joined cases T-79/89, T-84–6/89, T-89/89. T-91–2/89, T-94/89, T-96/89, T-98/89, T-102/89 and T-104/89, [1992] ECR II-315 and the appeal decision of the Court of Justice in Case C-137/92P *Commission* v *BASF AG* [1994] ECR I-2555.
45 Case C-137/92 P at para. 52.
46 ibid. at paras. 67–70.
47 Case 5/85 [1986] ECR 2585, 2614.
48 See Kapteyn and Verloren van Themaat, *Law of the European Communities*, p. 112.
49 Art. 8 of the Commission's Rules of Procedure.

Another way of ensuring that the weekly Commission meetings tackle only matters of some importance is for routine decisions, like the many technical agriculture regulations, to be delegated to the Commission member responsible for that area.[52]

In 1992 about 7,000 measures were adopted in this way. Article 11 of the Commission's Rules of Procedure authorizes the Commission to delegate its powers to members of the Commission or its officials; and the Commission has adopted an internal decision laying down the principles and conditions on which delegations of authority would be granted.[53] Decisions delegating authority must be adopted at meetings of the Commission and such delegations may be made only to designated persons for designated categories and everyday measures of management or administration. The Commission will only delegate powers where 'the principle of collective responsibility is fully respected'.[54] The Court accepts that a requirement of collective deliberation by the Commission in all cases would have a paralysing effect on the work of the Commission,[55] but the Court will not accept the delegation of decisions of principle such as decisions finding infringement of Article 85 EC.[56]

The twenty Commissioners and the personal staff in their cabinet are at the apex of the Community staff who work for the Commission. The Community civil service is not large. In 1994 the Commission had an authorized staff of 18,562 of whom all but 1,029 were in permanent posts.[57] By contrast the United Kingdom had 533,350 civil servants on 1 April 1994, including 6,034 in the Scottish Office, 10,183 in the Ministry of Agriculture, Fisheries and Food, and 11,616 in the Lord Chancellor's department.[58] The relatively small size of the Community's staff enables

50 See Art. 10 of the Rules of Procedure.
51 See Noel, *Working Together*, p. 51. For many years Emile Noel was Secretary-General of the Commission, the leading civil servant in the Commission who attends the Commission meetings.
52 ibid.
53 See Case 5/85, note 47 above, p. 2614.
54 Art. 11 of the Rules of Procedure.
55 See Case 5/85, note 47 above, p. 2615. See also Case C-200/89 *Funoc* v *Commission* [1990] ECR 1-3669, 3692.
56 Case C-137/92P above at para. 71.
57 See the *General Report on the Activities of the European Union 1994* (Luxembourg, EC Official Publications, 1995), p. 420. See also Ch. 3, note 5; Ch. 4, note 32; Ch. 6, note 9.
58 *See Civil Service Statistics 1994*, London, HMSO. *Public Expenditure, Statistical Supplement to the Financial Statement and Budget Report 1994–95* (1994, Cm 2519) indicates that the outturn for UK total central Government expenditure in 1992–3 was £158 billion, of which the net running costs of central Government were £17 billion. The proportion of UK Government running costs to total expenditure is about 10–11 per cent. If the Government's plans for 1995–6 are fulfilled the percentage would drop to just under 10 per cent.

administration costs to be kept comparatively low.[59] The staff are divided into over twenty directorates-general; e.g., competition, agriculture, external relations, etc. The Director-General and his or her senior staff report to the Commissioner who has been allocated the portfolio that covers their directorate-general.[60] Frequently a Commissioner will be responsible for a portfolio that covers more than one directorate-general.[61]

In preparing proposals for new legislation the relevant directorate-general will sometimes ask a committee of national experts to consider a draft before it is submitted to the *chefs de cabinets*, the Legal Service and then the Commission for approval.[62] Some of the committees are permanent – e.g. the Scientific and Technical Research Committee – and some contain representatives of the interest groups concerned. The experts are often national civil servants, but, of course, their views do not bind their respective Governments. This system helps the Commission to anticipate national reactions to their proposals and the draft could be amended in a way that makes its acceptance by the Council more likely.[63] The Commission will also use the consultation system where it has the power to take a decision or make a regulation itself if it feels the matter is important enough to justify it.

The Legal Service has about eighty lawyers and twenty lawyer-linguists, headed by the Director-General, who, in practice, attends meetings of the Commission to give legal advice. The Legal Service seeks to ensure that Commission proposals are in line with Community law, that the Commission's prerogatives are respected by the Council, that a coherent legal policy is adopted by all the Commission directorates-general, and that the drafts are accurate in all the Community languages.[64] Article 20 of the Commission's Rules of Procedure requires that: 'The legal service shall be consulted on all drafts of or proposals for legal instruments and on all documents which may have legal implications.'

59 In 1993 the Community's budget appropriations for administration were 4.9 per cent of the Community's total budgeted expenditure; see the *EC Financial Report 1993*. Most of the Commission staff are based in Brussels, but over 2,600 are still situated in Luxembourg; see Noel, *Working Together*, p. 51.
60 In 1989 there were 501 senior Commission officials from Director-General down to head of unit, but only 10 of them were women; see Hay, *The European Commission*, p. 8.
61 In the Commission of 1989–91 Karel Van Miert was responsible for Transport, Credit and Investments, and Protection and Promotion of Consumer Interests and in the 1995–2000 Commission, Emma Bonino is responsible for Consumer Affairs, Humanitarian Aid and Fisheries, although these subjects are handled in different directorates-general.
62 See Gordon-Smith, 'The Drafting Process in the European Community' (1989) StatL Rev 56, 57–8 and Buitendijk and van Schendelen, 'Brussels Advisory Committees: A Channel for Influence?' (1995) 20 ELRev 37–56.
63 See Noel, *Working Together*, pp. 52–3.
64 Gordon-Smith (1989) StatLRev, 56, 57–8.

LEGISLATIVE ROLE

INITIATION

The EC Treaty does not grant a general legislative power to the Community institutions; different Articles of the Treaty provide power to make legislation in specific fields and prescribe a variety of processes for making that legislation.[65] The Commission is nearly always required to initiate the legislative process by making a proposal.[66] The Commission exercises this power with due diligence.[67] There are a few exceptions to the Commission's right of initiative: the Court can request the Council to legislate on changes in the Court of First Instance's jurisdiction,[68] the European Parliament can draw up proposals for the Council on the procedure for its elections, and some legislation can be passed by the Council on the recommendation of the European Central Bank.[69] There are also other occasions where the Council legislates after the Commission has made a recommendation rather than a proposal.[70] The power to pass the legislation rests with the Council in nearly all cases.

The Council is not compelled simply to wait for a Commission proposal. It can request the Commission to undertake studies and submit to it any appropriate proposals for the attainment of any of the objectives of the Treaty.[71] The European Parliament was given a similar power under Article 138b of the EC Treaty by the amendments agreed in the Treaty on European Union. The Commission still retains discretion as to the content and timing of the proposal it makes to the Council.

While the Commission has the sole power to initiate legislative proposals, it is true that major political initiatives within the Community may

---

65 Art. 235 does give the Council a general legislative power to achieve 'one of the objectives of the Community' where the Treaty has not provided the necessary powers, but it requires a proposal from the Commission; see Ch. 5.

66 See the detailed list of Treaty provisions requiring a proposal from the Commission before legislation can be passed in Noel, 'The Commission's Power of Initiative' (1973) 10 CMLRev 123, 125, fn. 3.

67 In 1994 the college of Commissioners held 46 meetings and sent the Council 52 proposals for directives, 305 proposals for regulations and 201 proposals for decisions; see *General Report 1994*, at p. 420.

68 Art. 168a.

69 Arts. 106(6), 109.

70 See Ch. 5.

71 Art. 152. See also the more specific power, introduced at Maastricht, to request a proposal or recommendation from the Commission in relation to some aspects of economic and monetary policy in Art. 109d. Here the Commission is to submit its conclusions to the Council without delay.

come from the European Council.[72] The European Council set up a committee to 'study and propose concrete stages leading towards economic and monetary union' at Hanover on 27–8 June 1988 rather than giving the job to the Commission. This was possible because the creation of such a union required amendments to the Treaty and therefore the power of initiation had not been given to the Commission. The committee was chaired by the President of the Commission and included one other member of the Commission, but the majority was made up of the twelve governors of the central banks of the member states and three independent experts. Thus the so-called Delors Committee Report[73] was a plan not of the Commission but of this *ad hoc* group appointed by the European Council.

PARTICIPATION

In the normal situation where the Council is given the power to pass legislation on the basis of a Commission proposal the Commission is an active participant in the Council. At all Council meetings the Commission is represented by a Commissioner who acts as an honest broker to help to resolve deadlocks.[74] The Commission has the advantage that its proposals can be amended in the Council on the basis of unanimity only.[75] If the Council cannot obtain the required qualified majority or unanimity to agree to a Commission proposal, and cannot obtain unanimity to amend the proposal, the deadlock can be broken by the Commission altering its proposal in such a way that it can achieve the required vote in the Council.[76] If the Council is very keen to legislate in that area, then the

---

72 The threat to the Commission's right of initiative posed by the creation of the European Council is discussed in Bulmer and Wessels, *The European Council*, pp. 109–13.

73 *Report on Economic and Monetary Union in the European Community*, Luxembourg, EC Official Publications, (1989). The report was presented to the European Council prior to the meeting in Madrid in June 1989 and formed a basis for the intergovernmental conference on economic and monetary union that began in December 1990 and concluded at Maastricht in December 1991.

74 See Tugendhat, *Making Sense of Europe*, pp. 137, 158. The Council's Rules of Procedure, OJ 1993 L304, Art. 4(2) states that: 'The Commission shall be invited to take part in meetings of the Council.' The same Article does permit the Council by simple majority to exclude the Commission from its deliberations but this power is rarely, if ever, used.

75 Art. 189a(1). However, this restraint on the Council does not apply where the EC Treaty requires the Commission to make a recommendation rather than a proposal, e.g Art. 103 on economic policy.

76 Art. 189a(2). The Court has accepted that the Commission amendment need not be in writing because the Community legislative process is 'characterized by a certain flexibility necessary for achieving a convergence of views between the institutions'; see

Commission may be able to use the deadlock to negotiate a compromise that is nearer to its original proposal than would have been the case had the Council been able to amend the Commission's proposal by less than unanimity. There is, of course, another factor in the equation: the European Parliament may have a role in the legislative process.[77] In the consultation procedure the European Parliament has one reading only. The Council can ignore an opinion from the Parliament rejecting the proposal. If any amendments are proposed by the Parliament, they can be adopted by the Council only by unanimity. The Commission can, and often does, amend its own proposal to incorporate the views of the European Parliament.

In the cooperation procedure introduced by the Single European Act the first stage of the procedure is the same as the consultation procedure.[78] The Council adopts a common position on a proposal from the Commission after the European Parliament has considered the legislation at first reading. The European Parliament is then given a second reading, when it can consider the Council's common position. The European Parliament is able to reject the Council's common position. If it does so, then the Council can pass the legislation only by unanimity. If the Commission adopts an amendment to the common position, made by the European Parliament, then the Council can pass the amended version by qualified majority. If the Commission rejects an amendment made by the Parliament, then that amendment can be adopted by the Council only by unanimity.[79]

Thus, whether the legislation is passed under the traditional consultation procedure, whereby the European Parliament is consulted once, or under the cooperation procedure, the Commission is free to amend a proposal at any time, whereas Parliament or the Council itself can change the proposal only if its amendment is unanimously agreed by the Council. In the days when the Council passed legislation only by unanimity this may have been a relatively insignificant power, but now that majority[80] and qualified

---

Case C-280/93 *Germany* v *Council* [1994] ECR I-4973, 5054. The Court contrasted this informality with the much more formal approach necessary for Commission acts that are of direct concern to individuals; see Case C-137/92P *BASF* [1994] ECR I-2555, noted above.

77 As to the different types of legislative procedure, see Ch. 5.

78 At Maastricht two new legislative procedures were introduced: where the assent of the European Parliament is required, and the conciliation and veto procedure of Art. 189b. For more details on these and other legislative procedures, see Chs. 4 and 5.

79 Art. 189c.

80 This is not common but there were some examples in the EEC Treaty, e.g., Art. 128 on vocational training. The use of Art. 128 in relation to Council Dec. 87/569 was challenged in Case 56/88 *United Kingdom* v *Council* [1989] ECR 1615; [1989] 2 CMLR 789, but upheld by the Court of Justice. After Maastricht Art. 128 EEC was replaced by

majority voting are used the Commission needs only to amend its proposal sufficiently to command such a majority. It does not have to persuade all member states of the merits of its compromise.

COMPLETION

The Treaty has given the Commission powers to pass legislation in very few areas. Under Article 48(3)(d) the Commission can make regulations placing conditions on the right of a worker who is a national of one member state to remain in the territory of another member state after having been employed in that state. This power has been exercised in Commission Regulation 1251/70 of 29 June 1970.[81] The Commission can address directives to member states under Article 90(3) in relation to the application of competition policy to public undertakings and undertakings to which member states grant special or exclusive rights. The first such directive was not adopted until 1980 and concerned the transparency of financial relations between member states and public undertakings.[82] The Commission has also adopted directives under Article 90(3) dealing with the telecommunications terminal market.[83] The Commission can make a decision under Article 90(3) that a particular state measure is incompatible with the rules of the Treaty and specify the measures that the addressee state must adopt in order to comply with Community law. The Commission must, however, give the state a fair hearing before adopting the decision or it will be void.[84] The Commission also has the power to confirm or deny the validity of national legislation derogating from harmonization measures passed under Article 100a(1). Such measures are permitted only on one of the grounds referred to in Article 36, or relating to protection of the environment or of the working environment, if the

---

Arts. 126 and 127 EC, which use the Art. 189b procedure and the Art. 189c (cooperation) procedure respectively.

81 OJ Spec. Ed. 1970, L142/24, p. 402.

82 Dir. 80/723, OJ 1980 L195/35. The Court of Justice upheld the validity of this directive in Cases 188–190/80 *France, Italy & United Kingdom* v *Commission* [1982] ECR 2545. The directive was amended by Commission Dir. 85/413 (OJ 1985 L229/20).

83 In relation to Dir. 88/301 (the Telecommunications Terminals Directive) part of Arts. 2 and 9 and the whole of Art. 7 of the directive were declared void by the Court in Case C-202/88 *France* v *Commission*, [1991] ECR I-1223, noted by Wheeler (1992) 17 ELRev 67 and Slot (1991) 28 CMLRev 964. In relation to Dir 90/388 (the Telecommunications Services Directive) part of Arts. 1 and 2 and the whole of Art. 8 were annulled by the Court of Justice in Cases C-271, 281, and 289/90 *Spain, Belgium and Italy* v *Commission* [1992] ECR I-0000; [1993] 4 CMLR 110 (noted by Emiliou (1993) 18 ELRev 305).

84 See Cases C-48/90 and 66/90 *Netherlands and Others* v *Commission* [1992] ECR I-565.

national measures are not a means of arbitrary discrimination or a disguised restriction on trade between member states.[85] The Commission had significant powers in relation to a variety of safeguard clauses and the establishment of the customs union during the transitional period, but these powers are now of largely historical interest.

Most of the Commission's legislative powers have been delegated to it by the Council. The Commission has been entrusted with the power to pass many detailed regulations in relation to the common agricultural policy (CAP). The Council has passed regulations under Article 43 of the Treaty giving the Commission these legislative powers.[86] This form of delegated legislation is common.[87] Though much of the legislative power delegated by the Council to the Commission is of a technical nature, with little policy discretion, this is not always the case. Several significant Commission regulations on the application of Article 85(3) of the Treaty to different types of agreements have been passed under the authority of Council Regulation 19/65. These include Regulation 1983/83 on exclusive distribution agreements, Regulation 1984/83 on exclusive purchasing agreements, Regulation 2349/84 on patent licensing agreements, Regulation 4087/88 on franchise agreements and Regulation 556/89 on know-how licensing agreements.[88] The Commission has passed Regulations 417/85 and 418/85 concerning the application of Article 85(3) to specialization agreements and to research and development agreements under the authority of Council Regulation 2821/71.[89] The Council may also give the Commission power to exempt member states from the application of Community legislation within limits prescribed in the parent legislation.[90]

The Council is reluctant to delegate legislative powers to the Commission and to leave it entirely free to pass the legislation without the advice or, often, supervision of a committee of representatives of the member states. The Council passed a decision on 13 July 1987 under Article 145 of the Treaty as to the procedures for the exercise of implementing powers

85 See Art. 100a(4) and Case C-471/93 France v Commission [1994] ECR I-1829, discussed in Chap. 5.
86 See Snyder, Common Agricultural Policy, pp. 46–7.
87 In 1994 the Commission adopted 3,064 regulations, 3,635 decisions and 33 directives. In most cases the power to adopt these measures was delegated by the Council. See 1994 General Report, p. 720.
88 See OJ 1983 L173/1 and 173/5; OJ 1985 L113/34; OJ L359/46; and OJ 1989 L61/1. The significance of these Commission Regulations can be gauged by the attention devoted to them later in this book; see pp. 713–17.
89 See OJ 1985 L53/1 and 53/5. As amended by Reg. 151/93 OJ 1993 L21/8.
90 An example of this is the Commission Decision 94/785 of 2 December 1994, OJ 1994 L317/15, exempting the UK from having to apply Council Directive 89/684 on vocational training for certain drivers of vehicles carrying dangerous goods by road, in relation to the carriage of ammonium nitrate by farm vehicles between farmland occupied by the same person.

conferred on the Commission.[91] The decision prescribes the procedures that must be adopted if the Council intends to restrict the exercise of powers it delegates to the Commission. The Council need not place such restrictions on the Commission and can instead content itself with limiting the scope of the Commission's legislative power.[92] Apart from the special rules for safeguard measures, discussed below, the decision lays down three main procedures for the Commission's exercise of powers delegated by the Council.[93] The second and third procedures both have two variants.

Procedure I places no limitation on the Commission's power to pass the delegated legislation. It need only submit its draft to an advisory committee made up of representatives of the member states and chaired by a representative of the Commission. The chairperson can insist on a vote by the committee within a given time-limit. Even if the vote is adverse, the Commission is not bound by it. The Commission is, however, required to take the utmost account of the opinion of the committee. The use of advisory committees is, for obvious reasons, preferred by the Commission to management or regulatory committees. However, the Commission has repeatedly observed that the Council has tended to 'confine the implementing powers conferred on the Commission within tight limits'[94] and has agreed to advisory committees on far fewer occasions than the Commission has proposed them.[95]

Procedure II enables the Council to become involved if the measures adopted by the Commission are not in accordance with the opinion of a committee made up of representatives of the member states and chaired by a non-voting representative of the Commission. The Council can act only if the committee delivers an unfavourable opinion on the Commission's proposal by a qualified majority (using the weighted voting system prescribed for the Council in Article 149(2) of the Treaty). Under variant

---

91 Council Dec. 87/373 (OJ 1987 L197/33), passed under Art. 145 EEC as amended by the Single European Act. This is discussed in Ehlermann, 'Compétences d'Exécution Conférées à la Commission – la Nouvelle Décision-cadre du Conseil' (1988) RMC 232, and in detail by Blumann, 'Le pouvoir exécutif de la Commission à la lumière de l'Acte Unique Européen' (1988) Rev Droit Européen 23. See the report from the Commission to the European Parliament, 'Delegation of Executive Powers to the Commission', 28 September 1989 (SEC (89) 1591 final) and of 10 January 1991 (SEC (90) 2589 final).
92 See Council Dec. 87/373, Art. 1, note 91 above.
93 ibid., Art. 2.
94 This same quote is given in General Report 1992, p. 373, General Report 1993, p. 355 and General Report 1994, p. 411.
95 ibid. In 1992 the Commission proposed its use in all internal market measures 77 times whereas the Council used it 17 times and in 1993 the figures were 23 and 6. In 1994 the Commission suggested the use of an advisory committee 6 times in relation to instruments implementing Art. 100a of the EC Treaty but the Council adopted this procedure only twice.

(a) of Procedure II, after an adverse opinion of the committee the Commission may defer application of the measures for not more than one month, during which the Council may take a different decision by a qualified majority. Under variant (b) of Procedure II, after an adverse opinion of the committee the Commission shall defer application of the measures for a period laid down in the Council legislation that delegates the power to the Commission (the parent legislation) but not exceeding three months. During that period the Council can take a different decision from the Commission by a qualified majority. Thus in Procedure II, under either variant, the Commission's legislative powers can be taken back by the Council but only if both the committee and the Council are able to obtain a qualified majority. The type of committee envisaged in Procedure II is often referred to as a management committee.[96] In practice these committees are used frequently and rarely give an adverse opinion. Thus they present a very limited obstacle to the legislative power of the Commission.[97]

Procedure III imposes greater restrictions on the Commission's powers to pass delegated legislation. The composition of the committee is the same as in Procedure II, but it is commonly referred to as a regulatory committee[98] because the Commission can adopt the measures only if the committee gives a favourable opinion by a qualified majority. If the committee delivers no opinion or one that is not in accordance with the measures envisaged by the Commission, then the Commission shall without delay submit to the Council a proposal relating to the measures to be taken. Under variant (a) the Council has a period of time laid down in the parent legislation, not exceeding three months, during which it can act by a qualified majority. If the Council does not act within that time, then the Commission adopts its proposed measures. Variant (b) is similar to variant (a) except that the Commission cannot adopt the measures if the Council decides against them by a simple majority. The effect of Procedure III is that unless the committee gives positive approval to the Commission's proposal by a qualified majority, the Commission must submit the proposal to the Council, a situation similar to that where no delegation has taken place. The difference remains, however, that even under variant (b) of Procedure III the Commission does not require a qualified majority from

96 See Noel, *Working Together*, p. 21.
97 ibid; Noel records that out of 2,171 cases dealt with in 1992 by the management committees concerned with agriculture no adverse opinion was given. In 1989 there was one adverse opinion in an agricultural management committee. The Commission report to the European Parliament (SEC (89) 1591 final), referring to the period up to the end of 1988, said that in agricultural management committees 'no negative opinions have been delivered for several years now' (p. 9).
98 Noel, *Working Together*, p. 21.

the Council, as it would in primary legislation – it just has to avoid a negative vote by the Council. Thus the delegator is giving the delegate a little more power than it would have if no delegation were made.[99]

The question of which procedure and, indeed, which variant within a procedure, applies is determined by the parent legislation. The parent legislation may provide for the Commission to amend it by the delegated legislation within certain parameters and subject to an appropriate committee procedure.[100]

Where the Council delegates to the Commission the power to decide on safeguard measures,[101] the Commission is required to consult the member states before taking a decision, and to notify the Council and the member states of any decision.[102] Any member state can, within a time-limit laid down in the parent legislation, refer the Commission's decision to the Council. Under variant (a) the Council may, within the time-limit laid down in the parent legislation, take a different decision by a qualified majority. Under variant (b) the Council may confirm, amend or revoke the Commission's decision by a qualified majority; if it does not take any decision within the time-limit laid down by the parent legislation, then the decision of the Commission is deemed to be revoked. Thus the Council has delegated very little power in the context of variant (b).

Council Decision 87/373 does not affect the procedures for the exercise of the powers conferred on the Commission in acts that predate its entry into force.[103]

The Commission declared its unhappiness with variant (b) of Procedure III and with variant (b) of the procedure applicable to safeguard measures, and had this recorded in the Council's minutes. The Commission was concerned that these procedures unduly restricted its freedom of action and created a real danger that no decision would be taken. The Commission admitted that the variant (b) procedure (often referred to as the safety-net procedure) had not yet led to deadlock.[104] The European Parliament brought annulment proceedings against the Council's decision, but the

---

99 By December 1990 98 per cent of legislation involving a regulatory committee had been passed by the committee; see SEC (90) 2589 final. In the remaining 2 per cent of cases the Council nearly always passed the measure within the time-limit. Regulatory committees have been used frequently in relation to measures concerning the internal market, banking, the environment, and veterinary and plant health.
100 E.g. Council Dir. 79/409 on the conservation of wild birds was amended by Comm. Dir. 91/224 (OJ 1991 L115/41), and Council Dir. 67/548 was amended by Comm. Dir. of 5 March 1991 (OJ 1991 L180/79).
101 The Council can do this in the context of harmonization measures passed to secure the completion of the single internal market; see Art. 100a(4) of the Treaty.
102 See Council Dec. 87/373, Art 3.
103 See Art. 4 of the Decision.
104 See Ehlermann, (1988) RMC, p. 239; and SEC(89) 1591 final, pp. 3–4.

Court of Justice decided it did not have *locus standi*.[105] On 20 December 1994 an interinstitutional conference confirmed agreement on a *modus vivendi* between the Council, Parliament and the Commission on implementing measures for instruments adopted under the conciliation and veto procedure.[106]

EXECUTIVE ROLE

The Commission has Treaty-based executive powers in the field of competition policy under Articles 85–93, and of safeguard measures under Article 115.[107] The important powers are those whereby the Commission can decide that a member state or a firm is in breach of competition policy.[108] In this field the Commission must act within the powers given by the Treaty, as its decisions are subject to review by the European Court of Justice or the Court of First Instance, but it is not subject to supervision by the Council.[109]

The Commission has executive powers in administering the Community's structural funds.[110] The EEC Treaty gave power to the Commission to administer the European Social Fund, and provides for a committee, chaired by a member of the Commission and composed of representatives of Governments, trade unions and employers' organizations, to assist the Commission.[111] Article 130d EEC was introduced by the Single European

105 See Case 302/87 *European Parliament* v *Council* [1988] ECR 5615. The *locus standi* of the European Parliament under Art. 173 of the Treaty is considered in Ch. 8.
106 See EU Bull. 12–1994 and *1994 General Report*, p. 411.
107 Art. 115 has an application that will expire when the common commercial policy is fully operative but is still in use, e.g. Comm. Decs. C(90) 1437/1, 1437/2 and 1487, notified in OJ 1990 C179/3. The substance of Art. 115 remains the same as a result of the Treaty amendments agreed at Maastricht, though references to the transitional period and the introduction of the common customs tariff are removed. Art. 115 is discussed further in Ch. 16.
108 See Arts. 79(4) and 80(2) in relation to competition in transport, Art. 89 for competition generally, Art. 91 for dumping and Art. 93 for state aids. See Chs. 22–7.
109 Even in the context of competition policy many of the Commission's powers have been granted by the Council by way of regulation; e.g., Reg. 17/62 (OJ Spec. Ed. 1962, No. 204/62, p. 87).
110 See Scott, *Development Dilemmas in the European Community* (1995) and Frazer, 'The New Structural Funds, State Aids and Interventions on the Single Market' (1995) 20 ELRev 3–19.
111 Art. 124. The fund had a budget of 3,520 million ECU in 1989 and of 5,977 million ECU in 1993; see the *European Communities Financial Report 1989*, Luxembourg, EC Official Publications and the *EC Financial Report 1993*, Luxembourg, EC Official Publications.

Act to require the Commission to submit a comprehensive proposal to the Council to amend the structure and operation of the structural funds, with a view to defining the tasks, the priority objectives and the organization of the funds and ensuring the coordination of the funds with one another. The consultation procedure applied under the Single European Act. The Maastricht Treaty amendments now require the assent of the European Parliament to such a framework proposal. Indeed, Article 130d EC required the Council with the assent of the European Parliament to set up a Cohesion Fund to provide a financial contribution to projects in the fields of environment and trans-European networks in the area of transport infrastructure. The Fund will have resources of over 15 million ECU between 1993 and 1999 and is governed by Regulation 1164/94.[112] Only states with a per capita GNP of less than 90 per cent of the Community average can benefit from the Cohesion Fund: Greece, Ireland, Portugal and Spain.

Apart from the European Social Fund, the three other structural funds – the European Agricultural Guidance and Guarantee Fund, Guidance Section (EAGGF Guidance Section), the Financial Instrument for Fisheries Guidance (FIFG)[113] and the European Regional Development Fund[114] – were created by the Council and their administration delegated to the Commission, subject to advisory or management committees. The comprehensive proposal became Regulation 2052/88[115] which was substantially amended by Regulation 2081/93[116] and established five priority objectives:

1 promoting the development and structural adjustment of the regions whose development is lagging behind (an objective of all the funds except the fisheries one);
2 converting the regions, frontier regions or parts of regions (including employment areas and urban communities) seriously affected by industrial decline (an objective of the Regional Development Fund and of the Social Fund);
3 combating long-term unemployment and facilitating the integration into working life of young people and of persons exposed to exclusion

---

112 OJ 1994 L130/1.
113 Reg. 2080/93 OJ 1993 L193/1.
114 Implementing measures in relation to the Guidance Section can be taken by the Council under Art. 43 of the Treaty and in relation to the Regional Development Fund under Art. 130e of the Treaty. The former prescribes consultation procedure and the latter cooperation procedure. In 1993 the Guidance Section had 3,167 million ECU (1,465 million ECU in 1989) and the Regional Development Fund had 10,033 million ECU (4,710 million ECU in 1989); see the *European Communities Financial Reports for 1989* and *1993*.
115 OJ 1988 L185/9.
116 OJ 1993 L193/5.

from the labour market (an objective of the Social Fund);
4 facilitating the adaptation of workers of either sex to industrial changes and to changes in production systems (an objective of the Social Fund);
5 promoting rural development by:
   (a) speeding up the adjustment of agricultural structures in the framework of the reform of the common agricultural policy (an objective of the EAGGF Guidance Section and FIFG);
   (b) facilitating the development and structural adjustment of rural areas (an objective of all the funds except the FIFG).

In the framework of the review of the common fisheries policy, measures for the adjustment of fisheries structures come under Objective 5(a).[117]

In implementing Regulation 2052/88 the Commission is assisted by three committees. An advisory committee (i.e. Procedure I under Decision 87/373 discussed above) for objectives 1 and 2,[118] the European Social Fund Committee prescribed by Article 124 of the Treaty for objectives 3 and 4,[119] and a management committee composed of representatives of the member states for objectives 5(a) and (b).[120] The tasks of the committees in the framework of the management of the funds are established by Council decisions taken under Article 130e of the Treaty.[121] These detailed decisions prescribe which variant of Procedure II in Decision 87/373 applies to the management committee overseeing objectives 5(a) and (b).

ROLE AS GUARDIAN OF COMMUNITY LAW

The Commission is given power in Article 169 of the Treaty to initiate infringement proceedings against a member state that fails to fulfil its obligations under Community law.[122] The Commission also intervenes in all cases where the Court of Justice is asked for a preliminary ruling on the interpretation or validity of Community law.

Infringement proceedings have three formal stages. First, a letter of

---

117 Arts. 1 and 2 of Reg. 2052/88 as replaced by Arts. 1 and 2 of Reg. 2081/93.
118 See Reg. 2052/88, Art. 17 as replaced by Art. 17 of Reg. 2081/93.
119 See p. 63.
120 See Reg. 2052/88, Art. 17 as replaced by Reg. 2081/93.
121 See also Reg. 2052/88, Arts. 3(4) and (5) as replaced by Reg. 2081/93.
122 The subject is considered in more depth in Ch. 7. An accelerated procedure is prescribed in relation to state aids under Art. 93(2) of the Treaty, and under Art. 100a(4) in relation to member states improperly applying the 'major needs' exception to harmonization measures agreed by the Council to complete the single internal market.

formal notice from the Commission to the member state informing the state of the Commission's view that the state may be in breach of certain Community law obligations and asking for the state's formal response. Second, the Commission's reasoned opinion on whether or not there has been a violation of Community law by the member state after it has made its submissions to the Commission. Third, the Commission refers the case to the Court of Justice for a ruling on whether or not the member state has infringed its Community law obligations. Statistics show that most cases are resolved at one of the first two stages.[123] The total figures for infringement proceedings against all states between 1991 and 1994 demonstrate the point:

COMMISSION

	1991	1992	1993	1994
Letters of formal notice	853	1,216	1,209	974
Reasoned opinions	411	248	357	546
References to the Court	65	64	44	89

CONCLUSION

The extent of the Commission's powers to enact laws is almost entirely dependent on the Council's willingness to delegate its legislative power to the Commission. As with legislation in the United Kingdom, there is too much of it to be adopted by the full legislative process required for a regulation or a directive, hence the Council is compelled to delegate some legislative power to the Commission. As with United Kingdom Statutory Instruments,[124] most of this legislation is technical and of low policy content, but some of it is important. Where the full legislative process operates, the Commission is much less powerful than the Council. The Commission's role as initiator of legislation and participant in the Council

123 The figures are taken from the 'Eleventh Annual Report to the European Parliament on Commission Monitoring of the Application of Community Law 1993' (OJ 1994 C154) and from the *General Report on the Activities of the European Union 1994*, Commission (1995, Luxembourg, Official Publications) at p. 440. More detailed statistics are given in Ch. 7.
124 See Miers and Page, *Legislation*, Ch. 8.

combined with the restraints on the power of the Council to amend the Commission's proposals give the Commission real influence on the content of the final legislation. However, the conciliation and veto procedure and, to a lesser extent, the assent procedures introduced by the Maastricht Treaty amendments diminish that influence by enhancing the powers of the European Parliament. In these areas legislation will be a tripartite process, involving the Commission, the European Parliament and the Council, where the Commission is likely to be the weakest player.

The scope of the Commission's executive powers is determined by the Council, except in the key area of competition policy. The extent to which the Commission can allocate resources to reform agriculture and improve the economic situation of the poor regions is dependent on the size of the Community budget. The budget is determined by the Council and the European Parliament, and not by the Commission. The total size of the Community revenue in 1993 was 66 billion ECU (about £49.5 billion)[125] whereas the United Kingdom revenue for 1993 was £214 billion.[126] The Delors II Package agreed at the Edinburgh European Council in December 1992 envisages Community expenditure appropriations of 69 billion ECU in 1993, rising to 84 billion ECU in 1999, with the amount committed to the structural and cohesion funds rising from 21 billion ECU to 30 billion ECU in the same period. Thus, in the 1990s at least, a third of Community expenditure will be directed by the Commission to the poorer regions and people of the Community. In the 1980s the proportion so directed was less than a quarter of total expenditure.

The Commission's role as Community prosecutor is a vital one in being a neutral body that takes member states to the Court for failure to comply with Community law. If it were left to the member states to initiate such actions against other member states, there would be fewer actions and a deterioration in relationships between member states.[127]

So the Commission is a curious hybrid of a legislature, an executive and a law enforcer. It is not simply an international civil service like the Secretariat of the United Nations nor is it the government of Europe. The bulk of the Commission's legislative and executive power is held at the discretion of the Council. It is, therefore, the national Governments that retain control of the key legislative and executive powers either in their

125 See *European Communities Financial Report 1993.* By 1995 the Budget had grown to 81 billion ECU, see *1994 General Report,* p. 385.
126 See United Kingdom National Accounts, 1994 edition (1994, HMSO), p. 61.
127 The lack of cases brought under Art. 170 is evidence of this; see Ch. 7.

ability to act in their own countries in the many areas not within the Community's competence or in their ability to act in the Council.[128]

---

128 The Maastricht Treaty amendments give the European Parliament some real power to act as a block on the Council's legislative power in the context of the conciliation and veto procedure and the assent procedure, discussed in Chs. 4 and 5. The European Parliament and the Commission are still unable to force the Council to pass legislation against its will. The breadth of the Community's legislative competence is not finally resolved. Art. 235 was used before the Maastricht Treaty amendments to pass legislation that was at the margins of the Community objectives: e.g., legislation relating to tourism in Council Dec. 86/664 (OJ 1986 L384/52) and Council Dec. 89/46 (OJ 1989 L17/53). On the scope of Community legislative competence before Maastricht, see Usher, 'The Development of Community Powers after the Single European Act' in White and Smythe (eds.) European and International Law, pp. 3–18. On the post-Maastricht situation, see the brief consideration of Art. 235 in Ch. 5 and the discussion of the principle of subsidiarity in Chap. 1.

CHAPTER 3

Council

COMPOSITION

The Council of the European Communities was established by the Merger Treaty, taking the place of the Councils of the ECSC, EEC and Euratom, but acquiring the powers and jurisdictions of those Councils.[1] After the entry into force of the Treaty on European Union on 1 November 1993 the Council adopted the name Council of the European Union. It is the Council's role in the context of the European Community, not ECSC, Euratom, common foreign and security policy or justice and home affairs cooperation, that will be examined in this chapter. The Council is the institution in the Community that has the greatest legislative power. It consists of representatives of the member states drawn from the Governments of those states.[2] The Government representative attending the Council varies, depending on the subject-matter being discussed. The general Council is attended by foreign ministers, and the various specialist Councils are attended by the national ministers dealing with the issues in hand, e.g. agriculture ministers on agriculture, finance ministers on economic and financial affairs, and transport ministers on transport. This creates problems of coordinating the work of the various Councils. Agriculture ministers may want to increase farm prices when the finance ministers are trying to control the size of the Community budget.[3] These tensions have led to the development of mechanisms for budgetary discipline. More generally, the task of coordinating the work of the different Councils falls on the member state holding the presidency of the Council. Each state

1 Art. 1 of the Merger Treaty. See the *Guide to the Council of the European Union 1993* (1994, Luxembourg, EC Official Publications) produced by the General Secretariat of the Council.
2 Art. 146 EC explicitly requires that the member states must be represented at ministerial level in the Council and that the minister must be authorized to commit the Government of the member state.
3 See Tugendhat, *Making Sense of Europe*, p. 161, where he refers to the public dispute between these two Councils in October 1984.

holds the presidency for periods of six months in strict rotation.[4] This is rather short to ensure adequate coordination and therefore much is dependent on the work of the Secretary-General and the staff in the General Secretariat.[5] The general Council of foreign ministers can play a coordinating role, but may lack the political authority to reconcile conflicting specialist Councils.[6]

The Council meets when convened by its President. The presidency usually initiates this, but the Council can be convened at the request of one of its members or of the Commission.[7] The level of legislative production dropped markedly after its peak in the push to complete the single market legislative programme in 1992.[8] Until the Council's Rules of Procedure were altered in December 1993 none of its meetings were open to the public or televised. A very limited reform was undertaken as a result of the political agreement reached at the Edinburgh European Council in December 1992 to promote openness and transparency in the work of the Council. The Council's policy debates on the six-monthly work programme of the Council presidency and, if appropriate, on the Commission's annual work programme are the subject of public retransmission by audiovisual means.[9] The Council can decide unanimously on a case-by-case basis to permit the televising of its debates.[10] These changes are largely cosmetic and make for very dull television.

The Council can still be criticized on the ground that in a democratic society the legislature should operate under the scrutiny of the people and

4 See Council Decision 95/2 (OJ 1995 L1/220) which prescribes the order in which the member states hold the presidency. It formulated a new rotation to accommodate the new member states but also changed the order so that some of the larger member states will take up the presidency again sooner than would have been anticipated under the old rotation.

5 See Art. 21 of the Rules of Procedure of the Council, see OJ 1993 L304. The Council's establishment plan at the end of 1994 allowed for 2,289 permanent posts and 1 temporary post; see *General Report on the Activities of the European Union 1994*, Luxembourg, EC Official Publications, 1995, p. 420. Some coordination is also provided by Coreper, which is discussed below. The Council's Secretariat can correct the spelling and grammar of a legislative measure passed by the Council but cannot alter the content of any part of the measure, including the preamble; see Case 131/86 *United Kingdom* v *Council* [1988] ECR 905, 934–5.

6 See Tugendhat, *Making Sense of Europe*, pp. 162–3.

7 Art 147 EC. In fact, an incoming President will intimate seven months before the beginning of the presidency the dates envisaged for meetings of the Council during the presidency (see Art. 1 of the Rules of Procedure).

8 In 1994 the Council met 95 times, adopted 46 directives, 274 regulations and 148 decisions, see *1994 General Report* at p. 419, whereas in 1992 the Council met only 89 times but adopted 166 directives, 383 regulations and 189 decisions, see *1992 General Report* at p. 379.

9 Art. 6(1) of the Council's Rules of Procedure.

10 Art. 6(2) of the Council's Rules of Procedure.

yet the principal Community legislature operates in secret. Such secrecy may be vital if member states are to be willing to abandon their previously held positions in a compromise package agreed with the Commission. The Commission attends Council meetings as of right unless the Council decides by a simple majority to deliberate without them.[11] Commission participation at the Council is crucial to the Community legislative process and so in practice the Commission is not excluded.[12] Where the Council is discussing matters that are within the portfolios of several members of the Commission, they may all be present at the Council. As an example, at the economic and financial affairs Council on 12 March 1990 in Brussels (most Council meetings are held in Brussels, where the Council Secretariat is based, but some are held in Luxembourg and occasionally in the member state holding the presidency) the Commission was represented by the President, Jacques Delors, whose portfolio included monetary affairs; Vice-President Henning Christophersen, whose portfolio included economic and financial affairs: Peter Schmidhuber, whose portfolio was budget and financial control; and Christiane Scrivener, whose portfolio included taxation. Members of the Council and the Commission may be accompanied by and assisted by officials, but the Council may limit the numbers by a simple majority vote.[13] In practice each Council member will be supported by that member state's Permanent Representative (ambassador) or Deputy Permanent Representative to the Community and other officials. Where agreement is very hard to achieve, the Council may decide to exclude all officials and simply leave the ministers and the Commission to reach a solution.[14]

11 Art. 4(2) of the Council Rules of Procedure. Although the Rules refer to 'the Commission' being present at the Council, clearly all twenty Commissioners cannot attend, and therefore one or more Commissioners will be present on behalf of the Commission. Art. 109b(2) EC provides that from the start of its operations the President of the European Central Bank must be invited to participate in Council meetings when the Council is discussing matters relating to the objectives and tasks of the European System of Central Banks.
12 The role of the Commission in the Council is discussed in Ch. 2.
13 Art. 4(3) of the Council Rules of Procedure.
14 See Tugendhat, *Making Sense of Europe*, pp. 157–8.

VOTING

There are three systems of voting in the Council: simple majority, qualified majority and unanimity.[15] Clearly, the greater use that is made of some form of majority voting, the more the sovereignty of the individual member states is lost. If a state can be outvoted on the passing of Community legislation, then it can be in the position where that legislation is part of its own legal system against the wishes of the Government of that state. Where unanimity is required, the sovereignty of each member state is protected in that the Government minister present could prevent legislation being passed in the Council. The parliaments of the member states have lost some of their legislative sovereignty even when unanimity in the Council is required, because a Government minister may agree to something that would not be passed by the parliament of that country.

Until the Council's Rules of Procedure were altered in December 1993 all votes in the Council remained secret. Article 7(5) of the new Rules prescribes when the record of the votes shall be made public. When the Council is acting as legislator, or adopting a common position pursuant to Article 189b or 189c EC, then the record of the votes must be made public unless a simple majority of the Council decides otherwise.[16] The votes of the members of the Council or their representatives cast in conciliation committees set up under Article 189b EC must be made public.[17] In all other cases the Council, at the request of one of its members, can decide by simple majority to make the record of the votes public.[18] This is a potentially powerful change in the culture of the Council which will help national parliaments to hold their Ministers to account. It may, however, make it more difficult for Ministers to compromise from the positions they have adopted prior to the Council meeting. The price to be paid for greater transparency and openness in the voting

15 Occasionally the Treaty prescribes a different method, as in Arts. 44(6) and 104c(13), where variations on qualified majority voting are set out.
16 When the Council is acting as 'legislator' is defined in the Annex to Rules of Procedure, OJ 1993 L304/7, as being when it is adopting rules which are legally binding in or for the member states whether by means of regulations, directives or decisions with the exception of internal measures, administrative budgetary acts, and acts concerning inter-institutional or international relations.
17 It would be pointless to try and preserve secrecy here given that a number of MEPs are present at the time.
18 The exception is in relation to Council acts pursuant to Titles V and VI of the Treaty on European Union, common foreign and security policy and justice and home affairs cooperation. In these matters the record of votes can be made public at the request of one Council member but only by a unanimous decision of the Council.

record may be a slowing down in the pace of achieving or even a failure to achieve legislative agreement in the Council.

Another move towards greater transparency in the Council and Commission was made in December 1993 when these institutions agreed a Code of Conduct concerning Public Access to Council and Commission Documents.[19] The general principle established in the Code is that the public will have the 'widest possible access to documents held by the Commission and the Council'. Anyone can apply to the Commission or the Council for access to one of their documents. The institution must give a decision within a month. If the application is granted the person can consult the documents on the spot or have a copy sent at his or her own expense; the fee will not exceed a 'reasonable sum'. However, the Code allows the institutions to deny access to documents if the disclosure could undermine the protection of:

(a) the public interest (public security, international relations, monetary stability, court proceedings, inspections and investigations),
(b) the protection of the individual and of privacy,
(c) the protection of commercial and industrial secrecy,
(d) the protection of the Community's financial interests,
(e) the protection of confidentiality as requested by the natural or legal persons that supplied the information or as required by the legislation of the member state that supplied the information.

These exceptions could be construed very broadly but they are added to by another one which seems to give carte blanche to the institutions to protect the secrecy of their proceedings. They may refuse access 'in order to protect the institutions' interest in the confidentiality of its proceedings'.

The Council Decision on access to Council documents closely follows the Code and in Article 4 adopts word for word the exceptions set out in it.[20] The *Guardian* newspaper made use of the Council Decision to obtain information on the voting records in the Council. When a subsequent request was refused it decided to seek annulment of the Council's decision refusing it access to the documents. The case is pending before the Court of First Instance and raises very important questions about freedom of information within the Community.[21]

SIMPLE MAJORITY

Article 148(1) of the Treaty states: 'Save as otherwise provided in this

19 See OJ 1993 L340/41.
20 Decision 93/731 OJ 1993 L340/43.
21 See Case T-194/94 *Carvel and Guardian Newspapers* v *Council*, Proceedings 17/94.

Treaty, the Council shall act by a majority of its members.' In most cases the Treaty does provide for a different system of voting. It would be too much to expect the member states to surrender sovereignty over legislation to the extent that it could be passed by Government ministers from eight of the fifteen member states, especially when those eight states might include none of the five largest (France, Germany, Italy, Spain and the United Kingdom), whose combined population is over three-quarters of the Community's total population. Simple majority voting is, however, provided for in a few instances.

Under Article 128 EEC the Council could lay down general principles for implementing a common vocational training policy. This Article was the legal basis for Council Decision 87/569, which concerned an action programme for the vocational training of young people and their preparation for adult working life at a cost of 40 million ECU over five years.[22] The United Kingdom sought to annul this decision in the European Court of Justice on the ground that the measure should have had the additional legal basis of Article 235, which requires unanimity in the Council, because Article 128 EEC did not confer power on the Council to establish multi-annual programmes incurring significant expenditure. The Court of Justice upheld the validity of the decision on the ground that Article 128 EEC gave the Council power to adopt a common vocational training policy and hence it must have the means of action to carry out that common policy effectively by imposing obligations on the member states.[23] The provisions on Community vocational training policy were changed at Maastricht and simple majority voting was abandoned. The relevant provision is now Article 127 EC, and it requires the Council to act under the cooperation procedure.[24]

The Council's rules of procedure can be adopted by simple majority,[25] and a number of procedural decisions laid down in those rules are taken on the same basis, for example, the adoption of the agenda, the exclusion of the Commission and of officials, the opening of the voting procedure when it is not initiated by the President, whether or not to make the record of the votes public, the adoption of the minutes of the meetings and the authorizing of the production of a copy or an extract from the Council minutes for use in legal proceedings.[26] There are some instances in which the EC Treaty provides for certain procedural decisions to be taken by common accord of certain institutions. In Article 138c the detailed provisions

22 OJ 1987 L346/31.
23 Case 56/88 *United Kingdom* v *Council* [1989] ECR 1615, [1989] 2 CMLR 789.
24 Art. 189c, discussed in Chs. 4 and 5.
25 Art. 151(3).
26 Rules of Procedure, Arts. 2(5), 4(2) and (3), 5(2), 7(1) and (5), and 9.

governing the exercise of the European Parliament's right of inquiry are to be determined by common accord of the European Parliament, the Council and the Commission. In Articles 189b(7) and 189c(g) the time-limits laid down in the conciliation and veto procedure and in the cooperation procedure can be extended, for a limited period, by common accord of the European Parliament and the Council. In these cases one must assume that the Council can act by a simple majority. The EC Treaty also confers a power on the Council or the Commission to impose a time-limit within which the Economic and Social Committee and the Committee of the Regions must submit their opinions on a legislative proposal.[27] Here the Council can act by simple majority.

A simple majority is sufficient for the Council to request the Commission to undertake studies for the attainment of the common objectives of the Treaty and to submit appropriate proposals.[28] Prior to the ratification of the Maastricht Treaty amendments it was possible for international agreements to be concluded by the Council on the basis of a simple majority under Article 228 EEC. Post-Maastricht, Article 228 EC provides for qualified majority voting or unanimity.

The Council can by simple majority deliver an opinion convening an intergovernmental conference to consider amendments to the Treaty.[29] For amendments to be agreed at the conference, however, there must be common accord of the representatives of the Governments of the member states and they must be ratified by all the member states in accordance with their respective constitutional requirements. The power to initiate the process of Treaty amendments by a simple majority in the Council is significant. Once a conference is convened, it has its own momentum and participants want to be seen to be achieving something even if it is much less ambitious than some of the states advocating reform hoped for. This

---

27 See Arts. 198 and 198c.

28 Art. 152 of the Treaty. See also, post-Maastricht, the more specialized requests for a Commission proposal in relation to economic and monetary policy that can be made by the Council or a member state under Art. 109d. Under Art. 153 of the Treaty the Council can by simple majority determine the rules governing the committees provided for in the Treaty, e.g., the Committee of Permanent Representatives (Coreper); see Art. 151(1) of the Treaty. However, the Rules of Procedure of the Economic and Social Committee require the unanimous approval of the Council (Art. 196 of the Treaty).

29 Art. N(1) of the Treaty on European Union. The initiative to establish the intergovernmental conference in 1985 that led to the Single European Act was opposed at the European Council in Milan in June 1985 by Denmark, Greece and the United Kingdom, but it went ahead (see George, *An Awkward Partner*, pp. 180–83). The United Kingdom went along with the formal decision to convene the intergovernmental conference under the Luxembourg presidency at the foreign affairs Council on 22–3 July 1985 and then participated in the conference (see Taylor in Lodge (ed.), *The European Community*, p. 10).

can be seen by the willingness of the United Kingdom, Denmark and Greece to agree to the Single European Act although they all opposed any changes to the Treaty prior to the setting up of the conference. Another example is the concessions – in particular, the extension of the powers of the European Parliament[30] – made by the United Kingdom at Maastricht in December 1991 in order to avoid a breakdown and ensure a Treaty was signed.

QUALIFIED MAJORITY

The drafters of the EEC Treaty intended that after the end of the transitional period, from 1 January 1966 many legislative measures would be passed by qualified majority vote in the Council. However it was not until the 1980s that qualified majority voting became a regular feature of Council lawmaking. The so-called Luxembourg Compromise of January 1966 had the effect of stultifying the decision-making process in the Council, and, in practice, the Council operated by consensus. The period of the late 1960s and 1970s can be characterized as a time when states were not prepared to concede sovereignty to the Community and hence the wheels of the Community lawmaking process ground very slowly. In the 1980s the member states began to break out of the straitjacket of unanimity, and this trend was accelerated by the amendments to the Treaty made by the Single European Act providing for qualified majority voting in an increased number of areas. In 1986 around one hundred decisions were taken by this method.[31] By 1990, majority voting was becoming so normal that the Commission did not record the number of decisions taken by that method, but said that

The improvement in the Council's decision-making procedure which began with the signing of the Single European Act continued in 1990. Wherever necessary, decisions have been taken by a qualified majority, either by means of a formal vote or by establishing that a majority exists without resorting to a formal vote. The possibility of majority voting has introduced an element of flexibility in the position of the Member States, which are forced to reach a consensus.[32]

30 See Ch. 4. The United Kingdom also negotiated a protocol permitting it to opt out of the third stage of economic and monetary union, the adoption of a single currency. The United Kingdom had to concede that a date for the beginning of the third stage, no later than 1 January 1999, be written into the EC Treaty, Art. 109j(4); (see further Ch. 21). None the less the United Kingdom's opt-out protocol and the Agreement on Social Policy entered into by all the member states except the United Kingdom represent a worrying move towards fragmentation of the Community; see further Ch. 20.
31 See Noel, *Working Together* (1988), p. 27.
32 See the *XXIVth General Report on the Activities of the European Communities 1990*.

In 1994, the first full year of the Treaty on European Union being in force, the Council took 48 decisions by qualified majority in relation to internal legislative instruments only.[33] This apparent decline in the number of decisions taken by qualified majority may be explained by the fact that the single market legislation, most of which was subject to qualified majority voting, was largely completed before the end of 1993 and by the fact that votes may only be forced when there is some doubt as to whether a qualified majority exists within the Council for the particular measure.

The qualified majority voting system used in the Council is set out in Article 148(2) of the Treaty. A total of eighty-seven votes are allocated to the fifteen member states. The principle of equality of states is departed from and the more populous states are given more votes than the less populous ones. The distribution of votes is not, however, in accord with the population of the states, as proportionately the member states with smaller populations still have more votes than their populations warrant. Luxembourg, with a population of about 390,000, has two votes whereas the United Kingdom, France and Italy, with populations in excess of 55 million, and Germany, with a population of about 80 million, have only ten votes each.[34] To obtain a qualified majority sixty-two votes have to be cast in favour.[35] Thus it takes twenty-six votes to form a blocking minority, a minimum of three states; and it takes a minimum of eight states to achieve the required sixty-two votes for a qualified majority. The consequence is that member states have surrendered some sovereignty, as binding legislation that is opposed by one or more of the governments of the states can be passed. The weighting of the votes ensures that only measures that are supported by Governments representing a substantial majority of the Community's population can be passed.[36]

The fact that states can be bound by decisions that they oppose is not unique in international institutions, as the voting system in the United Nations Security Council demonstrates. A Security Council resolution can

---

Luxembourg, EC Official Publications, 1991, p. 359; the same words are repeated in the *XXVth General Report*, p. 363, with the substitution of 1991 for 1990.

33 *General Report on the Activities of the European Union 1994*, Commission (1995, Luxembourg, Official Publications) at p. 409.

34 The votes of the other member states are as follows: Spain (population about 40 million), 8; Belgium, Greece, Netherlands and Portugal (populations between 10 and 15 million), 5; Austria and Sweden (populations between 7 and 9 million), 4; Denmark, Finland and Ireland (populations between 3 and 5 million), 3.

35 These votes must come from at least ten states if it is a decision where the Council can act without a Commission proposal (see Art. 8 of Council Decision 95/1, OJ 1995 L1/1).

36 Even if the outvoted minority were Germany, Italy and the Netherlands, they have populations totalling around 151 million, and the total Community population is around 370 million.

be passed by nine of the fifteen states, provided that none of the five permanent members vote against it, and thereby veto it.[37] Such resolutions are binding not only on the dissenting minority in the Security Council, but also on all member states of the United Nations.[38] The powers of the Security Council are impressive in that they can impose mandatory economic sanctions and order military intervention, but its role is limited to the maintenance of international peace and security.[39] The Council of the EC does not have these defence powers,[40] but it has legislative powers across a much wider area. No state has a legal veto in the Council where the Treaty prescribes a form of majority voting. For the United Kingdom little or no loss of sovereignty is involved in its membership of the United Nations, as it has a veto in the Security Council as one of the five permanent members, but it has no veto in the Council under the legal framework prescribed by the EC Treaty, except where the Treaty requires unanimity. None the less, the United Kingdom claims that it can exercise a veto where its vital national interests are at stake when the Treaty provides for simple or qualified majority voting. This claim is based on the practice of the Council since the Luxembourg Compromise of January 1966.[41]

LUXEMBOURG COMPROMISE

The Luxembourg Compromise[42] was, in fact, an agreement to disagree that enabled France to resume normal business in the Council. It is not a legally binding agreement. France had adopted its notorious 'empty chair' policy in 1965, whereby it did not participate in the work of the Council for six months, for a number of reasons, including its disapproval of the planned introduction of majority voting in January 1966 when the transi-

---

37 UN Charter, Art. 27.
38 UN Charter, Art. 25.
39 See UN Charter, Art. 24 and Ch. VII.
40 Though, outside the framework of the European Community, in the context of Title V of the Treaty on European Union, Art. J4 provides for the 'eventual framing of a common defence policy, which might in time lead to a common defence'. Article J3 does allow for the possibility of qualified majority voting in the Council on joint action in relation to foreign and security policy, but not on issues having defence implications; see Art. J4(3).
41 See the statements of the United Kingdom Government to the United Kingdom parliament in HC Deb. 1982, Vol. 31, col. 770 and HL Deb. 1986, Vol. 479, col. 1007 and the discussion by Campbell, 'The Single European Act and The Implications' (1986) 35 ICLQ 932.
42 See Campbell, (1986) 35 ICLQ 932 and Vasey, 'Decision-making in the Agriculture Council and the Luxembourg Compromise' (1988) 25 CMLRev 725.

tional period was due to end. The Treaty had provided for unanimity on almost all matters during the transitional period. France insisted it had a veto on any matter where 'very important interests' were at stake, and this is its stated position in the Luxembourg Compromise. The other member states, five at the time, were prepared to concede only that they would, 'within a reasonable time', try to reach unanimity where very important interests of one or more states were at stake. If unanimity was not possible within a reasonable time, then those five states would invoke the majority voting system prescribed by the Treaty. The states acknowledged that their positions diverged, but they were prepared to resume the work of the Community.[43]

In practice the French position in the Luxembourg Compromise gradually prevailed and each state is able to exercise a veto in the Council where very important interests are at stake. The veto was, however, rejected in 1982 when the British agriculture minister attempted to veto the annual agricultural price-fixing agreement until the foreign ministers in their Council agreed the British contribution to the Community budget. The agriculture ministers ignored the veto and passed the price-fixing agreement by qualified majority.[44] This was not, however, regarded as a rejection of the concept of a veto. It was a rejection of the use of a veto to block a measure where no 'very important interest' was at stake in order to gain leverage in another area of Council decision-making.[45]

The ongoing existence of the practice of a veto was confirmed by its use by Germany in blocking a Council decision reducing the support prices for cereals and colza in 1985.[46] When Germany invoked the Luxembourg Compromise, Denmark, France, Greece, Ireland and the United Kingdom refused to vote against Germany even though they were all in favour of reducing the support prices for cereals and colza. Only Italy and the Benelux countries were prepared to take a vote after allowing a 'reasonable time' for further discussion.[47]

In 1986 Ireland managed to get an additional premium for Irish beef producers and in 1988 Greece won concessions for their farmers after these states had invoked the Luxembourg Compromise in the agriculture

43 See EEC Bull. 1966 no. 3, pp. 9–10.
44 The Danish and Greek ministers joined the British minister in refusing to take part in the vote. These three states can be regarded as the hard-core supporters of a veto.
45 See the explanation of the rejection of the 1982 veto by Sir Geoffrey Howe, then United Kingdom Foreign Secretary, in HC Deb. 1986, Vol. 96, cols. 320–21, and the discussion in Campbell, (1986) 35 ICLQ 932, 937–8.
46 See Vasey, 'The 1985 Farm Price Negotiations and the Reform of the Common Agricultural Policy' (1985) 22 CMLRev 649, and Vasey, (1988) 25 CMLRev 725.
47 See Vasey, (1988) 25 CMLRev 725, 728–9. If the Luxembourg Compromise is invoked, 'a reasonable time' means postponing a vote until the next Council meeting.

Council.[48] On the latter occasion Denmark, France, Ireland, Portugal and the United Kingdom explicitly stated that they would refuse to take part in a vote once Greece had invoked the Luxembourg Compromise.[49] Clearly there are enough member states who support the concept of a veto that the other states are unable to muster enough votes to push a measure through by qualified majority.

A state that invokes a veto where 'very important interests' are at stake in the decision being made by the Council can be confident that the measure will not be passed by qualified majority. If, however, the other states consider that the veto is not being invoked to protect very important interests at stake in the decision in hand, but rather as a tactic to help that state with other Community issues, then the veto may be ignored. No consensus exists in relation to the veto, because up to now Belgium, Italy, Luxembourg and the Netherlands have opposed it, Germany and Spain have been ambivalent, and the remaining member states have supported it. It is, therefore, too early to speak of the veto being a Community constitutional convention. On the one hand, a convention may be emerging because enough members of the Council feel bound by such a practice to make it effective. On the other hand, the Luxembourg Compromise veto may be fading from the scene of Community life as a result of the greater use and acceptance of qualified majority voting in the 1980s, particularly since the Single European Act was ratified. With the use of qualified majority voting being further widened by the Treaty amendments agreed at Maastricht in December 1991, it will become the increasingly routine method of conducting business in the Council. It may become more and more unusual for a state to claim a veto on the grounds that very important national interests are at stake. Such a claim may be particularly difficult to make when a state has relatively recently agreed to Treaty amendments permitting qualified majority voting in that area.

The Luxembourg Compromise veto is an important safeguard for states, but it has its limitations. The state invoking it must convince at least a blocking minority of member states that its very important interests are at stake in the decision concerned. The veto has to be actively invoked, as the days of acting by consensus only are past. The veto is rarely used in the Council[50] and even when it is, the state may not achieve the result it hoped

48 ibid., pp. 725, 727.
49 ibid., p. 729.
50 In an editorial in the *Common Market Law Review* in 1986, p. 744, it was stated that the Luxembourg Compromise 'has been invoked more than 240 times by civil servants [presumably at Coreper or working-party level] as against only ten times by governments'. It is impossible to verify these figures. Even if the veto has in the past been invoked below ministerial level, it seems unlikely that it will be in the future. The editorial supported the view of the then French Minister of European Affairs, Bernard

for. When Germany succeeded in blocking a cut in cereal and colza prices in the Council in 1985, the Commission used its emergency powers to adopt interim measures that largely reflected the cuts wanted by the majority of the member states.[51]

IOANNINA COMPROMISE

One of the most hotly debated issues in the discussions surrounding the accession of Austria, Finland and Sweden to the European Union was the appropriate size of the blocking minority when qualified majority voting applies in the Council. The solution adopted in the Act of Accession was to increase the blocking minority proportionate to the increase in the total number of votes brought about by the accession.[52] At the time of the negotiations Norway was involved (it was allocated three votes) so the blocking minority was increased from 23 to 27 votes. The United Kingdom and Spain were willing to agree to this increase only because a compromise was agreed under the Greek presidency at the informal meeting of foreign ministers in Ioannina, Greece, in March 1994. Unlike the Luxembourg Compromise this Ioannina Compromise was reduced to legal form in a Council Decision of 29 March 1994.[53] It was amended by a Council Decision of 1 January 1995[54] to take account of Norway's decision not to accede to the European Union. The substantive part of the Decision now provides that:

If members of the Council representing a total of 23 to 25 votes indicate their intention to oppose the adoption by the Council of a decision by qualified majority, the Council will do all in its power to reach, within a reasonable time and without prejudicing obligatory time limits laid down by the Treaties and by secondary law, such as Articles 189b and 189c of the Treaty establishing the European Community, a satisfactory solution that could be adopted by at least 65 votes. During this period, and always respecting the Rules of Procedure of the Council, the President undertakes, with the assistance of the Commission, any initiative necessary to facilitate a wider basis of agreement in the Council. The members of the Council lend him their assistance.

The intent of the Ioannina Compromise is that if there are enough votes to constitute a blocking minority under the pre-Accession rules but not

---

Bosson, that the Compromise should be invoked only by ministers. It would seem that the United Kingdom also adopts this policy.
51 Vasey, (1988) 25 CMLRev 725, 727 and 730–31.
52 See Art. 15 as substituted by Art. 8 of Council Decision 95/1 OJ 1995 L1/1.
53 OJ 1994 C 105/1.
54 OJ 1995 C1/1.

under the new rules then further efforts must be made to try and produce a solution which could not be blocked under the old voting rules. If the Council attempts to find a satisfactory solution that can be adopted by 65 votes but fails to do so and the measure is passed by between 62 and 64 votes it is very unlikely that states in the dissenting minority will be able to persuade the Court to strike down the measure. The Court will be reluctant to adjudicate on when the effort required by the Council to reach a compromise is sufficient to constitute doing 'all in its power'. It will also hesitate to engage in the essentially political question of what constitutes a 'satisfactory' solution. The Court may be more willing to give guidance on what constitutes a 'reasonable time' within which efforts to reach a compromise should be pursued before the matter is pushed through under the Treaty voting rules.

UNANIMITY

There are a considerable number of occasions when the EC Treaty requires the Council to act by unanimity.[55] Unanimity can be achieved with one vote in favour if all the other member states desist from voting against, as abstentions do not block a measure that requires unanimity.[56] A number of measures of a constitutional nature require unanimity:

changes in the number of judges and advocates-general in the Court;[57]

changes in the composition and jurisdiction of the Court of First Instance;[58]

changes in the number of Commissioners;[59]

recommendation of a uniform procedure for elections to the European Parliament;[60]

making a decision not to fill a vacancy in the Commission;[61]

amending Title III of the Statute of the European Court;[62]

appointing members of the Court of Auditors;[63]

concerning the Community's own resources;[64]

acceptance of a new member state;[65]

concluding an association agreement with another state or an international

55 Arts. 45(3), 51, 57(2), 73c(2), 75(3), 76, 93(2), 99, 100, 100c(1), 103a, 104c(14), 105(6), 106(5), 109, 109f(7), 109l(4) and (5), 121, 128(5), 130(3), 130b, 130d, 130i(1), 130o, 130s(2), 136, 138(3), 157(1), 159, 165, 166, 168a, 188, 188b(3), 189a(1), 189b(3), 189(c), (d), (e), 194, 201, 209, 217, 223(3), 228(2), 235; and 238.
56 Art. 148(3).
57 Arts. 165 and 166.
58 Art. 168a(2).
59 Art. 157(1)
60 Art. 138(3).
61 Art. 159.
62 Art. 188.
63 Art. 188b(3).
64 Art. 201.
65 Art. O of the Treaty on European Union.

agreement on a subject where any internal rules would have to be adopted by unanimity under the treaty;[66]

in certain circumstances, to amend the Statute of the European System of Central Banks;[67]

and to agree the conversion rates at which national currencies shall be irrevocably fixed and at which irrevocably fixed rate the ECU shall be substituted for these currencies.[68]

Some politically sensitive issues still require unanimity:

harmonization of indirect taxes;[69]

approximation of laws falling within the common market but outside the internal market;[70]

granting of Community financial assistance to a member state that is in difficulties;[71]

the general power to pass laws coming within the objectives of the Community;[72]

authorizing of state aids in exceptional circumstances;[73]

involving those provisions on the environment that are primarily of a fiscal nature or concern town and country planning or are measures significantly affecting a member state's choice between different energy sources.[74]

Some procedural decisions require unanimity:

to include an item on the Council agenda other than those included in the provisional agenda;[75]

to hold certain council meetings in public;[76]

---

66 Arts. 228(2) and 238.

67 Art. 106(5).

68 See Art. 109l(4). In this context only those member states without a derogation can vote. Member states with a derogation are those that do not fulfil the necessary conditions for the adoption of a single currency; see Arts. 109j(4) and 109k. If the United Kingdom decides not to move to the third stage at the same time as the first member states are ready to do so (before the end of the decade), then its opt-out protocol agreed at Maastricht makes it clear that Art. 109l(4) does not apply to the United Kingdom. It would not have a vote and could not prevent other member states from moving to a single currency. The protocol does allow for the United Kingdom to seek to move to the third stage, adoption of a single currency, (see para. 10) on the same basis as other member states that had a derogation (see Art. 109l(5)), i.e., unanimity of the member states without a derogation and of the member state seeking to join the single currency. For the Danish position, see pp. 774–9 of the 1st edition. Denmark has an opt-out Protocol from the third stage of EMU and has already indicated it will exercise that opt-out in a Decision agreed at the Edinburgh European Council in December 1992.

69 Art. 99.

70 Art. 100. Certain measures, listed in Art. 100a(2), are excluded from the scope of qualified majority voting allowed for in Art. 100a(1). These measures are fiscal provisions, those relating to the free movement of persons (as opposed to workers) and those relating to the rights and interests of employed persons.

71 Art. 103a.

72 Art. 235.

73 Art. 93(2).

74 Art. 130s(2).

75 Council Rules of Procedure, Art. 2(5).

76 ibid., Art. 6(2).

    to decide to use the written vote to adopt an act on an urgent matter;[77]

    to decide to adopt an act when it has not yet been translated into all the official languages of the Community;[78]

    to decide to publish certain directives, decisions, recommendations and conventions in the *Official Journal*;[79]

    to appoint the Council Secretary-General.[80]

Crucial to the institutional balance in the Community is the fact that unanimity is required in the Council for it to amend a Commission proposal[81] or to pass a measure under the cooperation procedure that has been rejected by the European Parliament.[82]

SUMMARY

Since the early 1980s qualified majority voting has been the norm in the Council, but in a few cases the Treaty prescribes simple majority voting and in rather more cases it requires unanimity. Even where a form of majority voting is prescribed by the Treaty, a state can still invoke the veto arising from the Luxembourg Compromise. Such an invocation is becoming very uncommon and although it is likely to be supported by sufficient states to prevent a qualified majority being achieved, it may produce only limited concessions for the state that invokes it.[83] The veto is now very much a weapon of last resort, which cannot be systematically invoked against every legislative proposal that a state opposes. Member states are obliged to accept that laws that they oppose will be passed. These laws cover a wide area of economic and social activity including the customs union, the four freedoms, the establishment of common policies in agriculture, fisheries and transport, and competition policy. The introduction of the Ioannina Compromise has cast further doubt on the efficacy of the Luxembourg Compromise. A state may find it increasingly difficult to persuade enough of the other member states to vote against their own interests to formulate a blocking minority just because it alleges that the

---

77 ibid. Art. 8(1). The fact that the United Kingdom did not consent to the use of the written vote by which the Council adopted Dir. 85/649 meant that this Art. was not complied with. The European Court found this to be an infringement of an essential procedural requirement within the meaning of Art. 173 of the Treaty and declared the Directive void in Case 68/86 *UK* v *Council* [1988] ECR 855.

78 ibid., Art. 10(1).

79 ibid., Art. 18(5).

80 ibid., Art. 21(1).

81 Art. 189a(1).

82 Art. 189c(c).

83 See Vasey, (1988) 25 CMLRev 732.

act threatens its very important national interests. Measures may only be blocked when a sufficient number of states to constitute a blocking minority, or at least to invoke the Ioannina Decision, share a common view that the measure is contrary to their national interests.

COMMITTEE OF PERMANENT REPRESENTATIVES

This Committee is commonly known by its French acronym, Coreper. Its existence within the scheme of the Community legislative process was formally recognized by Article 4 of the Merger Treaty, which says that 'a committee consisting of the Permanent Representatives of the Member States shall be responsible for preparing the work of the Council and for carrying out the tasks assigned to it by the Council'.[84]

The Committee, in fact, functions as two equal committees, called Coreper 1 and Coreper 2. The former is made up of the deputy Permanent Representatives (deputy ambassadors) of the member states to the Community, and the latter by the Permanent Representatives (ambassadors). Although the two Corepers are equal and not hierarchical, i.e., matters are not referred up from the deputies to the ambassadors, major political questions of an institutional nature are normally dealt with by the ambassadors. Coreper is chaired by the delegate of that member state whose representative is President of the Council.[85]

Coreper can set up working parties and instruct them to carry out such preparatory work or studies as it defines.[86] It is in the working parties that much of the detailed preparatory work is done. These will often be composed of one expert from each of the Permanent Representations (embassies) of the member states to the Community. These embassies are situated in Brussels, and the national civil servants working there become experts in the Community legislative milieu. They receive instructions from their Governments in their national capitals, but they also advise those Governments on the views of the other member states and of the Commission about a proposal. The Permanent Representations are the eyes and ears of the national Governments in Brussels.

---

84 Exactly the same wording is preserved in Art. 151(1) EC. In 1992 Coreper met forty-eight times; see Noel, *Working Together*, p. 54.
85 See Council Rules of Procedure, Art. 19(3).
86 See ibid., Art. 19(2). At any one time there are always more than 100 working parties; see *The Guide to the Council of the European Union*, p. 54.

A Commission proposal is discussed in the working parties and then in Coreper 1 or 2 in the presence of a representative of the Commission.[87] If agreement has been reached in the working party, then the proposal will appear in Part I of the agenda of Coreper 1 or 2, which, in turn, will put it on the Council agenda as an 'A' item if there is no dissent at that level. An 'A' item proposal will be formally passed by the Council unless a member state raises an objection at the Council, in which case it will be referred back to Coreper for further discussion before reappearing on the Council agenda.[88] On urgent questions Coreper may decide unanimously that the matter should be adopted by the Council by a written vote.[89]

If no agreement is reached in the working party, the matter will appear on Part II of Coreper's agenda. It may be that Coreper can resolve the differences and put the proposal on the Council agenda as an 'A' item. However, where Coreper is not able to do so, the proposal will be put as a 'B' item on the Council agenda, indicating that it needs further discussion and highlighting the points of disagreement.

The influence of the civil servants who sit on the working parties and in Coreper on the final decision-making of the Council is a matter of debate. Clearly they are often more attuned to what is politically possible in Brussels than their ministerial bosses, who may attend a Council meeting only once a month or even less frequently. None the less, members of the Permanent Representations must work within the political framework established for them by their political masters. An ambassador or deputy ambassador who not only takes decisions in Coreper but actively advises the minister in the Council meetings must be potentially very influential on that country's policy in Europe. However, the influence of ambassadors and deputy ambassadors at the highest level of decision-making is limited by the fact that they cannot attend the meetings of the European Council, although they will often be part of their state's delegation advising from the wings.[90]

---

87 The 1979 Council Rules of Procedure Art. 16(3) provided that 'unless the Council decides otherwise, the Commission shall be invited to be represented in the work of the Committee and of the working parties'. The 1993 Rules of Procedure are silent on the point.

88 See Council Rules of Procedure, Arts. 2(6) and (7).

89 See Council's Rules of Procedure, Art. 8(1).

90 See Bulmer and Wessels, *The European Council*, p. 108.

EUROPEAN COUNCIL

The European Council was not part of the institutional structure envisaged by the drafters of the EEC Treaty. Its birth can be traced to the 'summit' meeting of the heads of Government and of state and ministers of foreign affairs of the then nine member states, and the President of the Commission in Paris on 9–10 December 1974.[91] It was agreed in Paris that regular meetings of the heads of Government and of state, accompanied by the foreign ministers, should take place with a remit for progressing the work of the European Communities and of political cooperation. The European Council would meet three times a year to take an 'overall approach to the internal problems involved in achieving European unity and the external problems facing Europe'.[92]

The first European Council meeting was in Dublin on 10–11 March 1975. The role of the Commission at the European Council was gradually clarified at this and subsequent meetings, where the President of the Commission attended all the sessions at which heads of Government and of state were present and a Commission member attended all sessions at which the ministers of foreign affairs were present. The composition of the European Council and its existence as an entity separate from the Council were confirmed by Article 2 of the Single European Act.[93]

The European Council shall bring together the Heads of State or of Government of the Member States and the President of the Commission of the European Communities. They shall be assisted by the Ministers for Foreign Affairs and by a Member of the Commission. The European Council shall meet at least twice a year.

In practice, seven officials also attend the meetings of the European Council although they do not take part in the discussions: three civil servants of the Government holding the presidency of the Council, three members of the Council Secretariat (including the Secretary-General), and the Secretary-General of the Commission.[94] It is customary in the normal two-day European Council meetings for all the participants to meet

---

91 Previous 'summits' of heads of Government and of state of the member states had taken place but on a purely *ad hoc* basis in 1961, 1967, 1969, 1972 and 1973; see Bulmer and Wessels, *The European Council*, pp. 27–36.

92 Communiqué issued on 10 December 1974, EC Bull. 1974, (No. 12).

93 All member states are represented by the head of Government – e.g., the United Kingdom by the Prime Minister, and Germany by the Chancellor – except France, which is represented by the head of state, the President, who holds an executive and not merely ceremonial function under the French constitution.

94 See Bulmer and Wessels, *The European Council*, p. 50.

together at the beginning and the end, but for the heads of Government and of state and the President of the Commission to have a 'fireside chat' in the middle while the foreign ministers and a member of the Commission meet separately to draft the final communiqué.[95]

The reduction from three to two regular meetings of the European Council was agreed in 1986 to reduce the risk of the European Council being used as a referee to resolve difficult problems in the various specialist Councils.[96] However, in recent years the temptation for states holding the presidency of the Council to hold 'emergency' European Councils has been evident. Normally, each state holding the presidency hosts and chairs one European Council during its six months of office, but France, Ireland, Italy and Luxembourg each held two between July 1989 and June 1991. After the Netherlands and Portugal had restricted themselves to one European Council each between July 1991 and June 1992 the United Kingdom hosted two European Councils, in Birmingham in October 1992 and in Edinburgh in December 1992. The Belgians in the second half of 1993 and the Germans in the second half of 1994 continued the trend of having two European Councils, although the Danes and the Greeks resisted the temptation in the first half of those years. It would seem that on average three European Councils are held each year.

The role and powers of the European Council have evolved rather than being established by the Community Treaties. The Single European Act of 1986 did, belatedly, give the European Council the status of a body established by Treaty, but did not define its role or its method of voting and did not bring its decisions within the framework of the European Court's powers of judicial review.[97] At Maastricht the role of the European Council was elaborated slightly. Its composition is unaltered, but Article D of the Treaty on European Union states that: 'the European Council shall provide the Union with the necessary impetus for its development and shall define the general political guidelines thereof'. It also confirms that the chairing of the European Council rotates every six months with the presidency of the Council, and requires that the European Council submit a report to the European Parliament after each of its meetings, and a yearly written report on the progress achieved by the Union. Art. L of the Treaty on European Union confirms that the provisions on the European Council in Art. D of that Treaty are not subject to the jurisdiction of the European Court of Justice.

Despite its relatively late arrival on the Community scene and its uncertain institutional status, the European Council is the key forum for major political decisions in the European Community. In the modern

95 ibid., pp. 48–50.
96 Noel, *Working Together*, p. 31.
97 See Art. 31 Single European Act.

world it is heads of Government who have the political authority to take decisions with major financial or constitutional implications. Thus agreement at European Council level has been necessary to establish direct elections of the European Parliament,[98] for the creation of the European Currency Unit (ECU)[99] and the European Monetary System (EMS),[100] for budget rebates for the United Kingdom,[101] for budgetary reform,[102] to set up the intergovernmental conference that led to the Single European Act,[103] to set up the intergovernmental conferences on economic and monetary union[104] and on political union,[105] and to agree the Treaty on European Union.[106]

The European Council did not exercise a lawmaking power under the EEC Treaty.[106a] In principle it could have done so using the Treaty powers given to the Council, as there is nothing to prevent the Council being constituted by heads of Government. The European Council preferred to reach agreement at whatever level of detail was required to enable the legal measures to be finalized by the Council composed of ministers below head-of-Government level.[107] At Maastricht the European Economic Community became the European Community, and now the Community Treaty requires that certain Council decisions should be taken at the level of heads of state or of Government. In Article 109j(3) and (4) the Council,

98 The Paris summit of December 1974.
99 The Brussels European Council of December 1977.
100 This began with the Schmidt/Giscard d'Estaing proposal at the Copenhagen European Council in April 1978 and was concluded at the Paris European Council in March 1979; see Bulmer and Wessels. *The European Council*, pp. 63, 82–4.
101 A perpetual topic of discussion from Dublin in December 1979 until agreement was reached at the Fontainebleau European Council of June 1984; see George, *An Awkward Partner*, Ch. 5.
102 Brussels in February 1988 agreeing the Delors I package: see Kolte, 'The Community Budget: New Principles for Finance, Expenditure Planning and Budgetary Discipline' (1988) 25 CMLRev 487. See also the Delors II package agreed at Edinburgh in December 1992.
103 The European Council in Milan in June 1985 decided to establish an intergovernmental conference; see de Zwaan, 'The Single European Act: Conclusion of a Unique Document' (1986) 23 CMLRev 747. The Luxembourg European Council in December 1985 spent thirty hours finalizing the text of the Single European Act.
104 Strasbourg in December 1989.
105 Dublin in June 1990; see Jacque and Weiler, 'On the Road to European Union – A New Judicial Architecture: An Agenda for the Intergovernmental Conference' (1990) 27 CMLRev 185.
106 At Maastricht in December 1991.
106a Though it did reach a binding decision, which did not have its legal basis in the EEC Treaty, at the Edinburgh European Council in December 1992, see p. 17 above.
107 The Milan European Council in June 1985 took a decision to set up an intergovernmental conference, but the formal legal decision under Art. 236 EEC was adopted by the Council on 22 July 1985 after receiving favourable opinions from the Commission and European Parliament; see de Zwaan, (1986) 23 CMLRev 750–51.

composed of the heads of state or of Government of the member states, can set the date for the start of the third stage of economic and monetary union, the adoption of a single currency, and can determine which member states have fulfilled the economic and monetary conditions specified in Article 109j(2) to enable a single currency to be adopted.[108] This is not technically the European Council but rather the Council composed of the heads of state and of Government, because the President of the Commission is not a member of the Council though he is a member of the European Council. The European Council, including the President of the Commission, is given the task of reaching conclusions on the broad guidelines of the economic policies of the member states and of the Community.[109] It is envisaged that the Council, presumably acting at a ministerial level below that of heads of Government, will then adopt a recommendation setting out these broad guidelines.[110] Member states are required to conduct their economic policies with a view to achieving the objectives of the Community defined in Article 2 and in the context of these broad guidelines.[111]

The European Council's existence has implications for the other Community institutions. The Commission's institutional right of legislative initiative has to be seen in the light of the European Council's ability to launch political initiatives.[112] The European Council has set up *ad hoc* committees to report on different aspects of the development of the Community that can provide the basis for reform such as the Dooge Committee on European Union and the Adonino Committee on the People's Europe, which reported prior to the European Council agreeing in Milan in June

108 See the Protocol on the Convergence Criteria referred to in Art. 109j and, further, Ch. 21.
109 Art. 103(2). No guidance is given as to the voting rights in the European Council. Do the heads of Government and of state and the President of the Commission have to be unanimous as to the 'conclusions' or is some kind of majority sufficient?
110 ibid.
111 Art. 102a. The sanction against states that fail to comply with these broad guidelines appears to be simply adverse publicity; see Art. 103(4). On the other hand, there are real sanctions against member states that operative excessive government deficits defined in the Protocol on the Excessive Deficit Procedure agreed at Maastricht; see Art. 104c(11) EC, but these operate only from the beginning of the third stage of economic and monetary union, when the single currency is operative; see Art. 109e(3).
112 See Bulmer and Wessels, *The European Council*, pp. 109–13. In the context of the common foreign and security policy, which remains outside the European Community but within the Treaty on European Union, it is the European Council that has to 'define the principles of and general guidelines for the common foreign and security policy' (Art. J.8(1); see also Art. J.3(1)). The Council defines and implements these guidelines (Art. J.8(2); see also Art. J.3(2)). The Commission can make proposals to the Council (Art. J.8(3)), but it does now have the exclusive, or even the main, right of initiative. Each member state (Art. J.8(3)), the Council and the Political Committee, a substitute for Coreper in this context, have a right of initiative (Art. J.8(5)).

1985 on an intergovernmental conference; and the Delors Committee on Economic and Monetary Union, established by the European Council at its meeting in Hanover on 27–28 June 1988.[113] The European Council, rather than the Commission, can set the agenda for major reforms where Treaty amendments are being considered. Within the framework of the EC Treaty, however, the legislative measures that the European Council wishes to see adopted have to be drafted and proposed by the Commission, though some of the decisions on economic and monetary union are taken by the Council without a proposal from the Commission.[114] The Commission's position is safeguarded to some extent, by the fact that it is represented in the European Council by the President and another member of the Commission.

The political reality is such that a right of initiative that leads to initiatives simply being rejected or interminably delayed is not of much value. This was often the problem with the Commission's power of initiative prior to the creation of the European Council. The Commission is able to have direct access to the heads of Government at European Council meetings and to be part of the initiation of developments in the Community. Those developments that are within existing Community competence must come back to the Commission for legislative proposals.[115] If Treaty amendments are required, this is done by an intergovernmental conference, and the Treaty does not give the Commission the exclusive right of initiation in such a conference.[116] In practice, the Commission's views, along with those of every member state and the President of the Council, are fed into the conference and may be very influential.[117]

The Council has suffered a diminution of status by the setting up of the European Council and inevitably there is a danger that politically difficult

113 Discussed in Chs. 2, 21.

114 E.g. Art. 109j(3) and (4), where the decision to go ahead with the single currency and which member states qualify is taken by the Council at heads of Government level on the recommendation of the Council at a lower ministerial level. The Commission simply makes a report and a recommendation to help the Council in its decision-making. See also Arts. 104c(7), (9) and (11).

115 Except in the instance of the broad economic guidelines under Art. 103(2) EC discussed above.

116 Art. N of the Treaty on European Union.

117 In relation to the intergovernmental conference in 1985–6 that led to the Single European Act, de Zwaan claimed that 'the progress of the Conference was most influenced by the proposals submitted by the Commission. More particularly, the texts on the most fundamental areas of the Conference – internal market, European Parliament and cohesion – were in the first instance drawn up by the European Commission.' (1986) 23 CMLRev 747, 756. The Commission published its contributions to the intergovernmental conferences held in 1990–91 on economic and monetary union and on political union; see EC Bull. Supp. 2/91. A detailed study could be made comparing the Commission's proposals with the final text agreed at Maastricht.

decisions, such as reform of the CAP, are referred up to the European Council. This would be better than reform never being agreed because the specialist ministers are not prepared to sacrifice the interests of their 'consumers', e.g., agriculture ministers unable to agree significant cuts in farm subsidies.[118] However, the European Council can be reluctant to act as a court of appeal. In October 1990 the agriculture ministers met in the Council on several occasions but failed to agree on a package of cuts in farm subsidies of 30 per cent as the EC's negotiating position in the final rounds of talks of the GATT Uruguay Round.[119] Sadly, then, the European Council is sometimes better at agreeing to a grand design of European integration than the practical reality of cuts in agricultural subsidies that are electorally unpopular, at least in certain countries, but necessary for the future of world free trade.

118 See the views of Christopher Tugendhat, *Making Sense of Europe* (1986), p. 163.
119 See the *Times* editorial of 19 October 1990 and the report in *The Times* of 22 October 1990. The foreign ministers were unable to resolve the problem at their meeting on 22 October and yet the matter was only briefly considered at the European Council on 27–28 October without resolution. It was resolved by agriculture ministers in 1992 and the Commission negotiated a deal with the US. The Uruguay Round was eventually successfully concluded in 1994 and the new World Trade Organization (WTO) commenced operation in 1995.

CHAPTER 4

European Parliament

COMPOSITION AND STRUCTURE

The European Parliament began life as the Common Assembly of the European Coal and Steel Community on 10 September 1952 with seventy-eight members. It became the Assembly for all three Communities (ECSC, EEC and Euratom) on 19 March 1958 with 142 members. These members were delegates of their national parliaments, so they all had a dual mandate.[1] It was envisaged in the founding treaties of the Communities that the Assembly would propose a system for its own election by 'direct universal suffrage in accordance with a uniform procedure in all Member States' and that the Council would unanimously lay down the appropriate provisions for recommendation to the member states to be approved in accordance with their respective constitutional requirements.[2] The European Assembly originally made such proposals in 1960, but it was not until the summit of heads of Government and of state in Paris on 9–10 December 1974 that the political decision was taken to hold direct elections in or after 1978. The Assembly was asked for new proposals for direct elections and gave them in January 1975, but more than a year passed before the European Council reached agreement, on 12–13 July, on what would be contained in the Council decision. Finally, on 20 September 1976, the Council Decision and Act on Direct Elections was signed in Brussels.[3] It came into force on 1 July 1978 after all the member states had ratified it.[4]

1 Art. 138 EEC, Art. 21 ECSC and Art. 108 Euratom.
2 ibid.
3 Council Dec. 76/787, OJ 1976 L278.
4 The delay in ratification, which pushed direct elections back to 1979, was partly due to the time taken to pass the European Assembly Elections Act 1978 in the United Kingdom. Drawing up the large constituency boundaries for the seventy-eight seats in Great Britain was a lengthy process. Direct elections could have been held in 1978 had the House of Commons voted for a form of proportional representation, which was supported by the then Prime Minister, James Callaghan, as part of the Lib–Lab pact. On 28 November 1977 the House of Commons voted by a majority of eighty-seven against

The Council Decision and Act does not provide for a uniform electoral procedure, and until such a procedure can be agreed by the Council on a proposal from the Assembly each member state is free to adopt its own procedure.[5] Thus some variant of proportional representation is used throughout the Community except in Great Britain.[6] The decision does state that members are elected for a fixed period of five years and lists how many members are elected from each member state.[7] Membership of the Assembly is incompatible with a number of offices, including membership of the Commission, Court of Justice or a government of a member state.[8] The dual mandate is not precluded, but in practice the number of people who are members of both their national parliaments and the Assembly has declined to a small percentage.[9] The decision requires that voting is held in the member states some time between a Thursday morning and a Sunday night of a week unanimously chosen by the Council after consulting the Assembly. The first elections were held between 14 and 17 June 1979, and subsequent elections are held at five-year intervals. The Council can, unanimously, move the date of the election up to one month before or one month after the date that is five years from the previous election.[10] The votes are not counted until polling has ended in all the member states.[11]

---

proportional representation for the Assembly elections. The Labour members had a free vote and split 140 for and 115 against proportional representation, but the vote was lost, as the vast majority of Conservative MPs were against. This matter is discussed in George. *An Awkward Partner*, pp. 117–21.

5 See Council Dec. 76/787, note 3 above, Art. 7 and Art. 138(3) EEC. At Maastricht Art. 138(3) was amended so that the uniform procedure is not only proposed by the European Parliament but can be passed only by the Council acting unanimously after obtaining the assent of the European Parliament. A majority of the members of the European Parliament, not just those voting, must vote in favour of the uniform procedure in order for the Parliament's assent to be given.

6 In Northern Ireland the single transferable vote system is used.

7 See Council Dec. 76/787, note 3 above, Arts. 2 and 3. Germany has 99 seats; France, Italy and the United Kingdom 87; Spain 64; Netherlands 31; Belgium, Greece and Portugal 25; Sweden 22; Austria 21; Denmark and Finland 16; Ireland 15; and Luxembourg 6.

8 ibid., Art. 6.

9 In December 1979 31 per cent of the members of the Assembly held a dual mandate, but by July 1988 only 6 per cent held a dual mandate; see European Parliament, *Forging Ahead*, p. 112. As at 31 January 1990 the number of members holding a dual mandate was thirty-four (6.5 per cent); see Bradley, 'Legal Developments in the European Parliament' (1989) 9 YEL 235, 236.

10 See Council Dec. 76/787, note 3 above, Art. 10. The Council did this in relation to the date of the 1989 elections, contrary to the will of the European Parliament; see OJ 1988 C235/136 and OJ 1988 L210/25, and Bradley, 'Legal Developments in the European Parliament' (1988) 8 YEL 189, 203.

11 See Council Dec. 76/787, note 3 above, Art. 9(2).

The first directly elected Assembly met on 24 July 1979 with 410 members; it has since grown, with the accession of Greece, Portugal and Spain, to 518 members, with the adjustments made to incorporate former East Germany into the unified Germany to 567 members,[12] and with the accession of Austria, Finland and Sweden on 1 January 1995 to 626 members.[13] The Assembly called itself the European Parliament in 1962 but was given this name legally only when the Single European Act came into force on 1 July 1987.[14] Members of the European Parliament (MEPs) do not sit in national groupings, but in political groups. Rule 29(2) of the European Parliament's Rules of Procedure lays down a minimum of 13 MEPs to form a political group if they come from four or more member states, at least 16 if they come from three member states, at least 21 if they come from two member states, at least 26 if they come from one member state. MEPs who do not belong to a political group are known as non-attached members and they are provided with a secretariat.[15]

After the accession of Austria, Finland and Sweden on 1 January 1995, the largest political group was the Party of European Socialists (PES), with 221 members drawn from all the member states, but it could not be sure of majority support in the Parliament. The existence of ten groups with a broad range of political views meant that neither the left nor the right could be sure of a majority.[16]

The European Parliament elects its own President in a secret ballot by an absolute majority of the votes cast. If after three ballots no candidate has secured such a majority, then the fourth ballot is confined to the two candidates with the largest number of votes in the third ballot.[17] The President is elected for two and a half years. Like the Speaker of the House

---

12 See Council Decision of 1 February 1993, OJ 1993 L33/15.

13 See Art. 5 of Council Decision 95/1 of 1 January 1995, OJ 1995 L1/1.

14 See Art. 3(1) Single European Act and the ensuing Articles, which refer to the Assembly as the European Parliament.

15 See Rules of Procedure EP (9th ed., June 1994), Rule 30.

16 To the left of the PES is the Confederal Group of the European United Left (31 MEPs from eight member states). On the centre and right are the European People's Party (EPP; 173 MEPs from all 15 member states), the European Liberal Democratic and Reformist Party (ELDR; 52 MEPs from 13 member states), Forza Europa (29 MEPs drawn entirely from Italy), and the European Democratic Alliance (EDA; 26 MEPs from four member states). Four other groups are more difficult to fit on the political spectrum and these MEPs can hold the balance of power when an absolute majority is required: the Greens (25 MEPs from nine member states), the European Radical Alliance (ERA; 19 MEPs from five member states), Europe of the Nations (EN; 19 MEPs from three member states, largely France) and the non-affiliated group (31 MEPs from five member states). See The Week, 16–20 January 1995 (European Parliament).

17 See Art. 140 EC and Rules of Procedure EP, Rule 14.

of Commons, the President of the European Parliament chairs the proceedings of Parliament in plenary session, exercises administrative functions and represents Parliament in international relations, in administrative, legal or financial matters and on ceremonial occasions.[18] The President can delegate these functions to one of the fourteen Vice-Presidents elected by the Parliament.[19] The President has an important substantive role to play in the budgetary process.[20]

The President and Vice-Presidents together constitute the Parliament's Bureau. It also includes five more members elected by the Parliament, called quaestors, but they have no voting rights.[21] The Bureau has a number of administrative and financial functions laid down by the Parliament's Rules of Procedure, including the composition and organization of the Secretariat and the appointment of its head, the Secretary-General. It also authorizes committees of Parliament to meet at places other than the usual places of work and for rapporteurs to undertake fact-finding journeys.[22] It is hoped that in the election of the members of the Bureau an 'overall fair representation of Member States and political views' is achieved.[23] This is secured to some extent by candidates having the backing of the political groups, but it is still possible that certain political views or member states will be unrepresented on the Bureau.[24]

Since 1994 the Conference of Presidents, replacing the enlarged Bureau,[25] is responsible for making a number of key political decisions. It consists of the President of Parliament and the chairpersons of the political groups. The non-attached members delegate two of their number to attend the meetings but they do not have the right to vote. Although the Conference of Presidents tries to reach a consensus on all matters it can take decisions by a vote subject to a weighting based on the number of MEPs in each political group.[26] The Conference of Presidents takes decisions on the organization of Parliament's work and matters relating to legislative planning. It is the authority responsible for relations with other EC institutions and bodies, with national parliaments in member states, and with non-

18 See Rules of Procedure EP, Rule 19.
19 ibid., Rules 15 and 20.
20 On this and the President's role generally, see European Parliament, *Forging Ahead*, pp. 151–4. Since 1987 the President has had the opportunity to give the views of the European Parliament to the European Council just prior to their meetings commencing.
21 See Rules of Procedure EP, Rules 16 and 21.
22 ibid., Rules 22, 164, and European Parliament, *Forging Ahead*, pp. 155–6.
23 Rules of Procedure EP, Rule 13(3).
24 From January 1987 to June 1989 Denmark and Luxembourg were unrepresented in the Bureau, and Belgium had only a quaestor.
25 Its composition was the members of the Bureau plus the chairpersons of the political groups, see p. 82 of the 1st ed.
26 See Rule 23 of the Rules of Procedure EP.

member countries and non-Community institutions. The Conference of Presidents draws up the draft agenda of Parliament's part-sessions and makes proposals to Parliament as to the composition of committees of Parliament designed to ensure fair representation of member states and of political views.[27]

Plenary sessions are normally held for one week each month except in August. The sessions are usually held in Strasbourg, France.[28] Although the seat of the European Parliament was not finalized until 1992, it was *de facto* in Strasbourg for plenary sessions. This was confirmed by the European Court in *France* v *European Parliament*, where it upheld the Parliament's decision to build a debating chamber in Brussels but observed that it can hold plenary sessions outside Strasbourg only exceptionally.[29] On the other hand, over 70 per cent of committee meetings are held in Brussels, spread over two weeks each month.[30] Most of the remaining meetings are held in Strasbourg, but a few are held in Luxembourg. These are the places of work of the Parliament, but a committee can request to meet somewhere else,[31] and the President or, more usually, the Bureau can authorize this. Each committee has, on average, one such meeting a year. The third place of work of the Parliament, Luxembourg, is largely reduced to being the host to a large part of the Secretariat.[32] On 20 May 1983 the European Parliament decided to implement its resolution of 7 July 1981 and move the bulk of the Secretariat away from Luxembourg to Brussels and Strasbourg. However, in *Grand Duchy of Luxembourg* v *European Parliament*[33] the European Court ruled that the decision implementing the resolution was void, as it was contrary to Article 4 of the Decision of 8 April 1965 on the provisional location of certain institutions, which provided that 'the General Secretariat of the Assembly and its departments shall remain in Luxembourg'. More recently, in *Luxembourg* v *European Parliament*,[34] the Court dismissed Luxembourg's claim that two decisions and a resolution of the European Parliament were unlawful. These decisions and the resolution did not attempt to remove the Secretariat, or any of its directorates-general, from Luxembourg, but aimed to provide an adequate

27 See Rule of Procedure EP, Rules 24 and 137.
28 Parliament normally meets in plenary session for at least sixty days a year, spread over twelve part-sessions. In 1993 Parliament held 11 part-sessions in Strasbourg and 3 in Brussels (see *1993 General Report* at p. 359), in 1994 the figures were 10 and 4 and in 1995 the plan was to have 12 and 4 (see *1994 General Report*, pp. 414 and 417).
29 Cases 258/85, 51/86 [1988] ECR 4821, 4856.
30 See European Parliament, *Forging Ahead*, p. 168.
31 Rules of Procedure EP, Rule 11(3).
32 At 31 December 1994 the establishment plan of the Parliament's Secretariat provided for 3,249 permanent posts and 541 temporary posts. See *1994 General Report* p. 416.
33 Case 108/83 [1984] ECR 1945.
34 Cases C-213/88, C-39/89, [1991] ECR I-5643.

press office in Brussels, appropriately staffed offices and conference rooms in Brussels and Strasbourg, and a limited transfer of staff away from Luxembourg to the other two venues. The Parliament had acted within its margin of discretion in the exercise of its powers of internal organization. The Court accepted that the Parliament had to be in a position to maintain in the various places of work outside the place where its Secretariat is established the infrastructure essential for ensuring that it could fulfil in all those places the tasks that were entrusted to it by the treaties. This could not entail a partial transfer of any of the departments of the Secretariat away from Luxembourg.

It is very inefficient to have members, officials and documents travelling back and forth between three cities, but the three member states involved prevented the achievement of the common accord of the governments of member states needed to agree a single seat for the Parliament.[35] At the Edinburgh European Council meeting in December 1992 a decision of the representatives of the governments of the member states established that Strasbourg should be Parliament's seat and that twelve periods of monthly sessions should be held there annually. However, it also established that additional plenary sessions[36] and parliamentary committees should be held in Brussels. The General Secretariat of the Parliament and its Departments remain in Luxembourg.[37] The blame for this appalling arrangement must be laid firmly at the door of the Belgian, French and Luxembourg Governments and not of the European Parliament. The national self-interest in getting the jobs and prestige associated with having part of the European Parliament's operation outweighed the Community interest in reducing cost and increasing the Parliament's effectiveness by having all its activities in one place, logically Brussels where the other political institutions have their seat.

Parliament has a large number of standing committees dealing with a wide range of subject matters.[38] These committees have a function analo-

---

35 See Art. 216 EC.

36 In 1993 Parliament held three supplementary sessions in Brussels in September, October and December; see Westlake, *The Commission and Parliament* (1994), p. 103. In 1994 Parliament held four additional part-sessions in Brussels in February, March, September and November; see *General Report 1994*, p. 417.

37 See OJ 1992 C341/1.

38 As at June 1994 there were nineteen committees, dealing with: foreign affairs and security; agriculture, fisheries and rural development; budgets; economic and monetary affairs and industrial policy; energy, research and technology; external economic relations; legal affairs and citizens' rights; social affairs, employment and the working environment; regional policy, regional planning and relations with regional and local authorities; transport and tourism; environment, public health and consumer protection; culture, youth, education, and the media; development and cooperation; civil liberties and internal affairs; budgetary control; institutional affairs; rules of procedure, verification of

gous to that performed in the committee stage of the passage of a Bill through the House of Commons. Legislative proposals that come to the European Parliament are assigned to one of the standing committees and are thoroughly considered there.[39] The committee will put forward amendments to the proposal, or suggest its acceptance or rejection, accompanied by an explanatory statement or recommendation at a plenary session.[40] Parliamentary committees can be held in public if the committee so decides and are usually attended by a senior Commission official or the appropriate Commissioner. It is less common for the President of the Council to be represented, though he or she does attend the foreign affairs and security committee at least four times a year to discuss European political cooperation.[41]

The standing committees also perform a role that is more analogous to that of select committees in the House of Commons in that they make non-legislative reports which they hope will result in Parliamentary resolutions. In doing this the committees may set up fact-finding missions (subject to the approval of the Bureau), hear expert testimony, appoint a rapporteur or set up a subcommittee (subject to the approval of the Conference of Presidents) to examine a particular area within their remit.[42] This political, as opposed to legislative, work took up more than half of the committee time between the first direct elections and the coming into force of the Single European Act.[43] The Maastricht Treaty amendments gave explicit recognition to the role of these committees for the first time: Article 103(4) EC states that the 'President of the Council may be invited to appear before the competent Committee of the European Parliament' if the Council has made public its recommendations concerning the incompatibility of a member state's economic policies with the broad guidelines agreed under Article 103(2) EC; and Article 109b(3) EC provides that the President of the European Central Bank and other members of the

---

credentials and immunities; women's rights; and petitions. The powers and responsibilities of the standing committees are set out in Annex VI to the Rules of Procedure EP.

39 If the matter falls within the terms of reference of two or more committees, Parliament will designate the committee responsible but the others may be asked for their opinions; see Rules of Procedure EP, Rule 139(3) and European Parliament, *Forging Ahead*, p. 159. Only the committee responsible is able to table amendments in Parliament; see Rule 147(6).

40 Rules of Procedure EP, Rules 58, 66 and 67, 80 and 144(3). This is true of the consultation procedure, of both readings in the cooperation procedure, of the first and second readings in the conciliation and veto procedure, and of the assent procedure.

41 See European Parliament, *Forging Ahead*, p. 168, and Rules of Procedure EP, Rule 151.

42 See Rules of Procedure EP, Rules 139(5), 141, 145, 146 and 148, and European Parliament, *Forging Ahead*, pp. 162–6.

43 See European Parliament, *Forging Ahead*, p. 165.

Executive Board may be heard by the competent committees of the European Parliament.

SUPERVISORY ROLE

The most draconian power that the European Parliament has is to pass a motion of censure on the activities of the Commission. Such a motion must be carried by a two-thirds majority of the votes cast, representing a majority of the members of the Parliament. If such a motion were to be passed, the Commission would resign as a body.[44] The motion of censure can be tabled by one-tenth of the Members of Parliament and will not be debated for at least twenty-four hours. A further forty-eight hours must pass before the vote can be taken. Voting is by open vote by way of roll call.[45] A motion of censure has never been carried.[46] The closest vote yet came in December 1992 when MEPs from the Group of the European Right, the Greens and some of the non-attached members moved a motion of censure in relation to the Commission's negotiation of the EC-US oilseeds agreement in the context of the GATT Uruguay Round. The motion was defeated but 93 voted for it, 246 against, and 15 abstained.[47] It is something of a blunderbuss. Parliament cannot table a motion of censure against an individual member of the Commission; it has to be prepared to sack the whole Commission. It is unlikely that a two-thirds majority of Parliament will ever be sufficiently unhappy with the

---

44 See Art. 144 EC.

45 See Rules of Procedure EP, Rule 34. This means that 63 MEPs must back the motion of censure for it to be tabled. It used to be the case, prior to the coming into force of the TEU, that the Rules of Procedure permitted a political group to table a motion of censure.

46 Motions of censure were tabled on four occasions in the 1970s and votes were taken twice. The votes both related to agricultural matters and the majority against the motion of censure was overwhelming in each case; see European Parliament, *Forging Ahead*, p. 141. On the other two occasions the motions were withdrawn, once because the Commission produced the documents that Parliament had been insisting it should; see 1976 OJ Annex Debates No. 210 pp. 115–33. In February 1990 a motion of censure complaining generally about the Commission and in particular its handling of the CAP was tabled by the Group of the European Right. The motion was soundly defeated: the vote was 16 in favour, 243 against and 5 abstentions; see Bradley, (1990) 10 YEL 367, 381. In July 1991 the Group of the European Right were even more heavily defeated in a motion of censure relating to Commission policy on the former Yugoslavia: 8 in favour, 206 against, and 5 abstentions (see Westlake, *The Commission and the Parliament* (1994), p. 28).

47 See Westlake, ibid.

whole Commission to do this. The fact that Parliament, prior to the Maastricht Treaty amendments, had no control over the appointment of the new Commission was a deterrent against using the motion of censure. It is the Council that has the bulk of the legislative and budgetary power, and forcing the Commission to resign will not necessarily help the Parliament to exert more authority in either of these spheres.[48] The Commission does have the power to adopt or reject Parliament's amendments to the Council's common position under the cooperation procedure. If the Commission were to reject too many of Parliament's amendments, it might be an issue on which the motion of censure would be justified.

The Commission and Council both have a right to be heard by the Parliament.[49] The Commission must reply to questions put to it by the Parliament or its members.[50] The Council is not obliged by the EC Treaty to reply to questions, but it does do so in practice.[51] Since 1975 MEPs have been able to question the foreign ministers in relation to matters of European political cooperation. Question Time is a regular feature of each part-session of Parliament. No member may put more than one question to the Council and the Commission at a given part-session. The admissibility and order of questions at Question Time is determined by the President.[52] In addition to Question Time the Conference of Presidents can decide to put questions for the Commission and/or the Council on the agenda of Parliament at the request of a committee, a political group or at least 26 MEPs. The Commission must be given at least one week's and the Council at least three weeks' notice of the question before an answer is due. One of the questioners may speak to the question for not more than five minutes and one member of the institution concerned replies.[53] Written questions can be put down by any member. A member is allowed one priority question each month (one which requires no detailed research) which the Parliament insists should be answered within three weeks. Non-priority questions must, in the view of the Parliament, be answered within six weeks.[54] One of the effects of direct elections to the Parliament and the consequent expansion in the number of MEPs has been a significant increase in the number of questions asked at Question Time and in the number of written questions.[55] These questions have largely been

48 For another discussion of the motion of censure, see Ch. 2, p. 51.
49 Art. 140.
50 Art. 140.
51 The practice was confirmed by the Solemn Declaration on European Union of June 1983.
52 See Rule 41 and Annex II of the Rules of Procedure EP.
53 See Rules of Procedure EP, Rule 40.
54 See Rules of Procedure EP, Rule 42.
55 The total number of oral questions at question time in 1979 was 502 and this had risen to 813 by 1994. Comparing the same years, the number of written questions had

directed to the Commission, overwhelmingly so in relation to written questions, but the increase is also attributable to greater questioning of the Council.[56] This indicates that Parliament has made relatively little progress in the task of supervising the most powerful Community institution, the Council. This may be partly explained by the fact that the President of the Council is attempting to speak for a body of which he or she is just one of fifteen members, which meets relatively infrequently and is composed of different ministers. At least the Commissioner is speaking for a more collegiate body, bound together by collective responsibility, and has the advantage of being responsible for a particular area of Commission activity, which is the subject of the question.

The Commission is required by the EC Treaty to submit an annual general report, which is discussed in open session by the Parliament.[57] Of greater significance, however, is the Parliament's debate on the annual legislative programme of the Commission presented by its President at the beginning of each year. The European Parliament envisages that its President should negotiate the annual legislative programme with the President of the Commission. The President of the Parliament is to act on the basis of the conclusions of the Conference of Presidents. The programme should contain a timetable for the submission by the Commission of all the legislative proposals and documents to the Parliament and Council during the year.[58] This prospective debate is of more value in influencing the development of the Community than consideration of the Commission's general report on the previous year.

In stage three of economic and monetary union the President of the European Central Bank will be obliged to present an annual report on the activities of the European System of Central Banks and on the monetary

---

risen from 1,977 to 2,906; see European Parliament, *Forging Ahead*, pp. 139–41, and the *1994 General Report*, p. 416.

56 The number of questions to the Council at Question Time rose from 132 in 1979 to 248 in 1994, the number of written questions to the Council in the same years rose from 223 to 401; see European Parliament, *Forging Ahead* and the *1994 General Report*. Art. J.7 of the Treaty on European Union enshrines the right of the European Parliament to question the Council on the Union's foreign and security policy. The Parliament must hold an annual debate on progress in implementing the common foreign and security policy. See the similar rights of questioning and holding an annual debate in relation to cooperation in the fields of justice and home affairs, Art. K.6 of the Treaty on European Union.

57 Art. 143. According to Bradley (1990) 10 YEL 367, 391, the annual report is not debated in plenary session, but, rather, consideration is given to the appended reports on competition policy and on the monitoring of the application of Community law. See also Rules of Procedure EP, Rule 43.

58 Rules of Procedure EP, Rule 49. Cf. Westlake, *The Commission and Parliament* (1994) at pp. 19–20.

policy of both the previous and current year to the European Parliament, which may hold a general debate on that basis.[59]

The Council is under no obligation to report to Parliament, but its President does present the Council's programme to Parliament at the beginning of the six months of presidency and reports on what has been achieved at the end of the six months. Since the Solemn Declaration on European Union was adopted at the European Council in Stuttgart in June 1983 the President of the European Council has given a report to Parliament at least once every six months and an annual written report on progress towards European Union. These oral and annual reports from the European Council to the Parliament are now required by Article D of the Treaty on European Union.[60]

Some new requirements that Parliament be informed of certain matters were also written into the EC Treaty at Maastricht:

Council measures abolishing or amending a member state's unilateral measures against a third country in relation to capital movements and payments, Article 73g(2);

the Council's broad economic guidelines, (Article 103(2));

the results of multilateral surveillance of the economic policies of member states, Article 103(4);

Council measures granting financial assistance to a member state in difficulties, Article 103a(2);

Council sanctions on a member state that has not complied with a Council decision as to how it should reduce its excessive government deficit, Article 104c(11);

Council measures on the adoption, adjustment or abandonment of the ECU central rates within any future exchange-rate system with non-Community countries, Article 109(1).

Parliament is therefore kept informed of what the other political institutions are doing. The weakness of the system is the inability to question the European Council and the lack of any sanctions against it or the Council. Although the scrutiny of the Commission is much more comprehensive, it is hampered by the fact that Parliament's only sanction, apart from that of exposing wrongdoing or inefficiency by probing questions, the motion of censure, is too draconian and indiscriminate to be useful.

The European Parliament can set up committees of inquiry to investigate alleged contraventions of Community law or incidents of maladministration with respect to Community responsibilities. A quarter of the MEPs

59 Art. 109b(3) EC. The report is also submitted to the Commission, Council and European Council. See also Rules of Procedure EP, Rule 39.
60 See also Rules of Procedure EP, Rule 37.

must request the setting up of such a committee and it must report within nine months of being set up.[61] Committees of inquiry have investigated a number of issues, including the problem of stocks in the agricultural sector (1987), the handling and transport of nuclear material (1988), the problems of quality in the meat sector (1989), racism and xenophobia (1985 and 1990) and the extent of organized crime connected with drug trafficking (1991).[62] The non-legislative role of Parliament's standing committees, acting like House of Commons select committees, was considered above.[63] These two types of Parliamentary committees can do important work in exposing breaches of Community law, maladministration and inefficiency. Their work is hampered by their inability to insist on the cross-examination of members of the Council[64] and by the lack of attention paid by the media in Europe to their reports.

Another means of Parliamentary supervision of the other legislative institutions is by initiating, or intervening in,[65] legal action before the European Court. It has always been clear from Article 175 EC that Parliament has *locus standi* to bring actions for failure to act against the Council or the Commission: 'Member States and the other institutions of the Community may bring an action before the Court of Justice' [66] Much

---

61 See Rules of Procedure EP, Rule 136. At Maastricht this system was made part of the EC Treaty in Art. 138c. The Treaty adds the rider that the detailed provisions governing the exercise of the right of inquiry shall be determined by common accord of the European Parliament, the Council and the Commission. An inter-institutional agreement on this matter was reached on 20 December 1994; see *1994 General Report*, p. 416 and *The Week*, 16–20 January 1995 (European Parliament), pp. 19–22.

62 See European Parliament, *Forging Ahead*, p. 161 and Bradley, (1989) 9 YEL 235, 252 and (1990) 10 YEL 367, 383 and 396. Prior to the revision of Parliament's Rules of Procedure in June 1987 a committee of inquiry could investigate any matter that fell within the sphere of activities of the Communities.

63 See p. 99. A committee may have its own question time (Rule 149), it may hold public hearings and it may hear briefings from members of the Commission or Council in camera (Rule 151); see European Parliament, *Forging Ahead*, pp. 166–8.

64 The inter-institutional agreement on committees of inquiry of 20 December 1994 does not clarify what will happen if persons summoned to give evidence by a committee of inquiry refuse to attend or refuse to answer. Member states and Community institutions must submit documents to the committee save where 'prevented from doing so by reasons of secrecy or public or national security arising out of national or Community legislation or rules' (a potentially very broad exception).

65 On the general issue of the standing of the European Parliament see Bradley, 'The Variable Evolution of the Standing of the European Parliament in Proceedings Before the Court of Justice' (1988) 8 YEL 27–57; Dashwood, 'The European Parliament and Article 173 EEC: The Limits of Interpretation' in White and Smythe (eds.), *European and International Law*, pp. 73–82; and Bebr, 'The Standing of the European Parliament in the Community System of Legal Remedies' (1990) 10 YEL 171. By virtue of Art. 37 of the Protocol on the Statute of the Court of Justice the European Parliament can intervene in any case before the Court, but its submissions are limited to supporting the submissions of one of the parties. See also Art. 93 of the Court's Rules of Procedure.

66 Art. 4 EC expressly says that the Parliament is one of the institutions of the

more controversial was the question whether Parliament can bring actions for annulment under Article 173.

Initially, the European Court answered in the negative in the *Comitology* case in September 1988,[67] but less than two years later, in May 1990, it granted limited *locus standi* to Parliament in the *Chernobyl* case.[68] An action for the annulment of an act of the Council or the Commission brought by the Parliament is admissible provided that the action in question seeks only to safeguard Parliament's prerogatives and that it is founded only on submissions alleging their infringement. The Court found the *Chernobyl* case admissible. The Council had adopted a regulation under Article 31 of the Euratom Treaty, which requires that Parliament be consulted, but Parliament sought to annul it on the basis that it should have been adopted under Article 100a EEC, whereby the cooperation procedure would have been applicable. The Court decided that 'the Parliament's prerogatives include participation in the drafting of legislative measures, in particular participation in the cooperation procedure laid down in the EEC Treaty'.[69] This decision of the Court doubtless represents an activist judicial influence over the evolution of the Community's institutional balance, but showed little respect for the wording of Article 173(1) EEC[70] for its own decision in the *Comitology* case and for the fact that Article 173 EEC was not amended by the Single European Act although the granting of explicit *locus standi* for the Parliament had been mooted by the Commission in the intergovernmental conference.[71]

Citizens of, residents in, and legal persons having their registered office in one of the member states can petition the European Parliament on a matter that comes within the Community's fields of activity and that affects the person directly.[72] The Parliament has no powers to redress the

---

Community. The Parliament first exercised this right in Case 13/83 *European Parliament v Council* [1985] ECR 1513.

67 Case 302/87 *European Parliament v Council* [1988] ECR 5615.

68 Case C-70/88 *European Parliament v Council* [1990] ECR I-2041, discussed below at pp. 180–81.

69 ibid., p. 2073. In Case C-295/90 *European Parliament v Council* [1992] ECR I-4193, Parliament successfully sought the annulment of Dir. 90/366 on the right of residence of students because it was adopted under Art. 235 EEC rather than Art. 7(2) EEC/Art. 6(2) EC. The former requires the consultation procedure whereas the latter requires the cooperation procedure. See Bradley, (1992) 12 YEL 505, 506–508. Directive 93/96 on the right of residence for students was duly adopted using the correct legal basis on 29 October 1993 (OJ 1993 L317/59).

70 It gave the right to bring an action to a 'Member State, the Council or the Commission'. At Maastricht Art. 173 was amended to reflect the decision of the European Court. Now the European Parliament can bring an action for the purpose of 'protecting its prerogatives', see below at p. 227.

71 See Case 302/87, note 67 above, p. 5644, and Bieber, Pantalis and Schoo, 'Implications of the Single Act for the European Parliament', (1986) 23 CMLRev 767, 787 on the question of the standing of the European Parliament under Art. 173 EEC at the intergovernmental conference prior to the Single European Act.

72 Introduced into the Treaty framework at Maastricht; see Art. 138d EC; but the

grievance unless the matter relates to the internal working of the Parliament, but can use its influence with the other institutions and can publicize the case. The President of the Parliament assigns a petition to the committee responsible (the Committee on Petitions), which, if it finds the petition admissible, may refer the matter to the Ombudsman, may conduct hearings and may issue a report on the matter.[73] The number of petitions has grown significantly in recent years; in 1979–80 there were 57, in 1983–4 there were 100, in 1987–8 there were 484,[74] in 1989–90 there were 774 and in 1992–3 there were 900.[75] This increase led to the setting up of the committee on petitions in January 1987 which is assisted by a small team from the Commission's Secretariat-General.[76] If a petitioner reveals a failure on the part of a member state to comply with Community law, the committee will get in touch with the Commission, which may then initiate Article 169 EC proceedings.[77]

At Maastricht it was agreed to create another remedy for persons entitled to petition the European Parliament. They will be able to complain to a newly appointed Community Ombudsman concerning instances of maladministration in the activities of the Community institutions or bodies.[78] The Ombudsman can initiate an inquiry either on his or her own initiative, or in response to a complaint received directly from the person concerned or via an MEP. The Ombudsman has no jurisdiction where the alleged facts are or have been the subject of legal proceedings. If the Ombudsman finds maladministration, the matter will be referred to the institution concerned, which then has three months to respond to the finding. After considering the institution's response, the Ombudsman will forward a final report to the European Parliament and to the institution concerned. The person lodging the complaint must be informed of the outcome of the inquiries. Additionally, the Ombudsman will submit an annual report to the European Parliament.

Parliament had been hearing petitions since the establishment of the EEC; see European Parliament, *Forging Ahead*, pp. 145–7. In the EC Treaty 'Citizens' of member states are styled as 'Citizens of the Union' and given certain rights accordingly; see Arts. 8–8e EC. An inter-institutional agreement had been reached by the Council, Commission and European Parliament concerning the right of petition on 12 April 1989; see OJ 1989 C120/361 and Bradley, (1989) 9 YEL 235, 251.

73 Parliament's Rules of Procedure, 156–8.

74 See European Parliament, *Forging Ahead*, p. 146.

75 See Bradley, (1990) 10 YEL 367, 384 and Westlake, *The Commission and Parliament* (1994), pp. 46–7.

76 Westlake, ibid, at p. 16.

77 See Ch. 7. Such proceedings were initiated eight times in 1989–90 as a result of petitions to the European Parliament; see Bradley, (1990) 10 YEL 367, 384.

78 See Art. 138e. No complaints are permissible in relation to the Court of Justice and the Court of First Instance acting in their judicial role.

The Ombudsman has no formal powers to ensure that maladministration is corrected. The effectiveness of the post is dependent on the extent to which the Community institutions will respect the Ombudsman's assessment and act upon it. It may also depend on how effective the Ombudsman and the European Parliament are in interesting the media in cases of maladministration that are not rectified.

The European Parliament will appoint the Ombudsman after each election of the Parliament for the five-year lifetime of the Parliament.[79] The Ombudsman can be reappointed. The Ombudsman can be dismissed only by the Court of Justice at the request of the European Parliament if he or she no longer fulfils the conditions required for the performance of the duties of the office or is guilty of serious misconduct.[80] The Ombudsman is employed full time and must be completely independent in the performance of the duties of office. The European Parliament laid down the regulations and general conditions governing the performance of the Ombudsman's duties, after considering the Commission's opinion, and gaining the approval of the Council.[81] The Ombudsman has the same rank in terms of remuneration, allowances and pension as a judge at the Court of Justice and must meet the conditions required for the exercise of the highest judicial office in his or her own country or have the acknowledged competence and experience to undertake the duties of Ombudsman.[82] The seat of the Ombudsman is in Strasbourg and is assisted by a Secretariat, the principal officer of which is appointed by the Ombudsman.[83] The Community institutions and bodies are obliged to supply the Ombudsman with any information he or she requests and to give access to the files concerned. They may refuse to do so only on 'duly substantiated grounds of secrecy'. On the other hand member states are obliged to reveal information which may help to clarify instances of maladministration by Community institutions or bodies 'unless such information is covered by laws or regulations on secrecy or by provisions preventing its being communicated'.[84] This means that member states with very broad secrecy laws or other draconian laws can prevent the Ombudsman from gaining access to their information: no independent adjudication seems to be possible.

79 Rules of Procedure EP, Rule 159.
80 ibid., Rule 160. The Rules of Procedure indicate that Parliament hopes an Ombudsman would resign after an adverse vote in Parliament before the matter is referred to the Court of Justice.
81 See OJ 1994 L54, Westlake, *The Commission and Parliament* (1994), pp. 147–52 and Marias (ed.), *The European Ombudsman* (1994), pp. 135–46.
82 See Arts. 6 and 10 of the Decision.
83 See Arts. 11 and 13 of the Decision.
84 See Art. 3 of the Decision.

A two-year time bar operates in relation to complaints to the Ombudsman. Time begins to run from the date on which the facts on which it is based came to the attention of the complainant.[85]

LEGISLATIVE ROLE

COMPULSORY CONSULTATION

The system of compulsory consultation applies where the Commission proposal has a legal basis in the EC Treaty which specifies that the Parliament is to be consulted. In these circumstances Parliament has only one reading in which to consider the proposal and its views are not binding on either the Commission or the Council. Parliament is conscious of the power of the Commission to amend its own proposal right up until its adoption by the Council, and therefore Parliament's Rules of Procedure direct particular attention to methods of exerting influence on the Commission.

A Commission proposal is referred by the President of Parliament to the committee responsible,[86] e.g. a proposed directive on air pollution would be referred to the committee on the environment, public health and consumer protection. The responsible committee will examine the validity and appropriateness of the chosen legal basis,[87] whether the proposal respects the principle of subsidiarity and the fundamental rights of citizens, and whether sufficient financial resources are provided.[88] In performing these tasks the committee responsible is helping to ensure that the other political institutions respect the rule of law in any new legislation. The requirement to consider the principle of subsidiarity in relation to every legislative proposal should help to create a more decentralizing culture in the European institutions.[89] Parliament is concerned that the Council working parties reach compromises which result in the adoption by the Council of measures considerably different from the original Commission proposal being considered by Parliament. In order to combat this phenom-

---

85 Art. 2(4) of the Decision.
86 Rules of Procedure EP, Rule 51. The committee responsible should have been designated in the Annual Legislative Programme; see Rule 49.
87 Rules of Procedure EP, Rule 53. If the committee questions the legal basis then the opinion of Parliament's committee on legal affairs must be sought before the plenary session votes on any changes to the legal basis.
88 Rule 54.
89 The same requirement applies to the Commission and Council not only by virtue of Art. 3b EC but also as a result of the 1993 Inter-Institutional Agreement on Subsidiarity adopted in the margins of the Brussels European Council of October 1993; see Westlake,

enon the committee responsible requests the Commission and Council to keep it informed of any emerging compromises which will lead to substantial amendments of the Commission's proposal.[90] The Commission has undertaken to brief the committee responsible on the main guidelines emerging from the Council's discussions, especially when these diverge from the Commission's initial proposal.[91] The committee responsible may ask the Commission whether it intends to alter its proposal. If the Commission does so intend then the committee will not proceed until it is informed about the Commission's amendments. If the Commission says it does not so intend then this declaration will be annexed to the committee's report to provide justification for a request for reconsultation if the Commission does later alter the proposal.[92] The committee responsible will also try to get the Commission to state its position on all the amendments proposed by the committee before a vote is taken in a plenary session of Parliament. It may delay such a vote until it has won some concessions from the Commission.[93]

Parliament's greatest weapon under the consultation procedure is delay. The Council cannot adopt a proposal prior to receiving the Parliament's opinion[94] unless the need to adopt the legislation is urgent and Parliament fails to discharge its obligation to cooperate sincerely with the Council. In *European Parliament* v *Council*,[95] the Court decided that it was lawful for the Council to adopt a Regulation on 21 December 1992 extending the application of generalized tariff preferences in respect of certain products originating in developing countries without waiting for Parliament's opinion under the consultation procedure. In October 1992 Parliament had been asked for its opinion urgently so that the Council could pass the legislation before 1 January 1993. The Court decided that this request was justified given the harm that would be done to the developing countries if there was an interruption in the generalized tariff preferences applicable. The committee responsible draws up a report for the plenary session and recommends acceptance, rejection or amendment. If the plenary session votes to reject the proposal then the President will ask the Commission to withdraw it. If the Commission does not do so then Parliament will refer

---

above, pp. 145–46. The Commission is obliged to draw up an annual report to Parliament and the Council on compliance with the principle of subsidiarity, see pp. 12–15 above.

90 Rules of Procedure EP, Rule 55.

91 1990 Code of Conduct; see Westlake, above, pp. 123 and 125.

92 Rule 56.

93 Rule 57. The Commission has indicated that it regards this Rule as rather impractical and that it prefers to commit itself only after the plenary session has voted; see Westlake, *The Commission and the Parliament*, pp. 94–5.

94 See Case 138/79, *Roquette Frères* v *Council* [1980] ECR 3333, noted below.

95 Case C-65/93, judgment of 30 March 1995.

the matter back to the committee responsible which shall report back to the plenary session within two months.[96] If the Parliament votes to amend the proposal then the Commission will be asked to state its position on each of the amendments. The Parliament will delay issuing its formal opinion on the legislation until the Commission has done so. If the Commission does not accept all Parliament's amendments then the matter may be referred back by Parliament to the committee responsible for reconsideration. The committee has two months to report back to the Parliament and it can only table amendments seeking a compromise with the Commission.[97] After the Parliament has issued its formal opinion under the consultation procedure the committee responsible will monitor progress of the proposal until it is adopted or withdrawn. The committees can ask Parliament to call upon the Council to hold a conciliation procedure or reconsultation.[98]

The EEC Treaty required that Parliament be consulted about legislative proposals in a number of areas. In particular:

on any amendment to Article 14 on customs duties;
for legislation on the common agricultural policy under Article 43;
for the general programme on the abolition of existing restrictions on freedom of establishment under Article 54(1);
for legislation on freedom to provide services under Article 63;
for legislation on transport policy under Article 75;
on the approximation of laws under Article 100;
on certain aspects of the European Social Fund under Articles 126 and 127;
on certain financial measures under Article 209;
on international agreements under Article 228;
on legislation to achieve one of the objectives of the Community under Article 235;
on the calling of an intergovernmental conference to amend the Treaty under Article 236.

The Single European Act extended the consultation procedure to the following matters:

aspects of legislation on transport policy under Article 84;
legislation on the harmonization of indirect taxes under Article 99;
a comprehensive proposal for amendments to the structure and operational rules of the EEC structural funds under Article 130d;

96 Rules of Procedure EP, Rule 59. Parliament has interpreted this Rule in a way which prevents a proposal being referred back to the committee responsible more than once. This seems to be a recognition by Parliament that it cannot under the consultation procedure delay indefinitely the adoption of a measure it opposes.
97 Rules of Procedure EP, Rule 60.
98 Both of which are discussed below. See Rules of Procedure EP, Rule 61.

legislation on certain aspects of research and technology under Article 130q(1);[99]

legislation on the environment under Article 130s;

framework legislation for the delegation of legislative power to the Commission under Article 145;

the setting up of a Court of First Instance under Article 168a.

At Maastricht further changes were made. Some of the above examples of consultation were altered to another procedure, more favourable to the Parliament: the multiannual framework programmes on research and technological development moved to the Article 189b procedure,[100] Article 75(1) on the common transport policy, Article 125 (formerly Article 127 EEC) on implementing decisions relating to the European Social Fund, and Article 130s(1) on environmental measures have moved to the Article 189c cooperation procedure (certain environmental measures under Article 130s(2) still use the consultation procedure). A few new areas of consultation were added:

voting rights for nationals of other member states in local and European elections, Article 8b;

recommendations to member states to increase the rights accorded to citizens of the European Union, Article 8e;

regulations on state aids, Article 94;

determining the third countries whose nationals must be in possession of a visa when crossing the external borders of the member states, Article 100c;

detailed rules and definitions for the application of the protocol on the excessive deficit procedure and the adoption of the appropriate provisions to replace the protocol, Article 104c(14);

certain provisions under the Statute of the European System of Central Banks, Article 106(6);

the limits and conditions under which the European Central Bank (ECB) will be able to impose fines or periodic penalty payments on undertakings that fail to comply with the ECB's regulations and decisions, Article 108a(3);

formal agreements on an exchange-rate system for the ECU in relation to non-Community countries, Article 109(1);

during the second stage of economic and monetary union (EMU) the

---

99 The multiannual framework programme under Art. 130i EEC and the setting up of joint undertakings or other structures for the efficient execution of programmes of Community research, technological development and demonstration under Art. 130o EEC/Art. 130n EC.

100 See pp. 122–6.

conferring upon the European Monetary Institute (EMI) of any tasks for the preparation of the third stage not expressly given in the treaty, Article 109f(7);

whether the member states fulfil the necessary conditions for the adoption of a single currency, Articles 109j(2–4) and 109k(2);

measures in support of action on industry taken in the member states, Article 130(3);

specific actions on economic and social cohesion outside the framework of existing structural funds, Article 130b;

specific programmes for research and technological development, Article 130i(4).

International agreements can be concluded by the Council only after consulting the Parliament, unless the agreement is one concerning the common commercial policy under Article 113(3), where Parliament has no involvement.[101] When Parliament must be consulted, a time-limit may be imposed within which it must give its opinion. Certain international agreements require Parliament's assent.[102]

On the non-legislative front Article 109f(1) stipulates that the European Parliament is to be consulted in the second stage of EMU on the appointment of the President of the EMI, the forerunner of the ECB, and Article 109a(2) states that it is to be consulted in the third and final stage of EMU on the appointment of the President, Vice-President and other members of the Executive Board of the ECB.

If legislation is passed under one of the provisions that requires Parliament to be consulted without it being consulted, which means being able to express its opinion on the proposal, then an essential procedural requirement has been infringed. If the matter comes before the Court of Justice, it will declare the measure void under Article 173. This occurred in *Roquette Frères* v *Council*, in which the Court said that the consultation procedure:

is the means which allows the Parliament to play an actual part in the legislative process of the Community. Such power represents an essential factor in the institutional balance intended by the Treaty. Although limited, it reflects at Community level the fundamental democratic principle that the peoples should take part in the exercise of power through the intermediary of a representative assembly. Due consultation of the Parliament in the cases provided for by the

101 In practice the Council opts to consult Parliament on all matters based on Art. 113 except for some very urgent, purely technical or confidential measures, see Westlake, above, at p. 40.
102 See notes 193–7 below, Art. 228(3).

Treaty therefore constitutes an essential formality disregard of which means that the measure concerned is void.[103]

One of the ongoing problems facing Parliament is the tendency of the Council to reach a 'political agreement' on a legislative proposal before the Parliament has delivered its opinion. In order to remain within the letter of the law the Council then waits until Parliament gives its opinion before finally adopting the legislation.[104] This is not consistent with the spirit of consultation, and if the Parliament can obtain strong evidence that it has taken place in a specific case, it should be challenged by Article 173 proceedings.

OPTIONAL CONSULTATION

Parliament is also consulted about a number of the Commission's legislative proposals where the Treaty makes no such requirement. This type of optional consultation has increased in recent years and enhances the Parliament's role in the legislative process.[105] Optional consultation is not an acceptable substitute where the correct legal basis of the measure would have required compulsory consultation. In these circumstances one of Parliament's prerogatives is violated and the act can be annulled.[106] The Parliament has little or no formal role in the vast quantity of delegated legislation passed by the Commission under powers given by the Council.[107] The House of Lords Select Committee on the European Communities suggested that the Commission should lay such legislation before the European Parliament so that it has an opportunity to debate it.[108] This idea no doubt comes from the practice in the United Kingdom of laying

---

103 Case 138/79 [1980] ECR 3333, 3360. Parliament intervened in this case to support Roquette. It is now able to initiate proceedings under Art. 173 in these circumstances; see note 70 above.

104 See Bradley, (1989) 9 YEL 235, 246 and Westlake, *The Commission and Parliament* (1994), p. 34. Parliament has expressed its unhappiness about this practice in a resolution (OJ 1990 C324/125) discussed by Bradley, (1990) 10 YEL 367, 378–80. The Commission, in the 1990 Code of Conduct agreed between it and the Parliament, undertook to remind the Council not to reach political agreement on a proposal until it had received Parliament's opinion; see Westlake at pp. 123–4.

105 Examples of the Parliament being consulted where it is not required by the Treaty are given by Bradley, (1989) 9 YEL 235, 246, and relate to measures passed under Arts. 113 and 213 of the Treaty.

106 This principle was accepted in Case C-316/91 *Parliament v Council* [1994] ECR I-625 (para. 16), but in that case the measure had not been adopted under the wrong legal basis.

107 See Ch. 2. pp. 59–63.

108 See its Seventeenth Report, Political Union: Law-Making Powers and Procedures (Session 1990–91), para. 84.

delegated legislation before the United Kingdom parliament. If drafts of the Commission's delegated legislation were laid before the European Parliament, this could be a useful extension of optional consultation. However, failure to consult Parliament would not render the measure void if an action of annulment were brought under Article 173 unless the Court were to take the view that a concerted practice of consultation had developed in relation to that particular matter whereby the Parliament had a legitimate expectation that it would be consulted.[109] There are still a significant number of Treaty provisions that do not require Parliament to be consulted on legislative proposals.[110] This constitutes an unsatisfactory gap in the democratic legitimacy of the Community's legislative process.

RECONSULTATION

The obligation to reconsult the Parliament is not provided for by the EC Treaty. The Court of Justice initially accepted the principle of a requirement of reconsultation while denying its necessity in the cases before them.[111] In *Cabotage I* the European Court annulled Reg. 4059/89 owing to lack of reconsultation and established the following principle that in the context of the consultation procedure there is a requirement that: 'Parliament be reconsulted on each occasion when the text finally adopted, viewed as a whole, departs substantially from the text on which the Parliament has already been consulted, except in cases where the amendments essentially correspond to the wish of the Parliament itself'.[112] In *Cabotage I* the Commission's initial proposal was for freedom of cabotage in road haulage, i.e. that any road haulage carrier for hire or reward, established in a member state and authorized to operate such services

109 The concept of legitimate expectations is discussed in Ch. 8, pp. 258–9. The Court has said that the Council is 'always entitled to' consult Parliament and that this 'cannot be unlawful even if it is not mandatory'. Case 165/87 *Commission* v *Council* [1988] ECR 5545, 5562.

110 See Ch. 5, p. 125 and the Appendix.

111 See Case 41/69 *ACF Chemiefarma* v *Commission* [1970] ECR 661, 702; Case 817/79 *Buyl* v *Commission* [1982] ECR 245, 264–5; and Case C-331/88 *The Queen* v *Minister of Agriculture, Fisheries and Food and Secretary of State for Health, ex parte FEDESA and others* [1990] ECR I-4023, 4067.

112 Case C-65/90 *Parliament* v *Council* [1992] ECR I-4593 (para. 16) repeated in Cases C-13–16/92 *Driessen en Zonen and Others* v *Minister van Verkeer en Waterstaat* [1993] ECR I-4751 (para. 23); and Case C-388/92 *Parliament* v *Council* [1994] ECR I-2067 (para. 10) (*Cabotage II*). In Case C-280/93 *Germany* v *Council* [1994] ECR I-4973, 5054–6, the Court of Justice repeated the quotation in the text but substituted 'differs in essence' for 'departs substantially' and decided that the amendment made to the Commis-

internationally, should be allowed to operate national road haulage services in a member state other than the one in which he was established, whereas the adopted regulation laid down a Community cabotage quota and was only applicable on a temporary basis. In *Cabotage II*, the Commission's initial proposal was like its original proposal in *Cabotage I* except that it applied to road passenger transport services. The Court struck down Regulation 2454/92 because Parliament was not reconsulted even though the final version extended freedom of cabotage only to certain regular road passenger transport services in frontier areas involving the carriage of workers between home and work and pupils and students to and from their educational institution.

The Parliament's Rules of Procedure allow the President, at the request of the committee responsible, to call upon the Council to reconsult Parliament not only where the proposal on which Parliament originally delivered an opinion has been substantially amended but also where: 'through the passage of time or changes in circumstances, the nature of the problem with which the proposal is concerned substantially changes'.[113] It is not clear whether the Court of Justice will regard this ground as being sufficient to require reconsultation.

In relation to the principle that reconsultation is not required where the amendments essentially correspond to the wishes of Parliament the Court has observed that no reference can be made to the views of the committees of Parliament before the adoption of the legislative resolution ending the consultation procedure.[114]

CONCILIATION

As a result of the Joint Declaration of the Commission, the Council and the Parliament of 4 March 1975 a system of conciliation was established.[115] It applies only where three conditions are met: the legislative measure must be of general application, it must have 'appreciable financial implications' and it must relate to non-compulsory expenditure, i.e., acts 'of which the adoption is not required by virtue of acts already in existence'.[116]

---

sion's original proposal did 'not affect the very essence of the Regulation taken as a whole' and therefore reconsultation was not required.

113 Rule 62. The Parliament can also vote for a request for reconsultation on a proposal from a political group or at least twenty-six MEPs.

114 See Case C-388/92, above, at para. 17.

115 See OJ 1975 C89/1. See also Rules of Procedure EP, Rule 63.

116 See para. 2 of the Joint Declaration.

The scope of measures coming within the conciliation procedure is relatively narrow. It is designed to protect the Parliament's budgetary prerogatives. Parliament was given the last word on non-compulsory expenditure in the Community budget by the budgetary treaties in the 1970s and therefore it was agreed that it should have some enhanced say in legislative measures that have an appreciable impact on that part of the Community's budget.[117] Any of the three political institutions can call for the conciliation procedure to be invoked and it 'shall be initiated if the criteria laid down in paragraph 2 [of the Joint Declaration] are met and if the Council intends to depart from the Opinion adopted by the European Parliament'.[118] After the European Parliament has given its opinion in the consultation procedure, the conciliation takes place in a 'Conciliation Committee' comprising representatives of the European Parliament[119] and the Council, with the participation of the Commission. The aim of the procedure is to seek an agreement between the Council and Parliament, normally within three months. When the positions of the two institutions are sufficiently close, the Parliament may give a new opinion, after which the Council may take definitive action.[120]

The conciliation procedure has not been utilized very often.[121] It has certain inherent flaws: no provision is made for the situation where the political institutions diverge as to whether the criteria for establishing a conciliation process have been met, nor is the Council under any obligation to negotiate in good faith, as it is at liberty to pass the legislation in the form and with the content it wishes regardless of the views of Parliament. It is not even certain if the Council is under any legal obligation to comply with the terms of the Joint Declaration.

COOPERATION PROCEDURE

The Single European Act, which came into force on 1 July 1987, introduced the cooperation procedure.[122] The procedure then applied to:

117 Parliament has made significant efforts to extend the scope of the conciliation procedure, but so far the only concessions made by the other political institutions have been in relation to the Financial Regulations and the implementing measures for the Act concerning the election of MEPs by direct universal suffrage; see European Parliament, *Forging Ahead*, p. 137. See also Parliament's Resolution of 16 February 1989, OJ 1989 C69.
118 Para. 4 of the Joint Declaration.
119 The composition and procedure of Parliament's delegation is determined in the same manner as for the conciliation committee provided for in the Art 189b procedure discussed below; see Rule 75 of Parliament's Rules of Procedure.
120 Paras. 5–7 of the Joint Declaration.
121 For example, it was used twice in 1989; see Bradley, (1989) 9 YEL 235, 247.
122 See Arts. 6 and 7 Single European Act. See also Art. 149 EEC/Art. 189c EC; Rules of Procedure EP, Rules 64–68, 71–73.

legislation designed to prohibit discrimination on grounds of nationality, Article 7(2) EEC;[123]

legislation on freedom of movement for workers, Article 49;

directives on freedom of establishment, Article 54(2);

directives coordinating national law exceptions to freedom of establishment permitted by Community law on grounds of public policy, public security or public health, Article 56(2);

directives for the mutual recognition of diplomas, certificates and other evidence of formal qualifications, Article 57(1);

certain directives for the coordination of the provisions in member states concerning the taking up and pursuit of activities as self-employed persons, Article 57(2);

legislation for the approximation of laws for the achievement of the internal market, Article 100a(1);[124]

directives on the minimum requirements for health and safety of workers and for improving the working environment, Article 118a;

implementing decisions relating to the European Regional Development Fund, Article 130e;[125]

various provisions on research and technology, Article 130q(2) EEC.[126]

The Maastricht amendments moved the cooperation procedure from Article 149(2) EEC to Article 189c EC. Most of the provisions requiring the cooperation procedure under the EEC Treaty were upgraded to the conciliation and veto procedure set out in Article 189b EC,[127] but a few still apply the cooperation procedure.[128] At Maastricht a number of other provisions, which had previously simply required the consultation procedure, were made subject to the cooperation procedure: proposals for implementing the common transport policy, Article 75(1); implementing decisions relating to the European Social Fund, Article 125;[129] and Community action on environmental policy, Article 130s(1).[130] The Maastricht treaty amendments also moved measures on a vocational training policy from no consultation to the cooperation procedure.[131] Finally, some of the

---

123 Art. 6(2) EC.

124 Certain provisions are excluded from the scope of Art. 100a(1) by Art. 100a(2). See also Art. 100b.

125 The cooperation procedure does not apply to the major policy legislation on this and the other structural funds; see Art. 130d. In fact, prior to Maastricht the consultation procedure applied to Art. 130d and after Maastricht the assent procedure applies.

126 Art. 130o EC (2).

127 See Arts. 49, 54(2), 56(2), 57(1), 57(2) and 100a(1).

128 Arts. 6(2) EC, 118a, 130e, and 130o(2) EC.

129 Formerly Art. 127 EEC.

130 Though some particularly controversial matters remain within the consultation procedure under Art. 130s(2).

131 See Art. 128 EEC/Art. 127(4) EC.

new areas of Community competence introduced at Maastricht utilize the cooperation procedure:

certain measures on trans-European networks in the areas of transport, telecommunications and energy infrastructures, Article 129d(3);

measures on development cooperation (helping developing countries), Article 130w;

detailed rules for the multilateral surveillance of the economic policies of member states, Article 103(4);

measures specifying definitions for application of the prohibition on privileged access by Community institutions, national, regional and local governments, and other public authorities to financial institutions, Article 104a;[132]

measures specifying definitions for the prohibition on the Community or a member state being liable for the financial commitments of another member state, Article 104b;

measures harmonizing the denominations and technical specifications of coins issued by the member states after the adoption of the single currency.[133]

The first phase of the cooperation procedure is identical to the consultation procedure outlined above. There are no time-limits on Parliament to give its opinion at this first reading stage.[134] After Parliament has given its opinion, the Council, acting by a qualified majority, shall adopt a common position. There is no time-limit on the Council to adopt the common position but it can amend the Commission proposal only by unanimity.[135] Parliament argues that the provisions for reconsultation and conciliation can be applicable between its first and second reading.[136] This could occur

---

132 These measures were to be adopted before 1 January 1994. That deadline was complied with; see Reg. 3604/93, OJ 1993 L332/1.

133 Once the single currency is adopted, only the ECB will be able to authorize the issue of banknotes within the Community, though the national central banks may issue them; see Art. 105a(1) EC. Member states may issue coins subject to approval by the ECB of the volume of the issue (Art. 105a(2) EC).

134 Delay by Parliament in giving its opinion at first reading is one of the bargaining counters at its disposal. According to Bieber, Parliament 'generally takes six months to complete its consideration of proposals' at first reading; see 'Legislative Procedure for the Establishment of the Single Market' (1988) 25 CMLRev 711, 713.

135 See Art. 189a(1).

136 See Bieber, (1988) 25 CMLRev 717–18, and the example of reconsultation occurring in relation to the second directive concerning free movement of insurance services (88/357, OJ 1988 L172/1), where the first reading took place long before the introduction of the Single European Act (OJ 1978 C36/14) and the reconsultation was on 18 May 1988 (OJ 1988 C167/63). See also Parliament's Rules of Procedure, Rule 51(1) which suggests that the relevant Rules on reconsultation (62) and conciliation (63) apply to 'legislative proposals whether they require one, two or three readings'; and Bieber, above, at pp. 718, 720–21.

where the Council takes a long time to adopt the common position or that position is substantially different from the Commission proposal considered by Parliament at first reading. However, the Council seems to oppose the idea of reconsultation on first reading and suggests that a second reading is adequate.[137] It would seem unlikely that the Council is obliged to reconsult or agree to conciliation after the first reading in the context of the cooperation procedure,[138] where Parliament has an opportunity to express its opinion on the changed proposal at the second reading stage.

The Council has to forward its common position, with an explanation of its reasons, to Parliament.[139] At this second reading stage the common position is considered initially by the committee responsible for its scrutiny at first reading. The committee will make a recommendation to the Parliament as to the approach it should take at second reading.[140] If Parliament does not act within three months, or approves the common position, then the Council shall definitively adopt the measure in question in accordance with the common position.[141] If within the three-month period Parliament rejects the Council's common position by an absolute majority of its component members, at least 314, then the Council can pass the measure only by unanimity.[142] Furthermore, it must pass the measure within three months of Parliament's rejection of the common position or the Commission proposal shall be deemed not to have been adopted.[143]

Finally, if Parliament amends the Council's common position within the period of three months by an absolute majority of its component members, the proposal is referred back to the Commission.[144] Amendments to the common position can be tabled in Parliament only by the committee responsible, a political group or at least twenty-six MEPs. Parliament has imposed a restriction on the admissibility of amendments to the common position and given its President an unquestionable discretion to declare an amendment admissible or inadmissible. To be admissible an amendment must seek to restore wholly or partly the position adopted by Parliament in its first reading, or be a compromise amendment representing an

---

137 See Bradley, (1990) 10 YEL 367, 379 in the context of the amendments to the fourth and seventh Company Law Directives.
138 Or in the conciliation and veto procedure.
139 See Art. 189c(b). The Commission is obliged to inform the Parliament fully of its position.
140 Rules of Procedure EP, Rule 66.
141 Art. 189c(b) and Rules of Procedure EP, Rule 68.
142 See Art. 189c(c). A motion to reject the Council's common position can be tabled by the committee responsible, a political group or at least twenty-six MEPs and is voted on before any amendments; Rules of Procedure EP, Rule 71.
143 See Art. 189c(f). It is hard to imagine Parliament agreeing the one-month extension permitted by Art. 189c(g). It is not clear from what date the three-month period runs. Is it the date of the vote in Parliament rejecting the common position or the date on which the Council receives notice from Parliament of that vote?
144 See Art. 189(c)–(d).

agreement between the Council and Parliament, or seeks to amend a part of the text of a common position which was not included in – or differs in content from – the proposal submitted in first reading.[145] The Commission has one month to re-examine the proposal, taking into account the amendments proposed by Parliament. The Commission is under no obligation to accept any of Parliament's amendments, but if it rejects them, it must forward them to the Council with its opinion on them.[146] The Council can, within three months, adopt the Commission's re-examined proposal by qualified majority. Unanimity is required to adopt any of Parliament's amendments that were not accepted by the Commission or to amend the Commission's re-examined proposal in a way desired by the Council.[147] If the Council does not adopt the proposal within three months of receiving it from the Commission, then it shall be deemed not to have been adopted.[148] It should be borne in mind that until the Council has adopted the proposal definitively, the Commission is free at any stage of the above procedures to alter its proposal.[149]

The cooperation procedure increases the influence of the European Parliament on the Community legislative process. At the very minimum it gives Parliament more time to scrutinize legislation by the introduction of a second reading. The Commission may be more inclined to take Parliament's amendments on board, both at first reading and second reading, partly because it fears that a non-cooperative attitude might lead Parliament to reject a number of common positions and thereby make the adoption of those proposals difficult, as unanimity rather than qualified majority would be required in the Council.[150] Certainly, the statistical evidence of the use of the cooperation procedure shows that a significant proportion of Parliament's amendments are adopted by the Commission and ultimately by the Council. It seems that Parliament's amendments at first reading have a greater likelihood of being adopted.[151] Between the coming into force of the Single European Act in July 1987 and the end of December 1993, 332 proposals had been adopted under the cooperation procedure. More than 54 per cent of the amendments requested by Parliament at first reading were accepted by the Commission and more than 43 per cent by

145 See Rules of Procedure EP, Rule 72.
146 See Art. 189c(d). Parliament puts pressure on the Commission by requiring it to give reasons why it has not accepted Parliament's amendments; see Rules of Procedure EP, Rule 73.
147 See Art. 189c(d)–(e).
148 See Art. 189c(f). The Parliament and Council can by common accord extend the time-limit by one month; see Art. 189c(g).
149 See Art. 189a(2).
150 As discussed in Ch. 2, pp. 56–8, the Commission's influence on the legislative process is reduced when the Council can pass legislation only by unanimity. See the example of the proposed benzene directive on p. 121–2.
151 Both the Commission and Parliament are keen to emphasize the importance of the first reading; see Westlake, *The Commission and the Parliament*, p. 38.

the Council. More than 44 per cent of Parliament's second reading amendments were accepted by the Commission and 23.5 per cent by the Council.[152] Of course, quantitative analysis of the number of amendments accepted is easy to do, but it is far more difficult to assess qualitatively the impact of Parliament's amendments on the legislation that is finally adopted.

One example of the cooperation procedure producing a more environmentally friendly final directive than the Council had agreed as its common position, is the directive on emission standards for cars below 1.4 litres.[153] The Council's common position set the permitted levels of emissions of carbon monoxide and nitrogen oxide above those that would necessitate the fitting of catalytic converters to new cars with an engine size below 1.4 litres. In the second reading Parliament reduced the permitted levels of emissions to a point requiring the fitting of catalytic converters, and the Commission adopted these key amendments in its re-examined proposal.[154] The Council was unable to amend unanimously this re-examined proposal to raise the levels of emissions to a point where catalytic converters would not be necessary, as at least one member state was in favour of requiring them. Thus the Council had to either abandon the proposed directive and incur the wrath of the growing body of green voters throughout the Community, and leave an important legislative gap in the completion of the internal market, or accept the more stringent standards in the Commission's re-examined proposal which required the fitting of catalytic converters. The Council chose the latter option. The lesson of this example is that in the cooperation procedure Parliament can significantly amend legislation provided it has the support of the Commission and at least one member state and the Council feels obliged to legislate in the area covered by the proposal.

Rejection of the common position is an important weapon, which Parliament has used sparingly.[155] The first time Parliament rejected the Council's common position in October 1988, it involved a directive on the

152 See the *General Report 1993*, p. 355.

153 89/458, OJ 1989 L226/1. The comparable directive for cars over 1.4 litres is 91/441, OJ 1991 L242/1.

154 Catalytic converters reduce pollution in the atmosphere by converting carbon monoxide into carbon dioxide and by removing some of the other harmful products of car exhausts that contribute to acid rain. Admittedly, carbon dioxide is harmful to the ozone layer, and so Art. 6 of Directive 89/458, which provides for the Council to take measures by qualified majority to limit carbon dioxide emissions from motor vehicles, was added by the Council by unanimity when examining the Commission's re-examined proposal.

155 By the end of 1992 Parliament had rejected just four common positions and in two of these cases the Council was unable to obtain unanimity to pass the measure; see Westlake, *The Commission and the Parliament*, p. 37 and Bradley, (1992) 12 YEL 505, 522–523. No common positions were rejected in 1993, see *General Report 1993*, pp. 359–60, but two were rejected in 1994, see *General Report 1994*, p. 417.

protection of workers from the risk of exposure to benzene at work.[156] The Commission had modified the proposed directive in line with the Parliament's first-reading amendments, but a qualified majority could not be obtained in the Council for a common position based on that proposal. The Commission then amended its proposal radically in a way that did command qualified majority but not unanimous support in the Council and this became the common position. Parliament, when confronted with a common position that departed so much from its proposals at first reading and with a Commission that was willing to change its position substantially just to achieve a directive, rejected the common position. Predictably, the proposed benzene directive was not adopted, as the Council could not achieve unanimity.[157] Parliament may have been trying to keep the Commission honest by discouraging it from compromising too much in the Council and giving too little weight to Parliament's views. In certain circumstances it may be better to have no legislation than diluted legislation.

CONCILIATION AND VETO PROCEDURE

At Maastricht a new procedure, set out in Article 189b EC, was agreed, strengthening the powers of the European Parliament in the legislative process. It applies to the following matters:

legislation on freedom of movement for workers, Article 49;

directives on freedom of establishment, Article 54(2);[158]

measures for the approximation of laws that have as their object the establishment and functioning of the internal market, Article 100a;

incentive, not harmonization, measures in relation to education, e.g., the Erasmus and Tempus programmes on student mobility, Article 126(4);

incentive, not harmonization, measures on culture, Article 128(5);[159]

incentive, not harmonization, measures on public health, Article 129(4);

specific action that supports and supplements the policy pursued by the member states to protect the health, safety and economic interests of

---

156 The common position on the proposal of the committee on the environment was rejected by 276 votes to 47 with 3 abstentions; see *The Work of the European Parliament July 1988–June 1989*, Directorate-General for Research, European Parliament, p. 12.

157 See Bradley, (1988) 8 YEL 189, 199–200.

158 Art. 189b applies also in relation to particular aspects of freedom of establishment: coordination of the constraints in member states on the freedom due to public policy, public security or public health (Art. 56(2)), mutual recognition of diplomas, certificates and other evidence of formal qualifications (Art. 57(1)), and coordination of the provisions laid down by law, regulation or administrative action in member states concerning the taking up and pursuit of activities as self-employed persons (Art. 57(2)).

159 Here the Council has to act unanimously throughout the legislative process.

consumers and to provide adequate information for them, Article 129a(2);

guidelines covering the objectives, priorities and broad lines of measures envisaged in the sphere of trans-European networks in the areas of transport, telecommunications and energy infrastructures, Article 129d(1);

multiannual framework programmes on research and technological development, Article 130i(1);[160]

general action programmes setting out priority objectives to be attained in environmental policy, Article 130s(3).

The conciliation and veto procedure adopts the same first-reading approach of the cooperation procedure outlined above. The differences emerge when Parliament is thinking of rejecting or does amend the Council's common position at second reading. Where Parliament accepts or takes no decision within three months of receiving the Council's common position at second reading, then the Council will adopt the measure in question in accordance with its common position.[161] If Parliament intends to reject the Council's common position, then a proposal for a declaration by Parliament of intended rejection of the Council's common position must be passed by a majority of the component Members of Parliament (at least 314).[162] If the declaration is passed then the President of the Parliament will ask the Council if it intends to convene the conciliation committee. If the Council declines to do so then the President of the Parliament will announce in Parliament that the procedure is terminated and the proposed act shall be deemed not to have been adopted. This creates, for the first time, a veto for Parliament on Community legislation.[163] If a conciliation committee is set up during the second reading then the Parliament retains the option to reject or amend the common position.[164]

If Parliament merely proposes amendments to the Council's common position, these are forwarded to the Commission and then the Council.[165] The Council then has three months to adopt the measure, incorporating all Parliament's amendments. The Council acts by qualified majority in

---

160 Here the Council has to act unanimously throughout the legislative process.
161 Art. 189b(2)(a)–(b).
162 See Rules of Procedure EP, Rule 69. Such a proposal can be tabled only by a committee, a political group, or twenty-six MEPs.
163 See Art. 189b(2)(c) and Rules of Procedure EP, Rule 69. Parliament has five months in which to reject the Council's common position; Art. 189b(7). On 19 July 1994 Parliament, for the first time under Art. 189b, exercised its power to reject a common position of the Council. It did so in relation to the proposed directive concerning the application of ONP to voice telephony; see the *General Report 1994*, p. 139.
164 See Art. 189b(2)(c) and Rules of Procedure EP, Rule 70.
165 Art. 189b(2)(d).

relation to the amendments that the Commission has not expressed a negative opinion on, but by unanimity in relation to those where the Commission has expressed such an opinion. In the likely event that the Council does not adopt all Parliament's amendments, the President of the Council must, in agreement with the President of the European Parliament, convene a meeting of the conciliation committee.[166]

The conciliation committee will be made up of the members of the Council or their representatives and an equal number of MEPs. The Council is usually represented by the permanent representatives or deputy permanent representatives to the EC of the member states who sit in Coreper. The Parliament is represented by the same three Vice-Presidents (to provide continuity and expertise), the chairperson and rapporteur of the committee responsible and other MEPs appointed by the political groups, preferably from among the members of the committees concerned. The political composition of the delegation must correspond to the composition of Parliament by political groups.[167] In the margins of the October 1993 Brussels European Council an Inter-Institutional Agreement on arrangements for the proceedings of the conciliation committee under Article 189b was adopted.[168] It is a rather anodyne document but it does establish that the committee shall be chaired jointly by the President of the European Parliament and the President of the Council and that the co-chairpersons shall have a key role in deciding the agenda, in proposing joint texts and in approving the minutes of the meetings.

The Commission takes part in the proceedings of the conciliation committee with a remit to take all necessary initiatives to try to reconcile the positions of the Parliament and the Council. The Commission still has the power to alter the proposed act where this may help the process of conciliation.[169] The conciliation committee has the task of reaching agreement on a joint text by a qualified majority of the members of the Council or their representatives and by a majority of the representatives of the Parliament.[170] If within a period of six weeks the committee approves a joint text, the Council and European Parliament have a further six weeks in which to approve it. The Council acts by a qualified majority and the Parliament by an absolute majority of the votes cast. If either or both of the institutions fail to achieve the required majority, the proposed measure is deemed not to have been adopted.[171] Once again, the Parliament has a

166 Art. 189b(3).
167 See Rules of Procedure EP, Rule 75.
168 See Westlake, *The Commission and the Parliament*, pp. 143–4.
169 Art. 189a(2).
170 Art. 189b(4).
171 Art. 189b(5). No amendments may be tabled to the joint text; see Rules of Procedure EP, Rule 77.

veto on the legislation if it fails to approve the text agreed by the conciliation committee. This is precisely what happened on 1 March 1995 when the Parliament voted against the joint text agreed at the third conciliation committee meeting on 23 January in relation to the draft directive on the legal protection of biotechnological innovations.[172] The majority of MEPs objected to the joint text because it did provide for the possibility of patents being granted for elements of the human body even though its negotiators in the conciliation committee had secured the proviso that the human gene would have undergone a procedure whereby it was no longer connected with a specific individual.

For a high profile example of where the Parliament achieved its objectives in the conciliation committee, see the removal of a ban on motor bikes of over 100 brake horsepower in the joint text of 13 December 1994 which was approved by Parliament on Wednesday 18 January 1995.[173]

The final scenario is where the conciliation committee fails to approve a joint text within the time-limit of six weeks.[174] The Council has six weeks to confirm its original common position, acting by a qualified majority, or the measure will be deemed not to have been adopted.[175] If the Council does confirm its common position, the Parliament has a further six weeks in which it can veto the measure by an absolute majority of its component members.[176]

The key and novel feature of the Article 189b procedure is that the Parliament can always have the last word in blocking the legislation. The Council is for the first time prevented from passing legislation against the will of the Parliament. On the other hand, Parliament has no legal power to force the adoption of amendments that the Council does not want. Politically, it may have such power where the Council is anxious to conclude legislation on the particular topic and therefore wishes to avoid the Parliament exercising its veto. At least some of the member states, including Germany, are anxious to extend the scope of the Article 189b

172 The vote was 240 for, 188 against and 23 abstentions; see *The Times*, 2 March 1995.
173 See *The Week*, 16–20 January 1995 (European Parliament) pp. 22–3 and Directive 95/1/EC of the European Parliament and of the Council of 2 February 1995 on the maximum design speed, maximum torque and maximum net engine power of two- or three-wheel motor vehicles, OJ 1995 L52/1.
174 The period of six weeks mentioned here and in other parts of the Article, and the period of three months mentioned in the Article, can be extended for a further two weeks or one month respectively by common accord of the Parliament and the Council; Art. 189b(7).
175 It can adopt any of Parliament's amendments but only by unanimity; see Art. 189b(6).
176 The Parliament will request the President of the Council to justify its decision in a plenary session. No amendments can be made to the Council's text. See Rules of Procedure EP, Rule 78.

procedure. At Maastricht it was agreed that an intergovernmental conference would be convened in 1996 to examine those provisions of the Treaty on European Union for which revision is provided.[177] Article 189b(8) states that Article 189b is one such provision and that the Commission is to provide a report to the Council by 1996 on how the scope of the procedure may be widened.

The scope of Article 189b is not inconsequential. The number of Treaty Articles utilizing this procedure for legislation is greater than the number utilizing the cooperation procedure after the Single European Act.

In 1994, the first full year of the operation of the Article 189b procedure, the Parliament dealt with 18 first readings, 34 second readings and 8 third readings. In comparison the Parliament dealt with 33 first readings and 21 second readings under the Article 189c procedure (cooperation procedure), gave 11 assents and delivered 168 opinions under the consultation procedure.[178] Thus the work under the consultation procedure still outnumbers Parliament's work under all the other legislative procedures put together. It is not surprising therefore that the Parliament is keen to see the consultation procedure replaced by the Article 189b procedure in many more Treaty Articles as a result of the intergovernmental conference in 1996.

ASSENT

At Maastricht the member states agreed to give Parliament the power to assent to Community legislation outside of the budgetary process. In the Single European Act the concept of assent was introduced but only in relation to the accession of new member states and association agreements with third states. The power to block legislation by not giving assent applies to the following measures:

provisions facilitating the exercise of the rights of citizens of the European Union to move and reside freely within the territory of the member states subject to any limitations and conditions laid down in the provisions, Article 8a(2);

in stage three of economic and monetary union, provisions conferring upon the European Central Bank specific tasks concerning policies relating to the prudential supervision of credit institutions and other financial institutions with the exception of insurance undertakings, Article 105(6);

the amendment of certain Articles of the Statute of the European System of Central Banks, Article 106(5);

---

177 Art. N(2) of the Treaty on European Union.
178 See *General Report 1994*, p. 417.

defining the tasks, priority objectives and the organization of the Structural Funds, which may involve grouping the Funds, and defining the general rules applicable to the Funds and the provisions necessary to ensure their effectiveness and coordination with each other and with other financial instruments, Article 130d(1);

and proposals on a uniform procedure for elections to the European Parliament, Article 138(3).[179]

This is a modest list of proposals requiring the assent of Parliament.[180] In all these cases bar one[181] the Council must act unanimously in order for the measure to be passed. The combination of unanimity in the Council and assent in the European Parliament makes it difficult for any of the above measures to be passed.

In order to increase the possibility of a successful outcome Parliament has provided in its Rules of Procedure[182] for the possibility of a conciliation committee being convened before Parliament votes on the assent. The committee responsible can make an interim report to Parliament recommending amendment of the proposal and if the plenary session, by the majority necessary to give final assent, approves the amendment then the President shall request the Council to convene a conciliation committee. If the Council agrees to do so then the committee responsible will make its final recommendation for the assent of Parliament in the light of the outcome of the conciliation. Of course the Council is under no obligation to convene a conciliation committee, as it is not required by the EC Treaty, but it may do so if it believes that the likely alternative is Parliament failing to give its assent.

---

179 Here the Treaty specifies that assent requires a majority of Parliament's component members.

180 Apart from Art. 138(3), the Treaty is silent on the voting requirements in the Parliament to constitute assent. It is therefore a matter within the discretion of Parliament, but Rule 80 of its Rules of Procedure somewhat unhelpfully says that the majority required for the adoption of the assent 'shall be the majority indicated in the relevant article of the EC Treaty'. The implication is that, apart from Art. 138(3) measures, a simple majority of the votes cast is sufficient.

181 The one exception is Art. 106(5), where the Council can act by qualified majority provided it is acting on a recommendation from the ECB.

182 Rule 80.

INITIATION

The Maastricht Treaty amendments gave Parliament the same limited power of initiation that the Council has always enjoyed, i.e., the power to request the Commission to submit any appropriate proposals on matters on which the Parliament considers that a Community measure is required for the purpose of implementing the EC Treaty.[183] The content of the proposal remains a matter for the Commission, but at least Parliament now has an official outlet for its legislative ideas. The Parliament has set out the process whereby it can exercise this limited right of legislative initiative in Rule 50 of its Rules of Procedure. Parliament can by a majority of its component members adopt a resolution requesting the Commission to submit to it a legislative proposal on the basis of an own-initiative report from the committee responsible. However, the committee responsible can only prepare an own-initiative report with the authorization of the Conference of Presidents[184] and after it has established that such a proposal is not contained in the annual legislative programme, that preparations for such a proposal have not started or are unduly delayed, and that the Commission has not previously responded positively to earlier Parliamentary requests to bring forward such a proposal.

CONCLUSION

Parliament's legislative role was historically totally advisory, but the changes made by the Single European Act and the Treaty on European Union have given the Parliament some legislative teeth. Weaknesses remain: Parliament does not even have a right to be consulted about all proposed Treaty-based legislation. Where Parliament is consulted by the Council, either as of right under the Treaty or by the grace of the Council, it has no power to block the legislation and the success of its amendments is largely dependent on their being adopted by the Commission, which is under no obligation to do so. The traditional conciliation procedure is of limited application, has been little used and, even where applicable, provides no guarantee that the Council will not pass the legislation in a way contrary to the wishes of Parliament.

Thus the position of Parliament in the legislative process before the Single European Act was very weak and remains so where the traditional

183 Art. 138b. The Council's equivalent power is contained in Art. 152.
184 See Rule 148.

processes of no consultation, consultation (whether optional or compulsory, or even reconsultation) and conciliation are utilized. The cooperation procedure does represent a significant development in that Parliament can force a change in the voting procedure in the Council from qualified majority to unanimity by rejecting the Council's common position. This seems a largely negative power, but its existence may explain the healthy take up of Parliamentary amendments by the Commission, which does not wish to lose the negotiating position it has in the Council when qualified majority rather than unanimity is the voting system. The Treaty on European Union has taken matters further by providing Parliament with a veto on certain legislative proposals through the complex conciliation and veto procedure of Article 189b and the relatively simple assent procedure. The latter gives the Parliament less influence, as it operates in the context of one reading in Parliament. Parliament either has to assent to the measure as presented to it or reject it; this is not satisfactory and it is to be hoped that the Council responds positively to requests by Parliament to hold a conciliation committee within the framework of the assent procedure. The Article 189b procedure is very complex, but at least gives a framework for dialogue between the three institutions involved in the legislative process and sufficient power to each of the institutions to encourage compromise. In the areas where it applies the Council is no longer supremely dominant in the legislative process, as it has been accustomed to being.[185] The procedure does not, however, apply in many crucial areas of Community policy, e.g. economic and monetary policy, agriculture, fisheries, commercial policy, competition policy and state aids, where Parliament remains relatively weak.

The United Kingdom parliament has much greater formal powers than the European Parliament. All primary legislation has to be passed by parliament and legislation is introduced there. However, this disguises the fact that the United Kingdom Government initiates the vast majority of parliamentary legislation and that a large proportion of the legislation passed by parliament is in a form and has the content desired by the Government.[186] The European Parliament's ability to change Community legislation by getting its amendments accepted by the Commission and Council or to veto legislation is limited, but it is probably greater than the influence of Government backbenchers and the opposition parties in the

185 For a somewhat sceptical approach to significant increases in the European Parliament's legislative powers and a rejection of the notion that there is a democratic deficit in the Community, see the seventeenth report of the House of Lords Select Committee on the European Communities, *Political Union: Law-Making Powers and Procedures* (Session 1990–91).

186 See De Smith and Brazier, *Constitutional and Administrative Law* (1994, 7th ed.) by Brazier at pp. 251–5 and 291–3.

House of Commons and the House of Lords on United Kingdom legislation, when, as is normal, the Government can rely on an overall majority in the House of Commons.[187] The fact that legislation in the Community is not primarily a function of the European Parliament is not surprising to a United Kingdom reader used to the view that United Kingdom legislation 'is primarily a function of Government'.[188] In the Community, even after Maastricht, legislation may still be primarily a function of the Council, but the powers and influence of the Commission and Parliament can significantly shape the final product agreed by the Council.

ROLE IN ACCESSION AND ASSOCIATION AGREEMENTS

The Single European Act granted two important constitutional powers to the European Parliament in giving it a veto over the accession to the Community of new member states and over any new association agreements. Article 237 EEC stated that a European state could become a member of the Community with the unanimous approval of the Council, after consulting the Commission, and 'after receiving the assent of the European Parliament which shall act by an absolute majority of its component members'. At Maastricht it was agreed to repeal Article 237 EEC and to replace it with Article O of the Treaty on European Union. The new provision is, however, identical to the old one as to the procedure for a European state applying to become a member of the Union and hence of the European Community. Thus any applicant state requires to obtain the approval of at least 314 MEPs.

The European Parliament has established a procedure for dealing with applications for membership of the Community.[189] The application will be referred to the appropriate committee of Parliament for consideration, and that committee, a political group or at least twenty-six MEPs, may propose to Parliament that a debate is held before negotiations with the applicant state commence. Parliament may decide by a simple majority to

---

187 Examples of defeats of Government-sponsored bills are rare, e.g., the Shops Bill 1986, see 95 HC Deb. 584–702 (14 April 1986). Major amendments to Government bills that the Government did not wish to make are not common, e.g., the Law Reform (Miscellaneous Provisions) (Scotland) Bill 1989, which was shorn of some of its more controversial provisions in the 1990 Act of the same name due to a Government backbench revolt at committee stage.

188 De Smith and Brazier, *Constitutional and Administrative Law*, p. 251.

189 Rules of Procedure EP, Rule 89.

request the Commission and the Council to take part in such a debate. When the negotiations, which are conducted by the Commission and Council, are completed, Parliament will hold a further debate and take the vote on assent to the application required by the Treaty after receiving a report from the Parliamentary committee responsible.

At the time of writing several states had applied for membership of the Community – Turkey, Cyprus, Malta – and other states were seriously considering doing so. Parliament could exercise considerable leverage over the Council by threatening to block these applications. Although in 1988 Parliament approved a resolution stating that it would refuse to give its agreement to future applications to accede to the Community until substantial progress is made in reducing the Community's democratic deficit, i.e., until the European Parliament is given substantially more power,[190] it failed to carry through this threat in relation to the accession of Austria, Finland and Sweden on 1 January 1995. It gained no institutional concessions and yet voted by a very large majority for the accession.[191]

Prior to the coming into force of the Single European Act, the Council was obliged to consult the European Parliament on the conclusion of association agreements. Such agreements could be concluded with a non-member state, or a union of states or an international organization, and involve reciprocal rights and obligations, common action and special procedures.[192] Since 1 July 1987 the Council still concludes these agreements, acting unanimously. Until the Maastricht Treaty amendments it also required the assent of the European Parliament acting by an absolute majority of its component members, but the requirement of an absolute majority was dropped. On the other hand, it was added that Parliament and the Council may in an urgent situation agree upon a time-limit for the assent.[193]

Parliament can ask the Council to be consulted on the negotiating mandate that it intends to give to the Commission for the conclusion of a new or amended association agreement. It can also request the Commission to take part in a debate on its negotiating mandate before the negotiations commence. When the negotiations are concluded but before the agreement is signed, Parliament will vote on whether to give assent to the agreement.[194]

In the first two years after the coming into force of the Single European Act Parliament gave about thirty assents. It held up doing so in relation to

---

190 Resolution of 15 September 1988, OJ 1988 C262.
191 See OJ 1994 C205.
192 Art. 238 EEC, but Art. 238 EC does not contain a reference to a union of states.
193 See Art. 228(3).
194 Rules of Procedure EP, Rule 90.

certain agreements with Israel and Syria, and in doing so used the power of assent as a means of influence both on the Council and on the relevant states.[195] It is worth noting that no time-limit is imposed on Parliament giving its assent either under Article 238 EC or Article O TEU.[196]

At Maastricht amendments made to Article 228 extend the requirement of obtaining the assent of the European Parliament to a number of international agreements that are not association agreements; in particular to agreements establishing a specific institutional framework by organizing cooperation procedures, agreements having important budgetary implications for the Community, and agreements entailing amendment of an act adopted under the Article 189b procedure.[197] A time-limit for assent may be agreed by the Council and the European Parliament in urgent situations. Other international agreements are concluded by the Council after consulting the Parliament (though agreements under Article 113(3) EC can be made without Parliament being consulted), but in these cases the Council can impose a time-limit on Parliament for giving its opinion.

BUDGETARY ROLE[198]

Prior to the adoption of the Budgetary Treaties of 1970 and 1975 the European Parliament merely had a consultative role in relation to the budget of the European Community. The granting to the European Parliament of a greater measure of control over the Community's budget coincided with the adoption of a system of own resources to fund the Community.[199] The Budgetary Treaties were the first major extension of the powers of the European Parliament.

---

195 See *The Work of the European Parliament July 1988–June 1989*, pp. 14–15, and Bradley, (1988) 8 YEL 189, 198–9. In 1990 Parliament gave just two assents (see the *XXIVth General Report*, p. 364); and in 1991 there were three assents (see the *XXVth General Report*, p. 367).
196 Art. O of the Treaty of European Union is no different in this respect from Art. 237 EEC, the provision it replaced. The UK Government is not obliged by the UK constitution to obtain the consent of the UK parliament before ratifying any international agreement with another state or states. However, if the Government desires to give internal effect to the agreement in the law of the UK an Act of Parliament must be passed.
197 See Art. 228(3) EC.
198 See Arts. 199–209 EC; Rules of Procedure EP, Rule 85 and Annex IV.
199 See Decision of 21 April 1970 on the Replacement of Financial Contributions from Member States by the Communities' Own Resources (Dec. 70/243, OJ 1970 L94) and the First Budgetary Treaty signed in Luxembourg on 22 April 1970. The latest Own Resources Decision is 94/728 of 31 October 1994, OJ 1994 L293/9.

The crucial distinction in the budget is between that part which relates to compulsory expenditure[200] and that which relates to non-compulsory expenditure (NCE). In the Joint Declaration of 30 June 1982 of the European Parliament, Council and Commission on measures to improve the budgetary procedure compulsory expenditure is defined as 'such expenditure as the budgetary authority is obliged to enter in the budget to enable the Community to meet its obligations, both internally and externally, under the Treaties and acts adopted in accordance therewith'.[201] It constitutes a substantial proportion of the budget[202] and yet the Parliament's powers in relation to that part of the budget are much less than in relation to NCE. The Joint Declaration of 30 June 1982 established a system for determining the classification of each new budget item. The Presidents of the three institutions that agreed the declaration are to engage in dialogue when no agreement is reached on the classification.[203]

The budgetary procedure is commenced by the Commission putting forward the preliminary draft budget to the Council for the following calendar year no later than 1 September.[204] Thereafter the Council must agree to a draft budget, acting by a qualified majority, and submit it to the European Parliament for its first reading not later than 5 October.[205] The Parliament has forty-five days in which to act. It can amend the NCE parts of the budget by a vote of the majority of current MEPs, at least 314 members,[206] but it can propose modifications only to the compulsory expenditure parts of the budget, albeit by a simple majority of the members who vote. If the Parliament does not act within the forty-five days, the budget is deemed to be finally adopted.

Assuming Parliament does make amendments and propose modifications, the Council has fifteen days to act. It can, by a qualified majority, modify any of the amendments adopted by the European Parliament to the NCE parts of the budget. Modifications proposed by the European

---

200 See Art. 203(4).

201 This definition led to a broadening of the category of NCE; see Dankert, 'The Joint Declaration by the Community Institutions of 30 June 1982 on the Community Budgetary Procedure' (1983) 20 CMLRev 707.

202 When the *Fact Sheets on the European Parliament* were written in 1988 the proportion of compulsory expenditure was 77 per cent; En III/C/4. By the time of the 1995 budget the non-compulsory appropriations for commitments were 39.5 billion ECUs, almost 50 per cent of the total appropriations for commitments of 81 billion ECUs; see the *General Report 1994*, p. 392.

203 This tripartite dialogue is not always capable of resolving the issue; see Dankert (1983) 20 CMLRev 709–11.

204 Art. 203(3).

205 Art. 203(3)–(4).

206 Art. 203(4) and Rules of Procedure EP, Annex IV, Art. 3(8).

Parliament to reduce compulsory expenditure parts of the budget will stand unless they are rejected by a qualified majority of the Council. Modifications proposed by Parliament to increase compulsory expenditure will fall unless they are adopted by the Council by qualified majority. If the Council proposes no modifications to the Parliament's amendments on NCE and accepts the Parliament's modificatns on compulsory expenditure, the budget is deemed to have been finally adopted.[207] Otherwise the modified draft budget is then forwarded to Parliament for its second reading.

At second reading Parliament has no power to alter the parts of the budget relating to compulsory expenditure. However, it has fifteen days in which to amend or reject the modifications made by the Council to the Parliament's first reading amendments on NCE; to do so it needs a majority of its current members and three-fifths of those members who vote.

It can also reject the draft budget and ask for a new budget to be submitted; for this it needs a majority of the current MEPs and two-thirds of those who vote. If Parliament does not act within the fifteen-day period, the budget is deemed to have been adopted.

The system gives Parliament the last word on non-compulsory expenditure and the Council the last word on compulsory expenditure. Parliament, however, does not have an unlimited power to increase NCE. The Commission must declare before 1 May in the year preceding that to which the budget is to apply the maximum rate of increase in NCE. If the actual rate of increase established in the Council's budget is over half the maximum rate of increase, the Parliament may, by amendment, further increase the total amount of NCE to a limit not exceeding half the maximum rate. Thus if the maximum rate of increase was 10 per cent and the Council proposed an increase of 9 per cent, the Parliament could increase NCE by up to 14 per cent. The Council and Parliament can, however, agree to a greater maximum rate of increase than that proposed by the Commission.[208] If the Parliament increases NCE beyond the level of increase permitted by the EC Treaty, in the absence of an express agreement between the Council and Parliament, then the Council can successfully bring an action for annulment of the budget against the European Parliament. In *Council* v *European Parliament* the President of Parliament adopted a budget that contained increases in NCE of between 19.5 per cent and 29.7 per cent whereas the Council had proposed increasing the maximum rate of increase from 7.1 per cent to between 14.6

---

207 Art. 203(5).
208 Art. 203(9) The Council must act by qualified majority, and the Parliament requires a majority of its current members and at least three-fifths of the votes cast.

per cent and 20.5 per cent. The Court found the act of the President of the Parliament was void, as the increase in NCE was well in excess of the maximum rate of increase set by the Commission. This had not been altered because the proper voting procedure had not been gone through to achieve an agreement between the Council and Parliament on a greater maximum rate of increase.[209]

Clearly Parliament has very significant powers in relation to non-compulsory expenditure, albeit that it relates to just under half of the budget and the annual rate of increase is pegged by the Treaty. A medium term approach to financial planning in the Community has been developed by the inter-institutional agreements on budgetary discipline and improvement of the budgetary procedure agreed in 1988[210] and in 1993.[211] These inter-institutional agreements followed on the decisions reached at the European Council meetings in February 1988 and December 1992 as to the financial perspectives for the gradual increase in expenditure, within the limits of own resources, over the succeeding five-year periods. A key clause in both inter-institutional agreements states that:

The two arms of the budgetary authority agree to accept for each of the financial years from 1993 to 1999 [1988 to 1992], the maximum rate of increase for non-compulsory expenditure deriving from the budgets established within the ceilings set by the financial perspective.[212]

Parliament's power to reject the draft budget is of major constitutional significance and has been used to reject the 1980 budget, the 1982 supplementary budget and the 1985 budget. When this occurs, the previous year's budget continues to operate on a one-twelfth basis: Community expenditure in each month of the new financial year for which a budget has not been adopted is allowed up to the level of one-twelfth of the previous year's budget. Provision is made for the Council to increase these amounts in relation to compulsory expenditure and for the Parliament to increase them in relation to NCE.[213]

---

209 Case 34/86 [1986] ECR 2155. The Court's decision did not call into question the validity of payments made and commitments entered into in implementation of the 1986 budget. The Court preserved the effects of the budget up to its decision on 3 July 1986 in order to guarantee the continuity of the European public service and preserve legal certainty. In Case C-41/95 *Council* v *Parliament* the 1995 budget is being challenged.
210 OJ 1988 L185/33.
211 OJ 1993 C331/1, see Westlake, *The Commission and the Parliament*, pp. 32–4 and 153–8.
212 Para. 17 of the 1993 Agreement and para. 15 of the 1988 Agreement.
213 See Art. 204 and Pipkorn, 'Legal Implications of the Absence of the Community Budget at the Beginning of a Financial Year' (1981) 18 CMLRev 141.

CHAPTER 5

EC Legislation

One of the distinguishing features of the Community is the power entrusted by the member states to the political institutions to make laws. This chapter outlines the various types of Community legislation, considers some of its principal features and pulls together the threads of the previous three chapters to describe the lawmaking process.

TYPES OF EC LEGISLATION

REGULATIONS

A regulation has general application, is binding in its entirety and is directly applicable in all member states.[1] Regulations must be published in the *Official Journal* of the Community, and they come into force on the date specified in them or, if no date is specified, on the twentieth day following their publication.[2] Thus regulations are the most powerful lawmaking tools available to the Community institutions. Without any intervention by national governments or legislatures, regulations become part of the national legal system(s) of each member state.

In a large number of cases the political institutions are given a choice as to whether to enact a regulation or another form of legislation, a directive or a decision.[3] This choice is usually exercised by the Commission as part of its power of legislative initiation.[4] Remarkably, the EC Treaty specifies the use of regulations on only three occasions:

Article 48(3)(d) provides for Commission regulations placing conditions

1 See Art. 189.
2 See Art. 191. Measures passed under the Art. 189b procedure must be signed by both the President of the European Parliament and the President of the Council.
3 See Appendix.
4 However, Art. 108a, introduced at Maastricht, and the Statute of the European System of Central Banks enables the European Central Bank to pass certain regulations without requiring a proposal from the Commission.

on the rights of workers to stay in a member state, of which they are not nationals, after having been employed in that state;

Article 94 provides for Council regulations relating to state aids; and Article 209(a) provides for Council financial regulations relating to budgetary procedure and Community accounts.[5]

Powers to make regulations may be conferred on the Commission by a Council regulation.[6]

DIRECTIVES

A directive does not necessarily apply to all member states and, rather than being directly applicable in those states, allows them the choice of form and methods of implementing it in their national laws. Directives are, however, binding on the member states to which they are addressed as to 'the result to be achieved'.[7] There was no requirement in the EEC Treaty that directives be published in the *Official Journal*, simply that they be notified to those to whom they were addressed.[8] Directives were, however, frequently published in the *Official Journal*, and invariably so where they applied to all the member states. At Maastricht the EEC Treaty was amended to require the publication in the *Official Journal* of directives that apply to all member states.[9] Though the directive will take effect upon notification to the member states to which it is addressed, it will usually give the member states a specified period of time in which to implement the directive into their national laws. Since Maastricht, directives that are addressed to all member states take effect on the date specified in them or, in the absence thereof, on the twentieth day after publication.[10] Failure on the part of a member state to implement the directive completely or correctly within the stated time period may lead to individuals and legal persons being able to rely on the provisions of that directive in their dealings with that member state.[11]

Apart from the large number of occasions where the Treaty leaves open the choice of form of legislation,[12] it also stipulates the use of directives in a

5 Art. 24(2) Merger Treaty provides for the Council to lay down staff regulations for officials of the European Communities.
6 See, e.g., the provisions referred to in Ch. 2, at pp. 59–63.
7 See Art. 189.
8 See Art. 191 EEC.
9 Art. 191(2) EC.
10 Art. 191(2) EC.
11 The question of the direct effect of directives is considered at pp. 345–52.
12 See Appendix.

significant number of cases.[13] Where a choice is given, a directive may be appropriate if harmonization rather than uniformity is desired. Directives also have the merit of permitting time for member states to adjust their law to a new programme, e.g., the creation of the internal market between 1987 and 1993. Though a directive can be used in a way analogous to a decision affecting a particular state or states – indeed, sometimes the Treaty gives a choice between a directive and decision[14] – directives have primarily been used as a form of general legislation for the Community. In this context the ability of member states to implement the provisions of the directive into their national laws within the time-limit prescribed therein is crucial. The United Kingdom has a relatively good record in this matter whereas Greece, Italy and Portugal have comparatively poor records. Even the states with the poorest record have managed to implement more than four-fifths of the directives applicable to them.[15]

DECISIONS

A decision is binding in its entirety upon those to whom it is addressed.[16] Decisions come into effect when the requirement to notify them to those to whom they are addressed is complied with.[17] Although not required by the EEC Treaty, some of the more important decisions were published in the *Official Journal*. Since the entry into force of the Treaty on European Union decisions adopted under Article 189bEC must be and others may be published in the *Official Journal*.[18]

The Treaty provides for the exclusive use of decisions in many different contexts[19] in addition to the occasions where the Community institutions can choose to use a decision or another form of legislation. The Council

13 ibid.
14 The Commission can address either a directive or a decision to a member state where a public undertaking or certain other undertakings specified in Art. 90 are benefiting from laws in breach of the Treaty or are in breach of competition policy (Art. 90(3)) and where a member state whose average rates on turnover taxes for imported and/or exported products do not conform to the principles laid down in Arts. 95 and 96 (Art. 97). The Council can adopt a directive or a decision granting mutual assistance to a member state in balance-of-payments difficulties (Art. 109h(2)).
15 See Appendix. The problems that arise from delayed or inadequate implementation of directives are addressed in Ch. 11.
16 See Art. 189 of the Treaty.
17 See Art. 191.
18 Art. 191(1) EC.
19 See Appendix.

can also delegate power to the Commission to take decisions on matters within the competence of the Council.[20]

In general terms it can be said that decisions, unlike regulations, are not intended to have general application, but are directed at one or more member states or one or more undertakings. The idea that this is the general intention of the EC Treaty is reinforced by the terms of Article 173 concerning actions for annulment of Community legislation. Natural or legal persons, other than the Community institutions and member states, have limited *locus standi*. They can bring actions against decisions addressed to them 'or against a Decision which, although in the form of a Regulation', is of direct and individual concern to them. This permits the Court of Justice to treat regulations that are not of general application as being in reality decisions.[21]

RECOMMENDATIONS AND OPINIONS

The EC Treaty provides for the making of recommendations and opinions in a number of situations[22] and confers a general power on the Commission to make these provisions whenever it considers it necessary.[23] The Treaty is quite explicit that recommendations and opinions have 'no binding force'.[24] These provisions cannot have direct effect in national courts, as they are not binding, but it is competent for a national court or tribunal to refer to the European Court a question concerning their interpretation or validity.[25] Such a reference may be appropriate where the recommendation or opinion was the spur for the making of a particular provision of national law relevant to the case before the national court or tribunal or because a recommendation or opinion casts light on the interpretation of other provisions of Community law that are binding and relevant to the case in hand.

20 Art. 145 provides a general power for the Council to delegate lawmaking powers to the Commission. A general framework for such delegation was established in Council Dec. 87/373, discussed in Ch. 2, pp. 59–63. Art. 121 provides for the Council to assign to the Commission the implementation of common measures in social policy, in particular as regards social security for the migrant workers covered by the Treaty provisions on free movement of workers.
21 See the discussion in Ch. 8, pp. 228–37.
22 See Appendix.
23 See Art. 155.
24 See Art. 189.
25 See Case C-322/88, *Grimaldi* v *Fonds des Maladies Professionelles* [1989] ECR 4407, and the note by Arnull (1990) 15 ELRev 318.

CERTAIN FEATURES OF EC LEGISLATION

SUBJECT TO JUDICIAL REVIEW BY THE EUROPEAN COURT

All binding legislation is capable of being reviewed.[26] There is no equivalence between EC legislation and United Kingdom Acts of Parliament, the validity of which are not subject to review in the courts in the United Kingdom.[27] The Court of Justice can decide that a regulation, directive or decision is invalid if it goes beyond the powers granted in the EC Treaty, or those powers were misused or an essential procedural requirement was infringed. The Court has also developed general principles of law, e.g., proportionality, and will find Community legislation that fails to conform to those principles or otherwise infringes the EC Treaty to be invalid.

The lawmaking powers of the political institutions are constrained not only by the need to keep within the powers granted and procedures prescribed by the EC Treaty, but also by a potentially unlimited source of judge-made law. It is not good for legal certainty nor the respect due to legislation passed by the appropriate political institutions that a Court can strike it down on the basis of a principle it has just developed. One of the reforms of the Community should be to incorporate some or all of the general principles of law into the EC Treaty (Community constitution) and constrain the power of the Court to develop new principles. This does not mean that no new principles could be developed by the Court, but that much more rigorous criteria would have to be fulfilled before they could do so.[28]

26 The jurisdiction of the European Court of Justice to decide that EC legislation is invalid is considered in Ch. 8.

27 The United Kingdom courts may, however, disapply provisions of a United Kingdom Act of Parliament that conflict with directly effective Community law; see *R v Secretary of State for Transport, ex parte Factortame and others (No. 2)* [1991] 1 AC 603, [1990] 3 WLR 818, [1992] QB 680 and *Equal Opportunities Commission v Secretary of State for Employment* [1994] 1 All ER 910, discussed in Ch. 12, pp. 372–4.

28 For further discussion of general principles of law see Ch. 8, pp. 253–65. The Court has referred to the EC Treaty as the 'constitutional charter of a Community based on the rule of law' in Opinion 1/91, *Opinion on the Draft Treaty on a European Economic Area* [1991] ECR I-6079; [1992] 1 CMLR 245, 269.

EC LEGISLATION MUST HAVE A LEGAL BASIS

The preamble to a particular provision of Community law should state the legal basis on which it is made. This is not an absolute requirement, but it may be necessary to satisfy the requirement in Article 190 to state the reasons on which the legislation is based. The European Court stated in the *Generalized tariff preferences* case that

Admitted failure to refer to a precise provision of the Treaty need not necessarily constitute an infringement of essential procedural requirements when the legal basis for the measure may be determined from other parts of the measure. However, such explicit reference is indispensable where, in its absence, the parties concerned and the Court are left uncertain as to the precise legal basis.[29]

The choice of the legal basis for a provision of EC law must be based on objective factors that are amenable to judicial review.[30] It can be of major significance to the legislative procedure to be followed which legal basis is chosen. It may mean the difference between the European Parliament being consulted and being involved in the cooperation procedure[31] or between the Council acting by unanimity and some form of majority voting.[32]

In addition to the many provisions of the EC Treaty providing legal bases for Community legislation in specific areas there is a very broad lawmaking power in Article 235 of the Treaty[33] to attain one of the objectives of the Community. Thus far a liberal construction has been placed on what comes within the objectives of the Community in the use

---

29 Case 45/86, *Commission v Council (Generalized tariff preferences* case) [1987] ECR 1493, 1519–20. In that case the Council Regulations 3599/85 and 3600/85 on generalized tariff preferences had no specified legal basis, the preambles simply stating 'Having regard to the Treaty', and the Court was not able to determine from other parts of the measures what the precise legal basis was. The Court found the regulations to be void. One reason for doing so was the failure to comply with Art. 190 of the Treaty by virtue of the fact that the Court was left uncertain as to what the legal basis of the regulations was.

30 ibid., p. 1520 and Case C-70/88 *European Parliament v Council* [1991] ECR I-4529, 4564–5.

31 See, e.g., Case C-70/88, *European Parliament v Council* [1990] ECR I-2041, discussed in Ch. 4.

32 See, e.g., Case 56/88, *United Kingdom v Council* [1989] ECR 1615, [1989] 2 CMLR 789, discussed at p. 74; Case 68/86 *United Kingdom v Council* [1988] ECR 855, discussed at pp. 248–9; and Case 45/86, note 29 above. The situation where more than one legal basis seems to be appropriate for a measure is discussed in Ch. 8 at pp. 251–2.

33 See Usher, 'The Development of Community Powers after the Single European Act', in White and Smythe (eds.), *European and International Law*, p. 3.

of Article 235.[34] This was hardly surprising, given the general nature of the economic objectives specified in Article 2 EEC and the vague but all-embracing political objective of promoting 'closer relations between the States belonging to' the Community. Article 2 EC creates even broader objectives. It states that:

The Community shall have as its task, by establishing a common market and an economic and monetary union and by implementing the common policies or activities referred to in Articles 3 and 3a, to promote throughout the Community a harmonious and balanced development of economic activities, sustainable and non-inflationary growth respecting the environment, a high degree of convergence of economic performance, a high level of employment and of social protection, the raising of the standard of living and quality of life, and economic and social cohesion and solidarity among Member States.

The potentially unlimited legislative power of Article 235 is constrained by the requirement of unanimity in the Council to pass a measure under that Article. None the less it was used prior to the passing of the Single European Act to justify legislation on the environment,[35] on regional developments,[36] and on the European Currency Unit[37] before these topics had a specific legal basis within the Treaty. Even after the extension of the Community's specific legal competences in these and other areas by the Single European Act, Article 235 was still being used to extend EEC legislation into new areas prior to the Maastricht treaty amendments.[38] Further development of Community competence may take place after Maastricht using Article 235. However, it would seem inappropriate for Article 235 to be used to provide a legal basis for harmonization measures as regards matters that now have a specific legislative competence which precludes harmonization.[39]

The use of Article 235 is limited by the fact that it is a residuary power to be used, as the Court has said, 'only where no other provision of the Treaty gives the Community institutions the necessary power to adopt the

---

34 ibid., p. 17.
35 ibid., p. 5; an example being Directive 80/68 on the protection of ground water against pollution (OJ 1980 L20/43).
36 See, e.g., the creation of the European Regional Development Fund by Regulation 724/75 (OJ 1975 L73/1).
37 See Regulation 3181/78 (OJ 1978 L379/2).
38 See Usher, in White and Smythe (eds.), *European and International Law*, pp. 10, 15–18. Two examples are Council Decision 89/46 on an action programme for the European Tourism Year (OJ 1989 L17/53) and Council Decision 90/674 on the conclusion of the Agreement establishing the European Bank for Reconstruction and Development (OJ 1990 L372/1).
39 See education, Art. 126; vocational training, Art. 127; culture, Art. 128; and public health, Art. 129.

measure in question'.[40] In the *Generalized tariff preferences* case the Court took the view that the regulations should have been adopted under Article 113 of the Treaty as part of the common commercial policy. The Council had argued that the development-aid policy included in the regulations went beyond the scope of the common commercial policy while conceding that the part of the regulations dealing with tariff preferences came within it. Although the Council did not specify the legal basis for the regulations in their preambles, it intended that their legal basis was both Articles 113 and 235. If Article 113 had been adopted as the sole legal basis, then qualified majority voting would have been applicable in the Council rather than the unanimity required by Article 235. The Commission maintained that Article 113 was a sufficient legal basis on its own and the Court agreed, noting that a commercial policy that did not include development problems would be destined to become nugatory in the course of time.[41]

Where the legal basis selected for a piece of Community legislation requires majority voting in the Council, states in the dissenting minority may challenge the measure on the ground that it breaches the principle of subsidiarity. The principle of subsidiarity was introduced into the Treaty at Maastricht in Art. 3b EC, whereby Community action should be undertaken 'only if and so far as the objectives of the proposed action cannot be sufficiently achieved by the member states and can therefore, by reason of the scale or effects of the proposed action, be better achieved by the Community'. It may be that the Court of Justice will strike down legislation within the objectives of the Treaty on the basis that it conflicts with the principle of subsidiarity, but may restrict itself to procedural rather than substantive review.[42] The argument may be that the Community and the member states share competence to legislate in the area concerned and that the objectives of the particular legislative measure could be adequately achieved by national legislation. The Court may only sustain such an argument if the measure in question has not given reasons justifying why it was adopted in accordance with the principle of subsidiarity.[43]

---

40 See Case 45/86, note 29 above, p. 1520. See also Case 165/87 *Commission v Council* [1988] ECR 5545, 5562; Case 275/87 *Commission v Council* [1989] ECR 259; and Cases C-51, 90 and 94/89 *United Kingdom and Others v Council* [1991] ECR I-2757, 2790–1. For an example of where Art. 235 was justified, see Case 242/87 *Commission v Council* [1989] ECR 1425.
41 See Case 45/86, note 29 above, p. 1522. The Court was influenced by the growing link between trade and development since the adoption of the EEC Treaty, evidenced by the creation of UNCTAD and the incorporation into GATT of Part IV on trade and development.
42 See further Ch. 16, pp. 484–5.
43 See the discussion on subsidiarity in Ch. 1, pp. 12–15. Subsidiarity is in issue in two cases pending before the Court, Case C-84/94 *United Kingdom v Council* and Case C-233/94 *Germany v Parliament and Council*.

REASONS MUST BE GIVEN FOR EC LEGISLATION

Article 190 of the Treaty states:

Regulations, directives and decisions [adopted jointly by the European Parliament and the Council, and such acts] adopted by the Council or the Commission shall state the reasons on which they are based and shall refer to any proposals or opinions which were required to be obtained pursuant to this Treaty.[44]

The European Court has consistently interpreted Article 190 as requiring that legislation must include a statement of the facts and law that led the institution in question to adopt it, so as to make possible review by the Court and so that the member states and the nationals concerned may have knowledge of the conditions under which the Community institutions have applied the Treaty.[45] It has been argued that at least within the context of agricultural legislation the obligation contained within Article 190 has 'to a large extent lost its substantive value'.[46] The Court is willing to accept that legislation can be modified by later legislation without a formal amendment[47] and has accepted as a consequence of frequently modified and fragmented legislation that the reasons do not need to explain the often very complex matters of fact and law dealt with in the measure provided they disclose the essential objectives pursued by the institution.[48]

In the more high profile area of a Commission decision under Article 100a(4) permitting Germany to adopt stricter standards on the use of pentachlorophenol (PCP) than Directive 91/173 had laid down, the Court of Justice struck down the decision for non-compliance with the obligation to state reasons laid down in Article 190. It was not sufficient for the Commission in general terms to say that the objective of the German measure was the protection of health and the environment, two grounds of justification mentioned in Article 100a(4), and in particular was to protect citizens from the risks of cancer associated with dioxins. The Commission should have explained the reasons of fact and law on account

---

44 The words in square brackets were inserted at Maastricht.
45 See Case 158/80 *Rewe-Handelsgesellschaft Nord gmbH v Hauptzollamt Kiel* [1981] ECR 1805; Case 45/86, note 29 above; and Case C-41/93 *France v Commission* [1994] ECR I-1829.
46 See Barents, 'The Quality of Community Legislation' (1994) *Maastricht Journal of European and Comparative Law* 101, 112.
47 ibid., p. 111; see Cases C-143/88 and C-92/89 *Zuckerfabrik Süderdithmarschen* [1991]· ECR I-415 (para. 45).
48 Barents, at p. 112, see Case 250/84 *Eridania* [1986] ECR 117; Case C-27/89 *Scarpe*, [1990] ECR I-1701, see p. 250 below.

of which it considered that 'all' the conditions contained in Article 100a(4) were to be regarded as fulfilled in the case in point.[49] It may be that the Court's rigour in enforcing the requirement to state reasons will vary according to the political and economic significance of the measure in question. At least in relation to measures of importance the Court may apply similar rigour to ensuring that the preamble adequately justifies that the measure is in accordance with the principle of subsidiarity.

As seen above, in relation to the *Generalized tariff preferences* case, a failure to make it clear from the content of the legislation what its legal basis is will constitute a failure to comply with Article 190. Such a failure will be regarded by the Court as an infringement of an essential procedural requirement and hence grounds for holding the legislation to be invalid.

The Court can strike down legislation where the statement of facts leading the institution to adopt it is too vague[50] or where inadequate, even non-existent, reasons are given for the measures.[51]

TYPES OF LEGISLATIVE PROCEDURE

There is no uniform procedure for the making of Community legislation. Some of the various procedures that are used are outlined below. Cross-references are given to the chapters on the political institutions for discussion of their respective roles in the different procedures.

COUNCIL LEGISLATION BY THE CONSULTATION PROCEDURE

The key to this procedure is that the European Parliament must be consulted, or is consulted because the Council chooses to do so, on a legislative proposal.[52] The Commission initiates the proposal[53] and sends it to the Council, which consults the European Parliament by referring the

---

49 See Case C-41/93 *France* v *Commission* [1994] ECR I-1829, esp. paras. 31–7.
50 See Case 24/62 *Germany* v *Commission* [1963] ECR 63, discussed in Ch. 8, pp. 249–50.
51 See Case 158/80, note 45 above, and the cases referred to in Ch. 8, pp. 248–50.
52 See Ch. 4, pp. 108–14, where the Treaty provisions requiring Parliament to be consulted are listed.
53 See Ch. 2, pp. 51–4, on how the Commission arrives at such proposals.

proposal to it for its opinion.[54] Meanwhile, the Council is assisted by the detailed consideration given to the proposal by its working parties and Coreper.[55] Once the Council has received Parliament's opinion and the preparatory work of Coreper is completed, the Council can pass the legislation in accordance with the voting requirement prescribed in the provision providing the legal basis for the proposal.[56]

Parliament's opinion is not binding on the Council. Indeed, if the Council wishes to amend the Commission's proposal in any way, even to comply with Parliament's opinion, unanimity is required. However, the Commission may alter its proposal at any time in the legislative process prior to the Council adopting it. The Commission may choose to adopt some or all of the amendments suggested by the Parliament.[57]

Parliament should be reconsulted by the Council where substantial changes not requested by Parliament are made to a legislative proposal between the time of Parliament giving its opinion and the Council being ready to vote on the adoption of the proposal.[58]

COUNCIL LEGISLATION BY THE CONCILIATION PROCEDURE

This is a variation on the consultation procedure, which can apply to legislative proposals having appreciable financial implications for the non-compulsory part of Community expenditure. It was introduced by the Joint Declaration of the Commission, the Council and the Parliament of 4 March 1975 and is designed to give some protection to Parliament's budgetary prerogatives. Where the Council intends to depart from Parliament's opinion given in the consultation procedure, a conciliation committee can be established. The conciliation procedure is rather ineffective, principally because Parliament has no power at all in the process and thus is in such a weak bargaining position that the Council can ignore its views, and it has been rarely used.[59]

54 Within the European Parliament the proposal is referred to one of the standing committees. The full Parliament will vote on the proposal after hearing the recommendations of that committee; see Ch. 4, pp. 98–9 and 108–10.
55 See Ch. 3, pp. 85–6.
56 See Ch. 3, pp. 72–85.
57 See Ch. 2, pp. 56–8 on the Commission's participation in the legislative process.
58 See Case C-65/90 *European Parliament* v *Council* [1992] ECR I-4593; Case C-388/92 *Parliament* v *Council* [1994] ECR I-2067; and Ch. 4, pp. 114–15.
59 See Ch. 4, pp. 115–16.

COUNCIL LEGISLATION BY THE COOPERATION PROCEDURE

This is a very important procedure introduced by the Single European Act. It creates a second reading for Parliament, which is added to the single reading approach of the consultation procedure and enables Parliament to change the voting requirements in the Council from qualified majority to unanimity by rejecting the legislative proposal at the second reading.[60]

COUNCIL LEGISLATION WITHOUT CONSULTATION OF THE EUROPEAN PARLIAMENT

There are many instances in the EC Treaty where the Commission can make legislative proposals to be adopted by the Council without Parliament being consulted.[61] In relation to the more important proposals the Council usually voluntarily invokes the consultation procedure. However, there are a number of Community laws that are passed without being considered by Parliament, particularly in relation to urgent or trivial provisions of the common commercial policy under Article 113 of the Treaty. It is unacceptable that Parliament is dependent on the grace of the Council even to be consulted on a significant number of legislative proposals, particularly in relation to economic and monetary policy.

COUNCIL AND PARLIAMENT LEGISLATION UNDER THE CONCILIATION AND VETO PROCEDURE IN ARTICLE 189b EC

The conciliation and veto procedure is a vital step forward in the legislative process in the European Community. Introduced by the Treaty amendments agreed at Maastricht in December 1991 it came into operation on 1 November 1993. It introduces the possibility of a third reading in Parliament. For the first time the European Parliament has the power in several legislative fields to prevent legislation that it does not approve of from being passed. This ability to block legislation is, of course, a significant bargaining counter where the Council is keen to legislate in a matter governed by this procedure. The opportunities for mandatory conciliation, where the Parliament and the Council both have real bargaining power

60 See Ch. 4, pp. 116–22.
61 See Appendix.

and the Commission is present to help bring about an agreed text, puts the Parliament at the heart of the legislative process for the first time.[62]

COUNCIL LEGISLATION REQUIRING PARLIAMENT'S ASSENT

The Maastricht Treaty amendments introduced this new procedure whereby the Parliament has a veto on Council legislation. However, it applies to relatively few provisions and gives the European Parliament one opportunity only to consider the legislative proposal when it has to take it or leave it. The provisions in the EC Treaty do not build in an opportunity for Parliament to propose amendments. However, the Parliament has adapted its Rules of Procedure in a way which allows Parliament to request the Council to enter into conciliation if there is a sufficient majority in favour of any amendments.[63]

COUNCIL LEGISLATION NOT INITIATED BY THE COMMISSION

In a few instances the Council was able to legislate on its own initiative, but this was eliminated by the Single European Act.[64] There are some situations where the Council acts on a recommendation of the Commission rather than on a proposal, e.g. Article 109h(2). Significantly, the Council composed of heads of state or government can decide when the member states or a member state meets the economic requirements to enable the single currency to be established or a member state's currency to join it, on a recommendation from the Council composed of a lower level of government ministers.[65] The Commission's role is to make a recommendation to the lower-level Council. In these circumstances the Commission has less influence because it does not have the power to alter the 'recommendation' in the Council, as it is not a Commission 'proposal' within the meaning of Article 189a(2), and the Council does not require unanimity to depart from the recommendation, as it is not a 'proposal'

---

62 The details of this complex procedure and the provisions to which it applies are discussed in Ch. 4, pp. 122–6.

63 This procedure is discussed more fully in Ch. 4, pp. 126–7.

64 The main provision was Art. 84, allowing the Council to act unanimously in creating appropriate provisions for sea and air transport. The Single European Act amended the Article to require a proposal from the Commission, consultation of Parliament and qualified majority voting in the Council. The other powers of the Council were of a transitional nature; see Art. 28 (amended by the Single European Act) and Art. 136. These changes are discussed by Domestici-Met, (1987) RMC 556, 565.

65 See Art. 109j(2), (3).

within the meaning of Article 189a(1). The Council can, of course, request the Commission to submit to it appropriate proposals for the attainment of any of the common objectives of the Community, but this still leaves the content of the initial proposals and their legal basis in the hands of the Commission.[66]

The Maastricht Treaty amendments introduced the possibility that in the third stage of economic and monetary union the European Central Bank would be able to recommend legislation that the Council has the power to pass without the necessity of a proposal from the Commission. This will apply to certain provisions referred to in the Statute of the European System of Central Banks[67] and to certain provisions on the relationship of the single currency with currencies of third countries.[68] This could apply to the creation of, or changes to, an exchange-rate system between the ECU and currencies of third countries or to provisions on the general orientation of exchange-rate policy with third countries (the latter cannot prejudice the primary objective of the ESCB to maintain price stability). So in the third stage of EMU the Council will have a limited legislative role, but this cannot compromise the independence of the ECB on monetary policy.

The European Parliament has the power to initiate proposals for a uniform procedure in all the member states for its own elections. Here the Council has the power to lay down the appropriate provisions by a unanimous vote, but the new procedure must be approved by each of the member states in accordance with their respective constitutional requirements.[69]

In the institutional field the Council is empowered to make a number of changes acting unanimously. It can alter the number of members of the Commission.[70] At the request of the Court of Justice, the Council can increase the number of judges and advocates-general in the Court[71] and has set up a Court of First Instance. In relation to the setting up of this court, the Commission and European Parliament were consulted and the

---

66 See Art. 152. See also the more specialized power, introduced by the Maastricht Treaty amendments, granted to the Council or a member state to request the Commission to make a recommendation or a proposal on certain economic or monetary matters (Art. 109d).

67 See Art. 106(6) EC.

68 See Art. 109 EC.

69 See Art. 138(3) of the Treaty. As a result of the Maastricht Treaty amendments the Parliament not only has the power to initiate this procedure, but it must also give assent to the measure adopted by the Council.

70 See Art. 157(1) EC. The Council may decide not to fill a vacancy that arises in the Commission during the term of office: Art. 159.

71 See Arts. 165, 167.

Council acted unanimously.[72] The same procedure would be followed in altering the jurisdiction and the composition of the Court of First Instance and in making certain changes to the Statute of the Court of Justice.[73]

COMMISSION LEGISLATION MADE UNDER THE TREATY

The Commission has been authorized by the Treaty to enact legislation in a few areas.[74] They are of little significance in the overall scheme of Community legislation.

COMMISSION LEGISLATION MADE UNDER POWERS DELEGATED BY THE COUNCIL

Delegation of lawmaking power by the Council to the Commission is widespread, but tends to give relatively little policy discretion to the Commission. In addition, the Commission is often obliged to work with an advisory, management or regulatory committee set up by the Council.[75]

EUROPEAN CENTRAL BANK LEGISLATION

In the third stage of economic and monetary union, which, according to the Maastricht Treaty amendments, is to happen by 1 January 1999 at the latest,[76] the European Central Bank will have considerable power in running the new single currency, the ECU. It will have as its primary objective the maintenance of price stability.[77] The tasks of the ECB will be to define and implement the monetary policy of the Community, to conduct foreign exchange operations, to hold and manage the official foreign reserves of the member states and to promote the smooth operation

---

72 See Art. 168a(1) EEC as amended by the Single European Act and Decision 88/591 (OJ 1988 L319, corrected version in OJ 1989 C215).

73 See Art. 168a(2) EC, Decision 88/591, note 66 above, and Art. 188 as amended by the Single European Act. The Rules of Procedure of the Court of First Instance and the European Court are adopted by those courts (the latter simply by the European Court) but require the unanimous approval of the Council; see Arts. 168a(4) and 188.

74 Apart from Commission powers to take decisions during the transitional period or to authorize derogations by member states (e.g., Arts. 37(3), 46, 108(3), 115, 226), the key legislative powers are found in Arts. 48(3)(d), 90(3) and 97. Some of these are considered in Ch. 2, pp. 58–9.

75 These matters are considered at some length in Ch. 2, pp. 59–63.

76 See Art. 109j(4).

77 Art. 105(1).

of payment systems.[78] To carry out these tasks the ECB will have the exclusive right to authorize the issue of banknotes within the Community,[79] its members will act independently[80] and it will be able to make Community legislation, regulations and decisions, backed up by an ability to impose fines or periodic penalty payments on undertakings for failure to comply with obligations under those regulations and decisions.[81]

CONCLUSION

The bewildering variety of legislative procedures in the Community impedes the understanding of the Community lawmaking process. It is obscure to relatively well-informed law students, let alone the average man or woman in the street. Much could be gained by a radical overhaul of the EC Treaty to produce less variation.

This book has ignored the Economic and Social Committee on the grounds that its opinions are purely advisory and it is merely an appointed body.[82] Yet in many provisions of the EC Treaty consultation of the Economic and Social Committee is required as part of the legislative process.[83] The committee should be abolished. It is an unnecessary expense and complicates the legislative process. The views of industry and trade unions can be expressed by their respective collective European bodies and, like other pressure groups, they may influence one or more of the Commission, the European Parliament and the Council. Industry and trade unions should not be given an institutionalized voice in the legislative process. The Economic and Social Committee is, however, commended by Gordon-Smith,[84] for its useful role in drawing attention to ambiguities and inconsistencies in draft Community legislation.

At Maastricht a Committee of the Regions was established, which has an advisory role in certain measures.[85] Like the Economic and Social Committee, it is appointed by the Council and also has 222 members. In the case of both committees, the EC Treaty allows the Council to impose

---

78 Art. 105(2).
79 Art. 105a.
80 Not only the members of the Executive Board of the ECB but also the national central banks, whose governors serve on the Governing Council of the ECB, must be independent; see Arts. 107, 108 and 109e(5).
81 See Art. 108a, which empowers the ECB to make such legislation under certain provisions of the Statute of the European System of Central Banks.
82 See Arts. 193–8.
83 Arts. 49, 54, 63, 75, 79, 84, 99, 100, 100a, 118a, 121, 126, 127, 129, 129a, 129d, 130, 130b, 130d, 130e, 130i, 130o, 130s.
84 (1989) StatLRev 56, 68.
85 Arts. 198a–c.

a time-limit of not less than one month by which time they must give their opinion.[86] The Committee of the Regions must be consulted on legislative provisions under Articles 126, 128, 129, 129d, 130b, 130d and 130e EC. This small workload, its appointment by ministers of central government in the Council and its purely advisory role seem to make the Committee of the Regions an irrelevant waste of money.

As a minimum step in reform the Commission, as an unelected body, should not have any Treaty-based legislative powers and the European Parliament should have at least a right to be consulted on all Treaty-based legislation. For the sake of legislative efficiency and to ensure the passage of urgent legislation, e.g., under Art. 113 on the common commercial policy, it may be necessary to introduce a time-limit on Parliament, during which it must give its opinion or be deemed to have no opinion. This was done at Maastricht in relation to some international agreements to be concluded under Article 228(3). With regard to 'secondary legislation', EC legislation that is passed with a legal basis in another provision of EC legislation, consultation of Parliament may not always be necessary or practicable (e.g., the weekly Commission regulations relating to detailed and transient aspects of the CAP), but in many cases it would be appropriate. Relatively unimportant secondary legislation is passed in the United Kingdom where the United Kingdom parliament is not consulted because the statutory instrument is not laid before parliament or is laid but with no opportunity for a vote on it, whereas the more important statutory instruments are usually subject to negative or positive resolutions in the United Kingdom parliament.[87]

The conciliation and veto procedure should be extended, replacing the cooperation procedure entirely and leaving the consultation procedure in place for only the most urgent or trivial of measures. There is a danger that legislation will not be passed because of disagreements between the Council and Parliament. This should, however, be a price worth paying for advocates of a federal Europe, whereas for those opposing such a vision of Europe, the prospect of a reduction in the quantity of Community legislation should be attractive. The real concern about extending significant powers to the European Parliament to prevent the Council from legislating is that the Parliament may behave irresponsibly by blocking sensible progress in one area in order to force its wishes on the Council in another area. The only safeguard in a democracy against the abuse of the legislative process is for the electorate to return better MEPs at the next election. Up to the time of writing the degree of accountability of MEPs

86 Arts. 198, 198c.
87 See Miers and Page, *Legislation*, pp. 115–124.

was very low because so little attention was focused on their work by the media. Given real legislative power, media attention would come to the Parliament, turnout by voters at the elections would probably increase and more politicians of calibre who have established their reputation in national politics would be likely to stand for election.

At a more technical level EC legislation has the problem of being authentic in eleven languages and inevitably differences can arise in the translations.[88] In addition, compromise amendments are often drawn up at a late stage by the Commission or the Council, and this is not always conducive to clarity.[89] Some of the last-minute compromises in the inter-governmental conferences making Treaty amendments do not produce very coherent results;[90] an example is the acceptance at Maastricht of having two separate regimes on social policy, one contained in the Treaty – Articles 117–122 EC – and involving all the member states, and one contained in a protocol on social policy, which allows for the operation of an agreement on social policy involving all the member states except the United Kingdom yet still using the Community's institutional framework for lawmaking, excluding the United Kingdom's votes in the Council but not the votes of the two United Kingdom Commissioners in the Commission or of the United Kingdom MEPs.[91] A degree of uncertainty as to the meaning of some provisions of EC legislation is therefore almost inevitable.

Concern about the quality of EC legislation has grown in recent years and on 8 June 1993 the Council adopted a non-binding Resolution on the quality of drafting of EC legislation.[92] It addresses the need to produce clear, simple, concise and unambiguous legislation and for amendments, repeals and dates of entry into force, etc. to be clearly stated. Inconsistency with existing legislation should be avoided and an act amending an earlier act should not contain autonomous substantive provisions but only provisions to be directly incorporated into the act to be amended. However, the

---

88 The twelve official languages of the EC are Danish, Dutch, English, Finnish, French, German, Greek, Irish, Italian, Portuguese, Spanish and Swedish. However, because of difficulties of translation, and the fact that English is spoken by almost everyone in Ireland, an Irish translation is not made of Community regulations, directives and decisions, although the EC Treaty and EC Conventions, like the Brussels Convention and the Rome Convention, have an Irish text. Differences in the meaning of Community texts in the different languages have arisen in numerous cases; e.g. Case 29/69 *Stauder* v *Ulm* [1969] ECR 419 and Case 150/80 *Elefanten Schuh* v *Jacqmain* [1981] ECR 1671; see pp. 167–8.
89 See Gordon-Smith, (1989) StatLRev 56, a former member of the Council Legal Service, who says that 'occasionally some provisions will call to mind a horse designed by a committee' (p.68).
90 See e.g., the opaqueness of Art. 100a(4) EC, introduced by the Single European Act.
91 See pp. 644–6.
92 OJ 1993 C166/1.

measure is only a guideline and creates no enforceable obligations on the Community institutions.

The Community needs to develop a more systematic approach to codification of EC legislation, i.e. drawing together scattered existing legal texts into one text and repealing the others. It does happen[93] and was encouraged at the Edinburgh European Council in December 1992 but insufficient resources have been to devoted to ensuring that it is the norm. The inter-institutional agreement of 20 December 1994 on an accelerated procedure for the consolidation of legislation may help.[94] Even if these procedural problems were addressed, at least one commentator would still be anxious about the problem of 'low quality legislation' which he perceives to be 'above all a matter of substance'.[95]

93 E.g. the Council Regulation on the common organization of the market in fishery products, OJ 1991 L354/1.

94 See Bull. EU 12–1994, Point 1.7.1.

95 Barents, note 46 above, at p. 114. See also Advocate-General Mancini's colourful comment in Case 100/84, *Commission* v *United Kingdom* [1985] ECR 1169, 1173: 'I doubt whether Marguerite Yourcenar or Graham Greene would be prepared to read each morning a piece or two of Community legislation "pour prendre le ton" as Stendhal used to read articles of the *Code Civil*. In other words I admire the wisdom of the Community legislature but not its carelessness and too often imprecise language.' For an analysis of this case see Brown and Kennedy, *The Court of Justice* at pp. 305–7.

CHAPTER 6

Court of Justice

COMPOSITION AND STRUCTURE

Unlike the political institutions of the Community, the Court of Justice is not at all peripatetic. Although the representatives of the member states did not by common accord agree on the seat of the Court until 1992, as they were empowered to do by Article 216 EEC, they had taken a decision that the Court of Justice should remain in Luxembourg.[1] This rooting of the Court in Luxembourg is one factor in helping to give the Court a strong *esprit de corps*. Another important element is the collegiality of the Court.

There are fifteen judges[2] and nine advocates-general,[3] who are appointed by common accord of the governments of the member states for a renewable term of six years.[4] To be appointed to one of these offices a person has to either possess the qualifications required for appointment to the highest judicial offices in his or her respective countries or be jurisconsults of recognized competence. The latter ground allows for the appointment of academic lawyers.[5] Although in strict law the judges and

---

1 See Art. 3 of Decision 67/446/EEC (*Journal officiel des Communautes Européennes*, No. 152 of 13 July 1967, p. 18).

2 Art. 165 as amended by Art. 10 of Dec. 95/1, OJ 1995 L1/1.

3 Art. 166. Art. 11 of Dec. 95/1, above, provides that after 6 October 2000 there will only be eight advocates-general. The reason for the extra advocate-general between 1995 and 2000 is to accommodate Mr La Pergola who had just been appointed as the second Italian judge in October 1994 and had no place as a judge after 1 January 1995 when each of the fifteen member states appointed one judge. The hyphenated version of 'advocate general' has been used in the Treaties, although the non-hyphenated version has been used by the Court since 1982; see Brown and Kennedy, *The Court of Justice of the European Communities* (1994, 4th ed.), p. 60.

4 Art. 167.

5 Since September 1988 the advocate-general of British nationality has been Francis Jacobs, whose primary reputation had been formed as an outstanding academic lawyer in the field of European Community Law and who at the time of his appointment was the Professor of European Law at King's College, London. As a QC he also qualified on the first ground. The first two British judges, Lord Mackenzie Stuart (1973–88) and Sir

advocates-general could be of any nationality, in practice each member state will nominate one of its own nationals as a judge, and the five largest states – France, Germany, Italy, Spain and the United Kingdom – will each nominate an advocate-general. The remaining advocates-general are appointed by the smaller member states in accordance with a system of rotation. Belgium had an advocate-general from 1988 to 1994, Denmark from 1991 to 1997, Greece from 1994 to 2000 and Ireland from 1995 to 2000.[6] A disadvantage of the rotation system is that no matter how outstanding the person is, it is impossible for him or her to be reappointed at the end of six years (unless the state concerned is at the same time filling their regular appointment of a judge or advocate-general).

An odd number of judges is maintained in order to allow the full court to sit and to reach a majority decision. All decisions of the Court are signed by all the judges whether they were in the minority or the majority, so it is impossible to know whether the decision was reached by a bare majority or by unanimity.[7]

The Council has the power, acting unanimously on a request from the Court, to increase the number of judges and advocates-general.[8] In the past the size of the Court has been expanded upon the accession of new member states, but not on other occasions, to help it cope with extra business.[9] The creation of the Court of First Instance, discussed below, could mean that increased demand for judicial decisions may be absorbed

---

Gordon Slynn (1988–92), who were respectively judges in Scotland and England before being appointed to the Court, clearly qualified on the first ground. Sir Gordon Slynn was originally appointed as an advocate-general in 1981 and at that time was serving as the President of the Employment Appeal Tribunal. The current British judge, David Edward, a Scottish QC and former Professor of European Institutions at the University of Edinburgh, gained his judicial experience as a judge of the Court of First Instance from 1989 to 1992. The first British advocate-general, Jean-Pierre Warner, was appointed in 1973, having been junior counsel to the Treasury in Chancery matters from 1964 to 1972. Though he had never held judicial office in Britain, he did possess the qualifications required to be appointed as an English judge. In the 1991 Court at least five judges and three advocates-general had substantial reputations as academic lawyers before their appointment.

6 See the Joint Declaration of the member states of 1 January 1995, OJ 1995 L1/221. The remaining rotation is as follows: Luxembourg, Netherlands, Austria, Portugal, Finland and Sweden. For the most recent appointments see Dec. 95/4 OJ 1995 L1/223 and Dec. 95/8 OJ 1995 L17/14.

7 Judgments not infrequently suggest a lack of unanimity where they are brief, obscure, generalized and perhaps even contradictory; see the varied reasons given for the direct effect of directives in the *Van Duyn* and *Ratti* cases, discussed in Ch. 11, pp. 345–9.

8 See Arts. 165 and 166.

9 The Court started with seven judges, expanded to nine in 1973 (accession of Denmark, Ireland and the United Kingdom), to eleven in 1981 (accession of Greece), to thirteen in 1986 (accession of Spain and Portugal) and to fifteen in 1995 (accession of Austria, Finland and Sweden).

by increasing the jurisdiction of that court rather than expanding the number of judges in the Court of Justice.[9a]

Without doubt, the Court of Justice's workload has increased significantly over the years. The number of cases brought before it was 79 in 1970, 130 in 1975, 279 in 1980, 433 in 1985, 384 in 1990, 345 in 1991, 442 in 1992, 490 in 1993 and 354 in 1994. The dip in 1990 and 1991 may be partially explained by the fact that the Court of First Instance began to hear cases in November 1989 and the dip in 1994 can be explained by the substantial extension of the jurisdiction of the Court of First Instance in 1993–4. The large increase in the 1970s and 1980s was partly a result of the increase in the number of member states from six to twelve and partly due to the Court's own willingness to extend its jurisdiction by giving direct effect to many provisions of Community law,[10] which are then referred to the Court by national courts for a preliminary ruling under Article 177.[11]

The Court has coped with the increase in its workload in part by increasing the number of cases that it handles in a chamber rather than by a plenary session.[12] The EEC Treaty always allowed the Court to form chambers consisting of three or five judges, but originally insisted that cases brought before the Court by a member state or by a Community institution must be heard in plenary session.[13] Prior to 1974 the EEC Treaty did not allow preliminary rulings to be given by a chamber, but in that year the Council amended the third paragraph of Article 165 EEC to enable the Court's Rules of Procedure to grant jurisdiction to the chambers to hear preliminary rulings.[14] Initially, the change to Article 95 of the Court's Rules of Procedure was cautious,[15] but in 1978 the Court proposed that it should have complete discretion to refer any preliminary ruling that it saw fit to a chamber. The Court, however, has to gain the unanimous consent of the Council for any changes to its Rules of Procedure[16] and so

9a The Court of Justice and the Court of First Instance had 750 permanent staff and 87 temporary staff at 31 December 1994; see *General Report 1994*, p. 423.
10 See Ch. 11.
11 See Ch. 9.
12 In 1979 over 90 judgments were given by a plenary session of the Court, and over 40 by the chambers. Following the amendment to Article 95 of the Court's Rules of Procedure in 1979, a large number of cases have been decided by the chambers. In 1980 the Court decided 69 and the chambers 63; by 1983 the Court decided only 50 and the chambers 101; in 1986 the figures were 65 and 109, and in 1989 they were 72 and 116.
13 Art. 165 EEC.
14 The Council exercised this power under Art. 165 EEC, on a request from the Court, in Decision 74/584/EEC (OJ 1974 L318/22).
15 The amendment to Art. 95 in 1974 allowed chambers to hear preliminary rulings on matters 'of an essentially technical nature' or 'for which there was already an established body of case-law'; see OJ 1974 L350/1.
16 Art. 188.

the amendments agreed by the Council in 1979 did not go as far as the Court wished. They did, however, enable the Court to refer preliminary rulings to a chamber 'in so far as the difficulty or the importance of the case or particular circumstances are not such as to require that the Court decide it in plenary session'.[17]

The Court has, since then, been prepared to refer some fairly difficult and controversial questions of interpretation, where there was no precedent on the point, to a chamber.[18] Another factor enabling greater use of chambers has been, since 1981, the establishment of chambers of five judges. Such chambers are not much smaller than the smallest plenary session (seven judges).

Further changes were agreed at Maastricht so that under the EC Treaty the Court must sit in plenary session only when a member state or a Community institution is a party to the proceedings and requests a plenary session.[19] The entry into force of the Treaty on European Union led to further changes in the Rules of Procedure of the Court of Justice.[20] Article 95(1) now provides that: 'The Court may assign any case brought before it to a Chamber in so far as the difficulty or importance of the case or particular circumstances are not such as to require that the Court decide it in plenary session.'

The Court now has four chambers of three judges (two of which have four judges assigned but only three deliberate) and two chambers of seven judges (of whom only five deliberate on and sign the judgment in a particular case). Each chamber has a president, who is elected annually, and it seems that by convention the presidencies of the chambers rotate around all the judges apart from the President of the Court. Within the present constraints of the EC Treaty the Court has almost reached the limit on referral of cases to a chamber. Article 95(2) of the Court's Rules of Procedure as amended in 1991 allows a member state or Community institution to insist that a case be decided in plenary session not only, where it is a party to the proceedings, as the EC Treaty requires, but also where it is an intervener or, in a preliminary ruling, where it has submitted written observations. The Court faces the same problem in trying to change Article 95(2) of its Rules of Procedure or Article 165 EC: unanimity is required in the Council. At least one member state is likely to insist on the retention of the power to ensure that any case it is involved in will

---

17 Art. 95, read in conjunction with Art. 103 of the Rules of Procedure ECJ as amended by OJ 1979 L238/1.
18 E.g., Case 241/83 *Rösler* v *Rottwinkel* [1985] ECR 99, concerning the interpretation of Art. 16(1) of the EC Brussels Convention.
19 Art. 165 EC. No mention is made in the Treaty of any restriction on the chambers being able to hear preliminary rulings.
20 See the amendments of 21 February 1995, OJ 1995 L44/61, to the Rules of Procedure of 19 June 1991, OJ 1991 L176.

be heard in plenary session. The result is that a significant number of straightforward cases involving member states are heard in plenary session.[21] The Court indicates the degree of importance or difficulty it attaches to a case by the size of chamber or plenary session given to it. The least important cases that can be referred to a chamber are heard by a chamber of three, the more important cases by a chamber of five and only very important cases in plenary session. In relation to cases that cannot be referred to a chamber, the least important cases are heard by a plenary session of seven and the most important by the grand plenum (fifteen), with the intermediary cases heard by nine, eleven or thirteen.

The delivery of justice takes time in the Court of Justice. By the end of 1994 the average length of proceedings in references for a preliminary ruling was 18 months, in direct actions 20.8 months and in appeals from the Court of First Instance 21.2 months.[22] Owing to the complexity of the procedure before the Court involving written pleadings, interventions by third parties, oral hearings, advocate-general's opinion, etc. and the problems of translation it is difficult to imagine any significant improvement being brought about in these figures without a radical overhaul in the Court's procedures and structures.

PRESIDENT

The President of the Court is elected by the judges from among their number for a renewable period of three years.[23] The election is by secret ballot and the judge obtaining an absolute majority of the votes is elected. If on the first ballot no judge obtains an absolute majority, then a subsequent ballot is held and the judge obtaining the most votes is elected.[24] The President directs the judicial business and the administration of the Court. In particular, he or she presides at hearings and at the Court's deliberations,[25] fixes the dates and times of sittings of the Court[26] and

---

21 Indeed in 1991 and 1993 more cases were heard in plenary than by chambers for the first time since 1980. In 1991 118 judgments were given in plenary and 86 in chambers and in 1993 the figures were 103 and 100. The Court of Justice in its submission to the 1996 Intergovernmental Conference, see Proceedings of the Court of Justice No. 15/95, states that since the TEU entered into force in November 1993 it has been able to refer more cases to chambers because the member states and Community institutions 'have confined to exceptional cases their requests that the Court sit in plenary session'.

22 See *Proceedings of the Court of Justice* No. 34/94.

23 Art. 167 EC.

24 See Rules of Procedure ECJ, Art. 7 (OJ 1991 L176/10). If there is a tie in the second ballot, then the oldest of the judges involved in the tie is elected.

25 Rules of Procedure ECJ, Art. 8.

26 Rules of Procedure ECJ, Art. 25.

appoints a judge-rapporteur for every case.[27] The President also has important powers to order that a measure that is being contested before the Court be suspended and, in relation to any case before the Court, to prescribe any necessary interim measures.[28]

Up to now the presidency of the Court has been held by a national from each of the six original member states plus the United Kingdom, Denmark and Spain.[29] It may well be the case that the next time the job becomes vacant enough of the judges will feel that the President should come from Austria, Finland, Greece, Ireland, Portugal or Sweden for a judge from one of those states to be elected. The judges are free to ignore nationality and to vote for a candidate strictly on merit.

ADVOCATES-GENERAL

The role of the advocate-general has no equivalent in the legal systems in the United Kingdom. It does bear a strong resemblance to the role of the *commissaire du gouvernement* in the Conseil d'État in France, except that an advocate-general plays no part in the deliberations of the judges on the decision in a case.[30] The EC Treaty defines his or her[31] role as 'acting with complete impartiality and independence, to make, in open court, reasoned submissions on cases brought before the Court of Justice'.[32]

One advocate-general is assigned to each case by the First Advocate-General.[33] The latter job is held, by convention, in turn by each of the advocates-general for one year. An attempt is made to give an even

---

27 Rules of Procedure ECJ, Art. 10(2). It is on the basis of the judge-rapporteur's preliminary report at the end of the written procedure, and after hearing the advocate-general, that the Court decides to assign a case to a chamber or to a particular formation of the plenary session.

28 See Arts. 185 and 186 EC, Statute of the Court of Justice, Art. 36, and Rules of Procedure ECJ, Arts. 83–9.

29 The first President of the Court was an Italian, Massimo Pilotti (1952–8); followed in turn by a Dutchman, Andreas Donner (1958–64); a Luxembourger, Charles Hammes (1964–7); a Frenchman, Robert Lecourt (1967–76); a German, Hans Kutscher (1976–80); a Belgian, Josse Mertens de Wilmars (1980–84); a Scot, Lord Alexander Mackenzie Stuart (1984–8); a Dane, Ole Due (1988–94); and a Spaniard, Gil Carlos Rodríguez Iglesias (1994 onwards).

30 See Rules of Procedure ECJ, Art. 27, OJ 1991 L176/13.

31 Although there have been no female judges to date, Mme Simone Rozes of France was an advocate-general from 1981 to 1984, before becoming First President of the French Cour de Cassation (the highest civil court in France).

32 Art. 166.

33 Rules of Procedure ECJ, Art. 10, OJ 1991 L176/10.

workload to the advocates-general. Advocates-general of a given nationality can be assigned to cases involving parties of the same nationality[34] but do not appear to be assigned to cases brought by or against the state of which they are nationals.[35]

The opinion of the advocate-general is given orally at the end of the oral procedure,[36] invariably some time after the oral hearing. The style of the opinion varies to some extent, according to the legal background of each advocate-general. It will, in general, contain a full analysis of the relevant Community law and give the advocate-general's view as to how the Court should decide the case. Once the advocate-general has given the opinion, he or she plays no further part in the proceedings. The parties cannot comment on the opinion, and the next phase of the case is the secret deliberations of the judges, at which the advocate-general is not present.

The advocate-general's opinion will be considered by the Court but it is in no way binding on it. The opinion has the utility of ensuring that the issues of Community law are properly canvassed before the Court takes its decision. There is a risk that in some cases the parties may fail to address important issues of Community law in their arguments. This risk may be greater in the European Court, where the lawyers appearing there may do so only once in their careers and may not be experts in either the substantive or procedural aspects of Community law, than the risk of failure to address important issues of national law in the courts in the member states. It has to be said, however, that the judge-rapporteur not only prepares a public report for the oral hearing, containing a summary of the facts of the case and of the legal arguments presented in the case,[37] but also prepares a private preliminary report for the judges, which gives

---

34 E.g. AG Jacobs was assigned to Case C-355/89 *Department of Health and Social Security* v *C. S. Barr and another* [1991] ECR I-3479, a preliminary ruling from the Isle of Man and AG Darmon, of French nationality, was assigned to a preliminary ruling from the French Cour de Cassation, Case C-220/88 *Dumez France and Tracoba* v *Hessische Landesbank (Helaba) and Others* [1990] ECR I-49. This is not a new practice: AG Lenz, of German nationality, was assigned to Case 92/83 *3M Deutschland GmbH* v *Oberfinanzdirektion Frankfurt am Main* [1984] ECR 1587, a preliminary ruling from Germany.

35 Though Brown and Kennedy, *The Court of Justice of the European Communities* (1994, 4th ed.), p. 61, seem to suggest that this does happen.

36 Rules of Procedure ECJ. Art. 59, OJ 1991 L17/19. An advocate-general in the Court of First Instance can give his or her opinion in writing; see Rules of Procedure CFI, Art. 61, OJ 1991 L136/12.

37 Statute of the Court of Justice Art. 18 states that this report is read in the Court at the start of the oral procedure, but, in fact, it is made available in writing and taken as read. It is possible under Art. 44a of the Rules of Procedure ECJ for the oral part of the procedure to be dispensed with by the Court with the express consent of the parties (inserted by the 1991 amendments, OJ 1991 L176/2).

his view as to whether the case should be assigned to a chamber.[38] Later, after the advocate-general's opinion has been given, the judge-rapporteur prepares the first draft of the Court's judgment.[39] Thus, in practice, the advocate-general and the judge-rapporteur, assisted by their respective teams of legal secretaries,[40] both independently track the case they are assigned to and each thoroughly researches the issues of Community law involved in the case. The cynic would say that the role of the advocate-general in ensuring that the Court is fully briefed as to the relevant Community law is unnecessary; it could be left to the judge-rapporteur. However, that is to ignore other aspects of the advocate-general's role.

The advocate-general's opinion can serve the role that a judgment of a court of first instance does in a national legal system when an appeal court is considering its decision. It is generally regarded as desirable that judges who are in the highest court in a particular legal system do not pronounce on a case that has not been the subject of an earlier judgment by a lower court.[41] The hierarchical structure allows for mature reflection by the highest court, whose judgment will determine the law for subsequent cases. However, the European Court often will be deciding on questions of Community law that have not been previously decided by any court. The interposition of the advocate-general at least ensures that one judicial opinion has been expressed on the point of Community law before the Court has to do so.[42] The problem is that an advocate-general's opinion does not equate to a judgment by the Court of First Instance, which is definitive unless it is appealed to the European Court on a point of law only. In the latter case the Court starts from the Court of First Instance's decision. The Court of Justice is free to disregard the advocate-general's opinion and for a long time it was not the practice of the Court even to refer to it. However, in the 1990s the Court of Justice has referred approvingly to the reasoning of the advocate-general as part of its own

---

38 This private report is presented to the Court at a meeting of the judges at the end of the written procedure; Rules of Procedure ECJ, Art. 44, OJ 1991 L176/16. The case will have been provisionally assigned to a chamber by the President of the Court; see Rules of Procedure ECJ, Art. 9(2), OJ 1991 L176/10.

39 See Usher, *European Court Practice* (1983), pp. 178–9.

40 Each judge and advocate-general has three legal secretaries, who are not secretaries, but lawyers personally employed by a judge or advocate-general to do legal research on the cases allocated to that judge or advocate-general and to prepare a draft opinion. A legal secretary is similar to a law clerk in North America but often stays in the job for longer and is not necessarily newly graduated from law school.

41 This principle of 'double judicial control' is advocated by the Court of First Instance; see Court of First Instance, 'Reflections on the Future Development of the Community Judicial System' (1991) 16 ELRev 175.

42 See AG Warner expressing a similar view in 'Some Aspects of the European Court of Justice' (1976) 14 JSPTL 15, 18–19.

judgment,[43] has adopted a part of an advocate-general's opinion as part of its own judgment[44] or has simply taken on board the whole of the advocate-general's opinion.[45]

The job of the advocate-general can be justified in other ways. First, it can be said to be the best possible training ground for a judge of the Court. It is not unusual for an advocate-general to become a judge, particularly in Italy and the United Kingdom.[46] Sir Gordon Slynn was an advocate-general from 1981 until 1988, when he became a judge, Federico Mancini was an advocate-general from 1982 until he became a judge in 1988 and Claus Gulmann, from Denmark, was an advocate-general from 1991 until he became a judge in 1994. Second, the advocate-general's opinion may contain ideas that are adopted by the Court as part of Community law. The classic example of this is Advocate-General Warner's advocacy of the idea of the right to be heard as a general principle of Community law in *Transocean Marine Paint Association* v *Commission*.[47] This idea had not been put forward by the parties to the case but was adopted by the Court.[48] Third, even if the advocate-general's opinion is not followed by the Court in the instant case, it is published as part of the official reports of the Court's cases and can be used in argument in future cases or repeated by a subsequent advocate-general to persuade the Court to change its position.[49]

43 See eg. Case C-27/90 *SITPA* [1991] ECR I-133, 158; Case C-129/92 *Owens Bank Ltd* v *Bracco and another* [1994] ECR I-117 at para. 11; Case C-187/93 *European Parliament* v *Council* [1994] ECR I-2857 at para. 26; and Case C-76/93P *Scaramuzza* v *Commission* [1994] ECR I-5173 at para. 16.
44 See eg. Case C-36/92P *Samenwerkende Elektriciteits-produktiebedrijven NV (SEP)* v *Commission* [1994] ECR I-1911, where at para. 21 the Court adopted paras. 21 to 42 of the advocate-general's opinion as the basis for its rejection of the first five grounds of appeal.
45 See eg. Case C-284/91 *Suiker Export* v *Belgium* [1992] ECR I-5473; Case C-59/92 *Ebbe Soennischen GmbH* v *Hauptzollamt Hamburg St Annen*, judgment of 29 April 1993; Case C-377/92 *Felix Koch Offenbach Couleur und Karamel GmbH* v *Oberfinanzdirektion München*, judgment of 5 October 1993.
46 In fact, in the past two Italians served as judges before becoming advocates-general: Alberto Trabucchi, a judge from 1962 to 1973 and then an advocate-general for another three years, and Francesco Capotorti, a judge for a few months in 1976 and then advocate-general until 1982. Antonio La Pergola was briefly a judge from October 1994 to January 1995 when he had to accept a switch to being an advocate-general to retain an odd number of judges. As a result of the Norwegian people's rejection of membership of the Union fifteen member states each nominate one judge rather than the planned sixteen member states nominating one judge and an extra judge being appointed in rotation by the larger member states.
47 Case 17/74 [1974] ECR 1063.
48 See Warner's comment on this, (1976) 14 JSPTL 15, 20.
49 The Court of First Instance may refer to the opinion of an advocate-general in the Court of Justice in an earlier case; see Case T-3/90 *Prodifarma* v *Commission* [1991] ECR II-1, 14.

VOTING

The Court or a chamber must have an uneven number of judges sitting in the deliberations on a case.[50] After the Court has heard the advocate-general's opinion, it will subsequently meet in the deliberation room. What happens in the room is secret,[51] but it is known that the working language of the Court is French and that therefore the judges discuss their views in that language without the assistance of interpreters.[52] The views of each judge are given and after full discussion a vote is taken, starting with the vote of the most junior judge in terms of the order of precedence and finishing with the most senior.[53] As the Court's Rules of Procedure state: 'The conclusions reached by the majority of the Judges after final discussion shall determine the decision of the Court.'[54]

Although not mentioned in the Statute of the Court and the Rules of Procedure, the judge-rapporteur plays a significant part in the deliberations in that he or she will prepare the draft text of the decision and will amend it, or redraft it completely, to accommodate views commanding a majority among the judges.[55]

TENURE AND DISMISSAL

Judges and advocates-general are appointed by common accord of the Governments of the member states for six-year terms, which can be renewed.[56] As noted above, each Government is able to nominate its own judge. The five largest member states each nominate an advocate-general, and the other states take it in turns to nominate the remaining three advocates-general. This system would seem to allow for political bias in

---

50 Statute of the Court of Justice, Art. 15 and Rules of Procedure ECJ, Art. 26.
51 Statute of the Court, Art. 32.
52 See Lord Mackenzie Stuart, 'The Court of Justice: a Personal View' in Bates *et al.* (eds.), *In Memoriam J. D. B. Mitchell*, pp. 121–2. It may be that in chambers made up of judges who are more comfortable speaking in English rather than in French the former is used.
53 Rules of Procedure ECJ, Art. 27; the order of precedence is set out in the Rules of Procedure ECJ, Art. 6.
54 ibid.
55 See Lord Mackenzie Stuart in Bates *et al.* (eds.), *In Memoriam J. D. B. Mitchell*, p. 120.
56 Art. 167.

the appointment and reappointment of judges and advocates-general. It seems that in practice the people who have been appointed have gained their position on merit rather than on the acceptability of their views to their Government, although this is hard to verify. It is true that a number of judges and advocates-general have been career civil servants in the Ministry of Justice or Foreign Office of the state of which they are a national; for example, in the 1995 Court Judges Puissochet of France, Schockweiler of Luxembourg and Moitinho de Almeida of Portugal, and Advocate-General Elmer of Denmark. Such positions are, however, by definition politically neutral and they are servants of whatever Government is in power. In addition, some members of the the Court are lawyers who have held political office: in the 1995 Court Judge Murray from Ireland and Advocate-General Lenz of Germany. A large majority of members of the Court have a background as national judges (e.g., in the 1995 Court Judges Jann of Austria, Sevon of Finland, Kakouris of Greece, Hirsch of Germany, Kapteyn of the Netherlands, Ragnemalm of Sweden and Advocates-General Léger of France, Cosmas of Greece, La Pergola of Italy and Ruiz-Jarabo Colomer of Spain) or academics (e.g. in the 1995 Court Judges Joliet of Belgium, Mancini of Italy, and President Rodríguez Iglesias of Spain, and Advocates-General Jacobs of the United Kingdom and Tesauro of Italy). Of the other members of the 1995 Court Judge Gulmann of Denmark had a background in private practice before becoming an advocate-general, Judge Edward of the United Kingdom had been an advocate and academic before becoming a judge in the Court of First Instance and Advocate-General Fennelly of Ireland had been a barrister.

At the stage of reappointment it could be argued that a relatively short period of tenure leaves a member of the Court exposed to the risk of making decisions to please the Government of the state of which he or she is a national. Judges are relatively well protected from any backlash by Governments against their decisions, as nobody, apart from the judges, knows how an individual judge votes in the deliberation room. Hence a Government cannot be sure whether a judge has supported or rejected its contentions in cases.[57] The advocates-general are in a more vulnerable position because they must state their views in open court. Over a period of time it becomes clear what their position is on the controversial questions of Community law. The evidence tends to suggest that advocates-general from the four largest states often are reappointed or promoted. In relation to the United Kingdom Advocate-General Warner served for eight years before being made a High Court judge in England,

---

57 This point is made by Lord Mackenzie Stuart in Bates et al., (eds.), In Memoriam J. D. B. Mitchell, pp. 119–20.

Sir Gordon Slynn served as Advocate-General for seven years before becoming a judge in the Court. In 1992 he became a Lord of Appeal in Ordinary in the House of Lords, the United Kingdom's highest court in civil matters. Advocate-General Jacobs was appointed in 1988 and has subsequently been reappointed. In relation to Germany, Advocate-General Roemer served for twenty-one years, Advocate-General Reischl for eleven years and Advocate-General Lenz has been in office since 1984. In relation to France, Advocate-General Lagrange served for twelve years, but the subsequent office holders have generally served only one term before returning to high judicial positions in France or dying or retiring. In relation to Italy (which did not have an advocate-general until 1973) the tradition has been for a person to serve a time as a judge of the Court and then as an advocate-general or vice versa.[58] The problem faced by advocates-general from the smaller states is that their appointments cannot be renewed due to the rotation system. There does not seem to be any evidence of advocates-general tailoring their opinions to suit their respective Governments.

During the six-year term of office a judge or advocate-general can be removed from office only if in the unanimous opinion of the other judges and advocates-general he or she no longer fulfils the requisite conditions or meets the obligations arising from his or her office.[59] This procedure has never been used.

METHODS OF INTERPRETATION

It is a basic judicial function to have to ascertain the meaning of words in legal texts. All courts make choices as to the approach or approaches they adopt in doing so. Courts can lay emphasis on construing the words literally in order to ascertain their natural and ordinary meaning. They can ascertain the historical meaning of the words by examining documentation that reveals the intention of the authors of the legal text. Courts can place the words in issue in the overall context of the legal provision in which the words appear and in turn fit that legal provision within the scheme of the legal system as a whole. In doing so courts may construe the words in issue

---

58 See p. 163. Advocate-General Tesauro who took office in 1988 has been reappointed.
59 Statute of the Court of Justice, Art. 6. The judge or advocate-general concerned may make representations to the Court but is excluded from the deliberations; Rules of Procedure ECJ, Arts. 4, 5.

in the light of objectives stated in the legal provision or in related provisions. These different approaches can be categorized as literal, historical, contextual and purposive. Such categorization is somewhat artificial.[60] Judges in the European Court do not use these terms in the Court's decisions;[61] they are used by academics as an attempt to analyse the approach used by the Court. Judges may choose to use several methods of interpretation at the same time.[62]

LITERAL AND HISTORICAL INTERPRETATION

Any court will give consideration to the natural and ordinary meaning of the words of the text that requires interpretation. The European Court faces two main problems that limit the utility of this literal approach.

First, the plurilingual nature of Community law.[63] The EC Treaty is valid in twelve languages and most regulations and directives are valid in eleven languages.[64] As translation is not an exact science, this inevitably leads to variations in the meaning of words in the various texts. This can be illustrated by the case of Stauder v Ulm.[65] A Commission decision addressed to member states had a requirement that recipients of the Community's surplus butter at a cheap rate had to prove their entitlement to welfare benefits. The German and Dutch texts both required the person to give a coupon indicating their name whereas the French and Italian texts simply required that a coupon be given referring to the person concerned.[66] Stauder argued that it was a breach of his fundamental rights to have to reveal his name to those selling the cheap butter. The Court followed the more liberal provisions of the French and Italian texts so that Stauder did not have to reveal his name directly on the coupon. Other methods could be used to check his entitlement to the cheap butter.

It cannot be assumed that the Court will follow the meaning indicated

---

60 It is worth noting Lord Mackenzie Stuart's 'scepticism' about writing about the Court's methods of interpretation, given the 'dangers in over-analysis'; see *The European Communities and the Rule of Law*, p. 72.
61 See Kutscher, 'Methods of Interpretation as Seen by a Judge at the Court of Justice', Paper in the Court of Justice's Judicial and Academic Conference, Luxembourg, 1976, pp. 5–6.
62 ibid., p. 15.
63 See Neville Brown, 'The Linguistic Regime of the European Communities: Some Problems of Law and Language' (1981) 15 Valparaiso ULR, 319–41.
64 See Ch. 5, note 88. For a recent example of the Court examining different language versions of the Treaty see the analysis of Art. 228 in Case C-327/91 *France v Commission* [1994] ECR I-3641, 3676–7.
65 Case 29/69 [1969] ECR 419.
66 At the time there were only four official languages in the Community.

by the majority of language texts. In *Elefanten Schuh* v *Jacqmain*[67] the Court followed the French and Irish texts of Article 18 of the EC Brussels Convention and ignored the word 'solely' found in the English text and its equivalents in the Danish, Dutch, German and Italian texts. In English the relevant part of the Article provides that 'a court of a Contracting State before whom a defendant enters an appearance shall have jurisdiction. This rule shall not apply where appearance was entered solely to contest the jurisdiction.' In the French text the second sentence reads: '*Cette règle n'est pas applicable si la comparution a pour objet de contester la compétence* ...'. If the word 'solely' were given meaning, then a defendant would be deemed to submit to the jurisdiction of a court if he or she contested the merits of the case as well as the jurisdiction of the court. The Court did not regard this to be 'in keeping with the objectives and spirit of the Convention', as

a defendant who raises the issue of jurisdiction and no other might be barred from making his submissions as to the substance if the court rejects his plea that it has no jurisdiction. An interpretation of Article 18 which enabled such a result to be arrived at would be contrary to the right of the defendant to defend himself in the original proceedings, which is one of the aims of the Convention.[68]

The second reason why literal interpretation is of limited use to the European Court is the open-textured nature of many provisions in the EC Treaty and, to a lesser extent, in EC regulations and directives.[69] The level of detail is much less than a United Kingdom lawyer would expect from a statute and there is a general absence of clauses in the text defining the words used. One of many examples is Article 48 of the Treaty, which says that 'freedom of movement for workers shall be secured within the Community at the latest by the end of the transitional period'. Yet the key word 'workers' is not defined in the Treaty, and over thirty years later the Court is still deciding such fundamental questions as how long can a Community national seek employment in another member state and still benefit from the provisions on free movement of workers.[70] Clearly, a literal interpretation of the word 'workers' is of little help to the Court in dealing with concrete cases. Inevitably, open-textured provisions tend to be capable of more than one meaning.

---

67 Case 150/80 [1981] ECR 1671.
68 ibid., p. 1685. An inability to defend on the merits in the original proceedings means that no defence is possible because the system of recognition and enforcement in the other contracting states is almost automatic.
69 See Ch. 5, p. 153, on the problem of the lack of clarity of some EC legislation as a result of late political compromises in the Council to achieve the required majority.
70 See Case C-292/89, *R* v *Immigration Appeal Tribunal, ex parte Antonissen* [1991] ECR 1–745, [1991] 2 CMLR 373.

The combination of open-textured provisions and eleven or twelve different language versions makes it relatively unusual that there is no doubt that the words have one literal meaning that can be applied to resolve the case before the Court. Indeed, the fact that Community law is equally authentic in several language versions was highlighted by the European Court as a reason for a national court, against whose decision there is no judicial remedy, being cautious about deciding not to refer a case to the European Court on the ground that there is 'no scope for any reasonable doubt' as to the meaning of a provision of Community law.[71] None the less, there are examples of the Court deciding cases in accordance with 'grammatical and textual analysis'.[72] Usually the Court is faced with alternative constructions and requires another guide to determine which construction to follow.

The Court might be expected to turn to the documents that reveal the intentions of those who drafted the EEC Treaty. However, these documents are deliberately shrouded in secrecy. As Kutscher rightly says:

The Court cannot rely on preparatory work which provides a history of how the Treaties came into being. In so far as any such preparatory work exists at all . . . it has in any case not been published. Documents which are not generally accessible must, however, be ruled out as aids to interpretation for constitutional reasons.[73]

In the future the Court may gain some insight from the negotiations on the intergovernmental conferences in 1985–6, leading to the Single European Act, and in 1991, leading to the Treaty on European Union.[74] However, the evidence suggests that the Court will make limited use of such guidance even when it is available. In the intergovernmental conference that led to the Single European Act the member states had decided not to amend Article 173 EEC to give the European Parliament *locus standi* to bring actions for annulment. This was expressly noted by the Court in the *Comitology* case[75] when it refused to give the European Parliament *locus standi* under Article 173 EEC. None the less, the Court subsequently chose to give the Parliament limited *locus standi* under that

---

71 See Case 283/81 *CILFIT* v *Italian Ministry of Health* [1982] ECR 3415, 3430.

72 See Slynn, 'The Court of Justice of the European Communities' (1984) 33 ICLQ 409, 414.

73 'Methods of Interpretation', note 61 above, p. 21. Cf. note 80 below.

74 Some of the history of the negotiations on the Single European Act is available as a result of publications by individuals involved in the process, e.g., De Zwaan, 'The Single European Act: Conclusions of a Unique Document' (1986) CMLRev 747–65. In June 1991, at the end of its presidency of the Council, Luxembourg released to the press its draft Treaty of Union and this can be compared to the final document agreed during the Netherlands presidency in December 1991.

75 Case 302/87 *European Parliament* v *Council* (*Comitology*) [1988] ECR 5615, 5644.

Article, ignoring the evidence of the intention of the drafters of the Single European Act.[76]

The Court has made limited use of published *travaux préparatoires* in construing Community regulations and directives. The original proposal of the Commission is published in the *Official Journal*, as are the views of the European Parliament on the proposal. These sources have been found helpful by the Court in a few cases, such as *AIMA* v *Greco*,[77] but will not be relied on where they are contradictory or ambiguous, such as *Germany* v *Commission*.[78] In *United Kingdom* v *Commission*[79] the Court had regard to certain 'preparatory documents' in deciding upon the correct legal basis for Council Directive 86/113/EEC of 25 March 1986. These documents included a European Convention that had been approved by the Council in the name of the Community in 1978 and a Council Resolution of 1980, both of which were published in the *Official Journal*.[80] In interpreting the Common Customs Tariff headings the Court referred to the Rules for the Interpretation of the Nomenclature of the Common Customs Tariff before they were inserted into the text of the Common Customs Tariff.[81] In *Bahner* v *Hauptzollamt Frankfurt am Main-Ost*[82] the Court gave some weight to the Explanatory Notes to the Common Customs Tariff, which were not part of the Tariff.[83]

However, the crucial dialogue between the Council and the Commission and the deliberations of the Council are conducted in secret, so the published *travaux préparatoires* are of limited value. In *Antonissen*[84] Advocate-General Darmon refers to the secrecy of the deliberations of the Council. In this case a question was referred by the English High Court to the European Court as to whether a Council declaration entered in the minutes of the Council at the time of the adoption of Regulation 1612/68 and Directive 68/360 on the free movement of workers could be used as an

---

76 Case C-70/88 *European Parliament* v *Council* [1990] ECR 1–2041, noted by Bebr (1991) 28 CMLRev 663. This case is discussed below and in Chs. 4 and 8.
77 Case 36/77 [1977] ECR 2059, 2071.
78 Case 18/76 [1979] ECR 343, 383; see the discussion of this issue by Plender, 'The Interpretation of Community Acts by Reference to the Intentions of the Authors' (1982) 2 YEL 57, 92–7.
79 Case 131/86 [1988] ECR 905, 932.
80 The Court will not have regard to unpublished material; see Plender (1982) 2 YEL. 57, 94–5.
81 See Case 183/73 *Osram* [1974] ECR 477.
82 Case 54/79 [1980] ECR 311, 317–18.
83 For another example of the use of *travaux préparatoires*, see Case 61/80 *Coöperatieve Stremsel-en Kleurselfabriek* v *Commission* [1981] ECR 851, 869. Sometimes explanatory notes are made part of the Community legislation, e.g., Case 143/86 *Margetts and Addenbrooke* v *Cuddy* [1988] ECR 625, 642; then, of course, they are not *travaux préparatoires*.
84 Case C-292/89, note 70 above, [1991] 2 CMLR 373, 385.

aid in the interpretation of those provisions of Community legislation. In accordance with its then Rules of Procedure the Council had authorized the disclosure of the relevant part of the Council minutes containing the declaration for use by the English High Court in the *Antonissen* case. After quoting the declaration, the European Court said: 'However, such a declaration cannot be used for the purpose of interpreting a provision of secondary legislation where, as in this case, no reference is made to the content of the declaration in the wording of the provision in question. The declaration therefore has no legal significance.'[85] This is a very restrictive approach to the use of explanatory material adopted unanimously by the Council at the time of the adoption of the legislation.[86] It goes beyond the normal requirement of concurrent publication, which would have been sufficient to render the declaration irrelevant in the *Antonissen* case, to requiring an express mention of the declaration in the final text of the legislation.

The explanatory reports on the EC Brussels Convention are published in the *Official Journal* and have occasionally been referred to by the Court.[87] The Court has decided over seventy cases on the interpretation of the EC Brussels Convention, but in only a handful of cases has it been influenced by the reports. The Court first expressly referred to the Jenard Report in *Rinkau*[88] and has referred to it relatively infrequently since.[89] One example of where the Court gave a narrow literal construction of an Article in the Convention even when the official reports indicated the possibility of flexibility is *Rösler* v *Rottwinkel*.[90] The Jenard Report[91] and the Schlosser

---

85 ibid., pp. 399–400.
86 See a similar approach in Case 237/84 *Commission* v *Belgium* [1986] ECR 1247, 1256 and in Case 429/85 *Commission* v *Italy* [1988] ECR 843, 852.
87 The Jenard Report on the original Convention, its annexed Protocol and the 1971 Protocol are published in OJ 1979 C59/1; the Schlosser Report on the 1978 Accession Convention is published in OJ 1979 C59/71; the Evrigenis and Kerameus Report on the 1982 Accession Convention is published in OJ 1986 C298/1; and the Almeida Cruz, Desantes Real and Jenard Report on the 1989 Accession Convention is published in OJ 1990 C189/35.
88 Case 157/80 [1981] ECR 1391.
89 It has been of some assistance to the Court in construing Article 17 of the Convention in Case 150/80, note 67 above; Article 5(1) of the Convention in Case 133/81 *Ivenel* v *Schwab* [1982] ECR 1891; and Article 6(1) of the Convention in Case-189/87 *Kalfelis* v *Schröder, Münchmeyer, Hengst & Co.* [1988] ECR 5565. The Jenard Report, Schlosser Report and the Evrigenis and Kerameus Report were all referred to by the Court in its interpretation of Article 1(i)(4) of the Convention in Case 190/89 *Marc Rich & Co.* v *Società Italiana Impianti* [1991] ECR I-3855. For a complete list of cases where the reports have been referred to see *Anton & Beaumont's Civil Jurisdiction in Scotland: Brussels and Lugano Conventions* (1995, 2nd ed.) at p. 37.
90 Case 241/83 [1985] ECR 99 discussed in *Anton & Beaumont's Civil Jurisdiction in Scotland* at pp. 146–7 and 490–3.
91 OJ 1979 C59/1, at p. 35.

Report[92] indicated, respectively, that Article 16(1) need not be applied to disputes concerned either with rent or with short-term agreements for use and occupation of property, such as holiday accommodation, but the European Court applied the Article to both these types of dispute.

CONTEXTUAL AND PURPOSIVE INTERPRETATION

Given the limitations on the value of literal and historical interpretation, it is hardly surprising that the Court has turned to other methods of interpretation. As Hans Kutscher, a former President of the Court, has said extrajudicially: 'The literal and historical methods of interpretation recede into the background. Schematic and teleological interpretation ... is of primary importance.'[93]

Contextual and purposive interpretation 'are closely interlocked in the case-law of the Court'[94] and thus will be considered together here. This interlocking can be seen in a quote from the European Court's decision in the *CILFIT* case: 'Every provision of Community law must be placed in its context and interpreted in the light of the provisions of Community law as a whole, regard being had to the objectives thereof and to its state of evolution at the date on which the provision in question is to be applied.'[95]

In interpreting an individual Article of the EC Treaty the Court will often set it in its context in the Treaty and construe it in the light of the objectives set out in the Preamble and Articles 2 and 3 of the Treaty. Unlike United Kingdom statutes, the Court is not left to guess at the overall aims of the text it has to interpret.[96] The EC Treaty explicitly states its aims and, as reasons must be given for EC regulations and

---

92 OJ 1979 C59/71, at p. 120.
93 'Methods of Interpretation', note 61 above, p. 16. Schematic and teleological are similar to contextual and purposive. As in Lord Mackenzie Stuart (*The European Communities and the Rule of Law*, p. 76) purposive is preferred to teleological at least partly because it is more familiar to United Kingdom readers.
94 Kutscher, 'Methods of Interpretation', note 61 above, p. 40.
95 Case 283/81, note 71 above, pp. 3415, 3430.
96 Lord Mackenzie Stuart makes this point in *The European Communities and the Rule of Law*, p. 77. Gulmann, 'Methods of Interpretation of the European Court of Justice' (1980) Scand SL 189, 203, observes that the policies in the Preamble and early Articles of the EEC Treaty are more notable for their generality than their clarity, and Plender (1982) 2 YEL 57, 75) states that the objectives require to be reconciled and prioritized, quoting the Court in Case 28/66 *Netherlands v Commission* [1968] ECR 1, 12–13: 'Although the general objectives of the treaty, set out in Articles 2 and 3, cannot always be pursued simultaneously in their totality, the Community must continuously reconcile these objectives when considered individually and, when conflict arises, must grant such priority to certain general objectives as appear necessary, having regard to the economic facts or circumstances in the light of which it adopts its decisions.'

directives,[97] they can be readily found in the preamble to each piece of EC legislation.

An example of the contextual and purposive approach is seen in the Court's broad interpretation of the phrase 'any charges having equivalent effect' in Article 12.[98] In one of the earliest cases on this issue the Court elaborately set out the place of Article 12 in the scheme of the Treaty, noting that it is placed in the title relating to free movement of goods and in the part of the Treaty dealing with the foundations of the Community.[99] This served to emphasize that Article 12 should not be interpreted narrowly and in isolation as simply a ban on new customs duties and charges that are directly analogous to such duties, but rather extensively and in context as one part of the jigsaw in the creation of market integration.[100] The Court's case law on the related issue of the construction of 'measures having equivalent effect' to quantitative restrictions, which are required to be eliminated by Article 30, illustrates the same tendency to make sure that individual provisions are construed in a way that is consistent with achieving the aims of the Treaty, including the creation of a common market.[101] An example of contextual and purposive interpretation in relation to EC legislation is *Hoekstra* v *Bedrijfsvereniging Detailhandel*.[102] In construing the meaning of 'wage earner or assimilated worker' in Article 19 of Council Regulation No. 3 on social security for migrant workers the Court said that it had to refer to Article 51 of the Treaty, which was the legal basis for the regulation. The Court then put Article 51 in its context:

Article 51 is included in the Chapter entitled 'Workers' and placed in Title III ('Free movement of persons, services and capital') of Part Two of the Treaty ('Foundations of the Community'). The establishment of as complete a freedom of movement for workers as possible, which thus forms part of the 'foundations' of the Community, therefore constitutes the principal objective of Article 51 and thereby conditions the interpretation of the regulations adopted in implementation of that Article.[103]

The Court therefore gave a broad construction to the phrase in the regulation to include people who are not currently employed and are

---

97 See Art. 190 of the Treaty discussed at pp. 144–5 and 248–50.

98 See Ch. 13.

99 See Cases 2, 3/62 *Commission* v *Luxembourg and Belgium* [1962] ECR 425. The title 'Foundations of the Community' was deleted by the Treaty amendments made in Maastricht in December 1991. These provisions are now included in Part Three of the EC Treaty, Community Policies.

100 See further Brown and Kennedy, *The Court of Justice of the European Communities* (1994, 4th ed.), pp. 312–13.

101 See the discussion of the *Dassonville* case and its successors in Ch. 15. In *Dassonville* the Court did not emphasize the place of Art. 30 within the scheme of the Treaty, but it is a clear example of purposive interpretation.

102 Case 75/63 [1964] ECR 177.

103 ibid., p. 184.

temporarily resident abroad. It is an established part of the case law of the Court of Justice that preference should as far as possible be given to the interpretation of Community legislation which renders the provision consistent with the EC Treaty and the general principles of Community law.[104]

POLICY-MAKING

The Court is sometimes criticized for going beyond interpretation into the realm of policy-making. Scholars accept that policy-making by the European Court is inevitable;[105] the debate turns on when and to what extent it is appropriate. Hjalte Rasmussen, one of the leading writers who has been critical of the Court, has identified three circumstances where the Court makes policy choices.[106]

The first is where the legal provision in issue gives wide discretion to the judges. Two examples of this situation have been referred to above in considering the Court's approach to the interpretation of 'charges having equivalent effect' in Article 12 and 'measures having equivalent effect' in Article 30 of the Treaty. It is clearly a policy decision for the Court to determine whether a particular national measure is a charge having equivalent effect to a customs duty or a measure having equivalent effect to a quantitative restriction. It is generally accepted that such a policy choice is forced on the Court by the requirement to apply these skeletal provisions to concrete factual situations and that a broad choice that is consistent with the overall aims of the Treaty is justifiable. Rasmussen said the Court's

interpretation remains within the textual limitations established by the language of Article 30 ... Facing two incongruent definitions of the scope of Article 30's prohibition [it only prohibits national laws that discriminate against foreign products or it extends to non-discriminatory national laws that actually or potentially, directly or indirectly erect non-tariff barriers to intra-Community trade], the Court chose the one which the Treaty's spirit of integration inspired it. And that seems to me, juridically perfectly justifiable.[107]

---

104 See Cases 201, 202/85 *Klensch* v *Secrétaire d'État* [1986] ECR 3477, 3510; Cases C-90, 91/90 *Neu and Others* [1991] ECR I-3617, 3637; Case C-98/91 *Herbrink* [1994] ECR I-223, 253.
105 See e.g., Weiler, 'The Court of Justice on Trial' (1987) 24 CMLRev 555, 557; Cappelletti, 'Is the European Court of Justice "Running Wild"?' (1987) 12 ELRev 3, 4; and Hartley, *European Community Law*, p. 86.
106 *On Law and Policy*, Ch. 2.
107 ibid., pp. 26–7. See the cautious approach taken to Art. 30 by the Court of Justice in Cases C-267, 268/91 *Keck and Mithouard* [1993] ECR I-6097, discussed in Ch. 17, pp. 532–42.

The second situation is where the Treaty is silent on important points of law. An example of this is the development of the doctrine of supremacy of Community law. There is no statement in the Treaty on the question whether it has primacy over national law in the event of a conflict. This issue was tackled by the European Court in *Costa* v *ENEL*. It applied purposive and contextual interpretation to the Treaty to come to the conclusion that Community law has precedence over national law. The emphasis on the overall objectives of the Treaty is seen in the famous paragraph where the Court refers to the states having 'limited their sovereign rights' by creating a Community and conferring lawmaking powers on its institutions.[108] The Court also considered the consequences on various provisions of the Treaty if Community law did not have supremacy over national law.[109] Finally, the Court noted that the Treaty expressly provides for member states to act unilaterally in certain clearly defined cases[110] or to seek authority to derogate from certain of its provisions[111] and made the telling point that these provisions 'would lose their purpose if the Member States could renounce their obligations by means of an ordinary law'.[112]

The *Costa* case is an example of where the Treaty is silent on the specific issue but gives enough indications in the text as to what the answer to the question is.[113] A much more difficult question arose in the *Factortame* case on whether putative Community law rights have supremacy over clear provisions of national law.[114] The House of Lords asked the European Court whether it was obliged, or empowered, to grant interim protection to a party relying on Community law that is in conflict with a United Kingdom statute when that party's rights under Community law are not clear and are to be determined by the European Court in a preliminary ruling that is pending. The European Court referred to its own decision in the *Simmenthal* case[115] affirming that directly effective provisions of Com-

---

108 Case 6/64 [1964] ECR 585, 593.
109 Arts. 5(2), 7 and 189.
110 Arts. 15, 93(3), 223, 224 and 225.
111 Arts. 8(4), 17(4), 25, 26, 73, 93(2) and 226.
112 Case 6/64, note 108 above, p. 594.
113 Rasmussen, however, states that 'the Court probably pushed its gap-filling activities beyond the proper scope of judicial involvement in society's law and policy making [in] the judgments stating that . . . Community law must be considered the supreme law of the land'. (*On Law and Policy*, p. 28).
114 Case C-213/89 *R* v *Secretary of State for Transport, ex parte Factortame Ltd and others* [1990] ECR I-2433. For an alternative construction of the issue in the case, see Gravells, 'Disapplying an Act of Parliament Pending a Preliminary Ruling: Constitutional Enormity or Community Law Right?' (1989) PL 568.
115 Case 106/77 *Amministrazione delle Finanze dello Stato* v *Simmenthal SpA* [1978] ECR 629.

munity law 'render automatically inapplicable any conflicting provision of
. . . national law'. However, the European Court had to decide in the
Factortame case whether national courts should disapply national law in
favour of Community law by granting interim protection based on that
law when it has not yet been established that the Community law creates
rights for the applicants. The European Court filled this gap in Community
law by using the policy argument of effectiveness:

The full effectiveness of Community law would be . . . impaired if a rule of
national law could prevent a court seised of a dispute governed by Community law
from granting interim relief in order to ensure the full effectiveness of the
judgment to be given on the existence of the rights claimed under Community
law. It follows that a court which in those circumstances would grant interim relief,
if it were not for a rule of national law, is obliged to set aside that rule.

The Court said its interpretation was 'reinforced' by the need to avoid
impairment to the effectiveness of the system established by Article 177 of
the Treaty. However, Article 177 seems to offer no guidance to the Court
on the interpretation of the question in issue in *Factortame*. The concern of
the Court seems to be with enhancing the effectiveness of Community law
rather than being guided by textual or contextual indications.

The European Court is requiring national courts that are confronted
with a claim based on putative rights under the Community law and have
referred the question of the meaning of the Community law to the
European Court for a preliminary ruling to award interim relief, while the
case is pending before the European Court, where the party relying on
Community law has a case of sufficient cogency that, if the arguments
were based on national law, interim relief would be granted. In assessing
whether to award interim relief the national court is to ignore any national
law that might conflict with the Community law in question. It may be
that under national law interim relief is granted on the basis of a prima-facie
case. Is the effectiveness of Community law a sufficient justification for
insisting that a prima-facie case of a Community law right *must* take
precedence over a clear-cut national law right? It can be argued that the
'effectiveness' of clear provisions in national statutes should not be set aside
on the basis of prima-facie Community law rights that may turn out to be
inapplicable. Furthermore, legal certainty may point to a conclusion that
during the interim period in question the clear-cut provision should
prevail over the unclear provision.[116]

Another example of gap-filling is the European Court's decision in the
Zwartveld case.[117] A Dutch examining judge was engaged in a preliminary

116 Compare the approach of Gravells, (1989) PL 568. See further pp. 370–73.
117 Case C-2/Imm [1990] ECR I-3365, noted by Watson (1991) 28 CMLRRev 428.

investigation of Zwartveld in connection with alleged forgeries carried out in the Netherlands contrary to the Dutch criminal code. The judge wanted access to certain reports that had been made by Community fishing inspectors and to call the inspectors as witnesses. The Commission of the European Communities refused to release the reports. The judge then requested the European Court to order the Commission to supply him with the reports and to permit him to examine the inspectors as witnesses.

This request did not come within the scope of the system of preliminary rulings established by Article 177 of the Treaty, and the Treaty provided no other explicit mechanism for national courts to request the European Court to act. None the less, the Court emphasized that the Community is based on the rule of law and as such neither its member states nor its institutions should be able to avoid a review of the question whether measures adopted by them are in conformity with the Community's constitutional charter, the EC Treaty. The Court referred to Articles 5 and 164 of the Treaty to justify its jurisdiction to order the Commission to release the reports and to permit the inspectors to be examined as witnesses. Article 164 provides that in the interpretation and application of the Treaty the Court has to ensure that the law is observed.

Arguably, the Court should function within the limited heads of jurisdiction it has been granted in the Treaty[118] rather than using the very bland words of Articles 5 and 164 and its own notion of the rule of law to build a general jurisdiction to ensure that neither the member states nor the Community institutions can avoid a review of whether the measures adopted by them are in conformity with the Treaty.

The above cases are merely examples of the Court filling in gaps in Community law.[119] It would be wrong to suggest that the Court never exercises restraint. It decided not to extend the direct effect of directives to cases against individuals or legal persons who are not an emanation of the state.[120] The Court should exercise caution in filling in gaps in the Treaty,

---

118 This was the assumption of many leading writers on Community law. Hartley wrote: 'The European Court has no inherent jurisdiction: it has only such jurisdiction as is conferred on it by the treaties. There are a number of specific heads of jurisdiction and a case must be brought within one of them if the court is to hear it' (*European Community Law*, (2nd ed.), p. 56). On the question of inherent jurisdiction generally, see Arnull, 'Does the Court of Justice have Inherent Jurisdiction?' (1990) 27 CMLRev 683, and Ch. 10 below at pp. 335–6.

119 Another important example is the development of general principles of Community law, discussed in Ch. 8 at pp. 253–65.

120 See Case 152/84 *Marshall* v *Southampton and South-West Hampshire Area Health Authority* [1986] ECR 723 and confirmed in Case C-91/92 *Dori* v *Recreb Srl* [1994] ECR I-3325 discussed at pp. 347–9. Another example of judicial restraint is where the Court establishes a new principle in a judgment but limits its application: e.g., Case 43/

not least because of the basic principle of legal certainty. Rasmussen says that 'much gap-filling is undoubtedly usual judicial business. Yet, gap-filling may also constitute a transgression of judicial power.'[121] Rasmussen's main concern was that such a transgression would lead to 'non-compliance and other forms of defiance' by national courts and member states. The evidence of such non-compliance is, however, thin. The rebellions by the French Conseil d'État against the supremacy of Community law and by the German Bundesfinanzhof against the direct effect of directives have ended.[122] The House of Lords accepted the decision of the European Court in the *Factortame* case,[123] discussed above. The only sign of non-compliance is the fact that a number of findings have been made by the European Court of a violation of Article 171 of the Treaty; many of these can be explained by internal legislative difficulties in Italy, which, hopefully, have been remedied.[124]

A person should be able to ascertain what the law is and to regulate his or her conduct by it.[125] Weiler argues that because the Court consistently uses teleological interpretation its decisions 'become, on the whole, consistent, principled (within the rationale [of teleology]) and highly predictable'.[126] Weiler's use of the phrase 'on the whole' concedes that even assuming the Court will use teleological or purposive interpretation may not enable a person to predict the outcome of a case. The boundaries of such interpretation cannot be predicted with certainty. The 'effectiveness' of Community law was enough to justify supremacy of putative rights in

---

75 *Defrenne* v *Sabena* [1976] ECR 455, Case 24/86 *Blaizot* v *University of Liège* [1988] ECR 379, and Case C-262/88 *Barber* [1990] ECR I-1889 (all discussed at pp. 308–9). Finally, there are examples where the Court sets out a new idea but states that it is not applicable on the facts to the case before it. e.g., Cases C-143/88 and C-92/89 *Zuckerfabrik Süderdithmarschen* v *Hauptzollamt Itzehoe* [1991] ECR I-415, noted by Schermers (1992) 29 CMLRev 133 and discussed at p. 310.

121 *On Law and Policy*, pp. 28–9.

122 See Chs. 11, 12. However, see the discussion, in Chap. 12, of the German Federal Constitutional Court decision in *Brunner* v *European Union Treaty* [1994] 1 CMLR 57.

123 [1991] 1 AC 603, [1990] 3 WLR 818; see also note 114 above.

124 See Ch. 7, pp. 207 and 209.

125 It is interesting to note here the European Court of Human Rights' interpretation of the phrase 'prescribed by law' as it is used in Art. 10(2) of the European Convention on Human Rights to justify restrictions on freedom of expression: 'According to the Court's case law, 'foreseeability' is one of the requirements inherent in the phrase 'prescribed by law' in Article 10(2) of the Convention. A norm cannot be regarded as a 'law' unless it is formulated with sufficient precision to enable the citizen – if need be with appropriate advice – to foresee, to a degree that is reasonable in the circumstances, the consequences which a given action may entail' (*Müller* v *Switzerland* (1988) ECHR Series A, Vol. 133).

126 (1987) 24 CMLRev 555, 573.

Community law over clear-cut rights in national law in the *Factortame* case,[127] but was not enough to justify the direct effect of directives being applicable against individuals in the *Marshall* and *Dori* cases.[128]

The third situation where the Court exercises a policy choice is where it reaches a decision despite textual indications to the contrary. The Court's treatment of the position of the European Parliament in relation to Article 173 EEC provides a good example. At Maastricht the text of the Article was changed, but the earlier cases still illustrate the Court's capacity for departing from the text. Article 173 EEC granted to the European Court jurisdiction to review the legality of 'acts of the Council and the Commission ... in actions brought by a Member State, the Council or the Commission'. A simple reading of this provision would lead one to conclude that the Court does not have jurisdiction to review the legality of acts of the European Parliament and that the European Parliament does not have the capacity to bring an action to review the legality of acts of the Council and the Commission. However, the European Court departed from a literal interpretation of the Article in *Les Verts* v *European Parliament*[129] by accepting the admissibility of an action to review the legality of an act of the European Parliament. The European Court emphasized that the Community is based upon the rule of law, so that neither its member states nor its institutions can avoid a review of whether or not their acts are in conformity with the EEC Treaty, the Community's basic constitutional document.[130] The Court acknowledged that the wording of Article 173 EEC referred only to acts of the Council and the Commission, but stated that the scheme of the Treaty was, however, to open to review by the Court all measures adopted by the institutions that are intended to have legal force. The Court expressed the view that the European Parliament was not mentioned in Article 173 EEC because originally the Parliament did not have the power under the EEC Treaty to adopt acts intended to have legal force with regard to third parties. Subsequent amendments to the Treaty had given the Parliament increased powers, particularly in relation to the budget. It would be contrary to the spirit[131] and scheme of the Treaty to allow the Parliament to pass measures that are not subject to review under Article 173 that might encroach on the powers of the member states or other institutions or exceed the limits of the Parliament's powers.

---

127 Note 114 above.
128 Note 120 above and Ch. 11.
129 Case 294/83 [1986] ECR 1339.
130 The same reasoning was used later in the *Zwartveld* case, note 117 above.
131 The Court referred to Art. 164 of the Treaty; see the similar reliance on that Article in *Zwartveld*, note 117 above.

The Court was prepared to override the textual indications in Article 173 EEC in order to ensure that a Community institution acts within its powers under the Treaty. Here the Court is restraining an institution from acting beyond its powers and hence it is not motivated by the desire to expand the scope of Community law or of furthering European integration.[132] At Maastricht in December 1991 amendments were agreed to Art. 173 permitting the review of 'acts of the European Parliament intended to produce legal effects *vis-à-vis* third parties'.

In *European Parliament* v *Council* [133] the European Parliament sought the annulment of Council Regulation (Euratom) No. 3954/87 on the ground that it should have been adopted under Article 100a of the EEC Treaty rather than Article 31 of the Euratom Treaty. Had the former legal basis been chosen, then the cooperation procedure would have applied, whereas Parliament was merely consulted in accordance with Article 31 of the Euratom Treaty. The Court had previously refused to permit the European Parliament to bring an action for annulment under Article 173 EEC[134] and had said, *inter alia*, that Parliament's prerogatives can be protected by the Commission's duty under Article 155 of the Treaty to bring actions for annulment under Article 173 EEC, by natural or legal persons bringing actions under Article 173 EEC or pleading illegality under Article 184, and by the illegality of a measure being raised in a national court and that court referring the case to the European Court for a preliminary ruling under Article 177.

The Parliament pointed out to the Court that the Commission could not be expected to bring an action for annulment against the regulation to protect the prerogatives of the Parliament when the Commission had, when the regulation was a draft, rejected Parliament's request to change its legal basis. Parliament also argued that the prospect of the issue being raised by a natural or legal person in an action for annulment or of the matter coming before a national court and being referred for a preliminary ruling to the European Court was too uncertain to be regarded as an adequate safeguard of its prerogatives.

The Court, departing from its decision of less than two years before in the *Comitology* case, decided that the absence from the EEC Treaty (and the Euratom Treaty) of a provision enabling the Parliament to bring an action for annulment was a procedural gap that could not prevail over the fundamental interest in the maintenance of, and compliance with, the

---

132 The same point can be made in relation to the Court's decision in *Zwartveld*, note 117 above and in Case C-309/89 *Codorniu* v *Council* [1994] ECR I-1853, discussed below in Ch. 8 at pp. 232–4.

133 Case C-70/88, note 76 above.

134 Case 302/87, note 75 above.

institutional balance laid down in the Treaty. An action for annulment brought by the Parliament is admissible: 'provided that the action seeks only to safeguard its prerogatives and that it is founded only on submissions alleging their infringement'.[135] The Court decided that the case was admissible because the issue of the correct legal basis for the regulation was crucial in determining the level of participation of the Parliament in the legislative process.

The Court seems to be intent on creating an institutional balance that does not exist in the treaty. Article 173 EEC deliberately put the Parliament in an inferior position to the Commission and the Council, and this was not remedied by the Single European Act, a fact that was pointed out by the thirteen judges who decided the *Comitology* case.[136] Less than two years later nine judges felt confident to reverse the decision of their brethren.[137] It is surely not the Court's task, as an unelected body, to rewrite the Treaty to achieve an institutional balance of its own creation. It is for the member states in an intergovernmental conference to revise the Treaty and decide what additional powers, if any, the European Parliament should be given. Indeed, at Maastricht in December 1991 it was agreed to amend Article 173 to bring it into line with the Court's decision in Case C-70/88.[138] The European Parliament has *locus standi* for the purpose only of protecting its own prerogatives.[139]

The Court has occasionally given a decision that is contrary to the textual indications and restricts its own jurisdiction. In the *CILFIT* case the Court interpreted Article 177(3) EEC so that national courts against whose decisions there is no judicial remedy have a discretion not to refer questions of Community law to the European Court in certain circumstances.[140]

The Court does not often reach decisions that are contrary to the textual indications in the Treaty,[141] and should cease to do so. It is increasingly evident that intergovernmental conferences to amend the Treaty will become a fairly regular feature of the life of the Community. Such conferences are the appropriate forums for rewriting the Treaty, not the unaccountable decisions emerging from the secrecy of the deliberations

135 Case C-70/88, note 76 above, p. 2073.
136 Case 302/87, note 75 above.
137 This surprising reversal may be partially explained by the fact that only five of the nine judges sitting in Case C-70/88, note 76 above, sat in the *Comitology* case. At least one of those judges must have changed his mind or had been in a (inevitably silent) minority in the *Comitology* case.
138 Note 76, above.
139 See Ch. 8 at p. 227.
140 Case 283/81, note 71 above; discussed in Ch. 9 at pp. 301–3.
141 Some other examples are given by Rasmussen, *On Law and Policy*, pp. 29–31.

room of the European Court which may be based on a simple majority of the judges sitting on the case. Decisions that are based on the Treaty and have political consequences are acceptable, but political decisions with no textual foundations are not.[142]

PRECEDENT

The European Court is not bound by its own decisions, far less by an opinion of an advocate-general.[143] The ability of the Court to depart from its own decision is amply demonstrated by the granting of *locus standi* to the European Parliament under Article 173 EEC in May 1990, having refused it in September 1988.[144] None the less, the Court has sufficient regard for its own decisions that in the *CILFIT* case it allowed national courts from whose decisions there is no judicial remedy not to refer a question of Community law to the Court 'where previous decisions of the Court have already dealt with the point of law in question, irrespective of the nature of the proceedings which led to those decisions, even though the questions at issue are not strictly identical'.[145]

The position is that national courts can rely on a decision of the European Court on a particular provision of Community law as authoritative and follow it, or they may choose to refer the issue to the European Court for a preliminary ruling in the hope that the Court may depart from its previous decision.

Though the Court sometimes uses terminology and ideas it has already enunciated in a previous case without referring to that case,[146] it more

---

142 It is disturbing that a former judge of the European Court should freely admit that in deciding to give direct effect to Art. 12 of the Treaty in the landmark decision in Case 26/62 *Van Gend en Loos* v *Nederlandse Administratie der Belastingen* [1963] ECR 1, 'the judges had *"une certaine idée de l'Europe"* of their own, and that is the idea which has been decisive and not arguments based on the legal technicalities of the matter'; see Pescatore, 'The Doctrine of Direct Effect: An Infant Disease of Community Law' (1983) 8 ELRev 155, 157. It is, of course, possible to construe the *Van Gend en Loos* decision as one that does have textual foundations; see Ch. 11, pp. 341–3.

143 It would be very surprising if the European Court were bound by its own decisions given that in all the member states the highest court is not so bound. Even in the United Kingdom, since 1966, the House of Lords is not bound by its own decisions.

144 See pp. 180–81 and the examples given by Brown and Kennedy. *The Court of Justice of the European Communities* (1994, 4th ed.), pp. 346–7.

145 Case 283/81, note 71 above, p. 3429; discussed in Ch. 9 at p. 302.

146 For example, the idea that the Treaty is 'the constitutional charter of a Community based on the rule of law' was expressed by the European Court in Opinion 1/91 *Opinion on the draft Agreement on a European Economic Area* [1991] ECRI-6079; [1992] 1 CMLR

often does give references to its own case law.[147] Not surprisingly, the Court usually follows its previous decisions.[148] The Court may choose to distinguish a decision rather than overrule it. In *Ivenel v Schwab*[149] the European Court decided that in contracts of employment the 'obligation in question' in terms of Article 5(1) of the EC Brussels Convention was the one that 'characterises the contract'. In reaching this decision the Court distinguished the case of employment contracts from other contracts. The rule for other contracts had been laid down by the Court in *De Bloos v Bouyer*[150] – the 'obligation in question' being 'the contractual obligation forming the basis of the legal proceedings'. In *Shenavai v Kreischer*[151] the Court decided, after referring to the two previous cases, that the 'obligation in question' in contracts for the provision of services fell within the general rule in *De Bloos* and not the exception established for contracts of employment in *Ivenel*.

Two interesting questions that remain to be resolved are whether a chamber is bound by a decision of a plenary court and whether the Court of First Instance is bound by decisions of the European Court. In the *BASF* case[152] the Court of First Instance did not follow the reasoning of the Court of Justice in *Nakajima v Council*[153] in which the Court of Justice had stated that natural and legal persons could not rely on the failure of a Community institution to comply with its rules of procedure, because 'they are not intended to ensure protection for individuals'.[154] In the Court of Justice's decision on the appeal in the *BASF* case[155] the Court of Justice did not rebuke the Court of First Instance for departing from its reasoning in the *Nakajima* case and, without mentioning that case, departed from its reasoning by deciding that the failure to comply with the Commission's Rules of Procedure did constitute an

---

245, 269 without any reference to the origin of the use of the phrase in Case 294/83, note 129 above, at para. 23, and in Case C-2/Imm, note 117 above.

147 See Koopmans, 'Stare Decisis in European Law' in O'Keeffe and Schermers (eds.) *European Law and Integration*, pp. 17–18.

148 ibid., p. 18; Koopmans was then a judge in the European Court.

149 Case 133/81, note 89 above.

150 Case 14/76 [1976] ECR 1497.

151 Case 266/85 [1987] ECR 239. See further on the interpretation of Art. 5(1) in *Anton & Beaumont's Civil Jurisdiction in Scotland: Brussels and Lugano Conventions* (1995, 2nd ed.), pp. 98–9 and 454–63.

152 Cases T-79, 84–86, 89, 91, 92, 94, 96, 102 & 104/89 *BASF AG and Others v Commission* [1992] ECR II-315.

153 Case C-69/89 [1991] ECR I-2069, paras. 49 and 50, an 11-judge case.

154 See further on this point Arnull, 'Owning up to Fallibility: Precedent and the Court of Justice' (1993) 30 CMLRev 247, 263–4.

155 Case C-137/92P *Commission v BASF AG and Others* [1994] ECR I-2555, a 13-judge case discussed in Ch. 2 at p. 52.

illegality that *BASF*, a natural or legal person, could rely on and annulled the Commission decision.[156]

COURT OF FIRST INSTANCE

The Single European Act, which came into force in July 1987, inserted Article 168a into the EEC Treaty. It gave the Council the power, acting unanimously, to attach to the European Court of Justice a Court of First Instance. The Council did so by Decision 88/591 on 24 October 1988.[157] The Court of First Instance began to hear cases in November 1989. At this time 153 cases were transferred to it from the European Court.

The Court of First Instance is situated in Luxembourg and has its seat alongside the European Court.[158] It consists of fifteen members.[159] This has the advantage that, in practice, each member state can nominate one judge.[160] Somewhat belatedly the first women judges in either the Court of Justice or the Court of First Instance were appointed by Finland and Sweden upon their accession on 1 January 1995.[161] Although there are no advocates-general attached to the Court of First Instance, any of the members of that Court, apart from the President, 'may be called upon to perform the task of an Advocate-General'.[162] In such a case the member of the Court of First Instance chosen does the same job as an advocate-

---

156 Whether the Court of First Instance could legitimately distinguish the Court of Justice's decision in *Nakajima* was considered at some length by Advocate-General Van Gerven at pp. 2599–2605.

157 OJ 1988 L319/1 (a corrected version of the text is published in OJ 1989 C215/1). In accordance with Art. 168a, the Court had formally requested such a decision in September 1987 and the Commission and European Parliament had been consulted.

158 Council Dec. 88/591, Art. 1.

159 Council Dec. 88/591, Art. 2 as amended by Art. 10 of Council Dec. 95/1 OJ 1995 L1/1.

160 The first judge of British nationality was a Scot, David Edward. He was Professor of European Institutions at the University of Edinburgh and a Queen's Counsel of some renown in the Scottish Bar before being appointed to the Court of First Instance in 1989. It is to be hoped that David Edward's appointment at the time of Lord Mackenzie Stuart's retirement from the European Court is an indication that the British Government intends to ensure that at least one of the three judicial posts in Luxembourg within its gift is held by a Scots lawyer. This has been maintained by David Edward's elevation to the Court of Justice in 1992. His replacement as judge in the Court of First Instance is Christopher Bellamy, an English QC and co-author of a leading textbook on Community competition law.

161 Mrs Virpi Tiili and Mrs Pernilla Lindh, see Dec. 95/5 OJ 1995 L1/224.

162 Council Dec. 88/591, Art. 2, and Rules of Procedure CFI, Art. 2, OJ 1991 L136/1.

general in the European Court and does not take part in the judgment of the case. An advocate-general will always be appointed when the Court sits in plenary session.[163] If a chamber wants an advocate-general to be appointed to a particular case, then it must request a plenary session of the Court to appoint one and it may do so only where 'the legal difficulty or the factual complexity of the case so requires'.[164] The President of the Court designates the member of the Court who will act as an advocate-general in a particular case.[165]

The Court of First Instance normally hears cases in chambers of three or five judges. It operates with four chambers.[166] Each of the chambers operates in normal composition with three judges and in extended composition with five judges. Staff cases are normally assigned to chambers of three judges and all other cases to chambers of five judges.[167] The result is that members of the Court deal with the whole range of cases within the Court's jurisdiction.

Occasionally the Court may sit in plenary session.[168] The chamber to which the case is initially assigned by the President of the Court[169] must request a plenary session of the Court to decide that the case be heard by a plenary session of the Court. The plenary session of the Court may decide to do so only after hearing the parties (and the advocate-general) if 'the legal difficulty or the importance of the case or special circumstances so

163 Rules of Procedure CFI, Art. 17. Three rare examples of this occurring are Case T-51/89 *Tetra Pak Rausing SA* v *Commission* [1990] ECR 11–309, where H. Kirschner acted as advocate-general, and two related cases which were dealt with together although not joined, Case T-24/90 *Automec* v *Commission* [1992] ECR II-2223 and Case T-28/90 *Asia Motor France and Others* v *Commission* [1992] ECR II-2285 in which David Edward acted as advocate-general.

164 Rules of Procedure CFI. Arts 18 and 19. This has happened very rarely so far but see Case T-120/89, *Stahlwerke Peine-Salzgitter AG* v *Commission* [1991] ECR II-279 in which J. Biancarelli was the advocate-general, and the 14 polypropylene cartel cases which B. Vesterdorf, as the advocate-general, dealt with together but which were decided and reported separately by the Court of First Instance. The advocate-general's opinion can be found in Case T-1/89 *Rhône-Poulenc SA* v *Commission* [1991] ECR II-867.

165 ibid., Arts. 17 and 19.

166 CFI Decision 94/C 233/36, OJ 1994 C233.

167 See Rules of Procedure CFI, Art. 12, OJ 1991 L136/5 and part 4 of the CFI Decision 94/C 233/36 OJ 1994 C233. The appointment of three new judges from 1 January 1995 led to all of the chambers apart from the Second Chamber having four judges, to the First and Second Chambers in their extended composition having six judges and to the Third and Fourth Chambers in their extended composition having seven judges, see CFI Dec. 95/C 54/25, OJ 1995 C54/15.

168 ibid., Arts. 11, 14 and 51, OJ 1991 L136/1–23.

169 ibid., Art. 13.

justify'.[170] As with the European Court, the quorum for a plenary session is seven judges.[171]

The Court of First Instance reaches its decisions in secret and by majority vote in a similar fashion to the European Court.[172] The members of the Court can be removed from office only by the European Court.[173]

The qualifications required for appointment as a member of the Court of First Instance are lower than those required for appointment to the European Court. It is sufficient that the person be independent and 'possess the ability required for appointment to judicial office'. The Court of First Instance has a greater proportion of civil servants and practising lawyers than the European Court.[174] The members from Ireland, Italy and the Netherlands were holders of national judicial office; the members from Belgium and Portugal were academics; the members from Austria, Denmark, Germany, Luxembourg, Spain and Sweden were legal civil servants in their own countries; the Greek and United Kingdom judges were advocates/barristers; the Finnish judge was the Director-General of the Finnish National Consumers' Authority; and the French member was a lawyer with a private bank. Prior connection with the European Court was clearly of some value, as the member from Portugal was formerly an advocate-general, the Belgian, French, Greek and Italian members had been legal secretaries and the Danish member had been a lawyer-linguist.

The President of the Court of First Instance is elected by the members of the Court for a three-year appointment, which can be renewed.[175] The procedure is similar to that used to elect the President of the European Court.[176] The first President of the Court, José Luis da Cruz Vilaça of Portugal, was formerly an advocate-general in the European Court. Like

170 The Court sat in plenary session in Case T-51/89, note 163 above. This was an important competition case on the relationship between block exemptions under Art. 85(3) and the application of Art. 86; see p. 724. The other cases mentioned in the same note above were also important competition cases and are considered at pp. 272–3 and 758–61 below.

171 Rules of Procedure CFI, Art. 32, OJ 1991 L136/7.

172 See ibid. Art. 33, and p. 164.

173 The procedure for removing judges and advocates-general of the European Court (see p. 166) is applied to members of the Court of First Instance by Art. 44 of the Statute of the Court of Justice as inserted by Council Dec. 88/591. See the role of the members of the Court of First Instance in this process in Rules of Procedure CFI, Art. 5.

174 See p. 165 above for the composition of the European Court.

175 Although on the occasion of the appointment of the first President in 1989 the governments of the member states exercised a once and for all power under Art. 11 of Dec. 88/591 to choose the President themselves; see Brown and Kennedy, *The Court of Justice*, pp. 78–9. The members of the Court of First Instance showed their confidence in the man who had been chosen for them by re-electing him as President in 1992 under Art. 2(2) of Dec. 88/591 and Rules of Procedure CFI, Art. 7.

176 See p. 159.

the President of the European Court, the President of the Court of First Instance directs the judicial business and the administration of the Court and presides at plenary sittings and deliberations.[177] The President appoints a judge-rapporteur to each case, assigns each case to a chamber[178] and can be appointed as a president of a chamber (due to the relatively small number of cases heard in plenary session). Da Cruz Vilaça is President of the First Chamber as well as President of the Court.[179]

The jurisdiction of the Court of First Instance is limited by the constraints of Article 168a of the Treaty and by Council Decision 88/591 establishing the Court. The EEC Treaty made it impossible to give the Court of First Instance jurisdiction to hear and determine actions brought by member states or by Community institutions or questions referred by national courts for a preliminary ruling under Article 177. Such cases account for about two-thirds of the European Court's case load.[180] Within the limited area of the European Court's jurisdiction that could be transferred to the Court of First Instance the Council decided not to transfer jurisdiction in cases brought by natural or legal persons under Articles 173 and 175 EEC relating to measures to protect trade within the meaning of Article 113 of the Treaty in the case of dumping and subsidies. The European Court had requested that the Court of First Instance be given such jurisdiction, but the Council merely promised to re-examine the European Court's proposal after two years of operation of the Court of First Instance.[181] The Council did confer jurisdiction on the Court of First Instance in relation to staff cases (i.e., disputes between the servants of the Community and its institutions under Article 179 EEC[182]) and in actions brought against a Community institution by natural or legal persons under Articles 173 or 175 EEC relating to the implementation of competition rules applicable to undertakings.[183]

177 Rules of Procedure CFI, Art. 8.
178 ibid., Art. 13.
179 See OJ 1990 C199 and OJ 1994 C233.
180 See the analysis of the cases pending before the European Court at 31 October 1989 by Millett, *The Court of First Instance*, p. 35. Of the 622 cases pending, only 210 cases could have been transferred to the Court of First Instance within the terms of Art. 168a EEC.
181 See Council Dec. 88/591, Art. 3(3). As at 31 October 1989, twenty-two such cases were pending before the European Court.
182 For a brief discussion see Ch. 10, pp. 324–6 below.
183 See ibid., Art. 3(1). Art. 3(2) confers jurisdiction on the Court of First Instance to decide compensation claims under Art. 178 EC for non-contractual liability of the Community arising out of an action brought by the same natural or legal person for which it has jurisdiction under Art. 3(1) of the decision. As at 31 October 1989 there were 149 cases pending before the European Court that came within the jurisdiction of the Court of First Instance (plus two coal and steel cases covered by the jurisdiction given to the Court of First Instance under the ECSC Treaty): see Millett, *The Court of First Instance*, p. 35.

Any party to an action before the Court of First Instance has an automatic right of appeal to the European Court on a point of law. Article 51 of the Protocol to the Statute of the European Court provides that

An appeal to the Court of Justice shall be limited to points of law. It shall lie on the grounds of lack of competence of the Court of First Instance, a breach of procedure before it which adversely affects the interests of the appellant as well as the infringement of Community law by the Court of First Instance.[184]

There is a two-month time-limit on lodging appeals with the European Court. Member states or Community institutions can bring an appeal even though they were not parties to the case before the Court of First Instance or even interveners in the case.[185] If the appeal to the European Court is well founded, the Court shall quash the decision of the Court of First Instance. The European Court may itself give final judgment in the matter or it can refer the case back to the Court of First Instance for judgment. In such cases the Court of First Instance is bound by the European Court's decision on points of law.[186]

The Court of First Instance was established at least partly because of concern that the European Court was overloaded with cases. Sadly, it merely checked the inexorable increase in the European Court's case load. In 1990, the first complete year in which the Court of First Instance was operational, the European Court received only one less case than in 1989. Staff cases before the Court were reduced from forty-one in 1989 to none in 1990, but despite the fact that the Court of First Instance received a few competition cases, this was offset by a general increase in direct actions before the European Court and by sixteen appeals from the Court of First Instance. By the end of 1990 the backlog of cases pending before the European Court was almost back to where it was before the setting up of the Court of First Instance, and the position had deteriorated even further by the end of 1991.[187] The average length of proceedings before the European Court was still unacceptably long and no better than it had been before the setting up of the Court of First Instance.[188]

184 Inserted by Council Dec. 88/591, Art. 5. The President of the European Court may suspend the operation of the Court of First Instance's decision pending the outcome of the appeal; see Case C-345/90 P.R. *European Parliament* v *Hanning* [1991] ECR 1–231.
185 See Protocol to the Statute of the European Court, Art. 49, inserted by Council Dec. 88/591, Art. 5. Other interveners before the Court of First Instance can appeal to the European Court only where the decision 'directly affects them'.
186 ibid., Art. 54, as inserted by Council Dec. 88/591, Art. 5. See pp. 326–7.
187 At the end of 1988, prior to the setting up of the Court of First Instance, 605 cases were pending. The impact of transferring a large number of cases to the Court of First Instance during 1989 reduced the figure at the end of that year, temporarily, to 501. At the end of 1990 583 cases were pending. By the end of 1991 the figure had reached the alarming total of 640.
188 The average length of proceedings before the European Court in preliminary

The Court of First Instance received only fifty-nine cases in 1990, of which forty-three were staff cases. It managed to eat into the backlog of 153 cases handed on to it by the European Court in November 1989 by dealing with eighty-two cases, but it still had 145 cases pending before it at the end of 1990. The position deteriorated in 1991. The Court of First Instance received ninety-three cases, of which eighty-one were staff cases. Yet the Court managed to deal with only sixty-seven cases, thus 169 cases were pending before it at the end of the year.

The Court of First Instance, in suggesting proposed amendments to Article 168a EEC to be considered in the intergovernmental conference that concluded in Maastricht in December 1991, acknowledged that 'a point has been reached beyond which, unless care is taken, the law's delays will be such as to discourage those who seek the law's protection'.[189]

The Court of First Instance hoped that in the longer term it would be possible to transfer to it some cases brought by member states or Community institutions and some preliminary rulings. It advocated amending Article 168a EEC so that the Council would be competent, acting unanimously, to transfer all or some of these matters to the Court of First Instance without the necessity of Treaty revision.

The Treaty on European Union agreed at Maastricht amended Article 168a in a way that provides for the Council, acting unanimously on a request from the European Court and after consulting the Commission and the European Parliament, to transfer any area of the European Court's jurisdiction to the Court of First Instance, except for preliminary rulings under Article 177.

On 8 June 1993 the Council agreed to extend the jurisdiction of the Court of First Instance.[190] In addition to staff cases and competition cases brought by natural or legal persons other than a Community institution or a member state (non-privileged applicants) under Articles 173 or 175[191] the Court of First Instance was given jurisdiction in all other actions brought by non-privileged applicants under Articles 173, 175 and 178,[192] and under Article 181 where jurisdiction is conferred on the Court by an arbitration

---

rulings was 17.5 months in 1988 and 18.5 months in 1991, having dipped to 16.6 months in 1989. In direct actions the figures were even worse: 23.7 months in 1988 and 24.2 months in 1991, having dipped to 22.3 months in 1989.

189 'Reflections on the Future Development of the Community Judicial System' (1991) 16 ELRev 175.

190 Dec. 93/350 OJ 1993 L144/21.

191 Which could be combined with non-contractual liability claims under Art. 178, see Council Dec. 88/591, Art. 3(2), repealed by Art. 1(2) of Dec. 93/350.

192 Dec. 93/350, Art. 1(1) which created a new Art. 3(1) of Dec. 88/591. Actions under Art. 178 no longer need to be linked with actions under Arts. 173 or 175. Articles 173 and 175 actions are considered in Ch. 8 and Art. 178 actions in Ch. 10 at pp. 313–19.

clause in a contract concluded by or on behalf of the Community.[193] This Decision entered into force on 1 August 1993 and led to the transfer of 451 cases from the Court of Justice to the Court of First Instance in September 1993. Some 380 of these cases concerned claims against the Community for damages for the non-contractual liability of the Community arising from the adoption of illegal milk-quota regulations. However, the Decision deferred the transfer of cases brought by non-privileged applicants under Articles 173, 175 or 178 relating to measures to protect trade within the meaning of Art. 113 in the case of dumping and subsidies until a date to be fixed by a unanimous decision of the Council.[194] The Council Decision of 7 March 1994 fixed the date as 15 March 1994.[195] Shortly thereafter 14 cases were transferred from the Court of Justice to the Court of First Instance.

Even before this major transfer of cases and jurisdiction to the Court of First Instance it was unable to decide as many cases as it was receiving.[196] In 1993 the Court of First Instance received 596 cases but dealt with only 106, leaving 657 cases pending before it at the end of the year.[197] In 1994 the Court of First Instance received 409 cases[198] and dealt with 442,[199] leaving 618 cases pending at the end of the year.[200] The heavy burden of cases on the Court of First Instance is reflected in the fact that at the end of 1994 the average length of proceedings in direct actions was 23 months (over 2 months longer than the Court of Justice) but staff cases were dealt with relatively speedily in an average of 15.2 months.[201] In defence of the Court of First Instance, it must be said that many of its direct actions raise complex issues of fact and law, particularly in competition policy, which require lengthy consideration. The Court of First Instance gives noticeably longer judgments in these matters than the Court of Justice. This may be partly explained by the rare use of an advocate-general in the Court of First Instance and the feeling that the Court's judgment must be more fully reasoned to compensate for this.

REFORM OF THE JUDICIAL ARCHITECTURE

The European Court of Justice's initial contribution to the 1996 intergovern-

---

193 For a brief discussion of Art. 181 jurisdiction, see Ch. 10, pp. 329–30 below.

194 See Dec. 93/350, Art. 3.

195 Dec. 94/149 OJ 1994 L66/29, Art. 1 inserted a new Art. 3 into Dec. 93/350.

196 In 1992 it received 116 cases and decided 100.

197 The figures are taken from *Proceedings of the Court of Justice* No. 34/94. This left the CFI with more cases pending than the Court of Justice: the huge transfer of cases in September 1993 reduced its cases pending to 433.

198 Including 173 cases concerning the non-contractual liability of the Community with regard to milk quotas.

199 372 of them by order terminating the proceedings.

200 Of which 257 concerned the non-contractual liability of the Community with regard to milk quotas; see *Proceedings of the Court of Justice and Court of First Instance* No. 34/94.

201 *Proceedings* No. 34/94.

mental conference was published in May 1995.[202] It categorically asserted the importance of uniform interpretation of Community law and therefore that all national courts and tribunals should continue to be able to seek preliminary rulings under Article 177 and that the Court of First Instance should have no jurisdiction in such cases. The Court expressed doubts as to whether it would be appropriate for the European Parliament to have unlimited *locus standi* under Article 173 and to be able to request opinions under Article 228 given that such disputes could be settled at a political level. The publication of the Court's views might be regarded as judicial interference in essentially political questions. The Court opposed any alteration in the Community's judicial structure at the present time but could see merit, in the future, in the Court of First Instance having specialized chambers or perhaps for new specialized Community courts to be established. The Court would like to be able to amend its Rules of Procedure without needing the Council's approval. The Court of Justice is anxious to protect judicial independence and therefore would not object to the term of appointment of judges being extended from six years (though no figure is given) and the appointment becoming non-renewable. Although not mentioned by the Court this would remove a major impediment to having dissenting opinions. The Court opposes the suggestion that judicial nominees should be questioned by a parliamentary committee as it compromises judicial independence. The Court questions whether the restrictive *locus standi* under Article 173 for natural and legal persons is sufficient to enable them to protect their fundamental human rights and advocates codifying and streamlining the constitutive Treaties of the Union.

The Court of First Instance[203] rejected the idea of specialized courts but did not oppose the setting up of specialized chambers within the Court of First Instance. It favoured the appointment of assistant rapporteurs, experts in a particular specialism, who would draft the Court's judgment and, unlike legal secretaries, could be present at the Court's deliberations. This would be particularly desirable if cases could be decided by a single judge. The Court of First Instance would like to have more judges so that more chambers could be established. Unlike the Court of Justice it does not favour non-renewable appointments of judges and is not opposed to Parliament asking questions of judicial nominees as to their qualifications for the job.

In the long term it makes sense for all direct actions to be heard in the Court of First Instance including those brought by privileged applicants and for the European Court of Justice to become an appellate court in such matters and the only court dealing swiftly with requests from national courts for preliminary rulings. The European Court would still have a large enough workload. In 1994 it received 206 references for a preliminary ruling and 13 appeals from the Court of First Instance.

---

202 *Proceedings of the Court of Justice* No. 15/95.
203 ibid.

CHAPTER 7

Actions against Member States

The European Court has jurisdiction to hear cases brought against member states to ensure that they comply with their obligations under Community law, i.e. infringement proceedings. The principal head of jurisdiction is actions brought by the Commission under Article 169 of the EC Treaty. Special provisions apply in relation to general infringement proceedings brought by a member state under Article 170 and to infringement proceedings brought by the Commission or a member state in relation to state aids under Article 93(2), derogations from the single internal market[1] and distortions of competition caused by states taking essential security measures.[2] This chapter will focus on Article 169 infringement proceedings, which are by far the most numerous, but a brief treatment will be given to those brought by member states under Article 170 and to those against state aids under Article 93(2).

1 Arts. 100a(4) and 100b(2) of the Treaty; see Flynn, 'How well will Article 100a(4) work? A comparison with Article 93' (1987) 24 CMLRev 689. No case has yet been brought under Art. 100a(4) by the Commission or a member state to attempt to prevent a member state from making improper use of the power to derogate from internal market harmonization measures. However, in Case C-41/93 *France v Commission* [1994] ECR I-1829, France successfully challenged the Commission's decision under Art. 100a(4) permitting Germany to apply more stringent restrictions on PCP than Council Dir. 91/173 had provided for; see the discussion at pp. 144–5 above.

2 Art. 225 of the Treaty. The first case concerning this article was brought by the Commission against Greece and lodged in the Court of Justice in April 1994. In June 1994 the full Court of 13 judges, after hearing the case *in camera*, issued an order dismissing the Commission's application for interim measures; see Case C-120/94R *Commission v Greece* [1994] ECR I-3037. In the main action the Commission is arguing that Greece made improper use of its powers under Art. 224 in order to justify the unilateral measures it adopted on 16 February 1994 prohibiting trade with the Former Yugoslav Republic of Macedonia (FYROM) which were contrary to Art. 113. In the interim measures case the Commission did establish a prima-facie case of a breach of Community law but failed to demonstrate that there would be 'serious and irreparable harm' to the Community interest if interim measures were not adopted. The Commission was able to prove harm to FYROM but the Court was not prepared to take this into account in the proceedings for interim measures.

ACTIONS UNDER ARTICLE 169

Article 169 states:

If the Commission considers that a Member State has failed to fulfil an obligation under this Treaty, it shall deliver a reasoned opinion on the matter after giving the State concerned the opportunity to submit its observations.

If the State concerned does not comply with the opinion within the period laid down by the Commission, the latter may bring the matter before the Court of Justice.

Article 169 infringement proceedings can be broken down into four stages. First, informal discussions between the Commission and the member state; second, a letter of formal notice from the Commission to the member state; third, a reasoned opinion by the Commission; and fourth, the reference of the case to the European Court.

INFORMAL STAGE

Most cases of an alleged violation of Community law by a member state investigated by the Commission are initiated by a complaint from an individual or a company to the Commission, but a sizeable minority are detected by the Commission's own inquiries.[3] The Commission usually consults the member state at the level of officials. Typically, the director-general of the relevant Commission directorate will write to the permanent representative of the member state to the European Community.[4] The Commission will normally ask the member state to respond within a specified time and generally aims to conclude the informal stage within one year.[5]

---

3 The number of complaints from individuals registered by the Commission was 1,274 in 1990, 1,052 in 1991, 1,185 in 1992 and 1,040 in 1993; and the number detected by the Commission's own inquiries or with the assistance of a question or a petition in the European Parliament was 318 in 1990, 381 in 1991, 360 in 1992 and 300 in 1993; see the 'Eleventh Annual Report to the European Parliament on Commission Monitoring of the Application of Community Law 1993' OJ 1994 C154/1.

4 See Dashwood and White, 'Enforcement Actions under Articles 169 and 170 EEC' (1989) 14 ELRev 388, 396.

5 The Commission is not always able to abide by this self-imposed one-year time-limit and has admitted that 'this has proved impossible in many cases because of the complexity of the dossier'; see 'Tenth Annual Report to the European Parliament on

Although Audretsch's leading work[6] suggested that 85 per cent of cases were resolved at the informal stage, more recent figures suggest this has dropped to between 10 and 40 per cent.[7] A state either makes the necessary changes in its law to comply with the alleged violation or persuades the Commission that its laws are in compliance with Community law.

The informal stage can be important in determining the admissibility of an action before the Court. Relatively short periods for a state to respond to a letter of formal notice and to the Commission's reasoned opinion may be justified if there has been an extensive informal stage where discussions have taken place between the Commission and the member state. In Case 85/85[8] Belgium was given only fifteen days to submit its observations on the formal notice and fifteen days to comply with the reasoned opinion. The Court found these periods reasonable in the circumstances and the case admissible. It was influenced by the extensive informal stage, where the Commission had made the member state fully aware of the nature of the alleged violations of Community law. On the other hand, if the informal stage is truncated or non-existent, the Court may find such short periods unreasonable and declare the case inadmissible. In Case 293/85[9] the Court decided that the pre-litigation procedure was not validly carried out and the action was inadmissible. It was not justifiable in this case to give the member state only eight days to respond to the letter of formal notice and fifteen days to respond to the reasoned opinion. It was a relevant factor in this decision that 'the Kingdom of Belgium was not fully informed of the definitive views of the Commission before these proceedings were brought against it'[10] by the sending of the letter of formal notice. In determining whether the periods allowed are reasonable the Court takes account of 'all the circumstances of the case'.[11] One factor justifying short periods is where there is an urgent need to remedy a breach of Community law.[12] Such urgency will not avail the Commission

---

Commission Monitoring of the Application of Community Law 1992' OJ 1993 C233/1 at p. 7.

6 *Supervision in European Community Law*, p. 24; see also the summary of his views in Audretsch, 'Supervision in the EEC, OECD, and Benelux – A Difference in Degree, but also in Kind?' (1987) 36 ICLQ 838, 843.

7 In 1990 the Commission investigated 1,592 cases and issued 960 letters of formal notice, in 1991 1,433 cases and 853 letters, in 1992 1,545 cases and 1,216 letters, in 1993 1,340 cases and 1,209 letters, in 1994 the Commission issued 974 letters. See the 'Eleventh Annual Report' and the *General Report on the Activities of the European Union 1994* (Luxembourg, 1995), p. 440.

8 *Commission* v *Belgium* [1986] ECR 1149.

9 *Commission* v *Belgium* [1988] ECR 305.

10 ibid., p. 353.

11 ibid., p. 352.

12 ibid.

if it has been brought about due to its failure to take action earlier.[13] The Commission had known about the possible violation of Community law by Belgian law since a judgment of the European Court of 13 February 1985, but had not issued the letter of formal notice until 17 July 1985. This delay of five months had created urgency because under the Belgian law a minerval (supplementary enrolment fee for students from other member states) would be applied to students starting the new academic year in October 1985.

Deficiencies in the Commission's arguments in the letter of formal notice and reasoned opinion may be made up for by arguments used in Commission communications with the member state during the informal stage. In *Commission v United Kingdom*[14] the Court acknowledged that the Commission's letter of formal notice and reasoned opinion did not 'expressly assert', as the Commission did in its application before the Court, that differentiation of milk prices according to the intended use of the milk was contrary to a Community regulation irrespective of the consequences that that practice might have for the functioning of the common organization of the market. None the less, the Court held the application to be admissible because at the informal stage the letter sent to the United Kingdom permanent representation to the Community showed that 'the Commission was making it clear that the compatibility of a criterion for price differentiation with the Community rules could be assessed independently of its effects on the functioning of the common organization of the market'.[15]

LETTER OF FORMAL NOTICE

If the matter is not resolved at the informal stage, a letter of formal notice will be sent by the Commission to the member state. A member of the Commission may sign the letter, which is addressed to the foreign secretary of the state concerned. Since the late 1970s the Commission has been more rigorous in pursuing infringement proceedings under Article 169 and there is an upward trend in the number of letters of formal notice being issued.[16]

---

13 ibid.
14 Case 23/84 [1986] ECR 3581, [1987] 1 CMLR 607.
15 ibid., p. 3633. See also Case C-152/89 *Commission v Luxembourg* [1991] ECR I-3141, 3163.
16 The decision to prosecute infringements more vigorously was taken during the Commission presidency of Roy Jenkins, which began in 1977 (see Dashwood and White (1989) 14 ELRev 388, 399–400 and the references cited there). There were 335 letters of

The Commission normally gives a member state two months to reply to a letter of formal notice. In urgent cases the period can be shorter. The Commission tries to close the case or send a reasoned opinion within one year of issuing a letter of formal notice. It often needs more time because of the complexity of the case in question.[17]

The letter of formal notice defines the ambit of the case that is being brought against the member state. The Commission cannot widen the scope of the action, even at the stage of the reasoned opinion. In *Commission v Italy*[18] the letter of formal notice dealt only with Italian laws concerning the import of animal gelatin that is used in sweets. In the reasoned opinion the Commission extended the case to cover imports that use animal gelatin in preserved meat products and ice cream. The European Court decided that the action was inadmissible in relation to the preserved meat products and ice cream because the Italian Government had not been given a fair hearing in relation to those matters even though it had submitted observations on them in response to the Commission's reasoned opinion. The Court said that the letter of formal notice

is intended to define the subject-matter of the dispute and to indicate to the Member State which is invited to submit its observations the factors enabling it to prepare its defence . . . the opportunity for the Member State concerned to submit its observations constitutes an essential guarantee required by the Treaty and, even if the Member State does not consider it necessary to avail itself thereof, observance of that guarantee is an essential formal requirement of the procedure under Article 169.[19]

If a member state fails to cooperate with the Commission during an Article 169 investigation, this can constitute the basis for a later finding by the Court of a breach of Article 5 of the Treaty. In *Commission v Greece*[20]

---

formal notice in 1982, 503 in 1985, 516 in 1986, 572 in 1987, 569 in 1988, 644 in 1989, 960 in 1990, 853 in 1991, 1,216 in 1992, 1,209 in 1993 and 974 in 1994 (see the 'Seventh (OJ 1990 C232/1), Eighth (COM(91) 321 final) and Eleventh Annual Reports' and the *General Report 1994*).

17 See the 'Tenth Annual Report' at p. 8.
18 Case 51/83 [1984] ECR 2793.
19 ibid., p. 2804. See also Case 31/69 *Commission v Italy* [1970] ECR 25 and Case 211/81 *Commission v Denmark* [1982] ECR 4547. The Commission could, of course, initiate new infringement proceedings in respect of any matters beyond the scope of the original proceedings: e.g. Case C-157/89 *Commission v Italy* [1991] ECR I-57, 85, where a complaint rejected on procedural grounds in Case 262/85 *Commission v Italy* [1987] ECR 3073 was found admissible.
20 Case 240/86 [1988] ECR 1835. See also Case 272/86 *Commission v Greece* [1988] ECR 4875 and Case C-35/88 *Commission v Greece* [1990] ECR I-3125, [1992] 1 CMLR 548, 571, particularly serious cases of lack of cooperation because they persisted before the Court. An example of an alleged infringement of Art. 5 failing to be proved by the Commission is Case 192/84 *Commission v Greece* [1985] ECR 3967, 3979.

the Commission requested certain information relating to cereal imports from the Greek Government during the informal stage and again after the letter of formal notice had been issued. The failure by Greece to supply that information or even to give an adequate explanation as to why it could not be supplied constituted 'a failure to fulfil the duty incumbent on every Member State under Article 5 of the Treaty to facilitate the achievement of the Commission's tasks'.[21]

At least half of the cases that continue past the informal stage are resolved without the Commission having to issue a reasoned opinion.[22] It is a healthy feature of the enforcement system under Article 169 that the vast majority of cases are settled in the informal stage or during the first part of the formal stage.

REASONED OPINION

In the minority of cases where a settlement is not reached at an earlier stage the Commission will give a reasoned opinion as to how it considers the member state to be in violation of its obligations under Community law.[23] If the letter of formal notice establishes the scope of the action in terms of its subject-matter, then the reasoned opinion establishes the legal arguments that the Commission is relying on. In *Commission* v *Netherlands* the Court said: 'The Court has consistently held that an application must be founded on the same grounds and submissions as the reasoned opinion.'[24] Any attempt by the Commission to raise new grounds or submissions before the Court will be rejected.

21 Case 240/86, note 20 above, p. 1858. The Commission was unsuccessful on the substantive complaint that it was contrary to Arts. 30 and 106 EEC for importers of cereals to have to obtain a foreign-currency permit granted by a bank and approved by the Bank of Greece. Thus, had the Greek Government cooperated with the Commission's investigation, there would have been no finding of a breach of Community law.
22 It is possible to follow the trend of established infringements for each member state based on the year commenced since 1990 in the 'Eleventh Annual Report' at pp. 66–70.
23 The figures for reasoned opinions were: 157 in 1982, 223 in 1985, 164 in 1986, 197 in 1987, 227 in 1988, 180 in 1989, 251 in 1990, 411 in 1991, 248 in 1992, 352 in 1993 and 546 in 1994 (see the 'Seventh, Eighth and Eleventh Annual Reports' and the *General Report 1994*).
24 Case 290/87 [1989] ECR 3083, 3103. See also Case 211/81, note 19 above, in particular para. 14; Case 23/84, note 14 above, [1986] ECR at p. 3639, [1987] 1 CMLR at pp. 642–3; Case C-217/88 *Commission* v *Germany* [1990] ECR I-2879, 2902; Case C-52/90 *Commission* v *Denmark* [1992] ECR I-2187, 2215; and Case C-296/92 *Commission* v *Italy* [1994] ECR I-1, 12.

The extent to which the Commission's opinion must be 'reasoned' was considered by the Court in the *Pigmeat* case.[25] The Italian Government suspended imports of certain pigmeats from all countries. The Commission regarded this as contrary to Article 31 of the Treaty as it was a new quantitative restriction between member states. Italy failed to respond to the letter of formal notice. After the Commission delivered its reasoned opinion, but before the expiry of the time given by the Commission to comply with it, Italy asked the Commission to authorize protective measures under Article 226 of the Treaty due to serious economic problems in the Italian pigmeat market and to abandon its proceedings under Article 169. The Commission continued with the proceedings and brought the case before the Court. The Italian Government objected to the admissibility of the action on several grounds, including the lack of reasoning in the Commission's reasoned opinion. The Court stated that

the opinion referred to in Article 169 of the Treaty must be considered to contain a sufficient statement of reasons to satisfy the law when it contains – as it does in this case – a coherent statement of the reasons which led the Commission to believe that the State in question has failed to fulfil an obligation under the Treaty.[26]

It would seem that the Commission is simply expected to show in what way the member state's laws are in breach of Community law – in this case by saying they constitute a new quantitative restriction contrary to Article 31 of the Treaty – and is not required to rebut the arguments that the member state has made or may make in its defence. Of course, in this case the member state had made no arguments in its defence before the reasoned opinion was made by the Commission, so the Commission could hardly be expected to anticipate Italy's defence. In general, the Commission will give as cogently reasoned an opinion as possible because it is conscious that it cannot raise new grounds and submissions when the case comes before the Court. Lack of cogency in the reasoned opinion may be forgiven by the Court if the Commission has made the state aware of its grounds and submissions in the informal stage or in the letter of formal notice.[27]

The Commission will normally give the member state a period of grace of two months, but in urgent cases it may be just two weeks, to comply

---

25 Case 7/61 *Commission* v *Italy* [1961] ECR 317.
26 Case 7/61, note 25 above. p. 327. More recent case law has required 'a coherent and *detailed* statement of the reasons' (emphasis added); see Case 274/83 *Commission* v *Italy* [1985] ECR 1077, 1090 and Case C-247/89 *Commission* v *Portugal* [1991] ECR I-3659, 3689.
27 See p. 195.

with its reasoned opinion before the action is brought before the Court.[28] In *Commission v Ireland*[29] the Irish Government was given only five days to comply with the Commission's reasoned opinion. The Court disapproved of the Commission's behaviour, as there was no particular need for urgency:

It is indeed unreasonable, as Ireland has pointed out, to allow a Member State five days to amend legislation which has been applied for more than forty years and which, moreover, has not given rise to any action on the part of the Commission over the period which has elapsed since the accession of that Member State to the Community.[30]

Although the Court found the case to be admissible, as the Commission had given further time for the Irish Government to respond to the reasoned opinion and had delayed bringing the action before the Court,[31] it was clearly warning the Commission that, short of compelling arguments of urgency, it would be unlikely to accept such a short period to comply with a reasoned opinion in a subsequent case.

In the *Pigmeat* case it was established that the member state must take the necessary measures to change the law within that period of grace if it is to prevent the Commission from bringing the case before the Court. It is insufficient to ask the Commission to authorize the protective measures under Article 226 of the Treaty[32] within the time-limit laid down in the reasoned opinion or to change the offending national laws after the time-limit has expired but before the Court gives judgment.

REFERENCE TO THE EUROPEAN COURT

Prior to 1980 only about ten cases a year were referred to the Court under Article 169 of the Treaty.[33] The figures increased dramatically in the 1980s so that now about seventy cases a year is normal.[34] By the end of 1990

---

28 See Case 85/85, note 8 above, and Case 293/85, note 9 above. See also the 'Tenth Annual Report' at p. 8.
29 Case 74/82 [1984] ECR 317.
30 ibid., p. 338.
31 The reasoned opinion was given by the Commission on 9 November 1981 but it did not refer the case to the Court until 19 February 1982.
32 Protective measures under Art. 226 could be sought only during the transitional period. Thus the Article is now of historical interest. In this case the Commission decided not to authorize protective measures.
33 See Audretsch, *Supervision in European Community Law*, p. 353, and (1987) 36 ICLQ 838, 848.
34 There were 45 cases in 1982, 113 in 1985, 71 in 1986, 61 in 1987, 73 in 1988, 96 in

some 800 actions[35] had been brought before the Court under Articles 169 and 93, and of these 491 were brought between 1985 and 1990.[36] Although it is normal for considerably more than half the cases where a reasoned opinion has been given to be resolved without the case being referred to the Court,[37] the huge increase in the number of cases where letters of formal notice are issued inevitably leads to an increase in cases before the Court. The proportion of cases that start with a letter of formal notice and reach the Court continues to be under one-fifth[38] and in recent years is under a tenth.[39]

The Commission has a discretion whether or not to initiate proceedings against a member state under Article 169, and this discretion operates at each stage of the process. Thus the Commission is under no obligation to issue a letter of formal notice, even where the member state does not fully comply with its Community law obligations, and the same is true at the stage of the reasoned opinion or of referring the matter to the Court. This has been confirmed by the Court in a decision that ruled out the possibility of an action for failure to act under Article 175 of the Treaty on the basis of the Commission failing to initiate, or to carry through to a conclusion, Article 169 proceedings.[40] The Commission can bring the action before the Court at any time after the time-limit for compliance with the reasoned opinion has expired. In *Commission* v *Germany* a delay of over two years did not render the action inadmissible.[41]

1989, 77 in 1990, 65 in 1991, 64 in 1992, 44 in 1993 and 89 in 1994 (see 'Seventh, Eighth and Eleventh Annual Reports' and the *General Report 1994*).

35 See the *XXIVth General Report on the Activities of the European Communities 1990*, Luxembourg, EC Official Publications, 1991, p. 449.

36 See in note 34 above.

37 Compare the figures in notes 23 and 34.

38 Only crude comparisons can be made because the length of time between a letter of formal notice and reference to the Court varies from case to case. If one assumes an average one-year time-lag, then comparing the figures for letters of formal notice in one year with those for references to the Court in the following year shows that the proportion reaching the Court was 14 per cent in 1986, 12 per cent in 1987, 13 per cent in 1988, 17 per cent in 1989 and 12 per cent in 1990. Using the same method of calculation, there was a brief bulge in the mid-1980s when the percentage was higher: 19 per cent in 1984 and 22 per cent in 1985.

39 Applying the system used in the preceding footnote the proportion reaching the Court was 7 per cent in 1991, 8 per cent in 1992, 4 per cent in 1993 and 7 per cent in 1994.

40 Case 247/87 *Star Fruit Company* v *Commission* [1989] ECR 291, followed by the Court of First Instance in Case T-13/94 *Century Oils Hellas* v *Commission* [1994] ECR II-431. See also Evans, 'The Enforcement Procedure of Article 169: Commission Discretion' (1979) 4 ELRev 442.

41 Case C-317/92 [1994] ECR I-2039, 2057 following Case 7/68 *Commission* v *Italy* [1968] ECR 423, 428.

Even when the case has been referred to the Court it is not uncommon for it to be settled during the proceedings and for the Court not to give judgment; of the 649 cases that had been referred to the Court by the Commission under Articles 169 or 93 by the end of 1990 and which were no longer pending, 288 had not resulted in a judgment of the Court (about 44 per cent).[42] In those cases where judgment is given about one tenth only have been in favour of the member state.[43] A low success rate for member states before the Court is not surprising given that the vast majority of cases are settled at one of the earlier stages in the proceedings and thus nearly all of the weak accusations of the Commission are weeded out. The Court has also rejected a number of standard defences.

Any argument by the state that it is prevented from complying with Community law because of internal legislative difficulties will be rejected. The Court has said that 'a Member State may not plead provisions, practices or circumstances existing in its internal legal system in order to justify a failure to comply with [its Community] obligations'.[44]

The fact that a constituent part of the member state with legislative autonomy, not under the control of the national government or legislature, refuses to comply with Community law does not exempt the member state from liability under Article 169. In *Commission* v *Belgium*[45] the autonomous regions of Walloon and Brussels both failed to implement certain environmental directives and Belgium was found to have failed to comply with its Community obligations. The Belgian Government had argued that it could not force the legislatures of these regions to implement the directives, but the Court did not accept this as a defence. It is important to remember that it is the state that is found in violation of its obligations under Community law and not the central government of that state. Although central government defends the state before the Court, it is the state that is responsible for any 'agency of the State whose action or inaction is the cause of the failure to fulfil its obligations, even in the case of a constitutionally independent institution'.[46] Conversely, national legislation that in itself is in violation of a Community directive is not saved by the possibility that regional authorities may ensure that the directive is not violated by enacting appropriate local legislation.[47]

---

42 See the *XXIVth General Report*, note 35 above.
43 Of the 361 cases decided by the Court before the end of 1990 in actions brought by the Commission under Articles 169 or 93, 322 found in favour of the Commission in respect of at least one of its main claims, 35 were dismissed on the merits and only 4 were wholly inadmissible; see the *XXIVth General Report*, note 35 above.
44 Case 58/81 *Commission* v *Luxembourg* [1982] ECR 2175.
45 Cases 227–30/85 [1988] ECR 1, [1989] 2 CMLR 797.
46 Case 16/69 *Commission* v *Belgium* [1970] ECR 237, 243.
47 Case C-157/89, note 19 above, p. 88.

Thus it is possible that an Article 169 action may be brought because of a decision of a national court that fails to apply Community law properly. The Commission 'hesitates', 'given the universal principle of the independence of the judiciary, to find fault with a Member State on grounds of the conduct of one of its courts'.[48] None the less the Commission initiated Article 169 proceedings against France for the allegedly manifest error of application of Community law by the Cour de Cassation in failing to overturn the decision of a lower court in favour of the French prosecuting authorities. These proceedings reached the stage of a reasoned opinion.[49]

Member states are obliged to ensure that infringements of Community law are penalized in their legal systems under conditions analogous to those applicable to infringements of national law of a similar nature. The penalty must be effective, proportionate and dissuasive. Moreover, the national authorities must proceed with respect to infringements of Community law with the same diligence that they bring to bear in relation to corresponding national laws. A failure on the part of a member state to meet these standards – basically equal treatment in its enforcement of Community law and of national law – will constitute a breach of Article 5 of the Treaty and hence is a basis for Article 169 proceedings.[50]

A member state may be liable under Article 169 proceedings for the conduct of a private body, if it is subject to a sufficient degree of government control,[51] and for the conduct of a nationalized industry.[52]

48 'Sixth Annual Report to the European Parliament on Commission Monitoring of the Application of Community Law 1988' OJ 1989 C330/1, at p. 53.
49 See the 'Sixth Annual Report', at pp. 53–4, and the 'Seventh Annual Report', at p. 54, where it was suggested that the case was likely to be settled shortly, following discussions between the French authorities and the Commission. AG Warner, in Case 9/75 *Meyer-Buckhardt* v *Commission* [1975] ECR 1171, 1187, took the view that the Commission could bring Art. 169 proceedings against a member state where a national court of last instance fails to refer a question of Community law to the European Court contrary to Art. 177(3). However, he recognized that the Commission might exercise its discretion not to initiate such proceedings, given that they 'should not be lightly undertaken'.
50 See Case 68/88 *Commission* v *Greece* [1989] ECR 2965, 2985.
51 See Case 249/81 *Commission* v *Ireland* [1982] ECR 4005, (the 'Buy Irish' case) discussed in Ch. 15 at pp. 440 and 450.
52 Though the opinion of AG Lenz in Case C-247/89 *Commission* v *Portugal* [1991] ECR I-3659, noted by Gilliams (1992) 1 Pub Proc LRev 15 casts doubt on this. The Advocate-General did not think that Portugal was responsible for the procurement activities of ANA-EP, a Portuguese public enterprise in charge of the exploitation of airports. The Court did not decide the point, as it found another of Portugal's defences to be well-founded. The view of the Advocate-General seems difficult to reconcile with the view of the Court in Case C-88/89 *Foster* v *British Gas* [1990] ECR I-3313, that an individual can rely on the direct effect of a directive against a nationalized industry because that industry is an emanation of the state although an individual cannot so rely against another individual or private company (see further pp. 350–51). The Advocate-General's opinion on the liability of the state for the activities of public enterprises may have been peculiar to the context of public procurement.

A member state cannot invoke the doctrine of 'self-help' to justify failure to comply with Community law on the grounds that a Community institution or another member state had failed to comply with Community law. The Court established this in no uncertain terms in rejecting an argument by Luxembourg and Belgium:

In their view, since international law allows a party, injured by the failure of another party to perform its obligations, to withhold performance of its own, the Commission has lost the right to plead infringement of the Treaty. However, this relationship between the obligations of parties cannot be recognized under Community law.

In fact the Treaty is not limited to creating reciprocal obligations between the different natural and legal persons to whom it is applicable, but establishes a new legal order which governs the powers, rights and obligations of the said persons, as well as the necessary procedures for taking cognizance of and penalizing any breach of it. Therefore, except where otherwise expressly provided, the basic concept of the Treaty requires that the Member States shall not take the law into their own hands. Therefore the fact that the Council failed to carry out its obligations cannot relieve the defendants from carrying out theirs.[53]

The fact that a legislative proposal is before the Council that, if enacted, would terminate the infringements alleged by the Commission does not prevent the Commission from proceeding with an Article 169 action.[54]

A change in the administrative practice of a state without changing the formal law is not sufficient to comply with Community law in terms of an Article 169 action. In *Commission* v *France*[55] the *Code du travail maritime* was found to have a provision that required that a proportion of the crew of French merchant ships had to consist of French nationals. This provision was no longer enforced in practice and the French Government intended to repeal it. However, the Court insisted that the continued existence of this measure as part of French law discriminating against workers from other member states was contrary to Community law.

The Commission can continue to proceed with an action under Article

---

53 Cases 90, 91/63 *Commission* v *Luxembourg and Belgium* [1964] ECR 625, 631.
54 The Court decided this in rejecting an argument by the Irish Government in relation to the admissibility of several actions brought by the Commission against member states for failing to ensure freedom to provide services in the sector of co-insurance. See Case 220/83 *Commission* v *France* [1986] ECR 3663, 3705; Case 252/83 *Commission* v *Denmark* [1986] ECR 3713, 3745; Case 205/84 *Commission* v *Germany* [1986] ECR 3755, 3797; Case 206/84 *Commission* v *Ireland* [1986] ECR 3817, 3846.
55 Case 167/73 [1974] ECR 359. See also Case C-381/92 *Commission* v *Ireland* [1994] ECR I-215; Case C-80/92 *Commission* v *Belgium* [1994] ECR I-1019, 1034; and Case C-317/92 *Commission* v *Germany* [1994] ECR I-2039, 2057.

169 if the member state has complied with its reasoned opinion after the time-limit for compliance has expired, but not if the state has complied within the time-limit.[56] The reason why the Court permits such 'moot' judgments has been expressed repeatedly:

As the Court has consistently held ... the subject-matter of an action brought under Article 169 is established by the Commission's reasoned opinion and even where the default has been remedied after the period laid down pursuant to the second paragraph of that article has elapsed, an interest still subsists in pursuing the action. That interest may consist in establishing the basis for a liability which a Member State may incur, by reason of its failure to fulfil its obligations, towards those to whom rights accrue as a result of that failure.[57]

In Article 169 proceedings the burden of proof is on the Commission. As the Court said in *Commission v Netherlands*: 'In proceedings brought under Article 169 of the Treaty the Commission is required to prove the allegation that the obligation has not been fulfilled and may not rely on any presumption.'[58] The fact that fishing quotas were exceeded in 1983 and 1984 in the Netherlands was not enough to prove that the Netherlands had failed to take action to prohibit fishing for certain stocks, as the Commission had not proved whether the exceeding of the quotas was due to late action by the member state or to illegal catches made after the member state had acted. The Commission's application to the Court cannot simply cross-refer to the letter of formal notice and the reasoned opinion. It must specify the subject-matter of the dispute, the submissions and at least give a brief but accurate statement of the grounds on which the application is based.[59]

A member state can plead *force majeure*[60] in its defence, but this has been

56 See Case 240/86, note 20 above, pp. 1855–6. In this case the Commission's action was only partially admissible, as Greece had complied with part of the Commission's reasoned opinion within the time-limit and part outside. See also Case C-362/90 *Commission v Italy* [1992] ECR I-2353.

57 Case 240/86 above. See also Case 103/84 *Commission v Italy* [1986] ECR 1759; Case 309/84 *Commission v Italy* [1986] ECR 599; Case 39/72 *Commission v Italy* [1973] ECR 101; Case 7/61 note 25 above; Case C-263/88 *Commission v France* [1990] ECR I-4611; and Case C-29/90 *Commission v Greece* [1992] ECR I-1971.

58 Case 290/87 *Commission v Netherlands* [1989] ECR 3083, 3104. See also Case 96/81 *Commission v Netherlands* [1982] ECR 1791; Case C-62/89 *Commission v France* [1990] ECR I-925; Case C-244/89 *Commission v France* [1991] ECR I-163, 197; and Case C-249/88 *Commission v Belgium* [1991] ECR I-1275, 1310.

59 See Case C-347/88 *Commission v Greece* [1990] ECR I-4747; Case C-43/90 *Commission v Germany* [1992] ECR I-1909; and Case C-52/90 *Commission v Denmark* [1992] ECR I-2187.

60 See a general discussion of *force majeure* by Thompson, 'Force Majeure: The Contextual Approach of the Court of Justice' (1987) 24 CMLRev 259–71; and Magliveras, 'Force Majeure in Community Law' (1990) 15 ELRev 460.

interpreted very restrictively by the Court. In *Commission* v *Italy*[61] statistical returns in respect of the carriage of goods by road were not submitted by Italy from 1979 onwards in contravention of Community Directive 78/546. Italy relied on *force majeure* as its defence because a bomb attack on the Ministry of Transport's data-processing centre destroyed its vehicle register. The European Court said:

That argument cannot be accepted. Although it is true that the bomb attack, which took place before 18 January 1979, may have constituted a case of *force majeure* and created insurmountable difficulties, its effect could only have lasted a certain time, namely the time which would in fact be necessary for an administration showing a normal degree of diligence to replace the equipment destroyed and to collect and prepare the data. The Italian Government cannot therefore rely on that event to justify its continuing failure to comply with its obligations years later.[62]

A high proportion of Article 169 proceedings that are referred to the Court relate to failure to comply with a Community directive.[63] The Court has stated the general requirement for a state in implementing a directive:

The transposition of a directive into domestic law does not necessarily require that its provisions be incorporated formally and verbatim in express, specific legislation; a general legal context may, depending on the content of the directive, be adequate for the purpose provided that it does indeed guarantee the full application of the directive in a sufficiently clear and precise manner so that, where the directive is intended to create rights for individuals, the persons concerned can ascertain the full extent of their rights and, where appropriate, rely on them before the national courts.[64]

In *Commission* v *Italy*[65] the application was dismissed by the Court. Although the Italian legislation implementing the directives on feeding-stuffs did not use the wording of the definitions in the directives, the Court could find no practical or theoretical consequences from this that would jeopardize the attainment of the results to be achieved by the

61 Case 101/84 [1985] ECR 2629.
62 ibid., p. 2637.
63 See Table 7 of the 'Sixth Annual Report' and 'Seventh Annual Report'. In 1986 43 of the 71 cases, and in 1988 46 of the 73 cases related to directives. In the 'Eleventh Annual Report' at p. 6 the Commission highlights the fact that 244 of 352 reasoned opinions in 1993 related to an alleged failure by member states to notify national implementing measures. At p. 8 the Commission said it intended to 'Lay greater emphasis . . . on the quality of national implementing measures i.e. compliance with the requirements of directives.'
64 Case 363/85 *Commission* v *Italy* [1987] ECR 1733, 1742. See also Case 29/84 *Commission* v *Germany* [1985] ECR 1661.
65 Case 363/85, note 64 above.

directives. The differences between the Italian legislation and the directives were either merely terminological and of no substantive importance, or due to Italy not taking advantage of all the derogations permitted to the member states by the directives.

Apart from actions relating to failure to comply with Community directives, Article 169 proceedings are also competent where the state fails to comply with a provision of the Community Treaty, or a Community regulation or decision.[66] In addition a failure by a member state to comply with provisions of a Treaty concluded between the Community and a third state or states under Article 228 of the EC Treaty can be pursued under Article 169. In *Kupferberg*[67] it was less clear whether a violation by a member state of a treaty concluded jointly by the Community and the member states with one or more non-member states – a mixed agreement – was within the scope of Article 169 proceedings.[68] However in *Commission* v *Greece*[69] the Court, in Article 169 proceedings, decided that Greece had violated Article 3(1) of the second Lome Convention and hence had failed to fulfil its obligation under the EEC Treaty. Surprisingly, the issue of whether obligations under the Lome Convention (in practice, concluded as a mixed agreement) constitute obligations under the EEC Treaty was not discussed by the parties, advocate-general or the Court. In this context it may be that a failure by a member state to comply with an international agreement, including a mixed agreement, is in fact a breach of its obligations under Article 5 EC, whereby member states are to 'ensure fulfilment of the obligations *arising out of this Treaty or resulting from actions taken by the institutions of the Community*' [our italics].

It is not clear whether a failure by a member state to comply with the EC Brussels Convention, or any other convention concluded to give effect to Article 220 of the EC Treaty, comes within the scope of Article 169 proceedings.[70] This is likely to remain a theoretical problem, as it is improbable that the Commission would bring such proceedings unless a member state were to ratify a convention and fail to implement it into national law, or its national courts were persistently to ignore the conven-

---

66 But arguably not decisions of the representatives of the Governments of the member states meeting in Council: see Hartley, *European Community Law*, p. 306.

67 Case 104/81 *Kupferberg* [1982] ECR 3641, 3662.

68 See Hartley, *European Community Law*, p. 306.

69 Case 241/85 [1988] ECR 1037.

70 See Hartley, *European Community Law*, pp. 306–7, and Dashwood and White, (1989) 14 EL Rev 388, 390. These authors agree that breaches by member states of other subsidiary conventions negotiated between the member states within the auspices of the Community but not envisaged by Art. 220 do not come within the scope of Art. 169 proceedings. Such conventions include the EC Rome Convention of 1980 and the Community Patent Convention of 1976.

tion or the interpretations given to it by the European Court. Another unresolved question is whether a failure to comply with the general principles of law developed by the European Court constitutes a failure to fulfil an obligation under the Community Treaty within the meaning of Article 169. Most commentators take the view that it does and it seems probable that the Court would share this view.[71]

Statistics show that the member state that is persistently the worst offender in terms of infringement proceedings is Italy. Between one-fifth and a third of all references to the European Court in infringement proceedings are against Italy.[72] Italy has had persistent internal legislative difficulties in complying with Community law and, in particular, in implementing directives.[73] It is hoped that the passing of the so-called 'La Pergola Law' in Italy on 9 March 1989 will result in more satisfactory implementation of Community law in Italian law,[74] but the early signs were not encouraging: the Community Act of 1990 took nine months to go through the Italian parliament and was passed only in December 1990.[75] Between 1990 and 1993, Italy had 66 infringement proceedings referred to the Court, Belgium 34, Luxembourg 33, Greece 27, the Netherlands 19, Germany, Ireland and Spain 15, France 13, Portugal and the United Kingdom 5, and Denmark 4.[76] The publication of statistics by the Commission showing which states have the poorest record in compliance with Community law may help to shame those states into compliance. Publicity is an important enforcement tool, which the Commission has made more use of in recent years. In itself it is probably insufficient to deal with the recalcitrant member states. At Maastricht it was agreed to amend Article 171 of the Treaty to give the Court the power to impose fines or penalty payments on member states that persistently fail to comply with Community law, considered below.

71 See Hartley, *European Community Law*, pp. 307–8, and Dashwood and White, (1989) 14 ELRev 388, 390 and the other writers cited by them. Only Hartley expresses doubts and as he rightly says: 'This problem is not likely to arise very often.'
72 The number of references to the Court in infringement proceedings against Italy in recent years was as follows: 31 in 1985, 18 in 1986, 21 in 1987, 14 in 1988, 35 in 1989, 24 in 1990, 19 in 1991, 9 in 1992, 9 in 1993 and 12 in 1994 (see the 'Seventh, Eighth and Eleventh Annual Reports' and the *General Report 1994*). Compare these figures with the total number of references to the Court in infringement proceedings given in note 34 above.
73 See Gaja, 'New Developments in a Continuing Story: The Relationship Between EEC Law and Italian Law', (1990) 27 CMLRev 83, 89.
74 ibid., pp. 90–93, and see the expression of hope about this law by the Commission in the 'Seventh Annual Report', p. 6. Gaja says that: 'The main idea is that Parliament should approve each year a statute (called *legge communitaria*), which is specifically designed to ensure that Italian law is consistent with Community law.'
75 See Daniele, 'Italy and EEC Law in 1990' (1991) 16 ELRev 417.
76 'Eleventh Annual Report' at p. 64.

ACTIONS UNDER ARTICLE 170

Article 170 provides:

A Member State which considers that another Member State has failed to fulfil an obligation under this Treaty may bring the matter before the Court of Justice.

Before a Member State brings an action against another Member State for an alleged infringement of an obligation under this Treaty, it shall bring the matter before the Commission.

The Commission shall deliver a reasoned opinion after each of the States concerned has been given the opportunity to submit its own case and its observations on the other party's case both orally and in writing.

If the Commission has not delivered an opinion within three months of the date on which the matter was brought before it, the absence of such an opinion shall not prevent the matter from being brought before the Court of Justice.

The procedure for an action brought by one member state against another alleging failure to comply with Community law is self-explanatory. The Commission's role merely provides a delaying period of three months before the member state is free to refer the case to the Court. The burden of proof rests with the member state bringing the proceedings.

Article 170 has been invoked very rarely. Indeed, by the end of 1990 only two such cases had been referred to the Court and one of those was settled without the Court having to give judgment.[77] In the one case decided by the Court, *France* v *United Kingdom*,[78] it was held that the United Kingdom measures on mesh size for fishing nets were not in conformity with Community law.

Clearly, member states prefer the Commission to take actions against their fellow member states rather than doing so themselves. This saves the member state the cost involved in litigation, the difficulty of carrying the burden of proof and the diplomatic embarrassment attached to taking a close ally to court.

---

77 See *XXIVth General Report*, p. 499. The case that was settled without the Court's judgment was Case 58/77, *Ireland* v *France*. Since then Case C-349/92 *Spain* v *United Kingdom* was lodged in the Court of Justice on 3 October 1992 (OJ 1992 C256/14) but discontinued on 23 December 1992 (OJ 1992 C340/6).
78 Case 141/78 [1979] ECR 2923.

ENFORCEMENT OF ACTIONS AGAINST MEMBER STATES: ARTICLE 171

Article 171 EEC provided that 'if the Court of Justice finds that a Member State has failed to fulfil an obligation under this Treaty, the State shall be required to take the necessary measures to comply with the judgment of the Court of Justice'.

The Court's initial judgment in infringement proceedings[79] is declaratory. Though it is binding on the member state concerned, the Court has no powers to enforce its judgments by means of financial penalties. The result is that some member states are slow to comply with the Court's judgments. Indeed, by the end of 1993 eighty-two of the Court's judgments had not been complied with.[80] The only remedy prior to the Maastricht Treaty amendments coming into force on 1 November 1993 was for the Commission to initiate new infringement proceedings against the member state for a violation of the aspect of Community law that the Court has already ruled upon and for a failure to comply with Article 171 EEC by not complying with that ruling. This was a cumbersome process, as the whole Article 169 procedure had to be gone through again. Prior to Maastricht the Commission had expressed its concern about the high number of judgments of the Court not complied with and the number of proceedings it had to initiate alleging a violation of Article 171 EEC. In 1989, for example, the Commission brought twenty-six new procedures based on Article 171 EEC,[81] and said, 'This situation gives cause for concern as it undermines the fundamental principles of a Community based on law.' The Commission had also taken Article 171 EEC proceedings for a second time in relation to twelve cases,[82] a clear sign that the declaratory judgment under Article 171 EEC was not effective in relation to some cases.[83]

---

79 Whether under Arts. 169, 170, 93(2), 100a(4), 100b(2) or 225.
80 See 'Eleventh Annual Report' at pp. 169–173. Belgium had failed to comply with 18 judgments, Italy 16, France 10, Germany 9, Greece and Spain 6, Netherlands 5, Ireland and Luxembourg 4, the United Kingdom 3, Denmark 1 and Portugal 0.
81 See the 'Seventh Annual Report', p. 5.
82 See 'Intergovernmental Conferences: Contributions by the Commission (1991)', EC Bull. Supp. 2/91, p. 151.
83 The statistics at the end of December 1993 show that there were eight judgments which had been given against a member state in repeat infringement proceedings which had not been complied with. The four judgments concerning Belgium related to pension rights and environmental matters, the judgment concerning France related to retail prices of manufactured tobacco, the judgments concerning Germany and the

The European Court has not specified how long a period of time a member state is given to comply with a judgment against it and not fall foul of Article 171. In *Commission v Italy* the Court said:

Article 171 of the EEC Treaty does not specify the period within which a judgment must be complied with. However, it is beyond dispute that the action required to give effect to a judgment must be set in motion immediately and be completed in the shortest possible period. In the present case, such period has been greatly exceeded.[84]

The judgment of the Court in the original infringement proceedings[85] had been given on 15 November 1983, and in the subsequent infringement proceedings invoking Article 171 on 12 February 1987. This case indicates that compliance with a judgment of the Court should take place in considerably less than three years if a violation of Article 171 is to be avoided.

The United Kingdom Government advocated giving the Court sanctions under Article 171 to enforce its judgments in infringement proceedings. The sanctions could be imposed only in an action brought against a member state for failing to comply with the Court's judgment under the original infringement proceedings. These proposals were put forward at the intergovernmental conference on political union,[86] and appeared in the Luxembourg presidency's draft text in June 1991 even though the Commission had given the British proposals a lukewarm reception merely reserving the Commission's right to make proposals in due course for the introduction of financial penalties against member states in breach of their Community law obligations.[87] The Luxembourg draft proposals remained in place in the final version of Article 171 agreed at Maastricht in December 1991.

Netherlands both related to wild birds. At the same date the Commission had 29 Art. 171 proceedings in motion. Perhaps these will be settled before the Court gives a judgment given its new powers to impose a financial penalty under Art. 171(2) EC. The source of the statistics is the 'Eleventh Annual Report' at pp. 169–173.

84 Case 69/86 [1987] ECR 773, 780. See also Cases 227–30/85, note 45 above; Case C-328/90 *Commission v Greece* [1992] ECR I-425, 437; Case C-75/91 *Commission v Netherlands* [1992] ECR I-549, 555; and Case C-291/93 *Commission v Italy* [1994] ECR I-859, 864.

85 Case 322/82 *Commission v Italy* [1983] ECR 3689.

86 See EC Bull. Supp. 2/91, p. 151.

87 See ibid., pp. 151–2 for the Commission staff paper and p. 81 for the official Commission Opinion of 21 October 1990 on the proposal for amendment of the Treaty establishing the European Economic Community with a view to political union. Coincidentally, the Court on 19 November 1991 in Cases C-6/90 and C-9/90 *Francovich and others v Italy* [1991] ECR I-5357, decided in an Art. 177 preliminary ruling that in certain circumstances states must pay damages in their national courts to persons affected by the non-implementation of a Community directive; see Ch. 11, notes 70–76.

Under Article 171 EC financial sanctions cannot be invoked in the original infringement proceedings. However a failure to comply with the Court's judgment may lead to subsequent proceedings brought by the Commission for that failure to comply. The Commission must give the state an opportunity to submit its observations before issuing a reasoned opinion specifying the points on which the member state has not complied with the Court's judgment. The reasoned opinion will specify a time-limit for compliance by the member state. If the Commission is not satisfied that the member state has complied within the appointed period, then it may bring proceedings before the Court. The Commission must specify the amount of the lump sum or penalty payment that it considers to be appropriate for the member state to have to pay. If the Court finds that the member state has not complied with its judgment, it may impose a lump sum or penalty payment on it.

Clearly this is an important new power, which greatly enhances the armoury of the Court of Justice. It represents a very significant further move towards the European Court being the supreme court of the European Union. None the less, there is a risk that certain member states may continue to defy the Court by not complying with the financial sanctions in the same way they did not comply with the declaratory judgments. Mechanisms may have to be devised for ensuring that these financial penalties can be collected. Article 171 EC preserves the discretion of the Commission as to whether or not to institute, or to carry through, proceedings against a state for failing to comply with a judgment of the Court in infringement proceedings. The Court is under no obligation to impose a lump sum or penalty payment, but if it does do so, it is not limited by the figure suggested by the Commission.

ACTIONS UNDER ARTICLE 93(2)

Article 93(2) of the Treaty is part of the provisions on state aids. It states:

If, after giving notice to the parties concerned to submit their comments, the Commission finds that aid granted by a State or through State resources is not compatible with the common market having regard to Article 92, or that such aid is being misused, it shall decide that the State concerned shall abolish or alter such aid within a period of time to be determined by the Commission.

If the State concerned does not comply with this decision within the prescribed time, the Commission or any other interested State may, in derogation from the provisions of Articles 169 and 170, refer the matter to the Court of Justice direct.

The remainder of Article 93(2) permits the member state to apply to the Council to have the aid authorized as being compatible with the common market in derogation from the provisions of Article 92. The Council must act unanimously. The application freezes the infringement proceedings under Article 93(2) for three months. If the Council takes no decision within that time or decides against the member state, then the infringement proceedings can continue. Article 93(2) proceedings are in derogation from Article 169 proceedings and apply to the special problems created by state aid with regard to competition in the common market. The compatibility of aid schemes in relation to Community law provisions other than Article 92 – for example, agricultural subsidies – can be assessed in Article 169 proceedings.[88]

Member states must notify new or substantially altered state aids to the Commission under Article 93(3) of the Treaty. If the Commission believes that a member state has failed to comply with Article 93(3) by not informing it of any plans to grant aid, it can initiate proceedings under Article 169.[89] The Commission has a period of two months in which to decide to initiate the procedure under Article 93(2) or to decide that the aid is compatible with the Treaty.[90]

If the Commission has doubts about the compatibility of the aid, it initiates the Article 93(2) procedure by notifying the parties concerned to submit their comments, not just the member states but also undertakings affected by the aid.[91] Any attempt by the Commission to make a decision requiring a member state to recover aid from a beneficiary without going through the Article 93(2) procedure may be struck down by the Court on the ground that concerned parties, like the recipient of the aid, were not notified and thus were denied their right to be heard before the decision was made.[92] Although Article 93(2) is silent as to how long the Commission

---

88 See Case C-35/88, note 20 above, [1992] 1 CMLR 548, 566–7; Case 72/79 *Commission v Italy* [1980] ECR 1411, [1982] 1 CMLR 1; and Case 290/83 *Commission v France* [1985] ECR 439, [1986] 2 CMLR 546.

89 The Commission's procedure for dealing with non-notified new aid is set out in *Agence Europe* No. 5367, 9 November 1990, p. 10, and in Slot, 'Procedural Aspects of State Aids: The Guardian of Competition versus the Subsidy Villains?' (1990) 27 CMLRev 741, 751–2. See Case C-35/88, note 20 above, and Case 169/82 *Commission v Italy* [1984] ECR 1603, [1985] 3 CMLR 30.

90 The period of two months was fixed by the European Court in Case 120/73 *Lorenz v Germany* [1973] ECR 1471. A decision to permit the aid can be challenged under Art. 173: see Cases 166 and 220/86 *Irish Cement Ltd v Commission* [1988] ECR 6473 and Case 84/82 *Germany v Commission* [1984] ECR 1451.

91 See Case 60/79 *Producteurs de vins de table et vin de pays v Commission* [1979] ECR 2425.

92 See Case C-294/90 *British Aerospace and Rover v Commission* [1992] ECR 1–493, [1992] 1 CMLR 853.

can take before reaching its final decision, it must do so within a reasonable period.[93] If the Commission's final decision under Article 93(2) is that the state should abolish or alter the aid, it will be published in the L Series of the *Official Journal*.[94] The decision is clearly open to annulment proceedings under Article 173 of the Treaty. Consequently, a member state can challenge the validity of the decision only by taking such proceedings.[95] As the Court has consistently held: 'A Member State which is the addressee of a decision adopted under the first subparagraph of Article 93(2) may not call in question the validity of that decision in the course of legal proceedings commenced pursuant to the second subparagraph of that article.'[96]

The only defence open to a member state in proceedings before the Court under Article 93(2) is that 'it was absolutely impossible for it to implement the decision properly' within the time-limit specified[97] by the Commission in its decision.[98] Given this severe restriction on the member state's ability to contest the Commission's decision in Article 93(2) proceedings, the Court has encouraged cooperation between the Commission and the member state. If the member state has problems in giving effect to the

93 The Court has not defined the reasonable period as yet, but it found a delay of twenty-six months to be unacceptable in Case 223/85 *RVS* v *Commission* [1987] ECR 4617.

94 If the Commission decides to allow the aid, then this decision might not be published in the *Official Journal*, making it difficult for individuals adversely affected by it (competitors of those receiving the state aid) to challenge it under Art. 173, even if they have standing, as they may not be aware of it within the two-month time-limit. If the Commission decides to authorize the aid subject to certain conditions and later concludes that the state has breached those conditions, it must refer the matter directly to the Court under Art. 93(2) rather than attempt to impose a decision on the state requiring it to recover the aid from the beneficiary; see Case C-294/90, note 92 above. Audrestsch, *Supervision in European Community Law*, p. 221, gives figures for adverse decisions taken by the Commission under Art. 93(2): there were 14 in 1981, 13 in 1982, and 12 in 1983. It may be possible to bring an action in the national courts with the aim of obtaining a preliminary ruling from the European Court under Art. 177 on the validity of the decision.

95 If the member state challenges the decision in Art. 173 proceedings, it will find it very difficult to obtain the suspension of the Commission's decision in an application for interim measures; see case 303/88R *Italy* v *Commission* [1989] ECR 801 and Case 142/87R *Belgium* v *Commission* [1987] ECR 2589. The reason for this is that the member state cannot show 'serious and irreparable damage' to itself from having to withdraw state aid to an undertaking. The damage is to the undertaking and it would have to contest the decision and seek interim measures.

96 Case 52/84 *Commission* v *Belgium* [1986] ECR 89, 104. See also Case 52/83 *Commission* v *France* [1983] ECR 3707. At least after the expiry of the two-month time-limit on actions under Art. 173.

97 If the Commission simply specifies a date by which the member state is to notify it of the action taken to comply with the decision, then that date is deemed to be the date by which the government has to comply with the decision: see Case 213/85 *Commission* v *Netherlands* [1988] ECR 281, 299–300.

98 See Case 52/84, note 96 above, and Case 213/85, note 97 above, p. 300.

decision that the Commission may not have foreseen, it should submit them to the Commission with proposals for suitable amendments:

In such a case the Commission and the Member State concerned must respect the principle underlying Article 5 of the Treaty, which imposes a duty of genuine cooperation on the Member States and Community institutions; accordingly, they must work together in good faith with a view to overcoming difficulties whilst fully observing the Treaty provisions, and in particular the provisions on aid.[99]

Existing aids are monitored by the Commission in accordance with Article 93(1) of the Treaty. Unlike new state aids, the Commission does not have to operate within a time-limit of two months when deciding whether or not to invoke the contentious procedure under Article 93(2). The procedure is as described above from the moment the Commission gives notice to the parties concerned to submit their comments.

INTERIM MEASURES IN INFRINGEMENT PROCEEDINGS

Article 186 provides that 'the Court of Justice may in any cases before it prescribe any necessary interim measures'. This power clearly applies to infringement proceedings. In proceedings in 1977 under Article 93(2) the United Kingdom was still giving state aid to pig farmers contrary to the decision of the Commission under that Article. The Commission applied to the European Court for an interim order requiring the United Kingdom to cease infringing the decision pending the outcome of the proceedings before the Court. The Court ordered the United Kingdom to stop paying the aid 'forthwith'.[100] Interim measures have also been granted in a number of infringement proceedings under Article 169 of the Treaty.[101]

---

99 Case 52/84, note 96 above, p. 105. In this case the problem was that if Belgium recovered the aid from the undertaking that had received it, the undertaking would go into liquidation. The Court said this did not constitute a defence under Art. 93(2) but none the less encouraged a cooperative approach between the Commission and the member state. See also Case C-303/88 *Italy v Commission* [1991] ECR I-1433, 1485. More generally on state aids see Ch. 27 below, at pp. 874–80.

100 Joined Cases 31/77R *Commission v United Kingdom* and 53/77R *United Kingdom v Commission* [1977] ECR 921. The Court order was made on 21 May 1977 and the United Kingdom stopped paying the aid towards the end of June.

101 See Case 61/77R *Commission v Ireland* [1977] ECR 937, 1412; Case 154/85R *Commission v Italy* [1985] ECR 1753; Case 293/85R *Commission v Belgium* [1985] ECR 3521; Case 45/87R *Commission v Ireland* [1987] ECR 783, 1369; Case 194/88R *Commis-*

The Court's Rules of Procedure prescribe that the application for interim measures 'shall state the subject-matter of the proceedings, the circumstances giving rise to urgency and the pleas of fact and law establishing a *prima facie* case for the interim measures applied for'.[102]

The application is normally heard by the President of the Court, but he can refer it to the Court.[103] If the Commission fails to show that there is sufficient 'urgency'[104] to justify interim measures, the application will be dismissed. In *Commission* v *Italy*, the interim measure sought was for Italy to give Aer Lingus provisional authorization to operate a scheduled Manchester–Milan air service, pursuant to Article 8(1) of Council Decision 87/602/EEC. In order to show 'urgency' the Commission needed to show 'serious and irreparable damage' would be caused to Aer Lingus if the interim order was not granted. This was not done, as Aer Lingus had never operated such a service and therefore their loss was the anticipated profit from running it. The Court decided that the amount involved, 1,600,000 Irish pounds, 'cannot be regarded as sufficient to establish urgency'.[105]

Case 246/89R *Commission* v *United Kingdom* provides a good example of interim measures being granted in Article 169 proceedings.[106] This case was part of the series of cases concerning Anglo-Spanish fishing vessels registering in the United Kingdom in order to gain access to the British fishing quota under the EEC's common fisheries policy. In section 14 of the Merchant Shipping Act 1988 the United Kingdom had included *inter alia* certain nationality requirements before a fishing vessel could be registered in the United Kingdom. The vessel had to be British owned and any owner, charterer, manager or operator of the vessel had to be a British citizen of a company incorporated in the United Kingdom with at least 75 per cent of its shareholders being British citizens[107] and at least 75 per cent

---

sion v *Italy* [1988] ECR 5647; Case C-195/90R *Commission* v *Germany* [1990] ECR I-3351; and Case C-272/91R *Commission* v *Italy* [1992] ECR I-457.

102 Art. 83(2); see OJ 1991 L176/23.

103 Rules of Procedure ECJ Art. 85. The joined cases referred to in note 100 above and Case 61/77R and Case C-195/90R, note 101 above, were heard by the Court. The other cases referred to in note 101 above were heard by the President.

104 This can be where the Commission shows a lack of 'diligence' in pursuing the case, e.g. in Case C-87/94R *Commission* v *Belgium* [1994] ECR I-1395 the Commission only sought to suspend the contract in issue some three months after it was made aware of the facts; see pp. 1406–7.

105 Case 352/88R [1989] ECR 267. See also Case 57/89R *Commission* v *Germany* [1989] ECR 2849.

106 [1989] ECR 3125.

107 Or 'qualified companies', i.e. those that are incorporated in the United Kingdom and have 75 per cent of their ownership in the hands of British citizens or other qualified companies, and of which at least 75 per cent of the directors are British citizens.

of its directors being British citizens. These provisions prevented some British-registered fishing vessels, which had a significant proportion of ownership by Spanish citizens, from continuing to have access to the British fishing quota.

The Commission brought Article 169 proceedings, alleging that the nationality requirements in section 14 of the 1988 Act meant that the United Kingdom had failed to fulfil its obligations under Articles 7, 52 and 221 EEC. Pending the outcome of the Article 169 proceedings, the Commission sought an interim order requiring the United Kingdom to suspend the application of the nationality requirements as regards the nationals of other member states and in respect of fishing vessels that until 31 March 1989, the date the relevant provisions of the 1988 Act began to operate, were pursuing a fishing activity as registered British vessels and under a British fishing licence. Thus the order was to apply only to those vessels that were prevented from continuing to fish as British vessels solely by reason of the nationality requirements.[108]

The President of the Court first considered whether the Commission had demonstrated a prima-facie case. The President acknowledged that the United Kingdom may need to pass measures that ensure that there is a 'genuine link' between the vessels that are able to fish against the British quota and the British fishing industry:

However, there is nothing which would *prima facie* warrant the conclusion that such requirements may derogate from the prohibition of discrimination on grounds of nationality contained in Articles 52 and 221 of the EEC Treaty regarding, respectively, the right of establishment and the right to participate in the capital of companies or firms within the meaning of Article 58.[109]

The President decided that the Commission's application in the main proceedings 'does not appear to be without foundation and that the requirement of a *prima-facie* case is thus satisfied'.[110]

As regards the condition relating to 'urgency', the President decided that it must be assessed in relation to the necessity for an order to grant interim relief to prevent 'serious and irreparable damage'.[111] The President

---

108 There were other requirements in s.14 of the 1988 Act relating to the residence of the owner, charterer, manager or operator of the vessel in the United Kingdom, the principal place of business of a company in the United Kingdom and the management of the vessel from within the United Kingdom.

109 Case 246/89R, note 106 above, p. 3133.

110 ibid., p. 3134.

111 ibid.

held that for the fishing vessels that had been registered as British prior to 31 March 1989, the loss of that registration meant the cessation of their fishing activities, entailing serious damage. If the Commission were successful in its main proceedings, the damage suffered by the owners of the vessels in the interim would be irreparable.[112] The President acknowledged that for there to be urgency 'it is necessary that the interim measures requested should be of a nature to prevent the alleged damage'.[113] This condition was fulfilled in this case because the 'possibility cannot ... be excluded' that a number of the vessels affected by the nationality requirements would meet the other requirements of section 14 of the 1988 Act and hence be able to continue fishing against the British quota.

Finally, the President addressed the 'balance of interests' and concluded that the United Kingdom could maintain a genuine link between the vessels fishing against the British quotas and the British fishing industry, the legitimate objective it was trying to achieve in the 1988 Act, even with the suspension of the nationality requirements.

The President decided that the Commission had established a prima-facie case and the necessary urgency, and thus ordered the interim measures applied for. Within one month the United Kingdom passed the legislation necessary to comply with the President's order.[114]

It would seem that the Court will not grant interim measures in infringement proceedings where the Commission alleges that the member state has failed to comply with a judgment of the Court under Article 171 of the Treaty in previous infringement proceedings.[115] The reason for this is that the interim measures are not 'necessary', given that the order would substantially duplicate the Court's original judgment, which the member state is under an obligation to comply with.[116]

---

112 This may have been due to the fact that there was no means by which the United Kingdom could be ordered to compensate the owners of the fishing vessels concerned.

113 Case 246/89R, note 106 above, p. 3135.

114 The order was made on 10 October 1989 and s. 14 of the 1988 Act was amended with effect from 2 November 1989 by the Merchant Shipping Act 1988 (Amendment) Order 1989 (SI 1989 No. 2006).

115 See Joined Cases 24/80R and 97/80R *Commission v France* [1980] ECR 1319.

116 Hartley argues that in Joined Cases 24/80R and 97/80R, note 115 above, the Court did not prescribe interim measures because it did not want to see its order ignored by the French Government (*European Community Law*, p. 334). The case concerned the highly contentious French ban on imports of lamb and mutton from the United Kingdom. The matter was settled politically and the Court was able to avoid giving a final judgment.

The Court has recently had the opportunity to consider whether to grant interim measures in a case brought under Article 225 and it declined to do so for the reasons noted above.[117]

117 See Case C-120/94R *Commission* v *Greece* [1994] ECR I-3037, note 2 above.

CHAPTER 8

Judicial Review of EC Acts

Article 173 of the EEC Treaty provided for a system of judicial review of the legality of all acts of the Council and Commission other than recommendations or opinions. This was transformed by the European Court of Justice into a review of all 'measures adopted by the institutions, whatever their nature or form, which are intended to have legal effects'[1] including those adopted by the European Parliament.[2] The Article gives unrestricted *locus standi* to member states, the Council and Commission, and very restricted *locus standi* to natural or legal persons. The European Court of Justice gave the European Parliament standing to challenge the legality of EC legislation but only in so far as it is protecting its own prerogatives,[3] and this has been confirmed by the amendment to Article 173 agreed at Maastricht in December 1991. The grounds for challenging a measure seem quite limited: lack of competence, infringement of an essential procedural requirement, infringement of the EC Treaty or of any rule of law relating to its application, or misuse of powers. A strict two-month time-limit applies to the commencement of proceedings before the Court challenging an act under Article 173. As at 31 December 1990 just under 20 per cent – 801 – of the 4,116 cases brought to the European Court of Justice in relation to the EEC Treaty had been under Article 173, and of the 520 decided by the Court, just under 30 per cent – 150 – had been in favour of the applicant.[4]

The Treaty also provides for the possibility of challenging the legislative and administrative inaction of the Council or Commission under Article 175. This has proved to be of very limited value in practice: as at 31 December 1990 only forty-two cases had been brought before the Court (including five before the Court of First Instance) under Article 175, of

1 Case 22/70 *Commission* v *Council* (*ERTA* case) [1971] ECR 263, 277.
2 Case 294/83 *Les Verts* v *European Parliament* [1986] ECR 1339.
3 Case C-70/88 *European Parliament* v *Council* [1990] ECR 1–2041.
4 These figures include a handful of cases before the Court of First Instance. See *XXIVth General Report on the Activities of the European Communities 1990*, Luxembourg, EC Official Publications, 1991, p. 449.

which thirty had been decided and only three in favour of the applicant.[5]

Finally, Article 184 provides for a plea of illegality against EC Regulations. This is not an independent cause of action, but rather is a plea that can be made when an action is otherwise competently before the Court. It supplements Article 173, which does not permit natural or legal persons to challenge the validity of a true regulation.

ACTIONS UNDER ARTICLE 173

Article 173 EEC provided that

The Court of Justice shall review the legality of acts of the Council and the Commission other than recommendations or opinions. It shall for this purpose have jurisdiction in actions brought by a Member State, the Council or the Commission on grounds of lack of competence, infringement of an essential procedural requirement, infringement of this Treaty or of any rule of law relating to its application, or misuse of powers.

Any natural or legal person may, under the same conditions, institute proceedings against a decision addressed to that person or against a decision which, although in the form of a regulation or a decision addressed to another person, is of direct and individual concern to the former.

The proceedings provided for in this Article shall be instituted within two months of the publication of the measure, or of its notification to the plaintiff or, in the absence thereof, of the day on which it came to the knowledge of the latter, as the case may be.

Article 173 EEC was amended at Maastricht so that the Court can review the legality of acts 'adopted jointly by the European Parliament and the Council ... and of acts of the European Parliament intended to produce legal effects *vis-à-vis* third parties'. The former provision applies to measures adopted under the conciliation and veto procedure laid down in Article 189b EC. The latter provision is merely a recognition of existing Court case law on the interpretation of Article 173.[6] The amended version of Article 173 grants *locus standi* to the European Parliament and the European Central Bank but only for the purpose of 'protecting their prerogatives'.

5 See the *XXIVth General Report*.
6 See notes 33–7 below.

MEASURES THAT ARE REVIEWABLE

Article 173 EEC referred to measures of the Council and the Commission other than recommendations or opinions. The European Court noted in the *ERTA* case[7] that Article 189 of the Treaty provides that recommendations or opinions have no binding force. It concluded that Article 173 EEC treats as open to review by the Court all measures adopted by the Council and Commission that are intended to have legal effects. Conversely, the Court did not follow through on the use of Article 189 as an aid in interpreting Article 173 EEC by deciding that the latter applies only to regulations, decisions and directives.[8] This would be too restrictive an interpretation 'to ensure, as required by Article 164, observance of the law in the interpretation and application of the Treaty'.[9]

In the *ERTA* case the Commission was challenging the 'proceedings' of Council on 20 March 1970 concerning its conclusions on the attitude to be taken by the governments of the member states in the negotiations, under the auspices of the United Nations Commission for Europe, of the European agreement concerning the work of crews of vehicles engaged in international road transport (ERTA). The Court considered whether the power to negotiate and conclude this agreement was a matter within the competence of the Community or of the member states. Having decided on the former, the Court concluded that the Council's proceedings of 20 March were within the framework of the Community. The Council was laying down a course of action designed to be binding on the Community institutions and the member states. There was a risk that part of the Council's conclusions derogated from the negotiating procedure laid down in the EEC Treaty. The Court concluded that the Commission's action was admissible, as the Council proceedings of 20 March had 'definite legal effects both on relations between the Community and the Member States and on the relationship between institutions'.[10]

In *European Parliament* v *Council and Commission*[11] the Court of Justice confirmed that decisions adopted by the representatives of the member states collectively exercising the powers of the member states are not subject to review of their legality by the Court. This is true even though

7 Case 22/70, note 1 above.
8 See Ch. 5, pp. 136–9, on the types of legislation described in Art. 189.
9 Case 22/70, note 1 above, at p. 276.
10 ibid., p. 278. If the Commission enters into an international agreement with a non-member state then it will be reviewable if it produces legal effects; see Case C-327/91 *France* v *Commission* [1994] ECR I-3641, 3672.
11 Cases C-181 and 248/91 [1993] ECR I-3685, [1994] 3 CMLR 317, noted by L. Neville Brown (1994) 31 CMLRev 1347.

the decision is taken in the context of a meeting of the Council. The Court will look beyond the label attached to the measure to see if having regard to its contents and all the circumstances under which it was adopted, the act in question is in reality a decision of the Council. In this case the Court was satisfied that a decision of the 'member states meeting in Council' was not a decision of the Council within the meaning of Article 173 EC and was therefore not reviewable. The decision was to grant aid of 60 million ECU to Bangladesh and the Court noted that humanitarian aid was not a matter within the exclusive competence of the Community and therefore member states were free to take collective action outwith the framework of the EC while making use of a Community institution, the Commission, to coordinate the aid.

In *Cimenteries* v *Commission*[12] the Court found a Commission notice, carried out by a registered letter, to be a reviewable act under Article 173 EEC. Société Anonyme Cimenteries was one of seventy-four undertakings that had entered into an agreement called the 'Noordwijks Cement Accoord' in July 1956 that, *inter alia*, divided up the market in respect of the supply of cement and clinker by means of quotas. The undertakings notified the Commission of the agreement in October 1962 in accordance with EEC Regulation 17 on competition policy. On 14 December 1965 the Commission agreed that a notice should be addressed to the undertakings under Article 15(6) of Regulation 17. Such a notice was sent by registered letter on 3 January 1966. The undertakings brought an action under Article 173 EEC challenging the validity of the Commission's notice and registered letter.

The significance of the Commission's notice under Article 15(6) of Regulation 17 was that it removed the exemption from fines for breach of EC competition policy granted by Article 15(5) of the Regulation to notified agreements. The Commission's notification reflected its preliminary conclusion that the agreement breached Article 85(1) of the Treaty and that the application of the exempting provisions in Article 85(3) was not justified. It was, of course, possible that the Commission, when taking its final decision under Regulation 17, would find no breach of Article 85(1) of the Treaty or that the agreement was exempt from that paragraph by virtue of Article 85(3). If this occurred, then the Commission's notice under Article 15(6) of Regulation 17 would prove to have no adverse consequences, as no fine would be imposed. It was improbable that the Commission would change its mind, and the likely effect of the notice withdrawing exemption from a fine would be to force the undertakings to terminate the agreement. As the Court observed: 'The preliminary measure

12 Cases 8–11/66 [1967] ECR 75.

would thus have the effect of saving the Commission from having to give a final decision thanks to the efficacy of the mere threat of a fine.'[13]

The Court concluded that the Commission's notice and registered letter constituted a reviewable measure that deprived the undertakings of

the advantages of a legal situation which Article 15(5) attached to the notification of the agreement, and exposed them to a grave financial risk. Thus the said measure affected the interests of the undertakings by bringing about a distinct change in their legal position. It is unequivocally a measure which produces legal effects touching the interests of the undertakings concerned and which is binding on them. It thus constitutes not a mere opinion but a decision.[14]

The Court subsequently decided in *IBM* v *Commission*[15] that a letter sent by the Commission to an undertaking being investigated under Regulation 17 containing a statement of objections against the undertaking and requiring it to reply within a specified time was not a reviewable act. In this case IBM was being investigated by the Commission under Article 3 of Regulation 17 for a possible abuse of a dominant position contrary to Article 86 of the Treaty. Before the Commission could take its final decision it was required to send a statement of objections in writing to IBM and give it time to reply to them.[16] IBM brought an action under Article 173 EEC challenging the legality of the Commission's measures notified to them in the letter.

The Court expressed the view that, in principle, provisional measures intended to pave the way for a final decision are not reviewable.[17] Without referring to the *Cimenteries* case,[18] it distinguished the *IBM* case from it as follows:

A statement of objections does not compel the undertaking concerned to alter or reconsider its marketing practices and it does not have the effect of depriving it of the protection hitherto available to it against the application of a fine, as is the case when the Commission informs an undertaking, pursuant to Article 15(6) of Regulation No 17, of the results of the preliminary examination of an agreement which has been notified by the undertaking.[19]

---

13 ibid., p. 93; see further Ch. 24.
14 ibid., p. 91. The Court noted that Regulation 17 was silent as to the description of the measure taken under Art. 15(6). One of the reasons given for regarding a measure taken under that Article as a 'decision' was to protect the rights of individuals; see ibid., p. 92.
15 Case 60/81 [1981] ECR 2639.
16 See Reg. 17, Art. 19 and Reg. 99/63 on the hearings provided for in that Article, discussed in Ch. 24 at pp. 769–73.
17 Case 60/81, note 15 above, p. 2652.
18 Cases 8–11/66, note 12.
19 Case 60/81, note 15 above, p. 2654. It is true that the issuing of the statement of objections is an essential procedural requirement without which the Commission cannot

The Court concluded that the initiation of procedure under Article 3 of Regulation 17 and the statement of objections were not reviewable under Article 173 EEC, as they were simply procedural measures adopted preparatory to the final decision, which is reviewable under that Article.[20]

In *Automec* v *Commission*[21] the Court of First Instance decided that the Commission's preliminary observations in a competition investigation were not reviewable under Article 173. The Court of First Instance stated that the question of the admissibility of an application under Article 173 can be raised by the Court of its own motion.[22] In *SFEI* v *Commission*[23] the Court of Justice annulled the order of the Court of First Instance that the application was inadmissible on the ground that the letter from the Commission to SFEI was not a preliminary measure but was a decision to terminate its investigations of a possible infringement of Article 86 by La Poste which had been initiated by SFEI's complaint.

Although measures that are taken as part of the preliminaries leading up to a final decision are normally exempt from review, this does not apply to the releasing of confidential documents.[24] In *AKZO Chemie* v *Commission*[25] the Commission investigated a complaint against AKZO Chemie of an abuse of a dominant position under Article 86 of the Treaty. The complaint had been brought by a small competitor of AKZO called ECS. During the investigation the Commission obtained certain documents from AKZO and, on the request of ECS, sent some documents, which AKZO regarded as confidential, to ECS. AKZO brought an action under Article 173 to annul the Commission's action in transmitting certain confidential documents to ECS. The Court decided that the Commission's action

---

impose a fine on the undertaking; see Reg. 99/63, Art. 2. It does not, however, remove an immunity from fines applicable to a breach of competition policy in the period prior to the statement of objections being issued.

20 Case 60/81, note 15 above, p. 2654.

21 Case T-64/89 [1990] ECR II-367. See also Case T-113/89 *Neforma* v *Commission* [1990] ECR II-797. Further consideration as to the difference between non-reviewable letters from the Mergers Task Force and a reviewable statement of position by the Commissioner responsible can be found in Case T-3/93 *Air France* v *Commission* [1994] ECR II-121, 149–53.

22 Case T-64/89, note 21 above, p. 381.

23 Case C-39/93P [1994] ECR I-2681. See also a similar case turning on whether the letter from the Commission terminated its investigations or was simply a stage of it where the Court of First Instance decided on the former and found the case admissible, Case T-37/92 *BEUC and NCC* v *Commission* [1994] ECR II-285.

24 Nor does it apply to a 'decision' of the Commission not to allow a third party access to the non-confidential file in an anti-dumping investigation; see Case C-170/89 *BEUC* v *Commission* [1991] ECR I-5709, 5738–9.

25 Case 53/85 [1986] ECR 1965.

was not simply a preparatory measure in its investigation of a breach of Article 86, but was an independent decision of a definitive nature that the documents did not qualify for the confidential treatment guaranteed by Community law and could therefore be communicated. A challenge to the Commission's final decision in relation to a breach of Article 86 would not provide AKZO with an adequate degree of protection of its rights. In particular, it would neither prevent the Commission from repeating the release of confidential documents during the investigation nor render unlawful any use made by ECS of the documents. The procedures for the enforcement of competition law are discussed systematically in Chapter 24.

Provisions in the Acts of Accession of new member states are treated as primary law, like the EC Treaty itself, and are not reviewable.[26] Decisions of the European Council are outwith the scope of Article 173.[27] At the other end of the spectrum, a decision that is given orally can be reviewable under Article 173.[28]

In *Brother Industries* v *Commission*[29] a Commission memorandum to the member states stated that certain anti-dumping proceedings had been terminated because the goods originated in Japan rather than Taiwan. Brother Industries, a producer/exporter of the goods that were under investigation by the Commission, sought the annulment of this memorandum, as it would have adverse consequences if the anti-dumping duties applicable to Japan were to apply to its goods. The Court found the application inadmissible because the memorandum's contention that the goods originated in Japan was only a source of guidance to the national authorities and not binding on them when considering the origin of goods for the application of anti-dumping duties. Brother Industries had argued that the possibility that the national authorities might disregard the finding of Japanese origin made by the Commission was 'entirely theoretical' given the role played by the Commission in dumping matters.[30] It does seem unlikely that the national authorities would reach a different conclusion than the Commission after a detailed anti-dumping investigation by it. The case illustrates that for an act to be reviewable it must produce binding legal effects. Commission opinions, which are designed to influence

26 See Cases 31 and 35/86 *Laisa* v *Council* [1988] ECR 2285, concerning provisions in the Act of Accession of Spain and Portugal.
27 See Art. L TEU and Case T-584/93 *Rovjansky* v *Council* [1994] ECR II-585, 592. A legally binding decision was taken at the European Council in Edinburgh in December 1992; see the first edition of this book at pp. 774–9 and p. 17 above.
28 See Cases 316/82 and 40/83 *Kohler* v *Court of Auditors* [1984] ECR 641 and Case T-3/93 *Air France* v *Commission* [1994] ECR II-121, 154–5.
29 Case 229/86 [1987] ECR 3757.
30 ibid., p. 3761.

the national authorities on the interpretation of EC legislation, do not produce binding legal effects and are not reviewable.[31]

It would seem that a measure that in principle is not capable of producing binding legal effects will be reviewable if a Community institution uses it to attempt to do so, albeit by exceeding its powers. In *France v Commission*[32] Commission internal instructions 88/C264/03, relating to the supervisory powers of officials concerning product sampling under Regulation 729/70, were treated by the Court as measures attempting to have legal effects. The Court decided the case was admissible and that the instructions were void, as the Commission lacked the necessary powers to issue them.

Although Article 173, prior to the Maastricht Treaty amendments, referred only to acts of the Council and the Commission, the European Court decided in *Les Verts v European Parliament* that 'an action for annulment may lie against measures adopted by the European Parliament intended to have legal effects *vis-à-vis* third parties'.[33] The Maastricht amendments confirmed the Court's ability to review acts of the European Parliament intended to produce legal effects *vis-à-vis* third parties.

The contested measures in the 1986 *Les Verts* case concerned the allocation of appropriations in the budget of the European Parliament by its Bureau and enlarged Bureau for the expenses incurred by political parties contesting the 1984 European Parliament elections. In the 1988 *Les Verts* case[34] the Court, in a very cryptic judgment, decided that the contested measures were not reviewable, as they had only internal effects within the administration of the European Parliament and gave rise to no rights or obligations on the part of third parties. The measures involved were the financial implementing measures arising from the decisions of the Bureau and enlarged Bureau, which had been annulled by the European Court in 1986. The decisions in principle to allocate the budget appropriations to political parties taking part in the 1984 European Parliament elections were reviewable, but the decisions of the financial controller and accounting

---

31 See Case 151/88 *Italy v Commission* [1989] ECR 1255 and the cases referred to therein at p. 1261, para. 22; confirmed in Case C-50/90 *Sunzest v Commission* [1991] ECR I-2917.

32 Case C-366/88 [1990] ECR I-3571, [1992] 1 CMLR 205. See also Case C-303/90 *France v Commission* [1991] ECR I-5315, where the Commission adopted a Code of Conduct in relation to the obligations imposed on member states by Art. 23 of Reg. 4253/88 dealing with the financial control of the structural funds. The Court decided that the Code was reviewable as it imposed obligations on member states going beyond those required by the regulation and thus was intended to have legal effects of its own and on the substance annulled it on the basis that the Commission lacked the competence to adopt it.

33 Case 294/83, note 2 above, p. 1366. The reasoning of the Court is discussed in Ch. 6, pp. 179–80.

34 Case 190/84 *Les Verts v European Parliament* [1988] ECR 1017.

officer carrying out these decisions were merely internal measures not subject to review.

A decision by the European Parliament to set up a committee of inquiry is not reviewable, as it does not produce legal effects *vis-à-vis* third parties.[35]

Such a committee has no power to take binding legal decisions.[36] On the other hand, the declaration by the President of the European Parliament that the budget of the European Community has been finally adopted is a reviewable act under Article 173.[37]

LOCUS STANDI: PRIVILEGED APPLICANTS

The member states, Commission and Council have unlimited *locus standi* (standing) to bring an action under Article 173. It is not necessary for them to prove that they have an interest in bringing the proceedings.[38]

The European Parliament was not expressly mentioned in Article 173 EEC, but the European Court decided that it has *locus standi* to bring an action for annulment to safeguard its own prerogatives. The action must be brought exclusively on grounds based upon the infringement of those prerogatives.[39] This position was confirmed by the amendment to Article 173 agreed at Maastricht in December 1991.

LOCUS STANDI: NON-PRIVILEGED APPLICANTS

Natural and legal persons other than the member states, the Council, the Commission and the European Parliament have limited *locus standi* under

---

35 See Case 78/85 *Group of the European Right* v *European Parliament* [1986] ECR 1753. Any measure that relates to the internal organization of the European Parliament only cannot be challenged in an action for annulment; see Case C-68/90 *Blot and National Front* v *European Parliament* [1990] ECR I-2101.

36 See Ch. 4, pp. 103–4.

37 Case 34/86 *Council* v *European Parliament* [1986] ECR 2155.

38 See Case 45/86 *Commission* v *Council* [1987] ECR 1493, 1518; and Case 131/86 *United Kingdom* v *Council* [1988] ECR 905, 927.

39 See Case C-70/88, note 3 above. The reasoning of the Court is discussed in Ch. 6 at pp. 180–81. See also p. 105 above. In Case C-187/93 *European Parliament* v *Council* [1994] ECR I-2857, the Parliament was unable to challenge a Regulation on the ground that its legal basis should have included Art. 113 EC, the reason being that the Article does not provide for the European Parliament to be involved in any way in the drawing up of the acts envisaged in it and therefore its omission from the legal basis of the Regulation did not prejudice the prerogatives of the Parliament at all. See also Case C-70/88 *European Parliament* v *Council* [1991] ECR I-4529, 4567.

Article 173. These persons are categorized as non-privileged applicants. They have standing to challenge decisions that are addressed to them. Problems arise in relation to regulations and to decisions that are not addressed to the applicants. Although EC directives are not mentioned in this context in Art. 173, the Court has not rejected out of hand the admissibility of an action for annulment of a directive from a natural or legal person, treating a directive as a decision where it is not of general application.⁴⁰ It is likely that the Court will in future explicitly accept the principle that non-privileged applicants can challenge a directive on the same basis as they can challenge regulations.⁴¹ Applicants must prove that the measure is of direct and individual concern to them. The Court of Justice's case law on the *locus standi* of non-privileged applicants to challenge regulations will be considered before turning to the case law on decisions that are not addressed to the applicants. The Court's jurisprudence in this area has not always been consistent.

Regulations

In the first case concerning a challenge to a regulation by a natural or legal person under Article 173 EEC, *Producteurs de Fruits* v *Council*, the Court relied on the definitions of decision and regulation in Article 189 of the Treaty to establish the difference between them:

The criterion for the distinction must be sought in the general 'application' or otherwise of the measure in question.

The essential characteristics of a decision arise from the limitation of the persons to whom it is addressed, whereas a regulation, being essentially of a legislative nature, is applicable not to a limited number of persons, defined or identifiable, but to categories of persons viewed abstractly and in their entirety. Consequently, in order to determine in doubtful cases whether one is concerned with a decision or a regulation, it is necessary to ascertain whether the measure in question is of individual concern to specific individuals.⁴²

The Court subordinated the 'general-application' test to the 'individual-

---

40 See Case 160/88R, *Fédération européenne de la santé animale* v *Council* [1988] ECR 4121, [1988] 3 CMLR 534 (discussed below at p. 268). The matter was not resolved by the European Court in that case because the action was clearly inadmissible on another ground; see Case 160/88 [1988] ECR 6399. In Case C-298/89 *Gibraltar* v *Council* [1993] ECR I-3605, [1994] 3 CMLR 425, a full Court of 13 judges found an action brought by a non-privileged applicant against a directive inadmissible but not on the basis that such an action is in principle incompetent.
41 Arnull, 'Private Applicants and the Action for Annulment under Article 173 of the EC Treaty' (1995) 32 CMLRev 7, 47.
42 Cases 16, 17/62 [1962] ECR 471, 478.

concern' test, the latter being satisfied if the measure applies to a fixed and identifiable group of persons, a 'closed circle'. If a person could prove individual concern in relation to a measure entitled a 'Regulation', even if only part of it,[43] then the Court would regard the measure as not being a true regulation.

However, in *Compagnie Française Commerciale* v *Commission*[44] the Court did not give overriding priority to the individual-concern test. Even though the contested regulation contained a transitional provision that applied to a fixed and identifiable number of persons, including the applicant, and thus met the individual-concern test in relation to that provision, the Court found the application inadmissible. The transitional provision was regarded as an integral part of a true regulation, a legal measure of a general character.[45]

It was thought for some time that *Compagnie Française* was a rogue decision because in several cases[46] the Court reverted to its approach in *Producteurs de Fruits* and bypassed the 'general-application' test in favour of the 'individual-concern' test. However, the Court reverted to the *Compagnie Française* approach in the *Beauport* case in the 1980s[47] and in a series of cases required the applicant to show that the measure entitled as a 'regulation' was not truly of a legislative nature as well as establish that the measure was of individual concern, in that it applied to a fixed and identifiable group of persons.[48]

This dual requirement can be illustrated by the *Calpak* case,[49] in which Commission regulations concerning production aids for Williams pears preserved in syrup were challenged by some Italian producers. The particular provisions of the regulations concerned applied to a fixed and identifiable group: all producers of Williams pears in the marketing year 1978/9. Only such producers could apply for production aid for the marketing year 1979/80, restricted to 105 per cent of the amount produced during 1978/9. The Italian companies that challenged the regulations were among

---

43 ibid., p. 479.
44 Case 64/69 [1970] ECR 221.
45 ibid., pp. 226–7.
46 Cases 41–4/70 *International Fruit Company* v *Commission* [1971] ECR 411; Case 100/74 *CAM* v *Commission* [1975] ECR 1393; Case 88/76 *Exportation des Sucres* v *Commission* [1977] ECR 709; Case 123/77 *UNICME* v *Council* [1978] ECR 845; Case 112/77 *Töpfer* v *Commission* [1978] ECR 1019.
47 Cases 103–9/78 *Beauport* v *Council* [1979] ECR 17.
48 Case 162/78 *Wagner* v *Commission* [1979] ECR 3467; Cases 789–90/79 *Calpak* v *Commission* [1980] ECR 1949; Case 45/81 *Moksel* v *Commission* [1982] ECR 1129; Case 147/83 *Binderer* v *Commission* [1985] ECR 257; Case 26/86 *Deutz und Geldermann* v *Council* [1987] ECR 941; Case 253/86 *Agro-Pecuaria Vicente Nobre* v *Council* [1988] ECR 2725; Case C-244/88 *Usine co-operatives de déshydration du Vexin and Others* v *Commission* [1989] ECR 3811.
49 Cases 789–90/79, note 48 above.

the group of producers in 1978/9 and were adversely affected by the terms of the production aid for 1979/80 because their production in 1978/9 was well below average. The crucial part of the European Court's judgment is as follows:

> By virtue of the second paragraph of Article 189 of the Treaty the criterion for distinguishing between a regulation and a decision is whether the measure at issue is of general application or not . . .
>
> A provision which limits the granting of production aid for all producers in respect of a particular product to a uniform percentage of the quantity produced by them during a uniform preceding period is by nature a measure of general application within the meaning of Article 189 of the Treaty. In fact the measure applies to objectively determined situations and produces legal effects with regard to categories of persons described in a generalized and abstract manner. The nature of the measure as a regulation is not called in question by the mere fact that it is possible to determine the number or even the identity of the producers to be granted the aid which is limited thereby.[50]

Had the measures been decisions rather than regulations, then Calpak and the other Italian companies would have been able to demonstrate direct and individual concern and would have had *locus standi*. The measures were, however, true regulations in that they applied to a category of producers: anyone in the European Community that produced Williams pears in marketing year 1978/9. The fact that it is possible to count up all such producers and even list them does not mean that the character of the measure is not legislative.

Another case illustrating the point that being a member of a fixed and identifiable group was not sufficient in itself to give standing to challenge a regulation is *Deutz und Geldermann* v *Council*.[51] The Sixth Chamber noted that it was a matter of dispute between the parties as to whether the regulation that was being challenged applied to all producers and merchants of sparkling wines in the Community or whether it applied only to sparkling-wine producers who have traditionally used the *méthode champenoise*. The Court stated that even if the latter was the case, and the measure applied to a closed circle of persons:

> A measure does not cease to be a regulation because it is possible to determine the number or even the identity of the persons to whom it applies at any given time as long as it is established that such application takes effect by virtue of an objective legal or factual situation defined by the measure in relation to its purpose.[52]

50 ibid., p. 1961.
51 Case 26/86, note 48 above.
52 ibid., p. 951.

It was still a legislative measure that 'concerns the applicant only in its objective capacity as a sparkling-wine producer which has traditionally used a particular method of production in just the same way as any other producer or trader in the same position'.[53]

It may be clear that regulations that apply to such large categories of producers as those that grow Williams pears or make sparkling wine using the *méthode champenoise* are genuinely legislative and not simply disguised decisions. The general-application test is, none the less, subjective and it is difficult to predict when a regulation will fail to meet this standard. Even during the 1980s there were some examples of the Court bypassing the general-application test and simply considering whether or not the applicant was directly and individually concerned by the 'regulation'.

In *Agricola Commerciale Olio* v *Commission*[54] the applicants were challenging a regulation that retrospectively repealed an earlier regulation which had provided for the sale by lots of olive oil. The sale had already taken place and the applicants had been one of a fixed and identifiable group of successful purchasers. The applicants challenged the attempt by the Commission to revoke the sale. The Fifth Chamber of the European Court did not explicitly apply the general-application test, but rather found the case admissible on the ground that the measure was of direct and individual concern to the applicants. Nevertheless, the measure in question was surely a disguised decision and not a legislative measure of general application. It simply applied to the small group of successful purchasers in relation to a sale of olive oil that had already taken place.

In *Roquette Frères* v *Council*[55] the Court found the application admissible without referring explicitly to the general-application test. Regulation 1293/79 fixed the production quotas for certain isoglucose producers, including the applicant. The Court noted that in the annex to the regulation each undertaking was given a specific quota. The Court decided that each of these undertakings were the 'addressees' of the measure and were directly and individually concerned by it. It would seem that where a regulation applies to a general category of producers, in this case of isoglucose, but singles them out for individual treatment it ceases to be a true regulation and becomes a disguised series of decisions.

In *Sofrimport* v *Commission*[56] the Fifth Chamber did not refer to the general-application test but found the case partly admissible. The applicant was individually concerned only in so far as it was an importer of Chilean

53 ibid., p. 952.
54 Case 232/81 [1984] ECR 3881.
55 Case 138/79 [1980] ECR 3333, 3356.
56 Case C-152/88 [1990] ECR I-2477, 2507–2508.

apples whose goods were in transit when the relevant regulation was adopted.[57]

In May 1994 a nine-judge Court of Justice decided the *Codorniu* case.[58] This may prove to be a turning point in the Court's case law. Codorniu was a Spanish company that produced sparkling wines. It was the largest producer in the European Union of quality sparkling wines, the designation of which includes the term 'crémant', and held a Spanish graphic trade mark since 1924 for one of its products, 'Gran Crémant de Codorniu'. The only other significant producers in the Union of sparkling wine with the designation 'crémant' were in France and Spain. Codorniu sought the annulment of Regulation 2045/89 which reserved the term 'crémant' for quality sparkling wines made in France or Luxembourg while allowing wine producers from other member states who were using the term on 1 September 1989 to continue to do so for five years.

The Court of Justice decided that Regulation 2045/89 was a true regulation of a legislative nature and of general application. It applied to all Union producers of sparkling wines using the term 'crémant'. Nonetheless the Court was prepared to grant standing if certain producers could demonstrate they were individually concerned.[59] Codorniu could not show it was part of a fixed and ascertainable group as the regulation applied to all producers of 'crémant' sparkling wines in the Union. It could not prove that those affected by the transitional five-year period from 1 September 1989 were a fixed group that could have been identified by the Council when it passed the regulation in June 1989 as there was, theoretically at least, time for new producers to utilize the term 'crémant' before 1 September 1989. The Court decided that Codorniu was individually concerned because the regulation affected it in a way that differentiated it from other producers, i.e. it removed its right to use the Spanish graphic trade mark.[60]

---

57 In Case C-309/89 *Codorniu* v *Council* [1994] ECR I-1853, 1867, Advocate-General Lenz categorized *Sofrimport* as a departure from the need to be part of a fixed and identifiable group in order to prove individual concern. Such concern can be demonstrated if the applicant's situation is protected by particular clauses in the contested provision. In *Sofrimport*, Art. 3 of the parent regulation required the Commission to take account of the special provision of goods in transit to the Community when adopting protective measures for fruit and vegetables such as those in the contested regulation.

58 Case C-309/89, note 57 above, noted by J. Usher (1994) 19 ELRev 636 and D. Waelbroeck and D. Fosselard (1995) 32 CMLRev 257.

59 This abandoning of the 'general-application' test had been advocated by Advocate-General Lenz at pp. 1862–6.

60 Advocate-General Lenz had mentioned the existence of the trademark in his opinion (at p. 1872) but had not used it as the basis for saying that Codorniu was individually concerned. Rather he had applied the approach of the European Court in the context of an anti-dumping case, Case C-358/89 *Extramet Industrie* v *Council* [1991] ECR I-2501,

The *Codorniu* case is significant in that the Court has expressly acknowledged that a regulation can still be one of general application and yet non-privileged applicants can have standing because they are directly and individually concerned by it. This was a conclusion that the Court had already reached in anti-dumping cases.[61] The Court is also becoming more flexible in the avenues whereby an applicant can prove 'individual concern'. Removal of an intellectual property right by legislation can now be added to being part of a fixed and identifiable group, or being a participant in pre-legislative investigations,[62] or being expressly mentioned in the Regulation,[63] or being part of a group that is given certain rights in the parent legislation under which the contested measure is adopted.[64] It may now be possible for the Court to develop a consistent approach to *locus standi* albeit one that departs significantly from the wording of Article 173.[65] On the substance of the case Codorniu was successful as the Court regarded the limitation of 'crémant' to wine producers in France and Luxembourg as being unjustified discrimination on the grounds of nationality contrary to Articles 40(3) and 7 of the EEC Treaty.[66] Professor Usher has claimed that *Codorniu* 'would appear to be the first example of such a private direct action leading to the annulment of policy-making legislation'.[67] The Court of Justice may have been more willing to liberalize the *locus standi* provisions under Article 173 in May 1994 on the basis that the Court of First Instance had just been given jurisdiction to deal with all such cases brought by non-privileged applicants.[68] The burden of any opening of the floodgates will largely fall on the Court of First Instance in that the Court of Justice will hear only the appeals on points of law from that Court's decisions. One worry is that the delays in getting judgments will increase

---

which he described as the 'criterion of impact' (at p. 1869). Codorniu was individually concerned because it had a 'clearly distinguished position on the market' and was likely to be 'severely affected' by the measure.

61 See Cases 239 and 275/82 *Allied Corporation* v *Commission* [1984] ECR 1005, 1030 and Case C-358/89, note 60 above, p. 2531.

62 See the cases discussed below at pp. 235–6.

63 See Case 138/79, note 55 above.

64 See Advocate-General Lenz's analysis of Case C-152/88 *Sofrimport* v *Commission* [1990] ECR I-2477 above at note 57.

65 This departure from the wording was acknowledged by Advocate-General Lenz in *Codorniu* at p. 1865 but defended on the ground that 'it has the advantage of clarity and abstract logic'. Paul Craig, in an article written before *Codorniu*, 'Legality, Standing and Substantive Review in Community Law' (1994) 14 OJLS 507, defended an inconsistent approach on the basis that the approach to *locus standi* can legitimately vary depending on the substantive context of the case.

66 Now Art. 6 of the EC Treaty.

67 See Usher, op. cit., n. 58, at p. 640.

68 See Council Decision 93/350 (OJ 1993 L144/21) and Council Decision 94/149 (OJ 1994 L66/29), discussed at pp. 189–90 above.

as the Court of First Instance took about 23 months to decide direct actions in 1993 (the same time as the main Court) before its workload was greatly increased by the enlargement of its jurisdiction and the transfer of over 450 pending cases from the Court of Justice.[69] The Court of First Instance will have to make extensive use of three-judge chambers if it is to cope efficiently with considering the merits rather than just the admissibility of many direct actions.

Although *Codorniu* creates the possibility that the Court will treat the admissibility of all actions seeking the annulment of regulations in accordance with the same principles, it is still worth looking at the case law on anti-dumping regulations even if only as an exemplar of the new more liberal approach.

Anti-dumping regulations

Anti-dumping duties are imposed provisionally by the Commission and definitively by the Council by regulation on dumped products whose release for free circulation in the Community causes economic harm. A parent regulation outlines the procedure that is to be adopted and the rules to be applied in determining whether anti-dumping duty is applicable.[70] A product is regarded as having been dumped 'if its export price to the Community is less than the normal value of the like product'.[71] Such dumping can be acted against when it causes or threatens to cause material injury to an established Community industry or materially retards the establishment of such an industry.[72]

There are three categories of potential non-privileged applicants who may seek to annul an anti-dumping regulation: the producers and exporters of the product, the importers of the product and those who initiated the Commission's investigation of whether the product is being dumped by making a complaint.

Producers and exporters of a product on which an anti-dumping duty has been imposed have standing to challenge the part of the anti-dumping regulation that is exclusively applicable to them.[73] This is particularly the

---

69 In 1992, 168 cases were pending before the Court of First Instance but this had been increased to 657 by the end of 1993.
70 See Reg. 3283/94 (OJ 1994 L349), replacing Reg. 2423/88 (OJ 1988 L209/1), which replaced Reg. 2176/84 (OJ 1984 L201/1), which in turn replaced Reg. 3017/79 (OJ 1979 L339/1).
71 Reg. 3283/94, Art. 1(2).
72 Reg. 3283/94, Arts. 1(1) and 3(1).
73 See Case 240/84 *NTN Toyo Bearing* v *Council* [1987] ECR 1809. However, standing is not given in respect of those provisions of the regulation which impose anti-dumping duties on other undertakings, see Case C-156/87 *Gestetner* v *Council* [1990] ECR I-781 and Case C-174/87 *Ricoh* v *Council* [1992] ECR I-1335, 1389.

case where the producer/exporter is identified in the regulation.[74] Here the anti-dumping regulation amounts to a series of decisions against particular producer/exporters defining what the rate of anti-dumping duty will be rather than a legislative measure imposing a flat rate of duty on all producer/exporters of a type of product. The Court has suggested, albeit *obiter dictum*, that even in the latter type of case a producer/exporter that was 'concerned by the preliminary investigations' by the Commission into whether an anti-dumping duty should be imposed has *locus standi*.[75] If the Court were to apply these suggestions in an appropriate case it would represent a liberalization of the normal rules for *locus standi*. Such anti-dumping regulations do not apply to a fixed and identifiable group of persons. Any person who exports the product to the Community is affected by the duty; this includes any new exporter that was not in business at the time the anti-dumping regulation was passed.

An importer of a product that is subject to anti-dumping duty can challenge an anti-dumping regulation when it is associated with a producer/exporter of the product and was involved in the Commission's preliminary investigations of the anti-dumping duty.[76] This is particularly so where the export price used in determining the anti-dumping duty was calculated on the basis of the importer's selling price of the goods on the Community market.[77] On the other hand, if the importer was independent of the producer/exporter, then, until recently, its involvement in the preliminary investigations was not regarded as sufficient to give it *locus standi* to challenge the anti-dumping regulation.[78] However, in the *Extramet* case the Court extended *locus standi* even to independent importers who were involved in the preliminary investigations establishing the anti-dumping duty.[79] The Court focused on why Extramet was individually concerned rather than on whether the regulation was in

---

74 See Case 113/77 *NTN Toyo Bearing* v *Council* [1979] ECR 1185. Such a situation is similar to the *Roquette Frères* case, note 55 above.

75 See Cases 239, 275/82, note 61 above, p. 1030; Case 240/84, note 73 above, p. 1851; and Case 279/86 *Sermes* v *Commission* [1987] ECR 3109, 3114. In Case C-75/92 *Gao Yao* v *Council* [1994] ECR I-3141, the Sixth Chamber accepted that it was sufficient for producers and exporters to be 'concerned by the preliminary measures' to have standing but rejected Gao Yao (Hong Kong)'s application as it simply acted as a representative of Gao Yao China, one of the producers and exporters of the relevant goods in China against which a flat rate anti-dumping duty had been imposed, in the Commission's preliminary investigations.

76 See Case 113/77, note 74 above, para. 9 at p. 1204 and Cases C-305/86 and C-160/87 *Neotype Techmashexport* v *Commission and Council* [1990] ECR I-2945 and the cases referred to at p. 2998.

77 Cases 277, 300/85 *Canon* v *Council* [1988] ECR 5731, para. 8 at p. 5798.

78 See Case 307/87 *Alusuisse* v *Council and Commission* [1982] ECR 3463; Case 279/86, note 75 above; and Case 301/86 *Frimodt Pedersen* v *Commission* [1987] ECR 3123.

79 Case C-358/89, note 60 above, noted by Vermulst and Hooijer (1992) 29 CMLRev 380–404.

reality a decision. Extramet was distinguished from all other undertakings because it was the most important importer of the product subject to the anti-dumping measure, it was the ultimate consumer of the product, and it was seriously affected economically by the anti-dumping measure because there were very few producers of the product in countries against which the anti-dumping measure did not apply, and only one in the Community, which was its main competitor for the finished product.[80]

The *locus standi* of complainants is not clear. *Timex* v *Council and Commission*[81] is an important case on the point. Here Timex was the leading watch manufacturer in the European Community and had complained to the Commission about the dumping of watches from the Soviet Union in the Community. Its initial complaint was not investigated by the Commission, but later the British Clock and Watch Manufacturers' Association brought a complaint on behalf of its members, including Timex, which was investigated and led to anti-dumping duty being imposed. The Court took the view that the Association's complaint 'owed its origin to the complaints originally made by Timex'[82] and concluded that the 'contested regulation constitutes a decision which is of direct and individual concern to Timex'.[83] It is not clear, however, whether it would have been sufficient that Timex was the original complainant. In this case the conduct of the investigation procedure was largely determined by Timex's observations, the anti-dumping duty was fixed in the light of the effect of the dumping on Timex and this was made explicit in a reference to Timex in the preamble to the regulation.

It may be that the Court is moving towards a situation where a non-privileged applicant, whether a producer, importer or complainant, has *locus standi* to challenge an anti-dumping regulation if the applicant is named or specifically referred to in the regulation or if the applicant participated in the preliminary investigations or the applicant's prices were used by the Commission in establishing the anti-dumping duty. The *Extramet* case might imply even broader *locus standi*, extending to independent importers who are seriously affected by the anti-dumping regulation,[84] but it may be that the Court will still require the importer to have been a participant in the Commission's preliminary investigations. The *Codorniu* case shows that the Court is extending its liberalization of review of

80 AG Jacobs was prepared to give an independent importer standing where its participation in the Commission's preliminary investigations affected their outcome. Vermulst and Hooijer ((1992) 29 CMLRev 380) argue that it should be sufficient simply for the independent importer to have participated in the proceedings.
81 Case 264/82 [1985] ECR 849.
82 ibid., p. 865.
83 ibid., p. 866.
84 Note Advocate-General Lenz's theory of the 'criterion of impact' in Case C-309/89 above at note 60.

regulations beyond anti-dumping. Until this process of liberalization is completed inconsistencies will remain.

It does not seem sensible to give *locus standi* to an independent importer of goods covered by an anti-dumping regulation, such as Extramet, when importers of fruit covered by a Commission decision as to the level of import duty on that product do not have *locus standi*.[85] In the latter case it is because the importers are not part of a fixed and identifiable group and hence cannot show individual concern, and yet in the former case the importers are not fixed and identifiable. If this discrepancy is to be justified it must be on the basis that the importer was involved in the preliminary investigations by the Commission in establishing the anti-dumping duty. Even in such a case it is arguable that standing should be restricted to challenging the Commission's compliance, *vis-à-vis* the applicant, with the correct procedures during the investigation. The alternative, which would be preferable for upholding the rule of law and the rights of individuals, is for the Court to extend the liberalization seen in *Extramet* in relation to standing to challenge anti-dumping regulations to standing to challenge decisions that are not addressed to the applicant.

Decisions

It seems that the European Court will not look behind the label 'decision' on an EC measure to see if in fact it is an act of general application and hence not subject to review by non-privileged applicants.[86] If a decision merely confirms an earlier decision, then the action is inadmissible.[87] The crucial issue for non-privileged applicants is whether a decision that is not addressed to them is of direct and individual concern to them. A non-privileged applicant attacking a regulation also has to prove direct and individual concern.

Individual concern

The Court established the test for individual concern in the case of *Plaumann* v *Commission* and it has been followed in numerous subsequent cases:

85 See Case 25/62 *Plaumann* v *Commission* [1963] ECR 95 and Case 191/88 *Co-Frutta SARL* v *Commission* [1989] ECR 793, discussed on p. 238.
86 In Cases 142, 156/84 *BAT and Reynolds* v *Commission* [1987] ECR 4487, 4571, the Court did give some consideration to the content of a measure labelled as a decision to see if it was in substance a decision; there was no question of it being an act of general application.
87 Cases 166, 220/86 *Irish Cement Ltd* v *Commission* [1988] ECR 6473, 6503. See note 260.

Persons other than those to whom a decision is addressed may only claim to be individually concerned if that decision affects them by reason of certain attributes which are peculiar to them or by reason of circumstances in which they are differentiated from all other persons and by virtue of these factors distinguishes them individually just as in the case of the person addressed.[88]

In the *Plaumann* case the application was inadmissible. Plaumann, an importer of clementines into Germany, sought the annulment of a Commission decision addressed to Germany refusing to grant it authorization for the partial suspension of customs duties on clementines imported from third countries. The Court decided that Plaumann was not individually concerned by the decision because it affected all importers of clementines into Germany. This was not a fixed and identifiable group, because anyone, at any time, could begin to import clementines into Germany and would be adversely affected by the Commission's decision. The fact that Plaumann was one of about thirty-five existing importers of clementines into Germany did not suffice to create individual concern.

Importers of maize into Germany were more successful in challenging a Commission decision in the *Toepfer* case.[89] The decision in question was taken by the Commission on 3 October 1963. It retroactively authorized the German authorities to maintain protective measures to refuse certain maize import licences. The only people that could be affected by the decision were those persons, including the applicants, who had applied to the German authorities for a maize import licence on 1 October 1963. Thus when the Commission took its decision on 3 October, the number and identity of the importers had become 'fixed and ascertainable' and the Commission was in a position to know that the decision 'affected the interests and the position of the said importers alone'.[90]

To be individually concerned by a decision addressed to another person an applicant normally needs to show that he or she is part of a 'closed circle of persons who were known at the time of its adoption'. *Deutsche Lebensmittelwerke*[91] was brought by four German margarine manufacturers who supplied a substantial proportion of the margarine sold in West Berlin. They were concerned at the loss of sales of margarine precipitated by the Commission decision authorizing the sale of cheap Community

---

88 Case 25/62, note 85 above, p. 107. See also Case 231/82 *Spijker* v *Commission* [1983] ECR 2559, 2566; Case 97/85 *Deutsche Lebensmittelwerke* v *Commission* [1987] ECR 2265, 2286–7; Case 34/88 *Cevap and Others* v *Council* [1988] ECR 6265, 6270; Case 160/88R, note 40 above; Case 206/87 *Lefebvre Frère et Soeur* v *Commission* [1989] ECR 275, 288; and Case 191/88, note 85 above, p. 798.
89 Cases 106, 107/63 *Toepfer* v *Commission* [1965] ECR 405.
90 ibid., p. 411.
91 Case 97/85, note 88 above, p. 2287.

butter in West Berlin. A Court of nine judges decided the application was inadmissible: the applicants were not part of a 'closed circle', because the decision affected all suppliers of margarine on the West Berlin market – even new suppliers not known about when the decision was taken.

There are some cases where the Court has relaxed the 'fixed and ascertainable' rule. In *Control Data* v *Commission*[92] the Second Chamber concluded that the applicants had individual concern. The Commission had decided that two types of computers were not entitled, under the Common Customs Tariff, to be treated as of a scientific nature and hence free from import duty. The applicants were the sole importers of the particular types of computers into Belgium and were a wholly owned subsidiary of the US manufacturer of the computers. The computers could have been imported into other member states of the Community by other persons. Perhaps they would be only other subsidiaries of the parent company, because it might not have licensed any outsiders to import its products into the Community.[93] None the less no one could be certain that other importers might not be licensed by the parent company to sell the two types of computers in issue. Thus the applicants were not part of a 'fixed and ascertainable' group. The Court justified granting the applicants *locus standi* on the grounds that it 'would constitute an excessive degree of formalism'[94] to insist on the parent company, which clearly was individually concerned, bringing the action and, perhaps, because the Commission decision was in response to the applicants requesting zero rating for the two types of computers.

In *Piraiki-Patraiki* v *Commission*[95] the First Chamber was considering a Commission decision of 30 October 1984 authorizing France to impose a quota system on imports into France of cotton yarn from Greece between 1 November 1984 and 31 January 1985. The Court decided that the Greek exporters of cotton yarn to France who prior to 30 October 1984 had entered into contracts that were to be performed during the period when the quota system was to operate were individually concerned by the decision, because they were 'members of a limited class of traders identified or identifiable by the Commission and by reason of those contracts particularly affected by the decision at issue'.[96]

The Court's decision is a liberal one because the Commission decision as a whole did not apply to a fixed and ascertainable group of persons. It was possible, at least theoretically, that a Greek exporter could, after 30

92 Case 294/81 [1983] ECR 911.
93 See AG Slynn, ibid., p. 937.
94 ibid., p. 927.
95 Case 11/82 [1985] ECR 207.
96 ibid., p. 246.

October 1984, enter into a contract to sell cotton yarn that would be imported into France during the period of the import quotas. The Court was prepared to treat a sub-group of persons affected by the decision as being individually concerned.

It would seem unwise to read too much into the above two cases as they were both decided by only three judges. As noted above, in the context of regulations, there are some cases which demonstrate a move away from having to be part of a closed circle of persons to be individually concerned by a measure,[97] most significantly in the recent nine-judge decision in *Codorniu*. There are several judgments that show that the fixed-and-ascertainable test is departed from in relation to applicants who have been involved in Commission investigations into breaches of competition policy, into state aids or unlawful subsidies of products being imported into the Community.

Participants in Commission investigations

In *Metro* v *Commission*[98] the applicant was a self-service wholesaler (a 'cash and carry') dealing in electronic goods. It complained to the Commission about SABA refusing to allow such wholesalers, including itself, to sell its electronic goods, claiming that SABA was in breach of Articles 85 and 86 of the Treaty. Metro lodged its complaint in accordance with Article 3(2)(b) of Regulation No. 17.[99] After receiving the comments of Metro and SABA the Commission took a decision on 15 December 1975 that partially upheld Metro's complaint by making slight adjustments to the terms of SABA's distribution agreement with wholesalers, but not sufficiently to enable Metro to distribute SABA's products.

The European Court did not consider the question of whether Metro was part of a fixed and identifiable group to which the Commission's decision applied. Without doubt the decision affected any wholesaler who might have wished to distribute SABA's products. It was not possible for the Commission to know who, or how many, would be affected by the decision at the time it was taken. The Court's approach accorded special standing to complainants:

The contested decision was adopted in particular as the result of a complaint submitted by Metro and . . . it relates to the provisions of SABA's distribution system, on which SABA relied and continues to rely as against Metro in order to

97 See above at notes 57–65.
98 Case 26/76 [1977] ECR 1875.
99 It provides that those entitled to make application to the Commission complaining that an undertaking is infringing Art. 85 or Art. 86 of the Treaty are 'natural or legal persons who claim a legitimate interest'. See Ch. 24, pp. 756–62.

justify its refusal to sell to the latter or to appoint it as a wholesaler, and which the applicant had for this reason impugned in its complaint.

It is in the interests of a satisfactory administration of justice and of the proper application of Articles 85 and 86 that natural or legal persons who are entitled, pursuant to Article 3(2)(b) of Regulation No 17, to request the Commission to find an infringement of Articles 85 and 86 should be able, if their request is not complied with wholly or in part, to institute proceedings in order to protect their legitimate interests.[100]

When the Commission rejects by letter a complaint made under Article 3(2)(b) of Regulation 17, the complainant has *locus standi* to challenge the Commission's decision contained in the letter.[101] However, if the Commission does not take a final decision on a complaint made under Article 3(2)(b), the complainant does not have *locus standi* under Article 175 of the Treaty to force the Commission to take a final decision on the alleged infringement.[102]

In the context of the Merger Regulation[103] the Court of First Instance has given *locus standi* to Air France to challenge two decisions of the Commission concerning mergers by its competitors. In relation to the takeover of Dan Air by British Airways the Commissioner responsible had given an oral decision that it did not have a 'Community dimension' and therefore fell outside the scope of the Merger Regulation. The Court of First Instance decided that Air France was individually concerned by the decision.[104] The Commission's informal decision ruled out any need for the proposed concentration to be notified to the Commission under the Merger Regulation and hence deprived Air France of its procedural rights under Article 18(4) of the regulation if the Commission had decided there was a Community dimension and that proceedings should be initiated under Article 6(1)(c). In addition to the loss of procedural rights the Court of First Instance noted that Air France was the international air carrier most affected by BA's takeover of Dan Air.

As regards the common undertaking created by a transaction between BA and TAT, the French regional airline, Air France objected to the Commission's decision addressed to BA and TAT that they were not in breach of the Merger Regulation. The Court of First Instance accepted Air

---

100 Case 26/76, note 98 above, p. 1901. The Court's approach to admissibility of actions for annulment from complainants to the Comission about a breach of Arts. 85 or 86 was confirmed in Case 210/81 *Demo-Studio Schmidt* v *Commission* [1983] ECR 3045 and in the second *Metro* case, Case 75/84 *Metro* v *Commission* [1986] ECR 3021, 3080.
101 Cases 142, 156/84, note 86 above. See further Ch.24 at p. 758.
102 See Case 125/78 *GEMA* v Commission [1979] ECR 3173, 3190 and Ch.24, p. 759.
103 4064/89 (Corrected version published in OJ 1990 L257/90). See Ch.25 below.
104 Case T-3/93 *Air France* v *Commission* [1994] ECR II-121, 161–163.

France's claim that it was individually concerned by the decision on the basis of three factors.[105] First, Air France had responded to the Commission notification under Article 4(3) of the regulation that the notified concentration fell within the scope of the regulation. Second, Air France was the main competitor affected by the concentration and this was fully considered in the Commission's decision. Third, Air France was obliged by an agreement with the Commission and the French Government to give up the whole of its interest in TAT by a date before TAT and BA notified their concentration to the Commission.

It is difficult to extract clear principles from these cases as to when a competitor affected by a Commission decision under the Merger Regulation will be individually concerned. It is clearly not a requirement to be part of a fixed and identifiable group but whether it is sufficient to be a participant or potential participant in the preliminary investigations by the Commission remains to be seen. In Case T-2/93, the Commission and the United Kingdom Government invited the Court of First Instance to apply the principles laid down in the judgment of the Court of Justice in *COFAZ* v *Commission*[106] in the context of state aids. It is perhaps unfortunate that the Court of First Instance did not do so and couple significant involvement in the Commission's investigations with the merger significantly affecting the applicant's position in the market.

The position of natural and legal persons in challenging state aids is not so clearly set out as it is in relation to infringements of Articles 85 and 86 on competition. Article 93(2) of the Treaty simply provides that 'the parties concerned' can submit comments to the Commission if the latter decides to initiate an investigation into the lawfulness of a particular state aid. None the less it appears that natural or legal persons can be influential in persuading the Commission to initiate such investigations. This was the case in *COFAZ* v *Commission*,[107] where the French Trade Association, representing the applicants, submitted a complaint on 1 June 1983 to the Commission against the granting by the Netherlands of a preferential tariff for the supply of natural gas to Dutch producers of nitrate fertilizers. The complainants alleged that the preferential tariff was enabling the Dutch producers to undercut the French producers and increase the former's share of the French market from 9 per cent in 1980 to 21.7 per cent in 1982. The Commission initiated the procedure under Article 93(2) on 25 October 1983 and the French Trade Association was invited to submit comments and duly did so within the prescribed period. After changes made to the tariff by the Netherlands, the Commission decided on 17 April 1984 to

105 Case T-2/93 *Air France* v *Commission* [1994] ECR II-323, 340–342.
106 Case 169/84 [1986] ECR 391, discussed below.
107 ibid.

terminate the Article 93(2) procedure. COFAZ and other French nitrate fertilizer producers then brought an action under Article 173 for the annulment of the Commission's decision terminating the Article 93(2) procedure.

The European Court referred to the rights of complainants established in its case law on competition[108] and anti-dumping.[109] It concluded that where an applicant has been at the origin of the complaint that led to the Article 93(2) investigation and played a significant role in the Commission's investigations, then it will have *locus standi* provided that its position on the market is 'significantly affected by the aid' that is the subject of the Article 93(2) investigations.[110] At the admissibility stage it is sufficient for the applicant to adduce pertinent reasons to show that the Commission's decision 'may adversely affect their legitimate interests by seriously jeopardizing their position on the market in question'.[111] COFAZ was successful in doing so by showing the increase in Dutch exports to France between 1980 and 1982, and the application was admissible.

Although a trade association may initiate the complaint, the Court has decided that such associations do not have *locus standi* to bring an action under Article 173.[112] On the other hand, a body established by public law in the Netherlands to protect the interests of agricultural undertakings, taking into account the public interest, did have *locus standi* to challenge a Commission decision under Article 93(2) that a preferential tariff for natural gas to Dutch glasshouse growers should be discontinued.[113] The body concerned, Landbouwschap, had acted as negotiator of the gas tariffs in the Netherlands in the interests of the growers and had taken an active part in the procedure under Article 93(2) by submitting comments to the Commission and keeping in close contact with the responsible officials. Indeed, Landbouwschap was actually mentioned in the Commission's decision ordering the discontinuance of the preferential gas tariff. In Case 67/85, joined with Case 68/85, the Court decided that recipients of the preferential gas tariff had no *locus standi* because they had not been involved in the Article 93(2) procedures, had not negotiated the gas tariffs

---

108 ibid., pp. 414–15; see Case 26/76, note 98 above, and Case 210/81, note 100 above, discussed on pp. 240–41.

109 Case 264/82, note 81 above.

110 Case 169/84, note 106 above, p. 415.

111 ibid., p. 416.

112 Case 282/85 *DEFI* v *Commission* [1986] ECR 2469, following Cases 16, 17/62, note 42 above. However, the Court of First Instance in Case T-114/92 *Bureau Européen des Médias de L'Industrie Musicale* [*BEMIM*] v *Commission*, judgment of 24 January 1995, Proceedings 2/95, found an Art. 173 action from an association of undertakings admissible on the condition that it is entitled to represent the interests of its members and the conduct complained of is liable adversely to affect their interests.

113 Cases 67, 68 and 70/85 *Van der Kooy and Others* v *Commission* [1988] ECR 219, 268–9.

and were not mentioned in the decision. As the applicants were part of a group of growers that was not fixed and ascertainable, they lacked individual concern.[114]

If products that are imported into the Community are subsidized, the Community may under certain conditions impose a countervailing duty on the products to eliminate the advantage created by the subsidy.[115] If natural or legal persons complain to the Commission that the goods of their competitors outside the Community are being subsidized when imported into the Community, the Commission may initiate anti-subsidy proceedings. As with anti-dumping duty, any countervailing duty is imposed by regulation. However the Commission may, in response to a complainant, decide not to initiate an anti-subsidy investigation or to terminate such an investigation. In either case the complainant can bring an action under Article 173 to annul the Commission's decision not to investigate[116] or to terminate the investigation.[117] The Court is anxious to ensure that the procedural guarantees granted to complainants by the Community legislation on anti-subsidy proceedings are observed.[118]

Direct concern

Problems of direct concern arise in the situation where the application of a Community measure to the applicants depends on the exercise of discretion by a third party. In *Alcan* v *Commission*[119] the European Court held that the applicants lacked direct concern. Belgium and Luxembourg applied to the Commission for a quota of unwrought aluminium imports at a reduced rate of duty for 1968. The Commission decided on 12 May 1969 not to grant the application. Alcan and two other aluminium-refining companies who had imported unwrought aluminium during 1968 sought the annulment of the Commission's decision under Article 173. The Court decided that the applications were not directly concerned by the Commission's decision because even if the request of Belgium and Luxembourg had been granted by the Commission those two states would have had a discretion not to apply the reduced rate of duty to the imports made by the applicants. This is a particularly narrow interpretation of direct concern.

---

114 See ibid., pp. 267–8.
115 See Reg. 3284/94 (OJ 1994 L349/22).
116 Case 191/82 *Fediol* v *Commission* [1983] ECR 2913. See note 252 below.
117 Case 187/85 *Fediol* v *Commission* [1988] ECR 4155.
118 The procedural guarantees laid down in Reg. 3284/94 are quite elaborate; see Case 191/82, note 116 above, for a detailed discussion of the procedures contained in Reg. 3017/79, one of the statutory predecessors of Reg. 3284/94.
119 Case 69/69 [1970] ECR 385.

It is inconceivable that Belgium and Luxembourg would apply for a quota of imports of unwrought aluminium at a reduced tariff and then fail to use it. The persons who could benefit from the lower tariff were fixed and identifiable at the time the Commission's decision was taken in May 1969 because the decision applied only to imports made in 1968.

If the third party informs the applicant in advance of how it will exercise its discretion under the Community measure, then the applicant will be directly concerned. In *Bock* v *Commission*[120] Germany was authorized by Commission Decision 70/446 to exclude Chinese mushrooms from Community treatment. Bock was an importer of such mushrooms into Germany and it sought the annulment of the decision under Article 173. The Court decided that Bock was directly concerned by the decision even though Germany had a discretion not to use the authorization to exclude Chinese mushrooms from Community treatment, because Germany had fettered its own discretion by telling Bock that it would reject its application for a licence to import Chinese mushrooms as soon as it received the authorization from the Commission.

Another example of the Court adopting a less strict construction of direct concern is *Piraiki-Patraiki* v *Commission*.[121] The Commission decision authorizing France to institute a quota system on imports of cotton yarn from Greece was held to be of direct concern to the Greek exporters who brought the action. France had a discretion not to introduce such a quota system. The Court noted that this was 'entirely theoretical' because France had sought a system of import quotas more strict than that which was finally granted.[122]

Where the third party does have a genuine discretion in how it applies the Community measure, then those potentially affected by the measure do not have direct concern.[123] The *Mannesmann-Röhrenwerke* case[124] provides a typical example. The Community had entered into an arrangement with the United States concerning trade in steel pipes and tubes. Regulation 2335/85 allocated to Germany part of the Community's quota for export of those products to the United States. The applicants, German exporters of steel pipes and tubes, sought to annul the regulation. The Court did not consider whether the regulation was in reality a decision, but rather decided that the applicants were not directly concerned by the measure.

120 Case 62/70 [1971] ECR 897.
121 Case 11/82, note 95 above.
122 ibid., p. 242.
123 Case 333/85 *Mannesmann-Röhrenwerke* v Council [1987] ECR 1381; Case 55/86 *Arposol* v Council [1988] ECR 13; and Cases 89 and 91/86 *Étoile Commerciale and CNTA* v Commission [1987] ECR 3005.
124 Case 333/85, note 123 above.

245

The authorities in Germany had a discretion in deciding which undertakings would benefit from the German export quota.

GROUNDS OF REVIEW

Article 173 provides for four grounds of review: lack of competence, infringement of an essential procedural requirement, infringement of the Treaty or any rule of law relating to its application, and misuse of powers. Although the European Court does not always specify which ground it is relying on to annul a Community measure, it is helpful to examine each ground in turn.

Lack of competence

Lack of competence is applicable where the Community institution that has passed the Community measure in issue has done so in a way that exceeds the powers given to it by the Treaty or by the parent legislation under which the measure was passed.[125] There are very few examples of the Court upholding a plea of lack of competence,[126] but one example is *Germany and Others* v *Commission*.[127] Germany and four other member states sought to annul Commission Decision 85/381 on the basis that the Commission lacked competence to adopt the decision.[128] The decision set up a prior communication and consultation procedure on migration policies in relation to non-member states. The legal basis for the decision was Article 118 of the Treaty. That Article gives the Commission the task of 'promoting close cooperation between Member States in the social field'. The Commission is given the power explicitly to make studies, deliver opinions and arrange consultations. The applicant member states argued that the 'social field' mentioned in Article 118 did not extend to the

---

125 An example of the latter is Case 61/86 *United Kingdom* v *Commission* [1988] ECR 431, where the Court found that Commission Regulations No. 3451/85 and No. 9/86 were partially void because they exceeded the powers given to the Commission by Art. 9(3) of Council Regulation No. 1837/80. In a similar vein see Cases C-38 and 151/90 *Lomas and Others* [1992] ECR I-1781 and Case C-303/90 discussed above at note 32. The territorial scope of the Commission's powers to take competition decisions was called into question in the *Wood Pulp* case, Cases 89, 104, 116, 117 and 125–9/85 *Åhlström and Others* v *Commission* [1988] ECR 5193, but the Court found the decision to be within the Commission's competence; see Ch. 22, pp. 690–91.

126 The Court did do so in Case C-327/91 *France* v *Commission* [1994] ECR I-3641 when it decided that the Commission exceeded its competence when it concluded an international agreement with the United States because Art. 228 EC required it to be concluded by the Council. See also Case C-366/88 and Case C-303/90, note 32 above.

127 Cases 281, 283–5 and 287/85 [1987] ECR 3203.

128 The other grounds relied on by the applicants were rejected by the Court.

migration policies of the member states in relation to people from non-member states and that Article 118 does not give the Commission power to adopt binding decisions. The Court decided that the migration policies of member states in relation to people from non-member states did not fall entirely outside the scope of Article 118. The Court was influenced by the fact that the Council had passed several resolutions[129] since 1974 recognizing that the policies of the member states concerning immigration of people from non-member states does affect the Community's social policy, in particular because of its influence on the Community's employment market. The Court decided, however, that the part of Decision 85/381 relating to the cultural integration of workers from non-member states was void because 'migration policy is capable of falling within the social field within the meaning of Article 118 only to the extent to which it concerns the situation of workers from non-member countries as regards their impact on the Community employment market and on working conditions'.[130]

The Court decided that although Article 118 of the Treaty does not give the Commission an express power to take binding decisions, it does have such power where it is indispensable in order to carry out the task of promoting close cooperation between member states in the social field. The extent of that power, as determined by the Court, is to require the member states to notify essential information and to take part in consultations. The Commission exceeded its powers in part of the Decision by stating that the objective of the consultation is to ensure that the national draft measures and agreements on migration policy are in conformity with Community policies and actions.[131] The Commission has a power to make binding decisions only in relation to procedural matters under Article 118; it cannot pre-empt the outcome of the consultations by prescribing their objectives. In relation to the outcome of the consultations the Commission merely has a power under Article 118 to issue non-binding opinions.

The above case shows a careful balancing act by the Court in relation to the Commission's competence under Article 118. It is radical in that it reads into the Article a power to take binding decisions where the provision itself refers only to various non-binding measures, but the Court is properly cautious in ensuring that the Commission's power to take binding decisions is restricted to procedural matters. An indication of the importance of the case is the fact that it was decided by thirteen judges. It may be possible that the principle of subsidiarity introduced into the EC

---

129 See Cases 281, 283–5, 287/85, note 127 above, p. 3251. Council resolutions are non-binding measures.
130 ibid., p. 3252.
131 ibid., p. 3255; that part of the Decision was void.

Treaty at Maastricht in Article 3b will be used as a basis for arguing that the Community lacks competence to adopt particular measures. If the Court decides that the principle is justiciable, it might decide that a violation of it is an infringement of the Treaty rather than a lack of competence.

Infringement of an essential procedural requirement

Infringement of an essential procedural requirement arises where a Community measure has been passed without respecting the legislative process prescribed by the Treaty,[132] in contravention of the rules of procedure of the Community institution enacting the measure,[133] or where the requirements of Article 190 of the Treaty are not complied with because the measure does not have an adequate statement of reasons.[134]

In *Roquette Frères* v *Council* the Court established that it is an essential procedural requirement for the European Parliament to be consulted about a legislative proposal where the Treaty so requires. It is not enough for the Council simply to ask the Parliament for its opinion; it is usually necessary for it to wait for the opinion before passing the legislation. In *Roquette Frères* the Court pointed out that the Council had not exhausted the possibilities available to it for obtaining the opinion of Parliament. In particular, it did not request an extraordinary session of Parliament even though it can do so under Article 139 of the Treaty.[135] If, however, the need to pass the legislation is urgent and Parliament fails to discharge its obligation to cooperate sincerely with the Council then the Council is not obliged to wait for Parliament's opinion.[136] On the other hand, a failure to give an opinion at first reading in the Article 189b EC procedure could constitute a bar to the Council taking the matter any further because that Article gives the Parliament, expressly, a veto on making new legislation at later stages of the procedure.

In Case 68/86 *United Kingdom* v *Council*[137] the applicant sought to annul Directive 85/649 on the basis that it had been adopted by the Council

132 Case 138/79, note 55 above.
133 Case 68/86 *United Kingdom* v *Council* [1988] ECR 855; Case 131/86 note 38 above and Case C-137/92P *Commission* v *BASF AG and Others* [1994] ECR I-2555, noted at p. 52 above.
134 Case 24/62 *Germany* v *Commission* [1963] ECR 63; Case 158/80 *Rewe* v *Hauptzollamt Kiel* [1981] ECR 1805; Case 203/85 *Nicolet Instrument* v *Hauptzollamt Frankfurt am Main-Flughafen* [1986] ECR 2049. See further at pp. 144–5 above.
135 Case 138/79 note 55 above, p. 3361. The key passage from the Court's judgment is quoted in Ch. 4, p. 112.
136 Case C-65/93 *European Parliament* v *Council*, judgment of 30 March 1995, noted at p. 109 above.
137 Note 133 above.

using the written procedure even though the use of that procedure had been opposed by the applicant and Denmark. Article 6(1) of the Council's Rules of Procedure provided that a Community measure can be adopted by use of the written procedure only 'where all the members of the Council agree to that procedure in respect of the matter in question'.

The European Court decided that a breach of Article 6(1) constituted an infringement of an essential procedural requirement. Unfortunately, it gave no indication as to why it regarded compliance with Article 6(1) of the Council's Rules of Procedure as an 'essential' rather than 'inessential' procedural requirement.[138]

The United Kingdom was also successful in challenging a Council Directive in Case 131/86.[139] The General Secretariat of the Council altered the preamble to Directive 86/113 after it had been voted on and approved by the Council. The European Court accepted that the General Secretariat could correct spelling and grammar but could not alter the content of the measure in question. The Court regarded the changes in the preamble as affecting the content of the measure, given that it concerned the statement of reasons required by Article 190 of the Treaty.[140]

It has long been established that a failure to include an adequate statement of reasons in Community legislation is a breach of Article 190 of the Treaty and is sufficient cause for the Court to annul the legislation. It is not clear whether the Court regards it as an infringement of an essential procedural requirement or an infringement of the Treaty or both. It would seem to be both. In one of the early cases, *Germany v Commission*,[141] the Court laid down the purpose of the statement of reasons:

In imposing upon the Commission the obligation to state reasons for its decisions, Article 190 is not taking mere formal considerations into account but seeks to give an opportunity to the parties of defending their rights, to the Court of exercising its supervisory functions and to Member States and to all interested nationals of ascertaining the circumstances in which the Commission has applied the Treaty.[142]

The Commission decision, taken under Article 25 of the Treaty, authorized

---

138 This is particularly unsatisfactory in that AG Lenz advocated that the United Kingdom's action should be dismissed as unfounded; ibid., p. 891. Cf p. 183 above.
139 Note 38 above.
140 ibid., pp. 934–5.
141 Case 24/62, note 134 above. The parties argued the case on the basis that a failure to comply with Art. 190 constituted an infringement of an essential procedural requirement; see p. 145.
142 ibid., p. 69. Similar wording is used by the Court in Case 158/80 and Case 203/85, note 134 above; Case 45/86, note 38 above, p. 1519; Case 258/84 *Nippon Seiko v Council* [1987] ECR 1923; 1966; and Case 131/86, note 38 above, p. 935.

Germany to import 100,000 hectolitres of wine at a lower rate of duty than the common external tariff. Germany had applied to import 450,000 hectolitres at the reduced rate of duty. The Commission could make the authorization only 'provided that no serious disturbance of the market of the products concerned results therefrom'.[143] The Court found the Commission's statement of reasons to be inadequate, vague and inconsistent and hence in breach of Article 190. It was inadequate and vague in that it concluded that 'the production of the wines in question is amply sufficient' by referring to the unspecified information it had collected. It was contradictory in that it still allowed 100,000 hectolitres to be imported at the reduced rate of duty although it had concluded that the Community production of the wines was 'amply sufficient'.

Obviously the statement of reasons must not be vague or contradictory; rather it 'must disclose in a clear and unequivocal fashion the reasoning followed by the Community authority which adopted the measure in question'.[144]

The Court is prepared to accept a 'laconic' statement of reasons,[145] particularly in relation to regulations that fall within the general scheme of the body of measures of which they form part.[146]

The statement of reasons in the preamble to Community legislation should refer to its legal basis. Failure to make an explicit reference to the legal basis is an infringement of an essential procedural requirement where the legal basis cannot, with certainty, be determined from other parts of the measure.[147]

Reference to the wrong legal basis is also a ground for annulment of a Community measure, though it is not clear if the Court regards this as an infringement of an essential procedural requirement or of the Treaty.[148] Problems arise where more than one legal basis may be appropriate. In two cases brought by the United Kingdom against the Council the United Kingdom argued that the directives concerned should have been adopted under Article 100 of the Treaty as well as Article 43.[149] This would have

143 Art. 28(3) of the Treaty.
144 Case 258/84 note 142 above, at p. 1966, quoting from Case 203/85, note 134 above. An example of a statement of reasons that was inadequate due to being contradictory is Case 158/80, note 134 above, pp. 1833–4.
145 See Case 108/81 *Amylum* v *Council* [1982] ECR 3107, 3135; Case 203/85, note 134 above, p. 2059.
146 See Case 250/84 *Eridania* [1986] ECR 117; Case 55/87 *Moksel* v *Balm* [1988] ECR 3845, 3873; Case 167/88 *AGPB* v *ONIC* [1989] ECR 1653, 1686; Case C-27/89 *Scarpe* [1990] ECR 1-1701, 1733; and Case C-27/90 *SITPA* [1991] ECR 1-133, 158–9. The statement of reasons in such regulations is 'not required to specify the often very numerous and complex matters of fact or of law dealt with' in them.
147 Case 45/86, note 38 above, pp. 1519–20, discussed in Ch. 5, pp. 141–5.
148 It would seem to be both. Cf. Ch.5, pp. 141–3.
149 Case 68/86, note 133 above, and Case 131/86, note 38 above.

had the practical effect that the measures would have required unanimity rather than a qualified majority in the Council and could not have been adopted, as they were opposed by the United Kingdom and Denmark. The directives related to the prohibition of the use in livestock farming of certain substances having a hormonal action and the minimum conditions for keeping battery hens. The United Kingdom argued that these measures concerned not simply the common agricultural policy but also harmonized national laws regarding, respectively, consumer protection and animal welfare. The United Kingdom contended that in the past such measures had always been adopted by the Council using a dual legal basis of Articles 43 and 100. The Court decided that both directives contributed to the objectives of the common agricultural policy laid down in Article 39 of the Treaty and that

even where the legislation in question is directed both to objectives of agricultural policy and to other objectives which, in the absence of specific provision, are pursued on the basis of Article 100 of the Treaty, that article, a general one under which directives may be adopted for the approximation of the laws of the Member States, cannot be relied on as a ground for restricting the field of application of Article 43 of the Treaty.[150]

The Court stated that the choice of the legal basis for a measure must be based on objective factors that are amenable to judicial review. A Community institution cannot by practice create a binding precedent as to the correct legal basis.[151]

A dual legal basis for a measure can be the appropriate solution. In Case 165/87 *Commission v Council*[152] the Court decided that a dual legal basis of Articles 28 and 113 of the Treaty was appropriate for a Council decision concerning the conclusion of an international convention covering tariff nomenclature and the Community's external trade statistics. The Commission had argued that Article 113 on the common commercial policy was sufficient. However, the Court noted that neither Article 28 allowing the Council to change the duties in the common customs tariff, nor Article 113, which allows for the conclusion of tariff and trade agreements as part of the common commercial policy, 'expressly gives the Council power to establish a tariff nomenclature'.[153] The Court inferred a general power for the Council in relation to tariff matters on the basis of a combination of both Articles. This dual legal basis would have no consequences in the long term because, after the Single European Act came into force, both Articles

150 Case 68/86, note 133 above, p. 896, Case 131/86, note 38 above, p. 931.
151 Case 68/86, note 133 above, p. 898 and Case 131/86, note 38 above, p. 933.
152 [1988] ECR 5545.
153 ibid., p. 5560.

required a qualified majority in the Council. However, a dual legal basis will not be acceptable where it compromises the effectiveness of the cooperation procedure or, presumably, the conciliation and veto procedure or the assent procedure introduced in the Treaty agreed at Maastricht.

In the *Titanium Dioxide* case[154] the Commission sought the annulment of Council Directive 89/428 on the ground that its legal basis should have been Article 100a, which required the cooperation procedure, rather than Article 130s, which required unanimity in the Council following simple consultation of the European Parliament. The Directive concerned procedures for harmonizing the programmes for the reduction and eventual elimination of pollution caused by waste from the titanium dioxide industry. The Court acknowledged that it presented both the characteristics of a measure in relation to the environment within the meaning of Article 130s and that of a harmonization measure whose object was the establishment and operation of the internal market within the meaning of Article 100a. A dual legal basis would, however, require unanimity in the Council and hence deprive the cooperation procedure of its very substance by removing the European Parliament's power to influence the voting system in the Council. The Court decided that this was unacceptable and that therefore the measure must have one legal basis. The Court ruled that it should be Article 100a EEC, partly because Article 100a(3) explicitly refers to measures concerning environmental protection being within the scope of Article 100a EEC and states that such measures should be based on a 'high level of protection' of the environment. The Court also pointed out that Article 130r(2) stated that 'environmental protection requirements shall be a component of the Community's other policies'.[155]

The broad lawmaking power provided for in Article 235 of the Treaty can be used only 'where no other provision of the Treaty gives the Community institutions the necessary power to adopt the measure in question'.[156] In Case 165/87[157] the decision in question was adopted when

---

154 Case C-300/89 *Commission* v *Council* [1991] ECR I-2867, noted by Somsen, (1992) 29 CMLRev 140.

155 Maastricht amendments have changed the Treaty provisions discussed in this case. Art. 100a EC requires the conciliation and veto procedure of Art. 189b EC; Art. 130s(1) EC provides for the cooperation procedure set out in Art. 189c EC; and the relevant part of Art. 130r(2) EC provides that 'environmental protection requirements must be integrated into the definition and implementation of other Community policies'. The Court decided that Art. 130s rather than Art. 100a was the correct legal basis in two cases concerning waste, Case C-155/91 *Commission* v *Council* [1993] ECR I-939 and Case C-187/93 *European Parliament* v *Council* [1994] ECR I-2857, see p. 515 below.

156 Case 45/86, note 38 above, p. 1520 (the *Generalized Tariff Preferences* case) discussed in Ch. 5, p. 143. Case 224/87 *Commission* v *Council* [1989] ECR 1425 provides an example of where the use of Art. 235 as the legal basis was justified.

157 Note 152 above.

Article 28 required unanimity, hence the reliance by the Council in this case on Article 235 (which also requires unanimity) as well as Articles 28 and 113 did not lead to the decision being annulled even though the Court ruled that Article 235 was not an appropriate legal basis, because the decision could be based on Articles 28 and 113. In Case 275/87[158] a Council regulation of 13 July 1987 that had been based on Article 235 was annulled because the Court decided the proper legal basis was Articles 28 and 113, which both required qualified majority voting in the Council. The Single European Act had come into force prior to 13 July 1987, changing the voting requirements in Article 28 from unanimity to qualified majority.

Infringement of the Treaty or of any rule of law relating to its application

In relation to infringement of the Treaty there is considerable overlap with the two previous grounds of review. If a measure is passed that goes beyond the scope permitted by the Treaty, it can be struck down for lack of competence, but it is also an infringement of the Treaty. Likewise, if the measure is passed with an inadequate statement of reasons or without a clear legal basis or on the wrong legal basis, it can be struck down as an infringement of an essential procedural requirement but it is also, by not complying with Article 190, an infringement of the Treaty. The Court is doubtless aware of this point, which may explain its reluctance to specify which ground of review it is relying on, particularly in cases concerning the correct legal basis for a measure.

The Court's power to annul a measure because it infringes any rule of law relating to the application of the Treaty enables the Court to strike down legislation that is not in accord with the general principles of law that the Court itself has developed. It is not within the scope of this book to give a detailed account of the general principles of law,[159] but they will be described in brief using selected cases to help to illustrate their nature. The Treaty does not explicitly refer to general principles of law other than in the particular context of the non-contractual liability of the Community.[160] A more general foundation for general principles of law could be read into the seemingly innocent reference to 'the law' in Article 164 of

---

158 *Commission* v *Council* [1989] ECR 259; see also Case C-295/90, p. 608 below.
159 See Schwarze, *European Administrative Law*; Arnull, *EEC Law and the Individual*; Schermers and Waelbroeck, *Judicial Protection*, pp. 27–94; Hartley, *European Community Law*, pp. 137–64; Brown and Kennedy, *The Court of Justice of the European Communities*, pp. 323–42.
160 See Art. 215, which refers to 'the general principles common to the laws of the Member States', discussed in Ch. 10 at pp. 313–19.

the Treaty[161] – 'The Court of Justice shall ensure that in the interpretation and application of this Treaty the law is observed' – and to 'any rule of law relating to' the application of the Treaty in Article 173. The European Court has chosen not to articulate a legal basis in the Treaty for the general principles of law that it has developed. It is a source of judge-made law that is limited only by judicial self-restraint.[162]

Fundamental human rights

After an initial reluctance to develop human rights as a general principle of Community law,[163] the European Court espoused the notion for the first time in *Stauder* v *Ulm*.[164] The case turned on the interpretation of the different language texts of a Commission decision.[165] The liberal interpretation given by the Court to the decision avoided any possibility of a breach of fundamental human rights, but the Court established its acceptance of the concept by saying: 'Interpreted in this way the provision at issue contains nothing capable of prejudicing the fundamental human rights enshrined in the general principles of Community law and protected by the Court.'[166]

The Court developed the concept of fundamental human rights in the *Internationale Handelsgesellschaft* case by saying that the rights are 'inspired by the constitutional traditions common to the Member States'.[167] The Court clarified the significance of the constitutions of the member states, and recognized the influence of international treaties on human rights, in establishing Community fundamental rights in the landmark case of *Nold* v *Commission*:

As the Court has already stated, fundamental rights form an integral part of the general principles of law, the observance of which it ensures.

In safeguarding these rights, the Court is bound to draw inspiration from constitutional traditions common to the Member States, and it cannot therefore uphold measures which are incompatible with fundamental rights recognized and protected by the Constitutions of those States.

---

161 Advocate-General Warner did explicitly refer to Art. 164 as the basis for regarding the right to be heard as one of the rights that 'the law' upholds and that the Court must ensure is observed; see Case 17/74 *Transocean Marine Paint* v *Commission* [1974] ECR 1063.

162 For a comment on the dangers of this position, see p. 140.

163 Case 1/58 *Stork* v *High Authority* [1959] ECR 17, 26; and Cases 36–8, 40/59 *Geitling* v *High Authority* [1960] ECR 423, 438.

164 Case 29/69 [1969] ECR 419.

165 Discussed in Ch. 6, note 65.

166 Case 29/69, note 164 above, p. 425.

167 Case 11/70 [1970] ECR 1125, 1134.

Similarly, international treaties for the protection of human rights on which the Member States have collaborated or of which they are signatories, can supply guidelines, which should be followed within the framework of Community law.[168]

One issue that remains uncertain is the number of constitutions of the member states that must contain a particular fundamental right before the European Court will regard it as a general principle of law. It has been argued that it is sufficient for the right to be contained in the constitution of one of the member states for the Court to adopt it as a general principle of law.[169] The case of *Staatsanwalt Freiburg* v *Keller*[170] indicates the Court's reluctance to be seen to be declaring a Community measure invalid simply because it conflicts with a right contained in the constitution of a member state. It would seem that normally a right must be found in more than one constitution before it will be regarded as a general principle of law. The Court is prepared to consider explicitly individual provisions of national constitutions on fundamental rights in determining the scope of the Community general principle of law'.[171]

The most significant of the international treaties on human rights to which the Court has referred is the European Convention on Human Rights.[172] While the Court is not bound by the Convention, it has stated that 'the principles on which that Convention is based must be taken into consideration in Community law'.[173]

The Court of Justice has not, as yet, explicitly referred to the case law of the European Court of Human Rights concerning the Convention, but it has explicitly noted the lack of such case law on a particular subject.[174]

In the context of preliminary rulings under Article 177 it is possible for a national court to ask questions on the meaning of Community fundamental rights whenever it is dealing with national rules that are within the scope of Community law. The national court must ensure that the national

---

168 Case 4/73 [1974] ECR 491, 507.
169 See Hartley, *European Community Law* (2nd ed., 1988), p. 136 (in the 3rd ed., 1994 at p. 143, Hartley no longer favours that view having considered the consequences of it in the light of the Irish constitutional prohibition on abortion as an aspect of the fundamental right to life); Schermers and Waelbroeck, *Judicial Protection* (1987, 4th ed.), p. 30; and Advocate-General Warner in the *IRCA* case, Case 7/76 [1976] ECR 1213, 1237.
170 Case 234/85 [1986] ECR 2897; [1987] 1 CMLR 875.
171 See Case 44/79 *Hauer* v *Land Rheinland-Pfalz* [1979] ECR 3727, 3744–50, where the Court referred to the German, Italian and Irish constitutions in establishing the scope of the right to property.
172 The Court has also referred to the European Social Charter of 18 November 1961 and Convention 111 of the International Labour Organization of 25 June 1958 in Case 149/77 *Defrenne* v *Sabena* [1978] ECR 1365.
173 Case 222/84 *Johnston* v *Chief Constable of the RUC* [1986] ECR 1651, 1682.
174 Cases 46/87 and 227/88 *Hoechst* v *Commission* [1989] ECR 2859, 2924.

rules are compatible with Community fundamental rights.[175] Fundamental human rights have been relied on in numerous cases to challenge the validity of Community legislation. The Court has often considered the issue of principle but decided on the facts that the legislation does not breach any fundamental right.[176] A rare example of a successful challenge to Community legislation based on fundamental human rights is found in *R v Kirk*.[177] Captain Kirk boldly went where no Danish fisherman had gone before. He went fishing within the United Kingdom's twelve-mile coastal zone on 6 January 1983 and was arrested and charged under a United Kingdom Order in Council prohibiting Danish fishing boats from fishing inside this limit.[178] Kirk argued that he had a right as a Community national to fish anywhere in Community waters, and the Crown Court decided to refer the case to the European Court for a preliminary ruling.

Article 100 of the Act of Accession of the United Kingdom to the European Community had permitted the United Kingdom, in derogation from other provisions of Community law, to continue to exclude fishing boats from some other member states, including Denmark, from the United Kingdom's twelve-mile zone up to 31 December 1982. On 25 January 1983 the Council adopted Regulation 170/83 permitting the United Kingdom to maintain the derogation for another ten years as from 1 January 1983. Kirk, however, was fishing after the derogation under the

---

175 See Case 5/88 *Wachauf* v *Germany* [1989] ECR 2609; Case C-260/89 *ERT* [1991] ECR I-2925, 2964; Case C-159/90 *SPUC* v *Grogan* [1991] ECR I-4685, 4741; and Case C-2/92 *Bostock* [1994] ECR I-955. See also J. Temple Lang, 'The Sphere in which Member States are obliged to comply with the General Principles of Law and Community Fundamental Rights Principles', LIEI 1991/2, p. 23; and Weiler and Lockhart, '"Taking Rights Seriously" Seriously: The European Court and its Fundamental Rights Jurisprudence – Part I' (1995) 32 CMLRev 51, 63–82.

176 The cases arise in the context of preliminary rulings under Art. 177 as well as actions for annulment under Art. 173. See Case 98/79 *Pecastaing* v *Belgium* [1980] ECR 691, 716 (right to a fair hearing, Art. 6 of the European Convention on Human Rights); Cases 154, 205–6, 226–8, 263–4/78, and 31, 39, 83 and 85/79 *Valsabbia* v *Commission* [1980] ECR 907, 1010–11 (right to property, Art. 1 of the First Protocol to the European Convention on Human Rights); Case 136/79 *National Panasonic (UK) Ltd* v *Commission* [1980] ECR 2033, 2056–8 (right to privacy, Art. 8 of the Convention); Cases 100–103/80 *Musique Diffusion Française* v *Commission* [1983] ECR 1825, 1880–81 (right to a fair hearing, Art. 6 of the Convention); Cases 43 and 63/82 *VBVB & VBBB* v *Commission* [1984] ECR 19, 61–2 (freedom of expression, Art. 10 of the Convention); Case 222/84, note 173 above (right to a legal remedy, Arts. 6 and 13 of the Convention); Case 234/85, note 170 above (freedom to pursue a trade or profession); Case 265/87 *Schräder* v *Hauptzollamt Gronau* [1989] ECR 2237 (right to property, Art. 1 of the First Protocol); Cases 46/87 and 227/88, note 174 above (right to protection of privacy of business premises, Art. 8 of the Convention); Case C-100/88 *Oyowe and Traroe* v *Commission* [1989] ECR 4285 (freedom of expression); Case C-260/89, note 175 above, 2963–6 (freedom of expression, Art. 10 of the Convention).

177 Case 63/83 [1984] ECR 2689; [1985] 1 All ER 453.

178 SI 1982 No. 1849.

Act of Accession had expired and before the Council regulation had been adopted. At that time he had a right under Community law to fish in the United Kingdom's twelve-mile zone. The Court decided that the purported retroactivity of Council Regulation 170/83 could not have the effect of validating *ex post facto* the penal provisions in the United Kingdom Order in Council. The Court established that:

The principle that penal provisions may not have retroactive effect is one which is common to all the legal orders of the Member States and is enshrined in Article 7 of the European Convention for the Protection of Human Rights and Fundamental Freedoms of 4 November 1950 as a fundamental right; it takes its place among the general principles of law whose observance is ensured by the Court of Justice.[179]

Another example of a successful case based on human rights is *Razzouk and Beydoun v Commission*, which states that the principle of 'equal treatment of both sexes . . . forms part of the fundamental rights the observance of which the Court has a duty to ensure'.[180] This principle was applied to annul the Commission decision refusing to grant a widower's pension, because it treated 'surviving spouses of officials unequally according to the sex of the persons concerned'.[181] At Maastricht political recognition was given to the place of fundamental rights by Article F(2) of the Treaty on European Union:

The Union shall respect fundamental rights, as guaranteed by the European Convention for the Protection of Human Rights and Fundamental Freedoms signed in Rome on 4 November 1950 and as they result from the constitutional traditions common to the Member States, as general principles of Community law.

However, this provision is not part of Community law and is not justiciable by the European Court.[182]

The Council has requested an Opinion from the Court under Article 228 EC as to whether it would be competent for the Community to negotiate and conclude an agreement acceding to the European Convention on Human Rights.[183] The concern is whether the acceptance of the

179 Case 63/83, note 177 above, ECR at 2718; 1 All ER at 462.
180 Cases 75, 117/82 [1984] ECR 1509, 1530.
181 See also Case 374/87 *Orkem* v *Commission* [1989] ECR 3283, where an argument based on the rights of the defence was upheld and Case C-404/92P *X* v *Commission* [1994] ECR I-4737 in which a Commission decision not to appoint X to its staff was annulled because X's right to respect for his private life was violated when his refusal to take an Aids test was circumvented.
182 See Art. L of the Treaty on European Union. However, the Court of First Instance did quote Art. F(2) TEU in Case T-10/93 *A* v *Commission* [1994] ECR II-183, 201.
183 See Opinion 2/94 recorded as a new case in *Proceedings of the Court of Justice* No. 14/94.

jurisdiction of the European Court of Human Rights to adjudicate on questions of Community law would be incompatible with the role given to the Court of Justice by the EC Treaty.

Legitimate expectations

The Court will strike down Community legislation that infringes the legitimate expectations of concerned persons. In the *Staff Salaries* case[184] the Court annulled part of Council Regulation 2647/72, which had provided for a level of increase of the salaries of Community staff below that adopted by a decision of the Council some nine months earlier. The decision, which the Court found to be binding on the Council, provided for a system of increases in staff salaries for a period of three years. It referred to two indices and gave the Council some discretion in the application of them. However, the Court found that the Council had 'violated the rule relating to the protection of legitimate confidence'[185] in the regulation by providing for an increase below the level of the lower of the two indices referred to in the decision.

In *Mulder* v *Minister van Landbouw en Visserij*[186] the Court found parts of certain Community regulations relating to milk marketing to be invalid on the ground that they breached the principle of protection of legitimate expectations. Certain milk producers had opted out of delivering milk for five years under a Community scheme to reduce the excess supply of milk in the Community. At the end of the five-year period they found themselves unable to resume delivering milk because of provisions in EC regulations that did not take account of their situation but instead were based on milk marketing in a reference year during the five-year period when those producers marketed nothing. The Court said that where a producer

has been encouraged by a Community measure to suspend marketing for a limited period in the general interest and against payment of a premium he may legitimately expect not to be subject, upon the expiry of his undertaking, to restrictions which

---

184 Case 81/72 *Commission* v *Council* [1973] ECR 575.
185 ibid., p. 586. By the time of Case 112/77, note 46 above, pp. 1032–3, the English phrase was established as 'legitimate expectation' rather than 'legitimate confidence' (see the explanation of this in Usher, 'The Influence of National Concepts on Decisions of the European Court' (1976) 1 ELRev 359, 363). The Court found no breach of the principle, but confirmed its application to Art. 173 cases by saying that 'the principle in question forms part of the Community legal order with the result that any failure to comply with it is an "infringement of this Treaty or of any rule of law relating to its application" within the meaning of' Art. 173.
186 Case 120/86 [1988] ECR 2321, confirmed in Case 170/86 *von Deetzen* v *Hauptzollamt Hamburg-Jonas* [1988] ECR 2355.

specifically affect him precisely because he availed himself of the possibilities offered by the Community provisions.[187]

Challenges to Community legislation on the basis of a breach of legitimate expectations are quite frequent but rarely succeed. It is long established that 'traders cannot have a legitimate expectation that an existing situation which is capable of being altered by the Community institutions in the exercise of their discretionary power will be maintained'.[188]

This principle is particularly true in the area of the common organization of the markets in agriculture. Traders here may gain an advantage from Community legislation at one particular time, but economic circumstances may alter in a way that compels the Community institutions to change the legislation to their detriment.[189]

Legitimate expectations may arise where a Community institution gives an undertaking and then reneges on it[190] or where a Community institution acts in a particular way over a sufficiently long period as to establish a consistent practice and a legitimate expectation on the part of those affected by the practice that it will be maintained. The latter concept is debatable. It is derived from the GCHQ case[191] in the United Kingdom, where it applied to a consistent practice on the part of the Government in consulting trade unions at GCHQ before changing the terms and conditions of employment of the work-force there. It is not applicable to the choice of legal basis for a Community measure contrary to consistent prior practice.[192] It would seem unlikely that a consistent practice could impinge on a legislative measure (a true regulation or directive), but it may fetter the discretion of a Community institution in the context of a decision.

Proportionality

One of the leading cases on the application of the general principle of proportionality is commonly referred to as the *Skimmed-Milk Powder* case.[193] On 15 March 1976 the Council adopted Regulation 563/76 on the compulsory purchase of skimmed-milk powder. At the time the stocks of skimmed-milk powder held by the intervention agencies were very consid-

---

187 ibid., Case 120/86 at p. 2352, Case 170/86 at p. 2372.

188 See Case C-350/88 *Delacre and Others* v *Commission* [1990] ECR I-395, 426 and the many cases cited therein.

189 ibid. and Cases C-133, 300 and 362/93 *Crispoltoni* [1994] ECR I-4863, 4909.

190 This is similar to the situation in the *Staff Salaries* case, p. 258 above.

191 *Council of Civil Service Unions* v *Minister for the Civil Service* [1985] AC374.

192 Case 131/86, note 38 above, p. 933.

193 Case 114/76 *Bela-Mühle* v *Grows-Farm* [1977] ECR 1211.

erable and increasing. The regulation sought to reduce the stocks by making the grant of the aids provided for certain vegetable protein products as well as the free circulation in the Community of certain imported animal food products subject to the obligation to purchase specified quantities of skimmed-milk powder. The compulsory purchase of the powder was imposed at a price equal to about three times its value as animal feed. The European Court decided that the legitimate aim of reducing the skimmed-milk powder stocks could have been met without imposing an unnecessary burden on non-milk producers. A compulsory purchase price for skimmed-milk powder of three times its value as animal feed imposed a disproportionate burden on importers and users of animal feed. The Court found the regulation to be null and void.

It is now settled case law that in order to establish whether a provision of Community law complies with the principle of proportionality

it must be ascertained whether the means which it employs are suitable for the purpose of achieving the desired objective and whether they do not go beyond what is necessary to achieve it. Furthermore . . . if a measure is patently unsuited to the objective which the competent institution seeks to pursue this may affect its legality.[194]

Though the plea that Community legislation breaches the general principle of proportionality is often invoked, it is rarely successful. If the legislation requires forfeiture of all security granted by the applicant, even for minor, technical breaches of the contract, then the Court may uphold a plea of disproportionality. In the *Atalanta* case the Court found Article 5(2) of Commission Regulation 1889/76 contrary to the principle of proportionality. The Article provided that 'the security shall be wholly forfeit if the obligations imposed by the contract are not fulfilled'. The Court objected to this Article because it did not 'permit the penalty for which it provides to be made commensurate with the degree of failure to implement the contractual obligations or with the seriousness of the breach of those obligations'.[195]

Similarly, in *Man (Sugar)* v *IBAP*,[196] where the delay of a few hours in

---

194 Joined Cases 279, 280, 285 and 286/84 *Rau* v *Commission* [1987] ECR 1069, 1125–6. See also Case 138/78 *Stölting* v *Hauptzollamt Hamburg-Jonas* [1979] ECR 713; Case 122/78 *Buitoni* v *FORMA* [1979] ECR 677; Case 66/82 *Fromançais SA* v *FORMA* [1983] ECR 395; Case 181/84 *Man (Sugar)* v *IBAP* [1985] ECR 2889; Case 21/85 *Maas* v *Bundesanstalt für Landwirtschaftliche Marktordnung* [1986] ECR 3537. The phrase 'patently unsuited' is rendered 'manifestly inappropriate' in Case C-331/88 *Fedesa and Others* [1990] ECR I-4023, 4063 where 'even substantial negative financial consequences for certain traders' may be justified by the importance of the objectives pursued (p. 4064).

195 Case 240/78 *Atalanta* v *Produktschap voor Vee en Vlees* [1979] ECR 2137, 2151.

196 Case 181/84 [1985] ECR 2889.

applying for an export licence had led, in accordance with the relevant regulation, to the forfeiture of the whole security, the Court of Justice found a violation of the principle of proportionality. In both cases the Court suggested the absolute rule of total loss of security should be replaced with a discretionary rule making the level of forfeiture proportionate to the gravity of the breach of contract.

The Treaty on European Union gave a position within the EC Treaty to the principle of proportionality. The last paragraph of Article 3bEC states that: 'Any action by the Community shall not go beyond what is necessary to achieve the objectives of this Treaty.'

Equality of treatment/non-discrimination

Prohibitions of discrimination are found in specific provisions of the Community Treaty. These include Article 7 EEC/Article 6 EC prohibiting discrimination on grounds of nationality;[197] Article 40(3) prohibiting discrimination between producers or consumers in the Community in the context of the common agricultural policy;[198] and Article 119 prohibiting discrimination based on sex in the context of the pay of men and women. The European Court has said that these provisions are merely specific enunciations of 'the general principle of equality which is one of the fundamental principles of Community law. That principle requires that similar situations shall not be treated differently unless the differentation is objectively justified.'[199]

The Court has used the general principle of equality of treatment to extend the prohibition on overt discrimination by reason of nationality to 'all covert forms of discrimination which, by the application of other criteria of differentation, lead in fact to the same result'.[200] The Court has also used the equality of treatment principle to extend the scope of the prohibition of discrimination on grounds of sex in the context of pay to pension rights[201] and to allowances paid to Community officials.[202]

The *Skimmed-Milk Powder* case, discussed above,[203] is an example of inequality of treatment that could not be objectively justified. The animal-

---

197 See Case 293/83 *Gravier* v *City of Liège* [1985] ECR 593; Case 59/85 *Netherlands* v *Reed* [1986] ECR 1283; Case 186/87 *Cowan* v *Trésor Public* [1989] ECR 195.
198 See, e.g., Cases 103, 145/77 *Royal Scholten-Honig* v *IBAP* [1978] ECR 2037; Case 300/86 *Van Landschoot* v *Mera* [1988] ECR 3443.
199 See ibid., Cases 103, 145/77, at p. 2072, and Case 300/86. p. 3460.
200 Case 152/73 *Sotgiu* v *Deutsche Bundespost* [1974] ECR 153, 164.
201 See Case 1/72 *Frilli* v *Belgium* [1972] ECR 457, 466; Cases 75, 117/82 *Razzouk and Beydoun* v *Commission* [1984] ECR 1509, 1530.
202 Case 20/71 *Sabbatini* v *European Parliament* [1972] ECR 345.
203 See Case 114/76, note 193 above.

feed producers and importers were compelled to buy skimmed-milk powder at three times its value as animal feed. This discriminated in favour of skimmed-milk powder producers and against animal-feed producers in an unjustifiable way.

In *Weiser* v *Caisse nationale des barreaux français*, the Court described the principle of equal treatment as a 'fundamental right' which is binding on the Community authorities.[204]

Legal certainty/non-retroactivity

The Court has applied the general principle of legal certainty outside the context of non-retroactivity. It has said that 'certainty and foreseeability are requirements which must be observed strictly in the case of rules liable to entail financial consequences'.[205]

The principle of legal certainty was emphasized by the Court of First Instance and the Court of Justice in *BASF AG and Others* v *Commission*[206] as a reason for finding a Commission measure illegal where the Commission had not complied with its own Rules of Procedure and had failed to create an authenticated version of the measure.

In *Exportation des Sucres* v *Commission*[207] the European Court held that the principle of legal certainty precluded a Community measure from taking effect from a time before its publication. The regulation in question was published in the *Official Journal* of 1 July 1976. Due to a strike, however, that edition of the *Official Journal* was published and distributed on 2 July 1976. The Court decided that there was no reason to give the regulation retroactive effect by applying it from 1 July 1976 even though Article 2 of the Regulation stated that it shall enter into force on 1 July 1976. As the applicants applied for their licences on 1 July 1976, the regulation was not applicable to them.

The rule that Community legislation should not apply to a period before its actual publication is not absolute. In *Racke* v *Hauptzollamt Mainz* the Court stated that retroactive effect may exceptionally be allowed

---

204 Case C-37/89 [1990] ECR I-2395, 2420–21 and Weiler and Lockhart, above, note 175, at p. 90.
205 See Case C-30/89 *Commission* v *France* [1990] ECR I-691, 716; Case C-10/88 *Italy* v *Commission* [1990] ECR I-1229; Case 325/85 *Ireland* v *Commission* [1987] ECR 5041, 5088; Case 326/85 *Netherlands* v *Commission* [1987] ECR 5091, 5116; and Cases 92–3/87 *Commission* v *France and United Kingdom* [1989] ECR 405, 443. However, Barents has argued that the Court's case law on the requirement quoted in the text is 'more an ideal than a substantive standard' (1994) Maastricht J. of Eur. & Comp. L. 101, 111. For the problems of non-retroactivity in relation to the effects of preliminary rulings, see Ch. 9, pp. 307–10.
206 Cases T-79, 84–6, 89, 91–2, 94, 96, 98, 102 and 104/89 [1992] ECR II-315 and Case C-137/92P [1994] ECR I-2555.
207 Case 88/76, note 46 above.

'where the purpose to be achieved so demands and where the legitimate expectations of those concerned are duly respected'.[208] It decided that a two-week period of retroactive effect was justified, due in part to the special features of monetary compensatory amounts. Subsequent cases show that the exception may be becoming the rule.[209]

A particularly blatant example of retroactive effect being upheld by the Court is *Amylum* v *Council*.[210] Regulation 1293/79, which provided for a restrictive regime for the production of isoglucose, was struck down by the Court in *Roquette Frères* v *Council*[211] on the ground that the European Parliament had not given its opinion on the proposed regulation as required by Article 43 of the Treaty. Regulation 387/81 reproduced the provisions of Regulation 1293/79, which had been declared void by the Court on 29 October 1980, and purported to apply them from the date in 1979 when Regulation 1293/79 had come into force. Amylum brought an action under Article 173 for the annulment of Regulation 387/81, as it breached the general principle of legal certainty. Amazingly, the Court decided to uphold the validity of the Regulation. In doing so it decided that Amylum and other isoglucose producers had no legitimate expectation worthy of protection. The Court argued that the applicants should have anticipated that the Council would seek to impose some restrictions on isoglucose production because of the need to regulate the interdependent markets of liquid sugar and isoglucose. Furthermore, they should have been aware that Regulation 1293/79 was annulled only because of the failure to obtain Parliament's opinion and not on any of the substantive arguments against it.

The Court seems to have given very little weight to the principle of legal certainty. The applicants surely had a legitimate expectation that the effect of the decision in *Roquette Frères* would not be overturned retroactively. It really is an invitation to the Council to give little weight to consultation of the European Parliament if any adverse consequences can be swept away by subsequent legislation and a major deterrent to non-privileged applicants to challenge Community legislation.[212]

---

208 Case 98/78 [1979] ECR 69, 86. This formula has been repeated in numerous cases, e.g., Case 108/81, note 145 above, p. 3130, in Case C-337/88 *SAFA* [1990] ECR I-1, 18, in which a three-week period of retroactive effect was held not to be a breach of legal certainty in the circumstances, and in Case C-331/88 *Fedesa and Others* [1990] ECR I-4023, 4069, where two months of retroactivity was condoned. In Case C-248/89 *Cargill* v *Commission* [1994] ECR I-2987, 3012–14, the Court accepted the legality of a Commission regulation which amended an earlier regulation with retroactive effects on events that took place more than four years before.

209 See the cases noted above.

210 Case 108/81, note 145 above.

211 Case 138/79, note 55 above, discussed on pp. 231, 248 and in Ch. 4, p. 109.

212 In the context of the individual rights involved in staff cases the Court has ruled that

Right to a fair hearing

The Court of Justice decided in *Transocean Marine Paint* v *Commission* that there is a general rule of Community law that

a person affected by a decision taken by a public authority must be given the opportunity to make his point of view known. This rule requires that an undertaking be clearly informed, in good time, of the essence of conditions to which the Commission intends to subject an exemption[213] and it must have the opportunity to submit its observations to the Commission.[214]

The Commission had granted an exemption to the Transocean Marine Paint Association under Article 85(3) of the Treaty subject to a proviso requiring any links between members of the association and other companies in the paints sector to be notified to the Commission. This proviso was annulled by the Court because it was imposed by the Commission without the Association ever being given an opportunity to comment on the possibility of such a proviso being inserted into the Commission's decision.

The right to a fair hearing has been categorized in subsequent cases as a fundamental right[215] and thus is a specific example of fundamental human rights. The right to be heard applies in all proceedings initiated against a person which are liable to culminate in a measure adversely affecting that person.[216] In *Al-Jubail Fertilizer* v *Council*[217] the Court declared void an article of a Council regulation imposing anti-dumping duty on imports of urea originating in Libya and Saudi Arabia in so far as it imposed the duty on the applicants, because the applicants' right to a fair hearing had not been respected. The applicants, manufacturers of urea in Saudi Arabia, alleged that the Commission and the Council had failed to respect their right to a fair hearing in considering whether to impose anti-dumping

---

'the retroactive withdrawal of a legal measure which has conferred individual rights or similar benefits is contrary to the general principles of law'. See Case 159/82 *Verli-Wallace* v *Commission* [1983] ECR 2711, 2718–19; and Case T-123/89 *Chomel* v *Commission* [1990] ECR II-131, 141.

213 An exemption under Art. 85(3) of the Treaty stating that the provisions on competition policy in Art. 85(1) are not applicable.

214 Case 17/74, note 161 above, p. 1080. The implications of the right to be heard in the context of competition policy are considered further in Ch. 24.

215 Case 85/87 *Dow Benelux* v *Commission* [1989] ECR 3137; Case C-49/88 *Al-Jubail Fertilizer* v *Council* [1991] ECR I-3187.

216 See Case C-135/92 *Fiskano* v *Commission* [1994] ECR I-2885, 2909 and the cases cited therein.

217 Case C-49/88, note 215 above, noted by Vermulst and Hooijer (1992) 29 CMLRev 380–404.

duty on imports of urea from that country. The Court said that the Community institutions must provide the undertakings concerned, as far as is compatible with the obligation not to disclose business secrets, with information relevant to the defence of their interests:

In any event, the undertakings concerned should have been placed in a position during the administrative procedure in which they could effectively make known their views on the correctness and relevance of the facts and circumstances alleged and on the evidence presented by the Commission in support of its allegation concerning the existence of dumping and the resultant injury.[218]

The Court was not satisfied that the Commission and Council had discharged their duty to place at the applicants' disposal all the information that would have enabled them effectively to defend their interests. The Commission and Council both referred to letters allegedly sent to the applicants containing information that would have helped them to defend their interests. As the letters were not sent by registered post, it could not be established that the applicants had received them and thus the Court took no account of them.

Confidentiality/legal privilege

The right to a fair hearing includes a right of access for a party to the documentation on which the case against it is based. However, this right is limited by the countervailing right to preserve confidential information, particularly information obtained by a lawyer from his or her client.

The Commission must be careful not to betray the source of information about an alleged breach of competition policy in the course of ensuring that the party against whom the allegation has been made can exercise the right to a fair hearing.[219] The Commission has no right of access to documents relating to an undertaking's rights of defence that have been submitted by independent lawyers,[220] but the Court has allowed the Commission to have access to the advice of lawyers employed by the undertaking.[221]

---

218 ibid., para. 17.
219 See Case 53/85, note 25 above, and Case 145/83 *Adams* v *Commission* [1985] ECR 3539. See also Case C-36/92P *Samenwerkende Elektriciteits-produktiebedrijven NV (SEP)* v *Commission* [1994] ECR I-1911, discussed in Ch. 24 below at p. 763.
220 Case 155/79 *AM&S* v *Commission* [1982] ECR 1575.
221 ibid., p. 1612. See also *John Deere* Dec. 85/79 OJ 1985 L35/58, [1985] 2 CMLR 554.

Misuse of powers

The misuse of powers as a ground of illegality has proved to be of little relevance in practice. The Court has stated that 'a decision may amount to a misuse of powers if it appears, on the basis of objective, relevant and consistent facts, to have been taken for purposes other than those stated'[222] and more recently has refined the condition so that it has to be shown that the decision was 'taken with the exclusive purpose, or at any rate the main purpose, of achieving an end other than that stated or evading a procedure specifically prescribed by the Treaty for dealing with the circumstances of the case'.[223]

It is, of course, very difficult to prove that the main purpose lying behind a decision is not that stated in it. One successful example is *Giuffrida* v *Council*.[224] The applicant had unsuccessfully applied, in an internal competition, to be appointed as principal administrator at the Directorate-General for Regional Policy. He sought the annulment of the decision to appoint Emilio Martino on the ground that it was a misuse of powers. The conditions for admission to the competition for the post included a requirement that the successful candidate must have held the secretariat for meetings of Council working parties or committees on regional policy for at least four years. Only Emilio Martino could meet that requirement. Other evidence suggested that the competition had been created with the sole purpose of upgrading Emilio Martino in recognition of the work he was already doing. The Court decided that this rigging of the internal competition procedure constituted a misuse of powers and annulled the decision to appoint Emilio Martino.

TIME–LIMITS FOR BRINGING AN ACTION UNDER ARTICLE 173

For bringing an action of annulment Article 173 prescribes a relatively short time-limit of two months from the publication of the measure or of its notification to the plaintiff or, in the absence thereof, of the day on which it came to the knowledge of the latter. The two-month time-limit is extended to take account of the distance of the applicant from the Court in Luxembourg. A ten-day extension is granted in relation to the United.

---

222 Cases 18, 35/65 *Gutmann* v *Commission* [1966] ECR 103, 117; Case 69/83 *Lux* v *Court of Auditors* [1984] ECR 2447, 2465–6.
223 Case C-331/88 *Fedesa and Others* [1990] ECR I-4023, 4065; repeated in Cases C-133, 300 and 362/93 *Crispoltoni* [1994] ECR I-4863, 4902.
224 Case 105/75 [1976] ECR 1395.

Kingdom.[225] The two-month time-limit is also extended by a further fifteen days if the measure has been published in the *Official Journal*; if the measure is not published, then the time-limit begins the day following receipt of the notification of the measure by the applicant.[226] If the measure is neither published nor notified then time begins to run only when the third party concerned has precise knowledge of the content and grounds of the measure in question in such a way as to enable that person to institute proceedings.[227] The time-limit is strictly enforced[228] unless there are 'unforeseeable circumstances or *force majeure* which might have prevented [the applicants] from instituting proceedings within the prescribed period'.[229] An action for the annulment of a decision which merely confirms a previous decision not contested within the time-limit for bringing proceedings is inadmissible.[230]

A member state may be able to challenge a Commission decision totally lacking in any legal basis in the Community legal system outside the time-limit as part of its defence to an action for failure to fulfil Community law obligations brought by the Commission against the member state.[231]

An even more radical position was adopted by the Court of First Instance in *BASF AG and Others*,[232] when it decided that a Commission measure was in fact non-existent, by reason of the particularly serious and manifest defects that it exhibited, and that such a measure could be challenged without regard to time-limits. The Court of First Instance took the view that the non-existence of a Community measure is a matter of public interest, which the Community judges must raise of their own motion. On appeal the Court of Justice accepted that in 'quite extreme situations' an act may be legally non-existent if 'tainted by an irregularity

225 See Rules of Procedure ECJ, Annex II, OJ 1991 L176/7 at p. 32 and Rules of Procedure CFI, Art. 102(2), OJ 1991 L136/I at p. 19.
226 See Rules of Procedure ECJ, Art 81, OJ 1991 L176/7, p. 22 and Rules of Procedure CFI, Art. 102(1), OJ 1991 L136/1 at pp. 18–19.
227 Case T-465/93 *Murgia Messapica* v *Commission* [1994] ECR II-361, 374 and the cases cited therein.
228 Case 76/79 *Könecke* v *Commission* [1980] ECR 665; Case 152/85 *Misset* v *Council* [1987] ECR 223; Cases 281, 283–5, 287/85, note 127 above.
229 Case 352/87 *Farzoo and Kortmann* v *Commission* [1988] ECR 2281, 2284. The applicants put forward no such pleas in this case and their action was dismissed as being out of time. Sending an application by 'express delivery' – next day service – the day before the time-limit expired and its failure to arrive until three days after the expiry date did not constitute an unforeseeable circumstance or *force majeure* in Case C-59/91 *France* v *Commission* [1992] ECR I-525, 529.
230 Case C-12/90 *Infortec* v *Commission* [1990] ECR I-4265, 4269.
231 See Cases 6, 11/69 *Commission* v *France* [1969] ECR 523, 539.
232 Cases T-79, 84–6, 89, 91–2, 94, 96, 98, 102 and 104/89, note 206 above. As to why the Commission's measure was so defective see Ch. 2, p. 52.

whose gravity is so obvious that it cannot be tolerated by the Community legal order'. The Court annulled the measure but did not regard the Commission's failure to observe its own Rules of Procedure as enough to justify the Court of First Instance in regarding the measure as non-existent although it was sufficient to justify annulment.[233]

INTERIM MEASURES UNDER ARTICLE 173

An application for annulment under Article 173 of the Treaty may be accompanied by an application under Article 186 of the Treaty for interim measures. Although Article 185 of the Treaty makes it clear that actions brought before the Court of Justice do not have suspensory effect, this does not prevent applicants from seeking, as an interim measure under Article 186, suspension of the Community measure that they are challenging in the main action under Article 173.

The applicant must comply with Article 83(2) of the Rules of Procedure of the Court and state the circumstances giving rise to urgency and the pleas of fact and law establishing a prima-facie case for the interim measures applied for.[234] The Court, usually the President, will not normally consider whether the main action under Article 173 is admissible.[235] If, however, it is contended that the main action is manifestly inadmissible, the Court will consider the application for interim measures only if there are grounds for concluding prima facie that the main application is admissible.[236] In *Fédération européenne de la santé animale and Others* v *Council*[237] the President of the Court decided that there were no grounds for concluding prima facie that the main application was admissible, and dismissed the application for interim measures. The applicant had sought the suspension of Council Directive 88/146 prohibiting the use in livestock farming of certain substances having a hormonal action. The President noted that the directive was an act of general application, which cannot be challenged by non-privileged applicants under Article 173. He was pre-

---

233 Case C-137/92 P *Commission* v *BASF AG and Others* [1994] ECR I-2555.

234 OJ 1991 L176/7, p. 23. See also Rules of Procedure CFI, Art. 104(2), OJ 1991 L136/1 at p. 19.

235 Case 65/87R *Pfizer* v *Commission* [1987] ECR 1691. The rationale being that the President should be reluctant to prejudge the substance of the case, which will be decided by the Court.

236 Case 221/86R *Group of the European Right and National Front Party* v *European Parliament* [1986] ECR 2969; Case 82/87R *Autexpo* v *Commission* [1987] ECR 2131; Case 376/87R *Distrivet* v *Council* [1988] ECR 209; Case 160/88R, note 40 above; and Case C-117/91R *Bosman* v *Commission* [1991] ECR I-3353.

237 Case 160/88R, note 40 above.

pared to look behind the form of the legislation to see if, despite the label directive, it was a measure of direct and individual concern to the applicants. In this case it was clear that the measure applied to categories of persons envisaged in a general and abstract manner: all producers and distributors of substances having a hormonal action and all livestock farmers.

If the applicant can show grounds for concluding prima facie that the application is admissible, the next step is to prove the 'urgency' of the application for interim measures by showing that interim relief is necessary to prevent 'serious and irreparable damage to the party requesting the interim measure'.[238] If the only damage alleged is financial loss, it will not be regarded as serious and irreparable unless, in the event of the applicants' being successful in the main action, it could not be wholly recouped.[239] In principle such financial loss is capable of being recouped by an action for compensation on the basis of Articles 178 and 215(2) of the Treaty.[240]

An example of a successful application for interim measures is *Publishers Association* v *Commission*.[241] Commission Decision 89/44 had refused to grant an exemption under Article 85(3) of the Treaty to the Net Book Agreement, established by the Publishers Association in the United Kingdom in 1957, and had required the Association forthwith to take all the measures necessary to end the breach of Article 85. The Net Book Agreement applied to the majority of publishers in the United Kingdom and ensured that books were not sold below the agreed net price. The Agreement was notified to the Commission in June 1973, shortly after the accession of the United Kingdom to the Community, but the Commission did not rule on its incompatibility with Article 85 until 1989.

The Publishers Association brought an action under Article 173 for the annulment of the Commission decision and in the interim sought the suspension of its operation pending the Court's judgment in the main action. The President of the Court first ascertained whether the applicants had a prima-facie case in the main action. Such a case was made out in relation to the application for an exemption under Article 85(3). The

---

238 Case 191/88R *Co-Frutta Sarl* v *Commission* [1988] ECR 4551, 4555; Case 229/88R *Cargill* v *Commission* [1988] ECR 5183, 5189–90; Case 56/89R *Publishers Association* v *Commission* [1989] ECR 1693, 1698; Case T-19/91R *Vichy* v *Commission* [1991] ECR II-265.
239 Case 113/77R *NTN Toyo Bearing* v *Commission* [1977] ECR 1721; Case 229/88R, note 238 above, p. 5190; and Cases C-51 and 59/90R *Comos-Tank and Others* v *Commission* [1990] ECR I-2167.
240 Such actions are discussed in Ch. 10 at pp. 313–19. See Case 120/83R *Raznoimport* v *Commission* [1983] ECR 2573; Case 294/86R *Technointorg* v *Commission* [1986] ECR 3979; Case 229/88R, note 238 above.
241 Case 56/89R note 238 above.

President noted that in 1962 and 1969 the United Kingdom Restrictive Practices Court had upheld the Net Book Agreement as being of substantial benefit to the public even though the fixing of sales prices was in principle prohibited by the national legislation. The President was also satisfied that interim relief was required urgently to prevent serious and irreparable damage to the Publishers Association. Even the temporary abrogation of the Net Book Agreement would 'cause considerable commercial damage and lead to a development on the UK and Irish book markets which it would be impossible subsequently to reverse'.[242]

In balancing the risk to the Publishers Association with the Commission's interest in bringing an immediate end to the alleged infringement of competition policy the President noted that the Commission had shown no urgency in deciding that the Agreement was contrary to Community law. The Commission's interest in ending the Net Book Agreement forthwith could not override the Publishers Association's interest in preserving the Agreement, which may confer advantages on the public such as securing an adequate and varied supply of books of all kinds that could be irreversibly compromised by immediate implementation of the Commission's decision.[243]

EFFECTS OF ANNULMENT

If an action under Article 173 is well founded, the Court of Justice will declare the measure concerned to be void.[244] The Court has decided that it can rule that only part of a measure is void.[245] The Treaty explicitly allows the Court to state which of the effects of a regulation that it has declared void shall be considered definitive.[246] Two of the many examples of the Court using this provision are Case 81/72 Commission v Council[247] and Case 59/81 Commission v Council.[248] In both cases the Court annulled articles of a regulation fixing the price increases for Community staff but stated that they should continue to have effect until the Council passed new legislation in consequence of the judgment. The Court has extended this power into

---

242 ibid., p. 1700.

243 On 17 January 1995 the Court of Justice annulled the Commission's decision; see Case C-360/92P Publishers Association v Commission, The Times, 31 January 1995, discussed in Ch. 24 below at p. 788.

244 Art. 174(1) of the Treaty.

245 See the following examples: Cases 56, 58/64 Consten & Grundig v Commission [1966] ECR 299; Case 81/72, note 184 above; Case 17/74, note 161 above.

246 Art. 174(2).

247 Note 184 above.

248 [1982] ECR 3329. See also Case 45/86, note 38 above, p. 1522.

a general one by stating which of the effects of other Community measures remain in place even though the measure has been annulled. The Court's principal justification for doing so has been the need to uphold the general principle of law of legal certainty. For example, in *Simmenthal* v *Commission*,[249] a Commission decision was annulled but the Court preserved its effects in relation to everyone except the applicant because legal certainty required that those who had relied on the decision to tender successfully on the basis of the price stated in it should not be prejudiced, and in *Council* v *European Parliament*,[250] the declaration by the President of the Parliament that the 1986 budget had been finally adopted was annulled, but because it was already well into 1986 the Court decided to maintain legal certainty by preserving all the effects of the budget up to the date of the judgment.

ACTIONS UNDER ARTICLE 175 FOR FAILURE TO ACT

Article 175 of the Treaty states:

Should the *European Parliament*, the Council or the Commission, in infringement of this Treaty, fail to act, the Member States and the other institutions of the Community may bring an action before the Court of Justice to have the infringement established.

The action shall be admissible only if the institution concerned has first been called upon to act. If, within two months of being so called upon, the institution concerned has not defined its position, the action may be brought within a further period of two months.

Any natural or legal person may, under the conditions laid down in the preceding paragraphs, complain to the Court of Justice that an institution of the Community has failed to address to that person any act other than a recommendation or an opinion.

The Court of Justice shall have jurisdiction, under the same conditions, in actions or proceedings brought by the European Central Bank in the areas falling within the latter's field of competence and in actions or proceedings brought against the latter.[251]

---

249 Case 92/78 [1979] ECR 777, 811.
250 Case 34/86, note 37 above, p. 2212.
251 Amendments to Art. 175 EEC agreed at Maastricht are in italics. For the first time it is clear that the European Parliament can be challenged for failing to act. In relation to the European Central Bank's functions see Ch. 21.

Article 175 operates in tandem with Article 173 to ensure that the Council and the Commission not only act within the powers given by the Treaty but act on those powers. The effectiveness of Article 173 would be reduced, in the absence of Article 175, if the institutions were able with impunity to fail to make legislation or to take decisions. Article 175 at least forces the relevant institution to define its position. This position statement should, in turn, be reviewable under Article 173, at least by privileged applicants. For example, in *Fediol* [252] Fediol (the EC Seed Crushers' and Oil Processors' Federation) served notice on the Commission on 30 September 1981 under Article 175(2), calling upon it to initiate an anti-subsidy proceeding against Brazil in respect of imports of soya-bean-oil cake. After some correspondence, the Commission sent Fediol a letter on 25 May 1982 stating that it was not initiating such a proceeding. The Court permitted Fediol to challenge the Commission's decision not to initiate anti-subsidy proceedings in an action under Article 173 in order for it to protect its procedural rights. It was the case that the combined remedies of Articles 173 and 175 could not remove the discretion from the Commission not to reach a final decision on a complaint from an applicant that a third party is in breach of competition policy. [253] However, recent developments in the case law under Article 175 indicate that the Commission may have finally to reach a decision accepting or rejecting the complaint. [254]

The first paragraph of Article 175 gives standing to the member states and all the Community institutions, including the European Parliament, [255] to challenge the failure to make any type of Community act having legal effects. [256] The third paragraph of Article 175 applies to the standing of non-privileged applicants. Here the Court of Justice has decided to apply the same rules in relation to *locus standi* and to the type of measure that can

252 Case 191/82, note 116 above.
253 See Case 125/78, note 102 above, pp. 3189–90 and Case T-24/90 *Automec Srl* v *Commission (Automec II)* [1992] ECR II-2223; [1992] 5 CMLR 431 (para. 75).
254 See Case T-28/90 *Asia Motor France SA et al.* v *Commission* [1992] ECR II-2285; [1992] 5 CMLR 43 at paras 34–38, noted by Shaw (1993) 18 ELRev 427–41, although the point did not require to be decided in that case because the Commission had definitively rejected the complaint after the case was launched but before the Court's judgment. See also Case T-74/92 *Ladbroke Racing (Deutschland) GmbH* v *Commission*, judgment of 24 January 1995, *Proceedings* 2/95.
255 Confirmed by Case 13/83 *European Parliament* v *Council* [1985] ECR 1513.
256 Some scholars argue that non-binding Community acts can be challenged under Art. 175(1); see Schermers and Waelbroeck, *Judicial Protection*, p. 249; and Toth, 'The Law as it Stands on the Appeal for Failure to Act', 1975/2 LIEI 65, 80. This view is supported by the reasoning of the Court in the *Comitology* case, Case 302/87 *European Parliament* v *Council* [1988] ECR 5615, but that case has in other respects not been followed by the Court, see Case C-70/88, note 3 above, and is contrary to the so-called principle of unity between Arts. 173 and 175, see Hartley, *Foundations of Community Law*, pp. 400–3.

be challenged as it does in Article 173: 'The concept of a measure capable of giving rise to an action is identical in Articles 173 and 175, as both provisions merely prescribe one and the same method of recourse.'[257] However, in *Asia Motor France SA et al.* v *Commission*, the Court of First Instance decided that the Commission could be compelled to adopt a measure which does not have legal effects, in this case a letter under Article 6 of Regulation 99/63, even though the measure is not reviewable under Article 173.[258]

Paragraph two of Article 175 describes the procedure that must be followed. The applicant must ask the relevant Community institution to act. The institution has two months to define its position. If the institution is under no obligation to act, then it does not have to define its position, as its inaction cannot be an infringement of the Treaty. A classic example of this is where an applicant asks the Commission to initiate infringement proceedings against a member state under Article 169 of the Treaty. As the Commission is never under any obligation to bring such proceedings – it is within its discretion not to do so – an action for failure to act is inadmissible.[259]

The Community institution may define its position by saying that it is not going to act or that it is going to act in a different way from that hoped for by the applicant. The Court has repeatedly stated that 'Article 175 refers to failure to act in the sense of failure to take a decision or to define a position, and not the adoption of a measure different from that desired or considered necessary by the persons concerned.'[260]

The applicant may not like the definition of position made by the Community institution, but the remedy would be to challenge the decision not to act, or to act in a different way from that desired by the applicant,

---

257 Case 15/70 *Chevalley* v *Commission* [1970] ECR 975, 979. On the need for the non-privileged applicant to be directly and individually concerned by the act that the institution has allegedly failed to enact, see Case 246/81 *Bethell* v *Commission* [1982] ECR 2277 and Case 15/71 *Mackprang* v *Commission* [1971] ECR 797. As to the position under Art. 173, see pp. 221–46. Cases under Art. 175(3) are now within the jurisdiction of the Court of First Instance; see Case C-72/90 *Asia Motor France* v *Commission* [1990] ECR I-2181; Case T-3/90 *Prodifarma* v *Commission* [1991] ECR II-1, 13.

258 See Case T-28/90, note 254 above, at paras. 27–30. The Court of First Instance, at para. 42, confirmed that an Art. 6 letter is not reviewable under Art. 173 relying on Case T-64/89 *Automec Srl* v *Commission* [1990] ECR II-367 (*Automec I*) and Case 125/78, note 102 above. See also Case T-74/92, note 254 above.

259 Case 247/87 *Star Fruit Company* v *Commission* [1989] ECR 291, 301; and Case C-87/89 *Sonito and Others* v *Commission* [1990] ECR I-1981, 2009. See also Ch. 7, p. 200.

260 See Cases 166 and 220/86, note 87 above, p. 6503 (where the Commission refused to initiate an investigation under Art. 93(2) into the legality of certain payments made to a Northern Ireland cement company and in doing so rejected Irish Cement Ltd's formal complaint against the grant of aid to its rival); Case 8/71 *Deutscher Komponistenverband* v *Commission* [1971] ECR 705; and Case 125/78, note 102 above, p. 3190.

under Article 173, provided that the two-month time-limit is observed.[261] The Court has established that Article 175 cannot be used as a means to overcome the time-limits in Article 173. An applicant cannot bring an action for failure to act based on the fact that the institution did not respond when asked to revoke an act. Instead, the applicant must challenge the allegedly unlawful act under Article 173 within two months of it being passed.[262]

If the Community institution fails to define its position within two months of being requested to do so, then the applicant has a further two months within which it must bring the action before the Court. If the institution passes a measure while the case is pending before the Court, then the Court will not give a judgment. The Court can only require, by Article 176, the institution whose failure to act is contrary to the Treaty to take the necessary measures to comply with the judgment. If the institution has already taken those measures by passing the act then the subject-matter of the action has ceased to exist.[263]

COMMON TRANSPORT POLICY CASE

One of the leading cases on Article 175 is Case 13/83 *European Parliament* v *Council*,[264] which helps to illustrate the nature of the action. In a letter of 21 September 1982 the President of the European Parliament informed the Council of Parliament's intention to bring an action against the Council for failure to fix the framework of the common transport policy as required by Articles 3(e) and 74 of the Treaty and to take certain specific measures, including the introduction of freedom to provide services in the field of transport. The President of the Council replied on 22 November 1982 'without expressing an opinion at this stage on the legal aspects' of the letter from the President of the European Parliament. The reply acknowledged that the common transport policy was incomplete but listed the progress that the Council had made towards it. The Parliament did not regard the Council's reply as a definition of position and brought an action under Article 175 before the Court on 24 January 1983.[265]

The Court decided that the European Parliament's action was admissible. The Council's letter of 22 November 1982 did not constitute a definition

---

261 See, e.g., Case 191/82, note 116 above.
262 See Cases 10, 18/68 *Eridania* v *Commission* [1969] ECR 459, 483.
263 See Case 377/87 *European Parliament* v *Council* [1988] ECR 4017, 4048 and Case 383/87 *Commission* v *Council* [1988] ECR 4051, 4064.
264 Note 255 above.
265 The appropriate extension of time-limits because of distance applicable under Art. 173, see pp. 266–7, apply to Art. 175.

of position within the meaning of Article 175. It did not comment on the legal aspects of the letter from the European Parliament and simply listed the measures it had already taken to create a common transport policy. It failed to deny or confirm the alleged failure to act. It did not give the Council's views on the necessity or otherwise of legislating on the specific measures that Parliament thought were required to be taken.[266]

The Court then considered the substantive points made by the Parliament. It concluded that it is possible to challenge a failure by an institution to take several decisions, or a series of decisions where the adoption of such decisions is an obligation that the Treaty imposes on that institution. The applicant must state the measures that the institution has failed to take with a degree of precision that would make it possible for the institution to comply, pursuant to Article 176, with a judgment of the Court upholding the applicant's case:

Such a degree of precision is particularly required in view of the fact that in the system of legal remedies provided for by the Treaty there is a close relationship between the right of action given in Article 173, which allows unlawful measures of the Council and Commission to be declared void, and that based on Article 175, which may lead to a finding that the failure by the Council or Commission to adopt certain measures is contrary to the Treaty. In view of that relationship it must be concluded that in both cases the measures which are the subject of the action must be sufficiently defined to allow the Court to determine whether their adoption, or the failure to adopt them, is lawful.[267]

The Court decided that the applicant had not succeeded in doing this in relation to the allegation that the Council had failed to create a common transport policy. The Court was influenced by the fact that the Council has a broad discretion as to what the common transport policy should consist of and what the priorities are for bringing it about. The Court also noted the failure of the Parliament to specify the measures that should be taken, and in what order of priority, to achieve the common transport policy. The Court recognized the limits of the judicial function. It is meaningless for the Court to state in general terms that the Council should adopt a common transport policy. The Council would not know which measures must be taken to come into line with the Court's judgment and thus would not know how to comply with Article 176 of the Treaty. It would be totally inappropriate for the Court to attempt to flesh out the common transport policy of the Community.

On the other hand, the Court noted that the Parliament had specifically

266 Note 255 above, p. 1590.
267 ibid., p. 1592.

requested the Council to take measures to introduce freedom to provide services in transport, in particular, the matters mentioned in Article 75(a) and (b) EEC, which in accordance with Article 75(2) had to be laid down in legislation adopted by the Council during the transitional period and were not. The measures were 'common rules applicable to international transport' and 'the conditions under which non-resident carriers may operate transport services within a Member State'. The obligation to take such measures had a sufficient degree of precision that the Council would know what to enact in order to comply with the Court's judgment. Furthermore, the Council's discretion in this area is much more restricted than in other areas of the common transport policy, as it relates only to the means to be employed and not to the content of the policy.[268] The Court upheld Parliament's action in relation to these matters.

The Court noted that Article 176 of the Treaty does not prescribe a time-limit within which the institution that has failed to act must take the measures necessary to comply with the Court's judgment. The Court decided that the institution has 'a reasonable period' for that purpose and declined to speculate as to what would be the consequences if the institution continued to fail to act.[269]

PLEA OF ILLEGALITY UNDER ARTICLE 184

Article 184 states:

Notwithstanding the expiry of the period laid down in the *fifth* paragraph of Article 173, any party may, in proceedings in which *a Regulation adopted jointly by the European Parliament and the Council, or* a Regulation of the Council, of the Commission, *or of the European Central Bank* is at issue, plead the grounds specified in the *second* paragraph of Article 173 in order to invoke before the Court of Justice the inapplicability of that Regulation.[270]

It is not possible to found an action before the Court of Justice based on Article 184; rather it permits an applicant to plead that a regulation is inapplicable in proceedings brought before the Court under some other provision of the Treaty.[271] The Court has insisted on a connection between

268 ibid., pp. 1599–1600.
269 ibid., p. 1600.
270 Amendments agreed at Maastricht are in italics.
271 See Cases 31, 33/62 *Wöhrmann* v *Commission* [1962] ECR 501, 506–7; Case 33/80 *Albini* v *Council and Commission* [1981] ECR 2141, 2157; Cases 87, 130/77, 22/83, and 9, 10/84, *Salerno* v *Commission and Council* [1985] ECR 2523, 2536.

the main action and the plea that the regulation is inapplicable: 'The intention of [Article 184] is not to allow a party to contest at will the applicability of any regulation in support of an application. The regulation of which the legality is called in question must be applicable, directly or indirectly, to the issue with which the application is concerned.'[272]

It may be that the Court will accept the admissibility of a plea of illegality against a regulation only where in the main action a measure is in issue that has that regulation as its legal basis. This seems to have been the view of the Second Chamber in *Salerno* v *Commission and Council*:

The sole purpose of Article 184 is to protect parties against the application of an unlawful regulation where the regulation itself can no longer be challenged owing to the expiry of the period laid down in Article 173. However, in allowing a party to plead the inapplicability of a regulation, Article 184 does not create an independent right of action; such a plea may only be raised indirectly in proceedings against an implementing measure, the validity of the regulation being challenged in so far as it constitutes the legal basis of that measure.[273]

The utility of Article 184 is, therefore, to enable a non-privileged applicant to challenge the validity of a true regulation, which it does not have standing to challenge under Article 173, in the context of a challenge to the validity of acts implementing that regulation that are of direct and individual concern to the applicant. The implementing measures may themselves be unimpeachable, but could be rendered void by being based on a regulation that is inapplicable. For privileged applicants it would seem that the plea gives them a second opportunity to challenge the regulation if they failed to bring an action for annulment under Article 173 within the two-month time-limit. The plea would appear to be applicable to such applicants because Article 184 refers to 'any party' and the Court did not say it was inapplicable to such applicants in *Italy* v *Council and Commission*.[274] A successful plea of illegality does not render the regulation void, merely inapplicable to the applicant. As any implementing measures based on it would be likely to be found void by the Court, it is likely that the Community institutions would quickly replace the inapplicable regulation with an untainted one.

---

272 Case 32/65 *Italy* v *Council and Commission* [1966] ECR 389, 409. In that case there who was no necessary connection between Reg. 19/65, which Italy was seeking to annul in the main action, and Reg. 153/62 and the parts of Reg. 17/62, that Italy claimed were inapplicable in a plea of illegality under Art. 184. The inapplicability of the latter two regulations would not have any repercussions on the legality of the regulation contested in the main action. Thus the plea of illegality was inadmissible.
273 Cases 87, 130/77, 22/83 and 9, 10/84, note 271 above, p. 2536.
274 Case 32/65, note 272 above.

The Court has extended the scope of the plea of illegality to include measures of general application other than regulations. In *Simmenthal*[275] the Court decided that certain notices of invitations to tender were general measures that produced similar effects to a regulation and, as they could not be challenged directly by a non-privileged applicant under Article 173, should be subject to a plea of illegality when the applicant is contesting a decision implementing those notices that is of direct and individual concern to the applicant. Simmenthal's plea of illegality against the notices of invitation to tender was admissible, but unsuccessful on the merits.

It is not clear whether a member state can rely on a plea of illegality when defending an action brought by the Commission under Article 169. It may be possible to do so where the Commission claims that the member state has failed to comply with a provision of Community law that the member state alleges is not valid because its parent regulation is unlawful. What is clear is that a member state cannot use Article 184 in an enforcement action under Article 93(2)(2) to challenge the decision taken by the Commission under Article 93(2)(1) that the state aid is contrary to the provisions of the Treaty.[276] The reasons for this are that the Commission acts in this sphere by way of decision and not regulation[277*] and that the member state could challenge the Commission's decision under Article 93(2)(1) directly in an Article 173 action. The latter point may call into question the use of a plea of illegality in Article 169 proceedings.

275 Case 92/78, note 249 above, pp. 799–800.
276 Case 156/77 *Commission* v *Belgium* [1978] ECR 1881, 1896–7.
277 It is not an act of general application, unlike the notice of invitations to tender in *Simmenthal* above, as the decision is addressed to the member state concerned.

CHAPTER 9

Article 177: Preliminary Rulings

Article 177 of the Treaty enables national courts and tribunals to refer questions of Community law that require to be decided in a case pending before them to the European Court for a ruling. The Court's ruling on the points of Community law is then utilized by the national court or tribunal in reaching its decision on the case. Although the European Court does not give the final decision in the case when it exercises its jurisdiction under Article 177, this Article has proved to be the springboard for the development of some of the key concepts of Community law. The possibility of provisions of Community law having direct effect in the legal systems of the member states without any implementing measures can be traced to an Article 177 ruling in *Van Gend en Loos*,[1] and the doctrine that directly effective provisions of Community law have supremacy over conflicting provisions of national law has its origin in the Article 177 ruling in *Costa* v *ENEL*.[2]

Article 177 rulings have constituted almost half of the European Court's workload in actions brought under the Treaty.[3] The heavy volume of references from national courts and tribunals shows widespread penetration of Community law into litigation before these national bodies. It does mean, however, that the average length of time that a national court or tribunal has to wait for the Court's ruling is eighteen months: an unacceptably long period if justice is to be done.

The Court can be asked questions on the interpretation of the Treaty. It can be asked to interpret 'acts of the institutions of the Community' or to rule on their validity. A substantial majority of the cases referred to the

---

1 Case 26/62 [1963] ECR 1. Discussed in Ch. 11, pp. 341–3.
2 Case 6/64 [1964] ECR 585. Discussed at pp. 175 and 367.
3 Excluding staff cases. By 31 December 1990 2,057 cases had been brought before the Court under Art. 177 out of a total of 4,116 cases. Indeed, the proportion of Art. 177 cases that had been decided (1,699) out of the total cases decided (2,856) was nearer 60 per cent. The figures are contained in the Commission's *XXIVth General Report on the Activities of the Communities 1990*, Luxembourg, EC Official Publications 1991, p. 449. By 31 December 1994 2,893 cases had been brought before the Court for a preliminary ruling out of a total of 6,184 cases.

Court under Article 177 raise questions of interpretation rather than validity.[4] The Court sees the function of Article 177 as ensuring 'unity of interpretation of Community law' within all the member states.[5]

Article 177 provides that

The Court of Justice shall have jurisdiction to give preliminary rulings concerning:

(a) the interpretation of this Treaty;

(b) the validity and interpretation of acts of the institutions of the Community *and of the European Central Bank*;

(c) the interpretation of the statutes of bodies established by an act of the Council, where those statutes so provide.

Where such a question is raised before any court or tribunal of a Member State, that court or tribunal may, if it considers that a decision on the question is necessary to enable it to give judgment, request the Court of Justice to give a ruling thereon.

Where any such question is raised in a case pending before a court or tribunal of a Member State against whose decisions there is no judicial remedy under national law, that court or tribunal shall bring the matter before the Court of Justice.[6]

ARTICLE 177(1): SCOPE OF THE COURT'S JURISDICTION

The range of provisions upon which the Court can give a ruling under Article 177 is defined by the first paragraph. The meaning of subparagraph (a) is self-explanatory, and subparagraph (c) has proved to be of no practical importance to date. The meaning of 'acts of the institutions of the Community' in subparagraph (b) has, however, given rise to some discussion in the Court's case law. Clearly, this phrase is apt to cover the legally binding provisions referred to in Article 189 of the Treaty: regulations, directives and decisions. The Court has decided that it is apt also to cover the non-binding recommendations and opinions mentioned in that Article[7] and international agreements entered into by the Community under

---

4 Of the 2,057 cases referred to the Court by 31 December 1990, 275 raised questions of validity and 1,841 raised questions of interpretation. Of the 1,699 cases that had been decided by that date, 263 dealt with questions of validity and 1,462 with questions of interpretion. See the *XXIVth General Report*, p. 449.

5 Cases 28–30/62 *Da Costa* v *Nederlandse Belastingadministratie* [1963] ECR 31, 38.

6 The words in italics were added by the Maastricht Treaty amendments. The change permits rulings on the interpretation of acts of the ECB: see Ch. 21 on the powers of the ECB.

7 Case C-322/88 *Grimaldi* v *Fonds des maladies professionelles* [1989] ECR 4407, 4419.

powers given in the Treaty. In *Haegeman v Belgium* the Court decided that it had jurisdiction under Article 177 to give a ruling on the 1961 Association Agreement between the Community and Greece:

The Athens Agreement was concluded by the Council under Articles 228 and 238 of the Treaty as appears from the terms of the Decision dated 25 September 1961. This Agreement is therefore, in so far as it concerns the Community, an act of one of the institutions of the Community within the meaning of subparagraph (b) of the first paragraph of Article 177.[8]

Similar reasoning was adopted by the Court in relation to the Association Agreement between the Community and Turkey in *Demirel v Stadt Schwäbisch Gmünd*.[9] Other examples include *Bresciani v Amministrazione Italiana delle Finanze*,[10] where the Court interpreted the 1963 Yaounde Convention, and *Razanatsimba*,[11] where the Court interpreted the first Lome Convention, which were concluded by the Community under Articles 131 and 228 of the Treaty. In *Polydor v Harlequin Record Shops*[12] the Court interpreted the 1972 Agreement between the Community and Portugal, which was concluded by the Community under Article 228 of the Treaty. More controversially, the Court has decided that it can interpret the General Agreement on Tariffs and Trade (GATT) under Article 177 from 1 August 1968, the date on which the Community was substituted for its member states in relation to their commitments under GATT.[13]

The Court is even willing to give rulings on decisions. made by legislative bodies set up under such international agreements.[14] On the other hand the Court has no jurisdiction to interpret international agreements concluded solely by the member states. In *Hurd v Jones*[15] the Court

---

8 Case 181/73 [1974] ECR 449, 459.

9 Case 12/86 [1987] ECR 3719, 3750–51.

10 Case 87/75 [1976] ECR 129.

11 Case 65/77 [1977] ECR 2229.

12 Case 270/80 [1982] ECR 329.

13 See Case 267–9/81 *Amministrazione delle Finanze dello Stato v SPI and SAMI* [1983] ECR 801 and the criticism of the decision in this case by Hartley, *European Community Law*, pp. 272–3. See also Opinion 1/91 *Opinion on the Draft Agreement on the European Economic Area* [1991] ECR I-6079, [1992] 1 CMLR 245.

14 See the decisions of the Association Council established by the Association Agreement between the Community and Turkey, which were interpreted in Case C-192/89 *Sevince v Staatsecretaris van Justite* [1990] ECR 1–3461, noted by Schermers (1991) 28 CMLRev 183 and by Kuijper (1991) 28 CMLRev 1005. See also Case C-18/90 *Kziber* [1991] ECR I–199, noted by Weber (1991) 28 CMLRev 959 and by Neuwahl (1991) 16 ELRev 326.

15 Case 44/84 [1986] ECR 29, 76–7. See also Case C-379/92 *Peralta* [1994] ECR I-3453, 3494–5, in which the Court declined to rule on the compatibility of Italian legislation with the International Convention for the Prevention of Pollution from

stated that it had no jurisdiction to interpret the Statute of the European School and its protocols because they were based on international agreements concluded solely by the member states. However, the Court was able to rule on the meaning of Article 3 of the Act of Accession 1972.

The Court cannot give a ruling on questions of national law: in *Adlerblum* v *Caisse Nationale d'Assurance Vieillesse des Travailleurs Salariés*[16] the Court said: 'the classification under French social security legislation of a benefit awarded under the German Compensation Law . . . pertains to national law alone and thus does not come within the jurisdiction of the Court of Justice'. Therefore it is unable to rule explicitly that a provision of national law is not compatible with Community law. The Court has expressed its ability to circumvent this constraint:

Although the Court has no jurisdiction in proceedings under Article 177 of the EEC Treaty to rule on the question whether provisions of national legislation are compatible with the Treaty, it may provide the national court with all such criteria for the interpretation of Community law which may enable it to answer that question.[17]

If the national court asks a direct question as to whether or not certain provisions of national law are compatible with Community law (without specifying which provisions of Community law), the Court will reply by giving an interpretation of the provisions of Community law that seem to be relevant to the case from the information supplied by the national court.[18]

The Court is willing to give a ruling on a provision of Community law where it is being applied in a member state to situations that are not required to be covered by Community law. The Court gave a ruling on the meaning of provisions of Community law that were normally applicable to spouses of Community nationals working in another member state but had been extended by Belgian law to apply to foreign spouses of Belgian nationals working in Belgium.[19]

Ships as the Community has not assumed the powers previously exercised by the member states in the field to which the Convention applies.

16 Case 93/75 [1975] ECR 2147, 2151.

17 Case 97/83 *Melkunie* [1984] ECR 2367, 2382–3. See similar statements by the Court in Case 16/83 *Prantl* [1984] ECR 1299, 1324 and Case 237/82 *Jongeneel Kaas* v *Netherlands* [1984] ECR 483, 500.

18 See e.g., Cases 209–13/84 *Ministère Public* v *Asjes* [1986] ECR 1425, 1460–61.

19 Cases C-297/88 and C-197/89 *Dzodzi* v *Belgium* [1990] ECR I-3763, 3793–5. The Court said it would not give a ruling where the Art. 177 procedure was being abused by a 'contrived dispute' or where the 'provision of Community law referred to the Court for interpretation was manifestly incapable of applying' (para. 40). See also Case C-231/89 *Gmurzynska-Bscher* v *Oberfinanzdirektion Köln* [1990] ECR I-4003. Both cases are

If a person would have had standing to seek the annulment of a Community measure under Article 173 but failed to do so within the time-limit then the Court of Justice will not consider the validity of that measure in an Article 177 reference from a national court where the proceedings have been instigated by the person concerned.[20]

ARTICLE 177(2): NATIONAL COURTS AND TRIBUNALS THAT CAN REFER

The Court of Justice has dealt with the question of whether a body is a court or tribunal for the purposes of Article 177 on a case-by-case basis. If the parties choose in a contract that any disputes between them should be decided by arbitration, then the arbiter is not a court or tribunal within the meaning of Article 177. For example, in *Nordsee* v *Reederei Mond*[21] the Court was influenced by the fact that the parties had freely chosen by contract in 1973 to refer their disputes to arbitration in Germany and the German public authorities were not 'called upon to intervene automatically in the proceedings before the arbitrator'. On the other hand, if the law of a member state imposes an arbitration board on parties that cannot agree on a particular issue, and that law governs the composition of the board in a way that ensures it is not entirely within the parties' discretion, the board is a tribunal within the meaning of Article 177. In *Handels-og Kontorfunktio-naerernes Forbund i Danmark* v *Dansk Arbejdsgiverforening*,[22] for example, the Court noted that the jurisdiction of the Danish Industrial Board was not dependent on the parties' agreement. If the parties could not agree on the application of a collective agreement, then either party was entitled under Danish law to take the case to the Industrial Board. It was also significant that Danish law governed the composition of the board, determining the means by which the umpire was to be appointed when the parties could not agree.

It seems that a national body can constitute a court or tribunal within the meaning of Article 177 only if the national law requires, at least in practice, disputes to be settled before it and the law or the public authorities

---

noted by Delgado and Muñoa in (1992) 29 CMLRev 152. See also Case C-384/89 *Ministère Public* v *Tomatis and Fulchiron* [1991] ECR I-127. The Court's ruling must be binding in national law, see Case C-346/93, Ch. 10, note 116.

20 See Case C-188/92 *TWD Textilewerke Deggendorf GmbH* v *Germany* [1994] ECR I-833, noted by Ross (1994) 19 ELRev 640.

21 Case 102/81 [1982] ECR 1095, 1110–11.

22 Case 109/88 [1989] ECR 3199, 3224–5.

have some control over the composition of the body. In *Vaassen* v *Beambtenfonds Mijnbedrijf*[23] the Court permitted the 'Scheidsgerecht' (a Dutch arbitration tribunal for a fund established for non-manual workers in the mining industry) to refer a case under Article 177. The Scheidsgerecht was constituted under Dutch law, its members were appointed by a Dutch Minister, and the workers in the industry had to be members of the fund and had to resolve any disputes between themselves and the insurer before the Scheidsgerecht.

A body may meet these requirements even if it is not regarded as a court or tribunal under its own national law. In *Broekmeulen* v *Huisarts Registratie Commissie*[24] the Dutch Government stated that the Appeals Committee of the Royal Netherlands Society for the Promotion of Medicine was not a court or tribunal under Netherlands law. None the less the Court decided that the Appeals Committee could refer a case under Article 177. It took the view that, in practice, no one could work as a general practitioner in the Netherlands without being registered by the Royal Netherlands Society, and there was no right of appeal to the courts from a decision of the Appeals Committee refusing registration. Thus any doctor from another member state seeking to exercise the right to establish in the Netherlands was compelled to have his or her status decided by the Appeals Committee. In addition, the Court noted that the public authorities in the Netherlands had a significant degree of involvement in the composition of the Appeals Committee.[25] One-third of the committee was appointed by the Netherlands medical faculties, one-third by the Society's Board and one-third, including the Chair, by Government Ministers.

In *Corbiau*[26] the Court of Justice decided that the *Directeur des Contributions* (Director of Taxation) in Luxembourg was not a court or tribunal for the purposes of Article 177 and could not refer a question to the Court. The Court established that one of the requirements of being a court or tribunal for the purposes of Article 177 is that it must be in a third-party relationship with the person that took the decision which is the subject-matter of the proceedings. In this case Mr Corbiau was complaining about a decision made by the Luxembourg tax authorities to the Director of those authorities. The Director had an institutional connection with those who made the original decision.

If a national body exercises functions that are preliminary to its judicial function, the Court may accept a reference even though it is made at an

23 Case 61/65 [1966] ECR 261, 273.
24 Case 246/80 [1981] ECR 2311.
25 ibid., p. 2326.
26 Case C-24/92 *Corbiau* v *Administration des Contributions* [1993] ECR I-1277; *The Times*, 20 May 1993.

early stage in the proceedings. In *Pretore di Salo* v *Persons Unknown*[27] the *pretore* had not identified the alleged perpetrators of the pollution of certain fresh waters. In Italy a *pretore* acts initially as a public prosecutor and then as an examining magistrate. While the *pretore* was still acting as the public prosecutor in the course of a preparatory inquiry he decided to refer certain questions of Community law to the European Court. The Court, in accepting the reference, said:

The Court has jurisdiction to reply to a request for a preliminary ruling if that request emanates from a court or tribunal which has acted in the general framework of its task of judging, independently and in accordance with the law, cases coming within the jurisdiction conferred on it by law, even though certain functions of that court or tribunal in the proceedings which gave rise to the reference for a preliminary ruling are not, strictly speaking, of a judicial nature.[28]

The Court has repeatedly stated that although it may be in the interests of the proper administration of justice for a national court to hold an *inter partes* hearing before referring a case under Article 177 it is not a requirement. The President of an Italian district court is performing a judicial function within the meaning of Article 177 when adjudicating on an application in *ex parte* summary proceedings.[29] A national court hearing an appeal against an arbitration award is still a court for the purposes of Article 177 even if it has to decide the case according to what appears fair and reasonable.[30] Such a court is bound to apply the rules of Community law.[31] Article 177 provides that courts or tribunals in a 'Member State' can refer questions of EC law to the Court of Justice. The Court seems to have construed 'Member State' as including any territory to which the EC Treaty applies, even if only in part.[32] The territorial scope of the Treaty is defined by Article 227 and extends to the French overseas departments of Guadeloupe, French Guyana, Martinique, Réunion and Saint-Pierre and Miquelon, the overseas countries and territories listed in Annex IV to the Treaty,[33] the European territories for whose external relations a member state is responsible (Gibraltar), and the Channel Islands and the Isle of Man.[34]

27 Case 14/86 [1987] ECR 2545.
28 ibid., p. 2567.
29 See Case C-18/93 *Corsica Ferries* [1994] ECR I-1783, para. 12 and the long list of cases cited therein.
30 See Case C-393/92 *Almelo* [1994] ECR I-1477.
31 ibid. at p. 1515.
32 See Arnull, 'The Evolution of the Court's jurisdiction under Article 177 EEC' (1993) 18 ELRev 129, 132.
33 Including French Polynesia; see Cases C-100 and 101/89 *Kaefer and Procacci* v *France* [1990] ECR I-4647.
34 In relation to the Isle of Man, see Case C-355/89 *DHSS (Isle of Man)* v *Barr and Montrose Holdings* [1991] ECR I-3479.

ARTICLE 177(2): DISCRETION OF NATIONAL COURTS AND TRIBUNALS TO REFER

A national court or tribunal can request a ruling from the European Court on a question of Community law only 'if it considers that a decision on the question is necessary to enable it to give judgment'.[35] The European Court originally took a strict approach that it was not a matter for it to decide whether a ruling on the question of Community law was necessary to enable the national court to give judgment. In *Costa v ENEL*, the Court said: 'Article 177 is based upon a clear separation of functions between national courts and the Court of Justice, it cannot empower the latter either to investigate the facts of the case or to criticize the grounds and purpose of the request for interpretation.'[36]

The Court has on numerous occasions confirmed this separation of functions:

The Court has consistently held that Article 177 provides the framework for close co-operation between national courts and the Court of Justice, based on a division of responsibilities between them. Within that framework, it is solely for the national court before which the dispute has been brought, and which must assume the responsibility for the subsequent judicial decision, to determine in the light of the particular circumstances of each case both the need for a preliminary ruling in order to enable it to deliver judgment and the relevance of the question which it submits to the Court.[37]

There are however some circumstances where the European Court will not abide by the national court's view of the necessity of a ruling on Community law. The Court will give a ruling only where the national court or tribunal is called upon to give judgment in proceedings intended to lead to a decision of a judicial nature. The Court made this point in the *Borker* case,[38] in which the Court declined to give a ruling on a reference

---

35 Art. 177(2).

36 Case 6/64, note 2 above, p. 593.

37 Case C-127/92 *Enderby v Frenchay Health Authority* [1993] ECR I-0000, [1994] 1 CMLR 8 at para. 10. Cf. the similar wording in Cases C-332, 333 and 335/92 *Eurico Italia Srl v Ente Nazionale Risi* [1994] ECR I-711, [1944] 2 CMLR 580 at para. 17; Case C-67/91 *Asociación Española de Banca Privada* [1992] ECR I-4785, at para. 25; Case 278/82 *Rewe v Hauptzollämter Flensburg, Itzehoe and Lübeck-West* [1984] ECR 721, 753; Case 53/79 *ONPTS v Damiani* [1980] ECR 273, 281–2; and Cases 209–13/84, note 18 above, p. 1460.

38 Case 130/80 [1980] ECR 1975.

from the Conseil de l'Ordre (Bar Council) of the Cour de Paris. The Conseil de l'Ordre did not have before it a case that it was under a legal duty to try, but rather a request for a declaration relating to a dispute between a member of the Bar and the courts or tribunals of another member state.

The European Court has no jurisdiction to hear a reference for a preliminary ruling when at the time it is made the procedure before the national court or tribunal making the reference has already been terminated.[39]

The Court may decline to be used by parties who have no dispute between them but have colluded to litigate between themselves in a national court in order to get a ruling on a point of Community law. In *Foglia* v *Novello*[40] an Italian wine dealer, Mr Foglia, sold some cases of Italian liqueur wines to Mrs Novello, to be delivered as a gift to her friend in Menton, France. The contract included a clause that Novello was not to be liable for any duties on the wine that were claimed by the Italian or French authorities contrary to the provisions of the free movement of goods. Foglia engaged the Danzas company to take the goods to France and included a clause that Danzas would be liable for any duties claimed contrary to the free movement of goods. Danzas delivered the wine and presented a bill to Foglia including an amount to cover the consumption tax paid to the French authorities. Foglia paid the bill in full, without protesting to Danzas about the amount relating to the French tax, and sought to recover the whole amount from Novello. She declined to pay the amount relating to the French consumption tax and Foglia brought proceedings against her in the Italian courts to recover that amount. The Italian court of first instance referred questions to the European Court on the meaning of Articles 92 and 95 of the Treaty to enable it to ascertain whether the French law on consumption tax for liqueur wines was contrary to those provisions of the Treaty. In the written pleadings before the European Court Foglia and Novello both argued that the French legislation was incompatible with Community law. If this finding were upheld, then it would be Danzas who would have to bear the cost of the tax and not Foglia or Novello. On the basis of these facts the Court decided it had no jurisdiction to give a ruling, explaining that:

the parties to the main action are concerned to obtain a ruling that the French tax system is invalid for liqueur wines by the expedient of proceedings before an Italian

39 See Case C-159/90 *Society for the Protection of the Unborn Child* v *Grogan* [1991] ECR I-4685, 4737, [1991] 3 CMLR 849, 889 and Case 338/85 *Pardini* v *Ministero del Commercio con L'Estero* [1988] ECR 2041, 2075.
40 Case 104/79 [1980] ECR 745.

court between two private individuals who are in agreement as to the result to be attained and who have inserted a clause in their contract in order to induce the Italian court to give a ruling on the point . . .

The duty of the Court of Justice under Article 177 of the EEC Treaty is to supply all courts in the Community with the information on the interpretation of Community law which is necessary to enable them to settle genuine disputes which are brought before them.[41]

The Italian court decided to ask the European Court again for a ruling on the interpretation of Articles 92 and 95 and met with no success. However, it also asked a series of questions about the meaning of Article 177.[42] The Court of Justice ruled that it has a duty under that Article to confirm its own jurisdiction by examining, where necessary, the conditions on which the case has been referred to it by the national court. It explained that

the duty assigned to the Court by Article 177 is not that of delivering advisory opinions on general or hypothetical questions but of assisting in the administration of justice in the Member States. It accordingly does not have jurisdiction to reply to questions of interpretation which are submitted to it within the framework of procedural devices arranged by the parties in order to induce the Court to give its views on certain problems of Community law which do not correspond to an objective requirement inherent in the resolution of a dispute.[43]

The Court emphasized that it has to display 'special vigilance' when a question is referred to it by a national court with a view to it judging the compatibility of the law of another member state with Community law.[44] The Court noted that such disputes can be artificial in that the national court may not be in a position to provide effective protection of the individuals concerned and as the member state whose legislation is being impugned is not a party to the action in the national court its interests may not be properly defended. None the less, if the dispute between the parties is a genuine one, then the Court will give a ruling on provisions of Community law that will enable the national court to assess whether the provisions of law in another member state are compatible with Community law.[45]

In *Bertini* v *Regione Lazio*[46] the Court was asked by an Italian court

41 ibid., pp. 759–60.
42 Case 244/80 *Foglia* v *Novello (No. 2)* [1981] ECR 3045.
43 ibid., pp. 3062–3.
44 ibid., p. 3065.
45 See Case 46/80 *Vinal* v *Orbat* [1981] ECR 77, 91 and Case C-150/88 *Parfümerie-Fabrik 4711* v *Provide* [1989] ECR 3891, 3913.
46 Cases 98, 162, 258/85 [1986] ECR 1885.

whether Community law required a fixed student intake to be established at Italian medical schools. The Italian Government and the Commission urged the Court to treat the request as inadmissible because an answer to the question was unnecessary for the Italian court to decide the dispute before it, which concerned whether certain surgeons had been unlawfully dismissed by various Italian local health authorities. The Third Chamber of the Court thought it was regrettable that the national court had not given any reason why a ruling on the question of Community law was necessary to enable it to give judgment, but none the less decided to give a ruling. It stated that it is for the national court to weigh up the necessity of obtaining such a ruling and its 'assessment must be respected even if, as in this case, it is difficult to see how the answers which the Court is asked to give can influence the decision'.[47]

The Third Chamber seems to have construed *Foglia* v *Novello (No. 2)* restrictively.[48] It seems to have been prepared to give an academic ruling on a point of law that bore no relation to the resolution of the dispute before the Italian court, even though in *Foglia* the Court had indicated that it would not give such advisory opinions on Community law. The Third Chamber may have given a ruling for reasons of 'procedural economy' to stave off possible references in the twenty similar cases that were pending before the Italian courts.

The Court has subsequently been much stricter in rejecting references which request an advisory or hypothetical opinion, notably in the *Meilicke* and *Lourenço Dias* cases.[49] It has reiterated a long established test that it has no jurisdiction to rule on a question submitted by a national court where the interpretation of Community law bears: 'no relation to the actual nature of the case or the subject-matter of the main action'.[50] In addition it

---

47 ibid., p. 1897.

48 ibid., see Advocate-General Mischo's opinion at p. 1889.

49 Case C-83/91 *Meilicke* and *ADV/ORGA F.A. Meyer AG* [1992] ECR I-4871 (noted by Arnull (1993) 30 CMLRev 613–22 and by Kennedy (1993) 18 ELRev 121–9) and Case C-343/90 *Lourenço Dias* v *Director da Alfândega do Porto* [1992] ECR I-4673 (noted by Kennedy ibid.) In both cases the Court cited *Foglia* v *Novello (No. 2)* in support of its decisions.

50 See Case C-378/93 *La Pyramide* [1994] ECR I-3999, 4008 reiterating Case 126/80 *Salonia* v *Poidomani and Giglio* [1981] ECR 1563, 1576–7. Similar versions of the test are applied in Case C-428/93 *Monin Automobiles (No. 2)* [1994] ECR I-1707, 1714, Case C-18/93 *Corsica Ferries* [1994] ECR I-1783, 1818; Case C-343/90 above at para. 18; and Case C-286/88 *Falciola* [1990] ECR I-191, 195. In *Falciola* the Court issued an order stating that it had no jurisdiction to answer the questions referred to it by the Italian court. The questions were highly theoretical, relating to Arts. 5, 177 and 189 EEC, and an answer was not necessary to settle the dispute in the main action, which concerned Council Dirs. 71/304 and 71/305 and certain provisions of Italian law. See also Case 105/79 *Independence of the Judiciary* [1979] ECR 2257, where the Court issued an order saying it had no jurisdiction.

has specified that in order for it to establish whether it has jurisdiction, 'it is essential for the national court to explain the reasons why it considers that a reply to its questions is necessary in order to resolve the dispute'.[51] This requirement to contextualize the questions of Community law has been emphasised by the Court:

The need to provide an interpretation of Community law which will be of use to the national court makes it necessary that the national court defines the factual and legislative context of the questions it is asking or, at the very least, explains the factual circumstances on which those questions are based.[52]

Contextualisation is particularly important in certain areas, like that of competition, characterized by complex factual and legal situations.[53] However, the requirement is 'less pressing' where the questions relate to 'specific technical points' and the Court is able to give a useful reply without an exhaustive account of the legal and factual situation.[54] The legal and factual situation may be sufficiently well established from a previous reference for a preliminary ruling made by the same court and concerning the same producer that it does not have to be repeated.[55] In *Enderby*[56] the Court of Justice accepted a reference from the English Court of Appeal despite the objections of the German Government. The Court of Appeal asked questions relating to the burden of proof for showing objective justification that pharmacists ought to be paid more than speech therapists, the former being predominantly a male occupation and the latter almost exclusively female, without first establishing whether speech therapists and pharmacists do equivalent jobs and therefore deserve equal pay. The German Government argued that the Court should not rule on the questions asked because the two professions were not comparable and therefore there could be no breach of Article 119. The Court showed the limits of its willingness to turn down hypothetical questions by saying that:

---

51 Case C-378/93, above at para. 13 and Case C-343/90, above at para. 19.
52 Case 378/93 above at para. 14 and Cases C-320-2/90 *Telemarsicabruzzo* v *Circostel* [1993] ECR I-393, at para. 6; Case C-157/92 *Pretore di Genova* v *Banchero* [1993] ECR I-1085, at para. 4; and Case C-386/92 *Monin Automobiles (No. 1)* [1993] ECR I-2049, at para. 6.
53 See Case C-378/93, above at para. 15.
54 See Case C-316/93 *Vaneetveld* v *Le Foyer* [1994] ECR I-763, at para. 13. In that case the questions concerned whether an individual could rely on the direct effect of Directive 84/5 before the final date for implementation in national law. Clearly this was not possible.
55 See Cases C-133, 300 and 362/93 *Crispoltoni* [1994] ECR I-4863, 4900 referring to the previous case of Case C-368/89 *Crispoltoni* v *Fattoria Autonoma Tabbachi di Città di Castello* [1991] ECR I-3695.
56 Case C-127/92 above, at paras. 8–12.

Where, as here, the Court receives a request for interpretation of Community law which is not manifestly unrelated to the reality or the subject-matter of the main proceedings, it must reply to that request and is not required to consider the validity of a hypothesis which it is for the referring court to verify subsequently if that should prove to be necessary.[57]

The European Court has consistently held that a national court has a discretion as to the appropriate time to refer a case for a preliminary ruling. This discretion as to timing is not in any way fettered by the Court: 'The decision at what stage in proceedings a question should be referred to the Court of Justice for a preliminary ruling is . . . dictated by considerations of procedural economy and efficiency to be weighed only by the national court and not by the Court of Justice.'[58]

The Court has merely made a polite request that it might be convenient if national courts were to establish the facts in the case and to settle questions of national law before referring the case to the Court. This will enable the Court to take cognizance of all matters of fact and law that may be relevant to the interpretation of Community law that it is called upon to give. The *Pretore di Salo*[59] case is an example of the Court hearing a case at a very early stage, before the accused had even been identified. The Court heard the case despite its advice that the national court might do better to wait until the facts had been determined.

A national court always has the option of referring the same question on the interpretation of Community law it has asked in a previous case involving different parties.[60] An Article 177 ruling that a particular measure of Community law is invalid is held by the Court to be sufficient reason for any other national court to regard that measure as void for the purposes of a judgment that it has to give.[61] None the less, any such national court still has the discretion to refer a question to the European Court on the validity of the measure in question. The Court of Justice merely discourages such references unless questions arise as to the grounds, the scope and possibly the consequences of the invalidity established in the earlier case.[62]

---

57 ibid. at para. 12.
58 Case 14/86, note 27 above, p. 2568. Similar words were used in Cases 36, 71/80 *Irish Creamery Milk Suppliers Association* v *Ireland* [1981] ECR 735, 748, and Case 72/83 *Campus Oil Ltd* v *Minister for Industry and Energy* [1984] ECR 2727, 2745.
59 Case 14/86, note 27 above; see also Cases 36, 71/80, note 58 above.
60 Cases 28–30/62, note 5 above. See also Cases C-332, 333 and 335/92, note 37 above, at para. 15.
61 Case 66/80 *International Chemical Corporation* v *Amministrazione delle Finanze dello Stato* [1981] ECR 1191; Case 112/83 *Produits de Maïs* v *Administration des douanes et droits indirects* [1985] ECR 719, 747.
62 Case 66/80, note 61 above.

A national court can even seek more than one preliminary ruling from the European Court in relation to the same case. The Court has stated that

such a procedure may be justified when the national court encounters fresh difficulties in understanding or applying the [Court's] judgment, when it refers a fresh question of law to the Court, or again when it submits new considerations which might lead the Court to give a different answer to a question submitted earlier.[63]

The Court has no jurisdiction to give a second preliminary ruling where the national court is contesting the validity of the Court's decision in the first ruling.[64]

The European Court will give a ruling on a reference from a national court or tribunal even when the decision to refer the case to the European Court has been appealed to a higher national court or tribunal.[65] If, however, the European Court is made aware that the decision to refer the case to it has been quashed on appeal by a superior national court, it will remove the case from its register and give no ruling on the question(s) of Community law.[66]

A national court or tribunal cannot be prevented from referring a question of Community law to the European Court by a rule of national law that it is bound to follow the decision of a higher court on the same question of Community law.[67]

A national court or tribunal has a great deal of discretion as to the form of the question(s) it refers to the European Court: 'It is permissible for the national court to formulate its request in a simple and direct way leaving to this Court the duty of rendering a decision on that request only in so far as it has jurisdiction to do so.'[68]

The European Court is willing to abstract the questions of Community law from the questions referred by the national court. This can be illustrated by *Ministère Public* v *Asjes* where the Tribunal de Police de Paris asked for a 'ruling as to whether Articles L330–3, R330–9 and R330–15 of

---

63 Case 69/85 *Wünsche* v *Germany* [1986] ECR 947, 953; and Case 14/86, note 27 above, p. 2569.

64 Case 69/85, note 63 above.

65 Case 13/61 *de Greus* v *Boschvan Rijn* [1962] ECR 45, 50.

66 This happened in Case 31/68 *Chanel* v *Cepha* [1970] ECR 403 and has been confirmed by dicta of the Court in Case 166/73 *Rheinmühlen-Düsseldorf* v *Einfuhr- und Vorratsstelle Getreide* [1974] ECR 139, 147; and in Case 106/77 *Amministrazione delle Finanze dello Stato* v *Simmenthal* [1978] ECR 629, 642.

67 Case 166/73 *Rheinmühlen* v *Einfuhr- und Vorratsstelle Getreide* [1978] ECR 33, 39. Followed by Hidden J in *Feehan* v *Commissioners of Customs and Excise* [1995] 1 CMLR 193, 198–9.

68 Case 13/61, note 65 above.

the *Code de l'aviation civile* are in conformity with Community law'.[69] The European Court has no jurisdiction under Article 177 to determine whether provisions of national law are in conformity with Community law, and the national court did not ask for the interpretation of a specific provision of Community law. It would seem that the European Court had no jurisdiction to reply to the French tribunal. The Court was able to glean from the judgments requesting a preliminary ruling that the question was raised in connection with the Treaty rules on competition. It then proceeded to give an interpretation of specific provisions of Community competition law that it considered to be of assistance to the French tribunal.

The Court has expressed its liberal policy in this area as follows:

It is for the Court, when faced with questions which are not framed in an appropriate manner or which go beyond its functions under Article 177, to extract from all the information provided by the national court, in particular from the grounds of the decision referring the questions, the points of Community law which require interpretation or whose validity is at issue, having regard to the subject-matter of the dispute. In order to provide a satisfactory answer to a national court which has referred a question to it, the Court of Justice may deem it necessary to consider provisions of Community law to which the national court has not referred in the text of its question. However, it is for the national court to decide whether or not the rule of Community law, as interpreted by the Court of Justice pursuant to Article 177, is applicable in the case before it.[70]

The Court may decline to answer a question of Community law if it will have no bearing on the case before the national court. In *Produits de mais*[71] the Court declined to answer certain questions about the possible retrospective effect of its ruling of 15 October 1980 on the invalidity of Regulation 652/76 because they were irrelevant to the case before it, which was initiated in the national court after that ruling. The Court has the power, of its own motion, to consider provisions of Community law not referred to in the national court's question[72] but is not obliged to do so

---

69 Cases 209–13/84, note 18 above.

70 Case 35/85 *Procureur de la République* v *Tissier* [1986] ECR 1207, 1212. Cf. similar sentiments in Cases C-332, 333 and 335/92, note 37 above, at para 19 and Cases C-149 and 150/91, *Sanders Adour et Guyomarc'h Orthez Nutrition Animale* [1992] ECR I-3899, at para. 10.

71 Case 112/83, note 61 above.

72 See the dictum quoted above in Case 35/85, note 70 above, the approach of the Court in Cases 209–13/84, note 18 above and Case C-187/91 *Belgium* v *Belovo* [1992] ECR I-0000, judgment of 16 July 1992. See also an example of the raising of a ground of invalidity on the Court's own motion – lack of publication of a decision – in Cases 73, 74/63 *Handelsvereniging Rotterdam* v *Minister van Landbouw* [1964] ECR 1, 14 (the Court decided it was not a ground for rendering the decision invalid).

and to answer questions not asked by the national court.[73] In *Hauptzollamt Bielefeld* v *König*[74] the national court had questioned the validity of a regulation but on the ground only that it was issued after the expiry of the power conferred in Article 38 EEC. The Court said that it 'is not called upon to examine the compatibility with general principles of law of the provision in Article 2(1) of the Regulation, under which the Regulation was to "enter into force" on a date prior to its publication, this question not having been raised by the national court'.

THE APPROACH OF COURTS IN THE UNITED KINGDOM TO THEIR DISCRETION TO REFER

In *Bulmer* v *Bollinger*[75] Lord Denning MR laid down guidelines for English courts, other than the House of Lords, as to when it is appropriate for them to refer cases to the European Court for a preliminary ruling. He gave four guidelines as to whether a decision from the European Court is 'necessary' within the meaning of Article 177.

1 The decision on the question of Community law must be conclusive of the case.[76]
2 The national court may choose to follow a previous ruling of the European Court on the same point of Community law, but it may choose to refer the same point of law to the European Court in the hope that it will give a different ruling.
3 The national court may decline to regard a reference to the European Court as necessary on grounds of *acte clair*, where the 'point is reasonably clear and free from doubt'.[77]
4 'In general it is best to decide the facts first' before determining whether it is necessary to refer the point of Community law.[78]

If the national court decides that a reference is necessary, it still has a discretion whether or not to refer the case to the European Court. Lord Denning then listed six factors that national courts can take into account in exercising that discretion.

73 See Case 157/84 *Frascogna* v *Caisse des Dépots et Consignations* [1985] ECR 1739.
74 Case 185/73 [1974] ECR 607, 617.
75 [1974] Ch. 401, [1974] 2 CMLR 91.
76 *Bulmer* v *Bollinger*, note 75 above, p. 422. Hartley, *European Community Law*, persuasively argues that necessary 'should be interpreted to mean that the point *could* be decisive. In other words, it should be sufficient if a decision on the point is potentially decisive: it should not have to be proved that it would be decisive in all possible eventualities' (p. 291).
77 *Bulmer* v *Bollinger*, note 75 above, p. 423.
78 ibid., p. 423.

1 Bear in mind the length of time it takes to get a ruling from the European Court.
2 Do not overload the Court with too many references.[79]
3 Formulate the question clearly for the European Court.
4 Do not refer the case unless the point of Community law is difficult and important.
5 Bear in mind the expense to the parties of referring a case to the European Court.
6 Take into account the wishes of the parties and hesitate to refer where one or both of the parties does not wish it.[80]

Lord Denning's guidelines were given only limited support by the majority of the Court of Appeal. Lord Justice Stamp concurred with Lord Justice Stephenson, who said:

The guidelines should be few and firmly related to the basic requirement that the decision of the question raised must be necessary at the time the reference is requested to enable the court to give judgment at the end of the case. The best judge of that in any particular case is the court to which the Treaty submits the discretion, the judge who will have to give that judgment . . . He must exercise his right to refer sparingly and in case of serious doubt or difficulty only . . . He should also bear in mind the other considerations which Lord Denning MR has set out, but beyond that I would not go to guide the court of trial.[81]

Lord Denning's guidelines have been influential in a number of subsequent cases,[82] but they have not met with uncritical approval from the

79 ibid., p., 424. Lord Denning's argument was based on the fact that the Court had to sit in plenary sessions when dealing with preliminary rulings. This is no longer the case and chambers of the Court can hear these cases; see Ch. 6, p. 157.
80 In *Rochdale Borough Council* v *Anders* [1988] 3 CMLR 431, 435–6, Caulfield J decided not to refer the case to the European Court, but changed his mind when counsel for both parties argued in favour of a reference. In *Enderby* v *Frenchay Health Authority* [1991] 1 CMLR 626, 673, the Employment Appeal Tribunal took the very extreme, and erroneous, position that only the House of Lords should refer cases to the European Court, with one or two limited exceptions, including the fact that the parties consent to reference. The Court of Appeal overturned this decision and referred several questions to the European Court for a preliminary ruling, [1992] IRLR 15. In *Portsmouth City Council* v *Richards and Quietlynn Ltd* [1989] 1 CMLR 673, 708, Kerr LJ warned that the 'concept of so-called references by consent should not creep into our practice. All references are by the court. The court must itself be satisfied of the need for the reference.'
81 *Bulmer* v *Bollinger*, note 75 above, p. 430.
82 Although they do not slavishly follow Lord Denning's guidelines, see *R* v *Inner London Education Authority, ex parte Hinde* [1985] 1 CMLR 716; *R* v *Her Majesty's Treasury, ex parte Daily Mail and General Trust plc* [1987] 2 CMLR 1 *R* v *The Pharmaceutical Society of Great Britain, ex parte the Association of Pharmaceutical Importers* [1987] 3 CMLR 951; *R* v *Intervention Board for Agricultural Produce, ex parte the Fish Producers' Organisation Ltd* [1988] 2 CMLR 661; *Enderby* v *Frenchay Health Authority*,

courts. Mr Justice Bingham in endeavouring to follow the guidelines did add the caveat that he was conscious that the European Court is in a better position to determine questions of Community law than a national court. He noted the European Court's expert knowledge of Community law, its unique grasp of all the authentic language texts of that law, the ability of the Community institutions and member states to intervene before that Court and its greater familiarity with a purposive construction of Community law.[83]

After his elevation to Master of the Rolls, Sir Thomas Bingham attempted to express the essential points from earlier decisions, including *Bulmer* v *Bollinger*, as to when English courts other than the House of Lords should refer cases to the European Court:

if the facts have been found and the Community law issue is critical to the court's final decision, the appropriate course is ordinarily to refer the issue to the Court of Justice unless the national court can with complete confidence resolve the issue itself. In considering whether it can with complete confidence resolve the issue itself the national court must be fully mindful of the differences between national and Community legislation, of the pitfalls which face a national court venturing into what may be an unfamiliar field, of the need for uniform interpretation throughout the Community and of the great advantages enjoyed by the Court of Justice in construing Community instruments. If the national court has any real doubt, it should obviously refer.[84]

This dictum was followed by Leggatt LJ in *R* v *Secretary of State for the National Heritage, ex parte Continental Television BV*.[85] He entertained 'real doubt' about how to resolve the issues of Community law and therefore referred them to the European Court.

It has been argued that Bingham MR has reformulated Lord Denning's guidelines in *Bulmer* into three factors. First, the facts must be clarified. Second, the Community law provision must be critical to the final deter-

---

note 80 above; *R* v *Ministry of Agriculture, Fisheries and Food, ex parte Portman Agrochemicals Ltd* [1994] 3 CMLR 18, 25; *Feehan* v *Commissioners of Customs and Excise* [1995] 1 CMLR 193, 199; and in Scotland see *Prince* v *Secretary of State for Scotland*, 1985 SLT 74 (also reported as *Prince* v *Younger* [1985] 1 CMLR 723) and *Brown* v *Secretary of State for Scotland* [1988] 2 CMLR 836, 1989 SLT 402.

83 *Commissioners of Customs and Excise* v *Samex* [1983] 3 CMLR 194, 209–11. This caveat was repeated by the Court of Appeal as a factor favouring a reference to the European Court in *R* v *The Pharmaceutical Society*, note 82 above, pp. 970–71, and in *R* v *Intervention Board*, note 82 above, p. 676. Bingham J's points were accepted by Lord Clyde in the Scottish case of *Brown* v *Secretary of State for Scotland*, note 82 above, p. 849.

84 *R* v *International Stock Exchange, ex parte Else* [1993] Q.B. 534, 545; [1993] 1 All ER 420, 426; [1993] 2 CMLR 677, 715 analysed by Walsh, 'The Appeal of an Article 177 EEC Referral' (1993) 56 MLR 881.

85 [1993] 2 CMLR 333, 346.

mination of the case. Third, if the first two conditions are met a reference must ordinarily be made unless the natural court can resolve the Community law provision with complete confidence.[86] However, this reformulation should no more be read as a statute than Lord Denning's original guidelines. It was surely not the intention of Sir Thomas Bingham to suggest that in no circumstances can a reference be made unless the facts are clarified or unless the Community law issue 'is', not just 'may be', critical to the determination of the case. He said that he was not attempting to 'summarize comprehensively' the effect of the other leading cases including *Bulmer* v *Bollinger*.[87] He has done a great service in creating a presumption that national courts and tribunals should refer cases to the European Court when the facts are established, the question of Community law will decide the case and the court or tribunal is not completely confident as to how it should be decided. This is a *communautaire* approach consistent with the spirit of judicial cooperation that is needed if the Article 177 system is to do its job of ensuring uniform interpretation of Community law throughout the Community. It is, however, a rebuttable presumption in that the national court with doubts as to the meaning of Community law should 'ordinarily' refer the case but not always. In *R* v *Ministry of Agriculture, Fisheries and Food, ex parte Portman Agrochemicals Ltd*[88] Brooke J, after referring to *ex parte Else*, noted that he did not have 'complete confidence' that he could resolve the issues of Community law himself. Even though the facts had been established and the issue of Community law was determinative Brooke J declined to refer the case to the European Court. In doing so he gave careful consideration to Lord Denning's guidelines in *Bulmer* v *Bollinger*; in particular he was influenced by the fact that neither of the parties wished the case to be referred to the European Court and by the fact that 22 months after the date of his decision the issue between the parties would become academic in that the Ministry of Agriculture would then be able to make use of Portman's confidential data regardless of the outcome of the case. Given that a preliminary ruling took, at that time, between 18 months and two years to obtain it may have been given only when the matter had become academic as far as the parties were concerned. This is a good example of where the national court was wise not to seek a ruling even though it had doubts as to the meaning of Community law because the alternative would be that the European Court would end up giving what could be no more than an advisory opinion for future cases and justice being denied to the parties concerned.

86 See Szyszczak (1995) 20 ELRev 214, 222–3 and Walsh, note 84 above.
87 See *ex parte Else* above at note 84.
88 [1994] 3 CMLR 18, 25.

It is regrettable that the Court of Appeal does not always explain the criteria it has adopted for exercising its discretion to refer a case to the European Court even when the matter is controversial.[89]

Mr Justice Parker emphasized that Lord Denning's guidelines are not binding and cannot fetter the discretion of national courts. In particular, he observed that a national court can refer a question of Community law to the European Court before any facts have been found, although he recognized that it would be rare for such a course of action to be taken.[90] In Scotland Lord Cameron stated in *Prince* v *Secretary of State for Scotland* that

a reference to the European Court can competently be made when it appears that it *may* be necessary to do so at any appropriate stage of a litigation. Having regard, however, to our Scottish system of pleading, I would not normally be persuaded that such a necessity, with whatever degree of urgency that word be interpreted, should be held to arise until the pleadings have been adjusted and the real questions in dispute focused on the pleadings. I am fortified in this view of the matter by reference to the judgment of Lord Denning in the case of *Bulmer* v *Bollinger*. In particular, I should find it difficult to make such a reference where preliminary issues of title, competency and relevancy remained unresolved.[91] [our emphasis]

Several judges have placed a more liberal construction on the word 'necessary' than Lord Denning did by inserting the word 'reasonably' in front of it,[92] the implication being that it is enough if the ruling on the question of Community law may be determinative of the outcome of at least part of the case.[93] Warnings have been given about being too quick to assume that a matter is *acte clair*. Lord Justice Kerr said, 'The English authorities show that our courts should exercise great caution in relying on

89 A recent example is *R* v *Home Secretary, ex parte Gallagher* [1994] 3 CMLR 295, in which a 2–1 majority decided to refer the case. The majority in this case seemed to be of the view that on two points Gallagher had an arguable case under Community law and that in the absence of any clear authority from the European Court it was appropriate to refer the case to the Court of Justice.

90 *Bethell* v *SABENA* [1983] 3 CMLR 1, 4–5. The view that it may be appropriate to refer a case at an interlocutory stage before the facts have been found was repeated by Neill J in *An Bord Bainne Co-operative Ltd* v *Milk Marketing Board* [1985] 1 CMLR 6, 10.

91 Note 82 above, p. 78.

92 See *Polydor* v *Harlequin Record Shops* [1980] 2 CMLR 413, 428; *R* v *Plymouth Justices* [1982] QB 863, 869; *An Bord Bainne* v *Milk Marketing Board*, note 90 above, p. 10; *R* v *Inner London Education Authority*, note 82 above, p. 728.

93 This position is more in keeping with the interpretation of 'necessary' given by the European Court in Case 283/81 *CILFIT* v *Italian Ministry of Health* [1982] ECR 3415, see below at note 110, and in *Irish Creamery Milk*, note 58 above.

the doctrine of *"acte clair"* as a ground for declining to make a reference',[94] and Justice MacPherson stated that the *acte clair* test is whether the matter 'is so clear that there can be no doubt about the answer' and that a national court 'should be wary before saying that the matter is indeed thus clear'.[95] The reason for such warnings is that on more than one occasion the English courts have expressed a confident view about the meaning of a particular provision of Community law only to be proved wrong by a subsequent ruling by the European Court.[96] An example of extreme caution in the use of *acte clair* can be seen in *Johnson* v *Chief Adjudication Officer*.[97] In October 1992 the Court of Appeal referred two questions to the Court of Justice as to whether that Court's ruling in *Emmott*[98] had entitled Mrs Johnson to severe disablement allowance from an earlier date than the UK legislation provided for. In October 1993 the Deputy Registrar of the Court of Justice wrote to the Court of Appeal asking if it still wished the Court of Justice to give a ruling given its decision in the *Steenhorst-Neerings* case.[99] Although the ruling of the European Court in *Steenhorst-Neerings* clearly distinguished *Emmott* in a way unfavourable to Mrs Johnson the Court of Appeal decided not to withdraw the reference as the matter was not *acte clair*. It was possible that the European Court might distinguish the *Johnson* case from *Steenhorst-Neerings* given some factual differences between the cases.[100] A less cautious approach to *acte clair* was taken by Hidden J in *Feehan* v *Commissioners of Customs and Excise*.[101]

In England and Scotland it is possible for an appeal to be made against a decision of a court of first instance to refer a case to the European Court for a preliminary ruling under Article 177. In both jurisdictions the appellate courts will interfere with the discretion of the trial judge to refer the case to the European Court if the decision was 'plainly wrong'.[102] The

---

94 *R* v *The Pharmaceutical Society*, note 82 above, p. 971, giving the unanimous judgment of the Court of Appeal.

95 *R* v *HM Treasury*, note 82 above, p. 7.

96 See *Polydor* v *Harlequin Record Shops*, note 92 above, and *Henn and Darby* v *DPP* [1978] 1 WLR 1031, [1981] AC 850, see pp. 455–8 below.

97 [1994] 2 CMLR 829.

98 Case C-208/90 *Emmott* v *Minister for Social Welfare and Another* [1991] ECR I-4269; [1991] 3 CMLR 894.

99 Case C-338/91 *Steenhorst-Neerings* v *Bestuur van de Bedrijfsvereniging Voor Detailhandel, Ambachten en Huisvrouwen* [1993] ECR I-5475.

100 See [1994] 2 CMLR 829, 834–5. The European Court's decision in the *Johnson* case, Case C-410/92 *Johnson* v *Chief Adjudication Officer*, judgment of 6 December 1994, [1995] 1 CMLR 725, followed *Steenhorst-Neerings* and distinguished the *Emmott* case.

101 [1995] 1 CMLR 193, 199–200, illustrating a rather dubious reliance on the opinion of an advocate-general as providing the basis for concluding that the correct application of Community law was so obvious as to leave no scope for any reasonable doubt.

102 See *Bulmer*, note 75 above, [1974] Ch. 401, 431 (per Stephenson LJ) in England, and *Wither* v *Cowie*, 1991 SLT 401, 405–6; [1990] 3 CMLR 445 in Scotland. It is clear

first example of the English Court of Appeal overturning the decision of a lower court to refer a case to the European Court was in *R v International Stock Exchange, ex parte Else*.[103] The Court of Appeal did not specify the test applicable for doing so but did indicate that it was not 'necessary' to refer the questions of Community law to the European Court. Given the technical difficulty of the point perhaps it ought to have been referred. This decision may indicate a willingness on the part of the Court of Appeal to substitute its judgment for that of the first instance judge which may encourage more appeals against referral.[104] The Court of Appeal may be more deferential where it is accepted that a reference to the European Court is 'necessary' but the issue turns on whether the trial judge appropriately exercised his or her discretion to refer.

Although it has been mooted that only appellate courts should have jurisdiction to refer cases to the European Court, following the pattern of the 1971 Protocol to the Brussels Convention,[105] this has the disadvantage that in cases that clearly turn on a difficult question of Community law it introduces an extra delay of a fruitless appeal at national level before the matter can be resolved by the European Court.[106]

ARTICLE 177(3): THE OBLIGATION ON NATIONAL COURTS OF LAST RESORT TO REFER QUESTIONS OF COMMUNITY LAW TO THE EUROPEAN COURT

The language of the third paragraph of Article 177 is imperative. It states that courts or tribunals against whose decisions there is no judicial remedy

---

from the *Bulmer* case that in England it is possible to appeal against a decision of a court not to refer a case to the European Court under Art. 177 of the Treaty.

103 [1993] QB 534; [1993] 1 All ER 420; [1993] 2 CMLR 677.

104 See Szyszczak (1995) 20 ELRev 214, 225 and Walsh, (1993) 56 MLR 881, 885.

105 See Ch. 10, pp. 331–2, on the Brussels Convention and Jacobs, 'The European Court of Justice: some thoughts on its past and its future' (1995), The European Advocate 2, 8–9 criticizing the suggestion. See also the Court's opposition, p. 191 above.

106 This may be poignant in criminal cases where the consequences of delay are particularly serious. Lord Browne-Wilkinson suggested at the end of *R v Manchester Crown Court, ex parte D.P.P.* [1994] 1 CMLR 457, 464, which turned on the extent to which a national court is precluded from dealing with alleged fiddling of travelling expenses by an MEP because it is a matter to be resolved by the European Parliament, that if a similar case were to arise in the future it 'may well prove to be appropriate' for the trial judge to refer the point to the European Court.

under national law 'shall bring' a question of Community law before the Court of Justice. The Court has, however, limited the mandatory nature of Article 177(3). In the early case of *Da Costa* the Court said:

Although the third paragraph of Article 177 unreservedly requires courts or tribunals of a Member State against whose decisions there is no judicial remedy under national law – like the Tariefcommissie [who had referred the *Da Costa* case] – to refer to the Court every question of interpretation raised before them, the authority of an interpretation under Article 177 already given by the Court may deprive the obligation of its purpose and thus empty it of its substance. Such is the case especially when the question raised is materially identical with a question which has already been the subject of a preliminary ruling in a similar case.[107]

In the *Da Costa* case the questions referred to the Court were identical to questions referred to the Court by the Tariefcommissie in an earlier case that had been decided by the Court, Case 26/62,[108] but the parties were different. The *Da Costa* case was referred to the Court before the Court gave its ruling in Case 26/62. The Court stressed that Article 177 always allows a national court to refer questions of interpretation to the Court again. In this case no new factor was presented to the Court and it contented itself with referring the Tariefcommissie to its ruling in Case 26/62.

The significance of the *Da Costa* case is that it indicated that the Court was prepared to allow national courts against whose decision there is no judicial remedy to rely on the authority of a previous ruling from the Court rather than be compelled to refer the same question of interpretation to the Court. The extent of this relaxation of the mandatory nature of Article 177(3) became apparent in the leading case of *CILFIT* v *Italian Ministry of Health*.[109]

In *CILFIT* the Corte Suprema di Cassazione (Italian Supreme Court of Cassation) referred a question to the European Court on the interpretation of the third paragraph of Article 177. The Court of Justice stated that the courts or tribunals referred to in the third paragraph have the same discretion as courts or tribunals referred to in the second paragraph of Article 177 to ascertain whether a decision on a question of Community law is necessary to enable them to give judgment. The Court concluded that courts or tribunals referred to in the third paragraph of Article 177 'are not obliged to refer to the Court of Justice a question concerning the interpretation of Community law raised before them if that question is not

107 Cases 28–30/62, note 5 above, p. 38.
108 Note 1 above.
109 Case 283/81, note 93 above.

relevant, that is to say, if the answer to that question, regardless of what it may be, can in no way affect the outcome of the case'.[110] This can be categorized as the first *CILFIT* exception.

The Court then referred to its reasoning in the *Da Costa* case. It gave the exception to the mandatory nature of Article 177(3) outlined in that case a broad construction. This second *CILFIT* exception applies 'where previous decisions of the Court have already dealt with the point of law in question, irrespective of the nature of the proceedings which led to those decisions, even though the questions at issue are not strictly identical'.[111]

The Court of Justice, however, went further by creating a third *CILFIT* exception. The Court adopted the doctrine of *acte clair* by permitting national courts or tribunals covered by the third paragraph of Article 177 not to refer a case where the question of Community law is relevant to the outcome of the case and there is no previous ruling of the European Court on the point of law if 'the correct application of Community law [is] so obvious as to leave no scope for any reasonable doubt as to the manner in which the question raised is to be resolved'.[112]

The Court of Justice warned national courts and tribunals not to apply this *acte clair* doctrine too easily. It laid down the condition that the national court or tribunal must be convinced that the matter is equally obvious to the courts of the other member states and to the Court of Justice. The problem with this condition is that it is, at best, highly speculative. Few, if any, courts or tribunals in other member states may have ruled upon the point of law, and the Court of Justice will, by definition, not have done so. The Court of Justice reminded national courts and tribunals that in trying to predict how it would interpret the provision of Community law they should bear in mind the plurilingual nature of that law and the Court's use of contextual and purposive interpretation.[113]

The *acte clair* principle has been discussed extensively.[114] It is regrettable that the Court has allowed a gap to develop in the system for securing a uniform interpretation of Community law. This is the avowed aim of the Court:

In the context of Article 177, whose purpose is to ensure that Community law is interpreted and applied in a uniform manner in all the Member States, the

---

110 ibid., p. 3429.
111 ibid.
112 ibid., p. 3430.
113 ibid.; see also ch. 6, pp. 169, 172.
114 See, e.g., Rasmussen, 'The European Court's *Acte Clair* Strategy in *CILFIT*' (1984) 9 ELRev 242–59; Bebr, 'The Rambling Ghost of "Cohn-Bendit": *Acte Clair* and the Court of Justice' (1983) 20 CMLRev 439–72; and Wyatt, 'Article 177(3) – the Court cautiously endorses the *acte clair* doctrine' (1983) 8 ELRev 179–82.

particular objective of the third paragraph is to prevent a body of national case-law not in accord with the rules of Community law coming into existence in any Member State.[115]

It is now possible for national courts or tribunals against whose decision there is no remedy under national law to resolve a question of Community law for themselves without reference to the European Court. For example, in *R v London Boroughs Transport Committee*[116] the House of Lords decided that the case did not raise any Community law issues, because it concerned the regulation of local traffic, despite the fact that the Court of Appeal had held unanimously that the United Kingdom legislation was in breach of certain Community directives. Thus the House of Lords did not regard a reference to the European Court as being necessary to decide the case and declined to make such a reference. It may be said that this is not an example of *acte clair* but rather of the first *CILFIT* exception, where the national court regards the issue of Community law as 'irrelevant' to the case. The two exceptions do coalesce where the national court considers provisions of Community law, as it did here, and interprets them, without any assistance from the European Court, in a way that means they are irrelevant to the case. A different interpretation of the provisions of Community law – for example, the one given by the Court of Appeal in this case – would, of course, make them highly relevant to the case.

Another example where the House of Lords declined to refer a case to the European Court is *Finnegan v Clowney Youth Training Programme Ltd*,[117] in which their Lordships took the view that interpretation of national law was not a matter for the European Court under Article 177 and therefore it did not require to refer the case to the European Court. Here the House of Lords was not prepared to follow the European Court's line of reasoning from the *von Colson* case[118] that national courts are under a duty to interpret national law in the light of the purpose and wording of non-directly effective directives in order to achieve the result aimed for in the directive. The reason given was that the Northern Irish legislation in question was not designed to implement a directive. However, had the case been referred to the Court, it is likely that it would have found that

---

115 Case 107/76 *Hoffman-La Roche v Centrafarm* [1977] ECR 957, 973. The aim was reiterated by the Court in its initial contribution to the 1996 Intergovernmental Conference, see p. 191 above.
116 *R v London Boroughs Transport Committee, ex parte Freight Transport Association Ltd* [1992] 1 CMLR 5, 20–21 (HL), critically analysed by Weatherill, 'Regulating the Internal Market: Result Orientation in the House of Lords' (1992) 17 ELRev 299.
117 [1990] 2 AC 407, 416–17; see Ch. 11, p. 363.
118 Case 14/83 [1984] ECR 1891.

point irrelevant, and required the House of Lords to interpret the Northern Irish legislation consistent with the directive.[119]

Thus the matter of Community law at issue may never come before the Court of Justice.[120] The provision could be interpreted differently in various member states and still not be referred to the Court because the cases may not be reported and hence not referred to in the other member states as evidence of a need for a reference. A 'body of national case-law not in accord with the rules of Community law' could emerge. The danger of non-reporting, and the scope for disagreement on what constitutes *acte clair*, is evidenced by the House of Lords decision of 9 May 1985 in *In re Sandhu*, which discussed Article 177(3) in detail but was only inadequately reported in *The Times*.[121] Lords Templeman and Bridge of Harwich were prepared to decline to refer the case to the European Court on the ground that it was *acte clair* that Sandhu, as a non-Community national, had no right to remain in the United Kingdom once his EC-national spouse, who had been employed in the United Kingdom, had left him and the country. Lord Fraser of Tullybelton, whose opinion was agreed with by Lord Brandon of Oakbrook, did not regard the issue as *acte clair*. He took the view that a matter could not be 'obvious' if, as in this case, the conclusion could be reached only by 'a substantial chain of reasoning'. Also, he thought that Lord Templeman's interpretation of Community law was correct but was not 'so obviously correct as to leave no room for reasonable doubt'. Lord Keith of Kinkel declined to comment on the *acte clair* issue. The matter was resolved by all of their Lordships, except Lord Templeman, who stuck resolutely to his view that the matter was *acte clair*, declining to refer the case to the European Court on the basis of the second *CILFIT* exception because the point of law was decided by that Court in *Diatta* v *Land Berlin*[122] between the hearing by the House of Lords of the *Sandhu* case and the giving of its judgment. Even this conclusion is questionable, given that the *Diatta* case concerned the interpretation of Regulation 1612/68 whereas Sandhu was relying primarily on the wording of Directive 68/360, a matter not considered in *Diatta*.[123] The

---

119 See Case C-106/89 *Marleasing SA* v *La Comercial Internacional de Alimentacion SA* [1990] ECR I-4135; see further ch. 11, p. 356.
120 The issue of Community law discussed in *Finnegan*, note 117 above, was relevant in several other House of Lords cases, but none of them was referred to the European Court; see *Duke* v *Reliance Systems Ltd* [1988] AC 618; *Pickstone* v *Freemans Plc* [1989] AC 66; and *Litster* v *Forth Dry Dock & Engineering Co. Ltd* [1990] 1 AC 546 (all discussed at pp. 362–5). Admittedly, in the last two cases cited the House of Lords followed the approach called for by the European Court in the *von Colson* case, note 118 above.
121 10 May 1985. For the full report of the case see the LEXIS transcript, and for a discussion of it see Beaumont and Campbell 'Preliminary Rulings' (1985) 53 SLG 62–4.
122 Case 267/83 [1985] ECR 567.
123 See pp. 553–4 below.

Sandhu case illustrates that even where a final appellate court attempts to apply the guidelines laid down by the European Court in the *CILFIT* case, there is considerable scope for diverse opinion as to when the second and third exceptions should apply. It would be wrong to give the impression that the House of Lords consistently fails to refer cases to the European Court. Up to the end of 1993 it had referred fifteen cases.[124] In recent times the House of Lords has referred some controversial cases[125] and made sensible use of existing European Court case law without making a reference.[126]

The Court of Justice may have allowed an *acte clair* exception in response to the rebellions against the supremacy and direct effect of Community law of the French Conseil d'État[127] and the German Bundesfinanzhof.[128] It may have reasoned that a carefully circumscribed exception would bring these courts back into line whereas an outright rejection of *acte clair* may have reinforced the rebellion.[129] It seems that the rebellions in

---

124 See Brown and Kennedy, *The Court of Justice*, p. 415.

125 See e.g. *Webb* v *EMO Air Cargo (UK) Ltd* [1992] 4 All ER 929, discussed at pp. 365, 374, and *R* v *Secretary of State for the Environment, ex parte RSPB, The Times*, 10 February 1995, note 168 below.

126 See *Equal Opportunities Commission and Another* v *Secretary of State for Employment* [1994] 1 All ER 910, 920–3, noted by Beaumont (1994) 62 Scot. L. Gaz. 60–62. The House of Lords relied on European Court cases showing that it is for national courts to determine whether an indirectly discriminatory pay practice is founded on objectively justified economic grounds, see Case 170/84 *Bilka-Kaufhaus GmbH* v *Weber von Hartz* [1986] ECR 1607, and that the definition of pay in Article 119 includes 'redundancy' pay, see Case C-262/88 *Barber* v *Guardian Royal Exchange Assurance Group* [1990] ECR I-1889. The House of Lords decided not to refer a question on whether compensation for unfair dismissal constitutes pay within the meaning of Art. 119, even though it had not been decided by the European Court and was not *acte clair*, because it was not necessary for the disposal of the case. The Equal Treatment Directive (76/207) applied to the Equal Opportunities Commission's relationships with the government and it clearly prohibited discrimination as regards the right to compensation for unfair dismissal unless it is objectively justified.

127 In *Syndicat Général des Semoules de France* [1970] CMLR 395 the Conseil d'État did not accept the supremacy of Community regulations over subsequent national law and in *Minister of the Interior* v *Cohn-Bendit* [1980] 1 CMLR 543 it did not accept the direct effect of Community directives.

128 The German Federal Fiscal Court did not accept the doctrine of the direct effect of directives in *Re VAT Directives* [1982] 1 CMLR 527 and in a decision of 25 April 1985 in *Kloppenburg* [1989] 1 CMLR 873.

129 In Case 152/84 *Marshall* v *Southampton and South-West Hampshire Area Health Authority* [1986] ECR 723, the Court clarified for the first time the fact that directives cannot have horizontal direct effect; see Ch. 11, p. 347. This may have been another response by the Court to the rebellions in France and Germany against vertical direct effect. The Court had a firm legal argument for vertical direct effect of a directive, that a member state that fails to implement a directive timeously should not be able to profit from its own wrong, but would have had only policy arguments to justify horizontal direct effect of a directive.

France and Germany have ended and thus the Court's strategy may well have been vindicated.[130]

The European Court has decided that courts or tribunals are not required by Article 177(3) to refer a question of Community law that is raised in interlocutory proceedings even when there is no judicial remedy against the interim order under national law. This is so provided the parties can insist on proceedings being instituted on the substance of the case, during which the decision on Community law taken in the interlocutory proceedings can be challenged and may be the subject of a reference to the European Court.[131] A reference is not mandatory in interlocutory proceedings even if the substantive proceedings can be raised only in another jurisdiction within the Community.[132]

The courts or tribunals referred to in Article 177(3) are not only those that always sit as final appellate courts in each jurisdiction within the Community, like the House of Lords. This is apparent from a comment made by the European Court in *Costa* v *ENEL*.[133] That famous case on the supremacy of Community law was referred to the European Court by the Giudice Conciliatore in Milan, which had sole jurisdiction over the dispute because of the small amount of money involved. The Court said that this was a case governed by Article 177(3) because there was no judicial remedy against the decision of the Giudice Conciliatore in Italian law.[134] The implication of the *Costa* case is that any national court or tribunal that is adjudicating on a case where, under national law, there is no appeal against that decision falls within Article 177(3) for the purpose of that case, notwithstanding the fact that in many other matters the decisions of that court or tribunal are subject to appeal. In England the Court of Appeal has repeatedly stated that it is not a court or tribunal within the meaning of Article 177(3) because parties can always seek leave to appeal to the House of Lords.[135] The Queens Bench Divisional Court decided it could not reopen the question of whether or not to refer a case to the European Court after leave to appeal to the House of Lords had been denied by that House. The Court was *functus* in relation to that case and so Article 177(3) was not applicable, as the case was no longer 'pending' before the court.[136] This position is consistent with the view of

130 See Ch. 12, notes 34–8 and 49–52.
131 Case 107/76, note 115 above, p. 974.
132 See Cases 35–6/82 *Morson and Jhanjan* v *Netherlands* [1982] ECR 3723, 3734–5.
133 Case 6/64, note 2 above.
134 ibid. p. 592.
135 See *R* v *The Pharmaceutical Society*, note 82 above, p. 969 and *Generics (UK) Ltd* v *Smith Kline & French Laboratories Ltd* [1990] 1 CMLR 416, 435.
136 See *Magnavision* v *General Optical Council (No. 2)* [1987] 2 CMLR 262.

the European Court in the later cases of *SPUC* and *Pardini*.[137] In Scotland the High Court of Justiciary when hearing criminal appeals is a court within the meaning of Article 177(3), as no appeal is possible.[138]

TEMPORAL EFFECTS OF PRELIMINARY RULINGS

The European Court is of the view that, in general, a ruling on the interpretation of a provision of Community law is applicable 'even to legal relationships arising and established before the judgment'.[139] The Court's justification for this apparent retroactivity is that the Court's interpretation of the provision of Community law 'clarifies and defines where necessary the meaning and scope of that rule as it must be or ought to have been understood and applied from the time of its coming into force'.[140]

The Court is prepared, exceptionally, to restrict the effect of its ruling on existing legal relationships:

It is only exceptionally that the Court may, in application of the general principle of legal certainty inherent in the Community legal order and in taking account of the serious effects which its judgment might have, as regards the past, on legal relationships established in good faith, be moved to restrict for any person concerned the opportunity of relying upon the provision as thus interpreted with a view to calling in question those legal relationships.[141]

Typically, it will state that the ruling applies to such legal relationships only for those who had instituted legal proceedings prior to the ruling. For everyone else the ruling applies only from the date it was given. Only the Court of Justice can restrict the temporal effects of its ruling, and it has decided that it will do so only in the case in which the ruling was given, not in a subsequent case.[142] This can be illustrated by the case of *Barra* v

137 Cases C-159/90 and 338/85, note 39 above.
138 See *Geweise and Mehlich* v *Mackenzie*, 1984 SLT 449.
139 See Case 61/79 *Amministrazione delle Finanze dello Stato* v *Denkavit Italiana* [1980] ECR 1205; Cases 66, 127, 128/79 *Amministrazione delle Finanze* v *Salumi* [1980] ECR 1237, 1260–61; Case 811/79 *Amministrazione delle Finanze dello Stato* v *Ariete* [1980] ECR 2545, 2553; and Case 309/85 *Barra* v *Belgium* [1988] ECR 355, 375.
140 ibid.
141 In Case 811/79, note 139 above, at p. 2553, the Court repeated the same reasoning given in Case 61/79 and Cases 66, 127, 128/79, note 139 above.
142 See Case 811/79, note 139 above, at p. 2553; Case 61/79 and Cases 66, 127, 128/79, note 139 above.

Belgium,[143] in which the European Court declined to limit the temporal effect of the judgment it had given in *Gravier* v *Belgium*.[144] In *Gravier* the Court had ruled that, as a result of Article 7 EEC, it was illegal for Belgium to continue to charge a higher fee for vocational training courses to nationals of other member states than it did to Belgians.[145] In *Barra* the Court said that as it had placed no limit on the temporal effect of its judgment in *Gravier*, 'such a restriction cannot be made in this judgment'.[146] Thus nationals of other member states were able to recover the differential between their fees for vocational courses and those applicable to Belgian nationals for the period before the *Gravier* ruling.

On the other hand, in *Blaizot* v *University of Liège* the Court developed the *Gravier* ruling by deciding that, in general, university education constitutes vocational training and hence comes within the scope of the Treaty.[147] Thus the Belgian differential fee for nationals of other member states constituted discrimination contrary to Article 7 of the Treaty. The Court decided to limit the temporal effect of this ruling for reasons of legal certainty and in order to prevent throwing the financing of university education into confusion. The Court acknowledged that the scope of 'vocational training' in Article 128 EEC was being gradually developed and that as late as June 1985 the Commission had not indicated to the Belgian Government that university education would come within its scope.[148] The Court restricted the application of its ruling to the period after it was given except for students who had brought legal proceedings or submitted an equivalent claim before the date of the ruling.

In *Defrenne* v *SABENA*[149] the Court decided for the first time that Article 119 EEC had direct effect in relation to direct and overt discrimination in violation of the principle of equal pay for equal work for men and women. The Court also decided that its judgment could not be relied on to support claims relating to pay periods prior to the date of the judgment except as regarded those workers who had already brought legal proceed-

---

143 Case 309/85 [1988] ECR 355.
144 Case 293/83 [1985] ECR 593.
145 Vocational training comes within the scope of the EEC Treaty, as it is mentioned in Art. 128 (see also p. 74). See Art. 127 EC on vocational training, and Art. 6 EC (rather than Art. 7 EEC) in relation to non-discrimination on grounds of nationality.
146 Case 309/85, note 143 above, p. 375.
147 Case 24/86 [1988] ECR 379. The Court said all university courses were vocational except 'certain courses of study which, because of their particular nature, are intended for persons wishing to improve their general knowledge rather than prepare themselves for an occupation' (p. 404). In this case the Court decided that veterinary medicine courses were vocational.
148 For the slow handling of this issue by the Commission in its dealing with Belgium see Case 293/85 *Commission* v *Belgium* [1988] ECR 305, discussed in Ch. 7 at pp. 194–5.
149 Case 43/75 [1976] ECR 455, discussed in Ch. 20 at pp. 614, 616.

ings or made an equivalent claim. The Court took this exceptional approach because of the large number of claims for backdated pay that would otherwise have been submitted. This would have had serious financial consequences for many enterprises, possibly even creating bankruptcy or insolvency. The Court could not predict at what level pay would have been fixed had the equal pay provision been directly effective. Finally, the Court was influenced by the fact that the Commission had not initiated proceedings under Article 169 of the Treaty alleging that certain of the member states had failed to comply with Article 119 by not providing equal pay for men and women. This consolidated an incorrect impression as to the effects of that Article.

In the *Barber* case[150] the Court followed the example of the *Defrenne* case and restricted the direct effect of Article 119 in relation to pension entitlements, particularly contracted-out schemes, to the period after the date of the *Barber* judgment except in the case of workers or those claiming under the pension who had before that date initiated legal proceedings or raised an equivalent claim under the applicable national law. In reaching this view the Court examined the exemptions from equal treatment for men and women in the field of pensionable ages and occupational security schemes contained in certain Community directives. The Court concluded that member states and the parties concerned 'were reasonably entitled to consider that Article 119 did not apply to pensions paid under contracted-out schemes and that derogations from the principle of equality between men and women were still permitted in that sphere'.[151]

The Court of Justice has a discretion to decide on the temporal effects of a ruling of invalidity under Article 177 of the Treaty. The position was set out by the Court in the *Pinna* case:

When the Court makes use of the possibility of limiting the effect on past events of a declaration in proceedings under Article 177 of the Treaty that a measure is invalid, it is for the Court to decide whether an exception to that temporal limitation of the effect of its judgment may be made in favour of the party which brought the action before the national court or in favour of any other person who took similar steps before the declaration of invalidity or whether, conversely, a declaration of invalidity applicable only to the future constitutes an adequate remedy even for those persons who took action at the appropriate time with a view to protecting their rights.[152]

---

150 Case C-262/88 [1990] ECR I-1889; [1991] 1 QB 344, discussed in Ch. 20 at p. 619. A protocol was agreed at the Maastricht Summit clarifying the non-retrospective effect of the *Barber* judgment; its provisions are printed in [1992] 1 CMLR 3.
151 ibid. p. 1956 and p. 404.
152 Case 41/84 *Pinna* [1986] ECR 1, 26–27. See also Case 112/83, note 61 above, pp. 747–8.

In the *Pinna* case the Court decided that the invalidity of Article 73(2) of Regulation 1408/71 could be relied on to support claims regarding benefits for periods prior to the date of the *Pinna* judgment only by those who had already brought legal proceedings or made an equivalent claim prior to that date.[153]

INTERIM MEASURES

The general rule that a national court cannot declare acts of the Community institutions invalid is clear, as this is a matter exclusively for the European Court to determine.[154] It may be that the Court will make an exception to the rule where interim measures are sought before the national court while a ruling from the Court on the validity of the measure is pending.[155] In *Zuckerfabrik Süderdithmarschen* v *Hauptzollamt Itzehoe*[156] the Court accepted that a national court could suspend the operation of a national measure adopted in implementation of a Community measure. The suspension would operate only until the Court ruled on the validity of the Community measure. If such a ruling had not yet been sought from the Court, then the national court could suspend the national measure only if it sought such a ruling itself. The national court could order the suspension of the national measure if there was serious doubt as to the validity of the Community measure, if the matter was urgent, if there was a risk to the applicant of serious and irreparable harm, and the national court took due account of the Community's interest.

The conditions for suspension of a national measure laid down by the European Court are the same conditions as it applies itself in granting suspension of the validity of a Community measure in an application for interim measures during an Article 173 action. The Court suggested, *obiter dictum*, that it would permit national courts to suspend secondary Community legislation on the same conditions.

On the other side of the coin, it is expected that national courts may use

---

153 Case 41/84, note 152 above, p. 27. See also Cases C-38 and 151/90 *Lomas and Others* [1992] ECR I-1781, 1816–8 and Case C-228/92 *Roquette Frères SA* v *Hauptzollamt Geldern* [1994] ECR I-1445.
154 See Case 314/85 *Foto-Frost* v *Hauptzollamt Lübeck-Ost* [1987] ECR 4199, 4231. This was a factor taken into account by Henry J in deciding to refer a question on the validity of a Community directive to the European Court in *R* v *Minister of Agriculture, ex parte fédération européenne de la santé animale* [1988] 3 CMLR 207.
155 This question was left open in *Foto-Frost*, note 154 above, p. 4232.
156 Cases C-143/88 and C-92/89 [1991] ECR I-415, noted by Schermers (1992) 29 CMLRev 133.

interim measures to protect putative rights under Community law, pending an Article 177 ruling on the issues of Community law, as against clear provisions of national law. The European Court has barred national courts from denying interim relief to those who claim rights under Community law, where a preliminary ruling is pending on whether those rights exist, because those rights conflict with national law.[157]

The English courts have had to consider whether to grant interim relief while a case is pending before the European Court on several occasions but the leading case of *Factortame No. 2* is a rare example of the Court doing so.[158] In that case Lord Goff gave the leading judgment in the House of Lords. He applied the guidelines set out by Lord Diplock in the *Cyanamid* case.[159] First the applicant must establish that there is a 'serious issue to be tried'. Secondly, the Court will consider whether the applicant will receive an 'adequate remedy in damages' if the main action succeeds. If so, then normally no interim injunction is granted. If not then the court will consider whether the other party will receive an adequate remedy in damages if an injunction is granted but the applicant ultimately loses the main action. If the other party would receive an adequate remedy then normally the court will grant an interim injunction. If damages do not provide an adequate remedy then the court proceeds to the third stage and considers the overall 'balance of convenience'.

Lord Goff emphasized the need to preserve 'discretion' and rejected any suggestion that the applicant must show a 'strong *prima facie*' case that the relevant UK law is invalid. However, he did recognize the public interest in upholding existing UK legislation and in a key passage said:

the Court should not restrain a public authority by interim injunction from enforcing an apparently authentic law unless it is satisfied, having regard to all the circumstances, that the challenge to the validity of the law is, prima facie, so firmly based as to justify so exceptional a course being taken.[160]

In the *Factortame, Continental Television* and *BT* cases[161] the courts reached the 'balance of convenience' stage. Two key 'variables' affecting the

---

157 See Case C-213/89 *R v Secretary of State for Transport, ex parte Factortame* [1990] ECR 1–2433, discussed at pp. 175–6 and 372.
158 *R v Secretary of State for Transport, ex parte Factortame Ltd (No. 2)* [1991] 1 AC 603, [1990] 3 CMLR 375; *R v Secretary of State for the National Heritage, ex parte Continental Television BV* [1993] 2 CMLR 333 (QBD), [1993] 3 CMLR 387 (CA); *R v HM Treasury, ex parte British Telecommunications Plc* [1994] 1 CMLR 621 (CA); and *R v Secretary of State for the Environment, ex parte Royal Society for the Protection of Birds, The Times,* 10 February 1995 (HL).
159 *American Cyanamid Co v Ethicon Ltd* [1975] AC 396.
160 [1991] 1 AC 603, 674; [1990] 3 CMLR 375, 396.
161 See note 158 above.

exercise of the discretion that is vested in the court have been analysed by Sir Thomas Bingham MR.[162] One variable is the prospect of the applicant's case succeeding before the European Court. If the court thinks that the applicant's action is 'substantially more likely to fail than to succeed' then there is little prospect of the court granting interim relief.[163] On the other hand if it is 'fairly clear' from the European Court's existing case law that the applicant's action will succeed then it is very likely that an interim injunction will be granted.[164] The other variable analysed by Bingham MR is the public interest in not disapplying United Kingdom legislation. This is at its strongest when primary legislation of major political significance is at stake and at its weakest in relation to secondary legislation affecting very few parties other than the applicant.

The relative importance of the two variables can be assessed only tentatively from the existing cases. In *Factortame* primary UK legislation of some political significance was set aside primarily because it was highly likely that the applicants would succeed before the European Court.[165] In the *BT* case it was accepted that BT had a 'strongly arguable' case that the UK secondary legislation implementing an EC directive was unlawful and yet no interim relief was granted. This was so even though the other variable was at its weakest in that the UK legislation was secondary and its adverse consequences affected BT uniquely.[166] Although there are no 'absolutes, only variables'[167] it seems unlikely that interim relief will be granted unless it is probable that the applicant will get a favourable preliminary ruling from the European Court because only such a probability seems capable of overriding the public interest in not disapplying UK legislation even if it is narrowly focused and secondary.[168]

---

162 In *R v HM Treasury, ex parte British Telecommunications plc* [1994] 1 CMLR 621, 647.

163 See *R v Secretary of State for the National Heritage, ex parte Continental Television BV* [1993] 3 CMLR 387, 399.

164 See *Factortame (No. 2)*, cited above, and the analysis of that case by Bingham MR in *R v HM Treasury, ex parte British Telecommunications plc* [1994] 1 CMLR 621, 649: 'by the time the House of Lords granted interim relief in that case it was fairly clear what the answer to the underlying Community law problem was going to be'. For the outcome of *Factortame* see Ch. 12 below at p. 373.

165 Also because the applicants faced bankruptcy or at least massive losses in their fishing businesses if no interim relief was granted.

166 It was also relevant that although BT could have lost more than £10 million from denial of interim relief this would have done no more than 'dent its profits', [1994] 1 CMLR 621, 648.

167 ibid at p. 647.

168 The court will be more reluctant to grant an interim declaration than an interim injunction because in the former the party seeking interim relief is not required to give a cross-undertaking in damages whereas that is a normal condition of granting an interim injunction; see *R v Secretary of State for the Environment, ex parte RSPB, The Times*, 10 February 1995.

CHAPTER 10

Miscellaneous Aspects of the Court's Jurisdiction

In the last four chapters an overview of the European Court has been given and a reasonably detailed examination of its principal heads of jurisdiction; actions against member states, judicial review and preliminary rulings under Article 177 of the Treaty. This chapter will complete the picture of the Court's jurisdiction by briefly mentioning the other heads of jurisdiction. The treatment of each head of jurisdiction will be cursory, but references are given in the Select Further Reading to more detailed treatments elsewhere.

NON-CONTRACTUAL LIABILITY OF THE COMMUNITY

Articles 178 and 215(2) of the Treaty, which regulate the non-contractual liability of the Community, state:

The Court of Justice shall have jurisdiction in disputes relating to compensation for damage provided for in the second paragraph of Article 215. [Article 178]

In the case of non-contractual liability, the Community shall, in accordance with the general principles common to the laws of the Member States, make good any damage caused by its institutions or by its servants in the performance of their duties. [Article 215(2)]

The preceding paragraph shall apply under the same conditions to damage caused by the European Central Bank or by its servants in the performance of their duties.[1]

About 8 per cent of the cases brought before the Court under the EEC Treaty, excluding staff cases, concerned the non-contractual liability of the Community. However, as at 31 December 1990, in only 4 per cent of those cases (13 out of 329) had the Court found in favour of the applicant in respect of at least one of the applicant's main claims.[2]

[1] Words in italics added at Maastricht.
[2] See *XXIVth General Report on the Activities of the European Communities 1990*, Luxem-

The Court has established that the action for compensation provided for in Articles 178 and 215(2) is an autonomous form of action. It differs from an action for annulment under Article 173 in that its purpose is not to set aside a specific measure but to repair the damage caused by an institution.[3] Thus the Court has not imported the strict *locus standi* conditions of Article 173 into actions under Articles 178 and 215(2).[4] The Court has consistently held that Community liability depends on three requirements being fulfilled.

1 The institution against which the action is brought must have acted unlawfully.
2 The person bringing the action must have suffered damage.
3 There must be a direct link in the chain of causality between the wrongful act and the damage complained of.[5]

In relation to acts of general application the Community only incurs liability for damage suffered by individuals as a consequence of the act or omission[6] if there has been a 'sufficiently flagrant violation of a superior rule of law for the protection of the individual'.[7] Superior rules of law in this context constitute the Treaty and the general principles of law developed by the Court.[8] What constitutes a 'sufficiently flagrant' breach of the

bourg, EC Official Publications, 1991, p. 449. Since August 1993 the Court of First Instance has had jurisdiction over all non-contractual liability cases apart from those brought by a member state or Community institution; see Ch. 6 above, pp. 189–90.

3 See Case C-87/89 *SONITO and Others* v *Commission* [1990] ECR I-1981, 2010 and Case 175/84 *Krohn & Co. Import-Export* v *Commission* [1986] ECR 753, 770.

4 Actions can be brought by natural and legal persons against legislative acts; see, e.g., Case 5/71 *Schöppenstedt* v *Council* [1971] ECR 975, 983.

5 See Case C-87/89, note 3 above, p. 2011; Cases C-104/89 and 37/90 *Mulder and Others* v *Council and Commission* [1992] ECR I-3061, para. 12; Cases C-258, 259/90 *Pesquerias de Bermeo* and *Naviera Laida* v *Commission* [1992] ECR I-2901, para. 42; and Case C-146/91 *KYDEP* v *Council and Commission* [1994] ECR I-4199, para. 19. The idea that the Community institution must have acted wrongfully – must be at fault – is not specifically required by Art. 215(2). Although Lord Mackenzie Stuart has, extra-judicially, mooted the idea of no-fault liability ('The Non-Contractual Liability of the European Economic Community' (1975) 12 CMLRev 493, 501), it has not been adopted by the Court. This can be contrasted with the EC Directive on Product Liability (85/374 OJ 1985 L210/29), which provides for no-fault liability; see Weatherill, *Cases and Materials*, pp. 464–70.

6 See Case 50/86 *Grands Moulins de Paris* v *Council and Commission* [1987] ECR 4833, paras. 7–9; and Case C-146/91, note 5 above, at pp. 4241–7.

7 See Case 5/71 *Schöppenstedt* v *Council* [1971] ECR 975, 984. The case is noted in Weatherill, *Cases and Materials*, pp. 535–7. The test in the text applies not only to regulations but also to directives; see Case C-63/89 *Les Assurances du crédit* v *Council and Commission* [1991] ECR I-1799, 1846, noted by Curtin (1992) 17 ELRev 46–55.

8 These general principles are discussed at pp. 253–65 . They are not to be confused with the general principles of law referred to in Art. 215(2) in the narrower context of the principles common to the laws of the member states relating to non-contractual liability.

general principles of Community law is difficult to assess. In the *Skimmed-Milk Powder* case[9] the Court had found Regulation 563/76 to be unlawful in an Article 177 action. The Regulation had infringed the principles of proportionality and equality of treatment by imposing an obligation on the importers and users of animal feed to purchase skimmed-milk powder at a price three times its value to them as animal feed. None the less, when an action was brought under Articles 178 and 215(2) by some producers of animal feed who were adversely affected by the Regulation, the Court found that the damage done to them was not sufficiently serious for them to succeed in their action.[10] Very serious losses arising from a legislative act may be sufficient to succeed in an Article 178 action,[11] but only if the actions of the Community institution(s) making the act were 'verging on the arbitrary'.[12] In the *Bayerische HNL* case[13] the Court said 'the Community does not ... incur liability unless the institution concerned has manifestly and gravely disregarded the limits on the exercise of its powers'. A 'technical error' by the Community institution is not sufficient to found an action.[14] The requirement that the superior rule of law is 'for the protection of the individual' was discussed in *Vreugdenhil* v *Commission*.[15] The Court had declared in a preliminary ruling[16] that Article 13a of Regulation 1687/76 was invalid on the ground that in adopting that provision the Commission had exceeded its powers by disregarding a rule

---

9 Case 114/76 *Bela-Mühle* v *Grows-Farm* [1977] ECR 1211, discussed at pp. 259–62.

10 Cases 83, 94/76 and 4, 15, 40/77 *Bayerische HNL* v *Council and Commission* [1978] ECR 1209, 1225. The cost of skimmed-milk powder was a small proportion of the production costs for animal feed.

11 See the gritz and quellmehl cases, Cases 64, 113/76; 167, 239/78; 27, 28, 45/79 *Dumortier Frères SA* v *Council* [1979] ECR 3091. A breach of the principle of equality of treatment produced very serious losses for the producers of maize gritz who lost their Community subsidies and ceased to be treated equally with maize starch producers (see p. 3114). The case is noted by Rudden and Bishop, 'Gritz and Quellmehl: Pass It On' (1981) 6 ELRev 243–56.

12 See Cases 116, 124/77 *Amylum* v *Council and Commission* [1979] ECR 3497, 3561 and Case 143/77 *Koninklijke Scholten-Honig* v *Council & Commission* [1979] ECR 3583, 3627.

13 Cases 83, 94/76 and 4, 15, 40/77, note 10 above. See also Case C-63/89, note 7 above and Cases C-104/89 and 37/90, note 5 above. The latter case is particularly instructive because the test was met in relation to the original milk quota regulations but not in relation to the second version of the regulations. The breach of legitimate expectations was less severe in the latter case and the Council had taken account of a 'higher public interest' in a way that meant it did not manifestly disregard the limits of its discretionary powers. See the discussion of the case by Van Gerven, (1994) 1 Maastricht J. of Eur. & Comp. L 6 at pp. 25–7, and in his Advocate-General's opinion in the case.

14 See Cases 194–206/83 *Asteris* v *Commission* [1985] ECR 2815, 2828, and Case 20/88 *Roquette Frères* v *Commission* [1989] ECR 1553, 1589.

15 Case C-282/90, [1992] ECR I-1937.

16 Case 22/88 *Vreugdenhil and Another* v *Minister van Landbouw en Visserij* [1989] ECR 2049.

on the allocation of powers between the Community institutions; in particular it had exceeded the powers delegated to it by the Council by amending the scope of a Council regulation which the Council had determined in its entirety. Vreugdenhil then brought an action under Article 178 for compensation for damage allegedly suffered as a result of the adoption by the Commission of Article 13a. The Court stated that

the aim of the system of the division of powers between the various Community institutions is to ensure that the balance between the institutions provided for in the Treaty is maintained, and not to protect individuals. Consequently, a failure to observe the balance between the institutions cannot be sufficient on its own to engage the Community's liability towards the traders concerned.[17]

In order for a claim to succeed the substance of the measure must disregard a superior rule of law protecting individuals.[18]

In relation to acts that are not of general application, the applicant does not need to show that its effects were 'sufficiently flagrant' or that the Community institution acted in a way 'verging on the arbitrary'.[19] However, the applicant must show that the Community institution's decision was illegal before the Court will consider the other aspects of liability under Article 215(2).[20]

Problems can arise where a member state and a Community institution may be concurrently liable for a wrongful act.[21] This may happen, for example, in relation to aspects of the Common Agricultural Policy where the Community establishes the policy but a national intervention board carries it out. There was a tendency in such cases for the Court to require applicants to exhaust their remedies before the relevant national courts

---

17 At p. 1968.

18 Van Gerven, in 'Non-Contractual Liability of Member States, Community Institutions and Individuals for Breaches of Community Law with a view to a Common Law for Europe' (1994) 1 Maastricht J. of Eur. & Comp. L 6 at p. 27, says that 'an individual who has suffered loss or damage can ask for compensation only when he belongs to a group which the breached superior rule of law aims to protect'. As the title of Van Gerven's article implies, he favours the harmonization of the rules of Community law which regulate the non-contractual liability of Community institutions and member states, see p. 35. This implies the need for the *Francovich* case law on damages against the state, see pp. 352–5 below, to evolve along similar lines to the Court's case law on non-contractual liability under Arts. 178 and 215, but not necessarily identically, see p. 36.

19 See Case 175/84 note 3 above.

20 See Case C-200/89 *Funoc* v *Commission* [1990] ECR I-3669, 3695.

21 See, e.g., the sorry tale of delay in Cases 5, 7, 13–24/66 *Kampffmeyer* v *Commission* [1967] ECR 245, where the Court found the Commission to be liable for a wrongful decision authorizing the German Government to take safeguard measures but did not settle the amount of the damages until the applicants had concluded an action against the German Government in the German courts (noted in Schermers and Waelbroeck, *Judicial Protection*, pp. 355–6).

before coming to the European Court.[22] The Court now imposes such a requirement only where national rights of action provide an effective means of protection for the individual concerned and are capable of resulting in compensation for the damage alleged.[23] Where the national institution is merely carrying out the instructions of a Community institution, then Article 215(2) is applicable,[24] but if the national institution acts entirely independently of the Community institution, it is not applicable.[25]

Damages are awarded for specific losses, not economic loss arising from speculative transactions being thwarted.[26] The applicant must 'state the evidence from which the conduct alleged against the institution by the applicant may be identified'.[27] A failure to specify the damage is a bar to proceedings, which the Court may raise of its own motion.[28] It is possible to claim for imminent losses that are foreseeable with sufficient certainty but not for ones that may or may not happen in the future.[29] If the loss was passed on to others by the applicant, then this will be reflected in reduced or even no damages being awarded by the Court.[30] Indeed, the injured party must show reasonable diligence in limiting the extent of his or her loss or risk having to bear the damage.[31] The Court may decide that the applicant was contributorily negligent and apportion a proportion of the total damage to that negligence. In *Adams* v *Commission (No. 1)* [32] the Court decided that Adams had an equal responsibility with the Commission for the damage done to him. Adams was an employee of Hoffman la Roche in Switzerland. He had given certain confidential documents to the Commission that disclosed that Hoffman la Roche was in . breach of Article 86. Afterwards he left the company's employ and set up in a business in Italy. The Commission had not respected the confidentiality of

---

22 See Case 96/71 *Haegeman* v *Commission* [1972] ECR 1005; Case 46/75 *IBC* v *Commission* [1976] ECR 65; and Cases 67–85/75 *Lesieur* v *Commission* [1976] ECR 391, 406.
23 See Case 175/84, note 3 above, p. 769, in which this was not the case. See also Case 20/88, note 14 above, pp. 1586–7.
24 Case 175/84, note 3 above, pp. 767–8.
25 See Case 99/74 *Société des grands Moulins des Antilles* v *Commission* [1975] ECR 1531.
26 See Cases 5, 7, 13–24/66, note 21 above, p. 266.
27 See Case T-64/89 *Automec* v *Commission* [1990] ECR II-367, 390.
28 ibid.
29 See Case 147/83 *Binderer* v *Commission* [1985] ECR 257, 272; Cases 56–60/74 *Kampffmeyer* v *Commission and Council* [1976] ECR 711; Case 44/76 *Milch-, Fett- und Eier-Kontor* v *Council and Commission* [1977] ECR 393.
30 See Cases 27, 28, 45/79, note 11 above, p. 3115, though in that case the applicant had not been able to pass on the loss.
31 See Cases C-104/89 and 37/90, note 5 above, at para. 33.
32 Case 145/83 [1985] ECR 3539, noted by Meade, 'The Legal and Practical Implications of the Stanley Adams Case' (1986) 37 NILQ 370 and March Hunnings, 'The Stanley Adams Affair or the Biter Bit' (1987) 24 CMLRev 65.

the documents given to them by Adams and had returned them to Hoffman la Roche, who found out who the whistle-blower was. As a result, when Adams visited Switzerland he was charged with economic espionage, his wife committed suicide and he lost his business in Italy due to a loss in his credit rating. The Commission was clearly negligent in revealing confidential documents that might enable Hoffman la Roche to discover who the whistle-blower was, but Adams was contributorily negligent because he did not tell the Commission that the documents might reveal his identity to Hoffman la Roche and he returned to Switzerland rather than staying in the safety of Italy.

The amount of damages is something that the Court may leave the parties to reach an agreement on within a specified time period.[33] If the parties do not reach an agreement on the level of damages, then the Court will impose an amount of compensation which corresponds to the damage caused by the Community.[34]

The limitation period for an action under Article 178 is five years. The time-limit runs from the occurrence of the event giving rise to the proceedings.[35] This concept is interpreted generously by the Court in favour of the applicant, as time cannot begin to run before the injurious effects of the measure have been produced. It does not run from the date when the regulation came into force,[36] and it is interrupted if proceedings are instituted before the Court or if prior to such proceedings an application is made by the aggrieved party to the relevant institution of the Community. The Court is very unlikely to raise the limitation period of its own motion.[37]

If the damage is caused by one of the employees of a Community institution, then that institution is vicariously liable under Article 215(2) only if the employee was acting in the performance of his of her duties. The Court has had little opportunity to consider the scope of vicarious liability. It has ruled that if an employee is involved in an accident while

---

33 See Case 74/74 *CNTA* [1975] ECR 533, 551; and Case 145/83, note 32 above. The Commission agreed with Adams that he should receive £200,000 in damages and a further £200,000 in costs; see the *Guardian*, 18 September 1986, and Meade (1986) 37 NILQ 370, 383.

34 See Cases C-104/89 and 37/90, note 5 above, at para. 34. Van Gerven, in (1994) Maastricht J of Eur. & Comp. L 6 at p. 31, argued that this means that 'reparation must be made in full, that is to say that its aim must be to make good the loss of capital caused by the unlawful conduct (*restitutio in integrum*)'.

35 See the Statute of the Court of Justice, Art. 43.

36 See Cases 256, 257, 265 and 267/80 and 5/81 *Birra Wührer SpA* v *Council and Commission* [1982] ECR 85 and Case 51/81 *De Franceschi SpA Monfalcone* v *Council and Commission* [1982] ECR 117. For another generous construction of when time begins to run see Case 145/83, note 32 above, pp. 3591–2.

37 See Case 20/88, note 14 above, p. 1586.

driving a private car, the Community will be vicariously liable only in exceptional circumstances,[38] presumably in an emergency situation when the employee could not be at the correct place quickly enough without resorting to the use of his or her car.

REVIEW OF PENALTIES

Article 172 provides that 'Regulations *adopted jointly by the European Parliament and the Council and* by the Council pursuant to the provisions of this Treaty may give the Court of Justice unlimited jurisdiction in regard to the penalties provided for in such Regulations'.[39]

The principal example of such jurisdiction being conferred on the Court by the Council is in relation to competition policy under Article 17 of Regulation 17. It provides that 'the Court of Justice shall have unlimited jurisdiction within the meaning of Article 172 of the Treaty to review decisions whereby the Commission has fixed a fine or periodic penalty payment; it may cancel, reduce or increase the fine or periodic penalty payment imposed'.[40]

The Commission has a very wide discretion in fixing the level of fine imposed on an undertaking in breach of competition policy, and in reviewing that fine the Court has no constraints imposed on it. In the *Musique Diffusion Française* case the Court approved a level of fines sufficiently high to deter an undertaking from calculating that it would be better off breaching competition policy because the increased profits outweighed the level of fine imposed by the Commission.[41]

Another example of the application of Article 172 is found in Article 16 of Regulation 4064/89 on Merger Control,[42] which is identical to Article 17 of Regulation 17.[43]

The Council may give the European Central Bank power to impose

---

38 See Case 5/68 *Sayag* v *Leduc* [1968] ECR 395 and Case 9/69 *Sayag* v *Leduc* [1969] ECR 329 (discussed in Brown and Kennedy, *The Court of Justice*, pp. 173–4). The *Sayag* cases were decided in relation to Art. 188 of the Euratom Treaty, which is identical to Art. 215(2) EC.

39 The words in italics were added by the Maastricht Treaty amendments.

40 OJ Spec Edn. 1962, No. 204/62, p. 87. See the references for this section in Select Further Reading for a discussion of this provision.

41 Cases 100–103/80 [1983] ECR 1825, 1905–6, [1983] 3 CMLR 221, 333–4. See Ch. 24, pp. 782–5.

42 OJ 1989 L395, discussed in Ch. 25 at pp. 811–28.

43 Except that it refers to 'payments' rather than 'payment'.

fines or periodic penalty payments on undertakings.[44] However, it is not clear whether the Council will grant this power by regulation nor whether the Court will be given jurisdiction under Article 172 to review these penalties.[45]

OPINIONS UNDER ARTICLE 228

Article 228 of the Treaty regulates the procedure whereby agreements can be entered into between the Community and one or more non-member states or international organizations. Before such a draft agreement enters into force 'the Council, the Commission or a Member State may obtain the opinion of the Court of Justice as to whether an agreement envisaged is compatible with the provisions of this Treaty'.[46]

If the Court finds the draft agreement to be incompatible with the Treaty, then it can enter into force only if the Treaty is amended in accordance with the normal process laid down for such amendments,[47] or if the draft agreement is revised to be in accord with the Treaty. The Court has emphasized that its opinion under Article 228 is not advisory but, like all its other judgments, binding.[48]

The Court has been called on to give very few opinions under Article 228,[49] but in recent years it has been used more often. The Court gave a

44 See Art. 108a(3).
45 See Art. 106(6) EC and Arts. 34, 35 and 42 of the Protocol on the Statute of the European System of Central Banks and of the European Central Bank.
46 Even after the Maastricht Treaty amendments the European Parliament has no power to request an opinion from the Court under Art. 228 but it may be permitted to submit observations; see Opinion 1/94 *Re the Uruguay Round Treaties* [1994] ECR I-0000, [1995] 1 CMLR 205, at para. 35. The Court retains jurisdiction to give an opinion even though the international agreement has been signed as long as it has not been ratified, ibid. at paras. 9–12.
47 An intergovernmental conference to agree amendments unanimously, followed by ratification of the amendments by all the member states. See Art. N of the Treaty on European Union.
48 See Opinion 1/91 *Opinion on the draft Agreement on a European Economic Area* [1991] ECR I-6079, [1992] 1 CMLR 245, para. 61.
49 See Opinion 1/75 *Local Cost Standard Opinion* [1975] ECR 1355, [1976] 1 CMLR 90; Opinion 1/76 *Laying-Up Fund Opinion* [1977] ECR 741, [1977] 2 CMLR 295; Opinion 1/78 *Rubber Agreement Opinion* [1979] ECR 2871, [1979] 3 CMLR 639; Opinion 1/91, note 48 above; Opinion 1/92 *Opinion on the revised draft Agreement on the European Economic Area* [1992] ECR I-2821, [1992] 2 CMLR 217; Opinion 2/91 *Re ILO Convention 170 on Chemicals at Work* [1993] ECR I-1061, [1993] 3 CMLR 800; Opinion 1/94 *Re the Uruguay Round Treaties*, note 46 above; Opinion 2/92 *Third Revised Decision of the OECD on National Treatment*, Opinion of 24 March 1995. Opinion 2/94 on the competence of the Community to accede to the European Convention on Human Rights is pending before the Court of Justice.

very profound Opinion on the draft agreement on the European Economic Area on 14 December 1991.[50] In finding that agreement to be incompatible with the Treaty it reiterated some of the great principles of Community law, including its direct effect and supremacy.[51] The Opinion forced a fundamental rethink for the negotiators of the agreement between the member states of the European Community and the member states of the European Free Trade Association (EFTA) as to how to enforce the law applicable under that agreement. The proposed European Economic Area Court was not acceptable because it had jurisdiction to determine the respective competences of the Community and the member states, which, the European Court pointed out, is a matter within its exclusive jurisdiction under Article 219 of the Treaty.[52] The European Court found it unacceptable that judgments of the European Economic Area Court on provisions in the European Economic Area Agreement that were identical to the equivalent provisions in Community law might influence the judgments in the latter context. The thinking here related to the much more limited ambitions of the agreement than the Community and hence the same words might have been given a more restrictive meaning in the former context than in the latter. The likelihood of such prejudicial intermingling of the jurisprudence was strengthened by the fact that the members of the European Economic Area Court would include members of the European Court.[53] The European Court also rejected any possibility of it being given jurisdiction to hear preliminary rulings from the national courts of member states of EFTA if its rulings were not binding.[54] Finally the Court made it clear that any attempt to amend the Treaty to allow for a system of judicial supervision as proposed by the agreement would 'not cure the incompatibility with Community law of the system of courts to be set up by the agreement'.[55]

The draft agreement was revised to comply with the Court's Opinion 1/91. The idea of establishing a European Economic Area Court was abandoned. If national courts of EFTA countries were to be permitted to refer cases to the European Court for a preliminary ruling, the Court's decisions would be binding on them. The revised agreement provided for the EFTA countries to establish an EFTA Court and for the setting up of a Joint Committee. The former would be entirely separate from the European Court and would have jurisdiction only within the framework of EFTA. The Joint Committee would keep under constant review the

---

50 Note 48 above.
51 See the references to the case in Chs. 11 and 12 at pp. 342 and 367–8.
52 See Opinion 1/91, note 48 above, paras. 31–6.
53 ibid. paras. 37–53.
54 ibid. paras. 54–65.
55 ibid. para. 72.

development of the case law of the European Court and of the EFTA Court and act so as to preserve the homogeneous interpretation of the agreement. The European Court in Opinion 1/92 on the revised draft agreement found this system to be compatible with the Community Treaty provided that the 'principle that decisions taken by the Joint Committee are not to affect the case-law of the Court of Justice is laid down in a form binding on the Contracting Parties'.[56]

In November 1994 the Court of Justice gave a very important Opinion concerning the external competence of the European Community.[57] It decided that the Community has exclusive competence under Article 113 (common commercial policy) to conclude the Multilateral Agreements on Trade in Goods under the World Trade Organization (WTO) Agreement including the Agreement on Agriculture even though internal measures to implement the latter Agreement would be based on Article 43.[58] On the other hand the Court concluded that the Community and its member states are jointly competent to conclude the General Agreement on Trade in Services (GATS) and the Agreement on Trade-Related Aspects of Intellectual Property Rights (TRIPs). The Court first dealt with the Commission's argument that the Community had exclusive competence under Article 113. In relation to GATS the Court decided that cross-frontier supplies of services, where neither the supplier nor the consumer moves, is analogous to trade in goods and comes within the common commercial policy but the remaining aspects of GATS involving the movement of persons does not come within the common commercial policy.[59] Furthermore, the Court decided that international agreements in the field of transport are excluded from the scope of Article 113.[60] In relation to TRIPs the Court concluded that intellectual property rights 'do not relate specifically to international trade' and are outwith the scope of Article 113.[61] The legal bases for adopting EC legislation on intellectual property rights are Articles 100, 100a and 235. The Court decided that it is not competent for the Community to escape the internal constraints in relation to procedures and voting rules provided for by those articles by having exclusive competence to conclude international agreements harmonizing the protection of intellectual property.[62] The Court then addressed the Commission's arguments that the Community has exclusive competence to conclude GATS and TRIPs based on the Community's implied

---

56 Note 49 above, [1992] ECR I-2821, 2846; [1992] 2 CMLR 217, 241.
57 Opinion 1/94, note 46 above.
58 ibid. at paras. 22–34.
59 ibid. at paras. 41–7.
60 ibid. at paras. 48–53.
61 ibid. at para. 57.
62 ibid. at paras. 59–60.

external powers. In the context of transport the Court reiterated the formula from the *ERTA* judgment.[63] 'Only in so far as common rules have been established at internal level does the external competence of the Community become exclusive.'[64] In areas within the transport field in which common rules have not been adopted member states, whether acting individually or collectively, retain competence to enter into agreements with non-member states as long as they do not affect any common rules that have been adopted.

In the context of services the Court distinguished Opinion 1/76[65] and decided that external powers could not be exercised, and thus become exclusive, without any internal legislation having first been adopted.[66] The Community had adopted measures under Articles 100a, 235, 54 and 57(2) in the context of services but the coverage was not complete and therefore the Community did not have exclusive competence to conclude GATS.[67] The Court did define when the Community has exclusive external competence within the field of services:

Whenever the Community has included in its internal legislative acts provisions relating to the treatment of nationals of non-member countries or expressly conferred on its institutions powers to negotiate with non-member countries, it acquires exclusive external competence in the spheres covered by those acts.

The same applies in any event, even in the absence of any express provision authorizing its institutions to negotiate with non-member countries, where the Community has achieved complete harmonization of the rules governing access to a self-employed activity, because the common rules thus adopted could be affected within the meaning of the [*ERTA*] judgment if the Member States retained freedom to negotiate with non-member countries.[68]

In relation to TRIPs the Court applied similar reasoning to conclude that the Community did not have exclusive competence. Once again it narrowed the potential scope of the 'Opinion 1/76 doctrine', i.e. an exclusive external competence can be exercised/created even when no internal measures have been adopted if it is necessary for the Community to participate in the agreement in order to achieve one of the objectives set out in the Treaty. The Court said that: 'Unification or harmonization of

---

63 Case 22/70 *Commission* v *Council* [1971] ECR 263 at paras. 17 and 18.
64 Opinion 1/94 at para. 77.
65 Cited above at note 49.
66 Opinion 1/94 at paras. 82–6.
67 ibid. at paras. 87–98. The Court said that where harmonizing measures have been adopted under Art. 100a they may 'limit, or even remove, the freedom of the Member States to negotiate with non-member countries' (at para. 88). A similar point was made in relation to Art. 235 in para. 89.
68 ibid. at paras. 95–6.

intellectual property rights in the Community context does not necessarily have to be accompanied by agreements with non-member countries in order to be effective.'[69] Finally, the Court encouraged the member states and the Community institutions to engage in 'close cooperation' in exercising their joint competence in the fields covered by GATS and TRIPs within WTO.[70]

In this Opinion the Court of Justice has clearly shown a willingness to constrain the Community's exclusive competence by narrowing the *ratio decidendi* of Opinion 1/76. The Community's implied powers to act externally will, broadly speaking, have to be based on an actual exercise of internal competence rather than the simple existence of such competence. The Court has also shown a right and proper concern that the prerogatives of the institutions and the member states under Articles 100, 100a and 235 are respected by not permitting Article 113 to be used as a vehicle for harmonizing intellectual property measures internally by the back door method of concluding an international agreement.[71]

The Court's Rules of Procedure provide that its opinion under Article 228 of the Treaty may deal not only with the question whether the envisaged agreement is compatible with the Treaty, 'but also with the question whether the Community or any Community institution has the power to enter into that agreement'.[72]

An interesting quirk in the Court's procedure when dealing with opinions is the fact that the Court sits in closed session and gives its opinion, which has to be reasoned, after hearing the advocates-general.[73] Presumably all the advocates-general could give their individual opinions to the Court, but no matter how many opinions are given by the advocates-general, none of them is published.

STAFF CASES

Article 179 of the Treaty provides that 'the Court of Justice shall have

69 ibid. at paras. 99–100.
70 ibid. at paras. 108–9.
71 Art. 113 does not even require the Parliament to be consulted and qualified majority voting applies in the Council whereas Arts. 100 and 235 require unanimity in the Council and Art. 100a requires a joint act of the Council and Parliament under the conciliation and veto procedure.
72 See Rules of Procedure ECJ, Art. 107(2), OJ 1991 L176/28. See also para. 3 of Op 2/91, note 49 above.
73 See Rules of Procedure ECJ, Art. 108(2), OJ 1991 L176/28.

jurisdiction in any dispute between the Community and its servants within the limits and under the conditions laid down in the Staff Regulations or the Conditions of Employment'.

Disputes between the staff of the Community institutions and their employers have played a very significant part, in terms of volume, in the total workload of the Court and the Court of First Instance.[74] Staff cases, however, are essentially labour-law disputes of little or no significance to those who are not employed by a Community institution.[75] Since the setting up of the Court of First Instance these cases have been dealt with by that Court, normally by a chamber of three judges.[76] The European Court still hears appeals from the Court of First Instance in such cases but on a point of law only.[77] Litigation before the Court of First Instance is encouraged by the fact that the institutions bear their own costs in staff cases even if they win.[78] On the other hand, appeals to the European Court are discouraged by the fact that members of staff have to bear the institution's costs if they appeal unsuccessfully.[79] The Court can derogate from this rule and order the parties to share the costs where equity so requires.[80]

In practice, staff cases are not heard under the 'unlimited jurisdiction' of the Court provided for in Article 179 unless the disputes are of a financial character.[81] The Court merely exercises a review jurisdiction analogous to the one it exercises under Articles 173 and 175.[82]

---

74 As at 31 December 1990 7,085 cases had been brought before the Court or the Court of First Instance (including 15 under the Euratom Treaty and 535 under the ECSC Treaty), of which 2,444 – about 34 per cent – were staff cases; see *XXIVth General Report*, p. 448.

75 Since 1994 European Community staff cases have been reported in a separate section of European Court Reports. Abstracts of the judgments are published in English and the full reports in the language of the case. Cases raising issues of significance to Community law in general are still published in full in the main part of the ECR.

76 See Rules of Procedure CFI, Art. 12, OJ 1991 L136/5. The number of staff cases brought before the Court of First Instance has been as follows: 92 in 1989, 43 in 1990, 81 in 1991, 79 in 1992, 83 in 1993, and 81 in 1994.

77 See Ch. 6, pp. 184–90, on the jurisdiction and workload of the Court of First Instance and on the rules governing appeals to the Court of Justice.

78 Rules of Procedure CFI, Art. 88, OJ 1991 L136/17.

79 See Rules of Procedure ECJ, Art 69(2), OJ 1991 L176/20.

80 Rules of Procedure ECJ, Art. 122, OJ 1991 L176/30.

81 See Staff Regulations, Art. 91(1), as laid down by Art. 2 of Council Regulation 259 of 29 February 1968, JO 1968 L56/1, as amended; Schermers and Waelbroeck, *Judicial Protection*, p. 365; Conditions of Employment of Other Servants, Art. 73, as laid down by Art. 3 of Council Regulation 259, above, as amended. These and various other analogous provisions for staff of the European Investment Bank, of the European Centre for the Development of Vocational Training and of the European Foundation for the Improvement of Living and Working Conditions are set out in *Selected Instruments relating to the Organization, Jurisdiction and Procedure of the Court*, Luxembourg, EC Official Publications, 1990.

82 See Ch. 8.

Initially, the member of staff makes a complaint to the appointing authority against an act adversely affecting him or her, either where the said authority has taken a decision or where it has failed to adopt a measure prescribed by the Staff Regulations. The complaint must be lodged within three months. The authority must notify the person concerned of its reasoned decision within four months of the date on which the complaint was lodged. If at the end of that period no reply to the complaint has been received, this is deemed to constitute an implied decision rejecting it, against which an appeal to the Court of First Instance may be lodged.[83]

Only when this administrative procedure has been exhausted can a member of staff take his or her case to the Court of First Instance. The staff member has a maximum of three months in which to bring the case before the Court. The time runs from the date of notification of the decision of the appointing authority or, where no decision is taken by that authority, from the expiry of four months after the date of submitting the complaint to that authority.[84]

APPEALS FROM THE COURT OF FIRST INSTANCE

Decisions of the Court of First Instance can be appealed against to the European Court on a point of law.[85] In 1994 appeals took an average of 21.2 months. They occupy a relatively small part of the Court's workload. In 1993 there were 17 appeals out of 490 cases brought before the Court and in 1994 the figures were 13 out of 354. One reason for the small number of appeals so far was the dominance of staff cases in the workload of the Court of First Instance prior to the extension of the Court's jurisdiction in 1993–4.[86] There is a disincentive against appealing to the

---

83 See Staff Regulations, Art. 90(2).

84 See Staff Regulations, Art. 91. The staff member can bring an action before the Court of First Instance at the same time as his or her complaint is lodged with the appointing authority where interim measures or the staying of the execution of the contested act is sought. No decision is taken in the main action before the Court until the appointing authority has made its decision on the complaint or the four-month period has expired without it doing so.

85 Ch. 6, p. 188. See also the Rules of Procedure ECJ, Arts. 110–123, OJ 1991 L176/28–30.

86 In 1989 there were 92 staff cases brought out of a total of 169, in 1990 the figures were 43 out of 55, in 1991 81 out of 93, and in 1992 79 out of 116. However, in 1993 there were only 83 staff cases out of a total of 596 and in 1994 83 out of 145.

European Court for members of staff because they risk having to pay the costs of the institution against whom the appeal is made. Community staff incur no such risk when they bring their case before the Court of First Instance. Now that the Court of First Instance's jurisdiction has been extended significantly beyond staff cases, it may be that the Court of Justice will receive a larger number of appeals. Indeed, it is possible that the Court of Justice may evolve into an appellate court, hearing only appeals from the Court of First Instance and giving preliminary rulings in cases referred by national courts.

ACTIONS CONCERNING THE EUROPEAN INVESTMENT BANK AND NATIONAL CENTRAL BANKS

Article 180 EC provides:

The Court of Justice shall, within the limits hereinafter laid down, have jurisdiction in disputes concerning:

(a) the fulfilment by Member States of obligations under the Statute of the European Investment Bank. In this connection, the Board of Directors of the Bank shall enjoy the powers conferred upon the Commission by Article 169;[87]

(b) measures adopted by the Board of Governors of the Bank. In this connection, any Member State, the Commission or the Board of Directors of the Bank may institute proceedings under the conditions laid down in Article 173;[88]

(c) measures adopted by the Board of Directors of the Bank. Proceedings against such measures may be instituted only by Member States or by the Commission, under the conditions laid down in Article 173, and solely on the grounds of non-compliance with the procedure provided for in Article 21(2), (5), (6) and (7) of the Statute of the Bank;[89]

(d) *the fulfilment by national central banks of obligations under this Treaty and the Statute of the European System of Central Banks. In this connection the powers of the Council of the European Central Bank in respect of national central banks shall be the same as those conferred upon the Commission in respect of member states by Article 169. If the Court of Justice finds that a national central bank has failed to fulfil an obligation under*

---

87 See Ch. 7.
88 See Ch. 8.
89 ibid.

this Treaty, that bank shall be required to comply with the judgment of the Court of Justice.[90]

Under the EEC Treaty the European Investment Bank was governed by Articles 129 and 130.[91] This provided for the Bank to have legal personality, for its members to be the member states of the Community and for its task to be to contribute to 'the balanced and steady development of the common market in the interest of the Community'. The Bank fulfils that task by granting loans on a non-profit basis and giving guarantees to facilitate the financing of various projects. These projects include those for the development of less-developed regions of the Community, large-scale projects for modernizing or converting undertakings or which are of common interest to several member states.

The Maastricht Treaty amendments moved the provisions governing the Bank from Articles 129 and 130 EEC to Articles 198d and 198e EC and added the following paragraph: 'In carrying out its task, the Bank shall facilitate the financing of investment programmes in conjunction with assistance from the structural funds and other Community financial instruments.'

The Bank is able to borrow significant sums of money on the capital markets in order to lend money to private and public undertakings.[92] Most of the loans relate to projects within the Community,[93] but some are made under arrangements set up by international agreements between the Community and third states.[94]

Although the European Investment Bank plays a significant role in economic development, the jurisdiction of the Court of Justice under Article 180 of the Treaty has not proved to be of any significance to date. However, Article 180 is there to ensure that the Bank and the member states in their dealings with the Bank operate within the rule of law.[95]

Paragraph (d) of Article 180 EC gives the European Central Bank the right to take an action against national central banks that fail to fulfil their

[90] Paragraph in italics added by the Treaty amendments agreed in Maastricht in December 1991. On Art. 169, see Ch. 7.

[91] See Mathijsen, *European Union Law*, pp. 120–2.

[92] In 1993 the Bank borrowed more than 14 billion ECUs; ibid., p. 121.

[93] In 1993 the amount lent in the Community was over 17 billion ECU, of which 75 per cent went in loans for regional development; ibid., p. 121.

[94] In 1989 the Bank lent 612 million ECUs outside the Community. An example of such lending is provided by Case C-370/89 *SGEEM v EIB* [1992] ECR I-6211, which related to the laying of high tension electric cable in Mali under the third ACP-EEC Convention.

[95] Although the Art. 180 EC jurisdiction has not been used it was established in Case C-370/89, above, that the European Investment Bank is an 'institution' within the meaning of Art. 215(2) EC and hence its non-contractual liability is within the exclusive jurisdiction of the Court of Justice and Court of First Instance under Art. 178.

obligations under Community law in a way analogous to an Article 169 action against member states that fail to fulfil such obligations. The procedure is very similar to an Article 169 action. The European Central Bank must first notify the national central bank that it considers that bank has failed to fulfil one of its obligations. After receiving the national central bank's reply, the European Central Bank will issue a reasoned opinion. If the national central bank does not comply with that opinion within the specified time-limit, the European Central Bank may bring the matter before the Court of Justice.[96]

ARBITRATION

Article 181 of the Treaty states that 'the Court of Justice shall have jurisdiction to give judgment pursuant to any arbitration clause contained in a contract concluded by or on behalf of the Community, whether that contract be governed by public or private law'.[97]

Clearly, Community institutions are at liberty to seek to negotiate with contractors a clause appointing the Court of Justice as arbiter of any disputes arising under the contract. Thus far the Court has had to deal with very few arbitrations.[98]

The arbitration clause inserted in a contract concluded by or on behalf of the Community is likely to specify which state's law the Court is required to apply.[99] The Court will apply that law because Article 215(1) of the Treaty requires that 'the contractual liability of the Community shall be governed by the law applicable to the contract in question'. However, the Court will ignore any provision of national law which purports to exclude its jurisdiction.[100] Problems could arise if the contract

---

96 See the Protocol on the Statute of the European System of Central Banks and of the European Central Bank, Art. 35.6.

97 Since August 1993 the Court of First Instance has been granted jurisdiction over cases brought by natural or legal persons under Art. 181, see Ch. 6 above at pp. 189–90.

98 Nine arbitration cases had been brought before the Court under Art. 181 by the end of 1990. Some of the cases are as follows: Case 109/81 *Porta v Commission* [1982] ECR 2469; Case 318/81, *Commission v CO.DE.MI. SpA* [1985] ECR 3693; Case 118/84 *Commission v Royale Belge* [1985] ECR 1889; Case 123/84 *Klein v Commission* [1985] ECR 1907; Case 220/85 *Fadex v Commission* [1986] ECR 3387; Case 426/85 *Commission v Zoubek* [1986] ECR 4057; Case C-338/92 *Compagnie d'Entreprise CFE v European Parliament*, judgment of 20 October 1993; and Case C-42/94 *Advies v Parliament*, pending.

99 In Case 318/81, note 98 above, e.g., the Court had to apply Belgian law.

100 Case C-209/90 *Commission v Feilhauer* [1992] ECR I-2613, 2642.

did not expressly or impliedly state which law governs it. In that event the Court would surely apply the principles contained in the Rome Convention on the Law Applicable to Contractual Obligations to determine which law governs the contract.[101]

ACTIONS BETWEEN MEMBER STATES UNDER A SPECIAL AGREEMENT

Article 182 of the Treaty states: 'the Court of Justice shall have jurisdiction in any dispute between Member States which relates to the subject matter of this treaty if the dispute is submitted to it under a special agreement between the parties'.

This jurisdiction for the Court to deal with disputes between member states is distinct from its general jurisdiction in relation to such disputes under Article 170 of the Treaty.[102] It is not surprising that this specialized head of jurisdiction has not been used thus far, as only one judgment has been given under the general ground of jurisdiction in Article 170.[103]

JURISDICTION CONFERRED BY CONVENTIONS AND PROTOCOLS BETWEEN THE MEMBER STATES

Article 1 of the Protocol on Privileges and Immunities of the European Communities[104] explicitly confers jurisdiction on the Court of Justice: 'The property and assets of the Communities shall not be the subject of any administrative or legal measure of constraint without the authorization of the Court of Justice.' The Court has occasionally been called upon to exercise this jurisdiction.[105]

The Court of Justice has jurisdiction to give preliminary rulings on the interpretation of the EC Convention on Jurisdiction and the Enforcement

---

101 See pp. 333–4.
102 See Ch. 7.
103 See Ch. 7 at p. 208.
104 Signed on 8 April 1965 at the same time as the Merger Treaty, OJ 1967, No. 152, 13 July 1967.
105 See, e.g., Case 1/88SA *SA Générale de Banque* v *Commission* [1989] ECR 857; Case 1/87SA *Universe Tankship Company Inc.* v *Commission* [1987] ECR 2807.

of Judgments in Civil and Commercial Matters of 27 September 1968 (the Brussels Convention).[106] The jurisdiction was conferred on the Court by a protocol to the above Convention, which was signed on 3 June 1971 and entered into force on 1 September 1975.[107] Up to the end of 1994 national courts had referred eighty-six cases under the Protocol to the European Court for a preliminary ruling.[108]

The Court is dealing in this context with cases in the realm of private international law and its decisions have been extensively analysed by specialists in that field.[109] The Convention and the Court's unifying powers of interpretation under the Protocol have created uniform rules of international jurisdiction throughout the Community and have brought about the free movement of judgments.[110]

The provisions of the Protocol are very similar to Article 177 of the Treaty in that they make a distinction between discretionary and mandatory references.[111] The latter, however, applies only to the courts of last resort listed in Article 2(1) of the Protocol and not to any court that happens in the particular case to be one from whose decision there is no

---

106 OJ 1972 L299/32 (in French, German, Dutch and Italian). The Convention was signed by the six original member states of the Community and entered into force for them on 1 February 1973. The official report on the Convention is the Jenard Report (OJ 1979 C59/3). An Accession Convention for Denmark, Ireland and the United Kingdom was signed on 9 October 1978 (OJ 1978 L304/77) and entered into force for Denmark on 1 November 1986, for the United Kingdom on 1 January 1987 and for Ireland on 1 June 1988. The official report on the Convention is the Schlosser Report (OJ 1979 C59/71). The implementing legislation in the United Kingdom is the Civil Jurisdiction and Judgments Act 1982. An Accession Convention with Greece was signed on 25 October 1982 (OJ 1982 L388) and has been in force since 1 October 1989. An Accession Convention was signed at San Sebastian with Spain and Portugal on 26 May 1989 (OJ 1989 L285), which made some significant amendments to the original Convention. As at 31 December 1994 it was in force between France, Germany, Greece, Ireland, Italy, Luxembourg, the Netherlands, Portugal, Spain and the United Kingdom. The official report on the Spanish and Portuguese Accession Convention is the Almeida Cruz, Desantes Real and Jenard Report (OJ 1990 C189/35). A consolidated version of the Brussels Convention, as amended by all the Accession Conventions, can be found in OJ 1990 C189/2.

107 See OJ 1975 L204/28, in French, German, Dutch and Italian; the English version is found in OJ 1978 L304/50. The official report on the Protocol is the Jenard Report, note 106 above. For a consolidated version of the Protocol, taking into account the accession of Denmark, Ireland, the United Kingdom, Greece, Spain and Portugal, see OJ 1990 C189/25. All new member states of the Community are expected to enter into negotiations to accede to the EC Brussels Convention and to the Protocol.

108 As at 1 January 1995 all the member states of the Community were parties to the Protocol except Austria, Finland and Sweden.

109 See Select Further Reading.

110 The phrase 'free movement of judgments' was used by the Jenard Report, note 106 above, p. 42 and adopted by the Court in Case 145/86 *Hoffmann* v *Krieg* [1988] ECR 645, 666.

111 See Ch. 9.

judicial remedy.[112] Unlike Article 177, discretionary references cannot be requested by any national court or tribunal, but only by those sitting in an appellate capacity.[113] However, appeals against decisions authorizing enforcement of a judgment may be heard by a court of first instance acting in an appellate capacity,[114] and such a court can refer a question on the interpretation of the Convention to the Court under the Protocol.[115] Article 4 of the Protocol allows for the possibility of a competent authority in a state asking the Court for a ruling on the interpretation of the Convention in relation to a case that is already *res judicata*. Such an interpretation would provide guidance for future cases. This provision has not been used and is not one that the Court can view favourably, given its advisory nature and the Court's insistence that all its decisions are binding.[116]

The EC Brussels Convention was negotiated by the member states of the Community in fulfilment of the requirement in Article 220 of the Treaty that 'Member States shall, so far as is necessary, enter into negotiations with each other with a view to securing for the benefit of their nationals: ... the simplification of formalities governing the reciprocal recognition and enforcement of judgments of courts or tribunals and of arbitration awards'. Other attempts have been made to negotiate conventions under different aspects of Article 220. A convention on the mutual recognition of companies and legal persons was signed by the original six member states of the Community on 29 February 1968. Indeed, on 3 June 1971 the same states signed a protocol conferring jurisdiction on the European Court to grant preliminary rulings on the interpretation of the convention.[117] However, neither the convention nor the protocol have entered into force, as a result of the failure of the Netherlands to ratify them and both are now dead letters.[118] A draft Bankruptcy Convention was established in 1980, which contained provisions similar to the Protocol

---

112 It is not clear whether the exceptions to the mandatory reference under Art. 177 of the Treaty established in Case 283/81 *CILFIT* v *Italian Ministry of Health* [1982] ECR 3415 (see Ch. 9, pp. 301–2) are applicable in the context of the Protocol on the Interpretation of the EC Brussels Convention; it seems likely that they are.

113 See the Protocol, Arts. 2 and 3.

114 See EC Brussels Convention, Art. 37.

115 See the Protocol, Art. 2(3).

116 See Opinion 1/91, note 48 above, discussed on pp. 320–22. See also the Court's refusal to give a non-binding opinion under the Protocol in relation to the interpretation of Brussels Convention provisions used to resolve internal conflicts of jurisdiction within the United Kingdom under Sched. 4 to the Civil Jurisdiction and Judgments Act 1982 in Case C-346/93 *Kleinwort Benson Ltd* v *City of Glasgow District Council*, judgment of 28 March 1995, *The Times*, 17 April 1995.

117 See the Jenard Report, note 106 above, pp. 66–7.

118 See Lasok and Stone, *Conflict of Laws*, pp. 88–91.

on the interpretation of the Brussels Convention.[119] This convention, however, was shelved as no agreement could be reached on a final version that could be opened for signature[120] but recently efforts have been made to revive it. Negotiations are also under way for a Brussels II Convention concerning certain aspects of private international law of family matters and jurisdiction may be conferred on the Court of Justice.[121]

It is possible for the court to be given jurisdiction by the member states to interpret a convention that has no direct legal basis in the EC Treaty.[122] The Rome Convention on the Law Applicable to Contractual Obligations of 19 June 1980 is one such convention that has entered into force.[123] Its preamble merely states that the member states of the Community are 'anxious to continue in the field of private international law the work of unification of law which has already been done within the Community, in particular in the field of jurisdiction and enforcement of judgments'.[124] The Rome Convention came into force on 1 April 1991,[125] the same day as the implementing legislation for the United Kingdom, the Contracts (Applicable Law) Act 1990, came into force.[126]

In Brussels on 19 December 1988 the member states of the Community signed two protocols relating to the interpretation of the Rome Convention. The Second Protocol has to be ratified by all the member

---

119 ibid., Ch. 10.

120 See the Tizzano Report, OJ 1990 C219/1, at p. 4.

121 See 'Brussels Convention II: A New Private International Law Instrument in Family Matters for the European Union or the European Community' by Beaumont & Moir (1995) 20 ELRev 268–88.

122 Conventions in the field of justice and home affairs negotiated under Art. K.3(2)(c) TEU 'may stipulate that the Court of Justice shall have jurisdiction to interpret their provisions and to rule on any disputes regarding their application'.

123 OJ 1980 L266.

124 Another example is the Community Patent Convention of 15 December 1975 (OJ 1976 L17), which directly embodies a provision giving the Court of Justice powers to interpret it (Article 73). This convention has subsequently been modified, in particular by the Agreement on the Community Patent of 15 December 1989 (OJ 1989 L401). The Agreement provides for a Common Appeal Court but still leaves the possibility of that court or national courts requesting preliminary rulings from the European Court; see the Tizzano Report, note 120 above, pp. 4–5. See further in Ch. 26 at p. 855.

125 The Rome Convention came into force in Belgium, Denmark, France, Germany, Greece, Italy, Luxembourg and the United Kingdom. Subsequently, it has come into force in Ireland and the Netherlands. The official report on the Convention is the Giuliano and Lagarde Report, OJ 1980 C282. It has been the subject of a great deal of academic writings; see Select Further Reading.

126 See The Contracts (Applicable Law) Act 1990 (Commencement No. 1) Order 1991, SI 1991 No. 707. See the annotations to the 1990 Act by Morse in *Current Law Statutes* for the implementation of the Convention in the United Kingdom.

states before it enters into force.[127] It permits the Court of Justice to have jurisdiction to grant preliminary rulings on the interpretation of the Convention. The First Protocol comes into force when it has been ratified by seven member states, but only after the Second Protocol enters into force.[128] States that ratify the First Protocol permit their national courts to refer cases to the European Court of Justice for a preliminary ruling. Both protocols have been ratified by the United Kingdom but neither is yet in force.

Two protocols were adopted in order to permit individual member states not to allow their own national courts to refer cases on the interpretation of the Convention to the European Court and yet to permit other member states to go ahead.[129] This could have been achieved with one protocol but not without sacrificing the principle that the European Court's jurisdiction should be enlarged only with the agreement of all the member states.

The First Protocol is very similar to the Protocol on the Interpretation of the EC Brussels Convention, discussed above. The principal difference is that no mandatory references are provided for. Even courts of last resort, like the House of Lords, are not required to refer questions of interpretation on the Rome Convention to the European Court for a preliminary ruling. One of the reasons for this was the concern of the United Kingdom and some other member states that parties from outside the Community would no longer choose to litigate in their fora. Negotiators of international contracts would not include a clause conferring jurisdiction on the courts in England if it meant that their case would face the delay and expense involved in being referred to the European Court if one of the parties was determined to push the case to the House of Lords.[130]

---

127 OJ 1989 L48/17–18. Art. 3. As at 31 December 1994 it had been ratified by Greece, Ireland, Italy, Luxembourg, the Netherlands and the UK.
128 OJ 1989 L48/1–4, Art. 6. As at 31 December 1994 the First Protocol had been ratified by Greece, Italy, Luxembourg, the Netherlands and the UK.
129 One significant factor was that Portugal and Spain had not negotiated an Accession Convention in relation to the Rome Convention. They would not be in a position for some time to give powers to their own courts to refer questions on the interpretation of the Convention to the European Court. An Accession Convention was opened for signature at Funchal on 18 May 1992. As at 31 December 1994 it had been ratified by Italy, the Netherlands and Spain. Another factor was the declaration made by Ireland that it would not be in a position to ratify the First Protocol without a change in its constitution; see the Tizzano Report, note 120 above, at pp. 9–10, 15.
130 The Tizzano Report, note 120 above, attributes this concern to 'some Member States'; see p. 9.

INHERENT JURISDICTION

The traditional view of the European Court's competence is that it 'has no inherent jurisdiction'.[131] However some scholars are now detecting signs that the Court regards itself as having inherent jurisdiction to uphold the rule of law in the Community.[132]

In *Zwartveld and Others*[133] the European Court gave an order that clarified its powers of judicial control over the Community institutions. A Dutch examining judge was engaged in a preliminary investigation of Zwartveld and others in connection with alleged forgeries carried out at a fish market contrary to the Dutch criminal code. The judge wanted access to certain reports that had been made by Community fishing inspectors and to call the inspectors as witnesses. The Commission refused to release the reports to the judge, so he requested the European Court to order the Commission to supply him with the reports and to permit him to examine the inspectors as witnesses.

The European Court noted the obligation of sincere cooperation incumbent on member states according to Article 5 of the Treaty and extended the principle to the Community institutions. The Article states that

Member States shall take all appropriate measures, whether general or particular, to ensure fulfilment of the obligations arising out of this Treaty or resulting from action taken by the institutions of the Community. They shall facilitate the achievement of the Community's tasks.

They shall abstain from any measure which could jeopardize the attainment of the objectives of this Treaty.[134]

This obligation of cooperation is of particular importance where it concerns the judicial authorities of the member states, who are responsible for ensuring that Community law is applied and respected in the national legal system. The Court decided that there is an obligation on the Community institutions to provide national judges with assistance in carrying out investigations into infringements of Community law. The Court referred to Article 164 of the Treaty, which provides that in the

---

131 See Hartley, *European Community Law* (1988, 2nd ed.), p. 56 but contrast (1994, 3rd ed.) at p. 64.
132 See Arnull, 'Does the Court of Justice have Inherent Jurisdiction?' (1990) 27 CMLRev 683.
133 Case C-2/88 Imm [1990] ECR I-3365, [1990] 3 CMLR 457.
134 For an overview of the Court's jurisprudence on Art. 5, see Temple Lang, 'Community Constitutional Law: Article 5 EEC Treaty' (1990) 27 CMLRev 645.

interpretation and application of the Treaty the Court has to ensure that the law is observed. To do this it believes it has to guarantee judicial control of the compliance by Community institutions with the duty of sincere cooperation that is placed on them.

The Court ordered the Commission to send the reports to the judge and to authorize the inspectors to give evidence as witnesses before him, unless the Commission could submit to the Court imperative reasons relating to the necessity to avoid obstacles to the functioning and independence of the Community that could justify a refusal to do so. If the Commission attempted to give imperative reasons for non-disclosure, then the Court would rule at a later stage on whether it found these reasons convincing.

As a result of the Court's decision in *Zwartveld* national courts can request the European Court to order a Community institution to disclose evidence even though this falls outside the scope of the system of preliminary rulings established by Article 177 of the Treaty.

The European Court seems determined to give itself a general jurisdiction to ensure that neither the member states nor the Community institutions can avoid a review of the question whether the measures adopted by them are in conformity with the Treaty. The Court is anxious to ensure that the member states and Community institutions comply with the Community's 'constitutional charter', the EC Treaty, but the Court should be more careful itself to function within the limits of the jurisdiction it has been given by that Treaty.

CHAPTER 11

Direct Effect of Community Law

One of the tenets of Community law laid down by the European Court is that the Community constitutes a 'new legal order' that confers rights on individuals.[1] Certain provisions of Community law are directly effective in that they create 'individual rights which national courts must protect' without any need for implementing legislation in that member state.[2] The European Court has determined that a provision of Community law must be 'unconditional and sufficiently precise'[3] before it can produce direct effects.

The ability of individuals to rely on Community law before their national courts greatly enhances its enforceability. The alternative means of enforcement is, of course, an action against a member state brought by the Commission or another member state under Articles 169 or 170 for failure to fulfil its obligations under Community law. That process can be slow and, until the Maastricht treaty amendments, lacked any sanctions.[4] Furthermore, individuals benefit from such an action only when the state changes the internal law to comply with its Community law obligations, but that does not provide a remedy for the wrong done to them up to that time. On the other hand, national courts can quickly apply directly effective Community law and bring to bear the full force of their powers, including the award of damages, to enforce their orders.

1 Case 26/62 *Van Gend en Loos* v *Nederlandse Administratie der Belastingen* [1963] ECR 1. The importance of the new legal order in separating the Community from other international organizations was reiterated in the Court's *Opinion on the draft Agreement on a European Economic Area*, Opinion 1/91, [1991] ECR I-6079, [1992] 1 CMLR 245; see Ch. 10, pp. 320–21.
2 Case 26/62, note 1 above, p. 13.
3 See, e.g. Case 148/78 *Pubblico Ministero* v *Ratti* [1979] ECR 1629, 1642 and Case 8/81 *Becker* v *Finanzamt Munster-Innenstadt* [1982] ECR 53, 71.
4 See Ch. 7.

GENERAL CONDITIONS FOR COMMUNITY LAW TO HAVE DIRECT EFFECT

UNCONDITIONAL

A provision of Community law will not be unconditional if the right it grants is dependent on the judgment or discretion of an independent body, such as a Community institution or a member state. The test is a simple one and has survived unchanged for many years. In *Comitato di Coordinamento per la Difesa della Cava and Others* v *Regione Lombardia and Others* the European Court said: 'A Community provision is unconditional where it is not subject, in its implementation or effects, to the taking of any measure either by the institutions of the Community or by the Member States.'[5] The provisions on state aid illustrate this principle.[6] The final determination of whether state aid is compatible with the common market under Article 92 of the Treaty is the exclusive responsibility of the Commission, subject to the supervision of the Court of First Instance and/or the Court of Justice. Article 92 is not directly effective.[7] However, the last sentence of Article 93(3) does create direct effects which give the national courts a limited role to play in state aids.[8] Article 93(3) states:

The Commission shall be informed, in sufficient time to enable it to submit its comments, of any plans to grant or alter aid. If it considers that any such plan is not compatible with the common market having regard to Article 92, it shall without delay initiate the procedure provided for in paragraph 2. The Member State concerned shall not put its proposed measures into effect until this procedure has resulted in a final decision.

The national courts may be confronted with proceedings which require them to interpret and apply the concept of aid in Article 92 in order to decide whether the state aid introduced without being first submitted to

---

5 Case C-236/92 [1994] ECR I-483, para. 9, in which the Court cited its judgment in Case 28/67 *Molkerei-Zentrale Westfalen* v *Hauptzollamt Paderborn* [1968] ECR 143.
6 See Ch. 27 below.
7 See Case C-354/90 *FNCE* [1991] ECR I-5505, para. 14 and Case 78/76 *Steinike und Weinlig* v *Germany* [1977] ECR 595.
8 ibid.

the Commission should have been so submitted under Article 93(3). In doing so the national courts do not make a final decision on whether or not the state aid is compatible with the common market but simply preserve the rights of individuals until such a determination is made by the Commission.

The above shows the willingness of the Court to find an unconditional obligation in the midst of conditional ones and give it direct effect.[9]

The European Court may, however, decide that a provision is unconditional even where its application is conditional on the exercise of discretion by an independent body if that discretion is subject to judicial control. This can be illustrated by the case of *Van Duyn* v *Home Office*.[10] The Court decided that Article 48 of the Treaty has direct effect. The first two paragraphs provided that free movement of workers shall be secured within the Community[11] and that the freedom entailed the 'abolition of any discrimination based on nationality between workers of the Member States as regards employment, remuneration and other conditions of work and employment'. The third paragraph elaborates on the meaning of the rights conferred by the first two paragraphs but states that they are 'subject to limitations justified on grounds of public policy, public security or public health'.

It would seem that the right of an individual worker to move freely from one member state to another to take up employment is conditional on the person satisfying the public policy, public security and public health tests and thus Article 48 lacks direct effect. However, in the *Van Duyn* case the Court said:

The application of [the paragraph 3] limitations is, however, subject to judicial control, so that a Member State's right to invoke the limitations does not prevent the provisions of Article 48, which enshrine the principles of freedom of movement for workers, from conferring on individuals rights which are enforceable by them and which the national courts must protect.[12]

It is a fine line between conditions that do not prevent direct effect because they are subject to judicial control and the Court is able and willing to set the parameters of the operation of those conditions, and

9 For the opposite situation see the fact that Article 85(3) is conditional on a decision by the Commission and is therefore not directly effective, unlike the other key provisions on competition policy in the remainder of Art. 85 and in Art. 86, see Ch. 24 below.
10 Case 41/74 [1974] ECR 1337.
11 By the end of the transitional period, which had long since passed; see p. 22.
12 Case 41/74, note 10 above, p. 1347.

conditions that do prevent direct effect because they also are, ultimately, subject to judicial control but the Court is unable or unwilling to set the parameters.

SUFFICIENTLY PRECISE

In the *Regione Lombardia* case,[13] the Court briefly elaborated on what is meant by 'sufficiently precise' by saying that the obligation which the provision imposes is set out in 'unequivocal terms'.[14] Pescatore's view is that the requirement to be sufficiently precise is fulfilled if the provision of Community law furnishes 'workable indications to the national court'.[15] Article 119 of the Treaty provides an interesting example of a provision that is precise enough to be partly directly effective. In *Defrenne v SABENA*[16] the European Court drew a distinction between 'direct and overt discrimination' in the pay granted to men and women and 'indirect and disguised discrimination' in this area. The former is prohibited by Article 119 and is directly effective because it can be identified by national courts 'solely with the aid of the criteria based on equal work and equal pay referred to by the article'. The prohibition of the latter by Article 119 lacks sufficient precision to be directly effective. The Court said that disguised and indirect discrimination could be identified only by 'reference to more explicit implementing provisions of a Community or national character'.[17]

Direct and overt discrimination can be seen easily by straightforward legal analysis when a woman is paid less than a man for doing the same job.[18] Disguised and indirect discrimination is more subtle. It can arise where a woman is earning less pay than a man when they are doing

13 Case C-236/92, note 5 above, at para. 10.
14 ibid. The Court cited Case 152/84 *Marshall v Southampton and South-West Hampshire Health Authority* [1986] ECR 723 and Case 71/85 *Netherlands v Federatie Nederlandse Vakbeweging* [1986] ECR 3855. In *Marshall* the phrase 'unequivocal terms' is used in para. 52 and in the latter case the phrase 'unequivocally' is used in para. 18 but it is not so clear from those cases that the test for a provision being 'sufficiently precise' is that it should be 'unequivocal'.
15 Pescatore, 'The Doctrine of "Direct Effect": An Infant Disease of Community Law' (1983) 8 ELRev 155, 175.
16 Case 43/75 [1976] ECR 455, 473.
17 ibid., p. 473. The Court's case law on Art. 119 is explained in Ch. 20, where it is pointed out that in certain circumstances the prohibition on indirect discrimination in Art. 119 of the Treaty is capable of direct effect; see Ch. 20, notes 32 *et seq*.
18 As in Case 43/75, note 16 above. The same holds true where the man and the woman were not employed contemporaneously, see Case 129/79 *Macarthys Ltd v Smith* [1980] ECR 1275.

different jobs but the work is of equal value. The courts require detailed guidelines by way of implementing legislation to enable them to assess whether different jobs have equal value.[19]

CONCLUSION

The tests for a provision to have direct effect – that it is unconditional and sufficiently precise – boil down to a question of 'justiciability'. Pescatore defines that concept as meaning 'a rule can have direct effect whenever its characteristics are such that it is capable of judicial adjudication, account being taken both of its legal characteristics and of the ascertainment of the facts on which the application of each particular rule has to rely'.[20] The Court's case law on what is justiciable can evolve and a classic example is the development of Article 90(2) from a clearly non-directly effective provision to one that can have direct effect.[21]

DIRECT EFFECT OF DIFFERENT TYPES OF COMMUNITY LAW

TREATY PROVISIONS

In the *Van Gend en Loos* case[22] the Court for the first time determined that a Treaty provision had direct effect in the national courts. Van Gend en Loos imported ureaformaldehyde into the Netherlands on 9 September 1960 and was charged duty at the rate of 8 per cent. This was a level of duty 5 per cent higher than had been in place on 1 January 1958, when the EEC Treaty came into force. Van Gend en Loos objected to paying the extra 5 per cent, as it contravened Article 12 of the Treaty. The matter came before the Tariefcommissie, Amsterdam, which requested a preliminary ruling from the European Court under Article 177 as to whether

---

19 See Dir. 75/117, discussed in Ch. 20 at p. 625.
20 Pescatore, (1983) 8 ELRev 155, 176–7. In Cases C-6, 9/90 *Francovich and Others* v *Italy* [1991] ECR I-5357, (noted by G. Bebr (1992) 29 CMLRev 57 and by P. Duffy, 'Damages against the State: a new remedy for failure to implement Community obligations' (1992) 17 ELRev 133, the directive did not have direct effect because it did not make it possible for the national court to determine who was responsible for paying the guaranteed arrears of salary owed to the workers in a firm that is insolvent.
21 See the discussion in Ch. 27 below at pp. 864–6.
22 Case 26/62, note 1 above.

Article 12 created rights that individuals could rely on before their national courts.

The European Court examined the 'spirit' and the 'general scheme' of the EEC Treaty. The Treaty established institutions that were 'endowed with sovereign rights', and their powers affected individuals as well as states. A further factor indicating that the Treaty is intended to create rights that can be relied on in national courts is the setting up of a system whereby such courts can request a preliminary ruling on the interpretation of the Treaty and other legislative provisions from the European Court under Article 177.[23] The Court also noted that one of the objectives of the Treaty was the creation of a common market and that this implies that the Treaty is 'more than an agreement which merely creates mutual obligations between the contracting states'.[24]

The Court concluded that the Treaty had created a 'new legal order' in which 'independently of the legislation of Member States, Community law . . . not only imposes obligations on individuals but is also intended to confer upon them rights which become part of their legal heritage'.[25]

23 In Opinion 1/91, note 1 above, the Court noted that the European Economic Area (EEA) was to be established on the basis of an international treaty which, essentially, merely created rights and obligations as between the contracting parties (the EC member states and the EFTA member states) and provided for no transfer of sovereign rights to the intergovernmental institutions that it set up. Thus, although the EEA adopted many of the substantive provisions of the EC Treaty on the four freedoms and competition policy, the Court was concerned that its interpretation by the EEA Court would be incompatible with its own interpretation of provisions having the same wording. The EEA Agreement had a protocol that proposed that each EFTA state had the option of allowing its national courts to refer questions on the meaning of the provisions of the Agreement that are identical to Community provisions to the European Court of Justice for a preliminary ruling. However, the European Court was not happy with this system because it was optional and its ruling would not necessarily be binding on the relevant national courts. It has to be said that Art. 177 EC does not state that the European Court's rulings are binding on the national court that asks for it, though the mandatory nature of the third paragraph may imply it. The binding nature of an Art. 177 EC ruling, like the doctrine of direct effect, is a principle that has been developed by the Court itself. They are both reasonable though not necessary conclusions to be drawn from an examination of the Treaty as a whole. The Court here is reiterating the significance of giving legislative power to international institutions and conferring binding powers of interpretation on a supranational court to interpret those provisions so that they can be applied directly by national courts. Identical provisions on the four freedoms and competition policy do not have the same meaning outside that institutional and legal framework. See also Ch. 10 at pp. 320–22 and 332, note 116.

24 Case 26/62, note 1 above, p. 12. This argument now appears weak given the criticism of the draft Agreement on the EEA by the European Court. That agreement, by adopting the four freedoms and competition policy, sought to create a common market, yet the Court thought it, essentially, just created rights and obligations between the contracting states.

25 ibid. In Opinion 1/91, note 1 above, the Court repeated these ideas and stressed that

The above arguments have some force in justifying a conclusion that Community law can have direct effect. In particular, the creation of lawmaking institutions, with powers to make a species of legislation that is said to be directly applicable, and a judicial body empowered to give interpretative rulings for national courts on the Treaty and the legislation suggests that at least some Treaty provisions and legislation can be relied on in the national courts. It must be said, however, that it is possible that the judges in the Court were predisposed to arriving at the result of direct effect. This is the view of former Judge Pescatore. In relation to the *Van Gend en Loos* case he said: 'The important thing is to see what are the motives underlying this decision. The reasoning of the court shows that the judges had *"une certaine idée de l'Europe"* of their own, and that it is this idea which has been decisive and not arguments based on the legal technicalities of the matter.'[26]

Article 12 of the Treaty states that 'Member States shall refrain from introducing between themselves any new customs duties on imports or exports or any charges having equivalent effect, and from increasing those which already apply in their trade with each other.' The Court noted that the provision clearly prohibits any increases in customs duties and is not conditional on implementing legislation being passed in the member states. The fact that the obligation is expressly imposed on member states 'does not imply that their nationals cannot benefit from this obligation'.[27] Thus the Netherlands had imposed an additional 5 per cent duty unlawfully and Van Gend en Loos had a right not to pay it, which it could enforce in the Dutch courts.

Individuals are able to rely on the direct effect of Treaty provisions against other individuals (horizontal effect) as well as against a member state (vertical effect).[28]

---

the EC Treaty was not just an international agreement but was also the constitutional charter of a Community based on the rule of law.

26 (1983) 8 ELRev 155, 157. It may be observed that in *Van Gend en Loos* the Commission had favoured granting direct effect to Art. 12, but this had been opposed by the governments of the Netherlands, Belgium and Germany and by AG Roemer.

27 Case 26/62, note 1 above, p. 13.

28 Another example of vertical effect is Case 41/74, note 10 above, and examples of horizontal effect are provided by cases on Art. 119 like Case 129/79, note 18 above and discussed in Ch. 20, and cases on competition law; see Ch. 24. Some Treaty provisions are not capable of producing horizontal direct effect, e.g., Art. 30; see Ch. 15, pp. 449–50.

REGULATIONS

Article 189 of the Treaty provides that regulations are 'directly applicable in all Member States'. Thus regulations are automatically part of each national system without the necessity of any implementing legislation. It is not necessarily the case, however, that all provisions of regulations have direct effect, because they may not be 'unconditional and sufficiently precise'. This distinction between 'direct effect' and 'direct applicability' was recognized by Winter[29] and has gained acceptance by a number of scholars.[30]

The Court has not explicitly ruled on the question of whether there is a distinction between direct applicability and direct effect. It has made the following point in cases determining that directives can have direct effect: 'If . . . by virtue of the provisions of Article 189 Regulations are directly applicable and, consequently, *may* by their very nature have direct effects, it does not follow from this that other categories of acts mentioned in that Article can never have similar effects.' [our italics][31]

The implication of the Court's statement is that all regulations are directly applicable but that some regulations or provisions of regulations may not be directly effective. The Court has recognized that a regulation may provide for a Community institution or a member state to take implementing measures. In those circumstances the national court is at liberty to apply the implementing measures but in doing so should 'ascertain whether such national measures are in accordance with the content of the Community Regulation'.[32]

The Court has ruled that member states must not pass national measures implementing the provisions of a regulation that, in itself, meets the requirements to be directly effective.[33] The Court has accepted that member states can pass implementing measures that clarify doubts as to the

29 'Direct Applicability and Direct Effect: Two Distinct and Different Concepts in Community Law' (1972) 9 CMLRev 425–38.
30 See Steiner, 'Direct Applicability in EEC Law: a chameleon concept' (1982) 98 LQR 229; Schermers and Waelbroeck, *Judicial Protection*, p. 148; even Pescatore, (1983) 8 ELRev 155, 164, accepts that Winter's analysis is right although he notes that the problem has not aroused any difficulties in practice.
31 See Case 41/74, note 10 above, p. 1348. The wording is slightly different in subsequent cases: 'Regulations are directly applicable and, consequently, by their nature capable of producing direct effects' (see Case 148/78, p. 1641 and Case 8/81, p. 70, both note 3 above).
32 See Case 230/78 *Eridania* v *Minister of Agriculture and Forestry* [1979] ECR 2749, 2771, discussed by Pescatore, (1983) 8 ELRev 155, 164.
33 See Case 34/73 *Variola* v *Amministrazione Italiana delle Finanze* [1973] ECR 981, 990–91.

meaning of a regulation, but even here the interpretation is subject to a ruling by the European Court on the meaning of the regulation.[34]

In conclusion, regulations normally have direct effect and when they do national implementing legislation is unacceptable. When a provision of a regulation is not sufficiently precise or is too conditional to have direct effect, national implementing legislation is acceptable, but the national court must ensure that it is consistent with the meaning of the regulation as interpreted by the European Court.

DIRECTIVES[35]

Article 189 of the Treaty states that 'a Directive shall be binding, as to the result to be achieved, upon each Member State to which it is addressed, but shall leave to the national authorities the choice of form and methods'. In *Van Duyn* v *Home Office*[36] the Court established that directives could have direct effect, giving three reasons for this conclusion.

Firstly, the Court said, 'It would be incompatible with the binding effect attributed to a Directive by Article 189 to exclude, in principle, the possibility that the obligation which it imposes may be invoked by those concerned.'[37] This argument for direct effect is not wholly convincing in isolation. It is perfectly possible that a directive, like other measures, can impose a 'binding' obligation on a member state at an international level, and not impose a 'binding' obligation on a member state that an individual can rely on in the national courts.[38] Indeed, directives that are conditional or are not sufficiently precise are still 'binding' at the international level even though they cannot have direct effect.

Secondly, the Court stated that the 'useful effect' of a directive would

---

34 See Case 94/77 *Zerbone* v *Amministrazione delle Finanze dello Stato* [1978] ECR 99; cf. Case 50/76 *Amsterdam Bulb BV* v *Produktschap voor Siergewassen* [1977] ECR 137.
35 For an analysis of the direct and indirect effect of directives in the context of Community social policy, see Ch. 20 at pp. 632–5.
36 Case 41/74, note 10 above. The Court had earlier given direct effect to a directive in conjunction with Arts. 9 and 13(2) EEC and Council Decision No 66/532 in Case 33/70 *SACE* v *Italian Ministry of Finance* [1970] ECR 1213, 1223.
37 Case 41/74, note 10 above, p. 1348.
38 An example of this is the European Convention on Human Rights, which is binding on the United Kingdom at an international level but which does not have direct effect in the United Kingdom. Article 13 of the Convention requires each contracting state to provide an effective remedy in the national courts against violations of the Rights and freedoms set forth in the Convention. The European Court of Human Rights has not interpreted this as requiring contracting states to incorporate the Convention into internal law nor that the provisions of the Convention are directly effective in national law. See, e.g. *Observer and Guardian* v *United Kingdom* (1991) ECHR Series A, Vol. 216.

be 'weakened if individuals were prevented from relying on it before their national courts'.[39] This is a policy argument. The effectiveness of directives is enhanced by giving them direct effect. This policy argument could be used to justify horizontal direct effects. It can be argued, however, that the binding nature of directives and their effectiveness were intended, by the scheme of the Treaty, to be protected by the Commission or a member state taking a member state that fails to implement properly a directive to the European Court.[40]

Thirdly, the Court argued that Article 177 of the Treaty implies that directives may be invoked by individuals in the national courts. Of course, national courts can refer questions on the validity or interpretation of directives to the European Court for a preliminary ruling under Article 177.[41] However, it is also true that the European Court can be asked such questions in relation to recommendations and opinions, which are not binding and cannot have direct effect.[42] Furthermore, national courts can refer questions to the European Court under Article 177 on the interpretation or validity of directives that are not capable of producing direct effects. The Court is doubtless conscious of the weakness of this argument and has not repeated it.

The doctrine of the direct effect of directives had a shaky theoretical foundation and it was not clear if it extended beyond vertical effect. A more secure foundation was laid in the *Ratti* case.[43] The Court repeated the first two arguments given in the *Van Duyn* case but added a third. The Court referred to the concept of a 'defaulting Member State' and said that 'a Member State which has not adopted the implementing measures required by the Directive in the prescribed periods may not rely, as against individuals, on its own failure to perform the obligations which the Directive entails'.[44]

There is a strong legal argument for saying that in an action between an

---

39 Case 41/74, note 10 above, p. 1348.
40 See Ch. 7. However, Judge Mancini of the European Court defends the direct effect of directives on the ground that the Commission may not bring before the European Court every failure of a member state to implement properly a directive and that, even when it does, certain member states ignore the judgments given by the Court in infringement actions: see 'The Making of a Constitution for Europe' (1989) 26 CMLRev 595, 601–3.
41 See Ch. 9.
42 See Case C-322/88 *Grimaldi* [1989] ECR 4407, 4419.
43 Case 148/78, note 3 above.
44 ibid., p. 1642. This reasoning was repeated by the Court in Case 8/81, note 3 above, p. 71. The Court was aware at that time (see Pescatore, (1983) 8 ELRev 155, 170) that the principle that directives could have direct effect was not accepted by the French Conseil d'État in *Cohn-Bendit* [1980] I CMLR 543 and by the German Bundesfinanzhof (Federal Finance Court) in *Re Value Added Tax Directives* [1982] I CMLR 527.

individual and a member state the latter is barred from pleading that the individual cannot rely on the provisions of a directive after the time-limit for its implementation has expired without it being implemented properly. It is the fault of the member state if the directive is not implemented correctly and timeously, so it should not be able to profit from its own mistake.

Of course, this argument provides no support for directives being invoked against individuals, that is, having horizontal direct effects. The Court eventually ruled out such effects in the *Marshall* case.[45] It emphasized the fact that under Article 189 a directive is binding only in relation to each member state to which it is addressed. Thus a directive may not of itself impose obligations on an individual, natural or legal person, and provision of a directive may not be relied upon as such against such a person. In three cases in 1993 and 1994 advocates-general argued that the Court should reverse its decision in *Marshall I* and give horizontal direct effect to directives.[46] In doing so they had support from some academics[47] and at least one judge extra-judicially.[48]

A variety of reasons were advanced for giving horizontal direct effect to directives. The completion of the single market in January 1993 placed a premium on the need to create equality of the conditions of competition and on the prohibition of discrimination. This latter principle was reinforced by the entry into force of the Treaty on European Union in November 1993 creating the concept of Citizenship of the Union. That Treaty also amended Article 191 of the EC Treaty so that it is now a legal requirement that directives are published in the Official Journal.[49] The Court has given horizontal direct effect to Treaty provisions like Article 119 even though the wording of the article simply refers to an obligation on 'each Member State' and it should be prepared to do the same in relation to directives even though they are addressed to member states. It

---

45 Case 152/84 *Marshall* v *Southampton and South-West Hampshire Area Health Authority* [1986] ECR 723. Confirmed in Case 80/86 *Kolpinghuis Nijmegen* [1987] ECR 3969.
46 Advocate-General Van Gerven on 26 January 1993 in Case C-271/91 *Marshall II* [1993] ECR I-4367; Advocate-General Jacobs on 27 January 1994 in Case C-316/93 *Vaneetveld* [1994] ECR I-763; and Advocate-General Lenz in Case C-91/92 *Faccini Dori* v *Recreb* [1994] ECR I-3325.
47 e.g. Boch and Lane, 'European Community Law in national courts: a continuing contradiction' (1992) Leiden J. of Int. L. 171.
48 See Judge Schockweiler, 'Effets des directives non transpacées en droit national à l'égard des particuliers' in the Festschrift for Mr Diez de Velasco, *Hacia un nuevo orden international y europeo*.
49 See AG Lenz's opinion in *Dori*, note 46 above. The single market creates at least a floor of minimum rights but does not eliminate inequality in competition and differences in treatment of EU citizens in all sectors. In practice directives applying to all member states have always been published in the Official Journal.

would not be a radical departure from the existing state of the law because the obligation on national courts to construe national law consistent with non-directly effective directives in effect requires national courts to impose obligations on individuals which create consequences that are similar to horizontal direct effects.[50]

The full Court of thirteen judges in the *Dori* case emphasized that the basis of vertical direct effect of directives is the personal bar concept of preventing 'the State from taking advantage of its own failure to comply with Community law'.[51] The Court gave one new paragraph of supportive reasoning for not creating horizontal direct effect of directives:

The effect of extending that case-law to the sphere of relations between individuals would be to recognize a power in the Community to enact obligations for individuals with immediate effect, whereas it has competence to do so only where it is empowered to adopt regulations.[52]

This is an important constitutional argument for not further blurring the distinction between regulations and directives. The Treaty does discriminate between situations where the Community institutions can adopt regulations and where they can adopt directives. There are a few situations where only regulations can be used,[53] a significant number where only directives can be used,[54] and an even greater number where the Community institutions can choose either.[55] The representatives of the member states who negotiated the Treaty, and the amendments to it, must have had good reason for denying the Community institutions any choice of legal measure in the first two situations above. The implication of the Court's reasoning is that there would be a danger that Community institutions might pass directives with ridiculously short implementing periods if they knew that they would have horizontal and vertical direct effect as soon as the time-limit expired. By doing

---

50 AG Jacobs in *Vaneetveld*, note 46 above. The policy arguments for giving a liberal construction to the EC Treaty so that it creates rights for individuals are stronger than in relation to directives given that the former is the constitutional charter of the Community whereas the latter is a particular type of Community legislation with the characteristics specified in Art. 189. The obligation on national courts to construe national law consistent with non-directly effective directives is discussed below at pp. 355–8. It is important to note that national courts are required to do so only 'as far as possible' and therefore there is substantial scope for different results from those that would be reached by giving horizontal direct effect to directives.

51 Case C-91/92, note 46 above, at para 22.

52 ibid. at para. 24. The case is discussed by Coppel, 'Rights, Duties and the end of *Marshall*' (1994) 57 MLR 859–79.

53 See Ch. 5 above at pp. 136–7.

54 See the Appendix.

55 ibid.

so the Community institutions could render irrelevant the role of national parliaments in implementing directives and effectively equate them to regulations. This would impoverish the lawmaking process of the Community in a way inconsistent with the principle of subsidiarity.

The brevity of the Court's reasoning may indicate that it was split, leaving us with the lowest common denominator of the reasons supporting rejection of horizontal direct effects. It is likely that the Court exercised caution so as not to be accused of judicial activism shortly after the warnings issued by the German Constitutional Court in the *Brunner* case.[56]

Clearly, the direct effect of directives is not the norm, as it is for regulations, and can be relied upon by an individual only against a defaulting state. The expectation is that directives will be implemented into national law and that individuals will be able to rely on the national law. Where appropriate, such provisions of national law can be invoked against individuals. Reliance on the direct effect of a directive is impossible against a state until the time-limit for its implementation has passed, as prior to that date the state is not in default. In the *Ratti* case above, the individual had a valid defence in relation to one directive for which the time-limit for implementation had expired without it being implemented into Italian law, but not in relation to the other directive, for which the time-limit had not expired.[57] The European Court requires that directives are correctly and completely implemented.[58] An individual can rely against the state on any part of the directive that is unconditional and sufficiently precise and has not been adequately implemented into national law.[59] In the *Emmott* case[60] the Court decided that 'until such times as a directive has been properly transposed into national law, a defaulting Member State may not rely on an individual's delay in initiating proceedings against it in order to protect rights conferred upon him or her by the provisions of the directive and that a period laid down by national law within which proceedings must be initiated cannot begin to run before that time'. However, the reasoning in the *Emmott* case has subsequently been narrowed

---

56 See *Brunner* v *European Union Treaty* [1994] 1 CMLR 57, discussed at pp. 376–7 below.
57 Case 148/78, note 3 above. But a different position applies in relation to non-directly effective directives; see p. 358.
58 In Case 301/81 *Commission* v *Belgium* [1983] ECR 467, 479 the Court required 'sufficient' implementation, and in Case 145/82 *Commission* v *Italy* [1983] ECR 711, 719 said 'incomplete' implementation was inadequate. In Case 126/82 *Smit Transport* [1983] ECR 73, 88 and in Case 222/84 *Johnston* v *Chief Constable of the RUC* [1986] ECR 1651, 1691 the Court stated that directives needed to be implemented 'correctly'.
59 See Case 222/84, note 58 above, pp. 1690–91; and Case 271/82 *Auer* v *Ministère Public* [1983] ECR 2727, 2744.
60 Case C-208/90 *Emmott* [1991] ECR I-4269, para. 23 noted by Szyszczak (1992) 29 CMLRev 604.

by the Court.[61] It is now possible for a national limitation period to apply in relation to claims made under a directive prior to it being fully implemented in national law. It is competent for national law to limit the period prior to the bringing of the claim in respect of which the rights under the directive are applicable, even where that directive has not been properly transposed within the prescribed period in the member state concerned. Claims can be limited to the twelve-month period prior to their being lodged. If the limitation period has the effect of eliminating the Community law claim, as it did in *Emmott*, then it will be found to be unlawful.

In summary, the conditions that must be satisfied before an individual can rely on the direct effect of a directive are: the relevant provisions of the directive must be unconditional and sufficiently precise; the time-limit for implementation of the directive must have expired without the relevant part of the directive being correctly and completely implemented into the law of the member state; and the action must be against the state. This last condition requires further elaboration. The European Court has included within the concept of the state bodies such as local or regional government,[62] a Chief Constable of a police force[63] and public authorities providing health services.[64]

Some problems remain in identifying the scope of the state for the purpose of invoking directives. Nationalized industries and companies in which the state has a majority shareholding would seem to be under state control. It is not clear whether the European Court regards 'control' by the state as sufficient in itself. In paragraph 18 of *Foster v British Gas plc* the Court seemed to be saying that it was sufficient.[65] In addition, in paragraph 20 and in the ruling the Court seemed to create an alternative possibility for directives to be invoked by individuals against a body not itself under state control, but that has been made responsible, pursuant to a measure adopted by the state, for providing a public service under the control of the state and has for that purpose special powers beyond those that result from the normal rules applicable in relations between individuals.

61 Case C-338/91 *Steenhorst-Neerings* v *Bestuur van de Bedrijfsvereniging voor Detailhandel, Ambachten en Huisvrouwen* [1993] ECR I-5475 and Case C-410/92 *Johnson* v *Chief Adjudication Officer* [1995] 1 CMLR 725 judgment of 6 December 1994.
62 See Case 103/88 *Fratelli Costanzo* v *Commune di Milano* [1989] ECR 1839, 1871, in which the Court said that 'all organs of the administration, including decentralized authorities such as municipalities' are covered.
63 See Case 222/84, note 58 above, p. 1691, where the Court said that a Chief Constable was a 'public authority' who did 'not act as a private individual'. The Court regards the Chief Constable as a 'constitutionally independent' authority responsible for the maintenance of public order and safety who is none the less 'an emanation of the State'; see Case C-188/89 *Foster* v *British Gas plc* [1990] ECR I-3313, [1991] 1 QB 405, 427, at para. 19.
64 See Case 152/84, note 45 above, p. 749.
65 Case C-188/89, note 63 above.

That there are two separate criteria seems to be evident from the use of the disjunctive 'or' in paragraph 18 of the Court's judgment:

The Court has held in a series of cases that unconditional and sufficiently precise provisions of a Directive could be relied on against organizations or bodies which were subject to the authority or control of the State *or* had special powers beyond those which result from the normal rules applicable to relations between individuals. [our italics][66]

On the other hand, the conjunction 'and' is used in paragraph 22 and in the Court's ruling.

The House of Lords on receiving the European Court's judgment in *Foster* applied the criterion in the Court's ruling to see whether Foster could invoke the directive against British Gas prior to privatization.[67] British Gas met the relevant tests, as it was made responsible for supplying a public service by statute, that service was provided under the control of the state, and British Gas had special powers beyond those that result from the normal rules applicable in relations between individuals: indeed, it had a monopoly on the supply of gas.

The Court of Appeal has subsequently concluded in *Doughty* v *Rolls-Royce plc*[68] that a body being under the control of the state in terms of its ownership is not sufficient to enable an individual to rely on the direct effect of a directive against it. It construed the European Court's judgment in *Foster* and that of the House of Lords applying it as indicating that the power of control was only one of several cumulative criteria. Thus even though Rolls-Royce was wholly owned by the Crown at the relevant time, the Court of Appeal did not regard it as being made responsible, pursuant to a measure adopted by the state, for providing a public service, and it did not have any special powers beyond those that result from the normal rules applicable to relations between individuals. Rolls-Royce was merely one of several companies engaged in trading in a competitive environment. The Court of Appeal may be making the mistake warned against by Lord Templeman in *Foster* v *British Gas plc* of applying 'the ruling of the European Court of Justice, couched in terms of broad principle and purposive language characteristic of Community law, in a manner which is, for better or worse, sometimes applied to enactments of the United Kingdom Parliament'.[69]

Clearly, it is important that the European Court has an early opportunity to clarify whether state control is sufficient in itself to bring an undertaking

---

66 Case C-188/89, note 63 above.
67 *Foster* v *British Gas* [1991] 2 AC 306.
68 [1992] 1 CMLR 1045.
69 Note 67 above, p. 315.

within the ambit of the direct effect of directives. It seems that it should in the sense that the state is in default in not implementing the directive, is aware of what would be required to comply with the directive and has the power to change the operation of the body under its control to comply with it.

The scope of the direct effect of directives is important, but is not the only possible means for an individual to invoke the provisions of a directive before the national courts. An individual can, in certain circumstances, obtain damages against the state when it has failed to implement a directive properly. Also an individual can insist that the national court interprets any national law in the light of the purpose and wording of the provisions of a directive that do not have direct effect. The ability to obtain damages from a defaulting state and the rule of interpretation will be examined in turn.

Damages against the state for non-implementation of directives

In *Francovich and Others* v *Italy*[70] the European Court greatly increased the pressure on member states to implement directives timeously. The Court ruled that a member state is, in certain circumstances, obliged to make good damage to individuals arising from non-implementation of a directive.

The applicants were employees of undertakings that became insolvent, leaving substantial arrears of salary unpaid. They brought proceedings in the Italian courts against Italy for the recovery of the compensation provided for by Directive 80/987 on the approximation of the laws of the member states relating to the protection of employees in the event of the insolvency of their employer or, in the alternative, damages.

Directive 80/987 was to be implemented by the member states no later than 23 October 1983. Italy, however, failed to do so and in *Commission* v *Italy* was found to have failed to comply with its obligations under Community law.[71]

The Italian courts sought a preliminary ruling from the European Court. The Court first considered whether the relevant provisions of Directive 80/987 were directly effective. The Court applied the usual test for establishing direct effect: whether the provisions were unconditional and sufficiently precise. The directive provided guarantees for the payment of unpaid remuneration in the case of the insolvency of the employer. These guarantees were sufficiently precise and unconditional in relation to

70 Cases C-6, 9/90, note 20 above.
71 Case 22/87 [1989] ECR 143.

their content[72] and the people entitled to them but, unfortunately, not in relation to the person or persons obliged to pay the guaranteed sums. Thus the applicants could not rely on the direct effect of the Directive against the state even though the time-limit had expired without it being implemented.

Given that Directive 80/987 was not sufficiently precise in establishing who was liable to pay the guarantees contained in it, Community law, prior to the *Francovich* case, would have been of no avail to the applicants. The Court decided, however, that the principle of liability of a member state for damage caused to individuals by infringements of Community law for which it was responsible was inherent in the scheme of the Treaty. In particular, the obligation to make good such damage stemmed from Article 5 of the Treaty, which provides that 'Member States shall take all appropriate measures, whether general or particular, to ensure fulfilment of the obligations arising out of this Treaty'.

The Court also argued that the full 'effectiveness' of Community rules might be called in question and the protection of the rights that they conferred would be weakened if individuals could not obtain compensation where their rights were infringed by a breach of Community law imputable to a member state. This is an unconvincing policy argument. Articles 169–171 of the Treaty provide for an action to be brought before the European Court of Justice by the Commission or a member state against a member state that has failed to implement a directive. As a result of the Treaty amendments agreed in Maastricht the European Court has the power to fine a member state that fails to comply with a judgment of the Court under Article 171.[73] This is the way that the Treaty envisages the effectiveness of directives should be protected.

The Court's argument based on Article 5 of the Treaty carries more weight than the effectiveness argument. It is, nevertheless, a slender foundation on which to build a legal doctrine that member states are obliged to compensate individuals for damage caused to them by infringements of Community law imputable to the member states. The Community and Article 5 had existed for more than thirty years without the Court

---

72 The Court reached this conclusion even though the member states had a discretion to fix a ceiling on the amount guaranteed to be paid in order to avoid paying sums that were out of proportion to the social aim pursued by the Directive. The Court decided that a member state that had failed in its obligation to transpose a directive into national law could not frustrate the rights attributed by the Directive to individuals by relying on its power to limit the amount of the guarantee that it could have exercised if it had adopted the measures necessary to implement the Directive. This indicates a willingness on the part of the Court to find a provision directly effective when its conditionality has been removed by the failure of the member state to act.

73 See Ch. 7 at pp. 209–11.

granting such a remedy. The Court has left itself open to the accusation that it is engaged in judicial lawmaking.[74]

The Court laid down three conditions that must be fulfilled before an individual can claim damages against a member state for failing to implement or implement correctly or completely a directive:

1 The result laid down by the directive involves the attribution of rights attached to individuals.
2 The content of those rights must be capable of being identified from the provisions of the directive.
3 There must be a causal link between the failure by the member state to fulfil its obligations and the damage suffered by individuals.

It is a matter for each member state to determine the competent courts and appropriate procedures for legal actions intended to enable individuals to obtain damages from the state. The European Court has indicated that the procedures must be no less favourable to applicants than those relating to similar claims under internal law and must not be so organized as to make it practically impossible or excessively difficult to obtain damages from the state.

The results laid down by Directive 80/987 did indeed confer rights upon individuals, including a guarantee for employees that their claim for outstanding remuneration would be met, and the content of that right was identifiable from the provisions of the Directive. The third condition was also satisfied in *Francovich*, as the Court had already determined that Italy had failed to implement the Directive.[75] The non-implementation had the effect that no clarification had been made of who was the guarantor of the rights conferred by the Directive.

This case has obvious implications for insolvency and employment law. Community law does underwrite minimum protection for employees who are unpaid as a result of insolvency. If the national legislation does not conform to these guarantees, then employees who are adversely affected can claim damages from the state. *Francovich* has much wider implications. It provides a strong incentive for member states to implement directives properly and timeously. States will be anxious to avoid paying damages to individuals when implementation of the directive would confer rights on

---

74 For a general analysis of Art. 5, see Temple Lang, 'Community Constitutional Law: Article 5 EEC Treaty' (1990) 27 CMLRev 645. The Court is clearly determined to uphold the rule of law by ensuring that member states implement directives timeously and correctly. It is also keen to give individuals remedies to make their rights under Community law meaningful. The danger is that by creating a legal remedy on an unsure legal foundation it may undermine the rule of law.
75 Case 22/87, note 71 above.

the individuals *vis-à-vis* other individuals and leave the state free from financial liability.

When a state does fail to implement fully a directive, an individual now has two methods of seeking redress against the state. The individual can first of all argue that the directive has direct effects, and failing that can argue that the state must pay damages for the loss caused by the directive not being fully implemented.[76]

Interpretation of national law in the light of non-directly effective provisions of directives

The European Court first established the principle that national courts should interpret national law 'in the light of the wording and purpose' of a directive that lacked direct effect in the case of *Von Colson and Kamann* v *Land Nordrhein-Westfalen*.[77] Von Colson and Kamann were two female social workers who applied for a job in a German prison. Less well qualified males were appointed and the two women sought compensation for this sex discrimination. Under German law the local Labour Court was able only to award the women a trifling sum to cover their outlay in connection with the application. The Labour Court referred the case to the European Court for a preliminary ruling, asking *inter alia* what sanction was required by Directive 76/207 on equal treatment for men and women as regards access to employment when such sex discrimination takes place.

The European Court noted that Article 6 of the Directive requires member states to provide a means whereby victims of discrimination prohibited by the Directive can 'pursue their claims by judicial process' within their national legal system. The Court noted, however, that 'the Directive does not prescribe a specific sanction; it leaves Member States free to choose between the different solutions suitable for achieving its objective'.[78] This lack of an unconditional and sufficiently precise obligation meant that Directive 76/207 did not have direct effect as regards sanctions for discrimination.[79]

---

76 For an example of that approach see Case C-91/92, note 46 above, in which the *Francovich* conditions are reiterated and applied at paras. 27–9. Two cases testing the scope of the *Francovich* judgment are pending before the Court, see Case C-48/93 *Factortame III* and Case C-46/93 *Firma Brasserie du Pêcheur SA* v *Germany*. The extent to which *Francovich* may be a pointer towards a general liability in damages cast on member states that act in violation of Community law rights is considered by Ross, 'Beyond *Francovich*' (1993) 56 MLR 55 and Van Gerven, 'Non-contractual Liability of Member States, Community Institutions and Individuals for Breaches of Community Law with a View to a Common Law for Europe' (1994) 1 Maastricht J. of Eur. & Comp. L. 6, 12–24.

77 Case 14/83 [1984] ECR 1891.

78 ibid., p. 1907.

79 ibid., p. 1909.

The European Court then brought national courts within the ambit of the national authorities of the member states mentioned in Article 189 of the Treaty. Thus, for matters within their jurisdiction, national courts are bound to ensure that the result envisaged in a directive is achieved. The Court also included national courts, in matters within their jurisdiction, in the obligation on member states under Article 5 of the Treaty to take all appropriate measures to ensure fulfilment of their Treaty obligations.[80] The Court concluded that

in applying the national law and in particular the provisions of a national law specifically introduced in order to implement Directive No 76/207, national courts are required to interpret their national law in the light of the wording and purpose of the Directive in order to achieve the result referred to in the third paragraph of Article 189.[81]

In the ruling the Court appeared to qualify the obligation on the national court by stating that 'it is for the national court to interpret and apply the legislation adopted for the implementation of the Directive in conformity with the requirements of Community law, *in so far as it is given discretion to do so under national law*'. [our italics][82]

However, the European Court has not repeated this let-out clause in subsequent cases. The European Court has changed the qualifying words in subsequent cases to 'as far as possible'. Thus the extent to which it is 'possible' to construe national law consistent with non-directly effective directives becomes, potentially at least, a matter of Community law rather than national law.[83] Furthermore, the Court has specified that the duty to interpret national law in the light of the wording and purpose of the directive in order to achieve the result aimed for by the directive is applicable whether the provisions of national law concerned predate or postdate the directive.[84] Thus it is immaterial whether or not the national law is implementing the directive.[85] There is an exception in relation to criminal law: 'A Directive cannot of itself and independently of a law adopted for its implementation have the effect of determining or

---

80 ibid., p. 1909.
81 ibid.
82 ibid., pp. 1910–11.
83 See Case 222/84, note 58 above, p. 1690; Case 80/86, note 45 above, p. 3986; Case C-106/89 *Marleasing SA* v *La Comercial Internacional de Alimentación SA* [1990] ECR I-4135, 4159, noted by Stuyck and Wytinck (1991) 28 CMLRev 205; Case C-334/92 *Wagner Miret* v *Fondo de Garantía Salarial* [1993] ECR I-6911, para. 20; and Case C-91/92, note 46 above, para. 26.
84 See Case C-106/89, note 83 above.
85 See pp. 362–6 for the implications of the *Marleasing* decision for the case law of the House of Lords on the issue of interpreting national law in the light of non-directly effective directives.

aggravating the liability in criminal law of persons who act in contravention of the provisions of that Directive.'[86]

It is not clear to what extent national courts are required to depart from the wording of national law in order to achieve the result aimed for in a non-directly effective directive. In *Von Colson and Kamann* the Court acknowledged that Germany was not obliged to choose compensation as the sanction for sex discrimination in job applications.[87] Having chosen compensation as the method, it must be effective, not merely a nominal amount, and the national court is to interpret the national law in a way that ensures the adequacy of the compensation.[88] For a national court to ensure the 'effectiveness' of a non-directly effective directive may require a considerable departure from the wording of the national law.[89] The juxtaposition of a clear rejection of horizontal direct effect of directives and the repetition of the obligation on national courts to construe national law consistent with a non-directly effective directive in the *Dori* case shows that the latter is not intended to be a back-door method of achieving the former.[90] A *contra legem* interpretation of national law is not expected.[91] In other words a national court is not required to override the clear wording and intent of national law in order to make it comply with a non-directly effective directive. It is not often an easy task for a national court to know what is required to make the national law consistent with the result aimed for in the directive, given that a directive is equally authentic in eleven languages and may be conditional or lacking in precision. National courts will frequently find it necessary to refer the issue to the European Court for a preliminary ruling. That Court can give limited assistance in this context, as it is not within its jurisdiction under Article 177 to interpret national law. The Court can only clarify the meaning of

86 See Case 14/86 *Pretore di Salo* v X [1987] ECR 2545, 2570 and Case 80/86, note 45 above, pp. 3986–7.

87 Case 14/83, note 77 above, p. 1907. One alternative is to require the employer to offer a post to the candidate discriminated against.

88 ibid., p. 1909. In Case C-271/91 *Marshall II* [1993] ECR I-4367, [1993] 3 CMLR 293, the Court decided that in actions against the state or an emanation of the state the combined provisions of Arts. 5 and 6 of Directive 76/207 give rise, on the part of a person who has been injured as a result of discriminatory dismissal, to rights which that person must be able to rely on before the national courts. Each state can choose whether to provide a remedy of reinstatement or compensation but if it chooses the latter then an individual has an enforceable right to full compensation which may not be limited *a priori* in terms of its amount.

89 See *Litster* v *Forth Dry Dock & Engineering Co. Ltd* [1990] 1 AC 546, discussed on pp. 364–5.

90 Case C-91/92, note 46 above, at pp. 3356–7.

91 See Van Gerven, 'Non-contractual Liability of Member States, etc.' (1994) 1 Maastricht J. of Eur. & Comp. L 6,10.

the directive and leave it to the national court to interpret national law in a way that is consistent with that meaning.

It is dangerous to include national courts within the concept of a 'member state' for the purposes of Article 189. It is inappropriate constitutionally to require judges to implement directives into national law; this is a matter for the executive and the legislature. National judges, and, indeed, judges in the European Court, should be wary of usurping their legitimate role in interpretation by becoming legislators. Where provisions of directives are conditional and imprecise, the courts must not rewrite the provisions to remove the conditions and create precision. There is a role for interpreting national law in the light of provisions of directives that would be directly effective were the action against a state. It may also be appropriate where the legislature has attempted to implement the directive but has done so incompletely or incorrectly, even though the time-limit has not yet expired.[92]

DECISIONS

The European Court decided in the *Grad* case that Community decisions could have direct effect.[93] It employed very similar reasoning to that used later in the *Van Duyn* case[94] to justify the direct effect of directives. The Court took the view that when people other than the addressees are affected by a decision they may be able to rely on the decision's direct effects, invoking its binding nature and the need to make it effective:

It would be incompatible with the binding effect attributed to Decisions by Article 189 to exclude in principle the possibility that persons affected may invoke the obligation imposed by a Decision. Particularly in cases where, for example, the Community authorities by means of a Decision have imposed an obligation on a Member State or all the Member States to act in a certain way, the effectiveness (*'l'effet utile'*) of such a measure would be weakened if the nationals of that State could not invoke it in the courts and the national courts could not take it into consideration as part of Community law.[95]

It is not at all clear whether the direct effect of decisions can be invoked horizontally as well as vertically. When the decision is addressed to a member state and the state fails to comply with it, then reliance on the

92 The European Court did not require the expiry of the implementation period before the national court is obliged to interpret implementing legislation in accordance with a directive in Case 80/86, note 45 above, p. 3987.
93 Case 9/70 *Grad* v *Finanzamt Traunstein* [1970] ECR 825.
94 Case 41/74, note 10 above, pp. 296–7.
95 Case 9/70, note 93 above, p. 837.

decision by an interested individual against the state can be justified on the basis that the state is knowingly in default. However, it would seem unfair, and out of line with the Court's line of cases since *Marshall*[96] denying horizontal direct effect to directives, to permit an individual to rely on a decision addressed to a member state in an action against another individual. In *Bulk Oil* v *Sun International*[97] the European Court noted that certain Community decisions obliged member states to inform the other member states and the Commission before making any changes in their rules on exports to non-member countries. The Court said, however, that

that obligation . . . concerns only the institutional relationship between a Member State and the Community and the other Member States. In proceedings before national courts between natural or legal persons such persons cannot attack a policy or measure adopted by a Member State on the basis that that Member State has failed to fulfil its obligation to inform the other Member States and the Commission beforehand. Such a failure therefore does not create individual rights which national courts must protect.[98]

A different problem arises when an individual invokes a decision against one of the individuals to whom the decision is addressed. This sort of horizontal direct effect may be appropriate if the provision is unconditional, sufficiently precise and any time-limit for its implementation has expired.

INTERNATIONAL AGREEMENTS

The European Court has on rare occasions found provisions of an international agreement to which the Community is a party directly effective. In the *Bresciani* case the Court gave direct effect to Article 2(1) of the Yaounde Convention of 1963 on the elimination of customs duties and charges having equivalent effect where a directly effective provision of the EEC Treaty was incorporated into the Convention.[99] In the *Kupferberg* case the Court decided that Article 21(1) of the Free Trade Agreement between the Community and Portugal before it became a member state was directly effective. The Court found the prohibition on discrimination in taxation against goods imported from Portugal into the Community to be unconditional and sufficiently precise to be relied on by traders in the

---

96 See Case 152/84, note 45 above, discussed on pp. 347–9.
97 Case 174/84 [1986] ECR 559, 594.
98 For a similar judgment in relation to a Community directive obliging member states to inform the Commission of certain matters, see Case 380/87 *Enichem Base and Others* v *Comune di Cinisello Balsamo* [1989] ECR 2491, 2518.
99 Case 87/75 *Bresciani* v *Amministrazione Italiana delle Finanze* [1976] ECR 129, 141–2. The provision was Art. 13 of the Treaty.

courts in the Community.[100] In the *Sevince* case the Court decided that certain Articles of decisions of the Association Council set up by the agreement establishing an association between the Community and Turkey were directly effective.[101] In *ONEM* v *Kziber* the Court found Article 41(1) of the Cooperation Agreement between the Community and Morocco of 27 April 1976 to be directly effective.[102] In *Anastasiou and Others*[103] the Court concluded that provisions on the origin of products in the 1977 Protocol to the 1972 Association Agreement between the Community and Cyprus were directly effective.

On the other hand, the Court has decided several cases in which it has held an international agreement is not directly effective.[104] The Court has decided that the Community has been substituted for its member states in the General Agreement on Tariffs and Trade (GATT), yet it has, to date, declined to give direct effect to any provision of GATT.[105] However, in *Fediol* v *Commission*[106] the Court did find admissible a claim by the applicant relying on provisions of GATT referred to in Community Regulation 2641/84, although the applicant's claim was dismissed on the merits.

Clearly, the Court approaches the direct effect of an international agreement on a case-by-case basis. A provision of such an agreement will be directly effective only if it is unconditional and sufficiently precise. The Court applies a more restrictive approach to the interpretation of such agreements than it does to the Community Treaty, even where the wording is identical, because the Community is aiming for an ever closer union among its peoples and has created the necessary institutional framework to establish a new legal order.[107]

100 Case 104/81 *Hauptzollamt Mainz* v *Kupferberg* [1982] ECR 3641.

101 Case C-192/89 *Sevince* v *Staatssecretaris van Justitie* [1990] ECR I-3461, noted by Schermers (1991) 28 CMLRev 183 and Kuijper (1991) 28 CMLRev 1005.

102 Case C-18/90 [1991] ECR I-199, discussed in Ch. 18 and noted by Weber (1991) 28 CMLRev 959 and Neuwahl, 'Social Security under the EEC – Morocco Cooperation Agreement' (1991) 16 ELRev 326.

103 Case C-432/92 [1994] ECR I-3087, 3128.

104 An example is Case 12/86 *Demirel* v *Stadt Schwäbisch Gmünd* [1987] ECR 3719, where the Court did not find certain provisions of an association agreement between Turkey and the European Community to be directly effective.

105 See Cases 21–4/72 *International Fruit Company* v *Produktschap voor Groenten en Fruit* [1972] ECR 1219; Case 9/73 *Schlüter* v *Hauptzollamt Lörrach* [1973] ECR 1135; Case 266/81 *SIOT* v *Ministero delle Finanze* [1983] ECR 731; Cases 267–9/81 *Amministrazione delle Finanze dello Stato* v *SPI and SAMI* [1983] ECR 801.

106 Case 70/87 [1989] ECR 1781, 1830–31.

107 See Opinion 1/91, note 1 above; Case 270/80 *Polydor* v *Harlequin Record Shops* [1982] ECR 329, 348–50; Case 104/81, note 100 above, p. 3666.

DIRECT EFFECT OF COMMUNITY LAW IN THE UNITED KINGDOM

The United Kingdom paved the way for its accession to the European Community on 1 January 1973 by the passage of the European Communities Act 1972. Section 2(1) of that Act provides:

All such rights, powers, liabilities, obligations and restrictions from time to time created or arising by or under the [Community] Treaties, and all such remedies and procedures from time to time provided for by or under the Treaties, as in accordance with the Treaties are without further enactment to be given legal effect or used in the United Kingdom shall be recognized and available in law, and be enforced, allowed and followed accordingly; and the expression 'enforceable Community right' and similar expressions shall be read as referring to one to which this subsection applies.

The House of Lords in interpreting this subsection has used the phrase 'enforceable Community right' to refer to 'those rights in Community law which have direct effect in the national law of Member States of the EEC'.[108]

The effect of section 2(1) is to give the force of law in the United Kingdom to provisions of Community law that have direct effect no matter when those provisions were made – before or after the 1972 Act was passed – without any need for implementing legislation. The courts in the United Kingdom are required by section 3(1) of the 1972 Act to accept the views of the European Court as to which provisions of Community law have effect:

For the purposes of all legal proceedings any question as to the meaning or *effect* of any of the Treaties, or as to the validity, meaning or *effect* of any Community instrument, shall be treated as a question of law (and, if not referred to the European Court, be for determination as such in accordance with the principles laid down by and any relevant decision of the European Court or any court attached hereto). [our italics]

The principle of direct effect of Community law has caused no problems in the United Kingdom. The one area of difficulty has been in relation to the requirement to interpret national law in the light of the wording and

---

108 *R v Secretary of State for Transport, ex parte Factortame Ltd (No. 1)* [1990] 2 AC 85, 135; [1989] 2 WLR 997, 1006.

purpose of non-directly effective provisions of directives. This is an area where it is generally assumed section 2(1) of the European Communities Act 1972 does not apply[109] and that section 3(1) is relevant to the 'meaning' of the directive but not to the interpretation of national law dealing with the same subject matter as a non-directly effective directive.

In *Duke* v *Reliance Systems Ltd*[110] the House of Lords considered the interpretation of section 6(4) of the Sex Discrimination Act 1975 prior to its amendment by the Sex Discrimination Act 1986. The purpose of the latter Act was to comply with Directive 76/207 on Equal Treatment by preventing women being forced to retire at 60 when men retired at 65. Prior to the coming into force of the 1986 Act, Duke had been forced to retire at 60 although her male colleagues could continue to work until they were 65. Duke could not rely on the direct effect of the Directive because Reliance Systems was a private company and horizontal direct effect of a directive had been ruled out by the *Marshall* case.[111] Duke argued that the English courts should construe the unamended version of section 6(4) in a manner consistent with the Equal Treatment Directive and treat her forced retirement as an unlawful dismissal. Lord Templeman, giving the opinion of the House of Lords, noted the Sex Discrimination Act 1975 was passed before the Equal Treatment Directive of 1976 and therefore the Act could not have been intended to implement the Directive. He considered the European Court's decision in *Von Colson*[112] but he did not believe that it asserted 'power to interfere with the method or result of the interpretation of national legislation by national courts'.[113]

Lord Templeman was reluctant to give horizontal effects to the Equal Treatment Directive by the back door:

It would be most unfair to the respondent to distort the construction of the 1975 Sex Discrimination Act in order to accommodate the 1976 Equal Treatment

---

109 See the reasoning of Lord Templeman in *Duke* v *Reliance Systems Ltd* [1988] AC 618, 639–40, where he stated that s.2(4) of the 1972 Act applies only where Community provisions are directly effective. By implication, s.2(1) must be similarly restricted, as s.2(4) states that United Kingdom legislation is to be 'construed and have effect subject to the foregoing provisions of this section', including s.2(1). However, see a contrary interpretation of s.2(1) on p. 366.
110 Note 109 above.
111 See Case 152/84, note 45 above.
112 See Case 14/83, note 77 above.
113 *Duke* v *Reliance Systems Ltd*, note 109 above, p. 641. Here he may have been reminding the European Court of the limitation of the jurisdiction granted to it by Art. 177 of the Treaty. Indeed, this point was taken up by Lord Bridge when the House of Lords refused to refer *Finnegan* v *Clowney Youth Training Programme Ltd* ([1990] 2 AC 407, 416–17) to the European Court because it concerned the interpretation of national rather than Community law.

Directive . . .[114] As between the appellant and the respondent the Equal Treatment Directive did not have direct effect and the respondent could not reasonably be expected to reduce to precision the opaque language which constitutes both the strength and the difficulty of some Community legislation [in this instance] permitting differential retirement pension ages but prohibiting differential retirement ages.[115]

The House of Lords took the same approach in relation to the analogous provision to the Sex Discrimination Act 1975 for Northern Ireland, the Sex Discrimination (Northern Ireland) Order 1976.[116] Even though this order was passed after the Equal Treatment Directive, the House of Lords was not prepared to construe it consistently with the latter because it was not passed in order to implement the Directive. Lord Bridge said: 'To hold otherwise would be . . . effectively eliminating the distinction between Community law which is of direct effect between citizens of Member States and Community law which only affects citizens of Member States when it is implemented by national legislation.'[117]

On the other hand, the House of Lords has been willing to construe national legislation passed with the intention of implementing a Community directive in the light of its purpose and wording. In *Pickstone* v *Freemans Plc*[118] the Equal Pay (Amendment) Regulations 1983 were passed in order to fill a gap in the United Kingdom's implementation of Directive 75/117 on Equal Pay that had been exposed by the European Court in a case brought by the Commission under Article 169.[119] Here the House of Lords was prepared to adopt a purposive construction of section 1(2)(c) of the Equal Pay Act 1970, added by the Equal Pay (Amendment) Regulations 1983, in order to make it consistent with the United Kingdom's obligations under the Equal Pay Directive. Lord Oliver said that:

a construction which permits the section to operate as a proper fulfilment of the United Kingdom's obligation under the Treaty involves not so much doing violence to the language of the section as filling a gap by an implication which arises, not from the words used, but from the manifest purpose of the Act and the mischief it was intended to remedy.[120]

Thus the House of Lords made it clear that it is prepared to depart from

---

114 The 'unfairness' point was reiterated by Lord Bridge, giving the opinion of the House of Lords in *Finnegan*, note 113 above, p. 416.
115 *Duke* v *Reliance Systems Ltd*, note 109 above, p. 641.
116 *Finnegan* v *Clowney Youth Training Programme Ltd*, note 113 above.
117 ibid., p. 416.
118 [1989] AC 66.
119 Case 61/81 *Commission* v *United Kingdom* [1982] ECR 2601.
120 *Pickstone* v *Freemans Plc*, note 118 above, p. 125.

the normal meaning of an unambiguous provision in a United Kingdom statute in order to comply with a non-directly effective Community directive where the United Kingdom legislation is implementing the directive.

This willingness to adopt a purposive construction of United Kingdom legislation passed to implement a Community directive was seen again in the House of Lords decision in *Litster v Forth Dry Dock & Engineering Co. Ltd*.[121] The Transfer of Undertakings (Protection of Employment) Regulations 1981 were designed to give effect in the law of the United Kingdom to Community Directive 77/187. The Regulations applied, on a literal reading, only to those persons 'employed immediately before the transfer' of an undertaking. Litster and others had been employed by Forth Dry Dock & Engineering Co. Ltd but were dismissed at 3.30 PM on 6 February 1984. At 4.30 PM on the same day the business was transferred to Forth Estuary Engineering Ltd. The latter company argued that they had no liability under the 1981 Regulations because Litster and his colleagues were not employed by the former company immediately before the transfer of the business.

The House of Lords was prepared to imply certain words into the United Kingdom Regulations in order to make them consistent with the Directive as interpreted by the European Court. In *Bork International* v *Foreningen af Arbejdsledere i Danmark* the European Court had interpreted the relevant part of Directive 77/187 to mean that

the employees of the undertaking whose contract of employment or employment relationship was terminated with effect from a date prior to that of the transfer, contrary to Article 4(1) of the Directive, must be regarded as still in the employ of the undertaking on the date of the transfer with the result, in particular, that the employer's obligations towards them are automatically transferred from the transferor to the transferee in accordance with Article 3(1) of the Directive.[122]

Thus the House of Lords read into the Regulations after the words 'employed immediately before the transfer' the words 'or would have been so employed if he had not been unfairly dismissed'.[123]

Lord Templeman referred to the *Von Colson* case and said that it imposed a duty on the courts of the United Kingdom to 'follow the practice of the European Court of Justice by giving a purposive construc-

---

121 Note 89 above.
122 Case 101/87 [1988] ECR 3057, 3077.
123 With the caveat that he was dismissed in the circumstances described in Reg. 8(1). See *Litster*, note 89 above, Lord Oliver at p. 577, Lord Keith at p. 554 and Lord Templeman at p. 558.

tion to [United Kingdom] Directives and to Regulations issued for the purpose of complying with [Community] Directives'.[124]

In *Webb* v *EMO Air Cargo (UK)* Ltd[125] Lord Keith of Kinkel, giving the judgment of the House of Lords, acknowledged that

It is for a United Kingdom court to construe domestic legislation in any field covered by a Community directive so as to accord with the interpretation of the directive as laid down by the European Court, if that can be done without distorting the meaning of the domestic legislation.[126]

His Lordship noted that under the European Court case law the obligation to interpret national law consistently with a non-directly effective directive applies only if it is possible to do so and interpreted that qualification as meaning that 'domestic law must be open to an interpretation consistent with the directive whether or not it is also open to an interpretation inconsistent with it'.[127] The House of Lords referred the interpretation of Directive 76/207 to the European Court for a preliminary ruling which was given in July 1994.[128] By April 1995 the response of the House of Lords was still awaited. The Court's ruling meant that it was a breach of the equal treatment directive for an employer to dismiss a female employee who was pregnant who had been recruited for an unlimited term, even though she was specifically employed to cover for the maternity leave of another employee. The House of Lords must decide whether it can construe the Sex Discrimination Act 1975 consistently with the European Court's interpretation of the Directive. The delay in giving judgment may indicate that the House of Lords is divided on this crucial issue.

In *Duke* and *Finnegan* the House of Lords was concerned at imposing on individuals obligations arising from a directive that they could not have foreseen from reading the relevant United Kingdom legislation – the danger of giving horizontal direct effect to directives by the back door. This concern did not, however, prevent the House from doing that in the *Pickstone* and *Litster* cases. Having conceded this fundamental issue of

---

124 ibid., p. 558. On this occasion Lord Templeman quoted the part of the *Von Colson* case that omitted the let-out clause 'in so far as the national court is given discretion to do so under national law', whereas he had quoted the part containing that clause in the *Duke* case (note 109 above) and in the *Pickstone* case (note 118 above, p. 123). This may indicate a willingness to follow the European Court's subsequent case law, which omitted that let-out clause (see p. 356 and note 83 above), though it must be said that in *Finnegan* the House of Lords was fully aware of its own decisions in *Pickstone* and *Litster*.

125 [1992] 4 All ER 929.

126 ibid. at p. 939. See also p. 374 below.

127 ibid. at p. 940.

128 Case C-32/93 *Webb* v *EMO Air Cargo (UK)* Ltd [1994] ECR I-3567; [1994] QB 718; [1994] 4 All ER 115. The substance of the case is discussed at pp. 627–8 below.

fairness, it seems pointless for the House of Lords to rebel against the European Court over the question of whether the national legislation is implementing the Directive or not. The reason may be a concern to be faithful to the intention of the British legislature and a reluctance to be involved in judicial legislation, which would be improper.[129] However, it is reasonable for the House of Lords to assume that the United Kingdom Parliament intends its legislation to be in conformity with its obligations under Community law and wishes the courts to construe it in a way that maintains this position, particularly in relation to directives, where the United Kingdom is bound to implement them correctly and completely. In other words, an interpretation of ss.2 and 3 of the European Communities Act 1972 must be in accordance with the spirit of the evolving Community rather than in accordance with the letter of the statute. In any case it is arguable that s.2(1) applies to a broader category of Community law than simply directly effective Community law. It could be said that the obligation on the national courts to play their part in implementing directives by construing national law in accordance with their purpose and wording is one of the 'obligations and restrictions from time to time created or arising by or under the Treaties' that are to 'be given legal effect or used in the United Kingdom'. This 'obligation' is created by the European Court, 'under the Treaties', exercising its power under Article 164 to ensure that Community law is observed.

129 See discussion on pp. 357–8. This is an area where the United Kingdom courts are, arguably, not helped by s.2 of the European Communities Act 1972 and are not compelled by s.3 of the Act to change their construction of national legislation to comply with a non-directly effective directive.

CHAPTER 12

Supremacy of EC Law

The Treaty signed in Rome on 25 March 1957 establishing the European Economic Community did not explicitly establish the supremacy of Community law over the laws of member states. None of the subsequent amendments to the Treaty have altered this position. The European Court of Justice has, however, firmly established the primacy of Community law in its case law. The landmark decision was *Costa* v *ENEL*[1] in which the Court gave priority to Community law over provisions of Italian law. The court's comments on the nature of the Community are worthy of full citation:

> By creating a Community of unlimited duration, having its own institutions, its own personality, its own legal capacity and capacity of representation on the international plane and, more particularly, real powers stemming from a limitation of sovereignty or a transfer of powers from the States to the Community, the Member States have limited their sovereign rights, albeit within limited fields, and have thus created a body of law which binds both their nationals and themselves.
>
> The integration into the laws of each Member State of provisions which derive from the Community, and more generally the terms and the spirit of the Treaty, make it impossible for the States, as a corollary, to accord precedence to a unilateral and subsequent measure over a legal system accepted by them on a basis of reciprocity.[2]

The Court is conscious that the Community is unique. It goes beyond traditional international agreements establishing relations between contracting states and instead creates lawmaking institutions that can create rights and obligations for the nationals of the member states.[3] By 14 December 1991 the Court referred to the EC Treaty as the 'constitutional charter of a

---

1 Case 6/64 [1964] ECR 585. The reasoning of the Court is discussed in Ch. 6, p. 175.
2 ibid., pp. 593–4.
3 See Opinion 1/91 *Opinion on the draft Agreement on a European Economic Area* [1991] ECR I-6079, [1992] 1 CMLR 245.

Community based on the rule of law'.[4] The Court also modified its statement in the *Costa* case about the 'limited fields' within which states limit their sovereign rights to a statement that such rights are limited in 'ever wider fields'.[5] The Court here was conscious of the extension of Community competence agreed in the Single European Act and of the further extension agreed, subject to ratification, at the Maastricht summit on 9–10 December 1991, although the latter is not specifically mentioned in the Opinion. At that point in the evolution of the Community the Court maintained that two of the essential provisions of the Community constitution that had been firmly established were the primacy of Community law over the law of the member states and the direct effect of a whole series of Community law provisions.[6]

THE JURISPRUDENCE OF THE EUROPEAN COURT ON SUPREMACY

Having established the principle that Community law has supremacy over ordinary national laws in *Costa* v *ENEL*,[7] the Court was confronted, in the *Internationale Handelsgesellschaft* case,[8] with the question of whether Community law takes primacy over the constitutions of member states and in particular over the fundamental rights provisions contained therein. The Court emphasized the need to preserve the 'uniformity and efficacy of Community law' in all the member states. This would be sacrificed if member states could use their constitutions as a means to circumvent Community law obligations. The Court concluded that 'the validity of a Community measure or its effect within a Member State cannot be affected by allegations that it runs counter to either fundamental rights as formulated by the constitution of that State or the principles of a national constitutional structure'.[9]

So Community legislation has primacy over national constitutional law. Shortly afterwards the Court made the simple point that 'no provision

4 ibid., para. 21.
5 ibid.
6 ibid.
7 Case 6/64, note 1 above.
8 Case 11/70 *Internationale Handelsgesellschaft* v *Einfuhr- und Vorratsstelle für Getreide und Futtermittel* [1970] ECR 1125.
9 ibid., p. 1134. The Court did, of course, reassure the German courts that it would protect fundamental rights. If Community fundamental rights were breached by Community legislation, the Court would find the legislation to be invalid: see the discussion of fundamental human rights in Ch. 8, pp. 254–8.

whatsoever of national law may be invoked to override' Community law.[10] It was still an open question whether a member state could reserve to a particular national court, e.g., a constitutional court, the power to disapply national law in favour of Community law. This issue was dealt with by the European Court in the *Simmenthal* case.[11] Even a lowly court of first instance, like the Pretore di Susa in this case, is obliged to apply provisions of Community law, if necessary refusing of its own motion to apply conflicting provisions of national law. The national court must not wait for such provisions of national law to be set aside by legislation or by a constitutional court. Here the European Court is not requiring the national court to annul the provisions of national law that conflict with Community law but simply stating that it must not apply them. This principle was reiterated in *Albako* v *Balm*,[12] in which the Court held that where a national agency is implementing a Community decision, national courts are to disapply any provisions of national law that hinder the implementation of such a decision in order to uphold the principle of the primacy of Community law.

In the *Factortame* case the European Court decided that national courts must be capable of protecting putative Community law rights over clear provisions of national law pending the European Court's ruling on the precise nature of the Community law rights.[13]

RESPONSE OF THE MEMBER STATES

UNITED KINGDOM

The United Kingdom paved the way for its entry into the European Community by the passage through Parliament of the European Communities Act 1972. In a masterpiece of drafting, designed to minimize political controversy, the Act accepts the principle of the supremacy of directly effective Community law over laws in the United Kingdom. Prior to 1972 the basic principle of the constitution of the United Kingdom was parliamentary sovereignty. In the words of the late Professor Dicey that concept meant that 'Parliament has the right to make or unmake any law whatever; and further, that no person or body is recognized by the law of

---

10 Case 48/71 *Commission* v *Italy* [1972] ECR 527, 532.
11 Case 106/77 *Amministrazione delle Finanze dello Stato* v *Simmenthal* [1978] ECR 629.
12 Case 249/85 [1987] ECR 2345, 2360.
13 See Case C-213/89 *R* v *Secretary of State for Transport, ex parte Factortame Ltd and others* [1990] ECR I-2433, discussed in Ch. 6, pp. 175–6.

England as having a right to override or set aside the legislation of Parliament'.[14]

In the European Communities Act 1972, section 2(1), Parliament gave the force of law in the United Kingdom to directly effective Community law.[15] The subtle piece of parliamentary draftsmanship is contained in the apparently obscure section 2(4) of the Act. The relevant part of that subsection says: 'any enactment passed or to be passed ... shall be construed and have effect subject to the foregoing provisions of this section'.

Clearly, the natural interpretation of this provision is that all United Kingdom Acts of Parliament, whether passed before or after the European Communities Act 1972, are to have effect subject to the directly effective provisions of Community law, passed before or after the 1972 Act, given the force of law by subsection (1). This means that any conflicting provisions of United Kingdom Acts have to give way to directly effective Community law. Parliament can reassert its sovereignty only by repealing section 2(4) of the European Communities Act 1972 or by inserting a clause in a subsequent Act saying that the provisions of the Act must be given effect notwithstanding section 2(4) of the 1972 Act. It is difficult to conceive of the circumstances in which the United Kingdom Parliament would do either of these things while the United Kingdom remains a member state of the European Union.

After a period during which it was not clear whether the above construction of section 2 was correct,[16] the matter has been clarified by the House of Lords in the *Factortame* case. When the House of Lords was considering whether to refer the case to the European Court for a preliminary ruling Lord Bridge of Harwich, giving a speech concurred in by all their Lordships, made the following unequivocal observation:

By virtue of section 2(4) of the [European Communities Act 1972] Part II of [the Merchant Shipping Act 1988] is to be construed and take effect subject to directly

---

14 Dicey, *Law of the Constitution*, p. xviii. This includes the concept that Parliament cannot bind its successors (pp. 62–8), although it is a matter of academic debate whether the Treaty of Union between Scotland and England of 1707 imposed any restraints on the sovereignty of the United Kingdom Parliament; see *MacCormick v Lord Advocate* 1953 SC 396; Munro, *Constitutional Law*, Ch. 4; T. B. Smith, 'The Union as Fundamental Law' (1957) PL 99; MacCormick, 'Does the United Kingdom have a Constitution?' (1978) 29 NILQ 1; Mitchell, *Constitutional Law*, pp. 69–91.
15 See Ch. 11, p. 361.
16 See Trindade, 'Parliamentary Sovereignty and the Primacy of European Community Law' (1972) 35 MLR 375; Winterton, 'The British Grundnorm: Parliamentary Supremacy Re-examined' (1976) 92 LQR 591; *Macarthy's Ltd v Smith* [1979] 3 All ER 325 and [1981] QB 108, 200–202; *Garland v British Rail Engineering Ltd* [1983] 2 AC 751, 771; Hood Phillips, 'A Garland for the Lords; Parliament and Community Law Again' (1982) 98 LQR 524; Munro, *Constitutional Law*, pp. 127–32; S. De Smith and R. Brazier, *Constitutional and Administrative Law* (1989, 6th ed.), pp. 79–82, 106–8.

enforceable Community rights and those rights are, by section 2(1) of the Act of 1972, to be 'recognized and available in law, and ... enforced, allowed and followed accordingly; ...' This has precisely the same effect as if a section were incorporated in Part II of the Act of 1988 which in terms enacted that the provisions with respect to registration of British fishing vessels were to be without prejudice to the directly enforceable Community rights of nationals of any Member State of the EEC. Thus it is common ground that, in so far as the applicants succeed before the [European Court] in obtaining a ruling in support of the Community rights which they claim, those rights will prevail over the restrictions imposed on registration of British fishing vessels by Part II of the Act of 1988 and the Divisional Court will, in the final determination of the application for judicial review, be obliged to make appropriate declarations to give effect to those rights.[17]

The House of Lords accepted the primacy of directly effective Community Law over the clear provisions of a subsequent United Kingdom Act of Parliament. To put the above dictum in context it is necessary briefly to outline the history of the case up to that point. Factortame was one of a number of companies that owned fishing vessels that had been registered as British under the legislation in force prior to the passing of the Merchant Shipping Act 1988. These companies had strong Spanish connections, but they had an interest in their vessels being registered as British so that they would have access to the British fishing quota under the Common Fisheries Policy. The 1988 Act attempted to ensure a genuine link between vessels fishing against the British quota and the British fishing industry. Stringent British nationality, residence and management requirements meant that the vessels belonging to Factortame and the other companies no longer qualified to be registered as British. Factortame and the other companies brought an action for judicial review in the English courts, challenging the legality of certain provisions of the Act as contrary to EC law.

The Divisional Court referred the substantive questions of EC law to the European Court for a preliminary ruling[18] and granted interim relief to the applicants so that their vessels would continue to be registered as British pending the outcome of the European Court's preliminary ruling. The Secretary of State successfully appealed to the Court of Appeal against the order for interim relief and this decision was in turn appealed to the

---

17 *R* v *Secretary of State for Transport, ex parte Factortame Ltd and Others (No. 1)* [1990] 2 AC 85, 140. The case is discussed by Magliveras, 'Fishing in Troubled Waters: The Merchant Shipping Act 1988 and the European Community' (1990) 39 ICLQ 899; Gravells, 'Effective Protection of Community Law Rights: Temporary Disapplication of an Act of Parliament' (1991) PL 180; H. W. R. Wade, 'What Has Happened to the Sovereignty of Parliament' (1991) 107 LQR 1.

18 *R* v *Secretary of State for Transport, ex parte Factortame* [1989] 2 CMLR 353.

House of Lords by Factortame and the other companies. It was at this point that Lord Bridge of Harwich made the above *obiter dictum* accepting that if the preliminary ruling on the substantive issues found the Merchant Shipping Act 1988 to be in conflict with Community law, it would be the duty of the Divisional Court to give effect to the latter. The House of Lords decided as a matter of English law that the courts have no jurisdiction to grant an interim injunction against the Crown and that they could not confer upon the applicants rights based on Community law that were directly contrary to Parliament's sovereign will and that were 'necessarily uncertain until the preliminary ruling of the European Court' on the substantive question had been given.[19] The House of Lords sought a preliminary ruling from the European Court as to whether under Community law the English courts were obliged to grant interim relief to the applicants or were given power to do so pending the outcome of the European Court's ruling on the substantive questions of EC law. The European Court answered the question indirectly by saying that where a national court is dealing with a case concerning Community law and the sole obstacle that precludes it from granting interim relief based on Community law is a rule of national law, it must set aside the latter rule.[20]

The House of Lords chose to say nothing explicit about the supremacy of Community law, but gave effect to the Court's ruling.[21] Lord Bridge, alone, expressly affirmed the supremacy of Community law. He said that under the terms of the European Communities Act 1972

it has always been clear that it was the duty of a United Kingdom court, when delivering final judgment, to override any rule of national law found to be in conflict with any directly enforceable rule of Community law ... Thus there is nothing in any way novel in according supremacy to rules of Community law in those areas to which they apply and to insist that, in the protection of rights under Community law, national courts must not be inhibited by rules of national law from granting interim relief in appropriate cases is no more than a logical recognition of that supremacy.[22]

It surely is 'novel', and not a logical necessity of the supremacy of Community law, that the supremacy doctrine is extended to cases where, on the one hand, the Community law right is not clearly established, but rather there is a prima-facie case (not necessarily even a strong one) that

---

19 Note 17 above, pp. 142–3.
20 The European Court's ruling is discussed in more depth in Ch. 6, pp. 175–6. The issue of interim relief in the context of Art. 177 proceedings is discussed in Ch. 9, p. 311.
21 *R* v *Secretary of State for Transport, ex parte Factortame Ltd and others (No. 2)* [1991] 1 AC 603.
22 ibid., p. 659.

such a right exists and, on the other hand, the national legislation is very clear and precise.

The House of Lords set aside the rule of English law that an interim injunction cannot be granted against the Crown and the notion that parliamentary sovereignty cannot be overturned on the basis of 'necessarily uncertain' Community law rights. In doing so the House of Lords implicitly accepted the supremacy of putative Community law rights over English common law rules and, more significantly, over clear provisions of later United Kingdom primary legislation. It would seem that the House of Lords was not giving supremacy to directly effective provisions of Community law on the basis of section 2 of the European Communities Act 1972, as the nature of the Community law rights had not yet been definitively established by the European Court. Rather, the House of Lords seems to have felt bound to follow the ruling of the European Court to set aside the rules of national law that prevented the granting of interim relief based on Community law. In the absence of an explicit statement as to why the House of Lords followed the European Court's ruling one can only speculate. A possibility is that their Lordships had in mind section 3(1) of the European Communities Act 1972, which provides:

For the purposes of all legal proceedings any question as to the meaning or effect of any of the Treaties, or as to the validity, meaning or effect of any Community instrument, shall be treated as a question of law and, if not referred to the European Court, be for determination as such in accordance with the principles laid down by and any relevant decision of the European Court.[23]

The complex litigation concerning the qualifications of fishing vessels with Spanish connections to be registered as British has widespread ramifications for a number of aspects of Community law.[24] Not surprisingly, the European Court's ruling on the substantive questions of Community law raised in the *Factortame* case found that certain aspects of the Merchant Shipping Act 1988 were not compatible with Community law.[25]

---

23 The fact that Art. 177 rulings are binding on the national courts that seek them was reiterated by the European Court in Opinion 1/91, note 3 above, para. 61.

24 The related infringement proceedings, Case 246/89R *Commission* v *United Kingdom* [1989] ECR 3125 and Case C-246/89 *Commission* v *United Kingdom* [1991] ECR I-3905 are discussed at pp. 215–17 and 577 respectively. The importance of the *Factortame* case for interim relief in Article 177 proceedings is considered at p. 311, for the direct effect of Community law in the United Kingdom at p. 361 and for the approach to interpretation of the European Court at pp. 175–6.

25 See Case C-221/89 R v *Secretary of State for Transport, ex parte Factortame Ltd and Others (No. 3)* [1991] ECR I-3905; [1991] 3 CMLR 589; [1991] 3 All ER 709; [1991] 2 Lloyd's Rep. 648.

In *Equal Opportunities Commission and another* v *Secretary of State for Employment*,[26] Lord Keith of Kinkel, giving the judgment of the House of Lords on this issue, confirmed that the *Factortame* cases had established that a declaration could be obtained in judicial review proceedings that an Act of Parliament is incompatible with Community law.

His Lordship accepted that the Equal Opportunities Commission (EOC) could challenge the qualifying period set out in the Employment Protection (Consolidation) Act 1978 for the right not to be unfairly dismissed, the right to compensation and the right to statutory redundancy pay on the basis that this was a breach of Community law because it constituted indirect discrimination against women. The great majority of employees who failed to qualify for these rights because they worked for less than 8 hours or less than 16 hours a week were women. Lord Keith said:

The EOC is concerned simply to obtain a ruling which reflects the primacy of Community law enshrined in s. 2 of the 1972 Act and determines whether the relevant United Kingdom law is compatible with the equal pay directive and the equal treatment directive.[27]

The House of Lords upheld EOC's claim because the indirect discrimination was not objectively justified and the Government subsequently amended the legislation to comply with the judgment.

One area of potential difficulty remains. The extent to which it is 'possible' for the courts in the United Kingdom to construe national legislation consistent with non-directly effective directives may not coincide with what the European Court regards as possible. Certainly in the past the House of Lords did not accept this obligation when the legislation was not passed with the intent to implement a directive.[28] However, in *Webb* v *EMO Air Cargo (UK) Ltd*,[29] the House of Lords accepted that in principle it will try to construe domestic legislation consistent with a non-directly effective directive whether the domestic legislation came after or preceded the directive.[30] At the time of writing the House of Lords decision as to whether it could construe the Sex Discrimination Act 1975 consistently with the European Court's ruling in the *Webb* case was awaited.[31]

---

26 [1994] 1 All ER 910; [1995] 1 CMLR 391 noted by Beaumont (1994) 62 Scot. L. Gaz. 60.
27 ibid. at p. 920, and at pp. 401–2.
28 See *Duke* v *Reliance Systems Ltd* [1988] AC 618 and *Finnegan* v *Clowney Youth Training Programme Ltd* [1990] 2 AC 407, discussed in Ch. 11 at pp. 362–3.
29 [1992] 4 All ER 929, 939, discussed in Ch. 11 at p. 365.
30 In doing so it acknowledged the authority of Case C-106/89 *Marleasing SA* v *La Comercial International de Alimentación SA* [1990] ECR I-4135.
31 See Case C-32/93 *Webb* v *EMO Air Cargo (UK) Ltd* [1994] ECR I-3567 and the discussion in Ch. 11 at pp. 365–6.

GERMANY

Article 24 of the German constitution permits the transfer of sovereign powers to intergovernmental institutions. Thus, in general, the German courts had no difficulty in accepting the supremacy of Community law. However, one issue that did cause some theoretical difficulty was the question of whether Community law could take priority over the inalienable fundamental rights contained in the German Basic Law. In the *Internationale Handelsgesellschaft* case[32] the Bundesverfassungsgericht (German Constitutional Court) said that in the present state of evolution of the Community it would not renounce its right to uphold German fundamental rights even in the face of a conflict with Community law. The Constitutional Court therefore did not accept the ruling of the European Court that Community law must take priority even over German fundamental rights in the case before it,[33] though, in fact, it accepted that in that case the Community legislation did not violate German fundamental rights. The reservations noted by the Constitutional Court included the fact that the European Parliament was not at that time directly elected and that Community law did not include a precise catalogue of fundamental rights.

The German Constitutional Court has subsequently abandoned its reservations about the supremacy of Community law in the field of fundamental rights. In *Wünsche Handelsgesellschaft*[34] the German court decided that it would no longer examine the compatibility of Community legislation with German fundamental rights while the European Court continues adequately to protect fundamental rights. In other words, the German Constitutional Court is willing to trust the European Court to strike down Community legislation that is contrary to fundamental rights. The German court was doubtless influenced by the considerable development of the Community concept of fundamental rights by the European Court since its decision in *Internationale Handelsgesellschaft*[35] and by the direct elections of the European Parliament, which commenced in 1979.

The Bundesfinanzhof (German Federal Finance Court) did not accept the direct effect of Community directives, notably refusing to follow the

32 *Internationale Handelsgesellschaft* v *Einfuhr- und Vorratsstelle für Getreide und Futtermittel*, decision of 29 May 1974, BVerfGE 37, S.271; [1974] CMLR 540.
33 See p. 368 above.
34 *In re the Application of Wünsche Handelsgesellschaft*, also known as the *Solange II* case, decision of 22 October 1986, *Europaische Grundrechte-Zeitschrift*, 1987, p. 1; [1987] 3 CMLR 225, noted by Frowein (1988) 25 CMLRev 201.
35 Case 11/70, note 8 above, discussed in Ch. 8, pp. 254–8.

decision of the European Court in the *Kloppenburg* case.[36] The German Constitutional Court quashed this rebellion against the supremacy of Community law by overturning the German Federal Finance Court's decision in *Kloppenburg*.[37] The German Constitutional Court affirmed that it would quash a decision of a German court that failed to comply with a preliminary ruling from the European Court. It regards such a failure to comply with the European Court's ruling as a violation of Article 101 of the Basic Law. The Court will also find a breach of Article 101 if a German court in an indefensible manner disregards the obligation to refer a question for a preliminary ruling.[38]

On 12 October 1993 the German Constitutional Court gave judgment confirming the legality of Germany's ratification of the Treaty on European Union.[39] The Court affirmed that the European Court has the primary responsibility for protecting fundamental rights but hinted that if that Court failed to carry out the task adequately the German Constitutional Court would do so.[40] The Constitutional Court also asserted the right to review the legal instruments of European institutions and agencies to see whether they remain within the limits of the sovereign rights conferred on them.[41] This assertion of a general right to constrain the competence of the Union institutions undermines the supremacy of Community law and the sole competence of the European Court to determine the legality of acts of the institutions within the framework of the

---

36 Case 70/83 *Kloppenburg* v *Finanzamt Leer* [1984] ECR 1075 was not followed by the German Federal Finance Court on 25 April 1985 (*Europarecht* 1985, p. 191); [1989] 1 CMLR 873. See a similar rebellion in *Re Value Added Tax Directives* [1982] 1 CMLR 527.

37 Judgment of 8 April 1987 (*Europarecht* 1987, p. 333); [1988] 3 CMLR 1.

38 See *Re Patented Feedingstuffs*, judgment of 9 November 1987 [1989] 2 CMLR 902; *Re Value Added Tax Exemption*, judgment of 4 November 1987 [1989] 1 CMLR 113; and the eight-judge decision of 31 May 1990, noted by the Commission in its 'Eighth Annual Report to the European Parliament on the Commission Monitoring of Community Law 1990' (Com (91) 321 final), pp. 125–7).

39 *Brunner* v *European Union Treaty* [1994] 1 CMLR 57, noted by Foster, 'The German Constitution and EC Membership' (1994) PL 392–408; Herdegen, 'Maastricht and the German Constitutional Court: Constitutional Restraints for an "Ever Closer Union"' (1994) 31 CMLRev. 235–49; and Crossland (1994) 19 ELRev 202–14.

40 ibid. at paras. 13 and 23. The Constitutional Court had previously hinted that it may review the legality of an EC directive implemented into German law that is not compatible with German fundamental rights (see B Verf G 12 May 1989 (1990) NJW 974, discussed by Roth, 'The Application of Community Law in West Germany: 1980–1990' (1991) 28 CMLRev 137, 144).

41 ibid, at para. 49. In an earlier decision the Court had said that it may intervene if the powers of the *Länder* (regions) are transferred to the Community to an extent it finds unacceptable (see B Verf G 11 April 1989 (1990) NJW 974, discussed by Roth, above, at pp. 144–5).

European Communities. The Constitutional Court specifically warned that it would carefully review the use of Article 235 of the EC Treaty as a legal basis for measures. Legislation passed under that Article would not be binding in Germany if it was used as a basis for harmonization within the areas of new Community competence under Articles 126 to 129,[42] or if it constituted a *de facto* amendment to the Treaty.[43]

FRANCE

In France there is a divide between public law and private law reflected in the fact that the Conseil d'État is the highest public law court and the Cour de Cassation is the highest court dealing with disputes between private persons and their prosecution for crimes.[44] The Cour de Cassation has consistently upheld the supremacy of Community law over French law.[45] The same cannot be said of the Conseil d'État. In the past the Conseil d'État refused to question the validity of French legislation on the ground that it conflicted with Community law,[46] failed to accept the doctrine of the direct effect of Community directives, and in doing so disregarded its obligations under Article 177(3),[47] and even failed

---

42 ibid. at para. 64.

43 ibid. at para. 99. The latter is a particular concern as it would be a means for the Federal Government to expand the EC Treaty without gaining the appropriate internal constitutional approval for amendments to the EC Treaty which protect the interests of the *Länder*.

44 See Rudden, *A Source-Book on French Law*, p. 12.

45 See *Directeur Général des Douanes* v *Société des Cafés Jacques Vabre & Société Weigel et Cie* [1975] 2 CMLR 336; *Bouhabin Von Kempis* v *Geldof*, judgment of 1 December 1975, *Bulletin Civil*, III, No. 173, p. 282; *Leclerc* v *Syndicat des libraires de Loire-Océan*, *Gazette du Palais*, 1985, No. 359; and *Lener Ignace SA* v *Beauvois*, judgment of 12 May 1993, [1994] 2 CMLR 419, 424. The Cour de Cassation has exercised its discretion not to refer questions of Community law to the European Court, e.g. in *The Republic* v *Weckerle*, judgment of 15 February 1994, [1995] 1 CMLR 49 and in a case concerning Commission Directive 88/301 on competition in the markets for telecommunications terminal equipment, see [1993] *Recueil Dalloz-Sirey* 462. The Commission expressed doubts about the wisdom of the non-referral of the latter case in the 'Eleventh Annual Report' OJ 1994 C154/175.

46 See *Syndicat Général de Fabricants de Semoules de France*, judgment of 1 March 1968 (*Recueil Dalloz-Sirey*, 1968, p. 285), [1970] CMLR 395: *Union Démocratique du Travail*, judgment of 22 October 1979 (AJDA, 1980, p. 40); *Société Bernard Carant*, judgment of 27 April 1988, noted by the Commission in the 'Sixth Annual Report' OJ 1989 C330/54.

47 See *Minister of the Interior* v *Cohn-Bendit*, judgment of 22 December 1978 (*Dalloz*, 1979, J155), [1980] 1 CMLR 543 and numerous subsequent cases, including *Société de Courtage d'Assurance Renouf*, judgment of 10 June 1986; *Cabinet Mantout*, judgment of 16 June 1986; *Joseph Griesmar*, judgment of 23 December 1987, and *Consorts Genty*, judgment of 7 October 1987, noted in the 'Fifth Annual Report to the European

to comply with the European Court's judgment in the case before it.[48]

In recent times there have been signs that the Conseil d'État is moving towards an acceptance of the supremacy of Community law.[49] In the *Nicolo* case it assessed the legality of a French electoral statute against the EEC Treaty and by doing so may have signalled its willingness to accept the supremacy of Community law over French legislative measures.[50] Certainly in the *Boisdet* case the Conseil d'État accepted the supremacy of Community regulations over subsequent French legislation.[51] The Conseil d'État seems to have finally adhered to the direct effect of Community directives in two cases concerning tobacco prices. The companies were awarded FF 230,000 with compound interest from 1984 for the loss arising from having to comply with French legislation on tobacco prices, which was in violation of a 1972 Community directive.[52] The Conseil d'État has subsequently decided that French subordinate legislation which conflicted with the objectives of an EC directive was unlawful[53] but has surprisingly denied the vertical direct effect of EC directives in the context of a challenge to an administrative act rather than delegated legislation.[54] The Conseil d'État has, on the other hand, disapplied certain provisions of the

Parliament on Commission Monitoring of the Application of Community Law 1987', OJ 1988 C310/44; and *Association Club de Chasse du Vert Galant*, judgment of 2 March 1988, noted by the Commission in the 'Sixth Annual Report', OJ 1989 C330/55.

48 See *ONIC v Huileries de Pont-à-Mousson*, judgment of 9 May 1980, AJDA, 1980, p. 535, and *ONIC v Maiserie de la Beauce*, judgment of 26 July 1985, AJDA, 1985, p. 615.

49 See Cohen, 'The Conseil d'État: continuing convergence with the Court of Justice' (1991) 16 ELRev 144 and Roseren, 'The Application of Community Law by French Courts from 1982 to 1993' (1994) 31 CMLRev 315, 326–36.

50 Judgment of 20 October 1989, [1990] 1 CMLR 173, discussed in the 'Seventh Annual Report to the European Parliament on Commission Monitoring of the Application of Community Law 1989', OJ 1990 C232/54–5; by Pollard, 'The Conseil d'État is European – Official' (1990) 15 ELRev 267; and by Manin 'The *Nicolo* Case of the *Conseil d'État*: French Constitutional Law and the Supreme Administrative Court's Acceptance of the Primacy of Community Law over Subsequent National Statute Law' (1991) 28 CMLRev 499.

51 Judgment of 24 September 1990, [1991] 1 CMLR 3, noted by the Commission in its 'Eighth Annual Report', Com (91) 321 final.

52 See *SA Rothmans International France and SA Philip Morris France*; *Société Arizona Tobacco Products and SA Philip Morris France*, judgments of 28 February 1992, [1993] 1 CMLR 253, noted by Errera (1992) PL 340. For earlier signs of a changing attitude to the direct effect of directives in the Conseil d'État, see *Compagnie Alitalia*, judgment of 3 February 1989, [1990] 1 CMLR 248, and *Rassemblement des Opposants à la Chasse*, judgment of 7 October 1988, [1990] 2 CMLR 831.

53 *Union des Transporteurs en Commun de Voyageurs des Bouches-du-Rhône (UTCV) and Others*, judgment of 11 March 1994, [1994] 3 CMLR 121; and *Association Force Ouvrière Consommateurs*, judgment of 9 July 1993, [1994] 1 CMLR 721.

54 *Compagnie Générale des Eaux*, judgment of 23 July 1993, [1994] 2 CMLR 373.

French Tax Code as being contrary to an EC directive.[55] Since 1958 the Conseil constitutionnel has had the power to declare acts of the French Parliament unconstitutional.[56] It considers itself debarred, however, from ruling on the compatibility of an act with France's obligations under Community law.[57] On 9 April 1992 the Conseil constitutionnel ruled that the Treaty on European Union could be ratified by France only after a constitutional amendment which was subsequently adopted. In that ruling it was accepted that France could in certain circumstances transfer sovereignty to the European Union without a constitutional amendment.[58] France's membership of the European Communities is explicitly mentioned in the constitution for the first time as a result of the amendment to Article 88.

ITALY

The Italian Constitutional Court initially rejected the supremacy of Community law over subsequent national law.[59] Later it accepted the supremacy of Community law with a minor reservation that it might assert its power to uphold Italian fundamental rights if the European Court were, in general, no longer able to ensure adequate protection for fundamental rights in the Community legal order.[60]

The Constitutional Court has accepted the ruling of the European Court in the *Simmenthal* case[61] that it is not necessary for lower Italian courts to refer conflicts between Community law and national law to the Constitutional Court.[62] Indeed, Italian courts are legally bound not to apply domestic measures that are incompatible with Community law.[63] The Commission has expressed concern that the Italian Constitutional Court failed to refer two cases to the European Court in 1993 and in the

---

55 Judgment of 17 March 1993, [1993] *Les Petites Affiches*, No. 81, p. 19, noted in 'Eleventh Annual Report' OJ 1994 C154/176.
56 See Oliver, 'The French Constitution and the Treaty of Maastricht' (1994) 43 ICLQ 1–25 and Roseren, note 49 above, pp. 315–25.
57 See Oliver, note 56 above, at pp. 9–11.
58 See Oliver, note 56 above, at pp. 11–16.
59 No. 14 of 7 March 1964, *Costa v ENEL*, Foro it. 1964, I, 465.
60 No. 183 of 27 December 1973, *Frontini*, Foro it. 1974, I, 314: No. 170 of 8 June 1984. *Granital*, Foro it. 1984, I, 2063. See the note on the *Granital* case by Gaja (1984) 21 CMLRev 756, and, more generally, La Pergola and Del Duca, 'Community Law. International Law and the Italian Constitution' (1985) 79 AJIL 598, 614.
61 Case 106/77, note 11 above.
62 See *Granital*, note 60 above.
63 Judgment No. 389 of 11 July 1989, *Provincia di Bolzano v Presidente del Consiglio dei Ministri*, Foro it. 1989, I, 1076, noted by the Commission in the 'Seventh Annual Report' OJ 1990, C232/56.

latter of them made explicit reliance on the *CILFIT* exceptions when it might have been better advised to make a reference.[64]

In a way reminiscent of the French Conseil d'État, the Italian Consiglio di Stato has not yet accepted the direct effect of Community directives[65] and decisions.[66]

OTHER MEMBER STATES

There have been no rebellions against the primacy of Community law in the other member states. In Belgium the Cour de Cassation clearly accepted the supremacy of directly effective Community law in the *Fromagerie Le Ski* case.[67] In some member states the constitution explicitly accepts the primacy of international treaties over national law[68] and in others judicial interpretation of the constitution has arrived at the same result.[69] In these countries there is no theoretical obstacle to the courts accepting the primacy of Community law over national law.[70] In some of

64 Cases 6030 and 8390, 'Eleventh Annual Report' OJ 1994 C154/175.

65 Judgment No. 504 of 6 May 1980, noted in the 'Sixth Annual Report' OJ 1989 C330/54, 157. On the other hand, it seems that the Constitutional Court has accepted the primacy of directly effective directives in Judgment No. 64 of 2 February 1990, Foro it., 1990, I, 747, noted by Daniele, 'Italy and EEC Law in 1990' (1991) 16 ELRev 417, 424 and in the 'Eighth Annual Report' (Com (91) 321 final, p. 127).

66 Judgment of 2 December 1988, *Cooperativa Carrettieri la Rinascita*, noted in the 'Sixth Annual Report', OJ 1989 C330/54. The Consiglio di Stato seems to be reluctant to refer cases to the European Court for a preliminary ruling.

67 Judgment of 27 May 1971, Rev. Trim. Droit Européen 1971, p. 494, [1972] CMLR 330, 373. Some criticism has been made of the decision of the Belgian Conseil d'État not to refer *Mees v Belgian State* to the European Court for a preliminary ruling (*Journal des Tribunaux*, 1987, p. 188, [1988] 3 CMLR 137), but this does not appear to be a rebellion against the supremacy of Community law.

68 See Art. 28 of the Greek Constitution; Kerameus and Kremlis, 'The Application of Community Law in Greece 1981–1987' (1988) 25 CMLRev 141; Ioannou, 'Recent developments in the application of Community law in Greece' (1989) 14 ELRev 461; and Ioannou and Anagnostopoulou, 'The Application of Community Law in Greece (1989–1991)' (1994) 19 ELRev 412, 416–18; and Art. 94 of the Netherlands Constitution.

69 For Spain, see Art. 93 of the 1978 Constitution: the 'Sixth Annual Report', OJ 1989 C330/151; Santacruz, 'Spanish Adaptation to Community Law: 1986–88' (1991) 16 ELRev 149; and Liñán Nogueras and Roldán Barbero, 'The Judicial Application of Community Law in Spain' (1993) 30 CMLRev 1135. For Portugal, see Art. 8 of the Constitution; the Constitutional Court's judgment of 19 June 1984 in Case 107/83 D. R. II, 29 December 1984, p. 11. 681: the 'Sixth Annual Report', OJ 1989 C330/158; and Alves Vieira. 'The application of Community Law by Portuguese courts' (1991) 16 ELRev 346, 351. The direct effect of directives was accepted by the Coimbra Court of Appeal, judgment of 30 July 1987, No. 32–86; see the 'Fifth Annual Report 1987', OJ 1988 C310/44.

70 Liñán Nagueras and Roldán Barbero, above, highlight some inconsistencies in the Spanish courts in accepting the direct effect of directives and in the policy on referring

the member states no guidance can be obtained from the constitution as to the question of the supremacy of Community law and the relevant national courts have not ruled explicitly on the matter.[71]

CONCLUSION

The European Court's doctrine of the supremacy of Community law is very widely accepted by the courts in the member states. The only difficulties remaining are the need to ensure that the French Conseil d'État and the Italian Consiglio di Stato consistently accept the principle of the supremacy of Community law and, in particular, the doctrines of the direct effect of Community directives and decisions. The theoretical possibility still exists of a rebellion by the Constitutional Courts in Germany and Italy if they become dissatisfied with the general protection of fundamental rights in the Community legal order. That is an extremely unlikely eventuality, because of the development of the protection of human rights in the Community by the European Court and the political difficulties that such a decision would entail. In 1993 the threat of German rebellion was reawakened by the judgment of the German Constitutional Court in *Brunner* which reserved the right not to apply Community law whenever the Constitutional Court considers that the Community institutions have exceeded their competence. This is a very serious threat to the supremacy of Community law and may, for some time, have the effect of inhibiting

---

cases to the European Court under Art. 177(3). Cf. the decision of the Constitutional Court of 1 July 1992, *Re Municipal Electoral Rights* [1994] 3 CMLR 101. The Commission has noted that the administrative division of the Supreme Court giving judgment on 24 April 1993 in Case 6091/90 accepted the principle of the primacy of EC law over Spanish Constitutional law and disapplied Spanish legislation giving tax relief, see 'Eleventh Annual Report' OJ 1994 C154/176.

71 See Denmark, Luxembourg and Ireland. Though in Luxembourg the principle of the primacy of international treaty law has been accepted, judgment of the Cour Supérieure de Justice on 14 July 1954 Pas Lux XVI, p. 150, and this has been applied to Community law by the Conseil d'État in a judgment of 21 November 1984 *Bellion* v *Ministère de la fonction publique* Pas Lux XXVI, p. 174. In Ireland see the judgments of the Supreme Court in *Pigs and Bacon* v *McCarren* [1981] 3 CMLR 408; *Campus Oil Ltd* v *Minister for Industry and Energy* [1984] 1 CMLR 479; and in *Society for the Protection of Unborn Children* v *Grogan* [1990] 1 CMLR 689. See also Collins and O'Reilly. 'The Application of Community Law in Ireland 1973–1989' (1990) 27 CMLRev 315. The 'primacy' of Community law was accepted in an *obiter dictum* by the Irish Supreme Court in *Meagher* v *Minister for Agriculture and Food* [1994] 2 CMLR 654, 667, judgment of 18 November 1993, noted by Travers, 'The Implementation of directives into Irish Law' (1995) 20 ELRev 103.

the jurisprudence of the Court of Justice. Likewise, there is a theoretical possibility that the United Kingdom Parliament may repeal section 2(4) of the European Communities Act 1972 and thus undermine the supremacy of Community law. This will not happen for the foreseeable future, as all the major political parties in the United Kingdom are committed to continued membership of the Community and to upholding respect for Community law. There is some doubt as to how far national courts will be prepared to go in construing national law consistent with non-directly effective directives.

The European Court is not indulging in empty rhetoric when it talks of the primacy of Community law over the law of member states being one of the essential characteristics of the Community legal order. It is remarkable that the constitutional provisions, legislatures and judiciary in each of the member states by their acceptance of the principle have made it a reality. This has not been brought about by coercion or threat of financial sanctions,[72] but rather by the political and legal will to found a Community established on the principle of respect for the rule of law. A situation where the application of Community law varies from member state to member state would be a denial of the rule of law and would make the Community untenable.

---

[72] The Court was only given the power to fine member states who fail to comply with their Community law obligations in the Treaty amendments agreed at Maastricht.

CHAPTER 13

Article 12: The Abolition of Customs Duties

THE CUSTOMS UNION

Article 9 declares that

the Community shall be based upon a customs union which shall cover all trade in goods and which shall involve the prohibition between Member States of customs duties on imports and exports and of all charges having equivalent effect, and the adoption of a common customs tariff in their relations with third countries.

This provision makes it clear that the customs union has both internal and external aspects. The external aspect involves the adoption of the common customs tariff.[1] The internal aspect requires the elimination of customs duties and charges having equivalent effect on goods in free circulation within the Community. The internal aspect forms the focus of this chapter.

The prohibition on customs duties on intra-Community trade is achieved by virtue of Articles 12–17 of the Treaty. The abolition of customs duties is naturally indispensable to the establishment of a customs union, which is presented as the basis of the Community in Article 9 EC, but the Community has ambitions extending far beyond a customs union.[2] Article 2 EC refers to the establishment of a common market, and Articles 2 and 3 EC refer to common policy-making in many areas. Article 7a EC refers to the objective of completing the internal market by the end of 1992. The prohibitions that are the subject of examination in this chapter form only part of the range of Treaty rules that share the objective of liberating the movement of goods within a common market. Consequently, the scope of these provisions should not be assessed in isolation, but instead in conjunction with the Treaty rules governing Community trade law, which are discussed in the following chapters. In particular, Article 12 has elements in

1 For examination see Green, Hartley and Usher, *Single European Market*, Ch. 1.
2 See Ch. 1, esp. p. 21.

common with Article 95 because both contemplate control of fiscal charges imposed by member states that have the capacity to restrict inter-state trade.[3]

THE PROHIBITION ON CUSTOMS DUTIES

In focusing on the text of the provisions that are designed to eliminate customs duties on goods circulating between member states it will be observed that Articles 13–17 are concerned with the progressive reduction and elimination of customs duties during the course of the early develop-ment of the Community.[4] These provisions are now of historical interest only, although gradual reduction on similar principles occurs on the accession of new member states. The enduring core of the provisions may be found in the opening words of this section of the Treaty contained in Article 12: 'Member States shall refrain from introducing between them-selves any new customs duties on imports or exports or any charges having equivalent effect . . .'.

The Court has interpreted the prohibition contained in Article 12 strictly in ruling unlawful national levies imposed on imported or exported goods. In *Commission* v *Italy*[5] the Court considered the compatibility with Article 12 of an Italian tax on the export of art treasures. It was unarguable that a duty was levied on items crossing the Italian frontier. None the less, the Italian Government presented two arguments based on the Treaty rules on customs duties in order to persuade the Court that its system was compatible with Community law. Neither argument proved successful. Firstly, it was argued that the items on which the levy was raised were of artistic and cultural, not commercial, significance, and that for the purposes of Community law they did not count as 'goods' at all. The argument failed because the Court insisted that even items of artistic merit that can be valued in money and that are capable of forming the subject matter of commercial transactions do not escape the ambit of Article 12.[6] The Court's ruling was supported by the fact that the Italian authorities were

3 The demarcation between Articles 12 and 95 is considered more fully at p. 415.
4 The planned deadline for abolition was the end of 1969, but in fact Council Dec. 66/532 JO 1966 2971 advanced this date to the end of June 1968.
5 Case 7/68 [1968] ECR 423, [1969] CMLR 1.
6 The same approach to 'goods' would be taken in respect of the other provisions on the free movement of goods, such as Art. 95 (Ch. 14) and Art. 30 (Ch. 15). In Case C-2/90 *Commission* v *Belgium* [1992] ECR I-4431 [1993] 1 CMLR 365, examined at p. 516 below, the Court found laws governing the movement of waste fell within Art. 30.

prepared to make an economic assessment of the value of goods concerned in order to fix the amount of tax demanded, which revealed that even Italian law acknowledged the commercial nature of the items.

Secondly, it was submitted that the purpose of the tax was not to raise money for the national exchequer, but instead to retain national cultural artefacts within Italy. This function, it was argued, took the system outside the ambit of Article 12. The Court declined to follow this line of reasoning and found Italy in violation of the Treaty. It explained that Article 12 applied where the price of goods was inflated by a tax imposed by reason of the crossing of a frontier and where, accordingly, transfrontier trade was impeded. The purpose behind the tax could not alter the application of Article 12. As a matter of policy this seems entirely in accordance with the Treaty objective of market integration. In fact, an emphasis on *effect*, not *purpose*, is a stance that pervades EC trade law.[7]

Italy also sought to justify its scheme by reference to Article 36.[8] However, the Court refused to accept that that provision could be of any assistance as a means of justifying fiscal rules. Article 36 assists only the defender of non-fiscal trade barriers caught by Article 30.[9] A prohibition on the export of art treasures might conceivably be justifiable under Article 36,[10] but a fiscal levy cannot be so justified. This seems entirely correct. If a state has an interest in protecting its heritage, then surely that is a matter of pride in national identity, which cannot coherently be advanced by requiring exporters to pay for the privilege of denuding the galleries and museums of the nation.

An essentially similar judicial approach to Article 12 may be identified in *Sociaal Fonds voor de Diamantarbeiders* v *SA Ch Brachfeld & Sons*.[11] Belgian law required that 0.33 per cent of the value of imported diamonds be paid into a social fund. The fund was used to provide welfare benefits for workers in the industry. The matter reached the European Court by way of an Article 177 reference from a court in Antwerp before which Brachfeld, an importer, had argued that the levy contravened Article 12. Belgium denied the relevance of Article 12. The levy was not designed to raise money for the national exchequer – a typical function of the customs duty. Nor was it designed to protect domestic industry – also a typical function of the tariff barrier – for Belgium produces no diamonds of its own. The system improved welfare provision. The Court was not

---

7 See, e.g., p. 400 (Art. 95); p. 432 (Art. 30); p. 663 (Art. 85).
8 Ch. 16.
9 See further p. 474 on justifying trade barriers that possess both fiscal and non-fiscal elements.
10 See p. 476.
11 Case 2, 3/69 [1969] ECR 211, [1969] CMLR 335.

persuaded by these submissions and held the levy unlawful under Article 12. The prohibition contained in Article 12 is not dependent on the destination of the proceeds of the levy nor on the motive of the legislator. Instead, it bites where there is an obstacle to the free movement of goods resulting from the imposition of a pecuniary charge on goods by reason of their movement across a frontier. Judged from that objectively verifiable perspective, a violation of Article 12 had plainly been demonstrated in the case. Moreover, the clarity of the Article 12 prohibition so interpreted presented the Court with no difficulty in holding the provision directly effective.[12]

It may seem disturbing that a philanthropic system of welfare provision was held incompatible with Community law. However, the unacceptable element of the system was not its purpose but the method. Funds were raised through a levy on goods at point of importation. This creates an obstacle to trade. Had the welfare provision been secured through a more broadly based taxation system applied without reference to the fact of importation, then it may have proved possible to find the scheme compatible with Article 95.[13] Funding a welfare system through a sales tax on products made by the individuals benefiting from the scheme is, in principle, capable of conforming to Community law, because the rules would then constitute part of the state's internal taxation system. It would also be necessary to avoid the use of criteria that discriminate according to origin, which might require the state to show that the system applied broadly to employee protection and not simply in cases where imported goods could be burdened with the obligation to support workers.[14] Fiscal harmonization at Community level is slowly reducing the scope of permissible member state action in this area.[15]

12 This was first established in Case 26/62 *Van Gend en Loos* v *Nederlandse Administratie der Belastingen* [1963] ECR 1, [1963] CMLR 105. See generally Ch. 11, p. 341.
13 See Ch. 14; see also Burrows, *Free Movement*, pp. 15–16.
14 See further p. 401.
15 See further p. 420.

CEE: THE CHARGE HAVING EQUIVALENT EFFECT

The scope of Article 12 has been widened by the Court through its interpretation of the prohibited 'charge having equivalent effect' (CEE) to a customs duty. The Court has used the notion of the CEE to secure the abolition of charges imposed at frontiers even where those charges would not be classified as customs duties in the normal sense. In this way the Court has promoted the cause of market integration. It has already been seen in *Commission* v *Italy*,[16] the art treasures case, and in the *Sociaal Fonds*[17] decision that the Court analyses national rules with reference to their effect on trade rather than their object, and this theme underlies the following decisions on the meaning of the CEE.[18]

In a later *Commission* v *Italy* action,[19] which concerned not a levy on art treasures but a simple charge imposed on exports and imports, the Court defined the CEE in the following terms:

Any pecuniary charge, however small and whatever its designation and mode of application, which is imposed unilaterally on domestic or foreign goods by reason of the fact that they cross a frontier, and which is not a customs duty in the strict sense, constitutes a charge having equivalent effect ... even if it is not imposed for the benefit of the State, is not discriminatory or protective in effect and if the product on which the charge is imposed is not in competition with any domestic product.[20]

This formula was repeated by the Court in its judgment in *Sociaal Fonds*,[21] which was delivered on the same day, and it has remained fundamental to the Court's application of Article 12 ever since. This judicial definition, which is striking for its breadth, is illustrative of much of the Court's approach to Community trade law. Article 12, an exiguous provision, has been expanded by the Court in the light of the broad objects of the Treaty into a rigorous curtailment of national competence to act in a manner that impedes trade. The broad notion of the CEE is central to Article 12 and, in fact, the more restricted notion of the customs duty as normally

16 Case 7/68, note 5 above.
17 Cases 2, 3/69, note 11 above.
18 For a comprehensive survey of CEEs, see Gormley, Ch. 12, in Vaughan (ed.) *Halsbury's Laws*, vol. 52, para. 52.
19 Case 24/68 [1969] ECR 193, [1971] CMLR 611.
20 ibid., para. 9 of the judgment.
21 Cases 2, 3/69, note 11 above, para. 18 of the judgment.

understood has no independent importance, for it is plainly only a relatively small aspect of the wide ambit of Article 12. In *Commission v Italy* itself[22] the Italian Government denied that the sum demanded from importers and exporters constituted a customs duty, because it related to the funding of the preparation of statistical data on patterns of trade. It was not designed to raised money nor to protect home industry. The Court had no difficulty in holding the levy a CEE prohibited by Article 12. As with the Belgian levy on imported diamonds,[23] the charge amounted to an obstacle to trade arising by reason of passage across a frontier.

The cases so far discussed introduce a principle of Community trade law that will be seen applied to several other Treaty provisions concerned with the achievement of economic integration. The Court is primarily concerned to identify the *effect* of a national rule on the process of market integration. Legal response follows economic effect. Precise categorization according to legal form is not of central relevance before the European Court. This permits the Court to advance the spirit of integration enshrined in the Treaty without suffering constraint because of the diversity of national legal form and structure. Accordingly, the Court has accepted the invitation contained in Article 12 to develop its jurisprudence in a flexible manner through elaboration of the undefined notion of a 'charge having equivalent effect' to a customs duty. Close parallels will be observed with the Court's similarly flexible use of the notion of a measure 'having equivalent effect to a quantitative restriction' under Article 30 as a means of combating the range of non-fiscal obstacles to trade that member states have proved capable of devising.[24]

CEE: FEES FOR SERVICES CONFERRING A BENEFIT

The most significant group of cases decided in the light of the Court's effects-based approach to Article 12 is that concerning levies that are alleged to constitute fees paid in return for services rendered. In these cases the state does not simply demand a levy from an importer or exporter, for such a bare request is plainly incompatible with Article 12. Instead, the state alleges that the sum sought is not a duty at all, but instead payment in return for a benefit conferred on the importer and consequently a

22 Case 24/68, note 19 above.
23 Cases 2, 3/69, note 11 above.
24 See Ch. 15.

commercial transaction rather than a fiscal barrier to free trade. The Court has accepted the availability of escape from the Article 12 prohibition by this route in theory, but rarely in practice.

In *Commission* v *Italy* [25] the view of the Italian Government was that the sum demanded of traders represented payment for the compilation of statistical data on trade patterns, which would assist future business planning. It was accordingly submitted that no customs duty was involved and that the pecuniary charge was simply one part of a business deal: money in exchange for information. The Court accepted that if a genuine bargain existed, then Article 12 would not be infringed. However, that would be the case only if the trader received a specific, identifiable benefit in return for the sum paid, and that sum were proportionate to that benefit. The statistical service doubtless comprised a general benefit to the management of the economy, but not one traceable to an individual trader. Consequently, there was no true bargain. Italy was held in breach of its Treaty obligations.

Cadsky v *ICE* [26] reached the European Court by way of an Article 177 reference from a court in Bolzano. Cadsky, an exporter of salad vegetables from Italy to Germany, had brought an action before Italian courts for the recovery of small sums demanded by the Italian authorities to cover the expense of performing quality control of produce crossing the Italian frontier. The Court repeated its now standard definition of the CEE based on the obstructive effect of the unilateral imposition of a charge on crossing a border [27] and affirmed that the purpose of the charge is not relevant. It went on to accept that a proportionate fee extracted in return for a specific service may fall outside the definition of the CEE, because it constitutes a charge imposed as part of a commercial transaction, not because of passage across a frontier. However, the Court observed that this definition was not met in the case of a general system of quality control imposed on all goods, because there followed no sufficiently direct and specific benefit to the trader. Certainly, quality control might lead to a general improvement in the reputation of Italian vegetables and thereby enhance their competitive standing, but this objective should not be pursued through a mandatory system imposed on all traders irrespective of their particular preferences. [28]

In *Ford España* v *Spain* [29] the Court took the opportunity to emphasize

25 Case 24/68, note 19 above.
26 Case 63/74 *W Cadsky SpA* v *Instituto Nazionale per il Commercio Estero* [1975] ECR 281, [1975] 2 CMLR 246.
27 ibid., para. 5 of the judgment; and see p. 387.
28 The control itself may breach Art. 30, see p. 434; see p. 474 on the application of Arts. 12 and 30 to fiscal and non-fiscal elements in import/export control.
29 Case 170/88 [1989] ECR 2305. See similarly Case C-209/89 *Commission* v *Italy*, [1991] ECR I-1575.

that even if a benefit of the required specific nature can be identified, the state will fall foul of Article 12 unless the sum demanded is proportionate to the cost of supplying that benefit. Ford received a demand for 0.165 per cent of the declared vaue of cars and other goods imported into Spain. The Spanish authorities contended that the sum related to services rendered in connection with clearing the goods through customs. The matter reached the European Court by way of an Article 177 reference from a court in Valencia. The Court held that even if a specific benefit conferred on Ford could be shown, the flat-rate nature of the charge based on the value of the goods prevented the Spanish system being found compatible with Community law. The system was evidently *not* fixed according to the cost of the alleged service and thus could not meet the Court's test. Clearly, then, a fee must be assessed according to the particular costs involved in that deal before a true bargain will be held to exist.

A number of cases have provided the European Court with the opportunity to restate its views on submissions that a fee is simply payment for a specific benefit conferred on a trader. It has repeatedly accepted that in appropriate cases a charge may indeed be a legitimate fee and thus may fall outside Article 12. However, in its decisions it has consistently rejected submissions that particular contested charges meet those rigorous requirements.[30] A charge for storage connected solely with the completion of customs formalities is not lawful. If, however, a trader asks for and receives extra facilities, then a charge may lawfully be made, for a specific benefit has been conferred. In *Commission* v *Belgium*[31] Advocate-General Mancini concluded that the provision of warehousing facilities constituted a specific benefit for which a charge could be levied, but the Court found no benefit beyond the standard procedure for permitting clearance of customs. In *Commission* v *Italy*[32] the Court rejected the rather ambitious argument that compliance with Community directives that required customs posts to remain open for at least ten hours a day amounted to a specific benefit for which a fee could be imposed, because the working hours of Italian officials under domestic law were only six hours a day. It seems highly unlikely that the Court's formula could be satisfied in the absence of genuine negotiation between a trader or a group of traders and the national authorities. If a trader were to request a quality control certificate or the provision of storage facilities,[33] then the state would be

30 E.g., Case 43/71 *Politi SAS* v *Italian Ministry of Finance* [1971] ECR 1039; Case 29/72 *Marimex SpA* v *Italian Finance Administration* [1972] ECR 1309; Case 87/75 *Bresciani* v *Italian Finance Administration* [1976] ECR 129, [1976] 2 CMLR 62; Case 132/82 *Commission* v *Belgium* [1983] ECR 1649, [1983] 3 CMLR 600; Case 18/87 *Commission* v *Germany* [1988] ECR 5427, [1990] 1 CMLR 561.
31 Case 132/82, note 30 above.
32 Case 340/87 [1989] ECR 1483, [1991] 1 CMLR 437.
33 See para. 10 of the judgment in Case 132/82, note 30 above.

entitled to charge a proportionate fee. No customs duty would be in issue. However, a fee for a service *imposed* on a trader is treated as a charge having equivalent effect to a customs duty and is incompatible with Article 12.

The circumstances in which such disputes are likely to arise have been altered significantly by the completion of the internal market. The legislative initiatives that have resulted in the abolition of customs controls on goods are examined further in Chapter 15.[34] The disappearance of customs controls wipes out a major source of delay in intra-Community trade and, in addition, it removes the scope for levying a fee as part of passage through customs that may fall foul of Article 12. This signals the decline of Article 12's practical significance in EC law.[35] However, it should be recalled that the Court's definition of the CEE that is prohibited by Article 12 refers to charges imposed on goods 'by reason of the fact that they cross a frontier'.[36] This formula could be satisfied by state practices involving charges imposed independently of the formality of a customs control and therefore Article 12 retains some residual importance in the maintenance of the internal market.

CEE: FEES FOR SERVICES REQUIRED BY LAW

The cases involving fees in return for the conferral of an alleged benefit on the importer constitute the first major area in which the Court has accepted that a pecuniary charge may fall outside the notion of a CEE covered by Article 12. The second area in which the Court has in principle been receptive to such an argument is where the service for which a fee is charged is required by Community or international law. In this case, it remains incumbent on the state to demonstrate that the fee itself is proportionate to the costs of providing the service.

OBLIGATIONS UNDER COMMUNITY LAW

Bauhuis v *Netherlands*[37] involved a challenge to fees for veterinary inspections on swine imported into and exported from the Netherlands. The matter was complicated by the existence of Community legislation in the field, designed to facilitate the free movement of goods, which authorized

34 P. 437 below.
35 Although it will retain more relevance in EEA law; see p. 7 above.
36 Case 24/68, note 20 above.
37 Case 46/76 [1977] ECR 5.

states to take action to check the nature of the animals.[38] Some fees related to checks covered by such Community legislation; others related to unilaterally imposed national measures. The Court indicated that where the checks are mandatory under Community law as a means of enhancing the free movement of goods,[39] then fees levied to cover the costs of those checks are compatible with Community law.[40] They do not constitute CEEs, for they are simply a means of recouping the cost of performing an obligatory task. However, this is not so where there is no mandatory basis in Community law for the state's actions. Fees levied in such circumstances constitute CEEs on the same analysis as that observed in *Commission* v *Italy*[41] and *Cadsky* v *ICE*.[42]

This chapter began with a caution that the several rules concerning the free movement of goods should not be studied in isolation and it is here appropriate to anticipate subsequent discussion. The logic of the Court's approach in distinguishing between mandatory and permissible checks leads to the conclusion that where an inspection is lawful not under specific legislation but under Article 36 EC, the more general provision that admits of justification of non-fiscal barriers to trade,[43] the accompanying fee is *not* automatically lawful. Article 36 EC permits, but does not oblige, unilateral state action in defence of domestic interests and the Court has insisted that the costs of such action must in principle be borne by the state itself.[44] A fee can be justified only under the approaches discussed in this chapter, not under Article 36 EC generally.

OBLIGATIONS UNDER GENERAL INTERNATIONAL LAW

Checks may be made compulsory not only by Community legislation but also by the instruments of general international law. In *Commission* v *Netherlands*[45] the Court accepted that fees fall outside Article 12 if

---

38 See further p. 480.

39 Contrast Cases 80 and 81/77 *Ramel* [1978] ECR 927, in which Community legislation that authorized the levying of charges was held incompatible with Art. 13 in the absence of such an enhancement of trade.

40 See also Case 1/83 *IFG* v *Freistaat Bayern* [1984] ECR 349, [1985] 1 CMLR 453; Case 18/87, note 30 above.

41 Case 24/68, note 19 above.

42 Case 63/74, note 26 above; Case 314/82 *Commission* v *Belgium* [1984] ECR 1543, [1985] 3 CMLR 134.

43 See Ch. 16.

44 See further p. 474 below.

45 Case 89/76 [1977] ECR 1355.

they represent the cost of services that it is obligatory to provide under international conventions to which all member states are party. At issue was the International Plant Protection Convention 1951, which, the Court observed, is designed to liberalize trade by replacing diverse health controls in each state with a single check on which all states can rely. The Court drew an analogy between the function of the Convention and that of Directive 64/432,[46] the measure at issue in *Bauhuis*,[47] and applied the same approach to the role of Article 12. The Court emphasized once again that the state is not able to use such schemes as sources of general revenue. The fee must be proportionate to the cost of supplying the service.[48]

A RATIONALE FOR THE COURT'S APPROACH

In cases of inspections required by law the Court does not insist that a specific benefit to the importer be shown. The underlying assumption is that the trader enjoys the benefit of free trade consequent on the Community or international legislation that precludes unilateral member state action under Article 36 EC which restricts free trade.[49] Accordingly, it may be lawful to require the trader to fund the system in some circumstances. As a corollary, where the charge is imposed in respect of a regime that is merely permitted, rather than required, under Community law, whether by virtue of a directive or Article 36 EC, the Court has denied that any specific benefit is conferred on the trader.[50] The same applies to the operation of customs procedures.[51] Therefore the cost of the scheme falls on the member state.

It may appear anomalous that fees are lawful if related to mandatory acts, but not permissible acts.[52] However, it may be suggested that the distinction is tenable as a means of advancing the objective of market integration. One may presume that an inspection has been made mandatory under Community legislation because it serves the broader Community interest[53] and consequently it is proper that the state should be free of the obligation to fund the system. Where the inspection is merely permissive,

---

46 ibid., para. 12 of the judgment.
47 Case 46/76, note 37 above.
48 The decision in Case C-111/89 *Netherlands* v *Bakker Hillegom BV* [1990] ECR I-1735, [1990] 3 CMLR 119 runs parallel in this respect to that in Case 170/88, note 29 above.
49 See p. 480 below.
50 Dir. 71/118; Case 314/82, note 42 above, para. 12 of the judgment. Art. 36 EC; Case 63/74, note 26 above, para. 7 of the judgment.
51 Case 340/87, note 32 above.
52 See Timmermans, *Thirty Years of Community Law*, pp. 257–8.
53 See further p. 480 below.

one may take this as a recognition that the Community has no overriding interest in its performance and that a state that opts to undertake such a check is satisfying its own narrower interests.[54] In such circumstances it is proper that the costs should be met by the state rather than by the trader who is contributing to the acceleration of the integration of the market.

This is no more than an interim rationalization of a difficult area, and it is less than fully satisfactory. It may, for example, be thought logical that the costs of a mandatory check in the broader Community interest should not be borne by individual states; but logic does not dictate that the costs should then be cast upon the individual trader. Moreover, in such cases the precise level of the fee will in any event vary from state to state. Community legislation is required to resolve these anomalies.[55] Ultimately, the most satisfactory solution is likely to be some means of funding provided by the Community, but this is unlikely to occur until the Community enjoys a more general revenue-raising capacity.

CONCLUSION

There is no exception in the Treaty to justify charges contrary to Article 12. However, the Court's interpretation allows two types of levy that might appear to fall within the notion of the CEE prohibited by Article 12 to escape the prohibition. These are fees imposed to cover the costs of services that are of specific benefit to a trader, and fees imposed to cover the costs of services required under law that binds the member states. Strictly, in neither case is the Court finding an exception to Article 12. As a matter of Treaty interpretation it cannot do this, nor would it wish to, given its commitment to advancing the cause of market integration. In these instances the Court is prepared to find that the charge concerned is, in fact, not in the nature of a customs duty or a charge having equivalent effect at all. It falls outside Article 12; it is not an exception to it. If the fee and the service to which it relates are applied systematically on the same criteria to domestic goods within the domestic system, then the matter may fall for examination as part of a general system of internal taxation in

---

54 See Case 18/87, note 30 above, para. 11; Cases C-277/91, C-318/91 and C-319/91 *Ligur Carni Srl and Others* v *Unità Sanitaria Locale No XV di Genova and Others*, judgment of 15 December 1993.

55 ibid., Case 18/87 para. 15 of the judgment.

the light of Article 95, not Article 12.[56] Article 95 complements Article 12 as a means of controlling fiscal barriers to the free circulation of goods, but its focus is on the internal structure of the state's tax system. Articles 12 and 95 are mutually exclusive in their application.

[56] Case 70/79 *Commission* v *France* [1981] ECR 283; Case 314/82, note 42 above; Case 18/87, note 30 above. See further p. 415.

CHAPTER 14

Article 95: Prohibition on Discriminatory Internal Taxation

Article 95 states:

No Member State shall impose, directly or indirectly, on the products of other Member States any internal taxation of any kind in excess of that imposed directly or indirectly on similar domestic products.

Furthermore, no Member State shall impose on the products of other Member States any internal taxation of such a nature as to afford indirect protection to other products.

THE FUNCTION OF ARTICLE 95

Article 95 forbids internal taxation that discriminates against goods imported from other member states. It applies the basic Treaty rule against discrimination on grounds of nationality found in Article 6 EC to the area of national taxation. However, it goes no further than a rule against discrimination; it does not ensure equalization of tax treatment between member states. Tax regimes remain different state by state, subject only to a requirement of non-discrimination.

Although Article 95 was found in Part Three of the EEC Treaty, 'Policy of the Community', rather than Part Two, 'Foundations of the Community', it formed an important component in the fundamental task of securing the free movement of goods. This was confirmed by the amendments effected at Maastricht, which place Articles 9–136a inclusive in Part Three of the EC Treaty, 'Community Policies'. Article 95 is the second of the major Treaty provisions that serve to eliminate fiscal barriers to the free movement of goods. It complements the first, Article 12, in the sense that both are directed to the removal of fiscal impediments to the integration of the common market, but it operates at a different level.

Indeed, the Court has long held Articles 12 and 95 mutually exclusive.[1] Article 12 looks to the state's frontier controls, whereas the thrust of Article 95 is directed to the situation internal to a member state. It demands that systems of internal taxation shall apply without discrimination on the basis of the origin of goods. It would be fruitless to outlaw customs duties at the frontier if states could then prejudice the opportunities for imported goods through imposing on them a higher rate of internal taxation. Article 95 operates as a complement to Article 12 and as a key provision in the integration of a market in which competition on quality, not origin, prevails. In contrast to Article 12, Article 95's importance is in no way diminished by the completion of an internal market within which customs controls are eliminated.

DIRECT DISCRIMINATION

Examples of litigation involving national taxation that discriminates overtly against imported products are relatively rare. This is doubtless in part attributable to the unequivocal nature of the prohibition in Article 95. It may also be attributable to the deviousness of states capable of concealing discriminatory practices in more subtle form; this tendency is discussed below. However, unlawful direct discrimination was identified in *Lütticke GmbH* v *Hauptzollamt Saarlouis*.[2] Lütticke was an importer of powdered milk from Luxembourg into Germany. A claim for payment of tax issued by the German authorities was challenged on the basis that a German-produced product would not have been exposed to a similar demand. The European Court indicated that the challenge should succeed. The discrimination according to origin under the internal system of taxation constituted a simple violation of Article 95 and, indeed, such discriminatory treatment is plainly incompatible with the concept of a common market.

The Court's determination to eliminate fiscal discrimination has led it to insist that a system that treats imported products differently constitutes unlawful direct discrimination even where the system is capable of operating in some, even most, cases to the benefit of the imported product, provided that in some cases a detriment can be shown. In *Bobie Getränke-vertrieb* v *Hauptzollamt Aachen-Nord*[3] the *Biersteuergesetz*, the German tax on

---

1 See p. 415.
2 Case 57/65 [1966] ECR 205. See also Case C-47/88 *Commission* v *Denmark* [1990] ECR I-4509: and, on discrimination at different stages in the production process, Case 28/67 *Molkerei-Zentrale Westfalen/Lippe GmbH* v *Hauptzollamt Paderborn* [1968] ECR 143; Case 20/76 *Schottle* v *Finanzamt Freudenstadt* [1977] ECR 247, [1977] 2 CMLR 98.
3 Case 127/75 [1976] ECR 1079.

beer, was held incompatible with Article 95. The rate levied on home-produced beer varied in accordance with the output of the brewery. The higher the output, the higher the charge, in a range from 12 to 15 DM per hectolitre. The object of this sliding scale was to support small breweries through tax concessions. Imported beers were taxed at a flat rate of 14.40 DM per hectolitre irrespective of the size of the brewery. The effect of the tax therefore depended on the size of the brewer whose beer was being imported into Germany. A large brewer importing from another member state gained an advantage over a comparable German brewer by paying 14.40 rather than 15 DM per hectolitre. However, a small brewer suffered discrimination in comparison with a small German brewer: 14.40 rather than 12 DM. The European Court rejected the notion that an overall view should be taken of the effect of the system and held that a breach of Article 95 was established provided there existed any possibility of discrimination against the imported product. This condition was plainly satisfied, and therefore it fell to the German court to grant the declaration of incompatibility with Article 95 sought by the importers in the case and, subsequently, to the German authorities to amend their system in order to eliminate the taint of discrimination.

Even though the fact that importation was doubtless largely the preserve of the big brewer and that, consequently, the broad effect of the German tax regime was probably to advantage the importer, the Court was correct to insist on strict equality of tax rates imposed on identical products rather than accepting the legitimacy of a broad equivalence in the effect of the two different systems. Had a broad approach been preferred, supervision of national systems would have become extremely difficult. It is wise to preclude arguments about comparisons between taxation bases that are alleged to be broadly similar by insisting that where the same product is concerned precisely the same tax regime shall apply.[4]

In subsequent litigation the German Bundesfinanzhof observed that the intrusion of Community law into national competence to levy taxation goes no further than a rule against discrimination.[5] It therefore rejected the applicant's contention that the consequence of the *Bobie* decision was that all imported beer should be taxed at 12 DM per hectolitre and held lawful the practice of the German tax authorities in levying tax on the 12–15 DM sliding scale in accordance with the brewery's output. Community law, then, requires the removal of discrimination according to nationality in the imposition of taxation. However, it does not dictate the detail of the domestic system, which can, therefore, vary from state to state according

4 Cf. the pursuit of transparency as a means of effective supervision in an entirely different field in Case C-262/88 *Barber* v *GRE* on p. 624.
5 *Bobie Getränkevertrieb* [1988] 1 CMLR 482.

to national choice. Such divergence may lead to trade barriers when a state seeks to levy at the frontier the extra sums that are due on the item under its system, which differs from the system of the state of origin. Removal of such discrepancy is a matter for harmonization at Community level.[6]

The conditions of application of a tax

A prima-facie non-discriminatory tax may fall foul of Article 95 if the conditions attached to its application discriminate against goods imported from other member states. In *Commission* v *Ireland*[7] the Court held an Irish tax incompatible with Article 95. The tax itself was levied on the same criteria irrespective of the origin of goods, but whereas domestic producers were permitted several weeks' grace in paying the sum due, importers had to pay the duty immediately on importation. Article 95 requires non-discrimination in all aspects of the payment of the tax. Similarly, tax concessions granted under administrative procedures solely to domestic goods infringe Article 95.[8] However, there must be an outer limit to the application of Article 95, a point at which the conditions attached to the tax system are not properly adjudged part of the payment procedure and are instead general technical rules. This distinction is important for the purposes of Community law, because whereas fiscal rules are covered by Article 95 (or, if customs duties or charges having equivalent effect, Article 12), non-fiscal trade barriers are subject to the separate regime of Article 30.[9]

The point of demarcation between fiscal and non-fiscal barriers to trade was not addressed by the Court in *Drexl*,[10] although in the interests of legal certainty this omission was regrettable. Drexl, a German national, was prosecuted in Italy for importing a Volkswagen Golf motor car without paying the sum due as VAT. The car was confiscated as a penalty, although such a sanction would not have been applied to a comparable misdemeanour within Italy. This amounted to unjustified discrimination, which the Court indicated fell foul of Community law as

---

6 See pp. 420–27.
7 Case 55/79 [1980] ECR 481, [1980] 1 CMLR 734. See similarly Case C-287/91 *Commission* v *Italy* [1992] ECR I-0000, judgment of 3 June 1992.
8 Case 17/81 *Pabst and Richarz* v *Hauptzollamt Oldenburg* [1982] ECR 1331, paras. 19, 24 of the judgment.
9 See Ch. 15. In Case 74/76 *Iannelli and Volpi SpA* v *Meroni* [1977] ECR 557, para. 5 of the judgment, the Court insisted on sharp demarcation, without explaining the location of the margins. See similarly Case 222/82 *Apple and Pear Development Council* v *Lewis* [1983] ECR 4083. Case C-47/88 *Commission* v *Denmark* addresses demarcation in the case of tax levied on a product that is not made domestically; see pp. 417–19.
10 Case 299/86 [1988] ECR 1213.

an impediment to the free movement of goods. This was unquestionably the correct conclusion, but the Court's analysis proceeded from the assumption that Article 95, rather than Article 30, applied. Yet the sanction was not part of the fiscal charge on the product; rather, it was a means of securing an individual's compliance with a fiscal charge. It was part of the state's technical rules applied to importation, and consideration in the light of Article 30 seems more appropriate.[11] In fact, the initial error lay with the Italian court, which referred questions based only on Article 95. Perhaps the European Court would have been more rigorous in its scrutiny had the outcome been dependent on which Article of the Treaty was invoked. On the facts of *Drexl*, the result was unaffected by choice of Article 95 rather than Article 30, for the discriminatory practice plainly violated Community law.

Reverse discrimination

Finally, it should be observed that reverse discrimination is not objectionable from the perspective of Community law. In *Peureux* v *Directeur des Services Fiscaux*[12] the Court held that French rules on alcohol taxation, which placed home production at a disadvantage compared with imports, were unaffected by Articles 37[13] or 95. Community law insists that national law must treat imported products no less favourably than it treats domestic products, but, pending harmonization, discrimination against domestic goods lies outside the scope of Community law.[14] Article 95 does not forbid a state choosing to levy a higher tax on home-produced goods than is demanded of imports.[15]

INDIRECT DISCRIMINATION

Article 95 catches not only systems that discriminate according to origin, but also systems that on their face discriminate on the basis of other factors yet produce an effect that prejudices the imported product. The saga of the French road tax is perhaps the best-known example of the use of Article 95 to prohibit such indirect discrimination.

French road tax applied a sliding scale up to 1,100 French francs (FF) on

---

11 Cf., e.g., Case 212/88 *Levy* and other cases discussed on pp. 435–6. See comment by Lonbay (1989) 14 ELRev 48, 55.
12 Case 86/78 [1979] ECR 897.
13 Ch. 27, p. 873.
14 See Art. 30, p. 530; Arts. 48, 52, 59, p. 609.
15 Note, however, control of discriminatory tax treatment of exports, p. 419.

cars below 16-CV (horsepower) rating. Above 16 CV, the tax was levied as a lump sum at 5,000 FF. Obviously, there was a huge increase in the burden of the taxation system at the 16-CV level. A taxpayer who had bought a Mercedes in France found himself obliged to pay the flat rate levy of 5,000 FF on registration, for the car was so powerful that it was classified at 36 CV. The taxpayer, M. Humblot, sought repayment of the tax on the basis that it infringed Article 95.[16] It was shown that France produced no cars exceeding the 16-CV barrier. Thus, the disproportionately heavy burden on more powerful cars affected exclusively imported goods. Accordingly, the basis of the taxpayer's claim was that although the system discriminated according to the power of the car, the indirect effect of the system was to discriminate on grounds of nationality contrary to Article 95. The European Court took the view that such a system was capable of violating Article 95.

The French authorities responded to the damning judgment in *Humblot* by revising the categorization for tax purposes. However, in *Feldain* v *Directeur des Services Fiscaux*[17] the amended system of taxation was also held incompatible with the Treaty. The special rate of 5,000 FF for all cars above 16 CV had been replaced by nine separate tax bands graded according to the power of the car. However, the rate of increase in the level of the tax increased exponentially once the 16-CV threshold had been exceeded. Moreover, although 12–16 CV, the key area for French car production, was covered by just one tax band, the range 17–22 CV was covered by three bands representing increasing tax levels. Such a structure offered significant tax advantages to cars falling just beneath the 16-CV limit, which, of course, coincided with the bulk of French production. The discriminatory effect had been modified, but not eliminated.

Objective justification

An important point that is common to many Treaty provisions concerns a difference in approach to direct and indirect discrimination. A system, such as the French road tax system, that applies criteria that have an effect indirectly discriminatory on grounds of nationality remains susceptible to justification by the taxing state. An objectively justifiable reason that is unconnected with nationality is capable of explaining the selection of the factor that operates indirectly to discriminate on grounds of nationality.[18]

---

16 Case 112/84 *Humblot* v *Directeur des Services Fiscaux* [1985] ECR 1367, [1986] 2 CMLR 338.
17 Case 433/85 [1987] ECR 3536. The same grounds of judgment were given in Case 76/87 *Seguela* v *Administration des Impôts* [1988] ECR 2397, [1989] 3 CMLR 225.
18 See Art. 30 on p. 444; Art. 119 on p. 620.

Thus the Court declared in *Commission* v *Italy*[19] that 'in its present stage of development Community law does not restrict the freedom of each Member State to lay down tax arrangements which differentiate between certain products on the basis of objective criteria'.[20] In that case Italian tax law set a threshold based on cubic capacity for the application of higher rates to diesel-engined cars. The Commission considered that the choice of this basis led to the higher rate being applicable only to imports, thus disclosing an indirect discriminatory effect. The Court took the view that a system based on cubic capacity was not itself discriminatory on grounds of nationality. It indicated that the choice of such a criterion was capable of objective justification even if it had a discriminatory effect. However, the Court did not explore the notion in great depth, for it considered that in any event the Commission had failed even to prove the necessary discriminatory effect.[21] The Commission's economic analysis was faulty, for it looked only at the market for diesel-engined cars, whereas the competitive structure of the car market as a whole demanded assessment.[22]

Taxation of motor vehicles provides a useful example of the type of national rules that might be held objectively justifiable despite an effect indirectly discriminatory on grounds of nationality. Arguments of objective justification were weak in *Humblot*[23] and scarcely stronger in *Feldain*,[24] but cases with more merit may be envisaged. If a state is able to show that it taxes particular types of car at punitively high rates in order to encourage the use of more environmentally friendly models, which are given substantial tax concessions, then the Court would be prepared to hear submissions that the state's system is lawful even if it were shown that most of the models subjected to high rates of tax were imported.[25] If the heavy burden felt especially by imports is seen to be purely incidental to the primary lawful purpose of environmental protection, then no breach of Article 95 has occurred: it is not unlawful to discriminate according to capacity to pollute. Of course, this would not be so if the state exempted its own polluters from the regime; the system must be based on quality, not nationality.[26]

19 Case 200/85 [1986] ECR 3953, [1988] 1 CMLR 97.
20 ibid., para. 8 of the judgment.
21 The same fate befell the Commission in Case C-132/88 *Commission* v *Greece* [1990] ECR I-1567.
22 See similar calculations required under Art. 86, p. 728 below.
23 Case 112/84, note 16 above.
24 Case 433/85, note 17 above.
25 See the balance between environmental protection and free trade under Art. 30, p. 514 below.
26 See Case 21/79 *Commission* v *Italy* [1980] ECR 1; Case 142/80 *Amministrazione delle Finanze dello Stato* v *Essevi* [1981] ECR 1413; Case 277/83 *Commission* v *Italy* [1985] ECR 2049, [1987] 3 CMLR 324.

In *Commission* v *France*[27] the Commission failed to persuade the Court that a French system that taxed sweet wines produced in a traditional and customary fashion at a lower rate than liqueur wines was contrary to Article 95. The criterion for classification within the lower rate was in principle available to all products irrespective of origin and was not closed to imports.[28] There was consequently no direct discrimination on grounds of origin. Once it was shown that, if anything, indirect discrimination was in issue, it was open to France to demonstrate objective justification for the preferential treatment offered to natural sweet wines. It was shown that natural sweet wines tend to be produced in areas of low rainfall and poor soil, where the local economy is unusually dependent on wine output. It was consequently held objectively justifiable to confer tax concessions on such products in order to support economically weak areas.[29] It was thus accepted that the prohibition on discrimination under Article 95 still permits a state to use its tax system as a means of regional policy – provided only that the concession is kept open to all products, not just domestically produced goods.

The pattern, then, is that discrimination based directly on nationality is unlawful. However, discrimination based on factors unconnected with nationality but which tend indirectly to favour home-produced goods may be unlawful, but will be lawful if the state is able to submit an objectively justifiable reason unconnected with nationality for the choice of the factor. The effect prejudicial to imported goods is then shown to be incidental and overridden by the scheme's lawful function.[30] Thus, if the objective criterion of effect on trade of the scheme renders it potentially unlawful, the state is then able to submit subjective elements relating to the motive and function of the scheme in order to show that its primary purpose falls within an objective justification recognized by Community law.[31] The same indirect-discrimination/objective-justification model will be observed elsewhere in Community law.[32] Although further elaboration

---

27 Case 196/85 [1987] ECR 1597, [1988] 2 CMLR 851 noted by Lonbay (1989) 14 EL Rev 48.

28 Contrast, e.g., Case 277/83, note 26 above, in which the tax break was available only to Italian Marsala wine.

29 See also Case 148/77 *Hansen* v *Hauptzollamt Flensburg* [1978] ECR 1787; Case 140/79 *Chemial* v *DAF* [1981] ECR 1, [1981] 3 CMLR 350 (tax break as part of industrial policy: control of use of ethylene, a scarce resource); Case 46/80 *Vinal* v *Orbat* [1981] ECR 77, [1981] 3 CMLR 524.

30 See Schwarze, 'The Member States' discretionary powers under the tax provisions of the EEC Treaty' in Schwarze (ed.) *Discretionary Powers*, esp. pp. 147–8.

31 For a thorough discussion of the case law, see Danusso and Denton, 'Does the European Court of Justice look for a protectionist motive under Article 95?' [1990/1] LIEI 67. The authors believe the Court's primary concern is to establish the motive behind a tax system, and that this is a desirable approach.

32 See note 18 above.

at this point is inappropriate, it should be noted that this model permits the Court a potentially intrusive, and often legislatively ill-defined, role in judging whether member states' policy choices fall within the sphere of action permitted under Community law.[33]

Finally, it should be observed that the state must justify not only its object, but also the means of achieving it. The means must be apt to achieve the end in view and the burden imposed must be proportionate to the benefits sought. The principle of proportionality is familiar throughout Community trade law.[34] To use the example of *Humblot*,[35] even had the French Government been able to show a sound reason for imposing heavier burdens on more powerful cars, it would also have had to satisfy the Court that that policy could be achieved only by its rather peculiar leap to a high rate above the 16-CV threshold. One might normally expect that a state would be able to defend a sliding scale that, in its upper reaches, has an effect that discriminates against imported goods, provided there is objective justification for discouraging the use of products at the top end of the range. However, it is hard to visualize an erratic system such as that used in *Humblot* being justified as an appropriate mechanism.

DISCRIMINATORY REFUND OF TAXATION

It may be necessary to examine the use to which the proceeds of a tax are put in order to uncover a discriminatory effect. If the domestic industry is supplied with resources refunded out of a tax levied on all products, the effect is no different from a system that favours domestic goods in its initial application. Article 95 should be considered infringed. It is, however, necessary to examine carefully the circumstances of the refund. Article 95 forbids discriminatory internal taxation, but it does not assert a general power to control a state's spending policy. If sums have been levied as taxation and placed in the general treasury, then a payment to the benefit of a domestic producer is not subject to Article 95. Once the money is swallowed up by the state exchequer, thus destroying the direct link between money raised and money refunded in a particular case, the idea of an identifiable tax covered by Article 95 is lost. Consequently, such a subsidy in support of domestic industry from general revenue falls to be

---

33 See discussion by Easson, 'Fiscal Discrimination: New Perspectives on Article 95 of the EEC Treaty', (1981) 18 CMLRev 521. Danusso and Denton [1990/1] LIEI 67 expose inconsistencies in the Court's rulings.

34 See p. 455 in relation to Art. 30.

35 Case 112/84, note 16 above.

considered under the Treaty provisions on state aids contained in Article 92.[36]

However, if the money refunded to the advantage of the domestic product can be tied to the levy of a particular tax, then a breach of Article 95 may be revealed. The Court displayed an initial reluctance in *Rewe* v *HZA Landau-Pfalz*[37] to use Article 95 in such circumstances. However, that reticence was abandoned by the Court in *Commission* v *Italy*,[38] in which it accepted that 'in an interpretation of the concept of internal taxation for the purposes of Article 95, it may be necessary to take into account the purpose to which the revenue from the charge is put'.[39] Consequently, where proceeds of a prima-facie non-discriminatory tax are earmarked for the special benefit of home producers, the result is discriminatory. To the extent that the refund offers an advantage to the home industry, a breach of Article 95 has occurred; perhaps in addition to a breach of Article 92. However, in the absence of a specific link between the tax and the refund, the matter is a general subsidy subject to scrutiny only under Article 92.

In exceptional cases the refund may entirely nullify the effect of the tax imposed on the domestic product. In such a case all that is left is a charge imposed on the imported product. Consequently, Article 12 may be applicable. However, the Court has insisted that only where three criteria are met will Article 12 be relevant to a case of refunded taxation. Firstly, the refund must have the sole purpose of providing financial support for the specific advantage of the taxed domestic product. Secondly, the product taxed and the product receiving the benefit must be the same. Thirdly, the charge made must be made good in full. All three criteria must be satisfied before the Court will consider the matter a customs duty rather than an aspect of internal taxation. In *Interzuccheri* v *Ditta Rezzano e Cavassa*[40] an Italian levy on the sale of sugar was prima facie compatible with Article 95, for it was raised without reference to the origin of the sugar. However, the proceeds of the tax were used to benefit Italian sugar refineries and sugar-beet producers, and it was argued that in consequence

---

36 See further Ch. 27.
37 Case 45/75 *Rewe-Zentrale des Lebensmittel-Grosshandels GmbH* v *Hauptzollamt Landau/Pfalz* [1976] ECR 181, [1976] 2 CMLR 1.
38 Case 73/79 *Commission* v *Italy* [1980] ECR 1533; see also Cases C-78–C-83/90 *Société compagnie Commerciale de l'Ouest and Others* v *Receveur Principal des Douanes*, [1992] ECR I-1847.
39 ibid., para. 15 of the judgment.
40 Case 105/76 [1977] ECR 1029. See also Case 94/74 *Industria Gomma Articoli Vari* v *Ente Nazionale per la Cellulosa e per la Carta* [1975] ECR 699; Case 77/76 *Cucchi* v *Avez* [1977] ECR 987. The earlier approach in Case 77/72 *Capolongo* v *Maya* [1973] ECR 611 now seems abandoned.

the matter should have been considered in the light of Article 12, not Article 95. The argument failed because of the Court's insistence that all three criteria mentioned above should be satisfied. The taxed product was sugar, whereas the refund was to the advantage of beet producers and sugar processors. In consequence, sugar, as distinct from beet, recouped less than half of the original levy. The proceeds were directed more broadly than simply back into the pocket of the payer.

The Court should proceed to consider whether Article 95 is violated by such systems. After all, these are non-discriminatory taxes at point of application that in operation confer advantages on the home industry. However, the questions referred by the domestic courts in *Interzuccheri* and similar cases[41] focused on Article 12 and made no reference to Article 95, and, whereas one might have wished the European Court to take the initiative in drawing out the appropriate legal provisions, the Article 177 procedure is prone to allow analysis that is off course at national level to remain off course at Community level. After *Commission* v *Italy*,[42] however, which postdates *Interzuccheri* and in fact concerned the same Italian tax, it appears that the use of Article 95 is appropriate in cases of partial refund. This is confirmed by the Court's increasingly consistent reference to Article 95 in such circumstances.[42a]

THE RESPECTIVE ROLES OF ARTICLES 95(1) AND 95(2)

The cases considered in the preceding section all concerned instances of similar products being taxed at different rates because of their origin: *Bobie Getränkevertrieb*[43] concerned beer; *Humblot*,[44] cars; *Interzuccheri*,[45] sugar. The matter may, however, be rather more complicated. It is possible that in order to eradicate subtle discrimination a tax comparison needs to be made between products that are not similar, but comparable or competing. It is naturally more difficult to identify discrimination according to origin where the products of different origin themselves possess different character-

---

41 See note 40 above.
42 Case 73/79, note 38 above.
42a Case C-17/91 *G. Lornoy en Zonen* v *Belgium*, judgment of 16 December 1992; Case C-266/91 *Celulose Beira Industrial SA* v *Fazenda Publica*, judgment of 2 August 1993; Case C-72/92 *H. Scharbatke GmbH* v *Germany*, judgment of 27 October 1993.
43 Case 127/75, note 3 above.
44 Case 112/84, note 16 above.
45 Case 105/76, note 40 above.

istics. It is necessary to determine whether differences in tax levels are genuinely attributable to differences between the products. How, for example, is a domestic system of taxation of alcohol to treat, on the one hand, domestic beer and, on the other, imported wines or even strong spirits?

A reading of Article 95 paragraphs (1) and (2), set out at the beginning of this chapter, is required. These paragraphs envisage this very problem. The first outlaws discrimination where similar products are in issue; the second forbids indirect protection of products from competing imports. However, the paragraphs offer little in the way of precise guidance for the proper development of the law. That has been a job for the European Court and its work in this area in particular has been subjected to close critical analysis.[46]

ARTICLE 95(1): THE 'SIMILAR' PRODUCT

The first question that arises under Article 95(1) is what constitutes a 'similar' product for the purposes of a tax comparison. The European Court suggested in Fink-Frucht[47] that products are similar if they fall within the same tax classification. Subsequent case law indicates that this is correct, but that the reverse does not follow. Products in different tax categories may none the less be similar for the purposes of Article 95(1).[48] Article 95(1), then, goes beyond cars/cars, beer/beer, and sugar/sugar. The European Court has had the opportunity to develop its jurisprudence in this area in the large number of cases that it has been obliged to decide in relation to the taxation of alcoholic drinks. It is not surprising that alcohol has been a regular testing ground for the interpretation of Article 95, given member states' predilection for using such goods as a means of raising revenue through taxation. In such circumstances there have been regular disputes about how to tax the vast range of alcoholic drinks that share certain common features yet also display differences, particularly in flavour. Community law does not dictate the nature of domestic taxation. However, Community law's sole requirement, that discrimination on grounds of origin be eradicated, can effectively be enforced only by a close analysis of the structure of the domestic taxation scheme.

46 See, e.g., Easson (1981) 18 CMLRev 521; Schwarze, Discretionary Powers, pp. 141–8; Danusso and Denton [1990/1] LIEI 67; Barents, 'Recent Case Law on the Prohibition of Fiscal Discrimination under Article 95' (1986) 23 CMLRev 641.
47 Case 27/67 Fink-Frucht GmbH v Hauptzollamt München-Landsbergerstrasse [1968] ECR 223.
48 See, e.g., Case 45/75, note 37 above; Case 169/78 Commission v Italy [1980] ECR 385; Case 216/81 Cogis v Amministrazione delle Finanze dello Stato [1982] ECR 2701.

In *John Walker* v *Ministeriet for Skatter*[49] the Court was faced with the question whether liqueur fruit wine is similar to whisky for the purposes of the application of the rule against discrimination in Article 95(1). The Court considered it was first necessary to examine the objective characteristics of the product, which might include reference to alcohol content and method of manufacture. Secondly, the Court considered it appropriate to determine whether both products were capable of fulfilling consumer needs in a similar manner. Whisky has twice the alcohol content of a liqueur fruit wine. It is produced by distillation rather than fermentation. Where the intrinsic characteristics of the products are so fundamentally different, even the fact that whisky (however misguidedly) and liqueur fruit wines are both commonly diluted for consumption cannot affect the outcome. Such differences indicate that the products are not similar. The tax system then fell for consideration in the light of the second paragraph of Article 95.[50]

John Walker may usefully be contrasted with *Commission* v *Denmark*,[51] in which judgment was given on the same day. The Court's examination of the nature and function of wine deriving from the grape and wine deriving from other fruit led it to conclude that the products were similar and therefore had to be taxed at an equivalent level. The beverages were derived from the same basic product – agricultural produce – by means of the same process of fermentation and possessed the same alcohol content. Moreover, they fulfilled consumer needs in more or less the same way. A similar result was reached in *Commission* v *Italy*,[52] in which the Court rejected the submission of the Italian Government that Marsala wines were dissimilar to other liqueur wines and found a breach of Article 95(1) in the tax concessions granted to domestic Marsala wines but denied to similar imported products.[53]

Article 95(1) thus insists that the tax applied to product X be the same whether the product is domestically produced or imported. Origin neutrality is central. Even where a state wishes to tax product X at a rate lower than similar product Y, then, provided no discrimination according to nationality is involved, there is no breach of Article 95.[54] If indirect discrimination according to nationality follows from the differentiated

49 Case 243/84 [1986] ECR 875, noted by Denton (1986) 11 ELRev 309; Barents (1986) 23 CMLRev 641.
50 See p. 409.
51 Case 106/84 [1986] ECR 833.
52 Case 277/83, note 26 above.
53 In *Humblot, Case* 112/84, note 16 above, French submissions that luxury cars were dissimilar to normal cars were virtually ignored by the Court.
54 See further Wyatt and Dashwood, *European Community Law*, pp. 195–6; Schwarze, *Discretionary Powers*, pp. 147–8.

treatment of products X and Y, it is still open to the state to show objective justification for its system unconnected with nationality, as, for example, in the case of French naturally sweet wines.[55] However, such justification is never available to justify direct discrimination – where, for example, the lower rate granted to product X is granted only to domestic product X.[56]

ARTICLE 95(2)

In *John Walker* the Court, having rejected the argument that whisky and liqueur fruit wine were similar within Article 95(1), proceeded to the issue of whether the products were in competition. If so, Article 95(2) would forbid the Danish taxation system from offering indirect protection to domestic liqueur production at the expense of whisky, which is available in Denmark only as an imported product. However, the Court was satisfied that the Danish system was origin-neutral. Whisky was taxed within the general framework of taxation of spirits alongside other beverages, including many Danish-produced goods. The differential tax rates, viewed from this perspective, revealed no discrimination or protection of competing domestic products. No breach of Article 95(2) had been demonstrated.

Article 95(2), then, forbids the taxation of an import at a rate that confers protection on a domestic product in competition with that import.[57] The objectionable effect, and very often the true purpose of such a scheme, is to shield domestic production from competitive pressures. The result is the distortion of efficient competition contrary to the purpose of a common market.

The 'Spirits' cases

The Court's approach in *John Walker* is an elaboration of its stance in a series of important cases collectively known as the Spirits cases.[58] In these cases the Commission pursued with determination a number of member

---

55 Case 196/85, note 27 above. It may be possible in this way to justify heavy taxation of strong spirits as a means of combating alcohol abuse, even if most strong spirits are imported.

56 See cases at note 26 above.

57 Unless, perhaps, a similar (within Art. 95(1)) domestic product is also taxed at the heavier rate and any indirect effect that discriminates according to nationality is objectively justified; see note 54 and accompanying text above.

58 See Easson (1980) 5 ELRev 318 and (1981) 18 CMLRev 521, 531 ff.; Berlin (1980) 16 RTDE 460. See also Burrows, *Free Movement*, p. 18.

states whose taxation of alcohol was alleged to infringe Article 95. The typical issue concerned systems that set different levels for different drinks, but tended to offer particularly favourable rates to the traditional domestic product. France favoured cognac over whisky;[59] Italy, grappa over rum;[60] and Denmark granted tax advantages to aquavit compared with competing spirits, which were largely imported.[61] The United Kingdom was alleged to favour beer over wine.[62] The cases supply 'a fascinating guide to the drinking habits of Community citizens'.[63]

In the cases brought against France, Denmark and Italy the Court concluded that a breach of Article 95 had been established. In each case it adopted a rather cavalier approach to the distinction between the two paragraphs in Article 95. The Court chose not to specify whether the beverages in question were similar for the purposes of Article 95(1) or competing for the purposes of Article 95(2) because it was satisfied that the taxation systems under scrutiny failed to comply with the requirements of Article 95 however the relationship between the products was viewed. If not similar, the products were at least competing; if not discriminatory, the regime was at least protective.

Competition between wine and beer

Where the tax system obviously lacks origin neutrality, as in the bulk of the Spirits cases, it might seem acceptable to treat Article 95(1) and (2) as a single broad prohibition. The flaw in this 'globalized' approach[64] is that it obscures the proper response by the infringing state. If the products are similar within the meaning of paragraph 1 of Article 95, the state must equalize the taxes. If the products are competing within the meaning of paragraph 2, the protective effect alone must be removed, which may not mean equalization.

The troubling 'globalized' approach to Article 95 seemed to be rejected in the subsequent decision in *John Walker*,[65] in which the Court examined Article 95's two paragraphs separately and found no breach of Article

---

59 Case 168/78 *Commission* v *France* [1980] ECR 347.

60 Case 169/78 *Commission* v *Italy* [1980] ECR 385. See further Case 323/87 *Commission* v *Italy* [1989] ECR 2275, [1991] 1 CMLR 67.

61 Case 171/78 *Commission* v *Denmark* [1980] ECR 447. More recently, Greece was found to favour ouzo and brandy over typically imported spirits in Case C-230/89, [1991] ECR 1–1909.

62 Case 170/78 *Commission* v *United Kingdom* [1980] ECR 417; but see below, p. 411.

63 Easson (1980) 5 ELRev 318, 321.

64 Easson (1981) 18 CMLRev 521, drawn from Berlin (1980) 16 RTDE 460.

65 Case 243/84, note 49 above.

95(2) in the broad sweep of the system.[66] Furthermore, although a violation of Article 95(2) was ultimately established in *Commission* v *United Kingdom*, the Court was also forced in that case to analyse the two paragraphs of Article 95 with more circumspection than in the other Spirits cases. When the case was brought before the Court in 1980 as part of the package of Spirits cases, the Court refused to grant a declaration that the United Kingdom's wine/beer tax differential infringed Article 95.[67] It demanded further information about the nature of the competitive relationship between the two products. It was more than three years and two further sets of oral argument later that the Court finally obliged the Commission and held the United Kingdom in breach of the Treaty.[68] The problem was that wine, which is typically imported, and beer, typically home-produced, are plainly dissimilar yet arguably in competition with each other. The two paragraphs of Article 95 could not be conflated. The United Kingdom imposed a higher tax relative to price on wine than on beer. Yet to identify whether any protective effect prohibited by Article 95(2) flowed from the structure of the tax system required complex economic information about the nature of the market and the basis of the United Kingdom's chosen tax ratios. In 1980 the Court was not equipped with the required information to hold against the United Kingdom, in contrast to the clearer cases decided at that time against France, Denmark and Italy.

So in *Commission* v *United Kingdom* it was necessary to consider whether the discrepancy in taxation rates had any detrimental effect on sales of (typically imported) wine compared with (typically home-produced) beer. The Court was thus obliged to embark on a (by 1983 properly informed) analysis of the competitive nature of the relationship between the products. The United Kingdom laid emphasis on consumer habit and observed that beer is commonly drunk in public houses, whereas wine is drunk in the home. Consumers do not regard wine and beer as interchangeable and consequently any differential tax rate that might exist has no effect on the competitive structure of the market. The Court rejected the United Kingdom's arguments and found it in breach of Article 95(2). Impressed by the intervention of the Italian Government on this point, the Court found that there was an element of interchangeability between beer and wines at the cheap end of the market. Consequently the heavier tax on wine relative to price afforded indirect protection to beer contrary to

---

66 Although the *basis* of the separation, rather than the fact of performing it, is not convincing in *John Walker*, see Denton (1986) 11 ELRev 309. ,
67 Case 170/78, note 62 above.
68 ibid., Case 170/78 [1983] ECR 2265, [1983] 3 CMLR 512, noted by Easson, 'Cheaper wine or dearer beer?' (1984) 9 ELRev 57.

Article 95(2).[69] It is particularly interesting that the Court's discussion of the test of consumer substitutability indicated a certain scepticism about its value as a measure, at least where an analysis based purely on present rather than future trends is involved. Consumer resistance to a switch to wine may, in fact, be attributable to the higher price of wine. A state cannot be heard to deny the existence of a competitive relationship between products where it is its own protective tax rates that have prevented that competitive relationship ever having the opportunity to develop through the expression of consumer preference.[70]

The Court consequently concluded that 'the effect of the United Kingdom tax system is to stamp wine with the hallmarks of a luxury product which, in view of the tax burden which it bears, can scarcely constitute in the eyes of the consumer a genuine alternative to the typical domestically produced beverage'.[71] The United Kingdom was therefore obliged to amend its tax system in order to eradicate the element of protection granted to domestic beer production. Would this result, as the title of the annotation of the case in the *European Law Review* asks, in 'Cheaper wine or dearer beer?'[72] In fact, in the United Kingdom the consequence was both, as the Chancellor of the Exchequer eliminated the unlawful protective element by adjusting tax rates for beer upwards and those for wine downwards.[73] Perhaps the subsequent steady rise in British wine consumption demonstrates the truth of the Court's implied assumption that a latent wine-buying public existed in the United Kingdom, suppressed only by unfair tax rates.

Again, the limits of the intrusion of Community law into national competence should be observed. Pending Community harmonization,[74] a state remains free to set its own taxation levels. It is obliged only to eschew discrimination on grounds of nationality. The grant of tax advantages to particular products is unaffected by Community law except where an effect that discriminates in favour of or protects domestic products is in issue. Even where it is shown that one product is typically imported and the other typically home-produced Community law extends no further than insisting on an absence of discrimination in the system and the elimination of any protective effect in favour of the home product. It does not determine the actual rate itself.

---

69 The Court mentioned criteria other than price that also indicated protection of beer, such as level of tax per unit of volume. It declined to choose which criteria, if any, ought to govern such a tax system, which leaves states in a quandary as to how to meet the requirements of Art. 95(2).

70 See p. 497: the same perspective has been adopted in relation to the application of Art. 30.

71 Case 170/78 [1983] ECR 2265, 2292, para. 27 of the judgment.

72 Easson (1984) 9 ELRev 57.

73 But see note 69 above; the amended system remains as yet unchallenged.

74 See p. 420.

DISTINGUISHING ARTICLES 95(1) AND (2)

The Court applies an economic analysis for the purposes of both Articles 95(1) and (2). A product may fail to meet the requirement of similarity under Article 95(1), yet still compete with another product for the purposes of Article 95(2). The broad scope of Article 95, encompassing both paragraphs, thus takes in a wide range of products. There is a temptation to run the two paragraphs together and to consider the key distinction to be that at the margin, between competing products under the second paragraph and non-competing products that escape Article 95 entirely, rather than that between Articles 95(1) and (2). Where products, even if not similar, are competing, a breach of Article 95 is established if origin neutrality is absent. Several of the cases involving taxation of alcohol exemplify this approach.[75] Yet, as already suggested, this is not always an adequate analysis, not least from the perspective of the state called upon to amend its system. The consequences of Articles 95(1) and (2) are not identical. A domestic product must not be taxed at a lower rate than the similar imported product. Competing products must be taxed in such a way as to exclude a protective effect. In the latter case this will not necessarily mean exactly the same tax. As the Court observed in the Spirits cases, paragraph 2 of Article 95, in contrast to the precise comparability of paragraph 1, is 'based upon a more general criterion, in other words the protective nature of the system of internal taxation',[76] So in *Commission* v *United Kingdom*[77] there was no suggestion that beer had to be taxed at exactly the same rate as wine. What was required was that the taxation system adopt criteria that took objectively justifiable account of the nature of the products and removed the protective effect favouring beer.[78]

At this level, then, it is more difficult to show that a breach of Article 95(2) has occurred than a breach of Article 95(1). A simple comparison of rates may be made to reveal discrimination under Article 95(1). Under Article 95(2) a protective effect contained in tax rates that differ must be uncovered. In *Commission* v *Belgium*[79] the Court refused to hold a Belgian system of taxation applicable to beer and wine incompatible with Article 95(2). A value added tax (VAT) rate of 25 per cent was applied to wine,

---

75 Case 168/78, note 59 above; Case 169/78, note 60 above, Case 171/78, note 61 above; and see Case 319/81 *Commission* v *Italy* [1983] ECR 601, para. 17 of the judgment; Case 112/84, note 16 above, para. 14; Case 323/87, note 60 above, para. 13.
76 E.g., Case 168/78, note 59 above, para. 7 of the judgment.
77 Notes 62, 68 above.
78 See note 69 above.
79 Case 356/85 [1987] ECR 3299, [1988] 3 CMLR 277, noted by Lonbay (1989) 14 ELRev 48.

an imported product, whereas a VAT rate of only 19 per cent was applied to beer, a product in which Belgium boasts an enviable specialization. The domestic product bore a lighter tax burden than an imported product with which it competed.[80] However, the Court observed that there is a price differential between beer and wine. Belgian figures showed that a litre of beer costs on average 29.75 Bfr, whereas a litre of ordinary wine costs some 125 Bfr. Consequently, the Court was not satisfied that the minor VAT differential had any protective effect in favour of beer, because its elimination would still have left the prices far apart. This case would perhaps have been decided against Belgium had the Commission prepared its arguments with more care, for, after all, there existed a tax differential, albeit insubstantial, and no worthy reason was advanced for the discrepancy. However, the decision at least illustrates that the notion of protection under Article 95(2) may be more elusive than the direct comparisons that can be made under Article 95(1).[81]

The two paragraphs of Article 95 are in this sense distinct. Under Article 95(1) products, being similar, must be taxed at similar levels. Under Article 95(2) products are competing rather than similar. The Treaty requires that protection be eliminated. In practical application that means that differences in taxation must reflect objective differences in the nature of the product, or, at least, such differences must be so insubstantial as to involve no protective consequences. One would none the less conclude that the Court ought to take more care in its judgments to differentiate between the two paragraphs in order to ensure that states, even where plainly in breach,[82] effect the appropriate remedial action.[83]

DIRECT EFFECT

The economic complexities contained in Article 95(1) and, especially, in Article 95(2) might seem to defeat any argument that the provisions are directly effective. Yet the European Court has held both paragraphs directly effective.[84] Article 95 may be difficult to apply in individual cases where economic calculations must be undertaken, but the basic prohibition

---

80 The Court referred to Case 170/78, note 68 above, to support its view that beer and cheap wine may be in competition with each other.

81 The case may be seen as an example of a *de minimis* approach to Article 95; or, perhaps more accurately, as an illustration that minimal differences confer no protective effect and are therefore not caught by Art. 95(2) at all.

82 See cases at note 75 above.

83 See Lonbay (1989) 14 ELRev 48, 55; Easson (1981) 18 CMLRev 521, 535; Denton (1986) 11 ELRev 309; Danusso and Denton [1990/1] LIEI 67. See also note 69 above.

84 Case 57/65, note 2 above; Case 27/67, note 47 above.

is sufficiently clear in its nature and objective to be held capable of application by a national court. The Court has added that a national tax is unlawful under Article 95 only to the extent that it discriminates on the basis of nationality, but that in national proceedings based on the direct effect of Article 95 it is for the national court to determine whether to order refund of all or simply the discriminatory element of the tax under challenge.[85]

Article 95's direct effect is a valuable contribution to the process of market integration because two routes to effective enforcement are opened up; not simply Commission action under Article 169, but also individuals acting before national courts. In fact, the major provisions for securing the free movement of goods are all directly effective, which renders them invaluable weapons for individual traders confronted by obstructive national tactics.

THE RELATIONSHIP BETWEEN ARTICLES 12 AND 95

COMPLEMENTARY BUT MUTUALLY EXCLUSIVE

Articles 12 and 95 are complementary, yet mutually exclusive.[86] Both are concerned with the control of fiscal charges imposed on goods by member states. Both contribute to the process of market integration. However, although there is no loophole, in that a fiscal charge will fall under one or the other,[87] there is also no room for overlap between the two provisions. A fiscal charge is either considered a customs duty or a charge having equivalent effect thereto (Article 12), or else it forms part of a general system of internal taxation (Article 95). It is entirely logical and necessary that there should be no overlap, for the consequences of the application of the two Treaty provisions are different. A charge that is caught by Article

85 Case 34/67 *Luck* v *Hauptzollamt Köln-Rheinau* [1968] ECR 245; Case 74/76 *Iannelli and Volpi* v *Meroni* [1977] ECR 557. See also on the effect of Community law on national procedural law Case 68/79 *Hans Just I/S* v *Danish Ministry for Fiscal Affairs* [1980] ECR 501, [1981] 2 CMLR 714. Cf. A. Tatham, 'Restitution of charges and duties levied by the public administration in breach of EC law: a comparative analysis' (1994) 19 EL Rev 146.

86 Case 10/65 *Deutschmann* v *Federal Republic of Germany* [1965] ECR 469; Case 57/65, note 2 above.

87 Cases 2, 3/62 *Commission* v *Luxembourg and Belgium* [1962] ECR 425; Case 24/68 *Commission* v *Italy* [1969] ECR 193, para. 5; Cases 2–3/69 *Sociaal Fonds voor de Diamantarbeiders* v *SA Ch Brachfeld Sons* [1969] ECR 211, para. 10.

12 is unlawful, whereas a charge that falls to be considered under Article 95 is lawful except in so far as it contains an element that discriminates according to nationality. None the less, the demarcation between a customs duty and a charge forming part of a general system of internal taxation is not always simple to locate.

One may helpfully return to the Court's definition of a charge having equivalent effect that is caught by Article 12. In *Commission* v *Italy* the Court declared that 'any pecuniary charge . . . which is imposed unilaterally on domestic or foreign goods by reason of the fact that they cross a frontier . . . constitutes a charge having equivalent effect'.[88] Article 12, then, is applicable where the levy is attached to the fact of border crossing. In *Commission* v *France* the Court observed that Article 95 applies 'to a general system of internal dues applied systematically to categories of products in accordance with objective criteria irrespective of the origin of the products'.[89] As long as the charge in question can be accommodated within the internal structure, as long as it is based on criteria that are of general application to aspects such as quality or function rather than to the fact of crossing a border, then the matter falls to be dealt with in accordance with Article 95. It is then appropriate to assess whether the criteria are in any respect contaminated by discrimination on grounds of nationality or whether a protective effect is shown.

Consequently, even a charge levied in respect of a procedure carried out at a border is capable of assessment in the light of Article 95 rather than Article 12, provided the system is of general application. A fee attached to a border control may exceptionally be part of a general system of internal taxation if the same procedure is undertaken in the light of the same criteria in respect of home-produced goods. In *Commission* v *Belgium*[90] it was argued that this test was satisfied in respect of health checks and related fees on imported poultry. The Court accepted that had equivalence between internal and border checks been shown, Article 95 would have been in issue. In such a case the fee would have been levied *not* because of passage across a border, but because of the existence of a general internal system. However, after examination of the circumstances, the Court concluded that the border checks bore an insufficient similarity to the internal regime. It held accordingly that there was no general system, but

88 Case 24/68 [1969] ECR 193.
89 Case 90/79 [1981] ECR 283, para. 14. See also, e.g., Case 87/75 *Bresciani* v *Amministrazione Italiana delle Finanze* [1976] ECR 129, [1976], 2 CMLR 62; Case 132/78 *Denkavit* v *French State* [1979] ECR 1923, [1979] 3 CMLR 605; Case 32/80 *Officier van Justitie* v *Kortmann* [1981] ECR 251, [1982] 3 CMLR 46; Case 158/82 *Commission* v *Denmark* [1983] ECR 3573, [1984] 3 CMLR 658; Case 18/87 *Commission* v *Germany* [1988] ECR 5427, [1990] 1 CMLR 561.
90 Case 314/82 [1984] ECR 1543, [1985] 3 CMLR 134.

rather a special regime for imported goods. Consequently, the matter was subject to Article 12. The Court went on to hold Article 12 infringed.

By contrast the Court found a levy compatible with Article 95 in *Dansk Denkavit*.[91] The sum was demanded annually of all domestic producers and all importers on the same terms. It was designed to cover the costs incurred by the state in performing *ad hoc* inspections held lawful under Article 36.[92] The Court scrutinized the fiscal charge to determine its correct classification,[93] but concluded that it was satisfied that the charge was levied equally on all traders as such rather than on importers as a separate group. The matter was consequently judged in the light of Article 95 and held compatible with it.

THE EXOTIC IMPORT

One particular issue has caused difficulty in allocating a charge for consideration under the correct Treaty provision. Where a state does not itself produce a particular item and therefore has no tax applicable to domestic produce, it might seem that it would be automatically unlawful to tax the item when it is imported. Yet this would deprive a state of the opportunity to tax typically 'foreign' goods, which might seem to go beyond the Treaty's demand for no more than tax neutrality as far as origin is concerned. In *Commission v France*, mentioned above as the source of the Court's definition of the scope of Article 95,[94] French law imposed levies of 3 per cent of value on reprographic equipment such as offset printing machines, stencil duplicators and optical photocopiers sold in France, whether imported or home-produced. The large majority of such machines were imported, so in practice the levy was borne chiefly by importers. The Commission brought the matter before the Court under Article 169 and argued that France was acting in violation of Article 12 in imposing such a levy.[95] The Court declared that the fact that most goods subject to the tax were imported was not enough of itself to conclude the matter. Even a charge borne by an imported product where there is no similar domestic product may fall to be considered as an aspect of a general system of internal taxation within Article 95, not a charge having equivalent effect to a customs duty under Article 12, provided the charge relates 'to a general system of internal dues applied systematically to categories of

---

91 Case 29/87 [1988] ECR 2965, [1990] 1 CMLR 203.
92 See further p. 474 on inspections and related fees.
93 Case 29/87, note 91 above, para. 33 of the judgment.
94 Case 90/79, note 89 above.
95 And Art. 113 as far as machines from outside the Community were concerned.

products in accordance with objective criteria irrespective of the origin of the products'.[96] In assessing the French system the Court was impressed by the fact that the proceeds of the tax were used to support literature and indirectly to reimburse authors and publishers for the loss in sales suffered as a result of the widespread use of reprographic machines to copy texts. In addition, the Court noted that the structure of the tax also accommodated the book trade. In the light of this evidence the Court was prepared to accept that the tax was part of a considered attempt to address the problems created by the type of product subject to the levy. It was not tainted by discrimination or by protectionism and was accordingly lawful.

The Court had the opportunity to return to the point in *Cooperativa Cofrutta*.[97] The case concerned an Italian tax on bananas. Banana production in Italy is confined to Sicily and is insignificant, with the result that the tax was primarily applicable to imported goods. The litigation involved bananas originating in Columbia imported into Italy by Cofrutta from the Benelux countries.[98] The Court held that a tax should in these circumstances be considered in the light of Article 95, provided that it is part of a general system applying systematically to different categories of product. This reflects the approach adopted in relation to the French tax on reprographic equipment and, as suggested above, it seems entirely correct as a matter of policy, for otherwise a state would be prevented from taxing products that it does not itself grow or produce. In determining whether the Italian banana tax formed part of a broader internal taxation system the Court referred to the existence in Italian law of nineteen taxes on the consumption of a range of products including coffee, cocoa, sugar, margarine, tobacco and oils. These nineteen taxes were governed by common rules and shared the purpose of raising general revenue for the state.[99] None of the taxes was origin specific. This persuaded the Court that the banana tax formed 'an integral part of a general system of internal dues within the meaning of Article 95 of the Treaty'.[100] However, this did not conclude the matter. Having determined that the matter fell for assessment in the light of

---

96 Case 90/79, note 89 above, para. 14 of the judgment. See similarly Case C-343/90 *Manuel José Lourenço Dias* v *Director da Alfândega do Porto*, judgment of 16 July 1992.

97 Case 193/85 *Cooperativa Cofrutta* v *Amministrazione delle Finanze dello Stato* [1987] ECR 2085, noted by Lonbay (1989) 14 ELRev 48. See also Case 184/85 *Commission* v *Italy* [1987] ECR 2013, which deals with the same tax.

98 Belgium, Netherlands, Luxembourg. The case thus also decides that Art. 95 applies to all goods in free circulation in the Community irrespective of their original source; see also p. 487 Case 41/76 *Donckerwolcke* v *Procureur de la République* [1976] ECR 1921, [1977] 2 CMLR 535 (Art. 30) and, generally, p. 21.

99 Contrast Case 158/82 *Commission* v *Denmark* [1983] ECR 3573: groundnut tax held in breach of Arts. 9 *et seq.* due to the absence of the necessary 'much larger number of products determined by general and objective criteria'; para. 24 of the judgment.

100 Case 193/85, note 97 above, para. 13 of the judgment.

Article 95, it was then necessary to establish that no breach of the terms of Article 95 had occurred. At this point the Italian system was shown to fall foul of Community law. Bananas were considered dissimilar to table fruit typical of Italian production for the purposes of Article 95(1), but the Court was persuaded that bananas competed with other fruit for the purposes of Article 95(2).[101] This meant that Italian tax law could not afford indirect protection to domestic fruit through its level of taxation of bananas. The Court held that Italy's banana-tax law was set at relatively too high a level and that it consequently exerted a prohibited protective effect.[102] The Court concluded that a tax primarily imposed on imported goods was capable of being considered in the light of Article 95 and of complying with it, but that in the case the protective effect incompatible with Article 95(2) appeared fatal to the tax.

Article 95 does not control domestic taxation of imports where there is no similar or competing national product. In such circumstances neither discrimination nor protection may arise. However, in *Commission* v *Denmark*[103] the Court held that taxation of products outside Article 95 at a level that imperils the free movement of goods may be susceptible to control under Article 30. The scope of this ruling is unclear and may serve to blur the distinction between the treatment of fiscal and non-fiscal barriers to trade to the detriment of legal certainty.[104] In any event, such a levy may violate Article 12 in so far as it is shown to be imposed by reason of the product having crossed a frontier.[105]

THE APPLICATION OF ARTICLE 95 TO EXPORTS

Article 95 makes no reference to exports. In order to forbid disguised export subsidies Article 96 prohibits the repayment to an exporter of a sum exceeding the internal duty, but Article 96 does not bear directly on the problem of the internal system that makes special provision for goods for export. In the absence of explicit coverage in the Treaty it has been for

---

101 Cf. Art. 86, Case 27/76 *United Brands Co.* v *Commission* [1978] ECR 207, p. 729 below.

102 Case 193/85, note 97 above, p. 2099, AG Lenz examined the motive behind the tax; see Danusso and Denton [1990/1] LIEI 67, 88–9. However, the Court's analysis is based on effect and this approach seems more in tune with Community trade law generally; see, e.g., p. 432 on Art. 30.

103 Case C-47/88, [1990] ECR I-4509.

104 See note 9 above.

105 See notes 88 and 99 above.

the Court to develop an approach based on the intent of the Treaty.

There are two possible discriminatory practices: taxing exports at a lower rate than domestic products, and taxing exports at a higher rate. In the first case the Court has expressed the view that a preference given to exports is not incompatible with the Treaty. The discrimination is against the domestic market and consequently does not act as an impediment to cross-border trade. Such 'reverse discrimination' escapes the application of Community law.[106] However, taxation of exports at a higher level than goods destined for the home market is likely to discourage free trade between member states. For that reason the application of Community law is necessary. The Court has accordingly extended the explicit terms of Article 95 to cover fiscal discrimination against exports and in *Statens Kontrol v Larsen*[107] it insisted that Community law contains a general principle of tax neutrality with regard not only to imported goods, but also to goods for export. Consequently, a state that seeks to restrain the export of a valuable scarce commodity through tax disincentives acts in violation of Article 95. The Court's use of Article 95 in this context is a clear example of its willingness to seek its primary guidance from the broad objectives of the Treaty rather than the explicit terms of particular provisions.

FISCAL HARMONIZATION

THE NEED

Article 95 goes no further than an insistence that discrimination on grounds of nationality shall not contaminate the internal taxation systems of member states. However, such equal treatment of goods within each state is not sufficient to eliminate obstacles to trade within the Community. States operate different taxation systems.[108] Taxes imposed in a great variety of fields differ according to national preference. So, for example, in the case of excise duties on wine and beer the rates levied in the United Kingdom, Denmark and especially Ireland are far above the norm and many times greater than in some of the southern countries, where rates are the lowest in the Community. A comparable picture emerges from an analysis of the regime applicable to tobacco. VAT has been developed as a

---

106 Case 86/78, note 12 above. In exceptional circumstances such a situation may be susceptible to control under Art. 92 as a state aid; see p. 879.
107 Case 142/77 [1978] ECR 1543.
108 For a brief survey, see El-Agraa, *Economics of the European Community*, Ch. 14.

Community system,[109] yet it remains permissible for rates to differ from state to state. The United Kingdom, for example, has exemptions for certain products that are not applied in other states.

Thus, a product exported from Greece to Denmark cannot freely enter the Danish market or else it will evade Danish competence to levy internal taxation. It would also incidentally gain a substantial competitive advantage over a Danish product marketed in Denmark resulting not from the inherent nature of the product, but from the different approaches of the governments. Such tax discrepancies have for centuries contributed to the attraction of smuggling. The trade barrier maintained at the national border for the purposes of tax collection thus arises because of the existence of different national systems of taxation, even where those systems are internally non-discriminatory. States are entitled to demand sums from importers to reflect, for example, their chosen higher VAT rates, subject only to the Court's insistence that VAT levied on imports takes account of VAT paid but neither refunded nor refundable in the exporting state.[110] Article 95 eliminates internal discrimination within a member state, but not divergences between member states.[111] It does not go far enough to bring about full market integration.

OBSTACLES

Steps towards market integration must involve, at least, administrative coordination between national authorities and, at the most ambitious level, legislative action to harmonize the different tax regimes of the member states. In the event of fiscal equalization, fixing tax rates would ultimately become the preserve of the Community authorities. However, it is hardly surprising that this result, although doubtless a logical element in the creation of a common market, has evoked great concern and, in many cases, resistance at national level. Raising revenue is a cherished aspect of national sovereignty. Transfer of this power to the Community is a very visible and, to some, alarming manifestation of diminution in national sovereignty. Moreover, apart from concerns about relinquishing power, there are genuine practical difficulties in achieving fiscal harmonization at

---

109 See especially the Sixth Directive, 77/388 OJ 1977 L145/1. For background see McLennan, 'The Process of Harmonization of the Value-Added Tax in the European Community' (1991) 29 Col J Transnat L 69.
110 Case 15/81 *Schul* [1982] ECR 1409, noted by Barents (1986) 23 CMLRev 641, 655; Cases C-120/88, C-119/89 *Commission v Italy, Spain, Greece* [1991] ECR I-621, 641, 691. See Kapteyn and Verloren van Themaat, *Law of the European Communities*, p. 372; Green, Hartley and Usher, *Single European Market*, pp. 45-7.
111 Art. 30 is in this respect broader in its field of application; see Ch. 15.

Community level. The divergence between different national systems of taxation is not simply an unfortunate accident that can be corrected by the bureaucrats. Taxes are imposed for a great many reasons beyond the obvious objective of raising revenue for the state. Taxes reflect social concerns; they can act as a method of wealth distribution. Tax systems can be used as part of health policy, by increasing the tax load on products considered harmful, such as tobacco and alcohol. Pollution can be curbed by inducing better practice through tax concessions.[112] Regional policy is often based on tax inducement. Charities are helped through tax concessions. The functions of a taxation system, then, are manifold and it is quite wrong to view the types of national tax rules discussed in this chapter simply as revenue-raising mechanisms that act as troublesome distortions of free trade. Taxation involves politics, not simply economics. In fact, if the Community wishes to adopt common tax policies for the Community as a whole, it must address all the types of issue related to the function of taxation mentioned above. It must establish a policy on wealth distribution, regional policy, health policy and many other such matters because only by identifying the role of such objectives is it possible to formulate the structure of a tax system. Given the heterogeneity of political ideologies in the Community, as well as different national traditions in tax policy that divide even those of similar political persuasion, it has proved immensely difficult for the Community to make much progress in this area. Developments have generally been cautious and limited in their scope. The Community has concentrated on three areas: VAT, excise duties and corporation tax. The Community has left personal income tax well alone. Coordination of the operation of national systems has proved more feasible than the establishment of a common Community system. There is as yet nothing remotely comparable to a comprehensive Community tax system.

The delicacy of this area was reflected in the Single European Act. Article 8a EEC established the task of the completion of the internal market by the end of 1992.[113] Article 100a introduced qualified majority voting for measures related to the completion of the internal market in order to accelerate the process by, if necessary, overriding minority objections, yet measures related to fiscal harmonization were excluded from this advance by Article 100a(2). In the tax field unanimity remains necessary under either Article 100 or Article 99. Minority objections can still block progress, although in reality such is the complexity of this area that

112 Grabitz and Zacker, 'Scope for action by the EC Member States for the improvement of environmental protection under EEC law: the example of environmental taxes and subsidies' (1989) 26 CMLRev 423.
113 Ch. 1, pp. 8, 24. Art. 8a EEC is now Art. 7a EC.

objections have at some stage been presented on most issues by most member states. Unlike some issues relating to social policy, this is not an area where there exists a majority of agreed states and just one dissentient.[114] The amendments agreed at Maastricht effected no change to the requirement of unanimity for the adoption of fiscal measures.

DEVELOPMENTS

The 1985 White Paper on completing the internal market set out a range of ideas for dealing with fiscal barriers to trade.[115] These ideas have undergone significant refinement as a result of subsequent negotiations. Tax equalization is not a serious prospect and is in any event scarcely conceivable in the absence of a single currency.[116] Yet it is essential to eliminate border controls and to remove the inefficient trade distortions caused by differential tax rates. The task is to establish a structure that, while permitting states a degree of fiscal autonomy,[117] will not unduly inhibit the free flow of commerce between them.

Value-added tax

As the 1992 'deadline' approached the states were able to agree significant progress in the area of indirect taxation. In 1991 an agreement was reached in relation to the application of VAT in intra-Community trade from the start of 1993. This is a transitional plan and the intention was that it would be replaced by permanent arrangements from the start of 1997, subject to agreement in 1995 on long-term practical structures.[118] Reaching such agreement appears increasingly problematic.

Under the transitional plan transactions between persons subject to tax in different states are taxed in the state of importation, the state of the purchaser.[119] There is no border control. The administrative responsibility is taken away from national officials at border posts and transferred to the firms themselves. The seller invoices the goods without VAT. On periodic VAT returns it shows the level of intra-Community sales, providing

114 Ch. 20, p. 644; the dissentient is the UK.
115 COM (85) 310, Part III. See Easson, Ch. 10 in Bieber *et al.* (eds.) *1992*; Biehl, Ch. 11 in Bieber *et al.* (eds), *1992*; Van der Zanden and Terra, 'The Removal of Tax Barriers; White Paper from the Commission to the European Council/The Creation of an Internal Market; Follow up to the White Paper' [1989/1] LIEL 137.
116 For progress towards this objective see Ch. 21.
117 The principle of subsidiarity has been invoked in this sphere; see p. 12.
118 Dir. 91/680 OJ 1991 L376/1.
119 There are limited exceptions; e.g., mail-order selling is taxed in the country of origin.

supplementary information about total sales per client. On its tax return the buyer indicates total purchases from other member states and pays the VAT due. Larger companies complete a monthly declaration of transactions. A system has been established for collecting statistics on trade between member states direct from businesses.[120] This is known as INTRASTAT. This privatization of administrative functions is an imaginative attempt to achieve market integration by shifting the emphasis away from the relevance of physical borders, yet the possibilities of fraud are increased. The Community recognizes this potential problem and aims to establish anti-fraud mechanisms that do not impose undue burdens on business. In January 1992 the member states agreed measures to combat fraud that included the initiation of an automated information network linking national tax authorities.[121] The facilitation of cross-checking of tax records should restrict the opportunities for firms to arrange their trade so that deals slip through the tax net. Administrative cooperation/integration is thus being developed in response to commercial integration.[122]

Equalization of the VAT rates themselves has not occurred. Instead, a minimum standard rate of 15 per cent, with no fixed upper limit, has been set. There are very limited exceptions under which rates below 15 per cent may be set.[123] The absence of an upper limit is a concession that respects national tax autonomy, but it seems unlikely to lead to significant divergences between member states. Competition between regulators will cause the rates of the member states to converge. In general, no state will wish to take the option of setting an unusually high rate for fear of losing trade to its partners.[124]

The permanent system planned for 1997 envisages a switch from payment in the state of destination to payment in the state of origin. Payment of VAT on intra-Community purchases will be made in the state of origin, the state of the seller. Thus the exporter simply charges VAT to the customer in another member state and pays it to its own tax authorities. The customer deducts the VAT paid from its own tax payments. The Commission believes that this structure should remove any distinction between sales within a member state and sales between member states.

It is proving difficult to resolve the formidably complicated questions of

120 Reg. 3330/91 OJ 1991 L316/1.
121 Reg. 218/92 OJ 1992 L24/1.
122 Such administrative structures are required in many areas other than tax; see, e.g., links between agencies responsible for the enforcement of consumer protection laws, p. 526.
123 Dir. 92/77 OJ 1992 L316/1; Dir. 92/111 OJ 1992 L384/47. Existing zero rates, important to the UK, are permitted to remain in place for the time being.
124 See a comparable pattern in company law regulation, p. 600: the 'race to the bottom'.

detail that are indispensable to the envisaged switch from the transitional scheme to the permanent scheme. It is possible that it will be necessary to delay the switch. The Community legislation provides that the transitional scheme will continue automatically until the permanent system enters into force. Tellingly, Mme Scrivener, the responsible Commissioner, had expressed determination in the course of 1994 to present proposals for the permanent regime by the end of 1994, but in December 1994, shortly before the portfolio passed to Mario Monti, she admitted that this timescale had been too ambitious. She also commented that she considered the transitional arrangements had operated successfully.[125]

It remains to be seen how the Commission will proceed. It is possible that a delay will be beneficial. Extended experience under the transitional system may yield valuable insights into the practicality of the system. Although a permanent system based on the origin principle offers a less complex structure and enjoys 'the advantage of theoretical purity',[126] it may emerge that the transitional scheme is sufficiently workable in practice to justify abandonment of the tortuous pursuit of the planned permanent scheme.[127]

Excise duties

Excise duties, widely imposed on alcohol, tobacco and petrol, have long caused problems in the pursuit of market integration because of large variations in rates between the member states. Directive 92/12[128] established general arrangements for products subject to excise duty and on the holding, movement and monitoring of such products. These arrangements were refined in certain technical aspects by Directive 92/108.[129] A sharp distinction is drawn between the treatment of commercial cross-border trade and the activities of private consumers.

From the start of 1993 goods subject to excise duty have moved between 'bonded warehouses' within the member states, thereby eliminating border controls. Release of goods from the warehouses triggers the obligation to pay duty in the state of destination. Spot checks are designed to ensure fraud does not occur.

Private individuals have long been impeded from shopping across borders because of the obstacles arising out of differences between excise

---

125 *Financial Times*, 14 December 1994, p. 2. Cf. also, in this vein, Farmer and Lyal, *EC Tax Law* p. 337.
126 Farmer and Lyal, *EC Tax Law*, p. 337.
127 This possibility is mooted by Easson, *Taxation in the European Community*, p. 142.
128 OJ 1992 L76/1.
129 OJ 1992 L390/124.

duties. States have required an adjustment to be paid when goods are imported from another member state even where excise duty has already been paid in that other state, subject only to rather low concessionary allowances to individual travellers. In principle such barriers cannot survive the creation of an internal market. It was accordingly agreed that Community residents can bring home with them alcohol, tobacco, petrol, and other products bought in any member state.[130] These opportunities have been available since the start of 1993 and they represent one of the most tangible benefits of the internal market to the ordinary citizen. Naturally, consumers have seized their chance to cross borders in pursuit of prices lower than those on offer in their home market. Where the price differential is attributable to divergent tax rates, whether VAT or excise duties, a state that levies relatively high taxes will find its income depleted by the readiness of consumers to make their purchases elsewhere. The proliferation of outlets specializing in alcoholic drinks in the French Channel ports is a direct consequence of the removal of restrictions on consumer importation combined with the sharp discrepancy between French and British policies towards excise duties. A state unwilling to accept the shortfall in tax revenues may choose to raise rates, but this risks even higher levels of cross-border shopping. The alternative is a reduction in rates to competitive levels in order to remove the incentive to shop elsewhere.

However, it is necessary to establish when a large personal allowance is in reality a small commercial operation, in respect of which the bonded warehouse system mentioned above continues to apply. Notional upper limits have been set. These are designed merely to help to identify when activities are properly regarded as commercial. It remains the case that there is *no* limit placed on the importation of goods that are genuinely destined for private consumption.

The risks of fraud and the distortions in consumer buying patterns that flow from variation between rates state by state could be usefully reduced by harmonization of excise duties. Some progress was made in a flurry of Directives adopted in October 1992. These measures mirror the pattern of VAT harmonization by setting minimum figures, which preserve the opportunity for member states to fix higher rates. Directives 92/79 and 92/80[131] require the application of minimum duties on cigarettes and other tobacco products respectively. Directives 92/81 and 92/82[132] govern minimum rates for petroleum products. Directives 92/83 and 92/84[133] cover the harmonization of the structure and of the rates respectively of excise duties

130 Dirs. 92/12, 92/108, notes 128, 129 above.
131 OJ 1992 L316/8, 10.
132 OJ 1992 L316/12, 19.
133 OJ 1992 L316/21, 39.

on alcoholic beverages. Minimum rates are set for beer, wine and other defined categories of alcoholic beverage. The intractable nature of the job of harmonization in this area is strikingly revealed by the chosen minimum figure for excise rates levied on still and sparkling wine. It is zero. This reflects the vast gulf between states such as Italy and Greece, which do not tax wine, and those like the United Kingdom and Ireland which tax wine rather heavily. Taxation of alcohol may be presented as a measure of health policy, but the congruence of high-taxing states and low-producing states is no coincidence.[134] It is stretching language to regard a minimum rate set at zero as harmonization.

These measures represent the bare minimum that the member states were able to agree in advance of the planned deadline for the completion of the internal market. The member states were prepared to open their borders on the basis of these measures and to accept the distortions in trade that would flow from disparity between rates. As the market develops, it remains to be seen whether further steps towards alignment of excise duties are regarded by the member states as necessary and, if so, whether it is feasible to secure agreement on more ambitious schemes.

'Duty-free' shops at ports and airports offer goods that are not subject to tax and duty. Again, such arrangements seem incompatible with the successful completion of a single market. The benefit of such schemes would be lost to the consumer, but the price competition and cross-border shopping opportunities that would ensue from market integration would be more generally beneficial. However, as part of the package agreed in 1991 the Council decided that duty-free shopping could survive until 1 July 1999, although it declared that this should not delay the abolition of physical border controls.[135] 'Duty-free' will then be limited to the Community's external borders.

---

134 See Case 170/78, notes 62, 68 above, which led to adjustment of the UK's tax on wine. Art. 95, however, requires only non-discrimination.
135 Dir. 91/680, note 118 above. The allowances were increased by Dir. 94/4 OJ 1994 L60/14.

CHAPTER 15

Article 30: Prohibition on Quantitative Restrictions

SCOPE

Article 30 is the principal provision in the Treaty designed to eliminate national barriers to the free movement of goods that are not fiscal in character.[1] It forms a key component in the establishment of an economic area in which market forces operate freely without the restraint of national boundaries. It has been developed by the Court into a broad anti-protectionist charter. The vigour of Article 30 lies in its remarkable scope.[2] It covers tangible physical barriers to trade, such as formalities imposed at the frontier of a member state, and extends to more subtle barriers to trade, such as a government-sponsored campaign in favour of home-produced goods or a requirement that a manufacturer must have a presence in the state in which a product is marketed. Furthermore, Article 30 has been used to challenge national rules that apply equally to domestic and imported goods, such as those governing the permitted ingredients of foodstuffs. Such rules apply to all products, wherever produced, but have the effect of impeding the sale of products from other states where manufacture occurs in accordance with different traditions. Article 30 is capable of prohibiting national rules even in this area and consequently Community law may be used to challenge rules that on their face are quite irrelevant to cross-frontier trade. There are exceptional circumstances in which member states may legitimately maintain barriers to the free movement of goods, but the state wishing to make such an exceptional case bears a heavy burden of proof. Moreover, Community harmonization initiatives have steadily reduced the scope of unilateral member state action that may

---

1 Chs. 13 and 14 cover fiscal barriers. In Case 74/76 *Ianelli and Volpi* v *Meroni* [1977] ECR 557 the Court insisted on the need to maintain a distinction between the treatment of fiscal and non-fiscal barriers to trade under Community law. See also Cases C-78-83/90 *Société Compagnie Commerciale de l'Ouest and Others* v *Receveur Principal des Douanes*, [1992] ECR I-1847.
2 For a survey of the type of measure capable of falling within Article 30 see Mattera, 'Protectionism inside the EC', (1984) JWTL 283.

permissibly restrain trade. The completion of the internal market has involved determined legislative action to eliminate remaining obstacles to trade.

LEGISLATIVE INTERPRETATION

Article 30 is striking for its brevity:

Quantitative restrictions on imports and all measures having equivalent effect shall, without prejudice to the following provisions, be prohibited between Member States.

Article 34 applies a similarly worded prohibition to quantitative restrictions on exports. Article 36 provides member states with the opportunity to justify prima-facie breaches of Articles 30 and 34 in accordance with narrowly defined heads, such as the protection of public health and morality.

The idea of the 'quantitative restriction' or 'quota system' is well established in international trade law.[3] The typical case involves state A imposing a numerical limit on the imports of a certain product from state B. The purpose of such a system is commonly to offer protection to the industry of state A that produces the item in question. Such trade restrictions are, if anything, more prejudicial to free trade than the fiscal barriers discussed in Chapter 14, because they impose an absolute ban on trade beyond the stipulated ceiling of imports, rather than simply rendering importation more expensive. Indeed, in extreme cases state A may completely forbid any imports from state B. It is well established that in Community law both a partial restraint and an absolute ban on importation constitute 'quantitative restrictions' caught by Article 30.[4] Plainly, quotas run contrary to the very notion of a common market and their incompatibility with Article 30 is a fundamental tenet of the Community's substantive law. In practice, it has rarely proved necessary to challenge numerical quotas under Community law, for quotas on trade between member states were in the main abolished by virtue of international agreements during the 1950s.[5]

Article 30's remarkable evolution into an instrument for the removal of

---

3 See, e.g., Jackson, *World Trade*; McGovern, *International Trade Regulation*.
4 Case 2/73 *Geddo v Ente nazionale Risi* [1973] ECR 865, [1974] 1 CMLR 13. See further Case 34/79 *R v Henn and Darby* [1979] ECR 3795, p. 455 below.
5 Under the auspices of the GATT and the OEEC (later OECD).

a wide range of hindrances to the free movement of goods is attributable to the second limb of the Article 30 definition. It was always assumed that the quantitative restriction or quota, covered by the first limb, is unlawful; the majority of the case law and writing on Article 30 has concentrated on the second limb, the notion of the 'measure having equivalent effect' to the quantitative restriction, often abbreviated to the MEQR. Whereas the quota is well understood as an element of trade policy, the measure having equivalent effect is much harder to pin down. The European Court has elaborated the notion of the MEQR through a long line of case law to the point where it has become an instrument for tackling national laws that are far removed from the relatively simple idea of a numerical limit on imports. The objectives of the free movement of goods in particular and of market integration in general have been greatly advanced by eliminating a host of national rules that have an effect on trade on the basis that they constitute MEQRs contrary to Article 30.

In 1970 a Directive was adopted with a view to amplifying the meaning of Article 30.[6] As a matter of form,[7] the Directive applies only to measures to be abolished by the end of the transitional period, which expired at the end of 1969 for the original six states. However, the interpretative guidance contained in Directive 70/50 has endured beyond that deadline and two decades later the Directive is still an occasional visitor to the Court's judgments.[8] To read the Directive is to obtain a useful broad picture of the nature of Article 30 and the types of practice that are subject to it.

Articles 2 and 3 of the Directive establish a separation between two types of national measure that are capable of falling within the scope of Article 30 of the Treaty. Article 2 of the Directive covers rules that have come to be termed discriminatory or distinctly applicable; that is, rules that treat imported products less favourably than home-produced goods. The prohibition is triggered if imports are subjected to a condition that domestically produced goods are not expected to satisfy, or if different conditions are applied where the condition applicable to the import is more onerous. Article 2(3) of the Directive supplies a long illustrative list, ranging from fixing the prices of imports, to a requirement that imports be supported by guarantees, to the application exclusively to imports of rules relating to the size, shape or presentation of the product. In fact, nineteen different practices are mentioned in Article 2 of the Directive. None the less, the list is not exhaustive.

Article 3 suggests a still broader scope to Article 30's prohibition on

6 Dir. 70/50 JO 1970 L13/29.
7 The Directive was based on Art. 33(7) EEC.
8 E.g., Case 74/76, note 1 above; Case 145/88 *Torfaen BC* v *B&Q plc* [1989] ECR 765, p. 533 below.

MEQRs. It covers non-discriminatory, indistinctly applicable rules; rules that apply equally on their face to all goods irrespective of origin, but are nevertheless capable of impeding imports. Directive 70/50 concedes that rules that apply equally to domestic and imported products are simply a manifestation of the differences between the commercial laws of the member states themselves, and that therefore such rules normally do not constitute MEQRs. However, Article 3 indicates that where apparently equally applicable rules exert a restrictive effect on trade that 'exceeds the effects intrinsic to trade rules', then a breach of Article 30 may be established.

JUDICIAL INTERPRETATION

Directive 70/50 is valuable as a means of elaborating the nature and purpose of Article 30 of the Treaty. Its recognition that there is a distinction between two types of measure that are capable of falling foul of Article 30 is particularly useful. However, the Directive has been shown to be little more than a pointer. The evolution of Article 30 is primarily attributable to the jurisprudence of the European Court, rather than Community legislation. A cascade of case law has shaped Article 30 into a formidable and flexible instrument in the legal campaign against national rules that restrict the free circulation of goods in the Community. The Court's activity in this area provides a typical example of its general role as the innovative developer of the economic law of the Community, 'which is essentially evolutive and in constant need of adaptation'.[9] It is a process that has led English judges to remark with evident surprise on the Court's capacity for judicial lawmaking,[10] but it is inherent in the task of the Community's institutions in transforming the bare bones of the Treaty into a living, adaptable legal system.

In *Procureur du Roi v Dassonville* the Court set out what has come to be regarded as its standard definition of the scope of Article 30, stating that it prohibits as MEQRs 'all trading rules enacted by Member States which are capable of hindering, directly or indirectly, actually or potentially, intra-Community trade'.[11] The litigation arose from Belgian legislation

---

9 Mathijsen, *European Union Law*, p. 84.
10 In relation to Art. 30 see, e.g., May LJ in *R v Secretary of State for Social Security, ex parte Bomore* [1986] 1 CMLR 228, 234; Mustill LJ in *WH Smith v Peterborough CC* [1990] 2 CMLR 577, 585.
11 Case 8/74 [1974] ECR 837, [1974] 2 CMLR 436, para. 5 of the judgment.

that required an importer of Scotch whisky to hold a certificate of authenticity issued by the British customs authorities. Whisky had reached Belgium from Scotland via France, where no such certificate was required, and consequently the consignment was not accompanied by the necessary documentation. As a result of the certification requirement, the Belgian market was effectively closed to the whisky importer. It was argued that the Belgian law contravened Article 30. The matter was referred to the European Court under the Article 177 preliminary reference procedure. The Court took the opportunity to lay down the formula referred to above. It is plain that goods in free circulation within the Community were liable to meet a barrier in the event of importation into Belgium. Only importers of whisky direct from Scotland could readily satisfy Belgian law, which led to distortion in patterns of trade in Scotch whisky. The facts disclosed a clear restrictive effect on free trade, a breach of Article 30.

The striking feature of the Court's interpretation of Article 30 in *Dassonville* is that it concentrates on the *effect* of the national practice, not its form. The objectionable feature of the MEQR lies in its effect as an impediment to the integration of the market.[12] The precise legal form that the practice takes is not of direct relevance. The Court's approach in this landmark case is not incompatible with that found in Directive 70/50, but the Court in *Dassonville* appears to place a firmer emphasis on the vigour of Article 30 as a means of dismantling restrictive national rules. In its many subsequent decisions in cases that have raised Article 30 the Court has normally preferred to base its approach on this judicial interpretation of the Treaty rather than on Directive 70/50. The law focuses on the restrictive effect of the national rule. In this way Article 30 and, particularly, the flexible notion of the MEQR, is employed as a powerful means of challenging protectionism practised by member states, thereby securing the advancement of the Treaty objective of market integration.[13]

Although the *Dassonville* formula displays a sweeping scope, the Court suggested in its judgment that a limit may exist. In the absence of Community rules governing the relevant area, state action to suppress unfair practices may conform with Community law if 'reasonable'.[14] On the facts of the case this test did not appear to be satisfied, because procedures for proving origin were readily available only to direct importers of whisky, instead of being available generally to all traders. The

12 A connection should be made with the requirement of an effect on patterns of trade in Community competition law, discussed in Ch. 22.
13 See in particular Art. 2 EC; Ch. 1, p. 19.
14 Case 8/74, note 11 above, para. 6 of the judgment.

Belgian rules were unreasonably restrictive. The idea that reasonable measures may be lawful despite their hindrance to trade has come to be termed the 'rule of reason' within the *Dassonville* formula. Its importance as a potential escape clause for national rules that restrict intra-Community trade is plain, yet the precise nature of the 'rule of reason' was not articulated by the Court in *Dassonville*. The Court's subsequent creative treatment of available areas of residual national competence is a key issue in exploring the scope of Article 30.[15]

It should immediately be declared that the Court's approach sometimes lacks consistency. In part this is due to the impossibility of creating a consistent body of law out of the accidents of litigation. The Court cannot dictate the submission of ideal disputes on which it can supply model answers; it must work within the confines of the complicated material that reaches it as a result of trade disputes. In addition, however, the Court has at times contributed to the complexity of this area through some rather opaque decisions. The *Dassonville* definition itself, for example, straddles the distinction between discriminatory and equally applicable rules that is made in Articles 2 and 3 of Directive 70/50, and the application of *Dassonville* has led the Court into some difficulty in locating the outer margin of Article 30. The terms of the *Dassonville* formula could even be taken so far as to catch *any* rule that affects commercial freedom. In November 1993, the Court chose to 're-examine and clarify' its case law in *Keck and Mithouard*[16] where it stated that

the application to products from other Member States of national provisions restricting or prohibiting certain selling arrangements is not such as to hinder, directly or indirectly, actually or potentially, trade between Member States within the meaning of the *Dassonville* judgment (Case 8/74 [1974] ECR 837), provided that those provisions apply to all affected traders operating within the national territory and provided that they affect in the same manner, in law and in fact, the marketing of domestic products and of those from other Member States.[17]

A challenge to national trading rules is dependent on the demonstration of a special impact on imports. The outer limits of Article 30 in the light of *Keck* are examined more fully in Chapter 17.[18]

---

15 See further Ch. 17.
16 Joined Cases C-267 and C-268/91 [1993] ECR I-6097, [1995] 1 CMLR 101.
17 Para. 16 of the judgment.
18 Pp. 532–42 below.

THE DISTINCTLY APPLICABLE MEASURE

If a member state discriminates against imported products, then, prima facie, Article 30 is breached. The phrase 'distinctly applicable' refers to the fact that such discriminatory rules make a distinction between imported goods and domestic goods. This is in contrast to 'indistinctly applicable' rules, which make no such distinction (yet may nevertheless restrict trade) and are the subject of separate treatment.[19] The Court has had to deal with a large number of cases in which discriminatory, distinctly applicable practices have been held unlawful under Article 30. In accordance with the *Dassonville* formula, the Court concentrates on the restrictive effect of the national regulations rather than the legal form that they may assume. Consequently, examples of the Court's decisions are useful illustrations of the type of practice falling within the concept of the MEQR, but must not be considered in any sense exhaustive of the scope of Article 30. Equally, there is only a limited value in analysing Article 30 through sub-division of the case law according to the subject-matter of the national regulation under challenge, for the Court's primary concern is with the distortive effect of the measure, not with its form or content. The following analysis therefore is a broad portrayal of the nature and purpose of Article 30.

IMPORT RESTRICTIONS AND CUSTOMS CONTROLS

In *Denkavit Futtermittel GmbH* v *Minister für Ernährung*[20] veterinary inspections of imported feedstuffs were undertaken by the German authorities as a means of preventing the spread of disease. This was not a quota system, because no numerical limit on imports was in issue. It was, however, a measure having equivalent effect thereto, an MEQR. There was a restriction on trade between member states, covered by the *Dassonville* formula and detrimental to the stimulus of competition. There is no doubt that the imposition of such administrative burdens is in principle in breach of Article 30 in view of the restrictive effect on trade.[21] It is always open to member states to submit justifications for their action under Article 36. Health inspections may be upheld in this manner despite their restrictive effect, but it will be incumbent on the state to demonstrate the existence of

19 See Ch. 17.
20 Case 251/78 [1979] ECR 3369.
21 See also Case C-205/89 *Commission* v *Greece* [1991] ECR I-1361.

a genuine health risk and that the measures taken are no more restrictive than is necessary to combat the threat. In *Denkavit Futtermittel* this was left to be assessed by the national court, for the case was an Article 177 reference.[22] If the Community has established its own harmonized regime in the sector in question, reliance on Article 36 is in principle excluded. However, a member state may be able to find justification for its practices, depending on the terms of the harmonized rules.[23]

Bouhelier[24] involved Article 34, which is the provision parallel to Article 30 applicable to exports. The case arose out of a French requirement that watches for export be subjected to a quality inspection. No such test was demanded of watches produced for the home market. The effect was to hinder the free movement of goods between France and other member states, and the Court indicated that such a system infringes Article 34.

Import and export restrictions cost the Community economy money. They impose direct costs on traders and indirect costs on the competitive structure of the market by interfering with the stimulus of efficient competition. A strict application of Articles 30 and 34 is appropriate and the Court has consistently used them to prohibit regulations applied exclusively to goods crossing a frontier, even where those restrictions are of a relatively insignificant nature. A potential restrictive effect on imports is sufficient for Article 30 to apply and the Court appears to have set its face against any *de minimis* exception. So in *Commission* v *UK*,[25] a case that involved restrictions on the import of UHT milk, the Court declared that 'Article 30 precludes the application to intra-Community trade of national provisions which require, even as a pure formality, import licences or any other similar procedure'. Nor may a state escape a finding that it is in breach of Article 30 by arguing that exemption from its import formalities is freely given in the case of intra-Community trade. The very existence of an exemption system is liable to create uncertainty in the minds of importers and thereby to deter free trade. The operation of an administrative exemption procedure conceals and impairs the fundamental principle of unobstructed free movement, and consequently violates Article 30.[26] In establishing this firm stance against trade barriers the Court has gone beyond Article 2 of Directive 70/50, which appears to exclude mere formalities from the scope of Article 30. This provides an example of a

22 Art. 36 is examined in more detail in Ch. 16.
23 See further pp. 478–82.
24 Case 53/76 [1977] ECR 197, [1977] 1 CMLR 436.
25 Case 124/81 [1983] ECR 203, [1983] 2 CMLR 1.
26 Cases 51–4/71 *International Fruit Company* v *Produktschap voor Groenten en Fruit* [1971] ECR 1107; Case 68/76 *Commission* v *France* [1977] ECR 515; Case 27/80 *Fietje* [1980] ECR 3839; Case 124/81 note 25 above; Case C-304/88 *Commission* v *Belgium* [1990] ECR I-2801.

judicial insistence on the principle of free trade enshrined in Article 30 that surpasses the Commission's interpretative approach contained in Community legislation.[27]

Prior to the completion of the internal market, this did not mean that customs controls between member states were unlawful, but it did mean that any such impediments to trade required justification under Community law. As a matter of general observation such justification was found in the several areas in which the Community had not yet achieved comprehensive common rules through harmonization of national rules.[28] Thus, customs controls designed to facilitate the levy of internal taxation in conformity with the requirements of Article 95[29] were compatible with Article 30. The Court also accepted that the collection at frontiers of statistical data on the movement of goods within the Community could be justifiable.[30] The incomplete nature of the Community's external trade relations entitled states to impose controls on the movement of goods within the Community.[31] Finally, the protection of the interests contained in Article 36 were capable of being tied to the need to impose a control at the frontier, as suggested above in the discussion of *Denkavit Futtermittel*.[32] In all these cases, however, the trade restrictions imposed must be no more onerous than is necessary to achieve the end in view. The Court considered that 'these residuary controls must nevertheless be reduced as far as possible so that trade between Member States can take place in conditions as close as possible to those prevalant on a domestic market'.[33] Furthermore, any penalties imposed for breach of national administrative rules must not discriminate against imported goods[34] nor must they be disproportionately severe,[35] although penalties for the actual importation of goods where that is unlawful may be appropriately more severe than for mere errors relating to formalities and documentation.[36]

---

27 This apparent rejection of the interpretation provided in the Directive may be explained on the basis that the Directive applied only to the transitional period (see p. 430 above), since when a more rigorous stance has been appropriate. See also AG Capotorti on the Directive's 'prudence' in Case 120/78 *Rewe-Zentral AG v Bundesmonopolverwaltung für Branntwein* (Cassis de Dijon) [1979] ECR 649, 670, [1979] 3 CMLR 494, 501.
28 See Case 159/78 *Commission v Italy* [1979] ECR 3247, [1980] 3 CMLR 446.
29 See Ch. 14.
30 Case 159/78, note 28 above.
31 Case 41/76 *Donckerwolcke v Procureur de la République* [1976] ECR 1921; see further p. 486.
32 Case 251/78, note 20 above and Ch. 16.
33 Case 159/78, note 28 above, para. 7 of the judgment.
34 Case 52/77 *Cayrol v Rivoira* [1977] ECR 2261, [1978] 2 CMLR 253; Case 212/88 *Levy* [1989] ECR 3511, [1991] 1 CMLR 49.
35 Case 41/76, note 31 above; Case 203/80 *Casati* [1981] ECR 2595.
36 See discussion by Oliver, *Free Movement of Goods*, para. 7.12.

A key component in the 1992 manifesto was a commitment to eliminate these residual areas in which frontier formalities remained permissible. Article 7a EC committed the Community to the establishment of 'an area without internal frontiers' by the end of 1992.[37] Broadly, this objective was to be achieved by an initial harmonization of national practices leading subsequently to the introduction of systems of supervision that are administered at point of departure or destination and not in transit at national borders. However, border controls are so long established that the passage of the necessary Community legislation to coordinate policies both within the Community and at its external borders proved extremely difficult. A major breakthrough was achieved with the adoption in 1985 of a Single Administrative Document (SAD). This was designed to facilitate trade across borders by introducing the use of a common document that replaced different national requirements. The next stage was the move from reduction in the need for documentation to its abolition. This was achieved by the elimination of the Single Administrative Document by Regulation 717/91, which applied from the start of 1993.[38] This was designed to eliminate customs formalities within the Community,[39] although the SAD was still used in trade with non-EC countries. Regulation 717/91 was one of a large number of measures repealed by Regulation 2913/92 on the Community Customs Code.[40] The legislative programme designed to secure the removal of frontier controls operating because of differences between states' fiscal rules was examined in the preceding chapter.[41] Through the course of this chapter and the two that follow there will be regular encounters with elements of the intense legislative activity that brought about the conditions for removing customs controls and border checks as an integral part of the process of bringing the internal market project to fruition. Nevertheless, the creation of an area without internal frontiers involves more than the elimination of border controls on goods. The abolition of obstacles to the free movement of persons has been more problematic and requires separate examination.[42]

---

37 See further Ch. 1, p. 24.
38 OJ 1991 L78/1.
39 Apart from transitional arrangements affecting Spain and Portugal.
40 OJ 1992 L302.
41 Page 420 above.
42 See pp. 563–7.

EXAMPLES OF DISCRIMINATION

Italy required public authorities to purchase domestically produced motor
vehicles in order to be eligible for subsidies. This is a simple example of
discrimination in favour of domestic production. It reduces the opportunities for selling imported goods and thereby distorts the structure of the
Community market. This was held by the Court to constitute a violation
of Article 30.[43] In equally straightforward fashion the Court held in *Allen
and Hanburys* v *Generics*[44] that it was incompatible with Article 30 to make
available a legal remedy to prevent the marketing of an imported product
that infringed a patent where no such remedy would be available against
an infringing domestic product. Such rulings show how Article 30 reflects
the fundamental proscription of discrimination based on nationality contained in Article 6 EC.[45]

Schutzverband gegen Unwesen in der Wirtschaft v *Weinvertriebs GmbH*[46]
involved the importation of vermouth into Germany from Italy. The
background was that Italian law required that the alcoholic content of
vermouth marketed in Italy be at least 16 per cent by volume. Weaker
vermouth could be made in Italy provided that it was destined only for
export. German law, by contrast, contained no basic minimum alcohol
requirement for vermouth. However, foreign spirits could be marketed in
the Federal Republic only if the spirit could lawfully be sold in the state of
manufacture. The result of this rule was that, by making the required
reference back to Italian law, Italian vermouth of an alcohol strength
below 16 per cent could be excluded from the German market, even
though an identical German-made vermouth could lawfully be sold. This
was held to be an instance of discrimination forbidden by Article 30. The
reference in the German rules back to the rather peculiar state of Italian
domestic law was held irrelevant to the application of Article 30. Discrimination is properly assessed by reference to the law of the state of marketing
alone. The German rule applied only to imports, not to German products,
and such unequal treatment falls foul of Article 30.

The 'Irish Souvenirs' case, *Commission* v *Ireland*,[47] supplies a further

43 Case C-263/85 *Commission* v *Italy*, [1991] ECR I-2457. See also Case 72/83 *Campus
Oil* v *Minister for Energy* [1984] ECR 2727, considered at p. 462 in relation to
justification under Art. 36.
44 Case 434/85 [1988] ECR 1245, [1988] 1 CMLR 701; see p. 844 below.
45 The role of Art. 6 underpinning EC trade law is clearly recognized by the Court in
Joined Cases C-92/92 and C-326/92 *Phil Collins* v *Imtrat Handelsgesellschaft mbH* and
Patricia Im- und Export Verwaltungsgesellschaft mbH v *EMI Electrola GmbH*, judgment of
20 October 1993.
46 Case 59/82 [1983] ECR 1217, [1984] 1 CMLR 319.
47 Case 113/80 [1981] ECR 1625, [1982] 1 CMLR 706.

example of the application of discriminatory national legislation. Irish legislation required imported souvenir items considered typically Irish to be stamped either with an indication of their place or origin or with the word 'foreign'. The rules covered products such as models of wolfhounds, Irish round towers and shamrocks. Such souvenirs produced within the Republic of Ireland were unaffected by the legislation. The European Court held that the Irish rules infringed Article 30. They imposed an extra burden on imports and caused a diminution in sales opportunities for them. The *Dassonville* formula was satisfied. The submissions of the Irish Government were primarily directed to justifying the rules as legitimate measures of consumer protection, but, as will be discussed below,[48] its efforts were in vain and it was obliged to put an end to the Treaty infringement.

A member state cannot escape Article 30 by retaining legislation that applies to home-produced goods as well as to imports (thus avoiding the Irish Souvenirs trap) while in practice applying that legislation in a discriminatory manner. In *Commission* v *France*[49] the Court considered a French decree that postal franking machines required official approval. Until 1984 the law discriminated on its face against machines made outside France, but, as a result of Commission intervention, the law was changed to place goods from other member states on the same footing as French goods. However, there was substantial evidence that Pitney Bowes, a leading British manufacturer, had met obstruction over a number of years in its attempts to secure approval for the use of its machines in France. Even after the amendment of the decree it had seen no progress in its application. Pitney Bowes complained to the Commission, which instituted Article 169 proceedings.[50] France was eventually brought before the European Court. The Court held that such practices are capable of infringing Article 30. 'A systematically unfavourable attitude towards imported machines'[51] contravenes Article 30 even if concealed behind an apparently non-discriminatory law. The Court held that a practice of discrimination 'must show a certain degree of consistency and generality'[52] to constitute a violation of Article 30, but that the required consistency is to be assessed against the market under scrutiny. Discrimination against a single importer in a small market, such as that for postal franking machines, may suffice.[53]

48 See p. 502.
49 Case 21/84 [1985] ECR 1356, noted by Gormley (1985) 10 ELRev 449. Cf., under Art. 95, Case C-287/91 *Commission* v *Italy*, judgment of 3 June 1992.
50 See Ch. 7. Art. 30 is directly effective (e.g. Case 74/76, note 1 above), so it would also have been possible in principle to institute a challenge before French courts.
51 Case 21/84, note 49 above, para. 11 of the judgment.
52 ibid., para. 13 of the judgment.
53 See comment below, text to note 57, on the notion of a 'measure' covered by Art. 30.

France was held in breach of its Treaty obligations. Although it might prove difficult in practice to draw the demarcation between an isolated act that is not caught by Article 30 and an established practice that is, the logic of this decision conforms to the Court's fundamental *Dassonville* formula. It is the effect of the legislation rather than its form that governs the legal response, and the French practices clearly exerted a restrictive effect on imported goods.

THE CASE OF ENCOURAGING DISCRIMINATION

The 'Buy Irish' case,[54] another infringement action initiated by the Commission against Ireland, emphasizes the broad scope that the Court attaches to Article 30. The case involved a campaign to boost the sales of domestic products. A symbol was attached to Irish goods that indicated to shoppers the local origin of the goods. An information service, 'Shoplink', was established through which consumers were provided with information about how and where they could exercise a preference for Irish goods. The Irish Minister for Industry launched the scheme in 1978 with the declaration that it would challenge 'the continued erosion of home market sales by manufactured imports'.[55] His stated aim was to switch 3 per cent of total consumer spending from imports to Irish goods. The campaign was directed by the Irish Goods Council, a limited company. Government funding was the primary means of financial support for the Council. Its chair and members of its management committee were appointed by the Minister for Industry. The Commission's view that the system infringed Article 30 because it was capable of restricting the free movement of goods was tested before the European Court. The Court found itself confronted with a string of arguments by the defendant state that, in essence, involved attempts to curtail the scope of Article 30.

The first Irish argument was that the matter was insufficiently connected with the state to constitute a breach of Article 30. At issue, it was claimed, was a purely private campaign. Although the Court conceded that Article 30 is confined to the acts of public authorities, it held that the state was sufficiently involved in the scheme to bring it into the public domain.[56]

The second argument concentrated on the word 'measure' used as part of the MEQR under Article 30.[57] A measure, according to the Irish

54 Case 249/81 *Commission* v *Ireland* [1982] ECR 4005, [1983] 2 CMLR 99.
55 ibid., [1983] 2 CMLR 99, 106.
56 See further p. 450.
57 See text at note 53 above. See also Oliver, *Free Movement of Goods*, para. 6.10 *et seq.*

submissions in the case, implies a binding act issued by a public authority. The 'Buy Irish' campaign was no more than an attempt to persuade and it therefore lacked the necessary binding quality. The Court rejected this narrow view. The concept of a measure within Article 30 is capable of covering a broad range of state action, even if not formal, even if merely persuasive. What really mattered was the Irish Government's 'considered intention . . . to check the flow of imports from other Member States'.[58] The Court's response seems entirely correct as a matter of policy, for it ensures that Article 30 catches covert state attempts to induce discrimination using informal channels. Moreover, the Court's decision in this respect conforms to Directive 70/50. The recitals to the Directive declare that the word 'measure' includes recommendations issuing from a public authority that cause the addressee to pursue a certain conduct despite the lack of binding legal status.

Finally, the defendant state took refuge in statistics. The Court was informed that the percentage of imports sold in Ireland had risen during the period of the campaign. This was no MEQR; despite the Minister's hopes, it was a failure! The Court rejected the submission. It was pointed out that the *Dassonville* formula depends on the potential effect on trade. If a measure is *capable* of restricting imports it is prohibited by Article 30 and empirical evidence is therefore not necessarily relevant. The Court was doubtless eager to reach this result as a matter of policy in order to dissuade future litigants from assailing it with sheaves of data on trade figures, but the decision is in any event correct in principle. The statistically proven rise in imports in no way precluded the possibility that, in the absence of the 'Buy Irish' campaign, the rise in imports might have been still sharper. The statistics did not show that the scheme did not restrict imports.

The 'Buy Irish' decision represents a striking curtailment of national competence to promote domestic products. It forbids naked attempts to feed consumer prejudice against goods produced in other member states. However, the Court distinguished the 'Buy Irish' decision in *Apple and Pear Council* v *Lewis*.[59] The Council was set up under a United Kingdom statutory instrument and was financed by levies imposed under the same legal authority on growers in England and Wales. The Council's members were appointed by the Minister of Agriculture, Fisheries and Food. The Council's task was to promote the consumption of apples and pears. In addition to general advertisements, it promoted varieties typical of English and Welsh production, such as Cox and Bramley apples and Conference

---

58 Case 249/81, note 54 above, para. 23 of the judgment.
59 Case 222/82 [1983] ECR 4083, [1984] 3 CMLR 733.

pears. To this end it mounted advertising campaigns using the slogan, *inter alia*, 'Polish up your English'. Other activities included research projects and public relations. Several growers, presumably unimpressed with the Council's effectiveness, refused to pay the charges due to the Council under the statutory instrument. Sued before Tunbridge Wells County Court, they argued, *inter alia*, that the scheme was in breach of Article 30 because it involved discrimination against fruit originating in other member states. The matter reached the European Court by way of an Article 177 reference made by the county court.

The European Court began by pointing out that, given the statutory background, the campaign possessed a sufficient level of state involvement to fall within the ambit of Article 30. The Court proceeded to declare that it is contrary to Article 30 to induce consumers to prefer domestic goods over imports solely by reason of origin. Thereafter, however, the decision departs from the 'Buy Irish' judgment. It was held permissible to promote a product by reference to its particular qualities, even if those qualities are typical of national production. It would, for example, be justifiable to advertise to consumers the desirability of buying English fruit because it is pleasingly crisp and crunchy, but not simply because it is English in origin. The Commission, which chose to issue guidelines explaining its interpretation of this important area of law, believes that a balance must be struck between reference to quality and reference to origin; the former must constitute the primary focus of the campaign.[60] In practice it may prove difficult to draw a distinction between a campaign based on nationality and one based on a product characteristic that happens to be linked to nationality. However, it is fundamental to the idea of a common market that competition on quality is desirable whereas competition on nationality is not, and it is in this distinction that the explanation lies for the Court's willingness to differentiate in law between buying Irish and polishing up your English.

PRICE-FIXING

This selection of Article 30 case law reveals the breadth of national practices that are susceptible to challenge under Article 30. The key to these cases is the treatment of imported goods in a less favourable manner than domestic goods. However, Article 30 extends still further. The notion of discrimination covers not only the treatment of like products in an unlike manner, which was the issue in the cases examined above, but also

60 OJ 1986 C272/3.

the treatment of unlike products in a like manner. National law must not subject imports to the same regime applicable to domestic goods where that fails to take account of the distinct characteristics of the import.

The most important of the Court's decisions in this area relate to national price-fixing systems.[61] Price-fixing is a widely used means of economic regulation, and its potential unlawfulness under Community law represents a further clear example of the intrusion of Community rules promoting free trade into national legislative competence. From the perspective of Community law, the problem with price-fixing is that even if the rule is applied equally in law to all goods, wherever produced,[62] it may in fact have the effect of impeding imports by preventing the import from being traded at its market price, which may be outside the legally imposed price band. In *Riccardo Tasca*[63] the European Court held that a national rule that fixes maximum prices is capable of contravening Article 30. Although such a rule applies to all goods irrespective of origin, if the maximum price is fixed at such a low level that an importer can trade only at a loss, then the effect of the scheme is to discriminate against imports in violation of Article 30. In *Openbaar Ministerie v Van Tiggele*[64] the Court advanced its case law in this area to cover a minimum price-fixing system. If the minimum price is fixed at such a high level that the imported product is prevented from taking advantage of the fact that it is cheaper than the domestic product and could undercut the home market, then, again, a breach of Article 30 may be established. The national system cancels out the import's competitive advantage by precluding the reflection of lower costs in a lower retail price. The apparently even-handed national system is unlawful, because it fails to take account of the fact that the import is in a different situation from the domestic product.

For a system of price regulation to conform to the demands of Article 30 it must permit imports to derive benefit from any economic advantage that they may enjoy over domestic goods. Thus, the imposition of a maximum percentage profit figure would seem compatible with Community law, because it would operate in a genuinely neutral fashion. The

---

61 See Reich and Leahy, *Internal Market and Diffuse Interests*, pp. 43–9; Oliver, *Free Movement of Goods*, para. 7.65 *et seq.*

62 Overtly discriminatory price-fixing – like treated as unlike – violates Article 30. See e.g., Case 181/82 *Roussel v Netherlands* [1983] ECR 3849, [1985] 1 CMLR 834; Case 56/87 *Commission v Italy* [1988] ECR 2919, [1989] 3 CMLR 707. In cases before English courts contrast *R v Secretary of State for Social Services, ex parte Schering* [1987] 1 CMLR 277 (no discrimination: lawful) with *R v Secretary of State for Social Security, ex parte Bomore* [1986] 1 CMLR 228 (discrimination: unlawful).

63 Case 65/75 [1976] ECR 291, [1977] 2 CMLR 183.

64 Case 82/77 [1978] ECR 25, [1978] 2 CMLR 528; see also Case C-287/89 *Commission v Belgium*, [1991] ECR I-2233.

percentage criterion is equal in application and, in contrast to maximum and minimum price-fixing, the basis of calculation is the economic cost of production, which allows account to be taken of inherent price difference between imports and domestic goods. In *Commission* v *Italy*[65] the Court held that a system that required that the retailer's trading margin attached to the price of tobacco be set at 8 per cent was compatible with the Treaty.[66] The scheme operated without discrimination. Any producer was entitled to fix the price of tobacco in accordance with cost; thereafter an 8 per cent margin was added to all retail sales irrespective of the origin of the goods. In *Duphar* v *Netherlands*[67] the Court indicated that a limit placed on expenditure on medical preparations by the Dutch health service was compatible with Article 30, despite the fact that it might reduce sales of imported products, provided that there was no discrimination against imports.[68] State economic regulation of this type is lawful provided the imported product suffers no disadvantage. It is submitted that in the light of the Court's ruling in *Keck and Mithouard* [69] such fact patterns would today yield the same result, but that the Court would hold that such rules escape the reach of Article 30 by an explicit application of its *Keck* formula. Such provisions do not satisfy the *Dassonville* formula in so far as they 'apply to all affected traders operating within the national territory and . . . affect in the same manner, in law and in fact, the marketing of domestic products and of those from other Member States'.[70]

INDIRECT DISCRIMINATION

Discrimination may occur where the law applies a condition that is not based on national origin, but which, on closer inspection, tends to be satisfied more readily by home-produced goods. In *Commission* v *France*[71] French restrictions on the advertising of alcoholic beverages were held unlawful. The rules, which distributed various drinks to different categories, were not directly related to the origin of the product, but it was

---

66 The case was decided on the basis of Art. 37, p. 873 below. However, the approach appears equally applicable to Art. 30 and indeed the Court cited both *Tasca* and *Van Tiggele*.
67 Case 238/82 [1984] ECR 523, [1985] 1 CMLR 256.
68 See generally in relation to pricing in the pharmaceutical market Hancher, 'Creating the Internal Market for Pharmaceutical Medicines – An Echternach Jumping Procession' (1991) 28 CMLRey 821, 845–52.
69 Joined Cases C-267 and C-268/91, note 16 above.
70 See further Ch. 17, pp. 532–42.
71 Case 152/78 [1980] ECR 2299.

shown that the rules discriminated in practice against imports by subjecting imported products to control where competing national products escaped any restriction by virtue of their different categorization. It was an example of covert discrimination, in that like products were treated in an unlike manner. It was condemned as a measure unlawful under Article 30.[72] A materially distinct situation would have arisen where the rules introduced were genuinely even-handed between competing types of product but established categories of increasing level of restriction based on, for example, alcoholic strength; and where the products falling within the highest strength categories happened to be imported, because French production of goods of that type was minimal. This is indirect discrimination. Imported goods happen to be more heavily burdened, but the explicit basis of the differentiation is alcoholic strength, which is inherently nationality-neutral.

Faced with such a model, the European Court accepts that the choice of a criterion that indirectly affects imported goods more severely than domestic products may be capable of objective justification.[73] Thus, if it can be shown that there are objectively justifiable reasons for the rules in question unconnected with nationality, then the rules will be considered lawful. In effect, the state is able to argue that the direct burden that attaches to imported goods is purely incidental to the primary lawful purpose of the scheme. This makes it important to distinguish carefully between direct and indirect discrimination, for only the latter is susceptible to arguments of objective justification. Perhaps surprisingly, this argument has rarely been advanced to uphold rules covered prima facie by Article 30,[74] although it may be observed more frequently in connection with other Treaty provisions that forbid discrimination on grounds of nationality.[75] The jurisprudence is rather more developed in the context of defending employment practices that have an effect discriminatory on grounds of sex, but may be upheld for objective reasons unconnected with

---

72 The 'measure', a restriction on advertising, did not directly affect the sale of imports, but the Court had no difficulty in holding that the effect on marketing opportunities was sufficient to trigger the application of Art 30; see ibid, para. 11 of the judgment. See also Cases C-1, C-176/90 *APESA* v *DSSC*, [1991] ECR I-4151; and discussion of the impact of Cases C-267, 268/91 *Keck and Mithouard*, p. 539 below.

73 That is, prior to recourse to Art. 36, the explicit justification provision considered in Ch. 16.

74 But see Case 31/87 *Gebroeders Beentjes BV* v *Netherlands* [1988] ECR 4635, [1990] 1 CMLR 287.

75 E.g., Case 251/83 *Haug-Adrion* v *Frankfurter Versicherungs-AG* [1984] ECR 4277, [1985] 3 CMLR 266; Case 182/83 *Robert Fearon and Co. Ltd* v *The Irish Land Commission* [1984] ECR 3677, [1985] 2 CMLR 228. Cf. Case C-175/88 *Klaus Biehl* v *Administration des contributions du grand-duché de Luxembourg* [1990] ECR I-1779, [1990] 3 CMLR 143.

sex.[76] Under Article 30 rules that are in principle even-handed but tend to impede imports are normally analysed from the perspective of the 'rule of reason' developed by the Court in its *Cassis de Dijon* jurisprudence.[77] This is based on the restrictive effect of diversity between national rules rather than the notion of discrimination, but reflects the same idea that a state is entitled to demonstrate a justification for a rule that tends to protect a national market, provided that that reason is not tainted by nationality discrimination.[78]

ORIGIN-MARKING AND PRODUCT DESIGNATION

The decision in *Commission* v *United Kingdom*[79] provides a rather more extended notion of discrimination. The case involved origin-marking legislation of a rather more subtle nature than the scheme condemned in *Commission* v *Ireland*, the Irish Souvenirs case.[80] United Kingdom law required certain textile, electrical and other goods to be marked with or accompanied by an indication of their origin when offered for retail sale. The facts differed from the Irish Souvenirs case in that in the present case all goods were subject to the requirement, not just imported goods. However, the Court formed the view that the measure was non-discriminatory in form only. It led to discrimination against imported goods. The Court explained that the origin-marking requirement enabled the British consumer to assert any prejudice that he or she may hold against foreign goods. The discrimination was, in this sense, covert. This is unquestionably a rather extended notion of discrimination, but the Court felt able to reach its decision on the basis of the overall rationale of achieving 'economic interpenetration' within the Community.[81] The British origin-marking rules impeded this objective by placing a handicap on the sale of goods made in other member states.

Mandatory origin-marking thus appears to fall foul of Article 30. This does not preclude the ability of member states to take measures against false or misleading origin-marking, nor does it preclude the ability of

---

76 E.g., Case 170/84 *Bilka Kaufhaus* v *Weber* [1986] ECR 1607; see further Ch. 20. See also p. 400 in relation to Art. 95.

77 See Ch. 17.

78 Therefore, just as it is important to distinguish direct from indirect discrimination because of the broader justifications available in the latter case, so for the same reason it is important to distinguish distinctly from indistinctly applicable rules; see p. 502.

79 Case 207/83 [1985] ECR 1202, [1985] 2 CMLR 259, noted by Gormley (1985) 10 ELRev 434.

80 Case 113/80, note 47 above.

81 ibid., para. 17 of the judgment.

manufacturers to choose to apply indications of origin to their products if they feel that this will help sales.[82]

A related problem, that of the reservation of special product designations to national products, arose for decision in *Commission* v *Germany*.[83] The case concerned a German law that reserved several appellations, including *Sekt* and *Weinbrand*, to German-produced wines and spirits. Similar imported goods were obliged to adopt less familiar designations, with a consequential diminution in marketing prospects. The Court found the law incompatible with Article 30. It concluded that

these appellations only fulfil their specific purpose if the product which they describe does in fact possess qualities and characteristics which are due to the fact that it originated in a specific geographical area. As regards indications of origin in particular, the geographical area of origin of a product must confer on it a specific quality and specific characteristics of such a nature as to distinguish it from all other products.[84]

The Court considered that there was no intrinsic reason why the alcoholic drinks concerned could not be made outside Germany. Production in Germany conferred no special characteristic. It therefore held that the German legislation discriminated without objective justification against imports by denying them the opportunity to compete on equal terms with the domestic product.[85]

The corollary of the decision in *Commission* v *Germany* is that a state may reserve a designation to a product of a particular region if the product is in some way unique to that region and could not be made in a similar manner elsewhere. Naturally, claims of this nature are closely scrutinized for possible abuse. The basis of the approach in such an instance, if held permissible, would be that the named local product is objectively distinct from any other product and that consequently it is proper to reflect this objectively verifiable difference through the medium of product designation. In *Commission* v *Germany*, once the Court decided that the appellations *Sekt* and *Weinbrand* did not constitute genuine indications of origin, it ruled that the national measures infringed Article 30 and added briefly that they were incapable of justification under Article 36's concession to the protection of intellectual property.[86]

---

82 Subject to the application of the competition rules, Chs. 22, 23.
83 Case 12/74 [1975] ECR 181, [1975] 1 CMLR 340. See also Case 13/78 *Eggers* v *Freie Hansestadt Bremen* [1978] ECR 1935, [1979] 1 CMLR 562. Case C-47/90 *Établissements Delhaize Frères et Compagnie Le Lion SA* v *Promalvin SA and AGE Bodegas Unidas SA*, judgment of 9 June 1992.
84 Case 12/74, note 83 above, para. 7 of the judgment.
85 On laws against unfair competition generally, see p. 513; on trade-mark law, see p. 845.
86 Ch. 26.

A more permissive approach emerges from the Court's ruling in *Exportur SA v LOR SA and Confiserie du Tech.*[87] Even in the absence of objective differences between products, the Court was receptive to justification under Article 36 of rules that reserve designations. LOR and Confiserie, French producers of *turrón*, a type of nougat, used the statutorily protected designations Alicante and Jijona, which are Spanish towns. Under a 1973 Franco-Spanish Convention on protection of designations of origin, the designations in question were to be reserved in France to Spanish producers. Exportur, a Spanish firm, brought proceedings before French courts to stop the French firms using the designation. A reference was made to the European Court which considered that the rules of the Convention, which cannot prevail over those of the EC Treaty, were capable of impeding cross-border trade. The French firms were of the view that the quality of nougat was unconnected with its geographical origins and that therefore reservation of the designation to Spanish firms was incompatible with Community law. The Court did not contradict the submissions relating to the quality of the products. However, it referred to the important role of geographical designations as methods of providing information by producer to consumer even where the flavour of the product is not attributable to locality. The Court considered that the prevention of the use of geographical designations that take advantage of the reputation attaching to products of undertakings established in the locality referred to in the designation was caught by Article 30, but could be compatible with Article 36 as a method of protecting intellectual property. This would apply only where the designations had not acquired a generic connotation in the country of origin. *Exportur* suggests a shift away from reckless pursuit of market integration through the application of Article 30 towards a greater respect, manifested in the application of Article 36, for the role of product appellations in conveying information to consumers about a product's origin. This shift is also apparent in the Court's increasingly permissive approach to the use of trade marks to perpetuate segmentation of markets within the Community.[88]

Regulation 2081/92 on the protection of geographical indications and designations of origin is now of relevance in this field.[89] The Regulation envisages registration of protected designations of origin (PDO) and protected geographical indications (PGI) at Community level, in replacement of national systems. The designation of origin and the geographical

---

[87] Case C-3/91, judgment of 10 November 1992, noted by Brouwer (1993) 30 CMLRev 1209, discussing the divergent national practice in this area.
[88] Case C-10/89 *SA CNL-SUCAL v HAG*, Case C-9/93 *IHT Internationale Heiztechnik GmbH v Ideal Standard GmbH*, Ch. 26, pp. 845–7 below.
[89] OJ 1992 L208/1.

indication that are open to protection are defined in the Regulation. Its definition of 'geographical indication' covers 'the name of a region, a specific place or, in exceptional cases, a country used to describe an agricultural product or a foodstuff originating in that region, specific place or country and which possesses a specific quality, reputation or other characteristics attributable to that geographical origin'.[90] This formula is capable of interpretation in tune with the Court's case law. The Regulation cannot be applied in a manner that would conflict with Article 30.[91]

More generally, Community legislative activity in the field must respect the general principles of Community law, including a requirement of non-discrimination in allocation of appellations. *Codorniu SA v Council* is a case of prime importance on the admissibility of applications for annulment brought under Article 173 by non-privileged applicants.[92] The substance of the case involved a successful challenge by Codorniu, a Spanish producer, to provisions of Regulation 2045/89, applicable in the wine sector, that reserved the term *crémant* to French and Luxembourg wines even though the conditions for making *crémant* wines were capable of fulfilment by producers in other states and had been fulfilled for many years by Codorniu itself.

THE PERSONAL SCOPE OF ARTICLE 30

PUBLIC NOT PRIVATE

The Court has consistently adhered to the view that Article 30 applies only to measures adopted by the state, not to the conduct of private parties. There are strong policy arguments in favour of this distinction. For example, if a contract between two or more firms in different member states for the distribution of materials were held to affect inter-state trade (by precluding purchase from a source in another member state) and therefore capable of violating Article 30, then the competition rules of the Treaty, which contain complex provisions permitting such agreements if their benefit outweighs their cost,[93] would be deprived of any utility.[94] Article 30 must be kept distinct from Articles 85 and 86 in order to

---

90 Art. 2(2)(b) Reg. Art. 3 warns that generic names may not be registered.
91 Cf. Case 80–81/77 *Ramel v Receveur des Douanes* [1978] ECR 927, p. 481 below.
92 Case C-309/89 [1994] ECR I-1853. See Ch. 8, p. 232.
93 See Ch. 22.
94 Exemption under Art. 36 is confined to the public interest and is therefore inappropriate; see Ch. 16.

preserve the integrity of the scheme of the Treaty. There are practices, such as unilateral conduct by non-dominant undertakings, that are not intended to be caught by either set of provisions.[95] This is achieved by restricting the scope of Article 30 to measures adopted by the state, and restricting the scope of Article 85 to bilateral arrangements, and Article 86 to abusive dominance.[96]

Thus, if private firms agree to insist on the use of particular technical standards in contracts, then even if those standards are discriminatory on grounds of nationality, no breach of Article 30 has occurred. The firms may face challenge under Articles 85 and 86, and perhaps Article 6 EC, but in the absence of any state involvement Article 30 does not come into play. However, if the state were to intervene, for example by providing exclusive recognition in law for the privately drafted standards, then the control of Article 30 would apply to that state intervention.[97]

DEFINING THE STATE

Restricting Article 30 to state measures does not resolve the practical problems that may arise in defining exactly what constitutes the state for these purposes. Several cases that have been discussed above provide important indications of the Court's view. In *Commission* v *Ireland*, the 'Buy Irish' case,[98] one of the Irish submissions was that the Irish Goods Council, under the aegis of which the promotion of Irish goods was undertaken, was a private company and therefore immune from the application of Article 30. The Court accepted that Article 30 is confined to the acts of public authorities, but had little difficulty in holding that in the present case the element of Government involvement in funding and appointment of members was sufficient for the campaign to be considered to fall within the public sphere and therefore caught by Article 30. Similarly, in *Apple and Pear Council* v *Lewis*[99] the Court indicated that a body set up under a statutory instrument and funded by levies paid by private individuals under statutory obligation was subject to Article 30. The Council was financed by a charge imposed on growers, rather than by a direct Government subsidy as in the 'Buy Irish' case, which left it rather

---

95 Quinn and MacGowan, 'Could Article 30 Impose Obligations on Individuals' (1987) 12 ELRev 163, pp. 169–70. Note however the potential application of Art. 6 EC, which forbids discrimination on grounds of nationality.

96 See Chs. 22, 23; see esp. p. 673 on the narrow interpretation commonly placed on unilateral conduct.

97 See also WQ 862/83 OJ 1983 C315/15.

98 Case 249/81, note 54 above, considered at p. 440.

99 Case 222/82, note 59 above, considered at p. 441.

more remote from state control, but the European Court did not consider this a material distinction. The financial obligation was derived from legislation and consequently the Council was a public, not a private body. Article 30 was in issue. Plainly, the legal status of the body under domestic law is not determinative of its subjection to Article 30.

A body responsible for the regulation and disciplinary standards of a trade or profession may be bound by the obligations of Article 30 if it is accorded a measure of state support. The issue arose in *R v The Pharmaceutical Society, ex parte API*.[100] The Court considered the status of the Society, which is involved in the regulation of standards among United Kingdom pharmacists. The Society is an independent body, but it has certain functions conferred on it by statute. It maintains a register of pharmacists on which a pharmacist must appear in order to be entitled to practise. Its disciplinary committee has a statutory basis in the Pharmacy Act 1954 and it is empowered to remove pharmacists from the register for misconduct. Removal from the register would effectively destroy a pharmacist's ability to make a living. The Court held that the Society was bound by Article 30. Its activities and powers went beyond those of a typical private organization. Its disciplinary powers in particular gave it a general regulatory function in the public interest. The test, then, involves an assessment of the nature of the powers exercised and the manner of that exercise; it is a functional test.[101]

A court is a limb of the state for these purposes. Consequently it is possible that the award of a judicial remedy that hinders importation may be held contrary to Article 30.[102] Court proceedings to exclude imported products alleged to represent unfair competition or believed to infringe a national patent are capable of constituting MEQRs and therefore such measures require justification in accordance with the Treaty. Although such relief is typically sought by private parties, the barrier to trade in fact stems from the ruling of the court, which is equated with the state for these purposes.[103]

It is also plain that not only central but also regional and local government are subject to the obligations of Article 30. In *Commission v Ireland*, the Dundalk Water Supply scheme case,[104] the practices of the local

---

100 Case 266/87 [1989] ECR 1295, considered further at p. 467. See also Case 29/82 *Van Luipen* [1983] ECR 151. and Case C-292/92 *Hünermund and others v Landesapothekerkammer Baden-Württemberg*, judgment of 15 December 1993.
101 Other areas of Community law raise similar problems, and increasingly similar solutions are being applied. See, e.g., p. 350 on the scope of the direct effect of directives. See generally Curtin, 'The Province of Government' (1990) 15 ELRev 195.
102 E.g., Case 434/85, note 44 above.
103 Ch. 26 examines the application of Art. 30 in such cases in more depth.
104 Case 45/87 [1988] ECR 4929, considered at p. 499.

authority in Dundalk were held to violate Article 30. The Article 169 action instituted by the Commission was brought against the state, but this should not obscure the fact that the obligation to respect Article 30 rests directly on the local limb of government. Indeed, because Article 30 is directly effective,[105] an action before the Irish courts could have been brought against the Dundalk Council itself,[106] in contrast to the Article 169 action, which formally can be brought only against a state.[107] The direct action against the defaulting body may be more costly than alerting the Commission, but it is capable of yielding more immediate beneficial results as far as the complainant is concerned than the more indirect pursuit of Commission action under Article 169, particularly if the national court can be persuaded to grant interim relief to restrain the alleged violation of Article 30.

Finally, a state may interfere with the operation of the market through more indirect means, such as offering support to an unlawful private cartel.[108] In such circumstances the state may find itself in breach of Article 5 of the Treaty read with Articles 3(g) and 85. The provision of subsidies to domestic industry is controlled under Articles 92–4.

---

105 E.g., Case 74/76, note 1 above.
106 See Case 103/88 *Fratelli Constanzo* v *Milano* [1989] ECR 1839.
107 For an English example see *R* v *Wirral MBC, ex parte Wirral Taxi Owners Association* [1983] 3 CMLR 150, noted by Gormley (1983) 8 ELRev 141. See also the 'Sunday Trading' cases, Ch. 17, p. 533.
108 The responsibility of the state for obstructing the operation of the market is considered more fully in Ch. 27.

CHAPTER 16

Article 36

THE GENERAL PRINCIPLES OF INTERPRETATION

The prohibition contained in Articles 30 and 34 is subject to the possibility of justification under Article 36:

The provisions of Articles 30 to 34 shall not preclude prohibitions or restrictions on imports, exports or goods in transit justified on grounds of public morality, public policy or public security; the protection of health and life of humans, animals or plants; the protection of national treasures possessing artistic, historic or archaeological value; or the protection of industrial and commercial property. Such prohibitions or restrictions shall not, however, constitute a means of arbitrary discrimination or a disguised restriction on trade between Member States.

The structure of Article 36 offers a list of potential justifications and then issues a firm warning that any purported justification will be scrutinized carefully in order to ascertain that it is genuine. Article 36 permits the maintenance of barriers to intra-Community trade. It is in principle hostile to the fundamental principles of free trade within the Community and, in common with other derogation provisions, such as Article 48(3),[1] is to be interpreted narrowly. The second sentence of Article 36 encapsulates this policy approach and the Court has sustained this view in its decisions. The Court is absolutely unwilling to extend the scope of available heads of justification under Article 36 beyond those specifically laid down. In *Commission v Ireland*, the Irish Souvenirs case,[2] the Irish Government sought to justify its origin-marking rules as legitimate measures of consumer protection. The Court found this argument misconceived. Consumer protection is unavailable under Article 36 as a means of justifying

1 Ch. 18.
2 Case 113/80 [1981] ECR 1625, [1982] 1 CMLR 708; see p. 438 above.

discriminatory trade barriers that breach Article 30. Member states are allowed rather greater latitude in justifying rules that apply equally to all products, whether domestic or imported.[3]

In *Commission* v *Italy*[4] the defendant state endeavoured to justify its ban on the import of pigmeat on the basis that economic difficulties made it necessary to seek some temporary respite from the pressures of free trade. The Court held such general economic arguments unsustainable under Article 36. Submissions of the type advanced by Italy are fundamentally hostile to the concept of economic integration, and derogations on such grounds can be permitted only through the exercise of special Community procedures, never by unilateral state action.[5]

The Court's insistence that Article 36 offers only limited scope for permissible trade restriction was further emphasized in *Campus Oil* in which it declared that

the purpose of Article 36 ... is not to reserve certain matters to the exclusive jurisdiction of the Member States; it merely allows national legislation to derogate from the principle of free movement of goods to the extent to which this is and remains justified in order to achieve the objectives set out in the Article.[6]

Thus when the German Government argued in *Karl Prantl*[7] that any national rule supported by criminal sanctions should be considered a trade barrier justified as an element of public policy, the Court responded with a firm rejection. Such an approach would permit a state to mould the scope of Article 36 to its own taste through the unilateral application of its rules of criminal law. The proper approach involves establishing a Community definition of the scope of available derogations within which member states may be able to find justification for their action.

Combined with this strict approach is the requirement that a member state wishing to rely on an Article 36 derogation must show that its action corresponds to the particular circumstances of the case in question. In *United Foods* v *Belgium*[8] the Court considered action taken by Belgium in respect of imported fish as a means of protecting public health. The Court observed that any steps taken must take full account of the nature of the product subject to control. The detail of a rule may deprive it of the protection of Article 36 even though its broad objective falls within one of the heads of justification. Perishable products such as fish must be checked

---

3 See Ch. 17.
4 Case 7/61 [1961] ECR 317.
5 See p. 485.
6 Case 72/83 *Campus Oil* v *Minister for Industry and Energy* [1984] ECR 2727, [1984] 3 CMLR 544; see further p. 462.
7 Case 16/83 [1984] ECR 1299, [1985] 2 CMLR 238.
8 Case 132/80 [1981] ECR 995.

with all speed so that they do not deteriorate and become unfit for human consumption.

In accordance with the general theme of narrow interpretation of the Article 36 derogation the burden of proof rests on the national authorities wishing to curtail the free movement of goods to establish that the demands of Article 36 are met. The Court stated in *Leendert van Bennekom*[9] that '. . . it is for the national authorities to demonstrate in each case that their rules are necessary to give effective protection to the interests referred to in Article 36'. The European Court, or, in appropriate cases, the national court, thus assumes the task of scrutinizing the arguments presented by member states in support of their barriers.

The second sentence of Article 36 has been developed through interpretation by the European Court in the cases mentioned above and many others into approaches that may be rationalized as the principles of 'proportionality' and 'alternative means'. Action taken against imported products must impose a restriction that stands *in proportion* to the risk presented by the import; and it must not be possible to achieve the desired level of protection by *alternative means* that are less restrictive of trade. There are, then, two limbs to Article 36. A state must first establish the existence of a threat to an interest covered by the first sentence of Article 36. Thereafter, it is necessary to demonstrate in addition that the measures taken to protect the interest in question correspond to the demands of Article 36's second sentence, including the principles of proportionality and alternative means, which run throughout Community trade law.

SPECIFIC INTERESTS

PUBLIC MORALITY

Henn and Darby imported a selection of pornographic films and magazines into the United Kingdom from Rotterdam. They were prosecuted before Ipswich Crown Court for several offences relating to the import of obscene items, *inter alia*, under the Obscene Publications Act 1959 and the Customs and Excise Act 1952. Their defence was based squarely on Article 30. They argued that the seizure of their goods and the criminal prosecution brought against them constituted a barrier to the free movement of goods between member states prohibited by Article 30. Relying on the direct effect and supremacy of Community law, they claimed that Community

9 Case 227/82 [1983] ECR 3883, [1985] 2 CMLR 692.

law afforded them a complete defence to the charge under English Law.

The Crown Court convicted them. The conviction was upheld in the Court of Appeal,[10] where Lord Chief Justice Widgery refused to accept that Article 30 was of any assistance to the appellants. Article 30, he declared, concerns quantitative restrictions, which connotes a numerical limit placed on imports. It does not cover a total ban on imports, for no numerical limit is involved. This narrow literal interpretation is perfectly illogical, for a total ban is simply the lowest possible numerical ceiling. Moreover, such an analysis contradicts several important European Court decisions to the contrary.[11] Lord Widgery's judgment ignores even *Dassonville*.[12]

Henn and Darby appealed to the House of Lords, where they again failed,[13] but where Lord Diplock redirected the analysis of Article 30 on to its proper path. He believed that the appellants were plainly correct in their submission that Article 30 was in issue. Citing the *Dassonville* formula, he observed that the free movement of goods had unarguably been impeded. The troublesome point was whether the United Kingdom could justify its sanctions against such goods on the basis that they were necessary to protect public morality. Lord Diplock felt that the requirements of Article 36 were satisfied. However, at this point, Lord Diplock, alert to the vital need to secure authoritative interpretation of points of Community law,[14] made a preliminary reference under Article 177 to Luxembourg. The European Court began by confirming Lord Diplock's view that the Article 30 prohibition embraces not only partial but also total restrictions on imports.[15] Indeed, by this stage the United Kingdom did not seek to maintain the opposite view. The European Court proceeded to hold that a prohibition on the importation of obscene articles may be justifiable as a means of protecting public morality. The Court commented that such a ban would, however, be liable to be considered an instrument of arbitrary discrimination if there existed within the member state concerned a lawful trade in the articles denied access to that state's market from other member states.

It was therefore central to the United Kingdom's ability to rely on

---

10 *Henn and Darby* v *Director of Public Prosecutions* [1978] 1 WLR 1031, [1978] 3 All ER 1190 (CA).

11 E.g., Case 2/73 *Geddo* v *Ente nazionale Risi* [1973] ECR 865, [1974] 1 CMLR 13.

12 Case 8/74 *Procureur du Roi* v *Dassonville* [1974] ECR 837. Lord Widgery held in the alternative that if Art. 30 was in principle of assistance to the appellants, Art. 36 justified the application of domestic criminal law in their case. As explained in the text, this is a far sounder line of analysis.

13 [1980] 2 WLR 597, [1980] 2 All ER 166 (HL).

14 See Ch. 9.

15 Case 34/79 *R* v *Henn and Darby* [1979] ECR 3795, [1980] 1 CMLR 246.

Article 36 that the pornography in question was not freely available within the territory of the United Kingdom. In the absence of effective internal control of such obscenity it would be apparent that the alleged fear of declining standards of morality amounted to no more than a pretext for protecting domestic traders from competition. Notwithstanding some difficulty in determining the United Kingdom's approach to such goods, given differences between Scotland, Northern Ireland, England and Wales,[16] the House of Lords was plainly satisfied that the United Kingdom did operate an internal ban on the type of material that had been seized. Therefore, Article 36 justified the measures taken to prevent import of the goods and the seizure of the pornography was held compatible with Community law. Henn and Darby's convictions stood.

Several years later Conegate Ltd imported life-size inflatable dolls into the United Kingdom from Germany. Although the invoices for the goods described them as 'window display models', customs officers who inspected the consignment at Heathrow Airport found items described as 'love love dolls' and 'Miss World Specials'. They also discovered sexy vacuum flasks. The goods were seized. Their forfeiture was ordered by magistrates, who were told by counsel for the customs authorities that 'it is almost certain that the dolls were intended to be used as sex aids. I don't know about the sexy vacuum flasks.'[17]

Conegate argued that it was the victim of a violation of Article 30: its intra-Community trade had been interfered with. After *Henn and Darby* this argument could hardly be opposed. The United Kingdom, pursuing the precedent of *Henn and Darby*, submitted that its action constituted justified protection of public morality. The points of Community law were referred to Luxembourg under the Article 177 procedure.[18] The European Court observed that a member state is permitted by the Treaty to make its own assessment of the requirements of public morality within its territory. However, a state is guilty of arbitrary discrimination if it seeks to prohibit the importation of goods that could be made and marketed lawfully within its own territory. It was thus essential to examine the United Kingdom's internal regulation of such trade. The decision thus far follows *Henn and Darby*. In the United Kingdom with its separate legal systems, the law relating to such items was not absolutely uniform.

16 The Court indicated that, national diversity notwithstanding, for these purposes a unitary view of the nature of the UK's system could be taken by looking at the overall scope; it would have been more firmly integrationist, but potentially destructive of regional diversity, to insist that the UK could impose on imports restrictions no stricter than the most relaxed applied anywhere in the UK.

17 The *Guardian*, 22 January 1986.

18 Case 121/85 *Conegate* v *Customs and Excise Commissioners* [1986] ECR 1007, [1986] 1 CMLR 739.

There existed certain restrictions on the sale of such goods, including limits on public display and a requirement that shops stocking such goods be licensed for sale only to persons of 18 and over. The European Court observed that such controls did not amount to a prohibition on manufacturing and marketing the type of goods in which Conegate dealt. The United Kingdom was thus unable to rely on Article 36 to prohibit importation of the dolls. Its action was in breach of Article 30. The High Court quashed the forfeiture order and Conegate recovered its goods. Conegate was awarded costs, including those incurred in the European Court, but it agreed not to pursue an action for damages to compensate it for financial loss suffered as a result of the unlawful detention.[19]

The key distinction between *Henn and Darby* and *Conegate* lies in the element of discrimination against imported goods. Conviction in *Conegate* would have resulted in the application of harsher rules to an importer than a domestic trader, whereas it was concluded in *Henn and Darby* that there followed no such unequal treatment.[20] So Article 30 was successfully pleaded as a defence only in *Conegate*. The state, while retaining the power to select elements of morality it judges worthy of protection, remains within the ambit of the Article 36 justification only if it applies its rules without reference to the origin of offending products.[21] This means that different standards of morality apply in different member states, but that within a single state equal treatment of all goods is the rule.

---

19 See *Bourgoin* v *MAFF* [1986] QB 716, where the English Court of Appeal rejected a claim for damages based on violation of Art. 30; the grounds of the decision now seem weakened by the European Court's emphasis on the principle of effective remedies in Case C-213/89 *Factortame* and Cases C-6/90, C-9/90 *Francovich*, pp. 370, 352 above. In *Kirklees BC* v *Wickes Ltd* [1992] 3 All ER 717, 734, (HL) Lord Goff commented, albeit obiter, that 'since the decision of the European Court in *Francovich* . . . there must now be doubt whether the *Bourgoin* case was correctly decided'. Cf. *R* v *Secretary of State, ex parte EOC* [1993] 1 All ER 1022, 1031j (CA), [1994] 1 All ER 910, 924 (HL); and further p. 801 below on applications before national courts for damages for violation of the Treaty competition rules.

20 For an argument that the law in *Henn and Darby* did discriminate against imported goods, see Catchpole and Barav 'The public morality exception and the free movement of goods: Justification of a dual standard in national legislation?' [1980/1] LIEI 1. See also *Noncyp* v *Bow Street Magistrates Court* [1989] 1 CMLR 634 (CA), in which the court purported to follow *Henn and Darby* and distinguish *Conegate*; yet the decision appears extremely vulnerable to an argument that the law in fact discriminated against imported goods.

21 Van Rijn (1988) 25 CMLRev 600–1 argues that therefore where national law imposes controls at the stage of marketing, it is at that stage that control of imported goods should also be exercised; i.e., control at point of importation under customs legislation would constitute unlawful discrimination.

PUBLIC POLICY

If there is a temptation to see the nebulous concept of 'public policy' as a catch-all justification for national obstacles to the free movement of goods, then as a matter of Community law it must be resisted. In order to maintain the narrow scope that must be allowed to derogations from the fundamental principle of free movement the European Court has refused to adopt a broad approach.[22] A state cannot invoke the notion of public policy to embrace any domestic social or economic issue about which it may feel concerned.[23] Thus, as has already been mentioned, the German Government in *Prantl*[24] found the Court wholly unreceptive to the argument that national laws backed by criminal sanctions should be taken as justified by the demands of public policy even if they restrict trade. The state bears a much heavier burden if it is to uphold such rules. It must show that the interest that is the subject of protection is itself within Article 36. The form of protection chosen (the criminal law in *Prantl*) does not of itself bring the issue within the scope of public policy for the purposes of Article 36.

In conformity with this rigorous interpretation the Court has always shown itself unwilling to subsume specific types of welfare law under the broad rubric of public policy. In *Kohl* v *Ringelhan*[25] it was argued that although consumer protection does not figure explicitly within Article 36, barriers to trade introduced for such reasons are justifiable as legitimate measures of public policy. The Court rejected this submission. Public policy does not include the state's concern to protect the economic interests of its consumers.[26] The exclusion of consumer protection from the Article 36 list, already plain from the Court's judgment in the Irish Souvenirs case,[27] was affirmed. The Court repeated this view in *Leclerc* v *Au Blé Vert*,[28] where it once again rehearsed its familiar policy approach to the interpretation of Article 36: 'Since it derogates from a fundamental rule of the Treaty, Article 36 must be interpreted strictly and cannot be extended to objectives not expressly listed therein.'

---

22 See similarly Ch. 18 in relation to the free movement of persons.
23 AGs Warner (Case 30/77 *R* v *Bouchereau* [1977] ECR 1999, 2025, in relation to the same phrase in Art. 48(3)) and Slynn (Case 72/83, note 6 above, p. 2767) use the familiar English analogy of public policy as an 'unruly horse' as a reason for the Court to be wary of mounting the beast.
24 Case 16/83, note 7 above.
25 Case 177/83 [1984] ECR 3651, [1985] 3 CMLR 340.
26 Should it? See discussion at pp. 504–5.
27 Case 113/80, note 2 above.
28 Case 229/83 [1985] ECR 1, [1985] 2 CMLR 286.

Once again consumer protection was held inadmissible as a justification for a rule that discriminated against imported products. More esoteric arguments based on the protection of artistic creation and cultural diversity in the book trade met precisely the same fate. Such worthy goals should be pursued through methods that do not discriminate against imports.[29]

In fact, the Court has proved itself rather clearer on what Article 36's reference to public policy does not cover than on what it does. The majority of instances in which public policy has been advanced to support an impediment to cross-frontier trade have resulted in relatively curt rejection.[30] One of the few cases in which a fuller discussion of the notion is to be found is *Cullet v Centre Leclerc*.[31] French law imposed minimum retail prices for petrol. Garages owned by the Leclerc chain sold petrol below the statutory minimum. Cullet, a competing retailer, sought an injunction to restrain its rival's policy of undercutting the minimum price. Leclerc's defence rested on Article 30. It argued that the minimum price constituted a hindrance to cross-frontier trade and that therefore it was free to disregard the unlawful French regulations. This argument was tested before the European Court, to which the matter was referred as a preliminary reference under Article 177. It is well established that minimum price-fixing is capable of constituting an unlawful barrier to trade where cheaper imported goods are deprived by the fixed price of the opportunity to take advantage of the price differential in their favour.[32] The French Government then sought refuge in Article 36.

Arguments based on the protection of the organization of the French petroleum industry and the need to secure distribution throughout the territory were rejected as falling outside the scope of Article 36; they were essentially economic justifications.[33] More significantly, the French Government claimed that the abolition of the statutory controls would stimulate a petrol price war. This, it alleged, would carry the risk of fomenting social unrest, perhaps involving violence. Public policy and public security therefore justified the regulations despite their restrictive effect on trade. The French submissions aimed to accommodate the threat of civil disturbance caused by cross-frontier trade within Article 36's reference to public policy. This approach might seem peculiar, but a linguistic point should be taken here in at least partial explanation. The French term *'ordre public'*, of which public policy is in this context the usual English translation, is apt to

29 See Ch. 17 on the treatment of such rules under Art. 30.
30 For curt acceptance (on relatively trivial facts), see Case 7/78 *R v Thompson* [1978] ECR 2247, [1979] 1 CMLR 47.
31 Case 231/83 [1985] ECR 305, [1985] 2 CMLR 524.
32 Case 82/77 *Openbaar Ministerie v Van Tiggele* [1978] ECR 25, p. 443 above.
33 See Case 7/61, note 4 above.

mislead a Briton. The French phrase encompasses civil disturbance. The French submissions appear more cogent if the notion of public policy is read with a flavour of the English idea of preservation of 'law and order' in mind.[34]

Advocate-General Verloren van Themaat was unwilling to accept that the French argument possessed any valid basis. He observed that such an approach would come close to undermining the whole idea of the common market. It would provide private interest groups with an incentive to agitate against free trade in order to supply their Government with a justification for imposing restraints on imports. Civil disobedience would be encouraged by acceding to the French submissions. The Advocate-General held that far from restricting trade to avoid alleged unrest among the citizenry, France should instead prepare to take effective internal measures to combat any illegal action that might disrupt public order. It might be observed in addition that a member state that fails to offer proper protection to imports and importers from illegal action by its own nationals stands in breach of its Community obligations.[35]

The European Court reached the same conclusion as its Advocate-General and indicated that the French law was in violation of Article 30. However, the Court adopted a different approach. It avoided the Advocate-General's view that the submissions under Article 36 must in principle fail, and instead briefly considered the evidence presented. The Court held that it had not been shown that the abolition of the price controls would result in violence of such a level that it could not be controlled by the national authorities using their available resources. This precluded reliance on Article 36.

Thus, whereas the Advocate-General rejected the argument in principle, the Court preferred to examine its merits. Only then did it decline to find the trade barrier justifiable. Both approaches arrive at the same destination but by different routes. The Advocate-General's path holds attractions. There is much to be said in principle for the view that internal disorder should not be a ground for unilateral action to restrict imports. Otherwise, governments will be susceptible to domestic political pressures and potentially extreme action by private lobbies with an interest in the imposition of protectionist barriers. The maintenance of free trade under Community law would be better ensured by locating the responsibility for sanctioning such national measures within Community, not national, structures.[36]

---

34 See the same phrase under Art. 48(3), relating to the free movement of persons (p. 562 below), where a similar linguistic point is taken by AG Warner in Case 30/77, note 23 above, p. 2023.

35 Under Art. 5 and, in more specific instances, under Art. 30.

36 The exception in Art. 224, considered on p. 464, reflects this in part only by

However, the Advocate-General's approach would come very close to wiping out public policy as a justification under Article 36 altogether. The Court's stance in *Cullet* v *Centre Leclerc* appears to remain faithful to the Treaty by examining the French argument, but finding it unsupported by the evidence adduced. The usual strict rules of interpretation under Article 36 serve to exclude unduly liberal invocations of public policy. The Court respects the exceptional jurisdiction of the member states to act unilaterally in the event of extreme violent disorder requiring large-scale repressive measures, when the demands of Article 36 may be held to be satisfied in respect of import restrictions.

Overall, it is fair to conclude that the Court's approach to the public-policy exception under Article 36 conforms to its usual techniques of interpretation in the field of derogations from the basic principle of free movement. It has proved itself readier to explain what public policy does not embrace than what it does, but no member state can feel confident of success when it puts forward public policy as a justification for hindering the free flow of goods between member states.

PUBLIC SECURITY

The argument that the free movement of goods threatens public security has been infrequently advanced. This may be attributable to a sensitivity that has caused issues of security to be dealt with cautiously through legislative action and political negotiation rather than in the context of litigation concerned with free trade. The leading case emphasizes the delicacy of this area, for it is a European Court decision that appears in tenor unusually receptive to arguments based on Article 36. It is *Campus Oil* v *Minister for Industry and Energy*.[37]

Ireland possesses no natural reserves of crude oil. It has one refinery, Whitegate in County Cork, which is owned by the state. The refinery produces petroleum from imported crude oil. In order to maintain the refinery in operation Irish legislation required importers of petroleum to buy up to 35 per cent of their total needs from the Irish refinery. Prices were fixed by the responsible Minister.

The matter reached the European Court by way of an Article 177 reference made by the Irish court before which Campus Oil, an importer, challenged the system. A breach of Article 30 was readily established. A

---

requiring states to 'consult each other' where states act 'in the event of serious internal disturbance'.

37 Case 72/83, note 6 above, noted by Oliver (1985) 22 CMLRev 307, Minor (1984) 9 ELRev 340. Cf. Case C-347/88 *Commission* v *Greece*, [1990] ECR I-4747.

trader was not free simply to import a consignment of petroleum into Ireland. It was necessary to purchase part of the delivered bulk from the local source. It was submitted on behalf of the Irish Government that public security required the imposition of such an obligation on importers. Ireland claimed the right to protect its only refinery by providing it with captive consumers, because without such a system the refinery could not be kept in operation. Closure would deprive the economy of an assured supply of energy necessary to sustain vital national institutions and services.

It might have been predicted that the European Court would dismiss this argument as a variant on the general economic justification that it has never been prepared to accept under Article 36.[38] In fact, the Court instead adopted a significantly softer line. It was prepared to accept that concern about energy supplies could transcend matters of purely economic interest and intrude on the security of the nation.[39] In modern economic conditions energy sources are fundamentally important for the very existence of the state. Article 36 was available to Ireland. The state is obliged to abide by the demands of the second sentence of Article 36. It would have to be shown that the refinery was unable to find purchasers of its output at a competitive price in order to justify the element of compulsion on importers. Moreover, the amount of petroleum that an importer was obliged to buy would have to be shown to be no higher than necessary in order to sustain the refinery. The application of these principles of proportionality and of alternative means is a matter for the national court in the context of an Article 177 reference such as Campus Oil.

As in all Article 36 cases, the Court in Campus Oil was forced to balance the demands of free trade against national claims to legitimate protection.[40] The security of the state's energy supply is an area of peculiar sensitivity. Campus Oil is a hint that the Court is prone to exercise particular caution in upholding free trade against national protection where traditional functions of the state are involved.[41] This area can best be resolved by legislation to establish in a clearer manner the limits of national and Community competence. Only then can national concerns about security be allayed by a comprehensive Community system, thus removing the ability to rely on Article 36. However, the Community's progress towards

38 See p. 454, Case 7/61, note 4 above.
39 See also Case 118/86 Openbaar Ministerie v Nertsvoederfabriek Nederland BV [1987] ECR 3883; provided the action can be justified under an existing head under Art. 36, the incidental achievement of broader economic objectives does not preclude reliance on Art. 36.
40 Ch. 17 discusses in more depth the Court's work in locating the margin between lawful and unlawful barriers to trade.
41 However, more recently there has been increasing intervention in state monopolies via the different route of Arts. 86 and 90; see p. 862.

a common energy policy has proved slow.[42] The limited steps that have been taken to establish continuity of supply in time of crisis were advanced by the Commission as grounds for rejecting Irish reliance on Article 36 in *Campus Oil*. The Court held that the existing Community measures failed to offer unconditional assurances that an adequate supply would be maintained. National measures justified under Article 36 could not be ruled out. The Court here exhibits understandable diffidence when confronted by the regulatory gap in Community energy policy.

Campus Oil is a decision that should be limited to the peculiar situation that prevails in the energy market in the Community. Advocate-General Verloren van Themaat in *Cullet* v *Centre Leclerc*[43] was concerned to confine its scope as a justification for restricting trade. He gave several reasons for a narrow interpretation of the notion of public security itself and, moreover, stressed that measures taken must in any event meet the tests of proportionality and alternative means.[44] In its judgment in *Cullet* the Court chose not to develop the concept of public security, but in any event found that the measures in question had not been shown to be justified in the circumstances.

Beyond the area of the free movement of goods, Articles 223–5 of the Treaty provide for the protection of interests of national security. Article 223 refers to measures taken by a state in the 'essential interests of its security'; Article 224 to measures taken in the event of serious internal disturbance, war, threat of war or in order to undertake obligations accepted for the purpose of maintaining peace and international security. Misuse of these powers may be controlled directly before the Court by virtue of Article 225, which applies in derogation from Articles 169 and 170. As exceptions to the basic notion of market integration, these provisions are to be interpreted narrowly.[45]

The notion of public security under Article 36 and, more generally, Articles 223–5 of the Treaty are capable of justifying impediments to the free circulation of goods of military sensitivity within the Community.[46] Difficulties in this sphere are inevitable in the absence of a comprehensive common security and defence policy for the Union. However, there is a

---

42 See Slot, *Energy and Competition* (1994) 31 CMLRev 511.

43 Case 231/83, note 31 above.

44 Similarly, in Case C-367/89 *Ministre des Finances* v *Richardt* [1991] ECR I-4621 [1992] 1 CMLR 61 the Court paid special attention to the demands of proportionality, even though it accepted that public security might in principle justify administrative checks on strategically important computer goods in transit from France via Luxembourg to the Soviet Union.

45 E.g., Case 13/68 *Salgoil SpA* v *Italian Ministry for Foreign Trade* [1968] ECR 453.

46 Case C-367/89, note 44 above; and see, on Art. 225, Case C-120/94 R *Commission* v *Greece* [1994] ECR I-3037.

risk that product market integration will be unduly obstructed where states invoke security interests against trade in goods that may be used both for civil purposes and for purposes touching security interests. Legislation has been put in place to eliminate border controls on so-called 'dual use' goods. A 1994 regulation establishes a framework for a common regime for controlling the export of dual use goods. Authorization by a member state is required for export of dual use goods. The same criteria are to be applied by all the member states in handling applications for authorization.[47]

THE PROTECTION OF HEALTH AND LIFE OF HUMANS, ANIMALS AND PLANTS

It is not surprising that the Treaty concedes that health risks are capable of justifying the imposition of controls on imports. It is equally unsurprising that the European Court has shown itself determined to prevent spurious allegations of health risks being deployed as a device for introducing protectionism. If a member state claims to need protection from dangerous imported products, then it will have to satisfy the Court that its actions are genuinely motivated by health concerns, that they are apt to achieve the desired objective and that there are no other means of achieving protection that are less restrictive of trade.

Health protection

In several celebrated cases member states have been declared by the European Court to be guilty of erecting barriers to trade that are not justified as measures of health protection. In *Commission* v *United Kingdom*[48] a ban on the import of poultry meat and eggs was imposed. The United Kingdom Government alleged that the ban was necessary to prevent British flocks being infected with Newcastle disease, a severe contagious condition that affects almost all kinds of poultry, and consequently justified under Article 36. The Court found that the United Kingdom had introduced the import controls with remarkable haste. There was a marked lack of consultation with Community institutions and other member states. It observed that there were strong suspicions that the regulations were in fact designed to exclude French-produced turkeys from the United Kingdom market in the approach to Christmas 1981. The Court

47 Reg. 3381/94 OJ 1994 L367. On the background, Leslie, *Dual Use Goods and the European Community* (1994) XVII Boston Coll Intl & Comp LR 193.
48 Case 40/82 [1982] ECR 2793, [1982] 3 CMLR 497.

noted that British poultry farmers had lobbied vigorously for the introduction of such protection at the time. One may assume that health concerns were not their central motivation. The United Kingdom failed to convince the Court that it had instituted any seriously considered health policy such as would justify reliance on Article 36 and was consequently declared in breach of its Treaty obligations. This was an instance of protectionism, hostile to the very idea of a common market. French turkey producers subsequently instituted civil proceedings before the English courts based on the infringement of directly effective Community law. Part of their statement of claim was struck out in the Court of Appeal, but they won £3.5 million compensation from the United Kingdom authorities in an out-of-court settlement.[49]

This does not mean that the state is obliged to provide conclusive proof that the product will threaten public health in order to take advantage of Article 36. The Court treads warily in rejecting genuine fears about safety. In *Officier van Justitie* v *Koninklijke Kassfabriek Eyssen BV*[50] a cheese producer faced criminal proceedings for breach of a Dutch ban on the use of nisin, a preservative, in processed cheese. It was argued that the ban restricted free trade in cheese and therefore was in violation of Article 30. Other states were prepared to allow the use of nisin and it was submitted that this precluded Dutch claims that a health risk existed such as to justify action under Article 36. Research into the effects of nisin had been undertaken by national and international bodies, including the Food and Agriculture Organization of the United Nations and the World Health Organization. The scientific evidence was equivocal. Some sources suggested that nisin could be harmful and the Netherlands based its ban on such evidence. Other evidence suggested nisin was perfectly safe, and in some states this view was preferred. Different dietary habits in different states were thought relevant to the level of risk presented by nisin consumption, but the exact relevance of such factors remained obscure. The Court took the view that a state is entitled to protect its public from substances the safety of which is the subject of genuine scientific doubt. The existence of a risk, even if disputed, is sufficient to justify recourse to Article 36. The decision in *Eyssen*, then, implies that Article 30 does not drive protection down to the lowest national common denominator.[51] Real doubt about a product's

---

49 *Bourgoin* v *MAFF*, note 19 above. The settlement was announced in parliament, HC Deb Vol 102 col 116 (WA), 22 July 1986.
50 Case 53/80 [1981] ECR 409, [1982] 2 CMLR 20. See also Case 174/82 *Officier van Justitie* v *Sandoz BV* [1983] ECR 2445, [1984] 3 CMLR 43; Case 94/83 *Albert Heijn BV* [1984] ECR 3263; Case 247/84 *Leon Motte* [1985] ECR 3887; Case 304/84 *Ministère Public* v *Muller* [1986] ECR 1511.
51 See pp. 523–7 more generally on the issue of Art. 30 as a potential means of reducing existing national safety and quality standards.

safety may justify restrictive action under Article 36 even if other states have formed a different view.

Where a ban is imposed in these circumstances a state falls under an obligation to monitor scientific inquiry. If it becomes apparent that the fears about the safety of the product are, in fact, unjustified, then the restrictions on trade will lose legitimacy and will have to be abandoned.[52] It is a question of fact when genuine scientific dispute about a product's safety is replaced by a consensus that it is safe and therefore entitled to unrestricted free circulation.

In R v Pharmaceutical Society, ex parte API[53] the Court accepted that less tangible aspects of health protection, such as psychosomatic phenomena, may justify restrictions on trade. Imported pharmaceutical products had commonly been supplied to patients by pharmacists in substitution for more expensive similar domestic preparations prescribed by the patient's doctor. The Pharmaceutical Society took steps to suppress this practice. The API, an importers' association, challenged the Society's intervention, which had naturally led to a dramatic reduction in the sales of imported pharmaceutical products, on the basis that it infringed Article 30.[54] The Court accepted that the facts disclosed evidence of a breach of Article 30, but indicated a readiness to accept that the steps taken against product substitution might be justifiable in order to reassure the patient and thereby enhance his or her recovery from illness. The supply of a familiar, named drug is capable of providing the patient with comfort, which might be destroyed, or even replaced by anxiety, if a different drug is provided. Therapeutic similarity between medicines is not necessarily apparent to the patient. Consequently, measures of the type adopted in the case serve to preserve the doctor's choice of appropriate treatment and are capable of justification under Article 36 as measures taken to protect public health.[55]

---

52 See Case 54/85 Ministère Public v Mirepoix [1986] ECR 1067, esp. para. 16 of the judgment. More generally, Art. 5 imposes positive obligations on states to cooperate in achieving the objectives of the Community; in Case 272/80 Frans-Nederlandse Maatschappig voor Biologische Producten [1981] ECR 3277, [1982] 2 CMLR 470, examined at p. 470 below, the Court referred to a duty 'to assist in bringing about a relaxation of the controls existing in intra-Community trade' (para. 14 of the judgment); see also in relation to obstacles under Art. 52 Case 71/76 Jean Thieffry v Conseil de l'Ordre des avocats [1977] ECR 765, p. 594 below.

53 Case 266/87 [1989] ECR 1295, [1989] 2 CMLR 751, noted by Hancher (1989) 26 CMLRev 729, Weatherill (1990) 53 MLR 699.

54 An important undercurrent to the case is that national trade-mark law precluded the importers from simply changing the names of their products to match their UK therapeutic equivalents. Trade-mark law effectively distorted competition. See Ch. 26, and particularly p. 855, on harmonization of national laws in this area.

55 On the impact of Art. 30 on national control of the supply of medicines designed to

Proportionality and the domestic comparison

The member state bears the burden of showing that there is a genuine risk of a threat to health.[56] This implies the collection of adequate scientific information, involving, wherever possible, international verification of the problems that are alleged. The Court is prepared to examine the steps taken internally by the member state concerned to counter the alleged threat. If the risk is more or less ignored within the borders of the state, then a strong suspicion is raised that the threat is not genuine and that the state is engaged in a policy of devious protection of its home industry. The state will be called on to explain such discrepancy in treatment. In *Rewe-Zentralfinanz* v *Landwirtschaftskammer*[57] the German authorities subjected imported fruit and vegetables to inspections for the presence of San José Scale. Rewe, an importer, refused to allow its goods to be checked and claimed that the requirement contravened Article 30 of the Treaty. The matter was referred to the European Court by a court in Cologne. Justification for the obstacle to trade was presented. The Court trod familiar ground in accepting that such inspections are capable of being justified. However, if imports are subject to controls in circumstances where home-produced goods are free of any such constraint, then arbitrary discrimination may be detected. It was thus incumbent on the German authorities to satisfy the German court (this being an Article 177 reference) that San José Scale was a threat of sufficient magnitude to justify the measures adopted and that appropriate effective internal measures were in place to combat the same disease.

In common with the normal rules of interpretation under Article 36, the Court insists not only that a genuine health risk be proved, but also that the measures taken are proportionate and no more restrictive than is necessary to deal with the problem. So, for example, even if the United Kingdom had been able to persuade the Court that Newcastle disease presented a serious threat to animal health justifying interference with free trade,[58] the measures taken could not have extended to a complete ban unless the United Kingdom could demonstrate why less restrictive meth-

---

protect public health, see also Case 215/87 *Schumacher* v *Hauptzollamt Frankfurt am Main Ost* [1989] ECR 617, [1990] 2 CMLR 465; Case C-369/88 *Delattre*, [1991] ECR I-1487; Case C-347/89 *Bayer* v *Eurim-Pharm*, [1991] ECR I-1747; Case C-62/90 *Commission* v *Germany*, [1992] ECR I-2575. For analysis, including legislative developments at Community level, see Thompson, *The Single Market for Pharmaceuticals*.
56 Case 227/82, note 9 above.
57 Case 4/75 [1975] ECR 843, [1977] 1 CMLR 599. See also Case 215/87, note 55 above.
58 Case 40/82, note 48 above.

ods, such as inspections or licensing of imported goods, failed to offer adequate protection.[59]

Through its case law the Court is astutely developing a notion of good administrative practice in the conduct of cross-border trade.[60] One may observe a form of indirect judicial harmonization of national practice. Inspections and licensing systems are justifiable under Article 36 provided the state is able to show the existence of a real threat to health coupled to proof that less restrictive means of tackling the problem would be inadequate. States must actively consider how to satisfy legitimate concerns about health protection without impeding intra-Community trade any more than is necessary. Applying these principles, it is plain that complete prohibitions on imports will be justifiable under primary Community law only in exceptional circumstances.

Double checking

These principles have been applied to the problem of 'double checking' of goods crossing borders. The idea is simple. A product may be exposed to a requirement that it be checked in its country of origin and then again in its country of final destination. This amounts to a serious impediment to free trade. The importing state's check may be justifiable when viewed in isolation; for example, because the product in question has given rise to real problems in the past and may therefore lawfully be inspected to ensure that some associated disease has been effectively eradicated. But does the fact that a test directed to this issue has already been carried out in the state of manufacture exclude the ability of the importing state to impose its own controls?

In *Denkavit Futtermittel* v *Minister für Ernährung, Landwirtschaft und Forsten*[61] the Court indicated that it views double checking as thoroughly unsatisfactory. It urged national authorities to cooperate in order to avoid such burdens. Moreover, national authorities are obliged to ascertain whether documents raise a presumption that imported goods comply with national requirements. A parallel may be observed in cases arising under Article 52, where the Court has insisted that a host state must inquire whether professional qualifications obtained in another member state are equivalent to its own.[62] Yet the Court was forced to concede that a second check might in certain circumstances remain lawful, although a state

---

59 See Case 42/82 *Commission* v *France* [1983] ECR 1013, [1984] 1 CMLR 160 and Case C-128/89 *Commission* v *Italy* [1990] ECR I-3239, [1991] 3 CMLR 720.
60 See Reich and Leahy, *Internal Market and Diffuse Interests*, p. 57.
61 Case 251/78 [1979] ECR 3369, [1980] 3 CMLR 513.
62 Case C-340/89 *Vlassopoulou* v *Ministerium für Justiz, Bundes- und Europaangelegenheiten Baden-Württemberg*, [1991] ECR I-2357, p. 594 below.

would have to demonstrate that its measures were necessary and proportionate. In *United Foods*[63] the Court declared that a second check could not be upheld under Article 36 if less restrictive means could be found for securing the importing state's objective. This suggests that if an importer is already in possession of a certificate that declares the item free of the disease for which the importing state wishes to check, then the proposed check would in principle be unlawful.

The Court has advanced its jurisprudence in this area to the point where a second check will be difficult, though not impossible, to justify. In *Commission* v *United Kingdom*,[64] an Article 169 case rather than an Article 177 reference, the European Court itself assumed the function of holding that a presumption of accuracy should be applied to documents accompanying UHT milk. Of course, the type of product is relevant. *Commission* v *United Kingdom* concerned UHT milk, where the importer is in a strong position, because the product is hermetically sealed on production. It is difficult for the importing state to argue that there is a reason for rechecking a good that is not normally susceptible to tampering in transit. There may be greater scope for lawful inspection in the state of destination where impairment during transportation is more feasible. The burden of proof remains on the state that imposes the restrictions.

In *Biologische Producten*[65] the Court accepted that an approval system could be introduced even where the product had already been approved in another member state. However, it heavily qualified this stance by emphasizing that tests could not be carried out where the goods have already been subjected to the same tests in the state of origin, and where the results of those tests are available. This indicates that a product accompanied by a certificate that declares that it has been tested in its state of origin is in principle free to circulate throughout the Community without being subjected to further tests. The state of import can justify a second test if it shows that the first test failed to deal with, for example, a particular disease with which the product is associated or if it can demonstrate that the test was in some way defective. However, the burden is on the importing state, which must adopt measures that are the least restrictive of trade necessary to achieve protection, and there is a presumption in favour of adequacy of the first test. In pursuit of good administrative practice[66] the Court has also shown an increasing concern that national procedures be.

63 Case 132/80, note 8 above.
64 Case 124/81, [1983] ECR 203, [1983] 2 CMLR 1.
65 Case 272/80, note 52 above. See also Case 406/85 *Procureur de la République* v *Gofette and Gilliard* [1987] ECR 2525; Case C-373/92 *Commission* v *Belgium*, judgment of 8 June 1993.
66 See Reich and Leahy, *Internal Market and Diffuse Interests*, p. 57.

transparent and susceptible to challenge by the trader wishing to take advantage of the rights conferred by Community law.[67]

Such matters have become increasingly important as the integration of the market accelerates. There is an underlying idea that states should show mutual respect for each other's testing facilities, which, as the Court observed in *Wurmser*,[68] is a specific expression of a more general principle of mutual confidence between authorities of the member states.[69] In *Biologische Producten* the Court declared that 'the authorities of the Member States are ... required to assist in bringing about a relaxation of the controls existing in intra-Community trade',[70] which is capable of being interpreted as imposing a positive obligation on national bodies to co-operate actively with regulatory bodies in other member states.[71] This may be seen as a manifestation of the increasingly prominent and influential role played either explicitly or *sub silentio* by Article 5 of the Treaty.[72]

In many areas Community secondary legislation lays down specifically the nature of permissible controls. The fundamental objective of this legislative programme is to set common Community standards of health protection that eliminate the need to enforce different national systems. Such laws are central to the task of creating an internal market, which, according to Article 7a EC, comprises an area without internal frontiers. Accordingly, such Community harmonization legislation in principle excludes member state reliance on Article 36 to justify more rigorous checks.[73] In many sectors the legal assessment of national measures that restrict trade is performed in the light of secondary rather than primary Community law. For example, in *Commission* v *Italy*[74] the Court ruled

---

67 E.g., Case 54/85, note 52 above, para. 17 of the judgment, Case C-42/90 *Jeane-Claude Bellon* [1990] ECR I-4863; Case C-18/88 *Régie des Telegraphes* v *GB Inno*, [1991] ECR I-5941; Joined Cases C-46/90 and C-93/91 *Procureur du Roi* v *J.-M. Lagauche and others*, judgment of 27 October 1993.

68 Case 25/88 *Esther Bouchara, née Wurmser* [1989] ECR 1105.

69 The Cassis de Dijon line of authority has developed this idea far beyond mutual respect for administrative practice as a means of market integration; see Ch. 17.

70 Case 272/80, note 52 above, para. 14 of the judgment; see similarly Case 188/84 *Commission* v *France* [1986] ECR 419, para. 16 of the judgment.

71 See note 52 above; see also the Commission's observations on such duties submitted in Case 251/78, note 61 above, [1979] ECR 3369, 3381.

72 See Temple Lang, 'Community Constitutional Law: Article 5 EEC Treaty' (1990) 27 CMLRev 645. See further p. 594.

73 See, e.g., Case 5/77 *Tedeschi* v *Denkavit* [1977] ECR 1555, [1978] 1 CMLR 1; Case 251/78, note 61 above; Case 190/87 *Kreis Borken* v *Moormann* [1988] ECR 4689, [1990] 1 CMLR 656; Case C-128/89, note 59 above; Case C-83/92 *Pierrel SpA and others* v *Ministero della Sanità*, judgment of 7 December 1993. In some circumstances unimplemented legislation may be relied upon by individuals against the state to preclude the application of conflicting national law; see e.g., Case 148/78 *Pubblico Ministero* v *Ratti* [1979] ECR 1626 and, generally, p. 345 on direct effect.

74 Case C-294/92 [1994] ECR I-4311.

Italy in breach of its Community law obligations where it imposed requirements of prior authorization on all imports of plants susceptible to fire blight. Directive 77/93, as subsequently amended, regulated the field. It set up a system for checking plants in the state of origin, where a certificate was issued. The Directive permitted inspections in the state of destination only in specified circumstances, which were far more limited than those in which Italy purported to act. The Court stated that '. . . the aim of the directive is to remove barriers to trade while reorganizing phytosanitary inspections within the Community'. It ruled that in pursuit of that objective a system had been introduced by the Community under which it is the responsibility of the state of origin to check whether the products satisfy the relevant health requirements and under which permitted measures in the state of destination are strictly limited. The Court therefore interpreted the Directive as having replaced the power of states unilaterally to adopt inspection measures. Italy had failed to comply with its obligations under the Directive. The Court added that the Italian system obstructed trade in goods contrary to Article 30 and that the objective of the protection of plants under Article 36 could not be employed to justify the restrictions, because the harmonization Directive had eliminated the possibility of recourse to Article 36. The Court declared that '. . . [A]ppropriate checks must be carried out and the protective measures adopted within the framework outlined by the harmonization directive'.[75] Community legislative intervention may rule out more than the possibility of frontier checks. In *Ligur Carni Srl and others* v *Unità Sanitaria Locale No XV di Genova and others*[76] the Court ruled that Community legislative activity prohibited imported goods accompanied by a certificate issued by the exporting state in accordance with Community rules from being subjected to systematic checking in the municipality of the importing state through which the goods passed in transit and the municipality for which they were destined.[77]

Notwithstanding this general principle, some Community measures are not exhaustive, and outside their specified field of application permit member states to act subject to the normal control exercised by Article 36.[78] Moreover, some Community measures may provide express derogations even within their field of application that preserve a member state's

---

75 The Court referred to Case 5/77 *Tedeschi* v *Denkavit*, note 73 above.
76 Joined Cases C-277/91, C-318/91 and C-319/91, judgment of 15 December 1993.
77 Fiscal charges were also incompatible with EC law; Ch. 13, p. 394 above.
78 See, e.g., Case 125/88 *Nijman* [1989] ECR 3533, [1991] 1 CMLR 92. See also Case C-241/89 *SARPP* v *Chambre Syndicat des Raffineurs et Conditionneurs de sucre de France* [1990] ECR-I 4695; Case C-369/88, note 55 above.

independent competence, usually within defined limits.[79] All harmonization measures require careful scrutiny in order to ensure that their allocation of competence is accurately interpreted.[80] Some harmonization measures may imply a residual member state competence in the administration of the harmonized system. So in *Simmenthal* v *Italian Finance Administration*[81] the Court held frontier inspections of meat undertaken by the Italian authorities for the purpose of protecting public health to be unlawful. Directives 64/422 and 64/423 had introduced harmonized animal health rules, which had been implemented in all member states. Such a common system guaranteed that all member states had standardized their procedures in relation to, for example, health standards in slaughterhouses and in the storage and transport of meat. The Court observed that the directives had as their purpose the establishment of equivalent guarantees of health protection in each member state, with the result that the task of supervision was effectively transferred exclusively to the authorities of the state of export. The need for multiple systematic frontier inspections had been eliminated by the introduction of a Community regime and, in law, this precluded Italian reliance on Article 36 to justify unilateral action. However, the directives explicitly envisaged that a state could prohibit the importation of animals that inspection had revealed were contaminated by a notified disease. The Court accepted that this implied that it was permissible under Community law to check documents and, occasionally, to inspect consignments of meat. However, such checks must not constitute arbitrary trade barriers; that is, they must adhere to the principles of proportionality and alternative means.[82] The net result was that in order to facilitate the free movement of safe produce occasional checks could be undertaken by an importing state, but only to a limited extent in strict accordance with the terms of the Directives.

Harmonization legislation is designed to smooth the transformation of the market into a unified economic trading space, in which, in the long term, a common set of controls is exercised throughout the territory of the Community in accordance with need and efficiency, not the accidents of national frontiers. The passage of such legislation is a key component in

79 E.g. Case 4/75, note 57 above, in which the controls of San José Scale under Dir. 69/466 were interpreted as supplementing, not replacing, national measures. Stricter national controls could be justified, although the normal rules of interpretation under Article 36 must be adhered to (p. 468). The Treaty provision on which the legislation is based, rather than the terms of the legislation, may itself provide scope for derogation from the Community rule; see pp. 482–3 on Art. 100a.

80 Use of Art. 177 may be appropriate where the matter is raised at national level.

81 Case 35/76 [1976] ECR 1871, [1977] 2 CMLR 1; Case 46/76 *Bauhuis* v *Netherlands* [1977] ECR 5; Case 190/87, note 73 above.

82 See p. 455.

the process of bringing, first, the internal market and, subsequently, the common market to fruition, and therefore occupies much of the Community legislature's time. In the interim the development of the body of Community legislation and the extent to which it partially coexists with and partially supersedes national laws in a similar field represents an illuminating study in the problems of allocating competence between different levels in the evolving Community structure.[83]

Charging a fee for inspections

Suppose that a member state that requires an importer to subject goods to an inspection demands that the trader pay the cost of the inspection. There are then two elements to the impediment to importation: the fee, which is a fiscal charge, and the physical barrier presented by the inspection procedure. The EC Treaty establishes a demarcation between fiscal and physical barriers to trade. The former are considered under Articles 12 and 95,[84] the latter under Article 30. A system involving a fee charged for an inspection consequently requires assessment from the perspective of two separate Treaty provisions, which are not coextensive in their scope.[85] In accordance with the fundamental rule of interpretation that any derogation from the principle of free circulation of goods within the Community must be construed narrowly, both fee and inspection must be justified independently of each other in accordance with the relevant Treaty provision. An ability to justify one does not automatically offer a justification for the other. It is thus perfectly possible that an inspection held lawful under Article 36 may be accompanied by a levy held unlawful under Article 12, with the result that the importer is obliged to submit to the inspection but entitled to refuse to pay for it.

So in *Marimex* v *Italian Finance Administration*[86] the Italian Government's submission that a fee should be held compatible with Community law provided that the inspection to which the fee relates is justified under Article 36 met with rejection by the Court. The Court insisted that the lawfulness of the fee required assessment separately from the physical inspection, and that the fee, as a fiscal charge, had to conform with Article 12. Article 12 contains no explicit justification provision analogous to Article 36, but merely offers derogation through narrowly defined judge-

---

83 For broader discussion, see Select Further Reading, p. 904, *The effect of Community Legislation on National Competence.*

84 See Chs. 13, 14.

85 See Case 74/76 *Ianelli and Volpi* v *Meroni* [1977] ECR 557.

86 Case 29/72 [1972] ECR 1309; see also Case 46/76, note 81 above; Case 7/68 *Commission* v *Italy* [1968] ECR 423; Case 35/76, note 81 above; Joined Cases C-277/91, C-318/91 and C-319/91, note 76 above.

made 'exceptions'.[87] It is thus apparent that the treatment of an inspection and its related fee differs in Community law in a manner that corresponds to the difference in scope between the prohibition contained in Articles 30–36 and that contained in Article 12.

In *Commission* v *Belgium*[88] it was observed that if (as was not shown, but was assumed for the purposes of the case) an inspection was permitted by virtue of a Community directive, but not thereby made compulsory, a charge levied to cover the cost of the inspection would be unlawful under Article 12. The matter would be different if Community law required the inspection to be made, in which case a fee proportionate to the cost of the procedure could lawfully be made. This distinction emerges from the Court's jurisprudence under Article 12.[89] Thus, it is perfectly conceivable that the costs of a lawful inspection may fall on the importer if the inspection is made mandatory by Community law, but on the state if Community law merely authorizes the inspection. This seems rather anomalous, but perhaps reflects a presumption that it is only in the clearest cases, where impediments to trade are not just acceptable but essential to the Community itself rather than to individual member states, that costs should fall on the individual whose trading activities are furthering the objective of market integration. Similarly, where a state finds justification for an inspection under the terms of Article 36, it can require the trader to reimburse only the costs of protecting its own national interests provided the restrictive tests developed by the Court in relation to Article 12 are met.

Finally, if the fee charged relates to a general system of inspection and fees that applies within the member state to the marketing of all goods without making any distinction according to origin, then the fiscal charge falls to be considered under Article 95, not Article 12.[90] However, if there are special rules applicable only to imports, then the matter reverts to analysis under Article 12.[91]

---

87 See p. 388.
88 Case 314/82 [1984] ECR 1543, [1985] 3 CMLR 134.
89 See p. 393 above.
90 See Ch. 14. See, e.g., Case 29/87 *Dansk Denkavit* v *Landbrugsministeriet* [1988] ECR 2965, p. 417.
91 As in, e.g., Case 29/72, note 86 above; Case 314/82, note 88 above. See also Case 35/76, note 81 above; Case 46/76, note 81 above.

THE PROTECTION OF NATIONAL TREASURES POSSESSING
ARTISTIC, HISTORIC OR ARCHAEOLOGICAL VALUE

The cultural justification of protecting national treasures, which one would expect normally to relate to control of exports rather than imports, has received little attention in case law or academic writing. In *Commission v Italy*[92] the defendant state submitted that cultural artefacts were not to be considered goods in the economic sense at all and that therefore controls over the export of art treasures were wholly outside the scope of the economic objectives of the Treaty. The case was dealt with under Article 12, for a tax on export was involved, and the physical barriers also inherent in the system were not considered at all. However, the Court refused to accept the argument presented by the Italian Government and held that paintings possess an economic value and are capable of forming the subject of commercial transactions. They are therefore covered by the Treaty provisions forbidding fiscal barriers to the free movement of goods. It is submitted that the same analysis would apply to Article 30 and that controls over such goods would in principle contravene Article 30.[93] Justification for restricting the movement of such goods must be based on Article 36 and is subject to the usual narrow rules of interpretation.

In the absence of litigation on the point one can only speculate on the interpretation that the Court would be prepared to attach to this head.[94] By analogy with the Court's approach to public morality, one might suppose that there exists some latitude for member states to make their own determination of what constitutes a national treasure and that ideas may legitimately differ state by state. The concept of a nation is itself rather imprecise and certainly need not be coextensive with that of a member state, so it is probable that items of especial value to part of a state can be accommodated within the notion of a national treasure. None the less, drawing an analogy from the notion of public policy, Community law doubtless imposes an outer limit to the scope of justification. It would be incumbent on a member state to demonstrate why the item in question possesses such importance that it goes beyond mere high artistic quality and impinges on the cultural or historical heritage of the nation.[95] High value, an economic matter, is insufficient. Finally, in accordance with the

---

92 Case 7/68 [1968] ECR 423, [1969] CMLR 1.
93 Cf. Case C-2/90 *Commission v Belgium*, p. 516 below, where waste was regarded as subject to the rules on the free movement of goods.
94 See Oliver, *Free Movement of Goods*, para. 8.59 *et seq.*
95 In some cases it might be necessary to show why there is a link with that nation; which member state (if any) would be entitled to invoke this head in respect of a Van Gogh canvas? Or the Elgin Marbles?

familiar general rules of interpretation under Article 36, any attempt to rely on this justification will be scrutinized carefully in order to ascertain that a member state is not laying false claim to an alleged cultural item that it wishes to retain simply because the product is a scarce resource.

The existence under Article 36 of this head left open the possibility of its invocation in defence of border controls designed to forestall removal of treasures from national territory. Therefore, in the approach to the 1992 deadline for the completion of the internal market, attention was devoted to the creation of a Community regime that could accommodate national concerns in the field without the need to maintain border controls. This proved a complex task. Only in 1993 were important breakthroughs made, although the above discussion of the meaning of a national treasure is not superfluous, for the legislative measures adopted offer little elaboration of this definitional matter. Regulation 752/93 implements Regulation 3911/92 on the export of cultural goods.[96] A common system of export licences for cultural goods leaving the EC is established. The Regulation sets out the procedures governing the licensing system. Licences for export are to be made out on a form conforming to a specimen in the Annex to the Regulation. The member states operate under a common regime, to preclude the possibility that in the internal market items may be moved to the member state with the least stringent export regime and shipped from there out of the Community. Directive 93/7 is closely associated with the licensing system agreed to by the member states. The Directive deals with the return of illegally exported cultural items to the member state from which they have been exported. Principles governing return are set out in the Directive. The Directive encourages the development of administrative cooperation between the member states and provides an indicative list of measures that may be taken.[97] These measures have internal market policy as their primary focus and therefore they constitute, at most, an indirect form of Community cultural policy.[98] Article 128 EC, Title IX on *Culture* inserted by the Treaty on European Union, offers the prospect of more vigorous cultural policy-making. It envisages both the promotion of the culture of the member states and a European cultural identity, although the possibility of harmonization of laws is explicitly excluded by Article 128.

---

96 OJ 1993 L77/24, OJ 1992 L395/1 respectively.
97 OJ 1993 L74/74.
98 Voudouri, *Circulation et protection des biens culturels dans l'Europe sans frontières* [1994] RDP 479.

THE PROTECTION OF INDUSTRIAL AND COMMERCIAL PROPERTY

This head refers to rights such as patents, trade marks and copyrights, which are typically tied to the grant of exclusive territorial protection. The central feature of a patent held, say, in the United Kingdom is the right to exclude similar goods made elsewhere, including products made in other member states. National protection of industrial and commercial property raises severe problems for a legal regime that is committed to removing barriers to trade. The issues extend beyond Articles 30–36 and also encompass, particularly, the Community's competition rules.[99]

THE LEGISLATIVE ROLE

The Court accepts that Article 36 preserves the possibility of state action to protect the interests listed therein. Areas of morality, security and health, for example, remain susceptible to national action in their defence, notwithstanding the trade barriers that occur in consequence. Member states retain competence to select the aspects of public morality, for example, that they feel require protection. However, Community law sets the limits to such regulation where barriers to the free movement of goods that cannot be justified result in consequence. There is a heavy burden of proof on the state to demonstrate that the interest within Article 36 to which it is appealing is genuinely threatened by the import of goods from another member state. The member state must, in addition, satisfy the court that its action is apt to meet the threat and that its response is necessary and proportionate.

THE INTERIM NATURE OF ARTICLE 36

Article 36 operates as an interim protection pending the completion of the common market. It permits states to resist the impetus towards free trade in order to maintain and protect certain interests of particular sensitivity and importance. The subsequent introduction of harmonization legislation in the relevant area in principle removes the availability of justification

99 See Ch. 26.

under Article 36 and constitutes the next step towards a common market regulated by common rules. In theory, harmonization preserves the protection of the valuable interests referred to in Article 36, but it performs this function in the context of a Community-wide rule, which then facilitates free trade on common standards applicable in all member states. The development of harmonized rules possesses a dual objective in the development of the Community: protection of key interests *and* the establishment of free trade.[100]

The Commission originally felt that the termination of that interim power to rely on Article 36 to justify barriers to trade was central to the project of completing the internal market by the end of 1992. The Commission aspired to the introduction of a sophisticated regime of Community-wide regulation or, at least, mutually recognized national regulation by the end of 1992 that would preclude the need and the ability for member states to take unilateral action in derogation from the basic principles of free movement. However, a less radical compromise was achieved in the Single European Act in the shape of Article 100b, under which a Council decision is required.[101] The deadline at the end of 1992 did not automatically abolish legitimate reliance on Article 36.[102] Pending Council action,[103] the incomplete nature of the internal market will continue to provide a potential basis for valid justification of member state measures for some time to come. Equally, however, the amendments of the Single European Act do not subvert existing Community law on the elimination of national barriers to trade that cannot be justified.[104]

At the end of 1993, the Commission communicated to the Council and the Parliament its *Operational Conclusions reached in the light of the inventory drawn up pursuant to Article 100b*.[105] It asserts that Article 100b is not 'a second legal basis designed to harmonize notionally what has not been harmonized under Article 100a, but a provision aimed at facilitating the mutual recognition of non-harmonized national provisions'. On the basis

---

100 This dual objective may be observed in areas of harmonization policy other than the free movement of goods; see e.g., Case 43/75 *Defrenne* v *SABENA* in relation to sex discrimination, p. 614.
101 Ehlermann, 'The Internal Market following the SEA', (1987) 24 CMLRev 361, 399–402; Dehousse, 'Completing the Internal Market' in Bieber *et al.* (eds.) *1992*, p. 326; Reich, 'Protection of Diffuse Interests in the EEC', (1988) 11 JCP 395, 406; Bermann, 'The Single European Act', (1989) Col. J. Transnat.L. 529, 546–7.
102 For discussion, see Schermers, 'The Effect of the Date 31 December 1992' (1991) 28 CMLRev 275.
103 *Quaere* the use of Art. 175 (Ch. 8) to require action.
104 Under Art. 36 or as necessary to satisfy a mandatory requirement; see p. 508. The SEA did not introduce a new transitional period. For discussion see refs. at note 101 above; also H. Glaesner, 'The Single European Act' (1986) 6 YEL 283, 295–6.
105 OJ 1993 C353/4.

of information received from member states in drawing up its inventory, the Commission saw no need 'for any specific measures for the recognition of equivalence at Community level'. The Commission is particularly concerned to secure the transparent and effective management of the internal market, so that where blockages to free movement occur, the reasons may be appreciated and appropriate solutions devised. To this extent the Commission's focus is more on the administration of the existing rules than on new legislative initiatives. This practical edge is also apparent in the Sutherland Report of 1992, which is strongly motivated by the need to achieve effective administrative enforcement of the rules of the internal market.[106] In response, the Commission has prepared frameworks within which the application and effective management of the rules by national and Community institutions is intended to occur in partnership.[107]

THE FUNCTION OF LEGISLATION

The Community's legislative harmonization programme is a fuller and more mature approach to trade regulation than the application of Articles 30–36. The Court in applying Articles 30–36 is attempting to establish a margin between the lawful and the unlawful trade barrier, yet it is often performing this function with relatively little explicit background support from legislation. The margin has been set largely with reference to the Court's own conception of the trade-off between national regulatory competence and free trade. The Court's role is essentially negative. To uphold a restrictive national rule on the basis that it conforms to the demands of Article 36 admits of continuing partitioning of the market; to strike down a national rule as incompatible with Article 30 opens up the market but is essentially an exercise in 'negative harmonization' in the sense that free trade has been achieved through abolition of a rule rather than the creation of a common regulatory structure. The Court can influence the nature of legitimate national action through its interpretation of the scope of Article 36, yet its activity is typically in response to national practice. It cannot intervene directly to set common standards in advance. Harmonization is an altogether more positive contribution to the development of the Community and the common regulation of the single economic space. The legislature is able to establish a regime that breaks down market-partitioning national rules and replaces them with a Community

106 *The Internal Market after 1992: Meeting the Challenge* (Report to the EEC Commission by the High Level Group on the Operation of Internal Market).
107 E.g. COM (93) 256, COM (93) 632, COM (94) 29.

system that aims to accommodate diverse tradition within a flexible yet essentially unified framework.

From these basic concepts flow the principles of Community law on harmonization of laws motivated by the objective of market integration. Pending harmonization, Articles 30–36 apply to national trade barriers. A state may not escape the application of the Article 30 prohibition by arguing that it is awaiting the passage of harmonization legislation.[108] It is precisely during that interim period that Article 30 is designed to apply. As a corollary, once harmonization has been achieved, the application of Article 36 is, in principle, excluded.[109] A state may not justify a measure by reference to Article 36 if a harmonized Community regime has occupied the field. The purpose of harmonization is to facilitate free circulation within the Community and this must in principle exclude unilateral derogation. This also implies that a harmonized regime itself must conform to the demands of Article 30. In principle, the Community itself can no more breach Article 30 than can the member states. However, in the few cases involving challenge to the compatibility of Community legislation with Article 30,[110] the Court has indicated that since the Community legislature acts in the general interest of the Community, whereas national authorities act in the domestic interest, the application of Article 30 assumes a rather different character in this area. The Court has been prepared to accept that Community legislation that sanctions obstacles to free trade at national frontiers is compatible with Article 30, provided that the obstacles so created are necessary to ensure the effective operation of a Community-wide system and constitute less of a hindrance to trade than the pre-existing system based on national controls. Thus, Community legislation that serves to advance the process of economic integration is capable of being held in conformity with Article 30 despite the inclusion of provisions that permit national authorities to impose frontier controls.[111] The Court's approach should, however, be taken as an expression of the incomplete nature of the common market. The transformation of the individual markets of the member states into a unified area of economic activity demands that Community measures ignore national frontiers, except where reliance upon them is efficient and objectively justified. The

---

108 Case 193/80 *Commission* v *Italy* [1981] ECR 3019.
109 But harmonization legislation is frequently more complex than this simple model suggests; see further p. 473.
110 See, e.g., Case 15/83 *Denkavit Nederland* v *Hoofproduktschap* [1984] ECR 2171 (Reg. 1725/79); Case 37/83 *Rewe-Zentrale* v *Landwirtschaftskammer Rheinland* [1984] ECR 1229 [1985] 2 CMLR 586 (Dir. 77/93).
111 See Case 35/76, note 81 above; Case 46/76, note 81 above; Case 80–81/77 *Ramel* v *Receveur des Douanes* [1978] ECR 927. For discussion see Oliver, *Free Movement of Goods*, para 4.08 *et seq.*; Burrows, *Free Movement*, pp. 54–7.

Court's application of Article 30 to Community legislation may be expected to become more rigorous as the integration of the market accelerates.

THE POLICY OF HARMONIZATION

In many areas relating to harmonization policy there are fierce debates about the nature of the common regime under which the Community ought to operate, and even whether a common regime is needed at all. It has been observed that standards of public morality differ from state to state as a result of the protection of national rules under Article 36. This may cause goods lawfully produced and marketed in, say, Denmark to be excluded from the United Kingdom. Does a common market require a harmonized regime in this area; if so, how shall its content be identified? Such issues are, it will be noted, quite distinct from matters of public health, where subjective assessment of national tradition plays a much less prominent role. Thus it can be seen that the several heads of Article 36 neither are nor should be treated in an identical fashion under Community law.

Methods of harmonization have themselves undergone radical change. The diversity of the Community means that any attempt to create a single harmonized regime is likely to be fruitless. The task of achieving sufficient agreement is daunting. Moreover, the elimination of the remarkable diversity of the member states is, in any event, undesirable. It would stifle tradition and it would ossify existing practice, thereby deterring innovation by business. Therefore, the replacement of a range of national rules by a single, inflexible Community rule has become a discredited option in most circumstances. Adopting this perspective, the more modern approach is to accommodate different traditions within a flexible Community free-trade framework. This suggests that in some instances the Community may establish a minimum standard, above which states may adopt stricter rules if they so choose. This carries an implication of differentiated progress towards Community integration, albeit within a framework established by Community rules, but that may be both inevitable and desirable in a Community that is characterized by remarkable heterogeneity.

The Commission's policy of greater flexibility was expressed in its 'New approach to technical harmonization'.[112] This committed the Commission to setting basic rules governing health and safety of products but,

---

112 COM(85)19, adopted by the Council in its Resolution of 7 May 1985; OJ 1985 C136/1.

outside that area, the Commission was prepared to permit flexibility by manufacturers. This reduced the stifling effect of uniformity.[113]

In 1987 the Single European Act introduced legislative procedures that respected the ability of states to depart from norms established under Community legislation. Article 100a allows the adoption by qualified majority of measures designed, broadly, to contribute to the completion of the internal market, as defined in Article 7a EC. Some member states feared that the pursuit of free trade through the adoption of such legislation might jeopardize established national rules of social protection. Accordingly, Article 100a(4) was simultaneously introduced, which permits states, under defined procedures whereby the state must notify the Commission, to 'apply national provisions on grounds of major needs referred to in Article 36, or relating to the protection of the environment or the working environment'. The precise circumstances in which Article 100a(4) may be invoked remain shrouded in mystery.[114] Its only examination by the Court was rather unenlightening. The Court annulled a decision pursuant to Article 100a(4) in which the Commission had confirmed German rules imposing stricter controls on pentachlorophenol (PCP), a preservative, than were fixed by the relevant directive, 91/173.[115] The Court ruled the decision inadequately reasoned within the meaning of Article 190 EC.[116] It did not explore in depth the nature of Article 100a(4). However, for all its legal obscurity, the provision reflects a political commitment to the preservation of national regulations despite their obstructive effect where Community standards are considered inadequate.

Further manifestations of this policy may be observed outside the sphere of harmonization of rules directly relating to goods. The Single European Act introduced in Articles 130r-t a new title dealing with the environment and conferred legislative powers in the area on the Council. However, Article 130t provides that measures adopted 'shall not prevent any Member State from maintaining or introducing more stringent protective measures '. This provision is freer from interpretative doubt than Article 100a(4). It plainly recognizes that Community intervention introduces only a minimum standard, which states may choose to exceed.[117]

---

113 See further Ch. 17, p. 523.
114 For attempted unravelling see, e.g., Ehlermann (1987) 24 CMLRev 361, Bermann (1989) Col. J. Transnat. L. 529; Jacque (1986) 22 RTDE 575, 599–601; Flynn, 'How Will Article 100A(4) Work? A Comparison with Article 93' (1987) 24 CMLRev 689; D Waelbroeck (1989) 25 CDE 41, 54–60.
115 Case C-41/93 *France v Commission* [1994] ECR I-1829.
116 See Ch. 5, p. 144.
117 It is also provided in Art. 130t that measures must still conform to the basic principles of Art. 30. See p. 514 on the impact of Art. 30 on national environmental protection laws. Ch. 8, p. 252, deals with judicial supervision of the selection of

In a sense, such provisions detract from the notion of uniformity in a common market. Yet, more realistically, they reflect the notion that the Community cannot legislate in advance to cover all problems that may arise. They respect initiatives taken at national level and suggest the development of different levels of regulatory competence in the Community.[118]

The Maastricht Treaty introduced further such provisions. For example, a new title concerned with consumer protection follows the pattern set by the Single European Act's treatment of the environment. It empowers the Community to act in order to contribute to the attainment of a high level of consumer protection, but declares that such action shall not prevent any member state from maintaining or introducing more stringent protective measures.[119] Accordingly, it remains within the competence of the member states to adopt rules designed to protect the consumer even after the Community has acted in the field, provided only that any resulting obstacle to trade in goods remains justified under either Article 36 or, in respect of the economic interests of consumers, under the mandatory requirements that may justify indistinctly applicable rules.[120]

In conclusion, harmonization has implications extending far beyond its role as a method of preventing a member state from relying on Article 36 to obstruct the free movement of goods. The development of the Community's regulatory policy requires a rational basis for allocating competence between the different levels of government within the Community. In recent years a great deal of attention has been devoted to the 'principle of subsidiarity' as a guideline, although politicians using the phrase have tended to neglect to define it in precise terms.[121] The Maastricht Treaty amendments attempt to give shape to the principle by introducing Article 3b, which insists that Community activity shall be limited to where the 'objectives of proposed action cannot be sufficiently achieved by the Member States'. The specific words are additions to the principles set out in the Treaty, but the notion is not new in Community law. The Community has always in the past needed to respect the position of the member states in the development and administration of policy. Specific manifestations of the idea of subsidiarity in pre-Maastricht Community law may be found in Article 130r(4) EEC, which provided that 'the

---

the correct Treaty base for legislation that affects both the free movement of goods and the protection of the environment.
118 See Select Further Reading, p. 904, *The Effect of Community Legislation on National Competence.*
119 Art. 129a EC.
120 See p. 508.
121 For discussion, see Wilke and Wallace, *Subsidiarity.* See Ch. 1, pp. 12–15.

Community shall take action relating to the environment to the extent to which the objectives . . . can be attained better at Community level than at the level of the individual Member States';[122] and in the Mergers Regulation, which attempts in Articles 9 and 21 to ensure that even large 'Community dimension' mergers shall be regulated at national level where that is shown to be appropriate.[123] If Community lawyers have been applying the notions of subsidiarity for many years, without using the phrase as such, it remains to be seen whether the inclusion of the principle in the Treaty will permit challenges to Community legislative initiatives by states on the basis that they intrude on matters more efficiently dealt with at national level.[124] At present, Article 3b EC, although doubtless a focus for political debate, seems justiciable to a limited extent only.[125]

OTHER JUSTIFICATIONS

It has been explained that one aspect of the Court's narrow interpretation of Article 36 is its refusal to permit grounds based on broad economic policy to justify the introduction of trade barriers.[126] Economic difficulties concern the Community as a whole and, accordingly, action to adjust the operation of the common market cannot be taken unilaterally by a single member state. Measures must be adopted under procedures that ensure that the wider Community interest is taken into account.

Article 103 provided for the adoption of measures required to meet short-term economic difficulties (conjunctural policy). Articles 107, 108 and 109 allowed the adoption of measures to meet problems consequential on exchange-rate changes and balance-of-payments difficulties. Action could be taken through these procedures even where obstacles to trade ensued that would otherwise be incompatible with Community law. However, states were not permitted to act unilaterally, apart from in urgent situations referred to in Article 109. Community authorization was required. It was always envisaged that harmonization of policy-making between states would inevitably reduce the circumstances in which such

---

122 Repealed by TEU and now governed by Art. 3b EC.
123 Examined in detail in Ch. 25, p. 818.
124 Challenges by private parties may also be possible, although there would be formidable problems of *locus standi*; see Ch. 8.
125 Wedderburn calls it 'A principle of feline inscrutability and political subtlety' (1991) 54 MLR 1, 14. See Ch. 1, pp. 12–15.
126 See, e.g., Case 7/61, note 4 above.

procedures could be invoked and in the Maastricht Treaty the context in which they operate was substantially altered.[127]

ARTICLE 115

Nature and purpose

Article 115 provides a further procedure that may permit barriers to the free movement of goods within the Community. Article 115 is an important internal adjunct to the external common commercial policy. It applies to goods originating in third countries. Such goods, once imported into one member state, are, in principle, entitled to free circulation in every member state. That is the traditional theory of a customs union and it was expressly recognized by Articles 9 and 10.[128] Yet the external boundaries of the Community are not identical state by state, due principally to the as yet incomplete nature of the common commercial policy referred to in Article 113.[129] Even though external competence in commercial policy is, in principle, exclusive to the Community in order to achieve uniformity[130] it remains the case that different member states may be permitted or empowered by the Community to impose different quotas on the importation of goods from particular third countries.[131] There would be a risk that such concessions would be subverted if third-country goods could freely enter a state with a permitted quota via another member state. Article 115 is a procedure under which member states may request authorization to control the importation of third-country goods from other member states where deflection of trade occurs or economic difficulties arise. Article 115 thus envisages intra-Community barriers to trade in goods originating in third countries. External disunity causes internal disunity.

These principles were recognized and applied by the Court in *Tezi Textiel* v *Commission*.[132] Regulation 3589/82 did not create uniformity in the conditions for the importation of a range of textile products from outside the Community. Quotas were divided up between the member

---

127 This is examined in more depth in Ch. 21.
128 On the legal rules designed to achieve this end see Green, Hartley and Usher, *Single European Market*, Ch. 1.
129 ibid., Ch. 2. Cremona, 'The Completion of the Internal Market and the Incomplete Commercial Policy of the European Community' (1990) 15 ELRev 283.
130 Opinion 1/75 [1975] ECR 1355, [1976] 1 CMLR 85.
131 The limits of the lawfulness of such concessions are not clear. This is discussed by Cremona (1990) 15 ELRev 283.
132 Case 59/84 [1986] ECR 887.

states.[133] Under Article 115 the Benelux countries, which for these purposes had a single quota, were authorized by the Commission to require licences for the importation of products covered by the Regulation even from other member states. Tezi's business of importing into the Netherlands cotton trousers originating in Macao but in free circulation within the Community was impeded. It challenged the Commission's Article 115 authorization decision before the European Court. The Court insisted that Article 115 must be interpreted strictly as an exception to the nature and purpose of a common market.[134] There must be serious reasons for intervention and the restrictions must apply for a limited period only. Account must be taken both of the situation within a member state and of the Community interest. These requirements were satisfied and the application for annulment failed.

A lack of uniformity in external trade policy was thus reflected internally. An obstacle to the free circulation of goods within the Community was permitted. Article 30 is applicable in principle to prohibit all barriers to trade in goods between member states irrespective of origin,[135] but Article 115 envisages a special regime for third-country products. Partly in response to the consequent need to supervise trade patterns, the Court accepted that a requirement imposed by a member state that the origin of goods be declared is not incompatible with Article 30 where the importer knows or can reasonably be expected to know. However, more onerous administrative measures will be caught by Article 30 and require special authorization under Article 115.[136]

The invocation of such protective measures is possible only after Commission scrutiny and authorization. As the decision in *Tezi Textiel*[137] insists, in all cases the familiar principles of proportionality and alternative means apply. Intervention must be no more restrictive of intra-Community trade than is necessary in order to meet the objective. This implies close scrutiny of both the method and the duration of the control.

133 The validity of such quotas is controversial, see note 131 above. The Court might now be less amenable to such a system than it was in *Tezi Textiel*; see Case 51/87 *Commission* v *Council* [1988] ECR 5459 and the impact of Regs. 518/94, 519/94, discussed below.

134 See also Case 41/76 *Donckerwolke* v *Procureur de la République* [1976] ECR 1921; Case 52/77 *Cayrol* v *Rivoira* [1977] ECR 2261.

135 See., e.g., Case 41/76, note 134 above; Case 52/77, note 134 above; Case 212/88 *Levy* [1989] ECR 3511, [1991] 1 CMLR 49; Case C-128/89, note 59 above. See also p. 495, note 20.

136 See e.g., Case 41/76, note 134 above; Case 212/88, note 135 above. Oliver, *Free Movement of Goods*, paras. 7.13–7.14.

137 Case 59/84, note 132 above.

The future

There is a definitional point in this procedure that has caused much controversy. Article 115 can be invoked in relation only to third-country goods. Products originating in a member state are entitled to free movement, subject only to Article 36, which, as explained, is much narrower than Article 115 because it does not permit protection on economic grounds. This implies a sharp division between the status of non-Community and Community goods, yet the distinction may not always be easy to make, especially where products are in part manufactured outside the Community, then completed and assembled within the Community. Nissan cars made in the United Kingdom have been viewed as British by the United Kingdom, but as Japanese by France. The Community rules of origin are complex and do not yield a simple answer in such a case.[138] This is an area that requires determined political action to achieve consensus.[139]

The demise of Article 115 is dependent on the establishment of a comprehensive and uniform common commercial policy. In its 1988 decision in *Commission* v *Council*[140] the Court appeared to harden its stance against the validity of separate national quotas of the type at issue in *Tezi Textiel*. This advanced the cause of external unity and reduced the circumstances in which the Commission was susceptible to persuasion that barriers to trade between member states should be authorized under Article 115. It would appear impeccably logical that a quota system of the type envisaged by Article 115, which justifies frontier controls within the Community, cannot endure in a market characterized by an absence of internal frontiers. One would suppose that restrictions on importation should be permitted only in the context of agreements relating to third countries and the territory of the Community as a whole. The validity of such arrangements would then fall for examination in the light of international economic law and would neither directly affect nor be affected by the Community's internal trade law and policy.[141] Nevertheless, although it was amended, the essence of Article 115 survived the changes wrought to the EC Treaty by the Treaty on European Union. The Commission's intent was to make little use of it, but its existence reflected the persisting

---

138 The basic measure was Reg. 802/68 JO 1968 L148/1. This is now replaced by Reg. 2913/92 OJ 1992 L302/1. Parallel problems arise in fixing the state of origin in relation to the imposition of customs duties and anti-dumping duties.

139 A glimpse of the controversial nature of the structure of the international car market is provided by Case T-37/92 *BEUC* v *Commission*, examined in Ch. 24, p. 761.

140 Case 51/87, note 133 above. See Cremona (1990) 15 ELRev 283.

141 See generally Eeckhout, *The European Internal Market and International Trade: a Legal Analysis*. Opinion 1/94, examined at p. 322 above, represents an important statement of the respective competences of the Community and the member states in international trade relations.

obstacles to the completion of the common commercial policy. In 1994 the Community achieved a significant breakthrough with the making of Regulation 518/94 on common rules for imports[142] and Regulation 519/94 on common rules for imports from certain third countries, which in practice are former state-trading countries. Regulation 519/94 is notable in particular for establishing quotas for a range of products originating in China.[143]

These measures take the Community beyond the national quota systems envisaged by Article 115. Regulation 518/94 contains no list of permitted national derogations. It states that importation shall take place freely without quantitative restrictions. The effect of these measures is to permit the Community to develop its external trade policy hand-in-hand with its internal trade policy.[144] Nevertheless, even the 1994 regulations retain the possibility of a fragmentation in the common nature of the Community's policy and, by implication, create residual problems for the maintenance of uninterrupted internal trade. Where importation may cause serious injury to Community producers, controls may be imposed by the Commission. These may include safeguard measures 'limited to region(s) concerned if [the Commission] considers that such measures applied at that level are more appropriate than measures applied throughout the Community'. Such measures are to be temporary and exceptional. It is unclear how such special regional treatment can operate in an area without internal frontiers.

142 OJ 1994 L67/77. A separate regime in Reg. 517/94 governs textiles, OJ 1994 L67/1.
143 OJ 1994 L67/89.
144 The banana market has caused extraordinary difficulty for many years; it is now the subject of a special regime, Reg. 404/93 OJ 1993 L47/1, which was unsuccessfully challenged in Case C-280/93 *Germany* v *Council* [1994] ECR I-4973.

CHAPTER 17

Cassis de Dijon and the Development of Article 30

THE INDISTINCTLY APPLICABLE MEASURE

Article 30 forbids national rules that discriminate against imported products,[1] subject to the possibility that the member state may find justification for its practices under Article 36.[2] However, the scope of Article 30 extends beyond the discriminatory national rule. Even if a national rule on its face makes no distinction between domestic and imported products, it may still be subject to challenge under Article 30 if an effect that restricts interstate trade can be demonstrated.

AN EFFECT ON INTERSTATE TRADE

Suppose that a member state (say, France) introduces a regulation that requires that all widgets marketed within its territory be triangular. The regulation applies to all products marketed in France and makes no reference whatsoever to the place of manufacture of the product. It is a technical rule governing the composition of the product that makes no distinction between domestic and imported goods. However, imagine that in a neighbouring member state (say, Italy) widgets are lawfully made to a square design. Square, rather than triangular, widgets are simply the tradition in Italy. In practice, the result of the difference between the laws of the two member states is that importation from Italy into France is precluded: the square Italian widget cannot be sold in France. An Italian widget producer could penetrate the French market only if prepared to establish a special production run for triangular widgets. This would plainly place the Italian producer at a serious competitive disadvantage compared to the French producer and would consequently discourage

1 See Ch. 15.
2 See Ch. 16.

importation. The economic consequence is a partitioning of national markets that precludes manufacturers from realizing economies of scale by extending their production runs and inhibits the influence of effective competition between producers from different member states. Such distortions impede the attainment of efficient market structures and cost the Community a great deal of money.[3]

Rules of this nature are not based on discrimination. The French requirement that widgets be triangular applies to all products, French-produced or not. Yet the *Dassonville* formula, which is the Court's definition of the scope of Article 30,[4] is satisfied in such a case. This is a trading rule that is 'capable of hindering, directly or indirectly, actually or potentially, intra-Community trade'. The hindrance arises not because of any discrimination against the import, but simply because of the disparities between legal systems that exist within the Community. A French widget made for the French market need satisfy only one technical rule, whereas an imported Italian widget faces a dual burden of technical rules, Italian and French. This creates a restrictive effect felt especially by imported products, which is sufficient to trigger the application of the *Dassonville* formula independently of any suggestion of discrimination.[5] Advocate-General Slynn correctly observed in *Cinéthèque* v *Fédération Nationale de Cinémas Françaises*[6] that 'discrimination . . . although it may be sufficient, even conclusive, to bring a measure within Article 30, is not a necessary precondition for Article 30 to apply'.

The hypothetical widgets market may be trivial, but the legal principle contains wide-ranging implications. It is possible to use Article 30 to attack national technical rules that restrict the free circulation of a vast range of products. The isolation of national markets behind what are, in effect, protectionist technical rules governing product design is prevented. The Court first developed its approach to these market-partitioning rules that make no formal distinction between domestic and imported goods in *Rewe-Zentrale* v *Bundesmonopolverwaltung für Branntwein*.[7] The case is more commonly referred to by the name of the product with which the litigation was concerned: Cassis de Dijon.

3 For a summary see P. Cecchini, *The European Challenge*, Ch. 4; see also Ch. 1, p. 25 above.
4 Case 8/74 [1974] ECR 837; see Ch. 15, pp. 431–3.
5 See Ch. 15.
6 Cases 60, 61/84 [1985] ECR 2605, [1986] 1 CMLR 365.
7 Case 120/78 [1979] ECR 649, [1979] 3 CMLR 494. For contemporaneous comment on the case see, e.g., Oliver (1980) 17 CMLRev 109; Wyatt (1981) 6 ELRev 185; Dashwood [1981] 9 EIPR 268; Masclet (1980) RTDE 64; Mattera (1980) RMC 505.

THE COURT'S *CASSIS DE DIJON* PRINCIPLE

Cassis de Dijon is a blackcurrant liqueur, commonly drunk with white wine. It was lawfully produced in France and contained 15 to 20 per cent alcohol by volume. German law precluded the sale of any spirits of the category into which cassis fell unless they were of at least 32 per cent alcohol content. A prospective importer was consequently advised by the German authorities that although there was no objection to the importation of cassis into Germany from France, it could not be marketed there. The importer initiated proceedings before the German courts to establish the incompatibility of the German rule relating to alcohol strength with Article 30 of the Treaty.

The rule was not discriminatory. It applied to all fruit liqueurs marketed in Germany without making any distinction according to origin. It was an indistinctly applicable technical rule. However, the subject-matter of the case was ample demonstration that the rule restricted free trade across national frontiers within the common market. A product lawfully produced in France was excluded from the German market simply because the rules in Germany differed from the rules in France. An obstacle to trade that led to the partitioning of the common market arose as a result of the different traditions of two member states. As might have been expected in the light of the *Dassonville* formula, the Court was persuaded by the fact that the German rule exerted a restrictive *effect* on trade that Article 30 was indeed capable of applying. However, the Court established a principle in *Cassis de Dijon* that represented an important new initiative in its Article 30 jurisprudence. The Court began by declaring the member states' regulatory independence, provided that the Community has not itself moved into the field:

In the absence of common rules relating to the production and marketing of alcohol ... it is for the Member States to regulate all matters relating to the production and marketing of alcohol and alcoholic beverages on their own territory.[8]

The Court then declared this independence to be subject to the demands of Community law:

Obstacles to movement in the Community resulting from disparities between the national laws relating to the marketing of the products in question must be accepted in so far as those provisions may be recognized as being necessary in order to satisfy mandatory requirements relating in particular to the effectiveness of fiscal

8 Case 120/78, note 7 above, para. 8 of the judgment.

supervision, the protection of public health, the fairness of commercial transactions and the defence of the consumer.[9]

Thus, pending harmonization,[10] trade barriers arising from diversity between national laws are capable of falling foul of Article 30, even in the absence of discrimination against imports, but it is open to member states to show that technical rules that have the effect of restricting trade are justified as 'necessary in order to satisfy mandatory requirements'.[11]

Because no Community rules governing the alcohol strength of fruit liqueurs were in existence, it was for the German authorities to show that their national rules could be sustained on these grounds. The case had reached the European Court as an Article 177 reference, so it was not for the Court to decide the case. However, the Court left little doubt that such rules are incompatible with Community law. What was their purpose? The German Government submitted that the measure was part of a strategy for combating alcoholism. If weak spirits are available, drinkers may easily be lured towards addiction; far better to ban drinks that induce gradually increasing tolerance to alcohol. However, banning weak, not strong, drink in order to combat alcohol dependence is unconvincing and the Court's judgment reflects such scepticism. The Court observed that many relatively weak alcoholic drinks of different types are available and that strong drink is often diluted before consumption. The German rules lacked any coherent basis as an effective control on alcohol abuse.[12] The Court further emphasized that any measure taken to protect a 'mandatory requirement' must be proportionate to that end and must be the least restrictive of trade available. These principles are closely analogous to those that the Court has developed on the basis of the second sentence of Article 36.[13] The Court therefore indicated that where the alleged objective could be achieved by a less burdensome rule – for example, a requirement that drinks be labelled clearly to show their alcohol strength instead of the imposition of an outright ban – then a state is not entitled to maintain its unduly onerous rule. The assessment of proportionality and alternative means is for the national court to make in the context of an Article 177 preliminary reference.[14]

9 ibid.
10 See pp. 471, 478 on Community measures pre-empting national competence to regulate.
11 Where the rule *does* indirectly discriminate in favour of home-produced goods, the state retains the comparable escape clause of showing an 'objective justification'; see p. 444.
12 Cf. Cases C-1, C-176/90 *APESA* v *DSSC*, [1991] ECR 1–4151, relating to the application of Art. 30 to laws controlling *strong* drink.
13 See Ch. 16, p. 453.
14 See Ch. 9.

THE IMPETUS TOWARDS FREE TRADE

The decision in *Cassis de Dijon* is widely regarded as a fundamentally important advance in the Court's Article 30 jurisprudence. This is correct; yet the line of authority is not wholly novel. Directive 70/50[15] indicates that such indistinctly applicable rules are capable of falling within the scope of the Article 30 prohibition. Article 3 of the Directive covers 'measures governing the marketing of products . . . which are equally applicable to domestic and imported products, where the restrictive effect of such measures on the free movement of goods exceeds the effects intrinsic to trade rules'. It has already been observed that the *Dassonville* formula itself is capable of encompassing a rule of the type at issue in *Cassis* by virtue of its emphasis on the need to examine the effect of a measure rather than its form.[16] However, the Court's approach in *Cassis*, while not a novelty, is rightly described as a radical shift of emphasis in favour of free trade. It constitutes a more vigorous application of Article 30 as a means of removing national technical rules than was previously envisaged by the tentative terms of Directive 70/50[17] or even by *Dassonville*, where, the breadth of the Court's formula notwithstanding, the rule itself was distinctly applicable. The decision in *Cassis* reinvigorated Article 30 in an area where it had previously had minimal impact and where it had been widely assumed legislative harmonization of divergent national rules was required to eliminate obstacles to interstate trade. *Cassis de Dijon* is crucial to the integration of the market through the application of Article 30 by the courts. The decision comes close to establishing a presumption in favour of free trade throughout the Community in goods that have been lawfully produced and marketed in a member state, and that amounts to an incomparably firmer pro-integrative stance than that found in Article 3 of Directive 70/50, which contains more or less the reverse presumption. The Court concluded that

There is therefore no valid reason why, provided they have been lawfully produced and marketed in one of the Member States, alcoholic beverages should not be introduced into any other Member States; the sale of such products may not be subject to a legal prohibition on the marketing of beverages with an alcohol content lower than the limit set by the national rules.[18]

15 JO 1970 L13/29; see p. 430 above.
16 See p. 491 above.
17 In his Opinion in *Cassis* AG Capotorti expressed 'reservations . . . in relation to the compatibility of [Directive 70/50] with the prevalent strict interpretation of Article 30' (Case 120/78, note 7 above, ECR at 671, CMLR at 503). See also p. 431 above on the development of Art. 30 since the Directive.

This key passage in the Court's judgment introduces the important idea of 'mutual recognition' and the connected 'principle of equivalence'.[19] The idea is essentially that every member state must respect the traditions of other member states and that, consequently, once a product has been lawfully produced and marketed in one member state it is entitled to free circulation within the Community save in exceptional circumstances. In principle, it is no longer lawful to insist on compliance with detailed national technical rules as a condition of market access.[20] Protectionist practices disguised as national trade regulation have come under severe attack as a result of this judicially inspired approach. The depth of the impact of the Court's judgment as a means of promoting free trade can be more fully assessed after a discussion of the abundant case law that has followed the landmark decision in *Cassis de Dijon*.

CASSIS DE DIJON: SUBSEQUENT CASE LAW

In *Gilli and Andres*[21] a criminal prosecution was brought under Italian law against the importers of apple vinegar from Germany. Italian law prohibited the sale of vinegar unless derived from wine. The defendants relied on the *Cassis de Dijon* decision to show that the Italian rule violated Article 30. The prohibition on the sale of non-wine vinegar applied without distinction to all goods, wherever produced, yet its effect was to restrict the free circulation of apple vinegar produced and marketed in Germany, where, in contrast to Italy, no legal restrictions were imposed. A traditional German product was excluded from the Italian market.

The European Court, to which the matter was referred under Article 177, agreed that the facts were on all fours with its decision in *Cassis*.

---

18 Case 120/78, note 7 above, para. 14 of the judgment.
19 See Oliver, *Free Movement of Goods*, para. 6.55 *et seq*; see further pp. 519–23.
20 White submits that only goods originating in the Community, not third-country goods, may take advantage of the *Cassis* principle ('In Search of Limits to Article 30 of the EEC Treaty' (1989) 26 CMLRev 235, 259), but this seems irreconcilable with the basic notion of free circulation of all goods within a customs union (Art. 9(2), Case 41/76 *Donckerwolcke v Procureur de la République* [1976] ECR 1921, pp. 21, 486 above) and has not been widely accepted; see, e.g., Gormley, 'Some Reflections on the Internal Market and Free Movement of Goods' [1989/1] LIEI 9, 18; Oliver, *Free Movement of Goods*, para. 6.60. German courts treat the *Cassis* principle as applicable to all goods in free circulation irrespective of origin; see discussion by Tegeder (1994) 19 ELRev 86.
21 Case 788/79 [1980] ECR 2071, [1981] 1 CMLR 146. See also the parallel Article 169 proceedings in Case 193/80 *Commission v Italy* [1982] ECR 3019.

There existed no Community rules in the field and therefore member states retained competence to establish their own technical rules governing product composition, subject to the overriding demands of Community law. Where disparity between such national rules causes obstacles to trade, the state concerned is obliged to show that the restrictions are 'necessary in order to satisfy mandatory requirements'. There was no evidence that the product posed any threat to public health. Furthermore, the Court was clearly of the view that submissions that confusion might follow the appearance of new types of vinegar on Italian shelves must fail when tested against the principles of proportionality and alternative means. The confused consumer can be protected adequately by a system of labelling imposed on all products.[22] A system that effectively bans the import is excessive and therefore unjustifiable. The European Court explicitly commented that 'the principal effect of provisions of this nature is to protect domestic production'.[23] The Italian court that had made the reference to Luxembourg was plainly left with little choice but to acquit the defendants of the charge and thereby to permit the free circulation of the goods within the Community.

One of the most widely publicized applications of the *Cassis* principle to eliminate national technical rules that restrict trade came in *Commission* v *Germany*.[24] The case involved the *Reinheitsgebot*, the ancient and locally much-cherished German beer purity laws. These regulations have as their purpose the apparently laudable objective of preserving the high quality of traditional German beer. There were two limbs to the legislation under challenge in the case. In the first instance German law required that beverages entitled to use the name *Bier* be produced from four ingredients and four alone: barley, hops, yeast and water. Other beers could be sold, but not as *Bier*, which plainly hindered their sales opportunities. In the second instance beers containing additives could not be sold at all in German territory. The rules did not discriminate against foreign-produced beers; they made no reference to nationality whatsoever. As the German Government observed, in theory a foreign brewer could have made pure beer in the stipulated fashion and penetrated the German market. In practice, however, beers made according to the traditions and consumer preferences of other member states, perhaps containing different ingredients, perhaps containing additives, were not eligible for marketing in Germany. The beer purity laws were in fact classic *Cassis de Dijon* style

22 Labelling requirements may insist on the use of a particular language only where this is necessary to achieve protection; i.e., a state must show why symbols are inadequate to inform the consumer. See note 78 below.
23 Case 788/79, note 21 above, para. 10 of the judgment.
24 Case 178/84 [1987] ECR 1227, [1988] 1 CMLR 780.

rules in that they brought about the partitioning of the market as a result of the differences between the regimes operative in different member states. The German market was isolated from the rest of the common market and German brewers were to all intents and purposes immune from competition from foreign brewers.

The Commission felt sufficiently strongly about the incompatibility of the German rules with Article 30 to initiate proceedings under Article 169. The German Government contested the Commission's view that a breach of Article 30 had occurred and the matter was brought before the European Court. The Court observed that there existed no common Community rules in the area and proceeded to cite the operative paragraphs of its judgment in *Cassis* in order to demonstrate that the *Reinheitsgebot* restricted trade and therefore required justification. The German Government's defence of its legislation was based on two major arguments relating to public health and to consumer protection. In the first place the German Government submitted that the long-term health risks associated with the ingestion of additives were not fully understood and that therefore, given the high level of beer consumption in Germany, a ban on the use of additives in beer was a necessary aspect of public-health protection. The Court accepted that in certain specific cases it might be possible to demonstrate that a particular additive presented a risk and that in such circumstances a specific beer containing that additive could lawfully be excluded from the home market. However, the German rule, which imposed a blanket ban on all additives, took no account of evidence of a threat to health in individual cases and therefore went beyond what might be justifiable.[25]

The second argument, based on consumer protection, also failed to convince the Court. The submission that the free circulation of beers made according to a range of different traditions would leave the German consumer in a state of confusion about the composition of beers and that legislation governing product designation was consequently required was firmly rejected. The Court observed that 'the legislation of a Member State must not crystallize given consumer habits so as to consolidate an advantage acquired by national industries concerned to comply with them'.[26]

A consumer may, then, hold a preference for typical domestic goods.

---

25 Cf. Case 53/80 *Eyssen* [1981] ECR 409, discussed on p. 466, in which doubt about the safety of a particular additive was held to justify a ban on its use.
26 Case 178/84, note 24 above, para. 32 of the judgment. This dictum is drawn from the Court's judgment in Case 170/78 *Commission* v *UK* [1980] ECR 417, an Article 95 case; see p. 411 above. This is a useful reminder that, despite their differences in scope, the several Treaty provisions concerned with the free movement of goods share a unity of purpose: market integration.

However, national law must not bolster that preference by excluding differently made foreign goods. There is, of course, every likelihood that consumer preference for domestic goods is at least in part the result of past protectionism in favour of the home market, and it is precisely that national favouritism that the common market is designed to combat. The Court supplemented this important point of principle with reference to its well-established view on the requirements of proportionality and alternative means. Even if a genuine risk of consumer confusion worthy of protective measures could be shown, the German Government had failed to demonstrate why the matter could not be dealt with by measures less restrictive of the free flow of beer. The most obvious 'alternative means' would be found in a requirement that beers bear a label identifying clearly the nature of their ingredients, including, if relevant, their additive content.

THE CONSEQUENCE OF *CASSIS*: ENHANCING CONSUMER CHOICE

In assessing the implications of the Court's treatment of indistinctly applicable national rules it is essential to appreciate the consequence of rulings such as that in *Cassis*[27] and in *Commission* v *Germany*.[28] In holding the German *Reinheitsgebot* to be incompatible with Article 30, the Court is *not* denying the right of brewers to produce pure beer according to centuries-old tradition. The unlawful element of German law was the mandatory nature of the rules; the insistence that pure beer and only pure beer be sold in Germany. As a result of the judgment, beers made according to the different traditions that prevail throughout the Community are entitled to access to the German market, where they are then able to compete with traditional pure German beer. The consumer in Germany need not change his or her drinking habits, but if peculiar Belgian or British brews prove alluring, then there is no legal impediment to the importer wishing to satisfy (or stimulate) such curiosity, provided laws on, for example, labelling are complied with.[29]

The result of *Commission* v *Germany* is a small-scale reflection of the overall aim of economic integration in the Community. Competition between products is ensured on the German market, irrespective of origin. The previous isolation of the German beer market is removed and con-

---

27 Case 120/78, note 7 above.
28 Case 178/84, note 24 above.
29 The Court in *Commission* v *Germany* implies that such rules may be justifiable under the *Cassis* principle; see further p. 511.

sumer choice becomes the determining factor. The German consumer, rather than the German legislature, will decide which product, if any, occupies the dominant position on the market. It is perfectly conceivable that the traditional types of pure German beer will continue to dominate the market for the foreseeable future, and, of course, old habits will not die because of a European Court judgment. However, if the German brewer is to maintain a long-term grip on the German market, it will have to be through a process of persuading the consumer that traditional German beer is best[30] and not by sheltering behind the protectionist walls of the beer purity laws. The logic on which the decision is based is that the laudable objective of preserving the high quality of traditional German beer can be secured through consumer preference expressed in the market-place without the imposition of a mandatory rule, and that, if it emerges that the consumer was not, in fact, much impressed by traditional German beer and switches preference elsewhere, then the beer purity laws have been exposed as a measure that in reality protected the German brewing industry and not the consumer.

PUBLIC PROCUREMENT

The approach adopted by the Court since *Cassis de Dijon* has liberated the market for the traditional products of each member state. A narrow national perspective in drafting mandatory technical product standards is likely to conflict with Community law.[31] The application of the *Cassis* principle in a more specific commercial context is well illustrated by the Court's decision in *Commission v Ireland*,[32] which concerned public procure-ment.[33] The case revealed devious protectionism practised by a local authority[34] in Dundalk. The contract specification for the town's water supply augmentation scheme included a stipulation that asbestos cement pipes used in the construction project should conform to Irish Standard 188:1975, drafted by the Institute for Industrial Research and Standards. It was made clear to an interested firm that a tender based on the use of

---

30 See pp. 440, 447 on the lawfulness of public and/or private campaigns in support of typical German beer.
31 See, e.g., in relation to technical standards for consumer goods, Weatherill, 'Consumer Safety Legislation in the United Kingdom and Article 30 EEC' (1988) 13 ELRev 87, 94–8.
32 Case 45/87 [1988] ECR 4929, [1989] 1 CMLR 225.
33 An area in which there is important supporting secondary legislation designed to challenge long-standing assumptions of national preference; see Trepte, *Public Procurement in the EC*; Arrowsmith (ed.), *Public Procurement Law Review*.
34 See p. 449 on the personal scope of Article 30.

Spanish-made pipes would not be acceptable to the awarding authority, despite the firm's claim that the Spanish pipes were perfectly compatible with the overall requirements of the Irish standard, if not in precise conformity therewith, and that they were suitable for use in the project. The Commission took up the matter on receipt of a complaint about the Irish practices and the matter reached the Court.[35]

The Court ruled Ireland in breach of Article 30.[36] By insisting that domestic technical regulations be the norm in the negotiations, the Irish authorities were excluding products made lawfully and according to different standards in other states. It might have been open to the authorities to reject foreign-made pipes in individual cases on the basis that the quality of the goods fell short of the demands of the project, but the imposition of an inflexible requirement of conformity with Irish standards was unlawful because it relied on national traditions, not quality.

THE RATIONALE FOR THE COURT'S APPROACH

At this point it is necessary to consider more carefully the basis of the Court's approach in this line of authority. Plainly, Article 30 has been developed into a vigorous instrument for the elimination of protectionist barriers to free trade even in the absence of discrimination against imported goods, but where in the Treaty of Rome did the Court find authority for the *Cassis* principle? In particular, the phrase 'necessary to satisfy mandatory requirements',[37] which forms the operative part of the judgment in *Cassis* explaining when states may lawfully maintain restrictive technical rules,[38] was not to be found anywhere in the Treaty of Rome. Why are indistinctly applicable rules treated in a manner quite different from distinctly applicable rules; particularly, what has happened to Article 36, which the Court ignored in its judgment in *Cassis*?

35 See Ch. 7 on this procedure. Article 30 is directly effective, so it would have been open to the complainant firm (also) to pursue the matter before the Irish courts.
36 An interim ruling was awarded *ex parte* (Case 45/87R *Commission* v *Ireland* [1987] ECR 783, [1987] 2 CMLR 197), but refused *inter partes* ([1987] ECR 1369, [1987] 2 CMLR 563); see p. 214 on interim relief against member states.
37 German: *Zwingenden Erfordnisse*; French: *exigences impératives*; Italian: *esigenze imperative*. In English translation the word 'imperative' is sometimes preferred to mandatory, see, e.g., Case 178/84, note 24 above, para. 30 of the judgment. Neither 'mandatory' nor 'imperative' is entirely felicitous; the concept is closer to 'compelling' than 'compulsory'.
38 Case 120/78, note 7 above, para. 8 of the judgment, p. 492 above.

JUSTIFICATION

The idea that an indistinctly applicable national rule that restricts trade can be justified by a member state if the rule is shown to be 'necessary to satisfy a mandatory requirement' runs parallel to the idea that a national rule that discriminates indirectly against imports can be objectively justified.[39] In both instances successful justification takes the measure outside Article 30. It does not matter whether long-standing diversity between national rules has shaped the market in such a way as to protect home products or whether the state has imposed the rule on an existing market structure with the result that home products are favoured. In either event it is open to the state to attempt to justify a rule that exerts a market-partitioning *effect* as necessary to satisfy a mandatory requirement or as objectively justified.

The function of Article 36 is analogous in that it also defines the scope of member-state competence to impose lawful obstacles to the free circulation of goods. Article 36's place in Community law is distinct in that its role is to save measures incapable of benefiting from the mandatory requirements or objective justification and therefore caught within the Article 30 net; specifically, distinctly applicable or directly discriminatory rules only.

Article 36 is a Treaty provision; the notions of both the mandatory requirements and objective justification are judicial creations. This is, in fact, the key to this area of the law. The *Cassis de Dijon* line of authority is attributable to the remarkable creativity of the European Court, and the mandatory requirements constitute an aspect of judicial elaboration of the scope of Article 30. As in *Dassonville*, so in *Cassis* the Court has created a definition of Article 30 far removed from its explicit terms, yet rooted in the intent of the Treaty. It is a definition that the Court is prepared to develop through its jurisprudence. The idea of the mandatory requirement is, in fact, embedded in the very definition of the Article 30 prohibition. It is not really a justification for a measure found to contravene Article 30 at all; if necessary to satisfy a mandatory requirement, a measure is compatible with Article 30 in the first place. This indicates the close conceptual link between *Cassis* and the Court's judgment in *Dassonville*, where the Court similarly explained that a trading rule that is reasonable does not violate Article 30 even if a restrictive effect on interstate trade can be demonstrated.[40] In fact, the analogies between the judgments in *Dassonville* and

39 See p. 444 above.
40 See p. 432 above.

Cassis have led many commentators to effect a fusion between them by analysing the *Cassis* principle as a 'rule of reason'[41] that, if satisfied, takes the measure outside the scope of Article 30.[42] This approach has merit. Certainly, the functional similarities of *Dassonville* reasonableness and *Cassis* mandatory requirements demand acknowledgement. Yet caution is appropriate. The special characteristics of the *Cassis* line of authority, such as the principle of equivalence,[43] deserve their own special consideration and terminology. Conceptual similarity[44] should not lead one to overlook evidence of judicial refinement giving rise to important distinguishing features, and in *Cassis* the Court has taken Article 30 into new territory.[45]

DISTINGUISHING DISTINCTLY AND INDISTINCTLY APPLICABLE MEASURES

The basic distinction that the Court has established in this area holds that distinctly applicable measures are prohibited unless justified under Article 36, whereas indistinctly applicable measures are prohibited unless necessary to satisfy mandatory requirements. The next stage in solving the puzzle is in realizing that the scope of the mandatory requirements is broader than that of Article 36, and that mandatory requirements are unavailable to justify a distinctly applicable measure. These points emerge clearly from the Court's judgment in *Commission* v *Ireland*, the Irish souvenirs case.[46] In that case the Irish Government argued that it was necessary to require imported souvenirs to bear indications of origin in order to prevent the consumer from suffering confusion. The Court's decision in *Cassis* was invoked to demonstrate the relevance of consumer protection as a justification for trade barriers, for, as will be recalled, part of the German Government's case in *Cassis* was based on consumer protection, and, although the arguments failed on the facts, the availability of the ground

---

41 See also the use of this phrase in relation to agreements that, despite an apparently restrictive effect, may fall outside the application of Art. 85, p. 696. See also AG Verloren van Themaat's opinion in Case 286/81 *Oosthoek Uitgeversmaatschappij BV* [1982] ECR 4575, [1983] 2 CMLR 428, p. 512 below; drawing analogies with US law, he submits that the rule of reason describes 'a general principle of interpretation . . . in relation to strict prohibitions laid down by provisions of the EEC Treaty'.

42 See, e.g., Kapteyn and Verloren van Themaat, *Law of the European Communities*, p. 387.

43 See p. 519.

44 The judgments in *Dassonville* and *Cassis* are occupied with the same thematic issue, the outer margin of Article 30. The problem recurs in the Court's jurisprudence; see further p. 532.

45 See comment at p. 494 on whether *Cassis* is a novelty.

46 Case 113/80 [1981] ECR 1625, [1982] 1 CMLR 706; see p. 438.

of justification was not disputed in principle by the Court. In the Irish souvenirs case, however, the Court observed that there was a crucial distinction between the Irish rules in issue and the German rules relating to the alcohol strength of fruit liqueurs. The former discriminated against imports. The fact of discrimination constituted a material distinction between the present case and the decision in *Cassis* and precluded reliance on the *Cassis* principle. Because Ireland was guilty of discrimination against imports, it could look only to Article 36 to justify its rules. Article 36 does not cover consumer protection, except in so far as it may fall within the specific idea of protecting public health. More general conceptions of protecting the economic interests of the consumer, such as Ireland sought to invoke, are available as justifications for trade barriers only if the national rules in question apply without discrimination between domestic and imported goods.

The Court has had the opportunity frequently to emphasize this view. For example, in both *Commission* v *United Kingdom*[47] (mandatory origin-marking) and *Schutzverband*[48] (which dealt with German law on the strength of vermouth) the Court's ruling that the systems treated imports less favourably than domestic goods led it to reject the legitimacy of justification based on consumer protection. The objective of protecting the economic interests of the consumer may be perfectly worthwhile, but such regulation must be based on objective factors connected with the nature of the risk, not the origin of the product.

In *Commission* v *Germany*, the beer purity case,[49] the German Government pointed out that the stipulated ingredients of beer were not necessarily of German origin and that any brewer, irrespective of nationality or place of manufacture, could choose to observe the rules and thereby gain access to the German market.[50] This was designed to show that the rules were not protectionist in aim, but it failed to persuade the Court because of the restrictive effect that results from the application of even indistinctly applicable rules. However, the point made by the German Government was of legal relevance. Had the required ingredients been, say, typically Bavarian-grown, then the fact of discrimination would have curtailed available justifications to the list in Article 36, which does not include consumer protection. Given the absence of discrimination against imports, the German Government was permitted to take a stand in defence of its

47 Case 207/83 [1985] ECR 1202, considered at p. 446. See also, e.g., Case 177/83 *Kohl* v *Ringelhan* [1984] ECR 3651; Case 434/85 *Allen and Hanbury* v *Generics* [1988] ECR 1245, [1988] 1 CMLR 701; Case C-21/88 *Du Pont* v *Unità Sanitaria* [1990] ECR 889.
48 Case 59/82 [1983] ECR 1217, considered at p. 438.
49 Case 178/84, note 24 above, considered at p. 496.
50 See ibid., para. 26 of the judgment.

rules on the basis that they amounted to a measure of consumer protection, even though this proved ultimately fruitless. From the perspective of justification, then, it is important to distinguish between distinctly and indistinctly applicable rules.[51]

These principles were applied by the English Court of Appeal in *R v Secretary of State for Social Security, ex parte Bomore*.[52] The Minister sought to defend an NHS system under which chemists were reimbursed for the supply of medicines. The scheme discriminated against imported preparations, yet the Minister's argument had as its explicit basis the formula in *Cassis de Dijon*. The Court of Appeal held this argument misplaced. It was held that the presence of discrimination in the system precluded reliance on *Cassis*. Indeed, Lord Justice May held that the point was so clear and free from doubt that no reference to the European Court need be made.[53] A declaration that the scheme contravened Article 30 was granted on the application of an importer of pharmaceuticals.

It is firmly established that the scope of the mandatory requirements is broader than that of Article 36, but that only the indistinctly applicable, *Cassis*-style measure may take advantage of that wider scope. This means that discrimination is not a prerequisite to the application of Article 30, but that its presence confines the available justifications to those listed in Article 36. In the absence of discrimination a wider range of interests may be invoked to justify the practices.[54]

EXPLAINING THE COURT'S APPROACH

Exactly why the Court has devised the structure of the mandatory requirements through its interpretation of Article 30 and why it has developed this apparent 'favoured status' for indistinctly applicable rules is a matter for conjecture. The Court has never laid bare its underlying reasoning. One might argue that the Court should simply have broadened Article 36 to cover matters such as the protection of the economic interests

---

51 The Court erred in Case 16/83 *Prantl* [1984] ECR 1299, [1985] 2 CMLR 238 by allowing consumer protection arguments to be advanced to defend a distinctly applicable measure; it avoided the same mistake in relation to a similarly structured measure in Case C-21/88, note 47 above. See discussion of Case C-2/90 *Commission v Belgium*, p. 516 below, for an unusual approach to the distinction.

52 [1986] 1 CMLR 228.

53 He applied the Court's ruling in Case 283/81 *CILFIT* [1982] ECR 3415, considered at p. 301 above.

54 Marenco, '*Pour Une Interprétation Traditionelle de la Notion de Mesure d'Effect Équivalent à une Restriction Quantitative*' (1984) 19 CDE 291, attempts to establish that discrimination is the foundation of all the Court's Art. 30 jurisprudence, but the argument has not been widely accepted and is unconvincing.

of the consumer if it felt such interests were properly part of residual national competence. One might object that this constitutes an improper judicial redrafting of the Treaty, but perhaps it could have been accomplished through a more flexible reading of Article 36's reference to 'public policy'.[55] The major objection against this approach to Article 36 lies not in any literal difficulty in broadening the notoriously fluid concept of public policy in this fashion, but rather in its policy basis. Article 36 is a narrowly defined exception to the basic principle of the free movement of goods, as the Court has often been moved to remark.[56] The Court is not interested in extending it; quite the reverse. However, to rework the argument, if this is so, why did the Court allow arguments based on consumer protection to be advanced in Cassis de Dijon at all? It would be in conformity with a narrow interpretation of derogations to insist that Article 36 and Article 36 alone can justify any rule prima facie falling within the scope of Article 30. From this perspective, arguments of consumer protection should have been dismissed as inadmissible. The mandatory requirements, then, are a surprising softening of Article 30, albeit only in the area of the indistinctly applicable rules. The probable rationale for the Court's apparent weakening is that it formed part of a compromise. The Court in Cassis was aware that it was permitting the intrusion of Article 30 into national competence in a manner not previously envisaged, or at least not previously fully appreciated.[57] The concession that certain broader interests, such as consumer protection, may justify national rules of the Cassis type should be seen as an example of the Court cautiously cushioning the impact of a potentially alarmingly vigorous increase in the profile of Community obligations.[58]

The principal reason why it was long widely felt that Article 30 was inapplicable to the types of non-discriminatory but protectionist national laws now revealed to be susceptible to attack under the Cassis approach was that Community harmonization initiatives were expected to provide a solution to the problem of diverse national legislation. The Court's use of Article 30 in Cassis de Dijon was in part a reaction to the appallingly slow progress that was being made in securing free trade through harmonization.[59] Yet, to re-emphasize the caution referred to in the previous para-

---

55 See p. 459. The point is discussed by Dashwood in 'The Cassis de Dijon Line of Authority' in Bates et. al. (eds) In Memoriam J. D. B. Mitchell, pp. 145, 154.
56 See Ch. 16, pp. 453–5.
57 See Comm. Dir. 70/50, p. 430 above, and comment at p. 494.
58 See Rasmussen, On Law and Policy, for general discussion of the Court's 'political', creative capacity examined in Ch. 7 of this book; at p. 27 he discusses the 'renovation' of Art. 30. See also Verloren van Themaat on the 'softening' of Art. 30 in Bieber et al. (eds) 1992, pp. 114–19.
59 See p. 521 for discussion of harmonization post-Cassis.

graph, the Court accepted *sub silentio* that it bore both a political and a legal obligation to recognize that reasonable non-discriminatory national regulations deserve more careful consideration than the strictly limited provisions of Article 36 can provide.[60] Accordingly, the notion of the mandatory requirements as an aspect of a general principle of reasonable interpretation of Community prohibitions[61] manifests a judicial attempt to balance the often competing concerns of the national interest in protective legislation and the broader Community objective of market integration.

Taking account of, first, the idea that the mandatory requirements are wider than Article 36, and, second, that the mandatory requirements form part of the very definition of Article 30, one arrives at an important implication[62] of the Court's creativity. Once an indistinctly applicable measure has been shown to be contrary to Article 30 because it is not necessary to satisfy a mandatory requirement, it is possible but pointless to seek justification for the measure under Article 36. It is *possible* to seek Article 36 justification, because once one has determined that the measure is an obstacle to trade not necessary to satisfy a mandatory requirement, one has done no more than hold Article 30 applicable. Article 36 still remains available as a potential justification. It is, however, *pointless* to invoke Article 36 because the mandatory requirements, which the measure has by definition been held unnecessary to satisfy, embrace and surpass the whole field of Article 36. This provides an explanation for the peculiarity that Article 36 is not mentioned at all in the judgment in *Cassis*. By contrast, Article 36 *is* of practical value as a method of saving rules that discriminate against imports because such rules fall foul of Article 30 without the opportunity to embark on the interpretative route that the Court devised in *Cassis de Dijon*.

ARTICLE 36 AND THE MANDATORY REQUIREMENTS COMPARED

Of course, Article 36, on the one hand, and the mandatory requirements, on the other, share several common features. This reflects their functional similarity as expressions of the residual competence of the member states to impose obstacles to interstate trade. The principles of proportionality and alternative means appear to be integral to both approaches. This is entirely logical since both are in essence derogations from the basic

---

60 See Reich, *Internal Market and Diffuse Interests*, p. 61 *et seq.* Oliver, *Free Movement of Goods*, appears to take a different view; see, e.g., para. 6.80, esp. final sentence.
61 See note 41 above.
62 But only an implication! The Court's judgments in this area are rather underdeveloped in their analysis.

principle of the free movement of goods and therefore must be interpreted narrowly. So a state cannot justify a trade barrier if its measures are excessive in relation to the threat against which it purports to be acting, and it matters not whether the measure is distinctly or indistinctly applicable. Similarly, since the mandatory requirements encompass the heads listed in Article 36 (but go beyond it), where a member state's justification for its national rule is within the ambit of Article 36, the Court may consider it unnecessary to decide explicitly whether or not the measure under investigation is distinctly or indistinctly applicable, for the nature of the justification is in such cases unaffected by the distinction. Several cases concerned with public-health controls were decided by the Court with little apparent regard for the classification of the measure as discriminatory or not. The Dutch ban on nisin that was challenged in *Eyssen*[63] was indistinctly applicable, yet the Court's analysis makes little of this point and deals primarily with public-health justification under Article 36. The same approach may be observed in the Court's decision on Dutch law governing pasteurized milk in *Melkunie*.[64] So, sometimes, nothing turns on whether the measure is distinctly or indistinctly applicable, because the same justification would be presented whether or not the measure discriminates against imports.[65] The Court appears ready simply to refer to Article 36 in such cases. The Court's approach in cases such as *Eyssen* and *Melkunie* may seem to lack a certain intellectual rigour, but the point was of no practical moment.[66] The Court is normally more careful where arguments based on the protection of the economic interests of consumers are advanced.[67] However, frequently the distinction will be of indirect relevance even where a head of justification is advanced that is common both to the mandatory requirements and to Article 36. If, in a public-health case, the measures taken are shown to discriminate by applying to imports only, then it will be incumbent on the state to show why no effective internal measures have been taken to combat a threat alleged to be sufficiently serious to justify measures against imported goods.[68] Health controls that form part of a general internal programme will frequently be less susceptible to allegations that they constitute arbitrary discrimination.

---

63 Case 53/80, note 25 above, considered at p. 466 above.
64 Case 97/83 [1984] ECR 2367, [1986] 2 CMLR 318. See also Cases C-1, C-176/90, note 12 above; Case C-17/93 J. J. J. *van der Veldt* [1994] ECR I-3537.
65 See the opinions of AG Verloren van Themaat in Case 97/83, note 64 above and in Case 6/81 *Diensten Groep* v *Beele* [1982] ECR 707, [1982] 3 CMLR 102.
66 Note also that in both cases the national courts' questions concentrated on Article 36 alone.
67 See notes 46–8 above; but cf. Case 16/83, note 51 above, a rare error.
68 See p. 468.

THE MANDATORY REQUIREMENTS

The Court is responsible for the development of the notion of the mandatory requirements, and this endows it with a flexible jurisdiction to determine what types of interest may legitimately be pleaded in support of indistinctly applicable measures that cause obstacles to trade. However, it is fundamental to note that although the mandatory requirements are rather broader than Article 36, they are certainly no licence for the routine introduction of technical impediments to the free movement of goods. The Court examines purported justifications with caution and applies with rigour the principles of proportionality and alternative means. The Court's commitment to the creation of a barrier-free market remains strong.

CONSUMER PROTECTION

Examples of unlawful protectionism

In the field of consumer protection the Court's readiness in principle to accept arguments justifying trade barriers has been matched by its readiness to find that purported measures of national consumer protection in fact constitute disguised protectionism. The German rules that affected French Cassis de Dijon and 'impure' foreign beers were both struck down by the Court as unlawful obstacles to the free movement of goods. Consumer protection arguments were available in principle but unpersuasive on the facts. In *Walter Rau* v *de Smedt*[69] Belgian legislation requiring margarine to be marketed in cube-shaped packages was challenged as incompatible with Article 30. The legislation applied to all margarine irrespective of origin, but had the effect of excluding from the Belgian market margarine made in other member states according to different packaging techniques. The result of the legislation was the protection of the Belgian producer from external competition. Evidence showed that Belgian prices for margarine exceeded those normal in other member states and that the Belgian market was characterized by an absence of foreign producers, the classic symptoms of the isolated, protected market. The European Court, to which the matter was referred under the Article 177 procedure, held that a rule of this nature was capable of impeding interstate trade because of the diversity of national legislation in the area. The rule consequently fell foul of Article

69 Case 261/81 [1982] ECR 3961, [1983] 2 CMLR 496.

30 unless shown to be necessary to satisfy a mandatory requirement in the general interest. In support of the rule it was argued that the purpose of the packaging requirement was to inform the consumer of the nature of the product. The Court accepted that the protection of the consumer from confusion constituted a legitimate objective of national policy, but insisted that any measure taken with such an end in view should conform to the requirements of proportionality and alternative means. The Belgian rule in question was incapable of satisfying such tests. The consumer could be provided with information about the nature of the product by devices less obstructive of the circulation of goods within the Community, such as an obligation to label the product clearly. *Walter Rau* v *de Smedt* provides a clear example of the Court's readiness to hear arguments based on the protection of the economic interests of the consumer as possible justifications for indistinctly applicable measures that restrict trade, but its simultaneous determination to subject such arguments to close scrutiny in the circumstances of the case. Common-market theory demands the elimination of national protectionism, for the consumer ought to be the ultimate beneficiary of the stimulus of cross-border competition.

De Kikvorsch Groothandel[70] involved a criminal prosecution before the Dutch courts. The marketing of Berliner Kindl Weisse beer imported from Germany contravened two provisions of Dutch law. First, the imported beer contained more acid than permitted under Dutch law. Second, the strength of the original wort was displayed on the label of the bottle, which was forbidden by Dutch law. Both rules were plainly indistinctly applicable measures of the *Cassis* type. Both rules restricted trade in products made in a different member state according to different techniques. An obstacle to trade established, it was for the Dutch authorities to show that the rules were necessary to satisfy mandatory requirements if the criminal charges against the firm exploiting the principle of free circulation of goods in the Community were to be sustained.

The limit on acidity was designed to protect the typical taste of Dutch 'sour beer', to which the Dutch beer drinker was accustomed. Beer of a more acidic taste would be quite unfamiliar. The Court was firm in its rejection of such arguments as justifications for impeding free trade:

In particular, no consideration relating to the protection of the national consumer militates in favour of a rule preventing such consumer from trying a beer which is brewed according to a different tradition in another Member State and the label of which clearly states that it comes from outside the said part of the Community.[71]

---

70 Case 94/82 [1983] ECR 947, [1984] 2 CMLR 323.
71 ibid., para. 8 of the judgment. See para. 32 of the judgment in Case 178/84, note 24 above.

So, consumer preference for domestic products is no reason for the exclusion by law of unfamiliar products from other member states. Provided adequate labelling is provided, the consumer is not deprived of the opportunity of selecting his or her usual preference, and also has the chance of trying a change of taste. The Dutch rule protecting typical sour beer confined consumer choice and undermined the basic competitive structure of the Community market.

Having indicated that in the first instance any threat to the consumer interest could be dealt with by a system of labelling, the Court then proceeded to consider the second limb of the Dutch beer law, which prohibited the provision of particular information by labelling. The stipulated purpose of the ban on the wort figure was to avoid consumer confusion. Dutch law required the display on the label of the alcohol strength figure and it was argued that the wort figure, if also shown, would be apt to confuse. The Court held that a member state is entitled to take action to protect its consumers from misleading information even where the result of such intervention is a hindrance to the free circulation of goods in the Community.[72] Consequently, the prohibition of the supply of information on a label may in principle constitute a measure necessary to satisfy a mandatory requirement, but it is essential for the state wishing to defend such rules to demonstrate that there is a genuine risk of confusion likely to prejudice the consumer and that that risk can be removed only by a ban, rather than, for example, by a restriction on the manner in which the information can be displayed. Such an assessment belongs with the national court in the context of an Article 177 reference.

The importance of the informed consumer

Banning the provision of information is capable of restricting the free circulation of products in respect of which information is routinely provided in the country of origin. It is unlikely that such rules will be readily upheld given the priority that the Court attaches to the role of the informed consumer as a spur to the efficient operation of the market.

In *GB-INNO* v *CCL*[73] a Luxembourg law controlling the provision of information about the price of goods was held capable of restricting cross-border trade in goods originating in states where no such burdens were imposed and the Court displayed little sympathy for submissions that the consumer was served by such restrictions. The Court asserted the close link

---

72 The Community itself has acted in this field: Comm. Dir. 84/450 OJ 1984 L250/17.
73 Case 362/88 [1990] ECR I-667, noted by Gormley (1990) 27 CMLRev 825, 839–40. See also Case C-241/89 *SARPP* v *Chambre Syndicale des Raffineurs et Conditionneurs de sucre de France* [1990] ECR I-4695.

between consumer information and consumer protection[74] and left little doubt about the irreconcilability of the rule in question with Article 30. In *Schutzverband gegen Unwesen in der Wirtschaft* v *Y. Rocher GmbH*[75] the Court indicated that a German law prohibiting advertisements in which individual prices were compared, except where the comparison was not eyecatching, impeded the construction of a cross-border marketing campaign and was incompatible with Article 30. The Court focused on the fact that the law did not distinguish between true or false advertisements and that it was therefore apt to suppress the supply of accurate information to the consumer. A variant on the type of situation at issue in *De Kikvorsch Groothandel*[76] might provide a rare example of a legitimate restriction on the provision of information.[77] If one accepts that the provision of too much information in similar form might be apt to mislead and that therefore it is on balance in the consumer interest to suppress certain matters by law, then an information ban might be held necessary to satisfy mandatory requirements.[78] It would always remain incumbent on the national authorities to demonstrate that the system adheres to the principles of proportionality and alternative means. So, if it is compulsory to supply one set of facts on a label, but illegal to supply another because of the risk of confusion between the two sets of figures (as was argued in *De Kikvorsch Groothandel*), then justification not only for the ban on the

---

74 The Court drew on the 1981 Council resolution adopting a consumer protection and information policy, OJ 1981 C133/1. The point is reinforced by the title on consumer protection inserted by the Maastricht Treaty amendments, which makes specific reference to action to provide adequate information to consumers (Art. 129a EC).

75 Case C-126/91, judgment of 18 May 1993.

76 Case 94/82, note 70 above.

77 Where the information relates to matters of moral as well as commercial interest, there may be stronger arguments in favour of restriction; see in relation to Art. 59 Case C-159/90 *SPUC* v *Grogan* [1991] ECR I-4685 [1991] 3 CMLR 849, p. 580 below. See also Cases C-1, C-176/90, note 12 above, where the information suppressed related to a product capable of causing damage to public health (strong alcohol).

78 Consider an obligation to use only the language of the state of marketing on a label (see note 22 above); could a producer who (as is increasingly common) prints labelling bearing the same information in several different languages be required to produce a single-language label? Strong evidence of consumer prejudice resulting from confusion between different languages would have to be demonstrated. See Case 27/80 *Fietje* [1980] ECR 3839; Case 76/86 *Commission* v *Germany* [1989] ECR 1021, [1991] 1 CMLR 741; Case C-369/89 *Piageme* v *Peeters* [1991] ECR I-2971, which prompted the Commission to publish a communication concerning the use of languages in the marketing of foodstuffs, OJ 1993 C345/3; see also opinion of AG Mancini in Case 407/85 *Drei Glocken* v *USL Centro-Sud* [1988] ECR 4233, but beware that the Court reached a different conclusion from its advocate-general, p. 520 below. In Case C-51/93 *Meyhui NV* v *Schott Zwiesel Glaswerke AG* [1994] ECR I-3879 the Court ruled, contrary to the opinion of AG Gulmann in the case, that a provision in Dir 69/493 requiring that only descriptions in the language(s) of the country of marketing be used was valid in the light of the importance of providing information to the consumer.

display of the second set of figures but also for the compulsion to provide the first set of figures must be provided.

Compulsory systems of labelling that are imposed on traders are certainly measures that restrict free trade less than outright bans on the sale of products, yet they are still liable to close scrutiny under Community law because of their capacity to impede free trade. To require a producer to create a separate production run of labels for a particular member state[79] obstructs the ability to treat the Community as a unified market, albeit that the inhibition is less severe than requiring a separate production run for the item itself, as may be dictated by rules on composition. A state must explain why a mandatory, rather than a permissive, labelling system is required in the circumstances. Thus, national laws that impose an obligation to label fruit liqueurs with their alcohol strength[80] or beer bottles with their additive content[81] or gold and silver articles with a hallmark[82] are capable of partitioning the market, but a state may be able to find justification for such rules as a means of providing the consumer with the opportunity to act in the market-place in an informed manner. Ultimately, the problems of national diversity in this area will be most efficiently resolved by the introduction of basic Community rules.[83]

Lawful consumer protection: *Oosthoek*

Oosthoek[84] is one of the few cases in which the commonly observed invocation of the demands of consumer protection as a justification for indistinctly applicable obstacles to trade was treated favourably by the Court. Dutch legislation strictly controlled the offer for sales promotion purposes of 'free gifts' to buyers of encyclopaedias. The intent of the law was to protect the consumer from entering into a transaction, the terms of which were obscured by the existence of the inducement. The Dutch rule constituted a *Cassis*-type obstacle to trade, because it hindered the marketing opportunities in the Netherlands of traders in other member states whose packaging and selling techniques were based on the allure of the 'free gift'. Such traders had to adopt a wholly different policy in the Dutch market simply because Dutch law was more rigorous than that in other

---

79 See notes 22, 78 above.
80 Cf. Case 120/78 itself, note 7 above.
81 Cf. Case 178/84, note 24 above.
82 Case C-293/93 *Criminal Proceedings against Ludomira Neeltje Barbara Houtwipper* [1994] ECR I-4249.
83 See, e.g., Dir. 86/197 and Reg. 1576/89 on alcoholic drinks.
84 Case 286/81, note 41 above. See also Case 382/87 *Buet v Ministère Public* [1989] ECR 1235, noted by Gormley, 'Recent Case Law on the Free Movement of Goods: Some Hot Potatoes', (1990) 27 CMLRev 825, 837–9.

states. Oosthoek decided to ignore the law and pursued a sales policy based on the offer of inducements, which, although unlawful under Dutch law, was compatible with the law in Belgium, where the firm also operated. When prosecuted, it argued that the Dutch law contravened Article 30 as an unlawful barrier to trade. An Amsterdam court referred the point to Luxembourg. The European Court agreed that the rule in question constituted a barrier to trade, but indicated that it was receptive to arguments that the rule might be upheld as a legitimate means of protecting both the consumer from deception and the honest trader from unfair competition.[85] Although the final determination lay with the national court because the case was an Article 177 reference, the Court declared, in terms that clearly indicated a broadly favourable view of the lawfulness of the Dutch rules, that

it is undeniable that the offering of free gifts as a means of sales promotion may mislead consumers as to the real prices of certain products and distort the conditions on which genuine competition is based. Legislation which restricts or even prohibits such commercial practices for that reason is therefore capable of contributing to consumer protection and fair trading,[86]

UNFAIR COMPETITION

Apart from typical consumer-protection regulation, more general laws against unfair competition have been accommodated within the scope of interests constituting the mandatory requirements. In *Dansk Supermarked* v *Imerco*[87] the Court accepted that national legislation preventing unfair marketing practices – for example, rules prohibiting precise imitation of familiar products – could be justified as a legitimate means of ensuring fair competition despite the capacity of such rules to impede the importation of imitative goods from other member states.[88] Such rules are designed to suppress unfair competition in the interests both of the honest trader and the consumer and therefore may override the free movement of goods. So, the availability of an English 'passing-off' action brought against an import from another member state may be justified as necessary to satisfy

85 Many consumer-protection laws may equally well be seen as laws against unfair competition; outlawing unfair practices has the twin aim of protecting both the consumer and the fair trader.
86 Case 286/81, note 41 above, para. 18 of the judgment.
87 Case 58/80 [1981] ECR 181, [1981] 3 CMLR 590.
88 Cf. Case 6/81 *Diensten Groep* v *Beele* [1982] ECR 707. Cf. Case C-238/89 *Pall* v *Dahlhausen* [1990] ECR I-4827; application of rules against unfair competition held in breach of Art. 30. See also Case C-126/91, note 75 above.

a mandatory requirement. However, in *Prantl*[89] the Court insisted that any obstacle to trade had to be justified on an individual basis and that it would be impermissible to forbid the marketing of products made according to a fair and traditional practice in the state of export simply because such goods exhibited a similarity to domestic goods. The importation of goods from other member states in order to compete with domestic goods is not of itself an unfair practice; indeed, such developments are the basis of the common market. However, the insistence in *Prantl* on a fair and traditional practice suggests a need to show more than mere lawful manufacture in the state of origin and permits the importing state an ill-defined power to control deliberate attempts to undermine the fair operation of its market.

Unfair competition rules of this nature display a similar function to intellectual property rights in the sense that both are legal means of excluding potentially competing products from the market. However, unlike general unfair competition law, intellectual property law confers *exclusive* rights on the individual right holder to prevent the marketing of similar goods in a defined (usually national) territory.[90]

A NON-EXHAUSTIVE LIST

Consumer protection and the related field of securing fair competition have been the most frequently invoked 'mandatory requirements'. That fact should not obscure the importance of other interests that are capable of providing justification for indistinctly applicable national rules that operate as obstacles to trade. In *Commission* v *Denmark*[91] the Court was obliged to consider a national measure of environment protection that operated as a barrier to the free circulation of goods. The Danish system involved a requirement that beer and soft drinks be marketed only in containers that could be reused. Containers used required the approval of the Danish National Agency for the Protection of the Environment. Such approval would not be forthcoming for a container considered ill-suited to an adequate system of return and reuse. Severely limited exceptions

89 Case 16/83, note 51 above; the flaw in the decision identified above does not seem to detract from the general principle expressed by the Court.
90 See further Ch. 26.
91 Case 302/86 [1988] ECR 4607, [1989] 1 CMLR 619; see P. Kromarek, 'Environmental Protection and Free Movement of Goods: the Danish Bottles Case' (1990) 2 J Environ L 89; B. Jadot, '*Mesures Nationales de Police de l'Environnement, Libre Circulation des Marchandises et Proportionalité*' (1990) 26 CDE 408; Gormley (1990) 27 CMLRev 825, 844; T. Sexton, 'Enacting National Environmental Laws More Stringent than Other States' Laws in the European Community' (1991) 24 Cornell ILJ 563.

permitted the use of non-approved containers, but not if made from metal and only on condition that a deposit-and-return system had been instituted. The objective of the legislation was to encourage the reuse of scarce materials and thereby to reduce the quantity of discarded metal cans and other containers littering the streets. It was a measure of environmental protection. At the same time the Danish measures reduced the capacity of manufacturers in other member states to market in Denmark drinks in containers typically used in the home state that, in many cases, such as that of the widely used metal can, were incapable of complying with the Danish deposit-and-return system. The Danish environmental law had the effect of protecting the Danish drinks industry. There thus arose the classic trade-off that is at the heart of this area of the law: free circulation of goods or national social and welfare protection.

The Court held the approval system incompatible with Article 30. However, it accepted that Denmark's deposit-and-return system for empty containers could lawfully be implemented in accordance with Community law.[92] The Court thus chose national protection of the environment over the free movement of goods. The legal rationale for the decision lies in the Court's accommodation of environmental protection within the list of mandatory requirements that are capable of limiting the Article 30 prohibition and an acceptance that the deposit-and-return system amounted to an apt and proportionate method of achieving a better environment. The result is that the free flow of drink in containers into Denmark is hindered. The Danish system partitions the market lawfully and as other member states respond to the concerns of environmental protection doubtless further fragmentation will follow. Given the compatibility of the Danish system with Article 30, the trade barrier can be removed only through the introduction of specific Community rules in the field.[93] Such a harmonized regime would ideally, though perhaps unrealistically,[94] secure the legitimate

---

92 Contrast AG Slynn, who considered both schemes unlawful.

93 Some debate has arisen over the proper legal base for such measures. The Community first acquired formal competence in the field of environmental protection as a result of the Single European Act. The provisions, strengthened by the Treaty on European Union, are Arts. 130r-t EC. Difficulties arise in choosing between Art. 130s and Art. 100a, the internal market base. See Ch. 8, p. 252 above, on the Court's approach, which is rather erratic; Case C-300/89 *Commission* v *Council* [1991] ECR I-2867 suggests a priority for Art. 100a, Case C-155/91 *Commission* v *Council* [1993] ECR I-939 and Case C-187/93 *Parliament* v *Council* [1994] ECR I-2857 suggest preference for Art. 130s. The choice affects, *inter alia*, national competence to enact rules stricter than Community measures; Art. 130t is more permissive than Art. 100a(4), see Ch. 16, p. 483 above. See generally Emiliou, 'Opening Pandora's Box: The Legal Basis of Community Measures before the Court of Justice' (1994) 19 ELRev 488.

94 See p. 482 above on the inability of the Community to legislate in a manner that satisfies all competing interest groups.

concerns of protecting the environment from disposable drink containers throughout the Community and also facilitate free trade in such goods at those high standards of environmental protection.[95] A connected consequence is that producers in states previously lacking adequate environmental protection legislation will be relieved of their unfair competitive advantage over producers in other states who are subject to the costs of sophisticated regulation.[96]

The list of mandatory requirements that may be advanced in support of indistinctly applicable rules is not closed. This was already apparent in the *Cassis* judgment itself, when the Court declared that its list of protectable interests included *in particular* the effectiveness of fiscal provision *et al.*[97] It is therefore open to states to present arguments based on previously unrecognized conceptions of the general interest as justification for impeding free trade. *Commission v Denmark*[98] may provide an example of the increasing recognition in Community law of the modern rise of legitimate concern for the environment. The Court's decision, made in 1988, was doubtless in part stimulated by the inclusion of Environmental Policy in the Single European Act,[99] which entered into force in 1987, but such general developments in Community policy-making do not free the Court from the difficult task of balancing in individual cases the weight to be given to competing interests in the process of evolving Community integration.

Commission v Belgium[100] provided the Court with the opportunity to re-examine the application of Article 30 to environmental policy in an area partially covered by Community legislative activity. The rules challenged by the Commission as violations of Article 30 were introduced by Wallonia, a region of Belgium,[101] in order to prohibit the storage, tipping or dumping of waste originating in other member states or in other parts of Belgium. The Walloon authorities were concerned that areas with strict controls over disposal might target waste on Wallonia, with the result that Wallonia would suffer as a destination for so-called 'waste tourism'. The Court accepted that waste, having commercial value, counted as 'goods'

---

95 Subject to national derogations; see note 93 above.
96 It may be observed that this cuts both ways; a pro-environment stance is increasingly seen as a useful marketing ploy.
97 Case 120/78, note 7 above, para. 8 of the judgment. See also WQ 749/81, OJ 1981 C309/7.
98 Case 302/86, note 91 above.
99 Arts. 130r-t, which were developed further at Maastricht. The Court's decision in Case 240/83 *ADBHU* [1985] ECR 531 already acknowledged the protection of the environment as a fundamental objective of the Community.
100 Case C-2/90 [1992] ECR I-4431, [1993] 1 CMLR 365.
101 See Ch. 7, p. 201 above, on the application of the Art. 169 procedure to federal member states.

for the purposes of the application of Article 30.[102] There was no doubt that the Walloon rules impeded cross-border trade (in addition to trade within Belgium). That was their purpose. The Court found the measures justified on grounds of environmental protection. The Court stated that '[t]he accumulation of waste . . . constitutes a threat to the environment because of the limited capacity of each region or locality for receiving it'. It referred to Article 130r(2) EC, which provides that 'environmental damage should as a priority be rectified at source'. This, according to the Court, confirmed the importance of a policy designed to minimize transportation of waste. The Walloon rules conformed to good waste management practice and were upheld by the Court despite their obstructive effect on cross-border trade.

This describes the explicit course of the Court's ruling. However, there lurk beneath the surface a number of conundrums which have attracted much comment.[103] The rules in question were, one would suppose, discriminatory. Only Walloon-produced waste could be treated in Wallonia. The rule was origin-specific; the very objective of the policy was that it should be! Yet, on past judicial practice, the finding of discrimination should have limited Belgium to the list of justifications found in Article 36, which does not include environmental protection. Invocation of the *Cassis de Dijon*-inspired mandatory requirements, which permit environmental protection to be fed into the legal assessment of trade-restrictive rules, depends on the absence of discrimination according to the origin of goods.[104] The Court's answer was simple. It stated that the rules were *not* discriminatory. Once it had found in Article 130r(2) a basis for regarding treatment at source as a principle of Community policy, it felt able to conclude that '. . . having regard to the differences between waste produced in one place and that in another and its connection with the place where it is produced, the contested measures cannot be considered to be discriminatory'. It is submitted that it is not convincing to hold that because local responsibility is viewed as the norm, waste from different localities is therefore objectively different. This, if anything, is reasoning in reverse. It is notable that in the case Advocate-General Jacobs accepted that the rules discriminated between goods according to their origin.

Commission v *Belgium* is therefore a difficult judgment to fit within the legal trends in this area. It is submitted that the Court's unpersuasive characterization of the particular measure under scrutiny as non-discriminatory was a means to the end of securing conformity between the application of the law of the free movement of goods and the developing pattern of

---

102 Cf. Case 7/68, Ch. 13, p. 384 above.
103 E.g. Hancher and Sevenster (1993) 30 CMLRev 351; Von Wilmowsky (1993) 30 CMLRev 541; Geradin (1993) 18 ELRev 144. See also Select Further Reading, p. 906.
104 Pp. 502–4 above.

Treaty environmental policy. In using the *Cassis* principle, the Court showed flexibility in the practical application of what is, after all, its own creation. Even if one concludes that in upholding the apparently discriminatory Walloon rules the Court has accepted that *de facto* the mandatory requirements may be employed to defend even distinctly applicable rules, one must appreciate that the Court has explicitly denied that this is what it has done. The Court stated, in line with its previous approach, that an absence of discrimination is essential before the mandatory requirements may be taken into account. Therefore, one must suppose that the Court is unreceptive to a wholesale abandonment of the margin between distinctly and indistinctly applicable measures. Submissions based on defence of national laws as necessary to satisfy mandatory requirements should still respect the need to show to the Court's satisfaction that such laws fall within the category of indistinctly applicable laws. To this extent, it is submitted that the Court remains motivated by the desire to use Article 30 rigorously to police national rules that are hostile to market integration. Specifically, Article 36 will not be widened.[105] The Court is nevertheless receptive to the importance of protecting interests in the Community that compete with the promotion of the free movement of goods, pending the comprehensive treatment of such potential collisions in Community legislation. Community regulatory activity in the environmental field is increasing and, indeed, part of the Court's ruling in *Commission v Belgium* examined Belgian compliance with relevant Directives. Control of hazardous waste was examined in the light of Directive 84/631, where the Walloon rules were incompatible with the regime, which did not permit an absolute ban. The control of non-hazardous waste was not covered by existing rules and therefore fell to be considered in the light of Article 30 EC.

The Court's self-endowed capacity to enlarge the scope of the list of mandatory requirements furnishes it with the power to renew its approach to the legitimacy of national trade barriers in accordance with the evolution of societal concern for particular interests.[106] The Court can use the *Cassis* formula to sanction national social policy under Community law in areas where the adoption of relevant Community legislation lags far behind.[107] The Court has, however, consistently maintained that broad economic

---

105 Cf. p. 505 above.

106 Might the Court accommodate, e.g., national regional policy within the scope of the mandatory requirements? See generally Martin and Stehmann, 'Product Market Integration versus Regional Cohesion in the Community', (1991) 16 ELRev 216; and see pp. 403–4 in relation to Art. 95.

107 See comment at p. 524 on the Court's potential for creativity in setting the margin between lawful and unlawful trade barriers. See also its role in setting the outer margin of Community competence, p. 532.

justifications are not available to member states responsible for the creation of impediments to the free circulation of goods.[108] In this respect, at least, the bounds of the mandatory requirements are coextensive with those of Article 36.[109]

THE CONSEQUENCES OF *CASSIS DE DIJON*

The range of consequences that flows from the judgment in *Cassis de Dijon* and its subsequent amplifications has proved extremely broad. Many interest groups, including consumers, traders and the Community's legislature, are affected by the implications of the decision, and to some extent their concerns are interdependent. The following section is no more than a brief survey of some of the issues raised. It examines first the advantages and then the disadvantages of the Court's approach.

ADVANTAGES

Increased competition in an integrating market

The *Cassis* principle ensures increased consumer choice in the common market by guaranteeing in principle the free circulation of typical national products throughout the territory of the member states. This is the *Cassis* 'principle of equivalence', which insists that in the absence of specific evidence to the contrary a product lawfully made and marketed in one member state of the Community is entitled to access to the markets of all the other member states. The consumer should be able to pick and choose between the best of each member state's produce unhindered by the restraints of technical national rules governing product designation or composition. Free trade stimulates competition both in quality (upwards) and price (downwards). The injection of cross-border competition through the elimination of technical rules that isolate national markets is a constant theme of the Court's post-*Cassis* jurisprudence.[110]

The trader is enabled to abandon the constraints of production for relatively small national markets and take advantage of the reality of a

---

108 E.g., Case 238/82 *Duphar BV* v *Netherlands* [1984] ECR 523, [1985] 1 CMLR 256.
109 See Case 7/61 *Commission* v *Italy* [1961] ECR 454; p. 454 above.
110 The Court made particular reference to this objective in Case 178/84, note 24 above and Case 94/82, note 70 above.

Community-wide market-place with a population of some 370 million, which in many cases will allow dramatic reduction in unit costs. The disappearance of the shelter of national protectionism will force industries to restructure, but the logic of the common market is based on the realization of these economies of scale. Benefits accrue to the successful trader and ultimately to the general consumer.

So, in *Drei Glocken* v *Centro-Sud*[111] Italian rules restricting the marketing of pasta to products made from durum wheat were considered unnecessary to satisfy mandatory requirements.[112] This opens up the Italian market to importers of pasta made from other types of wheat. *Smanor*[113] involved a challenge to French rules that restricted the use of the designation 'yoghurt' to fresh fermented milk products. The effect was the protection of the French market from competition from imports of yoghurts made according to different methods, such as the use of deep-frozen fermented milk, for such products were obliged to adopt a different, locally unfamiliar designation. The Court indicated that such rules were capable of infringing Article 30, subject to final decision by the national court in the context of an Article 177 reference. In *Ministère Public* v *Deserbais*[114] the Court considered that French legislation setting a minimum fat content for Edam cheese was incompatible with Article 30. The rule excluded from the French market cheese made in other member states according to different preferences relating to fat content and was unsupported by any objective justification.[115] In all these cases any genuine and objectively justifiable fear of consumer confusion could be allayed by a labelling system, rather than a ban, as a means of providing the consumer with adequate information about the products he or she could select.[116] The breadth of post-*Cassis* case law is remarkable; the binding thread is the integration of the market and the free circulation of goods.[117]

---

111 Case 407/85, note 78 above, noted by Barents (1989) 26 CMLRev 103, Gormley, '"Actually or Potentially, Directly or Indirectly"? Obstacles to the Free Movement of Goods' (1989) 9 YEL 197, 201. See generally Brouwers, 'Free Movement of Foodstuffs and Quality Requirements: has the Commission got it wrong?' (1988) 25 CMLRev 237.

112 The case is notable for a fierce but unsuccessful defence of the Italian rules by Advocate-General Mancini.

113 Case 298/87 [1988] ECR 4489, noted by Gormley (1989) 9 YEL 197, 202.

114 Case 286/86 [1988] ECR 4907.

115 On fat in cheese see also Case C-210/89 *Commission* v *Italy*, [1990] ECR I-3697.

116 See discussion of labelling at p. 511. For criticism of the Court's view of the adequacy of labelling, see Lasa, 'Free Movement of Foodstuffs, Consumer Protection and Food Standards in the European Community: has the Court of Justice got it wrong?' (1991) 16 ELRev 391. See also Lister, 'The naming of foods: the European Community's rules for non-brand product names' (1993) 18 ELRev 179.

117 For further examples see Case 51/83 *Commission* v *Italy* [1984] ECR 2793, [1986] 2

Preservation of national tradition

Were national technical rules of this nature compatible with the Treaty, the obstacles to trade that they impose could have been eliminated only by establishing common Community rules on which interstate trade could proceed. The shaping of Article 30 into an instrument apt to cover such indistinctly applicable rules has the beneficial effect that there is now no need to resort to harmonization in order to secure the free flow of products affected by unlawful indistinctly applicable technical rules. The scope of Article 30 is increased, whereas the scope of required Community harmonization is correspondingly reduced. It should be appreciated that harmonization of such rules, even if achievable against the heterogeneous background of the Community, would have been profoundly undesirable because the establishment of common Community rules would tend to result in 'Euro-products'.[118] To use particular illustrations, if French rules on Edam cheese,[119] Italian rules on pasta[120] or German rules on beer[121] acted as lawful impediments to trade, they would eventually have had to be replaced by a Community concept of cheese, pasta and beer. This would rob the consumer of choice and destroy the Community's marvellous internal diversity. Consequently, the Court's decision to reinvigorate Article 30's application to indistinctly applicable rules in *Cassis* can be seen both as a response to the Community's long-term failure to achieve harmonization of national rules in this complex area[122] and as a reflection of a perception that harmonization would in any event constitute an undesirable suppression of national tradition.

The reaction of the Commission

The intractable nature of disparate national technical rules and indeed their apparent proliferation as a suspected protectionist device during the 1970s was viewed by the Commission as a major obstacle to the achievement of the aspirations of the Treaty of Rome. Consequently, the Commission's delight at the important new impetus towards the dismantling of such

---

CMLR 274 (animal gelatin in confectionery); Case 76/86 *Commission* v *Germany* [1989] ECR 1021 (milk substitutes); Case 52/88 *Commission* v *Belgium* [1989] ECR 1137, [1991] 1 CMLR 755 (edible gelatin); Case C-269/89 *Bonfait* [1990] ECR I-4169 (meat products); Case C-241/89, note 73 above (sweeteners).

118 See Mattera, '*L'Arrêt Cassis de Dijon*' (1980) RMC 505.
119 Case 286/86, note 114 above.
120 Case 407/85, note 78 above.
121 Case 178/84, note 24 above.
122 See p. 505 above.

rules provided by the Court in *Cassis* was hardly a surprise. The pre-existing situation, in which an extensive harmonization programme was expected, imposed a daunting workload on the Commission. For broader policy reasons it was undesirable because it imposed a stifling central regulatory structure on the Community. Harmonization of standards, particularly if compliance is mandatory, tends to operate in a conservative manner by discouraging technical innovation. *Cassis* contributed towards deregulation by shifting the focus in the area of many indistinctly applicable rules away from legislative harmonization towards Article 30 prohibition. This yielded free trade in goods irrespective of their lack of conformity with the different technical standards of the several member states and thereby stimulated interbrand competition. Such mutual recognition conforms to the increasingly prominent principle of subsidiarity, which insists that the Community should be allocated responsibility for decision-making only where that is shown to be more efficient than decentralized decision-making.[123] By the late 1980s respect for the strength of national tradition had become an increasingly influential element in Community policy-making, but the Court had already adopted this perspective a decade earlier in its *Cassis de Dijon* judgment.

The Commission took the opportunity to express its satisfaction with the judgment in *Cassis* and to sketch its subsequent policy in an important Communication issued in 1980.[124] The Commission observed that the basis of the Court's ruling was that 'any product lawfully produced and marketed in one Member State must, in principle, be admitted to the market of any other Member State'. Only under very strict conditions are exceptions permissible. Thus, many technical rules are now unlawful under the Court's criteria and the Commission has the task of challenging such rules under Article 30.[125] Harmonization work will be confined to the removal of national barriers to trade that remain lawful under the *Cassis* criteria. The Commission concluded that it was 'confident that this approach will secure greater freedom of trade for the Community's manufacturers, so strengthening the industrial base of the Community, while meeting the expectations of consumers'.[126]

---

123 See Ch. 1, pp. 12–15.
124 OJ 1980 C256/2, noted by Gormley (1981) 6 ELRev 454.
125 Art. 30 is directly effective, so challenge is not purely the preserve of the Commission, as *Cassis*, itself an Art. 177 reference, demonstrates.
126 The Commission's task of discovering the range of technical barriers to trade that may require either challenge under Art. 30 or harmonization was eased by Council Dir. 83/189 (OJ 1983 L109/8, amended by Council Dir. 88/182 OJ 1988 L81/75), which imposes obligations on states to notify the Commission of the introduction of technical rules. See pp. 479–80 above on the practical management of the internal market.

The impact on the completion of the internal market

In its 1985 White Paper on completing the internal market,[127] which was in essence the blueprint for the 1992 project,[128] the Commission once again declared its belief in the essential equivalence of the objectives of national standards and confirmed its intention to see unjustified national obstacles to trade struck down under Article 30.[129] Only outside the scope of this legally enforceable area of mutual recognition would harmonization be required. In addition, in relation to the harmonization programme itself, the Commission's determination to reduce the inflexible nature of Community legislation assumed a new dimension. Even in the limited area of rules held lawful after the application of the pro-integrative *Cassis* criteria – that is, national rules held necessary to satisfy mandatory requirements[130] – the Commission pledged itself, wherever possible, to limit its intervention to the field of health and safety. It would set basic Community performance standards for goods, but leave the elaboration of those rules to private standards-making bodies. This would, in turn, transfer decision-making about methods of manufacture to the efficient level, that of the manufacturer. Precise mandatory rule-making has thus been abandoned in many areas. The policy, known as the 'new approach to technical harmonization',[131] conforms to the policy concerns that underlie the decision in *Cassis*. As far as is consistent with basic standards of safety and health, goods that are made in one member state shall be free to circulate throughout the territory of the Community. The consumer is able to choose from a variety of products. Efficient competition is stimulated.

DISADVANTAGES

These very positive aspects suggest a community of interest in welcoming the *Cassis* judgment that one might sceptically consider too good to be true. It is certainly the case that there are a number of criticisms of the implications of the *Cassis* principle that need to be addressed. It should, however, be immediately noted that any discussion of *Cassis* should not

---

127 COM (85) 310.
128 See further Ch. 1, p. 24.
129 Note 127 above, para. 61 *et seq.*
130 Remember also rules justified under Art. 36; see Ch. 16.
131 OJ 1985 C136/1. See Pelkmans, 'The New Approach to Technical Harmonization and Standardization' (1986–87) 25 JCMS 249; Waelbroeck, '*L'Harmonisation des règles et normes techniques dans la CEE*' (1988) 24 CDE 243. The new approach is followed in, e.g., Dir. 88/378 on the safety of toys, OJ 1988 L187/1, Dir. 92/59 on general product safety OJ 1992 L228/24.

focus on the judicial role alone. Certainly there are aspects of the judgment that are open to criticism, but the decision was taken amid the pressure of a range of competing interests involving, *inter alia*, free trade, national competence to regulate the market and Community legislative initiatives. Many of the consequences of *Cassis* emerge and are moulded by the broader political economy of the Community, not just its Court. This suggests that an analysis of *Cassis* involves a need to consider the Community's general structure and purpose.

Negative harmonization

At the simplest level the Court is limited to defining which existing national practices are lawful and which are not. Judicial decisions that apply Article 30 are aspects of 'negative harmonization' in that they may achieve uniformity between member states, but only by the negative process of holding national laws incompatible with Article 30.[132] Positive action as a means of introducing Community rules, rather than simply bringing about an absence of national rules, is the preserve of the Community's legislature.

Consequently, the essential concern about *Cassis* resides in the fear that it has promoted free trade but that the terms on which such free trade will ensue are thoroughly uncertain. *Cassis* may have deregulated the market by eliminating many national technical barriers to trade, but it remains questionable whether the removal of national barriers without accompanying positive Community regulation is sufficient to secure the realization of a true common market. At a more fundamental level of policy, one must address the question of the extent to which the Community *ought* to regulate the market in a positive sense.

The risk that the principle of equivalence may be unduly emphasized

Some examples will illustrate the problem. As explained, the consumer has a great deal to gain from the elimination of technical rules governing product composition and designation because he or she can look forward to shopping in a more competitive environment. The 'principle of equivalence'[133] is thus a pro-consumer element in the *Cassis* judgment. However, the underlying assumption of equivalence deserves a sceptical hearing. The

---

132 See generally on negative harmonization, Reich, 'Community Consumer Law' in Bourgoignie (ed.) *European Consumer Law* above; Bourgoignie and Trubek, *Consumer Law*. Beyond Community law, see Tinbergen, *International Economic Integration*.
133 See p. 519.

Community's great strength is its diversity. That strength is founded on the assumption that standards are different from state to state. The policy base that, such diversity notwithstanding, each member state can boast a common core of health and safety standards earns limited support from the factual evidence of discrepancy in economic development between the member states.

The risk, then, is that the principle of equivalence is in many cases flawed because of an absence of genuine equivalence in fact. Whereas protectionist rules are properly eliminated by virtue of the Court's stance elaborated since *Cassis*, genuine rules of protection deserve to remain in place notwithstanding their inhibitive effect on the integration of the market pending the creation of sufficient confidence about basic standards in all states. Admittedly, the *Cassis* judgment provides a framework for making such assessments. An unsafe product originating in another member state is lawfully excluded from the market of the state of destination in accordance with the *Cassis* criteria.[134] This is, however, an inevitably rudimentary approach, given the limited nature of the Court's participation in the creation of the Community's regulatory structure. The Court can do no more than accept or reject a state's submissions in support of its rules, which is at best *ad hoc* policy-making. Moreover, although decisions on the balance between safety and free trade may be relatively easy to make in clear cases concerning unsafe goods, the Court faces much more difficult choices in connection with more intangible interests, such as the protection of the environment.[135] The legitimacy of national social protection is judged in the rather narrow context of its effect on interstate trade under Article 30. The basic risk inherent in the *Cassis* line of authority is that the Court has introduced a legal test that tends to tip the balance away from legitimate social protection towards a deregulated (perhaps unregulated) free market economy in which standards of, *inter alia*, consumer protection will be depressed.

Perceived inadequacy in positive harmonization

For the consumer, the risk of a free market in poor quality or, worse, dangerous products exists. The consequences for the Community are that, firstly, consumer confidence in the Community will be jeopardized, with

---

134 For an interesting example see Case 188/84 *Commission* v *France* [1986] ECR 419. The Court's appreciation of the different techniques for achieving product safety led it to hold national trade barriers lawful; the Court is not unaware of the policy concerns raised here. Dir. 92/59, note 131 above, now covers the field of product safety. See also Cases C-1, C-176/90, note 12 above, in relation to national controls on strong drink (the opposite of the *Cassis* rules themselves).

135 See p. 514. See also Lasa, note 116 above.

the result that national prejudice in purchasing decisions will persist, and, secondly, that member states accustomed to higher than average standards of social protection will refuse to abandon those standards.[136] Either or both reactions would have the potential to undermine the very enterprise of establishing a common market. This suggests that the Community must commit itself to achieving a balance between free trade and legitimate measures of protection in order to foster an environment in which integration will be truly welcomed. On its own Article 30 as interpreted by the Court in *Dassonville* and in *Cassis* and subsequently lacks the sophistication to supply that confidence.

The project to complete the internal market requires a method of accommodating national interests, which may justify trade barriers, within the Community framework. This suggests the need for a refined approach to the allocation of regulatory competence, recognizing the inability of the Community to regulate effectively in all matters. For example, cross-border free trade might be accompanied by cross-border regulation and enforcement of consumer and employee protection law.[137] A system of cooperation between the Community and its constituent member states is required, and it may be observed that this task is not helped, and perhaps hindered, by clinging to abstract notions of Community supremacy and pre-emption. As suggested in Chapter 16, discussion about the proper allocation of power and responsibility to different levels in the structure is nothing new to federations the world over.[138]

Aspects of the same problem of uncertainty in regulatory structure confront the cross-border trader. Many national technical rules are theoretically inapplicable to imported goods, but this may often not be conclusively shown until the outcome of extended litigation. A trader may be unwilling to embark on the long process of challenging a national technical rule[139] and will instead either simply avoid the market in question or adapt to its technical requirements. Even unlawful rules will continue to exert a protectionist effect and the integration of the market will be impeded. The problem, once again, is the negative aspect to judicial work in this area, which cannot create positive rules to regulate the Community-wide market on which the trader can rely with confidence. Indeed, Currall went so far as to declare that the judgment in *Cassis* would provide a 'glimpse of such

---

136 See Art. 100a(3) & (4); Art. 130t; Title on Consumer Protection in the EC Treaty, pp. 482–4 above.

137 See refs. under 'Consumer Protection' in Select Further Reading, and Ch. 20.

138 See Select Further Reading for Ch. 16, p. 904 below, refs. under *The effect of Community Legislation on national competence*. Cappelletti, Seccombe, Weiler (eds.), *Integration through Law*.

139 Weatherill (1988) 13 ELRev 87, 99–100; Burrows, 'Harmonisation of Technical Standards', (1990) 53 MLR 597, 598.

potential chaos that the fundamental necessity for speeding up harmonization would be appreciated'.[140] Judicial negative harmonization, in some
cases itself a response to legislative inertia,[141] may, then, provide a spur for
positive legislative (re)action to provide clarification.[142]

Such concerns carry an obvious implication that the Commission's
policy developed in response to the *Cassis* judgment contains unpersuasive
features. The deregulatory tenor of the judgment in *Cassis* may prove
insufficient *on its own* to provide the minimum that is required to stimulate
business activity in the wider market. A similar criticism may be directed
at the Commission's 'new approach to technical harmonization',[143] which
also struggles to achieve an acceptable balance between adequate basic
regulation and the impetus towards free trade.[144] Even though the new
approach is part of positive Community policy-making, its flexibility is
both its strength and its weakness. The same criticism can be levelled at the
Cassis approach to the legal status of indistinctly applicable rules. The point
is well made by Bermann: 'Reliance on the mutual recognition of national
standards at the expense of positive harmonization has a fashionable
deregulatory flavor. In the long run, however, harmonization is more apt
to create a uniform regulatory environment and produce the full advantages of a single market.'[145]

Future developments

Cassis de Dijon is an entirely welcome decision, but should form only part
of a comprehensive strategy for regulating the Community market. Negative must be supported by positive; the Court must be supported by the
legislature. Facilitating free movement is a first step; this may need to be
followed by protective legislation dealing with the consequences of that
free movement.[146] From this perspective springs the Community's social

---

140 'Some Aspects of the Relation between Articles 30–36 and Article 100 of the EEC
Treaty, with a Closer Look at Optional Harmonization' [1984] 4 YEL 169, 185.
141 See p. 505 in relation to *Cassis*. See generally Rasmussen, *On Law and Policy*.
142 See comments at p. 810 on the pressures that led to the adoption of the Merger
Regulation in 1989. See also the Court's perception of the division of function between
its role and that of the legislature made explicit in Case C-9/93 *IHT Internationale
Heiztechnik GmbH* v *Ideal Standard GmbH*, Ch. 26, p. 846 below.
143 See note 131 above.
144 Institutional aspects of the new approach add to the concern; see, e.g., Dehousse,
'1992 and Beyond: the Institutional Dimension of the Internal Market Programme'
[1989/1] LIEI 109.
145 In 'The Single European Act: a new Constitution for the Community?' [1989] Col.
J. Transnat. L 529, 540 n. 44.
146 On the facilitative/protective dichotomy see Taylor, *The Limits of European Integration*; McGee and Weatherill, 'The Evolution of the Single Market – Harmonization or
Liberalization?' (1990) 53 MLR 578.

policy in its broadest sense.[147] The mandatory requirements developed in *Cassis*, in common with the Article 36 list of justifications, are essentially an expression of the Community's gradual evolution.[148] Both the invocation of the necessity to satisfy mandatory requirements and the list of Article 36 justifications assume the absence of Community rules establishing exhaustive treatment of the relevant area. Thus *Cassis* represents a framework for judicial assessment of acceptable national values in the context of a Community dedicated to ultimate free trade, pending legislative reassessment. The Community at present faces the major difficulty that its legislative procedures are immature and that consequently many important legislative decisions that represent an integral part of establishing a comprehensive regulatory framework for the market are not being taken or are being blocked. Pelkmans, accordingly, insisted on the need to 'surpass the institutional evasiveness of the Single Act'.[149] Much the same observation can cogently be directed at the limitations of the pattern of the Treaty on European Union. Resolving this problem is an essential element in the development of the Community. It was explained in Chapter 16 that, partly in recognition of the relatively ill-defined institutional shape of Community regulatory competence, the Commission places an increasing emphasis on securing the practical administration of the existing rules. It is striving to engage in a dialogue with national and local bodies with a view to the construction of a reliable partnership within which the internal market can be successfully managed to the advantage of traders and consumers alike.[150]

THE SCOPE OF ARTICLE 34: *CASSIS* EXCLUDED

Discrimination against both imports and exports is unlawful under the apparently parallel provisions of Articles 30 and 34 respectively and in both cases justification under Article 36 is possible.[151] However, if one removes the element of discrimination in favour of domestic goods, are barriers to imports still treated in the same manner as barriers to exports?

---

147 Consider, e.g., employment protection rights; will workers take advantage of the ability to migrate unless assured of certain basic rights in the state of destination? See Ch. 20.
148 See p. 478.
149 In Bieber *et al.* (eds.), *1992*, p. 367.
150 Pp. 479–80 above.
151 See Chs. 15, 16.

Consider the case where national law imposes certain quality standards for products to be marketed in that state. An importer can, of course, challenge such rules as impediments to trade in goods made according to different traditions in other states by virtue of the *Cassis* line of authority. Could an exporter use the *Cassis* approach to argue that mandatory compliance with national rules amounts to a restriction on his or her ability to penetrate the markets of other member states where traditions are different?

ARTICLE 34 AND THE NEED TO SHOW DISCRIMINATION

The Court insists that Article 34 bites *only* in the event of discrimination against exports. *Cassis* does not apply. The leading case is *Groenveld v Produktschap voor Vee en Vlees*.[152] Dutch legislation prohibited all manufacturers of meat products from stocking or processing horsemeat. The purpose of the law was to promote confidence among export markets that Dutch sausages were not tainted by horsemeat. Groenveld, a Dutch firm involved in the import of and trade in horsemeat, decided to extend its business activities into the field of the manufacture of horsemeat sausages. This plan would place the firm in direct conflict with the Dutch law. Groenveld argued that the Dutch legislation precluded it from manufacturing and subsequently exporting horsemeat sausages and that, consequently, it contravened Article 34.

Advocate-General Capotorti accepted the argument presented on behalf of the firm. The rules were indistinctly applicable, but restricted trade and, applying the *Cassis* principle, no justification for the trade restriction could be demonstrated. However, the Court adopted an entirely different view. It insisted that Article 34 is exclusively concerned with 'the establishment of a difference in treatment between the domestic trade of a Member State and its export trade'.[153] It was therefore inapplicable to a rule such as that under challenge by Groenveld, which contained no discrimination between goods intended for the home market and those for export. The Court confirmed this approach in *Jongeneel Kaas*.[154] It rejected a submission that Dutch law on quality standards for cheese infringed Article 34. Despite a restrictive effect on the export of different-quality cheese, the absence of discrimination against exports precluded challenge on the basis of Article 34.

---

152 Case 15/79 [1979] ECR 3409, [1981] 1 CMLR 207.
153 ibid., para. 7 of the judgment.
154 Case 237/82 [1984] ECR 483, [1985] 2 CMLR 53. See also Case 286/81, note 41 above; Case 141/81 *Holdijk* [1982] ECR 1299, [1983] 2 CMLR 635.

One would have welcomed a clear explanation why the prohibition in Article 34 is dependent on the presence of discrimination, where, as has been apparent since *Dassonville* and unarguable since *Cassis*, Article 30 is capable of applying on condition that a restrictive effect on interstate trade be shown, irrespective of the element of discrimination. Indeed, it seems impossible to deny the trade restriction inherent in a rule such as that at issue in *Groenveld*. However the Court's conclusion that the *Cassis de Dijon* principle is exclusively an aspect of Article 30 and irrelevant to Article 34 is correct.[155] From the perspective of the completion of the common market, the objectionable feature of indistinctly applicable rules is that they are capable of imposing a 'dual burden' on goods that cross frontiers. That is, imports are subject to the technical rules of the state of origin and of the state of destination, where domestic products need satisfy only the rules of their own state. That second set of technical rules in the state of destination, an *extra* burden felt only by imports, obstructs trade. The Court in *Cassis*, mindful of the need to establish a barrier-free market, consequently insisted that national rules that create such impediments are subject to scrutiny under Article 30. The problem does not arise in relation to rules such as that in issue in *Groenveld* and in *Jongeneel Kaas*, where both goods for the domestic market and goods for export were subject to the same rule and, at that stage in the production process, to no other. There is no *Cassis*-style 'dual burden' felt by the export that provides effective protection for the domestic product. The situation under Article 34 is distinguishable from that which arises under Article 30 and therefore it is proper to refuse to extend *Cassis* into the sphere of Article 34.

An importer into the Netherlands might have been able to challenge the rules at issue in *Groenveld* and *Jongeneel Kaas*; an exporter from the Netherlands could have challenged rules of another member state if they impeded the importation of typical Dutch goods; but the exporter cannot challenge the non-discriminatory rules of its own state.

REVERSE DISCRIMINATION

A logical corollary to the Court's refusal to allow reliance on Article 34 save in cases of discrimination is that Article 30 is unavailable to challenge 'reverse discrimination'. *Groenveld* and *Jongeneel Kaas* establish that an exporter cannot invoke Article 34 against an indistinctly applicable national rule. This implies that an importer is in a better position than the exporter,

---

155 See Barents, 'New Developments in Measures Having Equivalent Effect' (1981) 18 CMLRev 271, 302.

because an importer could challenge the same indistinctly applicable rule on the basis of Article 30 and the *Cassis de Dijon* line of authority. If the domestic trader could then use Article 30 or, more generally, Article 6 to argue that the difference in treatment between exporter and importer constituted a barrier to the free movement of goods, then the Court's stance on Article 34 would be subverted. The Court has, however, maintained the logic of its position by denying that Articles 6 and 30 can be invoked to challenge discrimination by a state against its own nationals.

In *Ministère Public* v *Mathot*[156] the Court held unsustainable under Community law a challenge to a Belgian law that required domestic butter producers, but not importers, to display their name and address on packets. The Belgian law did not restrict imports of butter from other member states and discriminated only against home producers. Until such time as Community harmonization legislation might affect the field, Community law does not prevent such measures.[157]

Precisely the same approach is adopted under Articles 48, 52 and 59, where the Court has held that a national of a member state cannot invoke Community law against that state where he or she is treated less favourably than a migrant from another member state.[158] The Court has taken this line of authority one step further by holding that even discrimination against *imports* may be immune from challenge under Article 30 if the goods were imported solely as a ruse to win the protection of Article 30; that is, if the goods are in reality domestic goods. This implies that the Court may countenance a subjective inquiry into the circumstances of the passage across intra-Community frontiers. In *Leclerc* v *Au Blé Vert*[159] the Court refused to allow Article 30 to be used to challenge French price-fixing rules relating to books in circumstances where the books in question had been exported from France and immediately reimported solely in order to benefit from the Community rules on free movement.

The inapplicability of Community law to 'reverse discrimination' is unlikely to be of great practical importance, for it seems scarcely likely that member states will retain in place rules that abandon their own

---

156 Case 98/86 [1987] ECR 809. See also Cases 80, 159/85 *Nedelandse Bakkerij* v *Edah* [1986] ECR 3359, [1988] 2 CMLR 113; Case 355/85 *Driancourt* v *Cognet* [1986] ECR 3231, [1987] 2 CMLR 942; Case 160/86 *Ministère Public* v *Verbrugge* [1987] ECR 1783, [1989] 2 CMLR 51.
157 Once legislation is in place it must be interpreted with care in order to determine the residual scope of national competence. Community rules may preclude the application of stricter rules to domestic traders, see p. 471 above; by contrast, in Case C-11/92 *R* v *Secretary of State for Health, ex parte Gallaher and others*, judgment of 22 June 1993, noted by Weatherill (1994) 19 ELRev 55, the Court found that a Directive did not prevent a state setting stricter rules for its own producers alone.
158 See p. 609.
159 Case 229/83 [1985] ECR I, [1985] 2 CMLR 286.

producers to a competitive disadvantage in comparison with importers.[160] However, despite this rationalization, it should be observed that by providing importers with an opportunity to challenge quality standards that is not available to domestic producers the Court has embarked on an exercise in induced, if not forced, deregulation. Member states are encouraged to deregulate internally in order to avoid imposing burdens on their own producers. This may lead to inefficient results, in that states will be induced to abandon domestic regulation because they know that the costs of low-quality production will be felt primarily by consumers in other member states, whereas the benefits will accrue primarily to their own producers. This trend is liable to cause a downwards spiral in regulation without any assessment of the efficient level of regulation from the point of view of the whole Community. A positive Community commitment to create common basic Community standards to replace disappearing national rules is an essential supplement to the Court's stance on reverse discrimination.[161]

KECK AND THE LIMITS OF ARTICLE 30

IS THERE A LIMIT TO THE SCOPE OF ARTICLE 30?

The Court's broad interpretation of the scope of Article 30 has made a vital contribution to the elimination of barriers to trade and consequently to the integration of the market. But is *any* national rule that can be linked, however remotely, to an effect on trade caught by Article 30 and therefore unlawful, subject to a state showing justification for the measure? Consider building regulations that restrict the erection of shops where imported goods might be sold; rules requiring the owner of a firearm, which might be imported, to hold a licence; or spending limits imposed on a government department that reduce its capacity to purchase imported goods. All these rules have the potential to reduce sales opportunities for imported products.

It might seem absurd to bring these measures within Article 30, but the

---

160 A good example is provided by Part II Consumer Protection Act 1987, which enshrines the UK's shift away from mandatory compliance with domestic standards of manufacture for consumer goods towards a more flexible regime based on quality. This enables British traders to compete in the integrated market unconstrained by technical requirements that, in many cases, their competitors could have defeated by virtue of the *Cassis* principle of equivalence. See Weatherill, 'A General Duty to Supply Only Safe Goods in the Community: Some Remarks from a British Perspective' (1990) 13 JCP 79.
161 More generally on the inadequacy of 'negative harmonization' see p. 523.

Court's own *Dassonville* formula prohibits 'all trading rules enacted by Member States which are capable of hindering, directly or indirectly, actually or potentially, intra-Community trade'.[162] The rules mentioned unarguably restrict trade. However, they restrict trade in imported goods no more than they restrict trade in domestic goods; they impose an 'equal burden' on all goods. Moreover, they are not rules designed to regulate patterns of cross-border trade. They are of an application internal to a single member state. They do not isolate the market of one member state from the rest of the common market. For this reason it is desirable to locate an outer margin to the scope of Article 30. A common market requires free trade, but it does not require regulatory uniformity. National rules that do not partition the market should remain unaffected. This regulatory autonomy is an aspect of the principle of subsidiarity, which serves to confine Community intervention to instances where it is efficient.[163] Other federal jurisdictions have similarly had to confront in their own particular ways the problem of defining the limits of the law of market integration.[164]

However, it remains a difficult task to translate the perception that Article 30 must have an outer limit into an appropriate legal formula. The Court's expansive statement in *Dassonville* left it 'riding a tiger'.[165] It is wary of excessive intrusion on national competence, and recently it has attempted to tame the beast.

What was at stake in the exploitation of Article 30 as a means of challenging rules that affected trading generally, rather than initiatives designed to construct an integrated strategy for the Community market, is best explained through an examination of the most high-profile example of this expansionist trend – the 'Sunday Trading' cases.[166] *Torfaen Borough Council* v *B&Q plc* involved the Sunday trading laws in England and Wales.[167] The Shops Act 1950 forbade the sale on Sunday of items other than those specifically exempted in schedules to the Act. That list was full of anomalies. Gin could be sold, but not tea; pornographic magazines, but not Bibles; fresh milk, but not canned. B&Q, a garden and do-it-yourself store, was prosecuted for breach of the legislation. B&Q defended itself on

---

162 Case 8/74, note 4 above, discussed on. p. 432.
163 See Ch. 1.
164 See e.g. Staker, 'Free Movement of Goods in the EEC and Australia: a Comparative Study' (1990) 10 YEL 209; Sunstein, 'Protectionism, the American Supreme Court and Integrated Markets' in Bieber *et al.* (eds.), *1992*.
165 Dashwood, 'The *Cassis de Dijon* Line of Authority' in Bates *et al.* (eds.) *In Memoriam J. D. B. Mitchell*, p. 158.
166 Case 145/88 [1989] ECR 765, [1990] 1 CMLR 337, noted by Gormley (1990) 27 CMLRev 141.
167 There are no comparable laws in Scotland.

the basis that the Shops Act contravened Article 30. The store showed that the Sunday trading rules reduced its total weekly sales. This reduction applied to imported goods that B&Q offered for sale in its shops as well as to domestic goods and, consequently, reliance was placed on the *Dassonville* formula to defeat the prosecution. Magistrates in Cwmbran referred questions about the relevance of Article 30 to the European Court.

The Court pointed out that the rules contained in the Shops Act applied to all goods. Marketing imports was no more difficult than marketing domestic goods. The Court then proposed a two-step test for the application of Article 30. First, it was necessary to decide whether the rule pursued an aim that is justified under Community law. The Court was prepared to accept that shop opening hours 'reflect certain political and economic choices in so far as their purpose is to ensure that working and non-working hours are so arranged as to accord with national or regional socio-cultural characteristics'[168] and are in the present state of Community law a matter for the member states. The second limb of the test required the national court to assess whether the effects of the rules exceed what is necessary to achieve the desired objective. The Court concluded its remarkably brief judgment by ruling in answer to the magistrates' questions that Article 30 'does not apply to national rules prohibiting retailers from opening their premises on Sunday where the restrictive effects on Community trade which may result therefrom do not exceed the effects intrinsic to rules of that kind'.

In the United Kingdom the application of the European Court's ruling in *Torfaen* was chaotic. Many cases, involving B&Q and other stores, awaited the European Court's decision. Some courts took the view that the Shops Act was compatible with Article 30,[169] but others reached precisely the opposite conclusion.[170] The major problem was the application of the principle of proportionality, as aspect of Community trade law with which members of the English judiciary were clearly uncomfortable.[171]

The European Court's opaque ruling in *Torfaen* might be construed as

---

168 Case 145/88, note 166 above, para. 14 of the judgment.
169 E.g., *Torfaen* v *B&Q* itself, [1990] 3 CMLR 455; *Wellingborough Borough Council* v *Payless* [1990] 1 CMLR 773 (Crown Court).
170 *B&Q* v *Shrewsbury BC* [1990] 3 CMLR 535 (Crown Court). The High Court quashed a conviction for Sunday trading in *Payless DIY* v *Peterborough City Council* [1991] 4 All ER 193 for failure to adduce evidence to establish proportionality.
171 See especially Hoffmann J in *Stoke City Council* v *B&Q plc* [1990] 3 CMLR 31. Commentators have also misunderstood the nature of Community law; e.g., Diamond, 'Dishonourable Defences: The Use of Injunctions and the EEC Treaty – Case Study of the Shops Act 1950' (1991) 54 MLR 72. For perceptive analysis see Arnull, 'What Shall We Do on Sunday?' (1991) 16 ELRev 112.

an effort not to get involved in a largely domestic issue. Yet it seemed susceptible to disturbingly differing interpretations, and in December 1992 a further reference was made to the Court by the House of Lords in *Stoke-on-Trent and Norwich City Councils* v *B&Q*.[172] The European Court adopted a quite different approach. Rather than leave the matter in the hands of national courts, it decided in effect that the Shops Act was compatible with EC law. It stated that 'Article 30 is to be interpreted as meaning that the prohibition which it lays down does not apply to national legislation prohibiting retailers from opening their premises on Sundays.'[173]

THE BACKGROUND TO THE RULING IN *KECK*

The principal objection to the use of Article 30 in the Sunday trading saga was mentioned by the European Court in its first ruling, where it commented that the rules 'applied to domestic and imported products alike and did not put imported products at any disadvantage'.[174] The restrictive effect on trade arose because the Shops Act *existed*, not because it *differed* from laws in the state of origin of the imported products, which was the problem in *Cassis de Dijon*. However, notwithstanding this perception of an equal regulatory burden, the Court did not choose to question the assumption of the referring national court that the Shops Act exerted a sufficient impact on interstate trade to permit the invocation of Community trade law. Once the traders had crossed that threshold, it fell to the United Kingdom to justify its laws. The ease with which the criterion of an effect on interstate trade was satisfied represented a major tactical advantage to the traders in the litigation.

The Court's case law was widely perceived to have taken a wrong turning. Article 30 had been overextended. It had been pushed beyond application to national laws that impede market integration into the realms of national laws that did no more than affect the volume of sales of all goods to an equal extent.[175]

One method for reducing the confusion flowing from the intrusive depth of Article 30 was for the Court itself to rule on the compatibility of challenged national rules with Article 30. It did this in the second Sunday

---

172 Case C-169/91, judgment of 16 December 1992, [1993] 1 All ER 481.
173 Subsequent domestic reform has gone some way to improving the coherence of the law in this area; the Sunday Trading Act 1994 repealed the Shops Act 1950.
174 Case 145/88, note 166 above, para. 6 of the judgment.
175 See pp. 467–480 of the first edition of this book for an extended discussion of the case law and of attempts to achieve rationalization. See also Select Further Reading, p. 906 below.

trading case, *Stoke-on-Trent and Norwich City Councils* v *B&Q*.[176] Yet this promised only a case-by-case development that would bring little clarity to legal principle. In other cases, the Court chose to rule that no adequate effect on interstate trade had been established for the purposes of Article 30 and that therefore the state was not called on to show a justification recognized by Community law for its rules.[177] This too offered no general basis for reorientation. The Court was doubtless reluctant to act to curtail the reach of Article 30 lest it should prejudice the fundamentally pro-integrative thrust of that provision which it had carefully nurtured. Probably the lack of consistency in the Court's rulings also indicated that, beneath the single collegiate judgment emanating from Luxembourg, there were significant differences of opinion among the judges and the Advocates-General. However, increasingly the Court found itself urged to reassess its jurisprudence.[178]

The Court grasped the nettle in *Keck and Mithouard*.[179] Keck and Mithouard had resold goods at a loss. This violated a French law forbidding such practices. Keck and Mithouard submitted that the law restricted the volume of sales of imported goods and that it was therefore incompatible with Article 30. Any restrictive effect on trade affected *all* goods, not just imports. This placed the fact pattern on all fours with the Sunday trading cases, but the European Court proceeded to deal with the matter quite differently. The Court referred explicitly to 'the increasing tendency of traders to invoke Article 30 of the Treaty as a means of challenging any rules whose effect is to limit their commercial freedom even where such rules are not aimed at products from other Member States'.[180] It then declared it necessary to 're-examine and clarify' its jurisprudence. The Court stated that

the application to products from other Member States of national provisions restricting or prohibiting certain selling arrangements is not such as to hinder, directly or indirectly, actually or potentially, trade between Member States within the meaning of the *Dassonville* judgment (Case 8/74 [1974] ECR 837), provided that those provisions apply to all affected traders operating within the national territory and provided that they affect in the same manner, in law and in fact, the marketing of domestic products and of those from other Member States.[181]

The Court confessed that this statement runs 'contrary to what has

---

176 Case C-169/91, note 172 above. See similarly Case C-332/89 *Marchandise* [1991] ECR I-1027, Case C-312/89 *UDS* v *Conforama* [1991] ECR I-997.
177 See Case C-23/89 *Quietlynn Ltd* v *Southend on Sea BC* [1990] ECR I-3059; Case C-350/89 *Sheptonhurst* v *Newham BC* [1991] ECR I-2387.
178 See Select Further Reading, p. 906 below.
179 Joined Cases C-267 and C-268/91 [1993] ECR I-6097, [1995] 1 CMLR 101.
180 Para. 14 of the judgment.
181 Para. 16 of the judgment.

previously been decided', but it decided that rules of this nature fall outside the scope of application of Article 30.

THE IMPLICATIONS OF THE RULING IN *KECK*

Keck is the cautious decision that many commentators have expected and, to differing extents, encouraged since the Sunday trading saga highlighted the overextension of the *Dassonville* formula.[182] It seems that Article 30 is refocused on the objective of market integration. Its more general function of review of national economic regulation that does not partition markets is terminated. In this realignment the Court is groping towards a distinction between rules that affect patterns of trade across borders as such and rules that affect patterns of trade generally without any special reference to national borders. *Keck* appears intended to place the outer limits of Article 30 between these two categories; only the former is subject to review. The ruling is intended to release member states from the control of Article 30 when they exercise their competence to regulate markets in a manner that does not impede the interpenetration of national markets. The Court in *Keck* has adjusted the respective competences of the Community and of the member states in the sphere of economic regulation and, 'contrary to what has previously been decided', the member states enjoy competence untouched by Article 30 in the absence of an impediment felt especially by importers.

It is submitted that, at a general level, *Keck* deserves a welcome as a contribution to taming the Article 30 tiger[183] and to preventing Article 30 from becoming 'a busybody's charter for attacking national measures . . . with scarcely the most tenuous link with intra-Community trade'.[184] However, the detailed application of *Keck* is more troublesome. The phrase 'certain selling arrangements' in *Keck* is obscure.[185] It is submitted that this phrase should not be accorded undue emphasis and that it should not be taken to bear any technical meaning. What matters is the effect in law and fact of the national practice that is alleged to affect trade, not the form it may assume. It is submitted that, to this extent, the effects-based approach of the *Dassonville* formula survives. The significance of the phrase 'certain selling arrangements' lies only in the hint that rules affecting marketing alone are less likely to infringe the requirements of legal and factual equality than rules governing product composition.

182 Note 178 above.
183 Dashwood, note 165 above.
184 Gormley (1989) 9 YEL 199; see also ibid., p. 208 and (1990) 27 CMLRev 141.
185 *Modalités de vente* in the original French.

Establishing legal and factual equality in the effect of national rules, which insulates measures from challenge under Article 30, is likely to prove complex. It is submitted that the requirement of equality *in law* would not be met by discriminatory measures; they continue to fall within Article 30. The equality *in fact* test would not be met by rules of the *Cassis de Dijon* type, for they impose on imported products a dual burden of compliance with the regulatory rules of both the state of production and of sale, whereas domestic goods shoulder the burden of compliance with a single regulatory regime only. This is not equal application in fact. Therefore the *Keck* ruling does not alter the subjection to control under Article 30 of national rules which exert a protectionist effect in favour of home production. Disparity between national laws falls within the scope of Article 30 where it impedes cross-border trade and frustrates the realization of economies of scale in the Community market. By contrast, rules such as those at stake in the Sunday trading saga apply equally in law and in fact. Such a situation should now be disposed of on the basis that such national choices fall beyond the scope of application of Article 30. There is no impediment to market access that is felt especially by imported goods and *Keck* is motivated by the perceived need to abolish reliance on Article 30 in precisely these circumstances of equal application to all products irrespective of origin. A state is not called on to show justification recognized by Community law for its rules.

It will typically be relatively straightforward to show that rules governing the composition of products are unequal in their factual application, by reliance on the notion of the protectionist 'dual burden' of regulatory rules in the state of production and of marketing. As explained above, rules such as that at stake in *Cassis de Dijon* itself are equal in their application in law but not in fact. They are not excluded from review under Article 30 by *Keck*. Some rules governing methods of marketing *are* now excluded from the scope of Article 30. Those at stake in the Sunday trading cases and in *Keck* itself are prime examples. However, it is submitted that some marketing rules may still be subject to review under Article 30, where the marketing technique that is suppressed is shown to be part of a method used to construct an integrated marketing strategy that is apt to realize the economies of scale that underpin the theory of common markets. An example may be drawn from the application of Article 30 prior to the *Keck* ruling. In *Oosthoek* the Court stated that

Legislation which restricts or prohibits certain forms of advertising and certain means of sales promotion may, although it does not directly affect imports, be such as to restrict their volume because it affects marketing opportunities for the imported products. The possibility cannot be ruled out that to compel a producer either to adopt advertising or sales promotion schemes which differ from one

Member State to another or to discontinue a scheme which he considers to be particularly effective may constitute an obstacle to imports even if the legislation in question applies to domestic products and imported products without distinction.[186]

Such evidence is arguably sufficient to demonstrate that the national rule, although doubtless restrictive of a 'selling arrangement', did not in fact apply equally to all producers. The out-of-state producer was especially affected because of its inability to extend its preferred style of marketing campaign on to Dutch territory. The Dutch rule forced the development of a special commercial strategy for the Dutch market. The legal consequence of the rule's unequal factual application is that the state is called on to justify its law (which was successfully achieved in *Oosthoek*), rather than, as in *Keck*, being able to escape the scope of application of Article 30.[187]

Nevertheless, the status of pre-*Keck* rulings remains obscure. The Court's explicit admission that *Keck* conflicts with 'what has been previously decided' invites consideration of which cases are now overruled, but also invites regret that the Court did not make explicit the cases concerned. One cannot deny that rules such as that in *Keck* affect trade and the Court itself admitted in paragraph 13 of its judgment that such rules may restrict the volume of sales of products from other member states by depriving traders of a method of sales promotion. More is now required before the matter falls within the scope of Article 30. Traders are required to cross a threshold involving demonstration of inequality of effect in law or in fact before the onus shifts to the state to show justification. Inhibited commercial freedom is of itself insufficient to persuade the Court to embark on an Article 30 review of the national measure. This is a difficult test to apply, not least given the uncertain status of pre-*Keck* case law, and for this lack of clarity in its ruling the Court has earned some well-merited criticism.[188]

The Court's rulings subsequent to *Keck* confirm that it has significantly repositioned its approach to the scope of Article 30. In *Hünermund and others* v *Landesapothekerkammer Baden-Württemberg* the Court repeated its

186 Case 286/81, note 41 above, para. 15 of the judgment.
187 Cf. pre-*Keck*, Case 382/87 *Ministère Public* v *Buet*, note 84 above; Cases C-1, C-176/90 *APESA* v *DSSC*, note 12 above; Case C-126/91 *Schutzverband gegen Unwesen in der Wirtschaft* v *Y. Rocher GmbH*, note 75 above, which would, on this analysis, be disposed of even post-*Keck* on the basis that the state was required to justify its rules rather than that the rules affected traders equally in law and in fact. See pp. 473–6 in the first edition of this book for discussion of these matters, including analysis of Case 75/81 *Blesgen* [1982] ECR 1211, [1983] 1 CMLR 431, one of the first cases in which the Court addressed the issue of the outer limit of Art. 30.
188 E.g. Gormley, 'Reasoning Renounced? the Remarkable Judgment in Keck and Mithouard' [1994] Euro Bus L Rev 63. For further exploration of how the *Keck* test may operate see Chalmers, Poiares Maduro, Reich, Select Further Reading, p. 907 below.

view that Article 30 does not catch rules applying to all traders operating on the national territory and affecting in the same way, in law and in fact, the marketing of domestic products and those from other member states.[189] The case arose in the context of attempted reliance on Article 30 to challenge rules prohibiting pharmacists from advertising para-pharmaceutical products outside their pharmacies. By hampering product promotion, such rules doubtless restricted the volume of sales, including the volume of sales of imported goods, but this was insufficient to trigger Article 30. In *Tankstation 't Heukske vof and J. B. E. Boermans*[190] the Court repeated its *Keck* formula in the context of Dutch rules relating to the compulsory closing of petrol stations at stipulated times. The rules applied to all traders without distinguishing between products on the basis of origin. The effect on the marketing of imported and home-produced goods was the same.

However, since *Keck*, the Court has confirmed the continued vitality of the *Cassis* principle in relation to obstacles to trade caused by disparity between national laws governing product presentation and composition. *Verband Sozialer Wettbewerb eV* v *Clinique Laboratories SNC*[191] involved the prohibition under German law of the use of the name 'Clinique' for cosmetics. The Court pointed out that this forced the trader in goods that were lawfully marketed in other member states where use of the 'Clinique' name was permitted to use a different name for Germany. Traders consequently incurred additional packaging and advertising costs. The rule impeded the interpenetration of national markets. Once this finding was made, it fell to Germany to show justification for the rule. Submissions that consumers might be misled into believing that 'Clinique' products possessed medicinal properties did not persuade the Court.[192] It observed, *inter alia*, that the cosmetics were not available in pharmacies; and that consumers in other states were not misled by the use of the 'Clinique' name. This was an unjustified obstacle to cross-border trade in goods and to the development of an integrated commercial strategy for the territory of the whole Community.

Like *Keck* itself, these rulings were delivered in the context of the Article 177 procedure. The development of *Keck* will be supervised by the European Court, but much will depend on its practical application at national level. It offers national courts a firm legal basis on which to reject

---

189 Case C-292/92, judgment of 15 December 1993.
190 Case C-401/92 and C-402/92 [1994] ECR I-2199. Similarly Case C-69/93 and C-258/93 *Punto Casa SpA* v *Sindaco de Commune di Capena and others* [1994] ECR I-2355.
191 Case C-315/92 [1994] ECR I-317. See also Case C-320/93 *Lucien Ortscheit GmbH* v *Eurim-Pharm Arzneimittel GmbH*, judgment of 10 November 1994.
192 Cf. pp. 508–13 above on such justification under the *Cassis de Dijon* formula.

some of the more far-fetched attempts to invoke Article 30.[193] In assessing legal or, especially, factual equality in the effect of national rules, careful attention will need to be paid to the evidence presented by traders seeking to challenge a national measure. Empirical evidence may come to play a more prominent role in marginal cases. In *Walter Rau* v *de Smedt*, which concerned the compatibility with Article 30 of a Belgian law requiring margarine to be marketed in cube-shaped blocks,[194] the Court commented that '. . . the protective effect of the Belgian rules is moreover demonstrated by the fact . . . that despite prices appreciably higher than those in some other Member States there is practically no margarine of foreign origin to be found on the Belgian market'. Post-*Keck*, such market analysis may become more common as a means of proving factual inequality in the application of national laws. It is submitted that such evidence is sufficient, but not necessary, to permit reliance on Article 30. Even in the absence of statistical evidence, a potential hindrance should still suffice to allow a trader to deploy Article 30 where the dual burden of regulatory compliance is shown to be capable of leading to the sheltering of firms in the regulating state from competition. In its July 1994 ruling in *Criminal Proceedings against J. J. J. Van der Veldt*[195] the Court stated that national rules prohibiting the marketing of bread with a salt content of more than 2 per cent may exclude imported products from the market of the regulating state (Belgium, *in casu*). The rule may force importers 'to vary the method of manufacture according to the place where the bread . . . in question is to be sold and thus impede the movement of products lawfully produced and marketed in the Member States of origin'.[196] *Keck* does not signal a retreat in the role of the *Cassis de Dijon* formula in addressing market-partitioning caused by disparity between national laws, although it does demand that closer attention be paid to the identification of a market-partitioning effect.

Generally, it is probable that the climate of Article 30 cases at national level has been changed by *Keck*. The balance of power is tilted. The initial hurdle to be crossed by the trader is higher and this is likely to be of major practical significance in freeing states of the need to justify regulatory choices of purely local relevance. Only once the test of legal or factual inequality is satisfied does the focus shift to the state, which is then placed in the position of having to find a justification for the relevant rules.

---

193 For an especially remarkable example, see *Ex parte Wesson* [1992] 3 CMLR 377; the siting of road works outside a shop in Birmingham was challenged under Article 30.

194 Case 261/81 [1982] ECR 3961, p. 508 above.

195 Case C-17/93 [1994] ECR I-3537.

196 Para. 11 of the judgment. There was no adequate public health justification; cf. p. 507 above.

In conclusion, it is submitted that the ruling in *Keck*, as a concession to national competence untouched by Article 30, should be read in conjunction with the ruling in *Meng*,[197] in which the Court set outer limits to Articles 5 and 85 as instruments for subjecting national market regulation to the control of Community law. The Court, in adjusting the scope of Community trade law, appears unwilling to fill gaps in the Treaty in order to exercise a power of review over local regulatory choices that do not damage the realization of economies of scale in an integrating market. In the present state of Community law, the Court has declined the opportunity to develop a general theory of a constitutional framework governing public and private economic action. If there are to be further developments of such an ambitious nature, it seems that the impetus must come from legislative action or from the process of Treaty revision.[198]

---

197 Case C-2/91, judgment of 17 November 1993, examined in Ch. 27, p. 870.
198 See Reich, 'The November revolution of the European Court of Justice: Keck, Meng and Audi revisited' (1994) 31 CMLRev 459; Gerber, 'Constitutionalizing the Economy: German Neo-Liberalism, Competition Law and the "New" Europe' (1994) 42 AJCL 25; Bach, *Note* (1994) 21 CMLRev 1357.

CHAPTER 18

The Free Movement of Workers

Article 48 confers on workers the right of free movement between member states. Article 52 confers a similar right on the self-employed, which permits freedom of establishment. Article 59 confers a right freely to provide services across borders. All three sets of provisions envisage the liberation of factors of production within the common market. The Court has shrunk from treating the divisions in the Treaty as rigid, and has emphasized the areas of common ground between the three sets of provisions. In *Royer*[1] the individual's precise status was not clear, but the Court observed that all three freedoms are 'based on the same principles in so far as they concern the entry into and residence in the territory of Member States of persons covered by Community law and the prohibition of all discrimination between them on grounds of nationality'.[2] In *Walrave and Koch* v *Union Cycliste Internationale*[3] the Court considered it unimportant to decide whether work was being performed by an employee (Article 48) or an independent person (Article 52/59), because both work and services are covered equally by the prohibition against discrimination on grounds of nationality deriving from Article 6.

Accordingly, the similarities between the provisions are far more striking than their differences, although it will be seen that there are distinctions of detail in the scope of the applicable rules. The Court's own activity in this area has done much to establish common rules and principles that apply to the general phenomenon of migration within the Community. It has developed a nuanced structure of legal rules of far greater sophistication than might be suggested by the bare words of Articles 48–66. At a less tangible level, it has also done a great deal to liberate the free movement of services within the Community, a process of great significance for both natural and legal persons.

The Community legislature has played its own important role in this

---

1 Case 48/75 [1976] ECR 497.
2 ibid., para. 12 of the judgment. See also Case C-106/91 *C. Ramrath* v *Ministre de la Justice* [1992] ECR I-3351.
3 Case 36/74 [1974] ECR 1405.

area in enacting supporting legislation to amplify the basic Treaty rules. The scope of the legislation embraces rules that are doubtless designed to induce free movement, but that also serve to confer important social rights on migrants. These rules, adopted within the Community's first two decades, have been interpreted by the Court in a fashion favourable to market integration, as suggested above, and this has in some areas induced legislative initiatives to enhance individual rights still further. For example, in 1990 directives were adopted that granted certain rights of residence to migrating Community nationals whose status under Community law was previously dubious.[4]

This process reached a higher plane in the notion of Citizenship of the Union introduced into the Treaty at Maastricht, whereby every person holding the nationality of a member state shall be a citizen of the Union. These provisions represent a potentially exciting move towards the complete disassociation of EC law of persons from its economic focus in favour of a wider notion of the individual's position in society. However, as yet, the predominant thrust of the provisions is to exert a potential rather than an immediate impact.[5] For example, although Article 8 EC establishes 'Citizenship of the Union', Article 8(2) immediately creates a mood of a status tied to the pre-existing legal pattern in its declaration that 'Citizens of the Union shall enjoy the rights conferred by this Treaty and shall be subject to the duties imposed thereby.' Likewise Article 8a(1) provides that 'Every Citizen of the Union shall have the right to move and reside freely within the territory of the Member States', but this is expressly 'subject to the limitations and conditions laid down in this Treaty and by the measures adopted to give it effect'. Nevertheless, the future elaboration envisaged by Articles 8–8e is a potentially important shift in emphasis for the law of persons that is the subject of study in this chapter and the next. Much will depend on the commitment among the Community's political institutions, but the new provisions offer the opportunity to establish a dynamic constitutional dimension to the pattern of citizens' rights in the Union.[6] Some progress has been made. Article 8b, which deals with voting rights, has been the subject of legislative amplification. Article 8b(1) provides that citizens residing in states of which they are not nationals shall have the right to vote and to stand as a candidate at municipal elections in the state of residence under the same conditions as nationals of that state. Detailed arrangements are established by Directive 94/80.[7] Article 8b(2) contains a comparable provision dealing with Euro-

---

4 See p. 608 below.
5 Ch. 1, p. 15 above.
6 See Select Further Reading, p. 907 below.
7 OJ 1994 L368/38.

pean Parliament elections and it too has been converted into detailed legislation in the shape of Directive 93/109.[8] The provision that is potentially the most fruitful of all is Article 8e, which offers the Council the opportunity to adopt provisions by unanimity to strengthen or to add to rights laid down. Closa observed perceptively that 'the character of the union citizenship is determined by the progressive acquisition of rights stemming from the dynamic development of the Union . . .' The status has 'evolutive character'.[9] A gradual accretion of rights of a concrete character to the status of Citizenship of the Union will bring with it a gradual shift in perception of what is truly distinctive about nationality of one member state rather than another. Nevertheless, pending development of the nature of Citizenship of the Union, which exists as a status additional to, not in place of, national citizenship,[10] the pre-Maastricht pattern of law, which places economic activity at the core of EC law of persons, retains its central role.

THE NOTION OF A WORKER

Article 48 declares that workers are entitled to freedom of movement within the Community. Characteristically, the Treaty provides no definition of the 'worker' and the matter has fallen to the Court. Levin v Staatssecretaris van Justitie[11] concerned a British national who was refused a permit to reside in the Netherlands because the Dutch authorities considered her income from her work to be inadequate. The questions referred asked whether Article 48 covers a person whose activity yields an income less than the minimum required for subsistence under the legislation of the host state. This provided the Court with the opportunity to insist that the notion of 'worker' has a Community law content, and it rejected Danish and Dutch submissions that national criteria governing minimum wages and minimum number of hours worked should apply. The notion of a worker possesses a uniform Community meaning in order to preclude divergent interpretations at national level that would in effect allow unilateral modification of the scope of Community law. The Court

---

8 OJ 1993 L329/34.
9 Closa, 'The Concept of Citizenship in the Treaty on European Union', (1992) 29 CMLRev 1137.
10 See p. 775 of the first edition of this book for explanation of the need to clarify this point at the Edinburgh European Council of December 1992 in the light of apparent misapprehensions in Denmark.
11 Case 53/81 [1982] ECR 1035, [1982] 2 CMLR 454.

proceeded to hold that the definition cannot be restrictive in the light of the need to secure the economic development referred to in Articles 2 and 3 EC.[12] Such objectives would be undermined if Article 48 excluded those pursuing part-time work, for such activity is 'an effective means of improving ... living conditions'.[13] It is required only that the work involve 'the pursuit of effective and genuine activities to the exclusion of activities on such a small scale as to be regarded as purely marginal and ancillary'. Once this test is satisfied, 'the motives which have prompted the worker to seek employment in the Member State concerned are of no account and must not be taken into consideration'.[14] The Court's embracing of the concept of worker as a Community law concept is an important element in securing uniform protection throughout the Community of the rights arising under Article 48.

In *Levin* the Court insisted that a part-time worker is capable of falling within the scope of the Treaty whether he or she tops up the income received from other sources, such as personal wealth or income of another family member, or whether he or she simply makes do with a comparatively low wage. In *Kempf* v *Staatssecretaris van Justitie*[15] the Court went one stage further. A German working as a part-time music teacher in the Netherlands topped up his income with state supplementary benefits. He gave only twelve lessons a week, which might have been grounds for arguing that this was not 'effective and genuine' work. The Court refused to consider the point, because the referring court had, perhaps surprisingly, already declared that in this respect the *Levin* test had been satisfied.[16] The Court then decided that, provided effective and genuine part-time work is undertaken, the status of 'worker' cannot be denied just because remuneration is below the minimum national subsistence levels where reliance is placed on supplement 'by other lawful means of subsistence'. This is a marked extension of the *Levin* definition.

In *Steymann* v *Staatssecretaris van Justitie*[17] the Court showed flexibility in its definition of the wage/work bargain. A German in the Netherlands joined the Bhagwan Community, a quasi-religious commune. He acted as a plumber and participated generally in the commune's commercial activities. For its part, the commune provided for all the needs of its members. The Court declared that a migrant must be able to show an economic activity within the meaning of Article 2 of the Treaty to claim the

---

12 See generally Ch. 1, p. 19.
13 Case 53/81, note 5 above, para. 15 of the judgment.
14 ibid., paras. 17, 22 of the judgment.
15 Case 139/85 [1986] ECR 1741, [1987] 1 CMLR 764.
16 See Ch. 9 on the division of function under Article 177.
17 Case 196/87 [1988] ECR 6159, [1989] 1 CMLR 449.

favoured status of worker, but accepted that if the person's work is genuine and effective and an essential means of participating in the commune's goal of self-sufficiency, then that is work for which services are provided in return by the commune. This result can be contrasted with *Bettray v Staatssecretaris van Justitie*,[18] in which the Court considered that participation in the Dutch Social Employment Law scheme did not confer the status of worker. The scheme was designed to rehabilitate those handicapped for various reasons (drug addiction in Bettray's case) from participating in normal economic activity. The job was picked in accordance with the needs and abilities of the individual, as a means of assisting him or her ultimately to attain the reverse, 'normal' situation of being an individual picked in accordance with the needs of the job. The participant in such a scheme was not within the scope of Community law.

In *Lawrie-Blum v Land Baden-Württemburg*[19] the Court held that a trainee teacher conducting lessons for a few hours a week would be classified as a worker if the activities counted as 'effective and genuine'. The *Land* submitted that the activities were part of the training period that was merely preparatory to qualification as a teacher and did not constitute work. The Court disagreed: 'The essential feature of an employment relationship . . . is that for a certain period of time a person performs services for and under the direction of another person in return for which he receives remuneration.'[20]

A finding that an individual does not satisfy the Community law requirements to qualify as a worker is not fatal to the ability of that individual to rely on Community law. Persons other than workers have entitlements under Community law. However, the worker stands in a uniquely favoured position in claiming a wide panoply of social rights available under national law. Access to such benefits is dependent on being able to cross the *Levin* threshold. The next section examines the benefits to which the worker is entitled, and shows that the *Levin* threshold is not the end of the inquiry, for some workers are treated more favourably than others. Chapter 19 will show that many, but not all, of the advantages available to workers are extended to other migrants.

18 Case 344/87 [1989] ECR 1621.
19 Case 66/85 [1986] ECR 2121, [1987] 3 CMLR 389.
20 ibid., para. 17 of the judgment; see also Case C-3/87 *R v MAFF, ex parte Agegate* [1989] ECR 4459, [1990] 1 CMLR 366, and Case C-357/89 *Raulin v Netherlands Ministry of Education and Science*, [1992] ECR I-1027, noted by O'Keeffe (1992) 29 CMLRev 1215.

THE BENEFITS AVAILABLE

The bare Treaty provisions offer relatively little specific elaboration of the basic right of freedom of movement within the Community. Article 48(2) specifies the 'abolition of any discrimination based on nationality between workers of the Member States as regards employment, remuneration and other conditions of work and employment'. This is an amplification of the basic Treaty rule forbidding any discrimination on grounds of nationality within the scope of the Treaty, which is contained in Article 6. The scope of the rights is expanded in Article 48(3), which insists that the worker shall have the right (subject to exceptions considered below) to accept offers of employment actually made; to move freely within the territory of member states for this purpose; to stay in a member state for the purpose of employment in accordance with the provisions governing the employment of nationals of that state; to remain in the territory of a member state after having been employed there. A simple example of impermissible discrimination is provided by *Commission* v *France*.[21] The *Code du Travail Maritime* set a three-to-one ratio for the employment of French merchant seamen as opposed to non-French crew. This violated the fundamental rule of free movement, which entails the abolition of discrimination founded on nationality. For similar reasons, in *Commission* v *Greece*[22] restrictions on ownership of immovable property that applied to migrants from other member states but not to Greeks were held incompatible with the Treaty.

The scope of these rights is closely linked to the notion of labour as a factor of production in the liberalization designed to create a common market. Article 48 does not address the reality that such rights to cross borders will hardly be taken up unless migrants also enjoy associated rights; for example, to bring their families with them to live in the host state or to obtain access to social benefits made available to the host nation's own work-force. Article 49 envisages the adoption of measures of this nature and several important regulations and directives define further this area of Community law. These are measures that can be viewed as contributions to market integration, but the fact of conferral of rights on individuals also locates them in the more general sphere of social policy.[23]

---

21 Case 167/73 [1974] ECR 359. For a similar violation arising out of blatant nationality discrimination see Case C-179/90 *Porto de Genova* [1991] ECR I-5889 and Case C-37/93 *Commission* v *Belgium*, judgment of 1 December 1993.
22 Case 305/87 [1989] ECR 1461, [1991] 1 CMLR 611.
23 Explored more fully in Ch. 20.

REGULATION 1612/68

Regulation 1612/68 expands in Part One the worker's right to free movement. In three titles it deals with Eligibility for Employment (Articles 1–6), Employment and Equality of Treatment (Articles 7–9) and Workers' Families (Articles 10–12).

First title

The first title amplifies the basic Treaty rule of non-discrimination between nationals of different member states in respect of access to employment. In principle, jobs are open equally to nationals of all member states. France violated this principle in its *Code du Travail Maritime* in the case mentioned above.[24] Article 3(1) of the Regulation envisages that conditions of linguistic competence may permissibly be required in a particular post, even though the practical effect may be to exclude non-nationals. The Court in *Groener*[25] was prepared to accept that Irish-language competence could be a requirement for holding a college lectureship. However, it insisted that any such conditions must apply to all individuals irrespective of nationality and must be proportionate both to the end in view and in the manner of application.

Second title

The second title covers equality in the conditions of employment taken up. The broadest provision is Article 7(2), which stipulates that the migrant 'shall enjoy the same social and tax advantages as national workers'. This provision has been interpreted by the Court to cover equal availability of benefits arising outside the contract of employment. In *Ministère Public* v *Mutsch*[26] a roofer who was a Luxembourg national resident in a German-speaking municipality of Belgium found himself before a criminal court after an 'extended pub crawl'.[27] A Belgian citizen would have been entitled to choose to use the German language, but could Mutsch, a migrant? The matter was not directly linked to the contract of employment or, more generally, even to the work the migrant was performing. The Court held this unnecessary. Article 7(2) of the Regula-

---

24 Case 167/73, note 21 above.
25 Case C-379/87 [1989] ECR 3967, [1990] 1 CMLR 401, noted by MacMahon (1990) CMLRev 129.
26 Case 137/84 [1985] ECR 2681.
27 ibid., AG Lenz p. 2682.

tion covers advantages that are 'generally granted to national workers primarily because of their objective status as workers or by virtue of the mere fact of their residence on national territory'. This wide interpretation was justified by the Court as essential to bring about labour mobility, a fundamental Community objective. The Court held that choice of language before a court on the same conditions as nationals is an important element in the integration of a migrant into the host country.[28]

Article 9 of the Regulation provides specific rules on equal access to housing,[29] a matter that otherwise could doubtless be accommodated under the broad terms of Article 7(2). Article 7(4) declares that discrimination causes 'any clause of a collective or individual agreement or of any other collective regulation concerning eligibility for employment, employment, remuneration and other conditions of work or dismissal' to be null and void. Article 8 of the Regulation extends the rule of equality to membership of and participation in trade unions.[30] Both Article 7(4) and Article 8 demonstrate that the prohibition on discrimination on grounds of nationality extends into the private sphere. The Court confirmed this in *Walrave and Koch* v *UCI*.[31] Even rules emanating from private bodies must respect the equal rights of migrant workers where they regulate employment and the provision of services in a collective manner. The Court reached this conclusion both in view of the need to extend the impact of this basic Community law principle and in order to preclude inequalities in the application of Community law between states flowing from variations in the scope of the public sector.[32]

A state that protects workers from disadvantage where their employment is interrupted by compulsory military service must apply that concession not only to service with its own forces, but also to service with the forces of other member states in order to preclude national workers being more

---

28 See similarly on the right to equality Case 32/75 *Cristini* v *SNCF* [1975] ECR 1085, [1976] 1 CMLR 573 (access to cheap rail travel), Case 65/81 *Reina* v *Landeskreditbank* [1982] ECR 33 (interest-free loan granted on childbirth), Case 59/85 *Netherlands* v *Reed* [1986] ECR 1283, [1987] 2 CMLR 448 (permission to have non-national unmarried companion live with a worker), Case 235/87 *Matteucci* [1988] ECR 5589, [1989] I CMLR 357 (educational scholarship for study in another member state); but cf. Case 207/78 *Ministère Public* v *Even* [1979] ECR 2019 (war pension scheme not caught by Reg. 1612/68). See examination by O'Keeffe, 'Equal Rights for Migrants: the Concept of Social Advantages in Article 7(2) Regulation 1612/68' (1985) 5 YEL 93.

29 This provision was referred to by the Court in its judgment in Case 305/87, note 22 above, although the Commission's application related only to Art. 48 itself.

30 E.g., Case C-213/90 *ASTI* v *Chambre des Employés Privés* [1991] ECR I-3507.

31 Case 36/74, note 3 above, esp. paras. 17, 21 of the judgment.

32 Notice, however, the absence of direct controls that the Commission can exercise over a private party acting in violation of Art. 48. This suggests a role for remedies at national level. See generally Weatherill, 'Discrimination on Grounds of Nationality in Sport' (1989) 9 YEL 55.

favourably treated than migrants. As is indicated by the Court's ruling on such facts in *Südmilch* v *Ugliola*,[33] Community law does not interfere with national decisions to confer such advantages, provided only that the objective is achieved by means that do not lead to discrimination based on nationality. This may require a host state to apply its rules in a manner that reflects the migrant's objectively distinct situation. *Sotgiu* v *Deutsche Bundespost*[34] involved a separation allowance payable to those working away from their place of residence. A higher allowance was made to those working away from a place of residence within Germany than to those whose residence was outside Germany at the time of their initial engagement. The differentiation was thus based on residence, yet would in practice exert an effect distinct according to nationality, which led the Court to conclude that the scheme could fall foul of Community law. However, it is a familiar principle of Community law that the application of criteria that indirectly discriminate may be capable of justification on objective grounds.[35] Objective justification might be shown if, the Court suggested, the higher allowance was being paid because those living away from a home in Germany would be expected in due course to move their place of residence to their place of work, whereas those with residences outside Germany would be recognized as indefinitely separated from their place of residence. Final resolution of the compatibility of such a scheme with Community law lies with the national court under the preliminary reference procedure.

It is important to appreciate that the focus of these provisions is equality of treatment between migrants and workers of the host state. The Regulation does not establish a floor of rights for migrants that is uniform throughout the Community. The floor is that on which nationals of the host state already stand and that floor varies from state to state.[36] In order to improve standards and to achieve a common set of social advantages a more ambitious legislative commitment is required; this impinges on the field of social policy.[37]

Third title

The third title of Regulation 1612/68 draws distinctions between different classes of family members who may obtain rights as a result of their

---

33 Case 15/69 [1969] ECR 363, [1970] CMLR 194; also Case C-419/92 *Ingetraut Scholz* v *Opera Universitaria di Cagliari* [1994] ECR I-505, [1994] 1 CMLR 873.
34 Case 152/73 [1974] ECR 153.
35 See, e.g. Art. 95, p. 400; Art. 119, p. 620.
36 In all the cases at note 28 above access to the right depended on its availability to nationals of the host state.
37 See Ch. 20.

relationship with the worker. Article 10(1) confers a right on a spouse,[38] descendants who are under 21 or dependent, and dependent relatives in the ascending line to migrate with the worker and install themselves in the host state.[39] Article 10(2) requires only that member states 'shall facilitate the admission' of other family members if dependent on the worker or 'living under his roof in the country whence he comes'.[40] Both Articles 10(1) and (2) are subject to Article 10(3), which requires that the worker has available for the family housing 'considered normal for national workers' in the area where he or she works.[41] Article 12 adds that children of the worker residing in the host state shall enjoy non-discriminatory access to 'general educational, apprenticeship and vocational training courses'.[42]

These rights accrue irrespective of the nationality of the family member, but depend on the status of the worker. They are derivative rights only. So in *Morson and Jhanjan* v *Netherlands*[43] nationals of Surinam who wished to live with their children, who were Dutch nationals living and working in the Netherlands, were held to have no rights of their own, but merely those that they could derive through their children. Since the children had never worked in a member state other than their own, they had no Community law status for these purposes[44] and, accordingly, neither did their parents. The more extensive the Court's approach to individuals falling within Community law, the wider the impact on family members. The European Court took a broad view in *R* v *IAT and Surinder Singh, ex parte Secretary of State for the Home Department*.[45] A British national returned to the United Kingdom after working in Germany with her husband, an Indian national. The husband sought to rely on Community law to defeat the restrictions of British immigration law. The European Court ruled that even though this was an instance of a non-Community national claiming

---

38 But there is no absolute right to be joined by a cohabitee. Such a right may arise under Art. 7(2) of Reg. 1612/68, where a similar right is extended to national workers; see Case 59/85, note 28 above.

39 Dependent status is a factual matter. There is no call to determine why a person has recourse to the support of the worker; Case 316/85 *Centre Public* v *Lebon* [1987] ECR 2811.

40 See Wyatt and Dashwood, *European Community Law*, pp. 245–6 for an attempt to strengthen this apparently weak provision.

41 This condition applies only to the initial taking up of residence and cannot be reapplied thereafter; Case 249/86 *Commission* v *Germany* [1989] ECR 1263, [1990] 3 CMLR 540.

42 E.g., Case 9/74 *Casagrande* v *Landeshauptstadt München* [1974] ECR 773, [1974] 2 CMLR 423.

43 Cases 35 and 36/82 [1982] ECR 3723, [1983] 2 CMLR 221.

44 See further p. 610.

45 Case C-370/90, judgment of 7 July 1992, [1992] 3 CMLR 358, noted by White (1993) 18 ELRev 527.

rights through a British national against the British authorities, the move to Germany had interpolated a sufficient Community law element to convert the case into one in which EC law was of assistance to the non-national family member. Nevertheless, irrespective of nationality, it remains essential that the person through whom rights are claimed is economically active for these purposes. In *Brown* v *Secretary of State for Scotland*[46] the Court refused to allow a child to rely on Article 12 of the Regulation as a source of derivative rights in the United Kingdom, where his parents had ceased to live and work in the United Kingdom and had moved to France before he was born.

In *Diatta* v *Land Berlin*[47] a Senegalese woman married a French national living and working in Berlin. They subsequently separated and planned to divorce. When Diatta's application for an extension of her residence permit was rejected by the German authorities, she sought to rely on Article 10 of Regulation 1612/68. The Court declared that it would not interpret Article 10 restrictively. A family member who is not a national of a member state is entitled to remain in the host state even when not living permanently with the worker.[48] *Echternach and Moritz* v *Netherlands Minister for Education and Science*[49] concerned children of German families who had been educated in the Netherlands, where their parents worked. The parents returned to Germany, but the children wished to pursue college study in the Netherlands, because Dutch qualifications were not recognized in Germany. The Court stressed the importance of integrating family members into the society of the host state. This would be undermined if the child's status in the Netherlands were infringed when the parents finally chose to leave. The child was entitled under Article 12 of the Regulation to access to education and financial support on equal terms with Dutch nationals.

The rights of the family member flow exclusively through the worker, but the rationale of social integration implicit in *Diatta* and explicit in *Echternach and Moritz* means that the link through which rights derive need not be so tight as permanent cohabitation. Diatta pointed out that if cohabitation were mandatory, a worker could cause the expulsion of a non-national spouse in an instant by depriving him or her of a roof.[50] The Court did not address the point directly, but it is well founded and,

---

46 Case 197/86 [1988] ECR 3205, [1988] 3 CMLR 403. The case is discussed further on pp. 569, 607.

47 Case 267/83 [1985] ECR 567, [1986] 2 CMLR 164.

48 The Court referred also to Art. 11 of the Reg., which implies that the family member holding derivative rights may move independently throughout the host state; e.g., Case 131/85 *Gul* v *Düsseldorf* [1986] ECR 1573, [1987] 1 CMLR 501.

49 Cases 389, 390/87 [1989] ECR 723.

50 Case 267/83, note 47 above, para. 10 of the judgment.

further, the social integration rationale suggests that even a person who is not a national of a member state who is divorced by a worker does not inevitably and immediately lose derivative rights.[51]

DIRECTIVE 68/360

The rules on free movement are supplemented by Directive 68/360, which focuses on administrative matters. The fundamental point is that rights of entry, residence and equal treatment are conferred on workers directly by the Treaty. These are directly effective rights, which must be respected by national authorities, including courts. However, privileged status must be proved. Directive 68/360 sets out the documentation that a host state may demand of the migrant. Failure to obtain relevant documents may be the subject of penalties imposed by the national authorities. However, the Community law principle of proportionality remains applicable, and breach of administrative rules should lead to appropriate penalties. Fundamentally, the Court has made it clear that failure to respect rules concerning proof of status cannot be punished by denial of the status itself. A fine may be lawful under the Community law where deportation is not.

Article 3 of the Directive requires workers and family members covered by Regulation 1612/68 to be admitted to the host member state 'simply on production of a valid identity card or passport'. Visas may not be required, except in the case of family members who are not nationals of a member state. Article 4 of the Directive requires member states to grant the right of residence to workers on production of the document whereby entry to the territory was secured and a confirmation of engagement from the employer or a certificate of employment. The same right of residence shall be granted to family members covered by Regulation 1612/68 on production of the document whereby entry to the territory was secured, a document proving their relationship from the state of origin or the state from which they have come, and, where appropriate, a similar document testifying to dependence, as required by Article 10 of the Regulation.

Production of these documents compels the host state to grant the right of residence, and as a proof of this a 'residence permit' must be issued. Articles 6 and 7 of the Directive specify the rules that attach to the

---

51 The House of Lords' decision to the contrary in *Re Sandhu*, *The Times* 10 May 1985 seems dubious; an Art. 177 reference should have been made, see p. 304. The judgment of Comyn J in the High Court in favour of the divorced non-EC national spouse ([1982] 2 CMLR 553) accords more closely with the social integration rationale. See Steiner, *EC Law*, pp. 211–12; Saunders, 'Residence and the Non-EEC Spouse' (1990) SJ 591. The couple in Case C-370/90, note 45 above, were divorcing but the Court did not focus on this point.

residence permit. Normally, it must be valid for at least five years from date of issue, automatically renewable and valid throughout the territory of the issuing state, although adjustments are made in the case of temporary workers and the involuntarily unemployed.[52] Article 4(1) of the Directive clearly declares the residence permit to be *proof* of the right of residence; the source of the right is the Treaty itself. Accordingly, failure to obtain the permit cannot result in denial of the right of residence. In *R v Pieck*[53] the Court pointed out that there is no justification in the Treaty for general administrative measures beyond those needed in respect of the production of a valid identity card or passport, the documents referred to in Article 3(1) of the Directive.[54] A failure to acquire the permit as proof of status[55] through production of the relevant documents under Article 4 may be punished, but the principles of proportionality and of non-discrimination must be respected. The Court clearly considered that failure to hold the permit is a minor infraction and may lead neither to imprisonment nor to deportation.

REGULATION 1251/70

Regulation 1251/70 concerns the right of the worker to remain permanently in the territory of a member state after having been employed in that state. Once again, this right is both an aspect of inducing mobility of labour in the common market and also an aspect of conferring rights in the social sphere on individuals. Article 2 of the Regulation confers the right to remain on three different categories of worker: the worker who has reached pensionable age, the worker who is permanently incapacitated and the frontier worker. Each category has different qualifying periods relating to employment and/or residence before accrual of the right. Family members covered by Article 10 of Regulation 1612/68 also obtain the right to remain permanently once the worker has qualified and retain that right even after the worker's death. In limited circumstances the family may even be able to remain in the host state where the worker dies

---

52 Arts. 6(3), 7(2). There is no explicit reference to the position of the voluntarily unemployed, which implies that such persons lose their rights as workers.
53 Case 157/79 [1980] ECR 2171, [1980] 3 CMLR 220. See also Case 48/75, note 1 above; and Comm. Dir. 64/221, Art. 3(3), p. 560 below.
54 A variety of administrative systems have been tested before the Court, e.g., (lawful) Case 321/87 *Commission v Belgium* [1989] ECR 997; (unlawful) Case C-265/88 *Messner* [1989] ECR 4209, Case C-68/89 *Commission v Netherlands*, [1991] ECR I-2637. See Green, Hartley and Usher, *Single European Market*, pp. 131-4.
55 Note the special cases in Art. 8 where there is no need to obtain a permit: short-term workers, frontier workers, seasonal workers.

before crossing the qualification threshold.[56] Article 7 of Regulation 1251/70 adds that beneficiaries are also entitled to the right to equality of treatment established by Regulation 1612/68.[57]

SOCIAL SECURITY

The Court has consistently held that the objective of the free circulation of workers would be frustrated if a migrant were to lose social security benefits guaranteed under the law of a member state.[58] Regulation 1408/71 is the source of the Community's rules on social security entitlement. Amendments have extended these rights to the self-employed. Family members of both employed and self-employed persons are also covered. However, the notion of workers has for these purposes a meaning that is not coterminous with that which the Court applies to Article 48 generally. Under Article 1(a) of the regulation a beneficiary must be 'insured, compulsorily or on an optional basis, for one or more of the contingencies covered by the branches of a social security scheme for employed or self-employed persons'. It is insurance rather than the pursuit of 'effective and genuine activities'[59] that matters. In consequence, individuals other than migrant workers, including holiday-makers, may be entitled to benefit from equal treatment in social security matters.[60]

National social security law is notoriously complex and this is reflected in the Community provisions. It is relatively simple to describe the purpose of the provisions in terms of their role in the process of market integration and as the source of individual rights. It is much more difficult to explain in detail the impact of Regulation 1408/71. Since the primary objective of this book is to explain the policy that informs the development of the Community legal order, there is here no attempt to provide a practical guide to migrants' social security entitlements.[61]

Article 51 of the Treaty provides the basis for adoption of measures in

---

56 Art. 3(2). Evans argues that there might be a right to remain after the worker's death that is broader than the explicit terms of the legislation by virtue of the influence of the European Convention on Human Rights; 'Nationality Law and European Integration' (1991) 16 ELRev 190, 205.

57 See, e.g., Case 32/75, note 28 above.

58 E.g., Case 100/63 *Kalsbeek v Bestuur der Sociale Verzekeringsbank* [1964] ECR 565; Case 24/75 *Petroni v ONPTS* [1975] ECR 1149; Case C-186/90 *Durighello v INPS*, [1991] ECR I-5773.

59 Case 53/81, note 11 above.

60 E.g., Case 44/65 *Hessische Knappschaft v Maison Singer et Fils* [1965] ECR 965.

61 For a fuller survey see Wyatt and Dashwood, *European Community Law*, Ch. 11; Steiner, *EC Law*, Ch. 21.

the field of social security. It is based on two principles: first, arrangements to secure 'aggregation, for the purpose of acquiring and retaining the right to benefit and of calculating the amount of benefit, of all periods taken into account under the laws of the several countries' and, second, 'payment of benefits to persons resident in the territories of Member States'. These principles are supplemented in Regulation 1408/71 by specific expressions of the principle of non-discrimination on grounds of nationality. In addition, equality on grounds of sex is required by Directive 79/7.[62] This structure serves to 'abolish as far as possible the territorial limitations on the application of the different social security schemes'.[63] However, the Community rules do not attempt the formidable task of harmonizing the social systems of all the member states. That remains a distant prospect. The practical problems are severe and the striking of compromise solutions is not facilitated by the requirement of unanimity in Council for the adoption of measures under Article 51 EC. The absence of harmonization in this area is likely to remain a gap in the legal pattern of the internal market for some considerable time to come.[64] The scope of the rules is at present confined to the coordination of national systems in the pursuit of the objectives of integration pursued by the Community in this area.[65]

It is important to note that the provisions on social security do not exist in isolation. They are part of the general package of rights to which a migrant worker may lay claim. So although Regulation 1408/71 excludes from its scope 'social assistance', rights to such broader forms of benefit may be claimed by virtue of the principle of equal treatment under Article 7(2) of Regulation 1612/68.[66]

OTHER RIGHTS

The worker is entitled to rights beyond those relating to non-discrimination on grounds of nationality. Article 119 requires that men and women shall receive equal pay for equal work.[67] More broadly, the worker may be entitled to the protection of the fundamental rights recognized by Commu-

---

62 See Ch. 20; Cousins, 'Equal Treatment and Social Security' (1994) 19 ELRev 123.
63 Case 44/65, note 60 above, p. 971.
64 See Laske, 'The Impact of the Single European Market on Social Protection for Migrant Workers' (1993) 30 CMLRev 515.
65 See, e.g., Case 41/84 *Pinna* [1986] ECR 1; Case C-146/93 *Hugh McLachlan* v *CNAVTS* [1994] ECR I-3229.
66 See p. 549. E.g., Case 63/76 *Inzirillo* v *Caisse d'Allocations Familiales de l'Arrondissement de Lyon* [1976] ECR 2057; Case 207/78, note 28 above; and Case C-310/91 *Hugo Schmid* v *Belgian State*, judgment of 27 May 1993. See discussion by O'Keeffe (1985) 5 YEL 93.
67 It and the several supporting directives are examined in Ch. 20.

nity law. Respect for religious beliefs and non-discrimination on racial grounds are fundamental rights recognized both in the member states' and in the Community legal order.[68] The migrant, as a subject of Community law relying on the right to free movement guaranteed by the Treaty, may be consequently entitled to invoke such broader rights contained within the Community legal order against the host state. The precise scope of the armoury of protection on which the migrant can rely is unclear. General principles of Community law are binding on national authorities where they act within the scope of Community law. Where national authorities act outside the sphere of Community law, they are under no obligation to respect principles drawn from Community law. The matter falls within national competence. However, it is not clear precisely where the limits of Community law lie for these purposes.[69]

A helpful illustration is provided by *Konstantinidis* v *Stadt Altensteig*.[70] A Greek national working in Germany challenged a German requirement that he should register his name according to the Latin alphabet. Worse, the obligatory transliteration of his first name rendered it as 'Hrestos', rather than 'Christos' which Konstantinidis, born on 25 December, under-standably regarded as rather more appropriate. Advocate-General Jacobs considered that the German rules amounted to an interference with Konstan-tinidis' fundamental rights and proceeded to hold that this was contrary to Community law, which afforded the migrant worker the protection of a basic set of fundamental rights once he or she had chosen to exercise the right of free movement. By contrast, the European Court was not prepared to extend the scope of Community law beyond the specifically economic aspects of the individual's treatment. The Court recognized a violation of Community law principles only where the spelling Konstantinidis was obliged to employ distorted the pronunciation of his name and led to potential economic harm because of the risk of customer confusion.[71] In the absence of that economic consideration, the matter rested outside EC law and within national jurisdiction, subject, perhaps, to the control of the European Convention on Human Rights.

---

68 E.g. Case 130/75 *Prais* v *Council* [1976] ECR 1589. [1976] 2 CMLR 708.

69 See Clapham, 'A Human Rights Policy for the European Community' (1990) 10 YEL 309; Temple Lang, 'The Sphere in which Member States are obliged to comply with the general principles of law and Community fundamental rights principles' [1991/2] LIEI 23; De Burca, 'Fundamental Human Rights and the Reach of EC Law' (1993) 13 OJLS 283.

70 Case C-168/91, judgment of 30 March 1993, [1993] 3 CMLR 410, noted by Lawson (1994) 31 CMLRev 395 The matter was considered in the light of Art. 52 EC, rather than Art. 48, but this makes no difference in principle; p. 575 below.

71 The Court did not address the question of whether the German system discriminated against Greeks.

This is an area of the law in a dynamic evolution. Even though the *Konstantinidis* ruling represents a relatively narrow expression of the situations in which the migrant is entitled to draw on general principles of Community law, this is a fertile field in which it may be possible in future to nurture a developed pattern of minimum rights available to individuals. It may be possible to argue with some cogency that the protection of basic fundamental rights is critical to inducing labour mobility and that accordingly, even from the perspective preferred by the Court in *Konstantinidis*, a broad pattern of protection needs to be established in order to eliminate blockages to economic integration. More ambitiously, the Court may in future find itself once again invited to follow the route proposed by AG Jacobs. To conclude on a note of pragmatism, the effective enforcement of rights of this nature depends on the availability of adequate procedures at national level. Patterns vary state by state and Community legislative activity may be required to secure basic standards of proper procedure.

EXCEPTIONS

Article 48 mentions two separate sets of exception to the basic principle of free movement. These are contained in Article 48(3) – 'limitations justified on grounds of public policy, public security or public health' – and Article 48(4), which excludes 'employment in the public service'. The heads of justification under Article 48(3) resemble those under Article 36 pertaining to the free movement of goods, and, generally, these provisions are subject to an interpretation that runs parallel to all provisions that are hostile to the Community *Grundnorm* of market integration. Barriers to free circulation must be interpreted narrowly. For example, it has already been remarked that failure to comply with administrative rules relating to residence permits is not a sufficient reason for denying the basic right of free movement.[72] Moreover, the exceptions are capable of justifying only exclusion from a state, not discrimination in the terms and conditions of employment actually taken up.[73]

---

72 See p. 555.
73 Case 15/69 *Sudmilch* v *Ugliola* [1969] ECR 363, [1970] CMLR 194.

ARTICLE 48(3): LEGISLATIVE AMPLIFICATION

Directive 64/221 explains more fully the nature of the public-policy, public-security and public-health derogations from the principle of the free movement of workers contained in Article 48(3) of the Treaty. It includes several provisions that limit the capacity of a member state to invoke the exceptions. They may not be invoked to service economic ends.[74] Where public policy or public security is in issue, measures shall be based exclusively on the personal conduct of the individual concerned and, more narrowly still, cannot be taken on the grounds of previous criminal convictions in themselves.[75] The public-health exception is circumscribed by Article 4 of the Directive, which curtails the diseases or disabilities that may justify refusal of entry or of renewal of a first residence permit to those listed in an annex. Articles 6–9 impose procedural safeguards on the exercise of these exceptional powers. These rules reflect the notion that these provisions are not designed merely to integrate the market, but that they also give rise to rights vested in the individual that require protection. Article 6 requires that the person be informed of the grounds on which the decision is based, unless this runs contrary to the interests of the security of the state. Article 8 requires that the same legal remedies be made available to the would-be migrant as are available to nationals of the state in the matter of administrative acts (a rule of non-discrimination). Article 9 goes further and lays down a basic minimum protection applicable uniformly in all member states even in the absence of rights available as a result of Article 8.[76] Briefly, this is concerned to provide a two-tier protection in order to preclude a migrant being subjected to an unfavourable decision that cannot be challenged before a separate body, save in exceptional circumstances.[77]

ARTICLE 48(3): JUDICIAL INTERPRETATION

Against a general thematic background of hostility to obstacles to free movement a not entirely consistent line of case law has developed the interpretation of primary and secondary Community law in this area.[78]

---

74 Dir. 64/221, Art. 2(2)

75 ibid., Arts. 3(1), (2).

76 See, e.g., Case 98/79 *Pecastaing* v *Belgian State* [1980] ECR 691.

77 See, e.g., Case 131/79 *R* v *Secretary of State, ex parte Santillo* [1980] ECR 1585. *Quaere* whether this ruling was properly applied by the English courts: [1981] QB 778, noted by Gormley, 'The Application of Community Law in the United Kingdom 1976–1985' (1986) 23 CMLRev 287, 302–3.

78 For a comparison with the approach taken under the European Convention on

The decision in *Van Duyn* v *Home Office*

Van Duyn v *Home Office*[79] involved a challenge to a decision to refuse entry into the United Kingdom to a Dutch woman who had secured a post working for the Church of Scientology. An Article 177 reference was made by the English High Court. Article 3(1) of the Directive declares that action must be based exclusively on personal conduct. The European Court first ruled that the provision was directly effective and could therefore be pleaded before national courts. It then proceeded to hold that 'present association, which reflects participation in the activities of the body or of the organization as well as identification with its aims and designs' could amount to personal conduct.[80] This rather wide definition of personal conduct then led to the question of whether Van Duyn's conduct in the circumstances was sufficiently threatening to one of the interests recognized by Article 48(3). The United Kingdom considered Scientology contrary to the public good, but did not ban it; indeed a British national would not have been punished for taking up the very job offered to Van Duyn. The European Court declared that Article 48(3) is to be interpreted narrowly and is not at the unilateral disposal of a member state, but conceded that the circumstances in which recourse to public policy may arise will vary from state to state. It decided that where a state views an activity as socially harmful and has taken administrative measures against it, it is able to rely on the public-policy exception even where it does not consider it 'appropriate in the circumstances' to outlaw the activity.[81]

On two linked counts the Court's decision in *Van Duyn* displayed a surprisingly generous measure of discretion to the state in acting to repress conduct.[82] First, it envisaged control of an activity that was allegedly socially harmful, yet not shown to be dangerous; second, it envisaged steps taken against nationals of other member states in circumstances where no comparable measures would be taken internally. The Court pointed out in *Van Duyn* that absolute parity of treatment between migrants and the

---

Human Rights, see Hall, 'The European Convention on Human Rights and Public Policy Exceptions to the Free Movement of Workers under the EEC Treaty' (1991) 16 ELRev 466.
79 Case 41/74 [1974] ECR 1337, [1975] I CMLR 1.
80 ibid., para. 17 of the judgment.
81 ibid., para. 19 of the judgment.
82 The decision was perhaps designed to smooth a reluctant UK's gradual integration into the Community; see e.g., Dallen, 'An Overview of European Community Protection of Human Rights, with Some Special References to the UK' (1990) 27 CMLRev 761, 776. It came shortly after accession in 1973 and shortly before the referendum on continued membership in 1975.

state's own nationals is impossible, because a state cannot deny entry or residence to its own nationals, and concluded that this could justify the refusal of freedom of movement by migrants where nationals were not restricted. This analysis is evasive, for the United Kingdom was not even taking less repressive measures against its own nationals involved with the cult. This reveals arbitrary discrimination, which is irredeemable under Community law.

The Court's approach since *Van Duyn* v *Home Office*

Since *Van Duyn* the Court has significantly shifted its stance and now allows states a much narrower leeway, both by defining more carefully the type of threat that must be posed by the personal conduct and by requiring that that threat be combated effectively whatever its source. So in *R* v *Bouchereau*[83] a French national convicted in the United Kingdom of possession of drugs wished to rely on Community law to avoid deportation. The European Court was asked to rule on the scope of the United Kingdom's permissible reliance on the Article 48(3) exception. The Court echoes the Directive's insistence that a previous criminal conviction is of itself no basis for repressive measures. Conviction is relevant only as evidence of personal conduct that forms a threat to public policy. This indicates that a propensity to reoffend must be shown. The Court suggested that past conduct might be sufficient,[84] but it did not enlarge on the point and it would apply only in exceptional circumstances. The Court proceeded to consider the nature of 'public policy' itself.[85] It referred to *Van Duyn* as authority for the proposition that a narrow view of the notion must be taken and that its invocation depends on circumstances prevailing in particular states at particular times, but then, without further reference to *Van Duyn*, the Court established a test considerably more restrictive than anything to be found in that decision. A state wishing to rely on Article 48(3) must show a 'genuine and sufficiently serious threat to the requirements of public policy affecting one of the fundamental interests of society'.[86] That demands more than mere law-breaking. After the Court's ruling, the magistrate in London imposed a fine of £35 on M. Bouchereau but felt unable to hold that the possession of a relatively small amount of

---

83 Case 30/77 [1977] ECR 1999, [1977] 2 CMLR 800.
84 ibid., para. 29 of the judgment. For a questionable application by English courts, see *R* v *Secretary of State for the Home Department ex parte Marchon* [1993] 1 CMLR 207 (High Court), [1993] 2 CMLR 132 (CA).
85 The opinion of AG Warner is notable for a discussion of the difficulty in achieving a satisfactory English translation of the French notion of *ordre public*; the same problem arises in relation to Art. 36; see p. 461.
86 Case 30/77, note 83 above, para. 35 of the judgment.

drugs could be viewed as sufficiently grave to justify a recommendation of deportation.[87]

Rezguia Adoui and Dominique Cornuaille v *Belgium*[88] involved the Belgian authorities' refusal of residence permits to two French prostitutes. In Belgium prostitution was not unlawful, although connected activities, such as soliciting, were prohibited. The European Court referred to its own finding in *Van Duyn* that strict comparability between the measures taken by a state against its own nationals and against migrants is not possible, for a state cannot deport its own nationals. However, the Court added that that difference could not be used to justify arbitrary discrimination. It repeated the formulation given in *Bouchereau* of the scope of public policy and supplemented this with the observation that a state cannot expel a migrant worker where a national pursuing the same activity would not be subject to repressive measures or other genuine and effective measures designed to combat the activity.

Although this test is rather imprecise, the tenor of the judgment shows a much firmer commitment to non-discrimination than did that in *Van Duyn*.[89] A state in a position analogous to the United Kingdom in *Van Duyn* would today be obliged to provide persuasive evidence of the repressive nature of its internal controls in order to justify action taken against a national of another member state. More generally, despite the lack of comparability at the level of deportation, *Adoui and Cornuaille* shows that at the lower end of the criminal scale comparability can apply. In the case of a misdeed attracting a small fine under domestic law the nationality of the malefactor should be irrelevant.

The completion of the internal market

The law in this area has greatly reduced the ability of member states to exclude migrants from other member states. It follows that border controls on people travelling within the Community are increasingly difficult to justify.[90] The logical progression is stated in Article 7a: 'The internal market shall comprise an area without internal frontiers in which the free movement of goods, persons, services and capital is ensured in accordance with the provisions of this Treaty.'[91] This appears to mean nothing less than the unrestricted free movement of persons between member states. This would preclude the maintenance of border checks. On its own, it

87 ibid., [1977] 2 CMLR 800, 801.
88 Cases 115, 116/81 [1982] ECR 1665, [1982] 3 CMLR 631.
89 See Arnull, *EEC Law and the Individual*, pp. 95–6.
90 See also note 54 above.
91 See Ch. 1, page 24.

would not, in principle, preclude the power of member states to take internal measures against migrants by invoking the derogations recognized by Article 48(3), perhaps including deportation. However, deportation of citizens of the Union, even if considered lawful, loses much of its practical value once internal border controls have been dismantled.[92]

In Chapters 14 and 15 it was explained how the Community has succeeded in putting in place the legislative framework required to eliminate frontier controls on goods.[93] The removal of controls over people has been profoundly more difficult. The arguments surround ambiguities in the Treaty itself. Article 7a refers to an area without internal frontiers. Article 8a(1) provides that 'Every Citizen of the Union shall have the right to move and reside freely within the territory of the Member States.' On one view, this is sufficiently uncompromising to require the unrestricted free movement of persons between member states. However, Article 7a concludes with reference to free movement 'in accordance with the provisions of this Treaty' and Article 8a(1)'s statement is 'subject to the limitations and conditions laid down in this Treaty and by the measures adopted to give it effect'. This may be taken to justify continued border controls under Article 48(3), for example to counter drug smuggling, terrorist-related activity and the threat of rabies, at least until such time as effective safeguards have been put in place at Community level. The disputed personal scope of the right of free movement also causes problems of interpretation. On one view, the reference to 'persons' in Article 7a should be taken to mean *all* persons irrespective of nationality. So once an individual has entered Community territory that person is within a zone of free movement across borders and action to weed out those not entitled to be there cannot be tied to border checks. A contrary view holds that it is only Community nationals who enjoy free movement rights and that accordingly border checks remain justified in order to distinguish between categories of Community and non-Community nationals. On this view, such controls remain justified at least until such time as common external controls are agreed and effectively applied.

The matter remains unresolved and is the subject of intense debate among Community institutions and among member states. Long after the start of 1993 it was an empirical fact that border checks on people had not ceased within the Community. At the Edinburgh European Council in December 1992, it was asserted in the Conclusions of the Presidency that:

The European Council has had to take note of the fact that free movement of

---

92 See Vincenzi, 'Deportation in Disarray: the Case of EC Nationals' [1994] Crim LRev 163.
93 Pp. 423, 478.

persons within the Community, in accordance with Article 8a of the Treaty of Rome [now Art 7a EC], cannot be completely assured on 1st January 1993. The work necessary to achieve this result without creating dangers for public security and compromising the fight against illegal immigration, although having progressed, is still under way. Further progress is needed in particular to complete the ratification process of the Dublin Asylum Convention, to conclude the External Frontiers Convention and to complete negotiations on a Convention on the European Information System.

It is well known that the Government of the United Kingdom remains especially hostile to the surrender of border controls. British opposition may be capable of objective support based on the fact that the United Kingdom has one land border only, so that the natural shift of controls away from the accidents of political boundaries in many parts of the Community's territory is inappropriate in the United Kingdom. However, much of the British Government's opposition has a more strongly ideological tinge.

It will ultimately fall to the European Court to determine the legal validity of border checks on people. The Parliament was sufficiently dissatisfied with progress to institute an action under Article 175 in which it claimed that the Commission had wrongfully failed to take the necessary steps to put forward proposals to secure free movement.[94]

Pending a formal European Court ruling on the validity of a post-1992 policy of border checks, energy has been devoted to putting in place common controls at external borders and to establishing a high degree of internal coordination between national authorities to ensure that effective internal policing can be maintained in an environment in which reliance on systematic border checks is no longer permitted. Within the Community, there is a logic in a shift away from border controls towards administrative checks. This suggests a future of more intensive police cooperation and information-sharing. For the majority of the member states, this would be readily combined with compulsory identity cards, but this is a policy to which the United Kingdom maintains a strong antipathy. At the Union's external borders, a common policy on migration and asylum would seem appealingly logical. The Treaty on European Union creates Union structures within which these objectives can be pursued. Largely, the relevant provisions fall outside *Community* competence, which, given that the cooperation is strongly motivated by the Community objective of eliminating borders, represents one of several reasons for the lop-sided appearance of the Union built on distinct pillars.[95]

94 Case C-445/93 *European Parliament v Commission*, (1993) OJ C1/12.
95 See Ch. 1, p. 10.

Article K TEU, the pillar dealing with Cooperation in Justice and Home Affairs, serves as a forum for putting in place the level of effective cooperation that seems essential to underpin the open-borders policy. Article K is intergovernmental in nature. However, it offers a corridor in Article K.9 whereby matters subject to the intergovernmental pillar may be transferred by unanimous vote in Council to Article 100c in the EC pillar, where they will be dealt with under voting conditions decided at the time of the transfer. Article 100c, in its immediate post-Maastricht form, provides in its first paragraph that 'the Council, acting unanimously on a proposal from the Commission and after consulting the European Parliament, shall determine the third countries whose nationals must be in possession of a visa when crossing the external borders of the Member States'.[96] Article 100c(2) provides for the imposition of visa requirements on third-country nationals in the event of an emergency in that third country. Article 100c(3) requires that the Council shall, before the start of 1996, adopt measures relating to a uniform format for visas. This is to be done by a qualified majority in Council on a Commission proposal and after consulting the Parliament.

The Dublin Convention of 1990 is concerned with the determination of the state responsible for examining applications for asylum lodged in one of the member states.[97] However, by the end of 1994, ratifications by four of the twelve member states remained outstanding, precluding the Convention's entry into force.[98] It is important to appreciate that the Dublin Convention deals only with procedures for fixing the state that will decide an asylum application and does not govern the criteria for deciding whether or not the application should succeed. The Convention between the member states on the Crossing of their External Frontiers would complement the Dublin Convention, but its progress has been badly stalled by disagreements between Spain and the United Kingdom over the status of Gibraltar. The core of the draft 'External Frontiers Convention' is a set of common rules governing the position of nationals of non-EU states wishing to enter the EU and to move and reside within it.

The location of these developments outwith the EC pillar of the Union significantly confines the capacity of the Court, the Parliament and the Commission to exercise control over activities undertaken by the member states acting in the Council or the European Council. This is the nature of the non-EC EU. The chain of accountability for actions taken in the

---

96 Art. 100c(3) provides for a switch to qualified majority voting in Council from the start of 1996.
97 30 ILM 425.
98 Missing were Belgium, Ireland, Netherlands and Spain.

context of both the two intergovernmental EU pillars runs from national politicians in Council/European Council to their national parliaments. The efficacy of national parliamentary control over matters that are the subject of cooperation on a European scale is questionable.

A group of states have moved ahead of the relatively slow progress at Community level in the Schengen Agreement. This agreement, which bears the name of a town in Luxembourg, was entered into initially in 1985 by the Benelux countries, France and Germany and it envisaged the abolition of checks at common borders. A binding implementing convention was signed on 19 June 1990.[99] There were subsequent delays in its entry into force, in part attributable to technical difficulties in establishing administrative links between authorities that were adequate to underpin the operation of the system. However, the agreement eventually came into force on 26 March 1995. The states that were party to it with immediate effect were Germany, France, Belgium, Luxembourg, the Netherlands, Spain and Portugal. The dropping of internal checks was based on strengthened internal cooperation, founded on a computerized network of information-sharing, the SIS, the 'Schengen Information System'.[100]

At one level, the Schengen process offered a model for the Community as a whole. Travel between, say, Germany and France should in theory become as simple as travel between two German *Länder*. Nevertheless, even though it may seem churlish to criticize the Schengen states for boldly advancing a policy of open-borders, the system presents a threat to the integrity of the Community. After the agreement's entry into force, Schengen travel was distinct from non-Schengen but intra-Community travel. For example, a British national arriving in Germany might be treated less favourably than a French national. The Schengen Agreement is not EC law. It is international law. However, it is possible that the European Court will be asked to rule on the compatibility of such a two-tier system with the principles of the Community legal order, in particular Articles 6, 7a and 8a(1) EC.

ARTICLE 48(4)

Under Article 48(3) the Court has struggled to achieve a balance between the needs of market integration, the rights of the individual, the uniformity of Community law and the legitimate rights of the member states. A parallel development may be observed in the less frequently litigated

99 30 ILM 84.
100 See Select Further Reading, p. 908.

exception for 'employment in the public service' under Article 48(4).[101] In *Sotgiu* v *Deutsche Bundespost*[102] the Court stated that Article 48(4) has a uniform Community content in order to prevent uneven application of Community law between member states. In addition, it must be interpreted narrowly. In *Sotgiu* the Court concluded that this meant it could be invoked in respect of refusal to admit to an occupation, but not to justify discrimination in the terms of employment once taken up.

Two major Article 169 cases serve to illustrate the Court's support for the Commission's determination to confine the scope of the exception to a narrow core of jobs connected with the vital interests of the state. In *Commission* v *Belgium*[103] the Court confirmed the need for a uniform, but narrow, interpretation of Article 48(4). It held that it was necessary to examine the duties involved in the posts in question – a functional test. The Court looked for powers conferred by public law bearing a responsibility for safeguarding the general interests of the state. It found a breach of Article 48 where Belgians alone could take jobs as, *inter alia*, shunters, drivers and plate-layers with the Belgian national railway and as joiners and gardeners with the city of Brussels. However, considerations of state security could justify restrictions attaching to elevated administrative posts in the city of Brussels. In *Commission* v *France*[104] the Court found a breach of Article 48 where only French nationals could become nurses in public hospitals. It rejected the relevance of the post's designation under national law in order to preclude disunity in the scope of Community law between states. The Court preferred a test based on whether the functions and responsibilities were typical of the public service. The threshold was not crossed in the case.[105]

The Article 48(4) exception demands a special relationship of allegiance to the state. Judicial appointments would doubtless satisfy the test. It is probably that the higher echelons of the civil service, the police, and the army, navy and air force can also be confined to nationals. However, more mundane tasks do not fall within the notion of the public service simply because the state happens to be the employer.[106]

---

101 Handoll, 'Article 48(4) EEC and Non-National Access to Public Employment' (1988) 13 ELRev 223; Morris, Fredman and Hayes, 'Free Movement and the Public Sector' (1990) 19 ILJ 20.
102 Case 152/73, note 34 above.
103 Case 149/79 [1980] ECR 3881, follow-up judgment [1982] ECR 1845.
104 Case 307/84 [1986] ECR 1725, [1987] 3 CMLR 555.
105 See Case C-4/91 *Bleis* v *Ministère de l'Éducation Nationale*, [1991] ECR I-5627, in which employment as a secondary school teacher was held outside Art. 48(4).
106 It might be noted that there is absolutely no parallel between Art. 48(4) and the notion of the state for the purposes of establishing the scope of the direct effects of directives; see Case 152/84 *Marshall* v *Southampton AHA* [1986] ECR 723, considered in Ch. 11.

OTHER CATEGORIES

DIFFERENT CATEGORIES OF 'WORKER'

It has already been observed that the individual who is not a worker may none the less be able to claim rights under Community law by virtue of either Article 52 or Article 59.[107] However, even within the category of worker under Article 48, it would be misleading to suppose that the Court treats all individuals in precisely the same way. Identifying an individual as a worker[108] may be only the first stage of an inquiry into exactly what entitlements the individual may claim. The Court has shown itself prepared to subdivide the categories of benefits discussed above[109] in accordance with the type of worker making the claim. It is only relatively recently that it has become apparent that in some cases it is artificial to split the issue of defining the 'worker' from the scope of the advantages to which he or she may be entitled. The nature of the analysis under the first question governs the allocation of rights under the second question.

Brown v *Secretary of State for Scotland*[110] involved a man with dual French and British nationality, who had been born and educated in France. He went to work for eight months as a trainee engineer with a firm in Edinburgh in preparation for taking up an undergraduate place at the University of Cambridge. He was full-time and salaried, but it was a precondition for his post that he hold a university place. He duly took up that place and claimed entitlement to a maintenance grant on the same conditions as British students, relying on Regulation 1612/68. The Court referred to its key judgments in *Levin*,[111] *Kempf*[112] and *Lawrie-Blum*[113] and agreed that Brown was a worker. It accepted that the grant was a social advantage within Article 7(2) of the Regulation. However, the Court then turned against Brown by determining that the advantage was not available where the worker's status was attributable solely to admission to university in order to undertake studies.

The European Court's decision in *Brown* on the definition of worker conforms with the decisions in its leading cases, such as *Levin*. The departure occurs in elaborating the consequences of that status. It was apparent that the Court was adjusting the implications of the status of

107 See Ch. 19.
108 See p. 545.
109 See p. 548.
110 Case 197/86, note 46 above.
111 Case 53/81, note 11 above.
112 Case 139/85, note 15 above.
113 Case 66/85, note 19 above.

worker, because on the same day in *Lair* v *University of Hanover*[114] it held that an individual who had been working on and off in several different jobs in the host state *was* entitled to a grant as a social advantage under Regulation 1612/68 on choosing to enter university education. It insisted that this broad view of the right was essential in order to facilitate the mobility of workers. The Court added elements likely to cause problems of definition in the future when it held that the worker can claim the grant only where there is continuity between the previous work and the purpose of study – except where involuntary unemployment has forced the worker to retrain.

There is obviously a dividing line between the entitlements of different types of worker.[115] It seems that the simple act of crossing the 'worker' threshold does not conclude the question of the benefits then available. Entitlements vary. Cases such as *Levin, Lawrie-Blum* and *Bettray*[116] remain important authorities on the definition of worker, a status that yields the fundamental rights of entry and residence. Thereafter, access to social benefits on the same conditions as nationals of the host state differs between workers. It is far from clear whether Kempf, for example,[117] could have attended a Dutch university on precisely the same conditions as a Dutch national.

THE PERSON LOOKING FOR WORK

What of a person seeking a job? Already in *Levin*[118] the Court had suggested that an individual migrating in order seriously to look for work could be covered by Article 48. This was confirmed in *R* v *IAT, ex parte Antonissen*.[119] The case arose out of British rules that required nationals of other member states looking for work in the United Kingdom to leave after six months if unsuccessful. The European Court held that there is a right of entry and residence in order to look for work, but was less clear about the duration of that right. Council Minutes at the time of the adoption of Regulation 1612/68 referred to a right of three months' duration, but the Court refused to attach any legal significance to this

114 Case 39/86 [1988] ECR 3161, [1989] 3 CMLR 545.
115 For criticism, see Lonbay, 'Education and Law: the Community Context' (1989) 14 ELRev 363, 375–80.
116 Case 344/87, note 18 above.
117 See Case 139/85, note 15 above. See further Case C-357/89, note 20 above.
118 Case 53/81, note 11 above. See also Art. 5 Reg. 1612/68; and Case 48/75, note 1 above.
119 Case C-292/89 [1991] ECR I-745, [1991] 2 CMLR 373.

declaration. Community social security legislation[120] permits an unemployed person with an entitlement to benefits in his or her home state to retain that right for three months on moving to another state to seek work, but the Court did not consider that that right need be coextensive with a right to remain. In fact, the Court declined to stipulate a fixed length of time. It simply held that the United Kingdom's six-month limit seemed to be long enough to permit the migrant to seek work and that it therefore did not undermine the principle of free movement. The Court envisaged an exception where the person could show a genuine chance of employment even on the expiry of the six-month period.[121]

The ruling plainly raises several difficulties. It is merely a tentative step in establishing the law applicable to the job hunter. In *Dimitrios Tsiotras v Landeshauptstadt Stuttgart*[122] the Court crisply denied any right of residence to a Greek who had been unemployed in Germany at the time of Greek accession, who had remained unemployed thereafter and for whom it was objectively impossible to find employment. However, after *Antonissen*, active searchers for work may fall within Article 48. One of the issues that requires determination is the entitlements of such an individual. Plainly, there would be no right of financial support through the host state's university system! The Court had already commented briefly on the issue in *Centre Public v Lebon*.[123] It held that an individual seeking a job has a right of equal access to employment under Article 48 and Articles 2 and 5 of Regulation 1612/68, but no right to equal access to social and tax advantages under Article 7(2) of the Regulation. Rights to move with a family may be similarly beyond the person looking for a job.

NATIONALS OF NON-MEMBER STATES

The largest body of individuals falling outside these definitions is workers who are not nationals of member states. The issue of nationality remains in principle a matter of national, rather than Community, jurisdiction.[124] However, several million members of the Community work-force are

---

120 See p. 556 above.
121 AG Darmon also avoided a fixed time-limit; he submitted that the person must be engaged in an effective and serious search for work and that it is for the state to inquire whether this is or is not so.
122 Case C-171/91, judgment of 26 May 1993.
123 Case 316/85, note 39 above, noted by Greaves (1988) 13 ELRev 270.
124 E.g. Case C-369/90 *Micheletti v Delegación del Gobierno en Cantabria*, judgment of 7 July 1992. See also Art. 8(1) and the Declaration on Nationality of a Member State attached to the Treaty. See Green, Hartley and Usher, *Single European Market* pp. 101–9; Greenwood, 'Nationality and the Limits of the Free Movement of Persons in Community Law' (1987) 7 YEL 185; Evans, O'Leary, Select Further Reading, p. 907–8.

unable to claim rights as workers under Article 48 because they are not Community nationals.[125] Non-national members of the family of a national of one of the member states may obtain rights by virtue of Articles 10–12 of Regulation 1612/68, but these are derivative rights and consequently precarious.[126] Nationals of some states may be able to claim protection under association agreements, which may have effects comparable to the European Community Treaty.

ONEM v *Kziber*[127] involved the 1976 Cooperation Agreement between the Community and Morocco. The applicant, a Moroccan national resident in Belgium, claimed that the agreement guaranteed non-discriminatory treatment on grounds of nationality in the field of social security on terms analogous to those applied to Community nationals by virtue of Regulation 1408/71. The Court held that the provision in the agreement was of such a nature as to confer directly effective rights on the applicant. The Court conceded that the association agreement was less ambitious than the Treaty of Rome. This has been a basis for denying equivalence in substantive interpretation or constitutional impact between the Treaty and other instruments.[128] On a true interpretation of the agreement in question that reservation did not apply. A precise principle governing the legal status of an individual was concerned and interpretation in the light of Regulation 1408/71 was appropriate. The case may on this basis be contrasted with *Demirel* v *Stadt Schwäbisch Gmund*,[129] in which the Court found a provision of the Community–Turkey agreement insufficiently precise to confer directly effective rights on a Turkish national.

Generally however, external immigration policy remains in principle in the hands of national authorities. In *Germany, France, Netherlands, Denmark and United Kingdom* v *Commission*[130] the Court annulled part of the Commission's decision on the basis that it went beyond the Commission's powers under the Treaty. The decision required states to set up a procedure for communicating and consulting with the Commission on migration policies in relation to non-member states. The Court was prepared to accept that migration policy could fall within the social field specified by Article 118

125 Legal immigrants comprise approximately 3 per cent of the Community's population.
126 See p. 552 above.
127 Case C-18/90 [1991] ECR I-199, noted by Weber (1991) 28 CMLRev 959. See also Case C-58/93 *Zoubir Yousfi* v *Belgium* [1994] ECR I-1353; Case C-355/93 *Hayriye Eroglu* v *Land Baden-Württemberg* [1994] ECR I-5113.
128 E.g., Case 270/80 *Polydor* v *Harlequin* [1982] ECR 329, [1982] 1 CMLR 677; Opinion 1/91 *Opinion on the draft agreement on a European Economic Area* [1991] ECR I-6079 [1992] 1 CMLR 245; see further Ch. 10, p. 321.
129 Case 12/86 [1987] ECR 3719, [1989] 1 CMLR 421. See Case C-192/89 *Sevince* [1990] ECR I-3461.
130 Cases 281, 283–5, 287/85 [1987] ECR 3203.

to the extent to which it concerns the impact of workers from non-member countries on the Community employment market and on working conditions. However, the decision was annulled in respect of rules relating to broader cultural integration contained within it. The precise scope of the Community's powers in this field are not definitively settled,[131] for the decision focused more on Commission competence than on Community competence. The decision suggests a heavy emphasis on the third-country migrant as a factor of production rather than as a human being.

The creation of a Community without internal frontiers implies the development of common policies at the external frontier, or else migrants could avoid relatively restrictive immigration rules in state A simply by entering that state *via* the more generous state B. The same quest for external unity to complement internal unity was observed in relation to the free circulation of goods[132] and its application to persons has already been addressed in this chapter.[133] On this analysis it is not inherently inevitable that the external barriers of the Community will be high, merely that they will be uniform. However, there has been much criticism that the rules under development are pitched at a level that will forbid entry into the Community even by political refugees, quite apart from economic refugees or migrants. The Community finds itself in great difficulty in achieving a satisfactory compromise between the different views of the member states and then in persuading third countries that the result is not unfairly insular. European integration deserves a sceptical response if it advantages only (West) Europeans; Weiler has commented that 'we have made little progress if the *Us* becomes European (instead of German or French or British) and the *Them* becomes those outside the Community or those inside who do not enjoy the privileges of citizenship'.[134]

Equally contentious is the development of Community policies designed to offer social protection to third-country migrants who are lawfully resident within the Community. Proposals for measures to combat racism have been especially actively supported by the Parliament. Yet even with

131 E.g., see Weiler, 'The Transformation of Europe' (1991) 100 Yale LJ 2403, 2448 fn. expressing disagreement with Bradley. 'The European Court and the Legal Basis of Community Legislation' (1988) 13 ELRev 379, 384. See also Simmonds. 'The Concertation of Community Migration Policy' (1988) 25 CMLRev 177; Plender, 'Competence, European Community Law and Nationals of non-Member States' (1990) 39 ICLQ 599; Desolre. *'Compétence de la Communauté en général et de la Commission en particulier en matière de politique migratoire vis-à-vis des États tiers'* (1990) 26 CDE 453.

132 See Ch. 16, p. 486.

133 See p. 565.

134 (1991) 100 Yale LJ 2403, 2482. See also Ireland, 'Facing the True "Fortress Europe": Immigrant and Politics in the EC' (1991) 29 JCMS 572; and Select Further Reading, p. 908 below.

regard to Community nationals there is no comprehensive Community legislation forbidding race discrimination.[135] This issue connects with the problems of allocating competence for taking action that were ventilated in *Germany et al.* v *Commission*.[136] The outer limits of EC competence are ill-defined; it is especially difficult to pin down the demarcation between action that falls within the EC pillar of the Union and the pillar dealing with cooperation in justice and home affairs. Disputes about competence tend to obscure the substance of the matter.[137] Generally, calls for improved civil rights for non-Community nationals[138] appear to be gaining only limited support.

135 See the uncertain status of indirect protection mentioned at p. 558.
136 Cases 281, 283–5, 287/85 note 130 above.
137 On issues of competence, see further Chs. 5,8.
138 See, e.g., Wrench and Solomos (eds.), *Racism and Migration in Western Europe* (1995); Layton-Henry (ed.), *The Political Rights of Migrant Workers* (1989); Ireland (1991) 29 JCMS 572; also comment by O'Keeffe (1992) 17 ELRev 3, 16–19; Clapham (1990) 10 YEL 309.

CHAPTER 19

Freedom of Establishment and the Free Movement of Services

The basis of both Article 52 and Article 59 is a rule against discrimination on grounds of nationality. This rule may be relied upon by self-employed persons wishing to establish themselves in member states other than their own on the same terms as nationals of the host state. It may also be relied upon by individuals wishing to secure equal access to the market for the provision of services in a member state other than their own. It protects companies from discrimination where they wish to establish a permanent or temporary presence in a state other than that under the law of which they have been formed. The underlying objective of the elimination of discrimination that lies at the heart of both provisions is the promotion of market integration. This leads to the realization of economies of scale and the stimulation of competition within a common market.[1]

The Treaty provisions in this field are to be read in parallel, and much of the analysis below is equally applicable to both Articles 52 and 59. This is desirable, because the margin between the two will often be difficult to locate. One might take as an illustration the construction firm that regularly undertakes long-term projects in Belgium, although its base is located a short distance inside the Netherlands. It would be irrational if classification of such activity under Article 52 in preference to Article 59 or vice versa, were to lead to significant distinctions in legal entitlements. This is precluded by parallel interpretation of Articles 52 and 59. However, as a general observation, establishment under Article 52 involves a more permanent status in the host state than the provision of services under Article 59, and to a limited extent this is reflected in the tighter, although non-discriminatory, controls that may be permissibly exercised by a host state under Article 52 in contrast to Article 59.

---

1 See generally Ch. 1, p. 20.

THE RULE AGAINST DISCRIMINATION

THE DIRECT EFFECT OF ARTICLES 52 AND 59

Discrimination on grounds of nationality is unlawful. In *Van Binsbergen* v *Bestuur van de Bedrijfsvereniging voor de Metaalnijverheid* [2] the Court referred to Article 59 as a means of abolishing 'any discrimination against a person providing a service by reason of his nationality or of the fact that he resides in a Member State other than that in which the service is to be provided'. [3] *Reyners* v *Belgian State* [4] provides an example of the application of the rule against discrimination contained in Article 52. A Dutch national resident in Belgium held a Belgian legal qualification. He was denied admission as an *avocat* in Belgium because of rules restricting that profession to Belgians. His argument that he had rights to establish himself in Belgium was countered by the submission that Article 52 could not be directly effective because its implementation was dependent on the issue of specific directives regulating the professions envisaged by Articles 54(2) and 57(1) of the Treaty. The Court rejected this argument. It observed that the rule against discrimination on grounds of nationality contained in Article 7 EEC (now Article 6 EC) is a principle of the Community and that Article 52 is a specific implementation of that principle. Reyners was subject to conditions that would not have been applied to an identically qualified Belgian, a clear breach of the unambiguous rule against discrimination on grounds of nationality. The adoption of secondary legislation facilitates free movement, but the rule of equal treatment is independently enforceable. It is directly effective. Precisely the same approach applies to the application of Article 59. [5]

The rule of equal treatment irrespective of nationality applies where the migrant's qualification, though conferred in his or her home state, is recognized by the host state's authorities as equivalent to its own. *Thieffry* v *Conseil de l'Ordre des Avocats* [6] involved a Belgian holding a Belgian doctorate in law who wished to practise in France. His application for registration was rejected by the Paris Bar not because of his nationality, as

2 Case 33/74 [1974] ECR 1299.
3 ibid., para. 27 of the judgment.
4 Case 2/74 [1974] ECR 631.
5 See e.g., Cases 110, 111/78 *Ministère Public* v *Van Wesemael* [1979] ECR 35. However, Art. 61(1) provides that freedom to provide services in the transport sector is subject to the special regime of Arts. 74–84, which inhibits direct effect in that sector; e.g. Case C-17/90 *Pinaud Wieger Spedition* v *Bundesanstalt* [1991] ECR I-5253.
6 Case 71/76 [1977] ECR 765, [1977] 2 CMLR 373. See similarly Case 11/77 *Patrick* v *Ministre des Affaires Culturelles* [1977] ECR 1199.

in *Reyners*, but because he did not hold the required French legal qualification. However, the University of Paris I had recognized his Belgian qualification as equivalent to the French qualification required by the Bar. The European Court, asked to make a preliminary ruling under Article 177, referred to the general duty derived from Article 5 of the Treaty to apply national law and practice in accordance with the objectives of the Treaty, which include freedom of establishment. Specifically, it is impermissible to restrict that freedom on the grounds of failure to possess a national diploma where the individual holds a qualification recognized by competent national authorities as equivalent to the required national diploma.[7]

Commission v *United Kingdom*[8] provides an equally clear declaration that discrimination against companies that is rooted in nationality is impermissible. The United Kingdom imposed conditions on the registration of fishing vessels. Both the legal owners and the beneficial owners had to be British nationals or companies incorporated in the United Kingdom. Where ownership was vested in a company, at least 75 per cent of the shares had to be held by British nationals or by companies that fulfilled the same requirements, and 75 per cent of the directors of the company had to be British nationals. In addition the legal and beneficial owners had to be resident and domiciled in the United Kingdom. The system was held in violation of Community law.[9]

LEGISLATIVE AND JUDICIAL AMPLIFICATION

The rights to which the migrating individual is entitled are amplified by Directive 73/148, which concerns rights of entry and residence, and runs parallel to Directive 68/360 in the field of workers.[10] Directive 75/34 confers a right to remain on terms equivalent to Regulation 1251/70,[11]

---

7 Could Thieffry have relied on Community law had he been French? Probably; see p. 611.

8 Case C-246/89 [1991] ECR I-4585 [1991] 3 CMLR 706; see also Case C-221/89 *R* v *Secretary of State, ex parte Factortame* [1991] ECR I-3905 [1991] 3 CMLR 589; Case C-93/89 *Commission* v *Ireland* [1991] ECR I-4569 [1991] 3 CMLR 697.

9 On the background generally, see Magliveras, 'Fishing in Troubled Waters: the Merchant Shipping Act 1988 and the European Community' (1990) 39 ICLQ 899; Churchill (1992) 29 CMLRev 405; Noirfalisse, 'The Community System of Fisheries Management and the *Factortame* Case' (1992) 12 YEL 325. Case C-221/89, note 8 above, a challenge initiated at national level, generated important statements about the role of national courts as protectors of Community law rights; see Ch. 6.

10 See p. 554.

11 See p. 555. See Wyatt and Dashwood, *European Community Law*, pp. 283–4, on the implications of the use of a regulation in respect of workers, but a directive in respect of the self-employed.

although the Directive applies only to those permanently established under Article 52 rather than those temporarily present in another state by virtue of Article 59. However, there is no parallel in relation to Articles 52 and 59 to Regulation 1612/68, which secures equality in employment for the worker. The Court has thus been obliged to fall back on the more general rule of non-discrimination found in Article 6, and has used this to secure equality in aspects beyond the narrowly defined right to live and work.

In *Steinhauser* v *City of Biarritz*[12] a German artist resident in Biarritz discovered that only French nationals were allowed to rent lock-ups as business premises from the local municipality. The European Court indicated clearly that this restriction violated Articles 6 and 52. In *Commission* v *Italy*[13] access to publicly funded housing and reduced-rate mortgage loans was confined to Italian nationals. In response to the Commission's view that such rules violated Article 52 and Article 59, Italy submitted that there was no restriction on either basic freedom, because the effect was merely to limit availability of a facility that would indirectly assist a migrant. The Court found Italy in violation of the Treaty. The self-employed migrant needs not only business premises, but also housing. Restrictions on access to housing and financial support obstruct the pursuit of an occupation. The Court conceded that where the individual is already established in his or her home state and is providing services in the host state for a relatively brief period, there may be no need for permanent housing. Yet some migrants stay for an extended period in the host state, so an exclusion of all non-nationals from the benefits in question amounts to an unlawful obstacle to free movement. In *Commission* v *Greece*[14] the Court confirmed that the prohibition concerns not merely rules that relate to the pursuit of the occupation, but also rules relating to matters that assist in access to or exercise of the occupation. This extended notion allowed the Court to hold that Greek rules on ownership of immovable property, which discriminated according to nationality, were contrary to Articles 52 and 59 as obstacles to the effective exercise of the freedoms guaranteed by the Treaty.[15] These decisions suggest that there will be certain social benefits that the temporary migrant cannot claim from the host state. This category will comprise those benefits more properly claimed from the state of permanent establishment. This suggests a variation in entitlements.

12 Case 197/84 [1985] ECR 1819.
13 Case 63/86 [1988] ECR 29, [1989] 2 CMLR 601.
14 Case 305/87 [1989] ECR 1461, [1991] 1 CMLR 611.
15 Exceptionally and anomalously, a Protocol on the Acquisition of Property in Denmark attached to the Maastricht Treaty amendments permits Denmark to apply existing legislation restricting the acquisition of second homes.

between short-term and long-term migrants that corresponds to a similar variation between different types of worker.[16]

EXCEPTIONS AND LIMITATIONS

Articles 55, 56 and 66 contain derogations from the principle of free movement that run parallel to those applicable to workers under Articles 48(3) and (4). Directive 64/221[17] applies not only to workers, but also to the self-employed and the recipient of services. It is clear that economic ends relating, for example, to raising revenue, cannot justify restrictions on free movement.[18] Rules must be no more restrictive than is necessary to achieve the end in view.[19] In *Reyners*[20] the Court insisted that the public-service exception be construed narrowly. It could not cover the whole legal profession simply because it impinges on the state's administration of justice. Only activities involving 'a direct and specific connexion with the exercise of official authority'[21] may be sealed off from migrants.

Article 60(1) covers services 'only in so far as they are not governed by the provisions relating to freedom of movement for goods, capital and persons'. In *Webb*[22] the Court held that a business of supplying staff is dealt with under Article 59, even though persons are involved. Similarly, a firm providing services in another member state is entitled under Article 59 to use its own employees.[23] In *Sacchi*[24] the Court held that the transmission of television signals is dealt with under Article 59 although the circulation of more tangible items, such as films and recording equipment, falls within Articles 30–36. In *Customs and Excise Commissioners* v *Schindler and Schindler*[25] the Court considered restrictions on the provision of information pertaining to participation in a lottery from the perspective of the Treaty provisions on services. The risk that such economically comparable items

16 See pp. 569–70.
17 See p. 560.
18 Art. 2(2) Dir. 64/221; Case 352/85 *Bond van Adverteerders* v *Netherlands* [1988] ECR 2085, esp. para. 34 of the judgment.
19 E.g. ibid., para. 36 of the judgment.
20 Case 2/74, note 4 above; Case C-42/92 *A. Thijssen* v *Controledienst voor de Verzekeringen*, judgment of 13 July 1993.
21 ibid., para. 54 of the judgment.
22 Case 279/80 [1981] ECR 3305, [1982] 1 CMLR 406.
23 Case C-113/89 *Rush Portuguesa* v *Office National d'Immigration* [1990] ECR I-1417, noted by Gormley (1992) 17 ELRev 63. See also Case C-43/93 *Van der Elst* v *Office des Migrations Internationales* [1994] ECR I-3803.
24 Case 155/73 [1974] ECR 409, [1974] 2 CMLR 177. See also Case 52/79 *Procureur du Roi* v *Debauve* [1980] ECR 833.
25 Case C-275/92 [1994] ECR I-1039; see further p. 591 below.

may be subject to divergent legal rules is diminished by the similarities that may be observed between the several provisions concerned to liberate the factors of production within the common market. In Articles 30, 48, 52, 59 and 95, *inter alia*, the prohibition on discrimination is a common thread; so, too, the narrow interpretation of derogations from the fundamental principle of free movement. The Court has also devised an approach to non-discriminatory but protectionist technical barriers to trade that is broadly applicable throughout Community trade law. The *Cassis de Dijon* principle has been transplanted from the law relating to goods to that relating to services.[26]

The prohibition on discrimination applies only within the scope of Community law. Sport may be an economic activity, but in *Walrave and Koch* v *Union Cycliste Internationale*[27] the Court refused to hold discrimination that is based on considerations of purely sporting interest to be subject to Community law. Selection for a national representative team is made on the basis of factors that do not fall within the sphere of economic activity envisaged by Article 2 of the Treaty. The litigation in *Society for the Protection of Unborn Children* v *Grogan*[28] arose against the background of the right to life of the unborn child enshrined in Article 40.3.3 of the Constitution of Ireland. The Court examined a ban imposed under Irish law on the distribution by a students' association of information about the availability of abortions in the United Kingdom. Although the Court was prepared to accept that the provision of abortion services is an economic activity, this could not assist the students' association, because its interest in spreading the information was not commercial. It was acting purely gratuitously and it had no link with the provider of the service. The legal perspective would have been different had a challenge to the ban on advertising been launched by a supplier of abortion services or even by the association having accepted payment from a supplier for an advertisement. In such circumstances the commercial element would have brought the matter within the scope of Community law.[29] It would then have been necessary to balance the impact of Community law of market integration against the capacity of a state to defend its own legally protected standards of morality.[30] In order to secure the primacy of the latter, a protocol to the

---

26 See p. 494. See also p. 591 on the similar treatment of intellectual property rights under Arts. 30 and 59.
27 Case 36/74 [1974] ECR 1405, [1975] 1 CMLR 320. See also Case 13/76 *Dona* v *Mantero* [1976] ECR 1333, [1976] 2 CMLR 578.
28 Case C-159/90 [1991] ECR I-4685 [1991] 3 CMLR 849.
29 For discussion, see refs. in Select Further Reading, p. 909.
30 AG Van Gerven in Case C-159/90 took this approach and would have upheld the Irish rules. See further p. 586 below on the Court's approach to justifying rules that restrict trade.

Maastricht Treaty amendments declared that Community law should not 'affect the application in Ireland of Article 40.3.3 of the Constitution of Ireland'. However, the Irish Government quickly sought, unsuccessfully, to amend the protocol in order to make it clear that it did not wish to prevent Irish citizens leaving Ireland in order to receive abortion services in another member state. This followed controversial proceedings initiated by the Irish Attorney-General to restrain a young woman from leaving Ireland in order to secure termination of her pregnancy. It was submitted that she had a Community law right to travel. The matter was decided in the woman's favour by the Irish Supreme Court on a point of purely domestic constitutional law. The Irish Government indicated its intention to hold a referendum on changing the constitution in order to avoid the referendum on the acceptance of the Maastricht Treaty amendments becoming a test of feeling on the issue of abortion. The Irish people voted in favour of the Maastricht amendments in June 1992. A referendum on the abortion issue in December 1992 approved the right to travel. Moreover, although the protocol remains in place, a solemn declaration records Ireland's intent to respect the right to travel within the Community.[31]

The absence of commercial motivation means that state education is not considered as a service within Article 59, although the student is not unaffected by Community law.[32] A general matter that falls outside Community competence is 'reverse discrimination', discrimination by a state against its own nationals. The Court views such treatment as unaffected by Community law because there is no impact on interstate trade patterns.[33]

LEGAL PERSONS

As demonstrated by *Commission* v *United Kingdom*,[34] the rule against discrimination applies equally in principle whether a natural or a legal person wishes to secure establishment or provide services in another member state. Article 58 includes as beneficiaries of these provisions companies or firms constituted under the civil or commercial law of a member state and other legal persons governed by public or private law,

---

31 See refs. under Select Further Reading, p. 909 below. Findings of violation of Art. 10 of the European Convention on Human Rights have also prompted law reform in Ireland; *Open Door and Dublin Well Woman* v *Ireland* (Case No 64/1991/316/387–388).
32 See p. 605.
33 See further, p. 609.
34 Case C-246/89, note 8 above. See also Case C-330/91 *R* v *Inland Revenue Commissioners, ex parte Commerzbank AG*, judgment of 13 July 1993.

except those that are non-profit-making.[35] Thus, national rules relating to the conduct of companies are susceptible to challenge as barriers to trade where they discriminate on grounds of nationality. Companies are entitled to set up branches or subsidiaries in other member states on the same terms as those that apply to nationals or companies in that state. However, company law remains in many important respects the preserve of national law, and the Court has shown more caution in applying the rules of freedom of establishment in favour of legal persons than natural persons.

This may be illustrated by the ruling made in Article 177 proceedings in *R v HM Treasury, ex parte Daily Mail*.[36] The *Daily Mail* wished to move its residence from the United Kingdom to the Netherlands in order to obtain tax advantages. It submitted that Article 52 entitled it to carry out this move without having to obtain Treasury consent, which was required under British tax legislation. The European Court confirmed that freedom of establishment is a fundamental principle of the Community; that Article 52 is directly effective; that it covers companies within the meaning of Article 58 that wish to establish subsidiaries in other member states; and that it applies to restrictions on migration out of, as well as into, member states. However, the Court denied the existence of a precise parallel between natural and legal persons. 'Companies are creatures of law and, in the present state of Community law, creatures of national law.'[37] They are consequently subject to different rules in different states and, specifically, Community law as yet leaves untouched rules controlling transfers of the type planned by the *Daily Mail*. The Court concluded that Article 52 does not confer 'on companies incorporated under the law of a Member State a right to transfer their central management and control and their central administration to another Member State while retaining their status as companies incorporated under the legislation of the first Member State'.[38] The Court added to its rejection of the newspaper's case by refusing to hold that Directive 73/148 offers rights to legal, as well as natural, persons.

---

35 Art. 66 ensures the parallel application of Art. 58 in the sphere of the provision of services.
36 Case 81/87 [1988] ECR 5483, noted by Lever (1989) 26 CMLRev 327.
37 ibid., para. 19 of the judgment.
38 ibid., para. 24 of the judgment.

BEYOND DISCRIMINATION

Important though the suppression of discrimination is, the provisions examined above are inadequate to achieve a common market.

THE MARKET PARTITIONING IMPACT OF ARTICLES 52(2) AND 60(3)

Where a national of state B has a qualification issued in state B that is not recognized by state A as equivalent to its own requirements, free movement is frustrated. The Treaty seems to envisage that in these circumstances the migrant will not be entitled to free access to state A's labour market. Article 52(2) permits freedom of establishment 'under the conditions laid down for its own nationals by the law of the country where such establishment is effected'. The same notion appears in Article 60(3) in relation to the conditions on which services may be supplied. These provisos appear to leave the substance of market regulation in the hands of the national authorities. Although *Reyners*[39] and *Thieffry*[40] demonstrate that it is possible to combat any taint of discrimination, Article 52(2) indicates that there would have been no remedy for Thieffry in the absence of the university's recognition of the equivalence of his qualifications. Aside from such special circumstances, Articles 52(2) and 60(3) seem to envisage a migrant requalifying from scratch in each state where he or she wishes to work, which in practice would rule out cross-border migration, at least until the adoption of common Community rules governing qualifications.[41] This occurred in *Ministère Public* v *Auer*,[42] where the holder of an Italian veterinary medical qualification that had not been recognized as equivalent to French requirements was lawfully excluded from the French market as inadequately qualified. Precisely the same difficulty arises as a result of the existence of divergent rules of professional ethics between states and, more generally, because of variations between company law regimes, which, although non-discriminatory on grounds of nationality, none the less act as a serious impediment to access to the market of another member state. For example, a company may possess adequate capital to provide a service in

39 Case 2/74, note 4 above.
40 Case 71/76, note 6 above.
41 Examined at p. 596.
42 Case 136/78 [1979] ECR 437. See also Case C-61/89 *Bouchoucha* [1990] ECR I-3551; Case C-319/92 *Salomone Haim* v *KVN* [1994] ECR I-425.

its home state, but may find itself unable to provide the same service in another member state because its financial structure fails to meet the regulatory expectations of the target state. The result is the fragmentation of the common market, yet it is a result that seems to be envisaged by Articles 52(2) and 60(3).

Articles 52(2) and 60(3) hinder free movement, but respect national regulatory competence in important fields such as professional qualifications and standards. In other areas of the law of market integration the Court's boldest extension of the rules has come in its insistence that even non-discriminatory national rules that restrict free movement may fall foul of Community law. This will be recalled as the *Cassis de Dijon* jurisprudence arising out of Article 30 in relation to the free movement of goods.[43] There the Court held that national technical and administrative rules that cause barriers to free trade as a result of diversity between states require justification under Community law. In principle this approach is capable of application to Articles 52 and 59, which would mean that the object of national rules would have to be explained and their aptitude to achieve that end demonstrated. Articles 52(2) and 60(3) would remain in place, but national regulatory rules that exert a protectionist effect in favour of the domestic market would have to be balanced against the demands of market liberalization. They would require justification on grounds recognized by Community law.

The Court *has* accepted a *Cassis*-style analysis in examining the compatibility with Community law of national regulatory rules that partition the market. However, its precise impact is difficult to define. It will be recalled that a major drawback to the *Cassis de Dijon* formula is its unpredictable development through the accidents of litigation. The same holds true in this area. It seems that the arguments of market liberalization are likely to be more powerful where a given national rule obstructs the free movement of services rather than where it affects establishment. This seems to be attributable to the fact that the provider of services has a more transient presence in the host state and therefore should be more lightly regulated therein. The state of permanent establishment is normally taken as the primary regulator. However, examination of the Court's jurisprudence is called for in order to elucidate the nature of its approach.

43 See Ch. 17.

VAN BINSBERGEN: A PARALLEL WITH CASSIS DE DIJON

In 1974 the Court established in *Van Binsbergen v Bestuur van de Bedrijfsvernig-ing voor de Metaalnijverheid*[44] a method for subjecting national regulatory rules to the scrutiny of Community law of market integration. Only persons established in the Netherlands could act as legal representatives or advisers before Dutch social service courts. Van Binsbergen's adviser, a Dutch national, complied with this requirement at the commencement of proceedings, but on moving to Belgium was told that he was now ineligible. The exclusion was challenged as contrary to Articles 59 and 60, and an Article 177 preliminary reference was made to the European Court. The Court held that a requirement of a link between the place of permanent establishment and the place where services are provided runs contrary to the basic objective of Article 59. In fact, such a requirement would effectively transform the right to provide services into the mere right of establishment. However, there is no breach if the rule is 'objectively justified by the need to ensure observance of professional rules of conduct connected, in particular, with the administration of justice and with respect for professional ethics'.[45] The Dutch rule, which hindered transfrontier movement of services, had to be shown to be justified by the general good. The referring national court must also assess whether the objective could be attained by methods less restrictive of trade – the principles of proportionality and of alternative means.[46] On the facts of the case it was suggested that it might be possible to secure adequate supervision by requiring lawyers to have an address for service in the Netherlands, without imposing on them the more onerous requirement of permanent establishment in the Netherlands. As suggested above, the approach taken in *Van Binsbergen* is similar to the approach adopted by the Court in *Cassis de Dijon* in relation to technical barriers to the free circulation of goods within the Community, although it predates it by several years. Directive 77/249 elaborated some of these principles in relation to lawyers. In *Commission v Germany*[47] German rules requiring lawyers from other member states who provided services to clients in Germany to work in conjunction with a German lawyer were held in several respects to violate the Directive and Article 59.

Since *Van Binsbergen* the Court has taken the opportunity to refine its use of Article 59 in this area. The enforceability of national regulations that

44 Case 33/74, note 2 above.
45 ibid., para. 14 of the judgment.
46 See p. 455 in relation to Arts. 30, 36.
47 Case 427/85 [1988] ECR 1123, [1989] 2 CMLR 677.

impede the provision of services across borders is dependent on the state's ability to demonstrate overriding concerns in the public interest, which cannot be met by means less restrictive of trade. This applies to rules based on requirements of residence and establishment, as in *Van Binsbergen*, which are in a sense indirectly discriminatory on grounds of nationality, and also to genuinely even-handed rules that tend to partition the market simply because of diversity between national regimes. Both types of rule require an objective/public-interest justification. The approach has been elucidated through case law. Selected illustrations of the application of Article 59 follow, before a contrast is drawn with the rather less intrusive approach of the Court with respect to non-discriminatory technical rules that inhibit the freedom of establishment guaranteed by Article 52.

It must always be remembered that public-interest arguments of this nature can be advanced only where the rules do not discriminate directly on grounds of nationality.[48] Such discrimination restricts the availability of justification to the narrowly defined provisions of Articles 55, 56 and 66.[49]

THE COURT'S JURISPRUDENCE SINCE *VAN BINSBERGEN*

In *Coenen*[50] a Dutch national resident in Belgium was prevented from pursuing activities as an insurance broker in the Netherlands because he was not resident there. The Court pointed out that such a rule has an effect incompatible with the purpose of Article 59, which is to remove the requirement of a link between the place of establishment and the place where the service is provided. However, the Court admitted, as it had in *Van Binsbergen*, that a member state may adopt measures of control to prevent a person leaving state A for state B but directing his or her activities at state A and thereby avoiding state A's professional rules. The provision of services can be regulated, as Article 60(3) envisages. However, the controls must not discriminate on grounds of nationality; they must serve the public interest and they must be proportionate. The Court declared that a 'requirement of residence in the territory of the State where the service is provided can only be allowed as an exception where the Member State is unable to apply other, less restrictive, measures to ensure

---

48 See Case 352/85, note 18 above, noted by Blois (1990) 27 CMLRev 371 (rules prohibiting cable broadcasters from outside the Netherlands from using specified forms of advertising and subtitling held unlawful). See also Case C-17/92 *Federación de Distribuidores Cinematográficos* v *Estado Español*, judgment of 4 May 1993.
49 See p. 579.
50 Case 39/75 [1975] ECR 1547.

respect for those rules'.[51] The Court pointed out that where the provider has a place of business in the host state, the state normally has the capacity to supervise it and an additional requirement of permanent residence would accordingly be unlawful.

In *Webb*[52] a British national was engaged in supplying temporary staff to firms in the Netherlands. Under Dutch law he required a licence in order to provide such a service. Webb did not hold a Dutch licence and was the subject of criminal proceedings instituted by the Dutch authorities. He relied on his right to provide the service under Article 59 to defeat the charge. The Court took the view that a licensing control might be appropriate in view of the sensitive nature of the activity in question, which has not only economic implications but also social consequences for the individual staff concerned. However, that control must not be tainted by discrimination on grounds of the nationality of the provider or with respect to place of establishment. Moreover, the principles of proportionality and alternative means apply, which specifically require a state to 'take into account the evidence and guarantees already furnished by the provider of the services for the pursuit of his activities in the Member State of his establishment'.[53] Thus, where a supplier is shown to be subject to adequate supervision in its home state, the state in which it provides services is not entitled to subject it to extra, unnecessary controls.[54] This is an aspect of the duty to cooperate in the reduction of barriers to free trade that ultimately derives from Article 5 of the Treaty.[55]

Exhaustive exploration of the Court's jurisprudence would not be profitable. It is more important to extract recurrent themes from the Court's judgments, such as the central role played by the principle of proportionality. However, *Commission* v *Germany*[56] deserves attention as a fine example of the Court's typical approach. The case was one of four instituted by the Commission under Article 169 against member states in respect of national regulation of the insurance industry. The discussion below selects aspects of the decision in the action brought against Germany as a means of elaborating the development of the approach introduced in *Van Binsbergen*.[57]

51 ibid., para. 9 of the judgment. See also Case C-106/91 *C. Ramrath* v *Ministre de la Justice* [1992] ECR I-3351.
52 Case 279/80, note 22 above.
53 ibid., para. 20 of the judgment.
54 See also Cases 110 and 111/78, note 5 above; Case C-113/89, Case C-43/93, note 23 above.
55 See p. 594; and p. 471 in relation to Art. 30 EC.
56 Case 205/84 [1986] ECR 3755, [1987] 1 CMLR 69.
57 For comprehensive examination, see Edward, 'Establishment and Services: An Analysis of the Insurance Cases' (1987) 12 ELRev 231. Also Hodgin (1987) 24 CMLRev 273; and, more generally, Van Empel, 'The Visible Hand in Invisible Trade' [1990/2] LIEI 23.

Some, but not all, of the German rules regulating the conduct of insurance businesses were held to violate Article 59. The judgment has had a significant impact in reducing the obstacles faced by firms wishing to supply insurance services across borders. The liberalization of the market has increased the stimulus of competition. One of several matters examined by the Court was regulation of insurance cover in respect of risks situated in a member state in favour of a policyholder established or resident in that state provided by an insurer established in another member state that maintains no permanent presence in the policyholder's state and does not direct its business entirely or principally towards the territory of that state. The question whether a state can regulate such a provider of services is an important one, for provision of services in this manner is becoming technologically increasingly feasible, especially in the field of financial services. It is a market that is capable of rendering physical frontiers irrelevant. German law required insurers in these circumstances to be both authorized and established in Germany. This clearly restricted the ability of non-German insurers to operate in Germany. The Commission's challenge to the German rules was firmly supported by the United Kingdom, whose financial services industry is particularly strong and stands to gain much from the liberalization of markets in other member states.

The Court confirmed that national regulation applied to permanently established firms may not necessarily also be applied to temporary activities of firms established in other states. It also deduced from its existing case law that regulation that has the effect of restricting the free movement of services may be lawful where objectively justified by the general good, taking account of the protection offered by regulatory controls exercised in the state of establishment of the supplier. It then subjected the German requirements of establishment and authorization to this test. It began by acknowledging the sensitive nature of the insurance sector and the need to protect the consumer as policyholder, who will be severely prejudiced if on the occurrence of the claimable event payment is not forthcoming. The Court accepted that the need to impose conditions on insurance firms relating, for example, to available resources and methods of supervision was made out. The next issue was whether the protection was already secured by the state of establishment; if so, further controls in the state of supply could not be permitted. There had already been some Community legislative action in the field, but the Court did not find it adequate to secure the comprehensive level of protection for which a state was entitled to aim. The Court accepted the German submission that in the light of the diversity between national rules in this area a state remained entitled to lay down rules for ·services supplied in its territory, to the extent that such rules were necessary to achieve protection. The Court then examined the particular controls in question. It agreed with Germany that the authorization procedure was necessary in order to ensure effective supervision of insurers, although the Court insisted that the system must be administered with due regard for controls already performed in the state of establishment. The Court also added that the authorization procedure might not be justified in every sector of the insurance industry. It stated that it lacked the information to develop those observations in more specific fashion,[58] but clearly the Court was once again drawing attention to the demands of the principle of proportionality.

The Court reached a significantly different conclusion in respect of the requirement of establishment. As the Court pointed out, this is a much more serious impediment to market flexibility. It is hostile to the basic idea of Article 59, and a state bears a heavy burden in seeking to justify such a rule. Here Germany submitted that authorization alone was inadequate to secure effective protection. The Court was not persuaded. It took the view that a state was able to verify the presence of assets and inspect accounts and other such documents in the context of an authorization procedure, which would be sufficient to achieve protection, and which could be done without the added requirement of permanent establishment.

The decision establishes that disproportionate national rules will be incompatible with Community law, but it does not sweep away all national market regulation that may impede the completion of the common market. This may be seen as an undesirable restriction on modern commercial practice, which is increasingly international,[59] yet the Court's decision reflects the terms of Article 2 to the effect that free trade is not the Community's only goal. The decision respects the need to retain protection of the individual consumer and investor. The decision invites Community legislative action to advance the integration of the market through the adoption of common protective rules.[59a]

The decision in *Commission* v *Germany*[60] also invites litigation, before both the European Court and national tribunals, as a means of establishing the enforceability of specific national rules. Accordingly, the list of cases in which the Court has applied a *Cassis*-style approach to its interpretation of Article 59 continues to grow. In three cases in 1991 concerned with licensing requirements imposed on tour guides the Court was unable to find any link between the rules in question and their declared object of securing the effective dissemination of knowledge.[61] They were inapt to

---

58 The UK had submitted that protective rules cannot be justified in the field of commercial insurance, given the nature of the parties involved.
59 See especially Edward (1987) 12 ELRev 231, 252–5.
59a Developments are outlined at p. 597 below.
60 Case 205/84, note 56 above.
61 Cases C-154/89, C-180/89 and C-198/89 *Commission* v *France, Italy, Greece* [1991] ECR I-659, 709, 727. See also Case C-375/92 *Commission* v *Spain* [1994] ECR I-923.

achieve the end in view and consequently did not serve the public interest. They were unlawful obstacles to the freedom to supply services. The ruling released the market for tour guides from the grip of state direction and allowed the development of a competitive market for organized tours in which consumers could make their own choices about the type of guide required. Appreciation of this function locates Article 59 at the core of the process of building an integrated, competitive market.[62] *Säger* v *Dennemeyer* represents one of the Court's clearest expressions of the use of the deregulatory influence of the *Cassis de Dijon* principle in the services sector in parallel to its application to laws affecting product market integration.[63] Dennemeyer, a company registered in the United Kingdom, found that its business of providing patent renewal services was hindered in Germany by licensing requirements. Although the rules did not discriminate according to nationality, they hindered Dennemeyer's access to the German market and, in effect, they protected German-based suppliers of such services from competition. These are the symptoms of market partitioning caused by disparity between national rules in line with *Cassis de Dijon*.

The Court considered that the rules could be applied against Dennemeyer only where they were shown to be justified by 'imperative reasons relating to the public interest' and where the restrictive effect was no more severe than necessary to achieve the objective pursued. This involved demonstration that the concern underlying the rules was not adequately addressed by the regulatory system of the state of establishment of the service provider. The objective of the German rules was the protection of consumers from harm that could be inflicted by inadequately qualified advisers, but the German licensing system went beyond what was necessary to achieve this objective. The Court commented that Dennemeyer provided services 'essentially of a straightforward nature'. The restriction on trade was disproportionate and the rule fell foul of Article 59. The market was liberalized.

In line with the *Cassis de Dijon* formula, the ruling leaves open the possibility that justification for restrictive rules may successfully be advanced by a regulating state. The more profound the harm to which the consumer may be exposed, the stronger the state's justification for exercising regulatory control over the supplier. However, only in exceptional circumstances will the Court uphold national rules that require establishment as a precondition of activity on the national market. The Court remains alive to the economic damage to the process of market integration

---

62 This is the Commission's strong message in its summary of the Court's case law, *Commission interpretative communication concerning the free movement of services across frontiers* OJ 1993 C334/3.
63 Case C-76/90 [1991] ECR I-4221.

that would be wrought by conversion of the flexible Article 59 right to provide services into the Article 52 right of establishment.

An unusual case where the Court accepted the maintenance of restrictions on cross-border services is *Customs and Excise Commissioners* v *Schindler and Schindler*.[64] The Schindlers, acting as agents for a German lottery promoter, had sent advertisements and application forms from the Netherlands to the United Kingdom. These items were seized by the Commissioners under statutory powers connected with the British policy of suppressing large-scale lotteries irrespective of the nationality of the organizer or the member state where they originated. The European Court, to which an Article 177 reference was made, accepted that the facts disclosed a restriction on the provision of cross-border services within the meaning of Article 59.[65] However, it considered the rules justifiable as contributions to a range of public interests. The laws contributed to the prevention of crime; they served to ensure the honest treatment of gamblers; they forestalled a stimulation of gambling habits; they focused the operation of permitted lotteries on charitable, sporting and cultural purposes. The judgment mentions explicitly that it is dealing with the non-discriminatory situation prior to the 1993 Act that authorized the establishment of the National Lottery. The Court concluded that the controls were capable of justification 'in the light of the specific social and cultural features of each Member State, to maintain order in society'.[66] *Schindler* confirms that Community trade law does not automatically and inevitably cause the deregulation of national markets.

INTELLECTUAL PROPERTY RIGHTS

It should also be noted that in *Coditel* v *Ciné Vog*[67] the Court accepted that the free movement of services may be permissibly restricted through the exercise of national intellectual property rights. The matter arose in connection with the transmission of a film by cable broadcast from one

---

64 Case C-275/92 [1994] ECR I-1039, noted by Gormley (1994) 19 ELRev 642.
65 On the facts of the case, the Court saw no need to address the question of whether the approach to Art. 30 adopted in Cases C-267 and 268/91 *Keck and Mithouard*, Ch. 17 p. 536, also applies to Art. 59. It is submitted that it should. See now Case C-384/93 *Alpine Investments BV* v *Minister van Financien* [1995] All ER(EC)543.
66 Cf. Case C-353/89 *Commission* v *Netherlands* [1991] ECR I-4069; protection of cultural diversity may justify national rules that have the effect of partitioning the market (but not on the facts); Case C-23/93 *TV10 SA* v *Commissariaat voor de Media* [1994] ECR I-4795. Cf. AG Van Gerven in Case C-159/90, note 28, who, in contrast to the Court's approach, would have upheld the Irish rules despite their obstructive effect on trade.
67 Case 62/79 [1980] ECR 881.

member state to another, where rights over the film held by a third party in the receiving state were protected by law. The Court accepted that such cross-border trade may be restrained by the right holder. It is desirable that the approach taken to intellectual property rights that act as obstacles to the free movement of services should run parallel to that applicable in the field of the free movement of goods despite the absence of any exception under Articles 59–66 that is in the same terms as Article 36's reference to intellectual property rights.[68] The Court has secured this parallel interpretation.[69]

APPLICATION TO ARTICLE 52

The Court's model requires a state to demonstrate a justification recognized by Community law for rules that inhibit free movement, and then to satisfy the proportionality principle. The nature of the public-interest/rule-of-reason justification will depend on the circumstances of the case. The categories are not closed.[70] Providers of services cross borders temporarily or even, as *Commission* v *Germany*[71] shows, not at all. The imposition of national regulation on persons who are temporarily crossing borders while retaining establishment in another state to the same degree as on those permanently established in a state may be seen as disproportionate.[72] This will not always be so; in some cases the nature of the service will require control however it is provided. But, as a general principle, a state must take account of the proportionality principle in exercising its jurisdiction to regulate the market.

This suggests that challenges to non-discriminatory national rules that inhibit establishment are less likely to meet with success than challenges to obstacles to the provision of services. In fact, there are relatively few examples of the development of a *Cassis*-style approach to Article 52.[73] *Ordre des Avocats au Barreau de Paris* v *Klopp*[74] may provide one example. Klopp, a German national resident and a member of the Bar in Düsseldorf, was rejected by the Paris Bar, where he wished to set up a secondary

68 Kapteyn and Verloren van Themaat, *Law of the European Communities*, p. 450; Goyder, *EC Competition Law*, pp. 331–2.
69 The matter is explained more fully in Ch. 26.
70 See discussion by Arnull, *EEC Law and the Individual*, pp. 82–92.
71 Case 205/84, note 56 above.
72 See, e.g., para. 16 of the judgement in Case 279/80, note 22 above; also discussion by Lonbay, 'Picking over the Bones: Rights of Establishment Reviewed' (1991) 16 ELRev 507.
73 See Arnull, *EEC Law and the Individual*, pp. 73–9.
74 Case 107/83 [1984] ECR 2971.

establishment. Under the Bar rules an *avocat* had to establish chambers in one place only, which must be within the territorial jurisdiction of the regional court with which he or she is registered. The European Court held that Article 52 envisages a freedom to establish more than one place of work in the Community and, in response to the French arguments in support of the restriction that it was objectively necessary in the public interest to ensure a lawyer is readily available to court and clients, it pointed out that 'modern methods of transport and telecommunications'[75] permit such contact and that the host state is in any event entitled to apply its rules of professional ethics to the migrant. This is the familiar language of proportionality and the principle of alternative means. The Court's Article 59 ruling in *Van Binsbergen*[76] was referred to in *Klopp*, and it is possible that that approach by analogy may in future increase in importance as a means of reducing the market partitioning effect of Article 52(2).[77]

Even if a *Cassis*-style approach is introduced in relation to Article 52, many non-discriminatory national controls over establishment will be justifiable, thus maintaining barriers to trade.[78] The Court is likely to be wary of actively curtailing the scope of legitimate national regulatory measures designed to serve the public interest in order to avoid 'the chaotic-seeming spectre of crazy deregulation by virtue of Article 52'.[79] In *Gullung* v *Conseils de l'Ordre des Avocats*[80] a lawyer registered in Germany was refused admission to the French Bar for reasons relating to his character. The French requirement of registration at the Bar of the host state constituted an impediment to his ability to practise in France. The Court referred to Article 52(2) and observed that a member state is in principle free to regulate the exercise of the legal profession on its territory. Since all lawyers had to be registered to practise in France there was no discrimination and the rules were lawful. The Court remarked that the registration requirement 'seeks to ensure the observance of moral and ethical principles and the disciplinary control of the activity of lawyers and

---

75 Para. 21 of the judgment. The same point was made in relation to strict German rules controlling the provision of legal services by non-nationals in Case 427/85, note 47 above. See also Case C-351/90 *Commission* v *Luxembourg*, judgment of 16 June 1992, [1992] 3 CMLR 124.

76 Case 33/74, note 2 above.

77 Lonbay views its absence from the judgment in *Bouchoucha* (Case C-61/89, note 42 above) as 'bizarre', (1991) 16 ELRev 507, 509.

78 See Case 182/83 *Fearon* [1984] ECR 3677, in which the Court accepted that differentiation according to residence may be objectively justified and therefore compatible with Art. 52, even where it leads to indirect discrimination based on nationality. Contrast, however, the UK's unlawful rules in the *Factortame* saga, Cases C-221/89, C-246/89, note 8 above.

79 Lonbay (1991) 16 ELRev 507, 510.

80 Case 292/86 [1988] ECR 111.

thus pursues an objective worthy of protection'.[81] This observation was not made explicitly in terms of the *Cassis de Dijon* formula, but, adopting that approach to trade barriers, it seems probable that the rule is justifiable as a means necessary to protect the public interest. From this perspective, rules designed to ensure high standards of health protection, such as medical qualifications, are even more likely to remain untouched by the Court.[82]

It is submitted that little of principle turns on the formal categorization of an activity under either Article 52 or Article 59. The margin between establishment and provision of services is frequently ill-defined; consider, for example, the opera director spending a season lasting several months in another member state. Much the same comment may be made about the grey areas that lie between Articles 30 and 59; consider, for example, an instructor who visits other member states to teach courses of aerobic exercises with the assistance of video cassettes, which are then sold. In assessing the validity of national regulatory measures under the general principles of Community trade law, the key consideration is not the specific Treaty provision, but rather the balance between the ends served by those national rules coupled to the means used weighed against the impact of the rules on the process of market integration.

THE ROLE OF ARTICLE 5

Article 5 of the Treaty provides a potentially important instrument in deepening the market-integrative thrust of the law under both Articles 52 and 59. Article 5 had already been used by the Court in *Thieffry*[83] to require the application of national law and practice in accordance with the objectives of the Treaty, which include freedom of establishment. This secured free movement for those whose qualifications had been recognized as equivalent. More recent decisions assist in the procedure of actually obtaining that recognition of equivalence. *UNECTEF* v *Heylens*[84] involved a football trainer relying on Article 48, but the Court cited *Thieffry* and clearly considered that it was expressing a principle of general application. Heylens had applied to the French authorities to have his Belgian

---

81 ibid., para. 29 of the judgment.
82 See, e.g., the opinion of AG Darmon in *Bouchoucha*, Case C-61/89, note 42 above; and see p. 466 in relation to Art. 30. See also Case C-55/93 *Criminal Proceedings against Johannis Gerrit Cornelis van Schaik* [1994] ECR I-4837 (road safety as justification for restriction on use of out-of-state garages to issue test certificates).
83 Case 71/76, note 6 above.
84 Case 222/86 *Union Nationale des Entraîneurs et Cadres Techniques Professionels du Football* [*UNECTEF*] v *Heylens* [1987] ECR 4097.

diploma recognized as equivalent to the corresponding French qualification, but was rejected without reasons being given. The Court used Article 5 as the basis for imposing a duty to assess equivalence and as the foundation for a remedy of a judicial nature where the individual is refused the benefit of the claimed right. The imposition of a duty to give reasons for refusal is an essential element in securing that effective protection.

Vlassopoulou v *Ministerium für Justiz, Bundes- und Europaangelegenheiten Baden-Württemberg*[85] involved a Greek lawyer wishing to become established in Germany. Under German rules she was inadequately qualified. The Court insisted that the German authorities must cooperate with the Greek authorities in reviewing the adequacy of Vlassopoulou's Greek qualifications. This 'duty of good administration' is derived from Article 5 of the Treaty and runs parallel to the approach taken in the field of the free movement of goods, where cooperation in checking the safety of goods is demanded by the Court.[86] Requiring states to work together is likely to improve the integration of the market for legal services and also improves the position of individuals such as Vlassopoulou. Once again, this reflects the familiar twin thrust of the rules dealing with the free movement of labour.

The law has progressed beyond *Thieffry*, where recognition of equivalence had already occurred. Even in the absence of such recognition, a state must make inquiries of the adequacy of the migrant's qualifications. It must support its decision with reasons. The decision in *Vlassopoulou* follows *Klopp*[87] in tentatively suggesting that a *Cassis*-style approach should then be applied to the national rules. If the object is met by the home state's qualifications, then that should suffice to guarantee access to the market of the host state. The Court has not robbed the state of the basic power to exclude a migrant from its market as inadequately qualified, but it has developed the law in such a way that adequacy of qualifications must be assessed, the reasons for perceived inadequacy must be laid bare and they must be subject to the possibility of challenge.[88] The decision in *Vlassopoulou* may reflect a feeling that the *Cassis* approach to equivalence between differently achieved qualifications is on its own perilous in this field, because of judicial inability to make such assessments. It is wiser and less controversial to hand over the duty of inquiry to administrative

---

85 Case C-340/89, [1991] ECR I-2357), noted by Lonbay (1991) 16 ELRev 507, 511.
86 See p. 471 above.
87 Case 107/83, note 74 above.
88 Cf. Case C-19/92 *Kraus* v *Land Baden-Württemberg*, judgment of 31 March 1993, noted by Smith (1994) 19 ELRev 67; Case C-319/92, note 42 above; Case C-375/92, note 61 above.

authorities. *Heylens* and *Vlassopoulou* undermine the market partitioning effect of Article 52(2) by a more subtle route and in this field are perhaps more effective than the simple judicially applied *Cassis* approach. In the market for legal services the eventual outcome is hard to predict given the immense variety of traditions in the legal professions of the member states.[89]

THE FUNCTION OF LEGISLATION

The Court's jurisprudence shows that the rule of non-discrimination applies in advance of legislative action (*Reyners*,[90] *Van Binsbergen*,[91] *Van Wesemael*[92]) and that an act of recognition by competent authorities similarly triggers rights of free movement in advance of legislative action (*Thieffry*).[93] The Court has also extended the impact of the law into the field of national standards that act as obstacles to trade even in the absence of discrimination on grounds of nationality (*Van Binsbergen*).[94]

In the context of the free movement of goods *Cassis de Dijon* has long been seen as a welcome boost to the market integrative process in an area where legislation was not forthcoming due to a legislative log-jam and where legislation would have been undesirable in any event as an inhibition on national tradition.[95] The same favourable response is to some extent also deserved in the wake of the parallel jurisprudence applicable to persons and services. Yet both in relation to the problems of comparing the substance of national systems of qualifications and in relation to the procedural complexity of comparing national administrative practices[96] it may be that legislative support is needed in order to clarify the law. More generally, Articles 52(2), 60(3) and cases such as *Auer*[97] and *Commission* v *Germany*, concerning insurance[98] plainly indicate that in some areas national barriers to trade remain lawful and in such areas the market can be integrated only through a legislative initiative.

---

89 See discussion by Lonbay (1991) 16 ELRev 507, and, more generally, Donald-Little (ed.), *Cross-Border Practice Compendium.*
90 Case 2/74, note 4 above.
91 Case 33/74, note 2 above.
92 Cases 110, 111/78, note 5 above.
93 Case 71/76, note 6 above.
94 Case 33/74, note 2 above, and pp. 583-94.
95 See Ch. 17.
96 In relation to Art. 30, see pp. 471, 526 above.
97 Case 136/78, note 42 above.
98 Case 205/84, note 56 above.

THE GENERAL PROGRAMME AND SPECIFIC DIRECTIVES

There is, then, a role for the legislature. In Articles 53 and 63(1) the Treaty envisaged the adoption of general programmes, and in Articles 57 and 63(2), the adoption of directives. The former occurred in 1961 and there has been a string of the latter. The general programmes are policy statements.[99] They are not legislation as such, but the Court has often used them as an aid to interpretation.[100]

Great effort has been invested in the adoption of directives and there has been progress in liberalizing the market in relation to a number of particular professions.[101] The first *Ministère Public* v *Auer* case[102] had a sequel involving the same parties.[103] In 1978 directives were adopted by the Community relating to the taking up of the profession of veterinary surgeon. Under the terms of the directives Auer's Italian qualifications were adequate to allow him to practise throughout the Community. It was accordingly no longer permissible to bar him from the French market. The Community directives had occupied the field, thereby replacing divergent national standards. France had failed to implement the directives in time, but Auer, as a duly qualified migrant, was entitled to rely on them to secure access to the market of the host state by virtue of the principle of direct effect. Thus, once the Community has fixed standards by legislation, member states are no longer entitled to oppose freedom of establishment by applying stricter rules.[104] This is the normal principle of Community harmonization law designed to further the process of market integration.[105]

THE 'NEW APPROACH'

However, the process of fixing uniform terms for qualification requirements in tens, even hundreds, of different professions proved laborious, if

---

99 OJ 1974 Sp. Edn. 2nd Series IX pp. 3, 7.
100 E.g., Case 136/78, note 42 above; Case 63/86, note 13 above.
101 The list of directives is long; see e.g., Dirs. 80/154 OJ 1980 L33/1, 80/155 OJ 1980 L33/8 (midwives); Dir. 82/489 OJ 1982 L218/24 (hairdressers); Dir. 85/384 OJ 1985 L223/15 (architects). On lawyers, see Dir. 77/249 OJ 1977 L78/16 and Dir. 89/48 OJ 1989 L19/16, below; Skarlatos, 'European Lawyers' Right to Transnational Legal Practice in the European Community' [1991/1] LIEI 49.
102 Case 136/78, note 42 above.
103 Case 271/82 [1983] ECR 2727.
104 See similarly Case 246/80 *Broekmeulen* v *Huisarts Registratie Commissie* [1981] ECR 2311, Dir. 75/362 applied to a general practitioner.
105 Each directive requires careful interpretation to establish its allocation of competence; see generally pp. 478–82.

not impossible. More recently legislative initiatives in this area have followed the 'new approach', which insists on greater flexibility in the style of Community regulation. For professionals, the General Directive 89/48[106] is an extremely important means of diminishing the obstructive impact of Articles 52(2) and 60(3), thereby liberalizing the market and promoting professional mobility. It is based not on uniformity achieved through harmonization, but instead on mutual recognition of different systems supported by basic agreed standards. Moreover, it is based not on individual professions, but instead on coverage across the board.

The structure of the Directive can only be summarized here.[107] It aims to control the ability of states to exclude nationals from other member states from the pursuit of professional activities on the basis that they are inadequately qualified. Where an individual has in his or her home state acquired a higher education qualification of at least three years' duration, in principle that person is entitled to move to another state in order there to pursue the profession covered by the qualification issued in the home state. As a means of maintaining standards, there are defined circumstances where the host state may require the production of evidence of professional experience or may impose the need for an adaptation period. The migrant may choose to sit an aptitude test rather than fulfil the adaptation period, although the choice lies with the state not the individual where the profession requires precise knowledge of the law of the host state.

Directive 92/51 on a second general system for the recognition of professional education and training serves as a supplement to Directive 89/48.[108] Directive 92/51 covers recognition of the levels of education and training that escape the scope of application of Directive 89/48 either because they are of a shorter duration than, or a different nature from, that envisaged by Directive 89/48, which is confined to recognition of courses of at least three years' duration in higher education. Parallel principles apply.

THE EXAMPLE OF FINANCIAL SERVICES

Similar adjustments are visible in the process of eliminating the obstructive effect of divergent company and commercial regulatory regimes. In the field of the cross-border provision of financial services, several major directives designed to liberalize the market have been adopted and several are accompanied by ancillary measures designed to regulate the market.

106 Note 101 above.
107 See Select Further Reading, p. 909.
108 OJ 1992 L209/25.

The modern approach to such directives is based on the harmonization of essential standards only, home country supervision of firms and a notion of mutual recognition of each member state's rules. For example, Articles 52(2) and 60(3) envisage that a bank would require state authorization from each set of national authorities within the Community before it could treat the market as integrated. Now, a bank that obtains a licence from its home state according to the rules of its home state, which include certain elements derived from Community directives, is entitled in principle to trade freely throughout the Community. This structure is found in the Second Banking Directive,[109] which abandons the detailed quest for regulatory uniformity contained in the First Banking Directive,[110] and instead opts for a structure based on mutual recognition allied to home country control manifested in the issue of the single licence.[111] This reflects the theme of mutual recognition of standards and qualifications that forms an established part of the Court's jurisprudence under Articles 52 and 59.[112] Even under the Directive, the possibility that a state may exercise a residual power to regulate firms established elsewhere in the Community is not excluded, for provision is made to permit states exceptionally to invoke the 'general good' as a (rather nebulous) basis for control.[113]

The essential Community standards that must be incorporated into each state's regime are found in part in the Second Directive, but also in accompanying regulatory measures. These include the Own Funds Directive[114] and the Solvency Ratio Directive,[115] both of which deal with the capital to which a credit institution must have access. Directive 94/19 on deposit-guarantee schemes provides that member states shall put in place a scheme financed by the banking sector that guarantees to depositors a right to payment in the event of the failure of an institution.[116] Such ancillary

---

109 Dir. 89/646 OJ 1989 L386/1.
110 Dir. 77/780 OJ 1977 L322/30. On the contrast between the two methods, see Smits, 'Banking Regulation in a European Perspective' [1989/1] LIEI 61.
111 See Smits, [1989/1] LIEI 61; Van Gerven 'The Second Banking Directive and the Case Law of the Court of Justice' (1990) 10 YEL 57; Strivens, 'The Liberalization of Banking Services in the Community' (1992) 29 CMLRev 293. See generally Cranston (ed.), *The Single Market and the Law of Banking*; Usher, *The Law of Money and Financial Services in the European Community* (1994); Dassesse, Isaacs, Penn, *EC Banking Law* (1994).
112 See p. 586. See especially Usher, Ch. 1, in Cranston (ed.), *The Single Market and the Law of Banking*.
113 On the notion of general good, see Katz, 'The Second Banking Directive' (1992) 12 YEL 249; also refs. at note 111 above.
114 Dir. 89/299 OJ 1989 L124/16.
115 Dir. 89/647 OJ 1989 L386/14.
116 OJ 1994 L135.

measures were essential in order to regulate at Community level concerns that yielded at national level several different, market partitioning regimes. Market integration can be achieved only if national protective rules no longer act as trade barriers, which explains the establishment of common protective rules at Community level to replace diverse national, market partitioning rules. More broadly, the integrated market requires regulation in pursuit of, *inter alia*, consumer and investor protection, which offers a second, more positive justification for such Community intervention.

The insurance sector, the background to the richly illustrative decision in *Commission* v *Germany*,[117] has been the subject of intense legislative activity in pursuit of the objective of market liberalization. Community legislative activity aimed at coordination of national provisions has been separated into two strands – life insurance and non-life insurance. In both sectors, there have been three generations of directives.[118] The current legal structure follows the broad pattern of home state control as a basis for regulatory supervision of firms that are entitled to operate throughout the territory of the Community. This framework should yield a competitive market and enhanced consumer choice. The Community measures themselves include provisions designed to provide protection for consumers, including, for example, disclosure requirements to which firms are subject.

In both the banking and the insurance industries, ancillary measures impinge on social protection, which some would view as a means to market integration, others as a necessary consequence of market integration. In fact, what remains controversial is not so much the fact of Community-wide rules, but rather their content. There is much political disagreement about the role of law in a free market economy. A great deal of attention has been devoted to the phenomenon of the regulatory 'race to the bottom'.[119] This refers to the risk that in a federal structure companies may be induced to migrate to the state with the lightest regulatory regime and to supply the wider market from that base in order to cut the costs of complying with regulation. This is also known as the Delaware effect, for in the United States Delaware's regulatory regime was especially relaxed. If the pattern emerges, states will be induced to compete in reducing the burden of their regulatory regimes in order to attract firms to move to

117 Case 205/84, note 56 above.
118 Non-life: Dir. 73/239 OJ 1973 L228/3, Dir. 88/357 OJ 1988 L172/1, Dir. 92/49 OJ 1992 L228/1. Life: Dir. 79/267 OJ 1979 L63/1, Dir. 90/619 OJ 1990 L330/50, Dir. 92/96 OJ 1992 L360. See Usher; Dassesse, Isaacs, Penn, note 111 above; Page and Ferguson, *Investor Protection* (1992).
119 See, e.g., Bradley, '1992: The Case of Financial Services' (1991) 12 Northwestern J of Intl Law & Business 124 and refs. contained therein; Charny, 'Competition among Jurisdictions in Formulating Corporate Law Rules: An American Perspective on the "Race to the Bottom" in the European Communities' (1991) 32 Harvard Intl LJ 423.

their territory. That process may force measures of social protection below an appropriate level,[120] and/or it may lead to a backlash from states possessing more developed systems of regulation that refuse to accept free movement because it will undermine their own high standards. Some analysts are fully in favour of this competition between regulators; others argue for the imposition of certain uniform standards, although they may disagree about the level of those standards.[121] Such a debate is at present being conducted in several spheres of Community activity, including that of the regulation of financial services in particular and of companies in general.

COMPANY LAW

In the field of company law a substantial harmonization programme has been undertaken.[122] This was needed in view of the propensity for divergent company law regimes in different member states to partition the market by inhibiting exercise of the freedom of establishment. Article 54(3)(g) requires the Council to coordinate the safeguards that are required of companies with a view to making such safeguards equivalent throughout the Community. It provides the base for a series of directives that have narrowed the gaps between national company law. The impact of these measures is such that no company lawyer can operate without a secure knowledge of the Community dimension.

In addition to harmonizing national company law, the Community has begun to establish an independent body of Community company law. Such initiatives are achieved by regulation rather than directive, because they involve the creation of new legal rules rather than the harmonization of existing ones. The European Economic Interest Grouping (EEIG) Regulation is based on Article 235.[123] An EEIG may be set up by parties in two or more member states. It assists them to coordinate and develop activities ancillary to their main business. The EEIG cannot make profits for itself; any profits accrue to the participants and are taxed there. The

---

120 However that may be measured!
121 For the debate in Canada, see Daniels, 'Should Provinces Compete? The Case for a Competitive Corporate Law Market' (1991) 36 McGill LJ 130; and in Australia, see Ramsay, 'Company Law and the Economics of Federalism' (1990) 19 *Federal Law Review* 169. In the EC context, see Reich, 'Competition Between Legal Orders: A New Paradigm of EC Law?' (1992) 29 CMLRev 861.
122 See Dine, *EC Company Law* (1993); Werlauff, *EC Company Law* (1993); Werlauff, 'The Development of Community Company Law' (1992) 17 ELRev 207.
123 Reg. 2137/85 OJ 1985 L199/1. See Van Gerven and Aalders, *European Economic Interest Groupings* (1990).

EEIG is designed as a catalyst to cross-border activity between small- and medium-sized firms that might otherwise find existing legal forms inappropriate to their cross-border collaborative ventures. The EEIG is less ambitious than a jointly owned company, but more ambitious than a simple contract, and, by virtue of its status under Community law, reduces the problem endemic to cross-border collaboration that one party is forced to operate under an unfamiliar national legal system.

The proposed European Company Statute (ECS) is more ambitious. It would coexist with national law, yet in principle it would operate independently of it. It would allow the establishment of a European company on terms laid down in Community legislation. At the most ambitious level, it would remove the problem of incorporation under different national legal systems by providing a single Community vehicle for corporate activity. Progress in adopting the necessary legislation has been slow, in part due to disagreement over legal base. Current proposals locate the main regulation under Article 100a, but subsidiary provisions governing worker participation under a directive based on Article 54.[124]

Both the EEIG and the ECS are designed to provide a structure for the pursuit of commercial activities in the Community on a basis unhindered by national frontiers. However, neither is able fully to establish an entity autonomous of the influence of national law. Both are governed in part by common Community rules, but also in part by national law. Accordingly, both represent progress towards a corporate structure that has precisely the same nature in whichever member state it is active, but neither is yet totally free of the shackles of divergent national law.

Aspects of the company law harmonization programme impinge on social policy.[125] This is especially noticeable in relation to rules governing worker participation in companies.[126] This issue provides a particularly fine illustration of the truth that much of the controversy that surrounds the nature of the Community's company law programme is attributable to the fact that differences between national regimes are not matters of mere detail; they reflect fundamentally distinct perceptions of the function of the company in commerce and, more generally, in society.[127]

---

124 Current proposals may be found at OJ 1991 C138/8; see Wehlau, 'The Societas Europa: a Critique of the Commission's 1991 amended proposal' (1992) 29 CMLRev 473; and see further examination at pp. 640–41 below.
125 See Ch. 20.
126 See pp. 640–41.
127 See, e.g., *A Practitioner's Guide to European Take-Over Regulation and Practice*; Werlauff, *EC Company Law* (1993).

RECIPIENTS OF SERVICES

There are several other categories of individual whose status under the structure already explained is not immediately apparent, even though they participate in transfrontier economic activity. Some parties move to the state in which a provider of services is established in order to receive those services. This is the corollary of the normal case considered above under Article 59, where the provider moves to the state in which the recipient is established. Such recipients of services fall within the ambit of Community competence in order to ensure that the framework of Community law recognizes all forms of gainful cross-border activity. In *Luisi and Carbone* v *Ministero del Tesero*[128] the Court held that 'tourists, persons receiving medical treatment and persons travelling for the purpose of education or business' are to be regarded as recipients of services who enjoy the right of free movement under Article 59.[129]

The recognition that such persons are within the scope of Community law is only a first step. To what rights are these individuals entitled? To some extent, secondary legislation applies to these categories. Directive 73/148 confers on nationals of member states wishing to go to another member state as recipients of services a right of free movement and residence.[130] However, that provision is merely a starting point. It has not yet been established in what circumstances a state may prevent an individual leaving its jurisdiction in order to receive a service in another member state. Had it not resolved the matter under domestic law, the Irish Supreme Court might have had to address this point in the controversial proceedings involving abortion that confronted it in 1992.[131] The Court's approach to the rights of the individual within the host state has already been alluded to. It finds in Article 6 a basis for extending rights to individuals falling within the scope of Community competence. Such migrants are entitled to non-discrimination in the provision of benefits within the host state. It will be recalled that breaches of a combination of Articles 6, 52 and 59 were found in *Steinhauser* v *City of Biarritz* (access to rental of lock-ups),[132] *Commission* v *Italy* (access to housing and related benefits)[133] and *Commission* v *Greece* (ownership of immovable property),[134]

---

128 Cases 286/82 and 26/83 [1984] ECR 377, [1985] 3 CMLR 25.
129 ibid., para. 16 of the judgment.
130 Art. 1(1) (b).
131 See pp. 580–81.
132 Case 197/84, note 12 above.
133 Case 63/86, note 13 above.
134 Case 305/87, note 14 above.

in all of which non-nationals were denied equality of opportunity. However, the precise material scope of the right to equal treatment is difficult to define in advance. As is already apparent, it will not be identical in relation to every person who comes within the scope of Community competence. Through the accidents of litigation the Court has begun to develop the shape of the rights of the recipient of services.

In *Cowan* v *Le Trésor Public*[135] a British tourist 'mugged' in Paris was refused compensation by the French authorities because he was neither a French national nor a French resident. The European Court ruled that as a tourist he was receiving services and therefore was within the scope of Community competence by virtue of Article 59. This then led it to confer upon him a right to non-discriminatory treatment on grounds of nationality, which included a right to receive compensation for such injuries on the same terms as those applicable to nationals of the host state.

The French Government had argued that denial of a right of this nature did not prevent free movement. The provision of such a benefit goes beyond mere temporary economic migration and presupposes a closer bond with the state than mere presence as a recipient of services. Rejecting this restrictive approach, the Court preferred to find the protection of a person from harm on non-discriminatory grounds to be a corollary of the right to free movement. This plainly envisages a more extended notion of the need to ensure equal access to social benefits in order to eliminate impediments to migration. Case law will gradually lead to clearer definition of the scope of this right to equal treatment.[136]

The Court's activity is in effect an exercise in interpreting the scope of the Community's competence. Both the content of the judgments and the fact that the Court is making them are controversial. Legislation may be required to clarify and/or to extend the Court's rulings. The Parliament has called for a directive requiring states to introduce a system of criminal injuries compensation, as yet fruitlessly.[137] This would, in fact, go beyond providing a codification of *Cowan*, for that decision requires only non-discriminatory access to systems that are already in place. A directive would require states to establish systems even where they do not exist. It would lay a floor of rights.

---

135 Case 186/87 [1989] ECR 195, [1990] 2 CMLR 613, noted by Weatherill (1989) 26 CMLRev 563.
136 For discussion, see Weatherill (1989) 26 CMLRev 563; Lenaerts, '*L'Égalité de Traitement en Droit Communautaire*' (1991) 27 CDE 3, 28; Evans, 'Nationality Law and European Integration' (1991) 16 ELRev 190, 205–13. The situation should be distinguished from that in Case C-168/91 *Konstantinidis* v *Stadt Altensteig*, p. 558 above, where the migrant claimed a right under the general principles of Community law, not equality with nationals of the host state.
137 OJ 1989 C256/32 (noted (1989) 9 YEL 265).

STUDENTS

A student may be a recipient of services on precisely the same legal basis as that discussed above. However, 'services' are defined by Article 60 of the Treaty as 'normally provided for remuneration', which may exclude many forms of state education. In *Belgian State* v *Humbel*[138] the Court pointed out that the state's direct aim is not profit-making, but social, cultural and educational provision for the population. Moreover, education is, in general, publicly funded, notwithstanding that parents and/or pupils may make some financial contribution. Accordingly, the Court held that courses provided under the national education system do not normally amount to services within the meaning of Articles 59–66.[139]

VOCATIONAL TRAINING

The recipient of education may therefore be unable to rely on the provisions of Articles 59–66. This does not mean that he or she is excluded from the scope of Community competence. In *Gravier* v *City of Liège*[140] a French national who wished to study strip-cartoon-making on an arts course in Belgium was obliged to pay the *minerval*, a course enrolment fee, which Belgians did not have to pay. The Court referred to Article 128 EEC, which envisaged the development of a vocational training policy for the Community,[141] and observed that access to vocational training is a means of bringing about the key objective of the free movement of persons in the Community. The matter was thus capable of falling within the scope of the Treaty and Gravier could rely on Article 7 EEC[142] to claim equality with Belgian nationals in the conditions of access to the course.[143]

The Court in *Gravier* was willing to accept that the notion of vocational training covers 'any form of education which prepares for a qualification for a particular profession, trade or employment or which provides the

---

138 Case 263/86 [1988] ECR 5365, [1989] 1 CMLR 393; Case C-109/92 *S.M. Wirth* v *Landeshaupstadt Hannover*, judgment of 7 December 1993.
139 The case of private schooling would be different. See Case C-109/92, note 138 above.
140 Case 293/83 [1985] ECR 593, [1985] 3 CMLR 1, noted by Watson (1987) 24 CMLRev 89.
141 Art. 128 EEC was amended both numerically and substantively by the Maastricht Treaty amendments; it is now Art. 127 EC and is more explicit in its objectives.
142 Now Art. 6 EC.
143 See also Case 42/87 *Commission* v *Belgium* [1988] ECR 5445, [1989] 1 CMLR 457.

necessary training and skills for such a profession, trade or employment . . . even if the training programme includes an element of general education'.[144] In applying this interpretation in *Blaizot* v *University of Liège*[145] the Court confirmed its breadth. The Court decided that a six-year course, half of which was general education and half of which was specific to veterinary medicine, where completion of the first stage was a precondition for entry to the second, was capable of being viewed as a single course comprising vocational training.[146] Only 'certain courses of study . . . intended for persons wishing to improve their general knowledge rather than prepare themselves for an occupation' fall outside the scope of vocational training.[147] The focus is on studies providing the basis for the pursuit of a profession, not solely on the acquisition of a qualification required under legislative or administrative provisions. The vast majority of university and higher education courses are thus covered, and must be equally available to students of all member states.[148]

However, access to education cannot be equated with support during education. In *Brown* v *Secretary of State for Scotland*[149] the Court held that the provision of maintenance grants for students at present lies outside the scope of the Treaty. It remains a matter of national, not Community, competence. There is no right to equal treatment. Here are the limits of the *Gravier* principle. This caution had already been foreshadowed in *Gravier* itself, where the Court, reflecting concerns about the disruption to national education systems expressed by member states, had observed that its decision related only to access to education, not to the broader fields of its organization nor even its financing.

THE SCOPE OF ENTITLEMENTS

The precise scope of the right to equal treatment with nationals remains unclear. Article 6 allows arguments based on Community law to be advanced, provided it is shown that there is some basis for bringing the

---

144 Case 293/83, note 140 above, para. 30 of the judgment.
145 Case 24/86 [1988] ECR 379, [1989] 1 CMLR 57, noted by Arnull (1988) 13 ELRev 260.
146 For an integrated whole comprising vocational training where components viewed in isolation may not, see also Case 263/86, note 138 above.
147 Case 24/86, note 145 above, para. 20. The case, along with Case 309/85 *Barra* v *Belgium and City of Liège* [1988] ECR 355, is also important for the limits the Court was prepared to impose on claims for repayment of sums already paid based on the direct effect of Community law; see p. 307.
148 See refs under 'Students' in Select Further Reading, p. 910.
149 Case 197/86 [1988] ECR 3205, [1988] 3 CMLR 403.

matter within the scope of Community competence: Article 128 in *Gravier*,[150] Article 59 in *Cowan*.[151] But the definitions in this area are very difficult to pin down. The nature of the link that must be shown between the ability to circulate within the Community and the social benefits that may accordingly be claimed remains obscure. The least that can be said is that Article 6 is a valuable source of rights but it remains less well defined than the extensive rights to equal treatment available to the worker and his or her family under Article 48 and its supporting legislation, especially Regulation 1612/68,which has no direct parallel outside the case of the worker. The worker and his or her family would be entitled to equality in access to other forms of training, apart from simply vocational, and could claim maintenance grants on the same terms as nationals of the host state.[152] The decision in *Lair* v *University of Hanover*[153] contrasts with that in *Brown* v *Secretary of State for Scotland*.[154] In both cases the Court held that the provision of maintenance grants for students at present lies outside the scope of the Treaty. The matter is different where a worker undertakes study. In *Brown* the Court held that a worker who has achieved that status solely by virtue of admission to university in order to undertake the studies in question is barred from entitlement to the grant.[155] But in *Lair* the Court decided that in principle the 'normal' worker is entitled to such a benefit.[156] There is a graded structure of rights that may distinguish workers from other less favoured citizens and that may even distinguish between different types of worker.

Member states have expressed concern that they may be faced by excessive financial burdens as a result of migrating students. However, the decision in *Brown* allays some of those fears, both by holding maintenance grants unaffected by the *Gravier* rule of non-discrimination in provision of vocational training[157] and, less important, by depriving even a limited class of workers of rights to such grants. The Court in *Lair* also took care to

---

150 Case 293/83, note 140 above.
151 Case 186/87, note 135 above.
152 E.g. Case 9/74 *Casagrande* v *Landeshauptstadt München* [1974] ECR 773; Cases 389, 390/87 *Echternach and Moritz* [1989] ECR 723; Case C-308/89 *Di Leo* v *Land Berlin* [1990] ECR I-4185.
153 Case 39/86 [1988] ECR 3161, [1989] 3 CMLR 545.
154 Case 197/86, note 149 above.
155 See Ch. 18, p. 569.
156 See p. 570 on the obscure conditions attached by the Court to the link between the work and education.
157 Lonbay doubts that the distinction made by the Court in *Brown* has a sound legal basis and finds it a 'pragmatic . . . [limitation of] the logical scope of its *Gravier* ruling'; see 'Education and Law: the Community context' (1989) 14 ELRev 363, 373; see also Green, Hartley and Usher, *Single European Market*, p. 182; O'Leary (1993)30 CMLRev 639.

calm fears that its ruling may tempt individuals to cross borders, work briefly and then secure financial support for extended university education. The Court declared that such an abuse is not covered by Community law.[158] Presumably, in *Levin* terms[159] such work is ancillary to the pursuit of cheap education and the individual does not fulfil the requirements of worker status.

LEGISLATIVE INTERVENTION

Legislative intervention in this sphere has long been cautious. In accordance with the principle of subsidiarity, education is seen as a matter of national competence. Article 127 EC, the successor to Article 128 EEC, declares that the Community's vocational policy 'shall support and supplement the action of the Member States, while fully respecting the responsibility of the Member States for the content and organization of vocational training'.

Some legislation has been forthcoming. A right to reside in the host state conferred on students on vocational courses seems to be the logical consequence of the decision in *Gravier*.[160] *A fortiori* this should cover a right of entry. These entitlements are put on a firmer footing by Directive 93/96.[161] This measure confers rights of residence on students, their spouses and dependent children, provided the student is enrolled on vocational training courses in recognized educational institutions. There is no right to a maintenance grant. Directive 93/96 has a peculiar history. Its precursor is Directive 90/366, one of a package of three directives adopted in 1990 and due for implementation by the end of 1992. However, Directive 90/366 was annulled by the Court on application by the Parliament for incorrect choice of legal base.[162] The Court considered that Article 7(2), now Article 6(2) after Maastricht, was the proper legal base, rather than the Council's choice of Article 235. The Court ruled that the effects of the annulled measure should be maintained until the entry into force of a directive adopted under the correct legal base. Directive 93/96 was duly made to fill the gap. Its deadline for implementation expired at the end of 1993 from which time the annulled Directive finally perished. All three direc-

---

158 Case 39/86, note 153 above, para. 43 of the judgment; p. 507 above. AG Slynn was more specific; he suggested a minimum period of a year's work.
159 Case 53/81 [1982] ECR 1035; see Ch. 18, p. 545 above.
160 Case 293/83, note 140 above. See also Case C-357/89 *Raulin* v *Netherlands Ministry of Education and Science* [1992] ECR I-1027.
161 OJ 1993 L317/59.
162 Case C-295/90 *Parliament* v *Council* [1992] ECR I-4193, noted by Emiliou (1993) 18 ELRev 138. See Ch. 8, p. 250 above, on judicial supervision of legal base.

tives, 90/364, 90/365 and 93/96, confer rights only on those adequately supported in order to avoid becoming a financial burden on the state. Directive 90/364[163] grants rights of residence to those without the right under other provisions of Community law, which, given the requirement of adequate support, in effect confers rights on those with independent means. Directive 90/365[164] covers the right of residence of employees and the self-employed and their families who have ceased their occupational activity. Such legislation impinges on Union citizenship and should also be read in conjunction with the progress in the social policy field.[165] The significant conditions attached to the directives that require the individual to be able to support him- or herself independently reflect the potentially profound financial implications of legislation in this area.

Other legislation has been adopted of relevance to students.[166] ERASMUS is the best known of the Community's educational programmes.[167] It is designed to promote student mobility, inter alia, through the development of degree programmes involving study in more than one member state. The decision setting up the programme, based on Articles 128 and 235, was unsuccessfully challenged in Commission v Council.[168] Future developments will occur under the new SOCRATES scheme.

Judicial activism is unmistakable in this area, although decisions such as Brown[169] demonstrate some sense of restraint. However, much has depended on the accidents of litigation. Legal-base problems notwithstanding, legislative initiatives in this field are the desirable method of deepening Community intervention in educational policy.[170]

REVERSE DISCRIMINATION

The Court has consistently held that Community law forbids the treatment of migrants in a less favourable manner than nationals of the host state, but that it does not forbid a state from treating its own nationals less favourably than migrants. A national of state A cannot rely on the protection of Community law simply because state A, for whatever reason, chooses to

163 OJ 1990 L180/26.
164 OJ 1990 L180/28.
165 See Ch. 20; also Art. 8 EC, pp. 15, 544 above.
166 See refs. under 'Students' in Select Further Reading.
167 Dec. 87/327 OJ 1987 L166.
168 Case 242/87 [1989] ECR 1425.
169 Case 197/86, note 149 above.
170 See esp. Green, Hartley and Usher, Single European Market, pp. 190–93.

discriminate in favour of a national of state B. 'Reverse discrimination' is outside the scope of Community law.[171]

In *Morson and Jhanjan* v *Netherlands*[172] nationals of Surinam wished to live with their children, who were Dutch nationals living and working in the Netherlands. Refused permission by the Dutch authorities, they sought to rely on Articles 7, now 6, and 48. The Court held that those provisions concern the free movement of workers as an element in the establishment of a common market. They have no application to cases that lack any factor linking them with Community law, which includes the case of persons who have never exercised their right to cross borders to work. Had the children been migrant workers – for example, Germans in the Netherlands – the parents would certainly have been entitled to the protection of Community law by virtue of Article 48 and Regulation 1612/68.[173]

In *R* v *Saunders*[174] a British national convicted of theft before Bristol Crown Court was bound over on condition that she should return to Northern Ireland and keep out of England and Wales for three years. After Saunders had broken this condition, an Article 177 reference was made asking whether the restriction was compatible with Article 48. The Court found the matter to be 'wholly internal to a Member State' and therefore unaffected by the Treaty rules on the free movement of workers. A migrant worker could not have been subjected to such a restriction unless a national of the host state could have been subjected to the same restriction,[175] but in the absence of a cross-border element points of Community law were simply of no assistance.[176] Similarly, in *Moser* v *Land Baden-Württemburg*[177] a German national refused access to a teacher-training course sought to rely on Article 48 on the basis that the denial might deprive him of the chance of working in another member state in the future. The European Court viewed this as a purely hypothetical possibility and concluded that the matter was internal to Germany and unconnected with Community law.

---

171 See e.g, Case 44/84 *Hurd* v *Jones* [1986] ECR 29; Case 355/85 *Driancourt* v *Cognet* [1986] ECR 3231, [1987] 3 CMLR 942. In relation to Art. 95 see p. 400 above; Art. 30, p. 530 above.
172 Cases 35, 36/82 [1982] ECR 3723, [1983] 2 CMLR 221.
173 See p. 552.
174 Case 175/78 [1979] ECR 1129.
175 Case 36/75 *Rutili* v *Minister for the Interior* [1975] ECR 1219.
176 See also Cases C-54/88, C-91/88 and C-14/89 *Niño* [1990] ECR I-3537, [1992] 1 CMLR 83; Case C-332/90 *Steen* v *Deutsche Bundespost*, [1992] ECR I-341; Case 133/93 *Steen* v *Deutsche Bundespost* [1994] ECR I-2715.
177 Case 180/83 [1984] ECR 2539, [1984] 3 CMLR 720.

In *Ministère Public* v *Gauchard*[178] and in *Höfner* v *Macrotron*[179] the Court confirmed that the same approach applies in the field of freedom of establishment and the free movement of services respectively. A purely internal matter does not permit the invocation of arguments founded on Community law.

The limits of the notion of the wholly internal situation should be appreciated. In *Knoors* v *Secretary of State for Economic Affairs*[180] a Dutch national resident in Belgium and working there as a plumber was refused permission to work in the Netherlands because he did not have Dutch qualifications. The Netherlands submitted that a Dutchman could not rely on Article 52 against the Dutch authorities, an objection that would pre-empt any reliance on Community law. The Court accepted that Community law is inapplicable to purely internal situations, but denied that this was such a case. The national of a state who had resided in another state and obtained a qualification there is to be assimilated to the position of other persons claiming the freedoms conferred by the Treaty. A similar approach may be seen in cases arising under Article 59, such as *Van Binsbergen*[181] and *Coenen*,[182] both of which involved Dutch nationals resident in Belgium who wished to provide services in their state of origin.

It seems odd that reverse discrimination is not caught by Community law.[183] It is not a necessary interpretation of Article 6 EC, the fundamental source of the rule against discrimination on grounds of nationality. That provision prohibits any discrimination on grounds of nationality, without any explicit suggestion that the rule applies only to unfavourable treatment of nationals of other member states. It is, however, true that the Article's supplementary phrase 'within the scope of application of this Treaty' may be interpreted as an insistence that a cross-border element be present. There is no effect on interstate trade in the purely internal situation. Perhaps the Court's motivation lies in concern to avoid undue interference in the internal affairs of a member state, coupled with a perception that in any event the problem of reverse discrimination is unlikely to be serious, because a state has little incentive to discriminate against its own nationals.

---

178 Case 20/87 [1987] ECR 4879, [1989] 2 CMLR 489.
179 Case C-41/90, [1991] ECR I-1979; see also Case C-60/91 *Batista Morais* v *Ministerio Public*, [1992] ECR I-2085.
180 Case 115/78 [1979] ECR 399. See also Case 246/80, note 104 above; Case 292/86, note 80 above.
181 Case 33/74, note 2 above.
182 Case 39/75, note 50 above.
183 For discussion, see W. Pickup, 'Reverse Discrimination and Freedom of Movement of Workers' (1986) 23 CMLRev 135; C. Greenwood, 'Nationality and the Limits of the Free Movement of Persons in Community Law' (1987) 7 YEL 185, 193–205; Arnull, *EEC Law and the Individual*, pp. 51–62.

Yet the Court's approach gives rise to anomalies. Would Moser have been able to rely on Community law if he held a job offer from Belgium?[184] It is implicit in *Knoors* and explicit in *R v IAT and Surinder Singh, ex parte Secretary of State for the Home Department*[185] that a national of state A who works in state B and then returns to state A is *not* in a purely internal situation and is able to rely on Community law against his or her own state. In *Singh* this was to the advantage of a family member who was not a Community national. This ruling suggests that the Court is willing to chip away at the scope of the 'internal situation' which, rather anomalously, remains untouched by Community law principles. However, the matter remains unclear. The Court offered scope for further future complication when it suggested in *Knoors* that a state may have a legitimate interest in preventing nationals migrating in order to evade training requirements, which hints at a grey area of sham cross-border situations in the penumbra between the purely internal and the cross-border situation.[186]

Perhaps one can simply accept these cases as examples of the Court's rather erratic case-by-case development of the law. More broadly, it may be observed that as market integration accelerates and national borders lose economic relevance, the logic of the purely internal situation diminishes. Accordingly the importance of this odd area of law may simply wither away, even if the Court declines explicitly to reconsider its approach in principle.

184 Case 180/83, note 177 above.
185 Case C-370/90, judgment of 7 July 1992, p. 552 above; see also Case C-419/92 *Ingetraut Scholz* v *Opera Universitaria di Cagliari* [1994] ECR I-505, [1994] 1 CMLR 873.
186 See Case 39/86, note 153 above and, in connection with legal persons, Case C-23/93 *TV10 SA* v *Commissariaat voor de Media* [1994] ECR I-4795; the Court appears to envisage a similar exception for sham cross-border transactions under Art. 36; p. 531 above.

CHAPTER 20

Social Policy

THE NATURE OF COMMUNITY SOCIAL POLICY

Within a single state the scope of social policy is wide. Typically, it embraces, for example, regional policy, structural policy, cultural policy, education policy and health policy. Community social policy, however, has traditionally lacked such general scope. The bulk of the Community's social policy has developed from the focus on the creation of the common market and is, accordingly, directly linked to employment. The aspects of social policy examined in this chapter are primarily those that are connected with workers and the self-employed and, in this sense, the chapter should be read as a complement to the two that precede it. Indeed, the rights of free movement and equal treatment in social and tax matters, including social security, examined in the preceding two chapters, are themselves social rights in that they constitute benefits conferred on individual members of society. In *Reyners* v *Belgian State* the Court described the directives relating to freedom of establishment as instruments of 'economic and social interpenetration'.[1] This chapter examines additional social rights that may be enforced independently of the exercise of the right of free movement and the right to equality of treatment. Even workers who are not migrants are affected by the social policy of the Community. The final part of this chapter explores the extent to which Community social policy may be taken beyond employment-related rights. Legal notions of competence and political notions of subsidiarity constrain the Community from assuming full responsibility for matters such as regional policy and structural policy, culture, education and health, but the gradual evolution of the Community has ensured that Community social policy in the 1990s can no longer be narrowly defined solely with regard to the employment relationship.

The role of Community regulation in fields that may not appear to be

---

1 Case 2/74 [1974] ECR 631, para. 21 of the judgment; see pp. 577, 596 above.

directly linked to the liberalization of the factors of production within an integrating market has aroused fierce debate. The Court's views in *Defrenne* v *SABENA*[2] deserve immediate attention. The case concerned Article 119, which requires that men and women shall receive equal pay for equal work. In commenting on the function of Article 119 in the scheme of the Treaty the European Court exposed the broader underlying rationale for social policy in the Treaty:

Article 119 pursues a double aim. First, in the light of the different states of the development of social legislation in the various Member States, the aim of Article 119 is to avoid a situation in which undertakings established in States which have actually implemented the principle of equal pay suffer a competitive disadvantage in intra-Community competition as compared with undertakings established in States which have not yet eliminated discrimination against women workers as regards pay.

Secondly, this provision forms part of the social objectives of the Community, which is not merely an economic union, but is at the same time intended, by common action, to ensure social progress and seek the constant improvement of the living and working conditions of their peoples . . .[3]

The Court thus insisted on social objectives enshrined within Community law alongside the process of economic integration. Equal pay between the sexes under Article 119 provides only one example of this dual function. It is against this background that controversy has persisted about the appropriate nature and purpose of Community social policy.[4] The debate is sometimes loosely characterized as one conducted between the interventionists and the deregulators; between those who wish not simply to open up the common market to free trade but also to regulate that market *versus* those who would limit the role of law to the elimination of national barriers to trade. In fact, the debate is significantly more complicated than such slogans may imply. The issue is an aspect of diverse political traditions within the member states and does not necessarily proceed along left/right ideological lines. For example, the influence of the Christian Democrat tradition is much misunderstood in the United Kingdom, even by politicians occupying the same right-of-centre position on the political spectrum.

The controversy about the place of social policy in the Community has been fuelled by legal ambiguity. Article 2 of the Treaty of Rome declared that

The Community shall have as its task, by establishing a common market and

2 Case 43/75 [1976] ECR 455.
3 ibid., paras. 8–10.
4 See the items listed under the 'Nature of Community Social Policy' at p. 910 below.

progressively approximating the economic policies of Member States, to promote throughout the Community a harmonious development of economic activities, a continuous and balanced expansion, an increase in stability, an accelerated raising of the standard of living and closer relations between the States belonging to it.[5]

This suggested a core of common action, even in the social sphere. However, Article 7a EC, which sets out the goal of completing the internal market by the end of 1992,[6] seems much more concerned with deregulating, rather than regulating, the market. It declared that 'the internal market [which was to be completed by the end of 1992] shall comprise an area without internal frontiers in which the free movement of goods, persons, services and capital is ensured . . .' One view is that this provision must be read in the light of the broader notion of the common market and policy approximation mentioned in Article 2, but another view, espoused particularly by the United Kingdom, is that it represents a shift away from the notions of market regulation that characterized the first thirty years of the Community. These ambiguities were not resolved by the Treaty on European Union. In fact, the United Kingdom's isolation was placed on a more formal footing at Maastricht, where a protocol was negotiated that had the effect of permitting the United Kingdom to opt out of the deepened commitment to social policy undertaken by the other eleven, now fourteen, member states.[7]

It remains indisputable that the Treaty of Rome signed in 1957 contained a title explicitly devoted to social policy. That title contained two chapters. The first was entitled 'Social Provisions' and contained six Articles, 117–22. The second was entitled 'The European Social Fund' and contained six further Articles, 123–8. The Social Fund is used to combat unemployment, especially in the areas of greatest need.[8] Its impact has been limited by its relatively low allocation of resources.[9] Article 128 refers to the implementation of a common vocational training policy and has attained some importance in its own right as a method of establishing Community competence.[10]

The majority of the provisions in the 'Social Provisions' chapter were drafted in rather vague terms, and few offered explicit legislative competence. Article 118, for example, refers simply to the Commission's task of 'promoting close cooperation between Member States in the social field',

5 Art. 2 EEC was amended by the Maastricht Treaty; on Art. 2 EC, see p. 19.
6 See p. 24. The Maastricht Treaty converted Art. 8a EEC into Art. 7a EC.
7 See p. 644.
8 For a summary, see Kapteyn and Verloren van Themaat, *Law of the European Communities*, pp. 637–9.
9 See Ch. 2, p. 63.
10 See e.g., Case 293/83 *Gravier v City of Liège*, pp.605–6.

adding an illustrative list of matters such as employment, labour law and working conditions and the right of association.[11] The Single European Act had relatively little direct impact on these provisions. It inserted new Articles, 118a and 118b, which were relevant, in particular, to health and safety in the workplace. The revised EC Treaty, which emerged as a result of the negotiations at Maastricht, added references to initiatives in the spheres of education and vocational training, which were also of relatively minor impact, and added several new titles of relevance to social policy, although not contained within the social policy title itself, including Public Health[12] and Consumer Protection.[13] It also transformed the old Article 128 into Article 127, expanding the objectives referred to in it but making it more difficult for legislation to be adopted. Article 119 is the most specific and the most high-profile of the Articles in the title on social policy. It requires equality between the sexes in pay, and related secondary legislation has reinforced and extended this principle of sex equality.

COMMUNITY LAW OF SEX DISCRIMINATION

ARTICLE 119

Article 119 of the Treaty provides that 'each Member State shall during the first stage ensure and subsequently maintain the application of the principle that men and women should receive equal pay for equal work ...' Much of Community trade law applies only to situations that are shown to have a cross-border element,[14] but in the light of the Court's insistence in *Defrenne* v *SABENA*[15] that it is designed both to eliminate competitive distortion caused by discrepancies between social legislation in the member states and to secure social progress Article 119 may be invoked by *all* workers. Article 119 is accordingly uniformly available throughout the Community as a means of securing equality in pay with those of the opposite sex who are doing or who have been doing the same work.[16]

The decision in *Defrenne* v *SABENA* established two key characteristics of Article 119, which paved the way to its present vigour as an anti-

11 See further Ch. 8, pp. 246–7.
12 Art. 129 EC; see p. 33.
13 Art. 129a EC; see p. 33.
14 E.g., see Art. 30, Ch. 15; Art. 48, Ch. 18; Art. 85, Ch. 22.
15 Case 43/75, note 2 above.
16 The comparator need not be contemporaneously employed on the same work; see Case 129/79 *Macarthys* v *Smith* [1979] ECR 1275.

discrimination provision: Article 119 is directly effective, and the obligation applies both vertically and horizontally. An employee may enforce the principle of equal pay for equal work whether employed by a public body or a private party. The ruling meant that, in principle, Article 119 was enforceable by all employees against all employers in the original member states from the start of 1962 and in the United Kingdom, Ireland and Denmark from 1973. Given the entrenched nature of sex discrimination in pay in many states, there seemed every likelihood of a vast number of claims for a great deal of money being lodged before national courts throughout the Community. Principle yielded to pragmatism. The Court was persuaded by submissions relating to the immense financial disruption that its ruling would cause and accordingly held that the effect of the judgment would have no retrospective effect, except in respect of legal proceedings that had commenced before the date of the judgment (8 April 1976).[17]

The meaning of 'pay'

Article 119's reference to equal 'pay' raises definitional difficulties. The Article's second paragraph amplifies pay to mean 'the ordinary basic or minimum wage or salary and any other consideration, whether in cash or in kind, which the worker receives, directly or indirectly, in respect of his employment from his employer'. In response to this broad definition the Court has steadily widened the impact of Article 119 by steadily widening the definition of pay. Wages or salary are evidently included, as in *Defrenne* itself; so, too, entitlements such as bonus payments or sick pay.[18] In *Garland* v *BREL*[19] the Court held that pay covered travel facilities offered as a concession after retirement and that, accordingly, equality between the sexes was required. The absence of any contractual entitlement to the facilities was irrelevant. The Court's test depends not on legal form, but on the fact of conferring a benefit because of the employment relationship.

The Court has encountered particular problems in relation to pension schemes.[20] It has extended the notion of pay, and thus of Article 119 itself,

---

17 The Court is able to limit the temporal effects of its judgments in this way, but national courts are not; cf. Case 24/86 *Blaizot* [1988] ECR 379, [1989] 1 CMLR 57 and p. 307 above.
18 See e.g., Case 171/88 *Rinner Kuhn* v *FWW* [1989] ECR 2743, noted by Szyszczak (1990) 19 ILJ 114.
19 Case 12/81 [1982] ECR 359, [1982] 1 CMLR 696.
20 The case law is not examined exhaustively in this chapter. See e.g., Ellis, *European Community Sex Equality Law*, pp. 42–61; Nielsen and Szyszczak, *The Social Dimension of the European Community*, ch. 3.

in a manner that may be supported as dynamic, yet mistrusted as unpredictable and likely to cause commercial disruption. Naturally, pensions constitute pay where they are purely private in nature. However, many pension schemes operate in addition to the state scheme, have at least some state support, and in many cases are actually organized by the state. Practice differs from state to state. In *Defrenne* v *Belgium*[21] the Court held that a retirement pension established under a social security scheme created by legislation fell outside the notion of pay. Article 119 does not control benefits governed directly by legislation, with no element of agreement within the firm or the trade and where the system is compulsory for general categories of workers.

In *Bilka Kaufhaus* v *Weber*[22] the employer, Bilka Kaufhaus, had established a retirement pension scheme for its employees. Entitlements were payable under the contract of employment. The scheme was adopted in accordance with German legislation applicable to such pension schemes, but it had been set up voluntarily as a result of an agreement reached internally within the firm. It supplemented the benefits payable to employees under generally applicable national legislation with benefits that were financed entirely by the employer. The Court concluded that this was pay and subject to the requirement of equality between the sexes.[23] In *Rinner Kuhn* v *FWW*[24] German law required employers to pay six weeks' wages to an employee incapable of working, but allowed them to exclude specified part-time workers. In a sense this was a statutory sick-pay scheme, yet the Court held that pay within Article 119 was involved, given that it was payable by the employer by virtue of the employment relationship, the statutory background notwithstanding. In *Anna Adriaantje Vroege* v *NCIV Instituut voor Volkshuisvesting BV and Stichting Pensioenfonds NCIV*[25] the Court stated that access to an occupational pension scheme falls within Article 119 and is therefore subject to requirements of non-discrimination. It commented explicitly that this has been clear since *Bilka Kaufhaus*.

There is some difficulty in these cases in establishing a distinction between pay and general statutory welfare provision, and this problem is deepened by the process of transferring responsibility for social protection from the public to the private sector, which has been a particular feature of

---

21 Case 80/70 [1971] ECR 445. See also Case C-109/91 *Ten Oever* v *Stichting Bedrijfspensioenfonds voor het Glazenwassers-en Schoonaakbedrijf*, judgment of 6 October 1993.
22 Case 170/84 [1986] ECR 1607, [1986] 2 CMLR 701.
23 The application of the equality principle in the case is examined at pp. 621–2.
24 Case 171/88, note 18 above.
25 Case C-57/93 [1994] ECR I-4541; see also Case C-128/93 *Geertruida Catharina Fisscher* v *Voorhuis Hengelo BV and Stichting Bedrijfspensioenfonds voor de Detailhandel* [1994] ECR I-4583.

British policy through the 1980s. The issue of the margin between occupational and statutory schemes received further attention from the Court in *Barber* v *GRE*.[26] The plan in question was 'contracted out' of the general state scheme; that is, the parties had exercised a statutory option to replace the state pension, to which the employee had a legal entitlement, with a pension paid by the employer in substitute to, and improvement on, the state pension. In a sense the law required that a pension be paid to Mr Barber, yet in another sense the parties had chosen to take the matter into the sphere of their private contractual relationship. The European Court insisted that the pension constituted pay, because it was received by reason of the existence of the employment relationship. Accordingly, Mr Barber, who had been denied a pension where a female employee would have received one, had been the victim of discrimination on the grounds of sex within the meaning of Article 119. Had the matter fallen outside Article 119, it would have been subject to the exclusion from the principle of equality in the social security Directive 79/7 [27] relating to 'the determination of pensionable age for the purposes of granting old-age and retirement pensions'. Consequently, Mr Barber's claim would have failed had he been unable to show that the pension constituted 'pay'.

The *Barber* decision caused confusion.[28] The European Court declared that the unexpected nature of its ruling justified an application of the exceptional approach first taken in *Defrenne*.[29] It ruled that Article 119 could not be relied on 'in order to claim an entitlement to a pension with effect from a date prior to that of this judgment', except in respect of proceedings already initiated. The motivation of this ruling was plainly to curtail commercial disruption, but its precise impact was far from clear. Would it, for example, cover equality in respect of benefits received from the date of judgment? Or merely benefits received in respect of service after the date of judgment? Fears of broad financial implications led the member states to clarify and restrict the temporal effects of the judgment in a protocol to the Maastricht Treaty: '. . . benefits under occupational pension schemes shall not be considered as remuneration if and insofar as they are attributable to periods of employment prior to 17 May 1990'.

Decisions subsequent to *Barber* offered the Court the opportunity to bring its case law into alignment with the protocol. In *Ten Oever* v

---

26 Case C-262/88 [1990] ECR I-1889, [1990] 2 CMLR 513.
27 See p. 626.
28 For analysis, see Curtin, 'Scalping the Community Legislator: Occupational Pensions and "Barber"' (1990) 27 CMLRev 475; Shrubsall, 'Sex Discrimination and Pension Benefits' (1990) 19 ILJ 244; Fitzpatrick, 'Equality in Occupational Pensions – The New Frontiers after Barber' (1991) 54 MLR 271.
29 Case 43/75, note 2 above.

Stichting Bedrijfspensioenfonds voor het Glazenwassers-en Schoonaakbedrijf [30] it took that opportunity and ruled, in conformity with the terms of the protocol, that the direct effect of Article 119 may be relied on for the purpose of claiming equal treatment in occupational pensions only in relation to benefits payable in respect of periods of employment subsequent to 17 May 1990, the date of the *Barber* ruling, subject to an exception in favour of workers who have initiated proceedings before that date. Subsequent to *Barber*, the Court has clarified the legal parameters within which employers must operate in adjusting their schemes in the light of the requirements of Community equality law. For periods of employment between 17 May 1990 and the date on which measures are adopted to establish equality, equalization must be secured without depreciation of workers' entitlements already prevailing, but after equalization measures are taken, it is open to the employer to fix equality at any level, including levels that are significantly less favourable than those offered before the adjustment.[31] The temporal restriction, imposed in *Barber* to preserve legal certainty, does not apply to access to occupational schemes, because it has been clear since *Bilka Kaufhaus* that this matter falls within Article 119's rule of non-discrimination.[31a]

Indirect discrimination

Article 119 prohibits an employer from paying workers doing the same job rates that differ according to sex: it forbids direct discrimination. However, it goes further. Where a criterion selected for differentiation between workers is not sex, but particularly disadvantages one sex, then indirect discrimination has occurred. This is also subject to the control of Article 119. So if an employer chooses to pay higher wages to workers over six feet in height, this is likely to fall foul of Article 119 as discrimination that has an indirect impact based on sex. The notion of indirect discrimination has proved an important means of eliminating many established practices that have an effect that is sexually biased.

In *Jenkins* v *Kingsgate Ltd*[32] part-time employees received an hourly rate of pay that was lower than that received by full-time employees doing the same work. The part-timers were almost all female. Directly, the discrimination was based on the number of hours of work, but indirectly women

---

30 Case C-109/91, note 21 above; see also Case C-200/91 *Coloroll Pension Trustees Limited* v *James Richard Russell and others* [1994] ECR I-4389.
31 Case C-28/93 *Maria Van den Akker* v *Stichting Shell Pensioenfonds* [1994] ECR I-4527, criticized for its deregulatory effect by Deakin (1995) 54 CLJ 35.
31a Case C-57/93, C-128/93, note 25 above. On the lack of clarity in the Court's approach see Whiteford (1995) 32 CMLRev 801.
32 Case 96/80 [1981] ECR 911.

were the principal losers. The Court held that in such circumstances the choice of such a criterion for differential pay rates was capable of violating Article 119.

It is a general principle of Community trade law that indirect discrimination differs from direct discrimination in that it is susceptible to objective justification.[33] It is difficult to imagine that a height requirement as the basis for differential pay rates would be objectively justifiable, but it is more feasible that differential treatment of part-time and full-time workers could be upheld. In *Jenkins* v *Kingsgate Ltd*[34] the Court held that there was no violation of Article 119 'in so far as the difference in pay between part-time work and full-time work is attributable to factors which are objectively justified and are in no way related to any discrimination based on sex'. It left the matter to be resolved by the referring national court, suggesting that it might be open to an employer to show that economic reasons encouraged a preference for full-time work, irrespective of the sex of the worker.[35] Under the Court's formula the employer's intention in selecting a criterion of differentiation is irrelevant in identifying an effect that discriminates on the basis of sex, but the employer is entitled to refer to his or her motivation in choosing the criterion in attempting to demonstrate an objective justification.

The Court has been rather reticent in defining the nature of objective justification in this context. It is in accordance with the intent of Article 119 that only submissions that entirely divorce sex from overall capability shall be relevant. In *Danfoss* the Court itself declared that 'it is inconceivable that the quality of work done by women should generally be less good',[36] while accepting that paying extra to remunerate adaptability in hours and place of work may be objectively justified even where men tend to benefit from such a system, provided such incentives are important for the performance of specific tasks. Quality may be rewarded, but the assessment of quality may not be tainted by sex discrimination.

Bilka Kaufhaus v *Weber*[37] was mentioned above as an example of the subjection of an occupational pension scheme to the rule of equality in

---

33 See e.g., Art. 95, p. 400 above; Art. 30, p. 444 above. See generally Lenaerts, '*L'Égalité de Traitement en Droit Communautaire*' (1991) 27 CDE 3.

34 Case 96/80, note 32 above.

35 On the economic and social background to the distinction between full-time and part-time work, see, e.g., the debate between C. Hakim, 'Employment Rights: A Comparison of Part-time and Full-time Employees' (1989) 18 ILJ 69 and R. Disney and E. Szyszczak, 'Part-time work: Reply to Catherine Hakim' (1989) 18 ILJ 223.

36 Case 109/88 *Handels-OG Kontorfunktionaererernes Forbund i Danmark* v *Dansk Arbedjsgiverforening (acting for Danfoss)* [1989] ECR 3199, [1991] 1 CMLR 8, noted by Szyszczak (1990) 19 ILJ 114, para. 20 of the judgment.

37 Case 170/84, note 22 above.

Article 119. The complaint arose because part-time workers were able to obtain pensions under the scheme only after crossing a threshold of sufficient previous full-time work. Weber, a female part-time worker, did not qualify. She pointed out that women were more likely to work part-time than men due to family responsibilities and that, accordingly, the choice of criterion led indirectly to unlawful sex discrimination. The Court referred to its decision in *Jenkins* v *Kingsgate*[38] and confirmed that once an effect that discriminates on grounds of sex is shown, the practice remains capable of objective justification without reference to the sex of the workers concerned. Bilka submitted that it was economically justified for it to seek to attract full-time workers rather than part-time workers by remunerating full-time work more generously, because part-time workers' tendency to refuse to work Saturdays and late afternoons rendered them less economically valuable. The Court held that a national court should apply a three-fold test in assessing such purported objective justification. The measures taken must correspond to a real need on the part of the undertaking, they must be appropriate as means of achieving the end in view, and they must be necessary to achieve that end. Thus, the national court, having established an effect discriminatory on grounds of sex, would have to inquire into, for example, the suitability of other techniques for ensuring worker availability on Saturdays and late afternoons; and whether it is consistent with this test for a firm freely to take on part-time workers rather than full-time workers, yet then to treat them less favourably.

The complaint about sick pay in *Rinner Kuhn* v *FWW*[39] arose because employees whose contract required no more than ten hours' work weekly or forty-five hours' monthly were excluded from protection. Given the attraction of part-time work to women, a smaller percentage of women than men would cross the threshold. The Court, citing its decision in *Bilka Kaufhaus*, held that a breach of Article 119 was established unless there were objective factors justifying the differential treatment that were unrelated to discrimination on grounds of sex. The German Government had submitted that workers below the threshold were less integrated into the undertaking and less dependent on it. The Court retorted that these were mere generalizations and inadequate justification. More specific grounds of justification would be required. In *P. Kirsammer-Hack* v *Nurhan Sidal*[40] the Court was asked to consider German laws against unfair dismissal that made special provision in the case of part-time workers meeting the same criteria of number of hours worked as those affected in

---

38 Case 96/80, note 32 above.
39 Case 171/88, note 18 above.
40 Case C-189/91, judgment of 30 November 1993.

Rinner Kuhn. The Court was not convinced that a discriminatory effect based on sex was at stake in the rules in *Kirsammer-Hack*, but it stated that even were that to be the case, an objective justification for restricting the availability of employment protection rights could be found in the alleviation of constraints imposed on small businesses.[41]

Where a violation of Article 119 is established in a collectively agreed pay deal, the Court has stated that the national court shall disapply the offending provisions and extend to the victims of discrimination the same arrangements as are applied to other employees.[42] There is no need to await collective renegotiation. Where a workplace is governed by two (or more) collective agreements, which are, judged separately, non-discriminatory, there may still be unlawful discrimination where women under one agreement are treated less favourably than men under another. The Court pointed out in *Enderby* v *Frenchay Health Authority and the Secretary of State for Health* that, were it otherwise, employers could set up separate workplace bargaining processes that are internally non-discriminatory, but in effect discriminatory, and thereby evade the application of equality law.[43] However, the Court admitted the possibility that shortage of available candidates and a market-driven need to offer higher wages may constitute an objective justification for differences in pay between jobs that are of equal value.

Transparency and the burden of proof

The prohibition against indirect discrimination is capable of direct effect.[44] A national court must make the assessment, first, of the prejudice felt indirectly according to sex, and then of the opportunities for objective justification. However, such calculations will often be difficult to make, which precludes the potential for direct effect in some circumstances. This prompted legislative amplification in Directive 75/117.[45] The applicant will

---

41 In the UK the availability to full-time workers of certain employment protection rights after two years' service, whereas part-time workers required five years', was ruled incompatible with Community law by the House of Lords, as an instance of indirect discrimination against women that had not been shown to be objectively justified; *EOC* v *Secretary of State for Employment* [1994] 2 WLR 409, [1994] 1 All ER 910, see Ch. 12, p. 374.

42 Case C-33/89 *Kowalska* v *Hamburg* [1990] ECR I-2591; Case C-184/89 *Nimz* v *Hamburg* [1991] ECR I-297 noted by More (1991) 16 ELRev 320.

43 Case C-127/92 [1993] ECR I-5535, [1994] 1 CMLR 8.

44 See e.g. Case 96/80, note 32 above, paras. 14, 18 of the judgment; Case 170/84, note 22 above, para. 36; Case 171/88, note 18 above, para. 15. For discussion of the scope of direct effect in this context, see Arnull, 'Article 119 and Equal Pay for Work of Equal Value' (1986) 11 ELRev 625.

45 See p. 625.

also encounter problems of proof. In this respect the impact of the rules against discrimination was reinforced by the Court's ruling in *Danfoss*.[46] Although the same basic minimum wage was paid to all workers irrespective of sex, the employer enjoyed flexibility under a collective agreement to pay extra sums in accordance with matters such as training and long service. Although it was unclear exactly how these criteria were applied, it was clear that two female workers finished up receiving pay some 7 per cent lower than that of male workers in the same wage group. The Court held that in such circumstances the employer bears a burden of proof to explain how the wages are determined. Once a discriminatory effect is shown to emerge from a system that totally lacks transparency, the employer is required to make that system transparent. This ruling takes the notion of effective remedies seriously by refusing to allow lack of clarity to frustrate the claimant's capacity to secure judicial supervision of pay procedures. It thereby promotes the practical realization of the principle of equality.

In *Barber* v *GRE* the Court confirmed 'the fundamental importance of transparency and, in particular, of the possibility of a review by the national courts in order to prevent . . . discrimination based on sex'.[47] This prompted the Court to reject the notion that an employer could show equality between the sexes on an overall appraisal of pay packages, because of the difficulty of checking the validity of such a broad comparison. Instead, the Court insisted on equality term by term, a test that is readily invoked before a court.[48]

These judgments demonstrate the Court's readiness to intrude on national procedural autonomy in order to advance the effective application of the substantive rules of Community law.[49] In fulfilling this dynamic role the Court takes Community law into areas in which the legislature has been reluctant to tread. In 1988 a proposed directive dealing with the burden of proof in discrimination cases was blocked by opposition in the Council.[50]

---

46 Case 109/88, note 36 above. See also Case C-127/92 *Enderby*, note 43 above.
47 Case C-262/88, note 26 above, para. 33 of the judgment.
48 In English law the House of Lords had already reached the same conclusion in pursuit of the need for transparency in *Hayward* v *Cammell Laird* [1988] IRLR 257.
49 See Case C-213/89 *R* v *Secretary of State for Transport, ex parte Factortame* [1990] ECR I-2433, [1990] 3 CMLR 1, discussed on p. 176.
50 OJ 1988 C176. Nielsen and Szyszczak, *The Social Dimension of the European Community*, pp. 161–2. Prechal and Burrows, *Gender Discrimination Law*, pp. 296–300.

DIRECTIVE 75/117

Defrenne v *SABENA*[51] established that in some circumstances Article 119 creates directly effective rights enforceable before a national tribunal, but some instances of discrimination are incapable of control on the basis of Article 119 alone. Where a woman is paid less than a man doing a job that, though different, is of allegedly comparable economic worth, the discrimination can be uncovered only by performing an evaluation study that compares the nature of the jobs. This prevents the application of Article 119 directly by a national court before which a complaint is made, because Article 119 is not directly effective where the discrimination 'can only be identified by reference to more explicit implementing provisions'.[52] Directive 75/117[53] required member states to put in place methods whereby an evaluation of comparability could be undertaken at the request of an employee.[54] Directive 75/117 concerns equal pay for work of equal *value*. The Court considers that the Directive does not alter the scope of Article 119, but facilitates its practical application.[55] Accordingly, much of the above analysis of Article 119 is equally applicable to the Directive.[56]

DIRECTIVE 76/207

The adoption of Directive 76/207[57] effectively converted the Community rules into a system designed to challenge sex discrimination, rather than simply a set of rules concerned with equal pay. Directive 76/207 reaches beyond Article 119's requirement of equality in pay and requires *equal treatment* of men and women. The extended legislative coverage, buttressed by activist jurisprudence emanating from the Court, elevates equality between the sexes towards the status of a general principle of Community law.[58]

51 Case 43/75, note 2 above.
52 ibid.
53 OJ 1975 L45/19.
54 The UK's failure to meet its obligations in this respect was recorded in Case 61/81 *Commission* v *United Kingdom* [1982] ECR 2601, [1982] 3 CMLR 284; even thereafter the subsequent implementation was flawed and had to be 'rescued' by active interpretation in the light of Art. 119 and the Directive by the House of Lords in *Pickstone* v *Freemans* [1989] AC 66.
55 Case 96/80, note 32 above, para. 22 of the judgment.
56 E.g., the ruling in *Danfoss*, note 36 above, dealt explicitly with the Directive, but established a principle of general application.
57 OJ 1976 L39/40.
58 See Docksey, 'The Principle of Equality between Women and Men as a Fundamental

Scope

Equal treatment is a broad notion. It is defined in Article 2 of the Directive as meaning 'that there shall be no discrimination whatsoever on grounds of sex either directly or indirectly by reference in particular to marital or family status'. It requires equality between the sexes in, for example, recruitment, promotion and conditions governing dismissal. Selection of women over men for redundancy or compulsory retirement, for example, would fall foul of the equal-treatment principle. Indirectly unequal treatment would also contravene the Directive. Selection of part-timers over full-timers for redundancy or compulsory retirement, where this has a heavier impact on women than men, would also be unlawful except in so far as the employer can demonstrate an objective justification for discriminating against part-time workers.[59]

Although the equal-treatment principle under Directive 76/207 covers dismissal, Directive 79/7 excludes 'the determination of pensionable age for the purposes of granting old-age and retirement pensions' from the application of the equality principle. This appears to permit the United Kingdom to continue to pay old-age pensions to women at 60 and men at 65. However, in *Marshall* v *Southampton Area Health Authority*[60] the Court displayed a determination to interpret the exception narrowly. A woman had been required to retire earlier than a man would have been because of a policy linking retirement to the state pension age. The Court held that this did not fall within the exception. It was *not* a determination of age for the purposes of pension payment; it was a determination for the purpose of retirement. It fell outside the exception in Directive 79/7 and was contrary to the prohibition against unequal treatment under Directive 76/207.

A question that has posed some difficulty is whether and, if so, how discrimination on grounds of pregnancy is controlled under the Equal-Treatment Directive. There are at least three possible approaches. The first would deny that there is any issue of discrimination. There can be no comparison between a pregnant woman and a man, so there can be no objection to treating them differently. The second approach would treat the matter as potentially discriminatory. It would compare the employer's treatment of a pregnant woman with treatment of a man incapable of working for a similar period and would hold the employer to have acted

---

Right under Community Law' (1991) 20 ILJ 258; Watson, 'Equality of Treatment: a Variable Concept?' (1995) 24 ILJ 33.

59 See p. 620.
60 Case 152/84 [1986] ECR 723, [1986] 1 CMLR 688.

properly, provided the cases would be dealt with in the same way. The third approach would insist that discrimination on grounds of pregnancy is always direct discrimination because it is based on a uniquely female biological characteristic. In a rather unsatisfactory pair of cases the European Court adopted the third alternative, but diluted it with a hint of the second.[61] In *Dekker*[62] a woman was refused employment because she was pregnant. This was held to be direct discrimination prohibited by the Directive. An employer is precluded from seeking to escape liability by claiming that an incapacitated man would have been similarly treated, or by submitting that national law would render the recruitment of the woman economically unattractive because of the consequences of her absence on maternity leave. In *Hertz* v *ALDI*[63] a woman was dismissed because of her absences from work due to illness after her maternity leave. This was not held to be direct discrimination based on sex. It was based on illness, albeit originating in pregnancy, and both sexes may fall ill.

The juxtaposition of these cases, decided on the same day, sent confusing messages to national courts.[64] It is submitted that *Hertz* v *ALDI* should not be taken to qualify the basic principle established in *Dekker*, that discrimination because of pregnancy constitutes direct discrimination because of sex and is therefore unjustifiable.[65] Indeed, in *Hertz* the Court repeated that finding. *Hertz* was a case where the discrimination was *not* due to pregnancy and it shows merely that protection does not persist indefinitely after the woman has given birth. Admittedly, by leaving the time-limit to be fixed under national law, the Court may have left open the possibility of inequality in protection state by state, but such matters may be soluble only through a specific directive dealing with pregnancy and maternity leave.[66] In *Carole Louise Webb* v *EMO Air Cargo (UK) Ltd*[67] the Court ruled that a pregnant woman should not be compared with an indisposed man. Dismissal on account of pregnancy is direct discrimination. It decided that the dismissal of a pregnant woman recruited for an indefinite period cannot be justified on grounds relating to her inability to fulfil a fundamental condition of her employment contract. Although the presence of the

---

61 The English courts began with the first approach (*Turley* v *Allders Stores* [1980] ICR 66), but subsequently shifted to the second (*Hayes* v *Malleable Working Men's Club* [1985] IRLR 367).
62 Case C-177/88 [1990] ECR I-3841.
63 Case C-179/88 [1990] ECR I-3879.
64 For a range of comment, see Asscher-Vonk (1991) 20 ILJ 152; Shaw (1991) 16 EL Rev 313; Ellis [1991] PL 159; Nielsen (1992) 29 CMLRev 160.
65 Except, in principle, under the specific justifications in the Directive, examined below, none of which is applicable in such cases.
66 See Dir. 92/85, p. 640.
67 Case C-32/93 [1994] ECR I-3567, [1994] 2 CMLR 729, noted by Moore (1994) 19 ELRev 653.

employee was doubtless vital to the employer in securing proper performance of the contract and even though Webb had been hired to cover for the maternity leave of another employee, that could not prevail over the protection afforded by law to a woman during pregnancy and after childbirth. Any different system of priorities would wholly undermine the purpose of Directive 76/207. However, the Court restricted the explicit terms of its ruling to the position of a woman recruited for an unlimited period. This leaves open the possibility that a woman recruited on a fixed term contract might be vulnerable to a lawful dismissal if she becomes pregnant on the basis that the purpose of her recruitment has been frustrated. In *Habermann-Beltermann* v *Arbeitwohlfahrt, Bezirksverband*[68] the Court considered that termination of a contract on account of pregnancy was incompatible with the Directive and incapable of justification on the ground that a statutory prohibition on night-work by pregnant employees temporarily cut across the employee's duties as a night attendant in a home for the elderly. However, here too the Court referred to the fact that the contract was *not* for a fixed term. Further litigation on the impact of Directive 76/207 on pregnancy dismissals in the case of fixed term contracts seems inevitable. It is submitted that the purpose of the Directive, as a method of both removing competitive distortion and securing social progress,[69] would be no less subverted by permitting the dismissal of a woman from a fixed term contract when she falls pregnant than by permitting such a dismissal under a contract of indefinite duration.

Exceptions

Whereas the notion of equal treatment is broadly interpreted, any derogations from the notion are narrowly defined. Article 2(2) provides an exception where the sex of the worker is a determining factor by reason of the nature of the job, which is, in a sense, a legislative formulation of the judicially developed objective justification for practices that exert an indirect discriminatory effect.[70] Article 3(3) exempts from the principle of equal treatment provisions concerning the protection of women, particularly as regards pregnancy and maternity.

In *Johnston* v *RUC*[71] the police force in Northern Ireland was not prepared to employ women as full-time members of the reserve force because they were neither trained in the use of nor permitted to use

---

68 Case C-421/92 [1994] ECR I-1657.
69 Case 43/75 *Defrenne* v *SABENA*, note 2 above; p. 614.
70 See p. 620.
71 Case 222/84 *Johnston* v *Chief Constable of the Royal Ulster Constabulary* [1986] ECR 1651.

firearms. Several reasons for this inequality were advanced, such as the risk that women would become an increased terrorist target if armed, and the reduction in women officers' effectiveness in the social sphere of their duties. The Court insisted that derogations from the Directive must be interpreted narrowly. It held that the Article 2(2) exception could be invoked in relation to particular duties, not general activities, although it is acknowledged that the context in which the activity was pursued might be taken into account. Doubtless aware of the delicate circumstances, it admitted that in a situation characterized by serious internal disturbance the carrying of firearms by policewomen might create additional risks of their being assassinated. A situation might arise where the sex of the officer constituted a determining factor for performing the task, as required by Article 2(2) of the Directive. However, the employer is obliged to review the situation from time to time in order to satisfy itself that the exclusion remains justified, and the steps taken must be proportionate.

Remedies

Article 6 of the Directive contains an explicit commitment to the principle of effective remedies, which is itself part of the general Community legal order.[72] Article 6 declares that 'Member States shall introduce into their national legal systems such measures as are necessary to enable all persons who consider themselves wronged by failure to apply to them the principle of equal treatment ... to pursue their claims by judicial process after possible recourse to other competent authorities'. In *Von Colson and Kamann* v *Land Nordrhein Westfalen*[73] the Court interpreted this to require the availability in the national system of a sanction providing real and effective protection that would exert a deterrent effect on the employer. In *Marshall II*[74] the Court ruled that if a state chooses to put in place a system of compensation, limits placed by national law on the amount of compensation must be set aside in so far as they obstruct the availability of an effective remedy.

72 See pp. 176, 802.
73 Case 14/83 [1984] ECR 1891, considered further at p. 633.
74 Case C-271/91 [1993] ECR 1-4367, [1993] 3 CMLR 293, Ch. 11, p. 357.

DIRECTIVE 79/7

Directive 79/7[75] extends the principle of equal treatment into the sphere of social security. It is a specific application of the wider notion of equal treatment of the sexes with which Directive 76/207 is concerned.[76] Its requirement of equal treatment covers statutory schemes providing protection against sickness, invalidity, old age, accidents at work or occupational diseases and unemployment; and social assistance in so far as it is intended to supplement or replace these schemes. It applies to the working population, which is defined in Article 2 to embrace 'self-employed persons, workers and self-employed persons whose activity is interrupted by illness, accident or involuntary unemployment and persons seeking employment', and to 'retired or invalided workers and self-employed persons'.[77] Women meeting these criteria shall be treated no less favourably than men in the administration of the schemes covered by the Directive.

The Court has shown itself ready to adopt a broad interpretation of both the personal and the material scope of the Directive. For example, in *Drake* v *Chief Adjudication Officer*[78] it rejected United Kingdom submissions that an invalidity care allowance payable to a person engaged in caring for a severely disabled person fell outside the Directive because the recipient was a third party, not the actual invalid, and was in any event not part of the working population. The Court ruled that the benefit was part of a general statutory scheme providing protection against a stipulated risk and that the recipient, having given up work because of the invalidity of the person cared for, was for the purposes of the Directive part of the working population.[79] Sex discrimination in the conditions under which the benefit was granted had to be eliminated. Moreover, the Court has extended its familiar indirect discrimination/objective justification model into this area of equality law. In *Ruzius-Wilbrink*[80] it held that Dutch invalidity benefits that treated part-time workers less favourably than full-time workers were unlawful where a higher percentage of women than men worked part-time, unless objective justification unrelated to sex explained the differen-

75 OJ 1979 L6/24.
76 For discussion of Directive 79/7 and, in particular, its impact in the UK, see Luckhaus, 'Changing Rules, Enduring Structures' (1990) 53 MLR 655.
77 It does not apply to persons who have never been available for employment or who have ceased to be available for a reason other than illness, invalidity, old age, accident at work, occupational disease or unemployment; see Cases 48, 106 and 107/88 *Achteberg-te Riele and Others* v *Sociale Verzekeringsbank* [1989] ECR 1963, 1988, noted by Cousins (1992) 17 ELRev 55.
78 Case 150/85 [1986] ECR 1995.
79 Cf. more narrowly Cases 48, 106 and 107/88, note 77 above.
80 Case C-102/88 [1989] ECR 4311, [1991] 2 CMLR 202.

tial. The development of the nature of objective justification in the context of statutory social security schemes is likely to prove a sensitive task for the Court.[81]

A major feature of this Directive is its exclusion in Article 7 of 'the determination of pensionable age for the purposes of granting old-age and retirement pensions'. The narrow scope of this exception was established in *Marshall*.[82] Article 7 contains other exclusions: benefits or entitlements granted to persons who have brought up children; old-age or invalidity benefit entitlements granted by virtue of the derived entitlements of a wife; and increases granted in respect of dependent wives related to long-term invalidity, old-age, accidents at work and occupational disease benefits.

To the extent that the definition of pay under Article 119 has intruded into the sphere of social security, especially in relation to pension schemes,[83] it may be possible to use that Article rather than the Directive to secure equality. The claimant has some incentive to rely on Article 119 in preference to the Directive, as the former is not subject to the exceptions in the latter. This, it will be recalled, was especially important for Mr Barber.[84] Furthermore, Article 119 is plainly directly effective against both public and private employers, whereas the Directive is a more indirect source of rights, although the Court has indicated that it may be relied upon before a national court to challenge national provisions that are incompatible with it, which may have the practical effect of permitting a woman to claim that she must be treated in the same way as a man in a comparable situation.[85] However, despite the Court's extension of the notion of pay, many social security schemes remain outside Article 119 and it will be necessary to rely on the Directive and its domestic implementing measures to secure equality.

SUPPLEMENTARY DIRECTIVES

Directive 86/378[86] extends the principle of equal treatment to occupational pension schemes. It stands alongside Directive 79/7, which applies to statutory schemes, and should be interpreted in parallel. The Court's

81 E.g., Prechal and Burrows, *Gender Discrimination Law*, pp. 197–9. See Case C-229/89 *Commission* v *Belgium*, [1991] ECR I-2205.
82 Case 152/84, note 60 above.
83 See pp. 617–20.
84 Case C-262/88, note 26 above.
85 E.g., Case 286/85 *McDermott and Cotter* v *Minister for Social Welfare* [1987] ECR 1453; Case C-208/90 *Emmott* v *Minister for Social Welfare*, [1991] ECR I-4269.
86 OJ 1986 L225/40.

extended interpretation of 'pay'[87] under Article 119 has brought many occupational pension schemes within the scope of that basic prohibition and that has naturally both diminished the independent vigour of the Directive and curtailed the blocking effect of the exceptions within it.

Directive 86/613[88] applies the equal-treatment principle to the self-employed. It is a complement, in particular, to Directives 76/207 and 79/7.

COMMUNITY SEX DISCRIMINATION LAW BEFORE NATIONAL COURTS

Under Article 189 directives 'leave to the national authorities the choice of form and methods' of achieving the stipulated result. The elaboration of the principle of equal treatment thus rests with national implementing measures. However, inadequate implementation of directives by member states[89] has created obstacles for intended beneficiaries of the laws against discrimination and, in seeking to contribute to the correction of these flaws, the Court has delivered several judgments of constitutional importance beyond the field of equal treatment of the sexes. The constitutional status of a directive within a national legal order was discussed at length in Chapter 11, but it deserves consideration in the particular context of the equality directives, because resolution of the constitutional issues bears heavily on the practical effectiveness of the substantive rule of equality. Three remedial methods are identified below.

THE DIRECT EFFECT OF DIRECTIVES

It has already been seen in *Marshall* v *Southampton Area Health Authority*[90] that Ms Marshall's forced retirement at an age below that which would have applied to a man fell foul of Directive 76/207. The European Court held that she could rely on this directly before the English courts, which was essential to her claim, since the Sex Discrimination Act 1975 offered her no remedy because of a statutory exclusion of discrimination in 'provisions relating to death or retirement'. The United Kingdom had in this respect failed to implement the Directive. However, the basis for

---

87 See pp. 617–20.
88 OJ 1986 L359/56.
89 For a survey see Prechal and Burrows, *Gender Discrimination Law*, Ch. 6.
90 Case 152/84, note 60 above.

holding a directive directly effective, contrary to the explicit terms of Article 189, rested on the need to preclude a state from benefiting from its own unlawful failure to implement, and, accordingly, the Court determined that only employees of the state were entitled to invoke the Directive directly.

The Court has interpreted the 'state' broadly for these purposes. It included the Area Health Authority in *Marshall*, and in *Foster* v *British Gas*[91] the Court elaborated a test based on the function of the entity, not its legal form. The Court also enhanced the individual's position by ruling in *Emmott* v *Minister for Social Welfare* that national limitation periods do not begin to run against potential plaintiffs until such time as the state has properly implemented a directive.[92] However, the *Marshall* approach created the anomaly that those not employed by the state, however broadly defined, were unable to rely on an unimplemented directive that is intended to confer on them valuable rights. They must await implementation of Community law by the state.[93]

THE 'INDIRECT EFFECT' OF DIRECTIVES

In *Von Colson and Kamann* v *Land Nordrhein Westfalen*[94] the Court subverted the state/private dichotomy. Women refused posts in the prison service had been discriminated against on grounds of sex, but under German law their remedy was merely reimbursement of travelling expenses incurred in pursuing the posts. By contrast, Article 6 of Directive 76/207 obliges states to provide effective remedies, which the Court interpreted to mean a sanction offering real and effective protection exerting a deterrent effect on the employer. As in *Marshall*,[95] there was a gulf between national law and Community law, but in *Von Colson* the European Court, faced with this problem, did not proceed along the direct-effect route. Instead, it drew from Article 5 of the Treaty an obligation on state authorities to achieve the result envisaged by a directive. Courts, as organs of the state, were directed to interpret national law in the light of the wording and the purpose of a directive, which here required national law to be interpreted in order to provide effective protection. This method circumvents the issue of distinguishing between state and private employers, for it requires

91 Case C-188/89 [1990] ECR I-3133, see p. 350.
92 Case C-208/90, note 85 above. See Ch. 11, p. 350, on the Court's unwillingness to extend the ruling in *Emmott*, most notably in Case C-338/91 *Steenhorst-Neerings* v *Bestuur van de Bedrijfsvereniging voor Detailhandel, Ambachten en Huisvrouwen* [1993] ECR I-5475.
93 The UK filled the gap exposed in *Marshall* in the Sex Discrimination Act 1986.
94 Case 14/83, note 73 above.
95 Case 152/84, note 60 above. See also Case C-271/91 *Marshall II*, note 74 above.

national law in *all* cases to afford protection from discrimination consonant with that intended by Community law. It is not a matter of direct effect, but, through the medium of interpretation of national law by national courts, it is a matter of indirect effect. The Court subsequently insisted in *Marleasing* v *La Comercial Internacional*[96] that national courts should interpret all national law in the light of relevant directives, whether the national law in question predates or postdates the directive.

The advantage of this approach is that it is capable of eliminating the anomaly that only state employees may rely on a directive where national authorities have not met their obligation of implementation. The disadvantage is that it places a burden on national courts, which they may not be willing or able to fulfil. Individual victims of discrimination are reliant on national law, duly interpreted, not on Community law itself. The progress of Community law rests on the potentially very different interpretative techniques of national courts in different member states.[97]

In the United Kingdom the House of Lords has shown itself prepared to accept the task of interpreting provisions of national law in the light of Community law where it is satisfied that parliament intended the national legislation to conform to Community obligations. Thus, in *Pickstone* v *Freemans*[98] the rules governing equal pay for work of equal value introduced in the United Kingdom in 1983 were adjusted with reference to the intent of Directive 75/117. Where a domestic provision postdates a Community measure, the judges are willing to read it in the light of the relevant Community measure.[99] However, the House of Lords has declined to interpret pre-existing national law in the light of subsequently adopted Community provisions. In *Duke* v *GEC Reliance*[100] it was held that parliament could not have intended the Sex Discrimination Act of 1975 to conform to the subsequent 1976 Equal-Treatment Directive and therefore their Lordships refused to use the Community measure as an interpretative guide. An employee of a private firm was thus left without any remedy

---

96 Case C-106/89 [1990] ECR I-4135, [1992] 1 CMLR 305, noted by Stuyck and Wytinck (1991) 28 CMLRev 205.
97 The issue has attracted a great deal of comment, but the following analyses relate specifically to equality law: Wyatt, 'Enforcing EEC Social Rights in the United Kingdom' (1989) 18 ILJ 197; Fitzpatrick, 'The Significance of EEC Directives in UK Sex Discrimination Law' (1989) 9 Ox JLS 336; Shaw, 'European Community Judicial Method: Its Application to Sex Discrimination Law' (1990) 19 ILJ 228; Docksey and Fitzpatrick, 'The Duty of National Courts to Interpret provisions of National Law in accordance with Community Law' (1991) 20 ILJ 113.
98 [1989] AC 66, see note 54 above.
99 See also *Litster* v *Forth Dry Dock* [1990] 1 AC 546, [1989] 2 WLR 634. See further Ch. 11, p. 363.
100 [1988] AC 618, [1988] 2 WLR 359. See further Ch. 11, p. 361.

despite being subject to precisely the same type of discrimination as Ms Marshall, who, crucially, worked for the state.[101]

The European Court's decision in *Marleasing*[102] has demanded reassessment of these authorities.[103] However these issues are ultimately resolved, both employer and employee in such cases are in a sense 'innocent' parties, one of whom will suffer because of the legal uncertainty created by the non-implementation of the Directive.[104] The real miscreant is the state itself, which has caused these difficulties by failing to implement the Directive.[105] The Court has recently improved the opportunities for challenging the non-implementing state directly.

THE LIABILITY OF THE STATE

The approach elaborated in *Von Colson*[106] and *Marleasing*[107] asks courts to cure defects caused by state omissions, in advance of and independently of infringement proceedings initiated by the Commission under Article 169. *Francovich*[108] brings the correct target into focus. It establishes a potentially valuable deterrent sanction in damages against the non-implementing state. Where a private employee suffers loss due to non-implementation of a directive, it remains possible to rely on the indirect effect of the directive against the employer, which requires an excursion into the complexities of national interpretative techniques. It may, however, prove more valuable to sue the state itself. This route is certainly more likely to improve the observance of Community law obligations by the state.[109] It is to be hoped that the objective of matching the theory of Community sex-discrimination law with its practical application will in time no longer be obscured by constitutional debates about the nature of directives left unimplemented by member states.

101 See p. 350.
102 Case C-106/89, note 96 above.
103 See Ch. 11 for further examination of these cases.
104 *Duke* protects the employer, *Marleasing* the employee; neither decision explains adequately *why* such a preference has been made, although, as a matter of constitutional law, the European Court's view must, of course, prevail. The fulfilment of the intent of the Directive as a means of securing equality dictates a preference for the *Marleasing* pro-employee approach.
105 This, of course, motivated the Court to confine the scope of direct effect in *Marshall* itself; see p. 347.
106 Case 14/83, note 73 above.
107 Case C-106/89, note 96 above.
108 Case C-6, C-9/90 *Francovich and Others* v *Italy*, [1991] ECR I-5357 examined at p. 352.
109 It is, however, questionable whether such a general policy objective justifies the creation by the Court of a specific legal liability of this nature; see Ch. 11, p. 353.

BEYOND SEX DISCRIMINATION

HISTORY

The Community has always had an explicit commitment to social policy. Article 119 is simply the most precise of the provisions contained in the title, which comprised Articles 117-28 of the EEC Treaty. However, Community social policy has long been tied to the employment relationship, and the extension of Community activity in the sphere of social policy has been slow and often subject to fierce political opposition. Apart from Article 119, the original provisions were largely aspirational and inexplicit. Indeed, had it not been for the firm line adopted by the Court in *Defrenne* v *SABENA*[110] in relation to its direct effect, even Article 119 might have languished, more or less disregarded, as mere aspiration.

Up until the early 1970s Community social policy was limited to the task of achieving the free movement of persons. It was subordinate to, and dependent on, market integration. Politically, the raising of the profile of Community social policy may be traced to a Council resolution of January 1974, which adopted Commission proposals for a social action programme. This contained reference to the need for action in the fields of employment, living and working conditions and deeper participation by the social partners in Community decision-making. This reflected a feeling that the growth of the Community at the economic level should be reflected in initiatives at the social level. In part, this may be derived from the notion that without action to achieve social cohesion the process of integration is increasingly likely to meet opposition that will frustrate its completion. More broadly, there was a view that the integrated market itself needed regulation, independently of the specific task of integration, in order to distribute fairly the benefits of economic growth. Both perspectives enjoy some support in the original Treaty of Rome.[111] These political aspirations were transformed into legal norms in several important legislative acts, some of which dealt with the expanded sex-equality programme discussed above. In fact, the mid-1970s was the only period in its history when the Community moved forward rapidly and vigorously in the field of social policy. This political atmosphere was also doubtless a factor conducive to the Court's activism. *Defrenne* v *SABENA*, in which the direct effect of Article 119 was established, was decided by the Court early in 1976. However, political consensus in the Community is always fragile, given

110 Case 43/75, note 2 above.
111 See p. 615.

the regular likelihood of electoral change in one or more member states, and the support for the social dimension began to wane in the late 1970s. Economic recession contributed to the sapping of political will. The election in the United Kingdom in 1979 of a Conservative administration dedicated to the deregulation of the economy precipitated a significant breakdown in the consensus relating to social action within the Community.

LEGAL COMPETENCE

The problem of legal base

It is necessary to determine precisely what the Community is capable of achieving in the field of social policy. For all the political and economic interest in such questions, this is in many respects a fundamentally legal issue. The most appropriate starting point for the examination of the scope for development of Community social policy is the question of legislative competence. The Community, it should be remembered, lacks a general legislative competence. It may act only where a specific power to legislate may be identified in the Treaty – 'a legal base'.[112] There are many such bases, involving differing allocations of responsibility to the several institutions. In some cases the Parliament has a right to be consulted, in others it has an enhanced status under the cooperation procedure or the conciliation and veto procedure.[113] In some cases the Council may act by qualified majority, in others unanimity is the rule, which preserves the national veto. On occasion, a debate about the substance of a proposal may spill over into a question of legal base. Where states cannot agree on a measure, it will not be adopted if the appropriate legal base involves a requirement of a unanimous vote; the matter will be different if a majority base can be found. Legislative procedure is, accordingly, not just an abstract issue of legal technicality; it affects how the measure is adopted, and, where there is controversy, it might affect whether the measure is adopted.

The measures examined in the two preceding chapters used several different legal bases. Article 49 supplied a base for the adoption of legislation amplifying the rules relating to the free movement of workers. Article 51 provided the base for the adoption of legislation in the field of social security. Article 118 was used to establish by decision a prior communication and consultation procedure on migration policies in rela-

112 See Ch. 5.
113 See Chs. 4, 5.

tion to non-member states.[114] The directives that have already been the subject of examination in this chapter deserve attention from the perspective of legal base. Article 100 was the base for Directive 75/117, but Article 235 was used for Directives 76/207 and 79/7. Article 235 allows the Council, acting unanimously, to take appropriate measures 'if action by the Community should prove necessary to attain, in the course of the operation of the common market, one of the objectives of the Community and this Treaty has not provided the necessary powers'. This is the broadest of all the legal bases in the Treaty. Article 100 allows the Council to 'issue directives for the approximation of such provisions laid down by law, regulation or administrative action in Member States as directly affect the establishment or functioning of the common market'. It, too, requires a unanimous vote. Article 100a was added by the Single European Act as a base for the adoption of the legislation for the achievement of the objectives set out in Article 7a, the completion of the internal market.[115] The Council shall 'adopt the measures for the approximation of the provisions laid down by law, regulation or administrative action in Member States which have as their object the establishment and functioning of the internal market'. This is a power exercisable by qualified majority vote in Council – except in so far as provisions 'relating to the free movement of persons . . . [or] those relating to the rights and interests of employed persons' are concerned. In such cases, which embrace the social sphere, unanimity under Article 100 remains the rule.

Legislating to achieve the common market and the internal market

The use of Article 100/100a is based on the notion that the harmonization of legislation applicable to working conditions is necessary to ensure the effective functioning of the common market. This conforms to the Court's 'dual focus' approach to the nature of Community Social Policy adopted in *Defrenne* v *SABENA*.[116] The Community is equipped with competence to legislate in areas beyond the purely economic, albeit that a link to the functioning of the market must be demonstrated. Directive 75/117 provides a good illustration. A group of further directives that impinge on the social protection of workers have been made on this base. Three directives concern the protection of workers in the event of corporate-restructuring.[117] Directive 75/129 concerns the approximation of laws relating to

114 See Ch. 8, pp. 246–7.
115 See p. 24.
116 Case 43/75, note 2 above, and see p. 614.
117 Nielsen and Szyszczak, *The Social Dimension of the European Community*, Ch. 4.

collective redundancies.[118] It includes rules governing procedures and requiring consultation with workers' representatives. Directive 77/187 approximates laws relating to the safeguarding of employees' rights in the event of transfers of undertakings.[119] Its purpose is to ensure that a transfer of a business cannot occur without the position of the workers being taken into account and protected in specified ways. As far as possible, the employment relationship ought to be transplanted unchanged from the transferor to the transferee.[120] Directive 80/987 approximates laws relating to the protection of employees in the event of the insolvency of their employer.[121] It requires the provision of a minimum level of protection in the event of such insolvency.[122] Each of these directives contains a declaration in its preamble that differences between the existing laws relating to such matters in the member states exert a 'direct effect on the functioning of the common market', thereby demonstrating the reason why Article 100 may be used in order to introduce measures of a social nature.

Bases permitting qualified majority voting

The examination of legislation in this chapter is by no means exhaustive. However, in portraying the use of Articles 100 and 235 as legal bases for the adoption of legislation affecting employed persons, the policy debate about the scope of Community competence remains submerged. All three provisions require a unanimous vote. Questions of competence to adopt social policy measures will not be addressed explicitly. A dissentient state will simply veto the proposal. However, where a base permitting *qualified majority* voting is used instead, the veto disappears. States that disagree with the proposal and fear they may be outvoted may seek to challenge the Community's competence to act.

There are legal bases touching on social policy that may form the basis for subverting the veto held by one or a small minority of dissentient states. Article 118a(1) provides that 'Member States shall pay particular attention to encouraging improvements, especially in the working environment, as regards the health and safety of workers, and shall set as their objective the harmonization of conditions in this area, while maintaining

---

118 OJ 1975 L48/29, amended by Dir 92/56 OJ 1992 L245.
119 OJ 1977 L61/26.
120 E.g., Case 19/83 *Wendelboe* v *Music* [1985] ECR 457. See also Case 101/87 *Bork International* v *Foreningen af Arbejdsledere i Danmark* [1988] ECR 3057 and the House of Lords' decision in *Litster* v *Forth Dry Dock & Engineering Ltd* [1990] 1 AC 546, discussed in Ch. 11, p. 364.
121 OJ 1980 L283/23.
122 Italy's failure to implement this Directive formed the background to Cases C-6, C-9/90 *Francovich*, note 108 above.

the improvements made.' Article 118a(2) then authorizes the adoption of directives setting minimum requirements for gradual implementation in order to help achieve this objective. Such directives are to be adopted by the Council acting by qualified majority, utilizing the cooperation procedure.[123]

The most prominent Directive adopted under Article 118a was, in fact, adopted unanimously. Directive 89/391[124] is the 'Framework Directive', designed to improve the health and safety of workers. It contains broadly drafted objectives, and the intention was that it should be amplified by supporting directives of relevance to more specific aspects of health and safety. This quickly occurred through the adoption of five further directives concerning the workplace,[125] machines and work equipment,[126] personal protective equipment,[127] handling heavy loads,[128] and visual display units.[129]

The fact that measures concerned with health and safety within the meaning of Article 118a may be adopted without the unanimous agreement of all member states makes it rather important to define precisely when Article 118a may be used in preference to Article 100 or 235, which demand unanimity and thus allow a veto. The Court asserts that the choice must be based on objective factors amenable to judicial review,[130] but the limits of Article 118a are hard to define in advance. Article 118a EC has been used as the base for directives on the protection of pregnant workers,[131] the protection of young people at work[132] and on working time.[133] These measures may seem to disclose a rather extended notion of health and safety, but tactically it is necessary in order to lift a single state's veto. The opposing view is that these measures concern the completion of the internal market and are therefore subject to Article 100a(2). The broad approach taken to the scope of matters of health and safety under Article 118a is likely to result in legal challenges to the validity of these directives before the European Court.[134]

Article 54(3)(g), part of the provisions that deal with the right of

---

123 See Ch. 5, p. 147.
124 OJ 1989 L183/1; see Eberlie, 'The New Health and Safety Legislation of the European Community' (1990) 19 ILJ 81; Szyszczak, '1992 and the Working Environment' [1992] JSWFL 3.
125 Dir. 89/654 OJ 1989 L393/1, corrected OJ 1990 L211/15, OJ 1991 L59/23.
126 Dir. 89/655 OJ 1989 L393/13.
127 Dir. 89/656 OJ 1990 L393/18, corrected OJ 1991 L59/24.
128 Dir. 90/269 OJ 1990 L156/9, corrected OJ 1991 L59/24.
129 Dir. 90/270 OJ 1990 L156/14, corrected OJ 1990 L171/30.
130 E.g., Case 45/86 *Commission v Council* [1987] ECR 1493; see pp. 141, 250.
131 Dir. 92/85 OJ 1992 L348/92.
132 Dir. 94/33 OJ 1994 L216/12.
133 Dir. 93/104 OJ 1993 L307/93.
134 Dir. 93/104 has been challenged by the UK, C-84/94 *UK v Council.*

establishment,[135] provides the base for the company law harmonization programme, which has direct and indirect implications for workers. Worker participation in companies has long proved an issue of deep controversy touching on both substance and procedure.[136] Briefly, Germany has long insisted that any European regime must respect its entrenched worker participation structures. It feared a loss of domestic companies to the new model, if the European model offered lighter regulation.[137] States unaccustomed to such worker participation, including the United Kingdom, strongly opposed such perceived intervention in corporate governance. The Commission's attempts to resolve these disagreements in the context of the European Company Statute have latterly involved adaptation at both substantive level and procedural level. It has conceded that the diversity in legal tradition is insuperable and has accordingly put forward proposals for worker participation that offer a choice of three models, varying in their level of interventionism. Procedurally, worker participation proposals have been separated from the main regulation establishing the European Company. In its 1991 proposals the Commission presented the Company Statute in a regulation under Article 100a, whereas the related worker participation elements appear in a directive to be adopted under Article 54(3)(g).[138]

The tactical ploy of using Article 54 to circumvent the Article 100a unanimity requirement affecting a measure of social policy is obvious. The Court has insisted that legal bases cannot be selected at the discretion of the institutions and must be chosen according to objective factors amenable to judicial review.[139] Were the Commission's proposals to be adopted in Council under the Commission's chosen bases, a challenge by an outvoted state to the validity of the measure(s) may be anticipated.[140]

---

135 See Ch. 19.
136 Nielsen and Szyszczak, *The Social Dimension of the European Community*, Ch. 5.
137 See discussion of the regulatory 'race to the bottom', p. 600.
138 OJ 1991 C138/8.
139 See pp. 141, 250 and note 130 above.
140 See Ch. 19, p. 602 above. Cf. Dir. 94/45, p. 646 below.

THE UNITED KINGDOM'S APPROACH TO COMMUNITY SOCIAL POLICY

History

Throughout the 1980s the principal opponent of the extension of the Community's competence in the social sphere was the United Kingdom. Successive administrations under Mrs Thatcher pursued free-market economic thinking and adopted an approach to social policy that was, in comparison with governments in other member states, sceptical, if not hostile. Intervention in the labour market created, in Government parlance, 'burdens on business' that stifled innovation and enterprise to the detriment of wealth creation. To some extent the United Kingdom was able to persuade its partners of the need for regulatory restraint by governments. At the very least, it was able to secure guarantees that its views would not be overridden. Two illustrations may be taken from the Single European Act. Article 100a introduced qualified majority voting, but it has been explained that this was subject to an exception covering laws relating to 'the rights and interests of employed persons'. The United Kingdom thus maintained an effective veto over Community initiatives applicable to workers' rights. Less tangibly, Article 118a(2) is supplemented by the proviso that directives adopted thereunder 'shall avoid imposing administrative, financial and legal constraints in a way which would hold back the creation and development of small and medium-sized undertakings'. This may not be a justiciable norm, but it reflects United Kingdom policy concerns relating to the inhibiting effect of state intervention on economic growth.

The Single European Act was by no means a total concession to the United Kingdom perspective. For example, new provisions dealing with economic and social cohesion were introduced in Articles 130a-e.[141] The relatively limited reforms of the Single European Act suggested that the United Kingdom's view of the nature of social policy had been treated with toleration by its partners and accommodated within the Community structure. Yet the United Kingdom view seemed to find few, if any, active supporters, and as the programme designed to ensure the completion of the Community's internal market by the end of 1992 began to take clearer shape, it became evident that many sources viewed an increased commitment to social policy as an essential element in the project. Jacques Delors,

---

141 Kapteyn and Verloren van Themaat (ed. Gormley), *Law of the European Communities*, pp. 640–45. On recent developments, see Kenner, 'Economic and Social Cohesion' [1994/1] LIEI 1.

then President of the Commission, was prominent among this group, but his views were also shared by a number of member states able to make their views known directly in votes in the Council. Whether the basis of this approach was that harmonized social policy was an essential component of market integration or whether one was willing to accept that social policy had a legal life of its own in the Community, it became clear that the United Kingdom was becoming marooned in a position of increasing isolation.

The 'Social Charter'

One method of advancing Community social policy focused on the availability of legal bases permitting qualified majority voting, which could strip the United Kingdom of its veto.[142] However, more broadly, the next element in the drive to lend a higher profile to social policy came in the adoption of the Community Charter of the Fundamental Social Rights of Workers at Strasbourg in December 1989.[143] The Charter does not fit into any of the categories of Community act described in Article 189 of the Treaty. This does not necessarily deprive it of legal effect,[144] but it is at least an indication that its direct impact is likely to be limited. This minimalist impression is supported by its terms. These are largely vague and aspirational, and in many cases do no more than restate existing Community law and practice. In fact, the Charter was seen more as a policy commitment to future legislative initiatives than as a formal binding act in itself. It was a blueprint for social policy, to which the Commission responded by issuing an action programme.[145]

Eleven member states signed the Charter, but the United Kingdom refused. Mrs Thatcher viewed the Charter as an unacceptable inhibition on the flexible operation of the market. Formally, the United Kingdom's refusal might be regarded as having little, if any, legal consequence. The real battleground would be the capacity of the Community to adopt

---

142 See p. 640.
143 The text is reproduced in Blanpain, *Labour Law and Industrial Relations*, pp. 211–18. For discussion see Watson, 'The Community Social Charter' (1991) 28 CMLRev 37; Vogel Polsky, 'What Future is there for a Social Europe following the Strasbourg Summit?' (1990) 19 ILJ 65; Bercusson, 'The European Community's Charter of Fundamental Social Rights for Workers' (1990) 53 MLR 624; Hepple, 'The Implementation of the Community Charter of Fundamental Social Rights' (1990) 53 MLR 643; Szyszczak, '*L'Espace Sociale Européenne*: Reality, Dreams, or Nightmares' GYIL 33 (1990) 284.
144 See Cases 281, 283–5, 287/85 *Germany* v *Commission* [1987] ECR 3203, esp. para. 17 of the judgment. See further Ch. 8.
145 COM (89) 568. The Commission issues an annual report on progress in implementing the Charter; COM (91) 511 was the first such report.

specific directives emerging from the aspirations of the Charter even in the face of the United Kingdom's opposition, which would involve the complicated issue of the identification of an appropriate legal base permitting a qualified majority vote.[146] This matter was mentioned above in connection with the questionably broad use made of Article 118a, which allows qualified majority voting in Council, as the basis for directives.[147]

The social policy debate at Maastricht

The disagreement that surrounded the Charter foreshadowed deeper problems for the future. On the next occasion that the member states came to discuss extensions of Community competence, at Maastricht in December 1991, the United Kingdom found itself in a minority of one, but on this occasion at a more formal legal level. The member states were unable to achieve unanimous agreement on a deepened commitment to social policy suitable for inclusion in the Treaty. Accordingly, the matter was dealt with in a form that left the United Kingdom divided from the other eleven member states.

The eleven agreed several provisions concerned with social protection, working conditions and the promotion of dialogue between management and labour, envisaging the adoption of further measures to develop these policies. This agreement was annexed to the Protocol on Social Policy. The Protocol noted that eleven member states wished to pursue the plans laid out in the Social Charter of 1989 and that they had adopted among themselves an agreement to that end. It declared that the twelve had agreed to authorize the eleven 'to have recourse to the institutions, procedures and mechanisms of the Treaty for the purposes of taking among themselves and applying as far as they are concerned the acts and decisions required for giving effect' to the agreement. The Protocol added that the United Kingdom would not take part in the deliberations on and the adoption by the Council of Commission proposals relating to fields covered by the agreement entered into by the eleven and that it would not be bound by such acts.[148]

The United Kingdom Government led by John Major was insistent on having no part in this advanced social policy-making for fear of imposing costs on British industry that would jeopardize its competitiveness. This

146 For examination of aspects of the legal base problem in the context of the Social Charter, see Watson (1991) 28 CMLRev 37; Hepple (1990) 53 MLR 643.
147 P. 640 above.
148 Some of the measures to be adopted under the eleven's agreement must be adopted unanimously, whereas others require only qualified majority, in respect of which the figures are amended to take account of the United Kingdom's absence; 44 out of 66, now 52 out of 77, suffice; see p. 77–9.

special arrangement constitutes a rather remarkable demonstration of the United Kingdom's determination to veer away from an interventionist social programme, even if that also involves an element of veering away from the mainstream of Community decision-making.

The United Kingdom's Maastricht 'opt-out' appears to envisage that two streams of social policy legislation will flow in the Community. All twelve (now fifteen) member states will be party to the first stream. It will carry the legislation already susceptible to adoption under the legal bases examined above. The United Kingdom will participate in the debates, it will be able to block such rules where the legal base demands unanimity and it will be bound by the rules, like every other member state, where they become law. There will, however, be an additional stream of legislation that has its source in the agreement enshrined in the Protocol at Maastricht. This stream will concern the remaining eleven (now fourteen) member states alone. The United Kingdom will not be party to the negotiations, nor will it be subject to the rules ultimately agreed.

At the political level, the introduction of this two-speed Community in the social sphere may constitute a potentially serious impulse towards the fragmentation of Community solidarity. If only at the symbolic level, it seems inconsistent with the notion of citizenship of the Union solemnly agreed at Maastricht. At a more tangible level, the economic conditions prevailing in the single market will be distorted by the lighter regulatory regime in the United Kingdom. However, the legal problems with the two-stream model may prove more formidable still. The notion appears to be that there will be an inner ring of Treaty of Rome social policy in respect of which all twelve, now fifteen, member states are actively concerned, surrounded by an outer ring of more sophisticated Treaty of Maastricht social policy in respect of which the United Kingdom alone does not participate. This envisages fixing a line that the existing *acquis communautaire* of the fifteen cannot cross, and reserving development of further social policy to the remaining fourteen. Yet such a notion seems incompatible with the established character of Community law as a dynamic, evolving system that does not remain static. At a more fundamental constitutional level, it may be objected that the system envisaged by the Protocol infringes basic Treaty provisions such as Article 3g, which refers to the pursuit of undistorted competition, and Article 6, which insists on non-discrimination on grounds of nationality, a requirement that is violated by the Protocol's differential treatment of British workers.[149] The Maastricht Treaty amendments also introduced a commitment to the

---

149 See Select Further Reading, p. 911.

principle of subsidiarity.[150] It is not clear to what extent this constitutes a justiciable norm, but it is clear that it provides further scope for political and, perhaps, legal wrangling about the appropriate scope of Community social policy and, more generally, about regulatory techniques once the internal market begins to take clearer shape.[151]

The Social Policy Agreement was first used as the basis for the adoption of Directive 94/45 on the establishment of European Works Councils or a procedure in Community-scale undertakings and Community-scale groups of undertakings for the purposes of informing and consulting employees.[152] The objective of the Directive is to secure processes of information and consultation within firms through one of two methods, the Works Council or a less well-defined consultation structure that must be elaborated. Not all firms are subject to these requirements. There are threshold limits, based on the number of employees. It is estimated that approximately 1,000 companies will be subject to the Directive. The United Kingdom is alone in not being bound by the Directive, although British firms with subsidiaries in other member states will be caught if they are sufficiently large to cross the threshold limits.

It seems probable that the Protocol-plus-agreement will be regarded as a last resort.[153] The fragmentation to Community policy-making that is caused by British non-participation is sufficient to prompt efforts to secure agreement among all fifteen member states; or, where this proves impossible, to attempt to use Article 118a in the Treaty 'proper' as a legal base allowing a majority to proceed.[154] The existence of sufficient political will among the member states is indispensable to the adoption of new legislation, but much also depends on the astute presentation of initiatives by the Commission, in particular by the responsible Commissioner, Padraig Flynn, an Irishman. A White Paper on social policy, entitled *A way forward for the Union*, was published in late 1994.[155]

150 See pp. 12–15.
151 See Rhodes, 'The Future of the Social Dimension: Labour Market Regulation in Post-1992 Europe' (1991) XXX JCMS 23.
152 OJ 1994 L254/64, noted by McGlynn (1995) 24 ILJ 78; Carlin (1995) 20 ELRev 96. Cf. p. 641 above on the difficulty in securing progress in worker participation in companies.
153 See, e.g., COM (93) 600.
154 This yields dispute about the legal limits of Art.118a, cf. note 134 above.
155 COM (94) 333.

CHAPTER 21

Free Movement of Capital, and Economic and Monetary Union

A grasp of the impact of this area of Community law requires an appreciation of two sets of provisions that are physically separate in the Treaty, but depend on each other for their practical operation and for the fulfilment of their underlying objectives. The provisions concerned are, first, those dealing with the free movement of capital, and, second, those concerning economic and monetary policy. The importance of this area of law has been negligible for most of the period of the Community's existence, but the plans for economic and monetary union included in the Treaty agreed at Maastricht have elevated it to the very forefront of the Community agenda.

FREE MOVEMENT OF CAPITAL

This field was until 1 January 1994 governed by Articles 67–73 of the Treaty. The Treaty itself guaranteed free movement of payments[1] but it was not until 1990 that free movement of capital became a reality between persons resident in member states as a result of Council Directive 88/361.[2] This historical material is not analysed here.[3] Since 1 January 1994 the governing provisions in relation to free movement of capital are Articles 73b to 73g of the EC Treaty as inserted by the Treaty on European Union.[4] Article 73b sets out what appear to be guarantees of free movement

---

1 See Case 203/80 *Casati* [1981] ECR 2595.
2 See OJ 1988 L178/5. There were derogations for Ireland, Portugal and Spain until the end of 1992 and for Greece until 1 January 1995 (see OJ 1992 L407/1 and Art. 73e of the Treaty).
3 See the first edition of this book at pp. 573–9.
4 For an analysis of these provisions see Usher, *The Law of Money* (1994) and 'Capital Movements and the Treaty on European Union' (1992) 12 YEL 35–57 and Beaumont and Moir, *The European Communities (Amendment) Act 1993 with the Treaty of Rome (as amended) Text and Commentary* (1994), pp. 73–81.

of capital and payments not only between member states but also between member states and third countries. However, the guarantee is a qualified one as it is subject to a series of restrictions set out in Articles 73c to 73g.

FREE MOVEMENT OF CAPITAL BETWEEN MEMBER STATES

Article 73d sets out the grounds on which member states can restrict free movement of capital between themselves. Member states can discriminate in their tax law between 'tax-payers who are not in the same situation with regard to their place of residence or with regard to the place where their capital is invested'.[5] This appears to permit a member state to introduce new tax laws which restrict free movement of capital for non-residents who invest their capital in that state or for residents who seek to invest their capital in another member state. However, the member states agreed a non-binding declaration which was appended to the Treaty on European Union which restricted the member states to only having the power to retain any such tax laws which existed at the end of 1993. Apart from this political constraint on discriminatory tax laws member states are also prevented from adopting tax laws which 'constitute a means of arbitrary discrimination or a disguised restriction on the free movement of capital and payments'.[6] This provision has echoes of Article 36 and is likely to be interpreted by the Court in a similar way.[7] Usher has convincingly argued that the application of Article 36 principles to Article 73d(1)(a) is likely to mean that:

in order to justify differential tax treatment under that provision, not only must the measure be justified to protect the coherence of the tax system but it must also be shown that effective measures are taken at the domestic level in the national tax system to deal with the perceived problem.[8]

Article 73d(1)(b) sets out a much more general basis for member states to restrict free movement of capital within the Community. Member states have the right to:

take all requisite measures to prevent infringements of national law and regulations, in particular in the field of taxation and the prudential supervision of financial institutions, or to lay down procedures for the declaration of capital movements for

5 Art. 73d(1)(a) analysed by Usher, 'Capital Movements and the Treaty on European Union' (1992) 12 YEL 35, 50–53; and by Dassesse, 'The TEU, Implications for the Free Movement of Capital' (1992) 6 J. of Int. Banking Law. pp. 238–43.
6 Art. 73d(3).
7 See Ch. 16 above.
8 Usher, (1992) 12 YEL 35, 53.

purposes of administrative or statistical information, or to take measures which are justified on grounds of public policy or public security.

This provision reiterates Article 4 of Directive 88/361 and adds public policy and public security as new bases for restrictions on capital movements. The Court of Justice has consistently interpreted public policy and public security restrictively in other contexts.[9] Article 73(d)(1)(b) is also subject to Article 73d(3).[10] Given the close analogy with the terms of Article 36 it is likely that the burden of proof will rest on member states to show that the restrictions on capital movements are not contrary to Article 73d(3). States will probably be required to demonstrate that effective measures are being taken at the domestic level, where this is appropriate, and that the restrictions satisfy the proportionality test in that they are no more restrictive than is strictly necessary.[11]

Article 73d(2) preserves any restrictions on the right of establishment which are compatible with the EC Treaty.[12] These restrictions include the exception in the case of activities concerned with the exercise of official authority[13] as well as the permissible restrictions laid down in Article 56 that special measures may be taken as regards foreign nationals on the grounds of public policy, public security or public health.[14] Any measures or procedures justified by a member state under Article 73d(2) must meet the requirements of Article 73d(3) quoted above.

Notwithstanding the various restrictions to capital movements between member states which are still permissible it is probable that the Court of Justice will regard the basic principle of free movement of capital between member states as being directly effective. It remains to be seen whether the Court will follow the example of its interpretation of Articles 48, 52 and 59 and give horizontal and vertical direct effects to Article 73b or whether it will follow its interpretation of Article 30 and restrict the scope of direct effect largely to the vertical plane.[15] It used to be the case that the

---

9 See the discussion in Ch. 16. pp.459–65 on Arts. 36 and in Ch. 18. pp. 559–63 on Art. 48. Admittedly one of the rare instances where public policy has been successfully invoked under Art. 36 did relate to money, see Case 7/78 R v Thompson [1978] ECR 2247.

10 Quoted at note 6 above.

11 See the discussion by Usher, (1992) 12 YEL 35, 54–57, and the Court's case law on Art. 36 discussed in Ch. 16 above.

12 Art. 52(2) on the other hand gives a right to pursue activities as a self-employed person or as an owner or manager of a company, under the conditions laid down for the nationals of the country where such establishment is effected, 'subject to the provisions of the Chapter relating to capital'.

13 Art. 55 and Case 2/74 Reyners v Belgium [1974] ECR 631, discussed at p. 576 above.

14 See Ch. 19, p. 579 above.

15 For a discussion of this point see Usher, (1992) 12 YEL 35, 44–46.

Commission, and member states subject to a power of veto or amendment by the Commission, could take protective measures for a member state if movements of capital led to disturbances in the functioning of the capital market in that state.[16] However, these provisions were not used[17] and ceased to have effect from 1 January 1994. Instead member states made use of the powers in Articles 108 and 109 EEC relating to balance of payments difficulties and these have been retained in Articles 109h and 109i EC. The power of a member state to take unilateral action under the latter provision is subject only to veto or amendment by the Council acting by qualified majority. It cannot be altered by the Commission. These unilateral protective measures can limit free movement of capital between member states but they 'must cause the least possible disturbance in the functioning of the Common Market and must not be wider in scope than is strictly necessary to remedy the sudden difficulties [in the balance of payments] which have arisen'.[18] If a member state can persuade the Commission to authorize protective measures then the Treaty is silent as to any conditions that must be met.[19] Articles 109h and 109i will cease to apply from the beginning of the third stage of economic and monetary union except for states with a derogation.

FREE MOVEMENT OF CAPITAL BETWEEN MEMBER STATES AND NON-MEMBER STATES

Despite the symmetry of treatment of *intra*-EC free movement of capital and *extra*-EC free movement of capital in Article 73b it is clear that the latter is subject to many more restrictions than the former and is at this stage not capable of producing direct effects in national law.[20] The Article 73d restrictions, discussed above, apply equally well to movements of capital between member states and non-member states. Indeed, it is possible that the Court of Justice will give member states more latitude when interpreting Article 73d(3) in this context than when dealing with restrictions on capital movements within the EC.[21] Article 73c permits the

---

16 Art. 73 EEC.
17 Usher (1992) 12 YEL 35, 46.
18 Art. 109i(1).
19 Art. 109h(3). Although the Council has the power to revoke or change the Commission's authorization by qualified majority.
20 It is likely, however, that free movement of payments between member states and non-member states will be regarded by the Court of Justice as being directly effective given that the restrictions permitted by Arts. 73c and 73f apply only to 'capital' whereas the restrictions in Art. 73g explicitly refer to 'capital' movements and 'payments'. See Beaumont and Moir, *The European Communities (Amendment) Act 1993*, p. 81.
21 See Usher, *Law of Money*, pp. 182–3.

retention of any national or Community law measures that existed on 31 December 1993 restricting the movement of capital to or from third countries 'involving direct investment (including investment in real estate), establishment, the provision of financial services or the admission of securities to capital markets'. The mandate given to the Council to remove these restrictions by Community legislation is a rather weak one. Free movement of capital between member states and third countries is still only an 'objective' which the Council is to endeavour to achieve to 'the greatest extent possible'. The Council acts by qualified majority to liberalize free movement in this context and by unanimity if it wishes to take a 'step back'.

The Council is permitted to take short-term steps back by qualified majority voting under Article 73f. Such safeguard measures cannot last longer than six months and must be strictly necessary to combat serious difficulties for the operation of economic and monetary union caused by movements of capital to or from third countries. The collective nature of this article seems designed to cope with the period after the single currency is in operation. It could be used against a third country where massive inflows or outflows of money are affecting the interest rates set by the ECB in a way that is damaging to the real economy in the states that have adopted the single currency.

Article 73g(1) permits the Council to include a prohibition on or restriction of free movement of capital or payments between the Community and a third country as part of economic sanctions imposed under Article 228a.[22] Article 73g(2) permits member states to take unilateral action, as long as the Council has not taken collective action under paragraph 1, for serious political reasons and on grounds of urgency. The Council, by qualified majority, can amend or revoke such unilateral measures against third countries. The power of the state to act unilaterally is said to be 'without prejudice' to Article 224.[23]

CONCLUSION ON FREE MOVEMENT OF CAPITAL

The continuing possibility of restrictions imposed by states on capital movements demonstrates once again that the variations in economic policy between states stand in the way of an unqualified commitment to liberalization of capital movements. From this perspective, Community assumption of competence in the field of economic policy-making is not necessarily deserving of censure as regulatory centralization; it is essential in order to

22 The Treaty provision that links the Council's powers under the common foreign and security policy pillar of the TEU with its powers under the EC Treaty, see Beaumont and Moir, note 20 above, at pp. 81 and 212.
23 On Art. 224 see the brief discussion in Ch. 16 above, at p. 464.

achieve market integration. This is of importance in any assessment of the practical implications of the principle of subsidiarity.[24]

Other legislative initiatives examined elsewhere in this book should not be left out of account. Tax harmonization, for example, has an impact on capital movement.[25] In so far as there are differences in tax laws between the member states, there remain incentives for capital movements stimulated by concerns other than the efficient allocation of resources in a common market. Furthermore, the liberalization of the market for financial services both affects and is affected by the evolving structure of capital markets.[26]

ECONOMIC AND MONETARY UNION

THE FIRST STAGE

A committee under Commission President Jacques Delors prepared a report, the conclusions of which were endorsed by the European Council meeting in Madrid in June 1989.[27] The report insisted on the need for major initiatives at Community level in many areas of economic policy-making. It set out a three-stage programme for the realization of economic and monetary union. The first stage began on 1 July 1990 and had as its heart the pursuit of greater convergence between the economic performances of the member states in the context of the established task of completing the internal market in accordance with Article 8a. All the member states except Greece had entered the Exchange Rate Mechanism (ERM) of the European Monetary System (EMS) by 1992, although Portugal, Spain and the United Kingdom were, at that time, permitted a wider band of fluctuation from the central rate.[28] Considerable progress had been made towards free movement of capital in the Community largely as a result of Directive 88/361.[29] However, in September 1992 turbulence in international capital markets led to the suspension of sterling and the lira

24 See pp. 484–5 and, more generally, Ch. 1, pp. 12–15.
25 See p. 420.
26 See pp. 598–601.
27 See Marques Mendes, 'Economic Cohesion in Europe: the Impact of the Delors Plan' (1990–91) 29 JCMS 17; Gamble, 'EMU and European Capital Markets: Towards a united financial market' (1991) 28 CMLRev 319.
28 The EMS was established in 1979. It instituted the ERM which sets for each participating state a central currency rate expressed against the European Currency Unit (ECU). The ECU is calculated by reference to a basket of currencies of member states. In 1992 the wide fluctuation band against the central rate was 6 per cent whereas the normal band was 2.25 per cent.
29 See note 2 above.

from the ERM. Concerted action by France and Germany was necessary to save what remained of the ERM.

In 1993 renewed pressure came on the ERM and the traditional mechanisms of interest rate increases, selling foreign reserves of currency and devaluation of some of the weaker currencies were not enough to keep currencies within the 2.25 or 6 per cent fluctuation bands. Currency dealers continued to try and exploit the weakenesses in the system by speculating that the weaker currencies could not be sustained within such narrow bands in relation to the benchmark currency, the German mark. In order to keep currencies within the ERM it was decided in August 1993 to widen the normal fluctuation band to 15 per cent either side of the central bilateral rate.[30] Even this device, which largely eliminates any advantage the ERM may have in forcing economic convergence and leaves only a quasi-floating exchange-rate system, brought only temporary respite for the weaker currencies and by 1995 both the Spanish peseta and the Portuguese escudo had to be devalued within the ERM.

THE SECOND STAGE

The Treaty on European Union agreed at Maastricht in December 1991 prepared the ground for fundamentally important and wide-ranging changes in this field. The second stage of economic and monetary union began on 1 January 1994.[31] During this stage member states are to endeavour to avoid excessive government deficits. This is not a legally binding commitment and no sanctions can be taken to enforce it during the second stage.[32] Each member state is supposed to start the process leading to the independence of its central bank.[33]

The European Monetary Institute (EMI) was set up in Frankfurt,[34] comprising the governors of the national central banks plus a president appointed by common accord of the Governments of the member states at the level of heads of government or state. The President of EMI, Alexandre

---

30 See the *1993 General Report*, p. 22 and *European Economy, Annual Economic Report for 1994*, pp. 91–104. Although Germany and the Netherlands maintained a bilateral fluctuation band of 2.25 per cent.

31 Art. 109e(1).

32 Art. 109e(3), (4) and Art. 104c.

33 Art. 109e(5). During 1994 measures were taken to make the French and Spanish central banks independent, see *1994 General Report*, p. 25, and the UK Government gave the Bank of England greater independence by allowing it to decide the timing of interest rate changes and by publishing minutes of the meetings between the Governor of the Bank and the Chancellor of the Exchequer.

34 OJ 1993 C323/1.

Lamfalussy, a Belgian and former General Manager of the Bank for International Settlements in Basle, was selected from among persons of recognized standing and professional experience in monetary or banking matters.[35] The EMI does not have many legal powers, but it will prepare the ground for the much more powerful European Central Bank (ECB) to be set up in the third stage of economic and monetary union to run a single currency, the ECU. By 31 December 1996 at the latest the EMI will specify the regulatory, organizational and logistical framework necessary for the ECB to perform its task in the third stage. This framework is to be submitted to the ECB for decision at the date of its establishment.[36] The EMI is given the task of strengthening cooperation between the national central banks, monitoring the functioning of the EMS, and facilitating the use of the existing ECU.

THE THIRD STAGE

The Treaty provides that the third stage of economic and monetary union, when a single currency is established, must commence no later than 1 January 1999.[37] Prior to that date the Council, meeting in the composition of the heads of government or state, can decide by a qualified majority to set an earlier date for the commencement of the third stage if a majority of the member states achieve certain financial targets, which are the convergence criteria deemed necessary before they can be part of the single currency.[38] The financial targets are as follows:

1 an average rate of inflation, observed over a period of one year before the examination, which does not exceed by more than 1.5 per cent the average of the three best performing member states;[39]
2 the avoidance of an excessive government budgetary deficit, which is defined as meaning an annual budget deficit of less than 3 per cent of Gross Domestic Product (GDP) and an overall public debt ratio not exceeding 60 per cent of GDP;[40]
3 the member state's currency must have been within the normal fluctuation margins of the ERM of the EMS without severe tensions for at least two years prior to the period of the examination;[41]

35 Art. 109f.
36 Art. 109f(3).
37 Art. 109j(4).
38 Art. 109j(3).
39 Art. 1 of the Protocol on the Convergence Criteria referred to in Art. 109j.
40 Art. 1 of the Protocol on the Excessive Deficit Procedure referred to in Art. 104c.
41 Art. 3 of the Protocol on the Convergence Criteria referred to in Art. 109j.

4 the member state's average long-term interest rate, measured over a period of one year before the examination, does not exceed by more than 2 per cent the average interest rates in the three best performing states in terms of price stability (presumably in terms of inflation).[42]

The convergence criteria will not be easy to achieve. In 1994 only Luxembourg fulfilled all the criteria. All the other countries apart from Ireland[43] were reported on by the Commission to the Council because they had excessive government deficits.[44] The problem of accumulated government debt is particularly serious for Belgium,[45] Greece[46] and Italy.[47] In 1994 all the member states were borrowing more than 3 per cent of GDP apart from Ireland and Luxembourg. In relation to inflation, in 1994 only Greece with 10 per cent inflation was markedly out of line with the Community average of 3 per cent. In 1994 the Community average in long-term interest rates was around 8 per cent and the range was between Germany with 6.3 per cent and Portugal with 10 per cent. Only Portugal and Greece had significant problems in meeting the interest rate convergence criteria.[48] In early 1995 Greece, Italy and the UK remained outside the ERM and Portugal and Spain had to have their currencies devalued within it. It seems very unlikely that by 1998 all the member states will achieve the convergence criteria. In particular, it will be very surprising if Belgium, Greece and Italy achieve the targets because they are still increasing rather than reducing their accumulated government deficits. Portugal, Spain and Sweden also face major challenges to achieve all the targets.

At the time when the Council decides that a majority of the member states have achieved the convergence criteria set out above, or by 1 July 1998 at the latest,[49] the Council, acting by a qualified majority, must

42 Art. 4 of the Protocol on the Convergence Criteria referred to in Art. 109j.

43 Ireland was exempted by the Commission but this was controversial as statistics indicate that in 1994 it had a gross government debt of 93.1 per cent of GDP, see *European Economy*, 1994 No. 58, well above the 60 per cent target. The Commission took the view that the ratio was sufficiently diminishing and the 60 per cent target was being approached at a satisfactory pace, see Art. 104c(2)(b), but this seems a very lax interpretation of the convergence criteria.

44 See the excessive deficit procedure in Arts. 104c(5) and (6) and the Council's response as noted in the *1994 General Report*, pp. 24–5.

45 142 per cent of GDP in 1994.

46 154 per cent of GDP in 1994.

47 123 per cent of GDP in 1994.

48 The statistics are taken from *European Economy* 1994 No. 58.

49 See p. 659 regarding failure of a majority to achieve the criteria. In April 1995 the economics and finance ministers reached a broad consensus that the 'interim period' between the political decision as to which states qualify for the single currency and the start of the third stage should be prolonged. This would imply that the political decision will be taken no later than December 1997, even if the third stage does not commence until the last possible date on 1 January 1999.

decide which member states have fulfilled the convergence criteria and are thus ready to be part of the single currency. Any states that have not by then fulfilled the criteria will be granted a derogation and they will not be a part of the single currency and have no voting rights in relation to a number of the Treaty articles concerning the third stage.[50] Member states with a derogation can apply to join the single currency at least once every two years and will be accepted if they achieve the convergence criteria. The details of the convergence criteria referred to in Article 109j could be altered from those specified in the Protocol on the Convergence Criteria by provisions adopted by the Council, but only by a unanimous vote.[51]

THE EUROPEAN CENTRAL BANK (ECB)

The member states without a derogation will appoint the President, Vice-President and four other members of the Executive Board of the ECB for a non-renewable eight-year period of office.[52] The people appointed must be of recognized standing and professional experience in monetary or banking matters.[53] The ECB will replace the EMI. At the starting date of the third stage the member states without a derogation are to agree unanimously in the Council on the conversion rates at which their currencies shall be irrevocably fixed and at which irrevocably fixed rate the ECU shall be substituted for these currencies. The ECU will then become a currency in its own right.[54]

The ECB is to be independent, along the same lines as its model, the Bundesbank in Germany, as are the national central banks.[55] The Executive Board of the Bank will have day-to-day responsibility for the single currency.[56] The Executive Board members are joined by the governors of the national central banks of member states without a derogation to form the Governing Council of the ECB, which will formulate the monetary policy of the states party to the single currency, including intermediate monetary objectives, key interest rates and the supply of reserves.[57]

The ECB will have the main responsibility for controlling the new

---

50 Art. 109k.
51 Art. 6 of the Protocol on the Convergence Criteria referred to in Art. 109j.
52 Art. 109l.
53 Art. 109a.
54 Art. 109l(4).
55 Arts. 107, 108.
56 Art. 11 of the Protocol on the Statute of the European System of Central Banks referred to in Art. 106.
57 Arts. 10 and 12 of the Protocol on the Statute of the European System of Central Banks.

single currency, the ECU. Article 105(1) establishes the ECB's primary objective as the maintenance of price stability, and Article 105(2) gives it certain tasks: to define and implement the monetary policy of the states that are party to the single currency, to conduct foreign-exchange operations, to hold and manage the official foreign reserves of member states that are party to the single currency and to promote the smooth operation of payment systems. The ECB will have the exclusive right to authorize the issue of banknotes within the member states that are party to the single currency.[58] It will be able to make legislation, regulations and decisions in relation to certain matters, and will have the power to impose fines or periodic penalty payments on undertakings that fail to comply with that legislation.[59] The ECB legislation is subject to the usual procedures for judicial review in the EC Treaty under Article 173.

Although the ECB will be independent, there will be a degree of political accountability. The Bank must produce an annual report on its activities and on the monetary policy of both the previous and current year to the European Parliament, the Council, European Council and Commission. The President of the Bank must present this report to the Council and the European Parliament, and the latter can hold a debate on it.[60] In addition, the Parliament can invite the President and other members of the Executive Board to be heard by one of its committees with competence in this area.[61] However, the independence of the Bank is such that it can choose to ignore the views of the Parliament and its President and members of the Executive Board can refuse to answer particular questions from the members of the committee responsible in the Parliament. Even the Council and Commission have limited influence over the Bank. The members of the Executive Board are not concerned about reappointment, as their appointments are non-renewable, and thus will not be tempted to act in accordance with the wishes of the appointing governments. The governors of the national central banks, who are all members of the Governing Council of the ECB, are also free from government control because of the independence of the national central

---

58 Art. 105a. In April 1995 the economics and finance ministers accepted a report from the EMI that banknotes denominated in ECUs would probably not be in wide circulation until 2003 or 2004.

59 Art. 108a EC and Art. 34 of the Protocol on the Statute of the European System of Central Banks.

60 See Art. 109c(3) and Parliament's *Rules of Procedure* (1994) Rule 39.

61 Art. 109b(3). Rule 39 of Parliament's *Rules of Procedure* (1994) requires the President of the ECB, and in the second stage of EMU the President of the EMI, to appear before the relevant committee twice a year and makes it possible for the President and other Executive Board Members to be invited to make statements and answer questions at other meetings of the committee.

banks. The President of the Council and a member of the Commission can participate in the meetings of the Governing Council of the ECB but have no voting rights.[62] This guarantees that the Commission and Council are at least aware of the internal balances of power within the Governing Council of the ECB. The President of the Council also has the power to submit a motion for deliberation to the Governing Council of the Bank.[63] This right of initiation is of some value, but the Council cannot force its will on the Governing Council of the Bank.

The Council has some legislative powers in relation to monetary policy. The Council, acting under Article 109 on the basis of unanimity among the member states without a derogation, can conclude a formal agreement on an exchange-rate system for the ECU in relation to non-Community currencies. The Council, by a qualified majority of the member states without a derogation, can adopt, adjust or abandon the central rates of the ECU within such an exchange-rate system. In the absence of an exchange-rate system with non-Community currencies, the Council can, acting under Article 109(2) by a qualified majority of member states without a derogation, formulate general orientations for exchange-rate policy in relation to these currencies. However, these general orientations would be without prejudice to the ECB's primary objective of price stability. The Council also has the power, acting under Article 106(6) on a qualified majority of all member states, to adopt certain provisions referred to in particular articles of the Statute of the European System of Central Banks. More radically, the Council can, even against the will of the ECB, acting under Article 106(5) by qualified majority on a proposal from the Commission with the assent of the European Parliament, amend certain articles of the Statute of the European System of Central Banks. However, the articles that can be changed do not include the possibility of undermining the independence of the Central Bank and its ability to control the money supply and interest rates.

Whenever the Council is discussing matters relating to the objectives and tasks of the European System of Central Banks it must invite the President of the European Central Bank to participate, in a non-voting capacity, in its meetings.[64] This ensures that the Bank's case is properly represented in the Council and highlights the importance of the role of the President of the Bank.

62 Art. 109b(1).
63 Art. 109b(1).
64 Art. 109b(2).

PROGRESS TOWARDS THE SINGLE CURRENCY

Progress to a single currency is, in legal terms, irrevocable. This is clear from the EC Treaty itself but also from a protocol on the transition to the third stage of economic and monetary union. If by 1 January 1999 less than a majority of the member states meet the convergence criteria, then the single currency will be based on those few member states that do meet the criteria. Politically, however, it is hard to imagine the single currency going ahead in the unlikely event that Germany would not be part of it due to its failure to meet the convergence criteria. Treaty amendments to the timetable may be agreed at the next intergovernmental conference in 1996 but this seems unlikely given the requirement of the unanimous agreement of the member states.

At Maastricht the United Kingdom negotiated an opt-out Protocol giving it the right not to proceed to the third stage of economic and monetary union even if it were to satisfy the convergence criteria at the time the other states proceed to that stage. If the United Kingdom does opt out, it will be treated in the same way as a member state with a derogation. If at a later date the United Kingdom wishes to opt in to the single currency, it will be able to do so provided it meets the convergence criteria applicable at that time. Denmark also negotiated an opt-out Protocol at Maastricht and after the Danish people voted against the Treaty on European Union in the first referendum in 1992 the Danish Government indicated to the Community that it would exercise its right not to participate in the single currency and thus Denmark will be a member state with a derogation.[65]

If the single currency is established in the Community among some of the member states only, it will create a visible two-tier Community. This will be damaging to the idea of an ever closer union among the peoples of Europe that was found in the Preamble to the Treaty of Rome and confirmed in the Preamble to the Treaty on European Union agreed at Maastricht. On the other hand, if all member states are able to achieve the convergence criteria at the same time, or with only a short time gap, and the United Kingdom opts in to the single currency, this will be a huge step forward in the Community. It will bring major savings in transaction

---

[65] Section B of the decision taken at the Edinburgh European Council records that Denmark has notified the Council that it will not participate in the third stage of EMU as it is empowered to do by para. 1 of the Protocol on Certain Provisions Relating to Denmark annexed to the EC Treaty by the TEU. In terms of Community law, Denmark is able to reverse this notification by requesting that the procedure for abrogating a derogation under Art. 109k(2) is initiated (see para. 4 of the Protocol).

costs for individuals and companies. Perhaps more importantly, it will ensure that throughout the Community inflation is kept under control due to the European Central Bank having price stability as its primary objective and that excessive government budget deficits are avoided.[66] Indeed, during the third stage of economic and monetary union the Council will have the power, acting by a two-thirds majority of the votes of its members using the weighted voting system and excluding the votes of the member state being acted against, to impose sanctions on a member state that fails to correct an excessive government deficit.[67]

One of the main disadvantages of a single currency could be the inability to cope with different levels of unemployment in various parts of the Community by exchange-rate adjustments. The other mechanisms for coping with diverging employment levels are labour migration and large fiscal transfers from low unemployment countries to high unemployment countries. Labour migration has been a possibility since the Community was founded but the take-up rate has been very small, not least owing to the problems of language. The size of the Community budget is far too small to make any meaningful impact on high levels of structural unemployment in the poorer member states.[68]

The tensions within the ERM in 1992 and 1993 leading to the withdrawal of Italy and the UK and the widening of the fluctuation bands to 15 per cent showed the problems that confront a process of economic and monetary alignment between states, particularly when the economic position of the dominant economy, Germany, and the interest rates needed for that economy are not in line with the needs of the real economies in the other members of the ERM. The Bundesbank *de facto* determines the level of interest rates for all members of the ERM and yet does so with only the German economy in mind. This inherent instability in the ERM is a reason for moving to a single currency where the money supply and interest rates are set by the European Central Bank taking account of the real economy in all the states party to the single currency. Others see the instability of the ERM as a reason for not proceeding towards a single currency, preferring the short-term comfort of a more competitive (devalued) currency and the 'free market' solution of a floating exchange rate.

66 Art. 104c.
67 Art. 104c(9) and (11).
68 See the views of Eddie George, the Governor of the Bank of England, in *The Times*, 23 February 1995.

CHAPTER 22

Article 85: Cartels and Restrictive Practices

1. The following shall be prohibited as incompatible with the common market: all agreements between undertakings, decisions by associations of undertakings and concerted practices which may affect trade between Member States and which have as their object or effect the prevention, restriction or distortion of competition within the common market, and in particular those which:

(a) directly or indirectly fix purchase or selling prices or any other trading conditions;

(b) limit or control production, markets, technical development, or investment;

(c) share markets or sources of supply;

(d) apply dissimilar conditions to equivalent transactions with other trading parties, thereby placing them at a competitive disadvantage;

(e) make the conclusion of contracts subject to acceptance by the other parties of supplementary obligations which, by their nature or according to commercial usage, have no connection with the subject of such contracts.

2. Any agreements or decisions prohibited pursuant to this Article shall be automatically void.

3. Exemption — see p. 704 below.

Collusion between firms deprives the market of the stimulus of competition and thus distorts the efficient allocation of resources. Such collusion may involve a simple restriction on the parties to the agreement from competing with each other. It may include arrangements that treat the common market as divisible into national or localized component parts. Article 85 controls agreements between firms that are prejudicial to the operation of the common market, and is dedicated to the maintenance of competition between independent firms operating in an integrating market.

'Perfect competition', where the establishment of equilibrium between consumer demand and producer supply ensures maximum efficiency, is unattainable for many reasons. A more nuanced, pragmatic attitude to the market has to be taken. This is reflected in the notion of 'workable competition' as the objective of Article 85. Workable competition refers to the task of fashioning a market in which competition is induced and maintained where appropriate, but where curbs on its feasibility and desirability are acknowledged and allowed to impose pragmatic constraints on the purity of the vision of perfect competition.[1] The European Court referred in *Metro* v *Commission*[2] to

the existence on the market of workable competition, that is to say the degree of competition necessary to ensure the observance of the basic requirements and attainment of the objectives of the Treaty, in particular the creation of a single market achieving conditions similar to those of a domestic market.

The techniques of market regulation considered in this and the following chapters combine to keep the market operating in a state in which many economic and social interests are acknowledged but no single theory is allowed to dominate. Workable competition describes the melting pot of the modern Western economy.

THE SCOPE AND NATURE OF ARTICLE 85

Article 85(1) applies a basic prohibition to collaboration that impedes the influence of effective competition in the common market. Article 85(2) supplements the first paragraph by declaring that prohibited practices are void. This has important consequences before national courts, where prohibited agreements are accordingly unenforceable. The objective of the prohibition is to ensure that the efficient allocation of resources is not distorted. Yet, as suggested above, some forms of collaboration are beneficial even though they suppress competition. For example, collaboration may permit the widening of distribution networks or the promotion of deeper research programmes. Consequently, the basic prohibition contained in Articles 85(1) and (2) is subject to the availability of an exemption under Article 85(3) of agreements that meet specified criteria reflecting overall beneficial effect. The grant of exemption is the preserve of the Commission.

The types of practice that are capable of falling within Article 85 are many and varied. It is fundamentally important to notice that the definition

---

1 See similar issues in relation to dominant positions/monopolies, p. 721; intellectual property rights, p. 829.
2 Case 26/76 [1977] ECR 1875, 1904.

contained in Article 85(1) is very broad and flexible and, crucially, it is *effects based*. An agreement falls within the scope of Article 85 if it meets the tests relating, broadly, to the effect of the agreement on the patterns of trade within the common market. Neither the precise legal *form* of the agreement nor its actual *content* are of any direct relevance. Article 85(1) contains a useful illustrative list of the types of practice that are capable of falling within the scope of the prohibition. Thus, if a group of producers of widgets in several member states agrees to set a minimum selling price (example (a) in Article 85(1)) or to avoid intruding on each other's traditional territories (example (b)), then a prima-facie violation of Article 85 has occurred. Competition has been reduced to the detriment of consumer choice. However, even an agreement between the producers that cannot be fitted into any of the five examples, such as a franchising arrangement involving selected outlets, will still be incompatible with Article 85 if it distorts competition within the common market in accordance with the definition in the first part of Article 85(1). The list in Article 85(1), then, is not exhaustive.

In *Consten and Grundig* v *Commission*[3] the Court held incompatible with Article 85 a commercial arrangement that served to perpetuate existing national boundaries as obstacles to the free circulation of goods. Consten undertook to act as the exclusive dealer in France for the electrical products made in Germany by Grundig and was for these purposes permitted to register Grundig's trade mark, GINT, under French law. Consten promised not to handle competing brands. Grundig, for its part, supplied only Consten in France and made sure that other dealers that it supplied outside France undertook not to resell Grundig products in France or to a French customer. The net result of the arrangement between Consten and Grundig was that on the French market Consten enjoyed absolute protection from competition by other suppliers of Grundig goods.

The matter was taken up by the European Commission, which is responsible for the administration of the Community's competition rules. The Commission held that Consten and Grundig's agreement was incompatible with Article 85 because it sought to eliminate competition through the isolation of the French market from the rest of the common market. The agreement was accordingly unenforceable. The European Court, before which the firms sought annulment of the Commission's finding, upheld this decision.

The agreement between Consten and Grundig was both anti-competitive and market partitioning. It was anti-competitive in the sense that it

3 Case 56, 58/64 [1966] ECR 299, [1966] CMLR 418.

precluded the influence of competition in the supply of Grundig goods in a defined area, France. It was market partitioning because it served to create special conditions on the territory of a single member state, again, France. The common market's progress towards a market in which conditions of competition are unaffected by economically irrelevant national frontiers was plainly severely inhibited. Article 85, in this sense, has a parallel function to Article 30, which constrains states, rather than firms, from treating the common market as divisible into national units for trade purposes.

It is, however, instructive to note that as far as the development of the Community is concerned, the agreement between Consten and Grundig was not all bad. After all, it resulted in German-made goods being distributed in France, which is plainly in accordance with the objectives of market integration and enhanced consumer choice. It was, in fact, a vertical arrangement between traders at different levels of the production and supply chain. Vertical agreements do not necessarily extinguish competition. Quite the reverse; they may improve the operation of the market by stimulating fresh competition by virtue of the establishment of new links between supplier and distributor. Much more pernicious are horizontal agreements, which may eliminate competition between traders at the same level of the product supply chain, thereby curtailing the choice of those who must deal with a trader at that level. However, Article 85 makes no explicit distinction between horizontal and vertical arrangements and, in principle, embraces both.

It is plain that distribution agreements such as that between Consten and Grundig are capable of yielding significant benefits within a developing common market and that, accordingly, competition law must make a balanced and careful appraisal of such agreements.[4]

THE INTERVENTIONIST NATURE OF ARTICLE 85

One view of *Consten and Grundig* would hold that provided the Grundig products were subject to competition from other brands of electrical product on the French market, there is no need for any legal control. Interbrand competition protects the consumer, who is able to choose another brand of electrical product if Grundig goods are unsatisfactory in price or quality. Vertical deals, then, may be acceptable, indeed desirable,[5]

---

4 For further analysis of the calculation of the costs and benefits of such arrangements in the application of the legal control, see pp. 699–701.

5 Such deals may themselves serve to break up cartels simply by injecting fresh

provided interbrand competition thrives. By contrast, the suppression of interbrand competition through a horizontal restraint imperils the competitive structure of the market. Yet the vertical Consten/Grundig arrangement was held beyond redemption, because the beneficial effects of the deal as a means of spreading distribution were outweighed by Grundig's determination to protect Consten from any competition whatsoever in Grundig products, even deriving from indirect exports from Germany through a third country on to the French market. Because *cross-border* intrabrand competition was suppressed, the possibility of interbrand competition in France was no defence; the pervasive impulse of market integration in Community law defeated concern merely to secure competition. The evolution of the integrated market is driven by cross-border trade, and absolute territorial protection took Consten and Grundig's arrangement beyond the pale as far as Article 85 is concerned.

This analysis demonstrates that in the Community system the goal of market integration may call for a shift of emphasis unknown to domestic competition law systems concerned exclusively with economic efficiency. Accordingly, in the area of restrictive practices the Community is prone to adopt a more interventionist stance than is normal under US antitrust law. An economic analysis might lead one to hold a vertical agreement of the *Consten and Grundig* type relating to product distribution incapable of damaging the market, provided that the product in question remains subject to competition from other products serving a similar purpose – other brands of electrical product. A reduction in intrabrand competition is inconsequential provided interbrand competition remains strong. The US Supreme Court has shown itself prepared to declare such deals permissible under antitrust law.[6] In the Community the situation is different where such deals involve distribution systems that compartmentalize the common market along national lines. Even persisting interbrand competition is insufficient to allow the deal to escape the grasp of Article 85 where intrabrand competition across national boundaries is eliminated.[7] Thus, the objective of market integration compels EC law to adopt a more interventionist approach than is taken in a market that is already integrated. Similarly, the Community may be tempted to take a rather more favourable view of cross-border mergers than would be taken of a merger of a similar size within a single economic area, for the cross-border merger,

---

competition into a previously narrow market. Market integration is itself a form of competition policy.

6 433 US 36 (1977) *Continental TV v GTE Sylvania.* See generally Neale and Goyder, *The Antitrust Laws of the USA*; Frazer, *Monopoly, Competition and the Law*, esp. pp. 208–11.

7 Cases 56, 58/64, note 3 above.

although potentially destructive of competition, is living proof that the market is undergoing a process of integration.[8] Here, then, the pursuit of market integration induces a less interventionist approach than might be the norm in domestic systems.

Accordingly, analogies with domestic competition law systems, whether in Europe or in North America, may be misleading because Community competition law is not necessarily performing the same function as a domestic system. Community law may sanction agreements held unlawful under national systems of competition law, and perhaps vice versa, yet possess perfectly coherent reasons for reaching such apparently maverick conclusions. The objective of market integration alters legal and economic perspectives. Thus, it may not be until the EC market is treated by business as a genuine single market that precise analogies with US antitrust law will be appropriate.[9] A less interventionist attitude towards vertical deals, for example, may then be deemed appropriate. Such mature integration remains distant, and, indeed, the pressures caused by enlargement and the challenge of Eastern Europe may reinvigorate the integrative focus of Community law, thereby further delaying the validity of American analogies. However, even when the Community finally achieves economic integration comparable to that in the United States, there is no guarantee that there will be congruence in political choices about the functions of competition law on both sides of the Atlantic. The American competition law system is presently strongly influenced by the minimalist prescription of the Chicago school,[10] whereas the Community retains a more interventionist approach in, for example, its policy of support for small- and medium-sized businesses.[11]

---

8 See further Ch. 25.
9 See general discussion by D. Gerber, 'The Transformation of European Community Competition Law' (1994) 35 Harvard Intl LJ 97; Ehlermann, 'The Contribution of EC Competition Policy to the Single Market' (1992) 29 CMLRev 257, esp. 264–7; Frazer, 'Competition Law after 1992: the Next Step' (1990) 53 MLR 609; Faull, 'Effect on Trade between Member States and Community: Member State Jurisdiction' (1989) Fordham Corp L Inst 485; Green, 'Article 85 in Perspective: Stretching Jurisdiction, Narrowing the Concept of a Restriction and Plugging a Few Gaps', [1988] ECLR 190; Verstrynge, Ch. 1, in Slot and Van der Woude (eds.), Exploiting the Internal Market; Green, Hartley and Usher, Single European Market, Ch. 14.
10 See e.g. Bork, The Antitrust Paradox; Posner, 'The Chicago School of Antitrust Analysis' (1979) 127 U Pa LR 925. For brief survey see Frazer, (1990) 53 MLR 609.
11 See also pp. 709–11 on the more specific concern for the position of the consumer in the Community system.

COMPETITION LAW IN A COMMON MARKET

So the function of competition law in a common market extends beyond mere control of the anti-competitive consequences of collusion. It also looks to the objective of market integration, a matter of no concern within a national market. It would be fruitless to eliminate state-imposed market partitioning if commercial undertakings were permitted to reimpose those national boundaries in their private dealings. Accordingly, an agreement to carve up the common market along the lines of the member states and to stay out of competitors' territories in other states is the most serious of all breaches of Community competition law. The whole process of the Community's integrative task is subverted in such circumstances. Articles 85 and 86 thus serve to eliminate the economic relevance of national frontiers in a manner parallel to Articles 12, 30, 48 et al.[12] The competition rules thus form an aspect of general Community trade law. Furthermore, as state barriers to trade are dismantled in the pursuit of the integrated market, surveillance of private commercial activity becomes increasingly important in order to ensure that firms are not tempted to take advantage of the new open market by setting up cartels.

The objective of integration in a common market often coexists with the objective of securing economic efficiency; indeed, in the long term the two notions ought theoretically to be coterminous. Yet in the short term it is feasible that the two objectives may clash. How should the Community approach an agreement that is market-partitioning but efficient, or an agreement that furthers market integration but is inefficient? Rarely will the dilemma present itself so starkly,[13] yet the Community may be confronted with a choice of which notion to emphasize. It is in the resolution of this issue that the Community competition law system assumes an independent character, which, as explained, renders analogies with domestic competition law systems misleading. The brief discussion of *Consten and Grundig*[14] should serve as an introduction both to the type of balancing cost/benefit assessment that often has to be made in relation to restrictive trading agreements and also to the distinctive market-integrative flavour of EC competition law.

---

12 See the explanation of 'workable competition' at pp. 661–2.
13 But see Case 187/80 *Merck* v *Stephar* [1981] ECR 2063 discussed at p. 842; discussion of the *Distillers* proceedings by Whish, *Competition Law*, pp. 565–6, and by Whish and Sufrin, 'Article 85 and the Rule of Reason' (1987) 7 YEL 1, 15–16; also Green, Hartley and Usher, *Single European Market*, p. 217.
14 Cases 56, 58/64, note 3 above.

FURTHER ILLUSTRATIONS

Hundreds of different types of agreement have been held to fall within Article 85. It is possible to examine particular categories of deal separately in order to identify the nature of the applicable legal rules.[15] However, it is instructive simply to browse through the Commission's *Annual Report on Competition Policy*, which contains description of the Commission's activity.[16] Without the need to embark on an analysis of individual cases, one can in this way easily assimilate an overview of the nature and purpose of Article 85. A brief selection of decisions serves here as a useful illustration. Some of the deals are vertical, some horizontal – all are capable of being controlled under Article 85.

In *Solvay/ICI*[17] the Commission found that soda-ash producers had set up a horizontal *market-sharing* cartel. Solvay, a Belgian firm, agreed to keep out of the British and Irish markets; ICI agreed not to intrude on continental Western Europe. A heavy fine was imposed for conduct that is fundamentally hostile to the idea of a common market. In *Sperry New Holland*[18] an *export ban* imposed by a manufacturer of agricultural machinery on its national distributors was held to infringe Article 85(1). The vertical agreement partitioned the common market along national lines in addition to impeding competition between traders in the goods in question. In *Meldoc*[19] five dairy companies responsible for producing most of the milk consumed in the Netherlands set *minimum prices* and cooperated in a strategy designed to combat competition from producers in other member states wishing to penetrate the Dutch market. This was in breach of Article 85(1), for the scheme stifled competition and separated the Dutch market from the broader common market. The British Dental Trade Association[20] was held in breach of Article 85 because of practices that *discriminated* against producers and distributors from member states other than the United Kingdom. In *Irish Distillers Group*[21] the Commission used Article 85

---

15 Works designed specially for the practitioner tend to follow such a structure; see, e.g., Bellamy and Child, *Common Market Law of Competition*; Whish, *Competition Law*; Van Bael and Bellis, *Competition Law*.

16 A further useful source is the monthly *Antitrust Supplement*, published since the start of 1988 by the *Common Market Law Reports*: [198–, 9–] 4, 5 CMLR. Consult also the annual survey in the *Yearbook of European Law*; and the *European Law Review*'s annual *Competition Law Checklist*, first published to cover 1990.

17 Comm. Dec. 91/297 OJ 1991 L152/1, noted (1990) 10 YEL, 407, 456. The firms challenged the Commission's findings before the Court, Case T-30/91 OJ 1991 C153/16. See p. 785 on the Court's role.

18 Comm. Dec. 85/617, OJ 1985 L376/21, [1988] 4 CMLR 306.

19 Comm. Dec. 86/596, OJ 1986 L348/50.

20 Comm. Dec. 88/477 (*British Dental Trade Association*) OJ 1988 L233/15.

21 [1988] 4 CMLR 840.

to challenge and forestall a *joint bid* by three spirits producers for a rival company. The companies should have been bidding against each other instead of colluding in a manner that suppressed competition.[22] Its *Fatty Acids* decision[23] provided the Commission with the opportunity to hold that an agreement to exchange sales data restricts competition and is capable of being caught by Article 85(1).

Although these cases illustrate deals held incompatible with Article 85, many commercial agreements are accepted as justified restraints on competition. All the *collaborative arrangements* of the Eurotunnel project relating to the financing and construction of the Tunnel under the Channel had to be negotiated with the Commission in order to ensure that the venture was in conformity with Article 85.[24] Evidently, the Commission was persuaded that the benefits of the collaboration exceeded any detrimental effects caused by the absence of competition between independent firms. Perhaps the most obvious argument in favour of collaboration in a deal of this magnitude is that without joint activity the project would simply be beyond the capability of a firm acting on its own. From this perspective, a market is opened, not restricted. Subsequently, the Commission decided to issue exemptions under Article 85(3) in respect of agreements struck between several railway companies on use of the Tunnel for both goods and passenger services.[25] A *joint venture* between the German firm BBC Brown Boveri and NGK Insulators of Japan[26] designed to develop sodium-sulphur batteries was held to fall within Article 85(1), but was exempted under Article 85(3) by the Commission because of its contribution to technological advance.

The purpose of this brief survey has been to convey a flavour of the type of practices that are susceptible to control under Article 85. The list of examples of Commission interventions could be multiplied many times over. However, it is regrettably not the case that firms promptly change their ways once the Commission has established that particular practices fall foul of Article 85. Pernicious price-fixing and market-sharing arrangements continue to be uncovered. The maintenance of supervision of the market remains essential.

---

22 For scepticism about both the advisability of this approach and its likely future use, see (1990) ELRev *Competition Law Checklist* 18.
23 Comm. Dec. 87/1 OJ 1987 L3/17, [1989] 4 CMLR 445. See also Case T-34/92 *Fiatagri UK Ltd* v *Commission*, judgment of 27 October 1994.
24 Comm. Dec. 88/568 OJ 1988 L311/36 [1989] 4 CMLR 419 (construction; negative clearance, no breach of Art. 85(1), see p. 697 below).
25 Comm. Dec. 94/594 *ACI* OJ 1994 L224/28 (goods; five-year exemption on terms); Comm. Dec. 94/663 *Night Services* OJ 1994 L259/20 (passengers; eight-year exemption on terms).
26 Comm. Dec. (*BBC Brown Boveri/NGK Insulators*) 88/541, OJ 1988 L301/68, [1989] 4 CMLR 610.

In some, though not all, of these instances the Commission's findings were the subject of challenge before the European Court or the Court of First Instance, which has possessed jurisdiction in such cases since November 1989. The role of the Courts is examined more fully in Chapter 24. The commercial significance of rulings in competition cases frequently supplies a sufficient incentive to pursue judicial review. This is especially so where the Commission exercises its power to impose fines on firms that infringe the competition rules. The highest fine imposed on a single firm is 75 million ECUs, a figure which exceeds £50 million. The firm concerned was Tetra Pak, condemned by the Commission for a range of abusive practices prohibited by Article 86.[27]

ARTICLE 85(1): THE NATURE OF THE PROHIBITION

The definition of the prohibited practice covered by Article 85(1) contains several elements. The core of the prohibition is the requirement that the practice has as its 'object or effect the prevention, restriction or distortion of competition within the common market'. However, there is also the jurisdictional threshold requirement that the practice must 'affect trade between Member States'. Failure to satisfy this proviso means that the collaboration falls within the sphere of national law alone. At the more prosaic level lie definitional questions that confront all systems of competition/antitrust law: what is an 'undertaking' that is capable of participating in a prohibited practice? And what is the nature of the collusive venture that must have been pursued for Article 85 to bite? The provision refers to the notions of an 'agreement' and a 'concerted practice'.

These key definitional issues are not the subject of elaboration in the Treaty. There is no interpretation section that covers these phrases. It has been for the Commission, in the practice of its administration of the Treaty competition rules, and for the Court, in the exercise of a supervisory function over the Commission's decisions that is now exercised by the Court of First Instance, to develop the precise meaning and effect of Article 85. The flexibility of the terms used has allowed the institutions to mould the competition rules in a way that reflects conceptions of economic policy that are in some areas by no means uncontroversial.

The following analysis separates the various constituent elements of the

27 Comm. Dec. 92/163, page 783.

definition for the sake of convenience. However, the elements are to a significant extent connected and many decisions about the lawfulness of particular practices demand close consideration of more than one aspect of Article 85(1).

AGREEMENTS

It is perfectly obvious that a contract drawn up between commercial firms in which the parties promise, for example, to stick to their domestic markets and to set prices at an agreed level constitutes an 'agreement' for the purposes of the application of Article 85(1). It is equally obvious that most restrictive practices are likely to be conducted in a rather less blatant manner and that, accordingly, Article 85 and, indeed, competition/antitrust law generally must be capable of encompassing agreements of a rather less formal, often clandestine, nature.

The broad interpretation of an agreement

In *Cementhandelaren* v *Commission*[28] the Cement Dealers Association set 'target prices' for its members, who were all active on the Dutch cement market. The Commission concluded that the fixing of target prices amounted to an agreement within Article 85. The Association contested this finding before the European Court, where it argued that the target prices did not amount to fixed rates to which the participants had agreed, but merely constituted a basis for calculation of prices, which were determined independently. The arrangement, the Association claimed, was too loose and indisciplined to be caught by competition law. The Court upheld the Commission's finding that the arrangement fell foul of Article 85(1), observing that 'the fixing of a price, even one which merely constitutes a target, affects competition because it enables all the participants to predict with a reasonable degree of certainty what the pricing policy pursued by their competitors will be'.[29] So, in the view of the Court, the fixing of target prices allowed the parties to align their conduct. There was no binding code, there was no explicit agreement on a fixed price, yet the arrangement, however loose, drew the parties together in a manner sufficiently far removed from independence to fall within the scope of the Community provisions on restrictive practices.

The activities of trade associations are accordingly capable of control

28 Case 8/72 [1972] ECR 977.
29 ibid., para. 21 of the judgment.

under Article 85 as either 'agreements between undertakings' or 'decisions of associations of undertakings'.[30] Both notions are caught by Article 85(1). The Commission and the Court have tended to use them interchangeably[31] and differentiation is frequently pointless.[32]

Clearly, then, the notion of 'agreement' is to be interpreted broadly. The Community institutions have pursued this approach with rigour. In order to avoid detection secret cartels are not normally set up under contracts, nor are they often expressed in writing, but they are certainly subject to Article 85 as 'agreements'.[33] Agreements, written or oral, that are expressed to be informal and non-binding are also caught.[34] A failure to enforce an agreement by either legal or extra-legal means does not take it outside the scope of Article 85.[35] Reaching consensus about action to be taken on the market is sufficient to amount to an agreement. Firms do not escape Article 85(1) by showing a failure to implement a clause prohibiting exports. Such a clause is still capable of affecting trade between member states through its 'visual and psychological' effect.[36]

If legal form is irrelevant to finding an agreement, then so is motive. In *Duffy Group/Quaker Oats*[37] the Commission held that a deal that parti-

---

30 See also, e.g., Case 45/85 *Verband der Sachversicherer* v *Commission* [1987] ECR 405, [1988] 4 CMLR 264, noted by Shaw (1987) 12 ELRev 265; *London Exchanges* [1989] 4 CMLR 280. On trade associations generally, see M. Reynolds, 'Trade Associations and the EEC Competition Rules' (1985) 23 RSDIC 49; P. Watson and K. Williams, 'The Application of the EEC Competition Rules to Trade Associations' (1988) 8 YEL 121; B. Jacobi and P. Vesterdorf, 'Co-operative societies and the Community rules on Competition' (1993) 18 ELRev 271. On fining an association, see Cases T-39/92 and T-40/92 *Groupement des Cartes Bancaires 'CB' and Others* v *Commission* [1994] ECR II-49.

31 See, e.g., on the rules of an association, Comm. Dec. 78/59 *CBR* OJ 1978 L20/18, [1978] 2 CMLR 194 (Dutch bicycle traders' association treated as a decision); Comm. Dec. 84/191 *Nuovo CEGAM* OJ 1984 L99/29, [1984] 2 CMLR 484 (Italian insurers' association treated as an agreement).

32 Differentiation may occasionally be necessary in order to determine whether the association itself is in violation; see, e.g., Cases 89, 104, 114, 116–17, 125–9/85 *A. Ahlström and Others* v *Commission* (*Re Woodpulp Cartel*) [1988] ECR 5193, [1988] 4 CMLR 901 (Court quashed decision in so far as it related to a trade association).

33 Cases 41/69 *ACF Chemiefarma* v *Commission* [1970] ECR 661, 44/69 *Buckler* v *Commission* [1970] ECR 733, 45/69 *Boehringer Mannheim* v *EC Commission* [1970] ECR 769 (collectively, the *Quinine Cartel*).

34 E.g. Cases 41, 44, 45/69, note 33 above; Case 28/77 *Tepea* v *Commission* [1978] ECR 1391, [1978] 3 CMLR 392.

35 Case C-277/87 *Sandoz* v *EC Commission* [1990] ECR I-45, noted by Thompson (1990) 27 CMLRev 589, and Shaw (1991) 16 ELRev 258; Comm. Dec. 90/645 *Bayer Dental* OJ 1990 L351/46, [1992] 4 CMLR 61, noted (1990) ELRev *Competition Law Checklist* 31; (1990) 10 YEL 407, 414–17.

36 Case T-66/92 *Herlitz AG* v *Commission* [1994] ECR II-531, Case T-77/92 *Parker Pen Ltd* v *Commission* [1994] ECR II-549, paras. 40 and 55 of the judgments respectively, citing Case 19/77 *Miller* v *Commission* [1978] ECR 131.

37 Comm. Dec. 88/86 OJ 1988 L49/19, [1989] 4 CMLR 553. See also Case 32/78

tioned the toy market along national lines, which had been imposed by an economically powerful firm on a reluctant small supplier, constituted an agreement, notwithstanding the fact that the small firm had little choice in practice but to submit to the terms offered. The finding that an agreement existed then allowed the Commission to break up the arrangement,[38] although the respective responsibility for the violation of Article 85 was reflected in the imposition of a fine on the large firm but not on the small firm.[39] The irrelevance of motive in aligning conduct is further emphasized by the Commission's view that to agree while intending subsequently to cheat is to agree for the purposes of Article 85.[40] As a final example, in *Bayer AG v Sullhofer*[41] the Court held that an agreement concluded bona fide between two firms in order to put an end to litigation before a court did not escape the application of Article 85. The motive of dispute settlement could not of itself exclude the matter from the potential application of Article 85 where part of the agreed settlement involved a restriction of competition.

The distinction between bilateral and unilateral conduct

The activities of a single firm are not immune from EC competition law. If the firm occupies a dominant position on the market, then its activity may be subject to Article 86.[42] However, the unilateral conduct of a non-dominant firm prima facie falls outside the scope of Community competition law. It might, however, be observed that this principle is subject to the occasionally surprising willingness of the Community authorities to find a bilateral arrangement caught by Article 85 when one might have supposed mere unilateral conduct to exist.[43] In *AEG v Commission*[44] the Court held that a manufacturer's refusal to admit an applicant to a selective distribution system was not a unilateral act. The refusal had to be

---

BMW v Belgium [1989] ECR 2435, [1980] 1 CMLR 370; Comm. Dec. 85/617, note 18 above.
38 Note also that the imposition of an agreement by a dominant firm may itself infringe Art. 86; see Ch. 23.
39 See p. 782 on fines.
40 Comm. Dec. 86/399 *BELASCO* OJ 1986 L232/15, [1991] 4 CMLR 130, para. 86. The point was not addressed directly by the Court in rejecting the application for annulment of this decision in Case 246/86 *BELASCO v Commission* [1989] ECR 2117, [1991] 4 CMLR 96.
41 Case 65/86 [1988] ECR 5249, [1990] 4 CMLR 182.
42 See Ch. 23.
43 See comment by Green, 'Article 85 in Perspective: Stretching Jurisdiction, Narrowing the Concept of a Restriction and Plugging a Few Gaps' [1988] ECLR 190, 203.
44 Case 107/82 [1983] ECR 3151. See also Case 25/84 *Ford v Commission* [1985] ECR 2725, [1985] 3 CMLR 258.

assessed in the context of a distribution structure that involved several firms already accepted as part of the package. The system involved not just the manufacturer but also existing distributors, and, accordingly, the refusal could be seen as an aspect of a multilateral arrangement subject to Article 85.[45] So, too, in *Sandoz*[46] the Court upheld the Commission's view that the firm's distribution of invoices to its customers bearing the words 'not to be exported' constituted a tacitly agreed export ban caught by Article 85(1) rather than a gratuitous unilateral declaration. An agreement, then, can be discerned in a continuing business arrangement.[47]

Occasional difficulties have arisen in identifying the existence of an agreement where the participants are in some way economically linked. In *Christiani and Nielsen*[48] the Commission concluded that a Dutch firm wholly owned by a Danish company was not capable of entering into an Article 85(1) agreement with the parent company. The Dutch firm had been set up by the Danish undertaking in order to carry out its business on Dutch territory more efficiently. The Danish firm nominated the directors of the Dutch firm and was able to instruct that firm how to act. The subsidiary enjoyed no economic independence and, accordingly, the arrangements between the two firms were merely the allocation of responsibilities within a single undertaking. This, of course, means that even the existence of a formal contract between legally independent firms does not necessarily mean that an agreement under Article 85 is in place. For the purposes of Article 85 it is necessary to look behind the corporate veil and establish that the parties to that contract are not only legally but also economically separate. The Court has confirmed that the Commission's treatment of 'intra-enterprise conspiracy' is correct; there is no breach of Article 85 if the firms involved in the practices constitute a single economic unit.[49] The test is thus based on economic reality, not organizational

---

45 See p. 700 on selective distribution systems.
46 Case C-277/87, note 35 above.
47 See also Comm. Dec. 88/172 *Konica* OJ 1988 L78/34, [1988] 4 CMLR 848; Comm. Dec. 91/39 *D'Ieteren Motor Oils* OJ 1991 L20/42, noted (1990) ELRev *Competition Law Checklist* 33.
48 Comm. Dec. 69/165 JO 1969 L165/12, [1969] CMLR D36.
49 E.g. Case 22/71 *Beguelin* [1971] ECR 949, [1972] CMLR 81; Case 15/74 *Centrafarm v Sterling Drug* [1974] ECR 1147; Case 170/83 *Hydrotherm Geratebau v Andreoli* [1984] ECR 2999; Case 30/87 *Bodson v Pompes Funèbres* [1988] ECR 2479. See G. Assant, Anti-trust Intracorporate Conspiracies: A Comparative Study of French, EEC and American Laws' [1990] 2 ECLR 65. Note that this approach may take the agent/principal relationship outside the scope of Article 85, although this will depend on the precise nature of the relationship at issue; see, e.g., Cases 40–48, 50, 54–6, 111, 113–14/73 *Suiker Unie v Commission* [1975] ECR 1663, [1976] 1 CMLR 295. The Commission issued a notice on the matter in 1962; see Whish, *Competition Law*, pp. 552–5; Goyder, *EC Competition Law*, pp. 212–16.

structures which may reflect arbitrary legal or commercial patterns. A group of associated companies may for competition law purposes constitute a single undertaking.[50]

CONCERTED PRACTICES

The nature of the concerted practice

Article 85(1) goes further than the 'agreement', for it includes within its scope the notion of the 'concerted practice'. This plainly envisages a looser form of collaboration. In pursuing a concerted practice the parties may cooperate without ever having reached an agreement; or they may have abandoned an existing agreement without shaking off a persisting understanding that their behaviour would be aligned.[51]

In *Hasselblad* v *Commission*[52] the Court upheld the Commission's finding of a concerted practice involving Victor Hasselblad, a Swedish camera equipment manufacturer, and distributors of its products in several member states. Camera Care, a camera firm operating in London, had been a dealer in Hasselblad cameras but had lost the dealership in 1978. It had managed to acquire Hasselblad cameras for resale from Ireland, where it had bought up stocks marketed by Ilford, Hasselblad's authorized dealer for Ireland. Camera Care had had similar success in obtaining cameras from Telos, the Hasselblad authorized dealer in France. Hasselblad learned that Camera Care had obtained its goods from outside the United Kingdom as a result of inquiries made by Hasselblad UK, the United Kingdom distributor. Complaints were then directed by Hasselblad to Ilford and to Telos. Both stopped selling to Camera Care and began to sell only in their home markets.[53] The Court upheld the Commission's view that this was a concerted practice caught by Article 85. Hasselblad and its dealers had set up a scheme, initiated by Hasselblad's pressure, which prevented cross-border trade and stifled competition. A complaint, which is acted upon in a manner

---

50 The test may in practice be difficult to apply; consider, e.g., the problem of the partly owned subsidiary which enjoys limited economic independence; Comm. Dec. 91/335 *Gosme/Martell/DMP* OJ 1991 L185/23 [1992] 5 CMLR 586.

51 E.g. Case 51/75 *EMI* v *CBS* [1976] ECR 811, [1976] 2 CMLR 235, paras. 30–31; Comm. Dec. 91/297, note 17.

52 Case 86/82 [1984] ECR 883.

53 Both were subjected to economic pressure to respond to the complaints, but their reluctance was considered irrelevant to the finding of a concerted practice; see especially Comm. Dec. 82/367 OJ 1982 L161/18, [1982] 2 CMLR 233 para. 47. See also the irrelevance of motive in entering into an agreement, p. 672.

that leads to market partitioning, is thus evidence of a concerted practice forbidden by Article 85.[54]

The arrangement in *Hasselblad* was characterized as a concerted practice. Given the rather flexible approach discussed in the previous section, it seems arguable that the parties had, in fact, gone so far as to conclude an agreement. However, the fact that both the agreement and the concerted practice fall within the ambit of Article 85(1) means that in practice the need to locate a dividing line between them may be of no practical moment.[55] The Commission's decision in *Hasselblad* indicated that it saw no need to search for an agreement once it was satisfied that a concerted practice had been uncovered.[56] The key distinction is between the agreement/concerted practice and genuine independence, for that distinction is the outer margin of the application of Article 85 itself.

The problem posed by the oligopoly

The problem of identifying whether firms are in concertation or truly independent is especially acute in oligopolies.[57] Imagine a market that contains only a small number of producers, a market that is tightly knit. Obviously, the handful of producers will behave in a manner comparable to each other. They are subject to the same pressures. Most important, they are to some extent dependent on each other's behaviour. One firm is well aware that if it raises its prices, it may lose its market share to the other producers. Similarly, a firm knows that if another firm reduces its prices, it may have to follow or else risk losing market share. If there is no substitutable product and if the market is difficult to enter, because of, say, the high cost of establishing production facilities, the result is a market comprising only a few producers immune from the entry of new competitors to liberate the efficient forces of competition.

In economic jargon this is an oligopoly. The producers act in parallel. There is no explicit collusion in this model. Yet each party knows that to some extent it is dependent on the other producers. The dependence derives from market structure, not collusion. Yet the observable result of the parallel behaviour may be no different from outright agreement to behave in a set manner. The law must decide when such circumstances are caught by Article 85 as a 'concerted practice', and when the firms remain

---

54 See also Cases 100–103/80 *Musique Diffusion Française* v *Commission* [1983] ECR 1825, [1983] 3 CMLR 221; Comm. Dec. 91/532 *Toshiba* OJ 1991 L287.
55 M. Antunes, 'Agreements and Concerted Practices under EEC Competition Law: Is the Distinction Relevant?' [1991] 11 YEL 57.
56 Comm. Dec. 82/367, note 53 above, para. 46.
57 Whish, *Competition Law*, Ch. 14.

sufficiently independent to escape the application of competition law. It is a problem endemic in all systems of restrictive practices law.[58]

The European Court's approach in 'Dyestuffs'

The European Court's leading case is *ICI* v *Commission*, which concerned three separate price increases announced by Community dyestuffs producers.[59] The first increase was a 15 per cent rise in the price of most aniline dyes initiated by CIBA, an Italian firm, and followed by nine of the leading producers elsewhere in the Community within thirteen days. The producers concerned held some 80 per cent of the Community market between them. Subsequently, a 10 per cent increase in the price of dyes and pigments was announced in advance by BASF in Germany and copied by all the other firms on other national markets so that the increase came into force simultaneously, with the exception of the French market, constrained by governmental price controls, and the Italian market, suffering from severe recession. The third price rise was of 8 per cent, announced in advance and duly followed in all markets except the French, where a 'catch-up' 12 per cent increase was announced, and the Italian, where, again, there was no increase.

There were, then, undeniable elements of similarity in the conduct of the firms. However, faced with the threat of a finding that they had acted together in breach of Article 85, the dyestuffs producers submitted that in a market where the bulk of the production was concentrated in the hands of relatively few firms it was inevitable that action by one firm would cause the others to act. There was no concerted practice; instead, the firms were simply reacting to market pressures, including the decisions of their rivals, which affected all of them in more or less the same way.

The Commission and the Court both rejected this market structure explanation and found the firms guilty of involvement in a concerted practice in breach of Article 85. They had not entered into an agreement, but they had 'knowingly substitute[d] practical cooperation between them for the risks of competition'.[60] However, the institutions placed rather different emphases on the available evidence in reaching this conclusion.[61]

The Commission placed weight on circumstantial evidence that it had been able to accumulate.[62] Short of discovering actual documentation explaining the terms of a secret deal, there are other matters of fact that, if

58 On UK law, see ibid., pp. 139–44, 492–8.
59 Case 48/69 *Imperial Chemical Industries Ltd* v *Commission* [1972] ECR 619, noted by Korah (1973) 36 MLR 220; Mann (1973) 22 ICLQ 35.
60 ibid., para. 64 of the judgment.
61 See p. 681 on the burden of proof.
62 Comm. Dec. 69/243, JO 1969 L 195/11, [1969] CMLR D23.

discovered, point in the direction of the existence of an agreement or, at least, a concerted practice.[63] The existence of meetings and documents are factors, even if their content is unknown. The fact that the firms had notified price rises using similar phrases suggested a common source. The short time-gaps between the several announcements further indicated that a plan had been formed in advance and that this was not independent adaptation. In addition, the Commission was able to point to a meeting held in Basle[64] at which all the producers, except ACNA from Italy, were present. A single factor of this nature would be unlikely to provide a conclusive basis for a finding that a concerted practice had been pursued, but a combination of such evidence may suffice, particularly where no elements of evidence suggest the opposite, innocent conclusion.[65]

The Court agreed that the totality of available evidence should be assessed, but chose to place its emphasis on the evidence arising from the economic structure of the market. The Court was not convinced that this was a true oligopoly, in which firms would be expected to follow suit without collusion. There were enough producers for one to expect proper competition to break out. The fact that the market had not corrected itself in this way indicated that the firms themselves had raised obstacles to the operation of the market by collusion. Parallel behaviour, then, is not of itself proof of a concerted practice. A concerted practice will not be found if there exists a plausible explanation other than collusion for the parallelism.[66] However, parallel behaviour provides a strong indication of unlawful conduct where the market would not be expected to yield such an outcome.

From 'Dyestuffs' to 'Woodpulp'

The 'Dyestuffs' case establishes that it is permissible, indeed inevitable, to take account of a competitor's likely actions and reactions, but this must stop short of any taint of concertation that destroys independence. What may seem alarming is the slender dividing line between banned indirect contact and innocent responsiveness. In *ICI* v *Commission* both Court and Commission referred to the fact that the announcements in advance of

---

63 Joshua, 'Proof in Contested EEC Competition Cases', (1987), 12 ELRev 315, 328.
64 In Switzerland; see p. 689 on the reach of EC competition law beyond the Community's borders.
65 Nothing in principle prevents the Commission using 'hearsay' evidence; these are not criminal proceedings and fines are expressly stated to be non-criminal in nature; see p. 784; see also Wyatt and Dashwood, *European Community Law*, p. 397.
66 Case 395/87 *Ministère Public* v *Tournier* [1989] ECR 2521, [1991] 4 CMLR 248, para. 24 of the judgment; the case was an Art. 177 reference and therefore the economic inquiry was a matter for the national court.

pricing policy allowed the dyestuffs producers to eliminate all uncertainty about each other's plans. They were no longer competing independently; they were alert to competitors' plans. If the announcement of price rises, perhaps even indirectly communicated through, for example, trade journals, is capable of founding a finding of concertation, it is plain that the reach of Community competition law is remarkably extensive.

The Court followed its approach to the notion of the concerted practice in several important subsequent cases. The concerted practice refers to a form of cooperation between undertakings that, without having reached a stage where an agreement as normally understood has been concluded, knowingly substitutes practical cooperation achieved through direct or indirect contact for the risks of competition.[67] It is plain that any actor in a small, closely knit market must be wary of its connections with other participants in the oligopoly for fear of arousing Commission suspicion of concertation. Intelligent adaptation to rivals' strategies falls on the lawful side of the concerted practice line, but cooperation that suppresses independence, even if far short of a proper plan, even if merely a nod and a wink, is capable of violating Article 85. Both factual and economic evidence may be used in support of the inquiry.

The disturbingly slender division between unlawful collaboration and innocent parallel behaviour was revisited in the Court's 1993 ruling in *Ahlström (Woodpulp Cartel)*. This is one of the lengthiest sagas in the Court's history.[68] The challenged Commission Decision was made in 1984 and the case first came before the Court in September 1988 when the Court rejected submissions that the practices fell outwith the jurisdiction of the EC.[69] Then in March 1993 the Court ruled on the substance.[70] The central issue was whether the producers of woodpulp, used in paper

---

67 Case 40/73 note 49 above. The Commission's finding of a concerted practice was annulled for insufficient evidence in Cases 29, 30/83 *CRAM and Rheinzink v Commission* [1984] ECR 1679, [1985] 1 CMLR 688.

68 This explains why the European Court handled the case, even though today it would initially fall within the Court of First Instance's jurisdiction; Ch. 24. For the CFI's comparable approach to concertation, see the series of cases decided in three separate batches arising out of the *Polypropylene Cartel*: Cases T-1/, T-2, T-3/89 *Rhône-Poulenc, Petrofina, Atochem v Commission* [1991] ECR II-867, 1087, 1177; T-4, T-6, T-7, T-8/89 *BASF AG, Enichem Anic, SA Hercules, DSM NV v Commission* [1991] ECR II-1523, 1624, 1711, 1833; Cases T-9, T-10, T-11, T-12, T-13, T-14, T-15/89 *Hüls AG, Hoechst AG, Shell Ltd, SA Solvay, ICI plc, Montedipe SpA, Linz AG v Commission* [1992] ECR II-499, 629, 757, 907, 1021, 1155, 1275.

69 Joined Cases 89, 104, 114, 116, 117 and 125–129/85 [1988] ECR 5193, further considered at p. 690 below.

70 Joined Cases C-89/85, C-104/85, C-114/85, C-116/85, C-117/85, C-125–129/85 *A. Ahlström and Others v Commission*, judgment of 31 March 1993 [1993] 4 CMLR 407, noted by Jones [1993] 6 ECLR 273, Cumming [1994] JBL 165; see also (1993) ELRev *Competition Law Checklist* 12.

production, were guilty of collaboration on price. Much of the Commission Decision was annulled by the Court. Of widest importance was the Court's approach to Article 1(1) of the Decision, the infringement relating to general concertation on announced prices by firms from Finland, United States, Canada, Sweden and Norway.[71] The Court cited its earlier judgment in *Suiker Unie*[72] and referred to a concerted practice as the knowing substitution of practical cooperation for the risks of competition. Each actor is expected to determine policy in the market independently and Article 85(1) is targeted at deviation from that norm.

The Court excluded documentary evidence of concertation once it was satisfied that the Commission had improperly failed to identify all the undertakings alleged to be party to the concertation. This left only proof gleaned indirectly from market patterns.

The Court found that the simple fact of quarterly price announcements made to users did not 'lessen each undertaking's uncertainty as to the future attitude of its competitors'. In itself this normal market behaviour was no violation of Article 85(1). Presumably reciprocity of communication between producers would take the practices over the line into the realms of concertation.[73] More subtly, the Commission had identified not simply quarterly price announcements but their well-nigh simultaneous publication and an identical level of increase. This was a loud echo of the 'Dyestuffs' case. The Court accepted the relevance of parallel conduct in the search for proof of concertation, but repeated that the existence of plausible explanations for parallelism other than concertation precludes the allegation being sustained on such evidence. The Court carefully upheld the lawfulness of intelligent adaptation to the existing and anticipated conduct of competitors.

The Court had commissioned reports by two experts and it relied on their analysis of the state of the market to reject the Commission's findings. The near-simultaneity of the announcements was, according to the Commission, impossible without sharing of information among producers. But the Court saw this as a result of the very high level of transparency in a market where sellers and buyers of pulp had long-standing, close-knit networks. Pulp buyers – paper manufacturers, of whom there were in any event relatively few – typically diversified their sources of supply and, to gain price advantage, they typically disclosed to suppliers prices charged by competitors. The Court also pointed out that information on prices

71 Other parts of the ruling deal with procedural errors on the part of the Commission; and/or relate to trade associations in the sector.
72 Cases 40–48/73 *et al.*, note 49 above.
73 This is addressed in the Opinion of A G Darmon. See more generally Osti, 'Information Exchanges in the Obscure Light of Woodpulp' [1994] 3 ECLR 176.

spread rapidly even throughout an extended distribution chain as a result of modern use of instantaneous forms of communication such as telephone and fax. A dynamic trade press also played its part in achieving unusual market transparency.

Parallel prices were also explicable to the Commission only as the fruits of concertation. But the Court, again relying on its experts, found that the normal operation of a market bearing oligopolistic features provided a more plausible explanation. The Court was able to trace price levels from 1975 to 1981 and find market explanations for the features which the Commission had picked out as proof of concertation.

Much is expected of the Commission in future. It must establish a 'firm, precise and consistent body of evidence',[74] which plainly includes explanation of why other possible reasons for parallelism lack plausibility in the particular circumstances. The Court is ready carefully to check the interpretation of economic data (although it will be the Court of First Instance that today carries out that function). One may surmise that in future the deduction of concertation from evidence based solely on parallel conduct will occur in only the most blatant cases.

Alternative approaches to the oligopoly

In a genuine oligopoly, which did not exist in the 'Dyestuffs' case, the problem may be that in terms of economic effect there is absolutely no difference between a concerted practice and an intelligent response to market conditions. This might lead one to question whether the distinction made in Article 85 according to the existence of collusion is of any economic relevance. The system is open to criticism for concentrating on a symptom, not the disease.[75] The law induces oligopolists to operate without contacting each other, but fails utterly to tackle the oligopolistic economic interdependence that is the real problem. Is a better approach available? An oligopoly is unlikely to survive if new firms enter the market, so the law could profitably be directed at the elimination of barriers to entry to the market.[76] Indeed, cross-border economic integration is in itself an anti-oligopoly strategy, for it opens up markets to fresh competition.[77] A separate strategy would prevent the oligopoly coming into existence in the

---

74 Para. 127 of the judgment.
75 See, e.g., Franzosi [1988] ECLR 385.
76 For wider discussion of entry barriers, see p. 737. An aspect of such a policy may be to permit would-be entrants to form a cartel in order to facilitate penetration of the market; I. Forrester and C. Norall, 'Competition Law' (1990) 10 YEL 407, 467.
77 On this point and generally, see Krugman, 'Economic Integration in Europe: Some Conceptual Issues' in Jacquemin and Sapir (eds.) *The European Internal Market*.

first place. This might be achievable through the imposition of tighter controls on horizontal mergers in order to ensure that there remains a sufficient number of firms operating on the market in order to foster genuine competition. If the oligopoly is already in existence and entry barriers are high, it may be appropriate to break it up by forced dismantling of large firms or groups of firms. Yet these may be rather brutal instruments with undesirable side-effects. Suppressing anticompetitive agreements is much easier and less interventionist than eliminating obstinate oligopolistic structures. That latter task may have regulatory costs that exceed any benefits, which suggests that a system of workable competition has to tolerate some of the prejudicial effects of oligopolies.

This acquiescence in the existence of oligopolies may lead to the view that they should be controlled by curbing potential excesses in a manner comparable to control of monopolies. Attention has been devoted to the extent to which Article 86 can be employed on the basis that oligopolists occupy a position of joint dominance on the market. The legal position has been partly clarified by the ruling of the Court of First Instance in *Società Italiana Vetro SpA and others v Commission*, commonly referred to as the 'Flat Glass' decision.[78] The Court annulled the Commission's Decision dealing with practices in the flat glass industry. The Court found a number of serious procedural irregularities in the Commission's handling of the case.

The Court did not rule out the use of the notion of joint dominance as a means of controlling an oligopoly under Article 86. However, the Court disagreed with the way in which the Commission had found collaboration forbidden by Article 85 and then simply 'recycled' the same facts into an allegation of abuse of a joint dominant position contrary to Article 86.[79] The Court of First Instance insisted on a separation between the functions of Articles 85 and 86 and found the market analysis required in Article 86 cases sadly wanting in the Commission Decision in *Flat Glass*.[80]

It ruled that Article 86 is capable of controlling oligopolies on the basis that they may constitute positions of joint dominance. But it seems to have ruled out a finding of joint dominance where the links between the firms result purely from the structure of the market. There must be some 'economic link' between the firms in the oligopoly before they can properly be judged jointly dominant. The Court of First Instance explained that two or more independent firms may be

---

78 Cases T-68/89, T-77–78/89 [1992] ECR II-1403, [1992] 5 CMLR 302, noted by Pope [1993] 4 ECLR 172.
79 Para. 360 of the judgment.
80 Comm. Dec. 89/93 OJ 1989 L33/44.

. . . united by such economic links that . . . together they hold a dominant position vis-à-vis the other operators on the same market. This could be the case, for example, where two or more independent undertakings jointly have, through agreements or licences, a technological lead affording them the power to behave to an appreciable extent independently of their competitors, their customers and ultimately of their consumers.[81]

Oligopoly control under Article 86 via the concept of joint dominance is thus recognized in Community law, but only where these 'economic links' are shown to exist. In *Flat Glass* the Commission had not adduced the necessary proof.

The use of Article 86 to snare oligopolists has some attraction, but Article 86 lacks the sophistication necessary for the effective control of the complex phenomenon of the oligopoly. Its weaknesses are further examined in the context of the general examination of Article 86 in Chapter 23.[82]

UNDERTAKINGS

The broad interpretation of an undertaking

The term 'undertaking' goes undefined in the Treaty rules regulating competition.[83] In accordance with a policy that is readily identifiable elsewhere in Community law, the Community institutions have sought a broad definition of the notion in a manner that has maximized their competence. Provided the entity pursues an activity that falls within the broad objectives expressed in Article 2 EC, it is subject to the competition rules found in Article 85 *et seq.*

In *Italy* v *Council and Commission*[84] Advocate-General Roemer suggested a useful working definition that encapsulates the breadth of the notion: '. . . apart from legal form or the purpose of gain, undertakings are natural or legal persons which take part actively and independently in business and are not therefore engaged in a purely private activity . . .'[85] This is plainly a functional definition and depends for its application on the nature of particular entities. The Court has adopted an approach very similar to that mooted by the Advocate-General and has given a broad interpretation to

81 Para. 358 of the judgment.
82 See p. 725 below.
83 Contrast Arts. 52, 58 EC; Art. 80 ECSC.
84 Case 32/65 [1966] ECR 389.
85 ibid., 418.

the notion of an undertaking in a series of judgments during its development of Community competition law. The many economically active companies, partnerships, trade associations and cooperatives discussed in this and the following chapters are all undertakings covered by the provisions of Article 85. Even an individual acting independently as an economic actor is capable of fulfilling the definition of an undertaking.[86]

An entity engaged in commercial activity is capable of fulfilling the definition of an undertaking even in the absence of the pursuit of profit. In *Van Landewyck* v *Commission*[87] the Court held that FEDETAB, an association that represented the majority of cigarette manufacturers in Belgium and Luxembourg, was an undertaking subject to the competition rules, notwithstanding its own role as representative rather than independent profit-maker. The European Economic Interest Grouping is a vehicle for cross-border trade created under a regulation that expressly forbids it from having profit-making on its own account as an objective.[88] Yet there can be no doubt that an EEIG is an undertaking for the purposes of the competition rules, given its participation in the market, and both it and participating firms must be alert to Article 85.[89] A trade union might also fall within the notion of an undertaking for these purposes, which would lead to the awkward but as yet untested possibility of collective bargains struck with employers being subject to scrutiny as restrictive practices under Article 85.

Special sectors

Although in principle any undertaking participating in economic activity is subject to the competition rules, there are certain special types of body that require separate consideration.[90] Some undertakings are subject to particular regulatory rules found elsewhere than Articles 85–94. An obvious example is an undertaking involved in the coal or steel sector. Such bodies are capable of fulfilling the Article 85 EC test as undertakings, but are subject instead to the regime of the European Coal and Steel Treaty. Within the ambit of the European Community Treaty itself, agricultural

---

86 See Case 42/84 *Remia* v *Commission* [1985] ECR 2545, [1987] 1 CMLR 1; see also Comm. Dec. 76/743 *Reuter/BASF* OJ 1976 L254/40, [1976] 2 CMLR D44 (inventor and consultant); Comm. Dec. 78/516 *Unitel* OJ 1978 L157/39, [1978] 3 CMLR 306 (opera singers).
87 Cases 209–15, 218/78 [1980] ECR 3125.
88 Reg. 2137/85, Art. 3(1); see p. 601 above.
89 R. Drury and M. Schiessl, 'EC Competition Law Aspects of the EEIG' [1994] JBL 217.
90 Bellamy and Child, *Common Market Law of Competition*, Chs. 13–17; Whish, *Competition Law*, Ch. 10; Van Bael and Bellis, *Competition Law*, Ch. 10.

undertakings are similarly capable of meeting the definition of an undertaking covered by Articles 85 *et seq.*, but the special sensitivity of the agricultural sector persuaded the drafters of the Treaty to create a special regime, which has been elaborated under secondary legislation.[91] Other sectors are in principle subject to Article 85, but are treated in a manner distinct from the norm because enforcement of the competition rules is in some way limited. Thus, transport undertakings are in principle subject to Article 85, but were excluded from the scope of Regulation 17/62, which confers on the Commission its general powers to enforce the competition rules. Consequently, as the Court confirmed in *Ministère Public* v *Asjes*,[92] such undertakings were not subject to the normal enforcement procedures and, in the absence of parallel enforcement rules for that sector, in practice they enjoyed something close to immunity from the laws against anti-competitive practices.[93] The exceptional nature of the transport sector has to some extent been eradicated by the passage of legislation to provide for the enforcement of Articles 85 *et seq.* even in this sector as part of the Community's drive to complete the process of market integration and regulation.[94] Apart from such exceptional areas, however, a commercially active undertaking is normally presumed to be covered by Article 85 and subject to Commission enforcement procedures and the mere fact that there is no precedent for scrutiny of an entity in that sector is not relevant.[95]

Control of the state: a summary

In basing the scope of Article 85 on the context in which the body operates rather than its formal legal designation the Court has ensured that the notion of an undertaking is capable of covering commercial firms whether privately or state owned. A publicly owned firm may be subject to Article 85 provided its operations fall within the commercial sphere.[96] However, there are limits to the notion of the 'undertaking' to which the competition rules are applicable. The Court has accepted that bodies to which the State entrusts the management of a social security scheme fulfil

---

91 Art. 42 EC. See Bellamy and Child, *Common Market Law of Competition*, Ch. 14. For full treatment of this sector see Snyder, *Common Agricultural Policy*.
92 Cases 209–13/84 [1986] ECR 1457, [1986] 3 CMLR 173.
93 See further Ch. 24, which examines enforcement of the rules in more depth.
94 See p. 756.
95 Cases 209–13/84, note 92 above; Case 45/85, note 30 above.
96 Case 155/73 *Sacchi* [1974] ECR 409, [1974] 2 CMLR 177; Case 123/83 *BNIC* v *Clair* [1985] ECR 391; Comm. Dec. 85/206 *Aluminium Products* OJ 1985 L92/1, [1987] 3 CMLR 813.

an exclusively social function. They are not 'undertakings'.[97] Nor is the notion of an 'undertaking' satisfied by an international organization whose functions involve the establishment and collection of charges levied on users of air navigation services in accordance with international agreements.[98] Locating the outer margin to the notion of an 'undertaking' places an important limit on the incursion of the competition rules into the activities of non-profit-making public bodies charged with the task of fulfilling functions in the general interest. However, the Court's treatment of the 'undertaking' in this context is not entirely consistent. Where it has adopted a broader approach to the 'undertaking', concern has been raised that the Treaty competition rules have been improperly applied in areas regulated for non-economic reasons.[99] The Treaty of Rome shares with many legal systems an important yet sometimes ill-defined distinction between the public and the private spheres.[100] Intervention in the freedom of the market can be traced to private firms and to legislative enactment. Where the market for goods is concerned, the former are dealt with under Articles 85 and 86, the latter under Article 30. There are also interventions that may be traceable to actions part private, part public. The regulation of prices, for example, may be state policy, but that policy is carried out by commercial firms. So a firm may be pursuing governmental policy. It may be given governmental support, through financial or legislative backing, to enhance its ability to distort the market. The state may go so far as to require the firm by law to operate in a manner incompatible with the common market. Such activities, attributable both to firm and to state, all require Community supervision, for they are capable of impeding the operation of the market. Treaty provisions that may be relevant, apart from Articles 85 and 30, include Article 90, which concerns public undertakings; Article 92 (state aids); Article 37 (state commercial monopolies); and Article 5, the provision that imposes on member states the obligation to cooperate in the development of the Community and that in this context forbids states from requiring or even assisting firms to escape the full rigour of the competition rules. The matter of state participation in the market economy thus demands that attention be paid to several Treaty provisions.[101]

97 Cases C-159/91 and C-160/91 *C. Poucet and Others* v *Assurances Générales*, judgment of 16 February 1993.
98 Case C-364/92 *SAT Fluggesellschaft mbH* v *Eurocontrol* [1994] ECR I-43.
99 See Case C-41/90 *Höfner* v *Macrotron* and discussion at p. 862.
100 For discussion see Pescatore, 'Public and Private Aspects of Community Law' (1986) Fordham Corp L Inst 383.
101 The issue is analysed in more depth in Ch. 27.

AN EFFECT ON TRADE BETWEEN MEMBER STATES

A jurisdictional threshold

The agreement or concerted practice between undertakings must have an effect on trade *between member states* for Article 85 to apply. This is essentially a jurisdictional requirement. Community competition law applies only where this interstate criterion is satisfied.[102] If a restrictive practice has implications only within a single member state, then regulatory competence belongs solely at national level. However, the Community institutions have interpreted the requirement that there be an effect on trade between member states in such a way that the criterion has not proved a serious obstacle to the scope of application of Community law. The jurisdictional threshold is low. It is frequently possible to identify an effect on trade between member states even where the arrangements appear on first inspection to concern one state alone.

Consten and Grundig[103] provides a simple example of the required interstate element. The deal was designed to regulate and restrict the flow of goods across frontiers. Trade between member states was affected and therefore the agreement fell within the jurisdiction of Community competition law. Practices such as export bans, price-fixing for particular territories, and discrimination on grounds of nationality plainly have implications for trade between member states and consequently call for examination under Article 85. *Cementhandelaren*, in which the fixing of target prices was held to be an agreement covered by Article 85,[104] also sheds light on the ease with which the Community competition authorities are able to identify the required effect on trade between member states. It will be recalled that the association that set target prices comprised Dutch cement dealers alone. The prices related to commercial activity on the Dutch market alone. The scheme had no explicit application to imports and exports. It might therefore be thought that the collusion concerned the Netherlands alone and, if undesirable, fell for regulation by the Dutch authorities. However, the Court supported the Commission's finding that interstate trade was affected and that, accordingly, the Community authorities were empowered to intervene. The basis of this finding was that action on the Dutch market alone had inevitable implications for other markets. The state of

---

102 National competition law may also apply in such cases; on overlap and conflict, see Case 14/68 *Walt Wilhelm* v *Bundeskartellamt* [1969] ECR 1; comment by Faull, (1989) Fordham Corp L Inst 485; Whish, *Competition Law*, pp. 37–43; and p. 792 below.
103 Cases 56, 58/64, considered on p. 663, and note 3 above.
104 Case 8/72, note 28 above.

restricted competition on the Dutch market affected the ability of, say, German or Belgian cement producers to penetrate the Dutch market. So, similarly, in *Co-operative Stremsel-en Kleurselfabriek v Commission*[105] a national trade association that operated a system that committed members to trade with each other affected trade between member states by reducing opportunities for participation by importers. Arrangements of this type reduce competition and serve to compartmentalize national markets in a manner contrary to the objectives of market integration contained in the Treaty.

In adopting this approach the Court has greatly reduced the difficulty of finding the required interstate element. Provided that an impact on the patterns of trade across borders within the Community can be attributed with a sufficient degree of probability to the practice, then no matter that it is operated within a single state, there will be the required effect on trade between member states. The Court first relied on the test of an alteration in interstate trade patterns in *STM v Maschinenbau Ulm*[106] and has confirmed it many times since. It is a test that has also become increasingly influential in a slightly different guise in relation to the application of Article 30,[107] which serves as a useful reminder that the Community is showing signs of evolution towards a general law of market integration based on the common purpose of several provisions. From this perspective, it is notable that Articles 30 and 85 were formerly placed in different parts of the Treaty, but, after Maastricht, are both contained in Part Three, 'Community Policies', which covers Articles 9–136a inclusive. Given this 'patterns of trade' test, which is relatively easy to satisfy, it is likely that whereas an agreement between small firms within an isolated area of a single member state will escape Article 85 as purely internal in effect,[108] most agreements of any commercial significance will satisfy the interstate threshold. This is all the more so since it is clear that a single agreement must be judged not in isolation, but with reference to the effect of any broader network of which it forms part.[109] A realistic appraisal of the economic context must be adopted.

---

105 Case 61/80 [1981] ECR 851; see also Case 246/86, note 40 above.
106 Case 56/65 [1966] ECR 235, [1966] 1 CMLR 357.
107 See p. 432 above; cf. e.g., para. 10 of Case 158/86 *Warner Bros. v Christiansen* [1988] ECR 2605, [1990] 3 CMLR 684, with the *STM* Art. 85 test.
108 An isolated market was found in Case 22/78 *Hugin v Commission* [1979] ECR 1869 (no jurisdiction to apply Art. 86).
109 Case 23/67 *Brasserie de Haecht v Wilkin* [1967] ECR 407, [1968] CMLR 26; Comm. Dec. 89/515 *Welded Steel Mesh* OJ 1989 L260/1, [1991] 4 CMLR 13, noted by Jones and Van der Woude (1990) 15 ELRev 162, 163. See Case 193/83 *Windsurfing v Commission* [1986] ECR 611, [1986] 3 CMLR 489, which also tends to expand Community competence; cf. Case C-234/89. *Stergios Delimitis v Henninger Brau* [1991] ECR I-935 considered at p. 696.

Indeed, the Community's adoption of a test based on an effect on the structure of competition means that the interstate proviso will become steadily even easier to fulfil as the market continues to integrate. The logic of a single market is that practices have implications throughout the market and do not stop at national boundaries. In consequence, few agreements will affect a national market alone.[110] This, in turn, is likely to diminish the practical scope of application of domestic competition law.[111]

A test based on repercussions on the patterns of competition within the common market allows Article 85 to control even agreements that increase the level of trade between member states. This was apparent in *Consten and Grundig*,[112] which, after all, improved product distribution, and has been confirmed since.[113] The artificial nature of the patterns of trade that ensue is a sufficient basis for Community competence to control the deal, although, of course, it always remains open to the parties to such a deal to show that it should be permitted.[114]

Beyond the Community's borders

The Community's competition law is capable of supervising the conduct of firms based outside the member states, provided only that their agreements affect trade between member states. At the simplest level this asserts a power to control non-EC firms whose subsidiaries in the EC engage in restrictive practices. The law attributes responsibility for a subsidiary's activities to a parent that is in economic terms in control of the group structure,[115] and may impose appropriate sanctions on the parent. In the 'Dyestuffs' case, *ICI v Commission*,[116] several of the firms implicated in the concerted practice were non-EC firms operating through the medium of a subsidiary. The Court held them directly responsible for the collusion once satisfied that the parent and subsidiary were economically, if not legally, a single unit.

Where the non-EC firm has no direct presence in the Community, it is still possible to invoke the rules of competition law. So if a US firm enters

---

110 Green, [1988] ECLR 190, 192–5. However, it should not be *presumed* that all markets are European. Each market requires its own assessment; see e.g., Borrie in Fairburn and Kay (eds.), *Mergers and Merger Policy*, p. 251. Ch. 25, p. 823.
111 Alignment of national systems with the Community model may be induced; for discussion, see Faull, (1989) Fordham Corp L Inst 485, and Ehlermann, (1992) 29 CMLRev 257.
112 Cases 56, 58/64, note 3 above.
113 See, e.g., Comm. Dec. 88/518 *British Sugar* OJ 1988 L284/41 [1990] 4 CMLR 196.
114 Art. 85(1), p. 696 below; Art. 85(3), p. 704 below.
115 See p. 674.
116 Case 48/69, note 59 above. For criticism, see Acevedo (1973) 36 MLR 317, Mann (1973) 22 ICLQ 35, 42.

into an agreement with a German firm to share markets in the Community, both have participated in an agreement that affects trade between member states. In *Beguelin*,[117] an arrangement between Oshawa, a Japanese manufacturer of cigarette lighters, and Beguelin, the appointed French distributor, was held to infringe Article 85. Beguelin was restrained from re-exporting the products to other member states, whereas Oshawa's similarly tied distributors in other member states were forbidden from encroaching on the French market. Oshawa had, in fact, unlawfully established a network of deals that served to partition the common market along national lines. However, the case was an Article 177 reference and so did not decide the issue whether Oshawa, a Japanese firm, could have been subject to penalties imposed by the Commission for breach of Community law.

The next step is rather more controversial. Can the EC take action under Article 85 against non-EC firms having no direct or indirect presence in the Community but whose agreements have an *effect* within the Community? It has been explained that in *Cementhandelaren*[118] the Court accepted that firms in agreement on the Dutch market were caught by Article 85 because that agreement had an effect on the wider Community market. Suppose, however, that the firms are North American or Swiss and are in agreement on the North American or the Swiss market, but that their agreement has an effect on the Community market. The globalization of markets makes this an entirely probable proposition. In such a case, where there appears to be no territorial link, is the EC competent to assert jurisdiction over the firms concerned? The matter is difficult legally at least in part because the assertion of such jurisdiction is extremely sensitive politically. In *Ahlström (Woodpulp Cartel)*[119] it seemed that the Court would be obliged to answer this problem.

The parties were producers of bleached sulphate pulp, required for the manufacture of high-quality paper, based in the United States, Canada and Finland. It was alleged that the producers had aligned their conduct in several ways, including an agreement to fix prices charged to customers in the Community. For jurisdictional purposes, the Court was satisfied that the alleged price-fixing would have affected trade between member states *if* it were shown to have occurred – a matter of substance that would be addressed subsequently.[120] However, the applicants argued that it was

117 Case 22/71 [1971] ECR 949. See also Case 28/77, note 34 above.
118 Case 8/72, note 28 above.
119 Cases 89, 104, 116–17, 125–9/85, note 32 above. The cases have been extensively commented on and annotated; see, e.g., Van Gerven (1989) Fordham Corp L. Inst 451; Friend (1989) 14 ELRev 169; Lowe (1989) 48 CLJ 9; Lange and Sanders (1989) 26 CMLRev 137; Ferry [1989] ECLR 58; Mann (1989) 38 ICLQ 375; Collins (1992) 17 Yale J. Intl Law 249, 256.
120 See p. 679 above.

incompatible with international law to extend Community jurisdiction to firms whose collusion took place outside the Community, who had no Community base and whose only impact on the Community market was as a result of the *effect* of their conduct.[121] The Commission had been firmly of the view that this effect was sufficient to establish Community competence and Advocate-General Darmon's examination of authorities in international law led him to the same conclusion.[122] The Court's response was to avoid the emphasis on effect and instead to concentrate on the place of *implementation* of the agreement. The Court observed that a restrictive practice has two elements: formation and implementation. The Court considered the latter element decisive to Community competence, in order to preclude evasion of the law. The alleged woodpulp cartel, though formed outside the Community, was implemented within it and accordingly fell within the Community's jurisdiction under the territoriality principle uncontroversial in international law.[123]

The Court's judgment does not provide a clear answer as to whether EC competition law embraces the pure effects doctrine as understood under international law and espoused by the Commission. It avoids the use of the terms of the effects doctrine, but it is not apparent whether the choice of implementation as the key is meant to be materially different. If 'implementation' refers to no more than the *Beguelin* model of agreement performed within the Community mentioned above,[124] then there is no step forward. If it covers the agreement entirely external to the EC in all but effect, then the Court has taken an important step forward. The decision is not satisfactory; the Court has fudged the issue. The decision tells us that an agreement relating to terms of sale in the Community is caught by Article 85; but would an agreement not to sell also be caught? What of a non-EC cartel that works to hamper the activity of a Community-based firm operating outside the EC? Neither of these examples would seem to fall within the implementation test, but it is at least arguable that they are no less appropriate for control under Article 85 than the deals allegedly struck in *Woodpulp* itself. One must expect that the issue of the jurisdictional reach of Community competition law will trouble the Court and the Court of First Instance again in the future.

---

121 See, e.g., Rosenthal and Knighton, *National Laws and International Commerce*; Lowe, *Extraterritorial Jurisdiction*.
122 But see Lowe (1989) 48 CLJ 9 for criticism of his approach.
123 Cases 89/85 *et al.*, note 32 above, para. 18 of the judgment.
124 See p. 690 and Case 22/71, note 117 above.

'OBJECT OR EFFECT THE PREVENTION, RESTRICTION OR DISTORTION OF COMPETITION WITHIN THE COMMON MARKET'

Market distortion

The phrase 'object or effect the prevention, restriction or distortion of competition within the common market' is the substantive core of the Article 85 prohibition and it is rather less unwieldy than its length may initially suggest. 'Object or effect' are disjunctive;[125] either will suffice, although both are often present. It is appropriate to look first to 'object'.[126] The Court declared in *Consten and Grundig*[127] that 'there is no need to take account of the concrete effects of an agreement once it appears that it has as its object the prevention, restriction or distortion of competition'. The object of an agreement in this context may be judged objectively against its aims and structure, and may not necessarily be identical to the parties' actual intentions.[128] Even if the required object is missing, effect may readily form the basis of Commission decisions. The effect criterion implies an analysis of the market, but since the Court has accepted that only a capability to effect, rather than any actual effect, need be demonstrated,[129] this is not a difficult test to satisfy in many cases.[130] Commission and Court practice shows that 'prevention, restriction or distortion' are not really independent concepts and that 'distortion' alone covers the notion. Indeed, distortion of competition is the same idea as affecting trade (between member states), a phrase examined above in relation to its jurisdictional rather than its substantive relevance. The agreement, as explained, has to be shown to have an impact on (cross-border) trade patterns.[131]

The key, then, is that the collusion, whether vertical or horizontal, must distort the market. This is often perfectly evident in an agreement. Many agreements are entered into in the full knowledge and expectation that they will lead to market distortion. The examples provided in Article 85(1), such as price-fixing and market-sharing, are all perfectly simple

---

125 Case 56/65, note 106 above.
126 ibid.
127 Cases 56, 58/64, note 3 above.
128 Case 56/65, note 106 above; Cases 29, 30/83, note 67 above.
129 Case 19/77 *Miller Schallplatten* v *Commission* [1978] ECR 131. See Art. 30, p. 435 above; even unenforced restrictions may breach both Arts. 30 and 85 due to the legal uncertainty created, which may serve to impede cross-border trade.
130 For harder cases, see pp. 696–704.
131 Case 56/65, note 106 above.

illustrations of collusion that distorts the structure of the market. In *Consten and Grundig*[132] the parties' product distribution agreement had as both its object and its effect the distortion of the market by effecting compartmentalization along national lines. In *Fatty Acids*[133] the Commission held the exchange of production and sales data had a distortive effect on the market by diminishing the likelihood that individual firms party to the agreement would act without knowledge of each other's past performance and future plans. In *Zanussi*[134] the Commission upheld a system of after-sales guarantees attached to washing-machines only after the deletion of clauses providing that the guarantees were redeemable only in the state of purchase. Such restrictions tended to partition the market and to withhold from the consumer the opportunity that the manufacturer had already claimed to treat the market as unified.[135]

However, much more difficult problems arise where an agreement creates a market without restricting existing competition between firms. Where a manufacturer in state A agrees to supply a distributor in state B, a new market in those products has been created. Where two firms with separate commercial interests combine to develop a new field of interest, they are trying to establish a new market. It may be submitted that such deals cannot be seen as distortive of the market because, in their absence, there simply is no market. Proponents of this analysis favour the release of such deals from the application of competition law in the belief that intervention in such agreements cannot be efficient. However, the application of Article 85 in this area has been notably inconsistent.[136]

Minor agreements

Some agreements plainly have the effect of distorting the market, but that effect may be insignificant. Community law recognizes a *de minimis* argument on relation to Article 85. This is in contrast to Article 30, where a similar trade-pattern test is applied but without any saving *de minimis* gloss.[137] In Community competition law minor agreements are considered to lack the required distortive effect on trade patterns and fall outside the

---

132 Case 56, 58/64, note 3 above.

133 Comm. Dec. 87/1, note 23 above.

134 Comm. Dec. 78/922, 1978 OJ L322/26 [1979] 1 CMLR 81. See also Comm. Notice *Citroën* [1989] 4 CMLR 338.

135 See Fine 'EEC Consumer Warranties: a New Anti-trust Hurdle Facing Exporters' [1989] ECLR 233.

136 See pp. 696–704.

137 Although the Court has found different ways to curtail the reach of Art. 30, notably in Cases C-267 and C-268/91 *Keck and Mithouard*, p. 433 above.

Article 85(1) prohibition. In *Völk* v *Vervaecke*[138] Völk manufactured 0.2 per cent of the total German production of washing-machines. The firm had granted absolute territorial protection to its distributor in Belgium and Luxembourg, but the deal covered only 0.6 per cent of total sales in that territory. The Court held that even though absolute territorial protection had been established in *Consten and Grundig*[139] as inimical to EC competition policy, there would be no breach of Article 85(1) provided the effect was minimal. There is no reason for EC competition law to concern itself with such minor matters, for interbrand competition remains strong and the element of market partitioning is negligible.

This *de minimis* approach is sound in theory but is plainly capable of leading to confusion in practice because of the lack of predictability about the circumstances of its application. The Commission therefore issued a notice in which it set out the criteria that need to be satisfied before it will deem an agreement insignificant for these purposes. The Notice on Minor Agreements issued in 1986 and amended in 1994[140] is the most recent version of the Notice. There are two criteria that must be satisfied in order to establish the required insignificance: the parties must not hold more than 5 per cent of the relevant market,[141] and the parties' aggregate annual turnover must not exceed 300 million ECU.[142]

A Commission notice cannot alter the explicit terms of the Treaty, so the Notice on Minor Agreements merely reflects Commission enforcement policy. It is declared to be 'no absolute yardstick'. It does not bind the Court. Decisions are based on the structure of particular markets, not predetermined fixed thresholds. The parties to the 'Pioneer' cartel[143] claimed that their market shares in the supply of hi-fi equipment were only 3.38 per cent in France and 3.18 per cent in the United Kingdom. The Commission considered that the shares were between 7 and 10 per cent and 8 and 9 per cent of the respective markets. The Court was satisfied that the fragmented nature of the market gave the undertakings more than insignificant strength whatever their precise market share might

---

138 Case 5/69 [1969] ECR 295.

139 Cases 56, 58/64, note 3 above.

140 OJ 1986 C231/2 amended OJ 1994 C368/20.

141 This implies an examination of the availability of similar and competing products. The identification of a relevant market is central to the application of Article 86 and is considered further in that context at p. 728.

142 The figure was raised from 200 to 300 ECU by the 1994 amendment to the Notice, note 140 above. The Commission resisted commercial pressure, *inter alia*, to drop the turnover figure entirely and to raise the market share threshold.

143 Cases 100–103/80, note 54 above; see also Case 30/78 *Distillers* v *Commission* [1980] ECR 2229, [1980] 3 CMLR 121.

be. Indeed, they were among the largest of the many firms active in the hi-fi market. Therefore the Commission's application of Article 85(1) was upheld by the Court without any need to pin down the exact market share. Article 85(1) is directly effective,[144] which means that a national court too is able to apply the Notice, but is not bound by it. Nor does the Notice bind the Commission. It is mere guidance, as Advocate-General Warner observed in *Miller Schallplatten*.[145] Yet the Commission itself declares in the Notice that it will not impose fines in respect of agreements apparently covered by the Notice, but subsequently held contrary to Article 85(1). Moreover, the Advocate-General also suggested that a type of estoppel might be raised in favour of participants in a cartel if the Commission sought to apply Article 85 contrary to the terms of the Notice.[146] Presumably, the parties could then seek annulment of a Commission decision against them under Article 173 alleging breach of a legitimate expectation.[147] Such an expectation would be removed if the Commission advised the firms in advance that it considered the Notice inapplicable in the circumstances of a particular market structure. The Notice is, after all, mere guidance and, provided procedural guarantees are observed, it can be departed from where appropriate.

However, one can anticipate that the Notice will rarely be departed from. In practice, the Notice represents a reliable guide, although in some markets, such as those that are unusually fragmented, Commission advice should be sought in addition to simple reliance on the Notice.[148]

A final word of caution relates to the implications of the test for market distortion. The Commission and Court insist that the impact on trade patterns must be assessed realistically in the broad economic and legal context.[149] Accordingly, if an apparently minor agreement is part of a network, paragraph 16 of the Notice declares that it cannot be judged in isolation as capable of benefiting from the *de minimis* rule. The agreement's place within the network must be analysed in order to discover whether it exerts an appreciable influence on the patterns of trade. In *Municipality of Almelo and others* v *NV Energiebedrijf IJsselmij*[150] the Court analysed the Dutch electricity distribution system as a network of contracts involving, at different levels, generators, regional distributors, local distributors and consumers. At stake in the litigation was an obligation of exclusive

---

144 See further p. 789 below.
145 Case 19/77, note 129 above.
146 ibid., 158.
147 See Ch. 8.
148 See Ch. 24.
149 Case 23/67, note 109 above.
150 Case C-393/92 [1994] ECR I-1477.

purchasing borne by a local distributor. This restricted competition by preventing a local distributor from obtaining supplies from other sources, including those outside the Netherlands. Having regard to the legal and economic context, the cumulative effect of the prevalance of these clauses was to isolate the Dutch market from external competition. This was enough to trigger the prohibition in Article 85(1).[151] This will not always be the case. Even participation in a network of agreements may in some markets lack sufficient significance to be susceptible to control under Article 85, especially where there remains a large number of other outlets or sources in the market outside the network that are available to traders. Moreover, the Court insisted in *Stergios Delimitis*[152] that an apparently minor agreement that is part of a wider network will fall within Article 85(1) only if it makes a significant contribution to the cumulative effect. This insistence on demonstrating an appreciable impediment to market access seems to suggest a less intrusive role for Article 85 than previous judgments have indicated and may reflect an increased judicial deference to contractual freedom in markets shown to be competitive.[153]

A rule of reason

The term 'rule of reason' does not appear in Article 85(1), but it was suggested in relation to Article 30 that the Court is prepared to introduce such a rule as part of the process of interpreting the strict prohibitions of the Treaty in a flexible and pragmatic manner,[154] and this trend appears to have emerged in relation to Article 85 too. However, Commission and Court practice lacks consistency. It is far from clear whether it is correct to talk in terms of a generally applicable rule of reason or whether this approach is limited to particular types of deal. This caution notwithstanding, the concept is not difficult in the abstract. It is illogical to analyse agreements in terms of their distortive effect without consideration of the structure of the market as it would have developed in the absence of the agreement. After all, every contract restricts competition simply by tying the parties to deal with each other rather than a third party. Yet provided such a deal creates a market where one previously did not exist, and causes no appreciable restriction on competition, it may seem appropriate to deny

---

151 The Court left the referring national court to consider the possible application of Article 90(2) as a means of justifying the restrictions. See Ch. 27, p. 866.

152 Case C-234/89, noted by Kovar (1991) 27 Rev Trim Droit Européen 485; Shaw and Wheeler (1991) 16 ELRev 520; Lasok [1991] 5 ECLR 194.

153 A possible analogy may be drawn with the Court's more recent apparent restraint in Art. 30 cases; see note 137 above and p. 532.

154 See pp. 501–2.

the Community's jurisdiction under Article 85(1). Business should enjoy freedom of contract.

In *Remia*[155] the Court concluded that where the vendor of a business agrees to refrain from working in that field for a specified period, the restriction may fall outside Article 85(1) if it is a necessary element in the conclusion of the deal. Without the restraint, there would be no deal (because of the risk that the vendor would entice away existing customers) and therefore no competition to distort in the first place. The market was created, not distorted, by the arrangement and Article 85 is inapplicable. In *Eurotunnel*[156] the Commission considered that the deal to build the Tunnel struck by engineering firms did not restrict competition and therefore fell outside Article 85(1), given that no firm could have undertaken the project individually. There could have been no competition between individual firms to win such a large contract, so the consortium formed did not distort competition. One may propose a model whereby joint ventures that impose no appreciable restriction on competition between the parties, and include no taint of market-partitioning within the Community, are not subject to Article 85. However, it must be admitted that Commission decisions are not consistent, and the Commission has regularly preferred to find a market distortion in breach of Article 85(1), followed by analysis of the deal with reference to exemption under Article 85(3). This is unexceptionable where the venture restricts existing or potential competition, but the Commission has not always satisfactorily demonstrated that this has occurred,[157] which may lead it to intervene unnecessarily in the market. Finally, the grant of an exclusive licence has also been treated on the basis that it creates a market where one did not exist previously and therefore Article 85 has been held inapplicable.[158] In all such deals ancillary terms necessary to the conclusion of the agreement are also in principle unaffected by Article 85.

In such cases the rule of reason cannot be relied on if the restraints that are imposed go beyond what is necessary to conclude the deal. Additional

---

155 Case 42/84, note 86 above; see also Comm. Dec. 76/743, note 86 above.
156 Comm. Dec. 88/568, note 24 above. See similarly Comm. Dec. 90/446 ECR 90 OJ 1990 L228/31, [1992] 4 CMLR 54.
157 See, e.g., criticism of the approach taken in Comm. Dec. 88/541, note 26 above, by Korah, *EC Competition Law and Practice*, pp. 211, 258; and consider the different approaches in Comm. Dec. 90/410 *Elopak/Metal Box (ODIN)* OJ 1990 L209/15, [1991] 4 CMLR 832 (outside Art. 85(1)) and Comm. Dec. 90/46 *Alcatel/ANT* OJ 1990 L32/19 (breach Art. 85(1), but Art. 85(3) exemption granted), comment in (1990) ELRev *Competition Law Checklist* 11–14, 20–24; Forrester and Norall (1990) 10 YEL 407, 419–28. See generally Korah, *EC Competition Law and Practice*, Chs. 13, 14; Bellamy and Child, *Common Market Law of Competition*, Ch. 5; Van Bael and Bellis, *Competition Law*, pp. 294–334. See also p. 813 below in relation to mergers and related deals.
158 Case 258/78 *Nungesser* v *Commission* [1982] ECR 2015, [1983] 1 CMLR 278.

restraints that are imposed beyond the necessary core provisions of the transfer or the venture itself are market distortions that are caught by Article 85(1). In *Eurotunnel* the usage contracts went beyond the initial construction project and therefore required exemption under Article 85(3) rather than exclusion from Article 85(1).[159] Similarly, a *Remia*-style restrictive covenant that lasts an unreasonably long time is not saved by the rule of reason. In *Remia*[160] itself the Court upheld the Commission's finding that a ten-year period was excessive. Some commentators would question the yardstick used by the Commission in embarking on such interventionism. Better, it is argued, simply to allow the business parties to the deal to fix the appropriate length of the restraint; after all, the buyer has no incentive to offer too little, the seller no incentive to accept too much. The parties in negotiation *are* the market; they will fix the true market rate. This non-interventionist stance, popular among Chicago-school economists,[161] has attractions as a method of transferring decision-making competence from bureaucrats to those most intimately affected and therefore most likely to achieve the economically efficient outcome. It rules out intervention by the regulatory authorities, except, perhaps, where one party is economically dominant and able to impose oppressive terms or where the parties include undue restraints, such as price-fixing.[162] However, this is a perspective that the Community has not adopted. Community law forbids abusive dominance;[163] it also forbids a range of horizontal restraints.[164] However, it goes further still, in part because of pursuit of policies other than pure wealth-maximization,[165] and in part as a result of the influence of the objective of market integration, which demands that keener attention be paid to deals struck. So, in respect of an exclusive licence, Community law scrutinizes the duration of the grant,[166] as it scrutinized the duration of the restraint in *Remia*,[167] and it forbids minimum price-fixing under the

159 Comm. Dec. 88/568, note 24 above. Comm. Decs 94/594, 94/663, note 25 above.
160 Case 42/84, note 86 above.
161 E.g. Bork, *The Antitrust Paradox*; Posner (1979) 127 U Pa LR 925.
162 US law views certain such terms as fundamentally hostile to the market economy and therefore unlawful *per se*; see sources at note 6 above. Yet some of the Chicago school would be sceptical of controlling *any* vertical restraints; see note 10 above.
163 Article 86; see Ch. 23.
164 See, e.g., Korah, *EC Competition Law and Practice*, Ch. 7; and Van Bael and Bellis, *Competition Law*, Ch. 8.
165 Art. 2 EC; and see p. 702.
166 In Comm. Dec. 89/536 *German TV Films* OJ 1989 L284/36, [1990] 4 CMLR 841 the terms of an exclusive licence, including duration, were considered more restrictive than those inherent to the conclusion of such a deal, which meant that exemption under Article 85(3), rather than the rule of reason, was the gateway to legality.
167 Case 42/84, note 86 above.

licence.[168] However, in addition, the Court has also insisted that the licencee be protected from competition by traders based in that state only, not third-party parallel importers, thereby asserting the enduring influence of Community market integration.[169] Community law is therefore not capable of analysis in the light of US doctrine and dogma without appreciation of its thematic market-integration principle.

Distribution agreements

The rule of reason has proved particularly appropriate in its application to distribution deals. Where a manufacturer in state A agrees with distributors in state B to supply products, then at one level the collaboration distorts the market by tying the traders to each other. Yet such deals open up markets. They improve the range of products available and are consequently beneficial as a means of expanding consumer choice and promoting market integration. Where the distributorship is conferred exclusively on one trader in state B, the market has been opened up, albeit through the creation of a restricted number of outlets. Provided there exist competing products so that interbrand competition remains healthy, the consumer stands to profit. There are, accordingly, strong arguments for deeming such agreements immune from Article 85(1) altogether – unless, as in *Consten and Grundig*,[170] the parties have included an extra restriction, such as absolute territorial protection, through suppression of third-party importers. In *STM v Maschinenbau Ulm*[171] the Court considered an exclusive dealing arrangement capable of falling outside Article 85(1) altogether. It is necessary to assess whether, without the agreement, the market would have been penetrable at all. If not, the agreement opens up the market rather than distorting it.

The issue received little further attention because the Commission subsequently issued a block exemption regulation[172] covering exclusive distribution arrangements. Such an exemption is based on the criteria of Article 85(3) and was, on a strict reading, consequently superfluous in the case of agreements falling outside Article 85(1) altogether.[173] Yet the

---

168 Case 27/87 *Erauw-Jacquery* v *La Hesbignonne* [1988] ECR 1919; an Art. 177 reference, so it was for the national court to determine whether the facts disclosed a breach of Article 85.
169 Case 258/78, note 158 above.
170 Cases 56, 58/64, note 3 above.
171 Case 56/65, note 106 above.
172 See p. 713 on these measures.
173 See, e.g., Korah, *EC Competition Law and Practice*, pp. 269–72; Green, Hartley and Usher, *Single European Market*, pp. 241–2; in relation to know-how agreements, see Frazer, 'Vorsprung Durch Technik: The Commission's Policy on Know-How Agreements' (1989) 9 YEL 1, 5–6.

formalized criteria of the block exemption are more certain and reliable for business than the rule of reason, and the rule of reason has consequently lost its relevance in this area. However, the direct use of Article 85(1) has remained firmly on the agenda in respect of *selective* distribution, where no block exemption is in existence.[174] In *Metro* v *Commission*[175] the Court confirmed that a distribution network to which outlets were admitted provided they complied with defined criteria was capable of escaping the Article 85(1) prohibition altogether. The collaboration creates a market where one did not exist previously and thus is no distortion of competition within the meaning of Article 85(1). The apparent restriction on admission, then, is no more than an element in ensuring the workability of the arrangement. This, however, implies that any restraint imposed on a distributor that goes beyond what is strictly necessary in order to ensure that the system functions properly is subject to control under Article 85. Price-fixing or onerous conditions would be unlikely to be acceptable.[176] Moreover, the criteria for admission to the scheme must be objectively justifiable – for example, relating to the conditions of quality control and after-sales service that the distributor must respect – and the product must be of a nature that justifies the establishment of a selective distribution network.[177] In addition, the Community objective of market integration must be respected. It is, accordingly, familiar territory that the selective distribution scheme must not prevent parallel imports or otherwise seek to partition the market along national lines. There must be no taint of discrimination on grounds of nationality in the terms of admission or their application. *Metro SB-Grossmärkte GmbH & Co KG* v *Cartier SA* concerned selective distribution of Cartier watches.[178] The Court ruled that traders within a lawful selective distribution network are entitled to refuse to honour guarantees on products obtained outside the network. This permits the network a high degree of protection from external competition and may lead to inhibitions even on parallel trade in goods acquired outside the network. The Court is evidently receptive to the phenomenon of the selective distribution network and to the maintenance of its integrity, at least for high-quality products such as Cartier watches. It is submitted that it would be contrary to the consumer interest in a competitive market for

---

174 Except for the motor vehicle industry; Reg. 123/85.

175 Case 26/76, note 2 above.

176 But cf. the Chicago school, note 162 above. For a comparative survey, see Gyselen, 'Vertical Restraints in the Distribution Process: Strength and Weakness of the Free Rider Rationale under EEC Competition Law' (1984) 21 CMLRev 647.

177 '... justified in the case of high-technology products ... also ... for perfumes ... but not for plumbing fixtures', I. Forrester and C. Norall, 'Competition Law' (1989) 9 YEL 271, 277. See further refs. under 'Distribution agreements' in Select Further Reading. Whish, *Competition Law*, pp. 589–90.

178 Case C-376/92 [1994] ECR I-15.

the ruling in *Metro* v *Cartier* to be extended to justify refusal to honour guarantees on goods of lower prestige simply because they have been obtained outside the network.

In *Pronuptia* v *Schillgalis*[179] the Court accepted that a generally comparable approach was applicable to franchising agreements. There is no breach of Article 85(1) unless unacceptable additional restraints, such as price-fixing, are included in the deal.[180]

It has been observed on several occasions that horizontal agreements are considerably more dangerous to the structure of competition than vertical agreements.[181] Horizontal agreements suppress healthy interbrand competition between traders who ought to be fighting for each other's markets, whereas vertical agreements between, say, manufacturer and distributor frequently improve product availability without eliminating interbrand competition between traders operating at the same level. Competition law, then, ought to be capable of making a distinction between horizontal and vertical agreements. Explicitly, Article 85 makes no such distinction. Yet through the rule of reason it has proved possible to mould Article 85 into a more delicate instrument that is capable of taking account of such nuances. Selective distribution arrangements are vertical and, as a general rule, beneficial as a means of opening up markets, and the application of a rule of reason allows many such deals to escape legal interference. Horizontal arrangements, which do not create markets but rather confine their operation, are not normally susceptible to the rule-of-reason approach. One would only add the *Consten and Grundig* qualification that vertical agreements must not serve to partition the common market along national lines if they are to enjoy immunity from Article 85(1).

The status of the rule of reason

The rule of reason is familiar to antitrust lawyers in the United States, where the Sherman Act has long been applied on the basis that it contains a rule of reason, which exempts reasonable agreements from the scope of the prohibition.[182] However, there are grounds for supposing that the rule of reason is inappropriate for incorporation into EC competition law. Firstly, the US experience is not informed by the objective of market integration, which acts as a constant theme in EC trade law. Where market integration is imperilled, EC law may forbid restrictions on

179 Case 161/84 [1986] ECR 353, [1986] 1 CMLR 414.
180 Franchising is now subject to a block exemption; see p. 714.
181 See, e.g. pp. 664–6. See also Ehlermann (1992) 29 CMLRev 257, esp. 267.
182 See refs. at note 6 above. For a comparative survey see Peeters, 'The Rule of Reason Revisited' (1989) 37 JCL 521; also Whish and Sufrin (1987) 7 YEL 1, 4–20; Gyselen (1984) 21 CML Rev 647.

intrabrand competition despite continuing interbrand competition, whereas under US law the presence of the latter is a gateway to acceptability.[183] Even if one accepts the influential anti-interventionist Chicago school at face value,[184] its prescription is not directly transferable to the Community experience, where interventionism in the pursuit of market integration is necessary.[185]

Secondly, under the EC Treaty Article 85(3) already exists as an explicit exemption provision, so the introduction of an implicit justification procedure separate from that provision may seem unwarranted. The Sherman Act, by contrast, contains no explicit exemption, which may be thought to justify an activist judicial interpretative approach along the lines of the rule of reason.[186] This objection has weight from the perspective of preserving the independent vigour of Article 85(3), but it does not lead to the conclusion that a rule-of-reason approach under Article 85(1) should be completely ruled out. For example, if the commercial reality of a deal is that a market is opened up and no significant restriction on access by third parties is imposed, it is hard to find a convincing rationale for intervention. In fact, the existence of a rule of reason despite the existence of a separate exception runs parallel to Article 30 as interpreted through the *Cassis de Dijon* line of authority, which similarly sidesteps the exception provision in Article 36.[187] The Court aims to develop Community trade law in a flexible manner that reflects the practical demands placed on the system.

Finally, it is important to appreciate that there is a strong practical motivation for finding a quasi-exemption approach embedded within Article 85(1) itself. It improves the capacity of national courts to apply a flexible exemption-type approach, for Article 85(1) is directly effective whereas Article 85(3) is not.[188] That may diminish the Commission's

183 *Consten and Grundig* contrasted with *Continental TV* v *Sylvania*, see p. 665.
184 And many do not, even on the American side of the Atlantic! E.g., it has been criticized for its readiness to swop public for private market regulation, which may lead to unfairness and exploitation. See discussion by, e.g., Pitofsky, 'The Political Content of Antitrust' (1979) 127 U Pa LR 1051; Fox, 'The Modernization of Antitrust: a New Equilibrium' (1981) 66 Corn LR 1140; Hovenkamp, 'Distributive Justice and the Antitrust Laws' (1982) 51 Geo Wash LR 1. For a survey, see Page, 'Ideological Conflict and the Origins of Antitrust Policy' (1991) 66 Tul LR 1.
185 See AG Verloren van Themaat in Case 161/84, note 179 above. *Quaere* whether the US comparison might prove more influential post-successful integration; see p. 666.
186 See sources at note 6 above.
187 See Ch. 17; see esp. the views of AG Verloren van Themaat at p. 502.
188 See further p. 789. It is arguable that this practical problem would be better solved by making Art. 85(3) directly effective rather than by using the unpredictable Art. 85(1) rule-of-reason approach; Peeters, (1989) 37 AJCL 521 and, more fully, p. 796 below. There are also, admittedly, other procedural devices for improving enforcement before national courts without the need to resort to a rule-of-reason approach; see, e.g., 'Block Exemption' p. 713. See also discussion of the Commission's 1993 Notice, Ch. 24, p. 793.

immense workload as administrator of the exemption procedure. It may also release business from the administrative burden of securing Commission approval for pro-competitive deals.[189]

In conclusion, a rule of reason is acceptable within Article 85(1), provided that it is fully recognized that this is a *sui generis* Community rule of reason that accommodates, *inter alia*, the objective of market integration, which is absent from US law.[190] In order to emphasize this distinct function, Whish and Sufrin have intelligently argued in favour of the abandonment of the phrase 'rule of reason' and the adoption of a new vocabulary in Community competition law.[191] It may now be too late for this suggestion to be accepted, but the underlying point about the divergences between the systems is valid. However, other commentators favour an extension of the rule of reason towards the radical adjustment of Article 85 into a single control in place of the two-stage Articles 85(1)/(3) structure. It would be contrary to the Treaty to allow the rule of reason to apply universally to all restrictive practices, because such breadth of application would substantially diminish the Treaty commitment to, *inter alia*, consumer benefit found in Article 85(3).[192] Calls to clear deals under Article 85(1) based solely on a balance of the implications for competition may enjoy an internal logic, but they fail to respect the Treaty's commitment to wider matters under Article 85(3), which reflects the fundamental policy statements in Article 2. The perceived procedural advantages of a rule of reason also deserve cautious examination. A greater number of decisions at national level would prejudice uniformity in the application of the Community rules, and it is accordingly far from clear that increased certainty would follow a diminution in the Commission's role. In any event, a reduction in the Commission's administrative role might liberate business decision-making, but, as already suggested, it would also undermine the Commission's key role under the Treaty in ensuring respect for the matters contained in Article 85(3). Against this background of disharmony among commentators[193] one can simply admit

---

189 An influential and impressive study in this area is Forrester and Norall, 'The Laicization of Community Law: Self-Help and the Rule of Reason: How Competition Law is and could be applied' (1984) 21 CMLRev 11. For further discussion, see p. 796.
190 See p. 666; and AG Verloren van Themaat in Case 161/84, note 179 above. If comparisons with US antitrust law are apt to mislead, a better point of comparison may be Art. 30 EC; i.e., a focus on the market integrative emphasis of Community competition law rather than its attack on collusion may prove more illuminating.
191 (1987) 7 YEL 1.
192 Consider Whish, *Competition Law*, pp.205–11.
193 See, e.g., refs. under 'A rule of reason' in Select Further Reading. See further p. 796, and also, e.g., Slot and Van der Woude (eds.), *Exploiting the Internal Market*, in which Verstrynge emphasizes that flexibility should be achieved through Art. 85(3), not an Art. 85(1) rule of reason (p. 8), whereas Van Empel is significantly more receptive to an Art. 85(1) rule-of-reason approach (p. 22).

that business awaits a clear and consistent articulation of policy from both Commission and Court.

ARTICLE 85(3): EXEMPTION

THE NATURE AND STRUCTURE OF ARTICLE 85(3)

Article 85(1) contains a basic prohibition on collusion, supplemented by Article 85(2), which provides that agreements in violation of the first paragraph are automatically void. As frequently observed in the preceding pages, collusion is by no means always undesirable. Firms may, for example, be able to improve their efforts to develop new products by pooling their budgets and know-how, and it is in the public interest to foster progress of this type. Consequently, the third paragraph of Article 85 contains a provision under which collaborators may apply to the Commission for exemption of their arrangement from the prohibition in Article 85(1). The power to grant exemption under Article 85(3) is conferred exclusively on the Commission by Regulation 17/62,[194] which allocates to the Commission a pivotal role in administration and policy-making.

Article 85(3) reads as follows:

The provisions of paragraph 1 may, however, be declared inapplicable in the case of
– any agreement or category of agreements between undertaking;
– any decision or category of decisions by associations of undertaking;
– any concerted practice or category of concerted practices;
which contributes to improving the production or distribution of goods or to promoting technical or economic progress, while allowing consumers a fair share of the resulting benefit, and which does not:
(a) impose on the undertakings concerned restrictions which are not indispensable to the attainment of these objectives;
(b) afford such undertakings the possibility of eliminating competition in respect of a substantial part of the products in question.

The broad idea of exemption under Article 85(3) is plain enough. It envisages a balance between the costs and benefits of the restrictive practice. If the reduction in competition yields advantages that outweigh the disadvantages, then the law ought not to intervene. In fact, the criteria of Article 85(3), though based on this general perception, are rather more formalized than a broad cost/benefit analysis. They comprise four conditions – two positive, two negative – all of which must be satisfied for the grant of an exemption.

194 See further Ch. 24.

The two positive conditions are found in the middle paragraph of Article 85(3) set out above: the agreement must contribute to improving the production or distribution of goods or to promoting technical or economic progress. This formula invites a general appraisal of the economic context of the arrangement. Although some Commission decisions single out one particular aspect, the formula may be summarized as the requirement of an *economic benefit*. In addition, however, the second condition, the *consumer benefit* criterion, insists that the deal shall yield a fair share of its benefits to the consumer. This is plainly more broad aspiration than precisely measurable criterion, but at least the inclusion of this condition indicates a demand for a broader focus than the commercial interests of the parties themselves. It requires a steady trickle down of economic success as a precondition for exemption. It is also interesting that, although the consumer is ultimately the major intended beneficiary of the economic progress to which the Community is pledged,[195] Article 85(3) was one of the very few explicit references to the consumer found in the Treaty of Rome.[196] This is modified by the Maastricht Treaty amendments, which introduced a new title devoted to consumer protection, comprising Article 129a EC.

The two negative conditions are rather less easily reduced to a neat slogan, but are none the less reasonably straightforward in concept. Both are negative in that they insist that a particular result must *not* follow if exemption is to be awarded. The first negative condition requires that the terms of the deal do not impose restrictions that are not indispensable to the attainment of the objectives. This idea has already been seen in relation to the rule of reason under Article 85(1), where, for example, unreasonably long restraints prevent an agreement escaping Article 85(1),[197] and, in fact, this condition is no more than an application of a general principle of EC trade law, which requires that trade restrictions shall be no more onerous than is strictly necessary. So, as under Article 30, where trade barriers are unlawful if alternative means of meeting the objective are available that are less harmful to market integration,[198] here too under Article 85(3) clauses that fetter the parties more tightly than is necessary to achieve the claimed advantages of collaboration are unable to enjoy Article 85(3) exemption.

The second negative condition is also familiar from earlier discussion. It insists that the agreement shall not permit the elimination of competition

---

195 Consider Art. 2 EC.
196 See Art. 39(1)(e), Art. 40(3), Art. 86(b). Art. 100a(3) was added by the Single European Act.
197 See p. 697–8 above.
198 See p. 455.

in respect of a substantial part of the products in question. A *reduction* in competition may be acceptable where economic benefits are on offer in consequence, but *suppression* of competition is deemed a danger that lies beyond the Article 85(3) pale. Any benefits would be short-term in the absence of the stimulus of competition. It has already been remarked that a loss of intrabrand competition need not necessarily be resisted where interbrand competition remains effective, but a loss of both intrabrand and interbrand competition is pernicious.[199]

The four conditions are now examined separately, although it is obvious that the overall economic basis of Article 85(3) is dependent on the pattern established by the connections between them.[200] In order to reflect this linkage, the approach taken to particular agreements is traced through each condition.

ECONOMIC BENEFIT

The nature of the assessment

The Commission, in making an assessment under this condition, is called upon to look at the broad economic context of the collaboration. The Commission's investigation must first be directed towards an appraisal of the operation of the market in the absence of the agreement. If the market would have secured the claimed economic benefits itself under the influence of free competition, then the arguments in favour of permitting a collaborative approach are fatally undermined.[201] The Commission, then, is concerned to examine how the market would have operated without the agreement and to identify benefits unavailable without collaboration.

An exclusive distribution agreement restricts the freedom of action of the parties to look elsewhere and the freedom of third parties to deal in that product, but in the absence of exclusivity the parties may have felt unable to make the necessary investment in a new product for fear of 'free-riders' reaping profits without incurring costs.[202] The exclusive ties in the agreement thus yield otherwise unobtainable economic benefits in the shape of the penetration of new markets that permits increased choice and more efficient competition.[203] Firms that were previously in direct competition that agree to limit their activities to specialized areas of the production

---

199 See p. 665.
200 On burden of proof, see p. 769.
201 See, e.g., Comm. Dec. 91/130 *Eurosport* OJ 1991 L63/32.
202 See further p. 711–12.
203 Cf. the approach under the rule of reason, p. 699.

process and then to pool their results are thereby enabled to avoid inefficient duplication, which is likely to increase the quantity and quality of production.[204] In such a case it will be apparent that it is essential that the collaborating firms remain susceptible to the influence of competition from other independent producers, or else they will acquire severely anticompetitive virtual monopolies; this need for third-party competition is reflected in the second negative condition for exemption.[205]

In *SOPELEM/Rank*[206] the firms entered into a research and development agreement, allied to collaboration in the manufacture and distribution of film and TV camera lenses. The firms were able to divide up projects according to skills and experience and could achieve technical progress through such specialization. The Commission was satisfied that the agreement led to an increase in the range of products available on the market and to an improvement in the quality of those products. Such economic benefits would not have been forthcoming if the parties had gone their own way. Their research projects would have overlapped, which would have impeded the development of the broad product range achievable through collaboration.[207]

Crisis cartels

In the synthetic fibres market there was excess capacity and consequent overproduction, which provoked the manufacturers to enter into an agreement under which each would reduce capacity by agreed amounts. This was designed to leave the industry in a healthier state by bringing supply and demand into closer equilibrium. There was obviously an agreement caught by Article 85(1), for each party had surrendered its independence in respect of production and investment decisions. The

---

204 Comm. Dec. 73/323 *Prym-Werke* JO 1973 L296/24 [1973] CMLR D250. There is a block exemption in the area of specialization, p. 714 below, but this agreement fell outside its terms. For criticism of the decision, see Korah (1974) 23 ICLQ 447; see also criticism of the exemption of the specialization agreement in Comm. Dec. 72/291 *Lightweight Paper* JO 1972 L182/24, [1972] CMLR D94 by Korah (1973) CLP 36. The specialization agreement in Comm. Dec. 78/921 *WANO Schwarzpulver* OJ 1978 L322/26, [1979] I CMLR 403 was refused exemption, *inter alia*, because no useful improvement in quality was likely in the ancient art of making gunpowder.
205 See p. 712.
206 Comm. Dec. 75/76 OJ 1975 L29/20, [1975] 1 CMLR D72. There are literally hundreds of Commission decisions dealing with the economic benefit of particular agreements; for illustration only see, e.g., Comm. Dec. 77/543 *De Laval/Stork* OJ 1977 L215/II, [1977] 2 CMLR D69 (turbines and pumps); Comm. Dec. 83/390 *Rockwell/IVECO* OJ 1983 L224/19, [1983] 3 CMLR 709 (lorry axles) Comm. Dec. 93/48 *Fiat/Hitachi* OJ 1993 L20/10, [1994] 4 CMLR 571 (hydraulic excavators).
207 Notice the increasing list of block exemptions in this field, p. 714.

Commission, however, decided that the deal provided economic benefits within Article 85(3).[208] It led to a more efficient allocation of resources, as the parties themselves maintained. The arrangement encouraged specialization, which, in turn, permitted resources to be devoted to improving quality. It was central to the Commission's acceptance of the parties' submissions that the desirable reduction would not have been brought about without the agreement. Acting independently, no firm would have dared to have acted, for fear that it would have lost market share to another firm 'free-riding' on the first firm's cut in output. The Commission was accordingly persuaded that the agreement produced economic benefits, and that those benefits were unattainable in the absence of collaboration. The Commission added that the firms' cooperation made it easier 'to cushion the social effects of the restructuring' by setting up schemes to facilitate the retraining and redeployment of workers made redundant as a result of the cuts in capacity.

Article 85(3) is not a general mandate to pursue goals of wealth distribution, but such social provision can be accommodated within the notion of economic benefit under Article 85(3).[209] Environmental benefits may also form part of the Article 85(3) assessment.[210]

Cartels of this nature will be carefully scrutinized by the Commission. In markets in crisis there are strong arguments in favour of letting the influence of competition take its toll.[211] Overcapacity will drive firms from the market because of their simple inability to make profits, and this will itself serve to restructure the market. The major achievement of the participants in the synthetic fibres cartel was to persuade the Commission that their agreed reorganization yielded benefits over and above those that would have followed purely market-induced restructuring. The Commission accepted that the recent history of the industry demonstrated that the market had patently failed to achieve the capacity reductions that were necessary in order to restore an effective competitive structure. A cartel was therefore permissible in order to slim down the industry.

---

208 Comm. Dec. 84/380 (*Synthetic Fibres*) OJ 1984 L207/17, [1985] 1 CMLR 787, noted by Faull (1986) 11 ELRev 62, 64; see also Whish, *Competition Law*, pp. 458-9.

209 In Case 26/76, note 2 above, the Court held that the creation of employment may be a benefit within Art. 85(3); para. 43 of the judgment. For a rather narrow interpretation see Wyatt and Dashwood, *European Community Law*, pp 422-3. See also Whish, *Competition Law*, p. 229.

210 Comm. Dec. 91/38 *KSB/Goulds/Lowara/ITT* OJ 1991 L19/25; although, oddly, the Commission examined such benefits in connection with the second rather than the first positive condition for exemption. See Jacobs, *EEC Competition Law and the Protection of the Environment* [1993/2] LIEI 37.

211 For a strong attack on the *Synthetic Fibres* exemption, see Curzon Price in El-Agraa (ed.), *Economics of the EC*, p. 173: '. . . all firms in the industry share out the agony equitably - not on the basis of efficiency. They are spared the full implications of previous errors of judgement, while the efficient go unrewarded . . .'

In order to secure exemption such a crisis cartel must be limited strictly to the task of making the industry leaner and fitter. The inclusion of unnecessarily restrictive terms will take the agreement outside the scope of Article 85(3). The synthetic fibres cartel had, in fact, been obliged to delete production and delivery quotas from the agreement and to reduce its period of operation in order to secure a favourable response from the Commission. This is an application of the first of Article 85(3)'s negative conditions. Similarly, the cartel cannot be used to protect domestic industry from foreign competition; it must involve all those active on a particular market irrespective of nationality.[212]

Exemption of cartels of this nature is exceptional. The norm will remain market-driven adjustment. However, in *Stichting Baksteen*[213] the Commission was persuaded that agreed rationalization was the preferable method of reducing capacity in the Dutch brick industry. Under the plan, significant production capacity was closed down and restructuring, including provision for affected workers, was funded jointly by the 16 parties to the agreement. It appears that the Commission was satisfied that overcapacity was attributable to shifts away from the use of brick towards materials such as lightweight concrete and that such structural problems were best dealt with by planned rationalization rather than market solutions.

CONSUMER BENEFIT

The consumer is the intended beneficiary of economic growth in general, but this second positive condition asserts that in the area of restrictive practices the consumer is entitled to an identifiable slice of the benefits realized: 'a fair share of the resulting benefit'. This criterion is important, for it suggests that the Treaty has an interest not merely in the objective of creating wealth, but also in the distribution of that wealth. An unfair outcome in this sense deprives an agreement of exemptability even where the arrangement can be shown to be the most efficient means of increasing wealth.[214] However, it will be seen that the distributional flavour of this criterion has been significantly diluted by the Community institutions to the point where little more than lip-service is paid to any independent notion of consumer interest.

In *SOPELEM/Rank*[215] the consumer benefit was identified in the

---

212 Comm. Dec. 89/515, note 109 above.
213 Comm. Dec. 94/296 OJ 1994 L131/15.
214 Cf. US antitrust law; Peeters (1989) 37 AJCL 521.
215 Comm. Dec. 75/76, note 206 above.

availability of more and better products.[216] On this analysis the advantages identified as yielding an economic benefit were more or less identical with those that the consumer enjoyed as his or her fair share. This is a convincing approach to many agreements, such as distribution and specialization agreements and including *SOPELEM/Rank* itself, where the product attains a higher level of quality and is more widely available, and where, provided interbrand competition remains influential, prices will also be controlled.[217] Yet in some decisions the Commission has moved beyond holding similar advantages to be sufficient to satisfy both positive conditions to the point where it has found an economic benefit and then simply assumed that the consumer-benefit test is thereby also fulfilled in consequence, without any independent inquiry.

In *Synthetic Fibres*[218] the Commission accepted that the healthier and more efficient industry that emerged from the crisis cartel would lead to the conferral of a fair share of the benefits on the consumer, given the presence of continuing competition from other sources, including those outside the EC. Given economic advantage (the first positive condition) plus persisting competition (the second negative condition), it appears that the fulfilment of the second positive condition, the consumer-benefit criterion, is presumed to follow.[219] The Treaty is undoubtedly predicated on the belief that free competition in a common market will benefit the consumer, and this assumption explains the approach taken in *Synthetic Fibres* to consumer advantage. Yet Article 85(3) expects a more precise examination of the consumer benefit. This is suppressed by the Commission's approach, and the result is an assertion of the link between economic progress and consumer benefit rather than its demonstration.[220]

It is not suggested that the Commission has eradicated the consumer-benefit criterion. There are certainly cases in which a clear detriment to the consumer has been fatal to an application for exemption. In *VBBB/VBVB*[221] exclusive dealing and resale price maintenance in the Belgian and Dutch book trade was held to be incapable of exemption because the

---

216 Notice that the idea of the consumer covers any user of the product, not just the end user; the French text prefers *utilisateur* over *consommateur*.

217 See also Comm. Dec. 90/186 *Moosehead/Whitbread* OJ 1990 L100/32, [1991] 4 CMLR 391; Comm. Decs. 73/323, 72/291, 78/921, note 204 above, and Comm. Decs. 75/76, 77/543, 83/390, note 206 above.

218 Comm. Dec. 84/380, note 208 above.

219 See also, e.g., *Prym-Werke*, note 204 above.

220 See AG Verloren van Themaat in Case 75/84 *Metro* v *Commission* [1986] ECR 3021, 3067–8, where he criticizes the Commission's inadequate market analysis and its paternalist view of consumer preference. See also Evans, 'European Competition Law and Consumers' [1981] ECLR 425.

221 Comm. Dec. 82/183 OJ 1982 L54/36, [1982] 2 CMLR 344; decision upheld by the Court in Cases 43, 63/82 [1984] ECR 19.

Commission was unconvinced that the agreement led to an improvement that would have been unobtainable in the absence of the agreement, and because the limited advantages accruing to a minority of consumers were outweighed by the disadvantages suffered by the majority of consumers. It will be extremely difficult to show that the consumer benefits from price-fixing. In *Peugeot*[222] the Commission refused to exempt an agreement restricting the importation of cars into the United Kingdom because of, *inter alia*, the reduction in choice to the ultimate consumer and the maintenance of comparatively higher prices on the United Kingdom market. However, it is suggested that where evidence about the impact on the consumer is neutral, the Commission is close to applying a presumption that the condition is satisfied. This is not acceptable as a reading of Article 85(3), which insists that separate attention be devoted to the consumer interest.

NO RESTRICTIONS THAT ARE NOT INDISPENSABLE

As observed above,[223] the first negative condition is an application of the principle of alternative means that pervades Community trade law. Once one has identified the economic advantages that must accrue from the collaboration in order to satisfy the two positive conditions, one must then determine that the terms contained in the agreement are no more restrictive than is necessary to achieve those benefits. The availability of less onerous terms that would be equally effective in realizing economic gain is fatal to an application for exemption; so too is the inclusion of ancillary terms that tie the parties more closely than is necessary.[224] So, for example, had the synthetic-fibres cartel members agreed not only to fix their capacity reductions, but also their geographical spheres of operation and their prices, then exemption would doubtless have been unavailable.[225] The Commission has the ability to adopt an active policy in this respect because it possesses the power to attach conditions and obligations, including time-limits, to the grant of exemption under Article 85(3).[226]

The example of exclusive dealing has been used on several occasions in the course of this chapter, and *Consten and Grundig*[227] once again illustrates

---

222 Comm. Dec. 86/506 (*Peugeot*) OJ 1986 L295/19, [1989] 4 CMLR 371. See also Cases 25, 26/84 *Ford* v *Commission* [1987] ECR 2725, [1985] 3 CMLR 528.
223 See p. 705.
224 See Comm. Dec. 89/515, note 109 above.
225 The Decision explains that the cartel and the Commission.had in the past negotiated the removal of several terms of this nature.
226 Art. 8(1) Reg. 17/62; see p. 775.
227 Cases 56, 58/64, note 3 above.

the operation of this condition. Exclusivity is a defensible restriction. No distributor would take the risk of stocking and promoting an unfamiliar product from another state unless assured that he or she will enjoy a certain degree of protection from other outlets subsequently taking advantage of the profitable market he or she has created, perhaps at considerable expense. Yet there is an outer limit to the restrictions that are essential to the establishment of the distributorship.[228] Where, as in *Consten and Grundig*, the terms include an assurance of absolute territorial protection achieved by virtue of the suppression of parallel imports from third states, the restraint is excessive and therefore unlawful. It goes beyond what is necessary to the operation of the distributorship and, moreover, it is a restriction that serves to affirm market-partitioning in the common market.

NO POSSIBILITY OF ELIMINATING COMPETITION

The second negative requirement is an essential supplement to the positive conditions and, indeed, it is in a sense already an aspect of them. The basic assumptions of the theory of competition hold that economic benefits accruing from an agreement are likely to endure only provided that the parties remain susceptible to the influence of competition from other sources, which induces continued good performance. So in *SOPELEM/ Rank*[229] the improvement in the quantity and quality of products would have been temporary had the new partners found themselves immune from the discipline of competition. The finding that the condition of persisting external competition was met indicated that the firms would be forced to maintain the standards of economic progress in order to secure their place in the market.[230]

It should also be observed that it is implicit in this condition that it is possible to identify the nature of the competitive market within which the firms are in collaboration. Markets may be limited according to product and to geography. There may be no cause for concern if the only two widget producers in the Community collaborate, provided that there are plenty of independent gidget producers and provided gidgets are freely substitutable for widgets.[231] But if widgets are unique, irreplaceable products that other producers would experience great difficulty in manufactur-

---

228 See the rule-of-reason approach, p. 697–8.
229 Comm. Dec. 75/76, note 206 above.
230 See also Comm. Dec. 84/380, note 208 above.
231 Although the presence of such interbrand competition may not save the deal from falling foul of Art. 85 if cross-border intrabrand competition is impeded; see *Consten and Grundig*, note 3 above; more generally on the interventionism of Community competition law, see p. 664.

ing, then that deal between the only two producers would be catastrophic for the competitive structure of the market. So in *Tetra Pak*[232] the Commission's assessment of the possibility of exemption of a deal that restricted competition between producers of milk cartons drew it into a careful analysis of the extent to which particular types of product packaging techniques were interchangeable. In *Alcatel Espace/ANT*[233] the Commission explored the market for satellite production and concluded that collaboration was essential, given the range of skills required and the level of costs and risks incurred.[234] The Franco-German collaboration at issue would improve, not eliminate, competition, given the number of experienced US enterprises active in a market that was not geographically limited. These issues of market definition are of central relevance under Article 86.[235] They also arise in merger control. Effective competition is eliminated by the creation through merger of a European firm that will dwarf all other European firms only where non-European firms are unable to contest the market in which the merged entity will be active.[236]

BLOCK EXEMPTION

An application to the Commission for the grant of an exemption for a restrictive practice must be founded on the four conditions in Article 85(3). It is easy to see that if the Commission were obliged to evaluate each and every commercial agreement caught by Article 85(1) in the light of Article 85(3), then its workload would be intolerable. A number of schemes exist in order to make the administrative structure workable. At the forefront of the means of securing the effective administration of Article 85 is the *block exemption*.[237] In order to eliminate the need to secure a separate individual exemption on the Article 85(3) criteria for all agreements the Commission is able to rely on regulations that apply a block exemption to several categories of collaboration.[238] These block exemption

---

232 Comm. Dec. 88/501 OJ 1988 L272/27 [1990] 4 CMLR 47. The decision was upheld by the Court of First Instance in Case T-51/89 *Tetra Pak Rausing SA v Commission* [1990] ECR II-309, [1991] 4 CMLR 334.
233 Comm. Dec. 90/46 OJ 1990 L32/19, [1991] 4 CMLR 208.
234 It may, accordingly, be argued that the deal should have been held unaffected by Article 85(1) rather than exempted under Art. 85(3); cf. note 157 above.
235 See further Ch. 23.
236 See further Ch. 25.
237 For other mechanisms, such as negative clearance and comfort letters, see Ch. 24.
238 See Goyder, *EC Competition Law*, Ch. 5.

regulations contain a list of clauses that may or may not be included in particular types of agreement and are consequently essential guides for commercial planning. The block exemptions are based on Article 85(3); they constitute the concrete expression in relation to particular deals of the abstract requirements of the four conditions. If an agreement is of a type covered by a block exemption regulation, then rather than seek an individual exemption based on economic progress, consumer benefit *et al.*, the firms can instead consult the regulation that has already, in effect, translated the general criteria into specific acceptable ('white') and unacceptable ('black') clauses.[239]

Regulation 19/65 empowered the Commission to make regulations providing for the block exemption of particular types of agreement. The major block exemptions of general application are:

Reg. 1983/83 Exclusive Distribution agreements[240]
Reg. 1984/83 Exclusive Purchasing agreements[241]
Reg. 2349/84 Patent Licensing agreements[242]
Reg. 123/85 Motor Vehicle Distribution agreements[243]
Reg. 417/85 Specialization agreements[244]
Reg. 418/85 Research and Development agreements[245]
Reg. 4087/88 Franchising agreements[246]
Reg. 556/89 Know-How Licensing agreements[247]

Regulations 2349/84, 417/85, 418/85 and 556/89 were amended by Regulation 151/93[248] in order to secure more favourable treatment of joint ventures under the block exemptions. The principal motivation for this shift lay in the attempt to improve alignment between the treatment of cooperative joint ventures under Article 85 and the relatively more favourable treatment granted to joint ventures of a type that falls within the Merger Regulation.[249]

These measures are essential in planning commercial collaboration.[250]

---

239 The use of 'white' and 'black' in this fashion is needlessly offensive, but seems too well-established to eradicate.
240 OJ 1983 L173/1.
241 OJ 1983 L173/5.
242 OJ 1984 L219/15.
243 OJ 1985 L15/16.
244 OJ 1985 L53/1.
245 OJ 1985 L53/5.
246 OJ 1988 L359/46.
247 OJ 1989 L61/1.
248 OJ 1993 L21/8.
249 See further Ch. 25, p.813.
250 Other more specialized Regs. exist: e.g. Reg. 4056/86 OJ 1986 L378/14, which concerns liner conferences.

They are also invaluable for the practice of the Commission. It is inconceivable that it could deal with every agreement on an individual basis, but the block exemptions remove any such need in several important areas of commercial collaboration. Beyond this practical aspect, the regulations represent vehicles of Commission policy-making in rooting out anticompetitive practices and in advancing the cause of market integration.

The block exemptions are to some extent an uneasy compromise. Article 85(3)'s broadly phrased criteria are designed to allow firms flexibility in drafting beneficial agreements, and it may be objected that the block exemptions compromise that objective by encouraging firms to fit their agreement within predefined moulds. However, a firm unhappy with the *dirigiste* constraint of a block exemption is free to seek an individual exemption for a deal tailored to its own particular requirements. Moreover, the terms of the block exemption are based on Article 85(3) and ought therefore to reflect the flexibility inherent in it. It has been suggested that greater flexibility could be achieved through block exemptions biased more towards explanation of policy than listing specific terms,[251] but that might be unwelcome to drafters of commercial agreements eager for predictability.

The Regulations are limited in time. As the date for their expiry approaches, the Commission has typically found itself subjected to pressure from commercial parties to renew the exemption on more permissive terms. The debate about the extent to which the Commission will comply with such requests has been lively. Regulation 2349/84 on Patent Licensing expired at the end of 1994. The substance of the Commission's proposals to replace both that Regulation and Regulation 556/89 on Know-How Licensing by a single Technology Transfer block exemption generated a sufficiently active response to cause delay in the adoption of a new measure. In particular, the Commission's proposed introduction of maximum market share criteria as a means of distinguishing between agreements for the purposes of exemption attracted criticism for creating the very commercial uncertainty that the block exemption is designed to eliminate. The application of Regulation 2349/84 was extended by six months to 30 June 1995 while the Commission pondered the matter further.[252] Regulation 123/85 on Motor Vehicle Distribution expired on 30 June 1995 and consumer groups and the motor vehicle industry differed sharply on the future of competition policy in the area. The Commission once again found itself besieged by intense lobbying.[253]

---

251 See e.g. Korah *EC Competition Law and Practice*, pp. 277–80.
252 See notes by Korah (1994) 5 E Bus L Rev 167, Strivens [1994] *Lawyers' Europe* (Winter) 6.
253 See, from the consumer viewpoint, Locke and Bovis, 'The supply of new cars and the EU block exemption' (1994) 4 Consumer Pol Rev 38.

Since the block exemptions are no more than the practical expression of the requirements of Article 85(3), one can expect that the themes observed above will be reflected in the terms of the regulations. The preambles to the regulations base their explanation on the Article 85(3) criteria, so the pro-integrative element of cross-frontier collaboration is recognized, as are the connected advantages for the stimulation of competition brought about by cross-border activity. These elements are identified as contributions to increased consumer choice. It is, however, equally recognized that absolute territorial protection is anathema to Community competition policy and that the deals struck must observe this strict rule. Finally, the importance of persisting interbrand competition from third parties is emphasized. In the body of the regulations proper these policy objectives are reflected in the white and black clauses. The restrictions that are permissible in the operation of an exclusive distributorship appear in the list of white clauses. It is lawful to include a clause forbidding the supplier not to supply the contract goods to users in the contract territory; it is lawful to tie the distributor to obtain the contract goods for resale only from the supplier. However, the list of black clauses includes those that are designed to suppress importation by third parties from outside the contract territory, for such restrictions serve to eliminate competition and may partition the common market. An example of the balance that the regulation seeks to strike is found in the distinction between active and passive sales policy. The distributor may be restrained from actively selling the contract goods outside the contract territory, but must not be restrained from responding to unsolicited orders.[254] The more recent regulations include grey clauses, which, as one might expect, are clauses potentially permissible, but are of such a nature as to require some separate opportunity for Commission scrutiny.[255]

It should finally be observed that the block exemptions are not exhaustive. The fact that an agreement, whatever its content, cannot be accommodated within a regulation does not render it unlawful. The parties may still seek individual exemption from the Commission relying on the terms of Article 85(3). In *Alcatel Espace/ANT*[256] the collaboration encompassed not only research and development into satellite production, but also joint supply and marketing. The deal fell outside the Research and Development block exemption, which at the time did not envisage joint marketing.[257]

---

254 Art. 2(2)(c) Reg. 1983/83.
255 See p. 775.
256 Comm. Dec. 90/46, note 233 above. See also Comm. Dec. 88/563 *DDD/Delta Chemie* OJ 1988 L309/34. [1989] 4 CMLR 535.
257 As a result of the amendments of Reg. 151/93 n. 248 above, joint marketing plans may now fall within the exemption subject to ceilings placed on the parties' permitted market share. See in detail Whish, *Competition Law*, pp. 445–8.

The Commission was nevertheless prepared to grant an individual exemption for such unusually close collaboration, given that separate marketing was hardly feasible in a market where the customer expects close contact with and full knowledge of all parties that have participated in the development of such a technologically advanced product.

CHAPTER 23

Article 86: Abuse of a Dominant Position

Any abuse by one or more undertakings of a dominant position within the common market or in a substantial part of it shall be prohibited as incompatible with the common market in so far as it may affect trade between Member States. Such abuse may, in particular, consist in:

(a) directly or indirectly imposing unfair purchase or selling prices or unfair trading conditions;
(b) limiting production, markets or technical development to the prejudice of consumers;
(c) applying dissimilar conditions to equivalent transactions with other trading parties, thereby placing them at a competitive disadvantage;
(d) making the conclusion of contracts subject to acceptance by the other parties of supplementary obligations which, by their nature or according to commercial usage, have no connection with the subject of such contracts.

THE AIM OF ARTICLE 86

RATIONALES FOR CONTROLLING A DOMINANT POSITION

Article 86 forbids the abuse of a dominant position. It is the EC Treaty's monopoly provision. Its aim is the control of the activities of firms that enjoy such economic strength that they are immune from the influence of the normal constraints of a competitive market.

Where only one large producer is active in a market, that producer holds a monopoly and is able to deny the consumer any choice. The realization of efficiency through the exercise of consumer preference is thwarted. The monopolist, like the cartel, is able to trade without reference to the influence of competition, which is vital to a properly functioning market. Resource allocation is distorted. The dominant firm may raise prices with impunity. It is subject to little inducement to innovate or improve standards. There is no need to defend the market share; it is by definition more or less inviolable. The supplier is not led by demand and the economic benefits of the market economy are depressed and/or siphoned off into the pockets of the producer. Legal control is explicable as a means of redressing the inefficient outcome and curbing unfair wealth distribution.

The previous chapter explained how the market may itself be capable of curing the distortions of the cartel,[1] and the same may apply to a monopoly. The opportunity to acquire market share in the model described is likely to attract into the market a new firm that is prepared to offer an alternative product at a competitive price. Competition may therefore be latent and ready to emerge if consumer demand exists. If the market is so structured, legal intervention may be unnecessary. Yet the market-based cure is not always available. There may be obstacles to a firm entering the market in question. Production costs may be beyond those that the would-be market entrant is able to bear, or perhaps access to the essential raw material is controlled by the monopolist and is not freely available. Perhaps the monopolist has pursued a skilful advertising campaign that has induced consumers to believe its product is irreplaceable, even though the objective evidence may indicate otherwise. In all these instances the market is not constestable.[2] The competitive structure of the market is upset and the allocation of resources is not determined in accordance with consumer demand. Some response is called for; the technique adopted by EC law is to prohibit the abuse of a dominant position.

THE ABUSE OF A DOMINANT POSITION

The notion of the abuse of a dominant position within Article 86 is broad and flexible. It is capable of application to practices according to their prejudicial effect on the common market, irrespective of the precise nature of the conduct. The similarity to Article 85, and indeed to Community trade law generally, is immediately plain; it is the *effect* of the practice that is the focus of legal control. Also in common with Article 85, Article 86 includes a list of the type of practice that is subject to control, but the list is non-exhaustive.[3] Unfair pricing (example (a)), arbitary discrimination (example (b)) and restrictive tying arrangements (example (d)) are included as

1 See pp. 664, 681.
2 Emphasis on contestable markets as a key to efficiency has been a feature of much recent economic analysis; see further p. 737.
3 Case 6/72 *Continental Can v Commission* [1973] ECR 215, [1973] CMLR 199, para. 26 of the judgment: 'The list merely gives examples, not an exhaustive enumeration of the sort of abuses of a dominant position prohibited by the Treaty.'

potential abuses, but the Commission, supported by the Court, has used Article 86 to combat practices falling outside the illustrative list. The most remarkable example of the flexibility of the Article 86 prohibition is the accommodation of merger within the idea of an abuse.[4]

This chapter deals with a number of abusive practices controlled under Article 86, but a brief illustrative paragraph is useful as a means of providing a flavour of the provision. *United Brands* v *Commission*[5] is a decision that will be referred to on several occasions. The practices under scrutiny took place in the banana market. United Brands was found to have abused its dominant position by imposing arbitrary differential pricing levels for different areas of the common market, by imposing tight controls over resale by customers, which reduced the choice of the ultimate consumer, and by refusing to continue supplying a long-standing customer. It was in breach of Article 86 and was fined accordingly, although the Court annulled the Commission's separate finding that the firm had charged unfairly high prices. In *Commercial Solvents* v *Commission*[6] the dominant firm was found to have refused to supply a product to an established customer. This refusal was likely to have the effect of eliminating the customer from the market and Commercial Solvents planned to fill the gap itself. In the circumstances the Commission held that the effect on the market was sufficiently prejudicial to justify insisting that Commercial Solvents continue to supply its customer. In *British Sugar*[7] the Commission condemned practices that were designed to frustrate a smaller rival's attempts to broaden its sphere of activity. British Sugar had, *inter alia*, set price levels that bore no relation to economic cost and were in reality designed to obstruct the entry of competitors; it had tied customers to it through the offer of loyalty rebates, thereby stifling future competition by other suppliers; and it had pursued a policy of arbitrary refusal to supply against would-be entrants on to the market. Some of these practices prejudice the consumer directly, others indirectly; the scope of Article 86 is wide enough to accommodate both species of abuse.

It may be objected at this stage that Article 86 is an exercise in unwarranted interventionism. Are these not the legitimate business tactics of a profit maximizer? The important point, however, is that the controlled practices must be viewed in the context of the market dominance in which they occur. The market is devoid of the influence of healthy competition and therefore practices such as high prices, which would do no more than cost the firm its custom in a competitive market, are capable of remaining

---

4 ibid., see p. 710.
5 Case 27/76 [1978] ECR 207, [1978] 1 CMLR 429.
6 Cases 6, 7/73 [1974] ECR 223, [1974] 1 CMLR 309; see further p. 751.
7 Comm. Dec. 88/518 OJ [1988] L284/41, [1990] 4 CMLR 196.

uncorrected. Similarly, a refusal to deal may be simply an exercise of free will if the would-be customer can look elsewhere, but where the supply is under monopoly control, free will is backed up by economic power and the ability to harm the market structure by suppressing potential competition. In these circumstances resources may be misallocated, because the equilibrium of competitive supply and demand is distorted. Moreover, the dominant firm may be able to seize excessive profits. Hence there exist rationales for legal intervention in monopolies to promote efficient outcomes and to secure fair distribution of benefits.

DOMINANCE IS NOT UNLAWFUL

Article 86 accepts the existence of dominant firms, but asserts a power to control their conduct by forbidding abuse of that dominance. Dominance is tolerated, but its potential to foster inefficiency is subjected to supervision. As will be seen,[8] attempts to extend dominance may in themselves be found abusive, which indicates a determination to nurture any lingering competition even in a dominated market. Generally, then, dominated markets are seen as second-best to competitive markets.[9] Yet some dominant positions are not simply tolerated; they are welcomed. In some markets the absence of competition is not to be lamented. Competition is only a means to an efficient end, and some markets operate at their most efficient without the influence of competitive pressures. Some products and services constitute natural monopolies. The provision of water, for example, has long been thought to be a market where competition between suppliers would be simply inefficient. Duplication of supply networks – pipes, reservoirs – would cost more than any benefits that might accrue from careful control of distribution costs and reduced prices as a result of the effects of consumer choice. Similarly, a duplication of railway lines may be inefficient; yet in this instance the railway is not immunized from competition from other means of transport. There may be reasons why competition would be injurious to research and innovation. An inventor may be loath to spend time and money on a new product that would be of immense benefit to society if he or she knows that as soon as the product appears on the market the design will be immediately

8 See pp. 746, 748, 751.
9 This provides a rationale for controlling mergers, at least where only a few firms are active in a market, in order to forestall the creation of dominance. The divestment approach, whereby dominant firms would be forced to break up, would also emerge from this perception, but the cost of such a drastic interventionist policy may exceed the benefits, which suggests a preference for acquiescing in, but controlling, dominance on the Article 86 model.

copied by competitors, who will reap profits having incurred no costs (the 'free-rider' problem). The threat of competition deters expenditure on innovation. These examples of the undesirability of competition emphasize the role of workable, rather than perfect, competition as a guiding principle.[10]

Once it is accepted that competition will not and should not occur, as in natural monopolies, the function of the law becomes the control of potential adverse effects of the lack of competition for the economy. Thus price controls and safety standards may be imposed on suppliers of naturally monopolistic goods. This may be achieved by specific legislative controls. More broadly, Article 86 permits supervision of tactics pursued by monopolists that are deemed abusive. Article 86, then, does not outlaw dominance. However, whether the dominance is merely tolerated or positively welcomed, it is subject to a flexible prohibition against its abuse. In a sense, such regulation mimics the outcome that would obtain were the market open to the influence of competition.

None the less, the notion of abuse, although flexible, is simultaneously unstructured and potentially unsophisticated. It leaves a considerable degree of discretion vested in the competition authorities to supervise dominant firms in accordance with their own perceptions of proper market development. For example, although unfair pricing may be held abusive, the notion of unfairness is imprecise.[11] In the area of mergers it is apparent that abuse is an inadequate tool for the pursuit of a coherent policy. Specific legislation was essential, yet nearly two decades passed after the Court first held Article 86 applicable to mergers before agreement could be reached in this area.[12] Moreover, the idea of abuse leaves the Commission free to include aspects of policy, such as wealth distribution, that might be thought controversial elements in a competition policy.

Finally, the example of the inventor reluctant to innovate suggests a situation where the law should not simply tolerate or welcome dominance; here the law must go further and create it. By granting the inventor an exclusive right to make and sell the product in a territory for a stipulated period, the law recognizes that competition is inefficient and therefore provides for its suppression by granting the inventor a legally enforceable immunity from it. This is the field of intellectual property law – patents, copyrights, trade marks and allied rights.[13] However, even this desirable position of economic strength requires supervision, and Article 86, while

10 See pp. 661–2.
11 See p. 744.
12 See Ch. 25.
13 See Ch. 26.

not questioning the existence of the legal protection, demands that it is not abusively exercised.[14]

THE EC COMPETITION LAW SYSTEM

Articles 85 and 86 as complementary provisions

Broadly, Article 86 is directed at the control of potentially inefficient positions of economic strength. In some areas it serves to bring about the results that would obtain if competition did exist. The presence of competition would force prices down towards the efficient level; Article 86 insists that this be done even in the absence of competition.[15] Similarly, refusal to supply in a competitive market would occur only for objectively justifiable, non-arbitrary reasons; Article 86 imposes the same requirements even in the absence of competition. Article 86, then, is a complement to Article 85, which seeks efficiency through breaking up anticompetitive restrictive practices. Article 86 has as its broad objective the pursuit of efficient market outcomes, but it operates not at the level of the cartel, where two or more firms are involved, but at the level of the single, dominant firm.

The Court has insisted on the broad unity of purpose that exists between Articles 85 and 86. It considers that the two provisions 'seek to achieve the same aim on different levels, *viz*, the maintenance of effective competition within the Common Market'.[16] Both provisions, then, are concerned with the pursuit of efficiency and with the integration of the Community market. They act in tandem as a system.

It has been explained that Article 85 may in some circumstances confer a higher priority on market integration than a pure competition-only analysis would suggest.[17] Article 86 is on occasion used in a manner similarly surprising to those familiar with other competition law systems. For example, the Community may be tempted to take a more favourable view of cross-border mergers than would be taken of similar-sized mergers in a single economic area, because the cross-border merger, although potentially anticompetitive, is an instrument of market integration.[18] These competing concerns may give rise to a tension between mistrust of economic strength and the desire to promote truly integrated European commercial enterprises. The Commission has also been quicker to challenge firms practising

14 See p. 835.
15 In so far as the efficient level can be identified in the absence of competition; see further p. 744.
16 Case 6/72, note 3 above, para. 25.
17 Contrast (EC) Cases 56, 58/64 *Consten and Grundig* v *Commission* [1966] ECR 215 with (US) *Continental TV* v *GTE Sylvania* 433 US 36 (1977), p. 665 above.
18 See Ch. 25.

price discrimination between states than would be normal in other systems.[19] Once again, the concern is to root out the idea that the common market is divisible into its national elements.

The distinction between bilateral and unilateral conduct revisited[20]

Articles 85 and 86 are complementary but, in a sense, they are also mutually exclusive because where there is only one firm involved Article 86 alone is in issue; where two or more colluding firms are involved Article 85 is exclusively applicable. For example, where a firm cooperates with an economically independent subsidiary, then an agreement covered by Article 85 has been concluded. If the parent and subsidiary are in reality part of the same unit, then Article 85 is not in issue; Article 86 is – but only if the single unit occupies a dominant position. However, the demarcation between bilateralism under Article 85 and unilateralism under Article 86, though real, may require careful consideration in some areas, for it is possible that Article 86 will be relevant even where more than one firm is involved. If a dominant firm enters into agreements, particularly where those agreements are imposed by economic pressure on reluctant small firms, then the agreements themselves are capable of infringing Article 85 whereas the conduct of the dominant firm in securing such deals may itself count as an abuse of a dominant position.[21] Thus, participation in a restrictive practice may involve the abuse of a dominant position. These are independent infringements of the competition rules. Article 86's control of market dominance serves a function separate from Article 85's supervision of restrictive practices, despite the broad unity of purpose. Accordingly, even if the agreement is exempted under Article 85(3), its conclusion may in some circumstances involve an abuse of a dominant position.[22]

Moreover, it should be observed that the notion of collective dominance is apt to blur the line between Articles 85 and 86. The problems of controlling the oligopoly have been discussed.[23] Such firms are interdependent not as a result of collusion but because of market structure and Article 85 seems inappropriate as a means of control. The Court of First Instance in *Società Italiana Vetro SpA and others v Commission*[24] ruled that Article 86

---

19 See p. 747.
20 See Ch. 22, p. 673.
21 Case 66/86 *Ahmed Saeed* [1989] ECR 803, [1990] 4 CMLR 102, p. 749 below.
22 Case T-51/89 *Tetra Pak v Commission* [1990] ECR II-309, [1991] 4 CMLR 334, noted by James [1990] 6 ECLR 267; Daltrop and Ferry [1991] 1 ICCLR 24; Wheeler (1991) 16 ELRev 308.
23 See p. 676.
24 Cases T-68/89, T-77/89 [1992] ECR II-1403, [1992] 5 CMLR 302.

may be used in some circumstances to control oligopolies on the basis that the firms jointly occupy a dominant position on the market. As explained in Chapter 22,[25] the Court found in its decision that the Commission had committed serious procedural errors and it annulled the Decision condemning practices in the flat glass industry. On point of substance, the Court did not rule out the use of the notion of joint dominance as a means of controlling an oligopoly under Article 86. However, it insisted on both the demonstration of economic links between the firms alleged to enjoy joint dominance and on full market analysis to show dominant power. The Court of First Instance suggested that sufficient economic linkage could arise 'where two or more independent undertakings jointly have, through agreements or licences, a technological lead affording them the power to behave to an appreciable extent independently of their competitors, their customers and ultimately of their consumers'.[26]

In such circumstances, Article 86 seems to exists as a kind of half-way house between control of cartels, which is achieved under Article 85, and control of 'pure' structural oligopolies where joint dominance does not exist, which is not possible at all in EC law.[27] However, the 'economic link' test is murky. The notion, so defined, will be of significant value in the administration of competition policy only provided that the requisite economic links envisaged by the Court of First Instance are weaker than those required for a finding of a cartel within the meaning of Article 85 (and weaker than would convert the firms into a single economic unit), in order to permit the use of Article 86 in situations beyond the scope of Article 85. If economic linkage in this context means no more than agreements or concerted practices within Article 85, or the links that would convert the firms into a single economic entity, then Article 86 goes no further than Article 85. On the other hand, the Court of First Instance clearly envisages in 'economic links' something more concrete than the oligopoly in which firms are linked only by force of market structure.[28]

In *Municipality of Almelo and Others* v *NV Energiebedrijf IJsselmij*[29] the European Court approved the notion of a collective dominant position

---

25 P. 682.
26 Para. 358 of the judgment.
27 Control of oligopolies created by merger has not been treated by the Commission as dependent on the demonstration of economic links between the members of the oligopoly and is therefore more extensive; Ch. 25, p. 825.
28 So even where there are jointly dominant firms, firms 'in the slipstream' of the oligopoly would not be caught; Whish, *Competition Law*, p. 487. So the true oligopoly remains untouched. See also Bellamy and Child, *Common Market Law of Competition*, Ch. 9.036–9.039.
29 Case C-393/92 [1994] ECR I-1477.

occupied by a group of undertakings. The Court referred to undertakings linked 'in such a way that they adopt the same conduct on the market'. The case was an Article 177 ruling and the European Court accordingly left it to the referring Dutch court to decide whether the links between the electricity suppliers in question were 'sufficiently strong' for these purposes.[30]

Finally, even in cases where Article 86 is available – where there is joint dominance of the type envisaged by the Court of First Instance in *Società Italiana Vetro* – it must be remembered that in itself dominance, joint or single, is no cause for condemnation under Article 86. It is abuse of that position that is prohibited. Yet the vague notion of 'abuse' is not a useful means of controlling an oligopoly. Perhaps the jointly dominant firms may be obliged to surrender their economic links as part of a requirement not to abuse their position, yet if the market is of a truly oligopolistic structure, such a surrender will be largely irrelevant to finding a cure for the problem.[31]

Substantive similarities

Strictly, then, Articles 85 and 86 maintain a separate identity and are not mutually applicable; they are, however, certainly complementary. Taken together they serve as a broad charter for the control of anticompetitive behaviour. This parallel function is emphasized by the substantive similarities between the two Articles. The phrases employed in Article 86 mirror in several respects those in Article 85, and the Court has consistently affirmed that both provisions are subject to identical interpretation. So the notion of an 'undertaking' is to be read in precisely the same way in Article 86 as in Article 85.[32] An economically interdependent parent and subsidiary are a single undertaking for these purposes[33] and, if dominant, are caught by Article 86. Indeed, several of the leading Article 86 cases have involved non-EC parents held responsible for the activities of their EC subsidiaries.[34] The requirement that an 'effect on trade between Member States' be demonstrated is equally present in both provisions. Under Article 86 the Court has tended to use the notion of an impact on

---

30 Paras. 42, 43 of the judgment.
31 See R. Whish and B. Sufrin, 'Oligopolistic Market and EC Competition Law' (1992) 12 YEL 59; Rodger, 'Market Integration and the Development of European Competition Policy to Meet New Demands' [1994/2] LIEI 1.
32 See p. 683; see, e.g., Case 155/73 *Sacchi* [1974] ECR 409, [1974] 2 CMLR 177; Case T-68/89 et al. *Società Italiana Vetro SpA and others* v *Commission*, note 24 above.
33 See p. 674.
34 E.g., Case 6/72, note 3 above, (US); Case 27/76, note 5 above, (US); Case 85/76 *Hoffman la Roche* v *Commission* [1979] ECR 461 (Swiss).

the structure of competition as the test, but the approach in practice runs parallel to that under Article 85.[35] So the Commission in *British Sugar*[36] applied the test that the practice must have repercussions on the patterns of competition within the common market, familiar from *STM* v *Maschinenbau Ulm*[37] under Article 85, and added that an increase in trade does not prevent a finding that this criterion has been met, provided that the required distortion is demonstrated.[38] Finally, and less obviously, the phrase 'incompatible with the common market' in Article 86 has been applied by the Court in a manner clearly inspired by the same motivations that have informed its treatment of the idea of preventing, restricting or distorting competition within the common market that appears in Article 85. The flexibility of these terms has been used by the Commission and the Court to develop a control of anticompetitive practices that is spiced by a strongly market integrationist flavour.

The remainder of this chapter examines the substantive approach of the application of Article 86. Examination of the notion of abusing a dominant position logically invites a two-stage analysis. First, does the firm occupy a dominant position? If not, there is no breach of Article 86, and no breach of the competition rules generally, subject only to the Court's occasionally surprising ability to uncover an agreement caught by Article 85 in cases of apparently unilateral action.[39] If the firm holds a dominant position, then the second question must be asked: is it abusing that dominant position?

THE NOTION OF A DOMINANT POSITION

THE COURT'S DEFINITION

Article 86 controls only firms that are economically dominant. In *United Brands* v *Commission*[40] the Court defined the notion of a dominant position in the following terms. It declared that Article 86 'relates to a position of economic strength enjoyed by an undertaking which enables it to prevent effective competition being maintained in the relevant market by giving it

35 See p. 687 above; see, e.g., Cases 6, 7/73, note 6 above; Case 22/78 *Hugin* v *Commission* [1979] ECR 1869, [1979] 3 CMLR 345; Case T-65/89 *BPB Industries and British Gypsum* v *Commission*, judgment of 1 April 1993 [1993] 5 CMLR 32.
36 Comm. Dec. 88/518, note 7 above.
37 Case 56/65 *Société Technique Minière* v *Maschinenbau Ulm* [1966] ECR 235, p. 688 above, applied by the Court in relation to Art. 86 in, e.g., Case 27/76, note 5 above.
38 See Cases 56, 58/64, note 17 above, and p. 689 above.
39 E.g., Case 107/82 *AEG* v *Commission* [1983] ECR 3151; see p. 673 above.
40 Case 27/76, note 5 above.

the power to behave to an appreciable extent independently of its competitors, customers and ultimately of its consumers'.[41] Dominance, then, is reflected in immunity from the influence of normal competitive forces. This is, of course, entirely consonant with the rationale of Article 86. Legal control exists in this area precisely because of the potential for inefficiency as a result of the absence of competition;[42] it is logical to base the trigger for the application of the legal control on the need to demonstrate that absence of competition.

The test established in *United Brands* relates to market power that confers independence from competitive pressures. Market power can be assessed only with relation to the actual market in which a firm is operative. The only producer of widgets in the United Kingdom has no immunity from competition if there are ten United Kingdom gidget producers and gidgets are readily substitutable for widgets. Nor does the only United Kingdom widget producer enjoy dominance even if gidgets are no substitute for widgets if there are ten French widget producers already operating in the British market or able to do so. In such circumstances there is no market dominance. Competition will stimulate the market to work efficiently and there is no need for legal intervention in the pursuit of efficiency.[43] It is accordingly essential to identify the market in which the firm is operating before one can assess whether it is dominant and therefore subject to control under Article 86. As the case of the widget producer illustrates, the market may be defined according to product (widgets/gidgets) and according to geography (UK/France).

The identification of a dominant position involves two elements: on what market is dominance asserted – the 'relevant market' referred to in the *United Brands* definition – and is dominance of that relevant market established? Both issues are fertile fields of inquiry for the economic analyst.[44]

IDENTIFYING THE RELEVANT MARKET

The task of identifying the scope of the market in which the firm under scrutiny is operative is rather complex in its practical application, but the broad structure of the study that must be undertaken is not difficult to

---

41 ibid., para. 65.
42 See pp. 718–20 above.
43 Absent cartels and oligopolies; note also that there may exist distributional or social, rather than efficiency, rationales for intervention.
44 For examples, see refs. listed under 'The Notion of a Dominant Position' in Select Further Reading.

understand. Article 86 is concerned with the prejudicial effects of a lack of competition and it is accordingly vital to determine whether any such lack really exists. It does *not* exist if the firm's product is subject to effective competition from different products made by other firms that serve the same purpose. So one must identify the market for products that are interchangeable in assessing dominance, *not* just the firm's own products: interbrand competition is relevant. Nor is competition lacking if producers in other parts of the common market are capable of challenging the market share of the firm under scrutiny. So one must identify the geographic scope of the market in assessing dominance as well as the scope of the product market. It is essential to realize that if dominance does not exist and efficient competition is present, then the rationale for regulating against abuse of a dominant position in the pursuit of efficiency has been fatally undermined.[45]

The product market

In *United Brands*[46] the banana market came under examination. It was necessary to determine whether bananas were the market against which United Brands' conduct should be judged or whether the broader fresh fruit market should be taken into consideration. United Brands argued that bananas were readily interchangeable with other kinds of fruit and that accordingly any control that it might exert over the banana market did not confer on it independence from competitive pressures, because producers of other fruits were able to challenge its performance. This argument was rejected by both the Commission and the Court, which considered that bananas could be treated as a distinct market. They are not substitutable for other fruits and form their own relevant market. Fruit such as apples and oranges[47] are not substitutes because 'the banana has certain characteristics, appearance, taste, softness, seedlessness, easy handling, a constant level of production which enable it to satisfy the constant needs of an important section of the population consisting of the very young, the old and the sick'.[48] Banana consumers are not prone to significant shift in preference to other fruits.[49]

45 There may be other rationales for intervention, see note 43 above.
46 Case 27/76, note 5 above.
47 Other fruits that, unlike apples, oranges and bananas, are available only seasonally were considered incapable of competing effectively with the banana for that very reason. The market was thus judged across the entire year. However, seasonal fluctuations in the market may be taken into account in limiting market definition on a temporal basis where competition is effective for a specific period only.
48 Case 27/76, note 5 above, para. 31 of the judgment.
49 Arguably, the market should have been drawn more narrowly to distinguish branded from unbranded bananas; Korah, 'Abuse of a Dominant Position in the Banana Market'

The test that must be employed in identifying the relevant product market thus requires an examination of product substitutability. If the consumer is perfectly prepared to switch from product A to product B, then there is no prima-facie need to apply legal control to the conduct of either producer. If the price of product A is increased or its quality reduced, the consumer will simply switch to product B; competition exists as an incentive to the producers to act efficiently in response to consumer demand.[50] Only where there is no alternative product is there a market failure. One can check whether product A and product B are in competition and therefore form part of the same market simply by monitoring whether an increase in the price of one stimulates an increase in demand for the other.[51] If so, there is no prima-facie reason why the law should intervene, for the market is competitive. Of course, the correlation between price and demand is rarely perfect, for even similar products tend to differ to some extent in respect of quality and consumer perception, which may lead to distortion in the simplest model of interchangeability. However, the basic idea that one can test the scope of the product market by checking substitutability between products is the conceptual heart of market definition under Article 86, even though its practical application is doubtless often complex and sometimes controversial.

Naturally, as far as the undertaking is concerned, the wider the definition of the market, the less likely that its market share will be found to confer dominance. The Commission, alleging dominance, will typically draw the bounds of the market more narrowly than the firm would prefer. A constant theme in Article 86 cases is disagreement about market definition. Ultimately, the matter falls to the Court to decide. In *United Brands* the Court upheld the Commission's definition of the market in the face of United Brands' submissions that bananas did not form a market separate from that for fruit generally. Such a narrow definition of the market increased the probability of a finding that the firm occupied a dominant

---

(1975–76) 1 ELRev 322. Arguably, the market should have been drawn more broadly to include other fruits because UB had no means of directing an individualized selling policy at old, sick consumers for whom bananas were the only fruit; Korah, *EC Competition Law and Practice* p.72; Whish, *Competition Law*, pp. 255–6.

50 Provided the producers of A and B are truly independent; if they collude, Art. 85 may apply; if the products are produced by one and the same producer, Art. 86 may apply; if an oligopoly exists, both Arts. may apply; see pp. 681–3.

51 The economist's stock term is 'cross-elasticity'. See Rowley: '. . . coefficients of cross-elasticity of demand and/or supply beloved by the textbook writers, who never sully their hands on the real world . . .'; extracted in Ogus and Veljanowski, *Readings in the Economics of Law and Regulation*, p. 228.

position upon it.[52] In *Commercial Solvents*[53] the market was defined to cover only the raw materials (for which there was no substitute), excluding derivative products (for which several substitutes existed). A finding of dominance followed. However, in *Continental Can*[54] the undertaking was successful in persuading the Court to annul the Commission's decision that it had violated Article 86[55] on the basis that the Commission's analysis of the scope of the market was inadequate. The Commission had examined the firm's conduct in the markets for meat cans, fish cans and metal closures for glass jars. Continental Can argued that producers of other types of container and producers of metal cans for products such as fruit, vegetables and condensed milk were capable of achieving adaptation in order to enter its markets. This threat was part of the competitive environment in which Continental Can operated and it served to deny the firm independence from the influence of competition, actual or potential. The Court agreed that the Commission had failed adequately to explain why it had excluded potential competitors from its market definition and annulled the decision.

In *Hoffman la Roche*[56] the Court upheld the Commission's finding that several vitamins were not interchangeable because of their distinct properties and functions. Each vitamin occupied a separate market for the purposes of Article 86. In *Michelin v Commission*[57] it was held that producers of tyres for heavy vehicles and producers of car tyres operated in distinct markets. Interchangeability between the two markets was not feasible. The case is of particular interest because where *Continental Can* required an examination of capacity for substitutability of supply and *United Brands* looked to capacity for substitutability of demand, *Michelin* concerns both. Major differences in production techniques precluded producers of one type of tyre converting to suppliers of the other; the differences between the tyres themselves prevented users switching between them.[58] In *Hugin*[59] the Court upheld the Commission's finding that the relevant market was spare parts for Hugin cash registers, not, as Hugin argued, the cash register market in general. The novel design of the Hugin

52 It did; see p. 736.
53 Cases 6, 7/73, note 6 above.
54 Case 6/72, note 3 above.
55 The abuse was merger, see p. 807.
56 Case 85/76, note 34 above.
57 Case 322/81 [1983] ECR 3461.
58 Absence of both demand and supply substitutability was found in defining the market in Comm. Dec. 88/501 *Tetra Pak* OJ 1988 L272/27, [1990] 4 CMLR 47, upheld in Case T-51/89, note 22 above. Note that the decision also had to define the market for the purposes of Art. 85(3); p. 713.
59 Case 22/78, note 35 above.

machines meant that its parts were not interchangeable with those of other producers and Hugin could also rely on copyright law to suppress other sources of production of its parts.[60] Finally, it should be observed that the need to define a market by reference to interchangeability of product means that the holder of an intellectual property right does not necessarily dominate a product market. Although the protected product is, by definition, controlled by the holder of the right, there may be competing products that subject the right–holder to effective competition.[61] Article 86 is not applicable, nor is it required, in such circumstances.

When applying this approach to the area of transport, it is necessary to examine whether particular means of transport are distinct from possible alternatives due to characteristics that eliminate interchangeability and therefore competition. Certain scheduled airline flights are capable of being individualized in a manner that confers on them effective immunity from competition. An example may be found in specialized intercontinental flights.[62] Even within the Community, particular routes have been found to form distinct markets. In *British Midland/Aer Lingus* the Commission identified the Dublin–London Heathrow route as a distinct market.[63] Passengers were unwilling to use other airports, even in London, especially on journeys involving more legs than simply Dublin–Heathrow. Moreover, supply-side flexibility was largely non-existent, because of the absence of available slots at the notoriously congested Heathrow. Aer Lingus was found to dominate the route and a fine was imposed on it by the Commission for abusive practices designed to impede British Midland's efforts to maintain and increase its presence in the market.[64] In *Société Anonyme à Participation Ouvrière Compagnie Nationale Air France v Commission*,[65] a case arising in the area of merger control where comparable issues of detailed market definition are at stake,[66] the Court of First Instance upheld the Commission's definition of the market as air routes between Paris and London and Lyons and London. There was no substitutability between these two routes and other routes and very little between the two routes themselves.

60 For criticism of this narrow market definition, see p. 741. Hugin escaped a finding of breach because its activities did not affect trade between member states.
61 E.g., Case 78/70 *Deutsche Grammophon* v *Metro* [1971] ECR 487; see further p. 835.
62 Case 66/86, note 21 above. See Van Houtte, 'Relevant Markets in Air Transport', (1990) 27 CMLRev 521. See generally, on the regulation of this sector, Balfour, 'Air Transport: a Community success story?' (1994) 31 CMLRev 1025.
63 Dec. 92/213 OJ 1992 L96/34, [1993] 4 CMLR 596.
64 In particular, Aer Lingus was unwilling to 'interline' (loosely involving cross-recognition of tickets). On obligations of dominant firms to deal fairly with would-be competitors, see p. 750 below.
65 Case T-2/93 [1994] ECR II-323.
66 Ch. 25, p. 823.

Competition between different modes of transport may exist. The traveller between Paris and Brussels, for example, is probably able to substitute road or rail for air travel, which means that all form part of the same relevant market and are in competition with each other. Air fares are not independent of rail fares. By contrast, in *British Midland/Aer Lingus*[67] the Commission did not consider that any other form of transport between Dublin and London was fast enough to compete with air travel. Business travel from London to Paris is served by a relevant market comprising the airlines alone – until the Channel Tunnel is seen to provide a real alternative. Markets alter. In *Night Services* the Commission exempted under Article 85(3) an agreement between railway companies relating to passenger services through the Channel Tunnel.[68] Its market analysis led it to the conclusion that there was competition for business travel between air and train; and competition for leisure travel between rail, air, coach and sea.[69]

The geographic market

The cases discussed above relate to the identification of the product market in which the firm under scrutiny is operative. In addition, the geographic market requires identification. The firm's activities could, of course, encompass the whole of the EC and beyond and, indeed, the firm will be eager to define the market broadly here too in order to dilute the market power that it is alleged to possess. However, the market against which the firm's activity is properly judged may be much smaller. In *Michelin*[70] the Court accepted that market conditions were homogeneous on the separate Dutch market and that, accordingly, dominance should be assessed in that territory alone. The key is to identify a distinct market that is partitioned from the rest of the common market and on which competition is therefore unaffected by external influences. So in *United Brands*[71] the market was defined as the Community excluding the French, Italian and United Kingdom markets. The markets of the three excluded states operated under the influences of diverse traditions that rendered them distinct and separate. In the United Kingdom, for example, Commonwealth preference affected the structure of the market. This left the remaining six member states[72] as United Brands' market. In those six states homogeneous market

---

67 Note 63 above.
68 Comm. Dec. 94/663 OJ 1994 L259/20.
69 See p. 712-13 above on the need for market definition under Article 85(3).
70 Case 322/81, note 57 above.
71 Case 27/76, note 5 above.
72 The events occurred before the Community's second enlargement, which occurred when Greece joined in 1981.

conditions prevailed that allowed United Brands to treat the bloc more or less as a 'single market'[73] to which it applied a uniform marketing strategy. Just as the market for apples did not affect United Brands' policy towards bananas, nor did the state of the market in the United Kingdom affect its policy in Germany; the relevant market was for bananas in six of the nine member states.

As effective market integration proceeds it is likely that geographic markets in which firms operate will become ever broader. The basic policy of the common market involves the conversion of diverse national markets into a single Community-wide market and, accordingly, firms ought to become increasingly able and willing to adopt a homogeneous policy towards all the member states.[74] Admittedly, some markets will remain small, perhaps where bulky products and high transport costs are involved.[75] Other markets will remain limited by government regulation, such as the case of the conferral by law of an exclusive power to grant test certificates for cars in a single state.[76] However, such isolated markets will become exceptional as the Community market develops.[77] This is reflected in the Court of First Instance's decision in *Tetra Pak International SA* v *Commission*.[78] Tetra Pak had been found by the Commission to have engaged in a range of abusive practices and was fined 75 million ECU by the Commission,[79] the highest fine ever imposed on a single firm.[80] In Tetra Pak's unsuccessful application for annulment of the Commission's decision, one of its grounds related to the Commission's identification of a relevant market covering the whole Community. The Commission had found a more or less stable demand for the relevant products throughout the Community; the possibility that customers could obtain supplies in member states other than their own; and low transport costs that greatly facilitated cross-border trade in the goods. The Court of First Instance saw no reason to interfere with this market definition and rejected Tetra Pak's submission that a narrower market, comprising only north-western Europe, was in issue. The Commission's assessment had properly been

73 Case 27/76, note 5 above, para. 56 of the judgment.
74 Cf. Art. 85, p. 689 above.
75 E.g. *British Sugar*, Comm. Dec. 88/518, note 7 above.
76 'Administrative monopolies' found in Case 26/75 *General Motors* v *Commission* [1975] ECR 1367, [1976] 1 CMLR 95; Case 226/84 *British Leyland* v *Commission* [1986] ECR 3263, [1987] 1 CMLR 185. Provisions such as Arts. 5, 30 and 90 may affect such state practices; see Ch. 27; even where lawful, such monopolies will gradually be eroded by Community legislative initiatives.
77 Cf. Art. 9, Merger Control Regulation and analogous discussion in the context of market definition in merger control, Ch. 25, pp. 818, 823.
78 Case T-83/91, judgment of 6 October 1994.
79 Comm. Dec. 92/163 *Tetra Pak* OJ 1992 L72/1, [1992] 4 CMLR 551.
80 See p. 782 below on the Commission's powers and policy on fines.

carried out with reference to a homogeneous relevant market covering the whole territory of the Community.[81] Furthermore, it should be realized that the increasing internationalization of markets should itself act as a means of controlling previously dominated or oligopolistic markets simply by injecting fresh competition. Opening up markets should itself reduce the need for legal control of monopolies at national level.[82]

Article 86 refers to conduct in the common market or 'in a substantial part of it'. The relevant market must, then, cross this *de minimis* threshold. It is well established that the test for substantiality relates to economic importance, not acreage.[83] It is accordingly appropriate to determine the production level in the relevant market in relation to overall Community output.[84] The territory of a single member state may constitute a substantial part of the common market.[85] Furthermore, it is plain that this test allows even a part of a single member state's economy to constitute a relevant market caught by Article 86 if it is sufficiently substantial.[86] Control of the activities of a firm dominant in one region of a single state would be subject to the requirement that an effect on trade between member states be shown, but this test, as explained, has been interpreted in a broad fashion that extends Community competence even into areas of apparently

---

81 The Commission had taken a similar approach to Community-wide market definition in an earlier decision involving Tetra Pak, Comm. Dec. 88/501, note 58 above and p. 713. The point was not at issue in Case T-51/89, note 22 above, where the Court upheld the Commission's decision. See similarly on market definition Comm. Dec. 88/138 *Hilti* OJ 1988 L65/19, [1989] 4 CMLR 677 upheld by the Court of First Instance in Case T-30/89 *Hilti* v *Commission* [1991] ECR II-1439, [1992] 4 CMLR 16 and, on appeal, by the European Court in Case C-53/92 *Hilti* v *Commission* [1994] ECR I-667, [1994] 4 CMLR 614.

82 Similar comments may be directed at the impact of integration on merger control; Ch. 25.

83 Cases 40–48, 50, 54–6, 111, 113–14/73 *Suiker Unie* v *Commission* [1975] ECR 1663, [1976] 1 CMLR 295.

84 Unlike the guidance provided by the Commission in relation to Art. 85, p. 694, there is no percentage cut-off to the application of Art. 86; see, e.g., AG Warner in Case 77/77 *Benzine en Petroleum Handelsmaatschappij (BP)* v *Commission* [1978] ECR 1513, [1978] 3 CMLR 174.

85 The Netherlands sufficed in *Michelin*, Case 322/81, note 57 above; in Case 77/77, note 84 above, AG Warner observed that he 'would shrink' from denying Luxembourg constituted a substantial part of the common market. See also Whish, *Competition Law*: 'Politically it might be incautious to hold that a Member State forms an insubstantial part of the EEC' (p. 269).

86 Cases 40/73 *et al.*, note 83 above. In *British Sugar*, Comm. Dec. 88/518, note 7 above Great Britain was held to be the relevant geographic market and a significant part of the common market. More remarkable still, the port of Holyhead was regarded as a substantial part in the context of the rejection of an application for interim measures in Dec. 94/19 *Sea Containers/Stena Sealink* [1994] 4 CMLR 513, OJ 1994 L15/8. Cf. the approach taken by the English High Court in *Cutsforth* v *Mansfield Inns* [1986] 1 CMLR I; regional market held too small.

purely national jurisdiction.[87] However, even an economically substantial market within a single state is not a relevant market for the purpose of Article 86 if it has no special characteristics that distinguish it from the wider market. In *Alsatel* v *Novasam*[88] the Court refused to hold conduct in a region of France subject to control under Article 86 where the market properly defined was constituted by the whole of France. So one must first define the relevant market and only then check that it constitutes a substantial part of the common market.

ASSESSING DOMINANCE

Indicators of dominance

Having defined the relevant market, it is necessary to determine whether the undertaking dominates that market: is it able to behave independently of competitive pressures, in accordance with the *United Brands* test?[89] This is simply a question of economic power.[90] The factor that is the most obvious indicator of dominance is market share. If an undertaking holds the entire market share and is unchallengeable, it is plainly dominant in that market. So the determination that Hugin was operative in a distinct market for spare parts for Hugin cash registers led inevitably to a finding of dominance.[91]

Market shares below 100 per cent may also confer dominance. A 75 per cent share, for example, doubtless yields effective independence from competitive influence. However, the analysis is dependent on market structure and each case must be treated on its own facts. A share of less than 50 per cent of the market is capable of conferring dominance on a firm. In *United Brands* the firm held some 40–45 per cent of the market in which it had been operating, but this was considered sufficient to label it dominant, given that the rest of the market was deeply fragmented. The second largest producer after United Brands held only 16 per cent of the market. The Court's analysis ranged beyond market share. It commented

---

87 Case 56/65, note 37 above.
88 Case 247/86 [1988] ECR 5987, [1990] 4 CMLR 434, noted by Shaw (1989) 14 ELRev 96. The Court also studiously avoided the notion of collective dominance; see p. 724 above.
89 Case 27/76, note 5 above.
90 See refs. under 'The Notion of Dominant Position' in Select Further Reading, also Jones and Viehoff, 'Assessing Market Dominance' in Maitland-Walker (ed.), *Towards 1992*
91 Case 22/78, note 35 above; but was the market defined too narrowly? see p. 741. See also *Hilti*, Comm. Dec. 88/138, note 81 above.

on the attacks by small competitors that United Brands had withstood without losing market share. United Brands was additionally shown to exercise significant control over production and selling networks. Its vertically integrated structure enhanced its power.[92] The presence of competition, then, does not rule out a finding of dominance. The Court looks for indicators of dominance, including market share but also embracing the structure of the firm and its conduct.[93]

Profit-making is not an essential element in dominance. In *United Brands* the Court accepted that short-term losses are not necessarily inconsistent with dominance. A particularly telling pointer was United Brands' ability to maintain its market position even when its prices remained higher than any competitor.[94] The position would have been quite different had United Brands held 40–45 per cent of the market, or even more, but had been faced with a similarly powerful competitor active in the market that also possessed well-developed production and sales methods.[95] The firms would have been in competition and there would be no call for monopoly control.[96] It is accordingly possible that market shares of 30 per cent or even lower may confer dominance on a firm, where the market is severely fragmented and where economic independence is ensured by, for example, the firm's vertically integrated structure and its grip on technology superior to its rivals. But remember: the firm will stand condemned, if at all, not for possessing those advantages, but for abusing them.[97]

The notion of the contestable market

The idea that markets include present and potential competitors should be recalled.[98] This idea of latent competition is among the most difficult problems to be confronted in the identification of a dominant position. It was on the basis that the Commission had failed to consider producers capable of entering the market through adaptation that the Court granted Continental Can's application for annulment.[99] So, even where a firm is

92 See also Case 85/76, note 34 above; Case 322/81, note 57 above; Case C-62/86 *AKZO* v *Commission*, [1991] ECR I-3359, [1993] 5 CMLR 215, noted by Smith [1991] 5 ECLR 205, Levy (1992) CMLRev 415.
93 A useful indicator is whether the firm is an unavoidable trading partner in that market; Case 85/76 note 34 above; Case T-83/91, note 78 above.
94 Case 27/76, note 5 above, para. 128. Market retention *per se* is inconclusive, for it may simply indicate successful and efficient competitive conduct; see Case 85/76, note 34 above, esp. para. 44 of the judgment.
95 See, e.g., *Ashland Oil/Cabot* 14th *Report on Competition Policy* 109.
96 Laws controlling cartels and, perhaps, oligopolies may, of course, be relevant. See also the possibility of collective dominance, p. 724.
97 See p. 742 below.
98 See p. 728.
99 Case 6/72, note 3 above and p. 731.

the sole producer presently active in the market, this does *not* necessarily confer on it a dominant position, provided it is subject to the influence of potential competition. If, when it raises its prices, it will be challenged by a market entrant undercutting those prices, then the independence from competition that is the hallmark of dominance is missing. The lower the barrier to challenge, the more competitive the market and the harder legal intervention is to justify. Low-entry barriers mean flexible and competitive markets.[100] Under Article 86, then, market share means share of the contestable market, which includes recognition of latent competition; one must assess not simply whether the producer is unchallenged, but also whether it is unchallengeable. The latter is potentially pernicious and calls for legal intervention; the former need not be a cause for concern.

Much economic analysis in recent years has been devoted to study of the nature of barriers that surround apparently isolated markets.[101] For many years markets were analysed with reference to the barriers to entry that shielded them from effective competition. The high cost of investment and the difficulty of obtaining supplies, outlets or technological know-how were viewed as entry barriers. Other barriers arise from geography. The single EC producer of widgets is not dominant if readily challengeable by firms from outside the EC.[102] But the EC market may not be capable of penetration by outside firms where legal or economic obstacles (such as high transport costs) exist. On a different level, the firm or firms that have already scaled barriers guarding the market may themselves raise barriers by, for example, aggressive marketing campaigns to encourage loyalty to existing brands, perhaps allied to discounts granted to customers,[103] or by striving to destroy a new market entrant by deliberate overproduction[104] and predatory pricing.[105] Government-sanctioned entry barriers include intellectual property law[106] and licensing requirements regulating, for example, quality standards, which are not infrequently introduced by

100 Industrial policy may, accordingly, be directed to improving flexibility by dismantling entry barriers; Geroski and Jacquemin, 'Industrial change, barriers to mobility and European industrial policy', in Jacquemin and Sapir (eds), *The European Internal Market.*
101 See seminal work by Bain, *Barriers to New Competition.* See also Geroski and Jacquemin in Jacquemin and Sapir (eds), *The European Internal Market.* For a useful summary in the legal context, see Frazer, *Monopoly, Competition and the Law,* pp. 11–13; Green, Hartley and Usher, *Single European Market,* pp. 212–15.
102 See Comm. Dec. 90/46 (*Alcatel Espace/ANT*) OJ 1990 L32/19, [1991] 4 CMLR 208, p. 713 above; IV/M/017 *Aérospatiale/MBB* OJ 1991 C59/13, p. 824 below.
103 Which may count as an abuse under Art. 86; p. 748 below.
104 Geroski and Jacquemin in Jacquemin and Sapir (eds), *The European Internal Market,* pp. 312–13. See also Vickers, 'Strategic competition among the few', (1985) Ox Rev Ec Pol 1/3 I.
105 Forestalling the development of a competitive market may count as an abuse of a dominant position; see p. 745.
106 See p. 836; Ch. 26.

governments on the initiative of existing market participants eager for shelter from competition.[107] Where such barriers are significant, the market is likely to be dominated by an existing participant or participants immune from challenge. The pernicious effects of monopoly – high prices, low innovation, unfair distribution[108] – may follow.

More recently, scepticism has grown about the true significance of entry barriers. Consider the costs of investment, such as buying machinery and obtaining technology. Such costs are faced by *all* firms wishing to enter the market. In meeting such costs the new firm is doing no more than the present incumbent(s) had to do. Assuming an absence of governmental regulation acting as a barrier, the only barrier that would really matter would be the economies of scale, if any, obtained by the incumbent(s) to which the new firm could not aspire as an initially small-scale entrant. A different version of the modern scepticism about the height of entry barriers holds that costs of purchasing plant and technology are not costs at all, provided that the purchaser can recover the costs of purchase if and when it decides to leave the market. The real obstacle is not the cost of entry but the cost of exit; the loss of funds that have been irretrievably sunk into the venture is the real impediment to entry into the market. It is, then, exit costs that really protect markets. In their absence (and in the absence of artificial governmental barriers),[109] the market is contestable.[110] Whether or not it is *currently* contested does not matter. The contestable market needs no monopoly regulation.

The influence of the exit-cost thinking can be observed in part in Community competition law. In *United Brands*[111] the Court examined the barriers to market entry, which included the large capital sums required to establish banana plantations; the financial and technical difficulties of developing a distribution system, particularly problematic in the case of a perishable product; and the costs of setting up a retail network and supporting the initiative with advertising campaigns. The Court added that whereas existing actors enjoy economies of scale in running their operations, newcomers do not. In this analysis of barriers to entry the Court demonstrated at least some appreciation of the exit barrier approach by adding a reference to 'costs . . . irrecoverable if the attempt fails'.[112]

107 Such state barriers to trade are susceptible to challenge under Arts. 30, 48, 59 *et al.*
108 See p. 718.
109 Which may be controlled under other Treaty provisions, e.g. notes 76, 106, 107 above; intellectual property rights may prove especially obstructive.
110 See, e.g., Baumol, 'Contestable Markets: an uprising in the theory of industry structure', (1982) 72 Am Ec Rev 1; cf. Shepherd, '"Contestability" vs. Competition', (1984) 74 Am Ec Rev 572.
111 Case 27/76, note 5 above.
112 ibid., para. 122.

Perceived interventionism in Community law

On several occasions reference has been made to criticism that EC competition law is unduly interventionist,[113] and in this area too that charge has been laid. It is said that the Commission and Court tend to overstate the importance of barriers to market entry and that consequently they are prone to intervene in markets that are not really suffering from domination at all.[114] In *Michelin*[115] the competition authorities adopted a remarkably short-term perspective in stressing the time it would take a new arrival on the tyre market to establish itself. Such a barrier may be serious if the incumbent enjoys significant economies of scale that will be denied a new entrant for several years. In such circumstances the incumbent will maintain control for some considerable time and the market may not be contestable. However, the Court commented only briefly on the time and investment required to modify production plant in accordance with switches in demand between different types of tyre and declared the absence of elasticity of supply established.[116] But if the simple fact of time to establish oneself is treated as a decisive entry barrier without the need to demonstrate how the time-gap is significant, then there is a virtual denial of the idea of the market that is uncontested but contestable.[117] The Court adopted this more sophisticated approach in *Continental Can*,[118] and *Michelin* seems, in comparison, inadequately reasoned and unnecessarily interventionist. In *Hilti*[119] the Commission was satisfied that markets could be adjudged distinct where more than small cost changes were needed to achieve interchangeability, and in *Tetra Pak*[120] the Commission, finding a distinct market, stressed the absence of competition from other suppliers in the short term. Neither market definition was disturbed by the Court of First Instance[121] nor, on appeal in *Hilti*, by the European Court.[122] Yet transient

---

113 See, e.g., p. 665.
114 See, e.g., discussion by Green, 'Article 85 in Perspective: Stretching Jurisdiction, Narrowing the Concept of a Restriction and Plugging a Few Gaps' [1988] ECLR 190.
115 Case 322/81, note 57 above.
116 ibid., para. 41.
117 See, e.g., Korah, 'From legal form toward economic efficiency – article 85(1) of the EEC treaty in contrast to U.S. antitrust' (1990) 35 *Antitrust Bulletin* 1009, 1013–14. Korah, *EC Competition Law and Practice*, p. 74 criticizes the geographic market definition in *Michelin* too.
118 Case 6/72, note 3 above.
119 Comm. Dec. 88/138, note 81 above.
120 Comm. Dec. 88/501, note 58 above. See also, in merger control, IV/M/214 *DuPont/ ICI* OJ 1993 L7/13, [1993] 5 CMLR M41 (carpet manufacturers would not substitute nylon for polypropylene fibres).
121 Case T-30/89, note 81 above; Case T-51/89, note 22 above, where the Commission's market definition was not challenged before the Court.
122 Case C-53/92 note 81 above.

power is not dominance.[123] The decision in *Hugin*,[124] where spare parts for a firm's own brand of cash register was held to constitute a distinct market, has received criticism for its unconvincing treatment of product substitutability[125] and a consequent market definition that was narrow enough to permit unnecessary intervention.[126] The decision ignores the existence of other producers and a healthy competitive environment in the servicing of those machines. In particular, Hugin could not operate in its own market for spare parts immune from the risk that it would quickly lose its trade in new machines to other suppliers if it acted arbitrarily. This constraint on the firm's independence should have been taken into account in market definition; and should have broadened it.[127]

The identification of entry barriers is a controversial issue, but, in contrast to American law, which has its critics for an unduly wide approach to market definition resultant on downplaying entry barriers,[128] one is left with an assessment of Article 86 that classifies it firmly with the interventionist stamp.[129] If the Community authorities have paid attention to insignificant entry barriers, then they have treated markets as rather less contestable than much influential economic literature would advise. This, in turn, confers important powers to control firms' behaviour; powers unavailable under the American approach, which dilutes market power assessment and hence legal power to intervene. Yet it must be remembered that the Community is not integrated in the North American fashion and national markets may be truly less contestable as a result of long-standing differences, such as language and currency. Moreover, even if one admits

123 See especially Baden Fuller, 'Article 86 EEC: Economic Analysis of the Existence of a Dominant Position', (1979) 4 ELRev 423. See the Opinion of AG Warner in Case 77/77, note 84 above ([1978] ECR at 1538), where doubt is cast on the narrowness of the Commission's market definition because of its emphasis on temporary control. The Court did not decide the point in *BP*; it annulled the decision on the basis that no abuse had occurred; see p. 751.

124 Case 22/78, note 35 above.

125 Baden Fuller, 'Article 86 EEC: Economic Analysis of the Existence of a Dominant Position' (1979) 4 ELRev 423. See Case 77/77, note 84 above, for a market definition limited unconvincingly to a single firm; narrowness was due to the tie of customer to supplier in crisis economic conditions, but these were temporary.

126 But on the facts no intervention due to absence of jurisdiction: see note 60 above.

127 Fox, 'Monopolization and Dominance in the US and the EC: Efficiency, Opportunity and Fairness', (1986) 61 ND LRev 1981, 1003. See also Pathak, 'Vertical Restraints in EEC Competition Law', [1988/2] LIEI 15, 44–8. See the parallel criticism of an unduly short-term perspective taken in Case 77/77, note 125 above.

128 E.g. Pitofsky, 'New Definitions of Relevant Market and the Assault on Antitrust', (1990) 90 Col LR 1806.

129 Although, remember, this analysis goes to establishing dominance, which is not unlawful. A separate assessment of abuse still needs to be undertaken; see below.

that the Community is overly interventionist, this approach is not necessarily improper. It may be that just as Article 85 is used in some circumstances primarily as a means of securing market integration, perhaps at the expense of a pure competition-only focus,[130] so Article 86 is being used to mould markets in a manner required by the Community's special task of market integration. Intervening in markets that in the medium or long term would correct themselves may be perfectly defensible where the policy agenda includes objectives beyond wealth maximization, such as accelerating market integration or, more controversial, elements of industrial policy such as special support for small- and medium-sized firms. Yet those other policies ought to be transparent. In turning to general discussion of the notion of abuse under Article 86, it may prove useful to reflect whether the Commission and Court have deliberately adopted an interventionist approach in order to further the cause of, *inter alia*, market integration.[131]

ABUSE

If dominance is established, the second stage in the Article 86 analysis asks whether the dominant position that the firm holds has been abused. Dominance is not unlawful *per se*, but the dominant firm bears a 'special responsibility' not to distort the conditions of competition on the market.[132] The preceding discussion of the existence of a dominant position has been essentially structural in its examination of the market. Now, the analysis includes behavioural elements; what is the effect of what the firm has actually done (or failed to do)?

The notion of abuse is deliberately left undefined in Article 86. It is designed to be a flexible notion capable of application to a range of practices that have an injurious effect irrespective of the label that might be attached to them.[133] The list in Article 86 is a useful illustration, but it is by no means exhaustive. Article 86 controls dominant firms engaging in practices, such as unfair pricing, that involve the exploitation of the position of economic strength. It also controls anticompetitive practices,

130 See p. 665.
131 See, e.g., Whish, *Competition Law*, pp. 279–80; Pathak, [1988/2] LIEI 15; Ehlermann, 'The Contribution of EC Competition Policy to the Single Market', (1992) 29 CMLRev 257, esp. 261.
132 Case 322/81, note 57 above, para. 57.
133 Since the focus is the effect of the practice, abuse is assessed objectively; see, e.g., Case 6/72, note 3 above; Case 85/76, note 34 above.

such as the tying of customers through loyalty rebates, which are apt to secure the firm's already significant immunity from competition. But categorization of abusive practices, though certainly useful for the purposes of analysis, is not essential in the application of Article 86. Any abuse is caught.

There is no exemption provision in Article 86 analogous to Article 85(3),[134] but the unstructured notion of the abuse permits the Commission to accommodate a *de facto* justification procedure under Article 86. If a practice is desirable, it will not be deemed abusive. One of the most interesting, and at times controversial, aspects of Article 86 is the interventionist power that is conferred on the competition authorities as a result of its vague nature. Several instances of allegedly improper policy-making are discussed in the course of the following analysis.

Before examining some practices that have been condemned as abuses of a dominant position, brief mention might be made of the merger. In *Continental Can*[135] the Court held that a merger is in principle capable of constituting an abuse[136] and may accordingly be forbidden under Article 86. A controversial interpretation at the time, its potentially unpredictable capacity to obstruct business deals was long viewed as a weakness in Article 86. However, the entry into force in 1990 of the Merger Control Regulation has for most purposes ousted the application of Article 86 to mergers and accordingly discussion of the merger is left until Chapter 25. The following pages examine practices that are plainly subject to Article 86 control.

UNFAIRLY HIGH PRICING

The opportunity for a dominant firm to hoist its prices freely is perhaps the most immediately obvious attribute of market power and independence from competition. Such pricing needs to be controlled. It is likely to prove inefficient, for it will distort the allocation of resources. It is also likely to prove unacceptable on distributional grounds, for it transfers wealth from the consumer into the hands of the already powerful enterprise.

The concept of the unfairly high price is straightforward; its practical application to particular pricing policies may not be. In *United Brands*[137] the Court declared that it is an abuse to charge a price 'which is excessive because it has no reasonable relation to the economic value of the product

---

134 See pp. 704–17.
135 Case 6/72, note 3 above.
136 The decision was annulled for inadequate market definition, see p. 731.
137 Case 27/76, note 5 above.

supplied'.[138] The Court suggested that a comparison should be made between selling price and cost of production in order to calculate the profit made. It held that United Brands had not been shown to be guilty of abusively high pricing (although it had committed other abuses).[139] The Commission had failed to examine the cost of United Brands' production with adequate care.[140]

The Court's approach is open to criticism.[141] It insists that the profit margin should be identified. This is in itself a complex calculation, for it may require assessment of, for example, the implications of long-term capital expenditure in fixing production cost. After determination of the profit margin, the Court accepts that the taking of profits is permissible. However, it insists that there is an upper limit beyond which profits represent the fruits of abuse.[142] The level at which this limit should be set is dependent on the facts of the particular case, and the Court's test of 'reasonable relation' between price and value is thoroughly unpredictable. Ideally, one ought to compare the price actually charged with the price that would have been chargeable in a competitive market, but there are severe difficulties in fixing this latter value in the abstract independently of the market. For example, in *British Leyland*[143] the Court held the fee demanded by the dominant firm for the performance of an inspection 'disproportionate to the economic value of the service provided'.[144] This implies an unstructured calculation of economic value uninformed by the price the competitive market would actually stand. Admittedly, it will sometimes be possible to make a comparison with prices charged by other firms operating in the sector. In *Ministère Public* v *Tournier*[145] the market

138 ibid., para. 250.
139 Discriminatory pricing, see p. 747; market partitioning, see p. 750; refusal to supply, see p. 752.
140 See discussion by, e.g., Van Bael and Bellis, *Competition Law* p. 578.
141 See, e.g., Sharpe, 'Pricing by an undertaking in a dominant position' in Maitland-Walker (ed.), *Towards 1992*. See generally Whish, *Competition Law*, Ch. 15.
142 Consider whether a firm taking only low profits because its production is inefficient and costs high (the quiet life of the monopolist) is acting abusively. If not, does that mean that dominance may be caught where it is used to reap excessive profits but not otherwise, even though the price actually charged may be identical in both cases and thus equally inefficient?
143 Case 226/84, note 76 above; in Case 26/75, note 76 above, the Commission's finding of abuse on these grounds was annulled by the Court.
144 Case 226/84, note 76 above, para. 30 of the judgment. The point should not be taken in isolation; BL was pursuing a broader policy of unlawful market partitioning; see Van Bael and Bellis, *Competition Law*, pp. 581–2. The phrase in the text also appears in Case C-323/93 *Société Civile Agricole du Centre d'Insémination de la Crespelle* v *Coopérative d'élevage et d'Insémination Artificielle du Département de la Mayenne*; judgment of 5 October 1994.
145 Case 395/87 [1989] ECR 2521, [1991] 4 CMLR 248. See also Cases 110, 241 and 242/88 *Lucazeau* v *SACEM* [1989] ECR 2811.

was limited by governmental intervention to France alone, which allowed comparison between charges imposed on the French market with those charged on other similarly limited markets.[146] However, given the assumption that the firm under scrutiny dominates the market, this comparison will often prove unreliable or even impossible, especially where markets are not limited geographically. Sometimes assistance may be derived from legislation.[147] However, in practice, the limit is often likely to be settled as a result of informal negotiation between firm and Commission,[148] which confers on the Commission an alarmingly unconstrained power to mould the economy in its preferred image.

UNFAIRLY LOW PRICING

Unfair pricing may take forms other than high pricing. Unfairly low pricing may also constitute an abuse. This is the notion of predatory pricing through which an already strong firm may seek to protect or enhance its existing market strength by squeezing potential competitors out of the market. This is achievable by a drastic price reduction that the strong firm is able to bear, but which forces the smaller firm, unable to follow, to abandon its plans to compete. There are, of course, short-term benefits to the consumer in the price reduction, but the elimination of competition will soon cause such advantages to vanish. A policy of low pricing is often simply a means of securing an ability to (re)impose a policy of high pricing. Article 86 accordingly forbids such practices; they affect market structure by suppressing competition. In a sense, of course, such behaviour is an attempt to raise entry barriers in order to ensure the market is non-contestable.[149] It is therefore an abuse of a dominant position to act in a manner that will suppress competitive entry and prejudice market flexibility. Article 86 ties the hands of the dominant firm so that the market may correct itself and, by market entry, perhaps ultimately deprive the firm of dominance. Competition can then flourish.

146 The Court stated that objective reasons remain capable of justifying price differences so uncovered; see I. Forrester and C. Norall, 'Competition Law' (1989) 9 YEL 271, 311–12. See further p. 835 below on abusive exploitation of intellectual property rights. See also Case 66/86, note 21 above.
147 In Case 66/86, note 21 above, the Court's discussion of air fares was guided by Comm. Dir. 87/601, which lays down criteria to be followed in approving tariffs. It states that tariffs must bear a reasonable relation to the long-term costs of the carrier, taking into account consumer needs, a satisfactory return on capital *et al.*: *quaere* if this is any more helpful than the general *United Brands* test, from which it is plainly drawn.
148 See p. 773.
149 See p. 737.

Perhaps unexpectedly,[150] there has been rather more academic analysis of the phenomenon of predatory pricing than formal decision-making to condemn such practices.[151] However, in *Ahmed Saeed*,[152] an Article 177 reference, the Court observed that low pricing may infringe Article 86 because of the exclusionary effect on other participants in the market. In *British Sugar*[153] the Commission found that the firm was charging X for raw sugar and Y for derived retail sugar. But the margin Y minus X was less than the cost of transformation from raw to retail. Other firms without independent access to raw sugar were thus unable to compete with British Sugar's prices at the retail level. British Sugar had cut its price in such a way that it could see off potential competition. This was held abusive. However, after these legal skirmishes, the leading case on predatory pricing under Article 86 is now the Court's long-delayed 1991 decision in *AKZO Chemie*.[154] The Court upheld the key elements of a 1985 Commission decision[155] condemning AKZO for the adoption of a strategy of predatory pricing as a method of securing its dominance of the organic peroxyde market. Fixed costs are those incurred on production and are independent of the number of units produced. Variable costs refer to those that fluctuate according to the level of production. The Court determined that prices below average variable costs set by a dominant firm aimed at eliminating a competitor are unlawful. Prices below average total costs (fixed plus variable), though above average variable costs, appear less reprehensible, but are still unlawful if part of a scheme to undermine a competitor's position in the market.

It seems that the guiding principle in predatory pricing is the effect that it has on the structure of the market. To reduce or exclude competition is to distort it in a manner incompatible with the Treaty.[156] In *Tetra Pak International SA v Commission*[157] the Court of First Instance upheld the Commission's view that Tetra Pak had engaged in such a pricing policy with this anticompetitive objective in mind. However, the key problem, as in unfairly high pricing, is how one differentiates the competitive price from the anticompetitive price. When, for example, does low pricing designed to stimulate demand violate Article 86 because of its exclusionary

---

150 Perhaps the threat of predatory pricing has been a more common abuse/entry barrier than the execution.
151 For examples, see refs. under 'Unfairly low pricing' in Select Further Reading.
152 Case 66/86, note 21 above.
153 Comm. Dec. 88/518, note 7 above.
154 Case C-62/86, note 92 above.
155 Comm. Dec. 85/609 OJ 1985 L374/1.
156 See Art. 3(g) EC relied upon for similar reasons in relation to mergers, Case 6/72, note 3 above and p. 807, and refusal to deal, Cases 6, 7/73, note 6 above and p. 751.
157 Case T-83/91, note 78 above.

effect on potential competitors? A case-by-case approach is necessary, which can only mean unpredictability, and the Court's ruling in *AKZO* is likely to mean that in practice the Commission will frequently be able to act informally to control the pricing policies of dominant firms – as has already been observed in relation to unfairly high pricing.

DISCRIMINATORY PRICING

Unfair pricing may also extend to pricing policies that tend to treat the Community as divisible into separate national markets. It is here that the market integrationist flavour of Community competition law asserts itself. Discriminatory pricing has been condemned under Article 86 as part of this policy. United Brands was found to have acted in violation of Article 86 by setting different price levels at Rotterdam, point of entry into the EC, for customers in different states:[158] German banana distributors paid considerably more than Irish distributors. The Court appears to have believed that pricing in accordance with local market conditions is permissible only where the firm is closely involved with and taking commercial risks on the local market in question. United Brands, importing into Rotterdam, was not so involved and was held to have acted abusively by adjusting its banana prices with reference to local market conditions, to which it, as an importer into Rotterdam, had not been subject. This appears rather odd in that it would encourage the firm to develop more integrated distribution networks in the Community in order to take advantage of this local market concession, whereas other Article 86 decisions betray mistrust of vertical integration as a tool of enhanced dominance and suppression of competition.[159] The ruling against price discrimination in *United Brands* may thus be taken as an example of an intense, overriding concern to accelerate market integration, although that goal may be viewed with some scepticism by consumers in low-price states, such as Ireland, where banana prices were driven upwards as a result of the judgment requiring price equalization at Rotterdam. Here, then, is a fine demonstration of the tensions between different policy objectives in this area.

Whatever misgivings one may have about the Court's view of price

---

158 Case 27/76, note 5 above, criticized by Korah, *EC Competition Law and Practice*, pp. 100–101; Whish, *Competition Law*, pp. 534–5. See further criticism by Bishop, 'Price Discrimination under Article 86 EEC: Political Economy in the European Court' (1981) 44 MLR 282; Zanon, 'Price Discrimination under Article 86 of the EEC Treaty: the United Brands Case' (1982) 31 ICLQ 36.
159 E.g., Cases 6, 7/73, note 6 above and pp. 737, 752.

discrimination in *United Brands*, abuse of this nature will certainly be treated all the more seriously where it is part of a scheme to discourage parallel imports, which, as frequently observed,[160] are the very lifeblood of the Community's process of market integration. So United Brands' overall policy, which included imposing restrictions on resale on its customers and deliberately undersupplying in order to eliminate sales beyond the customer's own markets, allowed a 'rigid partitioning of national markets . . . at price levels which were artificially different'.[161] This was held a serious violation of Article 86.[162]

TIES AND DISCOUNTS

Article 86 may be breached where a dominant firm seeks to tie suppliers or customers to it under long-term obligations. A similar breach may occur where a dominant firm selling product A insists that customers must also buy products B and C from it at the same time. Example (d) in Article 86 itself indicates that the inclusion of supplementary obligations of this type may count as abuses.[163] More subtle ties may be secured through loyalty rebates, which grant the supplier or customer discounts provided it commits itself to dealing with the dominant firm (often exclusively) over a long period. At first glance such practices may appear perfectly proper tactics and, indeed, an efficient method of securing supply and establishing distribution networks. However, it must be realized that where one is examining the conduct of a *dominant* firm, such ties are severely detrimental to the competitive structure of the market. The dominant firm that is able to lure other firms into its web is enabled to seal off potential markets from any other small firms that seek to compete with it and simultaneously to foreclose the opportunities of potential market entrants. The tie that is achieved through the discount or loyalty rebate may prove severely anti-competitive. Once again, an abuse may be found in a practice that raises barriers to market entry.

However, although the rationale for controlling discounts is clear, the practical application of the idea is complex. Not all discounts can be condemned; it is perfectly normal to offer some degree of incentive to the regular customer, especially if a major buyer. In *Hoffman la Roche* v

---

160 See, e.g., p. 664 above.
161 Case 27/76, note 5 above, para. 233. See also Case T-83/91, note 78 above.
162 Even in the absence of dominance such networks are likely to infringe Art. 85.
163 See, e.g., Comm. Dec. 88/518, note 7 above; Comm. Dec. 92/163 *Tetra Pak* note 79 above, upheld in Case T-83/91, note 78 above.

Commission[164] the Court upheld Commission condemnation of the firm's practice of granting substantial discounts to customers buying all or most of their vitamin requirements from Roche. The rationale was that the few competing suppliers were deprived of available markets by these practices. The market structure, already distorted by dominance, sustained further damage. The Court suggested that such rebates are permissible only where they are genuinely based on the transactions in question; for example, as a means of passing on the fruits of economies of scale. So a quantity discount, based exclusively on volume purchased, may prove permissible whereas a discount fixed according to the percentage of the buyer's total requirements bought from the dominant firm would not. The former, but not the latter, reflects costs actually saved by the seller on the deal. In *Coca-Cola*[165] the Commission was concerned about the effect of the conduct of the Coca-Cola Export Corporation on the cola soft drinks market in Italy.[166] Commission inquiry led to the firm giving an undertaking to omit a series of provisions from its agreements with distributors. First, Coca-Cola agreed to stop granting a rebate to customers willing to buy only Coca-Cola and no other cola-flavoured drink. By deleting this obligation, interbrand competition was promoted. Second, a variety of target rebates was disallowed. These rebates were paid when a certain threshold of sales of Coca-Cola products was passed and plainly encouraged distributors to concentrate on Coca-Cola to the exclusion of other brands. Finally, the firm agreed to abandon rebate systems that induced customers to buy other Coca-Cola products in addition to Coca-Cola itself. The Commission was however prepared to allow Coca-Cola to maintain rebates conditional on the display of advertising material by distributors.

UNFAIR/INEFFICIENT CONTRACTS

It should be apparent that cases involving tying through discounts are bilateral arrangements. The contracts entered into are capable of falling foul of Article 85. At the same time, the actions of the dominant firm in extending its influence by concluding such deals may constitute the abuse of a dominant position. So Articles 85 and 86 are both applicable. In *Ahmed Saeed*[167] the Court held that where an agreement between separate firms to fix prices on a particular airline route or routes is in reality the

---

164 Case 85/76, note 34 above, noted by Zanon (1981) 15 JWTL 305. See also Case 322/81, note 57 above. Case T-65/89 *BPB Industries and British Gypsum* v *Commission*, judgment of 1 April 1993, [1993] 5 CMLR 32; Case C-393/92, note 29 above.
165 Notice [1989] 4 CMLR 137, noted (1990) 10 YEL 407, 434.
166 Note the narrow scope of the relevant market; see pp. 734–5.
167 Case 66/86, note 21 above.

result of overbearing pressure imposed by a dominant firm on other firms active in the market, then both Articles 85[168] and 86 are capable of being invoked. Even where the agreements are freely entered into by the smaller firms, there may be a breach of Article 86, because the rationale for control is the objectively verifiable suppression of competition achieved by the extended commercial activity of the dominant firm. However, the separate identity of the two provisions was emphasized in the first of the two *Tetra Pak* cases,[169] where the Commission, upheld by the Court, decided that even if the agreement in question has received exemption under Article 85(3), its conclusion may none the less involve a breach of Article 86. Article 86 is aimed at controlling market power and has a function separate from Article 85.

As one would expect, a particularly grave breach of Article 86 consists of setting up a network of agreements under which smaller firms agree to export bans.[170] The agreements infringe Article 85; the construction of the network violates Article 86. Such market partitioning achieved by the exercise of market power is likely to incur severe penalties, for it violates the fundamental integrationist objective of the common market. One of the several abuses in *United Brands* was found in the imposition of controls over customers that led to market partitioning even though no explicit export ban was imposed.[171]

Finally, even if the powerful firm that imposes the unlawful agreement is not dominant within Article 86, it may still find itself subject to more severe sanction for breach of Article 85 than its unwilling partner.[172]

REFUSAL TO SUPPLY

Article 86 deprives a dominant firm of the ability to pick and choose its customers. Arbitrary decisions about whether or not to supply are capable of being held in violation of Article 86 as abuses of a dominant position. The fear that motivates this control is, of course, that the economically strong firm will act in such a way as to maximize its own power, thereby excluding existing or potential competitors. The objective of exercising

---

168 See p. 673 on the application of Article 85 to imposed agreements.
169 Comm. Dec. 88/501, note 58 above, upheld in Case T-51/89 note 22 above. The second of the two cases is Comm. Dec. 92/163, note 79 above, upheld in Case T-83/91, note 78 above.
170 See, e.g., Comm. Dec. 88/138 and Case T-30/89 and Case C-53/92, note 81 above; Case 226/84, note 76 above.
171 See Case 27/76, note 5 above, paras. 130–62.
172 E.g., Dec., 88/86 *Duffy Group/Quaker Oats* OJ 1988 L49/19, [1989] 4 CMLR 553, p. 673 above.

control over supply decisions is to avoid damage to the market beyond that already inherent in dominance.

The leading case is *Commercial Solvents* v *Commission*.[173] Commercial Solvents (CS) had been supplying an Italian firm, Zoja, with aminobutanol, an essential element in Zoja's business of manufacturing ethambutol, a derivative substance used in the treatment of tuberculosis. Zoja was one of only three ethambutol producers in the Community. CS decided to begin making and selling ethambutol itself. It refused to supply Zoja. Zoja could no longer manufacture ethambutol. It complained to the Commission.

The Commission's finding that CS had violated Article 86 was upheld by the Court. First, CS was held to occupy a dominant position in the aminobutanol market throughout the Community. Second, it was held to have abused that dominant position by refusing to supply Zoja, its customer. That refusal was likely to drive Zoja from the market. The decision clearly asserts a striking power of intrusion into corporate tactics as part of an interventionist policy to shape desirable market structures.[174] The decision can usefully be contrasted with that in *BP*.[175] The dispute arose out of the steep oil price rises and output reductions of 1973/4. BP reduced its oil deliveries to its customers by a more or less standard rate of 13 per cent, but in the case of ABG, a casual Dutch customer, the reduction was 73 per cent. On this occasion the Commission's finding that BP had abused its dominant position was annulled by the Court, which concluded that no abuse had been committed.[176]

Can one construct a general principle of the abusive refusal to deal from these contrasting decisions? Plainly one cannot, in the sense that all Article 86 abuses require assessment against the particular markets in which they occur, but one can certainly identify at least three material distinctions between the decisions in *Commercial Solvents* and *BP* for the purposes of future advice. First, Zoja was a regular, established customer; ABG was merely a casual customer and, indeed, ABG had already been advised by BP that as a result of BP's restructuring plans it ought to seek alternative sources of supply. The established customer, then, may be entitled to expect more favourable treatment as a result of the existing commercial relationship. Second, the elimination of Zoja, a major producer of ethambutol, would be seriously disruptive to the structure of the market;[177] no such concern attached to the position of ABG, a small actor in a broad market.

173 Cases 6, 7/73, note 6 above. See, e.g., Pathak [1989] ECLR 78.
174 For comment on an alleged paucity of economic reasoning by the Court, see Pathak [1988/2] LIEI 15, 19–28.
175 Cases 77/77, note 84 above.
176 There were also reasons for doubting the Commission's finding of dominance, see note 125 above, but the Court did not address this issue.
177 Explicit reference was made to Art. 3(f) EEC (now Art. 3(g) EC).

Third, CS planned to take advantage of the gap in the market that its refusal had created by expanding its own operations, thus securing vertical enhancement of its market power; BP had no such motivation. The first element relates to the status of the parties; the second to the structure of the market; the third embraces both. Plainly, then, a range of facts is properly taken into account in determining whether or not a refusal to supply constitutes an abuse under Article 86.

United Brands had reduced supplies of bananas to Olesen, a Danish distributor, complaining that Olesen had been giving a priority to Dole, a rival brand of bananas. The Court was forceful in its response. It declared that a dominant undertaking 'cannot stop supplying a long-standing customer who abides by regular commercial practice, if the orders placed by that customer are in no way out of the ordinary'.[178] The Court based this duty firmly on the aspirations of Article 3(f) EEC,[179] reasoning that refusal to supply would, if unchecked, distort competition by causing its reduction. The Court accepted that even dominant firms are permitted to take 'reasonable steps' to protect their commercial interests,[180] but concluded that United Brands had acted abusively, for its measures were likely to render still more effective its dominance of the market by suppressing competition from other brands of banana.[181]

In *BPB Industries and British Gypsum v Commission*[182] the applicants challenged a Commission decision that imposed fines on them for granting priority to orders placed by customers who did not stock imported plasterboard. The Commission viewed this as a method of deterring trade with potential suppliers who would have been capable of injecting competition into the market that, on the Commission's analysis, was dominated by the applicants. The Court rejected the application for annulment.[183] The Court insisted that, where supplies are short, a dominant firm must choose criteria on which to fulfil orders that are objectively justified. It was not acceptable for the dominant firm to favour 'loyal' customers. The applicants' policy was discriminatory in the sense that it offered equivalent services on unequal terms. The Court made reference to the exclusionary, anti-competitive effect of these tactics in upholding the Commission's finding of abuse.

One is left, then, with broad indications of policy, but a need for a careful appreciation of the nuances of Commission and Court decision-

---

178 Case 27/76, note 5 above, para. 182.
179 Now Art. 3(g) EC.
180 Case 27/76, note 5 above, para. 189 of the judgment.
181 See comment by Pathak, [1988/2] LIEI 15, 28–43.
182 Case T-65/89, judgment of 1 April 1993, [1993] 5 CMLR 32. See comment at (1993) ELRev *Competition Law Checklist* 50.
183 Excepting one small aspect only relating to the time of the infringement.

making in attempting to predict the margin of legitimate action by the dominant firm.[184] There is plainly a 'duty . . . to deal equitably'[185] with regular customers. A firm may refuse to deal only if it has objective justification for that refusal; objectivity appears to embrace both justification related to the position of the parties and justification arising out of market structure. There is doubtless a flavour of the familiar principle of proportionality. The dominant firm may react to 'misconduct' by firms with which it is linked, but the response must be proportionate to the potential harm,[186] bearing in mind the fact that, by definition, there is an imbalance of economic power between the firms involved. Similarly, where a firm wishes to maintain quality control or safety standards, its conduct must be apt to achieve those ends and no more restrictive than necessary. Unduly onerous conditions are abusive.[187]

In *RTE, BBC, ITP v Commission*[188] the Court of First Instance upheld a Commission decision that extended existing practice on refusal to supply by condemning for the first time a failure to supply in the absence of a pre-existing commercial relationship.[189] In the past all three television companies had printed their own separate guides to forthcoming programmes and used copyright protection to prevent third parties entering the market; a lucrative monopoly. It was held that the companies must make available their listings to any interested third party on request on payment of a reasonable fee. Both Commission and Court of First Instance were strongly influenced by the benefit to the consumer that would follow the availability of a single guide. The Court of First Instance was accordingly prepared to permit intervention in what it saw as a market that malfunctioned by failing to meet consumer demand.[190]

In *RTE and ITP v Commission*[191] the European Court dismissed appeals by the companies. The Court commented that the companies, the only

184 For further decisions, see, e.g., Case 22/78, note 35 above; Case 311/84 *Centre Belge-Telemarketing* v *CLT* [1985] ECR 3261, [1986] 2 CMLR 558.

185 Goyder, *EC Competition Law*, p. 355.

186 Case 27/76, note 5 above, para. 190 of the judgment; Comm. Dec. 87/500 *BBI/ Boosey and Hawkes* OJ 1987 L286/36, [1988] 4 CMLR 67.

187 Comm. Dec. 88/138 upheld in Case T-30/89/Case C-53/92, note 81 above. See also Case 27/76, note 5 above, para. 158; Case T-83/91, note 78 above. See control of such terms under Art. 85, p. 700 above.

188 Cases T-69/89 [1991] ECR II-485, T-70/89 [1991] ECR II-535 and T-76/89 [1991] ECR II-575 respectively, noted by Forrester [1992] 1 ECLR 5, 15; Alexander and Mellor (1992) 41 ICLQ 202.

189 Comm. Dec. 89/205 OJ 1989 L78/43, [1989] 4 CMLR 757.

190 See also Case C-41/90 *Höfner* v *Macrotron* [1991] ECR I-1979; an abuse of Arts. 86 and 90 where the state had regulated the market in such a way as to prevent supply meeting demand; examined further in Ch. 27, p. 863.

191 Cases C-241/91 P and C-242/91 P, judgment of 6 April 1995, [1995] All ER (EC) 416.

sources of the indispensable raw material needed for compiling a weekly guide, had prevented the appearance of a new product for which there was a potential consumer demand. No justification for refusal to license existed. Referring to its *Commercial Solvents* ruling, the Court added that the companies' unwillingness to supply the raw material had secured for themselves the secondary market for weekly guides. The ruling upholds the Court of First Instance's strong assertion of the use of Article 86 to override a refusal to supply, even where backed by national copyright protection, where the market is underdeveloped from the consumer perspective.

More generally, the Commission and Court have evidenced their concern to sustain and/or create vestiges of competition in dominated markets by insisting that an undertaking that dominates the provision of an essential facility acts abusively where it refuses its potential competitors access to that facility without objective justification or where it grants them access on less favourable terms than it enjoys itself. As part of this regulatory trend, it is now clear that a dominant firm may not discriminate in favour of its own activities in markets related to those that it dominates.[192]

Ultimately, the application of Article 86 rests with the Commission's view of market reordering. The flexible discretion of the Commission is remarkable. It is apparent from examination of the law relating to refusal to deal and the other examples discussed above that the most striking feature of the concept of abuse is its flexibility. Yet that is its very virtue. It is not possible to apply an effective monopoly control without providing this breadth. What matters, then, is the nature of the legal and political control exercised over the institutions(s) that administer these flexible legal provisions.

192 Case 311/84, note 184 above; Case C-18/88 *RTT* v *GB-INNO* [1991] ECR I-5941; *Aer Lingus/British Midland*, note 63 above; *Sea Containers/Stena Sealink*, note 86 above.

CHAPTER 24

Enforcement of Competition Law

Conduct contrary to Articles 85 and 86 is unlawful. No prior decision to that effect is required. However, the procedures for investigating and discovering suspected unlawful behaviour require careful attention. In addition, the methods for then establishing authoritatively whether action is unlawful or not must be studied.

Community competition law shares the principle of 'dual vigilance' with Community law generally.[1] There are two levels of enforcement; the first at Community level, the second at national level based on the principle of direct effect. Articles 12, 30, 48 *et al.* are enforced at Community level by Commission supervision, leading, if necessary, to Article 169 proceedings, and at national level by private individuals invoking their direct effect before national tribunals. The Community level/national level structure is also apparent in competition law, where the Commission is responsible for administration but the provisions are also susceptible to enforcement before national courts. The pattern is, however, complicated in relation to Article 85 because although the first two paragraphs are directly effective, Article 85(3), the exemption provision, is *not* directly effective. This distorts the enforcement of Article 85 before national courts and may leave litigants at national level dependent on Commission attitudes to the applicability of Article 85(3). The independence of the two limbs of 'dual vigilance' is accordingly compromised. In addition, the Commission's powers of investigation are so much greater than those available to the private litigant that successful identification of unlawful action may not be feasible at national level. The complainant will have to look to the Commission for support.

This chapter first examines the nature of the powers conferred upon the Commission to ensure that the rules relating to restrictive practices and dominant positions are observed. Thereafter, it examines the opportunities for enforcement at national level. It concludes by explaining where the two levels interrelate and by offering practical advice to the victim of

1 Case 26/62 *Van Gend en Loos* [1963] ECR 1, discussed in Ch. 11.

anticompetitive conduct on how best to use the available avenues of redress.

ENFORCEMENT BY THE COMMISSION

Article 87 of the Treaty required the Council to adopt measures designed to give effect to the principles of Articles 85 and 86. This was done in Regulation 17/62. This measure is the major source of the Commission's powers to apply the competition rules and confers upon it the duty to administer the competition rules and to secure their uniform observance throughout the Community. Subsequent legislation, such as Regulation 99/63 governing the conduct of hearings, has amplified the nature of the Commission's powers and duties. Regulation 17/62 is of broad scope and permits control of most sectors of the economy. There are certain specific excluded sectors, such as air and sea transport,[2] which escaped Commission supervision for many years.[3] However, more recent legislation has brought even these sectors within the ambit of Commission control by virtue of measures comparable in function to Regulation 17/62.[4] Thus, the analysis in this chapter, which focuses on Regulation 17/62, is broadly relevant even to these sectors.

Supervision of competition is one of the Commission's most important administrative tasks. It is carried out by DG IV, the Directorate-General for Competition.[5] The following analysis examines the Commission's procedures step by step, starting with initiation of an investigation, continuing through powers of inquiry to the consequences of an investigation. Finally, the supervisory capacity of the Court is discussed.

INITIATION OF THE COMMISSION'S INVESTIGATION

The Commission need not await external impetus to initiate an investigation. Article 3(1) of Regulation 17/62 declares that it may commence an inquiry on its own initiative. Part of the job of Commission officials is to

---

2 So too agriculture; see Bellamy and Child, *Common Market Law of Competition*, Ch. 14.
3 See Cases 209–13/84 *Ministère Public* v *Asjes* [1986] ECR 1457, [1986] 3 CMLR 173.
4 E.g. (initially, though subsequently amplified) Maritime Transport: Comm. Reg. 4056/86; Air Transport: Comm. Regs. 3975/87, 3976/87. See generally Greaves, *Transport Law of the EC*. Bellamy and Child, *Common Market Law of Competition*, Ch. 15.
5 See p. 53 on the internal structure of the Commission.

keep abreast of the business press in order to alert themselves to areas that might require scrutiny. Other potential sources for the initiation of an investigation include member states, and natural or legal persons claiming a legitimate interest, who may apply to the Commission to undertake an investigation.[6] The Commission makes available Form C for such complaints.[7] In addition, the parties themselves may alert the Commission to their plans; Form A/B must be used.[8] As is explained below, it is rarely in the interests of the parties to an agreement to conceal the deal from the Commission. Incentives are provided to firms to advise the Commission of their plans.

Some difficulties have arisen in relation to the status of an applicant whose complaint the Commission declines to pursue. Article 3(2) of Regulation 17/62's reference to application by 'natural or legal persons who claim a legitimate interest' poses two obvious questions: what is a legitimate interest, and, what rights does such a person have if the Commission's response is unfavourable? On the first point the Commission has adopted a flexible approach. Complaints from a wide variety of sources, including rival firms, customers and consumer representative organizations, have been accepted. In *Kawasaki*[9] the Commission responded to a complaint by an individual consumer affected by an export ban and put an end to the practice. Broadly, the Commission is concerned to avoid technicality on this point. On the second issue mentioned above the complainant's ideal outcome is that the Commission hold the disputed practice unlawful.[10] However, the Commission may instead rule the practice lawful.[11] The Court held in *Metro* v *Commission*[12] that the complainant responsible for the initiation of the investigation has standing under Article 173(4) to challenge the final decision.[13]

Alternatively, the Commission may decline to pursue the matter at all. If this happens, the complainant enjoys a right to be informed of the

---

6 Reg. 17/62, Art. 3.

7 English courts have recognized the public interest in maintaining complaints as a source of information for the Commission by protecting such complainants from defamation claims; *Hasselblad Ltd* v *Orbison* [1984] 3 CMLR 540 (CA), on which see Joshua, 'Information in EEC Competition Law Procedures' (1986) 11 ELRev 409, 428–9. This may be an application of Art. 5 EC; Temple Lang, 'Community Constitutional Law: Article 5 EEC Treaty' (1990) 27 CMLRev 645, 663.

8 Except for applications for Art. 86 negative clearance; see p. 777.

9 Comm. Dec. 79/68 OJ 1979 L16/9 [1979] 1 CMLR 448.

10 On interim measures to halt the practice see p. 781.

11 Note also the possibility that the complaint may prompt the adoption of a regulation; in relation to a complainant's challenge to an anti-dumping regulation, see Case 264/82 *Timex* v *Commission* [1985] ECR 849, [1985] 3 CMLR 550.

12 Case 26/76 [1977] ECR 1875.

13 See Ch. 8 on Art. 173.

reasons. This is conferred by Article 6 of Regulation 99/63, a measure adopted to amplify the procedural aspect of the Commission's powers under the competition rules. The complainant may typically then submit further argument. The Commission has no legislative duty to respond at all to those further submissions. However, in practice it tends to offer reasons for its continued refusal to proceed and this statement is itself amenable to challenge under Article 173.[14] The Court of First Instance has developed the law to the point where the Commission is obliged to provide a final, reasoned rejection of the complaint, notwithstanding the absence of any legislative provision to this effect. The Italian firm Automec, in particular, has provided the Court with fertile material.

Automec found itself excluded from the selective distribution network for BMW cars. Pursuant to Article 3(2) of Regulation 17/62, it complained to the Commission that the network was incompatible with Article 85(1).[15] Correspondence between Automec and the Commission ensued. In the course of this, Automec brought an application to annul a letter of 30 November 1988. This was ruled inadmissible. The letter was merely preliminary in nature and did not constitute an 'act' susceptible to annulment.[16] Finally, by letter of 28 February 1990, Automec learned that the Commission would take the matter no further. The Commission informed Automec that even if the network were found to infringe Article 85(1), it lacked the power to compel a producer to supply a would-be customer in the manner requested by Automec. The Commission also advised Automec of the value of proceedings before Italian courts. The Commission observed that an Italian court, like the Commission, could apply Article 85 – the notion of 'dual vigilance'[17] – but that national proceedings could also yield to Automec the remedy of damages unavailable through a Commission investigation. The Commission concluded that it was entitled to accord different levels of priority to matters brought to its attention and that in this instance there was no sufficient Community interest in pursuing the matter more fully.

Automec then challenged the validity of the final rejection letter of 28 February 1990 before the Court of First Instance. This application is commonly referred to as 'Automec II'.[18] The Court of First Instance ruled that the Commission had not acted unlawfully in informing Automec that

14 This happened in Cases 142, 156/84 *BAT and Reynolds* v *Commission* [1987] ECR 4487, [1988] 4 CMLR 24, on which see p. 808.
15 On selective distribution, see p. 700 above.
16 Case T-64/89 *Automec* v *Commission* [1990] ECR II-367. See Ch. 8, p. 221, on acts subject to review.
17 Note 1 above.
18 Case T-24/90 *Automec Srl* v *Commission* [1992] ECR II-2223, [1992] 5 CMLR 431;

it had no power to require goods to be supplied. Only a national court may interfere with the rule of freedom of contract by ordering traders to contract with each other.[19] The Commission's role is to put an end to the violation of Article 85, which is achievable by several methods, including the abandonment of the network, at the choice of the parties.

On the point of priorities in dealing with a complaint, the Court of First Instance took the opportunity to state its view of the legal consequences of receipt of a complaint by the Commission.[20] Article 6 of Regulation 99/63 confers an explicit legislative right on the complainant to be informed of the reasons why the Commission proposes to reject a complaint. Article 6 also provides the complainant with a right to submit observations thereupon. However, there is no explicit reference to any right to a final decision thereafter. Moreover, the Court of First Instance referred to *GEMA v Commission*[21] as authority for the proposition that complainants do not have a right to a decision on whether or not the alleged infringement has occurred. It must follow that the Commission has no duty to conduct a full investigation.[22] The Court then explained that it viewed the setting of priorities as an essential component of the task of administration and that the Commission was therefore acting entirely within its powers in making such choices.

The inability of the complainant to force the Commission to embark on an investigation does not, however, mean that a Commission decision to close the file is unreviewable in a challenge brought by that complainant. Despite the absence of explicit legislative provision, the Court of First Instance insisted that the Commission must examine the factual and legal aspects of the complaint with due care and it must give reasons for closing the file based on its allocation of priorities. These requirements were satisfied in relation to the Commission's treatment of Automec. Of broadest importance for the future, the Court of First Instance in *Automec II* stated

---

Case T-28/90 *Asia Motor France SA and others* v *Commission* [1992] ECR II-2285, [1992] 5 CMLR 431, noted by Drijber (1993) 30 CMLRev 1237, Shaw (1993) 18 ELRev 427. See generally Vesterdorf, 'Complaints concerning infringements of competition law within the context of European Community Law' (1994) 31 CMLRev 77.

19 In this respect the Commission's capacity to remedy violations of Art. 85 seems to differ in practice from its capacity to remedy violations of Art. 86; eg Cases 6 & 7/73 *Commercial Solvents* v *Commission* p. 751 above. This aspect of *Automec II* is examined by Cumming [1994] 1 ECLR 32 and see further p. 780 below.

20 Paras. 71–98 of the judgment.

21 Case 125/78 [1979] ECR 3173; see also Case T-3/90 *Prodifarma* v *Commission* [1991] ECR II-1.

22 The Court of First Instance also referred to Case 247/87 *Star Fruit* v *Commission* [1989] ECR 291, [1990] 1 CMLR 733 where the European Court confirmed the Commission's discretion in Art. 169 proceedings; in that context complainants enjoy *no* special status conferred by legislation. See further Ch. 7.

that the Commission is entitled to take account of the 'Community interest' in choosing priorities, although Article 190 EC dictates that it must provide reasons for its perceptions in this regard. The 'Community interest' might embrace, according to the Court, the importance of the alleged violation for the operation of the market; the likelihood of establishing a violation; and the extent of investigation required. The Commission's reason in the case for declining to proceed was the availability to the complainant of proceedings at national level, which had indeed already been initiated by Automec. The Court checked whether the Commission had properly identified the scope of protection at national level. The Court pointed out that the national court could examine the network in the light of Article 85(1) and could assess whether it benefited from a block exemption under Regulation 123/85.[23] The national court is also able to protect the rights of individuals prejudiced by violation of the Treaty competition rules; and Automec had not shown that Italian law was deficient in the scope of available remedies. The Court therefore found no basis for annulling the Commission's letter and dismissed Automec's application.

The ruling in *Automec II* confirms that there is no duty to investigate alleged anti-competitive practices when a complaint is made. However, it establishes that a final decision on a complaint is required under Community law. That final decision may be extracted by means of an Article 175 action, if necessary, and it is susceptible to review under Article 173. However, the Court of First Instance allows the Commission considerable flexibility in choosing its priorities. This was absorbed by the Commission in its 1993 Notice on cooperation between national courts and the Commission[24] in which it set out its intention to concentrate on cases 'having particular political, economic or legal significance for the Community'.[25] An adequately reasoned explanation from this perspective of why the Commission prefers not to investigate the substance of a complaint is unlikely to be successfully challenged. So in *BEMIM* v *Commission* the Court of First Instance accepted that the Commission had acted properly in declining to pursue a complaint relating to practices that were essentially confined to the territory of a single member state, France.[26] The complainant is then left with the remaining possibility of pursuing the matter by proceeding at national level. This avenue is examined fully at p. 789 below.

23 Page 700 above.
24 OJ 1993 C39/6, considered further at p. 793 below.
25 Para. 14 of the Notice. In its *Annual Report on Competition Policy* for 1993 the Commission expresses an intention to use its discretion to refer complainants to national level 'with moderation' (p. 120).
26 Case T-114/92, judgment of 24 January 1995 and, similarly, Case T-5/93 *Roger Tremblay and others* v *SELL*, judgment of 24 January 1995.

However, the *Automec II* ruling left open the prospect of annulment of a refusal to proceed where the Commission's assessment is shown to be erroneous. For example, had it been shown in *Automec II* that the Commission had misapprehended the scope of protection at national level, its decision not to pursue the matter would have been flawed and susceptible to annulment. In *BEMIM* v *Commission* the Court asserted the proviso that adequate safeguards for the complainant must exist at national level, although there was in the case no specific evidence of inadequacy within the French system.[27] This secures the complainant's right to have the complaint properly considered. In *BEUC* v *Commission*[28] the Court of First Instance confirmed that it will review the Commission's reasons for rejecting a complaint. It annulled a decision not to pursue a complaint lodged by BEUC, a consumer representative organization.[29] BEUC had complained to the Commission about an agreement between the British Society of Motor Manufacturers and Traders (SMMT) and the Japan Automobile Manufacturers Association (JAMA) which restricted the export of Japanese cars to the United Kingdom. BEUC alleged violations of both Articles 85 and 86 EC. An exchange of correspondence between BEUC and the Commission ensued. In a letter of 17 March 1992 the Commission explained that it saw no Community interest in investigating the matter further. It commented that in July 1991 the Commission had come to an arrangement on motor vehicles with the Japanese authorities. In the light of this the Commission had no reason to doubt that the SMMT/JAMA arrangement would end by the start of 1993.

The Court of First Instance first ruled that the letter amounted to a final rejection of BEUC's complaint and that it was therefore susceptible to review. The Court of First Instance then identified a number of flaws in the Commission's reasons for declining to investigate. The Commission's belief that the agreement would come to an end before the start of 1993 was not supported by the documents inspected by the Court. There was significant evidence that the agreement might persist thereafter until as late as the end of 1999. This amounted to a manifest error of assessment on the part of the Commission such as to support the application for annulment. The Commission had also referred to the United Kingdom authorities' willingness to permit the agreement. The Court pointed out that it is well established in Community law that such permission is irrelevant to the

27 Case T-114/92 and Case T-5/93, note 26 above.
28 Case T-37/92 [1994] ECR II-285 noted by Shaw (1995) 20 ELRev 66, 91; Stroud [1994] 5 ECLR 272. See also Case T-7/92 *Asia Motor France* v *Commission* (No. 2) [1993] ECR II-669, [1994] 1 CMLR 30.
29 Bureau Européen des Unions de Consommateurs.

application of Article 85.[30] Nor was the reference in the decision to an absence of significant effect on interstate trade sufficiently well reasoned. The application for annulment was successful.

The Court of First Instance has moved far beyond the absence in Regulation 99/63 of any explicit right vested in a complainant to a formal reasoned rejection. In summary, the Commission is not obliged to investigate alleged infringements, but it must now offer a reasoned and reviewable decision when it finally declines to pursue a complaint. In order to provide such a decision, the Commission will in practice be obliged to engage in at least some initial inquiry into the matter.

Where the Commission has properly declined to proceed, the complainant must pursue the matter at national level. The scope of Community law applicable to such litigation has developed considerably in recent years. It is examined at p. 789 below.

THE POWERS OF THE COMMISSION

Regulation 17/62 confers on the Commission extensive powers to investigate firms that are suspected of acting in violation of the competition rules. These range from the collection of information by request to its accumulation through visits to premises, perhaps even unannounced. The Commission may also investigate sectors of the economy where anticompetitive conduct is suspected.[31] Even though the Regulation incorporates safeguards for the firm under investigation and even though many cases turning on the propriety of the Commission's behaviour have been brought before the Court, there remains concern about the breadth of the Commission's powers.[32] Without at this stage judging the merits of this debate, there is no doubt that the nature of the Commission's powers is distinct from those familiar to the lawyer in the United Kingdom.[33] Moreover, the significance for business of the Commission arriving unexpectedly 'on the doorstep' cannot be underestimated. Accurate legal advice is essential in such circumstances.

Regulation 17/62, Article 11

Acquisition of information is achieved by two separate procedures under

30 See Ch. 27, p. 873.
31 Reg. 17/62, Art. 12.
32 See Select Further Reading, p. 914, under *The Powers of the Commission*.
33 For a valuable comparative study, see Joshua, 'Proof in Contested EEC Competition Cases: A Comparison with the Rules of Evidence in Common Law', (1987) 12 ELRev 315, and 'Information in EEC Competition Law Procedures' (1986) 11 ELRev 409.

Regulation 17/62: Articles 11 and 14. Article 11 is the simple request for information and occupies two stages. First, the Commission lodges an informal request with the firm. If this is not complied with, the Commission may move to the second stage under Article 11(5), at which it requires the supply of the information. That request is backed by the sanction of a fine if ignored and, because of its legal consequences, it is a decision that the firm may challenge before the Court using Article 173(4).

Article 11 empowers the Commission to obtain 'all necessary information'. In *Samenwerkende* v *Commission*[34] the Court of First Instance held that there must be a link between the information requested and the infringement under investigation. Moreover, the obligation to supply information should not represent a burden on the firm disproportionate to the requirements of the investigation. On the facts of the case there was no reason to impugn the Commission's decision. The European Court dismissed an appeal by Samenwerkende.[35] Unusually, the judgment simply refers to Advocate-General Jacobs' Opinion for the reasons for rejecting submissions that the conditions for exercising the power under Article 11 were not met. The Advocate-General accepted that the Commission must reasonably suppose at the time of requesting that the document would help it to determine whether the alleged infringement had occurred. This seems to raise a slightly higher threshold than was envisaged by the Court of First Instance, but on the facts there was no evidence of the Commission having failed to comply with this requirement.[36]

The answer given by the firm must not mislead, but the Court decided in *Orkem* v *Commission*[37] that the request for information may not force the firm to admit the existence of a Treaty violation that it is the Commission's task to demonstrate. There is, then, protection against self-incrimination as an element in a fair hearing.[38]

The extent to which information gathered by the Commission remains confidential is of major significance to the firm under investigation. The European Court's ruling in *Samenwerkende*[39] explored issues of

---

34 Case T-39/90, [1991] ECR II-1497.
35 Case C-36/92 P *Samenwerkende Elektriciteits-produktiebedrijven NV (SEP)* v *Commission* [1994] ECR I-1911, noted by Shaw (1995) 20 ELRev 66, 87.
36 A complaint of disproportionate action in moving from Art. 11(1) to 11(5) was rejected in Case T-46/92 *The Scottish Football Association* v *Commission*, judgment of 9 November 1994.
37 Case 374/87 [1989] ECR 3283, [1991] 4 CMLR 502, noted by Kinsella [1991] E Bus LR 31.
38 In Case C-60/92 *Otto BV* v *Postbank NV*, judgment of 10 November 1993, noted by Cumming [1994] 6 ECLR 335, the Court declined to require that this principle be applied in proceedings at national level.
39 Case C-36/92 P, note 35 above.

confidentiality in some depth. The applicant's business was electricity generation and it used natural gas in the process. It had in the past acquired its gas from Gasunie, the Dutch state supplier, but it had been exploring the possibility of buying from Statoil, a Norwegian firm. One of the documents that the Commission requested concerned Samenwerkende's terms of business with Statoil. Were the Commission to transmit documents to the competent authorities of the member states, as provided for in Article 10(1) of Regulation 17/62, they would fall into the hands of, *inter alia*, the Dutch authorities. Samenwerkende claimed that the threat that confidential information about Statoil's terms would be released into, ultimately, the hands of the state-owned Gasunie justified its refusal to surrender the documents to the Commission.

The Court of First Instance disagreed with Samenwerkende. Its appeal to the European Court failed. Both Courts considered that Community law contained adequate protection for the undertaking's interest in confidentiality. However, the two Courts differed sharply on the precise location of that protection. The Court of First Instance had relied on Article 20 of Regulation 17/62. It envisaged tight restrictions on use of information transmitted to national authorities. The European Court in the so-called 'Spanish Banks' case[40] had held that national officials are obliged by Article 20(2) of Regulation 17/62 not to disclose information acquired as a result of the application of Regulation 17/62 where that information is covered by the obligation of professional secrecy. Accordingly such information may not be used as the basis for a decision at national level based on competition law, although it might provide the impetus for the initiation of a separate inquiry. However, in *Samenwerkende* the European Court disagreed with the Court of First Instance's view that this amounted to a sufficient safeguard. Once Dutch officials had seen Statoil's terms in the context of the administration of competition policy, they could not be expected to forget those terms if they found themselves involved in planning Gasunie's strategy. Article 20 of Regulation 17/62 did not adequately protect confidentiality. The European Court proceeded to find an adequate protection located in 'the general principle of the right of undertakings to the protection of their business secrets, a principle which finds expression in Article 214 of the Treaty and various provisions of Regulation No. 17, such as Articles 19(3), 20(2) and 21(2)'.[41] The Court then insisted that this principle governed the Commission's handling of transmission of documents to national authorities under Article 10 of

40 Case C-67/91 *Dirección General de la Defensa de la Competencia* v *Asociación Española de Banca Privada and others* [1992] ECR I-4785.
41 Para. 36 of the judgment, citing Case 53/85 *AKZO Chemie* v *Commission* [1986] ECR 1965; see page 768 below.

Regulation 17/62. The undertaking that claims the confidential nature of documents is entitled to receive from the Commission a decision on whether or not it proposes to release them to national authorities, and there must be opportunity for the undertaking to seek judicial review before the Commission implements its decision. This offered adequate protection to Samenwerkende's right to confidentiality and the Court therefore concluded that it was not justified in refusing to supply the contested documents to the Commission.

The Court's identification of a general principle of confidentiality represents an important method of safeguarding the interests of undertakings that are subject to a Commission inquiry. As a general principle, it applies to all aspects of investigations and there is no need to identify a specific provision in secondary legislation on which to base a claim to confidentiality.

It is submitted that effective protection of confidential information is better secured within the Commission than at national level. Once it is released to national authorities, control over its use is in practical terms limited. It is possible that the Court in *Samenwerkende* has responded to criticism that its 'Spanish Banks' ruling envisages an entirely unrealistic willingness of national authorities scrupulously to limit information supplied by the Commission to use in connection with Community competition policy.[42] It does not seem plausible that firms are adequately protected by the Court's instruction in 'Spanish Banks' to national authorities to start a fresh inquiry. Those authorities are, after all, fully aware by that stage of precisely what they are looking for in any such inquiry. Future developments in this area of judicial control seem likely both in defining the nature of the Commission's relationship with national authorities and in pinning down more precisely where the distinction lies between confidential information and mere commercially useful information.[43]

Regulation 17/62, Article 14

Article 14 of Regulation 17/62 is an immensely more powerful provision than Article 11. It forms the basis of the Commission's often well-publicized raids. Article 14(1) empowers the Commission to undertake 'all necessary investigations into undertakings' and specifies *inter alia* entering premises, the examination of books and asking for on-the-spot oral explanations. The officials may take photocopies of documents. Article 14(3)

---

42 Cf. Forrester and Norall (1992) 12 YEL 547, 631 who comment of 'Spanish Banks' that '[t]here are few practitioners who will not read this judgment with a certain chill'.
43 On this latter point see Joshua, 'Balancing the Public Interests: Confidentiality, Trade Secrets and Disclosure of Evidence in EC Competition Procedures' [1994] 2 ECLR 68.

declares that undertakings are to submit to procedures ordered by a Commission decision, although they have a right to seek review by the Court.[44] The nature of the Article 14 procedure and the safeguards that exist for the investigated firm have been developed by the Court in challenges to Commission practice.

First, it is clear that Article 14 is distinct from Article 11 in that it does *not* envisage a two-stage procedure. There is no need to give the firm an informal chance to comply before moving to the formal stage of the procedure. The Court declared in *National Panasonic v Commission*[45] that the Commission may choose between an initial request followed by formal action and immediate formal action. In the latter instance the firm is obliged to comply with the decision, even though it has no prior warning. This allows the Commission to catch the firm unawares, which may be important for effective enforcement, but may also be seen as a significant intrusion on the firm's right to privacy. In *Hoechst v Commission*[46] the firm was held to have acted unlawfully in excluding Commission officials investigating an alleged cartel on the basis that they did not possess a valid German search-warrant. The Court held that the decision under Article 14 is sufficient on its own to entitle the Commission to gain access, even though it is administrative rather than judicial in origin.

A firm that refuses to admit officials duly armed with an Article 14(3) decision faces two major consequences. The first is that entry may be secured with the assistance of the national authorities; Article 14(6) obliges the authorities to offer the necessary support. In English law this would mean an application for an injunction, perhaps of an interlocutory nature, perhaps even *ex parte*.[47] *Hoechst* emphasizes that in such proceedings it is proper to offer the firm the appropriate procedural safeguards under national law, but that the effective enforcement of the rules cannot be obstructed. This means that the national court may not question the Commission's decision that an investigation is needed.[48] However, the Commission officials may not gain immediate access if denied entry unless relevant national procedures have been followed.[49] The second consequence

---

44 Inadequate reasoning might form the basis for such a challenge, but this argument failed in Case 136/79 *National Panasonic* [1980] ECR 2033, [1980] 3 CMLR 169; Cases 46/87 and 227/88 *Hoechst v Commission*, [1989] ECR 2859, [1991] 4 CMLR 410, noted by Lauwaars (1990) 27 CMLRev 355; Shaw (1990) 15 ELRev 326 and Case 5/85 *AKZO v Commission* [1986] ECR 2585, [1987] 3 CMLR 716.

45 Case 136/79, note 44 above.

46 Case 46/87 and 227/88, note 44 above.

47 See Cases 46/87 and 227/88, note 44 above, para. 32 of the judgment.

48 Cases 46/87 and 227/88, note 44 above, para. 35 of the judgment. The appropriate forum for such a challenge is the Court of First Instance, see p. 785.

49 *Quaere* whether this suggests a need for harmonization of procedural rules to prevent discrepancies between states, or whether such divergence is an aspect of the principle of subsidiarity.

of the firm's refusal is that it will be subject to financial penalties.[50] Hoechst was fined 1,000 ECU for each of the fifty-five days between its initial denial of entry to the Commission officials and eventual access, gained with the help of the *Bundeskartellamt* using a warrant issued by a German court. This sanction undermines, perhaps even contradicts, the firm's ability to force the inspectors to pursue national procedures and respect national safeguards if denied entry, yet, short of permitting Commission officials the power to effect entry by force, it seems essential in order to ensure that Article 14 works effectively.

Article 14, then, implies a balance between effective Commission investigation and adequate protection for the rights of the firm. The Court has often been obliged to weigh that balance. It has endeavoured to meet some of the criticism of the power vested in the Commission by paying close regard to control founded in the protection of fundamental rights. In *Musique Diffusion Française* v *Commission*[51] it rejected the claim that the Commission was subject to Article 6 of the European Convention on Human Rights, which concerns the right to a fair trial before a tribunal, holding that the Commission was not a tribunal for these purposes. However, it added that the Commission is subject to the rules of Community law that offer protection to the party under investigation. The Court has increasingly acknowledged that these Community rules embrace many of the rights protected under the European Convention. Fundamental rights are embedded in the Community legal order and, if breached, will provide the basis for the annulment of a Commission decision.[52] In *National Panasonic*[53] the Court accepted the importance of adherence to fundamental rights, but found no violation on the facts. In *Hoechst*[54] the Court accepted that the firm had a right to a fair hearing, but held that the right had been respected. The Court also showed deference to the right to the inviolability of the home, but held that it applied to private dwellings, not to business premises.[55] However, it added that both natural and legal persons pursuing private activities are entitled to protection against arbitrary or disproportionate intervention by public authorities.[56] The Court is concerned to uphold fundamental rights in the Community legal order both as a matter of general principle and in the particular context of the

---

50 See p. 782.
51 Cases 100–103/80 (the 'Pioneer Cartel') [1983] ECR 1825, [1983] 3 CMLR 221.
52 Edward, 'Constitutional Rules of Community Law in EEC Competition Cases' (1989) Fordham Corp L Inst 384. See further Ch. 8.
53 Case 136/79, note 44 above.
54 Cases 46/87 and 227/88, note 44 above.
55 See also Case 85/87 *Dow Benelux* v *Commission* [1989] ECR 3137, [1991] 4 CMLR 410.
56 ibid., para. 19 of the judgment.

administration of Regulation 17/62, but found no violation on the facts of these cases.

Once the Commission officials have actually obtained entry to the premises, the firm may have an interest in shielding documents from their gaze. Here, too, the Court has striven to balance the needs of effective enforcement against the rights of the defence. In *AM & S v Commission*[57] the Court held that professional privilege attached to some, but not all, documents. Drawing on national rules governing confidentiality, it held that under Community law the Commission is not entitled to see documents relating to rights of defence that have been submitted by independent lawyers.[58] This privilege does not extend to in-house legal advice and, indeed, in *John Deere*[59] the Commission increased the level of the fine imposed when it gleaned from such documents that the firm had been advised that it ran the risk of violating EC competition law but chose to persist with the export bans regardless.[60] In *AKZO v Commission*[61] the Court held that the Commission owes a general duty of confidentiality in the conduct of its investigations. This is based on Article 214 of the Treaty and is amplified in Regulation 17/62.[62] The precise application of this duty will depend on the individual case and the balance between the effective administration of the Commission's powers and the legitimate interests of the firm and, in some cases, of third parties.[63] The role of the general principle of confidentiality in the context of transmission of information from Commission to national authorities was thoroughly examined by the European Court in *Samenwerkende Elektriciteits-produktiebedrijven NV (SEP) v Commission*, which was examined above in the context of information-gathering under Article 11 of Regulation 17/62.[64] It bears repetition that the Court's identification of the confidentiality principle as a general basis for the control of the exercise of the Commission's powers is of the highest practical significance.

When in the course of an investigation the Commission acquires information that suggests that breaches may have occurred other than those

57 Case 155/79 [1982] ECR 1575.
58 The Court insisted that the question whether a particular document is privileged or not is ultimately a question for it (now the Court of First Instance), reviewing a Commission decision, rather than a national tribunal.
59 Comm. Dec. 85/79 OJ 1985 L35/58 [1985] 2 CMLR 554.
60 See p. 782 on fines.
61 Case 53/85 [1986] ECR 1965, [1987] 1 CMLR 231, noted by Shaw (1987) 12 ELRev 199, 202.
62 See Arts. 19(3), 20, 21(2); Lavoie, 'The Investigative Powers of the Commission with respect to Business Secrets under Community Competition Rules' (1992) 17 ELRev 20.
63 See Case 145/83 *Adams v Commission* [1985] ECR 3539, [1986] 1 CMLR 506.
64 Case C-36/92 P, note 35 above.

referred to in the decisions authorizing the officials' actions, it may not make such broader use of the materials in that investigation.[65] However, the Commission is at liberty to initiate a fresh inquiry specifically based on the new information. The firm cannot then complain that its rights have been inadequately protected.[66]

The scope of the Commission's powers and the available sanctions strongly suggest that a firm that finds itself under investigation is well advised immediately to adopt a cooperative approach. This is wise if only to ensure that it is able quickly to appreciate and correct any misapprehensions that the Commission might entertain about its practices. It is essential to be aware that the Commission's procedure is *not* adversarial. The Commission is the adjudicator; there is no independent jury to impress.[67]

Regulation 17/62, Article 19, and Regulation 99/63

Article 19 of Regulation 17/62 provides rights to a hearing, which are amplified in Regulation 99/63. These must be respected before the Commission may adopt the measures referred to below.[68] Such rights are plainly key components of any system of procedural safeguard against administrative power. Since 1982 a Hearing Officer has supervised the conduct of the hearing in order to enhance the commitment to fair procedure.[69] The firm subject to investigation is entitled to be presented with a 'statement of objections' in which it is informed of the objections raised against it and to submit observations within the stipulated time-limit.[70] A hearing before the Hearing Officer is then arranged. The terms of reference of the Hearing Officer were clarified in a decision adopted by the Commission in December 1994.[71] The Officer's role is to contribute to the objectivity of the hearing and of any decision subsequently made. The terms of reference embrace not only the need to respect rights of defence, but also the importance of securing the effective application of the competition rules. There are two Hearing Officers in Directorate-General IV. One deals with mergers, the other with general competition cases.

The Commission cannot subsequently condemn the firm for practices

---

65 Reg. 17/62, Art. 20.
66 Case 85/87, note 55 above.
67 See further Korah, *EC Competition Law and Practice*, pp. 117–23; Joshua (1986) 12 ELRev 409, esp. 415–16.
68 See pp. 773–85.
69 Johannes, 'The Role of the Hearing Officer' (1989) Fordham Corp L Inst 347. For scepticism, see Van Bael and Bellis, *Competition Law*, pp. 749–75. See also Kerse, 'Procedures in EC Competition Cases: The Oral Hearing' [1994] 1 ECLR 40.
70 Reg. 99/63, Art. 2.
71 Dec. 94/810 OJ 1994 L330/67.

not included in the statement of objections on which it has had no opportunity to comment. Third parties with a legitimate interest enjoy qualified rights to a hearing.[72] The rights of third parties to participate may have to be balanced against the demands of confidentiality.[73] In *AKZO* v *Commission* the Court, alert to the risk that a complainant may abuse rights to participate in the conduct of investigation as a means to gain access to a competitor's plans, insisted that business secrets enjoy 'very special protection'.[74]

The Court considers that the provisions dealing with the right to be heard contained in Regulations 17/62 and 99/63 are simply applications of a general principle of Community administrative law.[75] In *Transocean Marine Paint* v *Commission*,[76] which concerned the renewal of an exemption on conditions, rather than an infringement decision, and was therefore not squarely covered by the hearing provisions of Regulation 99/63, the Court observed that in order to provide a genuine and effective hearing the parties must receive sufficient information about the nature of the Commission's intent. The case is remarkable for an example of the development of Community law through a comparative survey of national law in this area by Advocate-General Warner,[77] and culminated in the annulment of part of the Commission's Exemption Decision because the firm had been given inadequate advance notice of the Commission's views.

General principles and the European Convention

The Commission enjoys remarkably extensive investigative powers. This is necessary in order to secure the effective practical application of the competition rules, which are essential to the operation of the free and fair

---

72 Reg. 17/62, Art. 19(2); Reg. 99/63, Art. 5; note also Reg. 17/62, Art. 19(3).

73 See Cases 142, 156/84, note 14 above. Case T-65/89 *BPB Industries and British Gypsum* v *Commission*, judgment of 1 April 1993, [1993] 5 CMLR 32.

74 Case 53/85, note 18 above, para. 28 of the judgment; see Lavoie (1992) 17 ELRev 20; Vesterdorf, note 18 above; Doherty, 'Playing Poker with the Commission: Rights of Access to the Commission's File in Competition Cases' [1994] 1 ECLR 8. The same theme underlies the rulings in Case T-7/89 *Hercules* v *Commission* [1991] ECR II-1711 and Case C-36/92 P, note 35 above. A third party may also have rights to confidentiality; for a regrettable failure in this respect by the Commission see Case 145/83, note 63 above.

75 Case 85/76 *Hoffman la Roche* v *Commission* [1979] ECR 461; Cases 100–103/80, note 51 above. See further Ch. 8.

76 Case 17/74 [1974] ECR 1063.

77 See Usher, 'The Influence of National Concepts on Decisions of the European Court' (1976) 1 ELRev 359. See also the Court's technique in Case 155/79, note 57 above. See also Schwarze, 'Tendencies towards a Common Administrative Law in Europe' (1991) 16 ELRev 3.

market envisaged by Articles 2 and 3 EC. However, the exercise of these powers must be balanced by appropriate safeguards for those subject to Commission investigations and, ultimately, to penalties.[78] The examination above has revealed a general commitment by the European Court and the Court of First Instance to establish such protection. Rules relating to confidentiality and rights to a hearing, for example, exist as general principles of the Community legal order independently of the more limited provision made by Community secondary legislation.

The European Court has consistently declared its intention in the development of general principles of Community law to rely on principles of fundamental rights protection drawn from, *inter alia*, the European Convention on Human Rights.[79] In a number of the cases mentioned in this chapter, the Court has shown itself prepared to test Commission action against standards drawn from the Convention and mediated through Community law. It has not found the pattern of Community law wanting when measured against this standard, despite the remarkable concentration of power in the hands of the Commission under Regulation 17/62. In *Hoechst* v *Commission*[80] it found no violation of the rights envisaged by Article 8 of the Convention. In *Musique Diffusion Française* v *Commission*[81] it found no breach of rights drawn from Article 6 of the Convention. In the light of the judicial commitment to respect rights enshrined in the Convention as part of Community law,[82] the report of the European Commission on Human Rights in *Société Stenuit* v *France*,[83] which found French competition law procedures incompatible with the Convention, is of great interest to Community lawyers.

Article 6(1) of the European Convention provides that 'In the determination of his civil rights and obligations or of any criminal charge against him, everyone is entitled to a fair and public hearing within a reasonable time by an independent and impartial tribunal established by law.' The Commission decided that a 50,000 FF fine imposed on a member of an unlawful cartel was criminal in nature, notwithstanding its characterization in French law as administrative and its imposition by a Minister, not a court. There was no separation in French law between the investigating authority and the authority imposing the fine. The Commission ruled this

---

78 See p. 782 below on fines.
79 See Ch. 6, p. 254.
80 Cases 46/87 and 227/88, note 44 above.
81 Cases 100–103/80, note 51 above.
82 See also Art. F(2) TEU, although this appears incapable of direct application before the Court; Art. L TEU.
83 (1992) 14 EHRR 509. The company advised the Court of Human Rights of its wish to withdraw and the case was struck from the list prior to a Court ruling. See also *Niemitz* v *Germany* (1993) 16 EHRR 97.

in violation of Article 6(1) and rejected the argument that judicial review by the Conseil d'État, France's highest administrative court, sufficed for these purposes.

The Community cannot be challenged through the machinery of the Convention, for it is not party to it. However, there is every prospect that the European Court will be invited to absorb the *Stenuit* ruling into the Community legal order and to test the Commission's powers against that standard. The outcome is far from clear. Article 15(4) of Regulation 17/62 denies the criminal nature of fining decisions taken by the Commission, but this is not conclusive in the light of *Stenuit*. It is possible that the rigorous scrutiny of Commission decisions that is undertaken by both Courts in Luxembourg would satisfy Article 6 of the Convention.[84] However, an allegation that the structure of Regulation 17/62 and, in particular, the power of the Commission to deal with the whole investigation from initiation to imposition of fine should be ruled incompatible with general principles of Community law 'fed' by the European Convention would stimulate intriguing and important litigation.

Challengeable acts

As a matter of procedure, it should be noted that the firm dissatisfied with the Commission's conduct of the procedure should be careful to pick the correct moment to initiate a legal challenge before the European Court. In *IBM* v *Commission*[85] the firm applied under Article 173 to have the statement of objections annulled, but found its application rejected as premature. The statement of objections was not a definitive decision imbued with legal effect, but merely a preparatory step in a procedure that might culminate in such a decision. To allow challenge at such an early stage would distort the legal and administrative structure by forcing the Court to anticipate substantive issues not yet dealt with by the Commission. The Court has adopted the same approach in rejecting as premature a challenge to the procedure for handling a complaint lodged under Article

---

84 See particularly Joined Cases C-89/85, C-104/85, C-114/85, C-116/85, C-117/85, C-125–129/85 *A. Ahlström and Others* v *Commission*, 'Woodpulp', p. 679 above, where the European Court employed independent experts to examine the economic evidence; and Cases T-68/89, T-77–78/89 *Società Italiana Vetro SpA and Others* v *Commission*, 'Flat Glass', p. 682 above. See further on judicial supervision, p. 785 below.

85 Case 60/81 [1981] ECR 2639, [1981] 3 CMLR 635. See also Case T-113/89 *NEFARMA* v *Commission* [1990] ECR II-797 and Cases T-10/92, T-11/92, T-12/92 and T-15/92 *SA Cimentières CBR, Blue Circle Industries plc, Syndicat National des Fabricants de Ciments et de Chaux et Fédération de l'Industrie Cimentière asbl* v *Commission*, judgment of 18 December 1992.

3(2) of Regulation 17/62[86] prior to a formal disposal of the complaint.[87] Accordingly, the dissatisfied party should await the final formal decision on the practice or the complaint when it will be entitled to raise procedural defects as grounds for annulment. It is to the decision that emerges from the investigative procedure that the analysis now turns.

CONSEQUENCES

It is essential to appreciate that most Commission inquiries end in informal rather than formal consequences. Administrative expediency dictates that negotiations that lead to firms amending or abandoning their practices are preferable to formal decisions. Between 1986 and 1993 the number of formal decisions applying Articles 85 and 86 adopted by the Commission never fell below 11, but never rose above 25.[88] The annual number of informal settlements, some by comfort letter but the majority without a comfort letter, was typically several hundred in that period; for example, and not untypically, 832 in 1993. There has been a large backlog of cases, made up predominantly of applications for negative clearance or notifications for exemption, but including some complaints and own-initiative proceedings. Through the late 1980s, over 3,000 cases remained pending at the end of each year.[89] The Commission has devoted energy to reducing the backlog. In 1990 it brought the figure below 3,000 for the first time. At the end of that year, it was able to report that 2,734 cases were pending. The reduction was largely attributable to determined efforts to secure more informal settlements, although assistance was also derived from the adoption of some new block exemptions and, in the Commission's perception, to an increase in the application of the rules at national level. The figures continued to fall; 2,287 cases were pending at the end of 1991 and 1,562 at the end of 1992; by the end of 1993 the backlog was 1,231 cases and the Commission declared that 'the backlog clearing exercise is more or less complete, the number of cases pending cannot be expected to fall in future'.[90] However, given such statistics, it is no surprise that several Commission strategies to keep its workload within manageable proportions will be observed below. For example, the Commission prefers to reserve the laborious formal procedures for decisions which act as declarations of policy of broader relevance beyond the case in question. Comfort letters

86 See p. 757.
87 Case T-64/89, note 16 above. See also Case C-39/93 *SFEI* v *Commission* [1994] ECR I-2681 on the distinction between final rejection and preliminary observations.
88 1986: 21, 1987: 16, 1988: 25, 1989: 16, 1990: 11, 1991: 13, 1992: 20, 1993: 12 (see respective *Annual Reports on Competition Policy*, Luxembourg, EC Official Publications.
89 1986: 3,522, 1987: 3,427, 1988: 3,451, 1989: 3,239 (ibid).
90 *Annual Report on Competition Policy* for 1993, p. 120.

have assumed a practical importance that belies their uncertain legal status. A key issue is the extent to which administrative efficiency may be incompatible with legal safeguards and overall economic efficiency.

Commonly, the Commission's communication of misgivings about a particular practice leads to its amendment and the case is quickly closed. The formal procedures for hearings may not have to be exhausted. Further action may, however, be necessary. The following analysis progresses from formal decisions most favourable to the firm, through less formal and perfectly informal resolution that may, in practice, satisfy the firm, to formal decisions unfavourable to the firm.

Exemption

Exemption under Article 85(3) is available only in respect of an agreement covered by Article 85, not a dominant position regulated by Article 86, but for the collaborators it is plainly a desirable outcome. Their agreement is lawful. They may pursue their joint activity.

Article 4(1) of Regulation 17/62 requires the parties to notify their agreement to the Commission in advance in order to secure an exemption. This is a device to encourage the firms to cooperate with the Commission and to relieve the Commission of the impossible burden of seeking out every agreement concluded within the Community. Exemption is a prize that must be sought, for Community law does not confer automatic exemption on beneficial agreements. Administrative intervention is necessary.[91] The only exception to the rule that no agreement within Article 85(1) can be exempted in the absence of notification to the Commission appears in Article 4(2) of Regulation 17/62, which provides that specified agreements are exempted without the need to notify. The agreements covered are all small-scale and most are in any event now subject to block exemptions. Apart from this insignificant category, the rule remains that notification is a vital precondition for exemption. At national level this may cause difficulty for national courts asked to rule on the validity of agreements that have not been notified or, worse, notified but not yet dealt with by the Commission.[92]

The firms party to the agreement notify the terms to the Commission using Form A/B, which requires the production of information relating to general market structure and the particular status of the parties. From

---

91 See p. 796 for discussion of whether this administrative structure may deter efficient commercial planning and whether reform is possible, e.g., by curtailing the breadth of Art. 85(1) through the development of a rule of reason or by making Art. 85(3) directly effective.

92 See further pp. 790–98.

1 March 1995, a renovated version of Form A/B has been used.[93] The consequences of notification depend on whether the agreement falls within a block exemption adopted by the Commission or requires individual exemption. Where the agreement complies squarely with the permissible list of clauses in a block exemption regulation there is no need even to notify. The regulations are themselves means of reducing the Commission's workload by precluding the need to examine every agreement concluded within the Community. Since 1984 administrative expediency has been further promoted by the inclusion in regulations of 'grey clauses'; clauses that are neither automatically lawful (white) nor unlawful (black).[94] Such clauses should be notified, but the Commission is spared the need to examine them fully and formally, as it used to have to, thanks to the 'opposition procedure'.[95] This provides that the Commission has a stipulated period (six months) in which it may oppose the potentially lawful clause, thereby initiating proceedings to secure its elimination. Otherwise, the clause stands. Thus examination followed by inertia has constitutive effect, which is beneficial for the Commission's workload.

Where an agreement does not fall within the terms of a block exemption regulation, it is examined by the Commission in the light of the four conditions – two positive, two negative – for an Article 85(3) exemption. If the Commission is convinced that individual exemption is deserved, it grants the exemption by formal decision. As already mentioned, an informal outcome is much more likely, perhaps also involving informal discussion leading to amendment of the agreement. Article 8(1) of Regulation 17/62 permits a formal decision to include specific conditions and declares that it shall be issued for a specified period. So, for example, the Commission granted an exemption to an agreement between Continental Gummi-Werke and Michelin[96] to collaborate in developing a new tyre that was limited to the end of 1998 in respect of cooperation in research and development and 2008 in respect of exploitation of patents and know-how. The Commission added the requirement that the parties report instances of licences refused or granted to third parties and report bi-annually on the progress of the link. The joint venture between Enichem and ICI[97] was exempted subject to strict controls over the ability of the firms to deepen their power of joint influence in the sector in question.

---

93 Reg. 3385/94 OJ 1994 L377/28.
94 See note 239, p. 714.
95 Venit, 'The Commission's Opposition Procedure', (1985) 22 CMLRev 167; Waelbroeck, 'New Forms of Settlement of Antitrust Cases and Procedural Safeguards: Is Regulation 17 falling into abeyance?' (1986) 11 ELRev 268.
96 Comm. Dec. 88/555 *Continental Gummi-Werke/Michelin* OJ 1988 L305/33 [1989] 4 CMLR 920.
97 Dec. 88/87 *Enichem/ICI* OJ 1988 L50/18 [1989] 4 CMLR 54.

The Commission permitted collaboration to develop so far, but no further.[98] Exemptions granted in respect of collaboration on use of the Channel Tunnel have been limited in time and subjected to conditions.[99]

Naturally, the provision of misleading information at any stage invalidates the exemption. Article 8(3) provides that the exemption may be revoked with retrospective effect. The firm may then find itself fined on two counts: for provision of inaccurate information as well as for participating in the agreement in the first place.[100]

The firms party to the agreement may seem to be in limbo during the six-month period of the opposition procedure and the period pending a decision on an application for individual exemption. Uncertainty about the legal status of the deal would be commercially highly undesirable. However, during this spell, they enjoy immunity from fines,[101] so the agreement can be safely implemented pending final decision. The system, then, encourages the parties to work with the Commission using both incentives and safeguards.[102] There remains no duty to notify an agreement caught by Article 85, merely a duty not to infringe the Treaty rules, but factors such as the grant of exemption, unavailable without notification, and immunity from fines pending decision render it commercially sensible to notify. Even the administrative burden of notification is unlikely to be a good reason for not notifying; the burdens subsequently confronted in the absence of notification will probably be heavier. In addition, the firm may benefit from its reputation in Brussels as cooperative and helpful, although there is only limited evidence that DG IV is susceptible to capture by business.[103] Only if a firm wishes to conceal past or present malpractice from Community or national authorities is it likely to have a powerful incentive to avoid notification. The several secret horizontal cartels dis-

---

98 See Case 17/74, note 76 above, on granting a hearing before the imposition of such conditions.

99 Comm. Dec. 94/594 *ACI* OJ 1994 L224/28 (goods; five-year exemption on terms); Comm. Dec. 94/663 *Night Services* OJ 1994 L259/20 (passengers; eight-year exemption on terms).

100 See p. 782 on fines.

101 Unless the Commission issues a preliminary finding under Reg. 17/62 Art. 15(6) that Art. 85(3) of the Treaty is inapplicable. Such decisions clearly have legal effects and therefore seem to be susceptible to challenge under Art. 173, e.g., for inadequate reasoning, which may explain why they are little used; see Korah, *EC Competition Law and Practice*, p. 128 and see the successful application for annulment of an Art. 15(6) decision in Cases 8–11/66 *Cimenteries* v *Commission* [1967] ECR 75, considered at p. 222 above. See also the admissible but unsuccessful application in Case T-19/91 *Société d'Hygiène Dermatologique de Vichy* v *Commission* [1992] ECR II-415.

102 A national court is in a more uncomfortable position in this interim period if asked to rule on enforceability; see p. 792.

103 For a useful reading list on agency capture, albeit not in the Community context, see Baldwin and McCrudden, *Regulation and Public Law*, pp. 340–41.

cussed in Chapter 22 show that such practices remain a feature of the Community market.[104]

Negative clearance

Article 2 of Regulation 17/62 permits the Commission to certify that a practice gives rise to no grounds for action on its part on the basis of Articles 85(1) or 86. This procedure is known as a negative clearance. It provides the party or parties with a measure of security that the Commission considers the practices in question acceptable and that they may accordingly be implemented. As far as the Commission is concerned, the grant of a negative clearance allows it to close a case without a full formal decision. It is administratively expedient, but procedural safeguards remain. The decision must be published[105] and the opportunity for interested third parties to submit their observations must be respected.[106]

At Community level, then, the negative clearance is in practice as valuable as a formal exemption for the parties and accelerates procedures within the Commission. At national level, however, the negative clearance may be rather less desirable because of its limited formality. The key issue is the extent to which the national court, asked to apply the directly effective provisions of Articles 85 and 86, is bound by a negative clearance. If it departs from it, awkward disharmony in the application of the law to commerce may ensue.[107]

Comfort letters

Comfort letters are issued by Directorate-General IV and declare an intention to proceed no further in the matter. They might indicate that the Commission considers Article 85 or 86 inapplicable, or that Article 85(3) is thought applicable to exempt the agreement. Purely administrative in nature and signed by an official, they are issued without any of the formality contained in Regulation 17/62 and, indeed, they are not mentioned there at all. The comfort letter is not a formal decision recognized by legislation. On one view it is therefore incapable of being the subject of an application for annulment under Article 173. However, the Court in *AKZO v Commission*,[108] relying on its earlier decision in *IBM v Commis-*

---

104 The practical problems of dealing with DG IV may also undermine readiness to notify; see e.g., Brown, 'Notification of Agreements to the EC Commission: Whether to Submit to a Flawed System' (1992) 17 ELRev 323. See further pp. 796–8.
105 Art. 21 Reg. 17/62.
106 Art. 19(3) Reg. 17/62.
107 The matter is addressed in more depth at p. 792.
108 Case 53/85, note 61 above.

sion,[109] declared that acts that produce 'legal effects of such a kind as to affect the applicant's interests by clearly altering its legal position' are reviewable, and that test may fairly be said to be met by a comfort letter that closes the Commission's inquiry into the commercial practices, especially if one takes account of the letter's status before a national court.[110] The Commission itself has sought to enhance what it terms the 'declaratory effect' of comfort letters by its greater readiness to publish the essential contents of agreements in respect of which a letter is issued,[111] which further strengthens the view that the letter has an impact on the parties' legal position.

The comfort letter resembles the negative clearance in that it provides some security for the parties from the prospect of Commission intervention. Immunity from fines persists after the issue of the letter. The comfort letter also resembles the negative clearance in that it represents an administrative technique to lighten the Commission's workload. Like the negative clearance, then, its use has grown from the practical necessity of emptying Commission 'in-trays', but its development has brought some legal difficulty, especially in determining its relevance before national courts. As has already been observed in relation to the negative clearance, the national court may be unsure how much deference to accord the administrative decision. The Court has indicated that it may take the comfort letter into account in assessing the compatibility of a practice with Community law, but it is not bound by it.[112] The problem is at its most acute in relation to a comfort letter that declares the Commission's view that the agreement, though caught by Article 85(1), is worthy of exemption under Article 85(3). The national court may apply Article 85(1), for it is directly effective, but not Article 85(3), which is not. Strictly, then, the national court ought to hold the deal unlawful, even though the Commission's informal view is the very opposite. There are in practice likely to be methods of circumventing this impasse, but it remains a technical problem in the structure of the enforcement of competition law.[113]

However, at Community level, the comfort letter is valuable protection for the undertaking, for it reveals to it the Commission's attitude. Once the market alters, the Commission may change its view of the status of the practice, so the firm should be aware that its comfort letter is not indefinite security. The comfort letter is also unreliable if it has been obtained by the

---

109 Case 60/81, note 85 above. See more generally on acts susceptible to review, p. 221.
110 Korah (1981) 6 ELRRev 14, 30–34; see Venit, (1985) 22 CMLR 167, 192–9 in relation to the opposition procedure. The argument is developed further at p. 795.
111 OJ 1982 C343/4, OJ 1983 C295/6.
112 Cases 253/78, 1–3/79 *Procureur de la République* v *Giry* and *Guerlain SA* [1980] ECR 2327, [1981] 2 CMLR 99, noted by Korah (1981) 6 ELRev 14.
113 See further p. 792.

provision of misleading information. However, while circumstances remain unchanged, the undertaking seems able to hold the Commission to the promises in its comfort letter.[114] If the Commission changes its mind, the undertaking has a legitimate expectation that it will be informed, given the opportunity to submit observations and given an appropriate period to amend its practices. This is enforceable by application to the Court.[115]

Termination of infringements

If the Commission considers that a violation of either Article 85 or Article 86 has been committed, it will move to terminate the infringement. It has several techniques. Commonly, the first approach is informal, and this may yield success without the need for adherence to the full range of procedural safeguards discussed above.[116] Informal resolution of the issue is favoured by the Commission, able to minimize its paperwork, and by the firms, able to avoid complicated procedures, bad publicity and possible fines.

Article 3(3) of Regulation 17/62 allows the Commission to address 'recommendations' to the undertakings. If these are accepted by the firms, the matter may be closed, perhaps after Commission approval through exemption, negative clearance or comfort letter. The power to issue recommendations has been little used.

The resolution may typically involve steps to satisfy the several parties involved in the matter. Macron Fire, a small importer and supplier of fire hose in the United Kingdom, complained to the Commission that Angus Fire, a large firm active in the market, had violated Article 86 by pursuing pricing policies designed to exclude Macron from the market.[117] The Commission's initial view was that abuse had occurred. Angus responded by admitting no liability, but it gave assurances that it would in future comply with Article 86 and it made an *ex gratia* payment to Macron. Macron withdrew its complaint. The Commission closed the file.[118] So the settlement of an investigation may typically involve undertakings made by the firm under suspicion.[119] The legal status of the undertaking is nebulous; its breach would at least stimulate renewed Commission inquiry and may

---

114 See, e.g., AG Reischl in Case 31/80 *L'Oréal* v *De Nieuwe Amck* [1980] ECR 3775, [1981] 2 CMLR 235; Wyatt and Dashwood, *European Community Law*, p. 480.
115 See Ch. 8 for fuller discussion of the principle of legitimate expectation.
116 See especially on hearings pp. 769–70.
117 On such abuse see pp. 745–7.
118 Press Release IP (87) 340, 30 July 1987, [1987] 3 CMLR 715.
119 E.g., Cases 142, 156/84, note 14 above. See Waelbroeck (1986) 11 ELRev 268; Korah, *EC Competition Law and Practice*, p. 146.

cause an increase in any fine subsequently imposed.[120] However, resolution in this way is administratively desirable, cures market distortion rapidly and may often satisfy all interested parties.

Negotiated settlement may seem ideal, but naturally some cases are incapable of resolution in this way. If a formal decision is appropriate, Article 3 of Regulation 17/62 allows the making of a decision requiring that the infringement be brought to an end. Such formal decisions are likely to be required where the firm contests the Commission's view that the competition rules have been violated. It is probable that, by analogy with the Court of First Instance's view in *Automec II*[121] that the Commission is entitled to apply a 'Community interest' test in selecting which alleged infringements to investigate, it is also entitled to apply a comparable test in selecting cases that it will pursue to a formal decision. The Commission will be eager to adopt a formal decision where it believes that the matter is particularly important and it wishes to use a formal ruling as a guide for the future. Such concern may relate to future reliance on the ruling at national as well as Community level. The Commission adopted a formal decision condemning the deal in *Florimex/Bloemenveilingen Aalsmeer*[122] despite the abandonment of the disputed practice in order to lend support through its decision for actions commenced at national level in respect of that deal and others of a similar nature.[123] This is part of the Commission's policy of improving private enforcement of the competition rules as a complement to its own activities.[124]

The decision under Article 3 may involve a 'cease and desist' order addressed to the company. Termination may involve positive action and this may be specified in the Commission decision. In *Commercial Solvents* v *Commission*[125] the Commission's decision that Commercial Solvents' refusal to supply Zoja with aminobutanol was abusive under Article 86 was accompanied by the instruction that the abuse be terminated by supplying the substance within thirty days. The Court, before which annulment was sought, upheld the imposition of this positive obligation. The position is less clear cut under Article 85. In *Automec II*[126] the Court of First Instance ruled that the Commission had not acted unlawfully in stating that it had no power to require BMW to supply Automec with goods. Where a violation of Article 85 is shown, the Commission's function is to terminate

---

120 See p. 782.
121 Case T-24/90, note 18 above.
122 Comm. Dec. 88/491 OJ 1988 L262/27, [1989] 4 CMLR 500, paras. 164–8.
123 A similar approach may be observed in relation to private control of states acting in breach of Community law; see e.g., Case 240/86 *Commission* v *Greece* [1988] ECR 1835, paras. 12–15 of the judgment.
124 See p. 790.
125 Cases 6, 7/73 [1974] ECR 223, see p. 751 above.
126 Case T-24/90, note 18 above.

that violation. Unlawful aspects of, for example, a selective distribution network could be remedied other than by the imposition of an obligation to supply. The terms under which the network operates could be adjusted; or the scheme could be abandoned entirely. However, notwithstanding the ruling in *Automec II*, were circumstances to arise where the termination of a breach of Article 85 could be achieved only through an obligation to supply, it is submitted that the Commission would possess the power to make such an order under Article 3 of Regulation 17/62.

Interim measures

It may be important for the Commission to intervene even in advance of a formal decision requiring termination. Where the firm is unwilling to conform to the Commission's view expressed informally, it may be necessary to act quickly lest the cartel or abuse cause irreparable damage. The damage may be suffered by the economy generally, but the issue is more likely to present itself when an individual firm complains to the Commission because it fears for its own interests. Accordingly, the Commission has power to take interim measures in order to secure the termination of practices, pending final determination of the applicability of the competition rules.[127] This power is missing from Regulation 17/62 and it was left to the Court, in characteristically dynamic fashion, to deduce its existence as a means of ensuring that the machinery for enforcing the competition rules is effective.[128] In *Camera Care v Commission*[129] the Court decided that the Commission enjoyed the power to restrain a firm in the period pending final resolution of the merits of the case provided certain preconditions and safeguards were respected. There must be a prima-facie case of infringement.[130] The case must be urgent; the threat of harm must be serious and irreparable. The measures taken must be temporary, conservatory and proportionate. The safeguards of Regulation 17/62, particularly those relating to hearings, must be observed[131] and the decision must be

---

127 Temple Lang, 'The Powers of the Commission to Order Interim Measures in Competition Cases', (1981) 18 CMLRev 49; Piroche, *'Les mesures provisoires de la Commission des Communautes européennes dans le domaine de concurrence'* (1989) 25 Rev Trim Droit Européen 439; Whish, *Competition Law* pp. 297–300; Pais Antunes: *Interim Measures under EC Competition Law – Recent Developments* (1993) 13 YEL 83.

128 See Case C-213/89 R v *Secretary of State for Transport, ex parte Factortame* on effective remedies at the interim stage in a different context, p. 176.

129 Case 792/79 R [1980] ECR 119, [1980] 1 CMLR 334.

130 In Case T-44/90 *La Cinq v Commission* [1992] ECR II-1 [1992] 4 CMLR 449, the Commission was found to have interpreted this requirement too strictly by equating it with the need to show a clear and flagrant infringement.

131 This includes the requirement that the interim order does not go beyond the scope of any final order available under Art. 3 Reg. 17/62; decision annulled on this basis in Cases 228, 229/82 *Ford v Commission* [1984] ECR 1129, [1983] 1 CMLR 649.

susceptible to challenge before the Court. These powers are potentially effective and on occasion the Commission has needed only to put the procedures into motion in order to persuade the firms to comply with its view. The bid for Irish Distillers was dropped once the Commission evidenced an intent to adopt interim measures.[132] Complaints to the Commission by dependent customers in the United Kingdom led to interim measures being taken against Boosey and Hawkes requiring it, a dominant firm, to supply brass band instruments.[133] However, such measures may not be obtained quickly enough for the complainant and in such circumstances a complainant may be better advised to proceed at national level.[134]

As the Court recognized in *Camera Care*, it is a necessary balance to the Commission's access to interim relief that the undertaking too should be able to seek interim protection against the Commission pending full investigation of the merits of the case. Accordingly, interim proceedings before the Court initiated by the firm are also available.[135]

Fines

Simply putting an end to the unlawful action may not be sufficient. The imposition of fines may be valuable both as a means of removing profits made through anticompetitive conduct and as a means of deterring both the firm under investigation and other firms from pursuing similar conduct in the future. The power to fine is a key element in an effective enforcement strategy. Regulation 17/62 grants the Commission power to fine. Article 15(1) covers fines for the supply of misleading information and for refusal to comply with decisions requiring the production of information or submission to investigation under Articles 11 and 14; Article 15(2), more significantly, covers fines for breach of the substantive provisions of Articles 85 and 86 or a condition attached to an exemption. The fine can be imposed only for intentional or negligent infringement.[136] These provisions are supplemented by Article 16, which confers on the Commission the power to impose periodic penalty payments not exceeding 1,000 ECU

---

132 Press Release IP (88) 512, 17 August 1988, [1988] 4 CMLR 840. See also Dec. 94/19 *Sea Containers/Stena Sealink* OJ 1994 L15/8; port facilities were made available to competitor after the Commission announced an interest in taking interim measures.
133 Comm. Dec. 87/500 *BBI/Boosey and Hawkes* OJ 1987 L286/36, [1988] 4 CMLR 67.
134 See pp. 790, 803.
135 See further p. 788 in connection with the Court's broader jurisdiction to supervise the Commissions's administrative activity.
136 The Court held in Case 246/86 *Belasco* v *Commission* [1989] ECR 2117 and Case C-279/87 *Tippex* v *Commission* [1990] ECR I-261, citing Case 19/77 *Miller* v *Commission* [1978] ECR 131, that a breach is intentional if the firm knew or could not have been unaware that the conduct had as its object the restriction of competition.

a day on firms that refuse to comply with decisions relating to termination of violation, supply of information and submission to investigation.[137]

Under Article 15(1) the fine may not exceed 5,000 ECU.[138] In respect of the substantive violation, however, matters under Article 15(2) are more serious. The fine may reach 1 million ECU or 10 per cent of the turnover in the previous business year of each of the undertakings responsible, whichever is the higher. The Court interpreted this in *Musique Diffusion Française*[139] to mean 10 per cent of the entire turnover on all the products of the group of companies worldwide. This maximum will rarely be approached due to the demands of the principle of proportionality, and the Court itself in *Musique Diffusion Française* observed that it will rarely be appropriate to base a fine on total turnover, especially where the goods concerned represent only a small percentage. The Court of First Instance adopted this approach in *Parker Pen Ltd* v *Commission*[140] where it reduced a fine from 700,000 ECUs to 400,000 ECUs because the Commission had not taken into account the fact that the turnover accounted for by the products to which the infringement related was relatively low in comparison with the turnover accruing from total sales.

The Commission regards the power to fine as a crucial element in securing the effective application of the Treaty competition rules. The 75-million-ECU fine imposed on Tetra Pak for a range of abusive practices prohibited by Article 86 stands as the highest fine imposed on a single firm.[141] Tetra Pak's application for annulment was dismissed by the Court of First Instance in *Tetra Pak International SA* v *Commission*,[142] where it was observed that, despite the size of the fine, it amounted to only 2.2 per cent of the undertaking's total turnover in the business year prior to the making of the decision. It could not therefore be judged disproportionate. The highest aggregate fine imposed on a cartel is 248 million ECUs. This occurred in November 1994 and related to market-sharing and price-fixing by 33 cement manufacturers and also involved several trade associations.[143] Several individual undertakings party to the cartel were fined in excess of 10 million ECUs.

---

137 As in Cases 46/87 and 227/88, note 44 above.
138 See e.g., 4,000-ECU fine imposed in Comm. Dec. 86/506 *Peugeot* OJ 1986 L295/19 [1989] 4 CMLR 371; fine for failure to provide information reduced due to misunderstanding by the company and eventual compliance in Comm. Dec. 91/213 *Baccarat* OJ 1991 L97/16; serious repeated breach subject to full 5,000-ECU fine in Comm. Dec. 91/55 *Secretama* OJ 1991 L35/23, noted (1990) ELRev *Competition Law Checklist* 68.
139 Cases 100–103/80, note 51 above.
140 Case T-77/92 [1994] ECR II-549.
141 Comm. Dec. 92/163 *Tetra Pak* OJ 1992 L72/1, [1992] 4 CMLR 551.
142 Case T-83/91, judgment of 6 October 1994.
143 Dec. 94/815 *Cement* OJ 1994 L343/1. A challenge before the Court of First Instance was lodged in 1995.

The calculation of the fine is not governed in detail by the Regulation, but under Article 15(4) it shall not be of a criminal nature. There is immunity post-notification pending a Commission decision on an application for exemption.[144] Article 15(2) adds that the gravity and duration of the violation shall be taken into account. Beyond these considerations, the matter rests in the hands of the Commission. Even though decisions are susceptible to review by the Court, there must be concern that the Commission, having carried out the investigatory function, also possesses the function of imposing financial penalties, especially given the paucity of legislative guidance.[145] Increase in the level of fines can only serve to increase disquiet over this structure.

The Commission's fining policy has developed on a case-by-case basis. It weighs up factors. Circumstances likely to lead to an increase in the fine include where a deliberate choice to pursue a course of conduct known or suspected to be unlawful has been made;[146] where the unlawful practice is clearly covered by existing precedent – for example, a market-partitioning cartel[147] where the firms occupy a large slice of the market and therefore their conduct has especially significant economic implications.[148] The Commission has also increased fines where a firm has persisted with practices that it had earlier undertaken to abandon. The fine tends to be lower, or perhaps not imposed at all, where the practice has not previously been ruled in breach of the Treaty[149] or where the sector in question has not previously been subject to control.[150] The firm may also escape a fine where it has been forced into an unlawful agreement by an economically powerful partner on which it depends.[151] Within a cartel the Commission's fines will reflect the degree of responsibility that it attributes to each member, so peripheral members may escape a fine.[152] The Court has

---

144 But see note 101 above.

145 In Cases 100–103/80, note 51 above, the Court rejected the argument that this structure violates the European Convention on Human Rights or principles of Community law; see further p. 771, especially discussion of *Société Stenuit*.

146 E.g., Comm. Dec. 85/79, note 59 above; Case 27/76 *United Brands* [1978] ECR 207, paras. 298–301 of the judgment.

147 E.g., Cases 100–103/80, note 51 above; Comm. Dec. 94/815, n.143 above.

148 Obviously of particular relevance in relation to Art. 86; e.g. Comm. Dec. 92/163 *Tetra Pak*, note 141 above.

149 Comm. Dec. 88/518 *British Sugar* OJ 1988 L284/41, [1990] 4 CMLR 196, p. 748 above (delivered pricing as abuse); Case-62/86 *AKZO* v *Commission*, [1991] ECR I-3359, p. 746 above (predatory pricing, fine reduced by Court).

150 E.g., Comm. Dec. 88/589 *SABENA* OJ 1988 L317/47 (first ruling in the market for the supply of computerized reservation systems).

151 E.g., Comm. Dec. 88/86 *Duffy Group* OJ 1988 L49/19, p. 672 above.

152 See, e.g., Dec. 86/399 *BELASCO* OJ 1986 L232/15, [1991] 4 CMLR 130, upheld by the Court in Case 246/86, note 136 above.

refused to accept that implementation of a potentially exemptable agreement that the parties have failed to notify is a technical rather than a substantive violation and therefore deserving of a lower fine.[153] However, a fine might be reduced in the case of an agreement exemptable but not exempted due to non-notification on the basis that the consequences of the breach are not grave. The Commission is particularly prone to give a discount where the firm has cooperated with it in the investigation, abandoned its violation promptly and instituted a compliance programme for the future.[154] The Commission has in this way used its power to fine as an incentive scheme to facilitate its own enforcement strategy. Overall, the fine imposed is controlled by the principle of proportionality and the Commission could not fix one firm with a sum designed as an example in order to frighten the whole sector. However, the Court has approved a general policy of increasing fines where firms were calculating that profits from market division would exceed fines and where, accordingly, implementation of the Community's competition policy was proving ineffective.[155]

REVIEW BY THE COURT

Function

It has been observed at several points in the preceding discussion that the opportunity exists for a firm to challenge the decisions of the Commission before the Court of First Instance. The Commission is subject to legal supervision and Article 173 allows the firm that is the addressee of a decision to seek its annulment by that Court. The firm under investigation may accordingly challenge, *inter alia*, decisions under Article 11 of Regulation 17/62 requesting information, decisions under Article 14 requiring it to submit to investigations, and decisions requiring the termination of practices found to be unlawful. However, it may not challenge mere preparatory steps in the conduct of the investigation[156] and it must take care to observe the tight two-month time-limit for submission of Article

---

153 Cases 100–103/80, note 51 above, paras. 92–3 of the judgment.
154 E.g., Case 136/79, note 44 above; Comm. Dec. 84/282 *Polistil/Arbois* OJ 1984 L136/9. [1984] 2 CMLR 594, noted by Korah [1984] ECLR 203, Faull (1986) 11 ELRev 62; Comm. Dec. 85/79, note 59 above; Comm. Dec. 91/532 *Toshiba* OJ 1991 L287 Case T-77/92, note 140 above. All these decisions serve as useful illustrations of the wide range of factors that combine to fix the fine.
155 Cases 100–103/80, note 51 above, para. 106 of the judgment.
156 Case 60/81, note 85 above; Case T-64/89, note 16 above.

173 applications. Article 172 EC confers on the Court unlimited jurisdiction with regard to fines imposed by the Commission.[157] Third parties may also have access to the Court. A complainant has standing under Article 173 to challenge the final decision made by the Commission and a third party may also be able to act in protection of rights to a hearing.[158]

Much of the case law that has amplified the scope of the Commission's enforcement powers has been built up as a result of such annulment proceedings, in which the Court must balance the interests of the investigator and investigated. Where the complaint is that the Commission has failed to act, Article 175 may be employed. Article 215 allows a claim for compensation, but its invocation in this area has not been significantly more successful than generally,[159] although occasional blunders have fixed the Commission with liability.[160]

Judicial review is important as a safeguard over the exercise of the Commission's powers. The Court of First Instance is not strictly an appellate court in these circumstances. Article 173 provides the Court with a review function and it will annul the decision only if specified heads of illegality are established; lack of competence, infringement of the Treaty and so on.[161] In *Continental Can*[162] the European Court annulled the Commission's decision because of flaws in the economic analysis of market definition. So too in *United Brands*[163] the European Court annulled an inadequately explained finding of unfair pricing. But in many of the 'rule-of-reason' cases under Article 85(1), for example, the Court has accepted often opaque Commission decisions.[164]

The Court of First Instance, which has exercised jurisdiction in applications for annulment by private parties in the competition field since 1989, has won respect for its willingness rigorously to inquire into Commission practice. The intensity of judicial supervision seems to be on the increase.[165]

157 Elaborated in Art. 17 Reg. 17/62. See further Ch. 10.
158 See p. 770.
159 See Ch. 10.
160 E.g., Case 145/83, note 63 above.
161 On the position prior to the creation of the Court of First Instance, Usher, 'Exercise by the European Court of its jurisdiction to annul competition decisions' (1980) 5 ELRev 287. See generally Ch. 8 on Article 173.
162 Case 6/72, *Continental Can* v *Commission* [1973] ECR 215, [1973] CMLR 199.
163 Case 27/76, note 146 above.
164 See pp. 696–704.
165 See p. 772 above on the role of judicial control in securing compliance with rights under Community law drawn from the European Convention on Human Rights. In the United Kingdom, the influential House of Lords Select Committee on the European Communities concluded, after a thorough inquiry, that the presence of independent judicial control was a factor in supporting the continued allocation of power to the Commission to conduct the full investigation from initiation to decision; HL 7, 1993/94.

In *Società Italiana Vetro SpA and Others v Commission*[166] the Court of First Instance identified a number of serious procedural irregularities in the Commission's handling of the case and annulled the Commission's decision.

It remains possible to appeal on point of law from the Court of First Instance to the European Court.[167] In some cases the European Court has adopted a significantly different line from that taken by the Court of First Instance. In *Samenwerkende* the European Court's approach to preservation of confidentiality differed markedly from that of the Court of First Instance, although it did not set aside the decision.[168] In *BASF AG and Others v Commission* the Court of First Instance had found a Commission decision relating to an alleged cartel among PVC producers to suffer from such serious defects arising out of internal procedural rules that it was non-existent.[169] The European Court disagreed. It found that a decision *had* been made, but it annulled the decision for infringement of essential procedural requirements.[170] The Commission thereupon issued a further decision addressed to the same firms and the firms promptly brought renewed applications for annulment.[171]

In the past the European Court has attracted criticism for its 'amateur' efforts at economics.[172] Other commentators have called for more vigorous judicial supervision of the quality of economic analysis provided by the Commission.[173] This policy might stimulate more care in DG IV, but judicial second-guessing risks causing a shift in the institutional balance mapped out by the Treaty. However, it appears that a higher judicial profile is emerging. The Court of First Instance is developing a degree of specialist expertise. The European Court too seems to be concerned to maintain an active supervisory role in competition cases. In *Woodpulp*, a case that was within its jurisdiction because the litigation predated the creation of the Court of First Instance, it relied on independent experts in annulling a finding of concertation.[174] In *Publishers Association v Commis-*

---

166 Cases T-68/89, T-77–78/89 [1992] ECR II–1403, [1992] 5 CMLR 302, examined at p. 682 above.

167 Art. 168a(1) EC. See Ch. 6, p. 188.

168 Case C-36/92 P, examined at p. 764 above.

169 Cases T-79/89 et al. [1992] ECR II-315. See Ch. 2, p. 52 above on the Commission's Rules of Procedure.

170 Case C-137/92 P *Commission v BASF AG* [1994] ECR I-2555.

171 Dec. 94/599 *PVC* OJ 1994 L239/14, *(inter alia)* Case T-328/94 *ICI v Commission* pending before the Court of First Instance.

172 E.g. Bishop (1981) 44 MLR 282 examining Case 27/76, note 146 above.

173 Korah, *EC Competition Law and Practice*, Ch. 14.

174 Joined Cases C-89/85, C-104/85, C-114/85, C-116/85, C-117/85, C-125–129/85 *A. Ahlström and Others v Commission*, judgment of 31 March 1993 [1993] 4 CMLR 407, p. 679 above.

sion[175] the European Court set aside a judgment of the Court of First Instance[176] and annulled a Commission decision that the Net Book Agreement, a price-fixing arrangement in the British book trade, contravened Article 85. The European Court found that a number of aspects of the decision suffered from inadequate reasoning. It held that, *inter alia*, the Commission had failed to explain why the benefits of the arrangement that had persuaded the Restrictive Practices Court in the United Kingdom of its legality were of no relevance at Community level.

Interim measures

The Court has the power to take interim measures[177] to suspend a Commission decision pending a full hearing.[178] Article 185 EC permits the Court to suspend the application of a contested act, and Article 186 provides more generally the power to prescribe any necessary interim measures. A firm subject to interim measures taken by the Commission[179] may itself seek interim relief from the application of that decision before the Court. The Court is guided by the damage that is likely to be suffered by the addressee of the decision if the decision stands pending full hearing. Serious and irreparable harm must be shown. In *Publishers Association* v *Commission*[180] the Court suspended a decision holding unlawful the Net Book Agreement, a price-fixing cartel in the United Kingdom. The Court considered that there were prima-facie arguments against the decision and that if it were allowed to stand pending a full hearing, the matter would in practice be settled against the Agreement, for it would be too late to reinstate it.[181] A similar approach and result occurred in *R TE* v *Commission*.[182] An eventual ruling in favour of the applicants would have been fruitless; the harm irreparable. The Court weighs a delicate balance between competing interests, and its willingness to grant interim suspension must depend on the facts of individual cases.

Finally, the role of the European Court under Article 177 should be referred to. Where issues of competition law are raised at national level, a

---

175 Case C-360/92 P, judgment of 17 January 1995.
176 Case T-66/89 *Publishers Association* v *Commission* [1992] ECR II-1995.
177 See generally Ch. 8, pp. 268–70.
178 Pastor and Van Ginderachter, '*La Procédure en Référé*' (1989) 25 Rev Trim Droit Européen 561.
179 See p. 781.
180 Case 56/89 R [1989] ECR 1693.
181 The European Court eventually annulled the Commission decision in Case C-360/92 P *Publishers Association* v *Commission*, note 175 above.
182 Case 76/89 R [1989] ECR 1141, [1989] 4 CMLR 749. On final disposal of the case, see pp. 753, 837.

preliminary reference under Article 177 provides the Court with the opportunity to rule on the point of law raised. As in all Article 177 references, this is an important means of securing the uniform interpretation of Community law.[183] Mention of enforcement at national level immediately raises questions about the direct effect of Community law and the nature of the protection afforded to Community law rights before domestic tribunals. It is to this second level of enforcement, at national level rather than through the Commission, that analysis now turns.

ENFORCEMENT AT NATIONAL LEVEL

DIRECT EFFECT

In assessing the opportunities for domestic enforcement of Community law the first question to be addressed always concerns the direct effect of the provisions. In relation to the competition rules the situation has been established by the Court in important rulings dealing with the impact of Regulation 17/62[184] and can be clearly stated. Articles 85(1) and (2) are directly effective; so too is Article 86. All are enforceable before national courts by private individuals. Article 85(3), however, is not directly effective.[185] Whereas Articles 85(1), (2) and 86 envisage clear and unconditional prohibitions, the application of Article 85(3) belongs exclusively with the Commission by virtue of implementing Regulation 17/62.[186] A national court may rely on a Commission decision granting exemption under Article 85(3),[187] but it may not itself carry out the assessment under

---

183 Major decisions relating to the development of competition law made in Art. 177 rulings include Case 56/65 *Société Technique Minière* v *Maschinenbau Ulm* [1966] ECR 235, [1966] 1 CMLR 357; Case C-234/89 *Stergios Delimitis* v *Henninger Brau* [1991] ECR I-935; Case 311/85 *Vereininging Van Vlaamse Reisbureaus* v *Social Dienst* [1987] ECR 3801, [1989] 4 CMLR 213. See generally Ch. 9.

184 Especially Case 13/61 *De Geus* v *Bosch* [1962] ECR 45, [1962] CMLR 1. Prior to the introduction of Reg. 17/62 the application of Art. 85 was dependent on Arts. 88 and 89, thus precluding direct effect; this issue has long ceased to be of relevance in the area of agreements subject to Reg. 17/62, but caused occasional problems in sectors excluded from Reg. 17/62 until they were brought within the ambit of implementing regulations, allowing both Commission control and domestic enforcement as described here; see, e.g., air and sea transport Cases 209-13/84, note 3 above, Case 66/86, [1989] ECR 803.

185 Case 127/73 *BRT (Belgische Radio en Televisie and Société Belge des Auteurs, Compositeurs et Éditeurs)* v *SV SABAM and XIV Fonior* [1974] ECR 51; Case 31/80, note 114 above; Case C-234/89, note 183 above.

186 Art. 9(1).

187 Case 31/80, note 114 above, paras. 22–3 of the judgment.

Article 85(3). This inability makes the domestic enforcement of Article 85, though important in practice, more legally complicated than domestic enforcement of provisions such as Articles 12, 30 and 48.

Enforcement at national level supplements the alternative/additional route of complaining to the Commission in the hope that the Commission will take on the matter.[188] Indeed, the Commission is eager to encourage recourse to national courts.[189] It derives support in that quest from the Court of First Instance's ruling in *Automec II* that the Commission is entitled to prioritize cases according to the 'Community interest' in their pursuit.[190] There are three major motivations for the Commission's eagerness. The first reflects its oft-observed desire to contain its own workload; enforcement at national level may take some pressure off it. Second, the policing of the competition rules is rendered doubly effective by opening up control at national level. This will simply make the rules more widely respected and improve the operation of the market. More generally, however, enforcement at national level advances the general objective of integrating Community law within the national legal order. These factors suggest that it would be desirable to provide private parties harmed by anticompetitive practices with an incentive to litigate, perhaps on the model of the treble damages award available in American antitrust law, but, as will be observed below,[191] Community law has had a limited, though increasing, impact on the law of remedies in the member states.

USING THE TREATY RULES AS A DEFENCE

The sanction of nullity

Article 85(2) provides that agreements in breach of Article 85 are void. At national level this means that any agreement contrary to Article 85 is unenforceable. Indeed, any national legislative, administrative or judicial support for an unlawful agreement is itself incompatible with the Treaty.[192] Before English courts the unenforceability of a practice contrary to Article 85 could be established by an application for a declaration, which would require the court to test the agreement against the terms of Article 85(1).[193]

---

188 See p. 757.
189 See, e.g., Press Release IP (89) 884, 27 November 1989; 13th Report on Competition Policy, paras. 217, 218; 14th Report, para. 47. See also Comm. Dec. 88/491, note 122 above.
190 Case T-24/90, note 18 above.
191 See p. 799.
192 E.g., Case 311/85, note 183 above; see further p. 868.
193 For discussion of other jurisdictions see Mateo, '*L'Application de la Nullité de l'Article*

At a more passive level, a firm party to an unlawful agreement could simply refuse to comply and then defeat a breach of contract action by arguing that the contract is unenforceable. If a violation of Article 85 is established, it is for the national court to decide whether to hold the entire agreement unenforceable or to uphold those provisions untainted by the illegality, severing them from provisions incompatible with Community law.[194] Since Article 85(2) is directly effective, none of these possibilities is dependent on action taken against the alleged violation by the Commission, although that may occur independently.

Formal exemption

The principle that an agreement contrary to Article 85(1) is automatically void under Article 85(2) and therefore unenforceable at national level runs into difficulties when the possibility of exemption under Article 85(3) is added to the equation. An agreement exempted by the Commission[195] or falling within a block exemption[196] should be enforced by a national court. An agreement for which exemption has been refused and which has been held unlawful must not be enforced. These, however, are relatively simple cases. An unenviable task confronts the national court called upon to rule on the lawfulness of an agreement that has been notified to the Commission for an exemption, but on which no decision has yet been made.[197] The national court's ruling will be subsequently overtaken by a Commission decision that the agreement is either exempt or void, both of which operate retrospectively.[198] In the meantime the national court has to assess the lawfulness of the deal and, although it may suspend the proceedings in an attempt to avoid wrongly predicting the Commission's conclusion,[199] even suspension may mean a preservation of the *status quo* favourable to one party over the other, which may contradict the Commission's final

---

85.2 *du Traite CEE par les Juridictions Nationales (avec un Examen Particulier du Domaine des Transports Aériens)'* (1991) 27 CDE 317.

194 Case 56/65, note 183 above; Case 10/86 *VAG* v *Magne* [1986] ECR 4071, [1988] 4 CMLR 98. On English law see *Chemidus Wavin* v *TERI* [1978] 3 CMLR 5124 (CA). For a reference to German law see Case 65/86 *Bayer* v *Sullhofer* [1988] ECR 5249, [1990] 4 CMLR 182, para. 8 of the judgment. Notice that the law will differ in practice from state to state; see note 49 above.

195 Case 31/80, note 114 above.

196 E.g., Case 63/75 *Fonderies Roubaix* v *Fonderies Roux* [1976] ECR 111; Case 170/83 *Hydrotherm* v *Compact* [1984] ECR 2999. But it must fall squarely within; a national court may not exempt a deal similar to, but not covered by, a block exemption; Case C-234/89, note 183 above.

197 A parallel problem arises during the six-month duration of the opposition procedure; see pp. 774–5.

198 Exempt: Art. 6(1) Reg. 17/62; void: Art. 85(2) EC.

199 Case 127/73, note 185 above; Case C-234/89 note 183 above.

decision. Exceptionally, agreements concluded before the entry into force of Regulation 17/62 were considered void only from the date this was finally established; once notified to the Commission, they enjoyed a provisional validity pending an authoritative ruling.[200] No such agreements remain in force, but the principle that agreements falling for the first time within the Community's jurisdiction are void only when so declared, not automatically, may be of application when new member states join the Community.[201] Such old agreements apart, however, in the normal modern case the national court asked to rule on the enforceability of a notified agreement, but unable to rule on exemption directly, is faced with an awkward decision because the Commission's eventual ruling will have retrospective effect.

Informal exemption

Where the Commission has acted informally, not formally, to approve the agreement, the situation is even more complex. A negative clearance is not formally binding, but highly persuasive. The Court considers a comfort letter apt to be taken into account by a national court, but not binding on it.[202] A comfort letter declaring the Commission's view that no breach of Article 85(1) is in issue,[203] for example because of the 'rule of reason',[204] will probably be followed at national level and the agreement enforced. However, if the Commission's comfort letter declares that the Commission considers the agreement caught by Article 85(1) but exemptable under Article 85(3),[205] then the national court, taking account of, first, the letter and, second, the direct effect of Article 85(1) but not Article 85(3), must observe the first part, the prima-facie prohibition, but ignore the second part, the exemption. It then holds the agreement unlawful; the exact opposite of the Commission's view. The strict legal position thus makes the comfort letter, although desirable as a means of reducing the Commission's workload, distinctly dangerous for the firms party to the agreement.[206]

---

200 Case 48/72 *Brasserie de Haecht* v *Wilkin* (No.2) [1973] ECR 77; Case 59/77 *De Bloos* v *Bouyer* [1977] ECR 2359. The extent of provisional validity was reduced in Case 99/79 *Lancôme* [1980] ECR 2511, [1981] 2 CMLR 164; see Bellamy and Child, *Common Market Law of Competition*, para. 11.041. Note that the issue retained relevance in sectors excluded from the application of Reg. 17/62, see note 184 above.
201 Note that many deals will already be subject to the Community's rules; see pp. 689–91 on extraterritoriality.
202 Cases 253/78 *et al.*, note 112 above.
203 As in ibid.
204 See p. 696.
205 As in Notice *Rovin* OJ 1983 C295/7, [1984] 1 CMLR 128.
206 'A Trojan Horse': Korah, *EC Competition Law and Practice*, p. 116.

There are, then, two connected problems: the notified agreement on which the Commission has not ruled, and the agreement covered by a comfort letter suggesting exemption. In both instances the inability of the national court to apply Article 85(3) directly leaves it in a quandary and may cause a beneficial agreement to be held unenforceable, which is detrimental to economic efficiency within the Community. Given the Commission's heavy workload, its prioritization of cases with a 'Community interest' within the meaning of the *Automec II* judgment[207] and its predilection for informal settlements rather than formal decisions binding on national courts, these anomalies are capable of causing genuine problems in practice. The European Court has attempted to encourage practical cooperation between Community authorities and national courts in order to avoid such problems. In *Stergios Delimitis* v *Henninger Brau*[208] the Court insisted that a national court should suspend proceedings in respect of an agreement that has been notified where it suspects that exemption may be forthcoming or grant appropriate interim measures. Moreover, it may contact the Commission for guidance on likely outcome.

The Commission's 1993 Notice

In February 1993 the Commission published a Notice on cooperation between national courts and the Commission in applying Articles 85 and 86.[209] The Commission cannot displace the two Courts from their predominant authoritative position in overseeing the development of Community law. Nor can it amend Regulation 17/62. The Notice is necessarily built on and constrained by the existing legal pattern. It covers much of the material discussed above and it is, in particular, shaped by the European Court's ruling in *Stergios Delimitis*[210] and the Court of First Instance's ruling in *Automec II*.[211] However, the Notice is of importance as a means of clarifying the nature of the Commission's planned relationship with national courts. The Notice expresses the view that comfort letters stating that the conditions for exemption under Article 85(3) have been met may be taken into account by national courts as 'factual elements'.[212] The acute difficulty here lies in the Commission's inability to go so far as to require the national court to abide by the comfort letter's exemption. That would elevate the comfort letter into a *de facto* formal ruling on exemption,

207 Case T-24/90, note 18 above.
208 Case C-234/89, note 183 above.
209 OJ 1993 C39/6, [1993] 4 CMLR 12.
210 Case C-234/89, note 183 above.
211 Case T-24/90, note 18 above.
212 Para. 26 of the Notice.

which seems incompatible with the Court's pronouncements on its informal status.[213] Nevertheless, the Notice comes rather close to inviting national courts to uphold agreements falling within Article 85(1) that are informally regarded by the Commission as worthy of exemption under Article 85(3). Ultimately, however, the Notice's reference to comfort letters as 'factual elements' to be taken into account at national level amounts to a delicate sidestep around this core question.[214]

The Notice proceeds to address the particularly thorny status of a duly notified practice falling within Article 85(1), but covered by neither block nor individual exemption nor by a comfort letter. Where the national court assesses that the practice 'cannot be the subject of an individual exemption, it will take the measures necessary to comply with the requirements of Articles 85(1) and (2)'. However, where individual exemption is possible, suspension of the proceedings pending a Commission decision is appropriate and the national court is free to adopt any necessary interim measures according to the provisions of national law.[215]

The Commission is engagingly honest in the Notice. It accepts that the scheme is 'complex and sometimes insufficient to enable ... [national] courts to perform their judicial function properly'.[216] It suggests that it will offer assistance in line with the duty of Community solidarity in Article 5 EC, on which the Court relied in its ruling in *Stergios Delimitis*.[217] Within the limits of their national procedural law, national courts may ask for information on the timescale of the Commission's inquiry, including a likely date for a decision on the application for exemption. The Commission promises to endeavour to give priority to cases which are the subject of national proceedings that have been suspended. National courts may also consult the Commission on points of law. The Notice mentions, *inter alia*, the possibility of a non-binding 'interim opinion' on the likelihood of exemption on which the national court may choose to rely.[218] The Notice also envisages the transmission by the Commission of factual data, such as statistics and market studies, although the Notice makes explicit reference to the requirements of confidentiality to which the Commission is subject.

The Notice represents a valiant attempt by the Commission to improve the methods of effective application of Community competition law in the

---

213 E.g., in Case 253/78, note 112 above.
214 For an English example of the problems confronted by national courts, see *Inntrepeneur Estates Ltd* v *Mason* [1993] 2 CMLR 293 (High Court).
215 Para. 30 of the Notice.
216 Para. 32 of the Notice.
217 Case C-234/89, note 183 above, in which the Court drew on Case C-2/88 Imm *Zwartveld* [1990] ECR I-3365, [1990] 3 CMLR 457, discussed in Ch. 10, in developing Art. 5 EC as the source of obligations imposed on the Commission.
218 Para. 38 of the Notice.

face of some fundamental legal obstructions to coherent, two-tier enforcement at Community and national level. Plainly a number of the Commission's suggestions require elaboration in practice. The imaginative suggestion that national courts may request and use opinions and evidence supplied by Directorate-General IV implies a type of informal parallel to Article 177, involving the Commission rather than the Court. However, there are likely to be significant procedural obstacles rooted in national law to the admissibility of such material in judicial proceedings.[219] Some aspects of the Notice have been affected by subsequent judicial activity. The rulings on confidentiality in the 'Spanish Banks' case[220] and in *Samenwerkende*[221] deal with the capacity of the Commission to release information to national authorities. It should, however, be noted that the limits on disclosure envisaged in those decisions were drawn from the risk of application of the relevant material outside the realms of the application of Community competition policy. They do not necessarily constrain release of information in circumstances where the application of Articles 85 and 86 at national level is at stake.

In some circumstances a national court and, above all, an undertaking seeking absolute clarification will be fully satisfied only by a final, formal decision. The Commission may sometimes be prepared to provide this.[222] Its promise in the Notice to endeavour to give priority to cases which are the subject of national proceedings that have been suspended may suffice to resolve these issues in practice. Yet, especially in consequence of priorities in case handling chosen by reference to the 'Community interest', it remains possible that the Commission will not provide a formal decision. It is then possible that the Commission's refusal to adopt a formal decision would be challengeable under Article 173 or 175, as appropriate, by a party threatened at national level by, for example, a finding of unenforceability made against an agreement that the Commission regards informally as worthy of exemption. On one view, the Commission's refusal to supply a formal decision has affected the party's legal position (at national level), which should suffice to form the basis for an application for review before the Court of First Instance.[223] On another view, the party is affected only by the national court's ruling, not by the Commission's unwillingness to proceed to a formal decision. This would militate against judicial review

---

219 See Lasok, 'Assessing the Economic Consequences of Restrictive Agreements: A Comment on the Delimitis Case' [1991] 5 ECLR 194, 199–201 (written before the Notice, but anticipating some of the problems); Van Bael, 'The Role of the National Courts' [1994] 1 ECLR 3.
220 Case C-67/91, note 40 above.
221 Case C-36/92 P, note 35 above.
222 Comm. Dec. 88/491, note 122 above.
223 See p. 778.

at Community level. The matter is not settled. *NBV and NVB v Commission*[224] involved an application for annulment of a negative clearance granted in respect of the applicants' agreement. The applicants expressed a fear that they might suffer subsequent prejudice arising from the Commission's finding that aspects of the arrangement restricted competition without meeting the interstate criterion that is essential to the scope of Article 85(1).[225] The Court of First Instance ruled that the decision granting negative clearance was incapable of affecting the applicants' legal position in the manner required to permit a challenge. The mere risk of awkwardness in the future was inadequate. The application was inadmissible. However, it is submitted that this ruling does not rule out the possibility of an application against a Commission refusal to issue a formal decision, especially where the interested party is engaged in relevant litigation at national level. In *BEMIM v Commission*[226] the Court of First Instance commented that national courts are not bound by the Commission's informal appraisal of the applicability of Articles 85(1) and 86 and that therefore the Commission cannot affect the position of an individual in national proceedings. This dictum appears hostile to the ability of an individual litigant at national level to extract a formal Commission decision through application to the Court of First Instance, yet it does not address directly the question of whether an informal Commission view about exemption under Article 85(3) may exert a sufficiently unclear impact at national level to justify a challenge. It would then be difficult to show that the Commission has acted unlawfully, for its duty is to secure the administration of the competition rules, not to adopt formal decisions in every case. However, it might be argued that the Commission's failure to act formally under its exclusive powers to exempt an agreement has unlawfully compromised the parties' legal certainty at national level.

Adjusting the administration of Article 85

The problems examined here at length are primarily attributable to the structure of the administration of the competition rules. The exclusive power of the Commission to exempt and the consequent need to set up a system of notification exert a significant influence on competition law and practice. For example, there is an incentive for firms to avoid the system altogether by ensuring that their deals fall outside Article 85(1) or fall squarely within a block exemption. This may mean that commercial planning proceeds not on the basis of what is appropriate to the deal in

224 Case T-138/89 [1992] ECR II-2181.
225 P. 692.
226 Case T-114/92 and Case T-5/93, note 26 above.

question, but, in part, in accordance with what can be cleared with minimum formality.[227] Furthermore, the Commission, overburdened by the Regulation 17/62 edifice, has an incentive to devise methods for speeding up the process. Techniques examined in this chapter, such as block exemptions, the opposition procedure and comfort letters, combined with the clarification achieved by the 1993 Notice offer administrative convenience but do not address the basic problem of centralization of power. This is the result of the Commission's exclusivity under Article 85(3), guaranteed by Article 9(1) of Regulation 17/62 and consistently confirmed by the Court in rulings hostile to the notion that Article 85(3) is capable of direct effect.[228]

It has, accordingly, been suggested that the exclusivity conferred on the Commission may have been desirable in the early years of the Community, when rigorous supervision and direction were needed lest the Treaty system fail to take root, but that it is now time to seek radical reform based on more regular and effective enforcement at national level.[229] For example, it is tempting to extend the circumstances in which desirable deals are considered unaffected by Article 85(1), instead of exemptable under Article 85(3), in order to enhance the ability of national courts to uphold agreements on their own initiative and in order to reduce Commission intervention in commercial planning. This rule-of-reason shift has attractions if coherently developed, but here there is a risk that the rush towards administrative expediency will distort the development of the substantive law and tend to erase Article 85(3) altogether.[230] A different approach would include abandoning notification in favour of ad hoc Commission intervention to direct policy and would permit the enforceability of Article 85(3) by national courts.[231] This would seem superior to the extended rule-of-reason approach in that it would prevent the effective elimination of Article 85(3), yet the potential for legal disunity and commercial unpredictability that would follow different approaches to law

---

227 See, e.g., Korah, 'EEC Competition Policy: Legal Form or Economic Efficiency' (1986) 39 CLP 85.

228 E.g., Case 31/80, note 114 above; Case C-234/89, note 183 above.

229 See especially Forrester and Norall, 'The Laicization of Community Law: Self-Help and the Rule of Reason: How Competition Law Is and Could Be Applied' (1984) 21 CMLRev 11.

230 See pp. 701–3 above; for criticism see especially Whish and Sufrin, 'Article 85 and the Rule of Reason' (1987) 7 YEL 1; cf. Korah (1986) 39 CLP 85; Forrester and Norall (1984) 21 CMLRev 11.

231 See, e.g., Daltrop and Ferry, 'The Relationship between Articles 85 and 86: Tetra Pak' [1991] 1 ICCLR 24. See also Peeters, 'The Rule of Reason Revisited: Prohibition on Restraints of Competition in the Sherman Act and the EEC Treaty' (1989) 37 AJCL, 521 and, generally, Forrester and Norall (1984) 21 CMLRev 11, and Brown (1992) 17 ELRev 323.

and procedure in different states constitutes a serious drawback.[232] An even more fundamental overhaul of the system would involve the empowerment of national competition authorities to apply the Community rules and the creation of a decentralized pattern of administrative control.[233] At present this appears a remote prospect.

USING THE TREATY RULES AS A CAUSE OF ACTION

Participants in horizontal cartels will often be perfectly happy with their arrangement. They will have no incentive to go to law to deny the enforceability of their agreement, so the discussion in the previous subsection will be irrelevant. Any challenge to the agreement is likely to come from an affected third party wishing to maintain a challenge to the practice. Indeed, the victim of an anticompetitive practice may be interested not simply in putting an end to it, but also in securing compensation for loss suffered as a result of the unlawful conduct. This compensation is not available at Community level,[234] but it may be possible to pursue an action based on the violation of Community law before national courts.

The Commission's 1993 Notice draws explicitly on the *Automec II* ruling[235] in stating that 'there is not normally a sufficient Community interest in examining a case when the plaintiff is able to secure adequate protection of his rights before his national courts'.[236] The Notice moves beyond this statement of unwillingness to proceed at Community level to identify advantages to individuals and companies in proceeding at national level. These include the availability of compensation and the possibility of a more rapid grant of interim measures.

National remedies

The doctrine of direct effect ensures that the matter can be brought before national courts, but Community law does not dictate the remedies to be made available to vindicate those rights. The Court established in *Comet* v

---

232 See, e.g., debate between Kon, 'Article 85, para. 3: A Case for Application by National Courts' (1982) 19 CMLRev 541 and Steindorff, 'Article 85, para. 3: No Case for Application by National Courts' (1993) 20 CMLRev 125.

233 In this direction see Riley [1993] 3 ECLR 91. See also Editorial, (1995) 32 CMLRev 1.

234 Apart from the possibility that an informal *ex gratia* payment may be made as part of a settlement; see p. 779.

235 Case T-24/90, note 18 above.

236 Note 209 above, para. 15 of the Notice.

Produktschap[237] and *Rewe-Zentralfinanz* v *Landwirtschaftskammer*[238] that the provision of remedies remains within the jurisdiction of the national system, subject, first, to the requirement that the remedy must be available on conditions no less favourable than those applied to a similar right of action in purely national matters, and, second, that the conditions must not make it impossible in practice to exercise the rights under Community law which national courts are under a duty to protect. This formula has been repeated in materially similar terms by the Court in several subsequent cases.[239]

Remedies for breach of Community law thus differ from state to state.[240] This is in itself capable of causing disharmony in the practical impact of the competition rules within the Community and, in so far as such remedies prove inadequate, it will diminish the efficacy of the national route of enforcing Community law. Consequently, if the Commission's ambition to see more vigorous action at national level[241] is to be realized, it may be necessary for it to seek to harmonize and strengthen national remedies. Under US law, for example, treble damages are available in private actions for violation of antitrust law.[242] Advocates of release of the Commission's exclusivity under Article 85(3), discussed in the preceding subsection, also recognize the connected need to achieve improvement of procedures and remedies before national courts in order to establish credible sanctions against anticompetitive conduct.[243]

---

237 Case 45/76 [1976] ECR 2043, [1977] 1 CMLR 533.
238 Case 33/76 [1976] ECR 1989, [1977] 1 CMLR 533.
239 E.g. Case 61/79 *Amministrazione delle Finanze dello Stato* v *Denkavit Italiana* [1980] ECR 1205, [1981] 3 CMLR 694; Case 68/79 *Hans Just* [1980] ECR 501; Case 130/79 *Express Dairy Foods* v *Intervention Board* [1980] ECR 1887, [1981] 1 CMLR 451. See, e.g., Barav and Green, 'Damages in the national courts for breach of Community law', (1986) 6 YEL 55; Oliver, 'Enforcing Community Rights in English Courts', (1987) 50 MLR 881; Steiner, 'How to make the action suit the case', (1987) 12 ELRev 102; Ward, 'Government Liability in the UK for breach of individual rights in EC law', (1990) 19 Anglo-Am LR 1, 2–6; Weatherill, 'National remedies and Equal Access to Public Procurement', (1990) 10 YEL 243.
240 See Bridge, 'Procedural Aspects of the Enforcement of EC Law through the Legal Systems of Member States', (1984) 9 ELRev 28; Mateo (1991) 27 CDE 317; Kapteyn and Verloren Van Themaat, *Law of the European Communities* pp. 45–51. See subsidiarity, notes 49, 194 above.
241 See note 189 above.
242 See Neale and Goyder, *The Antitrust Laws of the USA* (1980); for Australia, see Brunt, 'The Role of Private Actions in Australian Restrictive Trade Practices Enforcement' (1990) 17 Melb ULR 582.
243 E.g., Forrester and Norall (1984) 21 CLMRev 11.

English and Scottish courts

In litigation before domestic courts it is for the domestic system to protect rights violated by anticompetitive conduct. What is the cause of action before English courts?[244] Lord Denning made an early foray into this area and suggested in *Applications des Gaz SA* v *Falks Veritas*[245] that a special tort ought to be created to cater for the special demands of Community law, but this now appears discredited.[246] Lord Diplock in *Garden Cottage Foods* v *Milk Marketing Board*[247] preferred to operate within the confines of existing torts and focused on breach of statutory duty: the statutory duty to observe Community law arising from the European Communities Act 1972. Other torts are less promising. Conspiracy depends on showing a high level of intent to harm the plaintiff,[248] not simply to advance the interests of the defendant, yet the latter is the normal objective of a violation of Articles 85 and 86. Unlawful interference with business is a tort that might assist, but its ambit awaits judicial elucidation.[249]

The most obvious remedy would be an injunction to restrain the allegedly unlawful conduct. In an urgent situation an application for an interlocutory injunction would be appropriate. However, the House of Lords established in *American Cyanamid* v *Ethicon*[250] that it is unlikely that a court would be prepared to award interlocutory relief where damages at trial would constitute effective protection for the plaintiff. The question then arises whether damages are, in principle, available in English law to compensate the victim of a violation of the Treaty competition rules. An affirmative answer was given by the House of Lords in *Garden Cottage Foods*.[251] The plaintiff dairy firm found the Milk Marketing Board unwilling to continue to supply it with bulk butter. It contended that the Board

244 Whish, 'The Enforcement of EC Competition Law in the Domestic Courts of Member States' [1994] 2 ECLR 60.
245 [1974] 3 All ER 51.
246 However, for an argument that the creation of special torts is not only desirable but necessary as a matter of Community law, see Davidson, 'Actions for Damages in the English Courts for Breach of EEC Competition Law' (1985) 34 ICLQ 178.
247 [1984] AC 130, [1983] 2 All ER 770, [1983] 3 WLR 143, [1983] 3 CMLR 43. See also Roskill LJ in *Valor* v *Applications des Gaz* [1978] 3 CMLR 87.
248 Although, despite earlier suggestions to the contrary, this need not be the predominant purpose of the conspirators; *Lonrho* v *Fayed* [1991] 3 WLR 188 (HL).
249 See Carty, 'Intentional Violation of Economic Interests: the Limits of Common Law Liability', (1988) 104 LQR 250.
250 [1975] AC 396.
251 Note 247 above. See, e.g., Goyder, *EC Competition Law*, pp. 440–42; Picanol, 'Remedies in National Law for Breach of Articles 85 and 86 of the EEC Treaty: A Review' [1983/2] LIEI 1; Jacobs, 'Damages for Breach of Article 86 EEC' (1983) 8 ELRev 353; Green, 'The Treaty of Rome, National Courts and English Law: The Enforcement of European Competition Law after Milk Marketing Board' (1984) 48 *Rabels Zeitschrift* 509.

held a dominant position in the supply of bulk butter and that its reluctance constituted an abuse of that dominance, contrary to Article 86. It sought an interlocutory injunction. The House of Lords held by a majority of 4–1[252] that damages are available to a party suffering loss as a result of breach of Article 86 on the basis of an action for breach of the statutory duty imposed by the European Communities Act 1972. This amounted to sufficient protection at trial for the plaintiffs and the injunction was therefore discharged. Damages, then, are available; interlocutory injunctions are correspondingly less likely to be awarded. Subsequently, the *Garden Cottage* approach has been followed,[253] although damages have not yet been awarded in any case. Interlocutory injunctions have been granted, but only where the court has been satisfied that damages will not be an adequate remedy at trial.[254]

Effective remedies at national level

If *Garden Cottage Foods* proves reliable authority that damages are available for breach of Article 86, then English law discriminates in favour of the litigant able to inject an element of Community law into his or her claim, because there is no domestic action yielding damages that would lie in these circumstances. This form of 'reverse discrimination' is not incompatible with Community law and may indeed be required by it in order to supply effective remedies to vindicate Community law rights at national level, which is the overriding concern in this area.[255] The matter is certainly not finally settled, not least because of troubling analogies that need to be drawn with the Court of Appeal's treatment of a claim for damages for loss suffered as a result of breach of Article 30 in *Bourgoin* v *Minister of Agriculture, Fisheries and Food*.[256] The majority, while accepting the direct effect of Article 30 before English courts, refused to accept the availability of an action for damages for breach of Article 30 *simpliciter*.[257] Lord Justices Parker and Nourse were of the opinion that the remedy before the English courts for breach of Article 30 lay in public, not

252 Lord Wilberforce delivered a powerful dissent.
253 *An Bord Bainne* v *Milk Marketing Board* [1984] 2 CMLR 584, noted by Shaw [1984] 43 CLJ 255.
254 *Cutsforth* v *Mansfield Inns* [1986] 1 CMLR 1; *Holleran* v *Thwaites plc* [1989] 2 CMLR 917. An application for an interim interdict was refused by the Court of Session in *Argyll Group* v *Distillers* [1986] 1 CMLR 764.
255 See especially Case C-213/89, note 128 above.
256 [1986] QB 716, [1985] 3 WLR 1027, [1985] 2 All ER 585. For analysis, see refs. at note 239 above.
257 Followed by the Court of Appeal in *An Bord Bainne* v *Milk Marketing Board* [1988] 1 CMLR 605.

private, law – by means of judicial review.[258] Lord Goff in the House of Lords' decision in *Kirklees BC* v *Wickes Ltd* commented, albeit obiter, that 'there must now be doubt whether the *Bourgoin* case was correctly decided'.[259] The explicit spur to this suggestion was the decision of the European Court in *Francovich*. National courts are increasingly receiving direction from the European Court, which made its concern for effective remedies at national level clear in *Factortame*.[260] The Court's views were reinforced in *Francovich*, which is explicitly concerned with the availability of damages at national level, albeit in connection with non-implementation of a directive.[261] The Commission's 1993 Notice refers to the access of individuals and companies

to all procedural remedies provided for by national law on the same conditions as would apply if a comparable breach of national law were involved. This equality of treatment concerns not only the definitive finding of a breach of competition rules, but embraces all the legal means capable of contributing to effective legal protection.[262]

The elaboration of the principles of liability established in the *Francovich* ruling is one of the major tasks of the European Court.[263] In *H. Banks & Co Ltd* v *British Coal Corporation*,[264] a damages claim arising out of alleged infringements of the competition rules of the European Coal and Steel Community Treaty, Advocate-General van Gerven analysed *Francovich* liability as part of the general system of Community law and favoured its application to violations by private parties. However, the Court, in a ruling carefully confined to the Coal and Steel Treaty, held that an action for damages before a national court could not be pursued in the absence of a Commission finding of violation. In spite of the cautious nature of this decision under the ECSC Treaty, it is submitted that although state liability may require cautious handling because of the potentially unlimited threat to the public purse, the Treaty competition rules are unusually well suited to the development of a Community law principle that damage shall be made good by parties responsible for causing loss in breach of the Treaty. Therefore the House of Lords' receptivity to the remedy of

---

258 The matter was not argued before the House of Lords, being the subject of a settlement involving a payment of £3.5 million to the plaintiffs, HC Deb Vol 102, col 116 (WA), 22 July 1986.
259 [1992] 3 All ER 717, 734.
260 Case C-213/89, note 128 above.
261 Cases C-6/90, 9/90 *Francovich and others* v *Italy*, [1991] ECR I-5357, [1993] 2 CMLR 66.
262 Note 209 above, para. 11 of the Notice.
263 See further p. 352.
264 Case C-128/92 [1994] ECR I-1209, [1994] 5 CMLR 30.

damages in cases of violation of EC competition law in *Garden Cottage Foods*[265] appears well-founded. The Commission, too, may seek to improve domestic enforcement by pressing for harmonization legislation covering procedures and remedies. However, this is a task of fiendish complexity. The entry of new member states increases the problems posed by heterogeneity of legal tradition.[266]

CHOOSING

'Dual vigilance' means that a firm prejudiced by conduct unlawful under the competition rules may complain to the Commission and hope that it will take action and may also pursue the matter at national level relying on the direct effect of the relevant provisions. Both routes may be pursued independently; one does not preclude the other.

Action at national level is the only method of securing compensation. The Commission may impose fines, but only the national court can require the payment of compensation by the malefactor to the victim. So, a claim for compensation should be pursued at national level. So, too, interim injunctions; these may be more quickly obtained at national level than through the Commission. In *Cutsforth* v *Mansfield Inns*[267] an interim injunction was awarded, with comment on the slow speed of action in Brussels.[268] The slowness is in part attributable to the heavy workload of DG IV and its consequent inability to deal promptly with all matters that come to its attention. However, even where the Commission resolves to act rapidly to adopt interim measures to halt a practice, the formalities that must be respected, such as hearings, ensure a time-lag. *Ex parte* awards are available only at national level. Before English courts, however, the opportunities for obtaining interlocutory relief have been diminished by the decision in *Garden Cottage Foods*[269] applying the principles of *American Cyanamid* v *Ethicon*.[270] This may encourage complaint to DG IV in Brussels.[271] The domestic litigant must also be aware of the risk of having

265 Note 247 above.
266 Discussed by Whish, *Competition Law*, p. 328; Weatherill (1990) 10 YEL 243. See also p. 799 above.
267 Note 254 above.
268 See also *Holleran* v *Thwaites*, note 254 above.
269 Note 247 above.
270 Note 250 above.
271 *A fortiori*, if, as Whish suggests (*Competition Law*, p. 298), the test for the award of interim relief may be rather less favourable to an applicant under English law than

to pay not only its own costs but also those of the other side. Winning at interlocutory stage but losing on the merits can be very expensive. In contrast, the Commission takes on the matter on its own behalf as guardian of the Community interest and bears its own costs.

So in some instances the domestic action may be more favourable to the victim. And if the Commission declines to pursue the matter despite a complaint and cannot be successfully challenged,[272] domestic action will have to be taken. But Commission investigation is likely to be the preferred route, especially where the victim wants no more than termination, rather than compensation. The Commission has extensive powers of investigation and is equipped with the power to fine. It is immeasurably better equipped to control anticompetitive practices than the private litigant. Indeed, it will often be the case that the Commission can discover and halt unlawful practices that would have been suspected but unprovable or simply undiscoverable using national procedures. It may then be that a litigant can rely on the Commission's authoritative ruling of illegality as the basis for a domestic action, perhaps for compensation. Where the Commission acts informally, the issues, as discussed, are complex and immediately raise the overlap between enforcement of Community law at two levels.[273]

In conclusion, the Commission's 1993 Notice on cooperation between national courts and the Commission deserves welcome for its attempt to bring transparency to Commission practice. Although the *Automec II* ruling, reflected in the Notice, points towards the Commission proving unwilling to pursue matters in which it perceives no 'Community interest', it is gratifying that the criteria that govern such choices have been made transparent. The opportunity for judicial review of the Commission's handling of its power to establish priorities is thereby enhanced. The ruling in *BEUC* v *Commission*[274] demonstrates the Court's role in this area. The Commission's commitment to support national courts, prompted by the ruling in *Stergios Delimitis*,[275] is also welcome, although the detailed procedures under which this relationship will operate require attention.[276] In the meantime, variation between the member states both in the capacity to ensure effective application of Community rules through national

---

Community law. Temple Lang observes that this discrepancy is undesirable, for it encourages shopping between Community and national fora, (1981) 18 CMLRev 49, 58.
272 See p. 762.
273 See p. 792.
274 Case T-37/92, note 28 above.
275 Case C-234/89 note 183 above.
276 P. 795 above.

procedures and in the attitude of the judiciary remains an impediment to the practical application of EC competition law that is inevitably concealed behind examination of Community law sources alone.[277]

---

277 See, on the UK and Italy, Behrens (ed.), *EEC Competition Rules in National Courts,* Part One.

CHAPTER 25

Law of Mergers

THE PROVISIONS OF THE TREATY

The Community law of mergers enjoys a chequered history. The Treaty of Rome contained no explicit provision applicable to mergers. This forms an odd contrast with its predecessor, the Treaty of Paris, which in Article 66 provided for merger control in the European Coal and Steel Community.[1] The omission may be attributable to political difficulty in agreeing an acceptable instrument. If so, this was an early manifestation of the endemic problem of political sensitivity that surrounds Community merger control. Whatever the reasons for the omission, it was highly unsatisfactory. Mergers are potentially beneficial vehicles for industrial restructuring designed to respond to the development of the common market, but they are capable of suppressing competition, particularly where they are concluded 'horizontally', between previously independent rivals.[2] The vital need for legal controls over mergers combined with the absence of provisions directly appropriate to that end led the Commission, supported by the Court, to mould first Article 86, then Article 85, to cover mergers. The distortions in law and in practice that this approach produced, coupled with an increase in merger activity throughout the Community as firms accelerated their cross-border expansion programmes in anticipation of the completion of the internal market by the end of 1992,[3] created a political environment conducive to the adoption of a specialized Community merger regime. This is now contained in the long-awaited Merger Control Regulation.[4] However, the Merger Control Regulation does not solve all the problems. In particular, it does not conclusively put an end to

1 See Downes and Ellison, *The Legal Control of Mergers*, pp. 2–3, Ch. 6; Bos, Stuyck and Wytinck, *Concentration Control in the European Economic Community*, Ch. 2.
2 See generally Chiplin and Wright, *The Logic of Mergers*; Fairburn and Kay (eds.), *Mergers and Merger Policy*; Bishop and Kay (eds.), *European Mergers and Merger Policy*.
3 See the Commission's Annual Reports on Competition Policy – e.g., 18th Report for 1988, pp. 233–45 – which provide statistics on such growth.
4 See pp. 811–12.

the relevance of the pre-existing law in this area. It is first necessary to examine the ways in which Community law has been applied to mergers in the past in order to identify the central policy concerns of the system.

ARTICLE 86

Article 86, examined in Chapter 23, is not explicitly concerned with mergers at all. It prohibits an abuse of a dominant position within the common market, which seems to connote behaviour of a directly exploitative nature. However, in an attempt to devise a means of asserting legal control over mergers the Commission has used the term 'abuse' to include a merger, thereby permitting control of such deals at Community level. This approach was first adopted in *Continental Can* v *Commission*,[5] in which the Commission condemned a merger as an abuse of a dominant position. On application by the firm, the Court annulled the Commission's decision on the grounds that the Commission had failed to supply a sufficient sophisticated economic analysis of the scope of the market against which Continental Can's activities were judged.[6] However, on the point of principle the Court confirmed the Commission's view that a merger may constitute an abuse under Article 86. Drawing on Article 3(f) EEC which declares that the activities of the Community shall include 'the institution of a system ensuring that competition in the common market is not distorted'[7] the Court held that, in view of the distortion consequent on a merger, such a deal falls foul of Community law where a dominant firm extends its power through merger in a manner that 'substantially fetters competition'.

The decision was of value in that it confirmed the ability in principle of the Commission to control mergers, but in practice it constituted little more than an artificial attempt to use Article 86 to cover a practice for which it is simply not suitable as a control. Article 86 permits only an unstructured calculation of the costs and benefits of the merger through the application of the vague notion of 'abuse'. The merger cannot sensibly be assessed simply as either abusive or non-abusive. The test of a substantial fettering of competition is difficult to apply, which may breed commercial uncertainty. Moreover, if the merger strengthens existing dominance, it may be controlled under Article 86, but this is impossible if the merger creates new dominance. So a firm holding 75 per cent of a market that merges with the holder of 5 per cent of the market is caught, whereas a 45

5 Case 6/72 [1973] ECR 215, [1973] CMLR 199.
6 See p. 731.
7 Now Art. 3(g) EC.

per cent market holder merging with its rival also holding 45 per cent is not caught.[8] Article 86 works in a manner that is irrelevant in economic terms.

Partly as a consequence of these complexities, there has been virtually no formal use of Article 86 in the field since *Continental Can*.[9] It has, however, supplied the basis for a significant level of informal work in this area by the Commission.[10] This has frequently involved modifications demanded of firms before the Commission is willing to indicate a favourable view of the merger.[11] This is scarcely satisfactory. The Commission is acting on the basis of its own concept of abuse without any clear guidance on the notion of the beneficial merger.

ARTICLE 85

Article 85, analysed in Chapter 22, focuses on restrictive practices, and its relevance to mergers and related deals is not immediately apparent. For twenty years the Commission adhered to its 1966 Memorandum, which seemed to rule out the application of Article 85 to mergers.[12] None the less, in 1987 the Commission, eager for instruments of merger control, earned the Court's support in using Article 85 in this area. The groundbreaking case was *BAT and Reynolds* v *Commission*.[13] Philip Morris and Rothmans were competing cigarette manufacturers. Morris agreed with Rembrandt, owner of Rothmans, that it would buy a stake in Rothmans. The terms of the deal gave Morris a 30 per cent interest in Rothmans and 24.9 per cent of the voting rights, plus certain ancillary rights. Rembrandt retained 43.6 per cent of the voting rights. The deal thus established a link between Morris and Rothmans, previously independent competitors. The Commission received undertakings from Morris that it would not seek to

---

8 A difficult task of market definition would have to be undertaken in reaching these figures; see p. 728.

9 For a rare example see Dec. 93/252 *Warner-Lambert/Gillette* OJ 1993 L116/21, [1993] 5 CMLR 559. See also Dec. 88/501 *Tetra Pak* OJ 1988 L272/27, [1990] 4 CMLR 47, upheld in Case T-51/89 *Tetra Pak Rausing SA* v *Commission* [1990] ECR II-309, [1991] 4 CMLR 334, where the objection was to the acquisition on merger of an exclusive patent licence, rather than to the merger *per se*.

10 See the Commission's Annual Reports on Competition Policy.

11 See, e.g., *Pilkington/BSN*, 10th Report on Competition Policy (1980) paras. 152–5.

12 See Bos, Stuyck and Wytinck, *Concentration Control in the European Economic Community*, pp. 69–70.

13 Cases 142, 156/84 [1987] ECR 4487, [1988] 4 CMLR 24. The case has been the subject of extensive academic comment; see, e.g., Korah and Lasok (1988) 25 CMLRev 33; Strivens [1988] 6 EIPR 163; Friend (1988) 13 ELRev 189; Brown [1988] JBL 351, 432, 514.

reinforce its position in order to exert influence over Rothmans. The Commission was satisfied that these arrangements conformed to the demands of Community competition law. However, the matter came before the European Court as a result of a challenge by dissatisfied third parties, BAT and Reynolds,[14] who were competing cigarette manufacturers alarmed at the link between Rothmans and Morris, which, they argued, was liable to restrict free competition. The Court held that Article 85 may apply

... where, by the acquisition of shareholding or through subsidiary clauses in the agreement, the investing company obtains legal or *de facto* control of the commercial conduct of the other company or where the agreement provides for commercial cooperation between the companies or creates a structure likely to be used for such cooperation. That may also be the case where the agreement gives the investing company the possibility of reinforcing its position at a later stage and taking effective control of the other company.[15]

Thus, in the case of an agreement that falls short of a full merger but involves the establishment of closer ties between competitors, Community law asserts a right to intervene to control the deal if the consequences may be anticompetitive. Article 85 is therefore widely available in the case of changes in corporate ownership through agreement. In a peculiar echo of *Continental Can* sixteen years previously, the Court, having established a significant new principle, held that the facts of the case disclosed no breach of Community law.[16] Morris's acquisition did *not* give it effective control. This was purely 'passive investment', lawful under Article 85. The importance of the case stemmed, of course, from the potential future application of Article 85 in this field. The Commission's hand was significantly strengthened in so far as control of transactions such as joint ventures, share transfer arrangements and partial and, perhaps, full mergers are concerned.

Immediately following this judgment the Commission abandoned its earlier reluctance to use Article 85 in the area of changes in corporate ownership. Thus, in *Carnaud/Schmalbach*[17] the Commission prevented the acquisition by Carnaud of a majority interest in Sofreb, because such an acquisition would have had the result that Carnaud would have come into collaboration with its competitor, Schmalbach,[18] which held a minority

14 See p. 757 on the position of complainants.
15 Cases 142, 156/84, note 13 above, paras. 38–9 of the judgment.
16 See Rasmussen, *On Law and Policy*, p. 137 on the Court's predilection for 'give and take' judgments of this nature.
17 [1988] 4 CMLR 262.
18 A subsidiary of the ubiquitous Continental Can.

interest in Sofreb. Remarkably, the Commission none the less then approved Carnaud's purchase of the whole of Sofreb, including Schmalbach's minority interest, on the basis that this kept Carnaud and Schmalbach at arm's length and thereby preserved unfettered competition.[19] A string of further decisions based on Article 85 confirmed the Commission's zeal in this area,[20] but such broad powers of intervention fell far short of a sophisticated regime for the supervision of mergers and related deals. In fact, Article 85 is no more an ideal instrument of control in this area than Article 86. Business is confronted by disturbing uncertainty in predicting what constitutes de facto control under the Court's BAT and Reynolds 'test'. Many other questions arise. For example, could Article 85 apply to a hostile take-over, where the firms are not in 'agreement'?[21] Could Article 85 apply to a full, rather than a partial, merger?[22] These are enduring problems. They were among the issues that contributed to the 1966 preference to avoid the use of Article 85 in this area.[23] Informal activity by the Commission is unsatisfactory, both because it is unpredictable and because it evades proper scrutiny and accountability. Once more, the only solution is the creation of a regime explicitly devoted to mergers. This is a matter of which the Commission was doubtless fully aware. The complexity that arises as a result of Court and Commission activity was in part designed as the prompt to the Council to produce the Mergers Regulation.

Enforcement

Precisely the same problems as have been noted above in connection with the substantive provisions arise again in connection with enforcement procedures. That is, the generalized procedures for enforcing competition law have to be used in the particular case of mergers, but prove unsuitable for that purpose. Regulation 17/62 is tied to the expectation of ex post facto supervision. This is acceptable in most areas to which competition law applies, such as the suppression of a restrictive practice contrary to Article

19 The Commission was satisfied that this deal, a full merger, did not fall foul of Article 86, for there was no market dominance.
20 E.g., British Airways/British Caledonian [1988] 4 CMLR 258. See also Dec. 93/252, note 9 above.
21 Perhaps the individual sale agreements by shareholders are caught, perhaps cumulatively, see Case 23/67 Brasserie de Haecht v Wilkin [1967] ECR 407, [1968] CMLR 26, pp. 695–6 above. This seems an artificial approach, but that may be no serious objection in this obscure area.
22 It seems illogical to use Art. 85 to control a de facto assumption of control, but not a 100 per cent assumption of control.
23 A fuller examination may be found in the 2nd edition of Whish, Competition Law, pp. 738–47.

85 or of unfair pricing prohibited under Article 86. However, it may be fiendishly difficult to unravel a merger if it is subsequently held to infringe Community law. Such difficulties are compounded by the direct effect of the relevant provisions, which allows their enforcement before national courts.[24]

In practice, the difficulties created by the absence of a priori control are to some extent circumvented by the informal practice of advance notification by firms of proposed deals for the Commission's consideration.[25] In extreme cases the Commission might be able to take interim measures to restrain a proposed merger.[26] However, these practices do not evade the basic difficulties of applying an inappropriate general regime to the special case of mergers. Interim measures are in any event useful only if the Commission actually knows of proposed deals. Informal practices also remain subject to the serious criticism that they reduce the transparency of the procedure, thereby diminishing the accountability of the Commission. What is needed, is, at least, a formal prenotification procedure with defined criteria under which mergers can be assessed.

THE MERGER CONTROL REGULATION

The inadequacies of existing Community law, some of which have been explained above, constitute an unarguable case for the introduction of legislation designed to provide a framework explicitly devoted to mergers in order to control their potential distortive impact on the Community market. This is the background to the Merger Control Regulation,[27] adopted on 21 December 1989, which entered into force on 21 September 1990.

The Regulation aims to establish a division between large mergers, which will be regulated at Community level, and smaller mergers, which remain the preserve of national authorities. Against that general background objective the Merger Control Regulation requires appraisal on four levels. First, what type of deal is caught under the Regulation? The second level concerns the scope of its application: what is the demarcation

---

24 See p. 789 above.
25 See, e.g., *British Airways/British Caledonian*, note 20 above.
26 Case 792/79 R *Camera Care* v *Commission* [1980] ECR 119, p. 781 above; see *Irish Distillers/GC&C*, p. 782 above, interim proceedings for breach of Art. 85 suspended after the receipt of undertakings to abandon a joint bid for a competitor.
27 Reg. 4064/89 OJ 1989 L395/1, corrected version published OJ 1990 L257/14.

between Community and national law competence to regulate concentrations/mergers? Double jeopardy – say, London and Brussels – or even treble jeopardy – say, London, Paris and Brussels – is disturbingly inefficient. The third level concerns the problems relating to the internal consistency of Community competition law, discussed above; does it solve the Article 85/Article 86 problem? At the fourth and final level, accepting that there is to be an explicit Community regime operating in some areas while national law prevails in others, what is the content of the Community regime: what criteria are to be used to judge the desirability of a merger? Experience of the Commission's handling of the Regulation since 1990 has provided insights into some of the practical aspects of these issues.[28] However, a number of difficulties await clarification and resolution. These four issues are examined in turn.

THE NOTION OF A CONCENTRATION

The Regulation controls 'concentrations' – commonly referred to as mergers. Article 3(1) of the Regulation defines the types of deal that are caught.[29] It covers two main types of transaction. First, a concentration within the meaning of the Regulation arises where 'two or more previously independent undertakings merge'. Second, a concentration arises 'where one or more persons already controlling at least one undertaking or one or more undertakings acquire, whether by purchase of securities or assets, by contract or any other means, direct or indirect control of the whole or parts of one or more other undertakings'. In December 1994 the Commission published two helpful Notices in this area. Commission Notices cannot displace judicial interpretation of the law, but the Notices serve to make Commission practice more transparent in this area. These are the Notice on the notion of a concentration[30] and the Notice on the notion of undertakings.[31] In the second category of concentration, the notion of acquiring 'control' is clearly of central importance. Article 3(3) of the Regulation defines control with reference to the possibility of exercising decisive influence, which may be achieved in some circumstances by acquisition of a minority shareholding. This test lacks legal precision and will be dependent for its application on an examination of the structure of

---

28 For discussion of evolving practice, see Select Further Reading for Ch. 25, p. 915.
29 Cook and Kerse, *EEC Merger Control*, Ch. 2; Downes and Ellison, *The Legal Control of Mergers*, Ch. 2; Bos, Stuyck and Wytinck, *Concentration Control in the European Economic Community*, Ch. IV. III; Jones and González Díaz, *The EEC Merger Regulation*, Chs, 1, 5.
30 OJ 1994 C385/5.
31 OJ 1994 C385/12.

the firms involved. In *Arjomari Prioux/Wiggins Teape*[32] acquisition of a 39 per cent shareholding was held to permit control, given that ownership of the remaining shares was widely dispersed. There was accordingly a concentration within the meaning of Article 3. In *Mediobanca/Assicurazioni Generali*[33] the Commission found that the acquisition of a 12.84 per cent shareholding did not confer decisive influence and that there was accordingly no merger. However, this is no iron rule. The Commission conceded that in circumstances where, for example, there was a sustained poor attendance at meetings by holders of the remaining shares, even an apparently small minority shareholding might suffice to permit control over a firm. Such unusual circumstances were not present in the deal in question.[34] The 1994 Notice on the notion of a concentration elaborates the Commission's approach to establishing an acquisition of control in, *inter alia*, such circumstances. It refers to the importance of examining the practice of recent years in order to determine whether a minority shareholder has a stable majority of the votes at the shareholders' meeting.[35]

In *Renault/Volvo*[36] the firms agreed to merge 25 per cent of their car manufacturing businesses and 45 per cent of their truck and bus divisions. The Commission held that the former did not constitute a concentration caught by the Regulation, whereas the latter did. The 25 per cent transfer would lead to neither sole control by one firm over the other nor common control. The Commission was also satisfied that the contractual ties between the firms did not rob them of independence. However, the 45 per cent link established in respect of trucks and buses was considered to lead to *de facto* permanent common control. In effect, a single economic entity had been created and this constituted a concentration within the meaning of the Regulation.

Joint ventures

The persistent problem of the application of competition law to joint ventures surfaces in defining concentrations for the purposes of the Regulation. Article 3(2) of the Regulation explains that where the joint venture performs 'on a lasting basis all the functions of an autonomous economic

---

32 IV/M/025 OJ 1990 C321/16 [1991] 4 CMLR 854, noted (1990) ELRev Competition Law Checklist 94.
33 IV/M/159, OJ 1991 C334/23, [1994] 4 CMLR M1.
34 An application for annulment under Art. 173 EC by shareholders in Generali was held inadmissible in Case T-83/92 *Zunis Holding SA and others* v *Commission*, judgment of 28 October 1993, [1994] 5 CMLR 154, noted by Brown [1994] 6 ECLR 296; an appeal to the European Court was lodged in December 1993, Case C-480/93.
35 Note 30 above, para. 14 of the Notice.
36 IV/M/004 OJ 1990 C281/2 [1991] 4 CMLR 297.

entity, which does not give rise to coordination of the competitive behaviour of the parties themselves or between them and the joint venture', it will be a concentration. Otherwise, the matter falls to be considered as an agreement subject to Article 85. The Commission produced guidelines on the distinction between collaborative joint ventures (Article 85) and concentrative joint ventures (Merger Regulation) in the course of 1990.[37] In December 1994 it published a revised version of the Notice.[38] This replaced the 1990 Notice and the new text reflects the experience accumulated by the Commission in its handling of merger control under the Regulation. Where the joint venture permits coordination of the parents' other activities, the joint venture remains subject to assessment in the light of Article 85. Depending on the extent to which it restricts competition, it may escape the ambit of Article 85 altogether or require exemption under Article 85(3).[39] Where most of the joint venture's sales or supplies are tied to one or both of the parents, it will not be seen to function as an autonomous entity, with the result that it will be subject to Article 85, not the Regulation. Similarly, the joint venture active in the parents' own markets or neighbouring markets is unlikely to have sufficient autonomy to be considered concentrative.[40] However, if, for example, a joint venture takes over an activity that was pursued by the parents and both parents withdraw from that area, and if the joint venture is a long-term plan with independent responsibility for its own commercial planning, then the structure is likely to be viewed as a concentration and will have to conform to the provisions of the Merger Regulation.[40a]

The 1990 Notice attracted criticism for an alleged excessive readiness to

37 OJ 1990 C203/10; [1990] 4 CMLR 721. See Downes and Ellison, *The Legal Control of Mergers*, Ch. 5. For criticism of the Commission's approach, see Pathak, 'The EC Commission's Approach to Joint Ventures', [1991] 5 ECLR 171; Sibree, 'EEC Merger Control and Joint Ventures' (1992) 17 ELRev 91; Fine, 'The Cooperative/Concentrative Dilemma of EC Merger Control – a Review of Commission Policy' (1994) XVII Boston Coll Intl and Comp Law 1; Hawk and Huser, 'A Bright Line Shareholding Test to end the Nightmare under the EEC Merger Regulation' (1993) 30 CMLRev 1155; and see Select Further Reading for Ch. 25 at p. 915.

38 OJ 1994 C385/1.

39 Ch. 22, p. 697 above. A Commission Notice, OJ 1993 C43/2, elaborates the treatment of cooperative joint ventures under Art. 85.

40 Eg. Dec. 93/48 *Fiat/Hitachi* OJ 1993 L20/10, [1994] 4 CMLR 571.

40a See, e.g., Comm. Dec. 75/95 *SHV/Chevron Oil* OJ 1975 L38/14; absence of actual or potential competition between the firms, no breach of Art. 85; such a structure would now probably fall within the Regulation. However, in Comm. Dec. 90/410 *Elopak/Metal Box* (ODIN) OJ 1990 L209/15, [1991] 4 CMLR 832 a joint venture of this type was held outside Art. 85 but not considered from the perspective of a concentration; see criticism (1990) ELRev Competition Law Checklist 11. For an example of a concentrative joint venture held compatible with the Reg., see IV/M/124 *BNP/Dresdner Bank* OJ 1991 C226/28.

identify potential coordination between parents and joint venture with the result that some joint ventures would be viewed unrealistically as cooperative. The 1994 Notice suggests a shift in favour of a more cautious examination of the nature of potential competitive relationships. It states that coordination between parents and joint venture is relevant 'only in so far as it is an instrument for producing or reinforcing the coordination between the parent companies'.[41] In the absence of such coordination, the joint venture would fall within the Regulation as concentrative, provided the remaining criteria are satisfied.

The importance that attaches to the identification of a joint venture as either concentrative or cooperative derives from the different control mechanisms. Concentrative 'JVs' are assessed under the Merger Regulation, cooperative 'JVs' in the light of Article 85. The substance of the test is not identical, nor are the procedural mechanisms. Most strikingly, the Merger Regulation has strict time-limits, whereas proceedings under Regulation 17/62 are notoriously open-ended.[42] The anomalously favourable procedures on offer to parties able to devise concentrative rather than cooperative structures were liable to distort business choices about preferred forms of collaboration. The Commission therefore devoted attention to closing the gap between treatment of the two types of JV. Sir Leon Brittan, during his spell as Commissioner responsible for Competition, initiated internal changes designed to ensure the conclusion of examination of cooperative JVs as rapidly as examination of concentrative JVs under the Merger Regulation.[43] This was accompanied by the making of Regulation 151/93.[44] This measure extends the scope of four Block Exemption Regulations, those dealing with Specialization, Research and Development, Patent Licensing and Know-How Licensing Agreements. The amendments achieved by Regulation 151/93 permit cooperative joint ventures concerned with specialization and research and development to benefit from block exemption even where not simply production but also joint distribution is envisaged, subject only to market share maxima.[45] Prior to the making of Regulation 151/93, firms planning, for example, to specialize and then jointly to distribute the fruits of collaboration would have been unable to rely on the block exemptions. They would have been tempted to devise a concentrative structure caught by the Merger Regulation simply in order to avoid the time-consuming uncertainty of an application

41 Para. 17 of the Notice.
42 Ch. 24.
43 This was facilitated by the publication of the 1993 Notice, n. 39 above.
44 OJ 1993 L21/8, Ch. 22, p. 714 above.
45 Individual exemption must be sought where the parties' share of the relevant market reaches 10 per cent. In the absence of distribution plans, 20 per cent is the threshold.

for individual exemption. Extensions to the Patent Licensing and Know-How Licensing Regulations permit licensing in the context of a joint venture, subject to market share maxima,[46] which was previously beyond the reach of the block exemption. Regulation 151/93 has in this manner reduced the administrative advantages of constructing a concentrative, rather than cooperative, joint venture.

DEMARCATION BETWEEN COMMUNITY LAW AND NATIONAL LAW

The Community dimension

Article 1 provides that the Regulation applies to concentrations/mergers that satisfy three criteria, two positive, and one negative.[47] The firms concerned must have a combined world-wide turnover in excess of 5,000 million ECU,[48] and a Community-wide turnover of at least 250 million ECU for at least two of the firms concerned (the two positive conditions). Finally, the negative condition: in order to exclude mergers that, though large, are principally of national relevance, the Regulation does not catch mergers where each of the parties derives two-thirds of its EC business in one and the same member state. Mergers meeting these three criteria are subject to Community, not national, jurisdiction. Other mergers are subject to national control alone. The first year of the Regulation's operation saw the review of forty-nine mergers by the Commission. This proved typical and the number has risen only slightly in subsequent years. Article 1(3) of the Regulation provided for review of these figures within four years of the adoption of the Regulation. The Commission anticipated that the Council would be persuaded to reduce these threshold figures.[49] This would increase the number of mergers falling within Community competence with a corresponding diminution in member-state competence. However, when the review took place, in 1993, several member states were adamant that they would not cede further power to the Commission

---

46 The same 10 per cent/20 per cent rule applies; note 45 above. See p. 715 above on the replacement of these two block exemptions by a new, single measure.
47 Cook and Kerse, *EEC Merger Control*, Ch. 3; Downs and Ellison, *The Legal Control of Mergers*, pp. 54–62; Bos, Stuyck and Wytinck, *Concentration Control in the European Economic Community*, Ch. IV.II; Jones and González Díaz, *The EEC Merger Regulation*, Ch. 2.
48 For banks and insurance companies, 10 per cent of total assets.
49 Sir Leon Brittan, *Competition Policy and Merger Control in the Single European Market*, esp. at p. 39.

and accordingly it was agreed that the Article 1 criteria would remain unchanged.[50] A further review is planned for 1996.

Article 23 of the Regulation envisages the introduction of a procedure for formal advance notification in order to meet the deficiencies of the standard procedures of Regulation 17/62, referred to above.[51] Regulation 2367/90 originally contained the relevant procedural accompaniment.[52] The Merger Regulation contains rules that govern procedures for investigation, hearings and enforcement. Articles 14 and 15 of the Regulation provide for the imposition of fines and periodic penalty payments respectively in the event of failure to observe the procedures of the Regulation. The Court has unlimited jurisdiction to review decisions fixing fines and periodic penalty payments.[53] These provisions have some similarities to the procedures in Regulation 17/62,[54] but are shaped with the particular demands of merger control in mind. Notification is made on Form CO, which requires the supply of detailed information about the firms concerned and the market in which they operate. Procedures on notification, time-limits and hearings were overhauled with effect from 1 March 1995 by Regulation 3384/94, which repealed Regulation 2367/90.[55] A streamlined Form CO was provided. This appears as an Annex to Regulation 3384/94.

On notification the merger is in effect frozen and the Commission is empowered to review the merger. It has one month in which to reach a decision. If it has doubts about the compatibility of the merger with the test contained in the Regulation, it may extend that period by four more months, at the end of which period the merger will be definitively cleared or prohibited. This imposes considerable administrative burdens on the Commission, but early public statements from the Merger Task Force in DG IV suggested optimism about its ability to meet these tight deadlines.[56] In practice, the deadlines have proved manageable and the Merger Task Force has won respect for its efficient handling of cases notified to it.[57] The vast majority have been cleared within the one month, 'Phase One' procedure. A short time-scale is essential to promote commercial certainty.

This structure appears to achieve the key goal of predictability through

---

50 COM (93) 385 (corrigendum COM (93) 385/2).
51 p. 810; Cook and Kerse, *EEC Merger Control*, Chs. 5, 6; Downes and Ellison, *The Legal Control of Mergers*, pp. 70–79 and Ch. 4; Bos, Stuyck and Wytinck, *Concentration Control in the European Economic Community*, Ch. IV.V; Jones and González Díaz, *The EEC Merger Regulation*, Ch. 15.
52 OJ 1990 L219.
53 Art. 16, Reg. 4064/89. See further Ch. 10.
54 See Ch. 24.
55 OJ 1994 L377/1.
56 Overbury, 'First Experiences of European Merger Control' (1990) ELRev Competition Law Checklist 79, 85.
57 See eg. Forrester and Norall (1992) 12 YEL 547, 610.

'one-stop shopping'. Where the merger meets the criteria for a Community dimension, the firms can look to the Commission for a definitive statement on the acceptability of the deal, without the need to look simultaneously to the national authorities.[58] Below the threshold the national rules apply. This desirably sharp demarcation is, however, subject to exceptions,[59] the product of entrenched political disagreement during negotiation.

Exceptions to one-stop shopping

In two cases national law may apply despite the fact that the merger crosses the thresholds of the Regulation. First, where there is dominance in a 'distinct national market', national laws may be applied if Commission authorization is received under Article 9 of the Regulation. This is the so-called 'German clause'. This exception may arise in a localized market isolated from the rest of the Community market. Such markets are likely to be unusual, especially as market integration deepens.[60] The Commission granted its first Article 9 authorization in February 1992. A firm was a target for two bidders, where one proposed deal would have a Community dimension, but the other would not. The market affected was chiefly within Britain and in such circumstances the Commission sensibly decided to authorize national control of the Community dimension concentration in order to permit both deals to be dealt with by one authority.[61] In late 1993 the Commission made a second authorization under Article 9 in rather less satisfying circumstances. In *CPC/McCormick/Rabobank/Ostmann*[62] the Commission claimed that the market in question, for the distribution of herbs and spices, exhibited peculiar local characteristics. However, the Commission had found itself precluded from investigating the deal by its miscalculation of deadlines under the Regulation and the main motivation for referral to the German authorities seems to have been the realization that this provided the only means for securing a review of the deal.

The second exception to the demarcation between Community and national control is found in Article 21(3). A member state may protect

---

58 Art. 21(2) Reg. 4064/89.
59 Cook and Kerse, *EEC Merger Control*, Ch. 7; Downes and Ellison, *The Legal Control of Mergers*, pp. 62–7, 79–83; Bos, Stuyck and Wytinck, *Concentration Control in the European Economic Community*, Ch. IV. VII; Jones and González Díaz, *The EEC Merger Regulation*, Chs. 3, 4; Bright, 'The European Merger Control Regulation: Do Member States still have an independent role in Merger Control?', [1991] 4 ECLR 139 and (cont.) [1991] 5 ECLR 184.
60 See p. 689, 734.
61 *Tarmac/Steetley* OJ 1992 C50/25, [1992] 4 CMLR 337.
62 IV/M/330, IP (93) 943, [1993] 5 CMLR 529.

interests affected by a merger other than those explicitly covered by the Regulation, particularly matters of public security,[63] plurality of the media and prudential rules and, exceptionally, other legitimate interests. The notion of other 'legitimate interests' is left undefined, but might conceivably embrace social or regional policy.[64] Commission authority is required for action to protect other legitimate interests, but not required in cases of reliance on the three stipulated public-interest justifications. Naturally, member-state action is subject to review by the Court. These derogations are doubtless to be interpreted narrowly. At the time of the Regulation's adoption, there were fears that member states' readiness to invoke Article 21(3) might come to destabilize the planned allocation of competence. However, in practice, no use of Article 21(3) was recorded by the end of 1994.

The two preceding paragraphs examined mergers with a Community dimension that may exceptionally be dealt with at national level. Articles 22(3)–(6) of the Regulation make inroads into the one-stop-shopping principle from the opposite direction. On the request of a member state that fears a merger will significantly impede competition on its territory, the deal may be examined by the Commission even though it falls beneath the Community dimension criteria.[65] This will occur only if a state chooses to refer the deal to the Commission. This provision was included at the request of states disappointed that the Community dimension threshold in Article 1 was not set lower. It permits them to invoke Community level supervision where they fear their domestic controls would prove inadequate.

The limitations of this so-called 'Dutch clause' were exposed in the British Airways/Dan Air merger. The Commission concluded that the deal did not cross the Article 1 threshold, but the Belgian authorities exercised their powers under Articles 22(3)–(6) to request the Commission to examine it. The Commission was competent to do so only in respect of competition on the territory of the requesting member state, Belgium, and was not able to consider the impact on the wider European and international transport market. The Commission felt that the successful entry of British Midland, in particular, into the market for routes between London and Brussels demonstrated that the merger did not create or strengthen a

---

63 Note also the separate exception provided by Art. 223(1) (b) EC relating to trade in arms, munitions and war materials.

64 Although compatibility with other provisions of Community law would be essential; see, e.g., regional policy and Art. 30 Case C-21/88 *Du Pont* v *Unità Sanitaria* [1990] ECR 889.

65 See Heidenhain, 'Control on concentrations without Community dimensions according to Article 22(2)–(5) Council Regulation 4064/89' (1990) Fordham Corp L Inst 413.

dominant position as a result of which effective competition in Belgium would be significantly impeded.[66]

Perfect one-stop shopping has plainly not been achieved. In fact, it was never really feasible, given that there remain separate regimes at national and Community level. In a contested take-over, for example, the bidder may be unable to discover the relevant turnover figures and will simply not know whether the proposed deal is caught by the Regulation. Even if the deal is consensual, the parties may be uncertain about exactly how turnover should be calculated for these purposes and therefore uncertain whether their deal is caught.[67] In practice, such cases will have to be taken up with both sets of competition authorities. However, the localized market and the public-interest exceptions in the Regulation, which preserve the possibility of national intervention, increase the likelihood that clean-cut one-stop shopping will be rare in practice for transfrontier mergers. It is wise for firms to alert their national authorities to proposed mergers even where they have a Community dimension in order to discover the likelihood of one of these provisions being invoked.[68] Thus, in the United Kingdom, Sir Gordon Borrie, then Director-General of Fair Trading, suggested that the Office of Fair Trading should be consulted in relation to any merger involving United Kingdom firms even where it clearly has a Community dimension. He envisages 'shopping briefly at two shops initially'.[69]

It is fair to conclude that inflexible demarcation rules would be undesirable. These incursions into one-stop shopping are desirable as means of allocating jurisdiction over a merger to the most appropriate set of authorities.[70] This is not always the Community authorities, even where the Regulation's turnover criteria are satisfied. In a sense the Regulation

---

66 IV/M278 OJ 1993 C68/5, [1993] 5 CMLR M61. The national authorities of the state most intimately affected by the deal, those of the UK, did not intervene in the merger.

67 E.g., *Arjomari Prioux/Wiggins Teape*, note 32 above; concentration notified to the Commission, but regulation held inapplicable due to thresholds not being met. Art. 5 Reg. 4064/89 deals with calculation of turnover; see Soames, 'The "Community Dimension" in the EEC Merger Regulation – The Calculation of the Turnover Criteria' [1990] 5 ECLR 213. The Commission's view that it lacked jurisdiction in the British Airways/Dan Air merger was challenged without success by a competing airline in Case T-3/93 *Air France* v *Commission* [1994] II-ECR 121, noted by Brown [1994] 6 ECLR 296. The Commission published a Notice on calculation of turnover in December 1994, OJ 1994 C385/21, which may bring clarification to this difficult area.

68 Note that Art. 19 Reg. 4064/89 is designed to keep national authorities abreast of developments at Community level.

69 *The Independent*, 9 June 1990 p. 21. See also *Mergers*, London, Office of Fair Trading, 1991, pp. 25–6.

70 Overbury (1990) ELRev Competition Law Checklist 79, 87; Sir Leon Brittan, *Competition Policy and Merger Control in the Single European Market*, esp. at p. 50. Jones (1990) Fordham Corp L Inst 385.

contains a compromise between clear rules and efficient rules. Moreover, cooperation between national and Community authorities should prevent serious confusion distorting the structure. At the time of the 1993 review it was mooted that a reduction in the Community dimension threshold figures in Article 1 of the Regulation might usefully be accompanied by an increase in the flexibility of the Commission's powers to refer mergers back to national authorities.[71] In the event, no adjustment was made to either set of provisions.[72] The appropriate division of function between Community and national authorities remains an agenda item for future reviews of the operation of the Regulation.

DEMARCATION AT COMMUNITY LEVEL

If the Merger Regulation is designed to rid Community law of the distortion caused by the application of Articles 85 and 86 of the Treaty to such transactions, then, ideally, the Regulation should ensure that it is the only Community rule available to control mergers; that the simultaneous application of the Treaty provisions is precluded. In principle, of course, this is not possible. Articles 85 and 86 cannot simply be placed in cold storage. As far as enforcement by the Commission is concerned, it would be possible to achieve this result in practice if the Commission simply declines to deal with mergers other than through the Regulation. However, this policy might be challengeable under Article 175, perhaps by the target of a hostile bid. Nor would a Commission policy of inaction remove the problem that the two Treaty Articles are directly effective and are therefore susceptible to pleading before national courts by firms who might see opportunities unavailable under the Merger Regulation.[73]

The Regulation attempts to achieve a solution. The application of Articles 85 and 86 is not − cannot be − suspended, but the operation of implementing Regulation 17/62 is. By virtue of Article 22(2) of the Merger Regulation, the Commission may not use its powers under Regulation 17/62 in respect of concentrations within the meaning of the Merger Regulation. So where there is a Community dimension to the concentration, only the Merger Regulation can apply; where there is no Community dimension, no regulation applies. Article 89 provides the Commission with a subsidiary enforcement competence available in the absence of specific powers such as Regulation 17/62, but the Commission

---

71 See eg. Siragusa [1993] 4 ECLR 139; Neven, Nuttall and Seabright, *Merger in Daylight*, Ch. 8.
72 Note 50 above.
73 See Ch. 24, p. 789 above.

has declared that it will not use Article 89 EC in respect of concentrations where the aggregate world-wide turnover is below 2,000 million ECU or the Community-wide turnover of each of at least two of the parties is below 100 million ECU.

On the domestic plane the disapplication of Regulation 17/62 has the result that Article 85(2)'s sanction of nullity is suspended, removing its enforceability before a national court. Article 85 is not directly effective in sectors where the Commission has no powers conferred upon it by implementing measures.[74] True, Article 86 remains directly effective, but, as a matter of practice, it will provide nothing beyond what is already available under the Regulation.[75] The test of legality is comparable and the attraction of using Article 86 to obtain interim relief against a merger from a national court will disappear, given that the same result is achieved by virtue of the prenotification and freezing procedure under the Regulation. The effective result is intended to be the exclusive application of the Regulation.[76]

There has been a great deal of speculation about the desirability and, indeed, the constitutionality of this device.[77] It is submitted that the scheme offers fertile ground for legal argument. The use of Article 175 to challenge the Commission's planned inaction under Article 89 may prove particularly attractive, especially as a spoiling tactic in a contested take-over. Litigation at national level relying on Articles 85 and 86 seems likely to be pursued, if only for the same reason.[78] These will be even more powerful means of attack if supplemented by submissions that Article 22(1) of the Regulation is unlawful as an impermissible diminution in the effect of basic Treaty provisions, Articles 85 and 86.[79] This argument seems especially compelling when applied to concentrations within the meaning of Article 3 of the Regulation, but below the Community dimension figures in Article 1, which, on the view advanced in the preceding paragraph, would be sheltered from the Merger Regulation, from Regulation 17/62 and from the direct effect of Article 85.

---

74 Case 209–13/84 *Ministère Public v Asjes* [1986] ECR 1425, p. 789 above.
75 Contra Downes and Ellison, *The Legal Control of Mergers*, p. 189.
76 Of course, where there is *no* concentration (e.g., joint ventures, p. 813 above), the old problems of applying Art. 85 remain.
77 E.g. Bos, Stuyck and Wytinck, *Concentration Control in the European Economic Community*, Ch. V; Downes and Ellison, *The Legal Control of Mergers*, Ch. 7; Fine, 'Merger Control: An Analysis of the New Regulation' [1900] 2 ECLR 47; Pathak, 'EEC Concentration Control: The Foreseeable Uncertainties' [1990] 3 ECLR 119; Bernini, 'Jurisdictional issues: EEC Merger Regulation: Member States laws and Arts. 85 and 86' (1990) Fordham Corp L Inst 611.
78 See, unsuccessfully, *R v Secretary of State for Trade and Industry, ex parte Airlines of Britain, The Times* 10 December 1992, noted by Levitt [1993] 2 ECLR 73.
79 Downes and Ellison, *The Legal Control of Mergers*, pp. 185–6.

Significantly impeding effective competition

The creation or strengthening[80] of a dominant position through merger will be declared incompatible with the common market where it significantly impedes effective competition in the common market or in a substantial part of it. Article 2(1) of the Regulation supplies a list of factors to be taken into account, based broadly on the notion of maintaining and developing effective competition and covering, *inter alia*, market structure, the firms' economic power, sources of supply and entry barriers. Many of these notions are familiar from Article 86, where parallel questions of market definition and dominance arise. Experience under Article 86 provides an insight into the nature and purpose of the Merger Regulation, although the test of significantly impeding competition is not identical to that found in Article 86.[81] The preamble to the Regulation declares that dominance is unlikely where the firms' combined market share is below 25 per cent. It is clear from Article 86 jurisprudence that market shares below 50 per cent can confer dominance.[82] However, every market bears its own peculiar features. It is necessary to determine the scope of the market in which the firms operate and to assess the structure of that market.

Markets will frequently be defined as Community-wide, but this need not necessarily be so.[83] In a number of decisions, smaller markets have been identified. *Nestlé/Perrier*, for example, concerned bottled source water.[84] This is a bulky but relatively inexpensive product. Transport costs are proportionately highly significant. Imports into France were negligible; past attempts to penetrate the French market had proved fruitless. This led the Commission to a finding that a planned merger should be assessed with regard to its impact on the French market alone. By contrast, in other decisions markets extending beyond the Community have been identified. Assessment against a background of an international or even global market has been judged appropriate. In *Aérospatiale Alenia/*

---

80 Note the inclusion of both solves the problem identified at p. 807.
81 Sir Leon Brittan, 'The Law and Policy of Merger Control in the EEC' (1990) 15 ELRev 351, 354. See analysis by Venit, 'Evaluation of concentrations under Regulation 4064/89: the nature of the beast' (1990) Fordham Corp L Inst 519; Downes and MacDougall, 'Significantly Impeding Effective Competition: Substantive Appraisal under the Merger Regulation' (1994) 19 ELRev 286.
82 E.g. Case 27/76 *United Brands* v *Commission* [1978] ECR 207, [1978] 1 CMLR 429.
83 Art. 2(1) Reg. 4064/89. See p. 734.
84 IV/M/190 OJ 1992 L356/1, [1993] 4 CMLR M17, considered further below at p. 825.

de Havilland[85] the Commission found no barriers to the importation of the relevant type of aircraft into the Community. Moreover, transport costs were negligible. The market was therefore global, excepting only China and Eastern Europe, where domestic industries using distinct methods met demand.[86] The Commission's concern, under this Regulation as under Article 86,[87] is to identify a market in which the conditions of competition are sufficiently homogeneous to allow a rational assessment of economic power.[88] Markets must be carefully examined in individual cases without preconceptions. Inaccurate market definition is liable to breed inefficient control.

Market share is just one relevant factor in assessing dominance; so too in assessing whether a significant impediment to effective competition has ensued. In *Renault/Volvo*[89] the Commission cleared the merger of the truck and bus divisions because it was satisfied that, big as the two parties were, they remained subject to competitive influences in a market populated by several large producers. In *Aérospatiale/MBB*[90] a merger between a French and a German manufacturer of civil helicopters was cleared, even though the merged firm would obtain some 50 per cent of the Community market. The Commission decided that markets in the USA and in the EC were open to penetration and that the market was accordingly global. The merged group would not be independent of competitive pressures, especially in the light of the potential impact of US competition. The Commission found the market to be contestable.[91] In *Eridania/Finebieticola*[92] a merger that would allow control of a large slice of the Italian sugar market was not opposed because of the presence of effective potential competition from producers outside Italy. The contestability of the market was shown by the fact that in 1990, a 1 per cent price rise in Italy had been accompanied by a doubling of imports.

---

85 IV/M/053 OJ 1991 L334/42, [1992] 4 CMLR M2, considered further below at p. 827.
86 The internationalization of markets dictates a need for cooperation in the application of national and transnational competition law. See Fidler, 'Competition Law and International Relations' (1992) 41 ICLQ 563. A 1991 agreement between the Commission and the Government of the United States was annulled on grounds of lack of competence in Case C-327/91 *France v Commission*, judgment of 9 August 1994.
87 P. 728 above.
88 See the statement of Commissioner Van Miert on consistent market definition under the Regulation, WQ 364/93 OJ 1993 C202/25.
89 Note 36 above.
90 IV/M/017 OJ 1991 C59/13.
91 Criticized by Fine, 'The Appraisal Criteria of the EC Merger Control Regulation' [1991] 4 ECLR 148, 158–9 for being too ready to assume the existence of competition.
92 Commission Press Release IP (91) 776; IV/M/78 *Torras/Sarrio* OJ 1992 C58/20, [1992] 4 CMLR 341.

Oligopolies and joint dominance

An issue of controversy familiar from Articles 85 and 86 has resurfaced in relation to the Regulation; namely, control of oligopolies. The Commission has maintained the view that the Regulation is capable of controlling mergers which do not confer dominant market power on the merged entity, but which nevertheless lead to a situation where effective competition is significantly impeded by the reduction in competition consequent on the merger. If the merged entity and a small number of other players will find themselves in an oligopoly, then the Commission has reasoned that the policy of the Regulation dictates that it should be interpreted in such a way as to allow supervision of the merger. Confining control to instances of single-firm dominance would open a loophole in the overall Treaty objective of maintaining effective competition, rooted in Article 3(g) EC. This is a view as yet untested before the Court. In fact, the whole issue of control of oligopolies and collective dominance under EC competition policy remains cloudy.[93]

In *Nestlé/Perrier*[94] the Commission concluded that a proposed merger would lead to the domination of the French market for bottled source water by Nestlé and BSN, an independent third party unconnected with the proposed merger. The decision asserts a power to control the deal under the Regulation even though the merged entity would not have secured a dominant position for itself, because of the presence of a rival, BSN. The Commission, having rejected Nestlé and BSN's submissions that it lacked jurisdiction to apply the Regulation in this fashion, none the less cleared the deal, but only on condition that Nestlé undertake to sell off some of its interests in order to inject fresh competition into the market.[95]

In *Mannesmann/Vallourec/Ilva*[96] the three firms involved agreed to create 'DMV', a concentrative joint venture in the seamless stainless steel tube sector. Post-merger, DMV would hold some 36 per cent of the relevant market; Sandvik, a Swedish company, would hold some 33 per cent; the remainder would be shared among smaller firms. Therefore the presence of Sandvik ensured that DMV could not attain sole dominance. The Commission, however, adhered to its view expressed in *Nestlé/Perrier* that

93 Ch. 22, 23, pp. 681, 724.
94 IV/M/190 OJ 1992 L356/1, [1993] 4 CMLR M17.
95 For comment, see Winckler and Hansen (1993) 30 CMLRev 787; Whish and Sufrin (1992) 12 YEL 59; Ridyard [1994] 5 ECLR 255. No interim measures were granted in a challenge by employees of firms to be sold off by Nestlé in Case T-12/93 R *Comité Central d'Entreprise de la SA Vittel* v *Commission*, judgment of 6 July 1993. But in another case of conditional clearing, interim measures were granted; Case T-88/94 R *Société Commerciale des Potasses et de l'Azote* v *Commission*, judgment of 15 June 1994.
96 IV/M/315 OJ 1994 L102/15.

the creation of a joint dominant position would be subject to control under the Regulation and would be blocked where it would significantly impede competition. However, on the facts, the Commission reached the decision that the market would *not* be so structured as to cause harm to effective competition on a lasting basis. Sandvik and DMV would not obtain an unacceptably damaging joint dominant position.

The Commission's use of the joint dominance concept represents an important development. It is one likely to provoke a challenge before the Court in due course. It is notable that in these two applications of the Merger Regulation to joint dominance the Commission has not emphasized the existence of the 'economic links' between the potential oligopolists which the Court of First Instance requires for the use of Article 86 in instances of joint dominance.[97] However, *Mannesmann/Vallourec/Ilva* attracted more controversy for its outcome than over the jurisdictional question of whether the Regulation can properly be employed in order to control mergers leading to joint dominance. The proposed creation of DMV was cleared only after a vote of the full Commission. The Decision asserts that the West European market is contestable by East European and Japanese producers and that therefore the apparent impediment to competition consequent on the merger is not sufficiently serious to warrant intervention. Sandvik and DMV are subject to constraint by potential competition. This conclusion sits uncomfortably with the analysis presented in the Decision at the stage of market definition, which identifies little likelihood of external penetration of the West European market. In fact the Merger Task Force had recommended that the deal be blocked. It did not share the belief in the contestability of the West European market embraced by the full Commission. The text of the final Decision is presented as an economic examination of the impact of the deal on the market, as required by Article 2 of the Regulation, but there are suspicions that the Commissioners who voted in favour of clearing the deal were motivated by domestic political concerns.[98] This incident has fuelled calls in Germany, in particular, for an EC competition authority independent of the Commission in particular and of any hint of political pressure in general.

---

97 Cases T-68, 77 and 78/89 *Società Italiana Vetro SpA et al.* v *Commission* [1992] ECR II-1403, [1992] 5 CMLR 301, p. 725 above.
98 See comment by Pathak (1993), ELRev Competition Law Checklist CC166, 179–80, Ridyard [1994] 5 ECLR 255, 261.

The (probable) exclusion of industrial policy

The Commission officials responsible for the application of the Regulation are firmly of the view that the criterion of control is the effect of the merger on competition.[99] More general social factors are excluded from the scope of the Commission's inquiry. Regional, structural or employment policy are not the Commission's business when it examines mergers. This deprives the Commission of any discretion to approve mergers once they have been found to be anticompetitive, and its ability to dictate industrial policy independently of the Council is excluded. However, it remains to be seen whether different officials in the future may be readier to inject a flavour of *dirigisme* into the test of a significant impediment to competition by relying on Article 2(1)(b)'s reference to 'the development of technical and economic progress . . .'[100]

In October 1991, in the first instance of a blocked merger, *Aérospatiale Alenia/de Havilland*,[101] the deal was held incompatible with the Regulation's criteria because of the large slice that the merged firm would obtain of the market for production of short-haul commuter aircraft. The Commission's decision was criticized for an unduly narrow product market definition that exaggerated economic power, which is a criticism based on application of the Regulation. The Commission was also criticized for failure to take account of the industrial and regional implications of the matter, which are criticisms more properly directed at the drafting of the Regulation rather than its application by the Commission. The affair highlights the political and economic sensitivity of the Commission's powers under the Merger Regulation. From the start of 1993 the Commission competition portfolio has been held by Karel Van Miert, a Belgian socialist. There are no signs that he wishes to pursue a more interventionist policy.

99 See, e.g., Brittan (1990) 15 ELRev 351; Brittan, *Competition Policy and Merger Control in the Single European Market*, p. 35; Overbury (1990) ELRev Competition Law Checklist 79, 83.

100 See e.g., Fine [1991] ECLR 148, 150–51; Halverson, 'EC Merger Control: Competition Policy or Industrial Policy? Views of a US practitioner' [1992/2] LIEI 49; Langeheine 'Substantive Review under the EEC Merger Regulation' (1990) Fordham Corp L Inst 481, 494–500; Venit (1990) Fordham Corp L Inst 519, 524–7. For a survey of policy see Holzler, 'Merger Control' in Montagnon (ed.), *European Competition Policy*.

101 IV/M/053 OJ 1991 L334/42 [1992] 4 CMLR M2, noted by Hawkes [1992] 1 ECLR 34; Forrester and Norall (1991) 11 YEL 450–55.

COMPROMISE

Much of the Regulation represents compromise solutions. The thresholds that demarcate Community from national competence are the result of disagreement between states such as the United Kingdom and Germany, content with their own law of mergers and eager to limit the Community's role and therefore bent on high thresholds, and smaller, legally less developed countries willing to maximize the Community's role and therefore eager to lower the figures. The four-year review procedure was part of this compromise.[102] The persisting differences of opinion may be judged by the failure of the review to lead to any change. The exceptions to one-stop shopping are further examples of compromise. Finally, the exclusion of social policy from the Commission's remit was achieved only after fierce debate. France, in particular, was eager to broaden the Commission's mandate. In the wake of the blocked *Aerospatiale Alenia/de Havilland* merger[103] the European Parliament adopted a resolution calling for a revision of the Regulation to take account of industrial, social, regional and environmental factors.[104] It should also be borne in mind that many of the compromises were not even the result of debate within the context of this single measure. It seems clear that concessions relating to the Mergers Regulation were 'traded off' for concessions in other areas of legislation under discussion in the approach to the completion of the internal market.[105] In the light of these bargains the final Regulation was hardly likely to satisfy all competing interest groups. Its future development seems likely to continue to reflect many of these hard-fought debates about policy choices. The application of the Regulation is also likely to form a major element in the institutional debate about the proper handling of competition policy by the Commission.[106]

102 See note 50 above.
103 Note 101 above.
104 OJ 1991 C280/140.
105 E.g., John Redwood, then a Minister in the DTI in the UK, is quoted as having insisted on the withdrawal of German objections to the Life Assurance Directive as a condition for agreeing to the Mergers Regulation; *The Independent*, 12 January 1990.
106 For discussion of this and other issues of policy for the future, see Goyder, *EC Competition Law*, Part III; Neven, Nuttall and Seabright, *Merger in Daylight*, esp. Ch. 8; Ehlermann (1995) 32 CMLRev 471.

CHAPTER 26

Intellectual Property

The astute inventor quickly takes out a patent in order to protect his or her invention. A patent confers on the inventor a legally enforceable monopoly in the exploitation of the new product or technique within a defined area. Imitative products can be excluded from the market. This is in one sense anticompetitive. The law enables the inventor to suppress competition. However, the patent is designed to reward, and thereby encourage, innovation by preventing the theft of ideas. Without the commercially valuable inducement of the protection of the patent, there would be little incentive to sink costs into the search for new gadgets, because the profits would be seized by a competitor who might have incurred no such costs. Society would be prejudiced by stunted innovation. In creating a patent regime the costs of restricting competition are outweighed by the benefits of stimulating new and valuable research. The generic term for patents and other techniques such as trade marks and copyrights, which similarly offer protection to the holder within a defined area, is intellectual (or industrial) property rights.

Such rights present problems under several provisions of Community law. Agreements between commercial parties relating to the exploitation of an invention on the markets of the member states run the risk of falling foul of Article 85. The exploitation of what may amount to a monopoly conferred by law may be susceptible to challenge under Article 86. The exercise of an intellectual property right typically involves asserting protection within a defined territory. A French patent holder may seek to exclude a similar German product. This naturally causes an obstruction to the free circulation of goods in the Community and requires scrutiny under Articles 30–36.

ARTICLE 85 AND
INTELLECTUAL PROPERTY RIGHTS

LICENSING AGREEMENTS

Assume A in one member state grants B in another member state a licence to exploit A's legally protected exclusive rights. B has acquired something he or she did not previously possess, so that cannot logically restrict competition. Indeed, the deal widens product distribution. This is sometimes termed the rule-of-reason approach and, if followed, it means Article 85 is inapplicable. The Court ruled in *Nungesser* v *Commission*[1] that even where the deal confers exclusive rights on the licensee for the territory of state B, there may be no violation of Article 85(1), for without such protection from rivals no licensee would take on the risk of investing in a product unknown in that territory. The Court has also held that a clause in a licence prohibiting sale and export of seeds over which the licensor holds exclusive rights may amount to an exercise of the rights themselves and therefore fall outside Article 85(1).[2] However, where extra restrictive clauses are included in the agreement, it might be possible to find a breach of Article 85(1). That invites consideration of the potential for exemption under Article 85(3). For example, in *Windsurfing* v *Commission*[3] clauses additional to the patent licence governing extended quality control and other ties were caught by Article 85(1); exemption under Article 85(3) was ruled unavailable by the Court for want of notification,[4] but was in any event disputed by the Commission. Where the extra restrictive clauses are designed to restrain parallel imports of the goods, there would be a clear breach of Article 85(1) that would be incapable of exemption under Article 85(3). This has been clear since the seminal decision in *Consten and Grundig* v *Commission*,[5] which insists that distribution deals that improve interbrand competition cannot completely suppress cross-border intrabrand competition. The Court confirmed its hostility towards market-partitioning in *Nungesser*, where it took the view that although exclusive licences permitting parallel trade might fall outside Article 85(1), the same could not apply to deals contaminated by clauses forbidding parallel trade.

---

1 Case 258/78 [1982] ECR 2015, p. 697 above. On the Commission's rather erratic approach prior to this case, see Korah, *EC Competition Law and Practice*, pp. 209–12.
2 Case 27/87 *Erauw-Jacquery* v *La Hesbignonne* [1988] ECR 1919.
3 Case 193/83 [1986] ECR 611.
4 On procedure, see pp. 774–6 above.
5 Cases 56, 58/64 [1966] ECR 299, see Ch. 22, p. 663.

Patent licensing

Generalizations about the application of Article 85 are hazardous, for much will depend on the structure of the particular market. However, the complex theology of either finding a clause non-restrictive of competition and therefore unaffected by Article 85(1) or finding it restrictive but exemptable under Article 85(3) is unlikely to be of great interest to the commercial person, and certainly business requires some clear and predictable rules in this area. Consequently, Regulation 2349/84 was introduced to provide a block exemption for patent licensing agreements.[6] The Regulation acts as a check-list. There must be two parties only. The agreement must relate to the licence of patents, although ancillary provisions relating to know-how and trade marks do not take the agreement beyond the scope of the Regulation.[7] Provided these conditions are satisfied, the agreement's clauses may be tested against the Regulation.

The Regulation's stipulated expiry date was at the end of 1994. The Commission published a draft replacement Regulation in the course of 1994.[8] The Commission's intention was to make a new Regulation exempting technology transfer agreements. This would go beyond the licensing of patents alone. The Commission also proposed some adjustments to the nature and scope of the exemption. The Commission found that in the course of 1994 a lively debate developed about the appropriate nature of the replacement regime. The Commission felt unable to issue a new Regulation that would come into force at the start of 1995. From that time, patent licensing was subjected to a transitional period of control under the rules of Regulation 2349/84 until such time as agreement could be reached on a new text. At time of writing the Commission had not finalized the text of the new measure that will succeed Regulation 2349/84. What follows is a brief survey of Regulation 2349/84.

Article 1 of the Regulation lists exempted restrictions. These are divisible into those restrictions that the licensor may permissibly undertake and those the licensee may undertake. The licensor may agree not to grant licences to other parties for the contract territory as long as the patent remains in force, and not to exploit the product itself within the contract territory. The licensee may undertake not to exploit the product in the

6 OJ 1984 L219/15. See Korah, *Patent Licensing and EEC Competition Rules: Regulation 2349/84.*
7 It does not cover plant-breeder's rights, which were at issue in *Nungesser*, note 1 above.
8 OJ 1994 C178/3, C187/16.

licensor's territory as long as the patents remain in force, not to manufacture or use the product in other licensees' territory, not actively to sell in other licensees' territories (a ban on active sales), not to sell at all into other licensees' territories where the product has been on the market for no longer than five years in the Community (a limited passive sales ban), and to use only the licensor's form of product presentation (typically a trade mark).

Article 2 contains a list of restrictions that are generally considered non-restrictive and not in principle contrary to Article 85(1) at all, but are exempted for the purposes of certainty. These include a minimum royalties clause, a restriction on exploitation to one field of use, an obligation to mark the product with the patentee's name and an obligation to conform to objectively justified minimum quality standards.

Article 3 contains the list of impermissible restrictions. These include clauses relating to royalties on non-patented products, price restrictions, product ties that lack objective justification, export restrictions beyond those clearly permitted by Article 1 of the Regulation and acts designed to curtail opportunities for parallel importers.

This is by no means an exhaustive examination of this important Regulation. However, it should be apparent how the basic principles of Articles 85(1) and 85(3) are applied in this area. The balance between the costs and benefits of commercial collaboration may be observed, with the thematic undercurrent of the promotion of market integration. The approach to active/passive resale by the licensee outside the contract territory is especially telling. The Regulation has to permit some restrictions on such trade, which protect the licensor and other licensees, or else patent licensing would be so commercially unattractive that it would scarcely occur. Some protective exclusivity is essential in providing the licensor with the incentive to invest in opening up a new market, just as exclusivity conferred on the licensee is equally essential as a means of inducing a licensee to take on the challenge of building a market for a new product. Such restrictions on intrabrand competition may be compatible with wider product distribution in the Community, resulting in interbrand competition to the benefit of the consumer. However, Community law is unrelentingly wary of territorial restrictions and, although for the reasons explained it dare not ban them altogether, it places limits on their permissibility. Hence, the licensor is not able unconditionally to forbid the licensee from selling outside the contract territory, and passive selling must remain possible in other licensees' territories after the expiry of the stipulated five-year period. Moreover, the Regulation supplements its mistrust of territorial segregation by requiring the parties not to impede third-party parallel importers of the contract goods.[9] This controls the freedom of the licensee

9 Art. 3(11) Reg. 2349/84. Note how this result was foreshadowed by the Court's

to refuse to sell to firms within its own territory, notwithstanding knowledge that the purchaser plans to export the goods. It would also control attempts by the licensor to limit production by licensees as a means of ensuring it can satisfy demand only on its home market.[10]

The broad policy thrust of the new regime will not differ radically from that under Regulation 2349/84. The existing list of permissible restrictions is highly likely to be maintained and, in some respects, supplemented. The list of impermissible restrictions is likely to be shortened. A novelty in the Commission's 1994 draft proposals[11] was the introduction of market share criteria. Firms crossing stipulated market share thresholds would be unable to enjoy the benefit of the block exemption. They would be obliged to seek individual exemption. The introduction of a market share threshold would run in parallel to other areas of Commission planning, notably Regulation 151/93, which extended the scope of four existing block exemption Regulations subject to conditions based on the size of the participants' market share.[12] The attraction of the introduction of market share criteria lies in the potential for releasing parties to small-scale deals from the costs of seeking exemption, while ensuring that deals with a potentially significant impact on competition are brought to the Commission's attention. The disadvantage lies in the difficulty in translating this broad policy into a pattern suitable for practical application. Frequently the calculation of market share is a complex and controversial matter. In areas of innovative technology there will often be arguments that markets should be narrowly defined and that parties to an agreement therefore hold high market shares. The application of the law is clouded by such uncertainty. Firms may be induced cautiously to undergo the burdensome individual notification procedure which the block exemption scheme is designed to circumvent.

Other block exemptions

Regulation 556/89 provides a block exemption on know-how licensing.[13] The structure of the Regulation is comparable to that which applies to patent licensing. The Commission's planned new Regulation exempting technology transfer agreements, considered above, is designed to cover know-how licensing as well as patent licensing. Therefore, although Regulation 556/89 is not due to expire until the end of 1999, it will probably be

---

decision in *Nungesser*, note 1 above, which predates the adoption of the Regulation. For a survey of the place of parallel imports in the scheme of the law, see Gonzalo de Ulloa, 'Licensing Contracts and Territoriality Clauses: Parallel Imports' [1991] 6 ECLR 220.

10 Art. 3(5) Reg. 2349/84.
11 Note 8 above.
12 See Ch. 22, p. 714; Ch. 25, p. 815.
13 OJ 1989 L61/1.

repealed before then by the Technology Transfer Regulation. Franchising, too, is subject to a block exemption, Regulation 4087/88.[14] The Court had already indicated in *Pronuptia de Paris* v *Pronuptia Schillgalis*[15] that such deals might fall outside Article 85 altogether, but that certain clauses might infringe Article 85(1) and thus require exemption. The adoption of a Regulation was important in the pursuit of commercial certainty. Although there is no block exemption covering trade-mark and copyright licensing, such deals should doubtless be drafted with reference to the approach set out in the Patent Licensing Regulation.[16] Other agreements in this area that are not formally within the Regulation should doubtless also be drafted with reference to the Commission's policy expressed therein.

OUTSIDE THE BLOCK EXEMPTIONS

Beyond the block exemptions individual clauses require careful scrutiny in the light of the normal rules under Article 85. For example, in *Ottung* v *Klee and Weilback*[17] the Court held that an obligation to pay royalties throughout the duration of an agreement, even after the expiry of the patent, will not breach Article 85(1) where the licensee may freely terminate the agreement on reasonable notice. The matter would be different where the obligation to pay even after the expiry of the patent arises in the absence of any right to terminate on reasonable notice or where the agreement otherwise seeks to restrict the licensee's freedom to manufacture or market the goods after termination. In the instructive decision in *Windsurfing* v *Commission*[18] the Court established, *inter alia*, that a clause allowing the licensor to terminate the agreement if the licensee manufactures goods in states where patent protection has not been obtained is a violation of Article 85(1).

Article 3(1) of the Regulation declares that agreement by the licensee not to challenge the validity of the licensor's industrial property right deprives the agreement of the benefit of exemption. The rationale lies in the undesirability of suppressing the ability to root out invalid rights, which unduly restrict the market contrary to the public interest.[19] In *Bayer AG* v *Sullhofer*[20] the Commission submitted that where such a no-challenge clause is part of a settlement of a genuine dispute about a right and where

14 OJ 1988 L359/46.
15 Case 161/84 [1986] ECR 353, [1986] 1 CMLR 414.
16 Van Bael and Bellis, *Competition Law*, pp. 280–86; Whish, *Competition Law*, pp. 640–42.
17 Case 320/87 [1989] ECR 1177, [1990] 4 CMLR 915.
18 Case 193/83, note 3 above.
19 See also Case 193/83, note 3 above.

the agreement is no more restrictive of competition than is necessary to achieve that settlement, there is no breach of Article 85(1). The Court rejected this view and held that in principle a no-challenge agreement is equally subject to Article 85(1) whether it is concluded in the context of a licensing agreement or the settlement of litigation. However, the Court complicated matters by also accepting that on the rather unusual facts of the case there was no breach of Article 85(1) because the licensee who agreed not to challenge the right had been granted a royalty-free licence as part of the settlement. The same would hold where royalties are payable but the technology is outdated and not used by the licensee.

In its decision in *Moosehead/Whitbread*[21] the Commission examined an agreement not to challenge a trade mark. It distinguished between not challenging the *ownership* of the mark and not challenging its *validity*. The former is in principle unaffected by Article 85(1), because the allocation of ownership between licensor and licensee is irrelevant as regards third parties who cannot in any event use the mark. The clause accordingly has no effect on competition. Clauses agreeing not to challenge validity are different because success in the challenge would propel the mark into the public domain, thereby removing a barrier to entry to the market that would have implications not just for the licensee but also for third parties. Such a clause does affect competition and is caught by Article 85(1) where it has an appreciable impact on trade. On the facts of the decision, however, the Commission declared that there was no appreciable impact on competition and therefore no breach of Article 85(1), because the trade mark, 'Moosehead' lager, was little known in the United Kingdom and therefore had little impact as an impediment to the competitive structure of the market.

ARTICLE 86 AND INTELLECTUAL PROPERTY RIGHTS

The holder of any intellectual property right must beware of abusing a dominant position. The normal approach to Article 86[22] applies; that is, first, the identification of a dominant position and, second, the abuse thereof. The holder of an intellectual property right is sometimes described as having acquired a legal monopoly, but that is not automatically coterminous with a dominant position. The holder of a patent for a new headache

20 Case 65/86 [1988] ECR 5249, [1990] 4 CMLR 182.
21 Comm. Dec. 90/186 OJ 1990 L100/32, [1991] 4 CMLR 391, noted by Subiotto [1990] 5 ECLR 226.
22 See Ch. 23.

cure will have to compete with the many other such cures on the market. A monopoly over one product does not preclude the existence of competing brands. However, even though the absence of intrabrand competition does not preclude the existence of interbrand competition, the acquisition of an intellectual property right tends to assist a firm to obtain dominance. If dominance is shown, the holder bears the familiar responsibility of avoiding abusive conduct, covering, for example, its policy on pricing and supply. In *Ministère Public* v *Tournier*[23] the French national copyright management society was accused of abuse in its behaviour towards discothèques that wished to use music over which it held rights. Its royalties were alleged to be unfairly high and arbitrarily fixed. The Court confirmed that such conduct could constitute a breach of Article 86, and suggested that a price comparison with other states might be relied upon as evidence of the legality of pricing practices. It conceded, however, that the mere fact of interstate price differences would not yield a finding of abuse where such differentials were attributable to objective differences.[24] In practice, the notion of unfairly high pricing is already a complex issue under Article 86[25] and its application to intellectual property rights, which to some extent exist in order to grant the inventor rewards expressed through profits, is likely to prove more controversial still.

It is important to achieve a balance between the ability of the holder of an intellectual property right to protect his or her market and the general interest in controlling dominated markets. *Volvo* v *Erik Veng*[26] involved a registered design, an exclusive right to make and import replacement car body panels that were irreplaceable by panels of different design. The right holder refused to license third parties to supply car body panels covered by the design. This was held not to be an abuse. The right holder was entitled to withhold licenses as part of 'the substance of his exclusive right'.[27] However, the European Court insisted that the dominant intellectual property right holder is not immune from the application of Article 86 and observed that an abuse might be found where, for example, the right holder arbitrarily refused to supply spare parts to independent repairers,

---

23 Case 395/87 [1989] ECR 2524, [1991] 4 CMLR 248, p. 744 above.
24 This is an application of the familiar Community law principle that it is not unlawful to apply different treatment to objectively distinct situations; see e.g., pp. 400, 620.
25 See p. 744.
26 Case 238/87 [1988] ECR 6211, [1989] 4 CMLR 122, noted by Friden (1989) 26 CMLRev 193, 204.
27 Having found no abuse, the European Court did not consider the (logically precedent) issue of dominance; the AG considered the matter, but rather briefly. Market definition is complex in such circumstances; see Case 22/78 *Hugin* v *Commission* [1979] ECR 1869, and Friden (1989) 26 CMLRev 193, 208.

imposed unfair prices for spare parts or terminated production of spare parts for models even where there was a demand.[28]

The Commission's investigation into the practices of three British and Irish television companies, RTE, BBC and ITP, subsequently taken before both Luxembourg Courts, confirms that the dominant right holder may not always be permitted freedom in choice of contracting partners. Equally, the saga confirms the complexity that surrounds the determination of the extent to which Article 86 may be used to curtail the enjoyment of intellectual property rights. The three television companies all refused permission for their copyright-protected programme listings to be reproduced, even on payment of a fee. Magill, which had hoped to produce a single television guide covering all channels for all Ireland, complained to the Commission that the firms were abusing a dominant position by refusing to license it to publish the material.[29] The Commission observed that the firms, by publishing their own separate guides and thereby preventing the appearance of a single guide, were suppressing the creation of a new market attractive to consumers.[30] The finding of abuse was upheld by the Court of First Instance.[31] It held that, although the exercise of an exclusive right is not of itself abusive, an abuse might occur where 'that right is exercised in such ways and circumstances as in fact to pursue an aim manifestly contrary to the objectives of Article 86'.[32] It then observed that 'preventing the production and marketing of a new product for which there is potential consumer demand' goes beyond what is necessary to fulfil the essential function of copyright protection.[33] The radical use of Article 86 to override the right to exclusive enjoyment which is characteristic of copyright in pursuit of the wider objective of creating a competitive market prompted the parties to take the matter on appeal to the European Court. Advocate-General Gulmann delivered his Opinion on 1 June 1994. He was of the view that the Court of First Instance's ruling should *not* be upheld. He considered that the Court of First Instance had used Article 86 improperly to curtail the scope of intellectual property rights. The European Court's ruling was much delayed, reflecting the sensitivity of the matter. It decided[34] to uphold the

28 Case 238/87, note 26 above, para. 9 of the judgment.
29 On complainants in competition procedures, see p. 757.
30 Comm. Dec. 89/205 *ITP, BBC, RTE* OJ 1989 L78/43, [1989] 4 CMLR 757.
31 Cases T-69/89 *Radio Times Editions*, [1991] ECR II-485 [1991] 4 CMLR 586; T-70/89 *British Broadcasting Corporation*, [1991] ECR II-535 [1991] 4 CMLR 669; T-76/89 *Independent Television Publications*, [1991] ECR II-575 [1991] 4 CMLR 745, noted by Forrester [1992] 1 ECLR 5, 15; Alexander and Mellor (1992) 41 ICLQ 202.
32 Case T-69/89, note 31 above, para. 71 of the judgment.
33 ibid., para. 73 of the judgment.
34 Cases C-241/91 P and C-242/91 P *RTE and ITP* v *Commission*, judgment of 6 April 1995, [1995] All ER (EC) 416.

Court of First Instance's ruling that an abuse had occurred. Citing *Volvo* v *Veng*, it confirmed that the exercise of copyright may be abusive in exceptional circumstances. In the light of the companies' refusal to allow the appearance of a new product for which there was a potential consumer demand, the European Court considered that the Court of First Instance had not erred in finding abusive conduct. The ruling asserts a more vigorous role for Article 86 in controlling the licensing policy of right holders than Advocate-General Gulmann preferred, but the Court has not provided a workable statement of principle. The position of right holders depends on the structure of particular markets and is not easy to predict.[34a]

In *Tetra Pak Rausing* v *Commission*[35] the Court of First Instance held that where a dominant firm took over another firm and thereby acquired, *inter alia*, an exclusive licence to exploit intellectual property, it had violated Article 86. This is an application of the Court's view that a dominant firm that extends its economic strength to the prejudice of competition may be caught by Article 86. The derivation is *Continental Can* v *Commission*,[36] where it was held that a merger may be abusive. The decision in *Tetra Pak* is especially striking in that the licence was covered by the block exemption on patent licensing, which had induced the firm to argue that a logically coherent application of the Treaty competition rules precluded the prohibition under Article 86 of an agreement permitted under Article 85. The Court insisted that there was no objection to the exclusive licence as such, but to the anti-competitive consequences of its acquisition in the dominated market under scrutiny. The decision emphasizes that Article 86 has a special function in controlling the market distorted by dominance and is in this sense aimed at a different situation from Article 85.

ARTICLES 30–36 AND INTELLECTUAL PROPERTY RIGHTS

Article 85 permits one party to a licensing agreement to protect a defined territory against the other. But what of the situation where a licensor is attempting to restrain imports not by its licensee, but by a third-party customer of the licensee? It is already clear from the above discussion that Community law is determined to curtail as far as possible results that are hostile to the principle of market integration and this is expressed in the

---

34a See generally on the law of refusal to supply, p. 750.
35 Case T-51/89 [1990] ECR II-309, [1991] 4 CMLR 334, pp. 724, 750 above.
36 Case 6/72 [1973] ECR 215, [1973] CMLR 199; p. 807 above.

block exemption regulations by the strict rules forbidding restraint of parallel imports.[37] The free circulation of parallel imports is typically secured by third parties who rely on the Treaty provisions dealing with the free movement of goods.

THE PROBLEM EXPLAINED, A COMPROMISE SOUGHT

An apparently irreconcilable conflict is encountered in applying the Treaty rules on the free movement of goods to intellectual property rights. Article 30, as interpreted by the Court in *Dassonville*,[38] prohibits 'all trading rules enacted by Member States which are capable of hindering, directly or indirectly, actually or potentially, intra-Community trade'. A patent that is used in, say, France to exclude a German product from the French market would seem to fall foul of this definition. Yet Article 36 declares that 'the provisions of Articles 30–34 shall not preclude prohibitions or restrictions on imports, exports or goods in transit justified on grounds of [*inter alia*] . . . the protection of industrial and commercial property', although it adds the proviso that 'such prohibitions or restrictions shall not . . . constitute a means of arbitrary discrimination or a disguised restriction on trade between Member States'. Moreover, Article 222 insists that 'the Treaty shall in no way prejudice the rules in Member States governing the system of property ownership'. Both Articles 36 and 222 point firmly towards the validity of market partitioning under national intellectual property law.

Exclusive territorial protection is characteristic of intellectual property rights,[39] yet this conflicts with the basic notion of economic integration on which the Treaty is based. The Court's work in this area needs to be appreciated in the light of this basic incompatibility. Some, but not all, of the oddities in the Court's approach can be traced to the basic problem left unresolved in the Treaty by Article 30 on the one hand, Articles 36 and 222 on the other.

Just as the Court under Article 86 has conceded that the existence of an intellectual property right is not abusive, but that its exercise might be, so too the Court has attempted to solve the Article 30 problem by drawing a

37 See p. 832.
38 Case 8/74 [1974] ECR 837, p. 431 above.
39 More generally, rules against unfair competition may permit territorial protection for traders, even though there is no exclusivity in the protection claimed; e.g., in English law the 'passing-off' action. Lacking exclusivity, such rules do not confer intellectual property rights, but may be justified despite being trade barriers subject in principle to Article 30; see, e.g., Case 16/83 *Prantl* [1984] ECR 1299, [1985] 2 CMLR 238; p. 513 above.

distinction between the existence of intellectual property rights and their exercise. The former cannot be challenged under the Treaty; the latter can. In this way the Court has tried to reconcile the incompatibility of national property rights with the pursuit of economic integration. The two are ultimately irreconcilable,[40] but the Court has reached a type of compromise. The exercise of an intellectual property right that causes market partitioning will be upheld only insofar as the 'specific subject-matter' of the right is being protected. The Court has defined the 'specific subject-matter' of patents in *Centrafarm* v *Sterling Drug*[41] as

the guarantee that the patentee, to reward the creative effort of the inventor, has the exclusive right to use an invention with a view to manufacturing industrial products and putting them into circulation for the first time, either directly or by the grant of licences to third parties, as well as the right to oppose infringements.

In the case of trade marks, *Centrafarm* v *Winthrop*[42] defined the specific subject-matter as

the guarantee that the owner of the trade mark has the exclusive right to use that trade mark, for the purpose of putting products protected by the trade mark into circulation for the first time, and is therefore intended to protect him against competitors wishing to take advantage of the status and reputation of the trade mark by selling products illegally bearing that trade mark.

No explicit definition of the specific subject matter of copyright has ever been given, but the concept appears to exist in parallel; a monopoly right over exploitation coupled to a corresponding right to restrain infringement.

The Court's notion is that there is a core to the intellectual property right on which it is possible to rely even if that impedes cross-border trade. That core is termed the 'specific subject-matter'. Within that core, Articles 36 and 222 prevail and free trade is subordinated to national protection. But beyond the core, beyond the assertion of the right's 'specific subject-matter', Article 30 prevails and free trade precludes the exercise of the rights. Exactly what the content of the core is has been developed through the Court's jurisprudence. The Court's approach is well seen in the cases where the Court has determined that the holder of a right in state A enjoys protection in state A. That is within the core and can be protected even if a trade barrier is the result. The owner of the right also enjoys the right referred to above to exploit the product for the first time outside

---

40 After all, confining the exercise of a right diminishes its existence; Wyatt and Dashwood, *European Community Law*, p. 574.
41 Case 15/74 [1974] ECR 1147, at p. 1162, [1974] 2 CMLR 480.
42 Case 16/74 [1974] ECR 1183, at p. 1194, [1974] 2 CMLR 480.

state A. But thereafter the right to protect the national territory is lost. Having chosen to step beyond the borders of home state A to sell in state B, the right holder must accept the consequences that others may choose to cross those borders in the opposite direction and to import the product sold in state B in state A. The right holder cannot prevent this. The right is 'exhausted'.

PATENTS

Exhaustion of rights

In *Centrafarm* v *Sterling Drug* a drug called Negram had been patented by Sterling Drug under British law and under Dutch law.[43] The United Kingdom price of pharmaceuticals was much lower than the price in the Netherlands, largely because of the economic power of the bulk buyer in the United Kingdom, the National Health Service. Centrafarm identified a commercial opportunity. It bought large stocks of the drug relatively cheaply in the United Kingdom and, even after taking account of its transport costs, it was able to undercut the price in the Netherlands and thereby obtain a profitable market share. This exploitation of interstate price differentials is good for the re-exporter, Centrafarm, good for the Dutch consumer able to buy more cheaply and good for the general process of market integration, but it is bad for the commercial interests of the producer. Sterling Drug responded by trying to prevent Centrafarm selling goods originating in the United Kingdom in the Netherlands by relying on its exclusive rights under patent law before the Dutch courts. The infringement action raised directly the conflict between free trade as practised by Centrafarm and reliance on national intellectual property rights owned by Sterling Drug. The Dutch court, wishing to establish whether Community law prevented Sterling Drug from asserting its rights, made a reference under Article 177 to the European Court. The Court defined the specific subject-matter of the patent and made it clear that Sterling Drug had in this case exhausted its rights by marketing the same product in two states. Having taken advantage of the wider market by choosing to operate in two states, the producer cannot then act to partition the market between those two states.

The judgment thus concentrates on whether the patent holder in state A has consented to marketing in state B. If this is so, it is impermissible to

---

43 Case 15/74, note 41 above. A large number of the relevant cases have involved pharmaceuticals. See generally, Hancher, 'The European Pharmaceutical Market: Problems of Partial Harmonization' (1990) 15 ELRev 9.

rely on intellectual property rights to prevent the free flow of the item back from state B into state A. The first exploitation of the product on another market exhausts the rights of protection on the home market. Conversely, where the product has been marketed outside state A by an unconnected third party rather than with the consent of the right holder, it is permissible to stand on exclusive rights under the patent before the courts of state A to keep out any imported goods.[44] The Court's emphasis on identifying whether rights have been exhausted is built on the logic that the producer who has chosen to integrate markets must accept the full consequences, both those favourable and unfavourable to its commercial interests, and it represents a laudable attempt to achieve a balance between Article 30 on the one hand and Articles 36 and 222 on the other.

In *Merck* v *Stephar*[45] Merck held a patent for a drug in the Netherlands and had marketed it there. It had also marketed the drug in Italy, but it had no patent there, because under Italian legislation as it then stood no such patent could be issued. A third party bought stocks in Italy and exported them to the Netherlands, where Merck attempted to rely on its patent. It argued that the case was distinguishable from *Centrafarm* v *Sterling Drug* on the basis that it, Merck, unlike Sterling Drug, had been denied the valuable opportunity of securing patent protection under Italian law. The European Court saw no such distinction. Merck had chosen to market its goods in Italy and had to accept the consequence that its rights were exhausted under Dutch patent law. The absence of patent protection in Italy made no difference. Merck had entered the Italian market willingly and fully aware of this deficiency.

The Court accepts that the right holder has a choice. He or she may stick to home territory and enjoy a monopoly in the protected goods. Once he or she chooses to expand by selling the product in another state, the free circulation of those goods between the states must ensue. If the producer chooses to take advantage of the wider market, then the impact of increased competition in that wider market must be accepted too. The Court's approach has attracted criticism. It allows the producer to sit tight and protect a home market. It even encourages that reticence, especially where the right is held in a high-price market, because the consequence of venturing forth into a new market is the loss of patent protection, as Merck discovered. That risks provoking market partitioning due to the reluctance of national patent holders to abandon cosy domestic isolation.[46]

---

44 The situation in Case 24/67 *Parke Davis* v *Centrafarm* [1968] ECR 55, [1968] CMLR 47, although in this early case the Court based its decision on Article 85 rather than Article 30.
45 Case 187/80 [1981] ECR 2063, [1981] 2 CMLR 463.
46 Korah, *EC Competition Law and Practice*, pp. 193–4. See also the outcome of the

Yet, as already observed, the Court is working with difficult materials. Embedded in the structure of the Treaty is an ambivalent approach to the status of intellectual property rights and no answer could satisfy all the competing interests.[47] Moreover, it is submitted that few traders will in practice confine themselves to a single national market. The lure of the wider market and its improved economies of scale will usually provide commercial incentives outweighing those that accrue from strength on a relatively small national market. Clearly, however, there is an incentive for the Community to seek resolution of these dilemmas through the adoption of harmonized rules[48] and an incentive for traders to support legislative initiatives that will improve the financial rewards of innovation by raising the relatively weak levels of protection available in some states.

The definition of consent

The Court's selection of 'exhaustion of rights' as the key element in distinguishing lawful from unlawful reliance on national patents leads to the vital definitional point of defining exactly when rights have been exhausted. Consensual marketing in state B was clearly the key in *Centrafarm* v *Sterling Drug* and in *Merck* v *Stephar*, but what exactly does 'consent' entail in this context?

In *Pharmon* v *Hoechst*[49] Hoechst owned patents for the drug Frusemide in Germany, the Netherlands and the United Kingdom. In the United Kingdom a compulsory licence was awarded for manufacture of the drug under the Patents Act. Under a compulsory licence a patentee is deprived of exclusivity by a state act, which permits the grant to third parties of a licence to exploit the patent provided a reasonable royalty is paid to the patent holder. The compulsory licence aims both to reward the inventor and to make more readily available to society the fruits of the invention. So Hoechst retained the patent but the drug was made by third parties licensed not by Hoechst but by the state. Pharmon, following Centrafarm's example, bought stocks of the drug made in the United Kingdom by DDSA, the licensee, and exported them to the Netherlands. Hoechst sought to exclude the imports by relying on the Dutch patent. The European Court held that exercise of Hoechst's Dutch patent was permissible. This decision favours national protection over free trade and gives a

Commission's investigations of Distillers' pricing policies discussed by Korah, '"Goodbye", Red Label: Condemnation of Dual Pricing by Distillers' (1978) 3 ELRev 62.

47 For an attempt see Marenco and Banks, 'Intellectual Property and the Community Rules on Free Movement' (1990) 15 ELRev 224, for example àt p. 250.

48 See further p. 854.

49 Case 19/84 [1985] ECR 2281.

narrow interpretation of the consent required before rights are exhausted. Hoechst had not manufactured the drug in the United Kingdom and so had not consented to its marketing there. Its choice to patent the drug in the United Kingdom did not amount to adequate consent, even though one might have anticipated that the initial consensual registration should be taken to encompass consent to all that might happen thereafter, including compulsory licensing. The Court, however, held that exhaustion of rights occurs only on consensual marketing, with the result that Hoechst had not exhausted its rights under national patent law.

Non-discrimination

It should finally be noted that the party seeking to protect itself under national patent law cannot obtain against an import a remedy unavailable in purely national proceedings. Even if rights have not been exhausted, it is not possible to exclude an imported product from the market if an infringing domestic product could not be so excluded. In *Allen and Hanburys* v *Generics*[50] the British patent had been adjusted under statute so that the patent holder could no longer claim exclusivity. Other firms could make the product, provided they paid a royalty to the patent holder. In these circumstances the European Court indicated that an injunction restraining the import of an infringing product, marketed in another state without the patent holder's permission, could not be awarded by an English court.[51] The import had to be admitted, although payment could be demanded in accordance with the rules equally applicable to domestic products.[52] This is no more than an application of Article 30's rule against unjustified discrimination.[53]

---

50 Case 434/85 [1988] ECR 1245, [1988] 1 CMLR 701.
51 It was submitted that it might be more difficult to check, e.g., quantities of imports for the purposes of calculation of royalties; the Court agreed that this might be so but that it could not justify a blanket rule.
52 See [1989] 2 CMLR 325 for the House of Lords' disposal of the case.
53 See also Case C-235/89 *Commission* v *Italy*, [1992] ECR I-777, [1992] 2 CMLR 709; Case C-30/90 *Commission* v *United Kingdom*, [1992] ECR I-829, [1992] 2 CMLR 709. The Court adopted a still broader approach to non-discrimination in Joined Cases C-92/92 and C-326/92 *Phil Collins* v *Imtrat Handelsgesellschaft mbH* and *Patricia Im- und Export Verwaltungsgesellschaft mbH* v *EMI Electrola GmbH*, judgment of 20 October 1993; copyright and related rights fall within the scope of application of the Treaty and therefore protection under national law must be available to nationals of all member states by virtue of the basic principle of non-discrimination now found in Art. 6 EC.

TRADE MARKS

Exhaustion of rights

Similar issues have arisen in relation to trade marks. *Centrafarm v Winthrop*[54] involved the same drug as *Centrafarm v Sterling Drug*,[55] Negram, but concerned an attempt by Winthrop, a Sterling Drug subsidiary, to rely on the trade mark, rather than the patent, to protect the Dutch market from imports from the United Kingdom. The Court concluded that the right holders' decision to market the product in more than one state precluded reliance on the right to maintain market partition. The trade mark, like the parent, was exhausted and the national court must uphold free trade over domestic intellectual property rights.

The definition of consent

It has already been explained in relation to patents that the focus on consensual marketing as the trigger to exhaustion of rights conceals the critical need to define precisely what is at stake in the notion of consent. The Court has also addressed this issue in the realm of trade marks and, in a manner comparable to that observed in *Pharmon v Hoechst*,[56] it has latterly shown a cautious restraint when asked to find the 'consent' necessary to disallow reliance on a national right. *IHT Internationale Heiztechnik Gmbh v Ideal Standard GmbH*[57] involved Ideal Standard trade marks held separately in France and Germany. In both countries, the trade mark derived from a common, American source. In 1984, the trade mark in France had been sold to an independent third-party buyer. The litigation arose out of attempts by the German trade-mark holder to rely on the right to exclude goods bearing the French version of the mark from the German market.

The European Court held that reliance on the German trade mark in these circumstances was permissible notwithstanding its obstructive effect on cross-border trade. The Court reached this result even though the trade marks had the same source and even though the situation stimulating litigation had arisen as a result of the *consensual* assignment of the French trade mark to a third party. Consent implicit in an assignment is less than the consent required to exhaust rights. The Court emphasized that the

54 Case 16/74, note 42 above.
55 Case 15/74, note 41 above.
56 Case 19/84, note 49 above.
57 Case C-9/93 [1994] ECR I-2789, noted by Tritton [1994] 10 EIPR 422.

marks were now held by economically independent firms. Were Community law to disallow reliance on a national trade mark in such circumstances, there might ensue a risk that consumers would be confused. The Court focused on the function of the trade mark in guaranteeing the origin of the product to the consumer. This took precedence over the drive towards product market integration.[58]

The *Ideal Standard* ruling establishes that the ability to rely on a national trade mark is lost only where the goods that the right holder seeks to exclude were marketed elsewhere in circumstances allowing the right holder to exercise control over the condition of the goods. Once economic separation occurs, protection under the national trade mark endures. The *Ideal Standard* ruling confirms and extends the ruling in 'HAG II', *SA CNL-SUCAL* v *HAG*,[59] which concerned division of a trade mark by governmental, rather than voluntary, action. The Court in 'HAG II' ruled in favour of reliance on a national right to exclude products made by a third party with which the right holder has no economic links even where the third party's goods bear a trade mark with a common origin to that of the right holder. 'HAG II', now extended by *Ideal Standard* to voluntary division, already indicated a retreat in the willingness of the Court to use Article 30 to integrate the European market notwithstanding the continued existence of national territorial protection. In 'HAG II' the Court overruled its 1974 ruling in 'HAG I', *Van Zuylen* v *Hag*,[60] in which it had controversially decided that where trade marks in different states held by different firms had a common origin, they could not be relied on in a way that would partition the market.

The decision always seemed unconvincing[61] and represented an over-eagerness on the part of the Court to further market integration at the expense of national protection. It was true, as the Court observed in the first *Hag* case, that exercise of the right 'would legitimize the isolation of national markets . . . would collide with one of the essential objects of the Treaty, which is to unite national markets in a single market'.[62] Yet the Treaty envisages this result in the sphere of intellectual property rights.

58 The separate undertakings should beware of entering into market-sharing agreements based on the mark for fear of violation of Art. 85; p. 849 below.

59 Case C-10/89 [1990] ECR I-3711, [1990] 3 CMLR 571, noted by Cornish (1990) 10 YEL 469; Joliet (1991) 27 Rev Trim Droit Européen 169; Oliver (1991) 54 MLR 587; Metaxas-Marangidis (1991) 16 ELRev 128; Alexander (1991) 28 CMLRev 681.

60 Case 192/73 [1974] ECR 731.

61 See, e.g., Kemp, 'The Erosion of Trade Mark Rights in Europe' (1974) 11 CMLRev 360 and Mann, 'Industrial Property and the EEC Treaty' (1975) 24 ICLQ 31. Cf. reply by Jacobs, 'Industrial Property and the EEC Treaty: A Reply' (1975) 24 ICLQ 643, now rejected by the author, who was the AG in Case C-10/89.

62 Case 192/73, note 60 above, para. 13.

Both 'HAG II' and *Ideal Standard* tend to push the margin a little further away from market integration and towards respect for national protection and, indirectly, towards the need for legislative intervention.

Repackaged products

The cases considered so far involve the importation of the product in its original state. It is not uncommon for an importer to add its own packaging to a product. Can a trade-mark holder use the trade mark to exclude a product consensually marketed in another state, where the product has been repackaged by a third party? In *Hoffman la Roche* v *Centrafarm*[63] Roche held the trade mark for Valium in both Germany and the United Kingdom. The price was much lower in the United Kingdom, so Centrafarm seized the opportunity to export from there to Germany, where it undercut prices. Roche asked the German courts to protect its trade mark against the imports. Had Centrafarm simply re-exported the drug in the form it was available in the United Kingdom, Roche would certainly have been powerless, as Winthrop was. However, Centrafarm had repackaged the goods into the larger boxes normal in Germany on which it had reprinted the Roche trade mark as well as its own details. The Court resolved the issue by admitting that in principle Roche could rely on its trade mark to protect the German market. The Court explained that the essential function of the trade mark is 'to guarantee the identity of the trademarked product to the consumer or ultimate user, by enabling him without any possibility of confusion to distinguish that product from products which have another origin'. Accordingly, where the repackaging is likely to lead to confusion about origin, it will be permissible to keep out the repackaged import. However, it follows that the trade-mark holder may not keep out a repackaged good where this consumer guarantee of non-interference is not undermined by the repackaging. This might occur where, for example, the original product has two layers of packaging and the inner layer remains untouched.[64] The Court explained more fully when it would be impermissible to rely on a trade mark to exclude even a repackaged product. Free trade prevails where three conditions are observed: first, the repackaging does not affect the original condition of the product; second, the owner of the right must be supplied with notice in advance of the marketing of the repackaged product; and, third, in order to protect the consumer from being misled, it must be plain who is responsible for the repackaging. If these conditions are met, the trade

63 Case 102/77 [1978] ECR 1139, [1978] 3 CMLR 217.
64 ibid., para. 10 of the judgment.

mark's guarantee to the consumer about the nature of the product remains intact and there is no justification for the producer of the original product to seek to exclude the product. The same approach was applied in *Centrafarm v American Home Products*,[65] where Centrafarm went still further by changing the trade mark on the import to take account of the fact that the drug was trade-marked as Serenid D in the United Kingdom and Seresta in Belgium.

In *Pfizer v Eurim-Pharm*[66] Pfizer held a trade mark in Germany and the United Kingdom for a pharmaceutical. In Britain the pills were packaged in blister strips stamped with the Pfizer trade mark inside an outer wrapper. Eurim-Pharm took off the wrapper and packed the strips in a box with a transparent window and sold them in Germany. Pfizer could rely on its German trade mark to exclude the imports only if the essential function of the trade mark had been compromised; that is, if Eurim-Pharm had failed to comply with the three-fold test. The transparent window allowed Pfizer's trade mark to be clearly visible and allowed the consumer to know the product itself was unaffected by the outer repackaging. Eurim-Pharm had alerted Pfizer and had added its own details, so the *Hoffman la Roche* test was met. The guarantee of origin was not impaired and Pfizer could not rely on its trade mark. Free trade prevailed.

The Court's reduction of the law to a three-part formula provides lessons for importers. The Court has in effect explained to the repackager exactly what it must do to secure access to new markets and has thereby smoothed the integrative process. In *Pfizer v Eurim-Pharm* the importer 'did its homework'.[67] But there are also lessons for holders of intellectual property rights. It would be possible to market goods in such a way that repackaging in conformity with the *Hoffman la Roche* formula is not possible and thereby to maintain market division. For example, different trade marks might be registered for the same product in different states, as in *Centrafarm v American Home Products*, and then pills might be packed in blister strips stamped with the trade mark, as in *Pfizer v Eurim-Pharm*. The repackager would need to alter the trade mark displayed to that familiar to consumers in the state of destination, yet tampering with the blister strips would affect the original condition of the product contrary to the *Hoffman la Roche* tests. Such a device could thwart the repackager and permit protection from cross-border competition by virtue of reliance on the trade mark. The profits available to the right holder able to achieve such protection make such a strategy tempting. Where such calculated registration of different trade marks or deliberate use of different packaging is seen

---

65 Case 3/78 [1978] ECR 1823, [1979] 1 CMLR 326.
66 Case 1/81 [1981] ECR 2913, [1982] 1 CMLR 406.
67 Steiner, *EC Law*, p. 115.

to be a device of artificial market segregation[68] the right holder might be deprived of the ability to rely on the right, by reference to the second sentence of Article 36, which forbids disguised restrictions on trade even where prima facie a head of justification has been established.[69] Such ruses might also be controlled under the competition rules. Article 85 catches agreements that partition the market and here may act as a control over devious attempts to evade the application of Article 30.

Similar but unconnected trade marks

It should finally be realized that this discussion concerns products consensually marketed by a right holder in more than one state or products bearing a trade mark with a common origin. The matter is different where the products are made by quite different parties but where the trade mark simply happens to be confusingly similar. In *Terrapin* v *Terranova*[70] a British building material was registered in the United Kingdom under the trade mark Terrapin. A similar product was registered in Germany as Terranova. The producers were totally separate. The question arose whether the British product could be excluded from the German market by the owner of the Terranova mark. Had these been Terranova's own products, bought in the United Kingdom and reimported to Germany, there would have been no scope for reliance on the trade mark. Rights would have been exhausted. However, because the products were different, the trade mark merely similar, the Court ruled that reliance on the trade mark was permissible provided there was a real risk of confusion that would justify the exclusion of the similar product. It was for the national court in the context of an Article 177 reference to decide on the depth of the risk of confusion. In *Deutsche Renault AG* v *Audi AG*[71] the alleged confusion was between Audi's German trade mark 'Quattro', applied to four-wheel drive vehicles, and Renault's 'Espace Quadra', also used for a four-wheel drive vehicle made in France. The European Court ruled that the determination of the criteria for deciding on the risk of confusion was

---

68 Registration of different names for the same product in different states is not necessarily unlawful even where it leads to the partitioning of the market; it might be objectively justifiable where, for example, the name used in one state would be obscene in another.

69 Case 102/77, note 63 above, para. 9 of the judgment; Case 3/78, note 65 above, paras. 19–23 of the judgment; Cases 266, 267/87 R v *Pharmaceutical Society, ex parte Association of Pharmaceutical Importers* [1989] ECR 1295, [1989] 2 CMLR 751, para. 20 of the judgment.

70 Case 119/75 [1976] ECR 1039, [1976] 2 CMLR 482.

71 Case C-317/92, judgment of 30 November 1993, noted by Smith (1994) 31 CMLRev 889, Würtenberger [1994] 7 EIPR 302.

a matter for the national system. The Court's refusal to identify Community law criteria represented a rather surprisingly cautious approach.[72] The Court was a little more forthcoming in *IHT Internationale Heiztechnik Gmbh* v *Ideal Standard GmbH*[73] where, although it confirmed that it was for national law to determine the criteria relevant to assessment of the risk of confusion, the Court added that the national court must comply with the prohibition against arbitrary discrimination and disguised restrictions on trade between member states found in the second sentence of Article 36. The Court observed that this proviso prevents a national court from 'conduct[ing] an arbitrary assessment of the similarity of products'.[74]

In cases where parties holding similar trade marks form links by agreement, Article 85 may apply. Were the parties to seek to reach a compromise in order to avoid confusion between their marks, they must take care to comply with Article 85. Where the agreement is a genuine resolution of true confusion it seems that there may be no breach of Article 85.[75] Where Henkel, owners of the Persil trade mark in Germany, Denmark, Italy and the Benelux countries, agreed to use red letters in a red oval, whereas Unilever, owners of the mark in the United Kingdom and France, opted for green letters, the Commission was satisfied that the firms were acting to preserve the existence of their trade marks and found no breach of Article 85(1). The removal of confusion allows both companies' products to be traded freely throughout the Community, and the Commission paid 'due recognition' to the sterling efforts of the firms to resolve their problems in the context of the rules of market integration.[76] However, where such agreements are horizontal, the parties must expect rigorous supervision and, fundamentally, the Commission is hardly likely to accept an agreement that envisages market partitioning. The Court recognizes the legality and utility of delimitation agreements designed to avoid confusion, but considers that Article 85 cannot be excluded 'if they are also for the purpose of market-sharing or other restrictions of competition'.[77]

---

72 See Reich, 'The November Revolution of the European Court of Justice: *Keck*, *Meng* and *Audi* revisited' (1994) 31 CMLRev 473.
73 Case C-9/93, note 57 above.
74 Para. 19 of the judgment.
75 Case 35/83 *BAT* v *Commission* [1985] ECR 363, [1985] 2 CMLR 470; see *SYNTHELABO/SYNTEX* IP (89) 108, noted by Jones and Van der Woude (1990) 15 ELRev 171. See Van Bael and Bellis, *Competition Law*, 290–93.
76 [1978] 1 CMLR 395.
77 Case 35/83, note 75 above, para. 33 of the judgment; see also Comm. Dec. 75/297 *SIRDAR* OJ 1975 L125/27, [1975] 1 CMLR D93 (breach of Art. 85(1), exemption unavailable).

COPYRIGHT

Exhaustion of rights

The doctrine of exhaustion of rights is also applicable to copyright.[78] In *Deutsche Grammophon* v *Metro*[79] Deutsche Grammophon had consented to the sale in France of records over which they held a right analogous to copyright in Germany. The price differential between France and Germany induced Metro to buy up stocks in France and undercut the price on the German market. It was held that Deutsche Grammophon had consented to the marketing of their products in France and could accordingly no longer block the marketing of those goods in Germany.

The definition of consent

In *Musik-Vertrieb Membran* v *GEMA*[80] the German right holder, having marketed goods in the United Kingdom, tried to restrain their re-introduction on to the German market. However, the right holder argued that in this case the price differential that made the reimportation attractive was not attributable to its own arbitrary pricing policies, but instead to statutory intervention. British rules allowed a significantly lower royalty sum to be added to the price due from a licensee than did German legislation. Records coming from the United Kingdom could undercut German prices simply because the law was different. The right holder argued that in these circumstances it should not be exposed to competition from the British goods, because it could not be held responsible for the statutory distortion of the market. It had not consented to a statutory regime over which it had no control. The importer should, at least, have to pay the extra statutory rate applicable in Germany.[81] However, rejecting this submission, the Court held that free trade must prevail. The British market had been entered willingly and the full consequences of that decision had to be accepted by the trader. The consent of the trader to widen the market was forthcoming and it could not be retracted to partition the market even in the face of statutory distortions between states for which the trader was in no way responsible.

---

78 Analogous protected design rights also attract a similar legal approach; see e.g., Case 144/81 *Keurkoop* v *Nancy Kean Gifts* [1982] ECR 2853.
79 Case 78/70 [1971] ECR 487, [1971] CMLR 631.
80 Cases 55, 57/80 [1981] ECR 147, [1981] 2 CMLR 44.
81 Cf. the situation in Case 395/87, note 23 above, where a rate *equally* applicable to both imports and domestic products was being sought.

This decision plainly pushes the law towards free trade and away from lawful national protection. Although, admittedly, the initial choice about stepping beyond the confines of a national market rests with the trader[82] the right holder thereafter has to accept the full consequences of deciding to enter the market of another state. Free trade is not delayed until the detail of national law has been harmonized, nor, indeed, until adjustment of the price variations that flow from the varying strengths of legal protection. Consent, then, is seen to relate to the initial decision to enter a market and encompasses subsequent developments on that market that might individually have been aspects to which consent would not have been given. In contrast, *Pharmon v Hoechst*[83] was a decision that gave greater emphasis to protection. It allowed a firm to enter a market but then to withhold consent from the marketing of products made under a compulsory licence, even though the grant of that licence could be seen simply as a consequence of that initial consensual market entry. Consent seems to relate only to consent to marketing.

EMI v Patricia Import[84] is also a decision that adopts a notion of consent weighted more in favour of protection of the right holder than free trade. EMI sought to exclude from Germany Cliff Richard records imported from Denmark. The records had been marketed perfectly lawfully in Denmark, because although EMI had held protection in Denmark parallel to that in Germany, the protection had expired after twenty-five years, whereas that in Germany would endure for five further years. The records had not been made or marketed by EMI in Denmark, but they had been lawfully marketed there after protection had expired, as EMI had known it certainly would. In favour of free trade it was submitted that the firm had entered Denmark, with its relatively short copyright period, with its eyes open and should be held to the consequences of that decision. Yet that would have the effect of reducing copyright protection in the Community to that of the least generous state, which might place an undue emphasis on free trade by undermining national choices about property rights.[85] Advocate-General Darmon saw this as a major risk 'for artistic creativity in the Community, an essential aspect of this Europe of culture which everyone desires'.[86] The Court insisted that 'consent' of the right holder, which would preclude reliance on a national copyright, cannot be found to encompass acts of third parties after the expiry of copyright protection,

---

82 As the Court insists at para. 25 of the judgment in Cases 55, 57/80, note 80 above.
83 Case 19/84, note 49 above.
84 Case 341/87 [1989] ECR 79, [1989] 2 CMLR 413.
85 In Case C-9/93 *IHT Internationale Heiztechnik Gmbh v Ideal Standard GmbH*, note 57 above, the Court made the same point explicitly in connection with trade-mark law.
86 ibid., [1989] ECR 79, 91. It might be noted that the Maastricht Treaty added a new title on culture.

even though the right holder must have known that this lawful manufacture and marketing would happen.

Consent, then, appears to relate to the actual marketing of the product in question and cannot be taken to apply to all matters that flow from the original choice to enter a market. That conforms to *Pharmon v Hoechst* and to *Ideal Standard*, but it sits uneasily with *Musik-Vertrieb* and, perhaps, *Merck v Stephar*.[87] *Warner Bros v Christiansen*[88] is a further decision that tends to favour the right holder. It permits the right to be divisible. Danish law grants a copyright holder two separate rights: to oppose sale of video-cassettes and to oppose their rental. British law recognizes only the right over initial sale; it confers no right to oppose rental once the product has been marketed. Warner Bros, a Danish firm, sold its product in the United Kingdom and then attempted to rely on its Danish right before Danish courts to restrain those products, imported from the United Kingdom, from being rented out in Denmark by Christiansen. It succeeded. The Court held that Warner Bros had consented to marketing the products in the United Kingdom and could not prevent the free circulation of the goods in Denmark, but it had not consented to the separate rental element. The Danish law's subdivision of the exclusive right could be maintained, even though British law made no such distinction. In effect, Warner Bros's consent was divisible and it had not exhausted the right to prevent rental. A broader view would have held that consent to marketing the video in the United Kingdom leads automatically to its release on to the wider market in all its manifestations, but the Court, rejecting an analogy with *Musik-Vertrieb Membran v GEMA*,[89] declared that marketing such a product in a state where rental rights cannot be protected (the United Kingdom) has no repercussions for the right to restrain rental in the home state (Denmark). Diversity between national laws persists, pending Community legislative activity.

87 Case 187/80, note 45 above.
88 Case 156/86 [1988] ECR 2605, noted by Friden (1989) 26 CMLRev 193, 195. See also Case 62/79 *Coditel SA v Ciné Vog Films* [1980] ECR 881, [1981] 2 CMLR 362, which creatively extends these principles into the field of the provision of services even though Arts. 59 *et seq*. contain no exception analogous to Article 36's reference to intellectual property. See Ch. 19, p. 591.
89 Cases 55, 57/80, note 80 above.

THE FUNCTION OF HARMONIZATION

The limits of the judicial role

The Court's attempt to draw a line between lawful and unlawful restraints on trade deserves credit. It was left a more or less impossible dilemma by the drafters of the Treaty and its own attempts to locate a margin should be judged against that background. However, having established that there must be a line and having located it in a particular place, based largely on the notion of 'exhaustion of rights', there are still cases that the Court seems to have placed on the wrong side of the line. That is, even if one accepts the logic of the Court's location of the margin, there are still cases that, applying the Court's criteria, seem wrongly decided. Logically, *Pharmon v Hoechst*[90] and *Musik-Vertrieb Membran v GEMA*[91] should be on the same side of the line, whichever side that might happen to be. Both involve consensual entry into a state, with commercially undesirable consequences attributable to governmental intervention. Yet Hoechst obtained protection, where GEMA did not. The Court has obviously adjusted its stance over twenty years, yet this has disturbed internal coherence in its jurisprudence.

The modern judicial approach tends to favour national protection over free trade. In so far as this interpretation of the basic Treaty rules is inadequate in the context of creating the common market, solutions must be found in a legislative response. An awareness of the role of legislation may be taken to underlie the Court's unwillingness in cases such as *EMI v Patricia Import*[92] and *Warner Bros v Christiansen*[93] to apply Article 30 in a way that would undermine national systems offering stronger protection to right holders than those operating in some other member states. In the *Ideal Standard* ruling[94] the Court made explicit its view that the imposition of a rule invalidating trade-mark assignments for part of the Community could be achieved only by legislative action under Article 100a EC and not by the application of Articles 30–36. The ultimate solution to these problems, which are embedded within the Treaty, lies in harmonization legislation. The first, and less ambitious, step is to harmonize the content of national intellectual property rights. This would allow the award of a similarly constituted right in each of the states. The more ambitious step

90 Case 19/84, note 49 above.
91 Cases 55, 57/80, note 80 above.
92 Case 341/87, note 84 above.
93 Case 156/86, note 88 above.
94 Case C-9/93, note 57 above.

would be the establishment of Community-wide protection. Exclusive territorial protection for the inventor would be secured within the Community, rather than a national market, thereby removing the problem of market partitioning. The variations in national rules are, as observed, capable of discouraging cross-border trade, which impedes the development of the Community market. Moreover, commerce can be expected to push for Community solutions to these problems.

Legislative developments[95]

The Convention on the grant of European Patents, concluded in Munich in 1973, established a European Patent Office, which is empowered to grant a bundle of national patents, thus avoiding the need to take out individual patents by separate procedures in every member state. It includes non-Community states. This is not a 'Community' patent, but rather a set of separate, albeit harmonized, national patents. Enforcement and infringement procedures remain governed by national law. Such harmonization of national systems is certainly a step forward, but the move towards a single Community system has been extremely tortuous. The Convention for a Community Patent was signed in Luxembourg in 1975, but an insufficient number of ratifications precluded its entry into force. In 1989 it was amended and member states were given until the end of 1991 to ratify the amended agreement.[96] However, no member states complied with this deadline. The ratification process proceeded slowly thereafter. By the end of 1994, only five member states had ratified the agreement. They were France, Germany and Greece (in 1992), Denmark (in 1993) and Luxembourg (in 1994). The proposed system would grant Community-wide protection in respect of specified matters. The inventor would obtain monopoly profits from a right of first exploitation on the Community market, but could not partition the Community market along national lines. Disputes would be dealt with through a judicial structure envisaged by the Convention, which includes national courts and a Common Appeal Court.

Commission Directive 89/104 is designed to approximate national trade-mark laws.[97] It lays down, for example, a common definition of the signs capable of constituting a trade mark. It contains a list of reasons that may be advanced for refusing a trade mark and for nullity of a mark. This is a limited harmonization of national law, not a Community trade mark as

95 This field is relatively fast moving; the *European Intellectual Property Review* (EIPR) provides a valuable source of up-to-date information and comment.
96 OJ 1989 L401/1; [1990] 2 CMLR 194.
97 OJ 1989 L40/1.

such. In a Council decision of December 1991 its deadline for implementation was deferred from December 1991 until the end of 1992.[98] The delay was connected to the failure to agree a regulation on a Community trade mark. This gap has been filled. A Community trade mark now exists. Regulation 40/94 on the Community trade mark[99] represents a limited breakthrough beyond the harmonization of national trade-mark laws to the creation of a Community trade-mark law, obtainable by registration. The Regulation is based on the objective of providing a legal structure which will encourage firms to operate on a Community, rather than national, scale. Although the Regulation establishes a trade mark of a unitary character available with equal effect throughout the whole Community, it does not replace national laws on trade marks. The Community trade mark will coexist with national trade marks. This permits firms to choose the structure that best suits their strategy, either the unitary Community right or a bundle of national rights.

The Regulation reflects the Court's case law on exhaustion of rights. Once the owner of a Community trade mark has consented to the marketing of trade-marked goods in the Community, it is not permissible for the owner to prohibit the use of the mark in relation to those goods by a third party, save where there exist 'legitimate reasons for the proprietor to oppose further commercialization of the goods, especially where the condition of the goods is changed or impaired after they have been put on the market'.[100] An Office for Harmonization in the Internal Market (trade marks and designs) is established to administer the rules. Challenges to its decisions may be brought before the Court of First Instance. The office is situated in Alicante in Spain. The majority of the Regulation's thirteen titles and 143 Articles are concerned with procedural matters. It seems highly likely that the office will have a heavy workload generated by opposition to trade marks in respect of which applications for registration are lodged. In particular, the potential clash between marks submitted to the office for registration under the Regulation and allegedly similar marks already protected in different ways in different states is likely to prove a fertile field for disputes about registration. Article 8 of the Regulation covers *Relative grounds for refusal*.[101] It provides that 'upon opposition by the proprietor of an earlier trade mark, the trade mark applied for shall not be registered' where the marks and the goods and services are identical or, doubtless more problematic in practice, where there is sufficient similarity to provoke 'a likelihood of confusion on the

98 Dec. 92/10 OJ 1992 L6/35.
99 OJ 1994 L11/1.
100 Art. 13 Reg.
101 Art. 7 Reg. covers *Absolute grounds for refusal* of registration.

part of the public'. For the purposes of opposition, 'earlier trade marks' include Community trade marks, national trade marks and trade marks registered under international arrangements having effect in a member state.

Progress in the area of copyright was stimulated by the Commission's 1988 Green Paper.[102] The Commission pursued the matter in its 1990 Action Programme.[103] A proposal for a directive on the legal protection of computer programs[104] excited a good deal of comment. In this area it is difficult to determine the extent of protection to which an idea and the technology designed to put into practice are entitled. This raises the familiar issue of striking a compromise between rewarding enterprise and avoiding undue suppression of competition. More specifically, differences in national law proved significant impediments to successful harmonization.[105] A directive was finally adopted in 1991 that established a partial analogy between protection of computer programs and copyright protection of literary works.[106] However, special provision was made for decompilation or reverse engineering, whereby it may be permissible for a program not simply to be used, but in addition to be analysed in order to discover how it is structured. This is allowed where necessary to achieve interoperability between the protected program and a program that has been separately devised.

A bigger step forward was taken with the adoption of Directive 93/98.[107] This directive harmonizes the duration of copyright and related rights. It fixes 70 years after the death of the author as the period of copyright protection and 50 years as the period for related rights (those held by performing artists, producers of sound recordings and film producers). This harmonized regime is more generous to right holders than systems previously available in some member states. Seventy years was the period preferred by Germany. It represents a significant extension for the United Kingdom, where 50 years was the norm under copyright law. This is naturally advantageous to those holding the rights, but it increases the period of suppressed competition that is characteristic of copyright protection. Striking a balance between the competing interests of right holders

---

102 COM (88) 172.

103 COM (90) 584. See comment by Groves [1991] E Bus LR 251.

104 OJ 1980 C91/5.

105 Cornish, 'Inter-operable Systems and Copyright' [1989] 11 EIPR 391; Lucas, 'Copyright in the European Community' (1991) 29 Col J Transnat L 145.

106 Dir. 91/250 OJ 1991 L122/42. See discussion by Dreier, 'The Council Directive of 14 May 1991 on the Legal Protection of Computer Programs' [1991] 9 EIPR 319; Berkvens and Alkemade, 'Software Protection: Life after the Directive' [1991] 12 EIPR 476.

107 OJ 1993 L290/9.

and of potential competitors and their customers is an endemic problem in intellectual property law. The 70-year period has attracted some criticism as unduly long.[108]

In the period leading up to and following the completion of the internal market the Commission continued to draft proposals for further legislation. It has enjoyed some success in securing the adoption of new measures. Directive 92/100 deals with rental rights and lending rights and certain rights related to copyright in the field of intellectual property.[109] Directive 93/83 concerns the coordination of rules concerning copyright and neighbouring rights applicable to satellite broadcasting and cable retransmission.[110]

Differences in national legal perspectives on the nature and purpose of intellectual property law and, in addition, the substantial commercial interests at stake combine to make the Commission's task in this area especially challenging.

108 See Parrinder, 'The Dead Hand of European Copyright' [1993] 11 EIPR 391.
109 OJ 1992 L346.
110 OJ 1993 L248.

CHAPTER 27

State Intervention in the Market

Article 222 declares that 'this Treaty shall in no way prejudice the rules in Member States governing the system of property ownership'. The fact that one member state chooses to place under public control an industry that another member state prefers to locate in the private sector is not of itself objectionable under Community law. Neither nationalization nor privatization are incompatible with primary Community law. However, the state remains subject to the rules forbidding discrimination on the grounds of nationality. If a programme of transfer of property ownership into either the public or the private sector were to favour a state's own nationals, then a breach of Community law would be established. Article 222 remains subject to the fundamental principles of the Community legal order.[1] This principle had important practical implications after German unification in 1990, when the transfer of the economy of the former East Germany into, largely, private hands, was scrutinized by the EC Commission to ensure that there was no state policy of favouritism towards German firms.[2]

Many of the primary rules of the law of market integration already examined in this book relate directly or indirectly to state measures. Articles 12 and 95 control fiscal barriers to the free movement of goods. Article 30 controls physical and technical barriers. Articles 48, 52 and 59 control obstacles to the free movement of persons and services. Even indistinctly applicable rules that partition the common market may violate these provisions, which ensures that Community law has an impact on regulatory measures that may appear to affect only the domestic market. However, in the modern mixed economy the state typically expects to involve itself in market regulation in many different guises, with many different objectives, including not only wealth creation but also wealth distribution. The state may claim exclusive power to operate in a particular

1 Case 182/83 *Fearon* v *Irish Land Commission* [1984] ECR 3677, [1985] 2 CMLR 228.
2 See Passavant and Nosser, 'The German Reunification – Legal Implications for Investment in East Germany' (1991) 25 Int Lawyer 875; also successive Commission Press Releases IP (91) 706, 836, 1174. Naturally, geography and language ensured that, in practice, many acquisitions were carried out by (West) German firms.

sector. It may fix prices in pursuit of, for example, price stability or protection of poorer members of society. It may induce private firms to operate in a particular manner, through persuasion or financial inducement. State subsidies of industry are a common device. The European Community Treaty contains a number of provisions designed to bring such strategies under the supervision of Community law. Against the general notion that state ownership and participation in the market are lawful, but that barriers to interstate trade must be controlled, Community law seeks to exercise control over state economic power where it leads to distortion of the structure or operation of the market.

Control of the state under Community law has always been a sensitive issue, given the faith that governments have long placed in market manipulation and given the extent of state involvement in crucial sectors of the economy such as transport, energy supply and communications. However, the caution of the past has recently been abandoned. A major plank of the policy of Sir Leon Brittan, the Commissioner responsible for Competition from 1989 to 1993, was the removal of entrenched state structures that are perceived to preclude the realization of an open, competitive market. The momentum has been maintained under Sir Leon's successor in DG IV, Karel Van Miert. The basis of the new impetus in this area is not that state ownership is unlawful, for that would conflict with the agnosticism expressed in Article 222. It is, instead, based on the notion that state ownership, although *per se* unobjectionable, is capable of leading to distortion of free and fair competition. A new title on industry was agreed at Maastricht, comprising Article 130 EC, which begins by requiring the Community and the member states to ensure 'that the conditions necessary for the competitiveness of the Community's industry exist' and concludes by declaring that 'this Title shall not provide a basis for the introduction by the Community of any measure which could lead to a distortion of competition'. Aspects of the application of this new policy emphasis have aroused both political controversy and legal complexity. This chapter outlines the Treaty provisions relevant to state intervention in the market and pays special regard to recent Commission and Court initiatives to reinvigorate those rules.

THE STATE AS A COMMERCIAL UNDERTAKING

ARTICLES 85 AND 86

An 'undertaking' for the purposes of the competition rules is defined with reference to its commercial activity, not its legal form.[3] The lawful

3 See p. 683.

existence of a publicly owned firm is guaranteed by Article 222, but the exercise of its economic strength is subject to the Treaty rules against anticompetitive conduct to which all undertakings are subject. Where British Telecommunications, as a nationalized enterprise, pursued allegedly abusive tactics in relation to its management of public telecommunications equipment and its provision of equipment to users on payment of a fee, the Court held that its business activities were subject to control under Article 86.[4] Where state trading organizations from Eastern Bloc countries entered into agreements with Western firms concerning, *inter alia*, price-fixing and market sharing, the Commission held that the organizations were undertakings for the purposes of Article 85 even though under national law they had no status separate from the state.[5] Their function was to trade in aluminium.

The Court's decision in *Sacchi*[6] confirms that the competition rules apply to public broadcasting organizations which pursue economic activity. In fact, in *Sacchi* the Court examined the conduct of the Italian state television firm, RAI, from the perspective of both Articles 86 and 90. Article 90 confirms that public undertakings are subject to the application of Articles 85 and 86. It is examined in more detail in the following section.

These rulings demonstrate that the Court has maintained a wide interpretation of 'undertaking' for the purposes of the application of Articles 85 and 86 (and, therefore, of Article 90). This allows significant areas of state activity that touch the economy to be subjected to the principles of Community competition law. The wider the notion of 'undertaking', the deeper the incursion of these rules into state activity. The Court has, however, accepted that some state functions do not meet the definition of an 'undertaking'. As explained in Chapter 22, bodies to which the state entrusts the management of a social security scheme fulfil an exclusively social function and are not 'undertakings'.[7] An international organization whose functions involved the establishment and collection of charges levied on users of air navigation services in accordance with international agreements was not viewed as an undertaking in *SAT Fluggesellschaft mbH v Eurocontrol*.[8] Control of the activities of such bodies may conceivably be exercised under the rules of free movement and non-discrimination, but not under the competition rules applicable to undertakings.

---

4 Case 41/83 *Italy v Commission* [1985] ECR 873, [1985] 2 CMLR 368.
5 Comm. Dec. 85/206 OJ 1985 L92/1, [1987] 3 CMLR 813.
6 Case 155/73 [1974] ECR 409, [1974] 2 CMLR 177.
7 Cases C-159/91 and C-160/91 *C. Poucet and Others v Assurances Générales*, judgment of 16 February 1993, p. 686 above.
8 Case C-364/92 [1994] ECR I-43.

ARTICLE 90

Article 90(1)

Article 90(1) declares that 'in the case of public undertakings and undertakings to which Member States grant special or exclusive rights Member States shall neither enact nor maintain in force any measure contrary to the rules contained in this Treaty, in particular to those rules provided for in Article 6 and Articles 85 to 94'. The importance of defining the notion of 'undertaking', mentioned above, is emphasized by appreciation that once an entity falls within that definition, the application of Article 90 to the member state is triggered. Article 90(1) confirms the control of anticompetitive conduct by public undertakings discussed in the previous section, but it also covers undertakings to which 'special or exclusive rights' have been granted. It recognizes that it is in principle compatible with the Treaty to confer such rights on an undertaking. However, the exercise of those rights is subject to the rules of the Treaty. So in *Sacchi*[9] the Court held that Article 90(1) ensured that the grant to RAI under Italian law of exclusive rights in respect of television broadcasts was not of itself incompatible with Community law. However, abuse of the position created by law or conduct that discriminates according to nationality is unlawful by virtue of the application of Articles 86 and 6 respectively.

Bodson v *Pompes Funèbres*[10] concerned the French practice of permitting local authorities to exercise exclusive powers to conduct funeral services. Some authorities offered the service themselves, whereas others licensed private firms to carry out these functions. The Court held that where market dominance is established, artificially high prices might be incompatible with Community law. Where a public authority fixes the prices, it violates Article 90(1) read with Article 86. Where a private firm fixes the prices, then Article 86 applies. A breach of Community law may also be established where the state has created the conditions of exclusivity that permit the firm to act abusively. *Höfner* v *Macrotron*[11] concerned German rules under which persons seeking work were put in contact with employers by a state-licensed agency, which possessed exclusive powers in the field. The activities of independent recruitment consultants were suppressed by the public monopoly. The Court held that the agency was an undertaking for the purposes of the competition rules. Any

9 Case 155/73, note 6 above.
10 Case 30/87 [1988] ECR 2479, [1989] 4 CMLR 984, noted by Shaw (1988) 13 ELRev 422.
11 Case C-41/90, [1991] ECR I-1979, noted by Slot (1991) 28 CMLRev 964. Shaw (1991) 16 ELRev 501.

state measure that maintained a law under which a body was forced to violate Article 86 was unlawful by virtue of Article 90(1). The Court considered that a Treaty violation had occurred, because the German rules restricted sources of supply in circumstances where the state was unable to meet demand and prevented private consultants pursuing the activity at all.

In one sense these cases confirm that, in the application of the competition rules, state participation in the market is treated in the same way as private activity. Article 90(1) means that there is no rule against the existence of a dominant position created by state acts, but rather a control of the consequences on the basis that the exercise of economic strength may be abusive. However, there is a fine line between existence and exercise, and recent practice suggests a greater readiness to find abuse in the state's reservation of certain activities to particular operators. In effect, the concession of Article 90(1) is in the process of being interpreted increasingly narrowly, to the point where Community law appears to question the very notion of exclusivity reserved by the state.[12]

Höfner v *Macrotron*[13] provides an example. In one sense the complaint was not about exclusivity, but about the distortive effect of inadequate supply. Yet the result was simply to require elimination of exclusive reservation to the state. *Porto di Genova* v *Siderurgica Gabrielli*[14] concerned the exclusive rights conferred by Italian law on recognized companies to load and unload goods from ships docked at Genoa. The Court held that the exclusivity conferred by the state brought the matter within Article 90(1). The Court conceded that the creation of a dominant position was not unlawful, but added that a breach of the Treaty was established where the undertaking was led to abuse that dominance in merely exercising its exclusive rights. The Court indicated that in the port of Genoa exclusivity led to payment being required for services not requested, disproportionate prices being levied and efficient modern technology neglected. The decision comes close to presuming that abuse is a natural consequence of the absence of the stimulus of competition caused by exclusivity. In the same week the Court found that monopoly rights over the Belgian telephone network had been abused where the firm reserved rights in relation to equipment connected to the network, thereby excluding without objective justification other suppliers.[15] All these decisions are capable of fatally undermining state reservation of exclusivity in many sectors, if necessary at

12 See Select Further Reading on Article 90, p. 916.
13 Case C-41/90, note 11 above.
14 Case C-179/90, [1991] ECR I-5889.
15 Case C-18/88 RTT v *GB-INNO,* [1991] ECR I-5941. See Ch. 23, p. 754 above.

the behest of private operators, who may rely on the direct effect of these provisions in order to gain access to hitherto uncontested protected markets.

Article 90(2)

Article 90(2) provides an exception to the application of the competition rules that is severely limited in its scope. It declares:

Undertakings entrusted with the operation of services of general economic interest or having the character of a revenue-producing monopoly shall be subject to the rules contained in this Treaty, in particular to the rules on competition, in so far as the application of such rules does not obstruct the performance in law or in fact, of the particular tasks assigned to them. The development of trade must not be affected to such an extent as would be contrary to the interests of the Community.

The discussion above has demonstrated the wide interpretation of the prohibition contained in Article 90(1). The competition rules are used with vigour to eliminate exclusive rights that forestall market access. In its practical effect, Article 90(1) is a major stimulus to the injection of market competition into areas previously controlled by the state. The liberalizing influence of Article 90(1) then renders the interpretation of Article 90(2) vital to determining the state's scope for preserving its regulatory choices.

There are two distinct hurdles to be crossed before Article 90(2) may be successfully invoked: the undertaking must be of a defined type, and the competition rules must obstruct the fulfilment of its tasks in the manner stipulated. In *BRT* v *SABAM* the Court insisted that, first and foremost, Article 90(2) represents a derogation from the basic rules of the Treaty and, accordingly, it must be interpreted narrowly.[16] The Court conceded that a private undertaking may fall within Article 90(2), but only where it has been entrusted with the operation of services of general economic interest by an act of a public authority. For example, in *Ahmed Saeed Flugreisen* v *Zentrale zur Bekampfung unlauteren Wettbewerbs*[17] the Court accepted that Article 90(2) was capable of covering carriers by air who were obliged by law to operate in the general interest routes that were not commercially viable. However, Article 90(2) cannot apply even to a *de facto* monopoly where the state has not assigned to it any task.

The immunity enjoyed by such entities is strictly limited, not least by the principle of proportionality. In relation to British Telecommunications the Court upheld the Commission's rejection of arguments founded on

---

16 Case 127/73 [1974] ECR 313, [1974] 2 CMLR 177, para. 19 of the judgment.
17 Case 66/86 [1989] ECR 803, [1990] 4 CMLR 102.

Article 90(2) where the firm was using statutorily conferred powers to prevent the development of competing private message-forwarding agencies. The Court accepted that third-party trade might reduce BT's revenue, but pointed out that the United Kingdom would obtain additional revenue from the activities of those third parties on its territory. The opening up of the market would not jeopardize the performance of the tasks entrusted to BT and Article 90(2) could not be invoked to curtail the application of Article 86.[18] In *Ahmed Saeed*[19] the airlines' arguments that price-fixing was necessary to support loss-making routes and therefore protected by Article 90(2) were not considered by the Court in the absence of adequate factual information.

Paul Corbeau[20] concerned a challenge to the monopoly over postal services held by a public agency in Belgium. The issues that especially troubled the referring national court revolved around the monopoly in the core letter delivery service. If that monopoly were lost, profits used by the state agency to cross-subsidize socially useful but loss-making ancillary services would vanish. 'Cherry-picking' private operators would be only too happy to compete in mail delivery in larger cities, but would either ignore geographically peripheral customers or, at best, charge them higher 'market' rates. The social function of the postal service, widely conceived, would be jeopardized. The European Court was asked whether Article 90(2) could justify the exclusion of competition so that profits can be used to cross-subsidize loss-making aspects of the business.

The Court acknowledged the role of cross subsidy. The Court commented that state intervention is permitted under Article 90(2) 'in so far as the restriction, or even the elimination, of competition from other companies is necessary to ensure the performance of the particular tasks' assigned to the undertaking.

The Court envisaged that some parts of the service must be removed from the shelter of the monopoly and opened up to competition where those services 'do not compromise the economic equilibrium of the service of general economic interest performed by the holder of the exclusive right'. Other aspects of the service will remain justifiably protected from the deregulated market by virtue of Article 90(2). On the one hand, the Court in *Corbeau* was remarkably quick to identify a violation of Article 90(1) in the operation of the monopoly, yet on the other hand it was

---

18 Case 41/83, note 4 above, Comm. Dec. 82/861 *British Telecommunications* OJ 1982 L360/36, [1983] 1 CMLR 457. See also Comm. Dec. 90/456 *Spanish Courier Services* OJ 1990 L233/19, noted (1990) 10 YEL 431.
19 Case 66/86, note 17 above.
20 Case C-320/91, judgment of 19 May 1993, noted (1993) ELRev Competition Law Checklist 94.

strikingly receptive to the potential availability of Article 90(2). This represents an important statement of the existence of limits to the remorseless liberalization of the market through the application of the competition rules. However, it leaves undefined the precise location of those limits in the particular context of Article 90(2). Perhaps they must be elaborated on a case-by-case basis. *Corbeau* was an Article 177 preliminary ruling so the Court did not have the task of deciding the case, merely of interpreting Community law.

It is apparently assumed by the European Court in *Corbeau* that Article 90(2) is directly effective. This follows from an earlier statement to this effect in *ERT v Dimotiki*.[21] The Court's view is rather surprising, given the complexity of the calculation envisaged by Article 90(2). In the past the Court appears to have withheld from national courts the power to apply Article 90(2), other than to rule it unavailable.[22] *Corbeau*, however, implies that the application of Article 90(2) is not the exclusive preserve of the Commission and in *Municipality of Almelo and others v NV Energiebedrijf IJsselmij*[23] the Court made explicit its view that a national court may consider whether the requirements of Article 90(2) are fulfilled with the result that a restriction on competition escapes the prohibitions contained in Articles 85 and 86.

This assertion of direct effect risks disunity state-by-state in the application of Article 90(2). Moreover, it offers the prospect of the politicization of the judicial process. It is possible that a national court confronted by attempted reliance on Article 90(2) is able to seek the assistance of the Commission in the manner already envisaged for the application of Articles 85 and 86 at national level.[24] The Article 177 preliminary reference procedure may also play a part in maintaining consistency in the application of Article 90(2), although the European Court offered little precise guidance in its rulings in both *Corbeau* and *Municipality of Almelo*.

Article 90(3)

Article 90(3) reads: 'The Commission shall ensure the application of the provisions of this Article and shall, where necessary, address appropriate directives or decisions to Member States.' It is a rarity in its conferral on the Commission of direct legislative competence.[25] The power has been

21 Case C-260/89 [1991] ECR I-2925, [1994] 4 CMLR 540.
22 Case 10/71 *Ministère Public v Muller* [1971] ECR 723; Case 127/73, note 16 above. The point was left unclear in both Case 66/86, note 17 above, and Case C-179/90, note 14 above.
23 Case C-393/92 [1994] ECR I-1477.
24 Ch. 24, p. 794 above.
25 See further Ch. 2, pp. 58, 138.

sparingly used and Article 90(3) long languished as a little regarded provision.[26] Breach of Article 90(1) was normally remedied through Article 169 proceedings or, less directly, under the influence of Article 177 in national proceedings.[27] That has changed under the influence of the new policy of greater interventionism in state enterprises, which has induced the Commission to add Article 90(3) to its range of instruments of market liberalization. It has begun to issue both decisions and directives. In *Netherlands/PTT* v *Commission*[28] the Court annulled a decision for failure to respect the right to a fair hearing of the parties affected, but no doubt was cast on the Commission's capacity in principle to proceed against violations of Article 90(1) by way of decisions adopted on the basis of Article 90(3).

In relation to the use of directives based on Article 90(3) a major test of the Commission's desire to pursue a more active policy came in its adoption of a directive designed to open up competition in the market for telecommunications terminal equipment.[29] The directive required the elimination of exclusivity conferred on operators, which the Commission considered was in violation of Article 90. The Commission's adoption of an Article 90(3) directive, bypassing Article 169 and methods under other Treaty provisions for adopting directives in Council, was plainly a challenge to vested state interests. The challenge was taken up by several states, which argued that such market restructuring could be achieved only through Council action. This permitted the Court to rule on the scope of Article 90(3).[30] The Court held that although Article 90 presupposes that the conferral of exclusive rights may be compatible with the Treaty, the legal status of particular monopolies depends on a close examination of their context. Where exclusivity cannot be justified, the Commission is entitled to proceed by way of directive under Article 90(3). Although the Court annulled part of the directive relating to control of the undertakings themselves on the basis that Article 90(3) could be directed only at state measures, the decision establishes that Article 90(3) is a further powerful weapon to be used against state support for monopolies.

---

26 However, it is the base for Dir. 80/723 OJ 1980 L195/35, noted by Page (1980) 5 ELRev 492 (see also note 82 below), which was challenged unsuccessfully in Cases 188–90/80 *France, Italy, UK* v *Commission* [1982] ECR 2545, [1982] 3 CMLR 144.
27 In Case 66/86, note 17 above, the Court confirmed that the application of Articles 90(1) and (2) is not foreclosed where the Commission fails to act under Art. 90(3).
28 Cases C-48/90 and C-66/90, [1992] ECR I-565.
29 Dir. 88/301 OJ L131/73.
30 Case C-202/88 *France* v *Commission*, [1991] ECR I-1223 [1991] 5 CMLR 552, noted by Platteau [1991] 3 ECLR 105; Slot (1991) 28 CMLRev 964; Wheeler (1992) 17 ELRev 67. See also Naftel [1993] 2 ECLR 105.

THE STATE AS REGULATOR OF THE ECONOMY

ARTICLE 5

Article 5 has been playing an increasingly prominent role in this area of Community law, as in others.[31] The Court in *INNO* v *ATAB*[32] declared that it 'provides that Member States shall abstain from any measure which could jeopardize the attainment of the objectives of the Treaty'. As an obligation of cooperation in the pursuit of those objectives, it may be interpreted as restraining the state from assisting violation of the competition rules by private parties. If a national court or national administrative authorities were to disregard the rules of Community competition law, by, for example, enforcing an agreement that the Commission had held incompatible with Article 85, there would be a breach of the basic duties contained in Article 5.[33] Several important cases have developed Article 5's flexible control in circumstances where the state has contributed to the pursuit of anticompetitive practices.

In *Vereininging van Vlaamse Reisbureaus* v *Sociale Dienst*[34] a Belgian travel agent gave discounts to customers. This violated the professional Code of Practice, which had been incorporated into Belgian law. The Association of Travel Agents was recognized under Belgian law as competent to seek a judicial order restraining the breach, and it initiated proceedings. The Court took the view that the Code, which involved price-fixing, was a naked horizontal cartel in breach of Article 85. The Association was accordingly attempting to enforce an unenforceable agreement, contrary to Article 85. As a separate breach, the Belgian state, in offering support to the cartel through its legal system, was itself in violation of Article 5 read in conjunction with Articles 3(g) and 85. The Court thus established that member states are bound neither to adopt nor to maintain in force any measures that could deprive Article 85 of its effectiveness. Requiring, favouring or offering support to an unlawful agreement constitute Treaty

31 See Temple Lang, 'Community Constitutional Law: Article 5 EEC Treaty' (1990) 27 CMLRev 645.
32 Case 13/77 [1977] ECR 2115, para. 30 of the judgment.
33 See pp. 792–6 on the duties of cooperation cast on both national courts and the Commission in the enforcement of the competition rules; the practical difficulties of respecting the demarcation between the application of national competition law and Community competition law envisaged by the Court in Case 14/68 *Walt Wilhelm* v *Bundeskartellamt* [1969] ECR 1 should not be underestimated; see, e.g. Whish, *Competition Law*, pp. 37–43.
34 Case 311/85 [1987] ECR 3801, [1989] 4 CMLR 213, noted by Shaw (1988) 13 ELRev 133.

violations.[35] The Court has elsewhere confirmed that precisely the same view is taken of measures supporting the abuse of a dominant position forbidden by Article 86.[36] These are important rulings, because they allow the defeat of agreements and unilateral practices even where they are supported by national law.

The profound complexity of the case law in this area is attributable to the Court's concern to establish a demarcation between the legal approach to the private and the public sphere, in order to adhere to the divisions that appear in the Treaty itself. State confirmation and reinforcement of a pre-existing private agreement is distinct from a newly introduced state measure to which private parties must adhere. In *Van Eycke* v *ASPA*[37] the applicant deposited money with ASPA and was told subsequently that he would receive less favourable interest rates than those originally advertised. A royal decree had placed a limit on the level of interest payable, because of the economic damage caused by high-deposit interest rates as triggers to high rates of interest payable on capital lending. Van Eycke sought a declaration that ASPA was not entitled to rely on the decree on the basis that it violated the competition rules by restricting competition on rates between private operators in the market. The Court determined that although Articles 85 and 86 are directed at undertakings, there is an obligation on states not to introduce measures – including legislation – that render ineffective the competition rules as applied to undertakings. This duty is derived from Article 5. Violation of the state's obligations could occur where the legislative act reinforces the effects of pre-existing private agreements incompatible with Article 85. It would not occur where there is no pre-existing arrangement, and where the state intervenes independently, although that may itself be controlled under other Treaty provisions.[38] It was not clear on the facts of *Van Eycke* v *ASPA* whether Belgium was guilty of unlawful intervention; the matter rested for final decision with the national court.

The Court added that violation could also occur where the state 'deprive[s] its own legislation of its official character by delegating to

---

35 See also, e.g., Case 229/83 *Leclerc* v *Au Blé Vert* [1985] ECR 1, [1985] 2 CMLR 286; Cases 209–13/84 *Ministère Public* v *Asjes* [1986] ECR 1425; Case 254/87 *Syndicat des Librairies de Normandie* v *L'Aigle* [1988] ECR 4457; Case 267/86 *Van Eycke* v *ASPA* [1988] ECR 4769; Case 66/86, note 17 above. See Slot, 'The Application of Articles 3(f), 5 and 85 to 94 EEC' (1987) 12 ELRev 179; Hoffman, 'Anti-competitive State Legislation Condemned under Articles 5, 85 and 86 of the EEC Treaty: How Far should the Court Go after Van Eycke?' [1990] 1 ECLR 11.

36 E.g., Case 13/77, note 32 above; Case 267/86, note 35 above; Case 66/86, note 17 above.

37 Case 267/86, note 35 above.

38 See especially Art. 30. p. 871.

private traders responsibility for taking decisions affecting the economic sphere'.[39] This had not occurred. The rules allowed the authorities to fix maximum rates; they did not delegate power to private traders. The implication is that state transfer of responsibility for price-fixing to an undertaking or group of undertakings may be incompatible with Articles 3(g) EC, 5 and 85.[40]

In *Leclerc* v *Au Blé Vert*[41] French legislation imposed on publishers and importers of books an obligation unilaterally to fix retail prices. Court proceedings were available to restrain breaches of the fixed price. The purpose of the law was to prevent price competition destroying cultural diversity in the book trade, but the question arose whether such a measure suppressed competition and thereby detracted from the effectiveness of Article 85. The Court reasserted the principle that the state is under a duty not to undermine the effectiveness of the competition rules as controls over the activities of private operators. The Court then noted that there existed no ruling on the compatibility with Article 85 of purely national price-fixing arrangements in the book trade and observed that some states permitted such arrangements out of respect for the peculiar nature of the book trade, where quantity may diminish quality.[42] There was accordingly no sufficiently clear violation of Article 85 that the state could be held to have supported in a manner incompatible with Article 5 read with Articles 3(f) EEC and 85.[43] The decision supports the view that state intervention to require or to encourage market distortion by private parties may be unlawful, but on the facts the violation of Article 85, on which is built the separate state violation, was not established.[44]

The limits of the control exercised by Article 5 read with the competition rules were defined more sharply by the Court's ruling in *Meng*.[45] Meng was a financial adviser in Germany. Several of his clients had entered into contracts with insurance companies. He had paid over to those clients commission that he had received from the insurance companies. However, payment of commission to clients in this fashion violated German law. Meng sought to rely on Community law to challenge what he regarded as a restriction on his ability to compete for custom.

---

39 Case 267/86, note 35 above, para. 16 of the judgment. See also Case C-153/93 *Germany* v *Delta Schiffahrts- und Speditionsgesellschaft mbH* [1994] ECR I-2517.
40 See analysis by Joliet, 'National Anti-Competitive Legislation and Community Law' (1988) Fordham Corp L Inst Ch. 16.
41 Case 229/83, note 35 above.
42 See Case C-360/92 P *Publishers Association* v *Commission*, p. 788 above.
43 The same approach was taken in Case 254/87, note 35 above.
44 See Cases 209–13/84, note 35 above, in contrast to Case 66/86 note 17 above (distinction based on existence of regulations implementing Art. 85).
45 Case C-2/91, judgment of 17 November 1993.

The Court confirmed that Articles 5 and 85 prohibit member states from introducing or maintaining measures which might render the competition rules ineffective. Encouragement or support for anti-competitive cartels or the delegation to private traders of responsibility for decisions affecting the economic sphere would count as violations of this Community law obligation. However, none of these situations matched Meng's case. At stake was state regulation of the market separated from any private arrangement of the type at which the competition rules are aimed.

One might question whether there is a rational economic basis to the Court's willingness to check such national regulation against Articles 5 and 85 where it has roots in a pre-existing private arrangement, but not in the absence of such a background. The effect of the rules on the market does not differ according to such historical matters. However, in *Meng* the Court was evidently in cautious mood in fixing the reach of Article 5. In its sensitivity to the scope of state regulatory competence that lies beyond the reach of EC trade law, the ruling in *Meng* has much in common with the Court's contemporaneous delicacy in refining the outer margins of Article 30.[46]

ARTICLE 30

The Court ensures that even though Articles 85 and 86 are directed only at undertakings, the Treaty forbids states as regulators from maintaining in force legislation capable of undermining the effectiveness of the competition rules.[47] In a sense the several strands of Community law examined in this chapter exercise a general control over states that act in a manner apt to compromise the objectives of undistorted competition contained in Article 3 of the Treaty.[48] However, although the perception that distortion is subject to general control may be useful, it is still necessary to be more precise in defining state liability in relation to specific Treaty provisions. The Treaty itself distinguishes between private rules supported by the state

---

46 Especially in Cases C-267/91 and 268/91 *Keck and Mithouard*, p. 536 above. See Reich, 'The "November Revolution" of the European Court of Justice: Keck, Meng and Audi Revisited' (1994) 31 CMLRev 459; Davies, 'Market Integration and Social Policy in the Court of Justice' (1995) 24 ILJ 46.
47 Case 267/86, note 35 above; Case 229/83 note 35 above, para. 14 of the judgment; Cases 209–13/84, note 35 above, para. 71 of the judgment; Case 66/86, note 17 above, para. 48 of the judgment.
48 See especially Case 13/77, note 32 above; Slot (1987) 12 ELRev 179: Van der Esch '*Dérégulation, Autorégulation et le Régime de Concurrence non Fausse dans la CEE*' (1990) 26 CDE 499. The relevant provision was Art. 3(f) EEC/Art. 3(g) EC.

and state intervention *per se*. The Court's point in cases such as *Van Eycke*[49] and *Meng*[50] is that where state intervention does not take the form of confirmation of, or support for, pre-existing agreements, it is not caught by Articles 5 and 85. However, if the act is an independent intervention that firms must then follow, it is still susceptible to control under Community law, but under different provisions. Article 30 in particular may control national measures that regulate the market, but act as barriers to trade in goods between member states. The point was implicit in *Van Eycke*, where the Court was not asked by the referring court to explore the consequences of a state measure imposing a ceiling on interest rates payable to depositors, where there was no pre-existing private arrangement. However, Article 30 was discussed explicitly in *Leclerc* v *Au Blé Vert*.[51] The Court found no violation of the competition rules but proceeded to point out that the obligation imposed on an importer of books to fix a price placed a burden on imports distinct from that imposed on domestic products. Within France the obligation was felt at a different stage of the production chain, on the publisher. The requirement discouraged the marketing of imported products and violated Article 30.

In *van Vlaamse Reisbureaus*[52] the Court was asked to consider possible breaches of Articles 30–34 by the state. It found no such breaches because the matter concerned the provision of services, not goods. This suggests that where goods are in issue and the state acts in a manner that leads to restrictions on trade, a breach of Article 30 may be found. An analogy with the Court's decision that a state-sponsored campaign to 'Buy Irish' was unlawful under Article 30 offers clear support for this view.[53] In addition, there seems no reason to doubt that a situation such as that at issue in *van Vlaamse Reisbureaus* could involve a violation of Article 59, for the state was responsible for distorting trade patterns in the supply of services. However, no questions relating to Article 59 were referred to the European Court by the Belgian court in that case.

The state's involvement in price-fixing may take forms other than offering legal support to a cartel, as in *van Vlaamse Reisbureaus*. The state may itself impose the prices under legislation. State price-fixing is compatible with Community law unless it disadvantages imports in comparison with domestic goods, when it is caught by Article 30, as in *Leclerc* v *Au Blé Vert*.[54] Such state measures are thus controlled under Article 30, and

49 Case 267/86, note 35 above.
50 Case C-2/91, note 45 above.
51 Case 229/83, note 35 above.
52 Case 311/85, note 34 above.
53 Case 249/81 *Commission* v *Ireland* [1982] ECR 4005, p. 440 above; see also Case C-202/88, note 30 above.
54 Case 229/83, note 35 above; see Ch. 15, p. 442 above.

private firms that fix prices under state compulsion will escape liability for violation of Article 85. However, in order to preclude evasion of the laws against anti-competitive conduct, this 'defence' of compulsion is narrowly interpreted. Where the firms enjoy any flexibility in their course of conduct, they too will be held to have violated the Treaty rules.[55] In *BNIC v Clair*[56] an organization was set up in the wine and cognac sector under statutory authority. Private parties were appointed by public authorities to a public body that regulated the trade. The public authority then made agreements reached binding on all traders concerned in the trade. The Court held that the public input did not prevent the agreements struck being held incompatible with Article 85.

ARTICLE 37

Article 37 requires member states that possess state monopolies of a commercial character to eliminate discrimination based on nationality regarding the conditions under which goods are procured and marketed. *Pubblico Ministero v Manghera*[57] concerned an exclusive right of importation of manufactured tobacco enjoyed by an Italian state monopoly. The Court held that Article 37(1) had direct effect and that an exclusive right to import would discriminate against exporters from other member states and was accordingly unlawful. Thus, a state monopoly limited to domestic products is unaffected by Article 37, but importers from other member states must be permitted free access to the market of the state in question. The court thus placed Article 37 alongside Article 30 as a means of securing the free movement of goods, and, although the Court's judgments have often lacked clarity, it appears that Article 37 has little, if any, vigour independent of Article 30 as an instrument designed to integrate the market for goods.

Article 37, like Article 90(1), acquiesces in the existence of monopoly power, but envisages close supervision of its exercise. In *Sacchi* the Court determined that Article 37's place in the Treaty demonstrates that it refers only to trade in goods, not the provision of services,[58] but cases such as *Höfner v Macrotron*[59] demonstrate how other provisions of Community

55 Case 13/77, note 32 above; Whish, *Competition Law*, pp. 341–6.
56 Case 123/83 [1985] ECR 391, [1985] 2 CMLR 430.
57 Case 59/75 [1976] ECR 91.
58 Case 155/73, note 6 above; see also Case 30/87, note 10 above. Likewise, Case 177/78 *Pigs and Bacon Commission v McCarren* [1979] ECR 2161, 2191, shows that Art. 37 has no application to agriculture, because Art. 38(2) gives priority to the rules for the organization of agricultural markets.
59 Case C-41/90, note 11 above; see also Case C-260/89 *ERT v Dimotiki*, [1991] ECR I-2925, [1994] 4 CMLR 540.

law control state monopolies in the provision of services. Article 37 is a further element in the general initiative against exclusivity conferred by the state discussed above. From this perspective it also represents a further example of the interrelation of provisions located in different parts of the Treaty that contributes to the daunting complexity of the application of Community law to state intervention in the market.

STATE AIDS

The function of state aid

State subsidy is a long-established method of regulation of the economy. It may be used to support an ailing industry because, for example, the state believes it would be injurious to the national interest to lose production in that sector. It may support an industry even though its economic efficiency is questionable where the decline of the industry would cause significant unemployment, especially if a distinct region were to be especially hard hit. Subsidy may be used as an instrument of industrial policy to develop activities in new technology, perhaps with a view to establishing a national champion capable of defending home markets and winning export markets.

Community law does not forbid state aids. However, it subjects such policy instruments to the requirements of the Community legal order. National industrial policy is not forbidden, but it must not be applied in a manner that discriminates on the basis of nationality or leads to unlawful obstacles to trade. In order to ensure that state aids are properly scrutinized in the light of the demands of Community law Articles 92–4 establish a special mechanism whereby the Commission must be notified of aids in order to assess their compatibility with the Treaty rules.[60] This provides the basis for a deeper level of cooperation between Community institutions and national authorities than is normal under the Commission's purely reactive Article 169 role.[61] The Commission has emphasized its firm determination to preside over the effective enforcement of the Treaty state-aid rules as a key component in the process of the completion of the internal market. This policy had the personal backing of Sir Leon Brittan and he pursued it through both substantive and procedural means. Karel Van Miert took on this portfolio in 1993 and has maintained a rigorous approach to the application of the rules in this sector.

60 Separate rules apply to aids in the field of agriculture, transport, and coal and steel; Bellamy and Child, *Common Market Law of Competition*, Chs. 14–17.
61 See Ch. 7.

The substance of the law relating to state aid

Article 92 contains the substantive rules on the lawfulness of state aids. Article 92(1) provides a basic prohibition, save as otherwise provided in the Treaty, against 'any aid granted by a Member State or through State resources in any form whatsoever which distorts or threatens to distort competition by favouring certain undertakings or the production of certain goods', provided an effect on trade between member states is shown. Article 92(2) then supplies a list of types of aid that *are* compatible with the common market, whereas Article 92(3) contains a list of those that *may* be considered to be compatible with the common market. The Article 92(2) list covers 'aid having a social character, granted to individual consumers, provided that such aid is granted without discrimination related to the origin of the products concerned', aid linked to natural disasters and aid related to the impact of the division of Germany. The list in Article 92(3) is broader. It covers 'aid to promote the economic development of areas where the standard of living is abnormally low or where there is serious underemployment', 'aid to promote the execution of an important project of common European interest or to remedy a serious disturbance in the economy of a Member State' and sectoral and regional aid that does not distort trading conditions to an unacceptable extent. The Council, acting by a qualified majority on a proposal from the Commission, is empowered to specify other categories of aid. The Treaty agreed at Maastricht added to the list aid to promote cultural conservation, where it does not affect competition in a manner contrary to the common interest. The Article 92(3) list permits the Commission considerable discretion. The Commission has declared that it will be receptive to submissions that aid should be considered compatible with the Article 92(3) criteria where the aid contributes to development in the general Community interest rather than the narrower national interest, where the aid is indispensable to achieving the development and, generally, where the costs of the aid are in proportion to the benefits.[62] The Commission will not permit aid systems that simply transfer economic woes from one member state to another.

In defining a state aid within the meaning of Article 92 the Court has pursued a theme familiar in Community trade law. It insists that the effect of a measure, not its form,[63] is decisive. Naturally, direct payment by a

---

62 *Twelfth Annual Report on Competition Policy*, Luxembourg, EC Publications, 1983. See also Case 730/79 *Philip Morris v Commission* [1980] ECR 2671, [1980] 2 CMLR 321; Case 310/85 *Deufil v Commission* [1987] ECR 901.

63 E.g., Case 173/73 *Italy v Commission* [1974] ECR 709, [1974] 2 CMLR 593, and see Quigley, 'The Notion of a State Aid in the EEC' (1988) 13 ELRev 242. See also effect, not form, in relation to Art. 30, p. 432; Art. 85, p. 692.

state to a firm is covered, but a wide definition has been adopted in order to control states that devise indirect methods for conferring beneficial treatment on firms. For example, these provisions are capable of catching support channelled through tax subsidy, reduced interest-rate loans, investment subsidy, purchase of shares at an inflated price or supply of assets at an undervalue. All these represent methods whereby a state may provide particular firms with funds or reduce their costs. The state comes under suspicion where it fails to behave as a normal investor.[64] Moreover, in this area as in others, the notion of 'state' encompasses regional and local organs of the state and bodies under the direction of the state.[65]

However, the Court has had the opportunity to place an outer limit to the reach of the state-aid provisions. The exemption of small businesses from laws against unfair dismissal is not a state aid, even though it may confer competitive advantages on such firms, for it is not an advantage afforded directly or indirectly from state resources.[66] It seems that competition between states in standards of labour regulation and, more generally, social regulation is not subject to control under the state-aid provisions.[67]

Procedural aspects

Article 93 establishes procedures whereby the Commission may supervise both existing and new aid. Article 93(1) charges the Commission to act in cooperation with the member states and to 'keep under constant review all systems of aid existing in those States'. Under Article 93(3) plans to grant or alter aid shall be notified in advance to the Commission, a procedure that serves to intensify cooperation between Commission and member states.

Where either existing or new aid is perceived to violate Article 92, Article 93(2) allows the Commission to pursue a special infringement procedure in derogation from that in Article 169.[68] Procedural guarantees must be observed in the pursuit of the inquiry. Such protection includes the right to a hearing, which the Court has confirmed as a fundamental right under Community law in proceedings where a decision is liable

---

64 See Case 323/82, note 65 below. See also Comm. Dec. 92/11 *Toyota* OJ 1992 L6/36.

65 E.g. Case 323/82 *Intermills* v *Commission* [1974] ECR 3809; Case 78/76 *Steinike and Weinlig* v *Germany* [1977] ECR 595. See the notion of state in relation to Art. 30, p. 450; in relation to the direct effect of directives, p. 350.

66 Case C-189/91 *P. Kirsammer-Hack* v *Hurhan Sidal*, judgment of 30 November 1993.

67 See also Cases C-72, C-73/91 *Sloman Neptune Schiffahrts* v *Seebetriebsrat Bodo Ziesemer*, judgment of 17 November 1993, and analysis by Davies, note 46 above. See Ch. 20, p. 642, on this type of regulatory competition.

68 See Ch. 7, p. 211 above.

adversely to affect a person's interests.[69] However, the Court has qualified this right by refusing to annul decisions unless the outcome might have been different were it not for the irregularity.[70] No time-limit is stipulated for the Commission's invocation of Article 93(2) once new aid has been notified to it, but the Court held in *Lorenz* v *Germany*[71] that the Commission should act within two months. Where the Commission does not act within two months, the aid may be implemented after this has been communicated to the Commission, although it may still be subject to Commission control under Articles 93(1) and (2) as an existing aid. Where the Commission concludes that there has been a violation of Article 92, it may require remedial action within a stipulated period. In the event of non-compliance, the matter may be brought directly before the European Court by the Commission or an interested state. In derogation from Article 92 a state is entitled to apply to the Council for a unanimous ruling that its aid shall be considered lawful, but such a decision must be justified by 'exceptional circumstances'. Such an application has the effect of suspending any Commission inquiry into the lawfulness of the aid for up to a maximum period of three months.

Article 93 does not make explicit the sanction for applying new aid without first notifying the Commission. Article 93(3) declares that 'the Member State concerned shall not put its proposed measures into effect until this procedure has resulted in a final decision', but it is not stated whether failure to respect the procedural requirement of notification would have any impact on the lawfulness of the aid itself. The Court has ruled that although the Commission may take interim measures to restrain the application of unnotified new aid, the aid is not rendered illegal *per se* because of the procedural flaw.[72] The Commission must examine the substance of the case. However, the Court ruled on the rather different position at national level in *Fédération Nationale* v *France*.[73] It declared that the national court that enforces Article 93(3) is not concerned with the compatibility of the aid with Article 92. That is a matter for the Commission and accordingly Article 92 is not directly effective. However, a national court should rule aid illegal where it has not been notified under

69 E.g. Case 259/85 *Commission* v *France* [1987] ECR 4393, and see more generally p. 264. For an example of violation, see Case C-294/90 *British Aerospace and Rover* v *Commission* [1992] ECR I-493 [1992] 1 CMLR 853, noted by Ross (1992) 17 ELRev 545.

70 Case 259/85, note 69 above; Case C-301/87 *France* v *Commission* [1990] ECR I-307 noted by Slot (1991) 16 ELRev 38; Case C-142/87 *Belgium* v *Commission* [1990] ECR I-959, [1991] 3 CMLR 213.

71 Case 120/73 [1973] ECR 1471.

72 Case C-301/87, note 70 above.

73 Case C-354/90, [1991] ECR I-5505; cf. Case 120/73, note 71 above.

Article 93(3), which is directly effective and gives rise to rights in favour of individuals that national courts must protect in the event of implementation without notification.[74] Any subsequent Commission decision that the aid conforms to the substantive criteria within Article 92 cannot be retrospective in effect.

Accordingly, a state that has failed to adhere to the obligation to notify under Article 93(3) may not submit before a national court that the aid is in any event compatible with Article 92. The Court has placed emphasis on the importance of upholding the useful effect of Article 93(3) and demonstrates concern to remove incentives to a state not to notify. This suggests a commitment to reinforce indirectly the supervisory role of the Commission in a field where there is no equivalent to Regulation 17/62. Such gradual institutional evolution is an important feature of deepening Community solidarity. In this sense Article 93(3) is a specific manifestation of the broad objectives of Article 5, which, on their own, lack the precision necessary for direct effect.[75]

Repayment of illegally granted aid may be required.[76] The Court has refused to accept that a firm can shelter behind a legitimate expectation that payment received from the state complies with the Community rules.[77] The firm must check that it is entitled to the aid and, where it is not, the Community authorities will insist that the aid is clawed back by the state, using national procedures, in order to remedy the damage done to the economy by the illegal subsidy. Only very exceptionally has the Court recognized that the firm may retain illegally paid aid; where, for example, the Commission has delayed unduly in adopting a decision under Article 93[78] or where recovery is completely impossible.[79] However, the Court's determination to interpret the latter exception narrowly may be judged by its view that a state must pursue repayment even where it will cause the recipient to be wound up.[80] The Court has further deepened the

---

74 It is possible that violation of the state-aid rules may trigger state liability towards competing firms that suffer loss under the principle established by the Court in Cases C-6/90 and C-9/90 *Francovich*, examined at p. 352 above.

75 E.g., Case 44/84 *Hurd* v *Jones* [1986] ECR 29, [1986] 2 CMLR 1; and see Temple Lang (1990) 27 CMLRev 645.

76 Morson, 'La Récupération des aides octroyées par les États en violation du Traité CEE'. (1990) 26 Rev Trim Droit Européen 409.

77 Case 310/85, note 62 above; Case 94/87 *Commission* v *Germany* [1989] ECR 175; Case C-142/87, note 70 above; Case C-5/89 *Commission* v *Germany* [1990] ECR I-3437, [1992] 1 CMLR 117.

78 Case 223/85 *Rijn-Schelde-Verolm (RSV) Maschinefabrieken en Scheepswerven NV* v *Commission* [1987] ECR 4617, [1989] 2 CMLR 259.

79 Case 52/84 *Commission* v *Belgium* [1986] ECR 89; Case 94/87, note 77 above.

80 Case 52/84, note 79 above; see also Case C-142/87, note 70 above; Case C-5/89, note 77 above.

impact of Article 5 by requiring the Commission and the member states to cooperate in overcoming legal and practical difficulties that hinder repayment.[81]

The state-aid procedures are rendered more effective by rules requiring states to supply the Commission with relevant information concerning financial relations between the state and public undertakings.[82] This obligation of transparency makes it considerably more difficult for the state to conceal illegal transfers from Commission scrutiny. As part of the process of tightening up control of subsidies the Commission attempted to introduce in 1991 extended reporting requirements imposed on public undertakings in the manufacturing sector with a turnover in excess of 250 million ECU.[83] This intervention was sufficiently controversial to stimulate a challenge to its validity before the Court. In *France v Commission* the Court annulled the Commission's act.[84] In the Court's view, the Commission had improperly used Directive 80/723[85] as the legal base. The Commission then amended the text while maintaining the essential features of the annual reporting system for public undertakings with a turnover exceeding 250 million ECU. It adopted Directive 93/84, amending Directive 80/723, on the basis of Article 90(3) EC,[86] which the Court had helpfully indicated in *France v Commission* was the appropriate provision.

Article 92 and other Treaty provisions

The state-aid provisions should not be seen in isolation. They impinge on other aspects of Community trade law. Where a state returns revenue raised from taxation on a particular product to domestic producers but not to importers that may lead to a violation of either Article 12 or Article 95.[87] If, however, the money disappears into the Treasury and producers are then supported out of general funds, the matter falls to be considered in relation to Articles 92–4. More generally, a discriminatory taxation system falls foul of Article 95 even where it may also count as an aid within Article 92.[88]

---

81 E.g. Case 94/87, note 77 above.
82 Dir. 80/723, note 26 above, adopted under Art. 90(3) (see p. 866), extended by Dir. 85/413 OJ 1985 L229/20. The validity of Dir. 80/723 was upheld by the Court in Cases 188–90/80, note 26 above.
83 OJ 1991 C273.
84 Case C-325/91, judgment of 16 June 1993.
85 Note 26 above.
86 Dir. 93/84 OJ 1993 L254/16, Notice OJ 1993 C307/3. On Art. 90(3) see p. 866 above.
87 See Ch. 14.
88 E.g. Case 73/79 *Commission v Italy* [1980] ECR 1533; Case 277/83 *Commission v Italy* [1985] ECR 2049; Cases C-78–83/90 *Société Compagnie Commerciale de l'Ouest v Receveur Principal des Douanes*, [1992] ECR I-1847.

Furthermore, the state-aid rules are not an exception to the rules in Articles 30–36. In *Commission v Italy*[89] the Court declared that Articles 30 and 92 share the common purpose of securing the free movement of goods under normal conditions of competition. Accordingly, Article 92 may not be employed to frustrate the provisions of Articles 30–36. A measure that hinders trade, actually or potentially, directly or indirectly, is judged in relation to Articles 30–36 and cannot be saved simply because it is part of a state aid. In *Commission v Ireland*, 'Buy Irish',[90] the Court found that the campaign in favour of home-produced goods was a measure prohibited by Article 30 distinct from the financial subsidy provided in support of the campaign. The whole scheme could not be defended on the basis of Article 92. Accordingly, it may be necessary to attempt to sever a measure from a connected subsidy in order to ensure that the correct Community rules, Articles 30 and 92 respectively, are applied to distinct aspects of a scheme.[91]

89 Case 103/84 [1986] ECR 1759.
90 Case 249/81, note 53 above; see also Case 74/76 *Iannelli and Volpi v Meroni* [1977] ECR 557; Case 18/84 *Commission v France* [1985] ECCR 1339; Case C-351/88 *Laboratori Bruneau v Unità Sanitaria*, [1991] ECR I-3641.
91 For the view that the Court has overemphasized market integration under Art. 30 to the detriment of regional policy-making under Art. 92, see Martin and Stehmann, 'Product Market Integration versus Regional Cohesion in the Community' (1991) 16 ELRev 216. See also Wishlade, 'Competition Policy, Cohesion and the Co-ordination of Regional Aids in the European Community' [1993] 4 ECLR 143.

EC Legislation

CHOICE OF TYPE OF LEGISLATION

Political institutions can choose between enacting a regulation, directive or decision under the following Treaty provisions:

Article 6(2), on anti-discrimination;

Articles 8b, 8c, 8e, on the rights of citizens of the Union;

Articles 20, 28, on changes in the common customs tariff;

Articles 43(2), 44(6), 45(3), 46, on common agricultural policy;

Article 49, on free movement of workers (choice between regulations and directives);

Article 51, on social security;

Article 55(2), 66, on 'certain activities' excluded from the scope of freedom of establishment and on freedom to provide services;

Article 59, on extending freedom to provide services to non-community nationals established within the Community;

Articles 73c, 73f, 73g, on capital and payments;

Articles 75, 79(3), 84, on the common transport policy;

Article 87, on competition policy;

Article 91, on dumping;

Article 93(1), on state aid;

Article 99, on harmonization of indirect taxes;

Article 100a, approximation of laws to achieve the internal market apart from fiscal provisions, those relating to free movement of persons and those relating to the rights and interests of employed persons;

Article 100c, on the third countries whose nationals must be in possession of a visa when crossing the external borders of the member states and on the format of such visas;

Articles 103(5), 103a, 104a, 104b, 104c, on economic policy;

Articles 105, 105a, 109, 109(4) and (5), on monetary policy;

Article 113(2), on measures implementing the common commercial policy;

Article 125 on the European Social Fund, which refers to 'implementing decisions';

Article 126, on incentive measures in education;

Article 127, on a common vocational training policy;

Article 128, on incentive measures in culture;

Article 129, on incentive measures in public health;

Article 129a(2), on specific action on consumer protection;

Article 129d, on measures and guidelines on trans-European networks;

Article 130(3), on measures on industry;

Articles 130b, 130d and 130e, on economic and social cohesion;

Articles 130g–130o on research and technology;

Article 130s, on environmental policy;

Article 130w, on development cooperation (assisting developing countries);

Article 138(3), on the uniform procedure for elections of the European Parliament;

Article 168a(2), on the jurisdiction of the Court of First Instance;

Article 223, on products that may not be affected by the Treaty due to military or security use;

Article 228a, on urgent measures to interrupt or to reduce, in part or completely, economic relations with one or more third countries;

Article 235, on legislation to attain one of the objectives of the Community.

DIRECTIVES

The Treaty stipulates the use of directives under the following provisions:

Articles 54, 56(2), on the freedom of establishment;

Article 57, on the mutual recognition of diplomas and other formal qualifications, and on the taking up and pursuit of activities as a self-employed person;

Article 63, on the freedom to provide services;

Article 100, on the approximation of laws that directly affect the common market;

Article 101, to eliminate distortions of competition in the common market;

Article 113(3), on Council directives guiding the Commission on how to negotiate with third countries in the area of the common commercial policy;

Article 118a(2), on the harmonization of health and safety of workers legislation.

IMPLEMENTATION OF DIRECTIVES
AS AT 31 DECEMBER 1993

Member state	Directives applicable	Directives for which measures have been notified	Percentage
Belgium	1149	1042	90.7
Denmark	1149	1096	95.4
France	1150	1032	89.7
Germany	1153	1025	88.9
Greece	1148	1011	88.1
Ireland	1148	1019	88.7
Italy	1149	1022	88.9
Luxembourg	1149	1042	90.7
Netherlands	1149	1062	92.4
Portugal	1146	1022	89.2
Spain	1147	1034	90.1
United Kingdom	1148	1060	92.3

Source: *Eleventh Annual Report to the European Parliament on Commission Monitoring of the Application of Community Law 1993* OJ 1994 C154/7.

Annex IV of the 'Eleventh Annual Report' also gives details in relation to each directive of whether proceedings have been initiated by the Commision against a member state for not implementing the directive or, alternatively, for not implementing it properly. These figures are reproduced in *Butterworths EC Implementation Service*.

DECISIONS

The Treaty stipulates the use of decisions under the following provisions:

Article 73g(2), decisions that a member state must amend or abolish urgent measures on the movement of capital and on payments as regards certain third countries;

Article 76, allowing a member state to give less favourable treatment for carriers who are nationals of other member states pending the adoption of the common transport policy;

Articles 79(4), 80, giving the Commission power to enforce a policy of non-discrimination as to country of origin or destination in the carriage of goods and to prevent state subsidy or protectionism in relation to undertakings involved in transport operations carried out within the Community;

Article 89(2), Commission decisions that competition policy has been breached;

Articles 92(3)(d), 93(2), on state aids held to be compatible with the common market by the Council;

Article 93(2), Commission decisions that aid granted by a state is not compatible with the common market and must be abolished or altered;

Article 100b, Council decisions in 1992 to recognize the provisions in force in one member state to be equivalent to those in force in another member state for the purposes of completing the internal market;

Article 104c(6), a Council decision that a member state has an excessive government deficit in its finances;

Article 104c(9), a Council decision on the measures necessary for deficit reduction in that member state within a certain time-limit, and Article 104c(11), a Council decision on the sanctions against the member state that fails to comply with the Article 104c(9) decision; the Council can take the decisions in Articles 104c(9) and 104c(11) only in the third stage of economic and monetary union; see Article 109e(3);

Article 109h(3), 109i(3), on the authorization of protective measures taken by a member state in balance-of-payments difficulties or on the suspending, amending or revoking thereof: from the beginning of the third stage of EMU these provisions will cease to apply;

Article 125, implementing decisions on the European Social Fund;

Article 130e, in relation to implementing decisions on the European Regional Development Fund.

The Council also has the power to take decisions in relation to certain institutional matters; for example, the organization of its General Secretariat, Article 151; the number of members of the Commission, Article 157(1); not to fill a vacancy in the Commission should it arise, Article 159(2); and the number of judges and advocates-general in the European Court and the Court of First Instance, Articles 165, 166 and 168a(2).

RECOMMENDATIONS AND OPINIONS

The Treaty provides for the use of non-binding recommendations and opinions under the following provisions:

Article 81, the Commission can make recommendations to member states on the reduction of transport charges for crossing frontiers;

Article 102, the Commission can recommend to the states concerned measures to avoid distortion in competition in the common market;

Article 103, allows the Council to adopt a recommendation on broad guidelines of the economic policies of the member states and of the Community and recommendations on how individual member states should make economic changes to comply with the guidelines;

Article 104c(7), Council recommendations as to how a member state should bring to an end its excessive government deficit in its finances; in stage 2 of economic and monetary union this non-binding approach is all that the Council has available, but in stage 3 it can take binding decisions and apply sanctions; see Article 104c(9), (11);

Article 109h, the Commission can recommend measures to be taken by a state in balance-of-payments difficulties; but in the third stage of EMU no such provision will exist;

Article 113(3), the Commission can make recommendations to the Council on the need to negotiate agreements with third countries;

Article 118b, the Commission can deliver opinions on matters related to the dialogue between management and labour at European level;

Article 126(4), the Council can make recommendations on education;

Article 128(5), the Council can make recommendations, unanimously, on culture;

Article 129(4), the Council can make recommendations on public health;

Article 155, the Commission can formulate recommendations or deliver opinions on matters dealt with in the Treaty if it considers it necessary.

COUNCIL LEGISLATION NOT INVOLVING PARLIAMENT

The Council can adopt legislative proposals made by the Commission under the following Treaty provisions without consulting Parliament:

Articles 20, 28, on the common customs tariff;

Articles 44–6, on certain aspects of agricultural policy;

Article 51, on the social security aspects of free movement of workers;

Article 55, on the exclusion of certain activities connected with the exercise of authority from the provisions on the right of establishment;

Articles 59, 66, on the narrowing or widening of the scope of the Treaty provisions on freedom to provide services;

Articles 73b–73g, on all aspects of free movement of capital;

Article 101, where differences in the laws of member states are distorting competition in the common market;

Article 103, on economic policy, which provides for the Council to adopt recommendations on broad guidelines for the economic policies of the member states and to recommend particular economic policies for individual member states without consulting Parliament;

Article 104c, which allows for the Council to make recommendations that a member state should reduce its excessive government financial deficit during stage 2 of economic and monetary union (EMU) and during stage 3 of EMU to take decisions ordering measures for the deficit reduction, backed up by sanctions if the decision is not complied with, without consulting the Parliament but rather simply informing it;

Article 109h(2), 109i(3), on mutual assistance for a member state with balance-of-payments difficulties, which will cease to apply from the beginning of the third stage of EMU;

Article 109l(4), on the adoption of the conversion rates at which the currencies entering the third stage of EMU are to be irrevocably fixed, the fixed rate at which the ECU is substituted for those currencies and the measures necessary for the rapid introduction of the ECU as the single currency of those member states, and Article 109l(5) for any member states who join the single currency later; here the Council acts on a proposal from the Commission after consulting the European Central Bank;

Article 113, on the common commercial policy;

Article 127, on a common vocational training policy; Parliament is involved in implementing a vocational training policy, not harmonizing the laws of the member states, through the cooperation procedure;

Article 223, on a list of products connected with military purposes in connection with which member states can take measures in derogation from the provisions of the Treaty;

Article 228a, on the interruption, reduction or severing of economic relations with one or more third countries.

Select Further Reading

Chapter 1   THE DEVELOPMENT OF THE EUROPEAN COMMUNITY

THE HISTORY OF THE COMMUNITY

Lord Cockfield, *The European Union: Creating the Single Market*.
Harrison, *Europe in Question*.
Kapteyn and Verloren van Themaat, *Law of the European Communities*, Chs I, II.
Lintner and Mazey, *The European Community*, Chs. 1, 2.
Nicoll and Salmon, *Understanding the New European Community*, Ch. 1.
Pinder, *European Community*.
Robertson, *European Institutions*.
Vaughan, *Twentieth Century Europe*.

THE OBJECTIVES OF THE COMMUNITY

El-Agraa (ed.), *Economics of the European Community*.
Hitiris, *European Community Economics*.
Kapteyn and Verloren van Themaat, *Law of the European Communities*, Ch. III.
Pinder, *European Community*.
Lintner and Mazey, *The European Community*, Chs. 3, 4.
Swann, *The Economics of the Common Market*.
Wise and Gibb, *Single Market to Social Europe*.

THE TREATY ON EUROPEAN UNION AND BEYOND

Booss and Forman, 'Enlargement: Legal and Procedural Aspects' (1995) 32 CMLRev 95.
Curtin, 'The Constitutional Structure of the Union: a Europe of Bits and Pieces' (1993) 30 CMLRev 17.

Curtin and Heukels (eds.), *Institutional Dynamics of European Integration*.

Dehousse (ed.), *Europe after Maastricht*.

Harmsen, 'A European Union of Variable Geometry: Problems and Perspectives' (1994) 45 NILQ 109.

McGoldrick, 'A New International Economic Order for Europe?' (1992) 12 YEL 433.

O'Keeffe and Twomey (eds.), *Legal Issues of the Maastricht Treaty*.

Peers, 'An ever closer waiting room?: The case for Eastern European accession to the European Economic Area' (1995) 32 CMLRev 187.

SUBSIDIARITY

The Principle of Subsidiarity (1994) XVI Fide Congress Vol. I.

Cass, 'The Word that saves Maastricht? The Principle of Subsidiarity and the Division of Powers within the European Community' (1992) 29 CMLRev 1107.

Emiliou, 'Subsidiarity: An Effective Barrier against the Enterprises of Ambition?' (1992) 17 ELRev 383.

Emiliou, 'Subsidiarity: Panacea or Fig Leaf?' in O'Keeffe and Twomey, eds., *Legal Issues of the Maastricht Treaty*, pp. 65–83.

Mackenzie Stuart, 'Subsidiarity: A Busted Flush?' in Curtin and O'Keeffe, eds., *Constitutional Adjudication in European Community and National Law*.

Steiner, 'Subsidiarity under the Maastricht Treaty' in O'Keeffe and Twomey, eds., *Legal Issues of the Maastricht Treaty*, pp. 49–64.

Chapter 2   COMMISSION

Bradley, 'Comitology and the Law: Through a Glass, Darkly' (1992) 29 CMLRev 693–721.

Buitendijk and Van Schendelen, 'Brussels Advisory Committees: A Channel for Influence?' (1995) 20 ELRev 37–56.

Hay, *The European Commission and the Administration of the Community*.

Lenaerts, 'Regulating the Regulatory Process: "Delegation of Powers" in the European Community' (1993) 18 ELRev 23.

Noel, *Working Together*.

Tugendhat, *Making Sense of Europe*.

Westlake, *The Commission and the Parliament*.

Chapter 3   COUNCIL

Bulmer and Wessels, *The European Council*.

General Secretariat of the Council, *Guide to the Council of the European Union*.

General Secretariat of the Council, *The European Council*, an information brochure.

Vasey, 'Decision-making in the Agricultural Council and the Luxembourg Compromise' (1988) 25 CMLRev 725.

Chapter 4   EUROPEAN PARLIAMENT

Bradley, 'Legal Developments in the European Parliament' (1988) 8 YEL 189; (1989) 9 YEL 235; (1990) 10 YEL 367; (1991) 11 YEL 383; (1992) 12 YEL 505.

Jacobs and Corbett, *The European Parliament*.

Marias, 'The right to petition the European Parliament after Maastricht' (1995) 20 ELRev 169.

Marias (ed.), *The European Ombudsman*.

Westlake, *The Commission and the Parliament*.

LEGISLATIVE ROLE

Bieber, 'Legislative Procedure for the Establishment of the Single Market' (1988) 25 CMLRev 711–24.

Bieber, Pantalis and Schoo, 'Implications of the Single Act for the European Parliament' (1986) 23 CMLRev 767, 779–86.

Dashwood, 'Community Legislative Procedures in the Era of the Treaty on European Union' (1994) 19 ELRev 343–66.

Forman, 'The Conciliation Procedure' (1979) 16 CMLRev 77–108.

Foster, 'The New Conciliation Committee, under Article 189b EC' (1995) 20 ELRev 185.

BUDGETARY ROLE

Dankert, 'The Joint Declaration by the Community Institutions of 30 June 1982 on the Community Budgetary Procedure' (1983) 20 CMLRev 701.

Kolte, 'The Community Budget: New Principles for Finance, Expenditure Planning and Budgetary Discipline' (1988) 25 CMLRev 487.

Pipkorn, 'Legal Implications of the Absence of the Community Budget at the Beginning of a Financial Year' (1981) 18 CMLRev 141.

Zangl, 'The Interinstitutional Agreement on Budgetary Discipline and Improvement of the Budgetary Procedure' (1989) 26 CMLRev 675.

Chapter 5   EC LEGISLATION

Barents, 'The Quality of Community Legislation' (1994) Maastricht Journal of European and Comparative Law 101.

Domestici-Met, 'Les Procédures Législatives Communautaires Après L'Acte Unique' (1989) RMC 556.

Gordon-Smith, 'The Drafting Process in the European Community' (1989) StatLRev 56.

Lang, 'The Place of Legislation in European Community Law' (1989) StatLRev 37.

Slynn, 'Looking at European Community Texts' (1993) 14 StatLRev. 12.

Usher, 'The Development of Community Powers after the Single European Act', in White and Smythe (eds.), European and International Law, p. 3.

Wainwright, 'The Future of European Community Legislation' (1994) 15 StatLRev 98.

Chapter 6   COURT OF JUSTICE

GENERAL

Arnull, 'Judging the New Europe' (1994) 19 ELRev 3–15.

Brown and Kennedy, The Court of Justice.

Harlow, 'Towards a Theory of Access for the European Court of Justice' (1992) 12 YEL 213–48.

Koopmans, 'The Future of the Court of Justice of the European Communities' (1991) 11 YEL 15–32.

ADVOCATES-GENERAL

Brown and Kennedy, *The Court of Justice*, Ch. 4.
Warner, 'Some Aspects of the European Court of Justice' (1976) 14
JSPTL 15.

VOTING, TENURE AND DISMISSAL

Mackenzie Stuart, 'The Court of Justice: A Personal View' in Bates *et al.,*
In Memoriam J. D. B. Mitchell, p. 118.

POLICY-MAKING/INTERPRETATION

Berlin, 'Interactions between the Lawmaker and the Judiciary within the EC',
LIEI 1992/2, 17–48.
Bredimas, *Methods of Interpretation and Community Law*.
Brown and Kennedy, *The Court of Justice*, Ch. 14.
Gulmann, 'Methods of Interpretation of the European Court of Justice',
(1980) Scand SL 187–204.
Kutscher, 'Methods of Interpretation as Seen by a Judge at the Court of
Justice', Luxembourg, paper in the Court of Justice's Judicial and
Academic Conference, 1976.
Lenaerts, 'Some Thoughts about the Interaction Between Judges and Politi-
cians in the European Community' (1992) 12 YEL 1–34.
Mackenzie Stuart, *The European Communities and the Rule of Law*, pp. 71–9.
Plender, 'The Interpretation of Community Acts by Reference to the
Intention of the Authors' (1982) 2 YEL 57–105.
Rasmussen, *On Law and Policy*, and critical reviews of this book by
Cappelletti, 'Is the European Court of Justice "Running Wild"?' (1987)
12 ELRev 3–17, and Weiler, 'The Court of Justice on Trial' (1987) 24
CMLRev 555–89, and the rejoinder by Rasmussen, 'Between Self-
Restraint and Activism: A Judicial Policy for the European Court'
(1988) 13 ELRev 28–38.
Slynn, 'The Court of Justice of the European Communities' (1984) 33
ICLQ 409, 413–18.

PRECEDENT

Arnull, 'Owning up to Fallibility: Precedent and the Court of Justice' (1993) 30 CMLRev 247–66.

Brown and Kennedy, *The Court of Justice*, Ch. 16.

Hartley, *European Community Law*, pp. 83–5.

Koopmans, 'Stare Decisis in European Law' in O'Keeffe and Schermers (eds.), *Essays in European Law and Integration*, pp. 11–27.

Slynn, 'The Court of Justice of the European Communities' (1984) 33 ICLQ 409, 422–5.

Toth, 'The Authority of Judgments of the European Court of Justice: Binding Force and Legal Effects' (1984) 4 YEL 1–77.

COURT OF FIRST INSTANCE

Arnull, 'Refurbishing the Judicial Architecture of the European Community' (1994) 43 ICLQ 296–316.

Brown and Kennedy, *The Court of Justice*, Ch. 5.

Court of First Instance, 'Reflections on the Future Development of the Community Judicial System' (1991) 16 ELRev 175.

Cruz Vilaça, 'The Court of First Instance of the European Communities: A Significant Step towards the Consolidation of the European Community as a Community Governed by the Rule of Law' (1990) 10 YEL 1.

Due, 'The Court of First Instance' (1987) 7 YEL 1.

Kennedy, 'The Essential Minimum: The Establishment of the Court of First Instance' (1989) 14 ELRev 7.

Millett, *The Court of First Instance*.

Schermers, 'The European Court of First Instance' (1988) 25 CMLRev 541.

Toth, 'The Court of First Instance of the European Communities' in White and Smythe (eds.), *European and International Law*, pp. 19–35.

Vesterdorf, 'The Court of First Instance of the European Communities after Two Full Years in Operation' (1992) 29 CMLRev 897.

Chapter 7 ACTIONS AGAINST MEMBER STATES

ACTIONS UNDER ARTICLE 169 EC

Audretsch, *Supervision in European Community Law*.
Brown and Kennedy, *The Court of Justice*, pp. 105–13.
Dashwood and White, 'Enforcement Actions under Articles 169 and 170 EEC' (1989) 14 ELRev 388–413.
European Commission, 'Eleventh Annual Report to the European Parliament on Commission Monitoring of the Application of Community Law 1993' OJ 1994 C154.
Hartley, *European Community Law*, pp. 303–22.

ACTIONS UNDER ARTICLE 170

Brown and Kennedy, *The Court of Justice*, pp. 113–14.
Dashwood and White, 'Enforcement Actions under Articles 169 and 170 EEC' (1989) 14 ELRev 388, 409.

ACTIONS UNDER ARTICLE 93(2)

Audretsch, *Supervision in European Community Law*, pp. 198–224.
Bellamy and Child, *Common Market Law of Competition*, Ch. 18.
Dashwood, 'Control of State Aids in the EEC: Prevention and Cure under Art. 93' (1975) 12 CMLRev 43, 53–7.
Gilmour, 'The Enforcement of Community Law by the Commission in the Context of State Aids: The Relationship between Articles 93 and 169 and the Choice of Remedies' (1981) 18 CMLRev 63.
Hancher, 'State Aids and Judicial Control in the European Community' [1994] 3 ECLR 134.
Schina, *State Aids under the EEC Treaty*, pp. 143–68.
Slot, 'Procedural Aspects of State Aids: The Guardian of Competition versus the Subsidy Villains?' (1990) 27 CMLRev 741–60.
Winter 'Supervision of State Aid: Article 93 in the Court of Justice' (1993) 30 CMLRev 311.

Dashwood and White, 'Enforcement Actions under Articles 169 and 170 EEC' (1989) 14 ELRev 388, 407–9.
Hartley, *European Community Law*, pp. 324–8.

Chapter 8 JUDICIAL REVIEW OF EC ACTS

Arnull, *EEC Law and the Individual*.
Schwarze, *European Administrative Law*.

ACTIONS UNDER ARTICLE 173

Brown and Kennedy, *The Court of Justice*, pp. 125–49.
Hartley, *European Community Law*, pp. 361–87.
Schermers and Waelbroeck, *Judicial Protection*, pp. 155–247.

Locus standi

Arnull, 'Private Applicants and the Action for Annulment under Article 173 of the EC Treaty' (1995) 32 CMLRev 7–49.
Bebr, 'The Standing of the European Parliament in the Community System of Legal Remedies' (1990) 10 YEL 171.
Craig, 'Legality, Standing and Substantive Review in Community Law' (1994) 14 OJLS 507–37.
Greaves, 'Locus Standi under Article 173 EEC when Seeking Annulment of a Regulation' (1986) 11 ELRev 119–33.

Fundamental human rights

Coppel and O'Neill, 'The European Court of Justice: Taking Rights Seriously?' (1992) 29 CMLRev 669–92.
Dauses, 'The Protection of Fundamental Rights in the Community Legal Order' (1985) 10 ELRev 398–419.
Mendelson, 'The European Court of Justice and Human Rights' (1981) 1 YEL 125–65.

Weiler and Lockhart, '"Taking Rights Seriously" Seriously: The European Court and its Fundamental Rights Jurisprudence' (1995) 32 CMLRev 51–94 and 579–627.

Legitimate expectations

Mackenzie Stuart, 'Legitimate Expectations and Estoppel in Community Law and English Administration' [1983/1] LIEI 53.

Schermers and Waelbroeck, *Judicial Protection*, pp. 65–8.

Sharpston, 'Legitimate Expectations and Economic Reality' (1990) 15 ELRev 103.

Proportionality

Herdegen, 'The Equation between the Principles of Equality and Proportionality' (1985) 22 CMLRev 683–96.

Schermers and Waelbroeck, *Judicial Protection*, pp. 77–80.

Schmitthoff, 'The Doctrines of Proportionality and Non-Discrimination' (1977) 2 ELRev 329–44.

Equality of treatment/non-discrimination

Herdegen, 'The Equation between the Principles of Equality and Proportionality' (1985) 22 CMLRev 683–96.

Lenaerts, '*L'Égalité de Traitement en Droit Communautaire*' (1991) 27 CDE 3.

Schermers and Waelbroeck, *Judicial Protection*, pp. 69–75.

Schmitthoff, 'The Doctrines of Proportionality and Non-Discrimination' (1977) 2 ELRev 329–44.

Legal certainty/non-retroactivity

Schermers and Waelbroeck, *Judicial Protection*, pp. 52–69.

Right to a fair hearing

Hartley, *European Community Law*, pp. 158–60.

Schermers and Waelbroeck, *Judicial Protection*, pp. 43–7.

Confidentiality/legal privilege

Forrester, 'Legal Professional Privilege: Limitations on the Commission's Powers of Inspection following the AM&S Judgment' (1983) 20 CMLRev 75–85.

Hartley, *European Community Law*, pp. 160–61.
Schermers and Waelbroeck, *Judicial Protection*, pp. 78–9.

INTERIM MEASURES UNDER ARTICLE 173

Borchardt, 'The Award of Interim Measures by the European Court of Justice' (1985) 22 CMLRev 203–26.
Schermers and Waelbroeck, *Judicial Protection*, pp. 475–9.

EFFECTS OF ANNULMENT

Hartley, *European Community Law*, pp. 449–52.
Schermers and Waelbroeck, *Judicial Protection*, pp. 273–7.

ACTIONS UNDER ARTICLE 175 FOR FAILURE TO ACT

Hartley, *European Community Law*, pp. 393–415.
Schermers and Waelbroeck, *Judicial Protection*, pp. 247–61.
Shaw, 'Competition complainants: a comprehensive system of remedies?' (1993) 18 ELRev 427–41.

PLEA OF ILLEGALITY UNDER ARTICLE 184

Barav, 'The Exception of Illegality in Community Law: A Critical Analysis' (1974) 11 CMLRev 366–86.
Hartley, *European Community Law*, pp. 416–26.
Schermers and Waelbroeck, *Judicial Protection*, pp. 261–5.

Chapter 9   ARTICLE 177:
PRELIMINARY RULINGS

Alexander, 'The Temporal Effects of Preliminary Rulings' (1988) 8 YEL 12–26.
Arnull, 'The Use and Abuse of Article 177 EEC' (1989) 52 MLR 622.

Arnull, 'References to the European Court' (1990) 15 ELRev 375.

Arnull, 'The Evolution of the Court's jurisdiction under Article 177 EEC' (1993) 18 ELRev 129–37.

Arnull (1993) 30 CMLRev 613–22.

Brown and Kennedy, *The Court of Justice*, pp. 193–226.

Collins, *European Community Law in the United Kingdom*, pp. 142–214.

Hartley, *European Community Law*, pp. 266–302.

Kennedy, 'First steps towards a European certiorari?' (1993) 18 EL Rev 121–9.

Oliver, 'Interim Measures: Some Recent Developments' (1992) 29 CMLRev 7.

Ross, 'Limits on Using Article 177 EC' (1994) 19 ELRev 640–44.

Schermers and Waelbroeck, *Judicial Protection*, pp. 266–72, 317–21, 390–446.

Szyszczak, (1995) 20 EL Rev 214 at pp. 222–5.

Walsh, 'The Appeal of an Article 177 EEC Referral' (1993) 56 MLR 881–6.

Chapter 10 MISCELLANEOUS ASPECTS OF THE COURT'S JURISDICTION

NON-CONTRACTUAL LIABILITY OF THE COMMUNITY

Bronkhorst, 'Action for Compensation of Damages under Articles 178 and 215, para. 2 of the EEC Treaty: Stabilization and Development' [1983/1] LIEI 99–114.

Brown and Kennedy, *The Court of Justice*, pp. 159–80.

Harding, 'The Choice of Court Problem in Cases of Non-Contractual Liability under EEC Law' (1979) 16 CMLRev 389–406.

Hartley, *European Community Law*, pp. 467–507.

Jones, 'The Non-Contractual Liability of the EEC and the Availability of an Alternative Remedy in the National Courts' [1981/1] LIEI 1–47.

Lysen, 'Three Questions on the Non-Contractual Liability of the EEC' [1985/2] LIEI 86–120.

Mackenzie Stuart, 'The Non-Contractual Liability of the European Economic Community' (1975) 12 CMLRev 493–512.

Schermers, Heukels, Mead (eds.), *Non-Contractual Liability of the European Communities*.

Schermers and Waelbroeck, *Judicial Protection*, pp. 328–65.

Van Gerven, 'Non-Contractual Liability of Member States, Community Institutions and Individuals for Breaches of Community Law with a View to a Common Law for Europe' (1994) Maastricht J of Eur and Comp L 6–40.

Wils, 'Concurrent Liability of the Community and a Member State' (1992) 17 ELRev 191–206.

REVIEW OF PENALTIES

Harding, 'The Use of Fines as a Sanction in EEC Competition Law', (1979) 16 CMLRev 591–614.

Schermers and Waelbroeck, *Judicial Protection*, pp. 365–75.

OPINIONS UNDER ARTICLE 228

Brown and Kennedy, *The Court of Justice*, pp. 227–43.

Gray, 'Advisory Opinions and the European Court of Justice' (1983) 8 ELRev 24, 31–9.

Schermers and Waelbroeck, *Judicial Protection*, pp. 376–81.

STAFF CASES

Brown and Kennedy, *The Court of Justice*, pp. 181–92.

ARBITRATION

Brown and Kennedy, *The Court of Justice*, pp. 157–9.

Hartley, *European Community Law*, pp. 459–63.

Schermers and Waelbroeck, *Judicial Protection*, pp. 375–6.

ACTIONS BETWEEN MEMBER STATES UNDER A SPECIAL AGREEMENT

Plender, 'The European Court as an International Tribunal' (1983) 42 CLJ 279–98.

Schermers and Waelbroeck, *Judicial Protection*, p. 376.

JURISDICTION CONFERRED BY CONVENTIONS AND PROTOCOLS BETWEEN THE MEMBER STATES

The Brussels Convention 1968

Anton with Beaumont, *Private International Law*, Chs. 8, 9.

Beaumont (ed.), *Anton & Beaumont's Civil Jurisdiction in Scotland*.

Collins, *The Civil Jurisdiction and Judgments Convention*.

Collins (ed.), *Dicey and Morris*, Pt 3.

Dashwood, Halcon and White, *A Guide to the Civil Jurisdiction and Judgments Convention*.

Droz, *Compétence judiciaire et effets des jugements dans le Marché Commun*.

Kaye, *Civil Jurisdiction and the Enforcement of Judgments*.

Lasok and Stone, *Conflict of Laws*, Chs. 5–7.

Mercier and Dutoit, *L'Europe judiciaire: Les Conventions de Bruxelles et de Lugano*.

North and Fawcett (eds), *Cheshire and North's Private International Law*.

O'Malley and Layton, *European Civil Practice*.

The Rome Convention 1980

Anton with Beaumont, *Private International Law*, Ch. 11.

Diamond, 'Harmonization of Private International Law Relating to Contractual Obligations' (1986) *Hague Recueil*, IV, 233.

D'Oliveira, '"Characteristic Obligation" in the Draft EEC Obligations Convention' (1977) 25 AJCL 303.

Fletcher, *Conflict of Laws*.

Lando 'New American Choice-of-Law Principles and the European Conflict of Laws of Contracts' (1982) 30 AJCL 19.

Lasok and Stone, *Conflict of Laws*, Ch. 9.

Nadelmann, 'Choice of Law Resolved by Rules or Presumptions with an Escape Clause' (1985) 33 AJCL 297.

North (ed.), *Contract Conflicts*.

North and Fawcett (eds.), *Cheshire and North's Private International Law*.

Plender, *The European Contracts Convention*.

INHERENT JURISDICTION

Arnull, 'Does the Court of Justice Have Inherent Jurisdiction?' (1990) 27 CMLRev 683.

Chapter 11   DIRECT EFFECT OF COMMUNITY LAW

Hartley, *European Community Law*, pp. 195–233.
Pescatore, 'The Doctrine of "Direct Effect": An Infant Disease of Community Law' (1983) 8 ELRev 155.
Schermers and Waelbroeck, *Judicial Protection*, pp. 138–54.

DIRECT EFFECT OF DIFFERENT TYPES OF COMMUNITY LAW

Treaty provisions

Collins, *European Community Law in the United Kingdom*, pp. 122–6.

Directives

Campbell, 'National Legislation and EC Directives: Judicial Cooperation and National Autonomy' (1992) 43 NILQ 330.
Coppel, 'Rights, Duties and the end of *Marshall*' (1994) 57 MLR 859–79.
Craig, 'Once upon a Time in the West: Direct Effect and the Federalization of EEC Law' (1992) 12 OJLS 453.
Curtin, 'The Effectiveness of Judicial Protection of Individual Rights' (1990) 27 CMLRev 709.
Curtin, 'The Province of Government: Delimiting the Direct Effect of Directives in the Common Law Context' (1990) 15 ELRev 195.
de Burca, 'Giving Effect to European Community Directives' (1992) 55 MLR 215.
Mead, 'The Obligation to Apply European Law: is Duke dead?' (1991) 16 ELRev 490.
Steiner, 'Coming to Terms with EEC Directives' (1990) 106 LQR 144.

Steiner, 'From Direct Effects to Francovich: shifting means of enforcement of Community law' (1993) 18 ELRev 3.

Tridimas, 'Horizontal Effect of Directives: a Missed Opportunity?' (1994) 19 ELRev 621.

International agreements

Bebr, 'Agreements concluded by the Community and their possible direct effect; from International Fruit Company to Kupferberg' (1983) 20 CMLRev 35.

Hartley, 'International Agreements and the Community Legal System' (1983) 8 ELRev 383.

Pescatore, 'The Doctrine of "Direct Effect": An Infant Disease of Community Law' (1983) 8 ELRev 155, 171–4.

DAMAGES AGAINST THE STATE

Lewis and Moore, 'Duties, Directives and Damages in European Community Law' (1993) PL 151.

Ross, 'Beyond *Francovich*' (1993) 56 MLR 55.

Steiner, 'From Direct Effects to Francovich', above.

Van Gerven, 'Non-contractual Liability of Member States, etc., (1994) 1 Maastricht J of Eur and Comp L 6, 12–24.

DIRECT EFFECT OF COMMUNITY LAW IN THE UNITED KINGDOM

Collins, *European Community Law in the United Kingdom*, pp. 99–122.

Chapter 12 SUPREMACY OF EC LAW

RESPONSE OF THE MEMBER STATES

European Commission, 'Sixth Annual Report to the European Parliament on Commission Monitoring of the Application of Community Law 1988' OJ 1989 C330/1, 146–60. For updates see the Annual Reports since then up to the 'Eleventh Annual Report' OJ 1994 C154/1, 175–6.

Germany

Crossland, 'Three major decisions given by the Bundesverfassungsgericht (Federal Constitutional Court)' (1995) 20 ELRev 202.

European Commission, 'Sixth Annual Report to the European Parliament on Commission Monitoring of the Application of Community Law 1988' OJ 1989 C330/1, 149–50.

Foster, 'The German Constitution and EC Membership' (1994) PL 392.

Herdegen, 'Maastricht and the German Constitutional Court: Constitutional Restraints for an "Ever Closer Union"' (1994) 31 CMLRev 235.

Roth, 'The Application of Community Law in West Germany: 1980–1990' (1991) 28 CMLRev 137, 141–5.

France

European Commission, 'Sixth Annual Report to the European Parliament on Commission Monitoring of the Application of Community Law 1988' OJ 1989 C330/1, 152–5.

Oliver, 'The French Constitution and the Treaty of Maastricht' (1994) 43 ICLQ 1.

Roseren, 'The Application of Community Law by French Courts from 1982 to 1993' (1994) 31 CMLRev 315.

Italy

Daniele, 'Italy and EEC Law in 1990' (1991) 16 ELRev 417.

European Commission, 'Sixth Annual Report to the European Parliament on Commission Monitoring of the Application of Community Law 1988' OJ 1989 C330/1, 156–7.

Gaja, 'New Developments in a Continuing Story: The Relationship between EEC Law and Italian Law' (1990) 27 CMLRev 83.

Petriccione, 'Supremacy of Community Law over National Law' (1986) 11 ELRev 320.

Schermers, 'The Scales in Balance: National Constitutional Court v. Court of Justice' (1990) 27 CMLRev 97.

Spain

Liñán Nogueras and Roldán Barbero, 'The Judicial Application of Community Law in Spain' (1993) 30 CMLRev 1135.

Chapter 13 ARTICLE 12: THE ABOLITION OF CUSTOMS DUTIES

Burrows, *Free Movement*, Ch. 1.
Gormley, Ch. 12 in Vaughan (ed.), *Halsbury's Laws* Vol. 52, esp. paras 49–54.
Green, Hartley and Usher, *Single European Market*, Ch. 3.

Chapter 14 ARTICLE 95: PROHIBITION ON DISCRIMINATORY INTERNAL TAXATION

Easson, 'Fiscal Discrimination: New Perspectives on Article 95 of the EEC Treaty' (1981) 18 CMLRev 521.
Easson, 'The Internal Market and the Elimination of Fiscal Frontiers' (1990) 10 YEL 147.
Easson, *Taxation in the European Community*.
Easson and Biehl, Chs. 10, 11 in Bieber *et al.* (eds.), *1992*.
El-Agraa, *Economics of the European Community*, Ch. 14.
Farmer and Lyal, *EC Tax Law*.
Gormley, Ch. 20 in Vaughan (ed.), *Halsbury's Laws*, Vol. 52.
Green, Hartley and Usher, *Single European Market*, Ch. 4.
Hitiris, *European Community Economics*, Ch. 5.
Schwarze, 'The Member States' discretionary powers under the tax provisions of the EEC Treaty' in Schwarze (ed.), *Discretionary Powers*.
Terra and Wattel, *European Tax Law*.
Tiley, 'The Law of Taxation in a European Environment' [1992] CLJ 451.

Chapter 15 ARTICLE 30: PROHIBITION ON QUANTITATIVE RESTRICTIONS

Burrows, *Free Movement*, Ch. 2.
Gormley, *Prohibiting Restrictions on Trade within the EEC*.
Green, Hartley and Usher, *Single European Market*, Ch. 5.
Kapteyn and Verloren van Themaat, *Law of the European Communities*, Ch. 7.3.
Oliver, *Free Movement of Goods in the EEC*, Chs. I–VII.
Wyatt and Dashwood, *European Community Law*, Ch. 8.

Chapter 16 ARTICLE 36

Burrows, *Free Movement*, pp. 54–82.
Gormley, *Prohibiting Restrictions on Trade within the EEC*, Ch. 6.
Green, Hartley and Usher, *Single European Market*, Ch. 7.
Kapteyn and Verloren van Themaat, *Law of the European Communities*, pp. 329–403.
Oliver, *Free Movement of Goods in the EEC*, Ch. VIII.

THE EFFECT OF COMMUNITY LEGISLATION ON NATIONAL COMPETENCE

Bieber, 'On the Mutual Completion of Overlapping Legal Systems: the Case of the European Communities and the National Legal Orders' (1988) 13 ELRev 147.

Cross, 'Pre-emption of Member State Law in the European Economic Community: a Framework for Analysis' (1992) 29 CMLRev 447.

Currall, 'Some Aspects of the Relation between Articles 30–36 and Article 100 of the EEC Treaty, with a Closer Look at Optional Harmonization' (1984), 4 YEL 169.

Lenaerts, 'Constitutionalism and the Many Faces of Federalism' (1990) 38 AJCL 205.

Mortelmans, 'Minimum Harmonization and Consumer Law' [1988] ECLJ 2.

Waelbroeck, 'The Emergent Doctrine of Community Pre-emption –

Consent and Redelegation' in T. Sandalow and E. Stein, *Courts and Free Markets*.

Weatherill, 'Beyond Preemption? Shared Competence and Constitutional Change in the European Community' in O'Keeffe and Twomey, *Legal Issues of the Maastricht Treaty*.

Weiler, 'The Transformation of Europe' (1991) 100 Yale LJ 2403.

Chapter 17   *CASSIS DE DIJON* AND THE DEVELOPMENT OF ARTICLE 30

THE INDISTINCTLY APPLICABLE MEASURE

Burrows, *Free Movement*, pp. 50–54, 57–61.

Gormley, *Prohibiting Restrictions on Trade within the EEC*, Ch. 3.

Green, Hartley and Usher, *Single European Market*, Ch. 6.

Kapteyn and Verloren van Themaat, *Law of the European Communities*, pp. 377–92.

Oliver, *Free Movement of Goods in the EEC*, Chs. VI–VIII.

THE MANDATORY REQUIREMENTS

Consumer protection

Bourgoignie and Trubek, *Consumer Law*, esp. pp. 159–72.

Goyens, 'Consumer Protection in a Single European Market: What Challenge for the EC Agenda?' (1992) 29 CMLRev 71.

Lewis, 'The Protection of Consumers in European Community Law' (1992) 12 YEL 139.

Micklitz and Weatherill, 'Consumer Policy in the European Community: Before and After Maastricht' (1993) 16 JCP 285.

Reich, 'Community Consumer Law' in Bourgoignie (ed.), *European Consumer Law*.

Reich, 'Protection of Consumers' Economic Interests by the EC' (1992) 14 Syd LR 23.

Stuyck, 'Free Movement of Goods and Consumer Protection' in Woodroffe (ed.), *Consumer Law in the EEC*.

Weatherill, '1992 and Consumer Law: Can Free Trade be Reconciled with Effective Protection?' (1988) 6 *Trading Law* 175.

Weatherill, 'The Role of the Informed Consumer in European Community Law and Policy' [1994] Consumer Law Journal 49.

Environmental protection

Demiray, 'The Movement of Goods in a Green Market' [1994/1] LIEI 73.

Geradin, 'Trade and Environmental Protection: Community Harmonization and National Environmental Standards' (1993) 13 YEL 151.

Kramer, 'Environmental Protection and Article 30 EEC Treaty' (1993) 30 CMLRev 111.

Lord Slynn, 'The European Community and the Environment' (1993) 5 Journal of Environmental Law 261.

THE CONSEQUENCES OF *CASSIS DE DIJON*

Bieber *at al.* (eds.), *1992*, esp. Part VII.

Dehousse, '1992 and Beyond: the Institutional Dimension of the Internal Market Programme' [1989/1] LIEI 109.

McGee and Weatherill, 'The Evolution of the Single Market – Harmonization or Liberalization?' (1990) 53 MLR 578.

Mortelmans, 'Minimum Harmonization and Consumer Law' (1988) ECLJ 2.

Reich, 'Protection of Diffuse Interests in the EEC and the Perspective of Progressively Establishing an Internal Market' (1988) 11 JCP 395.

THE LIMITS OF ARTICLE 30

Analysis pre-*Keck*

Chalmers, 'Free Movement of Goods within the European Community: an Unhealthy Addiction to Scotch Whisky?' (1993) 42 ICLQ 269.

Defalque, '*Le Concept de Discrimination en Matière de Libre Circulation des Marchandises*' (1987) 23 CDE 471.

Gormley, '"Actually or Potentially, Directly or Indirectly?" Obstacles to the Free Movement of Goods' (1989) 9 YEL 197.

Mortelmans, 'Article 30 of the EEC Treaty and Legislation Relating to Market Circumstances: Time to Consider a New Definition?' (1991) 28 CMLR 115.

Steiner, 'Drawing the Line: Uses and Abuses of Article 30 EEC' (1992) 29 CMLRev 749.

White, 'In Search of the Limits of Article 30 of the EEC Treaty' (1989) 26 CMLRev 235.

Wils, 'The Search for the rule in Article 30 EEC: much ado about nothing?' (1993) 18 ELRev 475.

Analysis post-*Keck*

Chalmers, 'Repackaging the Internal market – the Ramifications of the Keck judgment (1994) 19 ELRev 385.

Gormley, 'Reasoning Renounced? the Remarkable Judgment in Keck and Mithouard' [1994] Euro Bus L Rev 63.

Poiares Maduro, 'Keck: the end? the beginning of the end? or just the end of the beginning?' 1 (1994) Irish J of Eur Law 33.

Reich, 'The November revolution of the European Court of Justice: Keck, Meng and Audi revisited' (1994) 31 CMLRev 459.

Chapter 18 THE FREE MOVEMENT OF WORKERS

FREE MOVEMENT

Green, Hartley and Usher, *Single European Market*, Chs. 6–11.

Handoll, *Free Movement of Persons in the EU* (1995).

Johnson and O'Keeffe, 'From Discrimination to Obstacles to Free Movement. Recent Developments concerning the Free Movement of Workers' (1994) 31 CMLRev 1313.

Nielsen and Szyszczak, *The Social Dimension of the European Community* (1993), Ch. 2.

O'Keeffe, 'The Free Movement of Persons and the Single Market' (1992) 17 EL Rev 3.

Wyatt and Dashwood, *European Community Law*, Chs. 9, 11, 12.

CITIZENSHIP

Closa, 'The Concept of Citizenship in the Treaty on European Union' (1992) 29 CMLRev 1137.

Closa, 'Citizenship of the Union and Nationality of Member States' in O'Keeffe and Twomey (eds.), *Legal Issues of the Maastricht Treaty* (1994).

Evans, 'Nationality Law and European Integration' (1991) 16 ELRev 190.

O'Keeffe, 'Union Citizenship' in O'Keeffe and Twomey (eds.), *Legal Issues of the Maastricht Treaty* (1994).

O'Leary, 'Nationality Law and Community Citizenship: a Tale of Two Uneasy Bedfellows' (1992) 12 YEL 353.

INTERGOVERNMENTAL COOPERATION

Fijnaut, 'International Policing in Europe: Present and Future' (1994) 19 ELRev 599.

O'Keeffe, 'The Emergence of a European Immigration Policy' (1995) 20 ELRev 20.

SCHENGEN

Meijers (ed.), *Schengen*

O'Keeffe, 'The Schengen Conventions: a suitable model for European integration?' (1991) 11 YEL 185.

Schutte, 'Schengen: Its Meaning for the Free Movement of Persons in Europe' (1991) 28 CMLRev 549.

THIRD-COUNTRY NATIONALS

Evans, 'Third Country Nationals and the Treaty on European Union' [1994] EJIL 199.

Hailbronner, 'Visa Regulations and Third-Country nationals in EC law' (1994) 31 CMLRev 969.

Chapter 19   FREEDOM OF ESTABLISHMENT AND THE FREE MOVEMENT OF SERVICES

Green, Hartley and Usher, *Single European Market*, Chs. 8–13.
Kapteyn and Verloren van Themaat, *Law of the European Communities*, pp. 427–52.
Wyatt and Dashwood, *European Community Law*, Ch. 10.

BEYOND DISCRIMINATION

Arnull, *EEC Law and the Individual*, Ch. 4.
Art, Ch. 11 in Curtin and O'Keeffe (eds.), *Constitutional Adjudication*.
Marenco, 'The Notion of Restriction on the Freedoms of Establishment and Provision of Services in the Case Law of the Court' (1991) 11 YEL 111.

THE 'IRISH ABORTION' CASES

De Burca, 'Fundamental Human Rights and the Reach of EC Law' (1993) 13 OJLS 283.
O'Leary, 'The Court of Justice as a reluctant constitutional adjudicator' (1992) 17 ELRev 138.
Pearce, 'Abortion and the Right to Life under the Irish Constitution' [1993] JSWFL 386.
Spalin, 'Abortion, Speech and the European Community' [1992] JSWFL 17.
Wilkinson, 'Abortion, the Irish Constitution and the EEC' [1992] PL 20.

THE FUNCTION OF LEGISLATION

Green, Hartley and Usher, *Single European Market*, pp. 157–67.
Laslett, 'The Mutual Recognition of Diplomas, Certificates and Other Evidence of Formal Qualifications in the European Community' [1990/1] LIEI 1.
Edward, 'Freedom of Movement for the Regulated Professions' in White and Smythe (eds.), *European and International Law*

Pertek, 'Free Movement of Professionals and Recognition of Higher-Education Diplomas' (1992) 12 YEL 293.

STUDENTS

Flynn, 'Vocational Training in Community Law and Practice' (1988) 8 YEL 59.

Green, Hartley and Usher, *Single European Market*, ch. 13.

Lenaerts, 'Education in EC Law after Maastricht' (1994) 31 CMLRev 7.

Lonbay, 'Education and Law: the Community context' (1989) 14 ELRev 363.

Pertek, 'The Europe of Universities' (1991) 11 YEL 257.

Shaw, 'Twin Track Social Europe – the Inside Track' in O'Keeffe and Twomey, *Legal Issues of the Maastricht Treaty*.

Watson, Ch. 8 in Curtin and O'Keeffe (eds.), *Constitutional Adjudication*.

Chapter 20   SOCIAL POLICY

THE NATURE OF COMMUNITY SOCIAL POLICY

Blanpain, *Labour Law and Industrial Relations*, Pt. I.

Byre, *Leading Cases and Materials*, for a useful collection of sources.

El-Agraa (ed.), *The Economics of the European Community*, Ch. 18.

Hitiris, *European Community Economics*, Ch. 10.

Lodge (ed.), *The European Community*, Ch. 17.

Nielsen and Szyszczak, *The Social Dimension*, Ch. 1.

Swann, *The Economics of the Common Market*, Ch. 9.

COMMUNITY LAW OF SEX DISCRIMINATION

Ellis, *Sex Equality Law*, Chs. 2–5.

Ellis, 'The Definition of Discrimination in European Community Sex Equality Law' (1994) 19 ELRev 563.

Nielsen and Szyszczak, *The Social Dimension*, Ch. 3.

Prechal and Burrows, *Gender Discrimination Law*, Chs. 1, 3–5.

Wyatt and Dashwood, *European Community Law*, Ch. 21.

BEYOND SEX DISCRIMINATION

Blanpain, *Labour Law and Industrial Relations*, Pt. I.
Byre, *Leading Cases and Materials*, for a useful collection of sources.
Nielsen and Szyszczak, *The Social Dimension*, Ch. 4–6.

SOCIAL POLICY AFTER MAASTRICHT

Fitzpatrick, 'Community Social law after Maastricht' (1992) 21 ILJ 199.
Nielsen and Szyszczak, *The Social Dimension*, Ch. 7.
Shaw, 'Twin Track Social Europe – the Inside Track' in O'Keeffe and Twomey, *Legal Issues of the Maastricht Treaty*.
Szyszczak, 'Social Policy: a Happy Ending or a Reworking of the Fairy Tale?' in O'Keeffe and Twomey, *Legal Issues of the Maastricht Treaty*.
Szyszczak, 'Future Directions in European Union Social Policy Law' (1995) 24 ILJ 19.
Watson, 'Social Policy after Maastricht' (1993) 30 CMLRev 481.
Whiteford, 'Social Policy after Maastricht' (1993) 18 ELRev 202.

Chapter 21   FREE MOVEMENT OF CAPITAL, AND ECONOMIC AND MONETARY UNION

Beaumont and Moir, *The European Communities (Amendment) Act 1993 with the Treaty of Rome (as amended) Text and Commentary* (1994), pp. 13–15, 22–25, 41, 73–82, 95–131 and 235–60.
Fratianni, Von Hagen *et al.*, *The Maastricht Way to Economic and Monetary Union*, Essays in International Finance, No. 187, Princeton, Princeton University Press, 1992.
Usher, *The Law of Money*.
Usher, 'Capital Movements and the Treaty on European Union' (1992) 12 YEL 35–57.

Chapter 22 ARTICLE 85: CARTELS AND RESTRICTIVE PRACTICES

Bellamy and Child (ed. Rose), *Common Market Law of Competition*, Chs. 2–3.
Goyder, *EC Competition Law*, Chs. 6–8.
Green, Hartley and Usher, *Single European Market*, Chs. 14–17.
Korah, *EC Competition Law and Practice*, Chs. 1–3.
Van Bael and Bellis, *Competition Law*, pp. 23–67.
Whish, *Competition Law*, Chs. 1, 7.
Wyatt and Dashwood, *European Community Law*, Chs. 13, 14.

ARTICLE 85(1): THE NATURE OF THE PROHIBITION

A rule of reason

Joliet, *The Rule of Reason in Antitrust Law*, the classic European work.

For discussion and disagreement, see:

Korah, 'EEC Competition Policy – Legal Form or Economic Efficiency?'
(1986) 39 CLP 85, (1990) 35 *Antitrust Bulletin* 1009.
Steindorf, 'Article 85 and the Rule of Reason' (1984) 21 CMLRev 639.
Whish and Sufrin, 'Article 85 and the Rule of Reason' (1987) 7 YEL 1.

Distribution agreements

Bellamy and Child (ed. Rose), *Common Market Law of Competition*, Ch. 7.
Van Bael and Bellis, *Competition Law*, Ch. 3.
Whish, *Competition Law*, Ch. 17.

Chapter 23 ARTICLE 86: ABUSE OF A DOMINANT POSITION

Bellamy and Child (ed. Rose), *Common Market Law of Competition*, Ch. 9.
Goyder, *EC Competition*, Chs. 17–19.
Green, Hartley and Usher, *Single European Market*, Chs. 15, 18, 19.
Korah, *EC Competition Law and Practice*, Ch. 4.
Van Bael and Bellis, *Competition Law*, pp. 68–91, Ch. 9.
Whish, *Competition Law*, Ch. 8.

Wyatt and Dashwood, *European Community Law*, Ch. 15.

THE NOTION OF A DOMINANT POSITION

The Court's definition

Baden Fuller, 'Article 86 EEC: Economic Analysis of the Existence of a Dominant Position' (1979) 4 ELRev 423.

Frazer, *Monopoly, Competition and the Law*, Ch. 2.

Gyselen and Kyriazis, 'Article 86: Monopoly Power Measurement Issue Revisited' (1986) 11 ELRev 134.

Korah, 'The Concept of a Dominant Position within the Meaning of Article 86' (1980) 17 CMLRev 395.

For US perspectives, see:

Landes and Posner, 'Market Power in Antitrust Cases' (1981) 94 Harv LR 987.

Pitofsky, 'New Definitions of Relevant Market and the Assault on Antitrust' (1990) 90 Col LR 1806.

More generally on economic theory of market flexibility in the European context see:

Geroski and Jacquemin, 'Industrial change, barriers to mobility and European industrial policy' in Jacquemin and Sapir (eds.), *The European Internal Market*.

ABUSE

Unfairly low pricing

Martinez, 'Predatory pricing literature under European Competition Law: the AKZO case' [1993/2] LIEI 95.

Merkin, 'Predatory Pricing or Competitive Pricing: establishing the truth in English and EEC Law' (1987) Ox JLS 182.

Smith, 'The Wolf in Wolf's Clothing: the Problem with Predatory Pricing' (1989) 14 ELRev 209.

For US perspectives, see:

Beck, 'Intent as an Element of Predatory Pricing under section 2 of the Sherman Act' 78 Corn LR (1991) 1242.

Brodley and Hay, 'Predatory Pricing: Competing economic theories and the evolution of legal standards' 66 Corn LR (1981) 738.

Chapter 24 ENFORCEMENT OF COMPETITION LAW

ENFORCEMENT BY THE COMMISSION

Bellamy and Child (ed. Rose), *Common Market Law of Competition*, Chs. 11, 12.

Kerse, *EC Antitrust Procedure*.

Korah, *EC Competition Law and Practice*, Ch. 5.

Slot and McDonnell (eds.), *Procedure and Enforcement in EC and US Competition Law*.

Van Bael and Bellis, *Competition Law*, Ch. 11.

Whish, *Competition Law*, Ch. 9.

The powers of the Commission

Curtin, 'Constitutionalism in the European Community: the Right to Fair Proceedings in Administrative Law' in J. O'Reilly (ed.), *Human Rights and Constitutional Law*.

Joshua, 'Information in EEC Competition Law Procedures' (1986) 11 ELRev 409.

Van Bael, 'The Antitrust Settlement Practice of the EC Commission' (1986) 23 CMLRev 61.

ENFORCEMENT AT NATIONAL LEVEL

Bellamy and Child (ed. Rose), *Common Market Law of Competition*, Chs. 10, 11.

Goyder, *EC Competition Law*, Ch. 22.

Korah, *EC Competition Law and Practice*, Ch. 6.

Shaw, 'Decentralization and Law Enforcement in EC Competition Law' (1995) 15 *Legal Studies* 128.

Chapter 25 LAW OF MERGERS

Bellamy and Child (ed. Rose), *Common Market Law of Competition*, Ch. 6.

Sir Leon Brittan, *Competition Policy and Merger Control in the Single European Market*.

Bos, Stuyck and Wytinck, *Concentration Control in the EEC*.

Cook and Kerse, *EEC Merger Control*.

Downes and Ellison, *The Legal Control of Mergers*.

Goyder, *EC Competition Law*, Ch. 20.

Hawk (ed.), *EC and US Competition Law and Policy* (Proceedings of the 1991 Conference of the Fordham Corporate Law Institute), Chs. 26–30.

Jones and González Díaz, *The EEC Merger Regulation*.

Neven, Nuttall and Seabright, *Merger in Daylight*.

Whish, *Competition Law*, Ch. 20.

THE MERGER CONTROL REGULATION

Sir Leon Brittan, 'The Law and Policy of Merger Control in the EEC' (1990) 15 ELRev 351.

Collins, 'The Coming of Age of EC Competition Policy' (1992) 17 Yale J Intl L 249.

Downes and MacDougall, 'Significantly Impeding Effective Competition: Substantive Appraisal under the Merger Regulation' (1994) 19 ELRev 286.

Goyder, 'The Implementation of the EC Merger Regulation' [1992] Current Legal Problems 117.

Kovar, 'The EEC Merger Control Regulation' (1990) 10 YEL 71.

Overbury, 'First Experiences of European Merger Control' (1990) ELRev Competition Law Checklist CC79.

Pathak, 'EEC Merger Regulation Enforcement during 1992' ELRev Competition Checklist 1992, CC132.

Pathak, 'Market Definitions, Compatibility with the Common Market and Appeals from Commission Decisions under the Merger Regulation during 1993' ELRev Competition Law Checklist 1993, CC166.

Picat and Zachmann, 'Community Monitoring of Concentration Operations: Evaluation after over two years' application of Regulation 4064/89' [1993] 6 ECLR 240.

Siragusa and Subiotto, 'The EEC Merger Control Regulation: the Commission's Evolving Case Law' (1991) 28 CMLRev 877.

Venit, 'The Merger Control Regulation: Europe Comes of Age ... or Caliban's Dinner' (1990) 27 CMLRev 7.

Venit, 'Review of the Decisions under the Merger Regulation' ELRev Competition Law Checklist 1993, CC133.

Chapter 26   INTELLECTUAL PROPERTY

Bellamy and Child (ed. Rose), *Common Market Law of Competition*, Ch. 8.

Goyder, *EC Competition Law*, Chs. 15, 16.

Korah, *EC Competition Law and Practice*, Chs. 9, 10.
Reich and Leahy, *Internal Market and Diffuse Interests*, Ch. V.
Rothnie, *Parallel Imports*.
Singleton, *Introduction to Competition Law*, Ch. 9.
Van Bael and Bellis, *Competition Law*, Ch. 4.
Whish, *Competition Law*, Ch. 19.
Wyatt and Dashwood, *European Community Law*, Ch. 20.

Chapter 27   STATE INTERVENTION IN THE MARKET

Bellamy and Child (ed. Rose), *Common Market Law of Competition*, Ch. 13.
Goyder, *EC Competition Law*, Ch. 23.
Gyselen, 'State Action and the Effectiveness of the EEC Treaty's Competition Provisions' (1989) 25 CMLRev 33.
Gyselen, 'Anti-Competitive State Measures under the EC Treaty: Towards a Substantive Legality Standard' (1993) ELRev Competition Law Checklist 55.
Pescatore, 'Public and Private Aspects of Community Law' (1986) Fordham Corp L Inst 383.
Slot, 'The Application of Articles 3(f), 5 and 85 to 94 EEC' (1987) 12 ELRev 179.
Whish, *Competition Law*, pp. 330–46.
Wyatt and Dashwood, *European Community Law*, Ch. 19.

THE STATE AS A COMMERCIAL UNDERTAKING

Article 90

Bright, 'Article 90, Economic Policy and the Duties of Member States' [1993] 6 ECLR 263.
Ehlermann, 'Managing Monopolies: the Role of the State in Controlling Market Dominance in the European Community' [1993] 2 ECLR 61.
Hancher, 'Regulated Industries and Competition in Community Law' in Lonbay (ed.), *Frontiers of Competition Law*.
Pais Antunes, '*L'Article 90 du Traité CEE*' (1991) 27 Rev Trim Droit Européen 187.

Pappalardo, 'State Measures and Public Undertakings: Article 90 of the EEC Treaty Revisited' [1991] 1 ECLR 29.

Wainwright, 'Public Undertakings under Article 90' (1989) Fordham Corp L Inst 239.

THE STATE AS REGULATOR OF THE ECONOMY

State aids

Bellamy and Child (ed. Rose), *Common Market Law of Competition*, Ch. 18.

Green, Hartley and Usher, *Single European Market*, Ch. 21.

Hancher, Ottervanger and Slot, *EC State Aids*.

Schina, *State Aids under the EEC Treaty*.

Van Bael and Bellis, *Competition Law*, Part IV.

Wyatt and Dashwood, *European Community Law*, Ch. 18.

Procedural aspects

Hancher, 'State Aids and Judicial Control in the European Community' [1994] 3 ECLR 134.

Slot, 'Procedural Aspects of State Aids: the Guardian of Competition versus the Subsidy Villains?' (1990) 27 CMLRev 741.

Winter, 'Supervision of State Aid: Article 93 in the Court of Justice' (1993) 30 CMLRev 311.

Select Bibliography

Anton, A. E. and Beaumont, P., *Civil Jurisdiction in Scotland: Brussels and Lugano Conventions*, 2nd edn, Edinburgh, W. Green, 1995.

Anton, A. E. with Beaumont, P., *Private International Law*, 2nd edn, Edinburgh, W. Green, 1990.

Arnull, A., *General Principles of EEC Law and the Individual*, Leicester/London, Leicester University Press/Pinter, 1990.

Askham, T., Burke, T., and Ramsden, D., *EC Sunday Trading Rules*, London, Butterworths, 1990.

Audretsch, H. A. H., *Supervision in European Community Law*, 2nd edn, Amsterdam, North-Holland, 1986.

Bain, J., *Barriers to New Competition*, Cambridge, Mass., Harvard University Press, 1956.

Baldwin, R. and McCrudden, C., *Regulation and Public Law*, London, Weidenfeld and Nicolson, 1987.

Bates, T. St J. N., *et al.* (eds.), *In Memoriam J. D. B. Mitchell*, London, Sweet and Maxwell, 1983.

Beaumont, P. and Moir, G., *The European Communities (Amendment) Act 1993 with the Treaty of Rome (as amended) Text and Commentary*, London, Sweet and Maxwell, 1994.

Bellamy, C. and Child, G. (ed. Rose, V.), *Common Market Law of Competition*, 4th edn, London, Sweet and Maxwell, 1993.

Beseler, J. F. and Williams, A. N., *Anti-Dumping and Anti-Subsidy Law*, London, Sweet and Maxwell, 1986.

Bieber, R., Dehousse, R., Pinder, J. and Weiler, J. (eds.), *1992: One European Market?*, Baden-Baden, Germany, Nomos, 1988.

Bishop, M. and Kay, J., *European Mergers and Merger Policy*, Oxford, OUP, 1993.

Blanchet, T., Piipponen, R. and Westman-Clément, M., *The Agreement on the European Economic Area*, Oxford, Clarendon Press, 1994.

Blanpain, R., *Labour Law and Industrial Relations of the European Community*, Deventer, Netherlands, Kluwer, 1991.

Bork, R., *The Antitrust Paradox: A Policy at War with Itself*, New York, Basic Books, 1978.

Bos, P., Stuyck, J. and Wytinck, P., *Concentration Control in the EEC*, London, Graham and Trotman, 1992.

Bourgoignie, T. (ed.), *European Consumer Law*, Belgium, Centre de Droit de la Consommation, Louvain-la-Neuve, 1982.

Bourgoignie, T. and Trubek, D., *Consumer Law, Common Markets and Federalism*, Berlin, de Gruyter, 1987.

Bredimas, A., *Methods of Interpretation and Community Law*, Amsterdam, North-Holland, 1978.

Brittan, Sir Leon, *Competition Policy and Merger Control in the Single European Market*, Cambridge, Grotius, 1991.

Brown, L. Neville and Kennedy, T., *The Court of Justice of the European Communities*, 4th edn, London, Sweet and Maxwell, 1994.

Bulmer, S. and Wessels, W., *The European Council*, Basingstoke, Macmillan, 1987.

Burrows, F., *Free Movement in European Community Law*, Oxford, OUP, 1987.

Byre, A., *Leading Cases and Materials on the Social Policy of the EEC*, Deventer, Netherlands, Kluwer, 1989.

Cappelletti, M., Seccombe, M. and Weiler, J. (eds.), *Integration through Law*, Berlin, de Gruyter, 1986.

Cecchini, P., *The European Challenge: 1992, the Benefits of a Single Market*, Aldershot, Wildwood House, 1988.

Chiplin, B. and Wright, M., *The Logic of Mergers*, Hobart Paper 107, London, Institute of Economic Affairs, 1988.

Cockfield, Lord, *The European Union: Creating the Single Market*, Chichester, Wiley, Chancery Law Publishing, 1994.

Collins, L., *The Civil Jurisdiction and Judgments Act 1982*, London, Butterworths, 1983.

Collins, L., *European Community Law in the United Kingdom*, 4th edn, London, Butterworths, 1990.

Collins, L., (ed.), *Dicey and Morris, The Conflict of Laws*, 12th edn, London, Stevens, 1993.

Cook, J. and Kerse, C., *EEC Merger Control*, London, Sweet and Maxwell, 1991.

Cranston, R. (ed.), *The Single Market and the Law of Banking*, London, Lloyds of London Press, 1991.

Curtin, D. and Heukels, T. (eds.), *Institutional Dynamics of European Integration*, Dordrecht, Nijhoff, 1994.

Curtin, D. and O'Keeffe, D., *Constitutional Adjudication in European Community and National Law*, Dublin, Butterworths, 1992.

Dashwood, A., Hacon, R. J. and White, R. C. A., *A Guide to the Civil Jurisdiction and Judgments Convention*, Deventer, Netherlands, Kluwer, 1987.

Dassesse, M., Isaacs, S. and Penn, G., *EC Banking Law*, 2nd edn, London, Lloyds of London Press, 1994.

Dehousse, R. (ed.), *Europe after Maastricht*, Munich, Law Books in Europe, 1994.

De Smith, S. and Brazier, R., *Constitutional and Administrative Law*, 7th edn, London, Penguin, 1994.

Dicey, A. V., *Law of the Constitution*, 8th edn, London, Macmillan, 1927.

Dine, J., *EC Company Law*, Chichester, Wiley, Chancery Law Publishing, 1993.

Donald-Little, D. M. (ed.), *Cross-Border Practice Compendium*, London, Sweet and Maxwell, 1991.

Downes, T. A., and Ellison, J., *The Legal Control of Mergers in the European Communities*, London, Blackstone Press, 1991.

Droz, G. A. L., *Compétence judiciaire et effets de jugements dans le Marché Commun*, Paris, Librairie Dalloz, 1972.

Dudley, J. W., *1992: Strategies for the Single Market*, London, Kogan Page, 1990.

Easson, A., *Taxation in the European Community*, London, Athlone Press, 1993.

Eeckhout, P., *The European Internal Market and International Trade: a Legal Analysis*, Oxford, Clarendon Press, 1994.

El-Agraa, A. M. (ed.), *Economics of the European Community*, 4th edn, Hemel Hempstead, Philip Allan, 1994.

Ellis, E., *European Community Sex Equality Law*, Oxford, OUP, 1992.

European Commission, several authors, *Thirty Years of Community Law*, Luxembourg, Office for Official Publications of the European Communities, 1983.

European Parliament, *Forging Ahead*, 3rd edn, Luxembourg, EC Official Publications, 1989.

Fairburn, J. A. and Kay, J. A. (eds.), *Mergers and Merger Policy*, Oxford, OUP, 1989.

Farmer, P. and Lyal, R., *EC Tax Law*, Oxford, Clarendon Press, 1994.

Fletcher, I., *Conflict of Laws and European Community Laws*, Amsterdam, North-Holland, 1982.

Frazer, T., *Monopoly, Competition and the Law*, 2nd edn, Sussex, Wheatsheaf Books, 1992.

George, S., *An Awkward Partner: Britain in the European Community*, Oxford, Clarendon Press, 1990.

Gormley, L., *Prohibiting Restrictions on Trade within the EEC*, Amsterdam, Elsevier/North-Holland, 1985.

Goyder, D. G., *EC Competition Law*, 2nd edn, Oxford, OUP, 1993.

Greaves, R., *Transport Law of the European Community*, London, Athlone Press, 1991.

Green, N., Hartley, T. C. and Usher, J. A., *The Legal Foundations of the Single European Market*, Oxford, OUP, 1991.

Haas, E. B., *The Uniting of Europe*, 2nd edn, Stanford, Calif., Stanford University Press, 1968.

Halsbury's Laws of England, see Vaughan.

Hancher, L., Ottervanger, T. and Slot, P. J., *EC State Aids*, Chichester, Wiley, Chancery Law Publishing, 1993.

Handoll, J., *Free Movement of Persons in the EU*, Chichester, Wiley, Chancery Law Publishing, 1995.

Harrison, R. J., *Europe in Question*, 2nd edn, London, Allen and Unwin, 1975.

Harrop, J., *The Political Economy of Integration in the European Community*, Aldershot, Edward Elgar Publishing, 1989.

Hartley, T. C., *The Foundations of European Community Law*, 3rd edn, Oxford, OUP, 1994.

Hawk, B. (ed.), *EC and US Competition Law and Policy* (Proceedings of the 1991 Conference of the Fordham Corporate Law Institute), Irvington-on-Hudson, USA, Transnational Juris Publications, 1992.

Hay, R., *The European Commission and the Administration of the Community*, Luxembourg, Office for Official Publications of the European Communities, 1989.

Hitiris, T., *European Community Economics*, 3rd edn, Hemel Hempstead, Harvester Wheatsheaf, 1994.

Jackson, J. M., *World Trade and the Law of the GATT*, Indianapolis, Ind., Bobbs-Merrill, 1969.

Jacobs, F. G. and Corbett, R., *The European Parliament*, Harlow, Longman, 1992.

Jacquemin, A. and Sapir, A. (eds.), *The European Internal Market*, Oxford, OUP, 1989.

Joliet, R., *The Rule of Reason in Antitrust Law*, Dordrecht, Netherlands, Martinus Nijhoff, 1967.

Jones, C. and González Díaz, E., *The EEC Merger Regulation*, London, Sweet and Maxwell, 1992.

Kapteyn, P. J. G. and Verloren van Themaat, P. *Introduction to the Law of the European Communities*, 2nd edn, ed. Gormley, Deventer, Netherlands, Kluwer, 1989.

Kaye, P., *Civil Jurisdiction and the Enforcement of Judgments*, Professional Books, 1987.

Kerse, C., *EC Antitrust Procedure*, 3rd edn, London, Sweet and Maxwell, 1994.

Korah, V., *EC Competition Law and Practice*, 5th edn, Oxford, ESC, 1994.

Korah, V., *Patent Licensing and EEC Competition Rules: Regulation 2349/84*, Oxford, ESC, 1985.

Korah, V. and Rothnie, W. A., *Exclusive Distribution and the EEC Competi-*

tion Rules: Regulations 1983/83 and 1984/83, 2nd edn, London, Sweet and Maxwell, 1992.

Lasok, D., *Law and Institutions of the European Union*, 6th edn, London, Butterworth, 1994.

Lasok, P. and Stone, P. A., *Conflict of Laws in the European Community*, Abingdon, Professional Books, 1987.

Layton-Henry, Z. (ed.), *The Political Rights of Migrant Workers in Western Europe*, London, Sage, 1989.

Lindberg, L. N., *The Political Dynamics of European Economic Integration*, Calif., Stanford University Press, 1963.

Lintner, V. and Mazey, S., *The European Community*, Maidenhead, McGraw Hill, 1991.

Lodge, J. (ed.), *The European Community and the Challenge of the Future*, London, Pinter, 1989.

Lonbay, J. (ed.), *Frontiers of Competition Law*, Chichester, Wiley, Chancery Law Publishing, 1994.

Lowe, A. V., *Extraterritorial Jurisdiction*, Cambridge, Grotius, 1983.

McGovern, E., *International Trade Regulation*, Exeter, Globefield Press, 1986.

Mackenzie Stuart, *The European Communities and the Rule of Law*, (Hamlyn Lecture), London, Stevens, 1977.

Maitland-Walker, J. (ed.), *Towards 1992 – The Development of International Anti-trust*, Oxford, ESC, 1989.

Marias, E. (ed.), *The European Ombudsman*, Maastricht, European Institute of Public Administration, 1994.

Mathijsen, P. S. R. F., *A Guide to European Union Law*, 6th edn, London, Sweet and Maxwell, 1995.

Mayes, D. G. (ed.), *The European Challenge: Industry's Response to the 1992 Programme*, Hemel Hempstead, Harvester Wheatsheaf, 1991.

Meijers, H. (ed.), *Schengen*, Deventer, Netherlands, Kluwer, 1991.

Mercier, P. and Dutoit, B., *L'Europe judiciare: Les Conventions de Bruxelles et de Lugano*, Basle and Frankfurt, Helbing and Lichtenhahn, 1991.

Miers, D. R. and Page, A. C., *Legislation*, 2nd edn, London, Sweet and Maxwell, 1990.

Millett, T., *The Court of First Instance of the European Communities*, London, Butterworths, 1990.

Mitchell, J. D. B., *Constitutional Law*, 2nd edn, Edinburgh, W. Green, 1968.

Mitrany, D., *A Working Peace System*, Chicago, Quadrangle Books, 1966.

Monnet, J., *Memoirs*, trs. Mayne, London, Collins, 1978.

Montagnon, P. (ed.), *European Competition Policy*, Chatham House Papers, Royal Institute of International Affairs, London, Pinter Publishers, 1990.

Munro, C. R., *Studies in Constitutional Law*, London, Butterworths, 1987.

Neale, A. D. and Goyder, D. G., *The Antitrust Laws of the USA*, Cambridge, CUP, 1980.

Neven, D., Nuttall, R. and Seabright, P., *Merger in Daylight*, London, CEPR, 1993.

Nicoll, W. and Salmon, T. C., *Understanding the New European Community*, Hemel Hempstead, Philip Allan, 1994.

Nielsen, R. and Szyszczak, E., *The Social Dimension of the European Community*, 2nd edn, Copenhagen, Handelshojskolens Forlag, 1993.

Noel, E., *Working Together*, Luxembourg, Office for Official Publications of the European Communities, 1993.

North, P. M. (ed.), *Contract Conflicts*, Amsterdam, North-Holland, 1982.

North, P. M. and Fawcett, J. J. (eds.), *Cheshire and North's Private International Law*, 12th edn, London, Butterworths, 1992.

Ogus, A. I. and Veljanowski, C. G., *Readings in the Economics of Law and Regulation*, Oxford, Clarendon Press, 1984.

O'Keeffe, D. and Schermers, H. G. (eds.), *Essays in European Law and Integration*, Deventer, Netherlands, Kluwer, 1982.

O'Keeffe, D. and Twomey, P. (eds.), *Legal Issues of the Maastricht Treaty*, Chichester, Wiley, Chancery Law Publishing, 1994.

Oliver, *Free Movement of Goods in the EEC*, 2nd edn, London, European Law Centre, 1988.

O'Malley, S. and Layton, A., *European Civil Practice*, London, Sweet and Maxwell, 1989.

O'Reilly, J. (ed.), *Human Rights and Constitutional Law*, Dublin, Round Hall Press, 1992.

Page, A. C. and Ferguson, R. B., *Investor Protection*, London, Weidenfeld and Nicolson, 1992.

Pinder, J., *European Community: the Building of a Union*, Oxford, OUP, 1991.

Plender, R. *The European Contracts Convention: The Rome Convention on the Choice of Law for Contracts*, London, Sweet and Maxwell, 1991.

A Practitioner's Guide to European Take-over Regulation and Practice, Woking, Westminster Management Consultants Limited, 1990.

Prechal, S. and Burrows, N., *Gender Discrimination Law of the European Community*, Aldershot, Dartmouth, 1990.

Rasmussen, H., *On Law and Policy in the European Court of Justice*, Dordrecht, Netherlands, Martinus Nijhoff, 1986.

Reich, N. and Leahy, D., *Internal Market and Diffuse Interests*, Brussels, Story Scientia, 1990.

Robertson, A. H., *European Institutions*, 3rd edn, London, Stevens, 1973.

Rosenthal, D. E. and Knighton, W. M., *National Laws and International Commerce*, Chatham House Papers, London, Royal Institute of International Affairs, 1982.

Rothnie, W. A., *Parallel Imports*, London, Sweet and Maxwell, 1993.

Rudden, B., *A Source-Book on French Law*, 3rd edn, Oxford, Clarendon Press, 1991.

Sandalow, T. and Stein, E., *Courts and Free Markets*, Oxford, Clarendon Press, 1982.

Schermers, H. G., Heukels, T. and Mead, P. (eds.), *Non-Contractual Liability of the European Communities*, Dordrecht, Netherlands, Martinus Nijhoff, 1988.

Schermers, H. G. and Waelbroeck, D., *Judicial Protection in the European Communities*, 5th edn, Deventer, Netherlands, Kluwer, 1992.

Schina, D., *State Aids under the EEC Treaty*, Oxford, ESC, 1987.

Schwarze, J., *European Administrative Law*, London, Sweet and Maxwell, 1992.

Schwarze, J. (ed.), *Discretionary Powers of the Member States in the Field of Economic Policies and Their Limits under the EEC Treaty*, Baden-Baden, Germany, Nomos, 1988.

Singleton, E. S., *Introduction to Competition Law*, London, Longman, 1991.

Slot, P. J., *Technical and Administrative Obstacles to Trade in the EEC*, 1975.

Slot, P. J. and McDonnell, A. (eds.), *Procedure and Enforcement in EC and US Competition Law*, London, Sweet and Maxwell, 1993.

Slot, P. J. and Van der Woude, M. H. (eds.), *Exploiting the Internal Market: Cooperation and Competition toward 1992*, Deventer, Netherlands, Kluwer, 1988.

Snyder, F. G., *Law of the Common Agricultural Policy*, London, Sweet and Maxwell, 1985.

Steiner, J., *Textbook on EC Law*, 4th edn, London, Blackstone Press, 1994.

Swann, D., *The Economics of the Common Market*, 7th edn, London, Penguin Books, 1992.

Taylor, P., *The Limits of European Integration*, London, Croom Helm, 1983.

Terra, B. J. M. and Wattel, P. J., *European Tax Law*, Deventer, Kluwer Law and Taxation, 1993.

Thompson, R., *The Single Market for Pharmaceuticals*, London, Butterworths, 1994.

Tinbergen, J., *International Economic Integration*, Amsterdam, Elsevier, 1965.

Toth, A., *The Oxford Encyclopaedia of Community Law*, Oxford, Clarendon Press, 1990.

Trepte, P.-A., *Public Procurement in the EC*, Bicester, CCH Editions, 1993.

Tugendhat, C., *Making Sense of Europe*, New York, Columbia University Press, 1986.

Usher, J. A., *European Court Practice*, London, Sweet and Maxwell, 1983.

Usher, J. A., *The Law of Money and Financial Services in the European Community*, Oxford, Clarendon Press, 1994.

Van Bael, I. and Bellis, J.-F., *Competition Law of the European Community*, 3rd edn, Bicester, CCH Editions, 1994.

Van Gerven, D. and Aalders, C. A. V., *European Economic Interest Groupings*, Deventer, Kluwer Law and Taxation, 1990.

Vaughan, D., *Halsbury's Laws of England*, Vol. 52, London, Butterworths, 1986.

Vaughan, R., *Twentieth Century Europe*, London, Croom Helm, 1979.

Weatherill, S., *Cases and Materials on EC Law*, 2nd edn, London, Blackstone Press, 1994.

Werlauff, E., *EC Company Law*, Copenhagen, Jurist-og Okonomforbundets Forlag, 1993.

Westlake, M., *The Commission and the Parliament*, London, Butterworths, 1994.

Whish, R., *Competition Law*, 3rd edn, London, Butterworths, 1993.

White, R. C. A. and Smythe, B. (eds.), *Current Issues in European and International Law*, London, Sweet and Maxwell, 1990.

Wilke, M. and Wallace, H., *Subsidiarity: Approaches to Power-Sharing in the European Community*, RIIA Discussion Papers No. 27, London, Royal Institute of International Affairs, 1990.

Wise, M. and Gibb, R., *Single Market to Social Europe*, Harlow, Longman, 1993.

Woodroffe, G. (ed.), *Consumer Law in the EEC*, London, Sweet and Maxwell/Centre for Consumer Law Research, 1984.

Wrench, J. and Solomos, J. (eds.), *Racism and Migration in Western Europe*, Oxford, Berg Publishers, 1995.

Wyatt, D. and Dashwood, A., *European Community Law*, 3rd edn, London, Sweet and Maxwell, 1993.

Index

abuse of a dominant position
  abuse: 742–54: discounts: 738, 748–9;
    discriminatory pricing: 747–8;
    forestalling competition: 738, 746,
    748, 750–51, 779–80, 838; imposed
    agreements: 673, 724, 749–50, 784;
    market partitioning: 748, 784;
    merger: 720, 721, 722, 743, 838, *see*
    also merger; predatory pricing, *see*
    unfairly low pricing; refusal to
    supply: 750–54, 780, 800–801, 835–8;
    tie: 748; unfair contracts: 749–50, *see*
    also imposed agreements; unfairly high
    pricing: 722, 743–5, 836; unfairly low
    pricing: 738, 745–7, 784
  dominant position: 727–42: assessing
    dominance: 736–42; barriers to entry:
    682, 719, 737–42, 835; contestable
    market *see* barriers to entry;
    geographic market: 733–6; interven-
    tionism: 740–42; product market:
    729–33, 837–8; seasonal market:
    729; substantial part of the common
    market: 735–6; US law: 741
  flexibility as potential drawback: 722,
    742, 745, 754
  Merger Reg. analogy: 822
  natural monopolies: 721
  policy overview: 718–22
  see also competition rules, substance;
    intellectual property; oligopoly
accession agreements
  judicial review: 225
  Parliament's role: 130–32
  preliminary reference: 282
  transitional arrangements: 7, 22, 59,
    384, 792
acte clair see preliminary reference
Adonino Committee: 90
advertising: 444–5, 580
advisory committee procedure *see*
  Commission
advocate-general: 37, 155–6, 160–66, 182

Art. 228 Opinions: 324
  Court of First Instance: 162, 184–5
  qualifications for appointment: 155
  tenure and dismissal: 164–6
agency, competition law: 674
amending the Treaty *see*
  intergovernmental conference
anti-dumping: 35, 187, 190, 224, 225, 233
  judicial review: 225, 234–7, 757
  right to a hearing: 264
anti-subsidy: 35, 187, 190, 244, 272
arbitration: 283, 329–30
assembly, transformed into Parliament:
  4–5, 9, 95, *see also* Parliament
assent procedure: 57, 64, 67, 68, 126–7, 129,
  148, 252, 658
association agreements: 8, 130–32, 281,
  360, 572
Austria: 8, 42, 77, 81, 94–5, 131, 156,
  160, 165
balance of payments: 485, 650
banana market: 489
banking: 599–600, 656–8
bankruptcy convention: 332–3
Belgium: 77, 79–80, 94, 97–8, 165, 207,
  380, 567
Bellamy, Christopher: 184
Bonino, Emma: 54
border controls
  control under Art. 30: 434–7
  control under Art. 48: 563–7
  removed by tax harmonization: 423–7
  removed by harmonization of rules
    governing movement of persons:
    564–7
  removed by harmonization of technical
    rules: 437, 469, 472–3, 478–9, 480–81
Brittan, Sir Leon: 43, 44, 45, 47, 815,
  860, 874
Brussels Convention *see* Convention on
  Jurisdiction and the Enforcement of
  Judgments
budget: 69, 89, 116, 132–5

READ MORE IN PENGUIN

In every corner of the world, on every subject under the sun, Penguin represents quality and variety – the very best in publishing today.

For complete information about books available from Penguin – including Puffins, Penguin Classics and Arkana – and how to order them, write to us at the appropriate address below. Please note that for copyright reasons the selection of books varies from country to country.

In the United Kingdom: Please write to *Dept. EP, Penguin Books Ltd, Bath Road, Harmondsworth, West Drayton, Middlesex UB7 ODA*

In the United States: Please write to *Consumer Sales, Penguin USA, P.O. Box 999, Dept. 17109, Bergenfield, New Jersey 07621-0120*. VISA and MasterCard holders call 1-800-253-6476 to order Penguin titles

In Canada: Please write to *Penguin Books Canada Ltd, 10 Alcorn Avenue, Suite 300, Toronto, Ontario M4V 3B2*

In Australia: Please write to *Penguin Books Australia Ltd, P.O. Box 257, Ringwood, Victoria 3134*

In New Zealand: Please write to *Penguin Books (NZ) Ltd, Private Bag 102902, North Shore Mail Centre, Auckland 10*

In India: Please write to *Penguin Books India Pvt Ltd, 706 Eros Apartments, 56 Nehru Place, New Delhi 110 019*

In the Netherlands: Please write to *Penguin Books Netherlands bv, Postbus 3507, NL-1001 AH Amsterdam*

In Germany: Please write to *Penguin Books Deutschland GmbH, Metzlerstrasse 26, 60594 Frankfurt am Main*

In Spain: Please write to *Penguin Books S. A., Bravo Murillo 19, 1° B, 28015 Madrid*

In Italy: Please write to *Penguin Italia s.r.l., Via Felice Casati 20, I-20124 Milano*

In France: Please write to *Penguin France S. A., 17 rue Lejeune, F-31000 Toulouse*

In Japan: Please write to *Penguin Books Japan, Ishikiribashi Building, 2-5-4, Suido, Bunkyo-ku, Tokyo 112*

In Greece: Please write to *Penguin Hellas Ltd, Dimocritou 3, GR-106 71 Athens*

In South Africa: Please write to *Longman Penguin Southern Africa (Pty) Ltd, Private Bag X08, Bertsham 2013*

READ MORE IN PENGUIN

BUSINESS AND ECONOMICS

North and South   David Smith

'This authoritative study ... gives a very effective account of the incredible centralization of decision-making in London, not just in government and administration, but in the press, communications and the management of every major company' – *New Statesman & Society*

I am Right – You are Wrong   Edward de Bono

Edward de Bono expects his ideas to outrage conventional thinkers, yet time has been on his side, and the ideas that he first put forward twenty years ago are now accepted mainstream thinking. Here, in this brilliantly argued assault on outmoded thought patterns, he calls for nothing less than a New Renaissance.

Lloyds Bank Small Business Guide   Sara Williams

This long-running guide to making a success of your small business deals with real issues in a practical way. 'As comprehensive an introduction to setting up a business as anyone could need' – *Daily Telegraph*

The *Economist* Economics   Rupert Pennant-Rea and Clive Crook

Based on a series of 'briefs' published in the *Economist* , this is a clear and accessible guide to the key issues of today's economics for the general reader.

The Rise and Fall of Monetarism   David Smith

Now that even Conservatives have consigned monetarism to the scrap heap of history, David Smith draws out the unhappy lessons of a fundamentally flawed economic experiment, driven by a doctrine that for years had been regarded as outmoded and irrelevant.

Understanding Organizations   Charles B. Handy

Of practical as well as theoretical interest, this book shows how general concepts can help solve specific organizational problems.